INTERACTIVE CASEBOOK SERIES℠

PROPERTY

A Contemporary Approach

SIXTH EDITION

John G. Sprankling
Professor of Law
University of the Pacific
McGeorge School of Law

Raymond R. Coletta
Professor of Law Emeritus
University of the Pacific
McGeorge School of Law

Rachael E. Salcido
Professor of Law
University of the Pacific
McGeorge School of Law

The publisher is not engaged in rendering legal or other professional advice and this publication is not a substitute for the advice of an attorney. If you require legal or other expert advice, you should seek the services of a competent attorney or other professional.

Interactive Casebook Series is a servicemark registered in the U.S. Patent and Trademark Office.

© 2009, 2012 Thomson Reuters
© 2015, 2018, 2021 LEG, Inc. d/b/a West Academic
© 2024 LEG, Inc. d/b/a West Academic
 860 Blue Gentian Road, Suite 350
 Eagan, MN 55121
 1-877-888-1330

West, West Academic Publishing, and West Academic are trademarks of West Publishing Corporation, used under license.

Published in the United States of America

ISBN: 978-1-68561-481-2

WEST ACADEMIC PUBLISHING'S
EMERITUS ADVISORY BOARD

JESSE H. CHOPER
Professor of Law and Dean Emeritus
University of California, Berkeley

LARRY D. KRAMER
President, William and Flora Hewlett Foundation

GRANT S. NELSON
Professor of Law Emeritus, Pepperdine University
Professor of Law Emeritus, University of California, Los Angeles

JAMES J. WHITE
Robert A. Sullivan Emeritus Professor of Law
University of Michigan

WEST ACADEMIC PUBLISHING'S
LAW SCHOOL ADVISORY BOARD

MARK C. ALEXANDER
Arthur J. Kania Dean and Professor of Law
Villanova University Charles Widger School of Law

JOSHUA DRESSLER
Distinguished University Professor Emeritus
Michael E. Moritz College of Law, The Ohio State University

MEREDITH J. DUNCAN
Professor of Law
University of Houston Law Center

RENÉE MCDONALD HUTCHINS
Dean & Professor of Law
University of Maryland Carey School of Law

RENEE KNAKE JEFFERSON
Joanne and Larry Doherty Chair in Legal Ethics &
Professor of Law, University of Houston Law Center

ORIN S. KERR
William G. Simon Professor of Law
University of California, Berkeley

JONATHAN R. MACEY
Professor of Law,
Yale Law School

DEBORAH JONES MERRITT
Distinguished University Professor,
John Deaver Drinko/Baker & Hostetler Chair in Law Emerita
Michael E. Moritz College of Law, The Ohio State University

ARTHUR R. MILLER
University Professor and Chief Justice Warren E. Burger Professor of
Constitutional Law and the Courts, New York University

A. BENJAMIN SPENCER
Dean & Trustee Professor of Law
William & Mary Law School

To Gail, Doug, Tom, Alexis, Adeline, and Ben
J.G.S.

To Mom, Claudia, Sean and Mary, Julian and Sarah,
and my little ones—Eloise and Jonathan
R.R.C.

To Phil and Natalie
R.E.S.

Preface

This book is designed for you: the twenty-first century law student. Property has been part of the first-year curriculum for decades. Perhaps as a result, property casebooks tend to be somewhat old-fashioned in format and content. You will find that this book is different. It provides a modern approach to the traditional course.

What distinguishes this book?

- It presents the core concepts of property law in a streamlined format that is clear and easy to understand, while maintaining the intellectual challenge of the subject.

- The materials are as engaging and relevant as we could make them. We provide interesting background information about the cases, often in boxes inserted into the text. We also address two areas that are usually omitted from property courses: intellectual property and environmental law.

- And just as today's lawyer uses both physical books and electronic resources, you have access to both the hard copy of this book and an online version.

The ebook provides a wide range of resources not found in standard casebooks. Property is a visual subject. You will often understand the material better if you can see a photograph, a map, or a diagram. Accordingly, there are over 200 points in the ebook where you can click into a visual resource. It also contains a number of audio clips, ranging from popular songs to oral arguments before the Supreme Court. Finally, the ebook is hyperlinked to cases, statutes, law review articles, and other resources in Westlaw, so you can easily read the full text of all cited materials online, as modern lawyers do every day.

A few words about our subject: Property reflects the choices that each culture makes about how to allocate its resources. Its development is a product of—and a catalyst for—the economic, political, and social forces that shape a society. Many of the most challenging issues that we confront as a nation involve property law, such as encouraging economic development, preventing discrimination, protecting the environment, providing affordable housing, regulating land use, taking private property for public use, and using natural resources wisely.

We wish to thank everyone at West Academic—particularly Louis Higgins and Daniel Buteyn—for sharing our vision that this book and the other texts in the Interactive Casebook Series represent the future of American legal education.

In preparing this edition and prior editions, we were benefited by the insights of other colleagues who teach property or related courses. We particularly wish to thank Michael Blumm, Karrigan Börk, Donald Campbell, Scott Christman, Curt Cichowski, McKay Cunningham, Matthew Downs, Josh Eagle, Tabrez Ebrahim, Dave Eggert, Dave Fagundes, Dorothy Glancy, Michael Gottesman, George Gould, Shelby Green, James Grimmelmann, Ardath Hamann, Jennifer Harder, Tim Harris, Paul Hesse, Ron Hochbaum, Yolanda King, Maureen Kordesh, Sheldon Lyke, John Minan, Mike Mireles, Thomas Mitchell, Uma Outka, Robert Parrish, Heather Payne, Ngai Pindel, Eric Priest, David Sandino, Betsy Schmidt, Charles Sheppard, Sheila Simon, Allison Tirres, and Judith Wegner.

We also thank Dean Michael Hunter Schwartz and Associate Deans Frank Gevurtz, Mary-Beth Moylan, and Michael Vitiello for their inspiration and support.

John Sprankling thanks his wife Gail Heckemeyer for her loving encouragement, excellent photography, and careful proofreading, and thanks his son Doug Sprankling for more excellent photography. He thanks his co-authors for their creativity, expertise, and optimism.

Raymond Coletta thanks his partner Claudia Sobral Ramalho for her unwavering encouragement and soft understanding. And his co-authors for their patience, collegiality, and superb editing.

Rachael Salcido thanks her husband Phil Pogledich for his constant support and generous feedback, and her co-authors for their mentorship and commitment to excellence.

We welcome your comments, criticisms, and suggestions. Please write to us at the University of the Pacific, McGeorge School of Law, 3200 Fifth Avenue, Sacramento, CA 95817 or email us at jsprankling@pacific.edu, rcoletta@pacific.edu, or rsalcido@pacific.edu.

As authors, we own any errors in the text, at least until someone with better title comes along.

JOHN G. SPRANKLING
RAYMOND R. COLETTA
RACHAEL E. SALCIDO

March 2024

Features of This Casebook

Throughout the book you will find various text boxes on either side of the page. These boxes provide information that will help you to understand a case or cause you to think more deeply about an issue.

For More Information

These boxes point you to resources to consult for more information on a subject.

Food for Thought

These boxes pose questions that prompt you to think about issues raised by the material.

Take Note

Here you will be prompted to take special notice of something that deserves further thought or attention.

What About Your State?

These boxes provide Westlaw search terms that enable you to find the law of your state relevant to the material in the text.

FYI

A self-explanatory category that shares useful or simply interesting information relevant to material in the text.

See It

These boxes point you to visual information that is relevant to the material in the text.

Hear It

These boxes point you to an audio file that is relevant to the material in the text.

Go Online

If there are relevant online resources that are worth consulting in relation to any matter being discussed, these boxes will direct you to them.

Make the Connection

When concepts or discussions pertaining to information covered in other law school courses appear in this text, you will find this box to indicate the course in which you can study those topics. You may also be prompted to connect information in the current case to material you have covered elsewhere in this course.

It's Latin to Me

The law is fond of Latin terms and phrases; when you encounter these for the first time, this box will explain their meaning.

What's That?

These boxes explain the meaning of special legal terms that appear in the main text.

Practice Pointer

Here you will find advice relevant to legal practice typically inspired by the actions (or inactions) of legal counsel in the cases or simply prompted by an important issue being discussed.

Test Your Knowledge

These boxes point you to multiple choice quizzes that provide immediate feedback to help you gauge how well you're understanding the material. Many provide links to authoritative explanations from our Hornbook Series®.

Acknowledgments

We gratefully acknowledge receiving permission to reprint the following materials:

Douglas G. Baird, *Common Law Intellectual Property and the Legacy of* International News Service v. Associated Press, 50 U. Chi. L. Rev. 411 (1983).

Eric T. Freyfogle, *Owning the Land: Four Contemporary Narratives*, 13 J. Land Use & Envtl. L. 279 (1998). Reprinted with the permission of the Journal of Land Use & Environmental Law.

Howard Gensler, *Property Law as an Optimal Economic Foundation*, 35 Washburn L.J. 50 (1995). Reprinted with the permission of Howard Gensler and the Washburn Law Journal.

Michael Lewyn, *New Urbanist Zoning for Dummies*, 58 Ala. L. Rev. 257 (2006).

Philip Mechem, *The Requirement of Delivery in Gifts of Chattels and of Choses in Action Evidenced by Commercial Instruments*, 21 Ill. L. Rev. 341 (1926). Reprinted by special permission of Northwestern University School of Law, *Northwestern University Law Review*.

Thomas W. Merrill, *The Economics of Public Use*, 72 Cornell L. Rev. 61 (1986).

Margaret Jane Radin, *Property and Personhood*, 34 Stan. L. Rev. 957 (1982).

Joseph L. Sax, *Property Rights and the Economy of Nature: Understanding* Lucas v. South Carolina Coastal Council, 45 Stan. L. Rev. 1433 (1993).

Joseph L. Sax, *Some Thoughts on the Decline of Private Property*, 58 Wash. L. Rev. 481 (1983).

David A. Schultz, Property, Power, and American Democracy (1992).

Lior Jacob Strahilevitz, *The Right to Destroy*, 114 Yale L.J. 781 (2005).

Cass R. Sunstein, *On Property and Constitutionalism*, 14 Cardozo L. Rev. 907 (1993). Reprinted with the permission of Cass R. Sunstein and the Cardozo Law Review.

William Michael Treanor, *The Original Understanding of the Takings Clause and the Political Process*, 95 Colum. L. Rev. 782 (1995).

Audio clips of oral argument in the Supreme Court of the United States are provided courtesy of Oyez, a free law project by Justia and the Legal Information Institute of Cornell Law School. You are free to adapt, copy, distribute, or transmit those clips under the terms of the Creative Commons Attribution—NonCommercial 4.0 International License, https://creativecommons.org/licenses/by-nc/4.0/.

We thank Dr. Ananda Chakrabarty, Patrick Dewayne, Jr., William A. Fischel, Professor Eric E. Johnson from the Museum of Intellectual Property, Josh Martinez, Ogden Murphy Wallace PLLC, Glenn Prah, Robert H. Thomas, Phyllis Thomsen, and others for allowing us to reprint photographs. In addition, we appreciate permission to reprint the following photographs:

- Carahills Estate wedding chapel: image by Kaity Whitman of Photo Love.

- Grand Central Terminal: photograph by Eric Baetscher; reproduced under Creative Commons license at https://creativecommons.org/licenses/by-sa/3.0/.

- Ethel R. Lawrence Homes: photograph by Mark Lozier for Fair Share Housing Development.

- Shelley property: photograph by Nancy Francis; reproduced under Creative Commons license at https://creativecommons.org/licenses/by-sa/3.0/.

In some instances, we have reproduced images pursuant to the fair use doctrine, codified in 17 U.S.C. § 107. We believe that fair use is appropriate because:

- This book is written for educational purposes, and the images are designed to enhance the reader's understanding of the material.

- The book makes transformative use of the images by juxtaposing them with textual materials that place them in a new context, give them a new meaning, and allow them to serve a new purpose. In addition, this use comments on, or relates to the historical context of, or critically refers back to the original images. Finally, the images have been physically altered from the originals by being substantially reduced in size.

- The images have already been published, are widely available on the internet, and can be accessed for free by the public.

Acknowledgments

- It is highly unlikely that anyone who wanted a copy of any such image would choose to buy this book as a substitute given the price and size of this book.

Table of Contents

Preface v
Features of This Casebook vii
Acknowledgments ix
Table of Cases xxiii

Chapter 1 *The Concept of Property* 1

A. Why Recognize Property? 1
    1. Five Theories of Property 2
        a. Protect First Possession 2
        b. Encourage Labor 3
        c. Maximize Societal Happiness 3
        d. Ensure Democracy 5
        e. Facilitate Personal Development 6
        f. Conclusion 7
    2. Two Stories: The Fox and the Celebrity 7
        Pierson v. Post 8
        White v. Samsung Electronics America, Inc. 15
        White v. Samsung Electronics America, Inc. 19
B. What Is Property? 24
    1. Right to Transfer 26
        Johnson v. M'Intosh 27
        Moore v. Regents of the University of California 35
    2. Right to Exclude 46
        Jacque v. Steenberg Homes, Inc. 48
        State v. Shack 56
    3. Right to Use 63
        Tranfield v. Arcuni-English 65
        Prah v. Maretti 69
    4. Right to Destroy 76
        Eyerman v. Mercantile Trust Co. 77
Summary 87

Chapter 2 Owning Real Property 89
A. Adverse Possession 90
    1. Elements of Adverse Possession 91
       Gurwit v. Kannatzer 92
       Van Valkenburgh v. Lutz 99
    2. The Adverse Possessor's State of Mind 107
       Fulkerson v. Van Buren 108
       Tioga Coal Co. v. Supermarkets General Corp. 114
    3. Proving Adverse Possession 118
       Howard v. Kunto 119
       Other Procedural Issues 125
       a. Disabilities 125
       b. Identity of the Parties 126
B. The Vertical Dimension of Ownership 126
    1. Airspace Rights 127
       United States v. Causby 128
    2. Subsurface Rights 134
       Chance v. BP Chemicals, Inc. 135
C. Water Law 142
    Michigan Citizens for Water Conservation v. Nestlé Waters North America, Inc. 143
Summary 150

Chapter 3 Owning Personal Property 153
A. Rule of Capture 153
    State v. Shaw 154
    Popov v. Hayashi 159
B. Finders 165
    Armory v. Delamirie 166
    Hannah v. Peel 168
    McAvoy v. Medina 176
    Benjamin v. Lindner Aviation, Inc. 179
C. Adverse Possession of Chattels 185
    Reynolds v. Bagwell 185
    O'Keeffe v. Snyder 189
D. Gifts 197
    1. *Inter Vivos* Gift 197
       Gruen v. Gruen 198
    2. Gift *Causa Mortis* 208
       In re Estate of Oaks 208
Summary 214

Chapter 4 — An Introduction to Intellectual Property 217

- A. Common Law Approach 218
  - *Cheney Brothers v. Doris Silk Corp.* 219
- B. Copyrights 223
  - 1. Copyright Basics 223
    - *Eldred v. Ashcroft* 224
    - *Feist Publications, Inc. v. Rural Telephone Service Co., Inc.* 230
  - 2. Infringement 236
    - *Harper & Row, Publishers, Inc. v. Nation Enterprises* 237
    - *Selle v. Gibb* 247
- C. Patents 254
  - 1. Patent Basics 254
    - *Diamond v. Chakrabarty* 256
  - 2. Infringement 263
    - *Larami Corp. v. Amron* 264
- D. Trademarks 270
  - 1. Trademark Basics 270
    - *Qualitex Co. v. Jacobson Products Co., Inc.* 271
  - 2. Infringement and Dilution 278
    - *Jack Daniel's Properties, Inc. v. VIP Products LLC* 278
- E. Trade Secrets 286
  - 1. Trade Secret Basics 286
  - 2. Misappropriation 287
    - *PepsiCo, Inc. v. Redmond* 287
- Summary 292

Chapter 5 — Estates and Future Interests 295

- A. A Short History 296
- B. Modern Freehold Estates 298
  - 1. Fee Simple Absolute 300
    - *Cole v. Steinlauf* 301
  - 2. Life Estate 305
    - *White v. Brown* 306
    - *Woodrick v. Wood* 314
  - 3. Fee Tail 317
  - 4. Fee Simple Defeasible 319
    - a. Fee Simple Determinable 319
    - b. Fee Simple Subject to a Condition Subsequent 320
    - c. Fee Simple Subject to an Executory Limitation 321
      - *Paul Smith's College of Arts and Sciences v. Roman Catholic Diocese of Ogdensburg* 323
      - *Metropolitan Park District v. Unknown Heirs of Rigney* 329

C. Modern Future Interests 333
    1. Future Interests Retained by the Transferor 335
    2. Future Interests Created in a Transferee 337
        a. Remainders 337
        b. Executory Interests 342
D. Rules Furthering Marketability 344
    1. Rule in Shelley's Case 345
    2. Doctrine of Worthier Title 347
    3. Doctrine of Destructibility of Contingent Remainders 348
    4. Rule Against Perpetuities 350
        Jee v. Audley 354
Summary 360

Chapter 6   *Concurrent Ownership and Marital Property* 363

A. Concurrent Ownership 363
    1. Modern Concurrent Estates 364
        James v. Taylor 366
    2. Severance 369
        Tenhet v. Boswell 370
    3. Partition 374
        Ark Land Co. v. Harper 375
    4. Cotenant Rights and Duties 382
        Esteves v. Esteves 383
B. Marital Property 387
    1. Common Law Foundation 387
    2. Separate Property System 388
    3. Community Property System 389
    4. Tenancy by the Entirety 390
        Sawada v. Endo 391
    5. Defining Marital Property 397
        Guy v. Guy 398
    6. Unmarried Couples 404
        Gazvoda v. Wright 404
    7. Same-Sex Marriage 409
        Obergefell v. Hodges 410
Summary 416

Chapter 7   *Leasing Real Property* 419

A. Creating the Tenancy 420
    1. Selecting the Tenant 420
        *Texas Department of Housing and Community Affairs v. Inclusive
        Communities Project, Inc.* 420
        Neithamer v. Brenneman Property Services, Inc. 423

			Fair Housing Council of San Fernando Valley v. Roommate.com, LLC 430
	2.	Selecting the Estate 435
		a.	Term of Years Tenancy 436
		b.	Periodic Tenancy 436
		c.	Tenancy at Will 436
		d.	Tenancy at Sufferance 437
			Effel v. Rosberg 438
	3.	Negotiating the Lease 442
	4.	Delivering Possession 443
		Keydata Corp. v. United States 443
B.	Condition of the Premises 448
	1.	The Challenge of Substandard Housing 448
		In re Clark 449
	2.	Constructive Eviction 451
		Fidelity Mutual Life Insurance Co. v. Kaminsky 451
		JMB Properties Urban Co. v. Paolucci 456
	3.	The Implied Warranty of Habitability 461
		Wade v. Jobe 461
		Teller v. McCoy 466
C.	Transferring the Tenant's Interest 470
	Ernst v. Conditt 471
	Kendall v. Ernest Pestana, Inc. 480
D.	Ending the Tenancy 487
	1.	Abandonment 488
		Sommer v. Kridel 488
	2.	Security Deposits 494
	3.	Eviction 496
		Elk Creek Management Co. v. Gilbert 496
		Berg v. Wiley 502
Summary 508

Chapter 8 *Selling Real Property* 511

A.	The Purchase Contract 512
	1.	Statute of Frauds 513
		Hickey v. Green 514
	2.	Marketable Title 520
		Lohmeyer v. Bower 521
	3.	Equitable Conversion 527
		Brush Grocery Kart, Inc. v. Sure Fine Market, Inc. 527
	4.	Duty to Disclose 531
		Stambovsky v. Ackley 532

B.	The Closing	539
	1.	The Deed	540
		Rosengrant v. Rosengrant	540
		Vasquez v. Vasquez	547
	2.	Remedies for Breach	550
		Giannini v. First Nat'l Bank of Des Plaines	551
C.	Title Assurance	556
	1.	Title Covenants	557
		Brown v. Lober	560
	2.	Title Opinion Based on Search of Public Records	566
		a.	The Recording System	566
		b.	How to Search Title	567
		c.	Operation of the Recording System	569
			Luthi v. Evans	569
		d.	The Recording Acts	577
			Allen v. Allen	579
		e.	Chain of Title Problems	585
			Board of Education of Minneapolis v. Hughes	588
		f.	What Constitutes "Notice"?	592
			Raub v. General Income Sponsors of Iowa, Inc. ...	593
	3.	Title Insurance	598
		Riordan v. Lawyers Title Insurance Corp.	600
Summary	605

Chapter 9 *Financing Real Property* 609

A.	Creating the Obligation	610
B.	Providing the Security	614
	1.	Mortgage	614
	2.	Deed of Trust	618
	3.	Installment Land Contract	618
		Slone v. Calhoun	619
	4.	Equitable Mortgage	623
		Zaman v. Felton	624
C.	Foreclosing on the Security	630
	1.	Borrower's Rights Before the Foreclosure Sale	630
	2.	Judicial Foreclosure	630
	3.	Nonjudicial Foreclosure	631
	4.	Results of the Foreclosure Sale	631
	5.	Special Mortgage Priority Rules	633
D.	Exercising Rights After Foreclosure	634
	1.	Protecting the Borrower	634
	2.	Protecting the Lender	635
		Wansley v. First Nat'l Bank of Vicksburg	636

Summary 643

Chapter 10 *Private Land Use Planning* 645

A. Easements 646
    1. Creating Easements 647
        Emanuel v. Hernandez 650
        Berge v. State of Vermont 657
        O'Dell v. Stegall 663
        Kienzle v. Myers 670
    2. Interpreting Easements 676
        Marcus Cable Associates, L.P. v. Krohn 677
    3. Terminating Easements 684
        Preseault v. United States 684
    4. Negative Easements 691
B. Land Use Restrictions 693
    1. Traditional Approach 693
        a. Real Covenants 693
            Deep Water Brewing, LLC v. Fairway Resources Ltd. 697
        b. Equitable Servitudes 702
            Gambrell v. Nivens 702
    2. Restatement Approach 708
    3. Discriminatory Covenants 709
        Shelley v. Kraemer 709
    4. Termination of Covenants 715
        Vernon Township Volunteer Fire Department, Inc. v. Connor 715
    5. Common Interest Communities 722
        a. Enforcing Restrictions 723
            Nahrstedt v. Lakeside Village Condominium Association, Inc. 723
        b. Governing the Development 733
            Schaefer v. Eastman Community Association 734
Summary 739

Chapter 11 *Land Use Regulation* 741

A. Nuisance Law 742
    Boomer v. Atlantic Cement Co., Inc. 743
    Thomsen v. Greve 749
B. Basics of Zoning 756
    1. Constitutionality of Zoning 758
        Village of Euclid v. Ambler Realty Co. 759
    2. Typical Zoning Ordinance 767
    3. Nonconforming Uses 768
        Trip Associates, Inc. v. Mayor and City Council of Baltimore 769

C. Rigid Zoning or Flexible Zoning?..774
   1. Zoning Amendments 775
      Smith v. City of Little Rock...775
   2. Variances 782
      Detwiler v. Zoning Hearing Board of Lower Salford Township.............783
   3. Conditional Uses...789
   4. New Approaches to Land Use Regulation...789
D. How Far Can Land Use Regulation Go?..792
   1. Aesthetic Regulation...792
      State ex rel. Stoyanoff v. Berkeley..793
   2. "Family" Zoning..800
      Moore v. City of East Cleveland 801
   3. Growth Controls and Exclusion 806
      Southern Burlington County NAACP v. Township of Mount Laurel.......806
Summary..813

Chapter 12 *An Introduction to Environmental Law*....................817

A. Property and Ecology 817
   Just v. Marinette County 818
B. Water and Wetlands...821
   National Audubon Society v. Superior Court 822
   Sackett v. Environmental Protection Agency...829
C. Land Surface 838
   United States v. Monsanto Co. 839
   Babbitt v. Sweet Home Chapter of Communities for a Greater Oregon 847
D. Atmosphere..853
   Juliana v. United States..854
Summary..861

Chapter 13 *Eminent Domain*..863

A. Defining Public Use 864
   Hawaii Housing Authority v. Midkiff 865
B. Scope of Public Use 871
   Kelo v. City of New London 872
Summary..884

Chapter 14 *Takings*..887

A. Foundation Era 887
B. A New Doctrine 888
   Pennsylvania Coal Co. v. Mahon 888

C.	The *Penn Central* Standard		898
	Penn Central Transportation Co. v. City of New York		899
D.	Three Categorical Tests		913
	1.	Loss of All Economically Beneficial or Productive Use	914
		Lucas v. South Carolina Coastal Council	914
	2.	Exactions: Essential Nexus and Rough Proportionality	930
	3.	Physical Appropriation of Property	931
		Cedar Point Nursery v. Hassid	932

Summary 944

INDEX 947

Table of Cases

The principal cases are in bold type. Cases cited or discussed in the text are in roman type. References are to pages. Cases cited in principal cases and within other quoted materials are not included.

.88 Acres of Property, In re, 331
111-38 Mgmt. Corp. v. Benitez, 526
1000 Brickell, Ltd. v. City of Miami, 319
1973 John Deere 4030 Tractor, In re, 195
Abernathy v. Adous, 477
ABKCO Music, Inc. v. Harrisongs Music, Ltd., 246
Adams et al. v. Coon et al., 186
Adams v. Lamicq, 97
AIMCO Properties, LLC v. Dziewisz, 501
Albinger v. Harris, 207
Albrecht v. Clifford, 538
Alexander v. Boyer, 373
Allen, Ex Parte, 261
Allen v. Allen, 579
American Comm. Stores Corp. v. Newman, 477
American Electric Power Co., Inc. v. Connecticut, 854
American Furniture Warehouse Co. v. Town of Gilbert, 931
Anderson v. Gouldberg, 167
Andrus v. Allard, 918
Andy Warhol Foundation for the Visual Arts, Inc. v. Goldsmith, 244
Apple Group, Ltd. v. Granger Twp. Bd. of Zoning Appeals, 768
Apple Inc. Device Performance Litigation, In re, 55
Arkansas Game and Fish Commission v. United States, 927
Ark Land Co. v. Harper, 375
Arlington Heights, Village of v. Metropolitan Housing Development Corp., 811
Armory v. Delamirie, 166
Armstrong v. United States, 863
Association for Advancement of the Mentally Handicapped, Inc. v. City of Elizabeth, 805
Association for Molecular Pathology v. Myriad Genetics, Inc., 261
Authors Guild v. Google, 245
AVR, Inc. v. City of St. Louis Park, 774
Baatz v. Columbia Gas Transmission, LLC, 141
Babbitt v. Sweet Home Chapter of Communities for a Greater Oregon, 847
Babb v. Lee County Landfill SC, LLC, 748
Bartkowski v. Ramondo, 661

Beachwood Villas Condominium v. Poor, 739
Bean v. Walker, 623
Beard v. City of Ridgeland, 780
Bear Fritz Land Co. v. Kachemak Bay Title Agency, Inc., 604
Beck, Estate of, 82
Beers v. Brown, 669
Belle Terre, Village of v. Boraas, 800
Benjamin v. Lindner Aviation, Inc., 179
Berge v. State of Vermont, 657
Berg v. Wiley, 502
Berman v. Parker, 798
Bethurem v. Hammett, 526
BGW Development Corp. v. Mt. Kisco Lodge No. 1552, 556
Bikram's Yoga College of India, L.P. v. Evolation Yoga, LLC, 235
Bimbo Bakeries USA, Inc. v. Botticella, 291
Bird v. Bidwell, 655
Bjork v. Draper, 691
Black Hills Institute of Geological Research v. South Dakota School of Mines & Technology, 89
Black Jack, City of, United States v., 811
Board of County Commissioners of Teton County v. Crow, 765
Board of Education of Minneapolis v. Hughes, 588
Board of Supervisors of Cerro Gordo County v. Miller, 768
Boehringer v. Montalto, 140
Boomer v. Atlantic Cement Co., Inc., 743
Bostock v. Clayton County, 429
Brantley v. Wilson, 520
Briggs v. Southwestern Energy Prod. Co., 13, 140
Brock v. Yale Mortgage Corp., 583
Brown v. Branch, 519
Brown v. Lober, 560
Brown v. Town of Cary, 800
Brown v. Voss, 683
Brush Grocery Kart, Inc. v. Sure Fine Market, Inc., 527
Buchanan v. Warley, 766
Burch v. University of Kansas, 438
Burns v. McCormick, 518
Burns v. Town of Palm Beach, 800
California Building Industry Ass'n v. City of San Jose, 812
Callahan v. Carey, 435
Campbell v. Acuff-Rose Music, Inc., 243
Capers Estate, In re, 83
Carey v. Brown, 799
Carson v. Brown, 774
Caruso v. Young, 359
Castillo v. G & M Realty L.P., 86

Causby, United States v., 128
CDN, Inc. v. Kapes, 235
Cedar Point Nursery v. Hassid, 24, 61, 910, **932**
Centex Homes Corp. v. Boag, 555
Central Hous. Assocs., LP v. Olson, 500
CFS 915, LLC v. Unetixs Vascular, Inc., 631
Chamberlain v. Thompson, 302
Chance v. BP Chemicals, Inc., 135
Chaplin v. Sanders, 117
Chappell v. New York, N. H. & H. R. Co., 302
Cheney Brothers v. Doris Silk Corp., 219
Chevy Chase Land Co. v. United States, 689
Chicago Title Ins. Co. v. Kumar, 604
C & H Mfg., LLC v. Harlan County Indus. Dev. Authority, Inc., 177
Christian Louboutin S.A. v. Yves Saint Laurent American Holding, Inc., 276
Chuck v. Gomes, 380
Clare House Bungalow Homes, L.L.C., In re, 597
Clark, In re, 449
Cleburne, City of v. Cleburne Living Center, 805
Clickner v. Magothy River Ass'n, Inc., 669
Coffin v. Left Hand Ditch Co., 76
Cohen v. Clark, 458
Cole v. Steinlauf, 301
Commons v. Westwood Zoning Board of Adjustment, 788
Community Housing Improvement Program v. City of New York, 943
Cook v. University Plaza, 438
Cooper Industries, Inc. v. Leatherman Tool Group, 48
Corliss v. Wenner, 184
Country Bible Church v. County of Grant, 327
Craft, United States v., 397
Dahl and Angle, In re Marriage of, 86
Dann v. United States, 34
Davis v. Harmony Development, LLC, 555
Deep Water Brewing, LLC v. Fairway Resources Ltd., 697
Dembiczak, In re, 262
Dennen v. Searle, 304
Dennis v. Northwestern Nat'l Bank, 183
Detwiler v. Zoning Hearing Board of Lower Salford Township, 783
Diamond v. Chakrabarty, 256
Doctor v. Hughes, 347
Dolan v. City of Tigard, 930
Drost v. Hookey, 438
Dr. Seuss Enterprises, L.P. v. ComicMix LLC, 244
Dunbar v. Seger-Thomschitz, 196
East 13th Street Homesteaders' Coalition v. Lower East Side Coalition Housing Development, 124

Eastlake, City of v. Forest City Enterprises, Inc., 781
Edwards v. Harrison County Board of Supervisors, 775
Effel v. Rosberg, 438
Eiman v. Sullivan, 532
El Di, Inc. v. Town of Bethany Beach, 720
El Dorado Land Co., L.P. v. City of McKinney, 328
Eldred v. Ashcroft, 224
Elk Creek Management Co. v. Gilbert, 496
Emanuel v. Hernandez, 650
Environmental Law Found. v. State Water Resources Control Bd., 828
Equestrian Ridge Homeowners Ass'n v. Equestrian Ridge Ests. II Homeowners Ass'n, 694
Ernst v. Conditt, 471
Esteves v. Esteves, 383
ETW Corporation v. Jireh Publishing, Inc, 23
Euclid, Village of v. Ambler Realty Co., 741, 758, 759, 775
Eyerman v. Mercantile Trust Co., 77
Fair Housing Council of San Fernando Valley v. Roommate.com, LLC, 430
Fasano v. Board of County Commissioners, 781
FCC v. Florida Power Corp., 941
FCC v. Fox Television Stations, Inc., 794
Federal Hill Cap., LLC v. City of Providence, 804
Feist Publications, Inc. v. Rural Telephone Service Co., Inc., 230
Fidelity Mutual Life Insurance Co. v. Kaminsky, 451
Fink v. Miller, 721
First English Evangelical Lutheran Church v. County of Los Angeles, 928
Folsom v. Rowell, 339
Fontainebleau Hotel Corp. v. Forty-Five Twenty-Five, 75
Forshee v. Neuschwander, 732
Foster v. Board of Governors, 175
Fountain Valley Chateau Blanc Homeowners Ass'n v. Dept. of Veterans Affairs, 732
Francini v. Goodspeed Airport, LLC, 662
Francis v. King Park Manor, Inc., 429
Franzen v. Cassarino, 106
Fronczak v. Town of Ocean Park, 507
FTR Farms, Inc. v. Rist Farm, Inc., 380
Fulkerson v. Van Buren, 108
Funk v. Funk, 486
Gaida v. Planning & Zoning Commission, 780
Galvan v. Poon, 564
Gambrell v. Nivens, 702
Garcia v. Thong, 496
Garner v. Gerrish, 441
Gay, In re, 531
Gazvoda v. Wright, 404

George, Matter of, 635
Germaine v. Delaine, 368
Ghen v. Rich, 157
Giannini v. First Nat'l Bank of Des Plaines, 551
Gomes v. Harrison, 583
Goodridge v. Department of Public Health, 409
Google LLC v. Oracle America, Inc., 245
Graham v. John Deere Co., 262
Graver Tank & Mfg. Co. v. Linde Air Products Co., 269
Graves v. Dennis, 689
Gray v. Oxford Worldwide Group, 459
Greenberg v. Miami Children's Hospital Research Institute, Inc., 44
Griffeth v. Eid, 662
Gruen v. Gruen, 198
Guillette v. Daly Dry Wall, Inc., 587
Gurwit v. Kannatzer, 92
Guy v. Guy, 398
Hadacheck v. Sebastian, 888
Halbert v. Forney, 517
Hamil v. Casadei, 106
Hammond v. Hammond, 389
Hannah v. Peel, 168
Hansen, In re Estate of, 213
Harber v. Jensen, 675
Hardy, In re Estate of, 545
Harmon v. Misholy, 373
Harper & Row, Publishers, Inc. v. Nation Enterprises, 237
Harper v. Paradise, 598
Harris v. Capital Growth Investors XIV, 429
Hawaii Housing Authority v. Midkiff, 865
HawaiiUSA Federal Credit Union v. Monalim, 636
Held v. Montana, 861
Helena Sand & Gravel, Inc. v. Lewis & Clark Cty. Planning & Zoning Comm'n, 780
Hendle v. Stevens, 177
Hermitage Newark, LLC v. Arkansas Sand Co., 187
Heyn, In re Estate of, 206
Hickey v. Green, 514
Hilder v. St. Peter, 467
Hocking v. Title Insurance & Trust Co., 525, 604
Hoefer v. Musser, 544
Holbrook v. Taylor, 675
Holmquist v. King Cnty., 583
Horne v. Department of Agriculture, 943
Horne v. Harbour Portfolio VI, LP, 622
Howard v. Kunto, 119

Howard v. United States, 683
Hurley v. City of Niagara Falls, 174
Hurlocker v. Medina, 661
Iancu v. Brunetti, 277
Illinois Central R.R. Co. v. Illinois, 827
International News Service v. Associated Press, 218, 221
Iowa State University Research Foundation, Inc. v. ABC, 236
ITT v. Rayonier, Inc. v. Bell, 97
Jaber v. Miller, 477
Jack Daniel's Properties, Inc. v. VIP Products LLC, 278
Jackson v. Steinberg, 183
Jacque v. Steenberg Homes, Inc., 48
James v. Taylor, 366
Jancik v. Department of Housing & Urban Development, 427
Javins v. First National Realty Corp., 467
JBrice Holdings, LLC v. Wilcrest Walk Townhomes Ass'n, Inc., 732
Jee v. Audley, 354
JMB Properties Urban Co. v. Paolucci, 456
Johnson, In re Estate of, 374
Johnson v. Davis, 532
Johnson v. Johnson, 549
Johnson v. M'Intosh, 27
Juliana v. United States, 854, 861
Just v. Marinette County, 818
Kaiser Aetna v. United States, 46
Kelo v. City of New London, 872
Kendall v. Ernest Pestana, Inc., 480
Kewanee Oil Co. v. Bicron Corp., 286
Keydata Corp. v. United States, 443
Keystone Bituminous Coal Ass'n v. DeBenedictis, 896
Kienzle v. Myers, 670
Kilarjian v. Vastola, 555
Kingman Reef Atoll Development, LLC v. United States, 34
Kneller, Commonwealth v., 83
Knight v. Metro. Gov't of Nashville & Davidson Cnty., 931
Knopf v. Gray, 310
Koontz v. St. Johns River Water Management District, 931
Kosciusko County Cmty. Fair, Inc. v. Clemens, 694
Krueger v. AllEnergy Hixton, LLC, 749
Krummenacher v. City of Minnetonka, 787
Ladue, City of v. Gilleo, 800
Lafayette Place Assocs. v. Boston Redevelopment Auth., 517
Laguna Royale Association v. Darger, 732
Lamden v. La Jolla Shores Clubdominium Homeowners Ass'n, 739
Landis & Landis Construction, LLC v. Nation, 468
Larami Corp. v. Amron, 264

Table of Cases

Lehigh Gas-Ohio, LLC v. Cincy Oil Queen City, LLC, 89
LeMehaute v. LeMehaute, 545
Lerman v. Levine, 385
Lindholm v. Brant, 196
Lindsey v. Normet, 435
Littleton v. Plybon, 369
Lohmeyer v. Bower, 521
Long Beach Unified School Dist. v. Dorothy B. Godwin California Living Trust, 845
Long v. Marino, 408
Loretto v. Teleprompter Manhattan CATV Corp., 931
Lucas v. Hamm, 358
Lucas v. South Carolina Coastal Council, 914
Luthi v. Evans, 569
Lutz v. Van Valkenburgh, 107
MacDonald Properties, Inc. v. Bel-Air Country Club, 669
Mace v. Mace, 404
MacPherson v. Buick Motor Co., 532
Madero v. Luffey, 157
Magadini, Commonwealth v., 63
Mahoney v. Mahoney, 403
Marcus Cable Associates, L.P. v. Krohn, 677
Markstein v. Countryside I, L.L.C., 649
Marks v. Whitney, 827
Marsh v. Alabama, 62
Martinez v. City of Clovis, 812
Martin v. City of Alexandria, 787
Martin v. City of Boise, 435
Marvin M. Brandt Revocable Trust v. United States, 691
Marvin v. Marvin, 408
Mason v. Adams County Recorder, 714
Massachusetts v. Environmental Protection Agency, 853
Mastbaum v. Mastbaum, 374
Matal v. Tam, 277
Maui Electric Co., Ltd., In re, 860
McAvoy v. Medina, 176
McCarran Int'l Airport v. Sisolak, 133
McGrath v. Dockendorf, 207
Metro-Goldwyn-Mayer, Inc. v. American Honda Motor Co., 236
Metro-Goldwyn-Mayer Studios, Inc. v. Grokster, Ltd., 253
Metropolitan Park District v. Unknown Heirs of Rigney, 329
Metro Storage Int'l LLC v. Harron, 168
Meyer v. Law, 98
Michigan Citizens for Water Conservation v. Nestlé Waters North America, Inc., 143, 150
Millbrook Hunt, Inc. v. Smith, 649

Miller v. Vicksburg Masonic Temple, 141
Milliken v. Jacono, 538
Mirvish v. Mott, 205
Missionaries of Our Lady of La Salette v. Village of Whitefish Bay, 805
Mister Donut of America, Inc. v. Kemp, 598
Monsanto Co., United States v., 839
Moore v. City of East Cleveland, 801
Moore v. Regents of the University of California, 35
Moore v. Stills, 97
Morgan v. Kroupa, 183
M.P.M. Builders, LLC v. Dwyer, 683
Mugler v. Kansas, 887
Mulligan v. Panther Valley Property Owners Assn., 732
Murr v. Wisconsin, 6, 911, 925
Myerberg, Sawyer & Rue, P.A. v. Agee, 525
Myrick v. Peck Electric Co., 755
Nahrstedt v. Lakeside Village Condominium Association, Inc., 723
Naruto v. Slater, 228
National Audubon Society v. Superior Court, 822
National City Bank v. Case Western Reserve University, 82
National Wildlife Federation v. Norton, 853
Nectow v. City of Cambridge, 765
Neithamer v. Brenneman Property Services, Inc., 423
Neuman v. Grandview at Emerald Hills, Inc., 739
New York, City of v. Utsey, 437
New York Trust Co. v. Eisner, 295
NLRB v. Babcock & Wilcox Co., 942
Nollan v. California Coastal Commission, 930
Nome 2000 v. Fagerstrom, 117
Northwest Child Dev. Ctrs., Inc., In re, 320
Northwest Landowners Association v. State, 943
Oaks, In re Estate of, 208, 213
Obergefell v. Hodges, 410
O'Dell v. Stegall, 663
O'Keeffe v. Snyder, 189
Olmsted Falls, City of v. U.S. Environmental Protection Agency, 838
One Stradivarius Kieserwetter Violin, United States v., 186
Operation Rescue-National v. Planned Parenthood, 461
Orkin v. Taylor, 196
Page County Appliance Center, Inc. v. Honeywell, Inc., 755
Palazzolo v. Rhode Island, 909, 926, 928
Palm Springs, City of v. Living Desert Reserve, 328
Panavision, Int'l, L.P. v. Toeppen, 285
Pantry, Inc. v. Mosley, 486
Parcel of Real Property Known as 1500 Lincoln Avenue, United States v., 397
Parham v. CIH Properties, Inc., 468

Paul Smith's College of Arts and Sciences v. Roman Catholic Diocese of Ogdensburg, 323
Penn Central Transportation Co. v. City of New York, 83, 132, **899**
Pennsylvania Coal Co. v. Mahon, **888**
PepsiCo, Inc. v. Redmond, **287**
Pew v. Sayler, 381
Phenneger v. Kendrick, 544
Philadelphia, City of v. Galdo, 126
Philpot v. Fields, 440
Pierson v. Post, **8**
Playboy Enterprises, Inc. v. Welles, 285
Plymouth Coal Co. v. Pennsylvania, 895
Pocono Springs Civic Ass'n, Inc. v. MacKenzie, 178
Popov v. Hayashi, **159**
Porter, Marriage of, 403
Poyck v. Bryant, 468
Prah v. Maretti, **69**
Preseault v. United States, **684**
Property Acquisition Group, LLC v. Ivester, 635
PruneYard Shopping Center v. Robins, 62
Publications Int'l, Ltd. v. Landoll, Inc., 277
Qualitex Co. v. Jacobson Products Co., Inc., **271**
Raleigh Avenue Beach Assn. v. Atlantis Beach Club, Inc., 670
Rambod v. Tazeh, 207
Rancho Viejo, LLC v. Norton, 852
Raub v. General Income Sponsors of Iowa, Inc., **593**
Ray, Estate of, 304
Ray v. Beacon Hudson Mountain Corp., 124
Read's Landscape Constr., Inc. v. Town of West Warwick, 656
Reynolds v. Bagwell, **185**
Rhine, Town of v. Bizzell, 765
Richard Barton Enterprises, Inc. v. Tsern, 470
Riddle v. Harmon, 374
Rideout v. Knox, 64
Riordan v. Lawyers Title Insurance Corp., **600**
River Heights Assos. L.P. v. Batten, 720
Riverview Comm. Group v. Spencer & Livingston, 706
Rockafellor v. Gray, 565
Rodehorst Brothers v. City of Norfolk Board of Adjustment, 774
Rooks, In re Marriage of, 86
Rosengrant v. Rosengrant, **540**
Roslin Institute, In re, 262
Ross v. Hamilton, 408
Rucker v. Wynn, 508
Russakoff v. Scruggs, 656
Rutland v. Georgia Kraft Co., 96

Rutledge v. Feher, 339
Ryerson v. Brown, 870
Sackett v. Environmental Protection Agency, 829
Sainani v. Belmont Glen Homeowners Ass'n, Inc., 738
Sanborn v. McLean, 706
Sanders-Reed v. Martinez, 860
San Francisco, City & County of v. Sainez, 450
San Francisco Credit Clearing House v. Wells, 188
Sawada v. Endo, 391
Schaefer v. Eastman Community Association, 734
Schefer v. City Council of City of Falls Church, 765
Schenk v. City of Ann Arbor, 146
Schweiso v. Williams, 486
Selle v. Gibb, 247
Shack, State v., 56
Shands v. City of Marathon, 929
Shattuck v. Klotzbach, 519
Shaw, State v., 154
Shelby v. Shaner, 186
Shell Development Co. v. Watson, 258
Shelley v. Kraemer, 709
Shooting Point, LLC v. Wescoat, 683
Shore v. Maple Lane Farms, 755
Simpkins v. Speck, 754
Sinks v. Karleskint, 525
Sipriano v. Great Spring Waters of America, Inc., 149
Slavin v. Rent Control Board, 486
Sleboda v. Heirs at Law of Harris, 98
Sloan v. Johnson, 707
Slone v. Calhoun, 619
Smith Land & Improvement Corp. v. Celotex Corp., 846
Smith v. Bank of America, 373
Smith v. Butler Mountain Estates Property Owners Ass'n, 739
Smith v. Chanel, Inc., 222
Smith v. City of Little Rock, 775
Smith v. Cutler, 368
Smith v. Fair Employment & Housing Commission, 429
Solomon R. Guggenheim Foundation v. Lubell, 196
Sommer v. Kridel, 488
Southern Burlington County NAACP v. Township of Mount Laurel, 806, 813
Southwind Exploration, LLC v. Street Abstract Co., 567
Sowers v. Forest Hills Subdivision, 755
Spiller v. Mackereth, 385
Spur Industries, Inc. v. Del E. Webb Development Co., 748
Stambovsky v. Ackley, 532
Steinberg v. Columbia Pictures Industries, Inc., 254

Stephens, Partain & Cunningham v. Hollis, 639
St. Louis County National Bank v. Fielder, 549
Stop the Beach Renourishment, Inc. v. Florida Department of Environmental Protection, 929
Stoyanoff, State ex rel. v. Berkeley, 793
Strawn v. Canuso, 538
Suitum v. Tahoe Regional Planning Agency, 910
Sullivan v. Hernandez, 427
Swanner v. Anchorage Equal Rights Commission, 429
Tahoe-Sierra Preservation Council, Inc. v. Tahoe Regional Planning Agency, 927
Talk to Me Products, Inc. v. Larami Corp., 285
Taylor v. Northam, 722
Teller v. McCoy, 466
Tenhet v. Boswell, 370
Texas Department of Housing and Community Affairs v. Inclusive Communities Project, Inc., 420, 427
Thaler v. Vidal, 255
Thompson v. Whinnery, 661
Thomsen v. Greve, 749
Tiner v. Johnson, 311
Tioga Coal Co. v. Supermarkets General Corp., 114
Tranfield v. Arcuni-English, 65
Trip Associates, Inc. v. Mayor and City Council of Baltimore, 769
Turner v. Freed, 409
Two Pesos, Inc. v. Taco Cabana, Inc., 277
Tyler v. Hennepin County, 863
Union Cemetery Burial Soc'y of North Smithfield v. Foisy, 97
United Drug Co. v. Theodore Rectanus Co., 271
U.S. Patent & Trademark Office v. Booking.com B. V., 276
Van Ness v. Pacard, 90
Van Sloun v. Agans Brothers, Inc., 486
Van Valkenburgh v. Lutz, 99, 107
Vasquez v. Vasquez, 547
Vernon Township Volunteer Fire Department, Inc. v. Connor, 715
Village Commons, LLC v. Marion County Prosecutor's Office, 459
Villar, In re, 357
Von Saher v. Norton Simon Museum of Art at Pasadena, 197
Wade v. Jobe, 461
Waldorff Ins. & Bonding, Inc. v. Eglin Nat'l Bank, 598
Walker Rogge, Inc. v. Chelsea Title & Guaranty Co., 605
Walling v. Przybylo, 118
Wansley v. First Nat'l Bank of Vicksburg, 636
Warner-Jenkinson Co., Inc. v. Hilton Davis Chemical Co., 269
Warsaw v. Chicago Metallic Ceilings, Inc., 668
Washington State Grange v. Brandt, 351
Washington Wildlife Preservation, Inc. v. State of Minnesota, 689

Watchtower Bible and Tract Society v. Village of Stratton, 62
Waterman, Estate of, 125
West v. Louisville Gas & Electric Co., 682
Westwood Pharmaceuticals, Inc. v. National Fuel Gas Distribution Corp., 846
Wetzel v. Glen St. Andrew Living Cmty., LLC, 429
White Bear Lake Restoration Association v. Minnesota Department of Natural Resources, 828
White v. Auger, 327
White v. Brown, 306
White v. Samsung Electronics America, Inc., 15, 19
White v. Smyth, 386
White v. Western Title Insurance Co., 604
W.H.V., Inc. v. Associates Hous. Finance, LLC, 89
Wiesel v. 310 East 46 LLC, 468
Willard v. First Church of Christ, Scientist, 648
Williston Park v. 280 Hillside Ave. Rest. Corp., 773
Willson v. City of Bel-Nor, 800
Windsor, United States v., 409
Winecellar Farm, Inc. v. Hibbard, 311
Wishart, Estate of, 83
Woodrick v. Wood, 314
Woo v. Smart, 207
Wyatt, In re Estate of, 531
Zaman v. Felton, 624
Zambrotto v. Superior Lumber Co., 97
Zaschak v. Traverse Corp., 538
Zephier v. Agate, 178
Zimmer v. Sundell, 583

PROPERTY

A Contemporary Approach

SIXTH EDITION

Chapter 1

The Concept of Property

Look around you. Almost everything you see is owned by someone. In fact, life as we know it would be impossible without property. The book you are reading, the chair you are sitting on, the clothes you are wearing, the land surface underneath you, and the airspace which you occupy—all are governed by property rights.

As you begin to study property law, it is logical to ask two questions:

- Why do we recognize property?
- What is property?

The answers to these questions are closely intertwined. For example, the reasons *why* we recognize property influence *what* we consider to be property and vice versa. We begin to explore these questions in Chapter 1, but they raise fundamental themes that will recur throughout the entire book.

A. Why Recognize Property?

Suppose that a nut tree stands on top of a hill. Who owns the tree? It might be owned by the government as *public property* like a tree in a national park. It might be *private property*, that is, property owned by one or more private persons or businesses. Or perhaps the tree is not owned by anyone.

This course focuses on private property, which we will simply call "property." Our property law system is based on the concept that property is a human invention, not the result of divine gift or natural right. Thus, property exists only to the extent that it is recognized by the government, an approach called *legal positivism*. As the English philosopher Jeremy Bentham noted more than 200 years ago: "Before laws were made there was no property; take away laws, and property ceases." Because property is a human invention, it is necessarily based on reason. The justification for property is important because it determines the scope and extent of legally recognized property rights. Accordingly, *natural law theory*—the idea that certain rights naturally exist as a matter of fundamental justice regardless of government action—has little impact on modern property law.

Most people take property for granted, without questioning why it exists. In fact, if someone had asked you last week why our society recognizes private property, you might have had trouble coming up with a convincing answer. So, as a starting point, we will examine five theories that seek to justify the recognition of property rights. We will then explore how these theories apply to two specific cases.

1. Five Theories of Property

a. Protect First Possession

You are probably familiar with the adage: "first come, first serve." This concept is the heart of our first theory.

> ### Perspective and Analysis
>
> When the question arises as to why some people, rather than others, should own things, one of the issues which comes to mind is the question, "Who had it first?" The notion that being there first somehow justifies ownership rights is a venerable and persistent one. . . .
>
> **Lawrence C. Becker, Property Rights: Philosophic Foundations 24 (1977).**

The first possession approach offers a practical explanation for how unowned things become property. Suppose that our hypothetical nut tree is unowned. A is sitting under the tree when several nuts fall off, and he grabs them. Under this approach, A owns the nuts simply because he was the first person to take possession of them.

In a setting where resources were plentiful but people were few—like the early United States—this first-in-time approach accurately describes how unowned things came to be owned. Particularly during the nineteenth century, property rights in water, oil and gas, wild animals, and other natural resources were often allocated to the first possessor. The first-in-time concept has less relevance today because almost every tangible thing is already owned by someone, but you will see its lingering influence throughout the course. For example, all of us use this principle in everyday life. A parking space on a public street, a seat in a movie theater, or a place in a long line—all are allocated through an implicit first-in-time system.

Yet most scholars conclude that the first possession approach does not adequately justify property as a general matter. It describes *how* property rights arose, but not *why* it makes sense for society to recognize those rights. *See, e.g.,* Carol M. Rose, *Possession as the Origin of Property*, 52 U. Chi. L. Rev. 73 (1985).

b. Encourage Labor

Writing in the late 1600s, John Locke reasoned that each person was entitled to the property produced through his own labor. Assuming an unlimited supply of natural resources, Locke argued that when a person "mixed" his own labor (which he owned) with natural resources (which were unowned), he acquired property rights in the mixture. Returning to our hypothetical tree, assume that B picks all the nuts off the tree, puts them in a bag, and takes them home to eat. Under the labor theory, the nuts are now B's property because she acquired them through her labor. *See* Eric R. Claeys, *Labor, Exclusion, and Flourishing in Property Law*, 95 N.C. L. Rev. 413 (2017).

Labor theory has profoundly influenced American property law, as you will see throughout the course. But even at this early stage, you should consider its potential limitations. For example, how does labor theory apply in a modern legal system where almost everything is already owned? Hint: one potential application may be in the realm of newly created property, such as copyrights and patents.

> **Perspective and Analysis**
>
> To Americans [in the 1700s] . . . the writings of John Locke made a good deal of sense. Locke celebrated the common individual, arguing he possessed natural rights that arose in advance of any social order and trumped even the powers of the King. Preeminent among these individual rights was the right to property, which Locke justified by way of his well-known labor theory. As Locke interpreted the Bible, God originally gave the Earth to humankind collectively, as property in common, yet any individual who wanted could seize a thing from the common stock, including land, and make it his own simply by mixing his labor with it. Before the labor was added, the thing had no value. Once the labor was mixed in, value arose and the thing became private property.
>
> Locke's labor theory of property made particularly good sense in North America, more so than it did in England. Frontier colonists could easily see how labor was the key ingredient in the creation of value. Moreover, because land was plentiful, one person's occupation of land did not deny his neighbor the chance to gain land too. Back in England, a person had to buy property or inherit it, and one person's occupation of land did deny another the chance to use it. . . .
>
> **Eric T. Freyfogle, *Owning the Land: Four Contemporary Narratives*, 13 J. Land Use & Envtl. L. 279, 281–82 (1998).**

c. Maximize Societal Happiness

Under traditional utilitarian theory, as developed by Jeremy Bentham, we recognize property in order to maximize the overall happiness of society. Thus, it is a *means* toward an *end*. We distribute and define property rights in a manner that best promotes the welfare of all citizens—not simply those who own property. Thus, classic utilitarian theory would say that C owns our hypothetical nut tree not solely in order to benefit C, but because recognizing C's title will promote the welfare of all members of society. For example, if C's ownership is protected, C is able to use the nut tree in a manner that best serves the common good—perhaps harvesting the wild nuts for sale in the local market, using lumber from the tree to make valuable products, or preserving the tree to protect environmental values. Ownership gives C the security that he needs to use the tree effectively.

The law and economics variant of utilitarianism has powerfully affected modern property law scholarship. Under this approach, property is seen as an efficient method of allocating valuable resources in order to maximize one particular facet of societal happiness: wealth, typically measured in dollars.

> **Make the Connection**
>
> The law and economics approach views land only as a commodity in commerce, like any other raw material. Accordingly, it tends to ignore the non-monetary benefits of environmental preservation. In Chapter 12, you will explore an alternative view—an ecological approach to land ownership.

> **Perspective and Analysis**
>
> In order for an economy to reach its full potential, that is, to achieve an optimal level of production, there are three basic features which its system of property rights must have: universality, exclusivity, and transferability. The first requirement, universality, means that all valuable, scarce resources must be owned by someone. This requirement becomes obvious when illustrated with an example. Suppose that, as in India, cows were sacred and could not be killed or used for commercial purposes or consumption in any form.... An economy which is prevented from using cows and cow by-products certainly would be smaller than the same economy where cows could be so used....
>
> The second requirement is exclusivity. If an owner is unable to exclude others from the use and enjoyment of the property, then the owner has no incentive to improve the property.... Suppose an owner owned a piece of property which produces nothing. If the owner worked the land and planted crops, in time the land could produce a great crop of substantial value. But if the owner does not have the right to exclude others from the land, then ... marauding opportunists would simply wait until the crop was ready to be harvested, and come and take the fruits of the hard-working owner's land and labor. No owner would make such an undertaking....
>
> The final requirement for an optimal economy is transferability of property.... Suppose that there are two adjoining lots. The first lot has a restaurant which is very popular. The second lot has a small shack where

> the owner of the second lot lives. The restaurant owner would like to buy or lease the lot from the shack dweller. In a system which only allows exclusive ownership, the shack dweller cannot sell or lease his land. In fact, the shack dweller can never leave, because he cannot buy or rent another dwelling either. Everyone is stuck where they are with what they have. No gains from trade can be made....
>
> **Howard Gensler, *Property Law as an Optimal Economic Foundation*, 35 Washburn L.J. 50, 51–52 (1995).**

Under the law and economics approach, property exists to ensure that owners use resources in an *efficient* manner—that is, in a manner which maximizes economic value defined as a person's willingness to pay. As you would expect, this approach is more complex than we can cover in an introductory section. You will study more aspects of law and economics theory later in the course.

d. Ensure Democracy

Civic republican theory posits that property facilitates democracy. During the 1700s, elections to the British House of Commons were still affected by so-called "rotten boroughs"—electoral districts that contained only a handful of voters. Typically, these voters were tenants on farm land owned by a local patron who could control their votes, leading to sham elections. In contrast, Thomas Jefferson and others envisioned the new United States as a nation of free yeoman farmers who owned their own lands and could thus exercise the independent political judgment that was vital for true democracy. (In fact, at one time only property owners were eligible to vote in most states.) Under this approach, we would recognize D's ownership of our hypothetical nut tree and the surrounding land because this provides D with the economic security necessary to make political decisions that serve the common good.

> **Perspective and Analysis**
>
> The most fundamental point about the relationship between property and democracy is that a right to own private property has an important and salutary effect on the citizens' relationship with the state and—equally important—on their understanding of that relationship.... Personal security and personal independence from the government are guaranteed in a system in which rights of ownership are protected through public institutions.
>
> This theme has played a large role in republican thought. In the republican view, the status of the citizen implies a measure of independence from government power.... In fact, the republican tradition, read in the light of modern understandings, argues not for an abolition of private property, but instead for a system that attempts to ensure that everyone has some....

> A central point here is that in a state in which private property does not exist, citizens are dependent on the good will of government officials, almost on a daily basis.... They come to the state as supplicants or beggars rather than as rightholders. Any challenge to the state may be stifled or driven underground by virtue of the fact that serious challenges could result in the withdrawal of the goods that give people basic security. A right to private property, free from government interference, is in this sense a necessary basis for a democracy....
>
> **Cass R. Sunstein, *On Property and Constitutionalism*, 14 Cardozo L. Rev. 907, 914–15 (1993).**

The Supreme Court struck the same theme in *Murr v. Wisconsin*, 582 U.S. 383, 394 (2017) when it observed that "[p]roperty rights are necessary to preserve freedom...."

Civic republican theory is less prominent today than it was in the 1700s, in part because most citizens obtain economic security from wages earned at a job, not from farming their own land. Still, many scholars suggest that giving each person a "stake in society" through property ownership will provide political and social benefits to all.

e. Facilitate Personal Development

Based on the work of German theorist Georg Hegel, personhood theory argues that property is necessary for an individual's personal development. Under this view, each person has a close emotional connection to certain tangible things, which virtually become part of one's self—such as family photos, love letters, or perhaps a home. Suppose that E's family has owned our hypothetical nut tree for four generations; as a child, E literally grew up under the tree. Thus, E venerates the tree as almost an extension of herself. Under personhood theory, E's rights in the tree should merit special protection.

> ### Perspective and Analysis
>
> ... The premise underlying the personhood perspective is that to achieve proper self-development—to be a person—an individual needs some control over resources in the external environment. The necessary assurances of control take the form of property rights....
>
> Most people possess certain objects they feel are almost part of themselves. These objects are closely bound up with personhood because they are part of the way we constitute ourselves as continuing personal entities in the world. They may be as different as people are different, but some common examples might be a wedding ring, a portrait, an heirloom, or a house.
>
> One may gauge the strength or significance of someone's relationship with an object by the kind of pain that would be occasioned by its loss. On this

> view, an object is closely related to one's personhood if its loss causes pain that cannot be relieved by the object's replacement.... For instance, if a wedding ring is stolen from a jeweler, insurance proceeds can reimburse the jeweler, but if a wedding ring is stolen from a loving wearer, the price of a replacement will not restore the status quo—perhaps no amount of money can do so....
>
> Once we admit that a person can be bound up with an external "thing" in some constitutive sense, we can argue that by virtue of this connection the person should be accorded broad liberty with respect to control over that "thing."...
>
> **Margaret Jane Radin,** ***Property and Personhood,*** **34 Stan. L. Rev. 957, 957–61, 1013–15 (1982).**

All other things being equal, Professor Radin suggests that a right to personhood property should be given priority over a conflicting claim by the owner of non-personhood property. For example, she argues that a tenant's right to a rented apartment should be seen as personhood property. From the tenant's perspective, the apartment is a home; from the landlord's side, it is typically viewed in non-personhood terms as an investment. Accordingly, Radin advocates expanding the legal rights of residential tenants.

f. Conclusion

All five theories help form the foundation of American property law. But it is important to understand that no one theory is accepted as the only justification for property. Our property law system reflects a blend of different approaches, including these theories and others which you will encounter later in the book. Indeed, even these five theories overlap with each other.

---

2. Two Stories: The Fox and the Celebrity

We begin over 200 years ago, when the United States was a comparatively new nation, stretching from the Atlantic Ocean to the Rocky Mountains. With development clustered along the Atlantic Coast, over 95% of the country was a vast wilderness. Natural resources were abundant, and the human population was small. As you would expect, these conditions influenced the development of American property law.

Our first case concerns an unlikely dispute, set in the wilderness of early New York. Who owns the fox? And why?

Pierson v. Post

Supreme Court of New York

3 Cai. R. 175 (1805)

This was an action of trespass on the case commenced in a justice's court, by the present defendant against the now plaintiff.

The declaration stated that Post, being in possession of certain dogs and hounds under his command, did, "upon a certain wild and uninhabited, unpossessed and waste land, called the beach, find and start one of those noxious beasts called a fox," and whilst there hunting, chasing and pursuing the same with his dogs and hounds, and when in view thereof, Pierson, well knowing the fox was so hunted and pursued, did, in the sight of Post, to prevent his catching the same, kill and carry it off. A verdict having been rendered for the plaintiff below, the defendant there sued out a *certiorari*, and now assigned for error, that the declaration and the matters therein contained were not sufficient in law to maintain an action.

Red fox
Click here for larger photo

TOMPKINS, J. delivered the opinion of the court.

. . . The question submitted by the counsel in this cause for our determination is, whether Lodowick Post, by the pursuit with his hounds in the manner alleged in his declaration, acquired such a right to, or property in, the fox, as will sustain an action against Pierson for killing and taking him away?

The cause was argued with much ability by the counsel on both sides, and presents for our decision a novel and nice question. It is admitted that a fox is an animal *ferae naturae*, and that property in such animals is acquired by occupancy only. These admissions narrow the discussion to the simple question of what acts amount to occupancy, applied to acquiring right to wild animals?

If we have recourse to the ancient writers upon general principles of law, the judgment below is obviously erroneous. Justinian's Institutes, lib. 2. tit. 1. s. 13. and Fleta, lib. 3. c. 2. p. 175. adopt the principle, that pursuit alone vests no property or right in the huntsman; and that even pursuit, accompanied with wounding, is equally ineffectual for that purpose, unless the animal be actually taken. The same principle is recognised by Bracton, lib. 2. c. 1. p. 8.

Chapter 1 The Concept of Property

Puffendorf, lib. 4. c. 6. s. 2. and 10. defines occupancy of beasts *ferae naturae*, to be the actual corporal possession of them, and Bynkershoek is cited as coinciding in this definition. It is indeed with hesitation that Puffendorf affirms that a wild beast mortally wounded, or greatly maimed, cannot be fairly intercepted by another, whilst the pursuit of the person inflicting the wound continues. The foregoing authorities are decisive to show that mere pursuit gave Post no legal right to the fox, but that he became the property of Pierson, who intercepted and killed him.

> **FYI**
>
> Justinian was the Roman emperor from 527–565 A.D. By this time, the western part of the empire (including the city of Rome) had been lost. Justinian ruled over the eastern part of the empire from his capital in Constantinople. One of his major accomplishments was a complete revision of Roman law. Justinian's Institutes, cited here by the majority, was part of this effort. It was essentially a textbook that summarized legal principles.

It therefore only remains to inquire whether there are any contrary principles, or authorities, to be found in other books, which ought to induce a different decision. Most of the cases which have occurred in England, relating to property in wild animals, have either been discussed and decided upon the principles of their positive statute regulations, or have arisen between the huntsman and the owner of the land upon which beasts *ferae naturae* have been apprehended; the former claiming them by title of occupancy, and the latter *ratione soli*. Little satisfactory aid can, therefore, be derived from the English reporters.

> **It's Latin to Me**
>
> *Ferae naturae* means "wild animals." *Ratione soli* or "by reason of the soil" was an English doctrine that gave a landowner title to the natural resources (such as wild animals) found on his land.

Barbeyrac, in his notes on Puffendorf, does not accede to the definition of occupancy by the latter, but, on the contrary, affirms, that actual bodily seizure is not, in all cases, necessary to constitute possession of wild animals. He does not, however, *describe* the acts which, according to his ideas, will amount to an appropriation of such animals to private use, so as to exclude the claims of all other persons, by title of occupancy, to the same animals; and he is far from averring that pursuit alone is sufficient for that purpose. To a certain extent, and as far as Barbeyrac appears to me to go, his objections to Puffendorf's definition of occupancy are reasonable and correct. That is to say, that actual bodily seizure is not indispensable to acquire right to, or possession of, wild beasts; but that, on the contrary, the mortal wounding of such beasts, by one not abandoning his pursuit, may, with the utmost propriety, be deemed possession of him; since, thereby, the pursuer manifests an unequivocal intention of appropriating the animal to his individual use, has deprived him of his natural liberty, and brought him within his certain control. So also, encompassing and securing such animals with nets and toils, or otherwise intercepting them in such a manner as to deprive them of their natural liberty, and render escape impossible, may justly be deemed to give possession of them to those persons who, by their industry and labour, have used such means of apprehending them. . . . The case now under consideration is one of mere pursuit, and presents no circumstances or acts which can bring it within the definition of occupancy. . . .

We are the more readily inclined to confine possession or occupancy of beasts *ferae naturae*, within the limits prescribed by the learned authors above cited, for the sake of certainty, and preserving peace and order in society. If the first seeing, starting, or pursuing such animals, without having so wounded, circumvented or ensnared them, so as to deprive them of their natural liberty, and subject them to the control of their pursuer, should afford the basis of actions against others for intercepting and killing them, it would prove a fertile source of quarrels and litigation.

However uncourteous or unkind the conduct of Pierson towards Post, in this instance, may have been, yet his act was productive of no injury or damage for which a legal remedy can be applied. We are of opinion the judgment below was erroneous, and ought to be reversed.

LIVINGSTON, J. [dissenting]

> **FYI**
>
> Two years after *Pierson* was decided, the author of the majority opinion, Justice Tompkins, was elected the Governor of New York. Tompkins later served as Vice President of the United States under President Monroe from 1817 to 1825. President Jefferson eventually appointed dissenting Justice Livingston to the United States Supreme Court, where he served until 1832. Click here to see pictures of Justices Tompkins and Livingston.

My opinion differs from that of the court. Of six exceptions, taken to the proceedings below, all are abandoned except the third, which reduces the controversy to a single question.

Whether a person who, with his own hounds, starts and hunts a fox on waste and uninhabited ground, and is on the point of seizing his prey, acquires such an interest in the animal, as to have a right of action against another, who in view of the huntsman and his dogs in full pursuit, and with knowledge of the chase, shall kill and carry him away?

This is a knotty point, and should have been submitted to the arbitration of sportsmen, without poring over Justinian, Fleta, Bracton, Puffendorf, Locke, Barbeyrac, or Blackstone, all of whom have been cited; they would have had no difficulty in coming to a prompt and correct conclusion. In a court thus constituted, the skin and carcass of poor *reynard* would have been properly disposed of, and a precedent set, interfering with no usage or custom which the experience of ages has sanctioned, and which must be so well known to every votary of *Diana*. But the parties have referred the question to our judgment, and we must dispose of it as well as we can, from the partial lights we possess, leaving to a higher tribunal, the correction of any mistake which we may be so unfortunate as to make. By the pleadings it is admitted that a fox is a "wild and noxious beast." Both parties have regarded him, as the law of nations does a pirate . . . and . . . the memory of the deceased has not been spared. His depredations on farmers and on barn yards, have not been forgotten; and to put him to death wherever found, is allowed to be meritorious, and of public benefit. Hence it follows, that our decision should have in view the greatest possible encouragement to the destruction of an animal, so cunning and ruthless in his career. But who would keep a pack of hounds; or what gentleman, at the sound of the horn, and at peep of day, would mount his steed, and for hours together . . . pursue the windings of this wily quadruped, if, just as night came on, and his stratagems and strength were nearly exhausted, a saucy intruder, who had not shared in the honours or labours of the chase, were permitted to come in at the death, and bear away in triumph the object of pursuit? Whatever Justinian may have thought of the matter, it must be recollected that his code was compiled many hundred years ago, and it would be very hard indeed, at the distance of so many centuries, not to have a right to establish a rule for ourselves. In his day, we read of no order of men who made it a business, in the language of the declaration in this cause, "with hounds and dogs to find, start, pursue, hunt, and chase," these animals, and that, too, without any other motive than the preservation of *Roman* poultry. . . . If any thing, therefore, in the digests or pandects shall appear to militate against the defendant in error, who, on this occasion, was the foxhunter, we have only to say *tempora mutantur*; and if men themselves change with the times, why should not laws also undergo an alteration?

> **What's That?**
>
> *Arbitration* is a method of resolving disputes privately, outside of the judicial system. Typically, the disputing parties select one or more neutral third parties to hear and decide their case, and agree to be bound by the outcome. Arbitration is usually quicker, cheaper, and less formal than regular litigation.

> **It's Latin to Me**
>
> *Tempora mutantur* literally means "times change." In context, Justice Livingston is asserting that laws should change as times change.

It may be expected, however, by the learned counsel, that more particular notice be taken of their authorities. I have examined them all, and feel great difficulty in determining, whether to acquire dominion over a thing, before in common, it be sufficient that we barely see it, or know where it is, or wish for it, or make a declaration of our will respecting it; or whether, in the case of wild beasts, setting a trap, or lying in wait, or starting, or pursuing, be enough; or if an actual wounding, or killing, or bodily tact and occupation be necessary. Writers on general law, who have favoured us with their speculations on these points, differ on them all; but, great as is the diversity of sentiment among them, some conclusion must be adopted on the question immediately before us. . . .

Now, as we are without any municipal regulations of our own . . . we are at liberty to adopt . . . the learned conclusion of Barbeyrac, that property in animals *ferae naturae* may be acquired without bodily touch or manucaption, provided the pursuer be within reach, or have a *reasonable* prospect (which certainly existed here) of taking, what he has *thus* discovered an intention of converting to his own use.

When we reflect also that the interest of our husbandmen, the most useful of men in any community, will be advanced by the destruction of a beast so pernicious and incorrigible, we cannot greatly err, in saying, that a pursuit like the present, through waste and unoccupied lands, and which must inevitably and speedily have terminated in corporal possession, or bodily *seisin*, confers such a right to the object of it, as to make any one a wrongdoer, who shall interfere and shoulder the spoil. The justice's judgment ought, therefore, in my opinion, to be affirmed.

Points for Discussion

a. **Why Did Post Sue?**

If successful, Post would have recovered damages equal to the fair market value of the fox carcass. The carcass was worth perhaps four shillings, but local legend says that the parties spent over 1,000 pounds on the case—more than 5,000 times the amount at issue. Bethany R. Berger, *It's Not About the Fox: The Untold History of* Pierson v. Post, 55 Duke L.J. 1089, 1130, 1133 (2006). The dissent's suggestion that Pierson violated a "custom which the experience of ages has sanctioned" may provide a useful clue. Or perhaps personhood theory is helpful.

b. **A Case of First Impression**

The principal sources of law in our legal system, in priority, are (1) constitutions, (2) statutes, and (3) reported cases. But neither the majority nor the dissent relies on any of these key sources. The reason for this omission is simple. In 1805, the legal system of the young United States was relatively undeveloped, so there were no binding sources of law that directly resolved this particular case. Rather, it was a *case of first impression*, a situation where a court has considerably more latitude to reach an appropriate decision. Both the majority and the dissent rely on various *treatises*—summaries of the law written by venerable legal scholars such as Barbeyrac, Fleta, and Puffendorf—which may be persuasive to a court, but are not binding. Which side uses legal authority most persuasively?

c. First Possession

Pierson is a leading example of the first possession approach to property. Both sides agree that property rights in a wild animal are acquired by the first person to take possession of the animal, a principle called the *rule of capture*. So what issue did the parties differ on? And would it have made any difference if Post owned the land where Pierson killed the fox? Partly influenced by *Pierson*, later American courts adopted a first possession approach to allocating property rights in a variety of natural resources. For example, nineteenth-century judges reasoned that oil and natural gas were like wild animals because they moved underground in unknown ways in response to the laws of nature; therefore, by analogy to cases such as *Pierson*, ownership in such a resource should be given to the first person who physically possessed it. Many states still follow this approach. *See, e.g., Briggs v. Southwestern Energy Production Co.*, 224 A.3d 334 (Pa. 2020) (rule of capture applies to natural gas extracted by fracking). What are the benefits and costs of adopting a first possession approach to ownership of resources like wild animals, oil, or natural gas?

d. When Does Labor Matter?

Both Post and Pierson labored to catch the elusive fox: Post chased, and Pierson killed. Note that Post was aided in his chase by "dogs and hounds"—presumably dogs that were specially trained for hunting—so we might say that Post's labor included his prior investment in hunting technology. How should the case be resolved if we apply Locke's labor theory? And how much labor is needed? One scholar asks: "If I own a can of tomato juice and spill it in the sea so that its molecules . . . mingle evenly throughout the sea, do I thereby come to own the sea, or have I foolishly dissipated my tomato juice?" Robert Nozick, Anarchy, State and Utopia 175 (1974).

e. A Utilitarian Perspective

Both the majority and the dissent rely to some extent on public policies, which invoke the utilitarian approach. Which side makes the most convincing policy arguments? For example, the majority claims that its rule will benefit society in general by providing certainty. How so? To what extent are clear rules important in property law? *See* Carol M. Rose, *Crystals and Mud in Property Law*, 40 Stan. L. Rev. 577 (1988).

f. Civic Republican Theory?

There may be a thin strand of civic republican theory in the dissent's focus on protecting farmers' poultry from attacks by foxes. After all, the economic health of Jefferson's yeoman farmer was viewed by some as the keystone to effective democracy. The dissent argues for a rule that will provide "the greatest possible encouragement to the destruction" of foxes—and thereby promote American agriculture. Is the dissent's rule more effective than the majority's approach?

g. **Capture Hypotheticals**

Using the majority approach in *Pierson*, who holds title to the animals below?

> (1) Post shoots at a deer from a location 200 feet away; the shot grazes the deer's ear and temporarily stuns it. Pierson immediately snatches the deer and puts it in a large sack. Post arrives on the scene one minute later, while the deer is still stunned.
>
> (2) Motivated by environmental concerns, Post nets a wild rabbit, paints "Property of Post" on it, and then allows it to run free. Pierson shoots and kills the rabbit.
>
> (3) Post's dogs chase a fox into a shallow cave. But before Post can get to the cave, Pierson shoots the fox and mortally wounds it. Post arrives at the cave two minutes later.
>
> (4) Post's cow strays onto unowned land. Pierson finds the cow, places a rope around its neck, and leads it back to his own farm. Two days later, Post discovers the cow on Pierson's farm.

h. **Aftermath of *Pierson***

Today the "waste land" involved in *Pierson* is part of Southampton, New York—one of the nation's wealthiest resort communities. And although Pierson and Post are long dead, the famous case that bears their names lives on in American law: "Scholars cite it to illustrate everything from discrimination against transgendered persons to rights in fugitive home run balls. Outside the ivory tower, courts and lawyers use it to argue for contested forms of property from groundwater aquifers to the America's Cup trophy." Bethany R. Berger, *It's Not About the Fox*, supra at 1091–92.

Our second dispute concerns Vanna White, co-star of the television game show *Wheel of Fortune*. In many ways, *White* is the antithesis of *Pierson*. It arises almost two centuries later, in a high-tech industry located on the opposite side of the country, and concerns a type of intangible property—a celebrity's right of publicity. Yet the same perspectives on property that we explored in *Pierson* are key to understanding this quite different case. Is White entitled to control the use of her name and likeness? Why?

White v. Samsung Electronics America, Inc.

United States Court of Appeals, Ninth Circuit

971 F.2d 1395 (1992), *cert. denied*, 508 U.S. 951 (1993)

GOODWIN, SENIOR CIRCUIT JUDGE.

This case involves a promotional "fame and fortune" dispute. In running a particular advertisement without Vanna White's permission, defendants Samsung Electronics America, Inc. (Samsung) and David Deutsch Associates, Inc. (Deutsch) attempted to capitalize on White's fame to enhance their fortune. White sued, alleging infringement of various intellectual property rights, but the district court granted summary judgment in favor of the defendants. We affirm in part, reverse in part, and remand.

> **Practice Pointer**
>
> If the material facts are undisputed, a case can be resolved without a trial through a motion for *summary judgment*. Federal Rule of Civil Procedure 56(a) provides that summary judgment shall be granted if (a) "there is no genuine dispute as to any material fact" and (b) the party bringing the motion "is entitled to judgment as a matter of law."

> **FYI**
>
> Contestants on *Wheel of Fortune* have won over $200 million in prizes during the decades it has been on television. For more information about the program, including pictures of Vanna White, visit its website.

Plaintiff Vanna White is the hostess of "Wheel of Fortune," one of the most popular game shows in television history. An estimated forty million people watch the program daily. Capitalizing on the fame which her participation in the show has bestowed on her, White markets her identity to various advertisers.

The dispute in this case arose out of a series of advertisements prepared for Samsung by Deutsch. The series ran in at least half a dozen publications with widespread, and in some cases national, circulation. Each of the advertisements in the series followed the same theme. Each depicted a current item from popular culture and a Samsung electronic product. Each was set in the twenty-first century and conveyed the message that the Samsung product would still be in use by that time. By hypothesizing outrageous future outcomes for the cultural items, the ads created humorous effects. For example, one lampooned current popular notions of an unhealthy diet by depicting a raw steak with the caption: "Revealed to be health food. 2010 A.D." Another depicted irreverent "news"-show host Morton Downey Jr. in front of an American flag with the caption: "Presidential candidate. 2008 A.D."

The advertisement which prompted the current dispute was for Samsung videocassette recorders (VCRs). The ad depicted a robot, dressed in a wig, gown, and jewelry which Deutsch consciously selected to resemble White's hair and dress. The robot was posed next to a game board which is instantly recognizable as the Wheel of Fortune game show set, in a stance for which White is famous. The caption of the ad read: "Longest-running game show. 2012 A.D." Defendants referred to the ad as the "Vanna White" ad. Unlike the other celebrities used in the campaign, White neither consented to the ads nor was she paid.

Portion of Samsung ad
Click here for larger photo

Following the circulation of the robot ad, White sued Samsung and Deutsch in federal district court under: (1) California Civil Code § 3344; (2) the California common law right of publicity; and (3) § 43(a) of the Lanham Act, 15 U.S.C. § 1125(a). The district court granted summary judgment against White on each of her claims. White now appeals.

I. Section 3344

White first argues that the district court erred in rejecting her claim under section 3344. Section 3344(a) provides, in pertinent part, that "[a]ny person who knowingly uses another's name, voice, signature, photograph, or likeness, in any manner, . . . for purposes of advertising or selling, . . . without such person's prior consent . . . shall be liable for any damages sustained by the person or persons injured as a result thereof."

White argues that the Samsung advertisement used her "likeness" in contravention of section 3344. In *Midler v. Ford Motor Co.*, 849 F.2d 460 (9th Cir. 1988), this court rejected Bette Midler's section 3344 claim concerning a Ford television commercial in which a Midler "sound-alike" sang a song which Midler had made famous. In rejecting Midler's claim, this court noted that "[t]he defendants did not use Midler's name or anything else whose use is prohibited by the statute. The voice they used was [another person's], not hers. The term 'likeness' refers to a visual image not a vocal imitation." *Id.* at 463.

In this case, Samsung and Deutsch used a robot with mechanical features, and not, for example, a manikin molded to White's precise features. Without deciding for all purposes when a caricature or impressionistic resemblance might become a "likeness," we agree with the district court that the robot at issue here was not White's "likeness" within the meaning of section 3344. Accordingly, we affirm the court's dismissal of White's section 3344 claim.

II. *Right of Publicity*

White next argues that the district court erred in granting summary judgment to defendants on White's common law right of publicity claim. In *Eastwood v. Superior Court*, 149 Cal.App.3d 409, 198 Cal. Rptr. 342 (1983), the California court of appeal stated that the common law right of publicity cause of action "may be pleaded by alleging (1) the defendant's use of the plaintiff's identity; (2) the appropriation of plaintiff's name or likeness to defendant's advantage, commercially or otherwise; (3) lack of consent; and (4) resulting injury." . . . The district court dismissed White's claim for failure to satisfy *Eastwood's* second prong, reasoning that defendants had not appropriated White's "name or likeness" with their robot ad. We agree that the robot ad did not make use of White's name or likeness. However, the common law right of publicity is not so confined. . . .

The "name or likeness" formulation referred to in *Eastwood* originated not as an element of the right of publicity cause of action, but as a description of the types of cases in which the cause of action had been recognized. The source of this formulation is Prosser, *Privacy*, 48 Cal. L. Rev. 383, 401–07 (1960), one of the earliest and most enduring articulations of the common law right of publicity cause of action. In looking at the case law to that point, Prosser recognized that right of publicity cases involved one of two basic factual scenarios: name appropriation, and picture or other likeness appropriation. . . .

Even though Prosser focused on appropriations of name or likeness in discussing the right of publicity, he noted that "[i]t is not impossible that there might be appropriation of the plaintiff's identity, as by impersonation, without the use of either his name or his likeness, and that this would be an invasion of his right of privacy." . . . At the time Prosser wrote, he noted however, that "[n]o such case appears to have arisen." . . .

Since Prosser's early formulation, the case law has borne out his insight that the right of publicity is not limited to the appropriation of name or likeness. . . .

In *Midler*, this court held that, even though the defendants had not used Midler's name or likeness, Midler had stated a claim for violation of her California common law right of publicity because "the defendants . . . for their own profit in selling their product did appropriate part of her identity" by using a Midler sound-alike. *Id.* at 463–64.

In *Carson v. Here's Johnny Portable Toilets, Inc.*, 698 F.2d 831 (6th Cir. 1983), the defendant had marketed portable toilets under the brand name "Here's Johnny"—Johnny Carson's signature "Tonight Show" introduction—without Carson's permission. The district court had dismissed Carson's Michigan common law right of publicity claim because the defendants had not used Carson's "name or likeness." *Id.* at 835. In reversing the district court, the sixth circuit found "the district court's conception of the right of publicity . . . too narrow" and held that the right was implicated because the defendant had appropriated Carson's identity by using, *inter alia*, the phrase "Here's Johnny." *Id.* at 835–37.

These cases teach not only that the common law right of publicity reaches means of appropriation other than name or likeness, but that the specific means of appropriation are relevant only for determining whether the defendant has in fact appropriated the plaintiff's identity. The right of publicity does not require that appropriations of identity be accomplished through particular means to be actionable. It is noteworthy that the *Midler* and *Carson* defendants not only avoided using the plaintiff's name or likeness, but they also avoided appropriating the celebrity's voice, signature, and photograph. . . .

Although the defendants in these cases avoided the most obvious means of appropriating the plaintiffs' identities, each of their actions directly implicated the commercial interests which the right of publicity is designed to protect. As the *Carson* court explained:

> [t]he right of publicity has developed to protect the commercial interest of celebrities in their identities. The theory of the right is that a celebrity's identity can be valuable in the promotion of products, and the celebrity has an interest that may be protected from the unauthorized commercial exploitation of that identity. . . . If the celebrity's identity is commercially exploited, there has been an invasion of his right whether or not his "name or likeness" is used. *Carson*, 698 F.2d at 835.

It is not important *how* the defendant has appropriated the plaintiff's identity, but *whether* the defendant has done so. . . . *Midler* and *Carson* teach the impossibility of treating the right of publicity as guarding only against a laundry list of specific means of appropriating identity. A rule which says that the right of publicity can be infringed only through the use of nine different methods of appropriating identity merely challenges the clever advertising strategist to come up with the tenth.

Indeed, if we treated the means of appropriation as dispositive in our analysis of the right of publicity, we would not only weaken the right but effectively eviscerate it. The right would fail to protect those plaintiffs most in need of its protection. Advertisers use celebrities to promote their products. The more popular the celebrity, the greater the number of people who recognize her, and the greater the visibility for the product. The identities of the most popular celebrities are not only the most attractive for advertisers, but also the easiest to evoke without resorting to obvious means such as name, likeness, or voice. . . .

Viewed separately, the individual aspects of the advertisement in the present case say little. Viewed together, they leave little doubt about the celebrity the ad is meant to depict. The female-shaped robot is wearing a long gown, blond wig, and large jewelry. Vanna White dresses exactly like this at times, but so do many other women. The robot is in the process of turning a block letter on a game-board. Vanna White dresses like this while turning letters on a game-board but perhaps similarly attired Scrabble-playing women do this as well. The robot is standing on what looks to be the Wheel of Fortune game show set. Vanna White dresses like this, turns letters, and does this on the Wheel of Fortune game show. She is the only one. Indeed, defendants themselves referred to their ad as the "Vanna White" ad. We are not surprised.

Television and other media create marketable celebrity identity value. Considerable energy and ingenuity are expended by those who have achieved celebrity value to exploit it for profit. The law protects the celebrity's sole right to exploit this value whether the celebrity has achieved her fame out of rare ability, dumb luck, or a combination thereof. . . . Because White has alleged facts showing that Samsung and Deutsch had appropriated her identity, the district court erred by rejecting, on summary judgment, White's common law right of publicity claim. . . .

White v. Samsung Electronics America, Inc.

United States Court of Appeals, Ninth Circuit

989 F.2d 1512 (1993)

KOZINSKI, CIRCUIT JUDGE . . . dissenting from the order rejecting the suggestion for rehearing en banc.

I.

. . . Clint Eastwood doesn't want tabloids to write about him. Rudolf Valentino's heirs want to control his film biography. The Girl Scouts don't want their image soiled by association with certain activities. George Lucas wants to keep Strategic Defense Initiative fans from calling it "Star Wars." Pepsico doesn't want singers to use the word "Pepsi" in

> **What's That?**
>
> In a federal Court of Appeals, the case is heard by a panel of three judges. A party who loses an appeal may request that the case be reheard *en banc* (that is, by all the active judges of that court) in the hope of obtaining a different result.

their songs. Guy Lombardo wants an exclusive property right to ads that show big bands playing on New Year's Eve. Uri Geller thinks he should be paid for ads showing psychics bending metal through telekinesis. Paul Prudhomme, that household name, thinks the same about ads featuring corpulent bearded chefs. And scads of copyright holders see purple when their creations are made fun of.

Something very dangerous is going on here. Private property, including intellectual property, is essential to our way of life. It provides an incentive for investment and innovation; it stimulates the flourishing of our culture; it protects the moral entitlements of people to the fruits of their labors. But reducing too much to private property can be bad medicine. Private land, for instance, is far more useful if separated from other private land by public streets, roads and highways. Public parks, utility rights-of-way and sewers reduce the amount of land in private hands, but vastly enhance the value of the property that remains.

So too it is with intellectual property. Overprotecting intellectual property is as harmful as underprotecting it. Creativity is impossible without a rich public domain. Nothing today, likely nothing since we tamed fire, is genuinely new: Culture, like science and technology, grows by accretion, each new creator building on the works of those who came before. Overprotection stifles the very creative forces it's supposed to nurture.

The panel's opinion is a classic case of overprotection. Concerned about what it sees as a wrong done to Vanna White, the panel majority erects a property right of remarkable and dangerous breadth: Under the majority's opinion, it's now a tort for advertisers to *remind* the public of a celebrity. Not to use a celebrity's name, voice, signature or likeness; not to imply the celebrity endorses a product; but simply to evoke the celebrity's image in the public's mind. This Orwellian notion withdraws far more from the public domain than prudence and common sense allow. . . . It raises serious First Amendment problems. It's bad law, and it deserves a long, hard second look. . . .

III.

. . . The majority isn't, in fact, preventing the "evisceration" of Vanna White's existing rights; it's creating a new and much broader property right, a right unknown in California law. It's replacing the existing balance between the interests of the celebrity and those of the public by a different balance, one substantially more favorable to the celebrity. Instead of having an exclusive right in her name, likeness, signature or voice, every famous person now has an exclusive right to *anything that reminds the viewer of her*. After all, that's all Samsung did: It used an inanimate object to remind people of White, to "evoke [her identity]." 971 F.2d at 1399.

> **Food for Thought**
>
> Is Judge Kozinski right in concluding that "every famous person now has an exclusive right to *anything that reminds the viewer of her*"? If so, what are the implications of this right?

Consider how sweeping this new right is. What is it about the ad that makes people think of White? It's not the robot's wig, clothes or jewelry; there must be ten million blond women (many of them quasi-famous) who wear dresses and jewelry like White's. It's that the robot is posed near the "Wheel of Fortune" game board. Remove the game board from the ad, and no one would think of Vanna White. . . . But once you include the game board, anybody standing beside it—a brunette woman, a man wearing women's clothes, a monkey in a wig and gown—would evoke White's image, precisely the way the robot did. It's the "Wheel of Fortune" set, not the robot's face or dress or jewelry that evokes White's image. The panel is giving White an exclusive right not in what she looks like or who she is, but in what she does for a living.[18]

This is entirely the wrong place to strike the balance. Intellectual property rights aren't free: They're imposed at the expense of future creators and of the public at large. Where would we be if Charles Lindbergh had an exclusive right in the concept of a heroic solo aviator? If Arthur Conan Doyle had gotten a copyright in the idea of the detective story, or Albert Einstein had patented the theory of relativity? If every author and celebrity had been given the right to keep people from mocking them or their work? Surely this would have made the world poorer, not richer, culturally as well as economically. . . .

The intellectual property right created by the panel here . . . impoverishes the public domain, to the detriment of future creators and the public at large. Instead of well-defined, limited characteristics such as name, likeness or voice, advertisers will now have to cope with vague claims of "appropriation of identity," claims often made by people with a wholly exaggerated sense of their own fame and significance. . . . Future Vanna Whites might not get the chance to create their personae, because their employers may fear some celebrity will claim the persona is too similar to her own. The public will be robbed of parodies of celebrities, and our culture will be deprived of the valuable safety valve that parody and mockery create.

Moreover, consider the moral dimension, about which the panel majority seems to have gotten so exercised. Saying Samsung "appropriated" something of White's begs the question: *Should* White have the exclusive right to something as broad and amorphous as her "identity"? Samsung's ad didn't simply copy White's schtick—like all parody, it created something new. True, Samsung did it to make money, but White does whatever she does to make money, too; the majority talks of "the difference between fun and profit," 971 F.2d at 1401, but in the entertainment industry fun *is* profit. Why is Vanna White's right to exclusive for-profit use of her persona—a

---

[18] Once the right of publicity is extended beyond specific physical characteristics, this will become a recurring problem: Outside name, likeness and voice, the things that most reliably remind the public of celebrities are the actions or roles they're famous for. A commercial with an astronaut setting foot on the moon would evoke the image of Neil Armstrong. Any masked man on horseback would remind people (over a certain age) of Clayton Moore. And any number of songs—"My Way," "Yellow Submarine," "Like a Virgin," "Beat It," "Michael, Row the Boat Ashore," to name only a few—instantly evoke an image of the person or group who made them famous, regardless of who is singing. . . .

persona that might not even be her own creation, but that of a writer, director or producer—superior to Samsung's right to profit by creating its own inventions? . . .

[I]t may seem unfair that much of the fruit of a creator's labor may be used by others without compensation. But this is not some unforeseen byproduct of our intellectual property system; it is the system's very essence. Intellectual property law assures authors the right to their original expression, but encourages others to build freely on the ideas that underlie it. This result is neither unfair nor unfortunate: It is the means by which intellectual property law advances the progress of science and art. We give authors certain exclusive rights, but in exchange we get a richer public domain. The majority ignores this wise teaching, and all of us are the poorer for it. . . .

VII.

For better or worse, we *are* the Court of Appeals for the Hollywood Circuit. Millions of people toil in the shadow of the law we make, and much of their livelihood is made possible by the existence of intellectual property rights. But much of their livelihood—and much of the vibrancy of our culture—also depends on the existence of other intangible rights: The right to draw ideas from a rich and varied public domain, and the right to mock, for profit as well as fun, the cultural icons of our time.

In the name of avoiding the "evisceration" of a celebrity's rights in her image, the majority diminishes the rights of copyright holders and the public at large. In the name of fostering creativity, the majority suppresses it. Vanna White and those like her have been given something they never had before, and they've been given it at our expense. I cannot agree.

Points for Discussion

a. **Property Theory Revisited**

Consider again the five theories of property discussed earlier in this chapter. To what extent do these theories justify recognizing the right of publicity as a *general* matter? Notice that although *White* is a federal case, it relies on state law to define the right of publicity. Why? Under our federal system of government, state law generally determines what constitutes property. (This broad rule is subject, of course, to various exceptions; for example, federal law governs copyrights and patents.) Predictably, states often differ in defining property. For example, almost half of the states do not recognize the right of publicity as property. Why not?

b. **How Much Property?**

Law and economics theory endorses a property law system where every valuable resource is owned by someone. While agreeing that "private property . . . is essential to our way of life," Judge Kozinski cautions in his *White* dissent that "reducing too much to private property can be bad medicine." To what extent do these views conflict? How do our five theories bear on the question of how much private property is appropriate?

c. **Rights in Conflict**

Defining the *scope* of property rights in particular situations is often difficult, as *White* illustrates. California law clearly recognized the right of publicity as a general matter. The question was the scope of that right in a *specific* context—whether it should restrict conduct that merely reminds people of a celebrity. Judge Kozinski's dissent implies that a decision recognizing White's right on these facts would injure future creators and the public at large. How do the five visions of property help us define the appropriate scope of White's right? Which side makes the most convincing arguments here, the main opinion or the dissent?

d. **Dead Celebrities: From Einstein to Elvis**

In light of the different theories of property, consider what limits should exist on the right of publicity. For example, one question is whether the right of publicity should survive the celebrity's death. The estates of dead celebrities ranging from Elvis Presley to Marilyn Monroe have profited from agreements allowing advertisers to use their names and likenesses. For example, Albert Einstein's name and likeness generate over $12,000,000 each year. Is such a post-mortem right of publicity appropriate, considering our five theories? The states that recognize the right of publicity are divided on whether it survives death. Aside from this example, should other limits be placed on the right of publicity?

e. **The First Amendment**

The First Amendment to the Constitution provides: "Congress shall make no law . . . abridging the freedom of speech, or of the press. . . ." This provision does restrict the right of publicity—but to what extent? For example, consider this controversy arising out of Tiger Woods' legendary 1997 Masters golf tournament victory in Augusta, Georgia. Rick Rush, who calls himself "America's sports artist," created a painting entitled "The Masters of Augusta" to commemorate the event. It featured three views of Woods in different poses in the foreground, with images of past victors and the Augusta clubhouse in the background. The Sixth Circuit rejected Woods' right of publicity claim because the painting was an artistic transformation, not a literal depiction of his image: "[W]e conclude that the effect of limiting the right of publicity in this case is negligible and significantly outweighed by society's interest in freedom of artistic expression." *ETW Corporation v. Jireh Publishing, Inc.,* 332 F.3d 915, 938 (6th Cir. 2003). In light of this case, was *White* wrongly decided? *See also* Robert C. Post et al., *The First Amendment and the Right(s) of Publicity,* 130 Yale L.J. 86 (2020).

f. **Publicity Problems**

Has the right of publicity been violated in the following situations?

> (1) A sells a video football game that features virtual players. The jersey number for each virtual player is the same as a currently-enrolled college player, but the name and the likeness of the actual player are not used.
>
> (2) B writes a book about the impact of Martin Luther King, Jr. on the civil rights movement, which is sold to the public.
>
> (3) C invents a new dance style which reminds some people of the way Michael Jackson danced; C is paid to perform the dance on a television show.

g. Creation as a Source of Property

In *Pierson*, we saw that property rights may arise from first possession or *capture*. Note that this concept applies to rights in existing, unowned things. *White* introduces a different source of property: *creation*. All other things being equal, the law usually vests title in the person who creates an entirely new thing, such as an invention, a book, or a song. We will explore creation as a source of intellectual property rights in Chapter 4.

h. Aftermath of *White*

White originally sought $6.9 million in damages, but the jury ultimately awarded her only $403,000. Today *Wheel of Fortune* is still one of the most popular syndicated shows on television, and White's annual income (including revenue from product endorsements) is estimated to be over $10,000,000.

B. What Is Property?

An ordinary person conceives of property as *things*. If you were asked what property you own, you might list items such as books, clothes, a computer, and perhaps a car. In law, however, we define property as *rights among people concerning things*. For example, you hold legally enforceable *rights* in your computer, but do not own the *thing* itself. Thus, property is often described as a *bundle of rights* or, more informally, a *bundle of sticks*. The Supreme Court echoed this view in *Cedar Point Nursery v. Hassid*, 141 S. Ct. 2063, 2073 (2021), when it referred to the "sticks in the bundle of rights that are commonly characterized as property." Using this metaphor, the most important "sticks" in the bundle are:

> - The right to transfer
> - The right to exclude
> - The right to use
> - The right to destroy

The balance of this chapter will explore these four rights in depth. Note that the bundle of rights metaphor has come under attack in recent years. For an example of this critique, see Henry E. Smith, *Property as the Law of Things*, 125 Harv. L. Rev. 1691 (2012).

The idea that property consists of *rights* has important consequences, which we will see throughout the course. If you entered law school thinking about property as *things*, you will need to reconsider some of your assumptions. For example, take a moment to consider four key implications of the *rights* approach:

- *Property rights are defined by government*: As noted above, property is defined by government—the basic concept of legal positivism. In other words, A holds property rights in his farm only if and to the extent that they are recognized by government.

- *Property rights are not absolute*: Many people believe that "a person can do anything he wants with his own property." Not so. Property rights are *relative*, not *absolute*. Almost by definition, property rights sometimes conflict. Thus, B's right to use her land (for example, as a smelly pig farm) may interfere with C's right to use his adjacent land (for example, as a residence). Much of property law is devoted to reconciling disputes between different owners or between an owner and the community. As one scholar explains: "Some rights in the bundle conflict with other rights in the bundle; the property rights of one person impinge on, and interfere with, both the property and personal rights of others. Absolute property rights are self-defeating." Joseph William Singer, *Rent*, 39 B.C. L. Rev. 1, 34 (1997).

- *Property rights can be divided*: Property rights concerning a thing may be split among multiple holders, such that it may be difficult to identify a single "owner." For example, tenant D may have the right to use a leased apartment unit for a year, but not the right to destroy it, which is retained by landlord E. Similarly, borrower F who mortgages her property retains all the rights in the bundle, except that bank G holds a right to foreclose on the property if F fails to pay her debt.

- *Property rights evolve as law changes*: A core value of our property law system is *stability of title*—the concept that property rights should be certain and predictable. But the nature and scope of property rights do evolve slowly over time, as changing economic, technological, and social conditions gradually reshape the law. For example, the invention of the airplane ended the traditional notion that a landowner held title to all the airspace above her land. Thus, property law is a dynamic process, not a set of static rules.

Finally, if we define property as rights among people concerning things, does this mean that property owners owe any *duties*? As one professor notes: "Owners have obligations; they have always had obligations. We can argue about what those obligations should be, but no one can seriously argue that they should not exist." Joseph William Singer, Entitlement 18 (2000). *See also* Gregory S. Alexander, *The Social-Obligation Norm in American Property Law*, 94 Cornell L. Rev. 745 (2009).

---

1. Right to Transfer

A wants to sell her kidney to B. C's will devised farm land to D on condition that D never allow commercial development, but D now intends to build a shopping center. E and F, who have used in vitro fertilization to produce ten frozen human embryos from their genetic material, plan to donate one of the embryos to G. These situations share a common question: what is the scope of the right to transfer?

The right to transfer property—technically called *alienability*—is a cornerstone of the American legal system. As a general rule, any owner may freely transfer or *alienate* any of her property to anyone. But the scope of this right is sometimes limited for reasons of public policy. Occasionally, the law restricts *who* can transfer or obtain property; an insane person, for example, can do neither. More commonly, the law regulates *what* property can be transferred. For instance, some types of property cannot be transferred at all (such as rights to military pensions), while others can be given away but not sold (such as corneas). And, as you would expect, the law usually regulates *how* property may be transferred in order to avoid fraud, uncertainty, or other problems. For example, in general a will is not effective to transfer property at the owner's death unless it is in writing, signed by the owner, and appropriately witnessed by two people.

Advocates of the law and economics approach stress that the right to transfer is vital for efficiency in our market economy, because it helps to ensure that property is devoted to its most valuable use. For example, suppose A holds title to a large tract of land where he grows potatoes; the land is worth $2,000 per acre for agricultural use. But suppose that A's land is worth $50,000 per acre for industrial use, which would benefit society more than farming. If the law prevented A from selling his rights to entrepreneur B, then the land would remain locked into a low-value use.

So if the law favors the free alienation of property as a *general* matter, the question becomes: under what *specific* circumstances should alienation be restricted? To answer this question, we must examine the policies that underpin American property law.

The next case—*Johnson v. M'Intosh*—provides an excellent starting point for exploring the scope of the right to transfer and much more. Land speculation was rampant in the American colonies during the 1700s. The Crown officially prohibited private persons from purchasing land west of the Allegheny Mountains from Native American tribes. But this ban was often ignored, as shown by the events leading up to *Johnson*. In 1773, an investor group purchased 23,000 square miles of land in present-day Illinois from the Kaskakia, Peoria, and Cahokia tribes, in exchange for trade goods valued at $24,000. This tract was about the same size as the combined modern states of Maryland and Massachusetts. Two years later, another group purchased an even larger tract of land in present-day Illinois and Indiana from the Piankeshaw tribe in exchange for $31,000 in goods. These two investor groups merged in 1779 to form the United Illinois and Wabash Land Company. For the next 40 years, the Company lobbied state governments and the federal government to recognize its claimed land titles—without success. During this time, the federal government had acquired title to most of these lands from the same Native American tribes (in exchange for more trade goods), and had sold parcels to various buyers. Finally, in 1820, the Company turned to a new strategy: litigation. It arranged for a suit to be brought against William M'Intosh (who had allegedly bought some of the land from the government) on behalf of Joshua Johnson and his nephew, who were shareholders of the Company.

Land purchased by investor groups in *Johnson v. M'Intosh*

Johnson v. M'Intosh

Supreme Court of the United States

21 U.S. (8 Wheat.) 543 (1823)

. . . This was an action of ejectment for lands in the State and District of Illinois, claimed by the plaintiffs under a purchase and conveyance from the Piankeshaw Indians, and by the defendant, under a [later] grant from the United States. It came up on a case stated, upon which there was judgment below for the defendant. . . .

Mr. Chief Justice Marshall delivered the opinion of the Court.

The plaintiffs in this cause claim the land, in their declaration mentioned, under two grants, purporting to be made, the first in 1773, and the last in 1775, by the chiefs of certain Indian tribes, constituting the Illinois and the Piankeshaw nations; and the question is, whether this title can be recognised in the Courts of the United States?

The facts, as stated in the case agreed, show the authority of the chiefs who executed this conveyance, so far as it could be given by their own people; and likewise show, that the particular tribes for whom these chiefs acted were in rightful possession of the land they sold. The inquiry, therefore, is, in a great measure, confined to the power of Indians to give, and of private individuals to receive, a title which can be sustained in the Courts of this country.

As the right of society, to prescribe those rules by which property may be acquired and preserved is not, and cannot be drawn into question; as the title to lands, especially, is and must be admitted to depend entirely on the law of the nation in which they lie; it will be necessary, in pursuing this inquiry, to examine, not singly those principles of abstract justice, which the Creator of all things has impressed on the mind of his creature man, and which are admitted to regulate, in a great degree, the rights of civilized nations, whose perfect independence is acknowledged; but those principles also which our own government has adopted in the particular case, and given us as the rule for our decision.

Chief Justice John Marshall
Click here for larger image

> **Make the Connection**
>
> Legal positivism and natural law theory were discussed earlier in this chapter. Do these concepts affect Marshall's view of how the Court should decide this case?

On the discovery of this immense continent, the great nations of Europe were eager to appropriate to themselves so much of it as they could respectively acquire. Its vast extent offered an ample field to the ambition and enterprise of all; and the character and religion of its inhabitants afforded an apology for considering them as a people over whom the superior genius of Europe might claim an ascendency. The potentates of the old world found no difficulty in convincing themselves that they made ample compensation to the inhabitants of the new, by bestowing on them civilization and Christianity, in exchange for unlimited independence. But, as they were all in pursuit of nearly the same object, it was necessary, in order to avoid conflicting settlements, and consequent war with each other, to establish a principle, which all should acknowledge as the law by which the right of acquisition, which they all asserted, should be regulated as between themselves. This principle was, that discovery gave title to the government by whose subjects, or by whose authority, it was made, against all other European governments, which title might be consummated by possession.

The exclusion of all other Europeans, necessarily gave to the nation making the discovery the sole right of acquiring the soil from the natives, and establishing settlements upon it. It was a right with which no Europeans could interfere. It was a right which all asserted for themselves, and to the assertion of which, by others, all assented.

Those relations which were to exist between the discoverer and the natives, were to be regulated by themselves. The rights thus acquired being exclusive, no other power could interpose between them.

In the establishment of these relations, the rights of the original inhabitants were, in no instance, entirely disregarded; but were necessarily, to a considerable extent, impaired. They were admitted to be the rightful occupants of the soil, with a legal as well as just claim to retain possession of it, and to use it according to their own discretion; but their rights to complete sovereignty, as independent nations, were necessarily diminished, and their power to dispose of the soil at their own will, to whomsoever they pleased, was denied by the original fundamental principle, that discovery gave exclusive title to those who made it.

While the different nations of Europe respected the right of the natives, as occupants, they asserted the ultimate dominion to be in themselves; and claimed and exercised, as a consequence of this ultimate dominion, a power to grant the soil, while yet in possession of the natives. These grants have been understood by all, to convey a title to the grantees, subject only to the Indian right of occupancy. . . .

No one of the powers of Europe gave its full assent to this principle, more unequivocally than England. The documents upon this subject are ample and complete. So early as the year 1496, her monarch granted a commission to the Cabots, to discover countries then unknown to *Christian people*, and to take possession of them in the name of the king of England. Two years afterwards, Cabot proceeded on this voyage, and discovered the continent of North America, along which he sailed as far south as Virginia. To this discovery the English trace their title. . . .

[O]ur whole country [has] been granted by the crown while in the occupation of the Indians. These grants purport to convey the soil as well as the right of dominion to the grantees. In those governments which were denominated royal, where the right to the soil was not vested in individuals, but remained in the crown, or was vested in the colonial government, the king claimed and exercised the right of granting lands, and of dismembering the government at his will. . . . It has never been objected . . . to any . . . grant, that the title as well as possession was in the Indians when it was made, and that it passed nothing on that account. . . .

Thus, all the nations of Europe, who have acquired territory on this continent, have asserted in themselves, and have recognised in others, the exclusive right of the discoverer to appropriate the lands occupied by the Indians. Have the American States rejected or adopted this principle?

By the treaty which concluded the war of our revolution, Great Britain relinquished all claim, not only to the government, but to the "propriety and territorial rights of the United States," whose boundaries were fixed in the second article. . . . It has never been doubted, that either the United States, or the several States, had a clear title to all the lands within the boundary lines described in the treaty, subject only to the Indian right of occupancy, and that the exclusive power to extinguish that right, was vested in that government which might constitutionally exercise it.

Virginia, particularly, within whose chartered limits the land in controversy lay, passed an act, in the year 1779, declaring her

> exclusive right of pre-emption from the Indians, of all the lands within the limits of her own chartered territory, and that no person or persons whatsoever, have, or ever had, a right to purchase any lands within the same, from any Indian nation, except only persons duly authorized to make such purchase; formerly for the use and benefit of the colony, and lately for the Commonwealth.

The act then proceeds to annul all deeds made by Indians to individuals, for the private use of the purchasers. . . .

The United States, then, have unequivocally acceded to that great and broad rule by which its civilized inhabitants now hold this country. They hold, and assert in themselves, the title by which it was acquired. They maintain, as all others have maintained, that discovery gave an exclusive right to extinguish the Indian title of occupancy, either by purchase or by conquest; and gave also a right to such a degree of sovereignty, as the circumstances of the people would allow them to exercise.

The power now possessed by the government of the United States to grant lands, resided, while we were colonies, in the crown, or its grantees. The validity of the titles given by either has never been questioned in our Courts. It has been exercised uniformly over territory in possession of the Indians. The existence of this power must negative the existence of any right which may conflict with, and control it. An absolute title to lands cannot exist, at the same time, in different persons, or in different governments. An absolute [title] must be an exclusive title, or at least a title which excludes all others not compatible with it. All our institutions recognise the absolute title of the crown, subject only to the Indian right of occupancy, and recognise the absolute title of the crown to extinguish that right. This is incompatible with an absolute and complete title in the Indians.

We will not enter into the controversy, whether agriculturists, merchants, and manufacturers, have a right, on abstract principles, to expel hunters from the territory they possess, or to contract their limits. Conquest gives a title which the Courts of the conqueror cannot deny, whatever the private and speculative opinions of individuals may be, respecting the original justice of the claim which has been successfully asserted. The British government, which was then our government, and whose rights have passed to the United States, asserted title to all the lands occupied by Indians, within the chartered limits of the British colonies. It asserted also a limited sovereignty over them, and the exclusive right of extinguishing the title which occupancy gave to them. These claims have been maintained and established as far west as the river Mississippi, by the sword. The title to a vast portion of the lands we now hold, originates in them. It is not for the Courts of this country to question the validity of this title, or to sustain one which is incompatible with it.

> **Food for Thought**
>
> What does Marshall mean by saying: "Conquest gives a title which the Courts of the conqueror cannot deny"? How would the dispute have been resolved by a Native American court, if one had existed at the time?

Although we do not mean to engage in the defence of those principles which Europeans have applied to Indian title, they may, we think, find some excuse, if not justification, in the character and habits of the people whose rights have been wrested from them.

The title by conquest is acquired and maintained by force. The conqueror prescribes its limits. Humanity, however, acting on public opinion, has established, as a general rule, that the conquered shall not be wantonly oppressed, and that their condition shall remain as eligible as is compatible with the objects of the conquest. Most usually, they are incorporated with the victorious nation, and become subjects or citizens of the government with which they are connected. The new and old members of the society mingle with each other; the distinction between them is gradually lost, and they make one people. Where this incorporation is practicable, humanity demands, and a wise policy requires, that the rights of the conquered to property should remain unimpaired; that the new subjects should be governed as equitably as the old, and that confidence in their security should gradually banish the painful sense of being separated from their ancient connections, and united by force to strangers. . . .

But the tribes of Indians inhabiting this country were fierce savages, whose occupation was war, and whose subsistence was drawn chiefly from the forest. To leave them in possession of their country, was to leave the country a wilderness; to govern them as a distinct people, was impossible, because they were as brave and as high spirited as they were fierce, and were ready to repel by arms every attempt on their independence.

What was the inevitable consequence of this state of things? The Europeans were under the necessity either of abandoning the country, and relinquishing their pompous claims to it, or of enforcing those claims by the sword, and by the adoption of principles adapted to the condition of a people with whom it was impossible to mix, and who could not be governed as a distinct society, or of remaining in their neighbourhood, and exposing themselves and their families to the perpetual hazard of being massacred.

Frequent and bloody wars, in which the whites were not always the aggressors, unavoidably ensued. European policy, numbers, and skill, prevailed. As the white population advanced, that of the Indians necessarily receded. The country in the immediate neighbourhood of agriculturists became unfit for them. The game fled into thicker and more unbroken forests, and the Indians followed. The soil, to which the crown originally claimed title, being no longer occupied by its ancient inhabitants, was parcelled out according to the will of the sovereign power, and taken possession of by persons who claimed immediately from the crown, or mediately, through its grantees or deputies.

That law which regulates, and ought to regulate in general, the relations between the conqueror and conquered, was incapable of application to a people under such circumstances. The resort to some new and different rule, better adapted to the actual state of things, was unavoidable. Every rule which can be suggested will be found to be attended with great difficulty.

However extravagant the pretension of converting the discovery of an inhabited country into conquest may appear; if the principle has been asserted in the first instance, and afterwards sustained; if a country has been acquired and held under it; if the property of the great mass of the community originates in it, it becomes the law of the land, and cannot be questioned. So, too, with respect to the concomitant principle, that the Indian inhabitants are to be considered merely as occupants, to be protected, indeed, while in peace, in the possession of their lands, but to be deemed incapable of transferring the absolute title to others. However this restriction may be opposed to natural right, and to the usages of civilized nations, yet, if it be indispensable to that system under which the country has been settled, and be adapted to the actual condition of the two people, it may, perhaps, be supported by reason, and certainly cannot be rejected by Courts of justice. . . .

It has never been contended, that the Indian title amounted to nothing. Their right of possession has never been questioned. The claim of government extends to the complete ultimate title, charged with this right of possession, and to the exclusive power of acquiring that right. . . .

After bestowing on this subject a degree of attention which was more required by the magnitude of the interest in litigation, and the able and elaborate arguments of the bar, than by its intrinsic difficulty, the Court is decidedly of [the] opinion, that the plaintiffs do not exhibit a title which can be sustained in the Courts of the United States; and that there is no error in the judgment which was rendered against them in the District Court of Illinois.

Points for Discussion

a. **Bundle of Sticks**

According to Marshall, what rights did the Native Americans have before their 1773 and 1775 grants? If the Crown could extinguish the rights of the Native Americans at any time, were they truly "rights"?

b. **Theories of Property**

Pierson v. Post introduced a keystone principle of English property law: all things being equal, the law tends to vest title in the first-in-time possessor. The Native Americans were occupying and using the lands in question long before Europeans arrived in North America. Why weren't the Native Americans entitled to full ownership based on the first-in-time rule? Didn't they "capture" the land through labor before the Europeans appeared, just like Pierson killed the fox before Post arrived?

c. **Marshall's Rationale**

Exactly why didn't the Native Americans have the right to transfer title? Marshall's opinion mentions several possible reasons, including (1) prior payment ("they made ample compensation . . . by bestowing on them civilization and Christianity"), (2) abandonment ("[a]s the white population advanced, that of the Indians necessarily receded"), and (3) undue delay in claiming title ("if the property of the great mass of the community originates in it, it becomes the law of the land"). Are these themes relevant, or does the rationale lie elsewhere?

Marshall admits that the outcome of the case is inconsistent with "abstract justice" and "natural right." What is the appropriate role for a judge who is asked to apply a law that violates a fundamental principle of justice?

d. **Applying the *Johnson* Rule**

Suppose that you are an attorney for the State of Delaware. You learn that a Native American tribe sold and conveyed over 50,000 acres of tribal land to the state in 1805. Citing *Johnson*, the tribe now argues that the transaction was invalid and sues to obtain title. How would you advise your client?

e. **An "Efficient" Approach?**

Professor Eric Kades notes that in almost all instances the federal government acquired Native American lands by purchase—though often with the threat of force in the background. Eric Kades, *History and Interpretation of the Great Case of* Johnson v. M'Intosh, 19 Law & Hist. Rev. 67 (2001). So why was the outcome of *Johnson* important? By confirming that the Native Americans could transfer title to only one buyer, the decision ensured low purchase prices. As Kades explains, "it was collectively efficient for Europeans to make their governments the only legal entities empowered to buy Indian land. Single buyers (monopsonists) can drive prices down just as single sellers (monopolists) can drive prices up." *Id.* at 111. As a result, he concludes that purchase was cheaper than conquest.

f. **Fifty Years Later**

The Supreme Court decided this case in 1823, 50 years after the first grant in question. Why was the Native Americans' right to transfer relevant to a case occurring so many years later? Did this 50-year period affect the outcome of the case? Suppose that the Court had ruled in favor of the Johnson group. Marshall says that allowing the Native Americans to remain in possession of their lands would "leave the country a wilderness." Why is this relevant? For more information about the case, see Blake A. Watson, Buying America from the Indians: *Johnson v. McIntosh* and the History of Native Land Rights (2012).

g. **Chain of Title**

The succession of ownership over time is called a *chain of title*. Each different owner is a different link in the chain. Suppose that A acquires title to a house from B; B had previously obtained title from C, who had earlier received her title from D, and so forth. The chain of title for every parcel of real property in the United States can be traced backwards in time to a point where it was originally owned by a sovereign entity before being granted to a private owner. Most commonly, the sovereign who began the chain is the United States, as in *Johnson v. M'Intosh*; M'Intosh received his title through a deed from the federal government. However, a chain of title might also originate in the British crown, a state or colony, France, Spain or another foreign country that once claimed territory in the modern United States. The chain of title concept is important because—as a general matter—if two different people have competing title claims to the same property, the person with the better chain of title will prevail. You will study this doctrine in Chapter 8.

h. **Title by Discovery?**

Suppose A, a U.S. citizen, discovers a remote, uninhabited island that is outside of the sovereign territory of any nation. Can A obtain title by discovery? In *Kingman Reef Atoll Development, LLC v. United States*, 116 Fed. Cl. 708 (2014), the Court of Federal Claims rejected such a claim. It cited *Johnson v. M'Intosh* for the rule that "discovery of new land resulted in the discoverer's nation gaining both sovereignty over and title to the land," and that the discoverer "would have to seek a conveyance of title from the government in place." *Id.* at 750.

i. **Aftermath of *Johnson***

International law increasingly protects the rights of aboriginal peoples to their traditional lands. For example, in *Dann v. United States*, Inter-Am. C.H.R. Case No. 11.140 (2002), Carrie and Marie Dann and other members of the Western Shoshone claimed the United States violated their rights by extinguishing their aboriginal title to certain Nevada lands. The Inter-American Commission on Human Rights agreed, finding that the United States "failed to ensure the Danns' right to property under . . . the American Declaration [of the Rights and Duties of Man (1948)]." *Id.* at ¶ 172. *See also* Audrey Gledenning et al., *(Some) Land Back . . . Sort of: The Transfer of Federal Public Lands to Indian Tribes since 1970*, 63 Nat. Res. J. 200 (2023).

Consider the question of property rights in the human body. The Thirteenth Amendment to the Constitution abolished slavery in the United States. As a result, the human body cannot be sold. But what about body parts? If we view you as the "owner" of your body, do you have the right to sell your kidney?

Moore v. Regents of the University of California

Supreme Court of California

793 P.2d 479 (1990), *cert. denied*, 499 U.S. 936 (1991)

PANELLI, JUSTICE.

I. INTRODUCTION

We granted review in this case to determine whether plaintiff has stated a cause of action against his physician and other defendants for using his cells in potentially lucrative medical research without his permission. Plaintiff alleges that his physician failed to disclose preexisting research and economic interests in the cells before obtaining consent to the medical procedures by which they were extracted. The superior court sustained all defendants' demurrers to the third amended complaint, and the Court of Appeal reversed. We hold that the complaint states a cause of action for breach of the physician's disclosure obligations, but not for conversion. . . .

II. FACTS

. . . The plaintiff is John Moore (Moore), who underwent treatment for hairy-cell leukemia at the Medical Center of the University of California at Los Angeles (UCLA Medical Center). [The defendants included the Regents of the University of California (Regents), Dr. Golde (who treated Moore), and Shirley Quan (a researcher employed by the Regents).]

> **Practice Pointer**
>
> After a lawsuit is filed, the defendant may immediately challenge the legal sufficiency of the complaint. In California and many other states, this procedure is called a *demurrer*. In effect, the defendant argues: "Even if every fact asserted in the complaint is true, as a matter of law I should win this case." In *Moore*, the defendants filed a demurrer and won before any trial occurred, leading to Moore's appeal. Compared to a trial, a demurrer is inexpensive—and a successful demurrer means that the case will never be heard by a sympathetic jury.

Moore first visited UCLA Medical Center on October 5, 1976. . . . After hospitalizing Moore and withdrawing "extensive amounts of blood, bone marrow aspirate, and other bodily substances," Golde confirmed [the] diagnosis. [The defendants were aware that Moore's cells were unique and had substantial value, but did not inform Moore. Specifically, Moore's T-lymphocyte cells (a type of white blood cell) overproduced certain lymphokines, which are proteins that regulate the immune system; this overproduction enabled researchers to locate the genes responsible for those lymphokines. Golde recommended that Moore's spleen be removed to slow down the progress of the disease, and Moore agreed. Portions of the spleen—plus blood, skin, and other tissue removed from Moore during six years of follow-up visits—were used for research without Moore's knowledge. Using genetic engineering, the defendants developed a cell line from Moore's cells (called the "Mo cell line"), obtained a patent for it (U.S. Patent No. 4,438,032), and entered into a series of commercial agreements for rights to the cell line and its products. The market potential for these products was estimated to be three billion dollars. Moore sued for damages based on thirteen causes of action, including lack of informed consent, breach of fiduciary duty, and conversion. He alleged that the spleen, blood, and other bodily substances taken by the defendants were "his tangible personal property" and that the defendant's activities "constitute a substantial interference with plaintiff's possession or right thereto." The trial court sustained the defendants' demurrers, but the Court of Appeal reversed.]

III. DISCUSSION

A. Breach of Fiduciary Duty and Lack of Informed Consent

Moore repeatedly alleges that Golde failed to disclose the extent of his research and economic interests in Moore's cells before obtaining consent to the medical procedures by which the cells were extracted. These allegations, in our view, state a cause of action against Golde for invading a legally protected interest of his patient. This cause of action can properly be characterized either as the breach of a fiduciary duty to disclose facts material to the patient's consent or, alternatively, as the performance of medical procedures without first having obtained the patient's informed consent. . . .

B. Conversion

Moore also attempts to characterize the invasion of his rights as a conversion—a tort that protects against interference with possessory and ownership interests in personal property. He theorizes that he continued to own his cells following their removal from his body, at least for the purpose of directing their use, and that he never consented to their use in potentially lucrative medical research. Thus, to complete Moore's argument, defendants' unauthorized use of his cells constitutes a conversion. As a result of the alleged conversion, Moore claims a proprietary interest in each of the products that any of the defendants might ever create from his cells or the patented cell line. . . .

[W]e first consider whether the tort of conversion clearly gives Moore a cause of action under existing law. We do not believe it does. Because of the novelty of Moore's claim to own the biological materials at issue, to apply the theory of conversion in this context would frankly have to be recognized as an extension of the theory. Therefore, we consider next whether it is advisable to extend the tort to this context.

1. Moore's Claim Under Existing Law

"To establish a conversion, plaintiff must establish an actual interference with his *ownership* or *right of possession*. . . . Where plaintiff neither has title to the property alleged to have been converted, nor possession thereof, he cannot maintain an action for conversion." (*Del E. Webb Corp. v. Structural Materials Co.* (1981) 123 Cal.App.3d 593, 610–611, 176 Cal. Rptr. 284, emphasis added. . . .)

Since Moore clearly did not expect to retain possession of his cells following their removal, to sue for their conversion he must have retained an ownership interest in them. But there are several reasons to doubt that he did retain any such interest. First, no reported judicial decision supports Moore's claim, either directly or by close analogy. Second, California statutory law drastically limits any continuing interest of a patient in excised cells. Third, the subject matters of the Regents' patent—the patented cell line and the products derived from it—cannot be Moore's property.

Neither the Court of Appeal's opinion, the parties' briefs, nor our research discloses a case holding that a person retains a sufficient interest in excised cells to support a cause of action for conversion. We do not find this surprising, since the laws governing such things as human tissues, transplantable organs,[22] blood, fetuses, pituitary glands, corneal tissue, and dead bodies deal with human biological materials as objects sui generis, regulating their disposition to achieve policy goals rather than abandoning them to the general law of personal property. It is these specialized statutes, not the law of conversion, to which courts ordinarily should and do look for guidance on the disposition of human biological materials.

---

[22] See the Uniform Anatomical Gift Act, Health and Safety Code section 7150 et seq. The act permits a competent adult to "give all or part of [his] body" for certain designated purposes, including "transplantation, therapy, medical or dental education, research, or advancement of medical or dental science." (Health & Saf. Code, §§ 7151, 7153.) The act does not, however, permit the donor to receive "valuable consideration" for the transfer. (Health & Saf. Code, § 7155.)

Lacking direct authority for importing the law of conversion into this context, Moore relies, as did the Court of Appeal, primarily on decisions addressing privacy rights. One line of cases involves unwanted publicity. (*Lugosi v. Universal Pictures* (1979) 25 Cal.3d 813, 160 Cal. Rptr. 323, 603 P.2d 425; *Motschenbacher v. R.J. Reynolds Tobacco Company* (9th Cir. 1974) 498 F.2d 821 [interpreting Cal. law].) These opinions hold that every person has a proprietary interest in his own likeness and that unauthorized, business use of a likeness is redressible as a tort. But in neither opinion did the authoring court expressly base its holding on property law. Each court stated, following Prosser, that it was "pointless" to debate the proper characterization of the proprietary interest in a likeness. . . . For purposes of determining whether the tort of conversion lies, however, the characterization of the right in question is far from pointless. Only property can be converted. . . .

> **FYI**
>
> Consider the text of the key statutes cited by both the majority and the dissent:
>
> Cal. Health & Safety Code § 7153(a): Only the following persons may become donees of anatomical gifts for the purposes stated: (1) A hospital, physician, surgeon, or procurement organization, for transplantation, therapy, medical or dental education, research, or advancement of medical or dental science; . . . .
>
> Cal. Health & Safety Code § 7155(a): A person may not knowingly, for valuable consideration, purchase or sell a part for transplantation, therapy, or reconditioning, if removal of the part is intended to occur after the death of the decedent.

Not only are the wrongful-publicity cases irrelevant to the issue of conversion, but the analogy to them seriously misconceives the nature of the genetic materials and research involved in this case. Moore, adopting the analogy originally advanced by the Court of Appeal, argues that "[i]f the courts have found a sufficient proprietary interest in one's persona, how could one not have a right in one's own genetic material, something far more profoundly the essence of one's human uniqueness than a name or a face?" However, as the defendants' patent makes clear—and the complaint, too, if read with an understanding of the scientific terms which it has borrowed from the patent—the goal and result of defendants' efforts has been to manufacture lymphokines. Lymphokines, unlike a name or a face, have the same molecular structure in every human being and the same, important functions in every human being's immune system. Moreover, the particular genetic material which is responsible for the natural production of lymphokines, and which defendants use to manufacture lymphokines in the laboratory, is also the same in every person; it is no more unique to Moore than the number of vertebrae in the spine or the chemical formula of hemoglobin. . . .[30]

---

[30] By definition, a gene responsible for producing a protein found in more than one individual will be the same in each. It is precisely because everyone needs the same basic proteins that proteins produced by one person's cells may have therapeutic value for another person. . . . Thus, the proteins that defendants hope to manufacture—lymphokines such as interferon—are in no way a "likeness" of Moore.

The next consideration that makes Moore's claim of ownership problematic is California statutory law, which drastically limits a patient's control over excised cells. Pursuant to Health and Safety Code section 7054.4,

> [n]otwithstanding any other provision of law, recognizable anatomical parts, human tissues, anatomical human remains, or infectious waste following conclusion of scientific use shall be disposed of by interment, incineration, or any other method determined by the state department [of health services] to protect the public health and safety.

Clearly the Legislature did not specifically intend this statute to resolve the question of whether a patient is entitled to compensation for the nonconsensual use of excised cells. A primary object of the statute is to ensure the safe handling of potentially hazardous biological waste materials. Yet one cannot escape the conclusion that the statute's practical effect is to limit, drastically, a patient's control over excised cells. By restricting how excised cells may be used and requiring their eventual destruction, the statute eliminates so many of the rights ordinarily attached to property that one cannot simply assume that what is left amounts to "property" or "ownership" for purposes of conversion law. . . .

Finally, the subject matter of the Regents' patent—the patented cell line and the products derived from it—cannot be Moore's property. This is because the patented cell line is both factually and legally distinct from the cells taken from Moore's body. Federal law permits the patenting of organisms that represent the product of "human ingenuity," but not naturally occurring organisms. (*Diamond v. Chakrabarty* (1980) 447 U.S. 303, 309–310). Human cell lines are patentable because "[l]ong-term adaptation and growth of human tissues and cells in culture is difficult—often considered an art," and the probability of success is low. . . . It is this *inventive effort* that patent law rewards, not the discovery of naturally occurring raw materials. Thus, Moore's allegations that he owns the cell line and the products derived from it are inconsistent with the patent, which constitutes an authoritative determination that the cell line is the product of invention. . . .

2. Should Conversion Liability Be Extended?

. . . There are three reasons why it is inappropriate to impose liability for conversion based upon the allegations of Moore's complaint. First, a fair balancing of the relevant policy considerations counsels against extending the tort. Second, problems in this area are better suited to legislative resolution. Third, the tort of conversion is not necessary to protect patients' rights. For these reasons, we conclude that the use of excised human cells in medical research does not amount to a conversion.

Of the relevant policy considerations, two are of overriding importance. The first is protection of a competent patient's right to make autonomous medical decisions. That right, as already discussed, is grounded in well-recognized and long-standing principles of fiduciary duty and informed consent. . . . This policy weighs in favor of providing a remedy to patients when physicians act with undisclosed motives that may affect their professional judgment. The second important policy consideration is that we not threaten with disabling civil liability innocent parties who are engaged in socially useful activities, such as researchers who have no reason to believe that their use of a particular cell sample is, or may be, against a donor's wishes. . . .

To be sure, the threat of liability for conversion might help to enforce patients' rights indirectly. This is because physicians might be able to avoid liability by obtaining patients' consent, in the broadest possible terms, to any conceivable subsequent research use of excised cells. Unfortunately, to extend the conversion theory would utterly sacrifice the other goal of protecting innocent parties. Since conversion is a strict liability tort, it would impose liability on all those into whose hands the cells come, whether or not the particular defendant participated in, or knew of, the inadequate disclosures that violated the patient's right to make an informed decision. In contrast to the conversion theory, the fiduciary-duty and informed-consent theories protect the patient directly, without punishing innocent parties or creating disincentives to the conduct of socially beneficial research.

Research on human cells plays a critical role in medical research. This is so because researchers are increasingly able to isolate naturally occurring, medically useful biological substances and to produce useful quantities of such substances through genetic engineering. These efforts are beginning to bear fruit. Products developed through biotechnology that have already been approved for marketing in this country include treatments and tests for leukemia, cancer, diabetes, dwarfism, hepatitis-B, kidney transplant rejection, emphysema, osteoporosis, ulcers, anemia, infertility, and gynecological tumors, to name but a few. . . .

The extension of conversion law into this area will hinder research by restricting access to the necessary raw materials. Thousands of human cell lines already exist in tissue repositories. . . . At present, human cell lines are routinely copied and distributed to other researchers for experimental purposes, usually free of charge. This exchange of scientific materials, which still is relatively free and efficient, will surely be compromised if each cell sample becomes the potential subject matter of a lawsuit. . . .

> **Food for Thought**
>
> Compare this portion of the court's opinion to Judge Kozinski's dissent in *White v. Samsung Electronics America, Inc.* To what extent are these arguments similar? Different?

[T]he theory of liability that Moore urges us to endorse threatens to destroy the economic incentive to conduct important medical research. If the use of cells in research is a conversion, then with every cell sample a researcher purchases a ticket in a litigation lottery. Because liability for conversion is predicated on a continuing ownership interest, "companies are unlikely to invest heavily in developing, manufacturing, or marketing a product when uncertainty about clear title exists." ([U.S.

Congress, Office of Technology Assessment, New Developments in Biotechnology: Ownership of Human Tissue and Cells (1987)] at p. 27). . . .

If the scientific users of human cells are to be held liable for failing to investigate the consensual pedigree of their raw materials, we believe the Legislature should make that decision. Complex policy choices affecting all society are involved, and "[l]egislatures, in making such policy decisions, have the ability to gather empirical evidence, solicit the advice of experts, and hold hearings at which all interested parties present evidence and express their views. . . ." . . .

For these reasons, we hold that the allegations of Moore's third amended complaint state a cause of action for breach of fiduciary duty or lack of informed consent, but not conversion. . . .

ARABIAN, JUSTICE, concurring.

. . . Plaintiff has asked us to recognize and enforce a right to sell one's own body tissue *for profit*. He entreats us to regard the human vessel—the single most venerated and protected subject in any civilized society—as equal with the basest commercial commodity. He urges us to commingle the sacred with the profane. He asks much. . . .

It is true, that this court has not often been deterred from deciding difficult legal issues simply because they require a choice between competing social or economic policies. . . . The difference here, however, lies in the nature of the conflicting moral, philosophical and even religious values at stake, and in the profound implications of the position urged. The ramifications of recognizing and enforcing a property interest in body tissues are not known, but are greatly feared—the effect on human dignity of a marketplace in human body parts, the impact on research and development of competitive bidding for such materials, and the exposure of researchers to potentially limitless and uncharted tort liability. . . .

MOSK, JUSTICE, dissenting.

. . . The concepts of property and ownership in our law are extremely broad. . . .

Being broad, the concept of property is also abstract: rather than referring directly to a material object such as a parcel of land or the tractor that cultivates it, the concept of property is often said to refer to a "bundle of rights" that may be exercised with respect to that object—principally the rights to possess the property, to use the property, to exclude others from the property, and to dispose of the property by sale or by gift. . . . But the same bundle of rights does not attach to all forms of property. For a variety of policy reasons, the law limits or even forbids the exercise of certain rights over certain forms of property. For example, both law and contract may limit the right of an owner of real property to use his parcel as he sees fit. Owners of various forms of personal property may likewise be subject to restrictions on the time, place, and manner of their use. . . . Finally, some types of personal property may be sold but not given away, while others may be given away but not sold, and still others may neither be given away nor sold.

In each of the foregoing instances, the limitation or prohibition diminishes the bundle of rights that would otherwise attach to the property, yet what remains is still deemed in law to be a protectible property interest. . . . The same rule applies to Moore's interest in his own body tissue: even if we assume that section 7054.4 limited the use and disposition of his excised tissue in the manner claimed by the majority, Moore nevertheless retained valuable rights in that tissue. Above all, at the time of its excision he at least had *the right to do with his own tissue whatever the defendants did with it*: i.e., he could have contracted with researchers and pharmaceutical companies to develop and exploit the vast commercial potential of his tissue and its products. Defendants certainly believe that *their* right to do the foregoing is not barred by section 7054.4 and is a significant property right. . . . The Court of Appeal summed up the point by observing that "Defendants' position that plaintiff cannot own his tissue, but that they can, is fraught with irony." . . . As noted above, the majority cite no case holding that an individual's right to develop and exploit the commercial potential of his own tissue is *not* a right of sufficient worth or dignity to be deemed a protectible property interest. In the absence of such authority—or of legislation to the same effect—the right falls within the traditionally broad concept of property in our law. . . .

[O]ur society acknowledges a profound ethical imperative to respect the human body as the physical and temporal expression of the unique human persona. . . . The most abhorrent form of . . . exploitation, of course, was the institution of slavery. Lesser forms, such as indentured servitude or even debtor's prison, have also disappeared. Yet their specter haunts the laboratories and boardrooms of today's biotechnological research-industrial complex. It arises wherever scientists or industrialists claim, as defendants claim here, the right to appropriate and exploit a patient's tissue for their sole economic benefit—the right, in other words, to freely mine or harvest valuable physical properties of the patient's body. . . .

> **FYI**
>
> Before Henrietta Lacks died of cancer in 1951, doctors removed some of her tumor cells without her knowledge or consent and used them to develop an immortal cell line. For decades, scientists around the world have experimented with these "HeLa" cells, leading to major medical advances. See Rebecca Skloot, The Immortal Life of Henrietta Lacks (2010). In 2023, Lacks' descendants finally settled a lawsuit which will provide them with a share of the resulting profits. The case was primarily based on unjust enrichment, not conversion.

A second policy consideration adds notions of equity to those of ethics. Our society values fundamental fairness in dealings between its members, and condemns the unjust enrichment of any member at the expense of another. This is particularly true when, as here, the parties are not in equal bargaining positions. We are repeatedly told that the commercial products of the biotechnological revolution "hold the promise of tremendous profit." . . . In the case at bar, for example, the complaint alleges that the market for the kinds of proteins produced by the Mo cell line was predicted to exceed $3 billion by 1990. . . .

Yet defendants deny that Moore is entitled to any share whatever in the proceeds of this cell line. This is both inequitable and immoral. . . .

The inference I draw from the current statutory regulation of human biological materials, moreover, is the opposite of that drawn by the majority. By selective quotation of the statutes . . . the majority seem to suggest that human organs and blood cannot legally be sold on the open market—thereby implying that if the Legislature were to act here it would impose a similar ban on monetary compensation for the use of human tissue in biotechnological research and development. But if that is the argument, the premise is unsound: contrary to popular misconception, it is not true that human organs and blood cannot legally be sold.

As to organs, the majority rely on the Uniform Anatomical Gift Act (Health & Saf. Code, § 7150 et seq., hereafter the UAGA) for the proposition that a competent adult may make a post mortem gift of any part of his body but may not receive "valuable consideration" for the transfer. But the prohibition of the UAGA against the sale of a body part is much more limited than the majority recognize: by its terms (Health & Saf. Code, § 7155, subd. (a)) the prohibition applies only to sales for "transplantation" or "therapy." Yet a different section of the UAGA authorizes the transfer and receipt of body parts for such additional purposes as "medical or . . . dental education, research, or advancement of medical or dental science." (Health & Saf. Code, § 7153, subd. (a)(1).) No section of the UAGA prohibits anyone from selling body parts for any of those additional purposes; by clear implication, therefore, such sales are legal.[23] Indeed, the fact that the UAGA prohibits no sales of organs other than sales for "transportation" or "therapy" raises a further implication that it is also legal for anyone to sell human tissue to a biotechnology company for research and development purposes. . . .

It follows that the statutes regulating the transfers of human organs and blood do not support the majority's refusal to recognize a conversion cause of action for commercial exploitation of human blood cells without consent. On the contrary, because such statutes treat both organs and blood as property that can legally be sold in a variety of circumstances, they impliedly support Moore's contention that his blood cells are likewise property for which he can and should receive compensation, and hence are protected by the law of conversion. . . .

---

[23] By their terms . . . the statutes in question forbid only sales for transplantation and therapy. In light of the rather clear authorization for donation for research and education, one could conclude that sales for these non-therapeutic purposes are permitted. Scientists in practice have been buying and selling human tissues for research apparently without interference from these statutes. (Note, *"She's Got Bette Davis[s'] Eyes": Assessing the Nonconsensual Removal of Cadaver Organs Under the Takings and Due Process Clauses* (1990) 90 Colum. L. Rev. 528, 544, fn. 75.)

[Mosk concluded his dissent by arguing that recognizing a cause of action for nondisclosure was an "illusory" remedy, mainly because of the high burden of proof required.] First, "the patient must show that if he or she had been informed of all pertinent information, he or she would have declined the procedure in question." . . . The second barrier is still higher . . . : [the patient] must also prove that in the same circumstances *no reasonably prudent person* would have given such consent. . . .

Points for Discussion

a. **Bundle of Sticks**

Moore later told an interviewer: "What the doctors had done was to claim that my humanity, my genetic essence, was their invention and their property. They viewed me as a mine from which to extract genetic material. I was harvested." John Vidal, *Lambs to the Gene Market*, The Guardian, Nov. 12, 1994. Did Moore "own" his cells before he entered the UCLA Medical Center? Note that the majority frames the key issue as whether he "retained an ownership interest in them" *after* their removal.

b. **Change in Ownership?**

If Moore owned his cells before the operation, then how *exactly* did (1) he lose ownership and (2) the defendants acquire ownership? In considering these questions, consider the respective positions of the majority and the dissent on statutory interpretation. Who has the stronger argument? And which side has the stronger policy arguments? For an alternative approach to the issue, *see Greenberg v. Miami Children's Hospital Research Institute, Inc.*, 264 F. Supp. 2d 1064 (S.D. Fla. 2003) (where parents provided samples of tissue and blood from their children afflicted with Canavan disease to researchers who used the material to discover and then patent the disease's genetic sequence, parents were allowed to sue for unjust enrichment).

> **See It**
>
> In 1983—six years after the treatments began—Moore was asked to sign a form entitled "Informed Consent for Use of Blood and Bone Marrow Tissue for Medical Research." Click here to see how he filled out the form. Does this form affect your view of the *Moore* decision?

c. **Right to Transfer**

The dissent argues that Moore retained at least one stick in the bundle: the right to transfer his tissue to other researchers, presumably for a profit. Moore certainly had the right to donate his tissue or other body parts for research, transplantation, or other purposes—at least before the surgery—as the majority points out by its citation to California Health & Safety Code §§ 7151 and 7153. So should the majority have resolved this case by holding that Moore retained a limited right to transfer: the right to donate his tissue, but not to sell it? The dissent observes that "some types of personal property may be . . . given away but not sold. . . ." Property that falls into this category is said to be market-inalienable. Setting aside body parts for a moment, what types of property should be market-inalienable?

d. **Dueling Property Theories**

Who prevails if we apply the first-in-time theory? Or the labor theory? Put another way, if Vanna White is entitled to the publicity value she developed, why isn't Moore entitled to the tissue that grew in his body? On the other hand, might this case be closer to *Johnson v. M'Intosh*, in that Moore's rights in his tissue (like the Native Americans' rights to land) do not include the unfettered right to transfer?

e. **The Cell Line**

The majority suggests that even if Moore still owned his cells, he cannot own the cell line, which is "both factually and legally distinct" and the product of "inventive effort." The common law doctrine of *accession* provides that when a person uses his own labor or materials in good faith to fundamentally transform another's property, he acquires title to the final product. For example, suppose K mistakenly believes that he owns a particular log which is actually the property of L; if K uses the log to make baseball bats, K owns the bats but is liable to L for the value of the log. Even if Moore still owned his cells, did the defendants acquire title to the cell line based on accession? If so, they would owe Moore the fair market value of his cells. How would a court determine this value?

f. **Selling Body Parts**

People regularly sell their blood, hair, and sperm. Why shouldn't Moore be allowed to sell his tissue? Our nation faces a chronic shortage of transplantable human organs such as hearts, livers, and kidneys. Over 100,000 people in the United States are on the waiting list for organs, and 16 of them die each day. Economists suggest that the major reason for the shortage is simple: the law generally prohibits the sale of body parts for the purpose of transplantation. Because there is no economic incentive to provide an organ, the supply is small. Should we solve this problem by allowing body parts to be sold?

g. ***Moore* Problems**

Apply the principles from *Moore* in resolving the following hypothetical disputes:

> (1) A is rendered unconscious in an auto accident, and brought to a hospital where the surgeons remove her tissue as part of an operation to save her life. The surgeons later use her cells to create a valuable cell line. Who owns the cells?
>
> (2) B removes his own tissue at home, which he places in a jar on his window sill. A team of rogue doctors enters his yard, takes the jar, and uses the cells to create a valuable cell line. Who owns the cells?

> (3) C, a law student who has read *Moore* carefully, enters into an agreement to sell her rare cells to a research laboratory in exchange for 5% of the value of any future cell line based on those cells. After the lab uses the cells to create a valuable cell line, it repudiates the agreement and refuses to pay C anything. Who wins the ensuing lawsuit?

h. **Legislative Response to *Moore*?**

Suppose you are a member of the state legislature interested in developing a statutory response to *Moore*. What components would your statute contain? Should scientific researchers be forced to share the profits generated from human tissues? Can you craft a system that overcomes the majority's concern about chilling scientific research?

i. **Aftermath of *Moore***

Moore effectively lost his legal battle when the United States Supreme Court denied his petition for certiorari in 1991, ending his conversion claim. He then resolved his remaining claims in a confidential settlement. It is believed that Moore received between $200,000 and $600,000, though much of this was consumed by legal fees. Moore later became an advocate for patients' rights, testifying before Congress on the use of human biological materials in research and lobbying the European Parliament to reject a proposal to patent life forms. Moore's battle with cancer ended in 2001, when he died at the age of 56.

---

2. Right to Exclude

A's toy airplane lands in B's backyard. C, a homeless person on the brink of freezing to death, wants to enter D's vacant mansion. E plans to cross F's ranch to reach her favorite fishing spot. These hypotheticals pose the question: when can an owner exclude others from his land?

Each owner has a broad right to exclude any other person from his property. Indeed, the Supreme Court has characterized the right to exclude "as one of the most essential sticks" in the bundle. *Kaiser Aetna v. United States*, 444 U.S. 164, 176 (1979). For example, if you hold title to a tract of land you may—as a general matter—prevent anyone else from entering upon it. In practical terms, a landowner's right to exclude is implemented through the tort doctrine of *trespass*.

The United States inherited this absolutist view of the right to exclude—along with most of our property law—from England in the 1700s. The trespass doctrine has deep roots in early English common law. But its scope was expanded during the "enclosure movement." Traditionally, much of the agricultural land in England was held in a form of common ownership, and was farmed on a communal basis. Peasants often held certain special rights in these lands, such as the right to remove wood for fuel or the right to raise livestock. Accordingly, fields were unfenced, and people could walk freely through open, uncultivated lands. During the 1500s, however, changing economic and social conditions led to a process by which these common lands were "enclosed," that is, converted to parcels entirely owned by individual owners. The traditional rights that peasants had enjoyed were terminated, and communal farming died away. As a result, the landowner's right to exclude others from his land—even undeveloped rural property—gained new strength.

In the eighteenth century, Sir William Blackstone endorsed the absolutist view in his famous and popular treatise, Commentaries on the Laws of England.

> ### Perspective and Analysis
>
> ... Every unwarrantable entry on another's soil the law entitles a trespass...;... For every man's land is in the eye of the law, inclosed and set apart from his neighbor's: and that either by a visible and material fence, as one field is divided from another by a hedge; or, by an ideal invisible boundary, existing only in the contemplation of law, as when one man's land adjoins to another's in the same field. Every such entry or breach of a man's close carries necessarily along with it some damage or other: for, if no other special loss can be assigned, yet still the words of the writ itself specify one general damage, *viz*. the treading down and bruising his herbage.
>
> **William Blackstone, 3 Commentaries on the Laws of England 209–10 (1768).**

Under English common law, any intentional and unprivileged entry onto land in the possession of another person was a trespass. As Restatement (Second) of Torts § 158 reflects, modern American law still follows this approach:

> One is subject to liability to another for trespass, irrespective of whether he thereby causes harm to any legally protected interest of the other, if he intentionally... enters land in the possession of the other, or causes a thing or a third person to do so....

In this context, the defendant acts *intentionally* if he voluntarily enters onto the land. It is not necessary to prove that he had a subjective intent to trespass or that he otherwise acted in bad faith. Suppose that G voluntarily walks onto land that he believes is part of a public park, but which is actually private property owned by H. This is a trespass, regardless of G's good faith.

However, an entry made under a *privilege* is not a trespass. The most common privilege is *consent*: if O enters P's land with P's consent, no trespass has occurred. A privilege may also arise from *necessity*. For example, a police officer may enter S's land in hot pursuit of a fleeing thief. Similarly, the pilot who makes a forced landing on V's land after his airplane's engine stops is privileged to enter.

But why do we allow a landowner to exclude others from his land in the first place? Suppose A wishes to cross B's land for an important purpose (for example, to deliver a new home to a family in need of shelter) and can do so without causing any harm to B. Under these circumstances, why shouldn't the law permit A to enter over B's objection?

Jacque v. Steenberg Homes, Inc.

Supreme Court of Wisconsin

563 N.W.2d 154 (1997)

WILLIAM A. BABLITCH, JUSTICE.

Steenberg Homes had a mobile home to deliver. Unfortunately for Harvey and Lois Jacque (the Jacques), the easiest route of delivery was across their land. Despite adamant protests by the Jacques, Steenberg plowed a path through the Jacques' snow-covered field and via that path, delivered the mobile home. Consequently, the Jacques sued Steenberg Homes for intentional trespass. At trial, Steenberg Homes conceded the intentional trespass, but argued that no compensatory damages had been proved, and that punitive damages could not be awarded without compensatory damages. Although the jury awarded the Jacques $1 in nominal damages and $100,000 in punitive damages, the circuit court set aside the jury's award of $100,000. The court of appeals affirmed, reluctantly concluding that it could not reinstate the punitive damages because it was bound by precedent establishing that an award of nominal damages will not sustain a punitive damage award. . . .

> **What's That?**
>
> *Punitive damages* are awarded in certain tort cases to "punish the defendant and to deter future wrongdoing." *Cooper Industries, Inc. v. Leatherman Tool Group*, 532 U.S. 424, 432 (2001). In contrast, *compensatory damages* "are intended to redress the concrete loss that the plaintiff has suffered by reason of the defendant's wrongful conduct." *Id.*

I.

. . . Plaintiffs, Lois and Harvey Jacques, are an elderly couple, now retired from farming, who own roughly 170 acres near Wilke's Lake in the town of Schleswig. The defendant, Steenberg Homes, Inc. (Steenberg), is in the business of selling mobile homes. In the fall of 1993, a neighbor of the Jacques purchased a mobile home from Steenberg. Delivery of the mobile home was included in the sales price.

Steenberg determined that the easiest route to deliver the mobile home was across the Jacques' land. Steenberg preferred transporting the home across the Jacques' land because the only alternative was a private road which was covered in up to seven feet of snow and contained a sharp curve which would require sets of "rollers" to be used when maneuvering the home around the curve. Steenberg asked the Jacques on several separate occasions whether it could move the home across the Jacques' farm field. The Jacques refused. The Jacques were sensitive about allowing others on their land because they had lost property valued at over $10,000 to other neighbors in an adverse possession action in the mid-1980's. Despite repeated refusals from the Jacques, Steenberg decided to sell the mobile home, which was to be used as a summer cottage, and delivered it on February 15, 1994.

> **Make the Connection**
>
> A person who occupies another's land in a hostile manner for a period of time may acquire title to that land under the doctrine of *adverse possession*, which you will study in Chapter 2. The Jacques lost the earlier adverse possession case only because their attorney answered the complaint one day too late. As a result, they were reluctant to allow Steenberg Homes or anyone else to use their land.

On the morning of delivery, Mr. Jacque observed the mobile home parked on the corner of the town road adjacent to his property. He decided to find out where the movers planned to take the home. The movers, who were Steenberg employees, showed Mr. Jacque the path they planned to take with the mobile home to reach the neighbor's lot. The path cut across the Jacques' land. Mr. Jacque informed the movers that it was the Jacques' land they were planning to cross and that Steenberg did not have permission to cross their land. He told them that Steenberg had been refused permission to cross the Jacques' land. . . .

At that point, the assistant manager asked Mr. Jacque how much money it would take to get permission. Mr. Jacque responded that it was not a question of money; the Jacques just did not want Steenberg to cross their land. Mr. Jacque testified that he told Steenberg to "[F]ollow the road, that is what the road is for." Steenberg employees left the meeting without permission to cross the land.

Where the mobile home crossed the Jacques' land
Click here for larger photo

At trial, one of Steenberg's employees testified that, upon coming out of the Jacques' home, the assistant manager stated: "I don't give a –– what [Mr. Jacque] said, just get the home in there any way you can." The other Steenberg employee confirmed this testimony and further testified that the assistant manager told him to park the company truck in such a way that no one could get down the town road to see the route the employees were taking with the home. The assistant manager denied giving these instructions, and Steenberg argued that the road was blocked for safety reasons.

The employees, after beginning down the private road, ultimately used a "bobcat" to cut a path through the Jacques' snow-covered field and hauled the home across the Jacques' land to the neighbor's lot. One employee testified that upon returning to the office and informing the assistant manager that they had gone across the field, the assistant manager reacted by giggling and laughing. The other employee confirmed this testimony. The assistant manager disputed this testimony.

When a neighbor informed the Jacques that Steenberg had, in fact, moved the mobile home across the Jacques' land, Mr. Jacque called the Manitowoc County Sheriff's Department. After interviewing the parties and observing the scene, an officer from the sheriff's department issued a $30 citation to Steenberg's assistant manager. . . .

This case presents three issues: (1) whether an award of nominal damages for intentional trespass to land may support a punitive damage award and, if so; (2) whether the law should apply to Steenberg or should only be applied prospectively and, if we apply the law to Steenberg; (3) whether the $100,000 in punitive damages awarded by the jury is excessive. . . .

II.

Steenberg argues that, as a matter of law, punitive damages could not be awarded by the jury because punitive damages must be supported by an award of compensatory damages and here the jury awarded only nominal and punitive damages. The Jacques contend that the rationale supporting the compensatory damage award requirement is inapposite when the wrongful act is an intentional trespass to land. We agree with the Jacques. . . .

The general rule was stated in *Barnard v. Cohen*, 165 Wis. 417, 162 N.W. 480 (1917), where the question presented was: "In an action for libel, can there be a recovery of punitory damages if only nominal compensatory damages are found?" With the bare assertion that authority and better reason supported its conclusion, the *Barnard* court said no. The rationale for the compensatory damage requirement is that if the individual cannot show actual harm, he or she has but a nominal interest, hence, society has little interest in having the unlawful, but otherwise harmless, conduct deterred, therefore, punitive damages are inappropriate. . . .

However, whether nominal damages can support a punitive damage award in the case of an intentional trespass to land has never been squarely addressed by this court. Nonetheless, Wisconsin law is not without reference to this situation. In 1854 the court established punitive damages, allowing the assessment of "damages as a punishment to the defendant for the purpose of making an example." *McWilliams v. Bragg*, 3 Wis. 424, 425 (1854). The *McWilliams* court related the facts and an illustrative tale from the English case of *Merest v. Harvey*, 128 Eng.Rep. 761 (C.P. 1814), to explain the rationale underlying punitive damages.

In *Merest,* a landowner was shooting birds in his field when he was approached by the local magistrate who wanted to hunt with him. Although the landowner refused, the magistrate proceeded to hunt. When the landowner continued to object, the magistrate threatened to have him jailed and dared him to file suit. Although little actual harm had been caused, the English court upheld damages of 500 pounds, explaining "in a case where a man disregards every principle which actuates the conduct of gentlemen, what is to restrain him except large damages?" *McWilliams,* 3 Wis. 424 at 428.

To explain the need for punitive damages, even where actual harm is slight, *McWilliams* related the hypothetical tale from *Merest* of an intentional trespasser:

> Suppose a gentleman has a paved walk in his paddock, before his window, and that a man intrudes and walks up and down before the window of his house, and looks in while the owner is at dinner, is the trespasser permitted to say "here is a halfpenny for you which is the full extent of the mischief I have done." Would that be a compensation? I cannot say that it would be. . . .

McWilliams, 3 Wis. at 428. Thus, in the case establishing punitive damages in this state, this court recognized that in certain situations of trespass, the actual harm is not in the damage done to the land, which may be minimal, but in the loss of the individual's right to exclude others from his or her property and, the court implied that this right may be punished by a large damage award despite the lack of measurable harm.

Steenberg contends that the rule established in *Barnard* prohibits a punitive damage award, as a matter of law, unless the plaintiff also receives compensatory damages. . . . The Jacques argue that both the individual and society have significant interests in deterring intentional trespass to land, regardless of the lack of measurable harm that results. We agree with the Jacques. An examination of the individual interests invaded by an intentional trespass to land, and society's interests in preventing intentional trespass to land, leads us to the conclusion that the *Barnard* rule should not apply when the tort supporting the award is intentional trespass to land.

We turn first to the individual landowner's interest in protecting his or her land from trespass. The United States Supreme Court has recognized that the private landowner's right to exclude others from his or her land is "one of the most essential sticks in the bundle of rights that are commonly . . . characterized as property." *Dolan v. City of Tigard,* 512 U.S. 374, 384 (1994) (quoting *Kaiser Aetna v. United States,* 444 U.S. 164, 176 (1979)). . . . This court has long recognized "[e]very person['s] constitutional right to the exclusive enjoyment of his own property for any purpose which does not invade the rights of another person." *Diana Shooting Club v. Lamoreux*, 114 Wis. 44, 59, 89 N.W. 880 (1902).... Thus, both this court and the Supreme Court recognize the individual's legal right to exclude others from private property.

Yet a right is hollow if the legal system provides insufficient means to protect it. Felix Cohen offers the following analysis summarizing the relationship between the individual and the state regarding property rights:

[T]hat is property to which the following label can be attached:

> To the world: Keep off X unless you have my permission, which I may grant or withhold.
>
> Signed: Private citizen
>
> Endorsed: The state

Felix S. Cohen, *Dialogue on Private Property*, IX Rutgers Law Review 357, 374 (1954). Harvey and Lois Jacque have the right to tell Steenberg Homes and any other trespasser, "No, you cannot cross our land." But that right has no practical meaning unless protected by the State. And, as this court recognized as early as 1854, a "halfpenny" award does not constitute state protection.

The nature of the nominal damage award in an intentional trespass to land case further supports an exception to *Barnard*. Because a legal right is involved, the law recognizes that actual harm occurs in every trespass. The action for intentional trespass to land is directed at vindication of the legal right. The law infers some damage from every direct entry upon the land of another. The law recognizes actual harm in every trespass to land whether or not compensatory damages are awarded. Thus, in the case of intentional trespass to land, the nominal damage award represents the recognition that, although immeasurable in mere dollars, actual harm has occurred.

The potential for harm resulting from intentional trespass also supports an exception to *Barnard*. A series of intentional trespasses, as the Jacques had the misfortune to discover in an unrelated action, can threaten the individual's very ownership of the land. The conduct of an intentional trespasser, if repeated, might ripen into prescription or adverse possession and, as a consequence, the individual landowner can lose his or her property rights to the trespasser. *See* Wis. Stat. § 893.28.

In sum, the individual has a strong interest in excluding trespassers from his or her land. Although only nominal damages were awarded to the Jacques, Steenberg's intentional trespass caused actual harm. We turn next to society's interest in protecting private property from the intentional trespasser.

Society has an interest in punishing and deterring intentional trespassers beyond that of protecting the interests of the individual landowner. Society has an interest in preserving the integrity of the legal system. Private landowners should feel confident that wrongdoers who trespass upon their land will be appropriately punished. When landowners have confidence in the legal system, they are less likely to resort to "self-help" remedies. In *McWilliams*, the court recognized the importance of "'prevent[ing] the practice of dueling, [by permitting] juries [ ] to *punish* . . . insult by exemplary damages.' " *McWilliams*, 3 Wis. at 428. Although dueling is rarely a modern form of self-help, one can easily imagine a frustrated landowner taking the law into his or her own hands when faced with a brazen trespasser, like Steenberg, who refuses to heed no trespass warnings.

People expect wrongdoers to be appropriately punished. Punitive damages have the effect of bringing to punishment types of conduct that, though oppressive and hurtful to the individual, almost invariably go unpunished by the public prosecutor. *Kink v. Combs*, 28 Wis.2d 65, 135 N.W.2d 789 (1965). The $30 forfeiture was certainly not an appropriate punishment for Steenberg's egregious trespass in the eyes of the Jacques. It was more akin to Merest's "halfpenny." If punitive damages are not allowed in a situation like this, what punishment will prohibit the intentional trespass to land? Moreover, what is to stop Steenberg Homes from concluding, in the future, that delivering its mobile homes via an intentional trespass and paying the resulting Class B forfeiture, is not more profitable than obeying the law? . . .

In sum, as the court of appeals noted, the *Barnard* rule sends the wrong message to Steenberg Homes and any others who contemplate trespassing on the land of another. It implicitly tells them that they are free to go where they please, regardless of the landowner's wishes. As long as they cause no compensable harm, the only deterrent intentional trespassers face is the nominal damage award of $1, the modern equivalent of *Merest's* halfpenny, and the possibility of a Class B forfeiture under Wis. Stat. § 943.13. We conclude that both the private landowner and society have much more than a nominal interest in excluding others from private land. . . . Accordingly, assuming that the other requirements for punitive damages have been met, we hold that nominal damages may support a punitive damage award in an action for intentional trespass to land. . . .

In conclusion, we hold that when nominal damages are awarded for an intentional trespass to land, punitive damages may, in the discretion of the jury, be awarded. Our decision today shall apply to Steenberg Homes. Finally, we hold that the $100,000 punitive damages awarded by the jury is not excessive. Accordingly, we reverse and remand to the circuit court for reinstatement of the punitive damage award.

Points for Discussion

a. **Why Couldn't Steenberg Cross?**

Steenberg had a legitimate need to cross the Jacques' field: to deliver a new home to a neighbor with minimal cost and delay. It appears that the crossing caused no damage to the Jacques' land, which was covered with snow at the time. On these facts, why should the Jacques receive any damages? What policy reasons does the Wisconsin Supreme Court offer in support of the trespass doctrine? Do these policies apply to the facts of this case?

b. **The *Merest* "Gentleman"**

The *Jacque* court relied upon *Merest*, an 1814 decision from Great Britain which recounted the hypothetical tale of an intruder who disturbed a "gentleman" during his dinner. If you were counsel for Steenberg during the oral argument in *Jacque* and the court raised *Merest*, how would you respond?

c. **Why Prohibit Trespass?**

Trespassers may interfere with the efficient use of land. For instance, suppose farmer F establishes an apple orchard on his land; he plants young trees, nurtures them, and is finally ready to harvest his first crop. Unless F can exclude other people from his orchard, it is foreseeable that strangers may enter and pick all the apples, leaving F with nothing. As Richard Posner explains, without the right to exclude, a farmer like F has "no incentive to incur [the costs of farming] because there is no reasonably assured reward for incurring them." Richard A. Posner, Economic Analysis of Law 40 (9th ed. 2014). Posner argues that giving an owner "the unqualified power to exclude everybody else from using the resource" is a necessary step in maximizing economic value. *Id.* at 41. Of course, we all suffer if farmers lack the incentive to produce food. But should the law prohibit trespass that causes no harm at all, as apparently occurred in *Jacque*? Or are there good reasons for allowing the Jacques to exclude Steenberg, regardless of whether any damage occurs? In answering these questions, consider the various theories of property discussed earlier in this chapter.

d. **The Market Solution**

Steenberg's assistant manager asked Jacque "how much money it would take to get permission" to cross, apparently in an effort to purchase access; Jacque responded that "it was not a question of money." Why wasn't Jacque willing to sell Steenberg a temporary right to cross the land? Should Steenberg's apparent willingness to pay reduce the penalty for trespass (because it tried to buy access) or increase the penalty (because it ignored the owner's clear refusal)?

e. **Legislating the Right to Exclude**

Suppose that your state legislature is considering a bill that would give each landowner the absolute right to exclude any other person from her land. Would you favor or oppose such a bill? List (1) three public policies for your position and (2) three policies against your position.

f.   (Truly) Punitive Damages

Notice that the jury awarded the Jacques $1.00 in nominal damages. This award follows the general rule that a trespass occurs even if the intrusion does not cause any actual damage. Assuming that Steenberg is liable for trespass, is the $100,000 punitive damages award appropriate on the facts of this case? Would the outcome of this case be different if the trespasser was a fisherman who walked across the Jacques' property to fish in a publicly owned river? Why?

g.   Trespass in Cyberspace

Suppose X sends spam email to 10,000 people. Is he liable in trespass? The *trespass to chattels* doctrine governs liability for interference with possession of chattels that is less intrusive than conversion. For example, in *In re Apple Inc. Device Performance Litigation*, 347 F. Supp. 3d 434 (N.D. Cal. 2018), plaintiffs claimed trespass to chattels after Apple installed software updates on their phones allegedly in order to conceal a defect that reduced battery life. The court denied Apple's motion to dismiss the claim—even though plaintiffs had consented to the updates—because Apple had allegedly mispresented their purpose.

Once we recognize the right of a landowner to exclude others from his land as a general matter, the next question is: are there any exceptions?

During the 1960s, the plight of migrant farmworkers became front page news. Farmers in California, Florida, Texas, and other states employed seasonal workers to tend and harvest crops. Typically, these workers lived in temporary labor camps on land owned by the particular farmer who employed them. The living conditions in many camps were abysmal. For example, farmers in the "Garden State" of New Jersey employed over 12,000 workers each summer, mainly Black Americans who migrated from the south for the season. In an effort to prevent legal aid attorneys, antipoverty workers, and others from entering labor camps to investigate the problems, the New Jersey Farm Bureau distributed 4,000 "No Trespassing" signs to farmers across the state. Does a farmer have the right to exclude under these circumstances?

State v. Shack

Supreme Court of New Jersey

277 A.2d 369 (1971)

The opinion of the Court was delivered by WEINTRAUB, C.J.

Defendants entered upon private property to aid migrant farmworkers employed and housed there. Having refused to depart upon the demand of the owner, defendants were charged with violating N.J.S.A. 2A:170–31 which provides that "[a]ny person who trespasses on any lands . . . after being forbidden so to trespass by the owner . . . is a disorderly person and shall be punished by a fine of not more than $50." Defendants were convicted in the Municipal Court of Deerfield Township and again on appeal in the County Court of Cumberland County on a trial *de novo*. We certified their further appeal before argument in the Appellate Division.

Before us, no one seeks to sustain these convictions. The complaints were prosecuted in the Municipal Court and in the County Court by counsel engaged by the complaining landowner, Tedesco. However Tedesco did not respond to this appeal, and the county prosecutor, while defending abstractly the constitutionality of the trespass statute, expressly disclaimed any position as to whether the statute reached the activity of these defendants.

> **Practice Pointer**
>
> In a criminal prosecution, the prosecutor is normally employed by the state. This case involves an unusual procedure, authorized under New Jersey law, by which a landowner may retain a private attorney to prosecute a criminal trespass action.

Complainant, Tedesco, a farmer, employs migrant workers for his seasonal needs. As part of their compensation, these workers are housed at a camp on his property.

Defendant Tejeras is a field worker for the Farm Workers Division of the Southwest Citizens Organization for Poverty Elimination, known by the acronym SCOPE, a nonprofit corporation funded by the Office of Economic Opportunity pursuant to an act of Congress, 42 U.S.C.A. §§ 2861–2864. The role of SCOPE includes providing for the "health services of the migrant farm worker."

Defendant Shack is a staff attorney with the Farm Workers Division of Camden Regional Legal Services, Inc., known as "CRLS," also a nonprofit corporation funded by the Office of Economic Opportunity pursuant to an act of Congress, 42 U.S.C.A. § 2809(a)(3). The mission of CRLS includes legal advice and representation for these workers.

Differences had developed between Tedesco and these defendants prior to the events which led to the trespass charges now before us. Hence when defendant Tejeras wanted to go upon Tedesco's farm to find a migrant worker who needed medical aid for the removal of 28 sutures, he called upon defendant Shack for his help with respect to the legalities involved. Shack, too, had a mission to perform on Tedesco's farm; he wanted to discuss a legal problem with another migrant worker there employed and housed. Defendants arranged to go to the farm together. Shack carried literature to inform the migrant farmworkers of the assistance available to them under federal statutes, but no mention seems to have been made of that literature when Shack was later confronted by Tedesco.

> **See It**
>
> Click here for a modern photograph of Tedesco family land, taken in the approximate area where the farmworker camp was located; note the "No Trespassing" sign.

Defendants entered upon Tedesco's property and as they neared the camp site where the farmworkers were housed, they were confronted by Tedesco who inquired of their purpose. Tejeras and Shack stated their missions. In response, Tedesco offered to find the injured worker, and as to the worker who needed legal advice, Tedesco also offered to locate the man but insisted that the consultation would have to take place in Tedesco's office and in his presence. Defendants declined, saying they had the right to see the men in the privacy of their living quarters and without Tedesco's supervision. Tedesco thereupon summoned a State Trooper who, however, refused to remove defendants except upon Tedesco's written complaint. Tedesco then executed the formal complaints charging violations of the trespass statute.

I.

The constitutionality of the trespass statute, as applied here, is challenged on several scores.

It is urged that the First Amendment rights of the defendants and of the migrant farmworkers were thereby offended. Reliance is placed on *Marsh v. Alabama*, 326 U.S. 501 (1946), where it was held that free speech was assured by the First Amendment in a company-owned town which was open to the public generally and was indistinguishable from any other town except for the fact that the title to the property was vested in a private corporation. . . . There may be some migrant camps with the attributes of the company town in *Marsh* and of course they would come within its holding. But there is nothing of that character in the case before us, and hence there would have to be an extension of *Marsh* to embrace the immediate situation.

Defendants also maintain that the application of the trespass statute to them is barred by the Supremacy Clause of the United States Constitution, Art. VI, cl. 2, and this on the premise that the application of the trespass statute would defeat the purpose of the federal statutes, under which SCOPE and CRLS are funded, to reach and aid the migrant farmworker. . . . The brief of New Jersey State Office of Legal Services, *amicus curiae*, asserts the workers' Sixth Amendment right to counsel in criminal matters is involved and suggests also that a right to counsel in civil matters is a "penumbra" right emanating from the whole Bill of Rights . . . or is a privilege of national citizenship protected by the privileges and immunities clause of the Fourteenth Amendment. . . .

These constitutional claims are not established by any definitive holding. We think it unnecessary to explore their validity. The reason is that we are satisfied that under our State law the ownership of real property does not include the right to bar access to governmental services available to migrant workers and hence there was no trespass within the meaning of the penal statute. The policy considerations which underlie that conclusion may be much the same as those which would be weighed with respect to one or more of the constitutional challenges, but a decision in nonconstitutional terms is more satisfactory, because the interests of migrant workers are more expansively served in that way than they would be if they had no more freedom than these constitutional concepts could be found to mandate if indeed they apply at all.

II.

Property rights serve human values. They are recognized to that end, and are limited by it. Title to real property cannot include dominion over the destiny of persons the owner permits to come upon the premises. Their well-being must remain the paramount concern of a system of law. Indeed the needs of the occupants may be so imperative and their strength so weak, that the law will deny the occupants the power to contract away what is deemed essential to their health, welfare, or dignity.

Here we are concerned with a highly disadvantaged segment of our society. We are told that every year farmworkers and their families numbering more than one million leave their home areas to fill the seasonal demand for farm labor in the United States. The Migratory Farm Labor Problem in the United States (1969 Report of Subcommittee on Migratory Labor of the United States Senate Committee on Labor and Public Welfare), p. 1. The migrant farmworkers come to New Jersey in substantial numbers. The report just cited places at 55,700 the number of man-months of such employment in our State in 1968 (p. 7). . . .

The migrant farmworkers are a community within but apart from the local scene. They are rootless and isolated. Although the need for their labors is evident, they are unorganized and without economic or political power. It is their plight alone that summoned government to their aid. In response, Congress provided under Title III-B of the Economic Opportunity Act of 1964 (42 U.S.C.A. § 2701 et seq.) for "assistance for migrant and other seasonally employed farmworkers and their families.". . . Section 2862(b)(1) provides for funding of programs "to meet the immediate needs of migrant and seasonal farmworkers and their families, such as day care for children, education, health services, improved housing and sanitation (including the provision and maintenance of emergency and temporary housing and sanitation facilities), legal advice and representation, and consumer training and counseling." As we have said, SCOPE is engaged in a program funded by this section, and CRLS also pursues the objectives of this section. . . .

These ends would not be gained if the intended beneficiaries could be insulated from efforts to reach them. It is in this framework that we must decide whether the camp operator's rights in his lands may stand between the migrant workers and those who would aid them. . . .

A man's right in his real property of course is not absolute. It was a maxim of the common law that one should so use his property as not to injure the rights of others. Broom, Legal Maxims (10th ed. Kersley 1939), p. 238. . . . Although hardly a precise solvent of actual controversies, the maxim does express the inevitable proposition that rights are relative and there must be an accommodation when they meet. Hence it has long been true that necessity, private or public, may justify entry upon the lands of another. . . .

> **What's That?**
>
> Black's Law Dictionary defines a *maxim* as a traditional legal precept that has been "frozen into a concise expression." Courts cite maxims to denote fundamental principles.

The subject is not static. As pointed out in 5 Powell, Real Property (Rohan 1970) § 745, pp. 493–494, while society will protect the owner in his permissible interests in land, yet

> [s]uch an owner must expect to find the absoluteness of his property rights curtailed by the organs of society, for the promotion of the best interests of others for whom these organs also operate as protective agencies. The necessity for such curtailments is greater in a modern industrialized and urbanized society than it was in the relatively simple American society of fifty, 100, or 200 years ago. The current balance between individualism and dominance of the social interest depends not only upon political and social ideologies, but also upon the physical and social facts of the time and place under discussion.

Professor Powell added in § 746, pp. 494–496:

> As one looks back along the historic road traversed by the law of land in England and in America, one sees a change from the viewpoint that he who owns may do as he pleases with what he owns, to a position which hesitatingly embodies an ingredient of stewardship; which grudgingly, but steadily, broadens the recognized scope of social interests in the utilization of things. . . .
>
> To one seeing history through the glasses of religion, these changes may seem to evidence increasing embodiments of the golden rule. To one thinking in terms of political and economic ideologies, they are likely to be labeled evidences of "social enlightenment," or of "creeping socialism" or even of "communistic infiltration," according to the individual's assumed definitions and retained or acquired prejudices. With slight attention to words or labels, time marches on toward new adjustments between individualism and the social interests.

The process involves not only the accommodation between the right of the owner and the interests of the general public in his use of this property, but involves also an accommodation between the right of the owner and the right of individuals who are parties with him in consensual transactions relating to the use of the property. Accordingly substantial alterations have been made as between a landlord and his tenant. *See Reste Realty Corp. v. Cooper*, 53 N.J. 444, 451–453, 251 A.2d 268 (1969).

The argument in this case understandably included the question whether the migrant worker should be deemed to be a tenant and thus entitled to the tenant's right to receive visitors, or whether his residence on the employer's property should be deemed to be merely incidental and in aid of his employment, and hence to involve no possessory interest in the realty. These cases did not reach employment situations at all comparable with the one before us. Nor did they involve the question whether an employee who is not a tenant may have visitors notwithstanding the employer's prohibition. Rather they were concerned with whether notice must be given to end the employee's right to remain upon the premises, with whether the employer may remove the discharged employee without court order, and with the availability of a particular judicial remedy to achieve his removal by process. We of course are not concerned here with the right of a migrant worker to remain on the employer's property after the employment is ended.

We see no profit in trying to decide upon a conventional category and then forcing the present subject into it. That approach would be artificial and distorting. The quest is for a fair adjustment of the competing needs of the parties, in the light of the realities of the relationship between the migrant worker and the operator of the housing facility.

Thus approaching the case, we find it unthinkable that the farmer-employer can assert a right to isolate the migrant worker in any respect significant for the worker's well-being. The farmer, of course, is entitled to pursue his farming activities without interference, and this defendants readily concede. But we see no legitimate need for a right in the farmer to deny the worker the opportunity for aid available from federal, State, or local services, or from recognized charitable groups seeking to assist him. Hence representatives of these agencies and organizations may enter upon the premises to seek out the worker at his living quarters. So, too, the migrant worker must be allowed to receive visitors there of his own choice, so long as there is no behavior hurtful to others, and members of the press may not be denied reasonable access to workers who do not object to seeing them.

It is not our purpose to open the employer's premises to the general public if in fact the employer himself has not done so. We do not say, for example, that solicitors or peddlers of all kinds may enter on their own; we may assume for the present that the employer may regulate their entry or bar them, at least if the employer's purpose is not to gain a commercial advantage for himself or if the regulation does not deprive the migrant worker of practical access to things he needs.

And we are mindful of the employer's interest in his own and in his employees' security. Hence he may reasonably require a visitor to identify himself, and also to state his general purpose if the migrant worker has not already informed him that the visitor is expected. But the employer may not deny the worker his privacy or interfere with his opportunity to live with dignity and to enjoy associations customary among our citizens. These rights are too fundamental to be denied on the basis of an interest in real property and too fragile to be left to the unequal bargaining strength of the parties.

> **Make the Connection**
>
> In Chapter 14, you will study the later case of *Cedar Point Nursery v. Hassid*, 141 S. Ct. 2063 (2021), where the Supreme Court held that a regulation allowing union organizers to enter land owned by agricultural employers, without their consent, was a "taking" under the Fifth Amendment. The employees in that case did not reside on the land, unlike the situation in *State v. Shack*.

It follows that defendants here invaded no possessory right of the farmer-employer. Their conduct was therefore beyond the reach of the trespass statute. The judgments are accordingly reversed and the matters remanded to the County Court with directions to enter judgments of acquittal.

Points for Discussion

a. **Exclusion and Ownership**

As you saw in *Jacque*, a landowner has the legal right to exclude others from his private property. So exactly why didn't farmer Tedesco have the right to exclude Shack and Tejeras? In answering this question, consider the sources of law that the *Shack* court relied upon. Is it accurate to say that the farmworkers acquired a right in Tedesco's land—a right to allow others to cross the land? If so, how did they acquire that right?

b. **The Question of Purpose**

The *Shack* court states: "Property rights serve human values. They are recognized to that end, and are limited by it." What does this mean? Professor Joseph Singer has suggested that in *Shack* and similar cases, "non-owners have a right of access to property based on need or some other important social policy." Joseph William Singer, *The Reliance Interest in Property*, 40 Stan. L. Rev. 611, 675 (1988). Under Singer's approach, when could an owner exclude people from his land?

c. **Applying the *Shack* Standard**

Based on the standard used in *Shack*, has a trespass occurred in these situations?

> (1) A, B, and C, farmworkers living on Tedesco's property, decide to hold a large birthday party for their co-worker D. They invite ten friends from a nearby town, who enter the property to attend the party.
>
> (2) X owns a vacant apartment building in a large city. A group of homeless people enter the building through an unlocked door and begin living there as squatters. X discovers the squatters two months later.
>
> (3) T operates a casino in Atlantic City; he discovers that gambler G is "counting cards" in order to improve his odds of winning at blackjack. T asks G to "leave and never return." G enters the casino two days later and begins gambling.

d. **Farmworkers as Tenants**

The *Shack* court could have decided the case by ruling that the farmworkers were tenants and thus entitled to receive visitors under well-settled principles of New Jersey landlord-tenant law. After all, if you are a tenant, you presumably have the right to have guests come to your apartment without the landlord's consent. But the court rejected this approach as "artificial and distorting." Why?

e. **Free Speech in Public and Quasi-Public Places**

The court also bypassed the *Shack* defendants' free speech arguments. Just as the First Amendment constrains the power of government to regulate speech on public property, *Marsh v. Alabama*, 326 U.S. 501 (1946) extended this protection to the residents of a company-owned town. Based on state constitutional law, a number of courts have held that citizens cannot be excluded from privately owned shopping centers for exercising their free speech rights. *See, e.g., PruneYard Shopping Center v. Robins*, 447 U.S. 74 (1980) (upholding California Supreme Court decision based on state constitution). *See also Watchtower Bible and Tract Society v. Village of Stratton*, 536 U.S. 150 (2002) (striking down local ordinance that required a permit in order to enter private property to promote any "cause"). Was the farmworker camp in *Shack* comparable to a company-owned town or a shopping center?

f. **Aftermath of *Shack***

"We now might as well turn the country over to the Russians," Tedesco told a reporter after the *Shack* decision. He predicted that the ruling would lead New Jersey's remaining farmers to "clear out within six months." Ronald Sullivan, *New Jersey Rules Farmers Can't Prohibit Visits to Migrants*, N.Y. Times, May 12, 1971. But New Jersey farmers continue to grow vegetables today, mainly for the New York and Philadelphia metropolitan areas. Over 10,000 migrant farmworkers are employed in the region each summer—and many still have concerns about the housing conditions in the farm labor camps.

> ### Excluding the Homeless?
>
> In *Commonwealth v. Magadini*, 52 N.E.3d 1041 (Mass. 2016), police found Magadini, a homeless person, inside a commercial building on three occasions in February and March, 2014. He was "lying in a hallway by a heater during the evening, nighttime, or early morning hours of days described as 'cold' or 'very cold.'" *Id*. at 1046. The building owner had previously served him with a "no trespass" order. The jury convicted Magadini of criminal trespass after the trial judge refused to give an instruction on the defense of necessity.
>
> The Supreme Judicial Court of Massachusetts vacated the conviction, holding that Magadini was entitled to raise the necessity defense. It explained that the defense "exonerates one who commits a crime under the 'pressure of circumstances' if the harm that would have resulted from compliance with the law . . . exceeds the harm actually resulting from the defendant's violation of the law." *Id*. at 1047. The court concluded that the weather conditions created a "clear and imminent danger" to Magadini, citing a report that "life-threatening cases of hypothermia do not require extreme temperatures" and can occur when the temperature is between 32 and 40 degrees Fahrenheit. *Id*. at 1048 n. 9. It also found "no evidence that the defendant's presence did, or had the potential to, cause physical harm to any persons." *Id*. at 1050 n. 13. The court concluded: "Our law does not permit punishment of the homeless simply for being homeless." *Id*. at 1051. See Sara K. Rankin, *Punishing Homelessness*, 22 New Crim. L. Rev. 99 (2019).
>
> Do you agree with the outcome in *Magadini*? Would it make a difference if Magadini was found sleeping inside an unlocked garage while the homeowners were on vacation? Or if he was sleeping on the couch in their living room during their vacation? What is the right balance between protecting life and respecting property rights?

---

3. Right to Use

A's factory emits noise that stops B's hens from laying eggs. The putrid odor from C's pig farm wafts into D's home. The shadow from E's barn cuts off the sunshine to F's garden. These examples all raise the same issue: what is the scope of an owner's right to use land?

Traditionally, a landowner had the absolute right to use his property in any way he wished—as long as he did not harm the rights of others. This concept was embodied in the Latin maxim *sic utere tuo ut alienum non laedas*, broadly translated as: use your own property in a manner that does not injure another person's property. In practice, the principal limitation on an owner's right to use was the common law doctrine of *nuisance*, which is discussed in more detail below. Beginning in the 1880s, states began to prohibit the spite fence, often by adopting legislation which treated it as a statutory nuisance. And since the early twentieth century, statutes and local ordinances have imposed zoning and other use restrictions on almost all land in the United States, as you will study in Chapter 11.

What explains the traditional rule? In many ways, the right to use property is the core value of ownership. As Sir Edward Coke asked over 400 years ago, "what is the land but the profits thereof[?]" Because the economy of medieval England was based on agriculture, the ability to use land for farming, in particular, was vital. The concept that an owner was entitled to determine how to use his land presumably began as an assumption, evolved into a custom, and eventually emerged as a common law rule.

Of course, as a general matter, it makes sense to recognize the owner's relatively free right to use her land as she wishes. From a utilitarian perspective, it is fair to assume that the owner of land in an agricultural society knows best how to use it productively for the benefit of all, without any need for governmental interference. A farmer in Iowa, after all, is able to evaluate the soil quality, water needs, climate situation, and other factors that determine which crop is best for his land—far better than a distant official. Other property theories similarly justify a large degree of owner autonomy in land use decisions.

The cases below explore exceptions to the general rule that a landowner is entitled to use her land as she sees fit. Our first decision examines the *spite fence* doctrine. In many jurisdictions, a landowner cannot erect an unusually high fence along his property line for the purpose of annoying his neighbor. As Oliver Wendell Holmes, Jr.—a leading figure in American jurisprudence—remarked in *Rideout v. Knox*, 19 N.E. 390, 391 (Mass. 1889), an opinion upholding the constitutionality of a spite fence statute:

> [I]t is plain that the right to use one's property for the sole purpose of injuring others is not one of the immediate rights of ownership. It is not a right for the sake of which property is recognized by the law.

See It

Click here to see a photograph and a map depicting the famous Crocker spite fence.

The Crocker spite fence on San Francisco's Nob Hill was one of the early controversies that led to such reform legislation. Charles Crocker, a California railroad baron, tried to purchase all of the properties on a particular block in the 1870s, so that his planned mansion could occupy the entire parcel. When one owner refused to sell his three-story home, Crocker built a 30-foot-high fence close around it, which effectively shut out the light and air. A local newspaper later called the fence "the most famous memorial of malignity and malevolence in the city." *Famous Spite Fence Has Outlived Its Purpose*, S.F. Chron., Nov. 1, 1902.

Tranfield v. Arcuni-English

Supreme Judicial Court of Maine

215 A.3d 222 (2019)

MEAD, J.

Patricia Arcuni-English appeals from a judgment of the Superior Court (Knox County, *Wheeler, J.*) in favor of Richard Tranfield and Karla Doremus-Tranfield (the Tranfields) on their complaint alleging that Arcuni-English's installation of trees on the parties' boundary line [violated] . . . Maine's spite fence statute, 17 M.R.S. § 2801 (2018) . . . . We affirm the judgment.

I. BACKGROUND

The court found the following facts, which are supported by competent record evidence. In January 2016, the Tranfields purchased a parcel of land that abuts and is uphill from Arcuni-English's property. At that time, the Tranfield property had a slot view of the ocean out across Arcuni-English's property, but Arcuni-English was still afforded privacy by trees and overgrown shrubbery at lower levels on the parties' boundary line.

On the day the Tranfields moved in, Mr. Tranfield went onto Arcuni-English's property to ask if he could use some of her firewood. She was not home, and he took some wood. Arcuni-English saw him in her driveway, did not recognize him, and thought that he was stealing her firewood. Later, Mr. Tranfield was removing a tree near a shed on his property and limbing dead branches on his property along the parties' boundary line. Arcuni-English approached him, expressing anger that he was cutting trees without discussing it with his neighbors beforehand. Arcuni-English then told Mr. Tranfield that she would put up a ten-foot fence to block the Tranfields' view. Additionally, Arcuni-English expressed displeasure with the Tranfields removing

> **FYI**
>
> The trial court found that during the tree cutting incident, Arcuni-English told Tranfield: "What the hell are you doing? In this neighborhood, we don't do any cutting without discussing it with the neighbors first. You New Jersey people think you can come in and do anything you want! . . . I will put up a ten-foot fence to block your view."

a koi pond on their property and with the fact that their dogs had urinated and defecated on her property.

Later, while Arcuni-English was traveling, a local landscaper who works for both parties sent Arcuni-English a photograph of the parties' boundary line. The Tranfields had cleared much of the deadwood and debris on their property, thereby opening up a view of their house to Arcuni-English's property. Arcuni-English was devastated by the Tranfields' action on their property. She called the landscaper and told him that she needed trees and privacy, and they discussed how to do it.

In April 2016, the landscaper planted approximately twenty-four arborvitaes along the boundary line. These trees were ten to twelve feet in height; some shorter trees were also installed to create an additional row to fill in any gaps. The landscaper installed seven four-to-six-foot pine trees near a structure on Arcuni-English's property.

> **What's That?**
>
> *Arborvitaes* are dense, narrow evergreen trees—part of the cedar family. They are commonly used to create tall, fast-growing hedges in residential areas to protect privacy and provide windbreaks.

The Tranfields filed a complaint against Arcuni-English in the Superior Court alleging that the plantings constituted a nuisance and seeking damages and injunctive relief. A bench trial was held on September 29, 2017, and on February 9, 2018, the court entered a judgment in favor of the Tranfields. In determining that Arcuni-English had installed a spite fence, the court relied on the following facts, all of which are supported by competent evidence in the record:

> [T]he relationship between the Tranfields and Arcuni[-]English was poor from the first day the Tranfields moved to the neighborhood and tried to borrow firewood. The relationship became increasingly contentious . . . [and b]y the time[ ] Mr. Tranfield limbed the dead branches from the trees on his side of the property line opening up his property to . . . Arcuni[-]English's property, . . . Arcuni[-]English decided to take action . . . and she instructed [the landscaper] to put up trees and to bring back her privacy.
>
> Given an excuse, . . . Arcuni[-]English finally made good her threat to put up a fence to block the Tranfields' view, made when the Tranfields first moved into the neighborhood. Her dominant motive was to install a continuous green barrier between the two properties along the boundary line. The trees were installed without any advance notice to the Tranfields, along the portion of the boundary that would block their view and without considering other types of vegetation that could provide her privacy without blocking entirely the slot view that the Tranfields had or without totally closing in their back yard. The trees that were installed were 8 to 12 feet tall and will top out at 20 feet. They are 4 to 6 feet wide already creating a continuous wall of green. [Arcuni-English]'s motive was malicious and without that motive, she would not have installed the trees as she did, even to vindicate her privacy interest, which

could have been satisfied with a use of fewer and more contained trees and bushes. Arcuni[-]English, with a dominant malicious motive, installed a continuous green wall that was both dense and unnecessary to restore her privacy. Having considered the intense animosity that Arcuni[-] English held towards the Tranfields, the court determines that she installed a spite fence. . . .

The court ordered Arcuni-English to remove every other pine tree along the boundary line, remove the trees that were planted as an additional row to fill in gaps, and trim all of the arborvitae to a height no greater than ten feet. . . .

II. DISCUSSION

. . . Pursuant to 17 M.R.S. § 2801, "Any fence or other structure in the nature of a fence, unnecessarily exceeding 6 feet in height, maliciously kept and maintained for the purpose of annoying the owners or occupants of adjoining property, shall be deemed a private nuisance." The Tranfields, as the plaintiffs, bore the burden of demonstrating each of these elements by a preponderance of the evidence. *See Ma v. Bryan*, 997 A.2d 755, 758 (Me. 2010) (stating that it is the plaintiff's burden of proof to establish the elements of a cause of action). "For purposes of the [spite fence] statute, a plaintiff need not prove that malice, the purpose to annoy, was the sole motive for building the fence. The plaintiff need only prove that such was the dominant motive, meaning that without that malicious motive, the fence would not have been erected or maintained." *Peters v. O'Leary*, 30 A.3d 825, 829 (Me. 2011) (citation, quotation marks, and emphasis omitted).

Arcuni-English argues that the court erred in determining that the Tranfields demonstrated that she had a dominantly malicious motive. We disagree. The court's finding of malice is supported by the history of animosity between the parties; the court's determination that Arcuni-English's claimed reason for building a fence was not credible; Arcuni-English's installation of the fence without advance notice to the Tranfields; and the size, extent, and anticipated growth of the trees. *See Peters*, 30 A.3d at 829 (concluding that "[t]he court's finding of malice [was] supported by evidence of the number of trees planted; the size, extent, and anticipated rapid growth of the trees; . . . [the fence-builder]'s secrecy in making arrangements for the plantings; [and the fence-builder]'s own testimony regarding" interactions between the parties); *see also Obolensky v. Trombley*, 115 A.3d 1016, 1026 (Vt. 2015) (reasoning that the trial court properly considered the history of intense animosity and conflict between the parties and the credibility of the fence-builder's claimed reasons for building the fence). Although the court stated that it did "not doubt that her privacy was part of her concern," it determined that Arcuni-English's "motive was malicious and without that motive, she would not have installed the trees as she did, even to vindicate her privacy interest."

. . . In summary, the court did not err by determining that Arcuni-English's installation of trees on the parties' boundary line constituted a spite fence pursuant to section 2801 because her installation of more than thirty trees, which created a dense and continuous wall, was done with malice. Furthermore, the court crafted a fair and limited remedy based on its findings; the plantings that constituted a legitimate privacy barrier between the properties were allowed to remain. Arcuni-English's plantings will continue to provide the privacy that she previously enjoyed and, at the same time, the slotted view of the water from the Tranfields' property will be protected.

Points for Discussion

a. Role of Intent

Why does Arcuni-English's intent matter? Suppose she had acted in complete good faith in this case—having the trees planted solely in order to protect her privacy, even though they blocked the Tranfields' view. Would the case be decided in the same way? If not, why not? As a general rule, one element of proving a spite fence case is to show that the defendant acted out of malice. Some states require the plaintiff to prove that malice was the sole motive. In Maine and certain other states, it is only necessary to show that malice was the dominant motive.

b. "Other Structure in the Nature of a Fence"

The Maine spite fence doctrine is broader than the approach followed by most states because it covers a "structure" that is not a fence, but is in the "nature of a fence." The *Tranfield* court presumably reasoned that the row of trees was in the nature of a fence because it marked a boundary line. Other than trees and other vegetation, what else could be viewed as a "structure" in the nature of a fence? What about the fact that fences can serve functions other than marking boundaries, such as providing protection or confining animals? Is the Maine approach too broad?

The world's supply of oil is dwindling, while concern about global climate change is mounting. Under these circumstances, there is renewed interest in alternative energy sources such as solar energy. Experts predict that solar power could provide over 50% of the world's electricity by 2050. To what extent should property law accommodate this process? For example, suppose A installs a solar heating system on the roof of his home, only to discover that his neighbor B plans to build his new house in a manner that will cast shadow on the solar collector. How should we resolve the dispute that arises from these conflicting uses?

The common law doctrine of nuisance is the traditional method used to resolve land use conflicts. You will study nuisance law in Chapter 11, but here is a short preview. A *private nuisance* is an (1) intentional, (2) nontrespassory, (3) unreasonable, and (4) substantial interference with (5) the use and enjoyment of the plaintiff's land. Usually, the most difficult question is whether the conduct is unreasonable. The modern view is that conduct is unreasonable if the "gravity of the harm outweighs the utility of the actor's conduct." Restatement (Second) Torts § 826(a). In effect, the court must determine whether the defendant's conduct causes more harm than good. Should nuisance law apply to our solar energy dispute?

Prah v. Maretti

Supreme Court of Wisconsin

321 N.W.2d 182 (1982)

ABRAHMSON, JUSTICE.

This appeal [presents] an issue of first impression, namely, whether an owner of a solar-heated residence states a claim upon which relief can be granted when he asserts that his neighbor's proposed construction of a residence (which conforms to existing deed restrictions and local ordinances) interferes with his access to an unobstructed path for sunlight across the neighbor's property. This case thus involves a conflict between one landowner (Glenn Prah, the plaintiff) interested in unobstructed access to sunlight across adjoining property as a natural source of energy and an adjoining landowner (Richard D. Maretti, the defendant) interested in the development of his land.

The circuit court concluded that the plaintiff presented no claim upon which relief could be granted and granted summary judgment for the defendant. We reverse the judgment of the circuit court and remand the cause to the circuit court for further proceedings.

I.

According to the complaint, the plaintiff is the owner of a residence which was constructed during the years 1978–1979. The complaint alleges that the residence has a solar system which includes collectors on the roof to supply energy for heat and hot water and that after the plaintiff built his solar-heated house, the defendant purchased the lot adjacent to and immediately to the south of the plaintiff's lot and commenced planning construction of a home. The complaint further states that when the plaintiff learned of defendant's plans to build the house he advised the defendant that if the house were built at the proposed location, defendant's house would substantially and adversely affect the integrity of plaintiff's solar system and could cause plaintiff other damage. Nevertheless, the defendant began con-

> **See It**
>
> Click here to see photographs of: (a) the Prah and Maretti houses; and (b) the shadow that Maretti's house cast on Prah's solar collector.

struction. The complaint further alleges that the plaintiff is entitled to "unrestricted use of the sun and its solar power" and demands judgment for injunctive relief and damages.

After filing his complaint, the plaintiff moved for a temporary injunction to restrain and enjoin construction by the defendant. In ruling on that motion the circuit court heard testimony, received affidavits and viewed the site.

The record made on the motion reveals the following additional facts: Plaintiff's home was the first residence built in the subdivision, and although plaintiff did not build his house in the center of the lot it was built in accordance with applicable restrictions. Plaintiff advised defendant that if the defendant's home were built at the proposed site it would cause a shadowing effect on the solar collectors which would reduce the efficiency of the system and possibly damage the system. To avoid these adverse effects, plaintiff requested defendant to locate his home an additional several feet away from the plaintiff's lot line, the exact number being disputed. Plaintiff and defendant failed to reach an agreement on the location of defendant's home before defendant started construction. The Architectural Control Committee and the Planning Commission of the City of Muskego approved the defendant's plans for his home, including its location on the lot. After such approval, the defendant apparently changed the grade of the property without prior notice to the Architectural Control Committee. The problem with defendant's proposed construction, as far as the plaintiff's interests are concerned, arises from a combination of the grade and the distance of defendant's home from the defendant's lot line.

> **See It**
>
> Click here to see a diagram showing how Maretti's house would block the sunlight from Prah's solar collector.

The circuit court denied plaintiff's motion for injunctive relief, declared it would entertain a motion for summary judgment and thereafter entered judgment in favor of the defendant. . . .

III.

. . . The plaintiff presents three legal theories to support his claim that the defendant's continued construction of a home justifies granting him relief: (1) the construction constitutes a common law private nuisance; (2) the construction is prohibited by sec. 844.01, Stats. 1979–80; and (3) the construction interferes with the solar easement plaintiff acquired under the doctrine of prior appropriation. . . .[4]

---

[4] Under the doctrine of prior appropriation the first user to appropriate the resource has the right of continued use to the exclusion of others. The doctrine of prior appropriation has been used by several western states to allocate water, *Paug Vik v. Wards Cove*, 633 P.2d 1015 (Alaska 1981), and by the New Mexico legislature to allocate solar access, secs. 47–3–1 to 47–3–5, N.M. Stats. 1978.

We consider first whether the complaint states a claim for relief based on common law private nuisance. This state has long recognized that an owner of land does not have an absolute or unlimited right to use the land in a way which injures the rights of others. The rights of neighboring landowners are relative; the uses by one must not unreasonably impair the uses or enjoyment of the other. When one landowner's use of his or her property unreasonably interferes with another's enjoyment of his or her property, that use is said to be a private nuisance. *Hoene v. Milwaukee,* 17 Wis.2d 209, 214, 116 N.W.2d 112 (1962).

The private nuisance doctrine has traditionally been employed in this state to balance the rights of landowners, and this court has recently adopted the analysis of private nuisance set forth in the Restatement (Second) of Torts. . . .

Although the defendant's obstruction of the plaintiff's access to sunlight appears to fall within the Restatement's broad concept of a private nuisance as a nontrespassory invasion of another's interest in the private use and enjoyment of land, the defendant asserts that he has a right to develop his property in compliance with statutes, ordinances and private covenants without regard to the effect of such development upon the plaintiff's access to sunlight. In essence, the defendant is asking this court to hold that the private nuisance doctrine is not applicable in the instant case and that his right to develop his land is a right which is *per se* superior to his neighbor's interest in access to sunlight. This position is expressed in the maxim "cujus est solum, ejus est usque ad coelum et ad infernos," that is, the owner of land owns up to the sky and down to the center of the earth. The rights of the surface owner are, however, not unlimited. *U.S. v. Causby,* 328 U.S. 256, 260–1 (1946). . . .

Many jurisdictions in this country have protected a landowner from malicious obstruction of access to light (the spite fence cases) under the common law private nuisance doctrine. If an activity is motivated by malice it lacks utility and the harm it causes others outweighs any social values. This court was reluctant to protect a landowner's interest in sunlight even against a spite fence, only to be overruled by the legislature. Shortly after this court upheld a landowner's right to erect a useless and unsightly sixteen-foot spite fence four feet from his neighbor's windows, *Metzger v. Hochrein,* 107 Wis. 267, 83 N.W. 308 (1900), the legislature enacted a law specifically defining a spite fence as an actionable private nuisance. Thus a landowner's interest in sunlight has been protected in this country by common law private nuisance law at least in the narrow context of the modern American rule invalidating spite fences. *See, e.g., Sundowner, Inc. v. King,* 95 Idaho 367, 509 P.2d 785 (1973); Restatement (Second) of Torts, sec. 829 (1977).

This court's reluctance in the nineteenth and early part of the twentieth century to provide broader protection for a landowner's access to sunlight was premised on three policy considerations. First, the right of landowners to use their property as they wished, as long as they did not cause physical damage to a neighbor, was jealously guarded.

Second, sunlight was valued only for aesthetic enjoyment or as illumination. Since artificial light could be used for illumination, loss of sunlight was at most a personal annoyance which was given little, if any, weight by society.

Third, society had a significant interest in not restricting or impeding land development. *Dillman v. Hoffman*, 38 Wis. 559, 574 (1875). This court repeatedly emphasized that in the growth period of the nineteenth and early twentieth centuries change is to be expected and is essential to property and that recognition of a right to sunlight would hinder property development. . . .

Considering these three policies, this court concluded that in the absence of an express agreement granting access to sunlight, a landowner's obstruction of another's access to sunlight was not actionable. *Miller v. Hoeschler*, 126 Wis. 263, 271, 105 N.W. 790 (1905). These three policies are no longer fully accepted or applicable. They reflect factual circumstances and social priorities that are now obsolete.

> **Make the Connection**
>
> Modern law imposes limits on how most land can be used. You will study *Euclid v. Ambler Realty* in Chapter 11 and *Just v. Marinette County* in Chapter 12.

First, society has increasingly regulated the use of land by the landowner for the general welfare. *Euclid v. Ambler Realty Co.*, 272 U.S. 365 (1926); *Just v. Marinette*, 56 Wis.2d 7, 201 N.W.2d 761 (1972).

Second, access to sunlight has taken on a new significance in recent years. In this case the plaintiff seeks to protect access to sunlight, not for aesthetic reasons or as a source of illumination but as a source of energy. Access to sunlight as an energy source is of significance both to the landowner who invests in solar collectors and to a society which has an interest in developing alternative sources of energy.

Third, the policy of favoring unhindered private development in an expanding economy is no longer in harmony with the realities of our society. *State v. Deetz*, 66 Wis.2d 1, 224 N.W.2d 407 (1974). The need for easy and rapid development is not as great today as it once was, while our perception of the value of sunlight as a source of energy has increased significantly.

Courts should not implement obsolete policies that have lost their vigor over the course of the years. The law of private nuisance is better suited to resolve landowners' disputes about property development in the 1980's than is a rigid rule which does not recognize a landowner's interest in access to sunlight. As we said in *Ballstadt v. Pagel*, 202 Wis. 484, 489, 232 N.W. 862 (1930), "What is regarded in law as constituting a nuisance in modern times would no doubt have been tolerated without question in former times." We read *State v. Deetz*, 66 Wis.2d 1, 224 N.W.2d 407 (1974), as an endorsement of the application of common law nuisance to situations involving the conflicting interests of landowners and as rejecting *per se* exclusions to the nuisance law reasonable use doctrine.

In *Deetz* the court abandoned the rigid common law common enemy rule with respect to surface water and adopted the private nuisance reasonable use rule, namely that the landowner is subject to liability if his or her interference with the flow of surface waters unreasonably invades a neighbor's interest in the use and enjoyment of land. Restatement (Second) of Torts, sec. 822, 826, 829 (1977). This court concluded that the common enemy rule which served society "well in the days of burgeoning national expansion of the mid-nineteenth and early-twentieth centuries" should be abandoned because it was no longer "in harmony with the realities of our society." *Deetz, supra*, 66 Wis.2d at 14–15, 224 N.W.2d 407. We recognized in *Deetz* that common law rules adapt to changing social values and conditions.

Yet the defendant would have us ignore the flexible private nuisance law as a means of resolving the dispute between the landowners in this case and would have us adopt an approach, already abandoned in *Deetz*, of favoring the unrestricted development of land and of applying a rigid and inflexible rule protecting his right to build on his land and disregarding any interest of the plaintiff in the use and enjoyment of his land. This we refuse to do.

Private nuisance law, the law traditionally used to adjudicate conflicts between private landowners, has the flexibility to protect both a landowner's right of access to sunlight and another landowner's right to develop land. Private nuisance law is better suited to regulate access to sunlight in modern society and is more in harmony with legislative policy and the prior decisions of this court than is an inflexible doctrine of non-recognition of any interest in access to sunlight across adjoining land.

We therefore hold that private nuisance law, that is, the reasonable use doctrine as set forth in the Restatement, is applicable to the instant case. Recognition of a nuisance claim for unreasonable obstruction of access to sunlight will not prevent land development or unduly hinder the use of adjoining land. It will promote the reasonable use and enjoyment of land in a manner suitable to the 1980's. That obstruction of access to light might be found to constitute a nuisance in certain circumstances does not mean that it will be or must be found to constitute a nuisance under all circumstances. The result in each case depends on whether the conduct complained of is unreasonable.

> **Food for Thought**
>
> The majority suggests that recognition of a nuisance action for "unreasonable obstruction of access to sunlight" will not unduly hinder land development. Do you agree?

Accordingly we hold that the plaintiff in this case has stated a claim under which relief can be granted. Nonetheless we do not determine whether the plaintiff in this case is entitled to relief. In order to be entitled to relief the plaintiff must prove the elements required to establish actionable nuisance, and the conduct of the defendant herein must be judged by the reasonable use doctrine. . . .

CALLOW, JUSTICE (dissenting).

. . . The majority . . . concludes that this court's past reluctance to extend protection to a landowner's access to sunlight beyond the spite fence cases is based on obsolete policies which have lost their vigor over the course of the years. . . . The majority has failed to convince me that these policies are obsolete. . . .

I firmly believe that a landowner's right to use his property within the limits of ordinances, statutes, and restrictions of record where such use is necessary to serve his legitimate needs is a fundamental precept of a free society which this court should strive to uphold. . . .

I know of no cases repudiating policies favoring the right of a landowner to use his property as he lawfully desires or which declare such policies are "no longer fully accepted or applicable" in this context. The right of a property owner to lawful enjoyment of his property should be vigorously protected, particularly in those cases where the adjacent property owner could have insulated himself from the alleged problem by acquiring the land as a defense to the potential problem or by provident use of his own property. . . .

I believe the facts of the instant controversy present the classic case of the owner of a solar collector who fails to take any action to protect his investment. There is nothing in the record to indicate that Mr. Prah disclosed his situation to Mr. Maretti prior to Maretti's purchase of the lot or attempted to secure protection for his solar collector prior to Maretti's submission of his building plans to the architectural committee. Such inaction should be considered a significant factor in determining whether a cause of action exists. . . .

Because I do not believe that the facts of the present case give rise to a cause of action for private nuisance, I dissent.

Points for Discussion

a. Right to Use

Prah and Maretti each wanted to use his lot for a purpose that injured the other. Although the case assumes that Maretti's conduct is harming Prah, it may be equally valid to characterize the situation as Prah's conduct harming Maretti. Do you see why? How should the law resolve competing land use claims as a general matter? How strong are the policy arguments used by the majority and the dissent in this particular case?

b. Nuisance Law

The key issue on appeal in *Prah* was whether nuisance law was applicable to the dispute as a theoretical matter—not whether Maretti's house was in fact a nuisance. The Wisconsin Supreme Court remanded the case to the trial court to decide this factual question. How would you decide the case, using the Restatement standards set forth above? Note that the dissent's approach—like all "bright line" rules—has the virtues of certainty and predictability, perhaps at the cost of justice in the individual case. If the law requires a case-by-case determination of whether any proposed new home may be a nuisance to existing uses, how will this affect development? If you represented a client who wanted to build a new home on a vacant lot located south of an existing home with a rooftop solar collector, how would you advise her to proceed?

c. A Fundamental Right?

Should a landowner be entitled to build a house on his own land regardless of the wishes of neighbors, as long as the house complies with all laws? The dissent suggests that this is a "fundamental precept of a free society." What theory of property does this view reflect? In *Fontainebleau Hotel Corp. v. Forty-Five Twenty-Five*, 114 So. 2d 357 (Fla. Dist. Ct. App. 1959), the court refused to stop an oceanfront hotel from building a 14-story addition that would cast a shadow on the pool and sunbathing areas of an adjacent hotel. It relied on the "universally held" view that "where a structure serves a useful and beneficial purpose, it does not give rise to a cause of action . . . under the maxim *sic utere tuo ut alienum non laedas*, even though it causes injury to another by cutting off the light and air and interfering with the view that would otherwise be available over adjoining land in its natural state. . . ." *Id.* at 359.

d. The Coase Theorem

The *Coase Theorem* states that the initial allocation of a resource is irrelevant to economic efficiency—in the absence of transaction costs—because the affected parties will reach an efficient allocation through bargaining. *See* Ronald Coase, *The Problem of Social Cost*, 3 J.L. & Econ. 1 (1960). In this context, *transaction costs* refer to expenses of reaching and performing an agreement, such as the cost of searching for information, attorney's fees, and other negotiating costs. Why didn't Prah and Maretti negotiate a solution to their dispute without the need for litigation? Central to the law and economics approach is the assumption that each person is a *rational maximizer*, that is, one who seeks to rationally maximize his self-interest. Since Prah and Maretti were unable to bargain successfully, should the court have imposed an efficient bargain (e.g., by requiring Prah to pay Maretti in exchange for not blocking the solar collector)?

e. Capturing Sunshine

Did Prah "capture" the sunshine that flows across Maretti's land in the same way that Pierson captured the fox in *Pierson v. Post*? And wasn't Prah first-in-time, like Pierson? Or are these arguments inapplicable to the facts in *Prah*? Note that one of Prah's theories was *prior appropriation*, a doctrine used to allocate water rights in some western states. Under this approach, the first person who both (1) takes water from a river or other surface watercourse and (2) puts that water to beneficial use (e.g., for irrigating crops) acquires a permanent right to that water. The Colorado Supreme Court explained the policy basis for prior appropriation in the famous decision of *Coffin v. Left Hand Ditch Co.*, 6 Colo. 443 (1882): "to encourage the diversion and use of water . . . for agriculture" to ensure the productive use of land. Should the *Prah* court have adopted a prior appropriation approach to sunshine?

f. *Prah* Problems

How far does *Prah* stretch? In the problems below, should the court apply nuisance law or not?

> (1) A constructs a windmill in her back yard to generate electricity. B now proposes to build a home on his adjacent lot, which will partially block the flow of wind.
>
> (2) C builds a new home with large south-facing windows. The windows function much like a greenhouse, trapping warm air inside and thus reducing C's home heating bills; they also provide a lovely view of the countryside. D now plans to build a home on her adjacent lot, which will partially block the sunshine from C's windows (and also block the view).

g. Aftermath of *Prah*

The construction of Maretti's house was completed before the trial of Prah's nuisance claim could begin. Maretti later settled the case by a cash payment to Prah. Despite the partial blockage of sunlight caused by Maretti's house, Prah was still able to use his solar collector system to some extent; Prah later removed the collector from his roof. Ironically, while *Prah* was pending before the Wisconsin Supreme Court, the state legislature adopted a new Solar Access Act in order to encourage the use of solar energy. The act empowers municipalities to grant a solar access permit to a landowner who wishes to install a solar collector system; such a permit restricts the land development rights of neighboring owners. Wis. Stat. § 66.0403.

---

4. Right to Destroy

A plans to chop up the world-famous Rembrandt painting she owns. B, a former Supreme Court justice, wants to shred his legal papers before he dies. C's will directs his executor to demolish his mansion after he dies. Will the law intervene in any of these situations?

It is inevitable that most property will be destroyed. For example, if you ate an apple for lunch this week, you presumably destroyed the apple. After all, the apple was grown in order to be consumed. Or if you own a ramshackle, termite-infested house that has outlived its useful life, you might choose to demolish it in order to build a new one. In this sense, the right to destroy is a logical adjunct to the right to use.

But difficulty arises when an owner seeks to destroy property that retains substantial value, like a renowned painting, historic papers, or a new mansion. Of course, if the owner is insane or otherwise incompetent to handle his affairs—which might be evidenced by senseless destruction of property—a court is empowered to appoint a guardian or conservator to preserve the estate. Short of this extreme situation, however, what is the scope of an owner's right to destroy?

One important case dealing with the right to destroy arose in a wealthy St. Louis neighborhood known as "Kingsbury Place," a group of 63 homes located on two city blocks. In 1902, when development began, it was one of the first residential subdivisions in the United States. With homes ranging from mansions to large townhouses, Kingsbury Place has been described as "one of St. Louis' jewel communities and . . . one of the world's premier private places." Julius K. Hunter, Kingsbury Place: The First Two Hundred Years xiii (1982). Thus, "[t]he homes on Kingsbury Place and the people who built them . . . represent the finest application of Midwestern wealth to an elegant and sophisticated life-style at the turn of the century." *Id.* Number 4 Kingsbury Place was a two-story Mediterranean villa built in 1922 and owned by Louise Woodruff Johnston. Her will mandated that the home be destroyed after her death. A group of neighbors led by Edward Eyerman (who lived at No. 21 Kingsbury Place) brought suit to stop the demolition.

> **FYI**
>
> Famous Kingsbury Place residents have included William Danforth (founder of Ralston Purina), Ben Edwards (co-founder of A.G. Edwards and Sons), Francis Fowler (owner of the liqueur "Southern Comfort"), Saunders Norvell (president of the Remington Arms Company), and Sara Teasdale (American poet).

Eyerman v. Mercantile Trust Co.

Court of Appeals of Missouri

524 S.W.2d 210 (1975)

RENDLEN, JUDGE.

Plaintiffs appeal from denial of their petition seeking [an] injunction to prevent demolition of a house at #4 Kingsbury Place in the City of St. Louis. The action is brought by individual neighboring property owners and certain trustees for the Kingsbury Place Subdivision. We reverse.

Louise Woodruff Johnston, owner of the property in question, died January 14, 1973, and by her will directed the executor ". . . to cause our home at 4 Kingsbury Place . . . to be razed and to sell the land upon which it is located . . . and to transfer the proceeds of the sale . . . to the residue of my estate." Plaintiffs assert that razing the home will adversely affect their property rights, violate the terms of the subdivision trust indenture for Kingsbury Place, produce an actionable private nuisance and is contrary to public policy. . . .

Johnston's house
Click here for larger photo

Whether #4 Kingsbury Place should be razed is an issue of public policy involving individual property rights and the community at large. The plaintiffs have pleaded and proved facts sufficient to show a personal, legally protectible interest.

Demolition of the dwelling will result in an unwarranted loss to this estate, the plaintiffs and the public. The uncontradicted testimony was that the current value of the house and land is $40,000.00; yet the estate could expect no more than $5,000.00 for the empty lot, less the cost of demolition at $4,350.00, making a grand loss of $39,350.00 if the unexplained and capricious direction to the executor is effected. Only $650.00 of the $40,000.00 asset would remain.

> **See It**
>
> Click here to see pictures of the Kingsbury Place area near the Johnston house.

Kingsbury Place is an area of high architectural significance, representing excellence in urban space utilization. Razing the home will depreciate adjoining property values by an estimated $10,000.00 and effect corresponding losses for other neighborhood homes. The cost of constructing a house of comparable size and architectural exquisiteness would approach $200,000.00.

The importance of this house to its neighborhood and the community is reflected in the action of the St. Louis Commission on Landmarks and Urban Design designating Kingsbury Place as a landmark of the City of St. Louis. This designation, under consideration prior to the institution of this suit, points up the aesthetic and historical qualities of the area and assists in stabilizing Central West End St. Louis. It was testified by the Landmarks Commission chairman that the private place concept, once unique to St. Louis, fosters higher home maintenance standards and is among the most effective methods for stabilizing otherwise deteriorating neighborhoods. The executive director of Heritage St. Louis, an organization operating to preserve the architecture of the city, testified to the importance of preserving Kingsbury Place intact:

> The reasons [sic] for making Kingsbury Place a landmark is that it is a definite piece of urban design and architecture. It starts out with monumental gates on Union. There is a long corridor of space, furnished with a parkway in the center, with houses on either side of the street.... The existence of this piece of architecture depends on the continuity of the [sic] both sides. Breaks in this continuity would be as holes in this wall, and would detract from the urban design qualities of the streets. And the richness of the street is this belt of green lot on either side, with rich tapestry of the individual houses along the sides. Many of these houses are landmarks in themselves, but they add up to much more.... I would say Kingsbury Place, as a whole, with its design, with its important houses ... is a most significant piece of urban design by any standard.

To remove #4 Kingsbury from the street was described as having the effect of a missing front tooth. The space created would permit direct access to Kingsbury Place from the adjacent alley, increasing the likelihood the lot will be subject to uses detrimental to the health, safety and beauty of the neighborhood. The mere possibility that a future owner might build a new home with the inherent architectural significance of the present dwelling offers little support to sustain the condition for destruction.

We are constrained to take judicial notice of the pressing need of the community for dwelling units as demonstrated by recent U.S. Census Bureau figures showing a decrease of more than 14% in St. Louis City housing units during the decade of the 60's. This decrease occurs in the face of housing growth in the remainder of the metropolitan area. It becomes apparent that no individual, group of individuals nor the community generally benefits from the senseless destruction of the house; instead, all are harmed and only the caprice of the dead testatrix is served. Destruction of the house harms the neighbors, detrimentally affects the community, causes monetary loss in excess of $39,000.00 to the estate and is without benefit to the dead woman.

> **Food for Thought**
>
> Isn't it reasonable to assume that someone would have built a new house on the lot if the Johnston house had been demolished? After all, much of the majority opinion is devoted to explaining how desirable it is to live in the Kingsbury Place neighborhood. Why should the court intervene here?

No reason, good or bad, is suggested by the will or record for the eccentric condition. This is not a living person who seeks to exercise a right to reshape or dispose of her property; instead, it is an attempt by will to confer the power to destroy upon an executor who is given no other interest in the property. To allow an executor to exercise such power stemming from apparent whim and caprice of the testatrix contravenes public policy.

The Missouri Supreme Court held in *State ex rel. McClintock v. Guinotte*, 275 Mo. 298, 204 S.W. 806, 808 (banc 1918), that the taking of property by inheritance or will is not an absolute or natural right but one created by the laws of the sovereign power. The court points out the state "may foreclose the right absolutely, or it may grant the right upon conditions precedent, which conditions, if not otherwise violative of our Constitution, will have to be complied with before the right of descent and distribution (whether under the law or by will) can exist.". . . While living, a person may manage, use or dispose of his money or property with fewer restraints than a decedent by will. One is generally restrained from wasteful expenditure or destructive inclinations by the natural desire to enjoy his property or to accumulate it during his lifetime. Such considerations however have not tempered the extravagance or eccentricity of the testamentary disposition here on which there is no check except the courts. . . .

The term "public policy" cannot be comprehensively defined in specific terms but the phrase "against public policy" has been characterized as that which conflicts with the morals of the time and contravenes any established interest of society. Acts are said to be against public policy "when the law refuses to enforce or recognize them, on the ground that they have a mischievous tendency, so as to be injurious to the interests of the state, apart from illegality or immorality." *Dille v. St. Luke's Hospital*, 355 Mo. 436, 196 S.W.2d 615, 620 (1946). . . .

Public policy may be found in the Constitution, statutes and judicial decisions of this state or the nation. *In re Rahn's Estate*, 316 Mo. 492, 291 S.W. 120 (1927). But in a case of first impression where there are no guiding statutes, judicial decisions or constitutional provisions, "a judicial determination of the question becomes an expression of public policy provided it is so plainly right as to be supported by the general will." *In re Mohler's Estate*, 343 Pa. 299, 22 A.2d 680, 683 (1941). . . .

Although public policy may evade precise, objective definition, it is evident from the authorities cited that this senseless destruction serving no apparent good purpose is to be held in disfavor. A well-ordered society cannot tolerate the waste and destruction of resources when such acts directly affect important interests of other members of that society. It is clear that property owners in the neighborhood of #4 Kingsbury, the St. Louis Community as a whole and the beneficiaries of testatrix's estate will be severely injured should the provisions of the will be followed. No benefits are present to balance against this injury and we hold that to allow the condition in the will would be in violation of the public policy of this state. . . .

CLEMENS, JUDGE (dissenting).

... The simple issue in this case is whether the trial court erred by refusing to enjoin a trustee from carrying out an explicit testamentary directive. In an emotional opinion, the majority assumes a psychic knowledge of the testatrix' reasons for directing her home be razed; her testamentary disposition is characterized as "capricious," "unwarranted," "senseless," and "eccentric." But the record is utterly silent as to her motives.

The majority's reversal of the trial court here spawns bizarre and legally untenable results. By its decision, the court officiously confers a "benefit" upon testamentary beneficiaries who have never litigated or protested against the razing. The majority opinion further proclaims that public policy demands we enjoin the razing of this private residence in order to prevent land misuse in the City of St. Louis. But the City, like the beneficiaries, is not a party to this lawsuit. The fact is the majority's holding is based upon wispy, self-proclaimed public policy grounds that were only vaguely pleaded, were not in evidence, and were only sketchily briefed by the plaintiffs. ...

... The majority opinion bases its reversal on public policy. But plaintiffs themselves did not substantially rely upon this nebulous concept. Plaintiffs' brief contends merely that an "agency of the City of St. Louis has recently designated Kingsbury Place as a landmark," citing § 24.070, Revised Code of the City of St. Louis. Plaintiffs argue removal of the Johnston home would be "intentional . . . destruction of a landmark of historical interest." Neither the ordinance cited in the brief nor any action taken under it were in evidence. Indeed, the Chairman of the Landmarks and Urban Design Commission testified the Commission did not declare the street a landmark until after Mrs. Johnston died. A month after Mrs. Johnston's death, several residents of the street apparently sensed the impending razing of the Johnston home and applied to have the street declared a landmark. The Commissioner testified it was the Commission's "civic duty to help those people."

... As much as our aesthetic sympathies might lie with neighbors near a house to be razed, those sympathies should not so interfere with our considered legal judgment as to create a questionable legal precedent. Mrs. Johnston had the right during her lifetime to have her house razed, and I find nothing which precludes her right to order her executor to raze the house upon her death. It is clear that "the law favors the free and untrammeled use of real property." *Gibbs v. Cass,* 431 S.W.2d 662[2] (Mo. App. 1968). This applies to testamentary dispositions. An owner has exclusive control over the use of his property subject only to the limitation that such use may not *substantially impair another's right to peaceably enjoy his property. City of Fredricktown v. Osborn,* 429 S.W.2d 17[2, 3] (Mo. App. 1968). . . . Plaintiffs have not shown that such impairment will arise from the mere presence of another vacant lot on Kingsbury Place. . . .

Points for Discussion

a. **Property and Autonomy**

In essence, *Eyerman* asks: how much autonomy does an owner have over her property? The majority is concerned about the "waste and destruction of resources" inherent in allowing an owner to demolish property, while the dissent suggests that the only limitation on an owner's use of property is that "such use may not substantially impair another's right to peaceably enjoy his property." Which philosophical approaches to property do these views reflect? Which is closest to your own view?

b. **The Role of Intent**

In this case, there was no evidence about *why* Johnston wanted her home to be destroyed. Should this matter? Humans ordinarily make rational decisions, assuming that they are mentally competent. Assuming that Johnston was competent, why shouldn't the court enforce her decision? In *Estate of Beck*, 676 N.Y.S.2d 838, 841 (Sur. Ct. 1998), the court upheld the decedent's direction that her home be destroyed, noting that "[t]he clearly expressed provisions of a duly executed Will cannot be abrogated based on anemic assertions of vascillating public interest." If the owner's motive is relevant, what would be a suitable reason for destroying a house after its owner dies? *See, e.g., National City Bank v. Case Western Reserve University*, 369 N.E.2d 814 (Ohio Ct. Com. Pleas 1976) (suggesting that the decedent's desire to prevent her home from being desecrated by being turned into a business establishment after her death was an adequate reason to allow its destruction).

c. **Timing of Destruction**

The majority states that a living person may "dispose of his money or property with fewer restraints than a decedent by will." Why is the timing of destruction relevant? Suppose that Johnston—knowing she was near death—instructed a contractor to bulldoze her home before she died. Would the case have come out differently?

d. **Harming Neighbors**

How important to the outcome is the fact that the razing of Johnston's house would lower the value of nearby houses, and thus cause financial harm to neighbors? Does this case stand for the proposition that an owner cannot do anything on her own land that will lower the value of adjacent properties?

e. **Historic Preservation Ordinances**

The St. Louis landmarks ordinance mentioned in *Eyerman* was an early—and toothless—historic preservation ordinance, which did not expressly restrict an owner's ability to destroy. Today, state and local historic preservation ordinances are both widespread and more restrictive. For example, the entire French Quarter of New Orleans and large sections of downtown New York City are subject to such ordinances. The modern ordinance typically provides that the owner of covered property cannot make substantial modifications to the structure without government approval. The New York City landmarks ordinance was unsuccessfully attacked as a "taking" of private property under the Fifth Amendment in *Penn Central Transportation Co. v. City of New York*, 438 U.S. 104 (1978), which you will study in Chapter 14.

f.   Destruction of Animals

Suppose that O owns a healthy and valuable horse, which he decides to destroy for no particular reason. Representing a local animal rights group, you seek an injunction against the destruction, citing *Eyerman*. Would your argument succeed? A number of courts have refused to enforce provisions in wills that direct the killing of animals. *See, e.g., In re Capers Estate*, 34 Pa. D. & C.2d 131 (Pa. Ct. Com. Pleas 1964) (dogs) and *Estate of Wishart*, [1992] 129 N.B.R.2d 397 (horses). But is destruction of animals during the owner's lifetime a different situation?

In *Commonwealth v. Kneller*, 999 A.2d 608 (Pa. Super. Ct. 2010), the defendant dog owner convinced a friend to shoot and kill her dog, apparently out of spite. She was later convicted of conspiracy to commit cruelty to an animal, under a state statute which made it illegal for a person to "kill[ ] . . . any dog . . . whether belonging to himself or otherwise." On appeal, she claimed that the jury should have been instructed that the owner of an animal has a right to destroy her animal. The court upheld the conviction, citing with approval this phrase from an earlier opinion in the same case: "A sweeping policy conclusion that a dog owner can shoot a healthy, happy dog for no reason is not justifiable under the law, does not comport with the legislature's statutory scheme, is no defense to the crime of Cruelty to Animals, and would replace the call 'Lassie, come home' with 'Lassie, run for your life.'" *Id.* at 612.

g.   Kingsbury Place Today

The Johnston house still stands and is worth more than $1,000,000. Kingsbury Place is still considered to be one of the premier addresses in St. Louis. In 2007, it was listed on the National Register of Historic Places in recognition of its significance to American history. Although the Johnston house is included in the listing, federal law does not guarantee its preservation. The owner of a listed property has no legal obligation to maintain or restore it, although federal funds may be available to assist the owner's voluntary preservation effort.

The right to destroy attracted little scholarly attention until the 1990s. One of the most searching explorations is an article by Professor Lior Jacob Strahilevitz, simply titled *The Right to Destroy*.

Perspective and Analysis

. . . As a matter of everyday experience, the right to destroy one's own property seems firmly entrenched. Rational people discard old clothes, furniture, albums, and unsent letters every day. Most of this "junk" is worth little or nothing, so its destruction proves entirely uncontroversial. Indeed, it is difficult to imagine how a modern capitalist economy would function if owners were barred from destroying obsolete refrigerators, unfashionable clothes, or rough drafts of written work. Even in the context of valuable property, popular sentiment seems to tolerate substantial property destruction. For example, American cadavers are frequently buried wearing wedding rings, other jewelry, and expensive clothing. And no one took seriously historic preservationists' protests when a Chicago restaurant chain spent $113,824 to purchase and destroy the infamous "cursed" baseball that Steve Bartman deflected during game six of the 2003 National League Championship Series. . . .

When asked to resolve cases where one party seeks to destroy her property, courts have reacted with great hostility toward the owner's destructive plans. Despite the existence of a norm that tolerates the burial of wedding rings, courts might well refuse a decedent's humble request to wear such jewelry for eternity. If a testator orders her executor to destroy her home upon her death, the law probably will render the executor unable to carry out her wishes. And if a landlord requests the city's permission to demolish a venerable but badly burned building that has become an eyesore, a teetering hazard, and a financial burden, the government can thwart her wishes. Confronted with arguably hard cases and high stakes, many American courts have rejected the notion that an owner has the right to destroy that which is hers, particularly in the testamentary context. . . .

Those who wish to curtail the right to destroy base their argument almost exclusively on the resource waste that results from property destruction. Usable resources may be squandered; neighborhoods may empty; and historians may have more difficulty studying artistic, political, or cultural traditions. These are all substantial concerns. But . . . prohibiting people from destroying their property can result in waste too. Historic preservation laws can lock inefficient land uses into place. Rules barring patent suppression can discourage firms from investing in innovations. Rules requiring presidents to preserve all presidential papers can deter them from memorializing controversial or sensitive ideas. Particularly in cases involving high transaction costs, widely held prodestruction norms, or substantial adverse ex ante effects, the cure of preventing destruction is worse than the disease of allowing it.

. . . Rational people usually do not destroy valuable property intentionally. So where the government witnesses a rational person destroying her valuable property, it should presume that the destructive act furthers expressive objectives. This deferential approach still raises the question of

> whether expressive interests should trump the usual concerns about wasted resources and associated negative externalities.
>
> **Lior Jacob Strahilevitz,** *The Right to Destroy,* 114 Yale L.J. 781, 783–84, 852–53 (2005).

Points for Discussion

a. **A Qualified Right to Destroy?**

Professor Strahilevitz suggests that the government should presume that a destructive act by a rational person "furthers expressive objectives." In litigation, normally a presumption can be rebutted by evidence, so the practical effect of his approach would be to force the opponents of destruction to present evidence showing that the owner had a non-expressive intent. What are the benefits and costs of this approach? Suppose that the *Eyerman* court had adopted this view. Would this have affected the outcome of the case?

b. **Eminent Domain**

Government has the inherent power to take private property for public use upon payment of just compensation, consistent with the Fifth Amendment's Takings Clause and similar provisions of state constitutions. This power is known as *eminent domain*, which you will study in Chapter 13. For example, if the City of St. Louis wanted to preserve Johnston's house as a public museum, it had the undeniable right to take title to the property—upon payment of fair market value to Johnston's estate. Items with unique significance to the public in general, such as fine art or historic documents, can be similarly preserved by government purchase. Is eminent domain a better solution to the destruction problem than the approach presented by Professor Strahilevitz?

c. **Moral Rights of Artists**

The civil law system has long recognized that artists hold "moral rights" in their artwork—apart from copyright law—even after they sell their works. These protections include the right to prevent the current owner from destroying or significantly modifying the artwork. In 1990, Congress enacted the Visual Artists Rights Act (VARA), which provides similar protection. Under VARA, the author of a work of

> **What's That?**
>
> The legal systems of most nations are based either on the *civil law* or *common law* traditions. The civil law system originated in Roman law, and generally prevails today in Africa, Asia, Europe, and South America. The common law system, which developed in England, is used in the United Kingdom and former British colonies, including Australia, Canada, and the United States.

"visual art" created on or after June 1, 1990 has the rights, inter alia, to (1) prevent "any intentional distortion, mutilation, or other modification of that work which would be prejudicial to his or her honor or reputation" and (2) prevent "any destruction of a work of recognized stature." 17 U.S.C. § 106A(a)(3). *See, e.g., Castillo v. G & M Realty L.P.*, 950 F.3d 155 (2d Cir. 2020) (upholding $6.75 million award for willful destruction of murals created by graffiti artists).

d. Presidential Papers

Does the President of the United States have the right to destroy his or her presidential papers? During most of our nation's history, presidential papers were treated as private property—and were often destroyed by ex-presidents. Concerned that former President Nixon would destroy the infamous White House tapes that led to his resignation, Congress enacted a 1974 statute giving the General Services Administration custody of the tapes and other presidential papers. Nixon challenged the statute as an unlawful taking of his private property, claiming $200 million in damages; the case was eventually settled after his death for $18 million. To avoid similar disputes in the future, Congress adopted the Presidential Records Act of 1978 which specifies that "[t]he United States shall reserve and retain complete ownership, possession, and control of Presidential records. . . ." 44 U.S.C. § 2202. However, this legislation does not affect the property rights of other federal officials.

e. Human Embryos

Should a person have the right to destroy an embryo? Commentators have advanced three approaches to the legal status of an embryo: (1) viewing it as "property," (2) treating it as "life," and (3) according it a middle position of special respect. The issue arises most commonly in divorce proceedings, where one of the spouses wants to destroy frozen embryos created during the marriage.

In most states, courts will enforce a prior agreement between the spouses concerning disposition of the embryos. For example, in *In re Marriage of Dahl and Angle*, 194 P.3d 834, 842 (Or. Ct. App. 2008), the court concluded that "it is just and proper to dispose of the embryos in the manner that the parties chose at the time that they underwent the IVF process," thus allowing the wife to destroy the embryos.

Where the parties' embryo contract was ambiguous, the court in *In re Marriage of Rooks*, 488 P.3d 116, 121 (Colo. App. 2016) held that the trial court properly exercised its "inherent equitable power to determine whom to award the embryos to." After balancing the spouses' respective interests, the trial court concluded that the husband's interest in not having more children with the wife outweighed the wife's interest in having another child. Accordingly, it awarded the embryos to the husband, who planned to destroy them.

f. Problems in Destruction

In light of *Eyerman* and the other materials above, should the law recognize the owner's right to destroy under the following circumstances?

> (1) A owns a beautiful, world-famous painting by Claude Monet which, when publicly exhibited, helped millions of people develop a greater appreciation for fine art. A dies, leaving a will that instructs his executor to burn the painting and deposit its ashes in his grave.
>
> (2) B owns a 100-acre tract of prize-winning orange groves. On a whim, B decides to cut down the trees with a chain saw, which will reduce the value of the land by 90%.
>
> (3) C sells her Florida home for $2,000,000, and uses all the money to purchase rare stamps. As a "public art project," C then begins burning the stamps, one by one. C's four children protest this wanton destruction, but C ignores their pleas.

Summary

- **Theories of Property.** American property law reflects a blend of different theories, including the first possession, labor, utilitarian, civic republican, and personhood approaches. The law and economics variant of utilitarianism has been a particularly powerful influence in recent decades.

- **Legal Positivism.** In our legal system, property exists only to the extent that it is recognized by government. Thus, natural law theory has little impact on property law.

- **Property as a Bundle of Rights.** Property is commonly described as a "bundle of rights." The concept that property consists of *rights* rather than *things* has important consequences that we will study throughout the course. For example, property rights are relative, not absolute. Conflicts often arise between different owners, or between a particular owner and society in general, as the cases in this chapter demonstrate. The law resolves these conflicts by determining the relative scope and extent of each owner's rights in the particular situation.

- **Reasons for Property Rights.** The reasons that our society recognizes property are vital, because these reasons define the scope and extent of property rights. As the *State v. Shack* court explained: "Property rights serve human values. They are recognized to that end, and are limited by it." Under the utilitarian theory which this passage reflects, we recognize property rights not simply to benefit individual owners, but rather because private property benefits all of society.

- **Right to Transfer.** Although the law favors the free alienation of property, an owner's right to transfer is sometimes limited for public policy reasons. The law regulates what can be transferred, how transfers are made, and who can transfer or obtain property.

- **Right to Exclude.** The law generally protects an owner's right to exclude others from his property, subject to privileges such as consent and necessity. Other exceptions to the right to exclude may exist, depending on the jurisdiction.
- **Right to Use.** An owner is normally entitled to use her property as she wishes, as long as she does not injure the rights of others. The spite fence and nuisance doctrines help define the limits of the right to use.
- **Right to Destroy.** The scope of an owner's right to destroy is unclear. In practice, the law rarely intervenes to prevent destruction. But concern arises when an owner seeks to destroy property that has substantial value to society, and some courts have limited this right.

> **Test Your Knowledge**
>
> To assess your understanding of the material in this chapter, click here to take a quiz.

> **For More Information**
>
> For more information about the subjects covered in this chapter, please consult these sources:
> - Gregory S. Alexander & Eduardo M. Peñalver, An Introduction to Property Theory (2012).
> - Abraham Bell & Gideon Parchomovsky, *A Theory of Property*, 90 Cornell L. Rev. 531 (2005).
> - Thomas W. Merrill & Henry E. Smith, *What Happened to Property in Law and Economics?*, 111 Yale L.J. 357 (2001).
> - Carol M. Rose, *Property as the Keystone Right?*, 71 Notre Dame L. Rev. 329 (1996).
> - Christopher Serkin, *What Property Does*, 75 Vand. L. Rev. 891 (2022).
> - Joseph William Singer, *The Rule of Reason in Property Law*, 46 U.C. Davis L. Rev. 1369 (2013).

CHAPTER 2

Owning Real Property

Imagine that you are sitting in the living room of your country house on a leather chair enjoying the Picasso mounted on your wall and sipping a cool glass of water. Suppose you inherited your house 25 years ago from your mother, found the chair by the side of the highway last week, bought the Picasso six years ago from a friend recently found to be an art thief, and pumped the water from the well in your back yard. While you are clearly in possession of these things, do you hold title to any of them? Do you have any property rights at all?

In the United States, we generally divide property into two broad categories: *real property* and *personal property*. Real property consists of rights in land and things attached to land, such as buildings, fences, and trees. *See, e.g., Black Hills Institute of Geological Research v. South Dakota School of Mines & Technology,* 12 F.3d 737 (8th Cir. 1993) (Tyrannosaurus rex fossil embedded in land was real property). So in the example above, your country house and the land it sits on are real property. In contrast, personal property refers to rights in moveable items (such as chairs, pens, and computers) and intangible things (such as patents and shares of stock). *See, e.g., Lehigh Gas-Ohio, LLC v. Cincy Oil Queen City, LLC,* 66 N.E.3d 1226, 1234 (Ohio Ct. App. 2016) (safes and business inventory were personal property). The chair, the Picasso, and the glass of water are all personal property. Items of personal property that are physically attached to real property (such as chandeliers or smoke alarms) are called *fixtures*, and are generally treated as real property. *See, e.g., W.H.V., Inc. v. Associates Hous. Finance, LLC,* 43 S.W.3d 83 (Tex. App. 2001) (mobile home permanently affixed to land would be a fixture).

Traditionally, real property was the more important category. Property law in the United States was profoundly shaped by English law. For centuries, land constituted the foundation of economic, social, and political power in England. Accordingly, the real property law that evolved in England was extraordinarily complex, while personal property law was comparatively simple. Because the new United States inherited this system, our own vision of property law has long been dominated by real property principles—as the first-year course in Property usually reflects. This chapter will begin your study of real property, while Chapter 3 will introduce you to personal property.

The real property law that we inherited from England was based on conditions quite different from those prevailing in the United States. England was a mature agricultural economy where most land was privately owned and in productive use. In contrast, about 95% of the new United States was undeveloped, wild land owned by the federal government. The government sought to transfer these lands to private owners in order to facilitate national development—initially by allowing land purchases on credit and distributing free land to veterans, and later through the Homestead Act of 1862. The judicial system also played a role in this process. As the Supreme Court explained in one early case: "The country was a wilderness, and the universal policy was to procure its cultivation and improvement." *Van Ness v. Pacard*, 27 U.S. (2 Pet.) 137, 145 (1829). Thus, the need to develop land for productive use became a major theme in American property law.

In this chapter, we will examine three aspects of real property law: adverse possession; the vertical limits of ownership; and water law. The law in these areas has evolved over time in response to factors such as geography, technology, economic conditions, and social forces—and this evolution continues today. Each doctrine illustrates the central challenge in American property law: striking the appropriate balance between the rights of the owner and the interests of society in general.

A. Adverse Possession

Suppose A occupies B's land for 20 years. B never inspects his land, so he does not know about A's occupancy. Who owns the land? Surprisingly, the answer may be A—based on adverse possession.

Adverse possession is easily the most controversial doctrine in property law. As one authority noted: "Title by adverse possession sounds, at first blush, like title by theft or robbery, a primitive method of acquiring land without paying for it." Henry W. Ballentine, *Title by Adverse Possession*, 32 Harv. L. Rev. 135, 135 (1918). In effect, if A occupies B's land for a long enough period while meeting certain conditions, A acquires title to the land without B's consent. Why does the law recognize this doctrine?

Four justifications have been suggested for adverse possession:

- *Preventing frivolous claims*: Under the dominant view, adverse possession is seen as a special statute of limitations for recovering possession of land. Thus, like any other statute of limitations, it bars lawsuits based on stale, unreliable evidence, thereby protecting the occupant from frivolous claims. It also provides the occupant with security of title, thus encouraging the productive use of land.

- *Correcting title defects*: Technical mistakes often occur in the process of conveying title to land. For example, the property description in a deed might contain an error. Adverse possession resolves such problems by protecting the title of the person who actually occupies the land. Under this model, lengthy possession serves as proof of title.

- *Encouraging development*: Adverse possession may be viewed as a legal tool to encourage economic development. Under this view, it reallocates title from the idle owner to the industrious squatter, thus promoting the productive use of land.

- *Protecting personhood*: Supreme Court Justice Oliver Wendell Holmes, Jr. offered another explanation for adverse possession, which echoes personhood theory: "A thing which you have enjoyed and used as your own for a long time . . . takes root in your being and cannot be torn away without your resenting the act. . . ." Oliver Wendell Holmes, Jr., *The Path of the Law*, 10 Harv. L. Rev. 457, 477 (1897).

As you read the materials in this unit, consider which theory best explains the adverse possession doctrine.

1. Elements of Adverse Possession

In most jurisdictions, an occupant obtains title to land through adverse possession if her possession is: actual, exclusive, open and notorious, adverse and hostile, and continuous for the required period. Typically, the period for adverse possession is established by a statute, while the other elements stem from case law. A handful of jurisdictions also require that the occupant pay the taxes assessed against the land.

How much possession is required? This varies according to the character, nature, and location of the particular land. For example, in order for C to adversely possess a condominium unit in a large city, she would probably have to reside in the unit, because this is how a reasonable unit owner would behave. But D might adversely possess a tract of rural grassland just by having cattle graze on it occasionally, because this is an appropriate use for such property.

The precise phrasing of the adverse possession standards varies somewhat from state to state. A typical state requires these elements:

- *Actual possession*: At a minimum, the claimant must physically use the land in the same manner that a reasonable owner would, given its character, location, and nature. The claimant can also meet this standard by using the land more intensively than a reasonable owner would.

> - *Exclusive possession*: The claimant's possession cannot be shared with the owner or with the public in general.
>
> - *Open and notorious possession*: The claimant's possession must be visible and obvious, so that if the owner made a reasonable inspection of the land, he would become aware of the adverse claim.
>
> - *"Adverse and hostile" possession (some states also require "claim of right")*: This element is complex, and will be discussed in more detail below. All states agree that possession authorized by the owner does not meet this requirement. Beyond this point, states differ. Some find the element is met only if the claimant believes in *good faith* that he owns the land. In most states, the claimant's state of mind is *irrelevant*. A third view—now rare—requires *bad faith*, that is, the claimant must intend to take title from the owner.
>
> - *Continuous possession*: The claimant's possession must be as continuous as a reasonable owner's would be, given the character, location, and nature of the land.
>
> - *For the statutory period*: The period for adverse possession ranges from 5 to 40 years, depending on the state. The most common periods are 10, 15, and 20 years.

Our first case involves a successful adverse possession claim to a tract of "rough, brushy, wooded land" in central Missouri. Why did the owners lose their title?

Gurwit v. Kannatzer

Court of Appeals of Missouri

788 S.W.2d 293 (1990)

PER CURIAM:

The trial court after a court-tried case entered judgment quieting title in plaintiffs Monte and Martha Gurwit, husband and wife, to a certain 17-acre tract of land in Boone County. Defendants Eugene H. Gruender and Dorothy Gruender, husband and wife, and John R. Gruender and Karen Gruender, husband and wife, have appealed. . . .

The first question presented is whether the evidence supported the judgment of the trial court. The judgment was based upon the court's finding that the Gurwits had acquired title to the disputed tract by ten years' adverse possession under section 516.010, RS Mo 1986.

Chapter 2 *Owning Real Property*

[margin note: Parcel location]

The tract of land in dispute is located in Boone County, Missouri, and is described as: All that part of the East Half of the Southeast Quarter of Section 4, Township 50 North, Range 13 West, lying north and west of the Oak Grove School Road and south of Stidham Road, now vacated.

> **FYI**
>
> Section 516.010 provides: No action for the recovery of any lands, . . . or for the recovery of the possession thereof, shall be commenced . . . unless it appears that the plaintiff, his ancestor, predecessor, grantor or other person under whom he claims was seized or possessed of the premises in question, within ten years before the commencement of such action.

The Oak Grove School Road enters the east half of the southeast quarter of section 4 from the west at a point 382 feet north of the southwest corner of the 80-acre tract; curves to the northeast to its easternmost point 398 feet north and 391 feet east of the point where it entered; thence curves toward the northwest and proceeds in almost a straight line a distance of 1,266 feet to where it intersects with Stidham Road at a point 208 feet east and 1,518 feet north of the point where it entered the 80-acre tract. The disputed 17-acre tract is embraced then, on the south and [east], within the curve of Oak Grove School Road, with Stidham Road as its north boundary, and with the west line of the east half of the southeast quarter as its west boundary.

The plaintiffs Gurwit took possession of the property (if they did possess it, a disputed point in the case) in 1963. At that time they bought from Mr. and Mrs. Orval Putnam the half-quarter lying immediately to the west of the now disputed tract, to wit, the west half of the southeast quarter, except a four-acre tract in the southeast corner thereof, approximately 76 acres. (The excepted four-acre tract was triangular in shape and was cut off from the remainder of the half-quarter by the Oak Grove School Road. The road therefore furnished the boundary of the southeast corner of the 76-acre tract.) As the purchase was pending, Putnam conducted Monte Gurwit around the property to point out the boundaries. He pointed out the Oak Grove School Road as being the south and east boundary of the property, and Gurwit relied upon Putnam's representation.

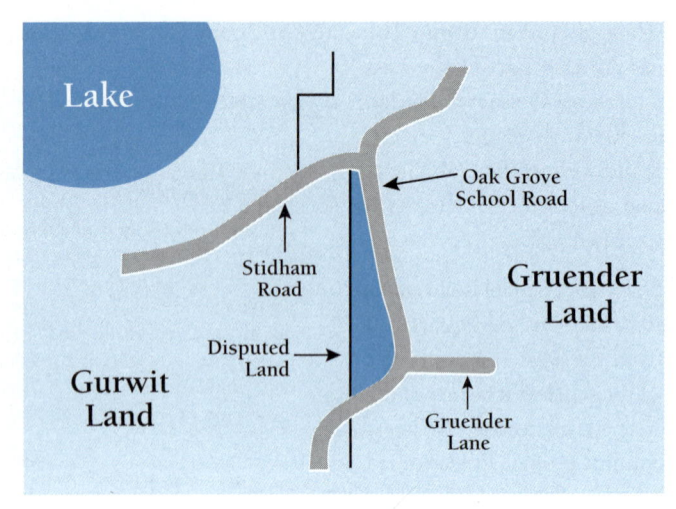

Map of land in *Gurwit v. Kannatzer*

The Putnams, however, did not have record title to the 17-acre tract and their deed to the Gurwits did not include it in the description. The deed described only the property in the west half of the southeast quarter.

The now disputed 17-acre tract was of the same character as the west half of the southeast quarter, which lay immediately to the west. It was rough, brushy, wooded land. There was no fence, monument or any kind of demarcation marking the west line of the east half of the southeast quarter, which was the west line of the now-disputed tract. The land was uncultivated and was used not even for pasture. With the addition of other land, the plaintiffs Gurwit had a primitive 300-acre recreational area, on which they built and stocked with fish a large lake.

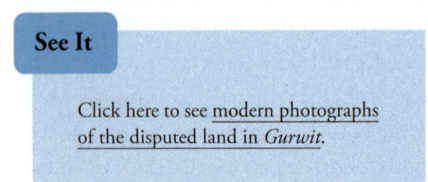

> **See It**
>
> Click here to see modern photographs of the disputed land in *Gurwit*.

The Gurwits, assuming they had a secure title, took possession of the 17-acre tract along with the land to the west thereof, and for the space of twenty years continued to possess it and exercise dominion over it in the manner we shall describe. They posted "no trespassing" and "no hunting" signs along the road. They cut firewood on the tract, and gave friends permission to cut firewood thereon. Gurwit assisted over a period of years to clean up the downed trees and brush along the road, which had been left there when the road was widened before the Gurwits purchased the land. For a time Gurwit planted plots of food for wildlife on the tract which included the disputed tract. He was not sure that any of the plots were on the disputed tract, but he did enter the tract from the road with the machinery he used in the operation.

The Gurwits' ownership of the 17-acre tract was apparently acknowledged by all. Defendants Mr. and Mrs. Eugene Gruender, who owned and occupied the property on the east side of the Oak Grove School Road, on occasion called the Gurwits about trespassers on the 17-acre tract. Defendant John Gruender, son of the Eugene Gruenders, once protested Gurwit's cutting a tree on his property lying north of vacated Stidham Road. Gurwit acknowledged his mistake, moved south of Stidham Road, onto the tract which is now disputed, and continued with his tree-cutting with the apparent approval of John Gruender.

In 1983 Eugene Gruender told Gurwit that Gurwit did not have record title to the 17-acre tract. Gurwit went to the assessor's office and verified what Gruender had told him. The 17-acre tract had in fact been included with Gruender's tax bills, and those of his predecessors in title, who owned that part of the east half of the southeast quarter of section 4 which lay east of the road. From 1983 on, Gurwit paid the taxes on the 17-acre tract.

Afterwards the Gurwits instituted this quiet title action, which included the 17-acre tract in question. The two Gruender families were made defendants. They filed answers and a counterclaim, seeking to have the title to the 17-acre tract quieted in themselves. From the judgment adverse to themselves the Gruenders have appealed.

In order to establish their title to the 17-acre tract by adverse possession, it was incumbent upon the plaintiffs to prove that their possession was hostile, that is under claim of right; actual; open and notorious; exclusive; and continuous over the statutory period. *Counts v. Moody*, 571 S.W.2d 134, 138 (Mo. App. 1978). *See also, Walker v. Walker*, 509 S.W.2d 102, 106 (Mo. 1974). . . . Appellants, the Gruenders, claim that the Gurwits' possession was not hostile, was not actual, was not open and notorious, was not exclusive and was not continuous over the statutory period. We hold, however, that each element of adverse possession was proved.

> **What's That?**
>
> A *quiet title* action is a lawsuit brought to establish the plaintiff's title to land. Typically, the plaintiff sues all persons who claim any right, title, or interest in the land, and the court issues a judgment that resolves the controversy. In this case, the Gurwits sought to quiet their title to four parcels of land, one of which was claimed by Kannatzer, the defendant named in the title of the case. However, Kannatzer had no claim to the 17-acre parcel involved in this appeal.

The Gurwits possessed and exercised dominion over the property as much as the character of the property admitted. The land, as noted, was unimproved and uncultivated. It had no buildings, no cross fences, and no fences along the road. The Gurwits did as they chose with the property, in the manner we have recounted above. Their possession was hostile, not in the sense that they fortified and stood ready to defend it by force of arms—though their posting of "no trespassing" and "no hunting" signs indicates most strongly a "hostile" possession. The intent of the Gurwits to possess, occupy, control, use and exercise dominion over the property satisfies the requirement of hostility. *Counts*, 571 S.W.2d at 139. . . .

The Gurwits' possession was actual. Possession . . . depends upon the nature and location of the property. The Gurwits lived some distance from the land. It was not necessary that they occupy or use every foot of the land at every minute. Their acts of dominion over the property were sufficient to establish the required possession. *Miller v. Medley*, 281 S.W.2d 797, 801 (Mo. 1955); *Teson v. Vasquez*, 561 S.W.2d 119, 126 (Mo. App. 1977).

The Gurwits' possession was open and notorious. Gurwit testified to the fact of his cutting firewood, picking up trash along the road, cleaning up the brush and trees left by the road widening project, all in the sight of passersby. No one having an adverse claim to the property could fail to have noticed that the Gurwits were claiming this property as their own. *Porter v. Posey*, 592 S.W.2d 844, 849 (Mo. App. 1979).

The Gurwits' possession was exclusive. "'Exclusive possession' means that the claimant must hold the possession of the land for himself, as his own, and not for another." *Walker*, 509 S.W.2d at 106.

The Gurwits' possession was as continuous as the nature of the property would admit. There were no doubt days or weeks when they were not physically present on the disputed tract, but continuous possession clearly does not require continuous occupation and use. *Teson*, 561 S.W.2d at 127.

We hold that the evidence amply supported the trial court's finding that the Gurwits' possession of the disputed tract was of a character that ripened into title with the passage of the statutory period of ten years. . . .

Points for Discussion

a. Justifying Adverse Possession

Do any of the justifications for adverse possession explain why—based on the facts of this case—the Gruenders lost their title? Notice the role of mistake. Before 1983, both sides mistakenly believed that the Gurwits owned the disputed tract. Should the Gruenders lose title simply because they made an error?

b. Actual Possession

Exactly why did the Gurwits meet the requirement of actual possession? Should the court have required evidence of more extensive use? For example, under Alabama law the adverse possession of woodlands requires "such a continuous and persistent cutting of timber or wood from the tract, as to be evidence of a claim of ownership." *Rutland v. Georgia Kraft Co.*, 387 So. 2d 836, 837 (Ala. 1980). But this appears to be a minority view. In most jurisdictions, activities such as gathering firewood, cutting small amounts of timber, grazing cattle or other animals, or removing minerals are considered sufficient "actual" possession of wild and undeveloped lands. However, the use of land solely for recreational purposes is not considered actual possession in some states. *See, e.g., Moore v. Stills*, 307 S.W.3d 71 (Ky. 2010) ("hunting, fishing, hiking, and riding four-wheelers" on forest land did not constitute actual possession).

c. **Exclusive Possession**

Suppose the Gruenders had collected firewood on the disputed property once each summer. Would the Gurwits' possession still be considered "exclusive"? In answering this question consider *Adams v. Lamicq*, 221 P.2d 1037 (Utah 1950). There, A and B relied on adverse possession in claiming title to an 80-acre tract of remote rangeland which they had used for grazing sheep during the winter. Record owner C, who had cultivated between 15 and 35 acres of the tract each summer, argued that the exclusive possession element was not met. Because their possession of the cultivated area was not exclusive, the court awarded A and B title *only* to the non-cultivated portion of the tract. Use of disputed property by third parties may also prevent an adverse claimant from proving exclusive possession. *See, e.g., ITT v. Rayonier, Inc. v. Bell*, 774 P.2d 6 (Wash. 1989) (claimant who moored his boat along the shore of the disputed tract did not have exclusive possession because other people used the land for the same purpose).

d. **Open and Notorious Possession**

The *Gurwit* court explained that the open and notorious requirement was met because the Gurwits' activities of cutting firewood and the like were "all in sight of passersby." Is such a fleeting glimpse enough or should a court require permanent, visible evidence of the adverse possessor's presence such as a fence? Did the Gurwits do anything that provided permanent notice of their possession? In *Zambrotto v. Superior Lumber Co.*, 4 P.3d 62 (Or. Ct. App. 2000), the court found that using a five-acre forest tract for occasional hiking and rattlesnake hunting was actual possession, but not open and notorious possession. It explained that "the nature and frequency of those activities hardly were sufficient to put [the owners] on notice that their title was being challenged." *Id.* at 66. Is *Gurwit* consistent with *Zambrotto*? Activities such as clearing brush, cultivating crops, storing equipment, building fences, and other structures, or posting signs are often used to satisfy the "open and notorious" requirement. *See, e.g., Union Cemetery Burial Soc'y of North Smithfield v. Foisy*, 292 A.3d 1205, 1216 (R.I. 2023) (storage of "scrap metal, vehicle chassis and appliances" was open and notorious possession).

e. **Continuous Possession**

The Gurwits' possession was deemed "continuous" even though there were "days or weeks when they were not physically present on the disputed tract." How often would a reasonable owner of such land use it? Because the required continuity is measured by a reasonable owner's conduct, sporadic uses of wild lands are usually deemed continuous. For instance, in *Sleboda v. Heirs at Law of Harris*, 508 A.2d 652 (R.I. 1986), this element was met when the adverse claimants visited the land twice each year to cut trees and gather firewood.

f. Adverse Possession Problems

Has adverse possession been established in these situations? Assume that the statutory period is 10 years.

> (1) A held title to a 200-acre tract of remote and unimproved desert land, which she never visited. Driving past the land one day, B noticed that rare and valuable cacti grew there; B spent 20 minutes digging out four small cacti, which he later sold. Over the next 10 years, he visited the property on five more occasions, each time removing a few cacti. B claims title to the tract.
>
> (2) C owned a home in a rural subdivision. D owned the house next door. All backyards in the subdivision were unfenced and covered by wild grass. Over the next 10 years, D occasionally watered the wild grass behind his house; he also mowed it three or four times each summer. D then discovered that part of the land he had been watering and mowing (a strip about 20 feet wide) was actually part of C's original lot. Over the years, C's children had played on this strip of land on 8 or 9 occasions. D claims title to the strip.
>
> (3) E and F owned large ranches; E's ranch was south of F's ranch. The boundary between the ranches was 1,000 feet long and was marked only by 10 metal posts. Late one night, E moved each of those posts north, 100 feet onto F's land, being careful to fill in the old post holes. E then planted grapevines on his own land and the part of F's land that he had taken. F did not notice that the posts were moved. Two years later in October, without asking permission, F entered the vineyard just south of the 10 metal posts and harvested 200 pounds of grapes. She repeated this every subsequent October. Ten years later, F learned that E had moved the fence posts.

g. Adverse Possession and Environmentalism

Is adverse possession obsolete? In *Meyer v. Law*, 287 So. 2d 37, 41 (Fla. 1973), the Florida Supreme Court commented:

> . . . [F]aced, as we are, with problems of unchecked over-development, depletion of precious natural resources, and pollution of our environment, the policy reasons that once supported the idea of adverse possession may well be succumbing to new priorities. A man who owns some virgin land, who refrains from despoiling that land, even to the extent of erecting a fence to mark its boundaries, and who makes no greater use of that land than an occasional rejuvenating walk in the woods, can hardly be faulted in today's increasingly "modern" world.

Suppose the Gruenders knew they owned the 17-acre parcel, but intentionally preserved it in natural condition to protect the environment. Would they still have lost the case?

h. Aftermath of *Gurwit*

Two years after the case was decided, the Gurwits sold all their land (including the disputed 17-acre tract) to the Missouri Department of Conservation. Now called the "Lick Creek Conservation Area," the land is open to the public for camping, fishing, hiking, hunting, and other uses. Anyone may gather nuts, berries, fruits, edible wild greens, and mushrooms there for personal consumption.

In a minority of states—including California, Florida, and New York—the traditional elements for adverse possession are supplemented by special statutory requirements. Our next case illustrates this minority approach.

In 1912, Mary and William Lutz, a newly married couple, decided to build a home in Yonkers, New York. Accordingly, they purchased two adjacent lots in the Murray Estate subdivision. The lots were located on the top of an extremely steep hill and, like the other lots in the subdivision, were covered with wild trees and brush—much like the disputed tract in *Gurwit v. Kannatzer*. The Lutzes began gardening on four other lots, which they did not own. The resulting controversy produced one of the most famous adverse possession decisions.

Van Valkenburgh v. Lutz

Court of Appeals of New York

106 N.E.2d 28 (1952)

[The Lutzes purchased Lots 14 and 15, on Leroy Avenue, where they built their home. Immediately southwest of their land were four vacant lots (Lots 19, 20, 21, and 22), "somewhat triangular in shape" with dimensions of 150 by 126 by 170 feet, fronting on Gibson Place. This triangular parcel was covered by "a wild natural growth of brush and small trees." Because Leroy Avenue was unpaved and steep, the Lutzes reached their home by parking on Gibson Place and then walking across the triangular parcel, along a walkway or "traveled way" that Lutz built for this purpose. By 1916, Lutz had cleared much of the triangular parcel and begun farming activities there, which continued until his death in 1948. He also built a one-room dwelling there for his brother Charlie.

Joseph and Marion Van Valkenburgh purchased property on the west side of Gibson Place in 1937, where they built a home. A feud developed between the Lutzes and the Van Valkenburghs, in part because of an incident where Lutz chased the Van Valkenburgh children off the triangular parcel, while waving an iron pipe and shouting, "I'll kill you." No one paid taxes on the triangular parcel, and it was accordingly auctioned off at a foreclosure sale for nonpayment of taxes in 1947, where the Van Valkenburghs bought it for $379.50. The Lutzes did not receive notice of the foreclosure sale. The Van Valkenburghs promptly demanded that the Lutzes vacate the land.

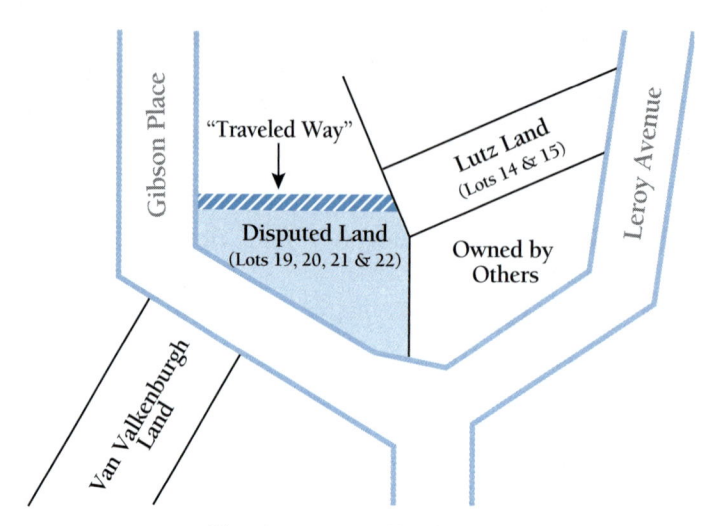

Map of land in *Van Valkenburgh v. Lutz*

Lutz then consulted an attorney. Based on his attorney's advice, Lutz filed a lawsuit against the Van Valkenburghs in 1947, alleging that (a) the Van Valkenburghs owned title to the triangular parcel but that (b) he was entitled to an easement to cross it. (An *easement* is a nonpossessory right to use land in the possession or ownership of another person.) Lutz won this case in January, 1948.

In April, 1948, the Van Valkenburghs sued the Lutzes to obtain possession of the triangular parcel and for related relief. The Lutzes hired a new attorney, who advised them to assert the defense of adverse possession. Note that the Lutzes were allowed to challenge the Van Valkenburgh's title despite the tax sale because they never received notice of the sale, as due process requires. Lutz died in August, 1948, leaving all of his property to his wife. In 1950, the case was tried before Hon. Frederick P. Close, Official Referee. He found that Lutz had acquired title to the triangular tract in 1935 by adverse possession. The Van Valkenburghs appealed.]

DYE, JUDGE.

. . . To acquire title to real property by adverse possession not founded upon a written instrument, it must be shown by clear and convincing proof that for at least fifteen years (formerly twenty years) there was an "actual" occupation under a claim of title, for it is only the premises so actually occupied "and no others" that are deemed to have been held adversely. Civil Practice Act, §§ 34, 38, 39.[1] The essential elements

---

[1] At the time, the relevant sections of the New York Civil Practice Act were:

§ 34. An action to recover real property or the possession thereof cannot be maintained . . . unless the plaintiff, his ancestor, predecessor or grantor, was seized or posof proof being either that the premises (1) are protected by a substantial inclosure, or are (2) usually cultivated or improved. Civil Practice Act, § 40.

Concededly, there is no proof here that the subject premises were "protected by a substantial inclosure" which leaves for consideration only whether there is evidence showing that the premises were cultivated or improved sufficiently to satisfy the statute.

We think not. The proof concededly fails to show that the cultivation incident to the garden utilized the whole of the premises claimed. Such lack may not be supplied by inference on the showing that the cultivation of a smaller area, whose boundaries are neither defined nor its location fixed with certainty, "must have been . . . substantial" as several neighbors were "supplied . . . with vegetables." This introduces an element of speculation and surmise which may not be considered since the statute clearly limits the premises adversely held to those "actually" occupied "and no others" (Civil Practice Act, § 39), which we have recently interpreted as requiring definition by clear and positive proof. . . .

> **Food for Thought**
>
> Why does the court emphasize that the boundaries of the cultivated area "are neither defined nor its location fixed with certainty"? As the attorney for Lutz, how would you have proven this at trial?

Furthermore, on this record, the proof fails to show that the premises were improved. Civil Practice Act, § 40. According to the proof the small shed or shack (about 5 by 10½ feet) which, as shown by survey map, was located on the subject premises about 14 feet from the Lutz boundary line. This was built in about the year 1923 and, as Lutz himself testified, he knew at the time it was not on his land and, his wife, a defendant here, also testified to the same effect.

The statute requires as an essential element of proof, recognized as fundamental on the concept of adversity since ancient times, that the occupation of premises be "under a claim of title" (Civil Practice Act, § 39), in other words, hostile . . . and when lacking will not operate to bar the legal title . . . no matter how long the occupation may have continued. . . .

---

sessed of the premises in question within fifteen years before the commencement of the action. . . .

§ 39. Where there has been an actual continued possession of premises under a claim of title . . . not founded upon a written instrument or a judgment or decree, the premises so occupied, and no others, are deemed to have been held adversely.

§ 40. For the purpose of constituting an adverse possession by a person claiming title not founded upon a written instrument or a judgment or decree, land is deemed to have been possessed and occupied in either of the following cases, and no others:

1. Where it has been protected by a substantial inclosure.
2. Where it has been usually cultivated or improved.

Similarly, the garage encroachment, extending a few inches over the boundary line, fails to supply proof of occupation by improvement. Lutz himself testified that when he built the garage he had no survey and thought he was getting it on his own property, which certainly falls short of establishing that he did it under a claim of title hostile to the true owner. The other acts committed by Lutz over the years, such as placing a portable chicken coop on the premises which he moved about, the cutting of brush and some of the trees, and the littering of the property with odds and ends of salvaged building materials, cast-off items of house furnishings and parts of automobiles which the defendants and their witnesses described as "personal belongings," "junk," "rubbish" and "debris," were acts which under no stretch of the imagination could be deemed an occupation by improvement within the meaning of the statute, and which, of course, are of no avail in establishing adverse possession.

We are also persuaded that the defendant's subsequent words and conduct confirms the view that his occupation was not "under a claim of title." When the defendant had the opportunity to declare his hostility and assert his rights against the true owner, he voluntarily chose to concede that the plaintiffs' legal title conferred actual ownership entitling them to the possession of these and other premises in order to provide a basis for establishing defendant's right to an easement by adverse possession—the use of a well-defined "traveled way" that crossed the said premises. In that action, *Lutz v. Van Valkenburgh*, 274 App. Div. 813, 81 N.Y.S.2d 161, William Lutz, a defendant here (now deceased), chose to litigate the issue of title and possession and, having succeeded in establishing his claim of easement by adverse possession, he may not now disavow the effect of his favorable judgment . . . or prevent its use as evidence to show his prior intent. Declarations against interest made by a prescriptive tenant are always available on the issue of his intent. . . .

On this record we do not reach the question of disseisin by oral disclaimer, since the proof fails to establish actual occupation for such time or in such manner as to establish title. What we are saying is that the proof fails to establish actual occupation for such a time or in such a manner as to establish title by adverse possession. Civil Practice Act, §§ 39, 40. . . .

The judgments should be reversed, the counterclaim dismissed and judgment directed to be entered in favor of plaintiff Joseph D. Van Valkenburgh for the relief prayed for in the complaint subject to the existing easement . . . with costs in all courts.

FULD, JUDGE (dissenting).

In my judgment, the weight of evidence lies with the determination made by the court at Special Term and affirmed by the Appellate Division. But whether that is so or not, there can be no doubt whatsoever that the record contains some evidence that the premises here involved were occupied by William Lutz, defendant's late husband, for fifteen years under a claim of title—and that, of course, should compel an affirmance.

The four lots in suit, located in the city of Yonkers, comprise a fairly level parcel of land, triangular in shape, with approximate dimensions of 150 by 126 by 170 feet. It is bounded on the north by a "traveled way," on the west and south by Gibson Place, an unopened street, and on the southeast by a vacant lot. Immediately to the east of the parcel, the land descends sharply to Leroy Avenue, forming a steep hill; on the hill are situated two lots, purchased by Lutz in 1912, upon which his family's home has stood for over thirty years.

Wild and overgrown when the Lutzes first moved into the neighborhood, the property was cleared by defendant's husband and had been, by 1916, the referee found, developed into a truck farm "of substantial size". Lutz, together with his children, worked the farm continuously until his death in 1948; indeed, after 1928, he had no other employment. Each year, a new crop was planted and the harvest of vegetables was sold to neighbors. Lutz also raised chickens on the premises, and constructed coops or sheds for them. Fruit trees were planted, and timber was cut from that portion of the property not used for the farm. On one of the lots, Lutz in 1920 built a one-room dwelling, in which his brother Charles has lived ever since.

> **See It**
>
> When the Lutzes began using the disputed land, it was covered by a "wild natural growth of brush and small trees," according to the court. Click here to see a modern photograph of land in similar condition; this photograph was taken of undeveloped land a few feet away from the triangular tract at issue in *Van Valkenburgh*.

Although disputing the referee's finding that the dimensions of Lutz's farm were substantial, the court's opinion fails to remark the plentiful evidence in support thereof. For instance, there is credible testimony in the record that "nearly all" of the property comprised by the four lots was cultivated during the period to which the referee's finding relates. A survey introduced in evidence indicates the very considerable extent to which the property was cultivated in 1950, and many witnesses testified that the farm was no larger at that time than it had ever been. There is evidence, moreover, that the cultivated area extended from the "traveled way" on *one side* of the property to a row of logs and brush—placed by Lutz for the express purpose of marking the farm's boundary—at the *opposite end* of the premises.

According to defendant's testimony, she and her husband, knowing that they did not have record title to the premises, intended from the first nevertheless to occupy the property as their own. Bearing this out is the fact that Lutz put down the row of logs and brush, which was over 100 feet in length, to mark the southwestern boundary of his farm; this marker, only roughly approximating the lot lines, extended beyond them into the bed of Gibson Place. The property was, moreover, known in the neighborhood as "Mr. Lutz's gardens," and the one-room dwelling on it as "Charlie's house;" the evidence clearly indicates that people living in the vicinity believed the property to be owned by Lutz. And it is undisputed that for upwards of thirty-five years—until 1947, when plaintiffs became the record owners—no other person ever asserted title to the parcel.

With evidence such as that in the record, I am at a loss to understand how this court can say that support is lacking for the finding that the premises had been occupied by Lutz under a claim of title. The referee was fully justified in concluding that the character of Lutz's possession was akin to that of a true owner and indicated, more dramatically and effectively than could words, an intent to claim the property as his own. Recognizing that "A claim of title may be made by acts alone quite as effectively as by the most emphatic assertions" (*Barnes v. Light*, 116 N.Y. 34, 39, 22 N.E. 441, 442), we have often sustained findings based on evidence of actual occupation and improvement of the property in the manner that "owners are accustomed to possess and improve their estates." *La Frombois v. Jackson*, 8 Cow. 589, 603. . . . That Lutz knew that he did not have the record title to the property—a circumstance relied upon by the court—is of no consequence, so long as he intended, notwithstanding that fact, to acquire and use the property as his own. As we stated in *Ramapo Mfg. Co. v. Mapes*, 216 N.Y. 362, 370–371, 110 N.E. 772, 775, "the bona fides of the claim of the occupant is not essential, and it will not excuse the negligence of the owner in forbearing to bring his action until after the time in the statute of limitations shall have run against him to show that the defendant knew all along that he was in the wrong. . . ."

> **FYI**
>
> The client is generally bound by the actions of his attorney. Otherwise, our legal system simply could not function. Thus, assuming that Lutz's admission in the first lawsuit was caused by his attorney's erroneous advice, the court will not permit his successor to challenge that admission in this second lawsuit. But the attorney might be liable for malpractice.

Quite obviously, the fact that Lutz alleged in the 1947 easement action—twelve years after title had, according to the referee, vested in him through adverse possession—that one of the plaintiffs was the owner of three of the lots, simply constituted evidence pointing the other way, to be weighed with the other proof by the courts below. While it is true that a disclaimer of title by the occupant of property, made before the statutory period has run, indelibly stamps his possession as nonadverse and prevents title from vesting in him . . . a disclaimer made after the statute has run carries with it totally different legal consequences. Once title has vested by virtue of adverse possession, it is elementary that it may be divested, not by an oral disclaimer, but only by a transfer complying with the formalities prescribed by law. . . . Hence, an oral acknowledgment of title in another, made after the statutory period is alleged to have run, "is only evidence tending to show the character of the previous possession." . . . Here, Official Referee Close, of the opinion that the 1947 admission was made by Lutz under the erroneous advice of his attorney . . . chose to rest his decision rather on evidence of Lutz's numerous and continual acts of dominion over the property—proof of a most persuasive character. Even if we were to feel that the referee was mistaken in so weighing the evidence, we would be powerless, to change the determination, where, as we have seen, there is some evidence in the record to support his conclusion.

In view of the extensive cultivation of the parcel in suit, there is no substance to the argument that the requirements of sections 39 and 40 of the Civil Practice Act were not met. Under those provisions, only the premises "actually occupied" in the manner prescribed—that is, "protected by a substantial inclosure" or "usually cultivated or improved"—are deemed to have been held adversely. The object of the statute, we have recognized, "is that the real owner may, by unequivocal acts of the usurper, have notice of the hostile claim, and be thereby called upon to assert his legal title." . . . Since the character of the acts sufficient to afford such notice "depends upon the nature and situation of the property and the uses to which it can be applied," it is settled that the provisions of sections 39 and 40 are to be construed, not in a narrow or technical sense, but with reference to the nature, character, condition, and location of the property under consideration. *See Ramapo Mfg. Co. v. Mapes, supra*, 216 N.Y. 362, 372, 373, 110 N.E. 722, 776. . . .

Judge Dye considers it significant that the proof "fails to show that the cultivation incident to the garden utilized the whole of the premises claimed." There surely is no requirement in either statute or decision that proof of adverse possession depends upon cultivation of *"the whole"* plot or of *every foot* of the property in question. And, indeed, the statute—which, as noted, reads *"usually* cultivated or improved"—has been construed to mean only that the claimant's occupation must "consist of acts such as are usual in the ordinary cultivation and improvement of similar lands by thrifty owners." *Ramapo Mfg. Co. v. Mapes, supra*, 216 N.Y. 362, 373, 110 N.E. 772, 776. The evidence demonstrates that by far the greater part of the four lots was regularly and continuously used for farming, and, that being so, the fact that a portion of the property was not cleared should not affect the claimant's ability to acquire title by adverse possession: any frugal person, owning and occupying lands similar to those here involved, would have permitted, as Lutz did, some of the trees to stand—while clearing the bulk of the property—in order to provide a source of lumber and other tree products for his usual needs. The portion of the property held subservient to the part actively cultivated is as much "occupied" as the portion actually tilled. The nature of the cultivation engaged in by Lutz was more than adequate, as his neighbors' testimony establishes, to give the owner notice of an adverse claim and to delimit the property to which the claim related. . . .

In short, there is ample evidence to sustain the finding that William Lutz actually occupied the property in suit for over fifteen years under a claim of title. Since, then, title vested in Lutz by 1935, the judgment must be affirmed. . . .

Points for Discussion

a. **The New York Approach**

Although the *Van Valkenburgh* opinion is remarkably silent on the point, New York law *also* requires that the claimant prove the traditional common law elements of adverse possession. *See Hamil v. Casadei*, 186 N.Y.S.3d 707 (App. Div. 2023). As a practical matter, the statutory and case law elements overlap substantially. For example, the "usual cultivation" that meets the statutory standard will normally also fulfill the elements of actual, open and notorious, and continuous possession.

b. **The Mysterious Owner**

The trial court found that Lutz acquired title by adverse possession in 1935, long before the Van Valkenburghs arrived on the scene. Who owned the triangular tract until 1935? Why do you suppose that owner never acted to evict Lutz?

c. **Exploring the Rationale**

The majority and the dissent differ sharply on whether Lutz acquired title by adverse possession. Which side is right? An appellate court will normally defer to the factual findings of the trial court, unless they are clearly unsupported by evidence in the record. To what extent did the majority defer to the trial court's findings?

d. **"Usually Cultivated"**

The dissent cites evidence that the Lutz garden occupied "nearly all" of the triangular tract. Why doesn't this meet the § 40(2) requirement that the land be "usually cultivated," according to the majority? In a later New York case, the court held that this requirement was met where the adverse claimants "mowed the lawn, planted grass and a vegetable garden, raked leaves, removed debris, and planted, transplanted and pruned trees and bushes within the disputed parcel." *Franzen v. Cassarino*, 552 N.Y.S.2d 789, 791 (App. Div. 1990). Is *Franzen* consistent with *Lutz*?

e. **Color of Title**

Most states provide enhanced protection for the adverse possessor whose claim is based on *color of title*. In this context, color of title refers to a deed, a judgment, or another document that is invalid for some reason. The standards for adverse possession based on color of title are easier to meet in many states. For example, the required period is often shortened for a claimant holding color of title. Georgia law illustrates the point: the claimant with color of title need occupy the land for only 7 years, while the normal period is 20 years. Ga. Code Ann. §§ 44–5–163, 44–5–164.

In addition, the successful claimant with color of title may be able to acquire more land. Suppose that Greenacre consists of 40 acres. If adverse possessor A occupies two acres of Greenacre without color of title and succeeds in his claim, he acquires title only to those two acres—as N.Y. Civil Practice Act § 39 provided. But if A holds color of title, then he is deemed to be in *constructive possession* of all 40 acres, so he will obtain title to all of Greenacre.

f. "Under a Claim of Title"

According to the majority, what state of mind must an adverse possessor have in order to make a "claim of title"? Good faith, bad faith, or what? Did Lutz meet any of these standards? The majority stresses the fact that in 1947 (12 years *after* Lutz's adverse possession was complete, according to the trial court), Lutz admitted in the first lawsuit that the Van Valkenburghs owned the triangular tract. In determining Lutz's state of mind *during* the adverse possession period, how much weight should the court give to a statement made *after* that period?

g. Comparing *Gurwit* and *Van Valkenburgh*

Gurwit and *Van Valkenburgh* both involved adverse possession claims to open, undeveloped lands. The claimants in *Gurwit* (whose activities were minimal) won. But the claimants in *Van Valkenburgh* (whose activities were extensive) lost. How can we reconcile these results in light of the theories used to justify adverse possession?

h. Aftermath of *Van Valkenburgh*

The Court of Appeals decision did not end the feud between the Lutz and Van Valkenburgh families. To collect their costs in the case, the Van Valkenburghs tried to force a sale of the Lutz home. *Van Valkenburgh v. Lutz*, 175 N.Y.S.2d 203 (App. Div. 1958). And brother Charlie unsuccessfully tried to challenge the Van Valkenburghs' title. *Lutz v. Van Valkenburgh*, 237 N.E.2d 84 (N.Y. 1968). The Van Valkenburgh family eventually sold the triangular tract and their home to the Prophet Elias Greek Orthodox Church. Today, the site of their home is occupied by an impressive church, while the triangular tract is part of the church parking lot. However, members of the Lutz family still reside in their original home. They access the home by crossing the church parking lot along the path of the former "traveled way."

> **See It**
>
> Click here for modern photographs of the church parking lot, where the Lutz garden was located. The "traveled way" ran along the left side of the lot.

2. The Adverse Possessor's State of Mind

The "adverse and hostile" element is the most puzzling aspect of adverse possession. At a minimum, all states agree that possession stemming from the true owner's consent does not meet this standard. For example, if A leases his land to B, B's possession is not "adverse and hostile."

But must the claimant also have a particular state of mind in order to be "adverse and hostile"? Courts disagree. In some states, the adverse possessor must believe in *good faith* that she is the owner of the land. Historically, some states required that the adverse possessor have *bad faith*—know she is not the owner and intend to take title from the owner—and echoes of this approach linger. But in most jurisdictions, the claimant's state of mind is *irrelevant*. Within this third group, some courts create confusion by insisting that the adverse possessor have a *claim of right*, which implies that some type of special mindset is required. But this requirement is essentially meaningless, because these courts reason that the claimant's objective conduct—measured by the other adverse possession requirements—demonstrates a claim of right. Which of these three approaches is best?

Fulkerson v. Van Buren

Court of Appeals of Arkansas

961 S.W.2d 780 (1998)

JENNINGS, JUDGE.

Appellant Floyd H. Fulkerson appeals the Pulaski County Circuit Court's judgment awarding title to a 4.5-acre parcel of real estate to appellee the Progressive Church, Inc. The church claimed title to the land by adverse possession. We reverse and remand.

The 4.5 acres at issue are situated in Pulaski County, near the town of Scott. The parcel is irregularly configured and has eleven sides. The northernmost part of the parcel abuts Old Highway 30 for approximately 115 feet. A single-story church building is situated near the highway. This building is the meeting place for appellee, the Progressive Church, Inc. When the litigation between the parties began, appellant Fulkerson had held legal title to the parcel since December 1949. Sometime in 1985, the congregation of the Progressive Church, without obtaining permission from Fulkerson, began using the church building on the property as their place of worship. Over the next several years, the congregation greatly improved the church building itself and the surrounding land. . . .

See It

Click here to see a map of the disputed land in *Fulkerson*.

In November 1994, Fulkerson sent to Reverend Van Buren a letter demanding that he and the church congregation immediately vacate the church building located on the parcel. The church did not vacate the premises. In May 1995, Fulkerson filed in Pulaski County Circuit Court a complaint in which he requested that the court eject the congregation from the church building and from the rest of the parcel at issue.... [The church filed a counterclaim, asserting] that it owned the parcel of land at issue by adverse possession.... In October 1996, trial was held in Pulaski County Circuit Court.... After hearing testimony from witnesses presented by both parties, the circuit court subsequently caused to be entered a judgment in which the court determined that the Progressive Church owned the parcel of land by adverse possession.

Church building in *Fulkerson v. Van Buren*
Click here for larger photo

The legal principles governing establishment of title to land by adverse possession are well established. We recently set forth these principles as follows:

> It is well settled that, in order to establish title by adverse possession, appellee had the burden of proving that she had been in possession of the property continuously for more than seven years and that her possession was visible, notorious, distinct, exclusive, hostile, and with intent to hold against the true owner. The proof required as to the extent of possession and dominion may vary according to the location and character of the land. It is ordinarily sufficient that the acts of ownership are of such a nature as one would exercise over her own property and would not exercise over that of another, and that the acts amount to such dominion over the land as to which it is reasonably adapted....

Moses v. Dautartas, 53 Ark. App. 242, 244, 922 S.W.2d 345 (1996).... For possession to be adverse, it is only necessary that it be hostile in the sense that it is under a claim of right, title, or ownership as distinguished from possession in conformity with, recognition of, or subservience to the superior right of the holder of title to the land. Possession of land will not ordinarily be presumed to be adverse, but rather subservient to the true owner of the land. *See Dillaha v. Temple*, 267 Ark. 793, 797, 590 S.W.2d 331 (1979). Therefore, mere possession of land is not enough to adversely possess the land, and there is every presumption that possession of land is in subordination to the holder of the legal title to the land. The intention to hold adversely must be clear, distinct, and unequivocal. . . .

The core of the church's proof of adverse possession of the 4.5 acres at issue was provided by appellee, Reverend Sylvester Van Buren. As noted above, the intent required for adverse possession is the intention to claim the land at issue under right, title, or ownership as distinguished from possession in conformity with, recognition of, or subservience to the superior right of the true owner of the land. We conclude that Reverend Van Buren's testimony shows that, from the time the congregation occupied the church building on the parcel until November 1994, the church congregation was unsure of the precise nature of its interest in the land and, moreover, recognized that Fulkerson owned the land.

On cross-examination, Reverend Van Buren testified that in 1990 or 1991 he first realized that the church did not have a deed to the land at issue. He testified further that, prior to this time, he made no assumptions about whether the church was on the land with permission or whether the church had purchased the land. Reverend Van Buren specifically stated in this regard, "I didn't know how or what kind of possession they had." In order to clarify the matter of the church's right to occupy the land, Reverend Van Buren contacted appellant Fulkerson. He asked Fulkerson to give a quitclaim deed to the church, which Fulkerson refused to do. Reverend Van Buren testified further that, after Fulkerson told him that he (Fulkerson) held legal title to the land, he (Van Buren) "accepted that as a fact.". . . With regard to the time at which the church congregation decided to claim the land at issue, Reverend Van Buren testified:

> **What's That?**
>
> A *quitclaim deed* conveys all the title the grantor has in the property—if any. Thus, the grantor does not represent or warrant that he has any title at all. A quitclaim deed is often used when the grantor wishes to release a weak or invalid title claim, in order to resolve an ownership dispute. You will study the different types of deeds in Chapter 8.

> Once the term adverse had been positioned and he [Fulkerson] had caused us to be evicted or had asked us out of the church and we had no other alternatives. I just wondered what we should do. It wasn't a decision that was made impulsively at that time. We made the decision that we wanted the land once we found out it wasn't ours. And as far as adverse, adverse only came into play when no other avenue worked.

When asked whether this decision would have been reached in 1994 to 1995, Reverend Van Buren replied, "If you say so, that's close."

Given this testimony by Reverend Van Buren, given that a possessor of land does not possess adversely if, while in possession, he recognizes the ownership right of the titleholder to the land, and given that proof of the possessor's intention to hold adversely must be clear, distinct, and unequivocal and must have lasted seven years, we conclude that the circuit court's finding of fact that the congregation of the Progressive Church possessed for seven years the requisite intent to possess the land at issue adversely to appellant Fulkerson is clearly against the preponderance of the evidence. Because the church congregation did not possess the land with the requisite intent for seven years, the church congregation did not adversely possess the land.

For the reasons set forth above, we reverse the Pulaski County Circuit Court's judgment in favor of appellee the Progressive Church, Inc., on its counterclaim for adverse possession. . . .

MEADS, JUDGE, dissenting.

The trial court determined that appellees established their claim for adverse possession of the tract of land they had occupied since 1985. Because I do not believe the trial court's findings of fact are clearly erroneous or clearly against the preponderance of the evidence, I would affirm.

Reverend Van Buren testified that he became pastor of the Progressive Church in 1985 and that he and other church members immediately began cleaning up the premises, which he described as a "wilderness" and "dumping site." The land was overgrown with vines and littered with storm debris, and the church building was infested with snakes. They cut down trees, cleared out debris, and cleaned up the highway frontage so that the building became visible from the road. They repaired the building by installing central heat and air, and by replacing the roof, siding, windows, and floor. They added a 40-foot building and office. After two years, the property was in "immaculate" condition, and the congregation received compliments for their efforts from the local community. When asked whether he had treated the property as his own, Reverend Van Buren asserted: "There's no way that I would have gone to this property and cleared it by hand . . . if I had assumed we didn't have business being there, the right to be there, or if the church didn't have the needed possession."

Reverend Van Buren further testified that he had no dealings whatsoever with appellant until sometime in the early nineties, when appellant stopped by the church, asked to speak to the preacher, complimented him on the church's efforts to improve the appearance of the church and grounds, but was silent as to his ownership of the site. It was not until 1992 that appellant, through his attorney, notified appellee that he (appellant) owned the land and was willing to negotiate a lease with the church. Subsequently, appellant personally spoke to Reverend Van Buren about a lease. Ultimately, appellant's attorney sent appellees a demand to vacate dated November 4, 1994, and filed the ejectment action in May 1995. All during this time, the Progressive Church steadfastly refused to negotiate with appellant, asserted its intent to remain in possession, and defied eviction efforts. Reverend Van Buren repeatedly asked appellant for a quitclaim deed to the premises. He contended there were never any "negotiations" with appellant for a lease, and "the only reason lease was mentioned is because Mr. Fulkerson dominated the conversation. You only talk about what Mr. Fulkerson wants to talk about. It doesn't matter what you say."

To establish adverse possession which ripens into ownership, the claimant must prove possession for seven years that has been actual, open, notorious, continuous, hostile, and exclusive, accompanied with an intent to hold against the true owner. *Utley v. Ruff,* 255 Ark. 824, 827, 502 S.W.2d 629, 632 (1973). The majority believes appellee failed to establish the requisite intent to hold against the true owner, because once appellant asserted his ownership and the church "recognized" appellant's ownership right, the church's occupancy ceased to be adverse, thus interrupting the seven-year statutory period. I disagree.

First, I do not believe the church recognized appellant's ownership. Church members began to occupy the premises in 1985, using the building regularly, without interruption, and without notice of appellant's ownership until 1992. After being notified of appellant's title and after receiving a demand to vacate and later an eviction notice, they continued to occupy the premises, using the building regularly and without interruption. By their actions, the congregation continued to repudiate appellant's ownership even through the date of trial and beyond. To date, they have been in continuous possession for almost thirteen years.

Second, I believe the church clearly demonstrated a hostile intent within the meaning of the law. As this court stated in *Walker v. Hubbard,* 31 Ark. App. 43, 787 S.W.2d 251 (1990):

> The word hostile, as used in the law of adverse possession, must not be read too literally. For adverse possession to be hostile, it is not necessary that the possessor have a conscious feeling of ill will or enmity toward his neighbor. Claim of ownership, even under a mistaken belief, is nevertheless adverse.

Id. at 46–47, 787 S.W.2d 251. Additionally, for possession to be adverse, it is only necessary that it be hostile in the sense that it is under a claim of right, title, or ownership as distinguished from possession in conformity with, recognition of, or subservience to, the superior right of the owner. *Barclay v. Tussey,* 259 Ark. 238, 241, 532 S.W.2d 193, 195 (1976). For the reasons stated in the previous paragraph, I cannot say that appellee's possession was "in conformity with, recognition of, or subservience to" appellant's rights. . . .

Points for Discussion

a. Why Did the Church Lose?

Does Arkansas law require *bad faith*, that is, the adverse claimant must (1) know that he is not the true owner and (2) intend to claim title anyway? Or is the Arkansas requirement more complex?

b. The Bad Faith Approach

In a provocative article, Professor Lee Anne Fennell argued that bad faith should be *required* for adverse possession. She suggested that the ultimate purpose of adverse possession is to maximize economic efficiency by shifting title from the current owner (who places a low value on the land, as evidenced by his lack of use) to an adverse possessor (who places a higher value on the land, as shown by his use). Accordingly, she reasoned that it makes sense to require that an adverse claimant expressly consider how much he values the land:

> If we define an inefficient trespass as one that harms the record owner more than it benefits the trespasser, then it follows that an encroachment becomes increasingly efficient . . . as the trespasser's valuation of an entitlement in the land grows relative to that of the record owner.

Lee Anne Fennell, *Efficient Trespass: The Case for "Bad Faith" Adverse Possession,* 100 Nw. U. L. Rev. 1037, 1073 (2006). How strong is this argument? Are there other reasons to require bad faith?

c. Productive Use of Land

Through hard work, the church members converted a neglected "wilderness" into an "immaculate" property suitable for religious services. Fulkerson, the record owner, apparently ignored all this activity for years—as if he had abandoned the property. In light of the justifications for adverse possession, should the church have won this case? More broadly, should the standards for adverse possession be lowered when the owner has abandoned the property? For example, there are over 20,000 abandoned houses in Detroit. Should we change the law to encourage urban pioneers to reclaim these properties? *See* Sally Brown Richardson, *Abandonment and Adverse Possession,* 52 Hous. L. Rev. 1385 (2015).

d. Legal Ethics and Adverse Possession

Suppose that you represent the Progressive Church in this case. You are aware that Reverend Van Buren's state of mind will be a central issue at trial. Should you explain the Arkansas law on the point before asking him about his intent? Or should you inquire about his intent before explaining the law? Consider the American Bar Association's Model Rule of Professional Conduct 3.4(b), which provides that an attorney shall not "counsel or assist a witness to testify falsely." Is that rule relevant here?

e. Breaking a Tie

If the evidence in a case is equally balanced on a particular point, a *presumption* can serve as a "tie breaker" that tips the balance toward one side. In *Fulkerson*, the majority uses the presumption that a non-owner's possession of land is not adverse to the owner. Should the law presume adversity in this situation? Would the case have come out differently if Arkansas law did presume adversity?

f. Aftermath of *Fulkerson*

The Progressive Church eventually moved to a new location a few miles away. Today, the former church building—bearing a "No Trespassing" sign—is unoccupied and deteriorating. The trees, vines, and other vegetation that the church members cleared away are slowly growing back.

Tioga Coal Co. v. Supermarkets General Corp.

Supreme Court of Pennsylvania

546 A.2d 1 (1988)

FLAHERTY, JUSTICE.

In September, 1978 Tioga Coal Company filed a complaint in equity against Supermarkets General Corporation seeking title by adverse possession to a strip of land known as Agate Street, located within Supermarkets' property and bordering Tioga's property. Agate Street is a paper street forty feet wide which was entered on the plan of the City of Philadelphia but was never opened to the public. It was stricken from the city plan in 1966. . . .

[At trial] the Chancellor determined . . . that some time around 1948 Tioga took control of a gate controlling access to Agate Street by putting its lock on the gate, and maintained the lock until approximately 1978, when the gate was removed. The court found that during the thirty year period between 1948 and 1978 Tioga controlled ingress and egress from Agate Street. . . .

The Chancellor also found that Tioga used Agate Street from 1948 through 1978 for its entire forty feet width from the gate northward for 150 feet. . . . Although the court found that Tioga's possession was "actual, open, notorious, exclusive and continuous" for a period in excess of the required twenty-one years, it determined that Tioga had failed to establish that its use or possession of Agate Street was hostile or adverse to the true owner of the land. . . . [The basis for this ruling was that Tioga thought the true owner of the land was the City, when in fact it was owned by defendant Supermarkets, such that Tioga did not "intend" to claim title against the actual owner. This ruling was affirmed on appeal by the Pennsylvania Superior Court.]

> **See It**
>
> Click here to see (a) a map of the disputed land and (b) a photograph of the disputed land.

B.

The elements of Pennsylvania's law of adverse possession are stated in *Conneaut Lake Park, Inc. v. Klingensmith*, 362 Pa. 592, 66 A.2d 828 (1949):

> It has long been the rule of this Commonwealth that one who claims title by adverse possession must prove that he had actual, continuous, exclusive, visible, notorious, distinct, and hostile possession of the land for twenty-one years. . . .

Id. 362 Pa. at 594–5, 66 A.2d at 829. With regard to the requirement of hostility, this Court has stated: "While the word 'hostile' has been held not to mean ill will or hostility, it does imply the intent to hold title against the record title holder." *Vlachos v. Witherow*, 383 Pa. 174, 118 A.2d 174, 177 (1955).

Intent, thus, has become a part of Pennsylvania law of adverse possession. . . . Exactly how Pennsylvania's state of mind requirement may be proved, however, is a matter of some uncertainty. . . .

Superior Court required that Tioga prove its subjective hostility by establishing that it directed its hostility toward the true owner [Supermarkets], not the mistaken owner of the land [the City]. . . . Tioga believed that Agate Street was owned by the City, and Superior Court was unwilling to imply hostility "where the claimant acknowledges the ownership of another." In Superior Court's view, therefore, what was required was that Tioga know who the true owner of the land was, meet all of the other requirements of actual, continuous, exclusive, visible, notorious, and distinct possession, and direct its hostility toward the true owner of the land.

. . . Tioga asserts that its taking and using the lands of another for longer than the required twenty-one years is "hostile" within the meaning of the law of adverse possession.

C.

Perhaps the reason that many appellate courts have been reluctant to rely on objective evidence of adverse possession without also considering the possessor's mental state of mind . . . is that they are reluctant to award title to a "land pirate." The thought of allowing a knowing trespasser to attain title to the land he has usurped is often regarded as unacceptable. There are, however, sound reasons to avoid entanglement with attempting to discern the mental state of adverse possessors. For one thing, discerning the mental state of an adverse possessor is, at best, an exercise in guesswork; and at worst, impossible. Beyond that, application of objective tests as to whether the land was adversely possessed promotes use of the land in question against abandonment. Also, as Justice Holmes points out in a letter to William James, the use of objective, as opposed to subjective tests, may involve an essentially equitable consideration that a person who has put down his roots on land develops an attachment to the land which is deserving of protection:

> The true explanation of title by prescription seems to me to be that man, like a tree in a cleft of a rock, gradually shapes his roots to his surroundings, and when the roots have grown to a certain size, cannot be displaced without cutting at his life. The law used to look with disfavor on the Statute of Limitations, but I have been in the habit of saying it is one of the most sacred and indubitable principles that we have, which used to lead my predecessor Field to say that Holmes didn't value any title that was not based on fraud or force.

Lerner, *The Mind and Faith of Justice Holmes,* 417 (1953). . . . In other words, as Holmes puts it, if an owner abandons his land and the land is possessed and used by another for the statutory period, beyond which the true owner no longer has a cause of action in ejectment, the trespasser has put down roots which we should not disturb.

> **FYI**
>
> Oliver Wendell Holmes, Jr. was a giant in American jurisprudence. As a scholar, a professor at Harvard Law School, the Chief Justice of the Supreme Judicial Court of Massachusetts, and—most importantly—as an Associate Justice of the United States Supreme Court for almost 30 years, he profoundly impacted our legal system. His book The Common Law influenced the development of both legal realism and the law and economics movement.

We believe that Justice Holmes' view of adverse possession represents sound public policy. Furthermore, this view is consistent with a requirement that adverse possession be characterized by hostility as well as the other elements of the cause of action, for it is inconceivable that if an adverse possessor actually takes possession of land in a manner that is open, notorious, exclusive and continuous, his actions will not be hostile to the true owner of the land as well as to the world at large, regardless of the adverse possessor's state of mind. We hold, therefore, that if the true owner has not ejected the interloper within the time allotted for an action in ejectment, and all other elements of adverse possession have been established, hostility will be implied, regardless of the subjective state of mind of the trespasser.

Judgment of Superior Court is reversed. . . .

McDermott, Justice, dissenting.

I dissent, and would affirm the Superior Court and the Chancellor below. There is no reason to change the law of this Commonwealth on the basis of a letter from Justice Holmes to William James. We have previously held with the prevailing opinion in this country that one must intend to take against the record title holder. . . .

The romantic notion that an interloper upon the land of another challenges the world bespeaks a time of wilderness and unrecorded land titles. In a modern organized state all titles are recorded and the "world" cannot bring an action in ejectment any more than a record title owner need periodically bring one against the "world." Recorded land titles should lie peacefully in their owners unless one who seeks to own them intends to own them by exercising exclusive, open, notorious, and hostile possession against the record title owner and not somebody else.

Points for Discussion

a. **Role of Intent**

   Do you agree with the majority's view that an adverse claimant's intent should be irrelevant? This is certainly the approach followed by most jurisdictions—and it represents the modern trend. When the Washington Supreme Court abandoned the good faith standard in *Chaplin v. Sanders*, 676 P.2d 431, 435 (Wash. 1984), it explained that the standard "does not serve the purpose of the adverse possession doctrine." What did the court mean?

b. **Land Piracy Revisited**

   Decisions such as *Tioga Coal Co.* and *Chaplin* seem to facilitate land piracy. Now that you are familiar with adverse possession law, suppose that you set out to adversely possess a remote and undeveloped parcel of land in a jurisdiction where intent is irrelevant. You take the minimum steps needed to meet the adverse possession standards (e.g., you periodically gather firewood, cut trees, etc.) for the required period. Would a court now recognize your title? Or should your prior knowledge of the law make a difference?

c. **The Court's Rationale**

   One reason for the majority's new standard is the difficulty of determining the adverse possessor's mental state. How strong is this argument? Courts routinely decide cases that involve a person's state of mind. For example, in a criminal prosecution the defendant's punishment will typically be more severe if he intended a crime than if he was merely negligent or reckless. Beyond this point, what other reasons does the court offer for changing Pennsylvania law?

d. **Native Americans and Ownership**

   In *Nome 2000 v. Fagerstrom*, 799 P.2d 304 (Alaska 1990), a Native American family claimed title to a forest tract by adverse possession. The record owner argued that the claimants lacked the required intent to claim title because they "thought of themselves not as owners but as stewards pursuant to the traditional system of Native Alaskan land usage." *Id.* at 310. Assuming that Alaska law requires an affirmative intent to claim title, would the intent to use land as stewards meet this standard? The Alaska Supreme Court bypassed this question by adopting the majority view that subjective intent is irrelevant.

e. Death(?) of Good Faith

A minority of states require that the adverse possessor act in good faith. What are the pros and cons of this approach? After reviewing over 800 appellate decisions on adverse possession, Professor R.H. Helmholz concluded that most courts *implicitly* require good faith in adverse possession cases, even if this is not an express requirement: "... [T]he results of most cases show that where courts allow adverse possession to ripen into title, bad faith on the part of the possessor seldom exists. Where the possessor knows that he is trespassing, title does not accrue to him simply by the passage of years." R.H. Helmholz, *Adverse Possession and Subjective Intent,* 61 Wash. U. L.Q. 331, 347 (1983). If Professor Helmholz is correct, should states *explicitly* require good faith for adverse possession?

In *Walling v. Przybylo*, 851 N.E.2d 1167 (N.Y. 2006), the New York Court of Appeals held that the plaintiffs (an attorney and his wife) had obtained title to part of their neighbors' lot by adverse possession, even though they knew they did not own that land. The case generated such adverse publicity that the New York Legislature adopted a statute that requires good faith for adverse possession without color of title: "a reasonable basis for the belief that the property belongs to the adverse possessor...." N.Y. Real Prop. Acts. § 501(3). The Sponsor's Memorandum in support of the legislation explained that: "Adverse possession ... should not be a doctrine which can be used offensively to deprive a landowner of his real property. This only encourages mischief between neighbors.... No good can come of it." Do you agree?

---

3. Proving Adverse Possession

Adverse possession claims normally arise in two procedural situations: the adverse possessor either brings a quiet title action to confirm his title (as in *Gurwit*) or raises the doctrine as a defense to an owner's lawsuit to recover possession (as in *Van Valkenburgh*). But judicial action is not necessary for an adverse possessor to obtain title. For example, if A occupies B's land for the required period and satisfies the adverse possession elements, A automatically acquires title to B's land when the period ends, without any litigation. In order to ensure that the public land records show that the adverse possessor has title, it is common for a successful claimant like A to bring a quiet title action; the court's judgment recognizing A's title can then

> **Practice Pointer**
>
> ABA Model Rule of Professional Conduct 3.1 provides that a lawyer "shall not bring or defend a proceeding ... unless there is a basis in law and fact for doing so that is not frivolous." Thus, if it is clear that A has satisfied all the requirements for adverse possession, B's attorney has an ethical obligation not to assert a frivolous defense. B's attorney will presumably advise B to give A a deed to the property in order to avoid litigation. On the other hand, B's attorney may assert any nonfrivolous defense to A's claim.

be entered in the public records. Alternatively, a former owner may avoid litigation by voluntarily giving A a deed. In this section, we will examine the mechanics of proving adverse possession.

The adverse possession periods of two or more successive occupants may be added together to meet the statutory period under the doctrine of *tacking*. Suppose F owns land in a jurisdiction with a 10-year adverse possession period. G occupies the land for 3 years and conveys her rights to H who occupies it for 8 more years. If G and H both satisfied the other adverse possession requirements, H may combine the two periods and receive credit for 11 years, thus obtaining title.

Our next case examines tacking in the context of an adverse possession claim to a summer beach cottage on the shore of Hood Canal in Washington. Hood Canal is a natural saltwater fiord just off Puget Sound. The parcels involved in this case are located in a forest area on the southeastern side of the canal, next to Twanoh State Park. They adjoin one of the warmest beaches in the state, which attracts crowds of swimmers and sunbathers each summer.

Howard v. Kunto

Court of Appeals of Washington

477 P.2d 210 (1970)

PEARSON, JUDGE.

Land surveying is an ancient art but not one free of the errors that often creep into the affairs of men. In this case, we are presented with the question of what happens when the descriptions in deeds do not fit the land the deed holders are occupying. Defendants appeal from a decree quieting title in the plaintiffs of a tract of land on the shore of Hood Canal in Mason County.

At least as long ago as 1932 the record tells us that one McCall resided in the house now occupied by the appellant-defendants, Kunto. McCall had a deed that described a 50-foot-wide parcel on the shore of Hood Canal. The error that brings this case before us is that 50 feet described in the deed is not the same 50 feet upon which McCall's house stood. Rather, the described land is an adjacent 50-foot lot directly west of that upon which the house stood. In other words, McCall's house stood on one lot and his deed described the adjacent lot. Several property owners to the west of defendants, not parties to this action, are similarly situated.

> **See It**
>
> Click here to see a photo of the Hood Canal.

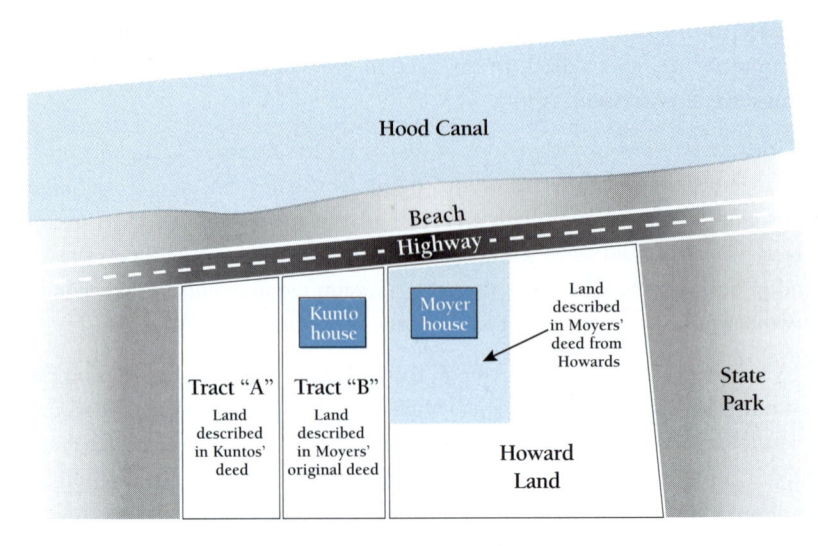

Map of land in *Howard v. Kunto*

Over the years since 1946, several conveyances occurred, using the same legal description and accompanied by a transfer of possession to the succeeding occupants. The Kuntos' immediate predecessors in interest, Millers, desired to build a dock. To this end, they had a survey performed which indicated that the deed description and the physical occupation were in conformity. Several boundary stakes were placed as a result of this survey and the dock was constructed, as well as other improvements. The house as well as the others in the area continued to be used as summer recreational retreats.

The Kuntos then took possession of the disputed property under a deed from the Millers in 1959. In 1960, the respondent-plaintiffs, Howard, who held land east of that of the Kuntos, determined to convey an undivided one-half interest in their land to the Yearlys. To this end, they undertook to have a survey of the entire area made. After expending considerable effort, the surveyor retained by the Howards discovered that according to the government survey, the deed descriptions and the land occupancy of the parties did not coincide. Between the Howards and the Kuntos lay the Moyers' property. When the Howards' survey was completed, they discovered that they were the record owners of the land occupied by the Moyers and that the Moyers held record title to the land occupied by the Kuntos. Howard approached Moyer and in return for a conveyance of the land upon which the Moyers' house stood, Moyer conveyed to the Howards record title to the land upon which the Kunto house stood. Until plaintiffs Howard obtained the conveyance from Moyer in April, 1960, neither Moyer nor any of his predecessors ever asserted any right to ownership of the property actually being possessed by Kunto and his predecessors. This action was then instituted to quiet title in the Howards and Yearlys. The Kuntos appeal from a trial court decision granting this remedy.

At the time this action was commenced on August 19, 1960, defendants had been in occupancy of the disputed property less than a year. The trial court's reason for denying their claim of adverse possession is succinctly stated in its memorandum opinion: "In this instance, defendants have failed to prove, by a preponderance of the evidence, a continuity of possession or estate to permit tacking of the adverse possession of defendants to the possession of their predecessors." . . .

Two issues are presented by this appeal:

(1) Is a claim of adverse possession defeated because the physical use of the premises is restricted to summer occupancy?

(2) May a person who receives record title to tract A under the mistaken belief that he has title to tract B (immediately contiguous to tract A) and who subsequently occupies tract B, for the purpose of establishing title to tract B by adverse possession, use the periods of possession of tract B by his immediate predecessors who also had record title to tract A?

In approaching both of these questions, we point out that the evidence, largely undisputed in any material sense, established that defendant or his immediate predecessors did occupy the premises, which we have called tract B, as though it was their own for far more than the 10 years as prescribed in RCW 4.16.020. . . .

We start with the oft-quoted rule that:

> [T]o constitute adverse possession, there must be actual possession which is *uninterrupted*, open and notorious, hostile and exclusive, and under a *claim of right* made in good faith for the statutory period.

(Italics ours.) *Butler v. Anderson*, 71 Wash.2d 60, 64, 426 P.2d 467, 470 (1967). . . .

We reject the conclusion that summer occupancy only of a summer beach home destroys the continuity of possession required by the statute. It has become firmly established that the requisite possession requires such possession and dominion "as ordinarily marks the conduct of owners in general in holding, managing, and caring for property of like nature and condition." *Whalen v. Smith*, 183 Iowa 949, 953, 167 N.W. 646, 647 (1918). . . .

We hold that occupancy of tract B during the summer months for more than the 10-year period by defendant and his predecessors, together with the continued existence of the improvements on the land and beach area, constituted "uninterrupted" possession within this rule. To hold otherwise is to completely ignore the nature and condition of the property. . . .

We now reach the question of tacking. The precise issue before us is novel in that none of the property occupied by defendant or his predecessors coincided with the property described in their deeds, but was contiguous.

In the typical case, which has been subject to much litigation, the party seeking to establish title by adverse possession claims *more* land than that described in the deed. In such cases it is clear that tacking is permitted.

In *Buchanan v. Cassell*, 53 Wash.2d 611, 614, 335 P.2d 600, 602 (1959) the Supreme Court stated:

> This state follows the rule that a purchaser may tack the adverse use of its predecessor in interest to that of his own where the land was intended to be included in the deed between them, but was mistakenly omitted from the description.

The general statement which appears in many of the cases is that tacking of adverse possession is permitted if the successive occupants are in "privity." *See Faubion v. Elder*, 49 Wash.2d 300, 301 P.2d 153 (1956). The deed running between the parties purporting to transfer the land possessed traditionally furnishes the privity of estate which connects the possession of the successive occupants. Plaintiff contends, and the trial court ruled, that where the deed does not describe *any* of the land which was occupied, the actual transfer of possession is insufficient to establish privity.

To assess the cogency of this argument and ruling, we must turn to the historical reasons for requiring privity as a necessary prerequisite to tacking the possession of several occupants. Very few, if any, of the reasons appear in the cases, nor do the cases analyze the relationships that must exist between successive possessors for tacking to be allowed. *See* W. Stoebuck, *The Law of Adverse Possession In Washington* in 35 Wash. L. Rev. 53 (1960).

The requirement of privity had its roots in the notion that a succession of trespasses, even though there was no appreciable interval between them, should not, in equity, be allowed to defeat the record title. The "claim of right," "color of title" requirement of the statutes and cases was probably derived from the early American belief that the squatter should not be able to profit by his trespass.

However, it appears to this court that there is a substantial difference between the squatter or trespasser and the property purchaser, who along with several of his neighbors, as a result of an inaccurate survey or subdivision, occupies and improves property exactly 50 feet to the east of that which a survey some 30 years later demonstrates that they in fact own. It seems to us that there is also a strong public policy favoring early certainty as to the location of land ownership which enters into a proper interpretation of privity.

> **Food for Thought**
>
> Why is there "a strong public policy favoring early certainty as to the location of land ownership"? In formulating your answer, consider how concern for certainty of title affected the decisions in *Johnson v. M'Intosh* and *Van Valkenburgh v. Lutz*.

On the irregular perimeters of Puget Sound exact determination of land locations and boundaries is difficult and expensive. This difficulty is convincingly demonstrated in this case by the problems plaintiff's engineer encountered in attempting to locate the corners. It cannot be expected that every purchaser will or should engage a surveyor to ascertain that the beach home he is purchasing lies within the boundaries described in his deed. Such a practice is neither reasonable nor customary. Of course, 50-foot errors in descriptions are devastating where a group of adjacent owners each hold 50 feet of waterfront property.

The technical requirement of "privity" should not, we think, be used to upset the long periods of occupancy of those who in good faith received an erroneous deed description. Their "claim of right" is no less persuasive than the purchaser who believes he is purchasing *more* land than his deed described.

In the final analysis, however, we believe the requirement of "privity" is no more than judicial recognition of the need for some reasonable connection between successive occupants of real property so as to raise their claim of right above the status of the wrongdoer or the trespasser. We think such reasonable connection exists in this case.

> **Make the Connection**
>
> Based on this decision, the Howards and the Yearlys lost any title claim to the Kunto lot. Did they have rights against anyone else? In Chapter 8, you will study techniques to protect the buyer's title such as deed covenants and title insurance policies.

Where, as here, several successive purchasers received record title to tract A under the mistaken belief that they were acquiring tract B, immediately contiguous thereto, and where possession of tract B is transferred and occupied in a continuous manner for more than 10 years by successive occupants, we hold there is sufficient privity of estate to permit tacking and thus establish adverse possession as a matter of law. . . .

Judgment is reversed with directions to dismiss plaintiffs' action and to enter a decree quieting defendants' title to the disputed tract of land in accordance with the prayer of their cross-complaint.

Points for Discussion

a. **Tacking Basics**

As the *Howard* court notes, most states allow tacking only if the successive occupants are in *privity*. This requirement is generally satisfied when one occupant transfers his rights in the property to a successor, for example, by a deed or a will. Conversely, suppose A abandons his occupancy after three years; B sees A leave the land, and begins to occupy it herself. In the eyes of the law, this is a succession of trespasses which will not justify B tacking on A's possession. Why does the law treat these two situations differently? Indeed, why is tacking ever allowed?

b. **Privity in** *Howard*

The facts in *Howard* fall somewhere between the two standard situations. The Kuntos did receive a deed, but the land described in that deed was different from the lot they claimed by adverse possession. So why were the Kuntos allowed to tack? In light of the purposes behind the privity requirement, what is the "substantial difference" the court mentions between the Kuntos and an ordinary trespasser? Note that there is wide variation among the states as to when tacking is permitted.

c. **Group Privity?**

In *East 13th Street Homesteaders' Coalition v. Lower East Side Coalition Housing Development*, 646 N.Y.S.2d 324 (App. Div. 1996), an organized group of squatters occupied four vacant, city-owned apartment buildings and later claimed title by adverse possession. The City had "sealed the buildings numerous times during the claimed period, and . . . the occupants had to break these seals, sometimes with a sledgehammer, to reenter the buildings." *Id.* at 326. Although the claimants argued that "there was a chain of possession of coalition members in all of the buildings during the requisite period," the court refused to allow tacking because "there is no evidence of privity between successive occupants of the apartments." *Id.* If all the occupants were members of the same group, should the court have found privity and thus permitted tacking?

d. **Tackle These Hypotheticals**

Under the *Howard* approach, is tacking allowed in the following situations? Assume the jurisdiction has a 10-year statutory period.

> (1) A occupies O's land for 6 years. A then tells his friend B: "You can be here if you want, but I'm leaving." B occupies the land for 5 more years.
>
> (2) C occupies O's land for 2 years. C then tries to convey the land to her sister D, but the deed C uses for this purpose is invalid. D occupies the land for 9 more years.

e. **Continuity Revisited**

Why did the Kuntos' summer occupancy satisfy the requirement of "continuous" possession? How would the court have ruled if the Kuntos (and their predecessors) had occupied the home for only 6 summers in 10 years? What if there was no house at all on the lot, but the Kuntos and their predecessors camped on the land for 6 weekends every summer? In *Ray v. Beacon Hudson Mountain Corp.*, 666 N.E.2d 532, 534 (N.Y. 1996), the continuity requirement was satisfied because the adverse possessor occupied a summer vacation cottage for "about one month per year."

f. Good Faith Improvers

Suppose X intends to build a house on her own lot, but due to a survey error inadvertently builds it on an adjacent lot owned by Y, as apparently happened in *Howard v. Kunto*. If X cannot meet the requirements for adverse possession, does she have any rights?

Most states provide limited relief to the *good faith improver*—one who improves land under the mistaken but good faith belief that she owns it. For example, statutes in many jurisdictions require the true owner to either (1) compensate the improver for the enhanced value produced by the improvement or (2) sell the land to the improver for its fair market value before the improvement. *See, e.g., Estate of Waterman*, 847 N.W.2d 560 (Iowa 2014).

g. Abolish Adverse Possession?

At the beginning of this unit, we explored the justifications offered for adverse possession. Now that you have studied the doctrine in detail, assume you are a member of your state's legislature which is considering a bill to abolish adverse possession. How would you vote on that bill and why?

Other Procedural Issues

a. Disabilities

What happens if owner A is unable to sue adverse possessor B during the state's 10-year statutory period because, for example, A is insane? The period for adverse possession will be extended due to A's *disability*. The most commonly recognized disabilities are imprisonment, minority, and lack of mental capacity. Some jurisdictions also protect the owner who is away on military service or who resides outside of the state.

States differ on how a disability affects the statutory period. For example, some jurisdictions suspend the running of the period until the disability is removed. But most states provide a limited period of time after the disability ends within which suit must be brought. For example, in our hypothetical above, assume a state statute allows an owner to bring suit within five years after her disability is removed. Suppose B's adverse possession period begins in 2009, and thus would normally end in 2019, ten years later. If A became mentally incompetent in 2004, and is cured in 2021, then A still has five years to sue to eject B, that is, until 2026. In many states, only a disability that exists at the beginning of the adverse possession period (such as A's incompetence here) will extend the statutory period. Note that death ends all disabilities; disabilities cannot be tacked; and a disability does not shorten the standard period for adverse possession.

To test your understanding of disabilities, consider this problem. Suppose owner C is ten years old in 2019. D begins adverse possession of C's land in 2019. C dies in 2022, and all his rights in the land are inherited by his heir H. However, H has been mentally incompetent since 2021. The normal adverse possession period is ten years, but an owner under a disability may bring suit within five years after his disability is removed. When is the earliest time that D can perfect title by adverse possession?

b. Identity of the Parties

The identity of the record owner may affect the availability and scope of adverse possession. Normally, we tend to think of adverse possession as a claim made against a private owner who holds *fee simple absolute* or complete title, which you will study in Chapter 5. But suppose the owner holds a lesser interest, such as a *life estate* (roughly equivalent to full ownership rights, but lasting only for the life of a specific person). In this case, the successful adverse possessor receives only what the owner had—a life estate. And adverse possession is not available at all against a person who does not hold the present right to possession of land, such as someone who has a future interest or a mortgage.

In most jurisdictions, adverse possession cannot be asserted against land owned by state or local governments. However, some jurisdictions permit adverse possession against land held by state or local governments if that land is used for a *proprietary* or nonpublic purpose. *See City of Philadelphia v. Galdo*, 217 A.3d 811 (Pa. 2019). In such a jurisdiction, for example, city-owned forest land used only for timber production may be subject to adverse possession, just as if it was owned by an individual; but a public park could not be adversely possessed.

B. The Vertical Dimension of Ownership

How far up do property rights extend? And how far down? We normally think of real property in terms of rights to the land surface. But some airspace and subsurface rights are obviously necessary for any meaningful use of the surface. If A builds a three-story house on her land, for example, the structure may rise 25 feet into the air, while its foundation penetrates 3 feet into the ground. But do A's rights extend upward and downward for 100 feet, 10 miles, 1,000 miles, or farther?

Early English courts grandly proclaimed that a landowner's title extended up to the "heavens" and down to the center of the earth. This concept was reflected in the Latin maxim *cujus est solum, ejus est usque ad coelum et ad inferos*. Under this view, a parcel of real property was seen as a long, slender column which stretched upward from our planet's center to the surface and then infinitely outward into space.

Over the last century, courts have modified the traditional approach in light of technological advances. The quaint notion that ownership extends to the "heavens" collapsed with the invention of the airplane. And new technology that allows ever-deeper drilling—coupled with modern scientific discoveries about the earth's interior—is leading to a reexamination of subsurface rights as well. (After all, the common law view means that each surface owner holds title to a slice of the earth's molten core, with a temperature of 5000° C!)

> **It's Latin to Me**
>
> The Latin maxim is usually translated as meaning that the rights of the surface owner extend upward to the heavens (*ad coelum*) and downward to the center of the earth (*ad inferos*).

Accordingly, the vertical dimensions of real property today are far less clear than they were in common law England. An owner is certainly entitled to the airspace immediately above his property. For example, a condominium is—in legal theory—the ownership of a cube of air space, surrounded by walls. Thus, landowner B may subdivide his land vertically by selling off condominium units within the airspace just above the surface. Similarly, owner C may sever part of his subsurface rights by giving a mining company the right to extract the coal just below the surface. But beyond such near-surface situations, the precise upward and downward limits of real property are now less clear than in the past.

1. Airspace Rights

The Fifth Amendment to the Constitution provides, in part: "[N]or shall private property be taken for public use, without just compensation." So if the federal government established a post office on land you owned, for example, you would be entitled to compensation. You will study this process—which is called *eminent domain*—in Chapter 13.

The next case examines whether the government effectively "took" part of the owners' airspace rights when military planes flew over the land at very low altitudes during World War II. The right at issue was an easement—a nonpossessory right to use land in the possession or ownership of another person, such as the right to use a private road across land owned by another. (You will study easements in depth in Chapter 10.) Here, the plaintiffs claim that the government took an easement for airplane transit through their airspace (an *avigation easement*) without their consent.

United States v. Causby

Supreme Court of the United States

328 U.S. 256 (1946)

MR. JUSTICE DOUGLAS delivered the opinion of the Court.

This is a case of first impression. The problem presented is whether respondents' property was taken within the meaning of the Fifth Amendment by frequent and regular flights of army and navy aircraft over respondents' land at low altitudes. The Court of Claims held that there was a taking and entered judgment for respondent, one judge dissenting. 60 F. Supp. 751. . . .

> **Make the Connection**
>
> The Fifth Amendment provides that private property may not be "taken" for public use without payment of just compensation. You will study takings in Chapter 14.

Respondents own 2.8 acres near an airport outside of Greensboro, North Carolina. It has on it a dwelling house, and also various outbuildings which were mainly used for raising chickens. The end of the airport's northwest-southeast runway is 2,220 feet from respondents' barn and 2,275 feet from their house. The path of glide to this runway passes directly over the property—which is 100 feet wide and 1,200 feet long. The 30 to 1 safe glide angle approved by the Civil Aeronautics Authority passes over this property at 83 feet, which is 67 feet above the house, 63 feet above the barn and 18 feet above the highest tree. The use by the United States of this airport is pursuant to a lease executed in May, 1942, for a term commencing June 1, 1942 and ending June 30, 1942, with a provision for renewals until June 30, 1967, or six months after the end of the national emergency, whichever is the earlier.

> **See It**
>
> Click here to see (a) a diagram of the farm involved in *Causby* and (b) a photo of some of the types of planes that flew over the farm.

Various aircraft of the United States use this airport—bombers, transports and fighters. The direction of the prevailing wind determines when a particular runway is used. The north-west-southeast runway in question is used about four per cent of the time in taking off and about seven per cent of the time in landing. Since the United States began operations in May, 1942, its four-motored heavy bombers, other planes of the heavier type, and its fighter planes have frequently passed over respondents' land buildings in considerable numbers and rather close together. They come close enough at times to appear barely to miss the tops of the trees and at times so close to the tops of the trees as to blow the old leaves off. The noise is startling. And at night the glare from the planes brightly lights up the place. As a result of the noise, respondents had to give up their chicken business. As many as six to ten of their chickens were killed in one day by flying into the walls from fright. The total chickens lost in that manner was about 150. Production also fell off. The result was the destruction of the use of the property as a commercial chicken farm. Respondents are frequently deprived of their sleep and the family has become nervous and frightened. . . . These are the essential facts found by the Court of Claims. On the basis of these facts, it found that respondents' property had depreciated in value. It held that the United States had taken an easement over the property on June 1, 1942, and that the value of the property destroyed and the easement taken was $2,000.

> **What's That?**
>
> The *Court of Claims* was a federal court that was established to consider claims for money damages against the United States government arising from the Constitution, a law, a regulation, or a federal contract. Today it is known as the United States Court of Federal Claims.

The United States relies on the Air Commerce Act of 1926, 44 Stat. 568, 49 U.S.C. § 171 et seq., as amended by the Civil Aeronautics Act of 1938, 52 Stat. 973, 49 U.S.C. § 401 et seq. Under those statutes the United States has "complete and exclusive national sovereignty in the air space" over this country. 49 U.S.C. § 176(a). They grant any citizen of the United States "a public right of freedom of transit in air commerce through the navigable air space of the United States." 49 U.S.C. § 403. And "navigable air space" is defined as "airspace above the minimum safe altitudes of flight prescribed by the Civil Aeronautics Authority." 49 U.S.C. § 180. And it is provided that "such navigable airspace shall be subject to a public right of freedom of interstate and foreign air navigation." Id. It is, therefore, argued that since these flights were within the minimum safe altitudes of flight which had been prescribed, they were an exercise of the declared right of travel through the airspace. The United States concludes that when flights are made within the navigable airspace without any physical invasion of the property of the landowners, there has been no taking of property. It says that at most there was merely incidental damage occurring as a consequence of authorized air navigation. It also argues that the landowner does not own superadjacent airspace which he has not subjected to possession by the erection of structures or other occupancy. . . .

It is ancient doctrine that at common law ownership of the land extended to the periphery of the universe—*Cujus est solum ejus est usque ad coelum*. But that doctrine has no place in the modern world. The air is a public highway, as Congress has declared. Were that not true, every transcontinental flight would subject the operator to countless trespass suits. Common sense revolts at the idea. To recognize such private claims to the airspace would clog these highways, seriously interfere with their control and development in the public interest, and transfer into private ownership that to which only the public has a just claim.

But that general principle does not control the present case. For the United States conceded on oral argument that if the flights over respondents' property rendered it uninhabitable, there would be a taking compensable under the Fifth Amendment. It is the owner's loss, not the taker's gain, which is the measure of the value of the property taken. Market value fairly determined is the normal measure of the recovery. And that value may reflect the use to which the land could readily be converted, as well as the existing use. If, by reason of the frequency and altitude of the flights, respondents could not use this land for any purpose, their loss would be complete. It would be as complete as if the United States had entered upon the surface of the land and taken exclusive possession of it.

We agree that in those circumstances there would be a taking. Though it would be only an easement of flight which was taken, that easement, if permanent and not merely temporary, normally would be the equivalent of a fee interest. It would be a definite exercise of complete dominion and control over the surface of the land. The fact that the planes never touched the surface would be as irrelevant as the absence in this day of the feudal livery of seisin on the transfer of real estate. The owner's right to possess and exploit the land—that is to say, his beneficial ownership of it—would be destroyed. . . .

> **Make the Connection**
>
> In medieval England, deeds were not used to transfer title to land. Rather, title was transferred through an elaborate ceremony called *feoffment with livery of seisin*. This technique became obsolete in 1677, when the Statute of Frauds mandated the use of deeds. You will study deeds in Chapter 8.

There is no material difference between the supposed case and the present one, except that here enjoyment and use of the land are not completely destroyed. But that does not seem to us to be controlling. The path of glide for airplanes might reduce a valuable factory site to grazing land, an orchard to a vegetable patch, a residential section to a wheat field. Some value would remain. But the use of the airspace immediately above the land would limit the utility of the land and cause a diminution in its value. . . .

We have said that the airspace is a public highway. Yet it is obvious that if the landowner is to have full enjoyment of the land, he must have exclusive control of the immediate reaches of the enveloping atmosphere. Otherwise buildings could not be erected, trees could not be planted, and even fences could not be run. The principle is recognized when the law gives a remedy in case overhanging structures are erected on adjoining land. The landowner owns at least as much of the space above the ground as he can occupy or use in connection with the land. *See Hinman v. Pacific Air Transport,* 9 Cir., 84 F.2d 755. The fact that he does not occupy it in a physical sense—by the erection of buildings and the like—is not material. As we have said, the flight of airplanes, which skim the surface but do not touch it, is as much an appropriation of the use of the land as a more conventional entry upon it. We would not doubt that if the United States erected an elevated railway over respondents' land at the precise altitude where its planes now fly, there would be a partial taking, even though none of the supports of the structure rested on the land. The reason is that there would be an intrusion so immediate and direct as to subtract from the owner's full enjoyment of the property and to limit his exploitation of it. While the owner does not in any physical manner occupy that stratum of airspace or make use of it in the conventional sense, he does use it in somewhat the same sense that space left between buildings for the purpose of light and air is used. The superadjacent airspace at this low altitude is so close to the land that continuous invasions of it affect the use of the surface of the land itself. We think that the landowner, as an incident to his ownership, has a claim to it and that invasions of it are in the same category as invasions of the surface. . . .

The airplane is part of the modern environment of life, and the inconveniences which it causes are normally not compensable under the Fifth Amendment. The airspace, apart from the immediate reaches above the land, is part of the public domain. We need not determine at this time what those precise limits are. Flights over private land are not a taking, unless they are so low and so frequent as to be a direct and immediate interference with the enjoyment and use of the land. We need not speculate on that phase of the present case. For the findings of the Court of Claims plainly establish that there was a diminution in value of the property and that the frequent, low-level flights were the direct and immediate cause. We agree with the Court of Claims that a servitude has been imposed upon the land. . . .

Mr. Justice Black, dissenting.

. . . It is inconceivable to me that the Constitution guarantees that the airspace of this Nation needed for air navigation is owned by the particular persons who happen to own the land beneath to the same degree as they own the surface below. No rigid constitutional rule, in my judgment, commands that the air must be considered as marked off into separate compartments by imaginary metes and bounds in order to synchronize air ownership with land ownership. I think that the Constitution entrusts Congress with full power to control all navigable airspace. Congress has already acted under that power. . . .

No greater confusion could be brought about in the coming age of air transportation than that which would result were courts by constitutional interpretation to hamper Congress in its efforts to keep the air free. Old concepts of private ownership of land should not be introduced into the field of air regulation. I have no doubt that Congress will, if not handicapped by judicial interpretations of the Constitution, preserve the freedom of the air, and at the same time, satisfy the just claims of aggrieved persons. The noise of newer, larger, and more powerful planes may grow louder and louder and disturb people more and more. But the solution of the problems precipitated by these technological advances and new ways of living cannot come about through the application of rigid constitutional restraints formulated and enforced by the courts. What adjustments may have to be made, only the future can reveal. It seems certain, however, the courts do not possess the techniques or the personnel to consider and act upon the complex combinations of factors entering into the problems. . . .

Points for Discussion

a. **How High?**

The majority states that a landowner "owns at least as much of the space above the ground as he can occupy or use in connection with the land." What is the source of this rule? Under this approach, how far upward do the surface owner's rights extend? One question is whether we measure the upper limit of an owner's airspace by facts applicable only to that owner or to owners in general. For example, if A owns a 50-story office building, are her airspace rights different from those of B, who owns a single-story house? Another issue is whether the upward boundary of airspace rights can change over time as social and economic conditions evolve.

b. **Other Approaches to Airspace Rights**

In addition to the approach adopted by the *Causby* majority, two other standards have been suggested: (1) the surface owner holds title upward only to a fixed height, usually 500 feet (typically the minimum altitude for aircraft flight under federal law); or (2) the surface owner's title extends infinitely upward to the "heavens," but aircraft have an easement to travel through this zone. Which approach is best?

c. **Value of Airspace**

Airspace rights may be quite valuable, especially in metropolitan areas. For example, *Penn Central Transportation Co. v. City of New York*, 438 U.S. 104 (1978) involved a 50-year lease of airspace rights over Grand Central Terminal in New York City valued at more than $150,000,000. You will study *Penn Central*—a landmark decision—in Chapter 14. In contrast, the value of airspace over most of the land surface of the United States is quite small.

d. **Toward a Better Rule**

Given the pace of technological change, what legal standard *should* govern property rights in airspace? The world is witnessing a boom in the construction of skyscrapers, as new technologies make it possible to construct higher and higher buildings. The tallest building in the world is the Burj Khalifa in Dubai which reaches 2,717 feet, while a skyscraper under construction in Saudi Arabia—the "Jeddah Tower"—would be even higher. Accordingly, we can anticipate that the height of buildings in the United States will continue to increase as well. How high should a landowner be allowed to build?

e. **What About Drones?**

Suppose A flies her drone 50 feet over B's land. Is A liable for trespassing into B's airspace? Today thousands of drones are utilized for tasks such as monitoring crops, surveying land, and taking videos. And the use of drones is expected to skyrocket in the near future. For instance, Amazon, DHL, Google, and other companies are hoping to have drones deliver products to customers' homes. Over the next decade, billions of dollars will be invested in drone-related products and services. Does the *Causby* approach adequately address this new technology? Recall Justice Black's admonition that the Court should not apply "[o]ld concepts of private ownership of land" to airspace because this would interfere with "the freedom of the air." Should drones be allowed to fly over privately owned lands? Conversely, should homeowners have the right to prevent such overflights? For a discussion of these issues, see Troy A. Rule, *Airspace in an Age of Drones*, 95 B.U. L. Rev. 155 (2015).

f. **Other Legal Controls on Airports**

Today most municipalities mitigate the *Causby* problem through land use regulation, typically by restricting the height of structures located near airplane flight paths. Courts have generally upheld such restrictions against constitutional attack. *But see McCarran Int'l Airport v. Sisolak*, 137 P.3d 1110 (Nev. 2006) (ordinance that imposed 150-foot height limit on private property near airport was a Fifth Amendment taking). Alternatively, low altitude flights might trigger nuisance liability under the standards discussed in Chapter 1. In fact, should the *Causby* court have based its decision on nuisance law, since the main problem was noise? What are the advantages and disadvantages of addressing airplane noise as a nuisance rather than a trespass?

g. **Airspace Hypotheticals**

How would these hypotheticals be resolved under the majority's view of airspace rights?

> (1) A hires a company to spray a chemical into the clouds 1,000 feet over B's land in order to prevent them from producing rain when they float over A's land, because this would harm A's mature wheat crop. B, whose young crops need water, argues that the spraying violated his airspace rights because he lost the rain these clouds would have produced over his land.
>
> (2) C is erecting a high-rise office building on land next to D's house. Temporary construction scaffolding on the 20th floor of C's building intrudes 3 feet into the airspace above D's land. D objects.

2. Subsurface Rights

A plans to install a fiber optic cable for electronic data that will pass 100 feet below the land surface owned by B. Under the traditional common law view, B's title extended downward to the center of the earth, so B could exclude A's cable. But how far down do B's rights go under modern law?

> ### Perspective and Analysis
>
> . . . For decades, the American legal system has answered this question with the solemn assurance that a landowner's title extends to everything between the land surface and the center of the planet. . . .
>
> This Article demonstrates that the center of the earth approach is mere poetic hyperbole, not law. Indeed, the law of subsurface ownership is so confused that it is impossible to know how deep property rights extend. Accordingly, this Article proposes a new subsurface ownership model that strikes an appropriate balance between the legitimate interests of the surface owner and the needs of society in general. . . .
>
> [T]he center of the earth theory has never been binding law. In cases involving underground uses within one hundred feet or so of the surface—such as disputes about building foundations or tree roots—courts have routinely recognized the surface owner's title. Beyond this point, however, the law is inconsistent at best. Broadly speaking, the deeper the disputed region, the less likely courts are to rely on the center of the earth theory. . . .
>
> **John G. Sprankling, *Owning the Center of the Earth*, 55 UCLA L. Rev. 979, 980–82 (2008).**

Our next case involves the Lima, Ohio plant of BP Chemicals, Inc. which produced acrylonitrile, a chemical used in the manufacture of products such as clear plastic wrap and plastic car parts. Over the course of 20 years—with the approval of the federal Environmental Protection Agency—BP disposed of almost four billion gallons of acrylonitrile-contaminated water by injecting it through wells into rock formations deep below the earth's surface. Acrylonitrile is recognized as a carcinogen: it is capable of causing cancer in humans after prolonged exposure. In 1991, when the case began, this plant was the largest polluter in Ohio according to EPA statistics. Assuming that these liquid wastes migrated into the subsurface below lands belonging to other owners, did a trespass occur?

Chance v. BP Chemicals, Inc.

Supreme Court of Ohio

670 N.E.2d 985 (1996)

ALICE ROBIE RESNICK, J.

This litigation commenced on July 17, 1991, when the named plaintiffs-appellants, Rose M. Chance, Eliza Avery, and Bessie Shadwick, filed a complaint in the Court of Common Pleas of Cuyahoga County on behalf of those whose interests in real property had allegedly been injured by the described operation of a chemical refining plant operated by defendant-appellee BP Chemicals, Inc. in Lima, Ohio. Appellants' claims focused on appellee's practice of disposing of hazardous waste byproducts from the manufacture of industrial chemicals through the use of "deepwell" injection technology. Appellants in essence claimed that the "injectate" placed under the surface of appellee's property by appellee had laterally migrated to be below the surface of appellants' properties and that the migration violated their rights as property owners.

> **See It**
>
> Click here to see modern pictures of the BP Chemicals plant involved in *Chance*.

Appellants sought recovery for trespass, nuisance, negligence, strict liability, and fraudulent concealment. The complaint prayed for one billion dollars in general and punitive damages and included a request for injunctive relief. . . .

Trial commenced on November 3, 1993, and a jury was seated. Testifying for appellants were property owners who were concerned about the possible presence of the injectate under their properties. Appellants' key expert was a hydrogeologist who had developed a model to determine the extent the injectate had laterally migrated away from appellee's property. On cross-examination, appellee's attorney challenged the expert's model as inaccurate. The witness in turn explained the reasoning behind decisions he had made in setting up his model, and also criticized the model on extent of migration developed by appellee's expert. In particular, appellants' witness did not accept the accuracy of data obtained by appellee through its use of a test well to monitor the site, and so did not incorporate that site-specific data into his model.

At the close of appellants' case in chief, the trial court granted appellee's motion for directed verdicts as to appellants' claims of ultrahazardous activity, fraud, and nuisance. The trial court thus limited the case to appellants' trespass claim. . . .

Appellee's presentation of its case included testimony of a geological engineer on the permeability and porosity of the substrata into which the injecting was done. This geological engineer's testimony explained why, in his opinion, appellee's site in Lima was suited to deepwell injection. Several impermeable (or barely permeable) layers of rock contained the injectate in the relatively permeable and porous, mostly sandstone injection zone in the Eau Claire geologic formation (beginning at a depth of approximately 2,430 feet) and the Mt. Simon formation (beginning at a depth of approximately 2,813 feet). The geological engineer testified that in his opinion the injectate was safely contained in the injection zone. On cross-examination, appellants' attorney observed that the real issue was the extent of lateral migration of the injectate, so that the witness's testimony that the injectate had not migrated upward was irrelevant to appellants' trespass claim.

> **See It**
>
> Click here to see a diagram showing how BP's injection wells functioned.

Another of appellee's expert witnesses was a hydrogeologist who had developed his own model of the extent of lateral migration. This witness was critical of the model developed by appellants' expert and of appellants' expert's view of the extent of lateral migration, opining that appellants' expert had erred by failing to take into account available site-specific data in developing his model. . . .

On November 18, 1993, the jury returned a general verdict in favor of appellee on the trespass claim and answered ten interrogatories. [The jury found, among other things,] (1) that the injectate was more than 2,600 feet below the surface of the earth; (2) that the model of appellee's expert best described the extent of its migration; (3) that appellants did not prove by a preponderance of the evidence that appellee had unreasonably interfered with the named plaintiffs' use of their properties; (4) that the named plaintiffs did not prove by a preponderance of the evidence that the deepwells had caused any actual and substantial damage to their properties . . . ; . . . (7) that no trespass as to the property owners had occurred, assuming portions of the injectate had migrated into the native brine flowing through the Eau Claire and Mt. Simon formations located more than one-half mile below the surface of their properties; . . . .

> **What's That?**
>
> A *general verdict* is a verdict by which the jury simply finds in favor of one party, without resolving specific factual questions. In many states, a jury may be asked to answer specific questions or *interrogatories* to supplement a general verdict, which is what happened here.

This case presents unique questions surrounding the process of deepwell disposal of wastes. We stress at the outset that, because appellee's operation of the wells is authorized by the relevant regulating bodies, this case does not involve the general propriety of deepwell waste injection. . . .

Our agreement with the conclusions reached by the court of appeals on [most issues in the case] leaves appellants' trespass claim as the principal issue to be resolved.

Trespass is an unlawful entry upon the property of another. *See Keesecker v. G.M. McKelvey Co.* (1943), 141 Ohio St. 162, 166, 47 N.E.2d 211, 214. In order to address the trespass issue, we first must examine the extent of the property interest owned by appellants involved here. . . .

Appellants argue in their Proposition of Law No. 1 that "[t]he owner of land has absolute ownership of all the subsurface property." If this proposition is correct, then as one of the incidents of absolute ownership, appellants have the right to exclude others. Appellants claim that while this court has recognized some limitations on absolute ownership of air rights by surface property owners, no such limitation exists on ownership of subsurface property rights by surface owners.

Appellants' argument implicates the ancient Latin maxim *cujus est solum, ejus est usque ad coelum et ad inferos,* defined in Black's Law Dictionary (6 Ed. 1990) 378, as "[t]o whomsoever the soil belongs, he owns also to the sky and to the depths. The owner of a piece of land owns everything above and below it to an indefinite extent." In *Winton v. Cornish* (1832), 5 Ohio 477, 478, this court appeared to adopt the position illustrated by that maxim, stating, "The word *land* includes not only the face of the earth, but everything under it or over it. He who owns a piece of land, therefore, is the owner of everything underneath in a direct line to the center of the earth and everything above to the heavens."

In *Willoughby Hills v. Corrigan* (1972), 29 Ohio St.2d 39, 49, 278 N.E.2d 658, 664, this court, citing the United States Supreme Court in *United States v. Causby* (1946), 328 U.S. 256, stated that "the doctrine of the common law, that the ownership of land extends to the periphery of the universe, has no place in the modern world." The court in *Willoughby Hills*, 29 Ohio St.2d at 50, 278 N.E.2d at 665, quoted from *Hinman v. Pacific Air Transp.* (C.A.9, 1936), 84 F.2d 755, 758: " 'We own so much of the space above the ground as we can occupy or make use of, in connection with the enjoyment of our land. This right is not fixed. It varies with our varying needs and is coextensive with them. The owner of land owns as much of the space above him as he uses, but only so long as he uses it.' "

Appellee claims that injectate is placed into the native brine in the Mt. Simon and Eau Claire formations, and that the native brine waters are "waters of the state" under R.C. 6111.01(H), and therefore are exclusively regulated by the state of Ohio. Appellee argues that the court of appeals correctly found that appellants have no possessory interest in these waters, and further argues that the alleged presence of injectate does not, as a matter of law, infringe any property right of appellants. To the extent that appellee appears to be arguing that the way the injectate disperses into the native brine serves to

> **Make the Connection**
>
> In some jurisdictions, underground water is considered to be property owned by the state, not by the owner of the land surface. You will study different approaches to property rights in groundwater later in this chapter.

insulate appellee from all liability in all circumstances, we reject appellee's contention. The native brine exists naturally in the porous sandstone into which the injecting is done. The injectate displaces and mixes with the brine in the injection zone. Appellants have a property interest in the rock into which the injectate is placed, albeit a potentially limited one, depending on whether appellants' ownership rights are absolute. If appellee's act of placing the injectate into the rock interferes with appellants' reasonable and foreseeable use of their properties, appellee could be liable regardless of the way the injectate mixes with the native brine.

Our analysis above concerning the native brine illustrates that appellants do not enjoy absolute ownership of waters of the state below their properties, and therefore underscores that their subsurface ownership rights are limited. As the discussion in *Willoughby Hills* makes evident, ownership rights in today's world are not so clear-cut as they were before the advent of airplanes and injection wells.

Consequently, we do not accept appellants' assertion of absolute ownership of everything below the surface of their properties. Just as a property owner must accept some limitations on the ownership rights extending above the surface of the property, we find that there are also limitations on property owners' subsurface rights. We therefore extend the reasoning of *Willoughby Hills,* that absolute ownership of air rights is a doctrine which "has no place in the modern world," to apply as well to ownership of subsurface rights. Furthermore, as we will discuss below regarding other considerations in this case, given the unique facts here we find that appellants' subsurface rights in their properties include the right to exclude invasions of the subsurface property that actually interfere with appellants' reasonable and foreseeable use of the subsurface.

Having determined that appellants' subsurface rights are not absolute, we must determine whether appellants proved an actionable trespass given the facts of this case. . . .

As discussed previously, the actual location of the injectate was vigorously contested by the parties throughout the litigation, with each side's experts testifying as to the models developed to illustrate the extent of the migration. The parties' experts disagreed as to the permeability and porosity of the rocks into which the injecting is done. Permeability and porosity are two factors upon which the models were based that would affect the extent of the lateral migration of the injectate. . . .

Another variable that figures in the equation involving lateral migration and the location of the injectate is the concentration of the injectate at any given point in the substrata as it intermixes with the native brine. As the injectate diffuses into the brine, its concentration decreases as the distance from the injection point increases. Therefore it is theoretically impossible to define an absolute perimeter on the extent of lateral migration, since any statement on the extent of migration must be in terms of a particular concentration level at that perimeter. . . .

All of these and more disputed variables went into the construction of the hypothetical models that attempted to illustrate the lateral extent of the migration. Given all these variables, there were great difficulties in appellants' establishing, as a factual matter, that a property invasion had occurred, so that appellants' claim must be regarded as somewhat speculative.

Appellants in essence argue that through its rulings, the trial court mistakenly imposed a requirement that they prove "actual" damages as an element of their trespass claim. Appellants argue that damages can be presumed in every case of trespass, and given that the bifurcation order left damages to be quantified at a future time, the trial court erred in requiring proof of any damages at all, much less of "actual" ones. We do not accept appellants' argument in this regard in the specific circumstances of this case, but find that some type of physical damages or interference with use must be shown in an indirect invasion situation such as this. Even assuming that the injectate had laterally migrated to be in an offending concentration under some of the appellants' properties, we find that some type of physical damages or interference with use must have been demonstrated for appellants to recover for a trespass. . . .

We find that appellants, given all the factors present in this case, did not, as a matter of law, establish an unlawful entry on their properties by appellee. Our ultimate conclusion that appellants did not prove an actionable trespass is dictated by considering the sum total of the circumstances of this case, as we have done in our foregoing discussion. Appellee operates the wells pursuant to required permits; appellants' subsurface property rights are not absolute and in these circumstances are contingent upon interference with the reasonable and foreseeable use of the properties; the trespass alleged is an indirect one and, due to the type of invasion alleged, physical damage or actual interference with the reasonable and foreseeable use of the properties must be demonstrated; appellants' trespass claim is a novel one, of a type previously unrecognized by any court. When all of the circumstances of this case are considered, appellants' evidence of trespass was simply too speculative. . . .

For all the foregoing reasons, the judgment of the court of appeals is affirmed.

Points for Discussion

a. The Scope of Subsurface Rights

The *Chance* court rejects the common law view that the surface owner's absolute title extends to the center of the earth. What are the policy arguments for and against the court's approach? After this case, how far downward does the surface owner's title extend in Ohio? Because property rights are generally defined by state law, the depth of subsurface ownership may differ in other states. Does this state-by-state variation pose any difficulties? *See* Joseph A. Schremmer, *Subsurface Trespass: Private Remedies and Public Regulation*, 101 Neb. L. Rev. 1005 (2023).

b. Interference with Reasonable and Foreseeable Use

Consider the meaning of the court's statement that a landowner has a right to exclude invasions only if they "actually interfere" with the owner's "reasonable and foreseeable use of the subsurface." What does this mean? How likely is it that a surface owner will be able to meet this test? In *Boehringer v. Montalto*, 254 N.Y.S. 276, 278 (Sup. Ct. 1931), the court held that "the title of an owner of the soil will not be extended to a depth below ground beyond which the owner may not reasonably make use thereof." Accordingly, it suggested that a public sewer line buried 150 feet deep did not violate the surface owner's property rights. *But see Briggs v. Southwestern Energy Prod. Co.*, 224 A.3d 334, 350 (Pa. 2020) (suggesting that entry of fracking fluids into another owner's land "miles beneath the surface of the earth" might be a trespass).

c. *Jacque* Revisited

In *Jacque v. Steenberg Homes, Inc.* (Chapter 1), the Wisconsin Supreme Court found trespass liability even though the Jacques' property had not been damaged. But the *Chance* court required proof of "some type of physical damages or interference with use" before the plaintiffs could recover in trespass. What explains this difference? Note that the jury foreman in *Chance* told a Cleveland newspaper that the evidence "showed that the injected liquids have migrated under [the plaintiffs'] residential properties but present no harm." *Jury Says BP Waste Disposal Does No Harm*, Plain Dealer, Nov. 19, 1993. Were the plaintiffs harmed?

d. *Chance* It

Using the *Chance* standard, has a trespass occurred in the following situations?

> (1) City builds and operates a subway tunnel that runs 300 feet below A's house. There is no vibration or other physical indication of the subway's presence that can be detected by anyone on the land surface. A has no plans to use his subsurface.
>
> (2) B designates his subsurface land as a "nature preserve," noting that it is a pristine natural area akin to a wilderness. Two years later, C injects salt water two miles underneath her land in order to create subsurface pressure that enhances production from her oil wells, a common procedure in oil fields. Some of the salt water migrates laterally underneath B's land, destroying an indigenous species of bacteria.
>
> (3) D installs a television cable that passes 50 feet below the land surface owned by E and others. E hopes to build a 6-story office building on his land. The planned underground parking garage for the building will extend 20 feet below the surface. Because the project is still in its preliminary stage, E does not yet know how deep the excavations for the parking garage will be.

e. Mitigating Global Climate Change

Carbon sequestration is a technique for mitigating the impact of climate change by removing carbon dioxide from the air, and then injecting it underground a mile or two deep for long-term storage. The U.S. Department of Energy estimates that the area of contamination from an injection of one million tons of carbon dioxide each year over 20 years might spread 15 square miles or more. Assume that you are an attorney for a new corporation that hopes to enter the carbon sequestration business. If your client buys a 10-acre parcel in Ohio and begins injecting carbon dioxide underground—knowing that it will migrate laterally underneath the lands of nearby owners—will *Chance* protect your client from trespass liability? Alternatively, in a state where the surface owner's absolute title is viewed as extending to the center of the earth, how likely is it that your client can purchase all the properties in a 15-square-mile area in order to avoid liability? For further discussion of this topic, see Alexandra B. Klass & Elizabeth J. Wilson, *Climate Change, Carbon Sequestration, and Property Rights*, 2010 U. Ill. L. Rev. 363.

f. Right to Support

The common law developed two doctrines that complemented the "center of the earth" theory. First, each landowner has the right to *lateral support*—to have his land in its natural condition supported by the adjacent parcels of land. Accordingly, if A's undeveloped land subsides because B excavates on her adjacent parcel, B is strictly liable for the damage. Second, each landowner also has the right to *subjacent support*—to have her land in its natural condition supported by the earth immediately below it. Thus, if A's undeveloped land subsides because C exercises his mineral rights by removing the coal beneath A's land, C is strictly liable for the damage. *See, e.g., Miller v. Vicksburg Masonic Temple*, 288 So. 3d 372 (Miss. Ct. App. 2019) (landowner liable for removing lateral and subjacent support from adjacent property).

g. Aftermath of *Chance*

In *Baatz v. Columbia Gas Transmission, LLC*, 929 F.3d 767 (6th Cir. 2019), the court extended the *Chance* approach to a different situation: subsurface storage of natural gas. Plaintiffs argued that defendant's intentional injection of gas into a region 3,000 feet below their properties was a trespass. But the Sixth Circuit rejected this claim because the plaintiffs "admitted that they have not used and do not intend to use their subsurface." *Id.* at 773.

C. Water Law

A drills a new well on his 500-acre estate in order to provide more irrigation water for his prize-winning rose garden. But he removes so much water that B's nearby well runs dry; B must now use trucks to haul in water for his thirsty cattle. Is A liable?

Water rights have long been characterized as real property. In many states, however, water resources are deemed to belong to the public; in these states, individuals may only acquire rights to use water for beneficial purposes (such as agriculture, homes, and industry) rather than full ownership.

Mark Twain once (allegedly) remarked that "in the west, whiskey is for drinkin' and water is for fightin'." The reason is simple: water is vital for the productive use of land. Due to the geography of the United States, water tends to be scarce in the west and plentiful in the east. This difference profoundly influenced the laws governing rights in *surface water*, such as lakes, rivers, streams and other watercourses. Three main approaches are used:

- *Riparian system*: Eastern states generally adopted this system, which assigns water rights to each landowner whose property adjoins a watercourse. Over time, most states following this view also adopted the *reasonable use doctrine*, which allows a riparian owner to take water for reasonable uses on her land, but not to unreasonably interfere with the uses of other riparian owners.

- *Prior appropriation system*: Under this system, followed by many western states, the location of the owner's land is irrelevant; instead, water rights are allocated to the first person to divert the water for *beneficial use*. This requirement ensures that an appropriator will not abuse her water rights, serving the same function as the reasonable use doctrine in riparian states.

- *Permit system*: Today many states require a permit for the diversion of surface water, so the government effectively regulates the amount of water that may be withdrawn.

The law governing rights in groundwater, however, developed quite differently. *Groundwater* is underground, dispersed water that percolates through permeable subsurface layers—in other words, the type of water usually produced by a well. In nineteenth-century England, blessed with plentiful surface water, groundwater was thought to be a minor and unreliable water source. Accordingly, England adopted the *absolute ownership rule* or *rule of capture*, by which the owner of the land surface could remove as much groundwater as he wished, even if this process caused severe injury to his neighbors. American courts generally adopted the absolute ownership approach, only to abandon it during the twentieth century when its consequences proved to be too harsh. Today, almost all states follow one of three approaches to groundwater ownership:

> - *Reasonable use approach*: The dominant view is that a surface owner may use groundwater only for a reasonable and beneficial (non-wasteful) use, a requirement that is nearly always met if the use takes place on the overlying land.
> - *Correlative rights*: The surface owner is entitled to a proportional share of the groundwater beneath his land.
> - *Permit system*: Title to groundwater is vested in the state, so the surface owner can obtain water rights only by securing a permit.

Unlike the absolute ownership rule, all three modern approaches effectively prevent any one landowner from injuring other owners by withdrawing too much groundwater.

Our next case examines rights to groundwater in connection with the bottled water industry. The largest producer of bottled water in the world is Nestlé Waters; its various brands—including Perrier—have about one-third of the market in the United States. One of its brands is Ice Mountain, which primarily sells bottled water in the Midwest; its water comes from various sources, including the wells at issue in the case below. Does a company have the right to pump groundwater in order to produce bottled water if this harms the interests of other water users?

Michigan Citizens for Water Conservation v. Nestlé Waters North America, Inc.

Court of Appeals of Michigan

709 N.W.2d 174 (2005)

SMOLENSKI, J.

I. Facts and Procedural History

The events leading to this appeal began when Nestlé's predecessor in interest, Great Spring Waters of America, Inc., a subsidiary of Perrier Group of America, Inc., began taking steps to construct a spring water bottling plant in Mecosta County. In December 2000, defendant purchased the groundwater rights to the Bollmans' property located north of the Osprey Lake impoundment and referred to as Sanctuary Springs. The Osprey Lake impoundment is a man-made body of water created by the damming of the Dead Stream. The Dead Stream originates from springs that are now obscured by the Osprey Lake impoundment. . . . Shortly after defendant announced its plans to build its spring water bottling plant, the nonprofit corporation

Michigan Citizens for Water Conservation (MCWC) was formed to represent the interests of riparian property owners in the vicinity of the proposed wells, as well as other interested persons.

In January and February 2001, defendant installed two wells on the Sanctuary Springs site. Two more wells were installed in July and August 2001. Permits to use the wells were issued by the Michigan Department of Environmental Quality (DEQ) in August 2001 and February 2002. The combined maximum pumping rate permitted for the four wells is 400 gallons per minute (gpm). . . .

> **FYI**
>
> Despite its ominous name, the Dead Stream is an ordinary stream which is commonly used for recreational purposes such as boating, fishing, and swimming. The plaintiffs included riparian property owners whose land adjoined the Dead Stream.

[MCWC and others filed a complaint alleging, among other claims, that "defendant's withdrawal of groundwater was unreasonable under the common law applicable to groundwater." At trial, the court found that "defendant's pumping had harmed and will continue to harm plaintiffs' riparian interests" in the Dead Stream. It ordered the defendant to "terminate all water withdrawals from Sanctuary Springs." Defendant appealed.]

III. Groundwater Claim

B. Michigan Water Law

. . . [W]ater law in Michigan . . . has developed along two distinct lines: (1) the law applicable to water use by riparian owners and (2) the law applicable to groundwater uses.

Under the common law, three main doctrines have developed for dealing with riparian water rights: the English common-law rule, also known as the natural flow doctrine; the reasonable use doctrine; and the appropriation or prior use doctrine. . . . Of these doctrines, the natural flow doctrine and the reasonable use doctrine are relevant to the development of water law in Michigan.

Under the natural flow doctrine, each riparian proprietor of a watercourse has a right "to have the body of water flow as it was wont to flow in nature," qualified only by the right of other riparian proprietors to make limited use of the water. Restatement, introductory note to §§ 850 to 857, p 210. . . .

Under the reasonable use doctrine, "a riparian owner may make any and all reasonable uses of the water, as long [as] they do not unreasonably interfere with the other riparian owners' opportunity for reasonable use." [Stoebuck & Whitman, The Law of Property (3d ed), § 7.4, p.] 423. "Whether and to what extent a given use shall be allowed under the reasonable use doctrine depends upon the weighing of factors on the would-be user's side and balancing them against similar factors on the side of other riparian owners. No list of factors is exhaustive, because the court will consider all the circumstances that are relevant in a given case." *Id*. While in theory no single factor is conclusive, "[d]omestic uses are so favored that they will generally prevail over other uses." *Id*. Furthermore, while the reasonable use doctrine generally allows water to be transported and used on nonriparian lands, such uses may be disfavored over uses on riparian land.

In *Dumont v. Kellogg*, 29 Mich. 420 (1874), our Supreme Court adopted the reasonable use doctrine for competing riparian owners. . . . After discussing the exceptions in which the natural flow rule might still apply, the Court went on to hold that, as between two riparian owners, the natural flow rule did not strictly apply because "it is manifest it would give to the lower proprietor superior advantages over the upper, and in many cases give him in effect a monopoly of the stream." *Id*. The Court concluded:

> It is therefore not a diminution in the quantity of the water alone, or an alteration in its flow, or either or both of these circumstances combined with injury, that will give a right of action, if in view of all the circumstances, and having regard to equality of right in others, that which has been done and which causes injury is not unreasonable. In other words, the injury that is incidental to a reasonable enjoyment of the common right can demand no redress. [*Id*. at 425.]

What constitutes a reasonable use must be determined on a case-by-case basis. . . . Hence, under Michigan's riparian authorities, water disputes between riparian proprietors are resolved by a reasonable use test that balances competing water uses to determine whether one riparian proprietor's water use, which interferes with another's use, is unreasonable under the circumstances.

As with riparian water law, there are three main common-law doctrines applicable to groundwater disputes. The first doctrine is referred to as the English rule or the absolute ownership rule, which was first stated in *Acton v. Blundell*, 152 Eng Rep 1223 (Exch, 1843). Under this rule, "a possessor of land may withdraw as much underground water as he wishes, for whatever purposes he wishes, and let his neighbors look elsewhere than the law for relief." [Stoebuck & Whitman, p.] 428.

In America, the most prevalent rule applicable to groundwater disputes is the doctrine of reasonable use. . . . However, the doctrine of reasonable use is not actually dependent on the reasonableness of the use; rather,

> [a]s the doctrine has developed, it generally has been held that all uses of water upon the land from which it is extracted are "reasonable," even if they more or less deplete the supply to the harm of neighbors, unless the purpose is malicious or the water simply wasted. But . . . when the question is whether water may be transported off that land for use elsewhere, this is usually found "unreasonable". . . . Authorities are not all agreed, but a principle that seems to harmonize the decisions is that water may be extracted for use elsewhere only up to the point that it begins to injure owners within the aquifer. [*Id*. at 428-29]

The last doctrine is a variant of the reasonable use doctrine developed in California, which is often called the correlative rights doctrine. . . .

The seminal case dealing with groundwater rights in Michigan is *Schenk v. City of Ann Arbor*, 196 Mich. 75, 163 N.W. 109 (1917). In Schenk, the city of Ann Arbor purchased land outside the city on which it planned to build a pumping station, and began pumping tests that drew approximately 3.8 million gallons of water daily for several weeks. Numerous persons commenced actions seeking to restrain the city from pumping, including the plaintiff, because of harms allegedly caused by the pumping. However, because the plaintiff in *Schenk* had successfully restored his water supply by lowering his well three feet, the trial court denied the plaintiff's request for an injunction, but granted damages for the actual harm already suffered.

. . . The Court then recited the rule of absolute ownership [but] . . . adopted the traditional reasonable use rule, which permits withdrawals of water whose use is not connected with the land from which it is withdrawn, but only to the extent that they do not interfere with an adjacent water user's reasonable use. . . .

. . . [I]n order to recognize the interconnected nature of water sources and fully integrate the law applicable to water disputes, we adopt the reasonable use balancing test first stated in *Dumont* as the law applicable to disputes between riparian and groundwater users.

C. Application of the Law

While the balancing test is a case-specific inquiry, there are three underlying principles that govern the process of balancing competing water uses. First, the law seeks to ensure a "fair participation" in the use of water for the greatest number of users. Hence, the court should attempt to strike a proper balance between protecting the rights of the complaining party and preserving as many beneficial uses of the common resource as is feasible under the circumstances. Second, the law will only protect a use that is itself reasonable. A plaintiff whose water use has little value or is excessive or harmful will be entitled to no protection. Third, the law will not redress every harm, no matter how small, but will only redress unreasonable harms. Therefore, a plaintiff must be able to demonstrate not only that the defendant's use of the water has interfered with the plaintiff's own reasonable use, but also that the interference was substantial. . . .

While the nature of the balancing test requires that the appropriate factors be ascertained on a case-by-case basis, . . . several factors can be discerned that will be relevant to every application of the test. These factors include (1) the purpose of the use, (2) the suitability of the use to the location, (3) the extent and amount of the harm, (4) the benefits of the use, (5) the necessity of the amount and manner of the water use, and (6) any other factor that may bear on the reasonableness of the use.

In the present case, plaintiffs alleged that defendant's groundwater withdrawals interfered with their riparian rights in the Dead Stream, including their right to utilize the stream for recreational boating, wildlife observation, swimming, and fishing. . . . [A] plurality of our Supreme Court has determined that recreational uses, including the use of riparian waters as a restful retreat, constitute reasonable uses, *Thompson* [*v. Enz*, 379 Mich. 667, 686, 154 N.W.2d 473 (1967)]. . . . Therefore, plaintiffs' use of the stream is a reasonable use worthy of protection.

It is also uncontested that defendant's use of the disputed water serves a beneficial purpose. Testimony established that defendant's bottling plant employed 140 persons at the time of the trial. This employment directly benefits the workers, their families, and the local community. Likewise, defendant's plant and equipment represent a significant investment in the community and are a source of tax revenue. The provision of water to the general public is also an economically and socially beneficial use of the water. . . . Consequently, we must balance the relevant factors to determine whether defendant's use of the water is unreasonable under the circumstances and in light of the harm inflicted on plaintiffs.

> **FYI**
>
> Under the riparian system, a landowner whose property adjoins a stream or other watercourse has the right to take water from the watercourse. But the rights of a riparian owner may extend more broadly, as the court indicates, to include using the adjacent watercourse for recreational purposes.

Plaintiffs . . . provide no evidence that defendant's water use has interfered or will interfere with their domestic water supplies. Likewise, defendant's use of the water is for commercial profit. Therefore, both uses are for artificial purposes and neither is entitled to a preference. However, plaintiffs' uses are directly related to the use and enjoyment of their riparian land, whereas defendant's use is not directly related to the land from which the water is withdrawn. Hence, plaintiffs are entitled to some measure of preference as local water users.

All parties agreed that defendant's water withdrawals will capture water that would otherwise have entered the Dead Stream. Hence, defendant's water withdrawals will have a direct effect on the amount of flow in the Dead Stream. . . . [T]he trial court found that even a modest drop in water level would have dramatic consequences for the stream. Finally, the established uses for the Dead Stream and the lakes to which it connects have traditionally been recreational rather than commercial in character. Considering these factors together, we conclude that the Sanctuary Springs location, with its direct connection to the Dead Stream, is not well suited for high-volume water extractions. . . .

In examining the degree of harm to the Dead Stream, the trial court found that it would lose approximately 24 percent of its base flow and 2 inches in stage beyond the stream's natural fluctuations given a withdrawal of 400 gpm. The trial court determined that this reduction in flow would raise the stream's temperature and cause the stream to become choked with plant life. . . . The trial court determined that these effects would impair the Dead Stream's aesthetic value and its usefulness as a fishery, and would impair recreational navigation of the stream. The loss of recreational use and the physical alteration of the Dead Stream will directly and substantially harm the riparian value of the Dead Stream. . . . On the other hand, defendant's bottling enterprise does have significant commercial benefits. . . . Overall, under the facts of this case, the harms inflicted on the riparian plaintiffs and the community in general are significantly offset by the economic benefits to society and the local community. . . .

> **What's That?**
>
> A withdrawal of 400 gallons per minute produces 576,000 gallons per day. This is enough to fill 36 average backyard swimming pools.

In examining the necessity of the manner and amount of defendant's water use, it must be noted that defendant chose the Sanctuary Springs location in order to facilitate its marketing of the extracted water as "spring water." Hence, defendant's options for locating its wells are limited by the nature of the required water source. However, while testimony established that any reduction in the withdrawal rate below 400 gpm will result in the loss of production and jobs, testimony also established that defendant has augmented the supply of water at other plants by shipping it in as needed. . . . Therefore, defendant does not need to maintain such a high pumping volume at the Sanctuary Spring site in order to continue operations. In contrast, plaintiffs' water uses do not remove water from the system, but do require a minimum level of water, which cannot be mitigated through changes in the manner of use. These factors weigh heavily against defendant's proposed pumping rate of 400 gpm.

Although defendant should be permitted to have a "fair participation" in the common water resources of the area, if defendant is permitted to pump at the maximum permitted rate, it will effectively appropriate for its own needs approximately 24 percent of the base flow of the Dead Stream. This is more than a fair participation. While plaintiffs might properly be required to suffer some harm to their use of the Dead Stream, it would be unjust to permit defendant to impose on plaintiffs the entire burden of the harms created by the depletion of the Dead Stream's flow while retaining all the benefits. . . . Therefore, taking all the factors outlined into consideration, we determine that defendant's proposed withdrawal of 400 gpm would be unreasonable under the circumstances.

. . . Therefore, we affirm the judgment in favor of plaintiffs on the groundwater claim, but remand to the trial court to determine the appropriate parameters of the injunction and modify it accordingly.

Points for Discussion

a. **Competing Groundwater Theories**

Why did states originally adopt the absolute ownership rule for groundwater ownership? Your study of *Pierson v. Post* (Chapter 1) may be helpful here. Is groundwater like a wild fox? Under today's conditions, what are the advantages and disadvantages of (1) the absolute ownership rule and (2) the reasonable use approach, as applied to groundwater?

One of the few states that retains the absolute ownership approach to groundwater is Texas. In *Sipriano v. Great Spring Waters of America, Inc.*, 1 S.W.3d 75, 80 (Tex. 1999), where ranchers claimed that groundwater pumping by a bottled water company had drained their wells, the Texas Supreme Court refused to abandon the doctrine and allowed the pumping to continue—even though it acknowledged that there were "compelling reasons for groundwater use to be regulated." But one concurring justice questioned the doctrine, citing a famous dictum by Oliver Wendell Holmes:

> It is revolting to have no better reason for a rule than that so it was laid down in the time of Henry IV. It is still more revolting if the grounds upon which it was laid down have vanished long since, and the rule simply persists from blind imitation of the past.

Id. at 82. Should Texas have adopted the reasonable use approach discussed in *Michigan Citizens*?

b. **Balancing Competing Water Uses**

Did the *Michigan Citizens* court strike the right balance? The defendant's plant employed 140 people, generated tax revenue for the community, and provided high-quality drinking water for the public—which the court agreed was "an economically and socially beneficial use of the water." In contrast, none of the plaintiffs were actually taking the water for a beneficial use; instead, they sought to protect recreational uses: boating, wildlife observation, swimming, and fishing. How much weight should these recreational uses be given when balanced against the benefits of the defendant's plant? Is the court also considering the environmental impacts of the pumping?

c. **Integrating Allocation of Surface Water and Groundwater**

Historically, states used different regimes to allocate surface water and groundwater, with little concern for their interrelationship. As *Michigan Citizens* illustrates, this approach is no longer adequate because groundwater withdrawals affect surface water and vice versa. Today most states have developed techniques to integrate these systems to at least some degree. *See* Barton H. Thompson, Jr., *Beyond Connections: Pursuing Multidimensional Conjunctive Management*, 47 Idaho L. Rev. 273 (2011).

d. **Negative Externalities**

Law and economics scholars approach the dilemma of conflicting land uses with the concept of *negative externalities*. Before acquiring its groundwater rights, Nestlé presumably weighed the benefits and costs of the planned project, and decided to proceed. But it apparently did not consider the effect that its project would have on riparian property owners. The impact on these owners is a *negative externality*—a cost that is not considered in the decision-making process. Law and economics theorists argue that efficiency is maximized if a company like Nestlé is required to *internalize* such costs—that is, to consider them in the decision-making process. You will learn more about negative externalities in Chapter 3.

e. **Aftermath of *Michigan Citizens***

Nestlé appealed the case to the Michigan Supreme Court. In *Michigan Citizens for Water Conservation v. Nestlé Waters North America, Inc.*, 737 N.W.2d 447 (Mich. 2007), that court upheld most of the appellate court's decision, but reversed the decision in part on the basis that plaintiff owners in certain areas had not proven injury and thus lacked standing to sue; it remanded the case to the trial court for further proceedings in light of this outcome. This eventually led to an out-of-court settlement under which the plaintiffs agreed that Nestlé could withdraw up to 218 gpm in the winter and an average of 125 gpm in the summer. MCWC vice president Jeff Ostahowski later commented: "There are some people who'd say that Nestlé taking 218 gallons instead of 400 is a victory. Well, they couldn't have taken 400 gallons. They've almost dried the aquifer as it is." Michael Jackman, *Nestlé's Push to Pump More Water Out of Michigan Meets Resistance*, Metro News, Dec. 21, 2016.

Summary

- **Adverse Possession Basics.** In order to obtain title to land by adverse possession in most jurisdictions, the occupant must prove these elements: (a) actual possession; (b) exclusive possession; (c) open and notorious possession; (d) adverse and hostile possession; (e) continuous possession; (f) for the statutory period. Some states add special statutory requirements.

- **Adverse and Hostile Possession.** The majority rule (and modern trend) is that the adverse possessor's state of mind is irrelevant. Thus, this element is satisfied so long as the owner has not authorized the occupancy. However, some jurisdictions require that the adverse possessor believe in good faith that he is the owner of the land.

- **Justifications for Adverse Possession.** Four justifications have been suggested for adverse possession. The dominant view is that adverse possession is a specialized statute of limitations. Other suggested justifications are correcting title defects, encouraging development, and protecting personhood.

- **Mechanics of Adverse Possession.** Proof of adverse possession may involve special doctrines: tacking, color of title, disabilities, and enhanced protection for certain owners.

- **Airspace Rights.** Under traditional theory, a landowner's title extended upward to the heavens, but this view collapsed with the invention of the airplane. Today, most authorities agree that the surface owner's rights do not extend upward indefinitely. One view is that the owner holds title only up to a fixed height, usually 500 feet.

- **Subsurface Rights.** The traditional view was that a landowner's title extended downward to the center of the earth, but modern courts increasingly question this view. Some courts suggest that the surface owner's rights extend downward only so far as to accommodate a reasonable and foreseeable use of the subsurface.

- **Rights to Groundwater.** Today almost all states have rejected the rule of capture approach to groundwater. The dominant view is the surface owner may withdraw groundwater only for reasonable uses on his overlying land.

> **Test Your Knowledge**
>
> To assess your understanding of the material in this chapter, click here to take a quiz.

For More Information

For more information about the subjects covered in this chapter, please consult these sources:

- Carol Necole Brown & Serena M. Williams, *Rethinking Adverse Possession: An Essay on Ownership and Possession*, 60 Syracuse L. Rev. 583 (2010).
- Joseph W. Dellapenna, *The Rise and the Demise of the Absolute Dominion Doctrine for Groundwater*, 35 U. Ark. Little Rock. L. Rev. 291 (2013).
- Wendie L. Kellington, *Drones*, 49 Urb. Law. 667 (2017).
- Nadav Shoked, *Who Needs Adverse Possession?*, 89 Fordham L. Rev. 2639 (2021).
- John G. Sprankling, *Owning the Center of the Earth*, 55 UCLA L. Rev. 979 (2008).

CHAPTER 3

Owning Personal Property

Remember how you were sitting in your living room on a leather chair in front of a Picasso when Chapter 2 began? Suppose that now you are also reading today's newspaper as your pet ferret lies in your lap. What are your property rights in each of these items? The chair was a lucky find on the side of a highway. The Picasso which you have possessed for six years was originally stolen by your friend. The newspaper was given to you by a neighbor. And the ferret was captured on a trip to Florida. The manner in which you acquired each item helps to define the bundle of rights you hold.

This chapter focuses on property rights in tangible personal property or *chattels*, while Chapter 4 will explore rights in intangible personal property. In this chapter, we will examine four different ways to acquire rights in chattels: (a) capture; (b) find; (c) adverse possession; and (d) gift. As you work through these materials, consider how the method of acquisition affects the scope of the property rights that the owner receives.

> **FYI**
>
> An item of tangible personal property is called a *chattel*. Blackstone noted that the word "chattel" was derived from the Latin "catalla," meaning beasts of husbandry. William Blackstone, 2 Commentaries on the Laws of England 385 (1766). The term's meaning was gradually expanded to include all movable property. The same Latin word is the source of our modern term "cattle."

A. Rule of Capture

F and his family live in a remote cabin, subsisting on the fish they catch. With his son S watching, F casts his lure into a nearby stream. A large trout swims by, opens its mouth, and is about to swallow the lure. As the lure brushes the inside of the trout's mouth, W, a day-hiking Wall Street banker, jumps into the stream and grabs the fish in his hands. Looking hungrily at his father, S exclaims, "Daddy, that man stole our fish!" Is S correct?

In Chapter 1, our main purpose was to explore the basic policies that underlie property law. In this context, we studied *Pierson v. Post*, which focused on the rule of capture. Here we will explore the rule of capture in greater depth as a foundational rule that applies to different types of personal property. You learned in *Pierson* that the rule of capture awards property rights to the person who brings a wild animal under her certain control. Under this ancient doctrine, *ferae naturae* are seen as unowned while roaming in their natural habitat. In our next case, *State v. Shaw*, the fish were still swimming freely in the waters of Lake Erie when Shaw and others seized them. So how could the court rule that the fish were already owned by other fishermen?

State v. Shaw

Supreme Court of Ohio

65 N.E. 875 (1902)

Exceptions to court of common pleas, Lake County.

Henry Shaw and others were indicted for grand larceny. The court directed a verdict for defendants, and the state excepted. . . .

The indictment is as follows:

In the court of common pleas of Lake County, Ohio, of the term of May, in the year of our Lord one thousand nine hundred and one. The jurors of the grand jury of the state of Ohio . . . do find and present, that Henry Shaw, John Thomas, and James Fostine . . . unlawfully and feloniously did steal, take, and carry away seven hundred and thirty pounds of fish, of the value of forty-one dollars, of the personal property of Morris E. Grow and John Hough. . . .

> **What's That?**
>
> *Larceny* is the carrying away of personal property belonging to another person with the intent to keep it forever. Grand larceny is typically larceny of a certain value, generally $200 or more. One cannot commit larceny of real estate. Why not?

In reply to an inquiry where they had got the fish, . . . defendant John Thomas said that "they lifted two pound nets west of the pier and got the fish." The testimony further tended to show that the two pound nets belonged to Grow & Hough. . . .

It also appears that the construction of these pound nets is such that the entrance to the net was about 35 feet deep, 8 rods long, and terminated in an aperture leading into the net, which was 2 feet 10 inches in diameter. This tunnel, as it is called, extended into the net, or pot,

> **See It**
>
> Click here to see a sample fishing net structure used in Lake Erie during the early twentieth century.

some 5 or 6 feet, and the pot was about 28 feet square, reaching, perhaps, 4 feet above the water. The evidence shows that the opening of the tunnel into the pot was the place where the fish entered, and that it was at all times left open. There is no evidence as to the quantity of fish escaping from the nets; it simply appears that it was possible for the fish to go out in the same way they got in. It was also in evidence that these nets were frequently disturbed by wind and storm, and at such times so disordered that fish escaped over the top. . . .

DAVIS, J.

> Fish are ferae naturae; yet,
>
> where the animals or other creatures are not domestic, but are ferae naturae, larceny may notwithstanding be committed of them, if they are fit for food of man, and dead, reclaimed (and known to be so), or confined. Thus . . . fish in a tank or net, or, as it seems, in any other inclosed place which is private property, and where they may be taken at any time at the pleasure of the owner, . . . the taking of them with felonious intent will be larceny. . . .

The trial judge seems to have directed the jury to return a verdict of "not guilty" on the theory that the fish must have been confined so that there was absolutely no possibility of escape. We think that this doctrine is both unnecessarily technical and erroneous. For example, bees in a hive may be the subject of larceny, yet it is possible for the bees to leave the hive by the same place at which they entered. To acquire a property right in animals ferae naturae, the pursuer must bring them into his power and control, and so maintain his control as to show that he does not intend to abandon them again to the world at large. When he has confined them within his own private inclosure, where he may subject them to his own use at his pleasure, and maintains reasonable precautions to prevent escape, they are so impressed with his proprietorship that a felonious taking of them from his inclosure, whether trap, cage, park, net, or whatever it may be, will be larceny. For such cases . . . the law does not require absolute security against the possibility of escape. . . .

In the present case the fish were not at large in Lake Erie. They were confined in nets, from which it was not absolutely impossible for them to escape, yet it was practically so impossible; for it seems that under ordinary circumstances few, if any, of the fish escape. The fish that were taken had not escaped, and it does not appear that they would have escaped, or even that they probably would have escaped. They were so safely secured that the owners of the nets could have taken them out of the water at will as readily as the defendants did. The possession of the owners of the nets was so complete and certain that the defendants went to the nets and raised them with absolute assurance that they could get the fish that were in them. We think, therefore, that the owners of the nets, having captured and confined the fish, had acquired such a property in them that the taking of them was larceny.

Exceptions sustained.

Points for Discussion

a. **Certain Control?**

In *Shaw*, the parties conceded that the entrance to the "pot" was always open, so that fish could escape by either (1) swimming out the same way they entered or (2) jumping over the top of the net. Given this, was the trial judge correct in directing the jury to return a verdict of "not guilty" because the fish could possibly escape? What degree of control did the *Shaw* court require? Certain control does not mean absolute control; but how much risk of escape is acceptable? With large hounds, fast horses, accurate guns, and the fox in sight, was Post's control in *Pierson v. Post* more certain than that of Grow & Hough? Should it matter that Grow & Hough's nets were so large that most fish would not notice their liberty was restricted?

b. **Location of the Capture**

Suppose Shaw captured fish swimming in a private pond on Grow & Hough's land. Or Pierson grabbed the fox in Post's backyard. How important is the *location* of the capture? The rule of capture primarily applies to wild animals seized on unowned land. Does it matter if the successful hunter was trespassing on privately owned land when he caught the animal? Usually, the answer is "yes." Suppose that a squirrel roams through L's backyard. Even though L has no certain control over the squirrel—and thus does not satisfy the rule of capture—the law views L as having a "better" interest in the squirrel than any trespasser could obtain. This result is necessary to meet an important policy goal—protecting a landowner's right to exclude.

If you grab and subdue a rhinoceros running wildly down the streets of your city, do you now own it? Should it matter that the area is not the rhino's natural habitat?

c. **Relativity of Property Rights**

As you saw in Chapter 1, title to property is *relative*, not absolute. Whether the law recognizes a particular person as the owner of a chattel depends on a number of factors, including the identity of the person against whom she is asserting her interest. Suppose that B trespasses on A's land and nets a wild squirrel. B carries the squirrel to her house, keeping it in her bedroom. C trespasses on B's property, captures the squirrel, and takes it to his cabin. Who has a better claim to the squirrel, B or C? How should B respond to C's assertion: "B, you never had any right to the squirrel"?

d. *Animus Revertendi*

Shaw concerned fish; *Pierson*, foxes. But what if these cases involved cattle? In order to encourage investment in cattle, horses, pigs, sheep, and other domesticated animals, the law recognizes an exception to the rule of capture. Thus, if B's cow wanders off B's ranch and onto C's land, B still owns the animal even if C wrestles it to the ground. Given the distinction between animals with *animus revertendi* (those with a "habit of returning") and *ferae naturae*, the correct classification of an animal becomes crucial. How should we classify D's pet fox, Millie? Should it matter that Millie wears a jeweled collar?

What about cats? In *Madero v. Luffey*, 439 F. Supp. 3d 493 (W.D. Pa. 2020), defendant Luffey alleged that officials wrongfully seized stray cats which he periodically fed and cared for; the key issue was whether Luffey owned the cats. The court reasoned that the determination of property rights in such cats should be determined on a case-by-case basis:

> Outdoor cats may, in many circumstances, be considered animals with an *animum revertendi*. . . . [I]t is not uncommon for cats which are considered pets by their owners to be permitted to wander outdoors. Provided that they have a habit of returning to their "home" and their owner considers them to remain his property during their forays into the wild, and the owner acts toward them in a manner which is consistent with ownership, the common law will recognize ongoing property rights in the animal. *Id.* at 506.

e. **The Role of Custom**

Law may be based on custom. For example, in allocating the property rights to a fin-back whale, one court examined the custom of whalers in Provincetown, Massachusetts, that a person who killed a whale with a bomb-lance owned it. This was so even though the whale sank, the whaler ceased pursuit, and another party found (and thus "captured") the carcass days later at a place far from the kill. In adopting this custom as its legal standard, the court noted that the rule worked well in practice, was needed for the continued viability of the whaling industry, and met the expectations of the community. *Ghen v. Rich*, 8 F. 159 (D. Mass. 1881). If the local custom of Ohio fishermen was that a person only owned the fish he successfully brought into his boat, was the court's decision in *Shaw* justifiable? Why did the customs of fox hunting not determine the outcome in *Pierson*, as Justice Livingston advocated in his dissenting opinion?

Courts must often choose between competing rules. In applying the rule of capture, courts commonly stress the goals of administrative efficiency, certainty, and social order. Which of these goals may be lost if a custom is adopted? When is it appropriate to use custom? *See* Richard A. Epstein, *Possession as the Root of Title*, 13 Ga. L. Rev. 1221 (1979), Robert C. Ellickson, Order Without Law: How Neighbors Settle Disputes (1991), and Angela Fernandez, *Fuzzy Rules and Clear Enough Standards: The Uses and Abuses of* Pierson v. Post, 63 U. Toronto L.J. 97 (2013).

f. **The Tragedy of the Commons**

While the rule of capture is an efficient tool when natural resources are plentiful, it is less successful when they are scarce. Do you see why? For example, if fishermen only gain property rights to fish inside their nets (per *Shaw*) and the fish population is decreasing, how will rational fishermen behave?

The problem of over-consumption was illustrated in Garrett Hardin's famous article, *The Tragedy of the Commons*, 162 Science 1243 (1968). Hardin imagined a commonly owned pasture on which each herdsman may keep as many cattle as he desires. As a rational individual, each herdsman will place as many cows as possible on the pasture since he receives all of the benefit of each additional cow, while the negative effects of its grazing are shared by the other herdsmen. In this situation, each herdsman will seek to exploit the pasture for his advantage because most of the costs of his exploitation are borne by others. Hardin explains: "Each man is locked into a system that compels him to increase his herd without limit—in a world that is limited. Ruin is the destination toward which all men rush, each pursuing his own best interest in a society that believes in the freedom of the commons." *Id.* at 1244.

g. Law and Economics

Chapter 2 introduced the concept of *externalities*, which we explore here in more depth. Put simply, externalities are costs and benefits associated with an activity that are imposed upon others not involved in the activity and not taken into account by the decision-maker. For example, if D cuts down a tree in a communal forest to use as firewood, D gains the benefit of the tree, but much of the cost is imposed on the other members of society who have each lost their proportional interest in that tree. Because each person will try to cut trees as quickly as possible, a "tragedy of the commons" will develop. Scholars suggest that many property rules have developed in response to externalities. *See* Harold Demsetz, *Toward a Theory of Property Rights*, 57 Am. Econ. Rev. 347 (1967).

Private property rights facilitate the efficient use of resources. If our forest is divided into privately owned parcels, each owner now has an incentive to use the trees on her land more efficiently because she bears all the costs arising from the destruction of each tree. For example, owner P may delay cutting immature trees because in the future he will be able to obtain more wood from the same trees when they mature. In short, privatization forces many externalities to be internalized. Similarly, a *cap and trade system*, where the government limits a company's emissions (the *cap*) but allows it to buy the ability to pollute more from companies that are not using their full allowances (the *trade*), can provide incentives to reduce carbon emissions, the primary cause of global climate change. Assigning maximum emission allowances to companies that emit carbon forces them to consider their external costs, allowing reductions to be achieved in the most efficient way. *See* Alan E. Friedman, *The Economics of the Common Pool: Property Rights in Exhaustible Resources*, 18 UCLA L. Rev. 855 (1971).

Should courts modify or abolish the rule of capture? Or is this the job of the legislature? Which body can best address the problem of externalities?

The rule of capture has a long history in American law. Originating as a rule for ownership of wild animals, it was extended over time to rights in water, oil, natural gas, hard rock minerals, and other resources. Over 200 years later, *Pierson* is still affecting our legal landscape. Indeed, Justice Tompkins might have cracked a broad smile upon learning that his opinion about the rights to a simple fox served as a legal basis for determining the owner of Barry Bonds' 73rd home run ball.

Popov v. Hayashi

Superior Court of California, County of San Francisco

2002 WL 31833731

McCarthy, J.

Facts

In 1927, Babe Ruth hit sixty home runs. That record stood for thirty four years until Roger Maris broke it in 1961 with sixty one home runs. Mark McGwire hit seventy in 1998. On October 7, 2001, at PacBell Park in San Francisco, Barry Bonds hit number seventy three. That accomplishment set a record which, in all probability, will remain unbroken for years into the future. . . .

When the seventy-third home run ball went into the arcade, it landed in the upper portion of the webbing of a softball glove worn by Alex Popov. While the glove stopped the trajectory of the ball, it is not at all clear that the ball was secure. Popov had to reach for the ball and in doing so, may have lost his balance.

Even as the ball was going into his glove, a crowd of people began to engulf Mr. Popov. He was tackled and thrown to the ground while still in the process of attempting to complete the catch. Some people intentionally descended on him for the purpose of taking the ball away, while others were involuntarily forced to the ground by the momentum of the crowd. . . .

Mr. Hayashi was standing near Mr. Popov when the ball came into the stands. He, like Mr. Popov, was involuntarily forced to the ground. He committed no wrongful act. While on the ground he saw the loose ball. He picked it up, rose to his feet and put it in his pocket. . . .

It is important to point out what the evidence did not and could not show. Neither the camera nor the percipient witnesses were able to establish whether Mr. Popov retained control of the ball as he descended into the crowd. Mr. Popov's testimony on this question is inconsistent

> **See It**
>
> Click here to see a video of Barry Bonds' 73rd home run, including the attempted catch by Popov.

on several important points, ambiguous on others and, on the whole, unconvincing. We do not know when or how Mr. Popov lost the ball.

Perhaps the most critical factual finding of all is one that cannot be made. We will never know if Mr. Popov would have been able to retain control of the ball had the crowd not interfered with his efforts to do so. Resolution of that question is the work of a psychic, not a judge. . . .

Legal Analysis

In the case at bar, Mr. Popov is not claiming that Mr. Hayashi damaged the ball or that he interfered with Mr. Popov's use and enjoyment of the ball. He claims instead that Mr. Hayashi intentionally took it from him and refused to give it back. There is no trespass to chattel. If there was a wrong at all, it is conversion.

Conversion does not exist, however, unless the baseball rightfully belongs to Mr. Popov. One who has neither title nor possession, nor any right to possession, cannot sue for conversion. The deciding question in this case then, is whether Mr. Popov achieved possession or the right to possession as he attempted to catch and hold on to the ball. . . .

Prior to the time the ball was hit, it was possessed and owned by Major League Baseball. At the time it was hit it became intentionally abandoned property. The first person who came in possession of the ball became its new owner. . . .

The focus of the analysis in this case is not on the thoughts or intent of the actor. Mr. Popov has clearly evidenced an intent to possess the baseball and has communicated that intent to the world. The question is whether he did enough to reduce the ball to his exclusive dominion and control. Were his acts sufficient to create a legally cognizable interest in the ball?

FYI

In earlier days, baseballs were themselves somewhat valuable, and teams routinely asked fans to return foul balls. As late as 1940, the Cleveland Indians required fans to return home run balls. Until recently, teams in Japan demanded that any foul ball be handed over to an usher, who gave the fan a small gift in return. *See* Paul Finkelman, *Fugitive Baseballs and Abandoned Property: Who Owns the Home Run Ball?*, 23 Cardozo L. Rev. 1609 (2002).

Mr. Hayashi argues that possession does not occur until the fan has complete control of the ball. Professor Brian Gray suggests the following definition: "A person who catches a baseball that enters the stands is its owner. A ball is caught if the person has achieved complete control of the ball at the point in time that the momentum of the ball and the momentum of the fan while attempting to catch the ball ceases. A baseball, which is dislodged by incidental contact with an inanimate object or another person, before momentum has ceased, is not possessed. Incidental contact with another person is contact that is not intended by the other person. The first person to pick up a loose ball and secure it becomes its possessor."[24]

Mr. Popov argues that this definition requires that a person seeking to establish possession must show unequivocal dominion and control, a standard rejected by several leading cases.[25] Instead, he offers the perspectives of Professor Bernhardt and Professor Paul Finkelman who suggest that possession occurs when an individual intends to take control of a ball and manifests that intent by stopping the forward momentum of the ball whether or not complete control is achieved.

Professors Finkelman and Bernhardt have correctly pointed out that some cases recognize possession even before absolute dominion and control is achieved. Those cases require the actor to be actively and ably engaged in efforts to establish complete control. Moreover, such efforts must be significant and they must be reasonably calculated to result in unequivocal dominion and control at some point in the near future.

This rule is applied in cases involving the hunting or fishing of wild animals or the salvage of sunken vessels. The hunting and fishing cases recognize that a mortally wounded animal may run for a distance before falling. The hunter acquires possession upon the act of wounding the animal not the eventual capture. Similarly, whalers acquire possession by landing a harpoon, not by subduing the animal. . . .

These rules are contextual in nature. They are crafted in response to the unique nature of the conduct they seek to regulate. Moreover, they are influenced by the custom and practice of each industry. The reason that absolute dominion and control is not required to establish possession in the cases cited by Mr. Popov is that such a rule would be unworkable and unreasonable. The "nature and situation" of the property at issue does not immediately lend itself to unequivocal dominion and control. It is impossible to wrap one's arms around a whale, a fleeing fox or a sunken ship.

The opposite is true of a baseball hit into the stands of a stadium. Not only is it physically possible for a person to acquire unequivocal dominion and control of an abandoned baseball, but fans generally expect a claimant to have accomplished as much. The custom and practice of the stands creates a reasonable expectation that a person will achieve full control of a ball before claiming possession. There is no reason for the legal rule to be inconsistent with that expectation. Therefore Gray's Rule is adopted as the definition of possession in this case.

The central tenet of Gray's Rule is that the actor must retain control of the ball after incidental contact with people and things. Mr. Popov has not established by a preponderance of the evidence that he would have retained control of the ball after all momentum ceased and after any incidental contact with people or objects. Consequently, he did not achieve full possession.

---

[24] This definition is hereinafter referred to as Gray's Rule.
[25] *Pierson v. Post*, 3 Caines R. (N.Y. 1805); *State v. Shaw* (1902) 67 Ohio St. 157, 65 N.E. 875.

That finding, however, does not resolve the case. The reason we do not know whether Mr. Popov would have retained control of the ball is not because of incidental contact. It is because he was attacked. His efforts to establish possession were interrupted by the collective assault of a band of wrongdoers. . . .

As a matter of fundamental fairness, Mr. Popov should have had the opportunity to try to complete his catch unimpeded by unlawful activity. To hold otherwise would be to allow the result in this case to be dictated by violence. That will not happen. . . .

Here Mr. Popov seeks, in effect, a declaratory judgment that he has either possession or the right to possession. In addition he seeks the remedies of injunctive relief and a constructive trust. These are all actions in equity. A court sitting in equity has the authority to fashion rules and remedies designed to achieve fundamental fairness.

Consistent with this principle, the court adopts the following rule. Where an actor undertakes significant but incomplete steps to achieve possession of a piece of abandoned personal property and the effort is interrupted by the unlawful acts of others, the actor has a legally cognizable pre-possessory interest in the property. That pre-possessory interest constitutes a qualified right to possession which can support a cause of action for conversion. . . .

Mr. Hayashi was not a wrongdoer. He was a victim of the same bandits that attacked Mr. Popov. The difference is that he was able to extract himself from their assault and move to the side of the road. It was there that he discovered the loose ball. When he picked up and put it in his pocket he attained unequivocal dominion and control.

If Mr. Popov had achieved complete possession before Mr. Hayashi got the ball, those actions would not have divested Mr. Popov of any rights, nor would they have created any rights to which Mr. Hayashi could lay claim. Mr. Popov, however, was able to establish only a qualified pre-possessory interest in the ball. That interest does not establish a full right to possession that is protected from a subsequent legitimate claim.

On the other hand, while Mr. Hayashi appears on the surface to have done everything necessary to claim full possession of the ball, the ball itself is encumbered by the qualified pre-possessory interest of Mr. Popov. At the time Mr. Hayashi came into possession of the ball, it had, in effect, a cloud on its title.

An award of the ball to Mr. Popov would be unfair to Mr. Hayashi. It would be premised on the assumption that Mr. Popov would have caught the ball. That assumption is not supported by the facts. An award of the ball to Mr. Hayashi would unfairly penalize Mr. Popov. It would be based on the assumption that Mr. Popov would have dropped the ball. That conclusion is also unsupported by the facts.

Both men have a superior claim to the ball as against all the world. Each man has a claim of equal dignity as to the other. We are, therefore, left with something of a dilemma.

Thankfully, there is a middle ground. . . .

The concept of equitable division has its roots in ancient Roman law. . . . [I]t is useful in that it "provides an equitable way to resolve competing claims which are equally strong." Moreover, "[i]t comports with what one instinctively feels to be fair.". . .

Mr. Hayashi's claim is compromised by Mr. Popov's pre-possessory interest. Mr. Popov cannot demonstrate full control. . . . Their legal claims are of equal quality and they are equally entitled to the ball.

The court therefore declares that both plaintiff and defendant have an equal and undivided interest in the ball. Plaintiff's cause of action for conversion is sustained only as to his equal and undivided interest. In order to effectuate this ruling, the ball must be sold and the proceeds divided equally between the parties. . . .

Points for Discussion

a. **Nature of the Action**

Popov brought an action for *conversion*: the wrongful exercise of dominion over the personal property of another. What legal assumptions underlay Popov's suit? As plaintiff, Popov had the burden of proof. Did a preponderance of the evidence support his claim of possession?

b. **Analogy to the Rule of Capture**

Popov never obtained certain control over the ball. Accordingly, if we apply the rule of capture, he did not acquire title. But is a baseball analogous to a wild animal? What did the court mean when it stated that "rules are contextual in nature"? In *Shaw*, the court tolerated a certain amount of risk that fish might escape from the net. Should the *Popov* court have accepted a similar risk that the ball might escape from Popov's glove?

c. **A "Pre-Possessory Interest"**

How would you frame the rule adopted by the court? The court's reference to a pre-possessory interest suggests something more than "intending to have," but something less than "having." Under this analysis, would Post receive a pre-possessory interest in the fox by pursuing and "almost" killing it? Can you think of any other examples of pre-possessory interests? Does the concept of a pre-possessory interest make sense?

d. **Questioning the Opinion**

The judge's opinion mentions ancient Roman law, hunting and fishing cases, salvage rules for sunken ships, and whaling customs—and the testimony of several law professors. Why should any of these authorities be influential in determining ownership of a baseball? Do they suggest that the ball should belong to someone other than Popov or Hayashi? What about Barry Bonds (he "created" the home run by his labor, and his personal "relationship" with the ball generated all of the ball's value); the San Francisco Giants (the ball never left its stadium); or Major League Baseball (it purchased the ball for the game that became part of baseball history)?

e. The Role of Custom

Is there a "common law of baseball" that governs the ownership of a ball that clears the outfield fence? Was it important for the court to define possession in a manner that baseball fans will respect? The judge noted that the "custom and practice of the stands creates a reasonable expectation that a person will achieve full control of a ball before claiming possession." Should this custom doom Popov's claim?

f. Abandoned Property

The court treated the ball as *abandoned* property—property in which the owner has voluntarily relinquished its rights. Why? When sitting in the stands during a baseball game when a foul ball or home run is hit, do you generally think: "There goes another abandoned ball"?

g. Equitable Division

The judge reasoned that awarding the ball to one party over the other would be unfair. If Popov would have caught the ball but for the wrongful actions of other fans, wasn't Hayashi the beneficiary of a series of unlawful (and perhaps criminal) acts? If so, shouldn't he return the ball to the victimized Popov?

Do you agree with the judge's Solomon-like verdict of selling the ball and splitting the profits? Or was this merely a ruse to avoid a difficult decision? While equitable division is often utilized in divorce proceedings, it is rarely used to allocate ownership rights in abandoned property.

h. Aftermath of *Popov*

Nineteen months after Barry Bonds' 73rd home run ball first grazed Popov's glove, it was sold in a televised auction for $450,000—far less than the estimated value of $1.5 million. The ball was purchased by comic book creator Todd MacFarlane, who had previously spent $3 million to purchase Mark McGwire's 70th home run ball. Unfortunately, Popov hired his attorney on an hourly fee basis; his legal bill totaled over $473,000, far more than the $225,000 he received from the sale. Hayashi was more prudent: he retained his counsel on a contingent fee basis. The *Popov* case became the subject of the 2005 documentary *Up for Grabs*.

> **What's That?**
>
> A *contingent fee* is a payment arrangement where the client is responsible to pay only if he wins the case or agrees to a settlement. The fee is usually a percentage of the judgment or settlement. Contingent fee arrangements allow litigation to be brought by people who otherwise could not afford it.

Nearly three years after his 73rd home run, Bonds hit his 700th career home run. Steve Williams gained possession of the ball after another scramble in the bleachers. He was then sued by Timothy Murphy, who claimed that he owned the ball because he had locked it behind his knees while at the bottom of the pile of fans, moments before Williams grabbed it. The trial court dismissed Murphy's lawsuit, and the ball was later sold at auction at Overstock.com for $804,129.

B. Finders

Have you ever lost or misplaced something? Or found something? Did you think you owned the item that you found? In everyday life, chattels are frequently lost and found. A finder's rights are governed by a number of factors, including the type of item and the place where it was found.

There are four categories of "found" chattels:

- *Lost property*: Property is lost when the owner unintentionally and involuntarily parts with it.
- *Mislaid property*: Property is mislaid when the owner voluntarily and knowingly places it somewhere, but then unintentionally forgets it.
- *Abandoned property*: Property is abandoned when the owner knowingly relinquishes all right, title, and interest to it.
- *Treasure trove*: Property is treasure trove when the owner concealed it in a hidden location long ago. Treasure trove is usually limited to gold, silver, coins, or currency.

As you read the following cases, think about why the category of the found item should affect the court's decision. Remember that each item here has a prior owner, quite unlike unowned things that are governed by the rule of capture.

Our next case involves considerable drama. A poor chimney sweep appeared before the highest court in England, presenting his case against a famous goldsmith, Paul de Lamerie.

Armory v. Delamirie

King's Bench

93 Eng. Rep. 664 (1722)

The plaintiff being a chimney sweeper's boy found a jewel and carried it to the defendant's shop (who was a goldsmith) to know what it was, and delivered it into the hands of the apprentice, who under pretence of weighing it, took out the stones, and calling to the master to let him know it came to three halfpence, the master offered the boy the money, who refused to take it, and insisted to have the thing again; whereupon the apprentice delivered him back the socket without the stones. And now in trover against the master these points were ruled:

1. That the finder of a jewel, though he does not by such finding acquire an absolute property or ownership, yet he has such a property as will enable him to keep it against all but the rightful owner, and consequently may maintain trover.

2. That the action well lay against the master, who gives a credit to his apprentice, and is answerable for his neglect.

> **FYI**
>
> Paul de Lamerie opened his London workshop in 1712 at the age of 24. Four years later, he was selected as the official goldsmith to George I. He eventually had 13 employees in his workshop and operated a retail store that sold gold, silver, and jewelry. Click here to see the De Lamerie collection at the Victoria and Albert Museum in London.

3. As to the value of the jewel several of the trade were examined to prove what a jewel of the finest water that would fit the socket would be worth; and the Chief Justice directed the jury, that unless the defendant did produce the jewel, and shew it not to be of the finest water, they should presume the strongest against him, and make the value of the best jewels the measure of their damages: which they accordingly did.

Points for Discussion

a. Framing the Issue

In *Armory*, the court held that a finder's property interest gives him priority against everyone *except the rightful owner*. But is this wording too restrictive? Who is a "rightful owner"? Suppose that F first found the jewel on the sidewalk, and then hid it for safekeeping in the place where the chimney sweep discovered it. F's rights to the jewel would be superior to the sweep's rights, even though F was not the original owner. As we have seen, property rights are relative: the chimney sweep has better title than the goldsmith; F has better title than the sweep; and the original owner has better title than F. How could the court's rule be modified to more clearly describe a finder's property interest? Remember that a court's task is to determine the rights of the parties before it, not to determine the item's ultimate owner.

b. **Who "Owned" the Jewel?**

Why didn't the goldsmith (through his apprentice) have a better property right to the jewel since (1) the chimney sweep was not the original owner and (2) the goldsmith had present possession? In the United States, an argument asserting that a person other than one of the litigants has superior title (a *jus tertii* defense) is usually unsuccessful. The court must determine which of the parties actually before it has better title; the potential rights of a nonparty are irrelevant.

> **It's Latin to Me**
>
> *Jus tertii* is Latin for "third party rights." When a person in possession of property pleads that title is in someone other than her predecessor in possession, she raises a *jus tertii* defense.

Which of the following is correct: (1) the chimney sweep owned the jewel; (2) the sweep's possession was prima facie proof of ownership; or (3) the sweep was a prior possessor and thus had a better right than the goldsmith? What is the relationship between ownership and possession?

c. **Chimney Sweep as Thief**

Would it make a difference in *Armory* if the sweep had stolen the jewel? Generally, courts say "no." One famous case involved a trespasser who illegally cut down trees on another's land. When X, a third party, wrongfully took possession of the same logs, the court held that the trespasser's title—although based on illegal conduct—had priority over X's claim. As the court emphasized, "[a]ny other rule would lead to an endless series of unlawful seizures and reprisals in every case where property had once passed out of the possession of the rightful owner." *Anderson v. Gouldberg*, 53 N.W. 636, 637 (Minn. 1892). Do you agree? Why should the law protect a thief?

d. **Liability to the Rightful Owner**

Once the goldsmith paid the chimney sweep the value of the jewel as the court mandated, did the goldsmith own the jewel? What if the rightful owner demanded her jewel from the goldsmith one week later? Generally, a subsequent possessor's full payment to the finder bars any later action by the true owner against the possessor. However, the true owner can compel the successful finder to transfer the payment to her. What concerns does this scenario present?

e. **Trover**

Armory was a lawsuit in *trover*, a common law action where the plaintiff seeks damages for the wrongful taking of personal property. Alternatively, the sweep might have brought an action in *replevin*, a lawsuit to recover possession of personal property. Why did the sweep sue in trover rather than replevin? Today these common law forms of action are obsolete. In most states, they have been replaced by statutes that govern the recovery of personal property.

f.   "A Jewel of the Finest Water"

The court awarded Armory the value of a "jewel of the finest water." *Water* was a standard for assessing the color and transparency of a jewel. A jewel of the *finest water* had the best quality—and thus the most value. So did the goldsmith pay too much? What factors might influence a court to award the sweep less than fair market value? Consider Armory's property interest at the moment of the find. Was his ownership complete?

Armory is the source of the modern rule that "when damages are at some unascertainable amount below an upper limit and when the uncertainty arises from the defendant's wrong, the upper limit will be taken as the proper amount." *See, e.g., Metro Storage Int'l LLC v. Harron,* 275 A.3d 810 n. 33 (Del. Ch. 2022).

g.   Aftermath of *Armory*

After his brief moment of fame in this case, Armory disappeared from history. But de Lamerie continued his successful business until his death in 1751. In this era, a goldsmith worked in both gold and silver. De Lamerie was especially known for his ornate silver plate creations such as coffee pots, tureens, wine vessels, and silverware. Almost two centuries after his death, one British authority noted that de Lamerie is "by common consent acknowledged to be the greatest exponent of his art in this country." W.W. Watts, *Paul de Lamerie,* Burlington Magazine, Aug. 1935. Today de Lamerie's creations are still displayed in art museums in Great Britain and the United States.

———

In *Armory*, the court held that the finder owned the jewel, not a later possessor. But what if the dispute was between a finder and the owner of the land where the jewel was found? Why might a court award title to the landowner?

Hannah v. Peel

King's Bench

1 K.B. 509 (1945)

On December 13, 1938, the freehold of Gwernhaylod House, Overton-on-Dee, Shropshire, was conveyed to the defendant, Major Hugh Edward Ethelston Peel, who from that time to the end of 1940 never himself occupied the house and it remained unoccupied until October 5, 1939, when it was requisitioned, but after some months was released from requisition. Thereafter it remained unoccupied until July 18, 1940, when it was again requisitioned, the defendant being compensated by a payment at the rate of £250 a year. In August, 1940, the plaintiff, Duncan Hannah, a lance-corporal, serving in a battery of the Royal Artillery, was stationed at the house and on the 21st of that month, when in a bedroom, used as a sick-bay, he was adjusting the black-out curtains when his hand touched something on the top of a window-frame, loose in a crevice, which he thought was a piece of dirt or plaster. The plaintiff grasped it and dropped it on the outside window ledge. On the following morning he saw that it was a brooch covered with cobwebs and dirt. Later, he took it with him when he went home on leave and his wife having told him it might be of value, at the end of October, 1940, he informed his commanding officer of his find and, on his advice, handed it over to the police, receiving a receipt for it. In August, 1942, the owner not having been found the police handed the brooch to the defendant, who sold it in October, 1942, for £66, to Messrs. Spink & Son, Ltd., of London, who resold it in the following month for £88. There was no evidence that the defendant had any knowledge of the existence of the brooch before it was found by the plaintiff. The defendant had offered the plaintiff a reward for the brooch, but the plaintiff refused to accept this and maintained throughout his right to the possession of the brooch as against all persons other than the owner, who was unknown. By a letter, dated October 5, 1942, the plaintiff's solicitors demanded the return of the brooch from the defendant, but it was not returned and on October 21, 1943, the plaintiff issued his writ claiming the return of the brooch, or its value, and damages for its detention. By his defence, the defendant claimed the brooch on the ground that he was the owner of Gwernhaylod House and in possession thereof. . . .

Gwernhaylod House

> **FYI**
>
> Hannah's annual military salary would be worth only about $9,000 today, while the broach would be worth over $8,000. Peel, on the other hand, was a wealthy descendant of King Henry VII. At one point, the Peel family owned more than 5,700 acres in Wales.

BIRKETT, J.

There is no issue of fact in this case between the parties. As to the issue in law, the rival claims of the parties can be stated in this way: The plaintiff says: "I claim the brooch as its finder and I have a good title against all the world, save only the true owner." The defendant says: "My claim is superior to yours inasmuch as I am the freeholder. The brooch was found on my property, although I was never in occupation, and my title, therefore, ousts yours and in the absence of the true owner I am entitled to the brooch or its value." Unhappily the law on this issue is in a very uncertain state and there is need of an authoritative decision of a higher court. Obviously if it could be said with certainty that this is the law, that the finder of a lost article, wherever found, has a good title against all the world save the true owner, then, of course, all my difficulties would be resolved; or again, if it could be said with equal certainty that this is the law, that the possessor of land is entitled as against the finder to all chattels found on the land, again my difficulties would be resolved. But, unfortunately, the authorities give some support to each of these conflicting propositions. . . .

The case of *Bridges v. Hawkesworth* . . . was in fact an appeal against a decision of the county court judge at Westminster. The facts appear to have been that in the year 1847 the plaintiff, who was a commercial traveller, called on a firm named Byfield & Hawkesworth on business, as he was in the habit of doing, and as he was leaving the shop he picked up a small parcel which was lying on the floor. He immediately showed it to the shopman, and opened it in his presence, when it was found to consist of a quantity of Bank of England notes, to the amount of £65. The defendant, who was a partner in the firm of Byfield & Hawkesworth, was then called, and the plaintiff told him he had found the notes, and asked the defendant to keep them until the owner appeared to claim them. Then various advertisements were put in the papers asking for the owner, but the true owner was never found. No person having appeared to claim them, and three years having elapsed since they were found, the plaintiff applied to the defendant to have the notes returned to him, and offered to pay the expenses of the advertisements, and to give an indemnity. The defendant refused to deliver them up to the plaintiff, and an action was brought in the county court of Westminster in consequence of that refusal. The county court judge decided that the defendant, the shopkeeper, was entitled to the custody of the notes as against the plaintiff, and gave judgment for the defendant. Thereupon the appeal was brought which came before the court composed of Patteson J. and Wightman J. Patteson J. said: . . . "The case, therefore, resolves itself into the single point on which it appears that the learned judge decided it, namely, whether the circumstance of the notes being found inside the defendant's shop gives him, the defendant, the right to have them as against the plaintiff, who found them." After discussing the cases, and the argument, the learned judge said: "If the discovery had never been communicated to the defendant, could the real owner have had any cause of action against him because they were found in his house? Certainly not. The notes never were in the custody of the defendant, nor within the protection of his house, before they were found, as they would have been had they been intentionally deposited there; and the defendant has come under no responsibility, except from the communication made to him by the plaintiff, the finder, and the steps taken by way of advertisement. . . . We find, therefore, no circumstances in this case to take it out of the general rule of law, that the finder of a lost article is entitled to it as against all persons except the real owner, and we think that that rule must prevail, and that the learned judge was mistaken in holding that the place in which they were found makes any legal difference. Our judgment, therefore, is that the plaintiff is entitled to these notes as against the defendant."

It is to be observed that in *Bridges v. Hawkesworth* . . . there was no suggestion that the place where the notes were found was in any way material; indeed, the judge in giving the judgment of the court expressly repudiates this and said in terms "The learned judge was mistaken in holding that the place in which they were found makes any legal difference." It is, therefore, a little remarkable that in *South Staffordshire Water Co. v. Sharman*, Lord Russell of Killowen C.J. said: "The case of *Bridges v. Hawkesworth* stands by itself, and on special grounds; and on those grounds it seems to me that the decision in that case was right. Someone had accidentally dropped a bundle of banknotes in a public shop. The shopkeeper did not know they had been dropped, and did not in any sense exercise control over them. The shop was open to the public, and they were invited to come there." That might be a matter of some doubt. Customers were invited there, but whether the public at large was, might be open to some question. Lord Russell continued: "A customer picked up the notes and gave them to the shopkeeper in order that he might advertise them. The owner of the notes was not found, and the finder then sought to recover them from the shopkeeper. It was held that he was entitled to do so, the ground of the decision being, as was pointed out by Patteson J., that the notes, being dropped in the public part of the shop, were never in the custody of the shopkeeper, or 'within the protection of his house.'" Patteson J. never made any reference to the public part of the shop and, indeed, went out of his way to say that the learned county court judge was wrong in holding that the place where they were found made any legal difference.

Bridges v. Hawkesworth has been the subject of considerable comment by text-book writers and, amongst others, by Mr. Justice Oliver Wendell Holmes, Sir Frederick Pollock and Sir John Salmond. All three agree that the case was rightly decided, but they differ as to the grounds on which it was decided and put forward grounds, none of which, so far as I can discover, were ever advanced by the judges who decided the case. Mr. Justice Oliver Wendell Holmes wrote: "Common law judges and civilians would agree that the finder got possession first and so could keep it as against the shopkeeper. For the shopkeeper, not knowing of the thing, could not have the intent to appropriate it, and, having invited the public to his shop, he could not have the intent to exclude them from it." So he introduces the matter of two intents which are not referred to by the judges who heard the case. Sir Frederick Pollock, whilst he agreed with Mr. Justice Holmes that *Bridges v. Hawkesworth* was properly decided wrote: "In such a case as *Bridges v. Hawkesworth*, where a parcel of banknotes was dropped on the floor in the part of a shop frequented by customers, it is impossible to say that the shopkeeper has any possession in fact. He does not expect objects of that kind to be on the floor of his shop, and some customer is more likely than the shopkeeper or his servant to see and take them up if they do come there." He emphasizes the lack of de facto control on the part of the shopkeeper. Sir John Salmond wrote: "In *Bridges v. Hawkesworth* a parcel of banknotes was dropped on the floor of the defendant's shop, where they were found by the plaintiff, a customer. It was held that the plaintiff had a good title to them as against the defendant. For the plaintiff, and not the defendant, was the first to acquire possession of them. The defendant had not the necessary animus, for he did not know of their existence.". . .

With regard to *South Staffordshire Water Co. v. Sharman*, the first two lines of the headnote are: "The possessor of land is generally entitled, as against the finder, to chattels found on the land." I am not sure that this is accurate. The facts were that the defendant Sharman, while cleaning out, under the orders of the plaintiffs, the South Staffordshire Water Company, a pool of water on their land, found two rings embedded in the mud at the bottom of the pool. He declined to deliver them to the plaintiffs, but failed to discover the real owner. In an action brought by the company against Sharman in detinue it was held that the company was entitled to the rings. Lord Russell of Killowen C.J. said: "The plaintiffs are the freeholders of the *locus in quo*, and as such they have the right to forbid anybody coming on their land or in any way interfering with it. They had the right to say that their pool should be cleaned out in any way that they thought fit, and to direct what should be done with anything found in the pool in the course of such cleaning out. It is no doubt right, as the counsel for the defendant contended, to say that the plaintiffs must show that they had actual control over the locus in quo and the things in it; but under the circumstances, can it be said that the Minster Pool and whatever might be in that pool were not under the control of the plaintiffs? In my opinion they were. . . . The principle on which this case must be decided, and the distinction which must be drawn between this case and that of *Bridges v. Hawkesworth*, is to be found in a passage in Pollock and Wright's 'Essay on Possession in the Common Law,' p. 41: 'The possession of land carries with it in general, by our law, possession of everything which is attached to or under that land, and, in the absence of a better title elsewhere, the right to possess it also.'" If that is right, it would clearly cover the case of the rings embedded in the mud of the pool, the words used being "attached to or under that land." Lord Russell continued: "And it makes no difference that the possessor is not aware of the thing's existence." . . . Then Lord Russell . . . continued: "It is somewhat strange"—I venture to echo those words—"that

> **See It**
>
> Click here to see an 1890 image of Minster Pool, where the defendant in *South Staffordshire Water Co.* found the rings in question.

> **It's Latin to Me**
>
> *Locus in quo* is Latin for "the place in which." It refers to the place where the cause of action arose. In a finder's case, this is the location of the find.

there is no more direct authority on the question; but the general principle seems to me to be that where a person has possession of house or land, with a manifest intention to exercise control over it and the things which may be upon or in it, then, if something is found on that land, whether by an employee of the owner or by a stranger, the presumption is that the possession of that thing is in the owner of the locus in quo.". . . *South Staffordshire Water Co. v. Sharman* which was relied on by counsel for the defendant, has also been the subject of some discussion. It has been said that it establishes that if a man finds a thing as the servant or agent of another, he finds it not for himself, but for that other, and indeed that seems to afford a sufficient explanation of the case. The rings found at the bottom of the pool were not in the possession of the company, but it seems that though Sharman was the first to obtain possession of them, he obtained them for his employers and could claim no title for himself.

The only other case to which I need refer is *Elwes v. Brigg Gas Co.*, in which land had been demised to a gas company for ninety-nine years with a reservation to the lessor of all mines and minerals. A pre-historic boat embedded in the soil was discovered by the lessees when they were digging to make a gasholder. It was held that the boat, whether regarded as a mineral or as part of the soil in which it was embedded when discovered, or as a chattel, did not pass to the lessees by the demise, but was the property of the lessor though he was ignorant of its existence at the time of granting the lease. . . .

It is fairly clear from the authorities that a man possesses everything which is attached to or under his land. Secondly, it would appear to be the law from the authorities I have cited, and particularly from *Bridges v. Hawkesworth*, that a man does not necessarily possess a thing which is lying unattached on the surface of his land even though the thing is not possessed by someone else. A difficulty however, arises, because the rule which governs things an occupier possesses as against those which he does not, has never been very clearly formulated in our law. He may possess everything on the land from which he intends to exclude others, if Mr. Justice Holmes is right; or he may possess those things of which he has a de facto control, if Sir Frederick Pollock is right.

There is no doubt that in this case the brooch was lost in the ordinary meaning of that term, and I should imagine it had been lost for a very considerable time. Indeed, from this correspondence it appears that at one time the predecessors in title of the defendant were considering making some claim. But the moment the plaintiff discovered that the brooch might be of some value, he took the advice of his commanding officer and handed it to the police. His conduct was commendable and meritorious. The defendant was never physically in possession of these premises at any time. It is clear that the brooch was never his, in the ordinary acceptation of the term, in that he had the prior possession. He had no knowledge of it, until it was brought to his notice by the finder. A discussion of the merits does not seem to help, but it is clear on the facts that the brooch was "lost" in the ordinary meaning of that word; that it was "found" by the plaintiff in the ordinary meaning of that word, that its true owner has never been found, that the defendant was the owner of the premises and had his notice drawn to this matter by the plaintiff, who found the brooch. In those circumstances I propose to follow the decision in *Bridges v. Hawkesworth*, and to give judgment in this case for the plaintiff for £66.

Points for Discussion

a. **Owner's Rights**

The *Hannah* court cites Lord Russell for the general principle that "where a person has possession of house or land, with a manifest intention to exercise control over it and the things which may be upon or in it, then, if something is found on that land, whether by an employee of the owner or by a stranger, the presumption is that the possession of that thing is in the owner of the locus in quo." Peel owned Gwernhaylod House and leased it to Hannah's employer. So why didn't Peel win?

b. **Peel's Expectations**

The court could have ruled that Peel had constructive possession of all lost articles on his property, but it did not. Why? How did the court balance the policies of protecting the finder's expectations, rewarding the finder, encouraging honesty, and protecting the landowner's expectations? Would the case have come out differently if Hannah were a trespasser?

c. **Role of Precedent**

Armory was a well-established precedent when the court considered Hannah's claim. Under the *Armory* standard, who should have won in *Hannah*? The *Hannah* court referred to a number of other cases in its opinion, including *Bridges*, *South Staffordshire*, and *Elwes*. Did these cases apply consistent rules? How effectively did the court use these cases to support its decision?

d. **"Prying Eyes and Fingers"**

Suppose that homeowner O hires contractor C to perform repairs; C finds a hidden cache of money beneath the floor. Who owns the money? One might argue that C is much like Hannah—a person legally entitled to be present on land owned by another. But do different policies apply in this situation? Ruling that a homeowner had constructive possession of all lost, mislaid, or abandoned property located on the premises, the court in *Hurley v. City of Niagara Falls*, 280 N.Y.S.2d 182, 185 (Sup. Ct. 1967) observed:

> To hold otherwise would expose such privately owned and occupied residential property to the prying eyes and fingers of the very large number of public invitees, as well as social guests, who today by necessity must come onto private residential

property for delivery of commodities, servicing of utilities and appliances, inspection, maintenance and repairs. . . .

e. Rights and Duties of Finders

The *Hannah* court recognized the finder's title to the broach. But what bundle of rights did Hannah have as a finder? Could he use the brooch? Could he sell it? And did he have a responsibility to care for it? While a finder has rightful possession, he does not have unqualified ownership; he is a *bailee*. Under the law of bailments, a finder is obligated to (1) keep the chattel safe and (2) return it to the prior possessor on demand.

f. Bailments

A restaurant guest hands his car keys to the attending valet. A farmer borrows his neighbor's tractor. A homeowner leaves her dog with a friend while she goes on vacation. Each of these acts creates a *bailment*—the rightful possession of goods by one who is not the owner. The person who delivers the chattel is called a *bailor*, while the one who receives it is called a *bailee*.

There are three basic types of bailments: (1) those for the mutual benefit of both the bailor and the bailee; (2) those for the primary benefit of the bailee; and (3) those for the primary benefit of the bailor. *See, e.g., Foster v. Board of Governors,* 342 P.3d 497, 501 (Colo. App. 2014). When a bailment is for mutual benefit, the bailee has the duty to take reasonable care of the property. Thus, in the example above, the valet is responsible for any damages he causes by driving the car negligently. When the bailment is for the primary benefit of the bailee, extraordinary care is required. Thus, our hypothetical farmer must return the tractor in the same condition that he received it. When the bailment is for the primary benefit of the bailor, the bailee is liable only if the property is damaged because of gross negligence or bad faith. For instance, if the dog died because the neighbor left it in a closed car on a sweltering day, the neighbor would be liable. Which bailment arises when a finder discovers a lost item?

g. Sharing the Find

The court assumed that ownership of the brooch had to be awarded to *either* Peel *or* Hannah. Judges rarely hold that found property should be shared. Why not? Recall *Popov*, where the court awarded each party an equal share in Barry Bonds' home run baseball and equitably divided the proceeds from its sale. What are the advantages of this approach? *See* R.H. Helmholz, *Equitable Division and the Law of Finders,* 52 Fordham L. Rev. 313 (1983).

Suppose there was a large party in Gwernhaylod House the night before Hannah's discovery. And imagine that Hannah found the brooch on a table where many guests had placed their purses, hats, and shawls. Why might these additional facts change the result in *Hannah*?

McAvoy v. Medina

Supreme Judicial Court of Massachusetts

11 Allen 548 (1866)

TORT to recover a sum of money found by the plaintiff in the shop of the defendant.

At the trial in the superior court, before Morton, J., it appeared that the defendant was a barber, and the plaintiff, being a customer in the defendant's shop, saw and took up a pocket-book which was lying upon a table there, and said, "See what I have found." The defendant came to the table and asked where he found it. The plaintiff laid it back in the same place and said, "I found it right there." The defendant then took it and counted the money, and the plaintiff told him to keep it, and if the owner should come to give it to him; and otherwise to advertise it; which the defendant promised to do. Subsequently the plaintiff made three demands for the money, and the defendant never claimed to hold the same till the last demand. It was agreed that the pocket-book was placed upon the table by a transient customer of the defendant and accidentally left there, and was first seen and taken up by the plaintiff, and that the owner had not been found.

The judge ruled that the plaintiff could not maintain his action, and a verdict was accordingly returned for the defendant; and the plaintiff alleged exceptions.

DEWEY, J.

It seems to be the settled law that the finder of lost property has a valid claim to the same against all the world except the true owner, and generally that the place in which it is found creates no exception to this rule. *Bridges v. Hawkesworth,* 7 Eng. Law & Eq. R. 424.

But this property is not, under the circumstances, to be treated as lost property in that sense in which a finder has a valid claim to hold the same until called for by the true owner. This property was voluntarily placed upon a table in the defendant's shop by a customer of his who accidentally left the same there and has never called for it. The plaintiff also came there as a customer, and first saw the same and took it up from the table. The plaintiff did not by this acquire the right to take the property from the shop, but it was rather the duty of the defendant, when the fact became thus known to him, to use reasonable care for the safe keeping of the same until the owner should call for it. In the case of *Bridges v. Hawkesworth* the property, although found in a shop, was found on the floor of the same, and had not been placed there voluntarily by the owner, and the court held that the finder was entitled to the possession of the same, except as to the owner. But the present case more resembles that of *Lawrence v. The State*, 1 Humph. (Tenn.) 228, and is indeed very similar in its facts. The court there took a distinction between the case of property thus placed by the owner and neglected to be removed, and property lost. It was there held that "to place a pocket-book upon a table and to forget to take it away is not to lose it, in the sense in which the authorities referred to speak of lost property."

We accept this as the better rule, and especially as one better adapted to secure the rights of the true owner.

In view of the facts of this case, the plaintiff acquired no original right to the property, and the defendant's subsequent acts in receiving and holding the property in the manner he did does not create any.

Exceptions overruled.

Points for Discussion

a. **Classification of Property**

The common law often resolved disputes by categorizing found items as either lost or mislaid. The *Hannah* court assumed the brooch was lost, while the *McAvoy* court assumed the pocketbook was mislaid. Why? Wouldn't most people think the brooch was mislaid? And how do we know that the pocketbook didn't fall out of a customer's pocket as he bent over to reach another item on the table? Do the circumstances of a find prove whether an item was placed intentionally or dropped unintentionally? *See Hendle v. Stevens*, 586 N.E.2d 826 (Ill. App. Ct. 1992) (court was unable to determine whether currency found in loose soil was lost or mislaid).

b. **Basis for the Rule**

As a general rule, a mislaid chattel belongs to the owner of the *locus in quo*, not the finder. This gives the item to the person most likely to ensure its return to the true owner, as the *McAvoy* court noted. If the shopkeeper had rented his shop, who would have the best claim to the money, the shopkeeper or the landlord?

c. **Abandoned Property**

Suppose that O misses a key putt while playing golf, hurls his putter into a nearby pond, and shouts "I'll never play golf again!" O has abandoned his putter. *Abandonment* is the intentional relinquishment of a known right. *See, e.g., C & H Mfg., LLC v. Harlan County Indus. Dev. Authority, Inc.*, 600 S.W.3d 740 (Ky. Ct.

App. 2020) (company abandoned manufacturing equipment); *Zephier v. Agate*, 957 N.W.2d 866 (Minn. 2021) (ex-girlfriend did not abandon pet dog by arranging for ex-boyfriend to care for it while she relocated to California). Normally, abandoned property becomes the property of the finder. But some argue that all abandoned items should belong to the state. Which is the better view? Why?

The doctrine of abandonment generally does not apply to real property—although some interests in real property, such as easements and leases, can be lost by abandonment. *Pocono Springs Civic Ass'n, Inc. v. MacKenzie*, 667 A.2d 233 (Pa. Super. Ct. 1995). While title to real property cannot be lost by mere nonuse, it can be lost by adverse possession (Chapter 2) or through a foreclosure sale (Chapter 9).

d. Law of Shipwrecks

The discovery of sunken ships filled with treasure has occupied the imagination of countless Americans. Traditionally, either salvage law or finders law applies. Salvage law provides the finder with a reward, but not ownership; finders law gives the finder ownership of her discovery. In maritime cases, finders law applies only if the shipwreck is abandoned. These common law principles were partially superseded by the Abandoned Shipwreck Act of 1987, 43 U.S.C. §§ 2101–2106. Under this act, abandoned shipwrecks that are "embedded" within the three-mile territorial limit belong to the United States, which in turn relinquishes title to the appropriate state. Shipwrecks that are not embedded in this manner are still subject to the traditional common law rules. *See* M. June Harris, *Who Owns the Pot of Gold at the End of the Rainbow? A Review of the Impact of Cultural Property on Finders and Salvage Laws*, 14 Ariz. J. Int'l & Comp. L. 223 (1997); Sabrina L. McLaughlin, *Roots, Relics and Recovery: What Went Wrong with the Abandoned Shipwreck Act of 1987*, 19 Colum.-VLA J.L. & Arts 149 (1995).

Modern cases continue to grapple with the four-part classification system that began this section. But how can a court accurately determine whether a found item was lost, mislaid, abandoned, or concealed as treasure trove? The nature of the item and the location of the find are helpful facts, as you saw in *Hannah* and *McAvoy*. For example, people do not generally place money on the ground, and they rarely throw it away. Therefore, courts usually presume that money found on the floor is lost, not mislaid or abandoned. Using similar logic, a rare book discovered on a table is typically seen as mislaid, while a diamond ring found in a drawer is not deemed abandoned. In our next case, which facts support the court's conclusion that the property was mislaid?

Benjamin v. Lindner Aviation, Inc.

Supreme Court of Iowa

534 N.W.2d 400 (1995)

TERNUS, J.

... In April of 1992, State Central Bank became the owner of an airplane when the bank repossessed it from its prior owner who had defaulted on a loan. In August of that year, the bank took the plane to Lindner Aviation for a routine annual inspection. Benjamin worked for Lindner Aviation and did the inspection.

As part of the inspection, Benjamin removed panels from the underside of the wings. Although these panels were to be removed annually as part of the routine inspection, a couple of the screws holding the panel on the left wing were so rusty that Benjamin had to use a drill to remove them. Benjamin testified that the panel probably had not been removed for several years.

Inside the left wing Benjamin discovered two packets approximately four inches high and wrapped in aluminum foil. . . . The currency was predominately twenty-dollar bills with mint dates before the 1960s, primarily in the 1950s. The money smelled musty.

Benjamin took one packet to his jeep and then reported what he had found to his supervisor, offering to divide the money with him. However, the supervisor reported the discovery to the owner of Lindner Aviation, William Engle. Engle insisted that they contact the authorities and he called the Department of Criminal Investigation. The money was eventually turned over to the Keokuk police department.

Two days later, Benjamin filed an affidavit with the county auditor claiming that he was the finder of the currency under the provisions of Iowa Code chapter 644 (1991). Lindner Aviation and the bank also filed claims to the money. The notices required by chapter 644 were published and posted. *See* Iowa Code § 644.8 (1991). No one came forward within twelve months claiming to be the true owner of the money. *See id.* § 644.11 (if true owner does not claim property within twelve months, the right to the property vests in the finder).

Benjamin filed this declaratory judgment action against Lindner Aviation and the bank to establish his right to the property. . . . The district court held that chapter 644 applies only to "lost" property and the money here was mislaid property. The court awarded the money to the bank, holding that it was entitled to possession of the money to the exclusion of all but the true owner. The court also held that Benjamin was a "finder" within the meaning of chapter 644 and awarded him a ten percent finder's fee. *See id.* § 644.13 (a finder of lost property is entitled to ten percent of the value of the lost property as a reward).

Benjamin appealed. He claims that chapter 644 governs the disposition of all found property and any common law distinctions between various types of found property are no longer valid. He asserts alternatively that . . . the trial court should have found that the property was treasure trove or was lost or abandoned rather than mislaid, thereby entitling the finder to the property. . . .

Whether the money found by Benjamin was treasure trove or was mislaid, abandoned or lost property is a fact question. . . . Therefore, the trial court's finding that the money was mislaid is binding on us if supported by substantial evidence. . . .

We think there was substantial evidence to find that the currency discovered by Benjamin was mislaid property. . . .

The place where Benjamin found the money and the manner in which it was hidden are . . . important here. The bills were carefully tied and wrapped and then concealed in a location that was accessible only by removing screws and a panel. These circumstances support an inference that the money was placed there intentionally. This inference supports the conclusion that the money was mislaid. *Jackson v. Steinberg*, 200 P.2d 376, 378 (Or. 1948) (fact that $800 in currency was found concealed beneath the paper lining of a dresser indicates that money was intentionally concealed with intention of reclaiming it; therefore, property was mislaid, not lost). . . .

We also reject Benjamin's assertion that as a matter of law this money was abandoned property. Both logic and common sense suggest that it is unlikely someone would voluntarily part with over $18,000 with the intention of terminating his ownership. The location where this money was found is much more consistent with the conclusion that the owner of the property was placing the money there for safekeeping. . . .

Finally, we also conclude that the trial court was not obligated to decide that this money was treasure trove. Based on the dates of the currency, the money was no older than thirty-five years. The mint dates, the musty odor and the rusty condition of a few of the panel screws indicate that the money may have been hidden for some time. However, there was no evidence of the age of the airplane or the date of its last inspection. These facts may have shown that the money was concealed for a much shorter period of time. . . .

Because the money discovered by Benjamin was properly found to be mislaid property, it belongs to the owner of the premises where it was found. Mislaid property is entrusted to the owner of the premises where it is found rather than the finder of the property because it is assumed that the true owner may eventually recall where he has placed his property and return there to reclaim it. . . .

Type of airplane involved in case
Click here for larger photo

We think that the premises where the money was found is the airplane, not Lindner Aviation's hangar where the airplane happened to be parked when the money was discovered. The policy behind giving ownership of mislaid property to the owner of the premises where the property was mislaid supports this conclusion. If the true owner of the money attempts to locate it, he would initially look for the plane; it is unlikely he would begin his search by contacting businesses where the airplane might have been inspected. Therefore, we affirm the trial court's judgment that the bank, as the owner of the plane, has the right to possession of the property as against all but the true owner.

Benjamin claims that if he is not entitled to the money, he should be paid a ten percent finder's fee under section 644.13. The problem with this claim is that only the finder of "*lost*" goods, money, bank notes, and other things" is rewarded with a finder's fee under chapter 644. Iowa Code § 644.13 (1991). Because the property found by Benjamin was mislaid property, not lost property, section 644.13 does not apply here. The trial court erred in awarding Benjamin a finder's fee. . . .

Affirmed in part; reversed in part.

SNELL, JUSTICE (dissenting).

. . . After considering the four categories of found money, the majority decides that Benjamin found mislaid money. The result is that the bank gets all the money; Benjamin, the finder, gets nothing. Apart from the obvious unfairness in result, I believe this conclusion fails to come from logical analysis.

Mislaid property is property voluntarily put in a certain place by the owner who then overlooks or forgets where the property is. . . . The property here consisted of two packets of paper currency totaling $18,910, three to four inches high, wrapped in aluminum foil. Inside the foil, the paper currency, predominantly twenty dollar bills, was tied with string and wrapped in handkerchiefs. . . .

These facts satisfy the requirement that the property was voluntarily put in a certain place by the owner. But the second test for determining that property is mislaid is that the owner "overlooks or forgets where the property is.". . . I do not believe that the facts, logic, or common sense lead to a finding that this requirement is met. It is not likely or reasonable to suppose that a person would secrete $18,000 in an airplane wing and then forget where it was. . . .

The scenario unfolded in this case convinces me that the money found in the airplane wing was abandoned. Property is abandoned when the owner no longer wants to possess it. . . . The money had been there for years, possibly thirty. No owner had claimed it in that time. No claim was made by the owner after legally prescribed notice was given that it had been found. Thereafter, logic and the law support a finding that the owner has voluntarily relinquished all right, title, and interest in the property. Whether the money was abandoned due to its connection to illegal drug trafficking or is otherwise contraband property is a matter for speculation. In any event, abandonment by the true owner has legally occurred and been established.

I would hold that Benjamin is legally entitled to the entire amount of money that he found in the airplane wing as the owner of abandoned property.

Points for Discussion

a. Categories of Found Objects

Benjamin provides a nice summary of the four major classifications of found property. But the most important element distinguishing the four categories—the intention of the prior owner—is almost always unknown. Do the location and nature of the find provide reliable evidence of the owner's intent? *See* John V. Orth, *What's Wrong with the Law of Finders & How to Fix It*, 4 Green Bag 2d 391 (2001).

> **FYI**
>
> Perhaps Oscar Wilde understood the problem. In one of his most famous plays, the colorful Miss Prism states, "The manuscript unfortunately was abandoned. I use the word in the sense of lost or mislaid." *The Importance of Being Earnest*, Act II.

It is common for hikers to place objects they find lying along the trail (like hats, rings, and water bottles) on top of a rock or branch so they are readily visible to passersby. Have they changed the classification of these objects from lost to mislaid?

b. Exploring the Decision

Did the owner of the plane in *Benjamin* prevail because the money was mislaid? Or did the court label the money as mislaid in order for the owner to prevail? Given the number of variables (*type of property*: lost, mislaid, abandoned, treasure trove; *character of the finder*: invitee, trespasser, employee, resident owner; and *place of the find*: home, business, public place) and the equities inherent in differing fact patterns, courts have wide latitude in reaching a decision. Is society better served if a court mechanically applies the common law categories or if it takes a more practical, ends-oriented approach?

c. **Lost Pets**

Suppose X finds a lost dog. X cares for it and unsuccessfully tries to find the owner. One year later, the owner shows up and demands the dog. Under *Armory*, what result should follow? Ruling that the finder gets the dog, the Vermont Supreme Court reasoned in *Morgan v. Kroupa*, 702 A.2d 630, 633 (Vt. 1997):

> Recognizing . . . the substantial value that society places on domestic animals, it is proper that the law encourage finders to take in and care for lost pets. A stray dog obviously requires care and shelter, and left unattended could pose hazards to traffic, spread rabies, or exacerbate an animal overpopulation problem if unneutered. A rule of decision that made it difficult or impossible for the finder to keep the animal after many months or years of care and companionship might deter these salutary efforts, and would not be in the public interest.

One justice dissented, noting that an "unfortunate consequence of the Court's opinion will be to give those who operate the nation's black market in stolen pets an easier means to gain title and profit from pets that are not their own." *Id.* at 636. How would you rule?

d. **Found Meteorites**

In 2010, a meteorite crashed into the offices of two doctors in Lorton, Virginia, who gave it to the Smithsonian Museum of Natural History; they received a $5,000 payment in return. The doctors leased their office space and claimed that they, as finders of the meteorite, were its rightful owners. Their landlords argued that the meteorite belonged to them because it entered through the exterior of the building and embedded itself in the floor. Who has the best claim to the meteorite? How should finders' law address natural, unowned objects? Meteorites are extremely valuable to science, offering insights about the origin of the universe. The Lorton meteorite has been valued at $50,000.

e. **Employee Finders**

When an employee finds an object during the course of his employment (as in *Benjamin*), the court usually awards the item to the employer on the theory that the employee's actions were performed on behalf of the employer. Therefore, money found in a hotel room drawer by a maid was awarded to the hotel (*Jackson v. Steinberg*, 200 P.2d 376 (Or. 1948)); and a large envelope containing money found by a bank attendant on the floor of the safety deposit vault was awarded to the bank (*Dennis v.*

Northwestern Nat'l Bank, 81 N.W.2d 254 (Minn. 1957)). But what if the maid found the money while on her break? Or the attendant found the envelope in the bank lobby?

f. Treasure Trove

Under English common law, the crown owned all treasure trove. In the United States, a few states give treasure trove to the finder, essentially treating it as lost property. However, as a general rule, most courts hold that items embedded in the soil are the property of the landowner, as in *Elwes*. So why should treasure trove be treated differently? Most jurisdictions reject the treasure trove doctrine entirely and give such property to the owner of the land where it was found. *See, e.g., Corliss v. Wenner*, 34 P.3d 1100 (Idaho Ct. App. 2001).

g. Finders Problems

Who owns the items found in the problems below?

> (1) X buys a safe at an auction and asks Y to sell it at a weekend garage sale. While Y is showing the safe, he finds a wad of cash stuffed between the inner lining and the outer metal wall.
>
> (2) C, a contractor, agrees to demolish D's building and to remove all resulting debris. After demolition, while C is moving debris into a dump truck, he discovers valuable bearer bonds inside part of an old wall.
>
> (3) Farmer F employs two neighborhood boys to clean his barn. Underneath the chicken coop, the boys discover an old, rusted can filled with silver dollars.
>
> (4) G rents an apartment from H. G finds a sack filled with uncut diamonds wedged underneath the bottom shelf in one closet.

h. Statutory Approaches

Over one-third of the states have adopted some form of lost property statute. The typical statute requires the finder to: (1) notify the police or other government officials; (2) deposit the found article with them; and (3) publish notice of the find. If the owner fails to claim the property within a certain period (commonly 6–12 months), title is irrevocably vested in the finder. What advantages do these statutes have over the common law approach? *See generally* Cal. Civil Code §§ 2080–2080.9; Mass. Gen. Laws ch. 134, §§ 1–7.

i. Finders Keepers?

The old adage "finders keepers, losers weepers" is a simple and predictable rule. It avoids the ambiguities inherent in determining the status of the found article and provides concrete encouragement for finders. Is this the best approach?

C. Adverse Possession of Chattels

Suppose that eight-year-old H secretly takes a small painting from his friend F's garage. Twenty years later, H becomes a successful businessman and places the painting in the lobby of his office building. H occasionally lends the painting to museums for display. H sells the painting for $45,000 to B, who places it in his home. While visiting B, F's parents see the stolen painting and demand its return. Is B obligated to return the painting?

Title to personal property may be obtained by adverse possession. The basic concept is the same as for adverse possession of real property: the statute of limitations bars the prior owner from bringing an action to recover possession, thus vesting title in the adverse claimant. But courts often apply somewhat different rules to adverse possession of personal property, as the following cases illustrate.

Our next case arose when a father paid $10 to buy a used violin for his six-year-old daughter. He did not know that the violin had been stolen from its true owner—and was quite valuable.

Reynolds v. Bagwell

Supreme Court of Oklahoma

198 P.2d 215 (1948)

GIBSON, J.

On the 10th day of March, 1938, defendant in error, as plaintiff, instituted this action in replevin against plaintiff in error, as defendant, for the recovery of a violin, violin bow and violin case. It is alleged in plaintiff's petition that the property was stolen from plaintiff in January 1933, and that in March 1938 plaintiff discovered it in the possession of defendant and made demand therefor which was refused. It is further alleged that defendant's possession, acquired immediately after the theft, was not open, notorious and in good faith and that it was sought to conceal the identity of the violin by wilful alteration of its appearance. For answer defendant filed general denial and further alleged that he purchased the property in good faith and for value, that same had been in his possession without concealment for more than five years and

> **FYI**
>
> The violin at issue was made by Gennaro Gagliano, a famous craftsman working in Naples during the 1700s. Plaintiff Bagwell, a music professor at Oklahoma City University, had purchased the violin for $1,800. Today a Gagliano violin is worth more than $200,000.

plead the statute of limitation as a bar to plaintiff's action. The case was tried to a jury, resulting in a verdict for plaintiff upon which judgment was rendered.

Plaintiff's ownership of the property, the theft thereof, and defendant's purchase thereof and possession for more than the statutory period of limitation, are recognized facts. The sole question involved is whether the statute of limitation is a bar to plaintiff's action.

The applicable statute, 12 O.S. 1941 § 95, prescribes the period of two years. Construing the statute, in *Shelby v. Shaner*, 28 Okl. 605, 115 P. 785, we declared:

> The statute of limitations as to personal property, though stolen, when held in good faith for value, openly and notoriously, runs in favor of such adverse possession so as to bar a recovery by the true owner after the expiration of two years.

And in *Adams et al. v. Coon et al.*, 36 Okl. 644, 129 P. 851, we said:

> The statute of limitations, as to lost personal property, or personal property in the hands of a thief, begins to run from the time of the wrongful taking or possession, and not from the time when the owner first had knowledge thereof, provided there was no fraud or attempt at concealment; and if such fraud or concealment exists it must, in order to avail the owner, be the act of the thief or finder of the property.

The possession of defendant having begun more than two years before the action was instituted the statute is a bar unless there has been fraud or concealment. There is no evidence of fraud other than might be reflected in the fact of concealment, if any. . . .

. . . [A] similar case is *United States v. One Stradivarius Kieserwetter Violin*, 2 Cir., 197 F. 157, 158, [where the court stated:]

> The concealment which prevents the running of the statute must be some act which places the property in a situation which tends to prevent its discovery. Something must be done which prevents or hinders the governmental authorities from obtaining, in the exercise of ordinary diligence, information concerning the property. Whether a fraudulent motive must in all cases be shown need not be determined. But there must always be acts of an affirmative character. Mere failure to give information is not enough. Silence with or without knowledge is not concealment.

The evidence reflects that the violin was purchased by an established dealer in musical instruments in the city of Norman and by him sold to defendant for use of his daughter in taking violin lessons; that it was kept in the sitting room of the home; carried back and forth and used by the daughter in taking lessons from several music teachers. There is no evidence of any intent to secrete the same from the view of any one. The only fact in evidence that could be held indicative of an intent to conceal the violin, and to any degree effective as such, is that the original varnish thereon had been removed resulting in a radical change in the appearance. Emphasis is placed on the removal of the original varnish as an act of concealment. According to the evidence this change was not made until three or four years after defendant acquired the violin and it follows that such act if otherwise sufficient could not toll the statute that had already run.

Reversed with direction to dismiss.

Points for Discussion

a. **Traditional Rule**

Reynolds illustrates the traditional common law approach to adverse possession of chattels. What elements did the court cite as necessary? In most states, the required elements are quite similar to those applicable to real property: the claimant's possession must be actual, exclusive, open and notorious, hostile, and continuous for the statutory period. *See, e.g., Hermitage Newark, LLC v. Arkansas Sand Co.*, 599 S.W.3d 654 (Ark. Ct. App. 2020). But some courts modify the traditional adverse possession standard when dealing with chattels because of an important distinction: chattels are movable, while land is not. Why is this distinction relevant?

b. **Open and Notorious**

Many jurisdictions require the adverse claimant to possess the chattel in an open and notorious manner. In *Reynolds,* the defendant's daughter kept the violin in the sitting room of her home, and only took it outside when going to music lessons. Was this open and notorious? Is this element satisfied when the possessor: (1) uses the item as an ordinary owner would; (2) displays it regularly in a public forum; or (3) uses it in a way that would notify the owner of the location of his property?

c. **Good Faith**

Reynolds asserted that he bought the violin "in good faith and for value," without knowledge of the theft. If he knew about the theft at the time, would the court have ruled differently? What if he had stolen the violin?

d. **Concealment**

The *Reynolds* court addressed a major barrier to the recovery of stolen chattels: concealment. Concealment is not relevant to real property because land cannot be hidden or moved. But a stolen chattel may be kept in a location that provides little, if any, notice to the true owner. What constitutes concealment? And why does it stop the running of the statute of limitations? In *Reynolds*, the original varnish on the violin had been removed, causing a "radical change in the appearance." Why wasn't this concealment? What if the defendant had painted the violin pink?

e. **Statute of Limitations**

Oklahoma law provided a two-year limitations period for recovering possession of personal property, but a 15-year period for real property. Most states require an action for the recovery of personal property to be brought within two to six years after the claim accrues, a period usually shorter than that applicable to real property. Why is the period for personal property shorter?

f. Policy Perspectives

As you saw in Chapter 2, a number of policies have been suggested to justify adverse possession of real property: avoiding stale claims, correcting title defects, encouraging the productive use of property, and protecting personhood. To what extent do these policies apply to chattels? Are other policies more relevant?

g. Tacking

Suppose that Reynolds kept the violin for only one year and then sold it to F, who kept it for an additional year. May F add both periods of possession together in order to satisfy the two-year limitations period? The weight of authority in the United States allows tacking as long as there is privity between the possessors. But some courts refuse to permit tacking. They usually reason either that (1) each transfer by an individual without title constitutes a separate conversion so the period begins anew or (2) tacking would increase the difficulty that the owner has in finding her property. In *San Francisco Credit Clearing House v. Wells*, 239 P. 319, 322 (Cal. 1925), the court disallowed tacking, and explained that:

> [P]ersonal property . . . is of an ambulatory and movable character, and easy of concealment. Less baneful consequences would probably flow from a rule that would require a fixedness or stability of possession before an owner of property, without fault on his part, could be deprived of its use and enjoyment than that which would follow the confusion of "tacking" the possessions of many holders of various durations, residing in various neighborhoods and with the situation further embarrassed by the difficulties of identification.

The traditional adverse possession standard may make it difficult for an owner to recover his chattel, as *Reynolds* illustrates. The main problem is that the limitations period may expire before the owner learns where the missing chattel is located. Accordingly, many states have modified the common law approach by adopting a *discovery rule*: the limitations period begins to run only when the owner discovers (or reasonably should have discovered) where the chattel is. As you read our next case, consider whether this rule strikes the right balance between an owner's right to recover her property and the possessor's right to repose.

O'Keeffe v. Snyder

Supreme Court of New Jersey

416 A.2d 862 (1980)

POLLOCK, J.

This is an appeal from an order of the Appellate Division granting summary judgment to plaintiff, Georgia O'Keeffe, against defendant, Barry Snyder, d/b/a Princeton Gallery of Fine Art, for replevin of three small pictures painted by O'Keeffe. *O'Keeffe v. Snyder*, 170 N.J. Super. 75, 405 A.2d 840 (1979). In her complaint, filed in March, 1976, O'Keeffe alleged she was the owner of the paintings and that they were stolen from a New York art gallery in 1946. Snyder asserted he was a purchaser for value of the paintings, he had title by adverse possession, and O'Keeffe's action was barred by the expiration of the six-year period of limitations provided by N.J.S.A. 2A:14–1 pertaining to an action in replevin. Snyder impleaded third party defendant, Ulrich A. Frank, from whom Snyder purchased the paintings in 1975 for $35,000.

The trial court granted summary judgment for Snyder on the ground that O'Keeffe's action was barred because it was not commenced within six years of the alleged theft. The Appellate Division reversed and entered judgment for O'Keeffe. A majority of that court concluded that the paintings were stolen, the defenses of expiration of the statute of limitations and title by adverse possession were identical, and Snyder had not proved the elements of adverse possession. Consequently, the majority ruled that O'Keeffe could still enforce her right to possession of the paintings.

The dissenting judge stated that the appropriate measurement of the period of limitation was not by analogy to adverse possession, but by application of the "discovery rule" pertaining to some statutes of limitation. He concluded that the six-year period of limitations commenced when O'Keeffe knew or should have known who unlawfully possessed the paintings, and that the matter should be remanded to determine if and when that event had occurred. . . .

I.

O'Keeffe contended the paintings were stolen in 1946 from a gallery, An American Place. The gallery was operated by her late husband, the famous photographer Alfred Stieglitz. . . .

In 1946, Stieglitz arranged an exhibit which included an O'Keeffe painting, identified as Cliffs. According to O'Keeffe, one day in March, 1946, she and Stieglitz discovered Cliffs was missing from the wall of the exhibit. O'Keeffe estimates the value of the painting at the time of the alleged theft to have been about $150.

About two weeks later, O'Keeffe noticed that two other paintings, Seaweed and Fragments, were missing from a storage room at An American Place. She did not tell anyone, even Stieglitz, about the missing paintings, since she did not want to upset him. . . .

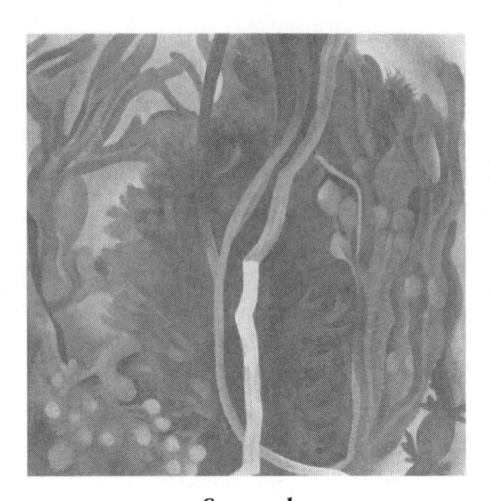

Seaweed
Click here for larger photo

There was no evidence of a break and entry at An American Place on the dates when O'Keeffe discovered the disappearance of her paintings. Neither Stieglitz nor O'Keeffe reported them missing to the New York Police Department or any other law enforcement agency. Apparently the paintings were uninsured, and O'Keeffe did not seek reimbursement from an insurance company. Similarly, neither O'Keeffe nor Stieglitz advertised the loss of the paintings in Art News or any other publication. Nonetheless, they discussed it with associates in the art world and later O'Keeffe mentioned the loss to the director of the Art Institute of Chicago, but she did not ask him to do anything because "it wouldn't have been my way." O'Keeffe does not contend that Frank or Snyder had actual knowledge of the alleged theft.

Stieglitz died in the summer of 1946, and O'Keeffe explains she did not pursue her efforts to locate the paintings because she was settling his estate. In 1947, she retained the services of Doris Bry to help settle the estate. Bry urged O'Keeffe to report the loss of the paintings, but O'Keeffe declined because "they never got anything back by reporting it." Finally, in 1972, O'Keeffe authorized Bry to report the theft to the Art Dealers Association of America, Inc., which maintains for its members a registry of stolen paintings. The record does not indicate whether such a registry existed at the time the paintings disappeared.

In September, 1975, O'Keeffe learned that the paintings were in the Andrew Crispo Gallery in New York on consignment from Bernard Danenberg Galleries. On February 11, 1976, O'Keeffe discovered that Ulrich A. Frank had sold the paintings to Barry Snyder, d/b/a Princeton Gallery of Fine Art. She demanded their return and, following Snyder's refusal, instituted this action for replevin.

Frank traces his possession of the paintings to his father, Dr. Frank, who died in 1968. . . . Frank does not know how his father acquired the paintings, but he recalls seeing them in his father's apartment in New Hampshire as early as 1941–1943, a period that precedes the alleged theft. Consequently, Frank's factual contentions are inconsistent with O'Keeffe's allegation of theft. Until 1965, Dr. Frank occasionally lent the paintings to Ulrich Frank. In 1965, Dr. and Mrs. Frank formally gave the paintings to Ulrich Frank, who kept them in his residences in Yardley, Pennsylvania and Princeton, New Jersey. In 1968, he exhibited anonymously Cliffs and Fragments in a one day art show in the Jewish Community Center in Trenton. . . .

Frank claims continuous possession of the paintings through his father for over thirty years and admits selling the paintings to Snyder. Snyder and Frank do not trace their provenance, or history of possession of the paintings, back to O'Keeffe.

As indicated, Snyder moved for summary judgment on the theory that O'Keeffe's action was barred by the statute of limitations and title had vested in Frank by adverse possession. For purposes of his motion, Snyder conceded that the paintings had been stolen. On her cross motion, O'Keeffe urged that the paintings were stolen, the statute of limitations had not run, and title to the paintings remained in her. . . .

III.

Our decision begins with the principle that, generally speaking, if the paintings were stolen, the thief acquired no title and could not transfer good title to others regardless of their good faith and ignorance of the theft. . . . Proof of theft would advance O'Keeffe's right to possession of the paintings absent other considerations such as expiration of the statute of limitations.

Another issue that may become relevant at trial is whether Frank or his father acquired a "voidable title" to the paintings under N.J.S.A. 12A:2–403(1). That section, part of the Uniform Commercial Code (U.C.C.), does not change the basic principle that a mere possessor cannot transfer good title. . . . Nonetheless, the U.C.C. permits a person with voidable title to transfer good title to a good faith purchaser for value in certain circumstances. . . . If the facts developed at trial merit application of that section, then Frank may have transferred good title to Snyder, thereby providing a defense to O'Keeffe's action. . . .

> **What's That?**
>
> The Uniform Commercial Code is one of several uniform acts that seek to harmonize the law of sales in the United States. The UCC was drafted by a group of attorneys, judges, and law professors as a set of laws recommended for adoption by states. It primarily deals with personal property transactions. Each state is free to enact all or part of its provisions; it has been enacted in some form by all 50 states.

On this appeal, the critical legal question is when O'Keeffe's cause of action accrued. The fulcrum on which the outcome turns is the statute of limitations in

N.J.S.A. 2A:14–1, which provides that an action for replevin of goods or chattels must be commenced within six years after the accrual of the cause of action.

The trial court found that O'Keeffe's cause of action accrued on the date of the alleged theft, March, 1946, and concluded that her action was barred. The Appellate Division found that an action might have accrued more than six years before the date of suit if possession by the defendant or his predecessors satisfied the elements of adverse possession. As indicated, the Appellate Division concluded that Snyder had not established those elements and that the O'Keeffe action was not barred by the statute of limitations. . . .

IV.

. . . The purpose of a statute of limitations is to "stimulate to activity and punish negligence" and "promote repose by giving security and stability to human affairs". *Wood v. Carpenter,* 101 U.S. 135 (1879); Tevis v. Tevis, 79 N.J. 422, A.2d 1189 (1979); *Fernandi v. Strully,* 35 N.J. 434, 173 A.2d 277 (1961). A statute of limitations achieves those purposes by barring a cause of action after the statutory period. . . .

To avoid harsh results from the mechanical application of the statute, the courts have developed a concept known as the discovery rule. *Lopez v. Swyer,* 62 N.J. 267, 300 A.2d 563 (1973). . . . The discovery rule provides that, in an appropriate case, a cause of action will not accrue until the injured party discovers, or by exercise of reasonable diligence and intelligence should have discovered, facts which form the basis of a cause of action. *Burd v. New Jersey Telephone Company,* 76 N.J. 284, 386 A.2d 1310 (1978). The rule is essentially a principle of equity, the purpose of which is to mitigate unjust results that otherwise might flow from strict adherence to a rule of law.

This Court first announced the discovery rule in *Fernandi,* 35 N.J. at 434, 173 A.2d 277. In *Fernandi,* a wing nut was left in a patient's abdomen following surgery and was not discovered for three years. The majority held that fairness and justice mandated that the statute of limitations should not have commenced running until the plaintiff knew or had reason to know of the presence of the foreign object in her body. The discovery rule has since been extended to other areas of medical malpractice. . . .

Similarly, we conclude that the discovery rule applies to an action for replevin of a painting under N.J.S.A. 2A:14–1. O'Keeffe's cause of action accrued when she first knew, or reasonably should have known through the exercise of due diligence, of the cause of action, including the identity of the possessor of the paintings. . . .

In determining whether O'Keeffe is entitled to the benefit of the discovery rule, the trial court should consider, among others, the following issues: (1) whether O'Keeffe used due diligence to recover the paintings at the time of the alleged theft and thereafter; (2) whether at the time of the alleged theft there was an effective method, other than talking to her colleagues, for O'Keeffe to alert the art world; and (3) whether registering paintings with the Art Dealers Association of America,

Inc. or any other organization would put a reasonably prudent purchaser of art on constructive notice that someone other than the possessor was the true owner.

V.

... To establish title by adverse possession to chattels, the rule of law has been that the possession must be hostile, actual, visible, exclusive, and continuous....

[P]roblems with the requirement of visible, open, and notorious possession readily come to mind. For example, if jewelry is stolen from a municipality in one county in New Jersey, it is unlikely that the owner would learn that someone is openly wearing that jewelry in another county or even in the same municipality. Open and visible possession of personal property, such as jewelry, may not be sufficient to put the original owner on actual or constructive notice of the identity of the possessor.

The problem is even more acute with works of art. Like many kinds of personal property, works of art are readily moved and easily concealed. O'Keeffe argues that nothing short of public display should be sufficient to alert the true owner and start the statute running. Although there is merit in that contention from the perspective of the original owner, the effect is to impose a heavy burden on the purchasers of paintings who wish to enjoy the paintings in the privacy of their homes....

The limited record before us provides a brief glimpse into the arcane world of sales of art, where paintings worth vast sums of money sometimes are bought without inquiry about their provenance. There does not appear to be a reasonably available method for an owner of art to record the ownership or theft of paintings. Similarly, there are no reasonable means readily available to a purchaser to ascertain the provenance of a painting. It may be time for the art world to establish a means by which a good faith purchaser may reasonably obtain the provenance of a painting. An efficient registry of original works of art might better serve the interests of artists, owners of art, and bona fide purchasers than the law of adverse possession with all of its uncertainties.... Although we cannot mandate the initiation of a registration system, we can develop a rule for the commencement and running of the statute of limitations that is more responsive to the needs of the art world than the doctrine of adverse possession.

> **FYI**
>
> In 1976, the International Foundation for Art Research established the Art Loss Register to help deter international art theft. The ALR is now the world's largest private database for stolen art. There are many other registries, such as the FBI's National Stolen Art File, a computerized index of stolen art and cultural properties.

We are persuaded that the introduction of equitable considerations through the discovery rule provides a more satisfactory response than the doctrine of adverse possession. The discovery rule shifts the emphasis from the conduct of the possessor to the conduct of the owner. The focus of the inquiry will no longer be whether the possessor has met the tests of adverse possession, but whether the owner has acted with due diligence in pursuing his or her personal property.

For example, under the discovery rule, if an artist diligently seeks the recovery of a lost or stolen painting, but cannot find it or discover the identity of the possessor, the statute of limitations will not begin to run. The rule permits an artist who uses reasonable efforts to report, investigate, and recover a painting to preserve the rights of title and possession. . . .

By diligently pursuing their goods, owners may prevent the statute of limitations from running. The meaning of due diligence will vary with the facts of each case, including the nature and value of the personal property. For example, with respect to jewelry of moderate value, it may be sufficient if the owner reports the theft to the police. With respect to art work of greater value, it may be reasonable to expect an owner to do more. In practice, our ruling should contribute to more careful practices concerning the purchase of art. . . .

Our ruling not only changes the requirements for acquiring title to personal property after an alleged unlawful taking, but also shifts the burden of proof at trial. Under the doctrine of adverse possession, the burden is on the possessor to prove the elements of adverse possession. . . . Under the discovery rule, the burden is on the owner as the one seeking the benefit of the rule to establish facts that would justify deferring the beginning of the period of limitations. . . .

We reverse the judgment of the Appellate Division in favor of O'Keeffe and remand the matter for trial in accordance with this opinion.

Points for Discussion

a. Use of Precedent

The *O'Keeffe* court used medical malpractice cases as precedent for applying a discovery rule to the adverse possession of chattels. What does a nut "left in a patient's abdomen following surgery" have to do with stolen paintings? What factors are similar in these cases?

b. Owner's Diligence

The discovery rule shifts the focus from the possessor's conduct to the owner's conduct. Rather than considering whether the adverse possessor has met a list of requirements, this approach asks whether the owner has pursued her property with due diligence. What facts suggest that O'Keeffe will meet this standard at trial? What facts harm her position?

c. Two Innocent Parties

The *O'Keeffe* court stated that the discovery rule becomes "a vehicle for transporting equitable considerations into the statute of limitations for replevin." What does this mean? How should the law choose between an innocent victim of theft and an innocent purchaser for value? The Oklahoma Supreme Court adopted the discovery rule in *In re 1973 John Deere 4030 Tractor*, 816 P.2d 1126 (Okla. 1991) for policy reasons similar to those expressed by the *O'Keeffe* court, effectively overruling its earlier decision in *Reynolds v. Bagwell*. See generally Ashton Hawkins et al., *A Tale of Two Innocents: Creating an Equitable Balance Between the Rights of Former Owners and Good Faith Purchasers of Stolen Art*, 64 Fordham L. Rev. 49 (1995).

d. Applying U.C.C. § 2–403

When the court remanded the case for trial, it highlighted an important issue: whether Frank or his father had *voidable title* to the paintings. Uniform Commercial Code § 2–403 provides:

> (1) A purchaser of goods acquires all title which his transferor had or had power to transfer except that a purchaser of a limited interest acquires rights only to the extent of the interest purchased. A person with voidable title has power to transfer a good title to a good faith purchaser for value. When goods have been delivered under a transaction of purchase the purchaser has such power even though
>
>   (a) the transferor was deceived as to the identity of the purchaser, or
>
>   (b) the delivery was in exchange for a check which is later dishonored, or
>
>   (c) it was agreed that the transaction was to be a "cash sale", or
>
>   (d) the delivery was procured through fraud punishable as larcenous under the criminal law.
>
> (2) Any entrusting of possession of goods to a merchant who deals in goods of that kind gives him power to transfer all rights of the entruster to a buyer in ordinary course of business.
>
> (3) "Entrusting" includes any delivery and any acquiescence in retention of possession regardless of any condition expressed between the parties to the delivery or acquiescence and regardless of whether the procurement of the entrusting or the possessor's disposition of the goods have been such as to be larcenous under the criminal law.

Under § 2–403, what if O'Keeffe gave the paintings to Stieglitz for safekeeping and Stieglitz secretly sold them to Frank's father? Would the fact that Stieglitz was a gallery owner be relevant? Would it make any difference if Stieglitz had stolen the paintings?

e. **Good Faith Purchaser**

A good faith purchaser (also referred to as a *bona fide* purchaser) is one who gives valuable consideration for an item without knowledge of adverse claims. As you will see, the law provides added protection for the good faith purchaser in a number of different contexts. *See, e.g., Lindholm v. Brant,* 925 A.2d 1048 (Conn. 2007) (defendant who paid $2.9 million to art dealer for Andy Warhol painting was a good faith purchaser and thus owned the painting). This reflects a strong public policy in favor of encouraging a vibrant market and thereby enhancing the flow of goods. How does U.C.C. § 2–403 provide confidence to purchasers?

f. **Void v. Voidable Title**

Under U.C.C. § 2–403, who owns the chattel in each situation below?

> (1) X steals an antique chair from his neighbor Y, and places it on Craigslist. X sells the chair to an unknowing B for $150.
>
> (2) M purchases an historic table from O, and immediately sells the table to P for a nice profit. Unfortunately, M's account is overdrawn and his check to O bounces.
>
> (3) D takes his Elizabethan bureau to a furniture store to be repaired. The salesperson at the store makes a mistake and sells the bureau to an interested customer, C.

g. **"Demand-and-Refusal" Approach**

In *Reynolds*, the statute of limitations ran from the time of the theft. In *O'Keeffe*, the limitations period began only when the owner discovered, or by exercise of reasonable diligence should have discovered, the location of the missing item. New York embraces a different rule, commonly known as the "demand-and-refusal" rule. Under this approach, the statute is tolled until the owner demands the return of her property from a good faith purchaser. *See Solomon R. Guggenheim Foundation v. Lubell,* 569 N.E.2d 426 (N.Y. 1991). Note that this rule does not require analysis of the owner's diligence. Which approach gives the greatest protection to the original owner? Which approach do you favor?

h. **Looted Art**

Courts have struggled with applying the discovery rule to art looted by the Nazis. Many suits are barred by statutes of limitations because the pieces were displayed in galleries or sold at public auction. *See, e.g., Orkin v. Taylor,* 487 F.3d 734 (9th Cir. 2007) (actress Elizabeth Taylor made a highly publicized purchase of a Van Gogh, loaned it to museums, and tried to sell it at public auction); *Dunbar v. Seger-Thomschitz,* 638 F. Supp. 2d 659 (E.D. La. 2009) (defendant's mother registered her purchase and loaned the painting to museums).

The federal government has directed states to use "good faith efforts" to return such looted artworks to their rightful owners, but has not mandated changes to the discovery rule. When California adopted a statute that extended the discovery period until 2010 for art taken during the Holocaust, the Ninth Circuit held that it was unconstitutional because it conflicted with the federal government's power to conduct foreign affairs. *Von Saher v. Norton Simon Museum of Art at Pasadena*, 592 F.3d 954, 957 (9th Cir. 2009). As a result, in states using the discovery rule the statute of limitations runs from the point at which a person would have reasonable notice of the artwork's current holder. For an interesting analysis of the barriers to recovery, see Jennifer Anglim Kreder, *Fighting Corruption of the Historical Record: Nazi-Looted Art Litigation*, 61 U. Kan. L. Rev. 75 (2012).

i. Aftermath of *O'Keeffe*

Shortly after the court remanded the case, the parties settled. "Seaweed" went to O'Keeffe, "Fragment of the Rancho de Taos Church" went to Snyder, and "Cliffs: My Backyard" was sold to pay attorneys' fees. O'Keeffe died six years later at the age of 98. Her ashes were spread over Perdernal Mountain, New Mexico—a distant mesa she viewed each day from her home. The Georgia O'Keeffe Museum in Santa Fe is dedicated to preserving her artistic legacy.

D. Gifts

1. *Inter Vivos* Gift

Have you ever received a birthday gift from a friend? How did you know that it was a legally enforceable transfer? What if your friend wanted the gift back a week later because she needed the money? Or because you had an argument?

The law governing gifts is surprisingly complex. Broadly speaking, a *gift* is the immediate transfer of property rights from the *donor* (the person making the gift) to the *donee* (the person receiving the gift), without any payment or other consideration. Our first type is the *inter vivos gift*—the ordinary gift of personal property that one living person makes to another, like the gift at a birthday party. The essential elements for a valid *inter vivos* gift are donative intent, delivery, and acceptance.

> **What's That?**
>
> An *inter vivos gift* is the usual type of gift made during the donor's lifetime. In contrast, a *testamentary gift* is effective only after the donor dies; it is usually made by a will.

- *Donative intent*: The donor must intend to make an immediate transfer of property.
- *Delivery*: The property must be delivered to the donee, so that the donor parts with dominion and control.
- *Acceptance*: The donee must accept the property—although acceptance of a valuable item is usually presumed.

Because no consideration is paid, no contract arises between the parties. Therefore, a promise to make a gift in the future is unenforceable without some form of consideration. Generally, an *inter vivos* gift cannot be revoked.

Suppose B wants to give her painting to C, but also wants to retain possession of the painting during her lifetime. How should we describe B's state of mind? Does she intend to give C an interest in the painting *now*? Or does she intend to give C an interest in the *future* when she dies? These questions are important because a valid gift arises only if B intends to give C an interest immediately. A gift intended to take effect in the future—for example, when the donor dies—is invalid.

In our next case, a father wanted to give his son a birthday present: a valuable painting. But the father kept the painting in his home until he died decades later. As you read the case, consider which facts suggest that the father intended to make an immediate gift and which facts indicate otherwise.

Gruen v. Gruen

Court of Appeals of New York

496 N.E.2d 869 (1986)

Simons, J.

Plaintiff commenced this action seeking a declaration that he is the rightful owner of a painting which he alleges his father, now deceased, gave to him. He concedes that he has never had possession of the painting but asserts that his father made a valid gift of the title in 1963 reserving a life estate for himself. His father retained possession of the painting until he died in 1980. Defendant, plaintiff's stepmother, has the painting now and has refused plaintiff's requests that she turn it over to him. She contends that the purported gift was testamentary in nature and invalid insofar as the formalities of a will were not met or, alternatively, that a donor may not make a valid inter vivos gift of a chattel and retain a life estate with a complete right of possession. Following a seven-day nonjury trial, Special Term found that plaintiff had failed to establish any of the elements of an inter vivos gift and that in any event an attempt by a donor to retain a present possessory life estate in a chattel invalidated a purported gift of it. The Appellate Division held that a valid gift may be made reserving a life estate and, finding the elements of a gift established in this case, it reversed and remitted the matter for a determination of value (104 A.D.2d 171, 488 N.Y.S.2d 401). That determination has now been made and defendant appeals directly to this court, pursuant to CPLR 5601(d), from the subsequent final judgment entered in Supreme Court awarding plaintiff $2,500,000 in damages representing the value of the painting, plus interest. We now affirm.

> **What's That?**
>
> The owner of a *life estate* has title to property for a period equal to the length of one particular life. At death, the life estate ends, and the holder of the future interest takes possession. If the future interest holder is a transferee (that is, someone other than the person who created the life estate), his interest is called a *remainder*.

Schloss Kammer am Attersee II
Click here for larger photo

The subject of the dispute is a work entitled "Schloss Kammer am Attersee II" painted by a noted Austrian modernist, Gustav Klimt. It was purchased by plaintiff's father, Victor Gruen, in 1959 for $8,000. On April 1, 1963 the elder Gruen, a successful architect with offices and residences in both New York City and Los Angeles during most of the time involved in this action, wrote a letter to plaintiff, then an undergraduate student at Harvard, stating that he was giving him the Klimt painting for his birthday but that he wished to retain the possession of it for his lifetime. This letter is not in evidence, apparently because plaintiff destroyed it on instructions from his father. Two other letters were received, however, one dated May 22, 1963 and the other April 1, 1963. Both had been dictated by Victor Gruen and sent together to plaintiff on or about May 22, 1963. The letter dated May 22, 1963 reads as follows:

> Dear Michael:
>
> I wrote you at the time of your birthday about the gift of the painting by Klimt.
>
> Now my lawyer tells me that because of the existing tax laws, it was wrong to mention in that letter that I want to use the painting as long as I live. Though I still want to use it, this should not appear in the letter. I am enclosing, therefore, a new letter and I ask you to send the old one back to me so that it can be destroyed.
>
> I know this is all very silly, but the lawyer and our accountant insist that they must have in their possession copies of a letter which will serve the purpose of making it possible for you, once I die, to get this picture without having to pay inheritance taxes on it.
>
> Love,
>
> s/Victor.

Enclosed with this letter was a substitute gift letter, dated April 1, 1963, which stated:

> Dear Michael:
>
> The 21st birthday, being an important event in life, should be celebrated accordingly. I therefore wish to give you as a present the oil painting by Gustav Klimt of Schloss Kammer which now hangs in the New York living room. You know that Lazette and I bought it some 5 or 6 years ago, and you always told us how much you liked it.
>
> Happy birthday again.
>
> Love,
>
> s/Victor.

Plaintiff never took possession of the painting nor did he seek to do so. Except for a brief period between 1964 and 1965 when it was on loan to art exhibits and when restoration work was performed on it, the painting remained in his father's possession, moving with him from New York City to Beverly Hills and finally to Vienna, Austria, where Victor Gruen died on February 14, 1980. Following Victor's death plaintiff requested possession of the Klimt painting and when defendant refused, he commenced this action.

The issues framed for appeal are whether a valid inter vivos gift of a chattel may be made where the donor has reserved a life estate in the chattel and the donee never has had physical possession of it before the donor's death and, if it may, which factual findings on the elements of a valid inter vivos gift more nearly comport with the weight of the evidence in this case, those of Special Term or those of the Appellate Division. The latter issue requires application of two general rules. First, to make a valid inter vivos gift there must exist the intent on the part of the donor to make a present transfer; delivery of the gift, either actual or constructive to the donee; and acceptance by the donee. . . . Second, the proponent of a gift has the burden of proving each of these elements by clear and convincing evidence. . . .

Donative Intent

There is an important distinction between the intent with which an inter vivos gift is made and the intent to make a gift by will. An inter vivos gift requires that the donor intend to make an irrevocable present transfer of ownership; if the intention is to make a testamentary disposition effective only after death, the gift is invalid unless made by will (*see, McCarthy v. Pieret*, 281 N.Y. 407, 409, 24 N.E.2d 102; *Gannon v. McGuire*, 160 N.Y. 476, 481, 55 N.E. 7; *Martin v. Funk*, 75 N.Y. 134, 137–138).

Defendant contends that the trial court was correct in finding that Victor did not intend to transfer any present interest in the painting to plaintiff in 1963 but only expressed an intention that plaintiff was to get the painting upon his death. The evidence is all but conclusive, however, that Victor intended to transfer ownership of the painting to plaintiff in 1963 but to retain a life estate in it and that he did, therefore, effectively transfer a remainder interest in the painting to plaintiff at that time. Although the original letter was not in evidence, testimony of its contents was received along with the substitute gift letter and its covering letter dated May 22, 1963. The three letters should be considered together as a single instrument . . . and when they are they unambiguously establish that Victor Gruen intended to make a present gift of title to the painting at that time. But there was other evidence for after 1963 Victor made several statements orally and in writing indicating that he had previously given plaintiff the painting and that plaintiff owned it. Victor Gruen retained possession of the property, insured it, allowed others to exhibit it and made necessary repairs to it but those acts are not inconsistent with his retention of a life estate. . . . Victor's failure to file a gift tax return on the transaction was partially explained by allegedly erroneous legal advice he received, and while that omission sometimes may indicate that the donor had no intention of making a present gift, it does not necessarily do so and it is not dispositive in this case.

Defendant contends that even if a present gift was intended, Victor's reservation of a lifetime interest in the painting defeated it. She relies on a statement from *Young v. Young*, 80 N.Y. 422 that " '[a]ny gift of chattels which expressly reserves the use of the property to the donor for a certain period, or . . . as long as the donor shall live, is ineffectual' " (*id.*, at p. 436, quoting 2 Schouler, Personal Property, at 118). The statement was dictum, however, and the holding of the court was limited to a determination that an attempted gift of bonds in which the donor reserved the interest for life failed because there had been no delivery of the gift, either actual or constructive (*see, id.*, at p. 434; *see also, Speelman v. Pascal*, 10 N.Y.2d 313, 178 N.E.2d 723). The court expressly left undecided the question "whether a remainder in a chattel may be created and given by a donor by carving out a life estate for himself and transferring the remainder" (*Young v. Young, supra,* at p. 440). We answered part of that question in *Matter of Brandreth,* 169 N.Y. 437, 62 N.E. 563, *supra*) when we held that "[in] this state a life estate and remainder can be created in a chattel or a fund the same as in real property." The case did not require us to decide whether there could be a valid gift of the remainder.

Defendant recognizes that a valid inter vivos gift of a remainder interest can be made not only of real property but also of such intangibles as stocks and bonds. . . . That being so, it is difficult to perceive any legal basis for the distinction she urges which would permit gifts of remainder interests in those properties but not of remainder interests in chattels such as the Klimt painting here. The only reason suggested is that the gift of a chattel must include a present right to possession. . . . Insofar as some of our cases purport to require that the donor intend to transfer both title and possession immediately to have a valid inter vivos gift (*see, Gannon v. McGuire,* 160 N.Y. 476, 55 N.E. 7, *supra*; *Young v. Young,* 80 N.Y. 422, 430, *supra*), they state the rule too broadly and confuse the effectiveness of a gift with the transfer of the possession of the subject of that gift. The correct test is " 'whether the maker intended the [gift] to have *no effect* until after the maker's death, or whether he intended it to transfer *some present interest*' " (*McCarthy v. Pieret,* 281 N.Y. 407, 24 N.E.2d 102, *supra* [emphasis added]; *see also,* 25 N.Y. Jur., Gifts, § 14, at 156–157). As long as the evidence establishes an intent to make a present and irrevocable transfer of title or the right of ownership, there is a present transfer of some interest and the gift is effective immediately. . . .

Defendant suggests that allowing a donor to make a present gift of a remainder with the reservation of a life estate will lead courts to effectuate otherwise invalid testamentary dispositions of property. The two have entirely different characteristics, however, which make them distinguishable. Once the gift is made it is irrevocable and the donor is limited to the rights of a life tenant not an owner. Moreover, with the gift of a remainder title vests immediately in the donee and any possession is postponed until the donor's death whereas under a will neither title nor possession vests immediately. Finally, the postponement of enjoyment of the gift is produced by the express terms of the gift not by the nature of the instrument as it is with a will. . . .

Delivery

In order to have a valid inter vivos gift, there must be a delivery of the gift, either by a physical delivery of the subject of the gift or a constructive or symbolic delivery such as by an instrument of gift, sufficient to divest the donor of dominion and control over the property. . . . As the statement of the rule suggests, the requirement of delivery is not rigid or inflexible, but is to be applied in light of its purpose to avoid mistakes by donors and fraudulent claims by donees. . . . Accordingly, what is sufficient to constitute delivery "must be tailored to suit the circumstances of the case" (*Matter of Szabo,* 176 N.E.2d 395). The rule requires that " '[t]he delivery necessary to consummate a gift must be as perfect as the nature of the property and the circumstances and surroundings of the parties will reasonably permit'". . . .

Defendant contends that when a tangible piece of personal property such as a painting is the subject of a gift, physical delivery of the painting itself is the best form of delivery and should be required. Here, of course, we have only delivery of Victor Gruen's letters which serve as instruments of gift. Defendant's statement of the rule as applied may be generally true, but it ignores the fact that what Victor Gruen gave plaintiff was not all rights to the Klimt painting, but only title to it with no right of possession until his death. Under these circumstances, it would be illogical for the law to require the donor to part with possession of the painting when that is exactly what he intends to retain.

> **FYI**
>
> Michael S. Gruen, a graduate of UCLA Law School, practices law in New York City. He gave the oral argument on behalf of the appellant before the U.S. Supreme Court in *Loretto v. Teleprompter Manhattan CATV Corp.*, a famous land use case that is discussed in Chapter 14.

Nor is there any reason to require a donor making a gift of a remainder interest in a chattel to physically deliver the chattel into the donee's hands only to have the donee redeliver it to the donor. As the facts of this case demonstrate, such a requirement could impose practical burdens on the parties to the gift while serving the delivery requirement poorly. Thus, in order to accomplish this type of delivery the parties would have been required to travel to New York for the symbolic transfer and redelivery of the Klimt painting which was hanging on the wall of Victor Gruen's Manhattan apartment. Defendant suggests that such a requirement would be stronger evidence of a completed gift, but in the absence of witnesses to the event or any written confirmation of the gift it would provide less protection against fraudulent claims than have the written instruments of gift delivered in this case.

Acceptance

Acceptance by the donee is essential to the validity of an inter vivos gift, but when a gift is of value to the donee, as it is here, the law will presume an acceptance on his part (*Matter of Kelsey*, 26 N.Y.2d 792, 257 N.E.2d 663, *affg. on opn. at* 29 A.D.2d 450, 456; *Beaver v. Beaver*, 117 N.Y. 421, 22 N.E. 940, *supra*). Plaintiff did not rely on this presumption alone but also presented clear and convincing proof of his acceptance of a remainder interest in the Klimt painting by evidence that he had made several contemporaneous statements acknowledging the gift to his friends and associates, even showing some of them his father's gift letter, and that he had retained both letters for over 17 years to verify the gift after his father died. Defendant relied exclusively on affidavits filed by plaintiff in a matrimonial action with his former wife, in which plaintiff failed to list his interest in the painting as an asset. These affidavits were made over 10 years after acceptance was complete and they do not even approach the evidence in *Matter of Kelly* (285 N.Y. 139, 33 N.E.2d 62 [dissenting in part opn.], *supra*) where the donee, immediately upon delivery of a diamond ring, rejected it as "too flashy"....

Accordingly, the judgment appealed from and the order of the Appellate Division brought up for review should be affirmed, with costs.

Points for Discussion

a. **Present Transfer of a Future Interest**

The *Gruen* court concluded that Victor intended a present transfer of a future interest, rather than a future transfer of a present interest. What does this mean? Is there any difference between Victor telling Michael: (1) "I give you the painting when I die" and (2) "I give you the painting but I want to keep it until I die"? Note that Michael never took possession of the painting during his father's life. It remained firmly in his father's control during moves from New York City to California and finally to Austria. Should this matter?

American property law allows an owner to separate her title into different segments based on *time*. For example, one person can have the immediate right to possession (a *present interest*), while another can have the right to possession at a future date (a *future interest*). A common example is the lease. The tenant is entitled to present possession of the leased property, while the landlord has the right to possession of the property in the future when the lease ends. The holder of a future interest—such as a landlord—holds a valuable property right which can be sold or given away. In *Gruen*, what interest did Michael have in the painting?

> **Make the Connection**
>
> Chapter 5 will introduce the system of estates in land and future interests. This system began in feudal England and was later adopted in the United States. It continues to be a fundamental part of American property law today.

b. **Types of Delivery**

The common law recognized three types of delivery: manual, constructive, and symbolic.

> • *Manual delivery*: Manual delivery occurs when the donor physically transfers possession of the item to the donee. For example, A manually delivers a pen to B by handing him the pen. Traditionally, manual delivery of a gift is required if practicable.

- *Constructive delivery*: Constructive delivery requires that the donor physically transfer to the donee an object that provides access to the gifted item. For example, C could hand D the key that opens up the item, such as a locked desk. Constructive delivery is allowed if manual delivery is impracticable or impossible. Was constructive delivery available in *Gruen*? How could Victor have used this method to deliver the painting?

- *Symbolic delivery*: For symbolic delivery, the donor physically transfers to the donee an object that represents or symbolizes the gifted item, like the letters in *Gruen*. *See, e.g., Mirvish v. Mott*, 965 N.E.2d 906 (N.Y. 2012) (physical delivery of picture of sculpture with gift language written on reverse side was valid delivery of sculpture). For example, a note from E stating that "I give my 100 shares of Apple, Inc. to F" may be enough to deliver the shares to F. But what if the stock certificates were in E's pocket when she wrote the note? In many jurisdictions, symbolic delivery is allowed only if manual delivery is impracticable or impossible.

c. Why Require Delivery?

If a person clearly manifests his intent to make a gift, why should the law insist on delivery? Restatement (Third) of Property: Wills and Other Donative Transfers § 6.2 Comment yy adopts the position that a gift of personal property is valid without delivery "if the donor's intent to make a gift is established by clear and convincing evidence." However, as a general matter, courts still insist that a gift must be delivered.

Perspective and Analysis

In a widely-cited article, Professor Philip Mechem summarized the policies underlying the delivery requirement:

> In the first place, the delivery makes vivid and concrete to the donor the significance of the act he is doing. Any one can realize the psychological difference between a man's saying he gives something, yet retaining it, and saying he gives it and seeing it pass irrevocably out of his control. The *wrench* of delivery . . . the little mental twinge at seeing his property pass from his hands into those of another, is an important element to the protection of the donor. . . .
>
> Secondly, the act of manual [delivery] is as unequivocal to actual witnesses of the transaction as to the donor himself. . . . If he hands over the property, he has done an act that will settle many doubts. . . .
>
> Thirdly, and lastly, the fact of delivery gives the donee . . . at least prima facie evidence in favor of the alleged gift. . . . If the donee comes out of the sick room and says the bonds have been given to him he will be more

credited, and more reasonably, if he has them in his possession. It is easier to fabricate a story than to abstract the property.

Philip Mechem, *The Requirement of Delivery in Gifts of Chattels and of Choses in Action Evidenced by Commercial Instruments*, 21 Ill. L. Rev. 341, 348–49 (1926). *But see* Chad A. McGowan, *Special Delivery: Does the Postman Have to Ring at All—The Current State of the Delivery Requirement for Valid Gifts,* 31 Real Prop. Prob. & Tr. J. 357 (1996) (criticizing Mechem's approach).

d. Hypotheticals on Delivery

In which of the situations below has O delivered the gift to P?

(1) O calls P into O's bedroom. Pointing to a gold pen on the desk, O declares, "I give you my pen."

(2) Pointing to his bedside drawer, O declares, "I want you to have my drawer and everything inside it." O hands P a key that unlocks the drawer; inside are a diamond ring and the title to O's car.

(3) O declares, "P, I want you to have my Van Gogh. It's in my office in Rome, Italy. Pick it up whenever you want."

(4) Handing P his bank book, O declares, "All the money is now yours."

(5) Taking 200 shares of Google stock from his safe and handing them to P, O declares, "I want you to have all of these when I die. Keep them safe."

(6) O lends a book to his neighbor P, who takes it home. Several days later, O finds that he has a second copy of the book. O calls P and declares: "Keep that book I lent you. It's yours!"

e. Acceptance

Courts generally presume that a valuable gift has been accepted. But sometimes acceptance is disputed. In *Gruen*, what facts suggest that Michael accepted the gift? What facts suggest that he did not? Indeed, the mere fact that a gift is beneficial to a donee usually is sufficient to satisfy this element.

f. Gift by Check

Suppose E hands F a check on E's personal savings account for $250 saying, "F, this is for you." Is this a completed gift? The majority rule is that no gift occurs until the check is cashed, because the donor retains dominion and control of the funds. A check is merely an instrument authorizing the bank to pay the holder from a specified account. The donor can stop payment, write another check for the same funds, or die, thereby preventing any gift. *See In re Estate of Heyn,* 47 P.3d 724 (Colo. Ct. App. 2002) (donor only parts with control of the funds when her bank accepts the check);

Woo v. Smart, 442 S.E.2d 690 (Va. 1994) (check is simply an unenforceable promise to make a gift).

g. Testamentary Gifts

In *Gruen*, the court noted the distinction between an *inter vivos* gift and a gift made by a will (a *testamentary gift*). An *inter vivos* gift transfers an interest to the donee *now*, while a testamentary gift transfers an interest to the donee only in the *future* when the donor dies. A testamentary gift is valid only if it satisfies the Statute of Wills, which requires a writing signed by the donor and witnessed by two or more people. You will learn more about wills in Chapter 5.

> **What's That?**
>
> The Statute of Wills was enacted by the English Parliament in 1540. For the first time in English history, it enabled a landowner to determine who would receive his property when he died. Under the prior common law rule of *primogeniture*, the first-born son automatically inherited all the property. The Statute established the formal requirements for a valid will.

Michael and his stepmother disagreed on the nature of Victor's intent. Which facts support the stepmother's claim that Victor intended a testamentary gift? Would Victor's letters satisfy the Statute of Wills?

h. Aftermath of *Gruen*

After the Court of Appeals decision, Michael received a note in the mail from his stepmother, enclosing a receipt from a Swiss bank. He flew to Zurich, presented the receipt, and received the painting. Michael immediately sold it at auction for over $5 million; a decade later it was resold for $23.5 million. Today it is owned by the Galleria Nazionale d'Arte Moderna in Rome. *See* Susan F. French, Gruen v. Gruen: *A Tale of Two Stories*, in Property Stories 75 (Gerald Korngold & Andrew Morriss eds., 2d ed. 2009). Klimt's paintings continue to appreciate. In 2016, Oprah Winfrey sold a Klimpt painting for $150 million, one of the highest sums ever paid for a painting.

i. Engagement Rings and Revocable Gifts

While generally inter vivos gifts are irrevocable, engagement rings are a special category. In almost all states, the gift of an engagement ring is subject to an implied condition that the marriage occur. Thus, the gift does not become absolute until the marriage ceremony. *See McGrath v. Dockendorf*, 793 S.E.2d 336 (Va. 2016). *But see Albinger v. Harris*, 48 P.3d 711 (Mont. 2002) (gift of an engagement ring was complete upon delivery, and completed gift was not revocable).

Many jurisdictions follow a no-fault approach to the disposition of engagement rings: the ring is returned to the donor if the engagement is broken, regardless of who is at fault. *See, e.g., Rambod v. Tazeh*, 125 N.Y.S.3d 449 (App. Div. 2020). Other jurisdictions consider who was at fault in ending the engagement, giving the ring to the other person. Thus, if the donor was at fault, the donee keeps the ring; if the donee was at fault, the donor regains the ring. Does this distinction make sense? *See* Ruth Sarah Lee, *A Legal Analysis of Romantic Gifts*, 67 U. Miami L. Rev. 595 (2013).

---

2. Gift *Causa Mortis*

The doctor tells F, an elderly man with a brain tumor, that he has one month to live. Fearing death, F tells his son S that he wants him to have his expensive Rolex watch. F hands S the watch, and S gratefully thanks F for the gift. A few weeks later, F miraculously recovers and is declared to be tumor-free. Who owns the Rolex?

A gift *causa mortis* is a gift of personal property made by a living person in contemplation of death. There are four essential elements for a gift *causa mortis*: donative intent, delivery, acceptance, and the donor's anticipation of imminent death. It is important to understand that a valid gift *causa mortis* is immediately effective when it is made. However, unlike its counterpart the *inter vivos* gift, the gift *causa mortis* is revocable. The donor may revoke it at any time before her death. But can a person contemplating suicide make a valid gift *causa mortis*?

> **It's Latin to Me**
>
> A *gift causa morti*s is also referred to as *donatio mortis causa* (Latin for "on the occasion of death"). It originated as a method to transfer property rights between husband and wife, thereby avoiding some of the more onerous elements of succession law.

In re Estate of Oaks

Court of Appeals of Wisconsin

944 N.W.2d 611 (2020)

STARK, P. J.

Shortly before he died by suicide, David Oaks wrote a note giving all of his "worldly belongings" to Lynne Stouff, his longtime romantic partner. Based on that note, the circuit court awarded Oaks' entire estate to Stouff, pursuant to the doctrine of gift causa mortis. On appeal, Oaks' estate ("the Estate") argues the court erred because a gift causa mortis can never occur when the donor dies by suicide. . . .

We reject the Estate's argument that a gift causa mortis can never occur in the context of a donor's suicide. While a gift made in anticipation of a donor's suicide may not always qualify as a gift causa mortis, the doctrine applies in this case, where the undisputed facts show that Oaks' suicide was the result of a present mental illness. . . .

CHAPTER 3 *Owning Personal Property*   209

BACKGROUND

Stouff and Oaks were in a romantic relationship for over twenty-three years—from February 1995 until Oaks' death on March 8, 2018. They never married, but they lived together for approximately ten years—from 2008 until Oaks' death. Oaks had been divorced twice and had an adult daughter, Cheri Wardell, who was not Stouff's offspring. It is undisputed that Oaks and Wardell did not have a "close relationship" and were "estranged for many years" prior to Oaks' death.

In the early morning hours of March 8, 2018, Oaks fatally shot himself in the head in the home he shared with Stouff, while Stouff was asleep upstairs. Stouff woke when she heard a loud bang, and when she went downstairs to investigate, she found two handwritten notes on a table. The first note read:

3-7-18

> Lynne Stouff has been my companion and my crutch for a long while.
>
> As I leave this existence I want all worldly belongings to be assigned to Lynne.
>
> David Oaks

The second note read:

> Lynne—
>
> This is all I can go with this—Thank you for being there for me all these years.
>
> I love you.

First note
Click here for larger photo

Second note
Click here for larger photo

It is undisputed that Oaks died intestate—that is, without a valid will. It is further undisputed that Oaks died unmarried and that Wardell was his only child. As such, Oaks' entire estate would normally pass to Wardell under the general rules of intestate succession, as set forth in WIS. STAT. § 852.01 (2017–18).

Wardell filed a petition for formal administration of Oaks' estate on May 23, 2018. An order for formal administration was issued two days later, and Wardell was named the Estate's personal representative. Stouff subsequently filed several claims against the Estate. As relevant to this appeal, Stouff contended she was entitled to Oaks' entire estate under the doctrine of gift causa mortis based on the first note Oaks left before he died. . . .

The circuit court ultimately issued a written decision granting Stouff's summary judgment motion. . . . Based upon the undisputed facts, the court determined Stouff had established each of the elements of a gift causa mortis, and she was therefore entitled to the entirety of Oaks' estate. . . . The Estate now appeals, arguing the court erred by granting Stouff's summary judgment motion.

DISCUSSION

"The general rule is that a testamentary disposition (a disposition that takes effect upon the death of the person making the disposition) must comply with the statutory requirements for the execution of wills." *Meegan v. Netzer*, 2012 WI App 20, 9, 339 Wis. 2d 460, 810 N.W.2d 358. However, a gift causa mortis operates as an exception to that general rule. *Id*. Under the doctrine of gift causa mortis, "a gift made during the life of the donor becomes effective upon the donor's death if certain requirements are met." *Id.*, 1. Specifically, in order to establish a gift causa mortis, a claimant must prove that: (1) the donor had an intention to make a gift effective at death; (2) the donor made the gift "with a view to the donor's death from present illness or from an external and apprehended peril"; (3) the donor died of that ailment or peril; and (4) there was a delivery of the gifted property. *Id.*, 10 (citation omitted). . . .

> **Make the Connection**
>
> Traditionally, a will must be signed by at least two witnesses who saw the decedent sign it. Oaks' first note was not a valid will in Wisconsin because his signature was not witnessed. But in many states the note would be enforced as a *holographic will*—a will written entirely in the handwriting of the decedent and signed by him. You will study holographic wills in Chapter 5.

The Estate . . . concedes Stouff can prove that Oaks gifted property to her in anticipation of his death. However, the Estate argues Stouff cannot prove Oaks gifted that property in anticipation of his death from a present illness or external peril because suicide is not a present illness or external peril. Further, because Oaks died as a result of suicide, the Estate argues he did not die from a present illness or external peril. For these reasons, the Estate contends a gift causa mortis can never occur in the context of a donor's suicide.

While the Estate concedes that no Wisconsin case to date has addressed this issue, it asserts that "[h]istorically, the common law has maintained that a gift causa mortis made in contemplation of the donor's suicide is void." The Estate further contends that various other jurisdictions have followed this historical rule and have held that "death by suicide does not satisfy the requirement that a gift be made in expectation of imminent death from illness or impending peril."

We do not find the Estate's argument in this regard persuasive. In making its argument, the Estate fails to distinguish between the manner of a donor's death and the ultimate cause of the donor's death. While the manner of death may be suicide, that suicide may, in some cases, have been caused by a present mental illness—for instance, depression. Accordingly, even in a case in which the donor died by suicide, a party may be able to show that the donor made a gift in expectation of his or her death from a present mental illness, and that the present mental illness caused the donor's death. Thus, contrary to the Estate's contention, the fact that a donor died by suicide does not automatically prevent a party from establishing that the donor made a gift causa mortis. . . .

The New Jersey Supreme Court reached a similar conclusion in *Scherer v. Hyland*, 75 N.J. 127, 380 A.2d 698 (1977). There, the donor was "acutely depressed" during the weeks leading up to her death by suicide. *Id.* at 699. Before her death, she left a note stating that she bequeathed all of her possessions to her romantic partner. *Id.* at 699–700. Under those circumstances, the court concluded the donor had made a gift causa mortis. The court expressly rejected the appellant's contention that suicide is "not the sort of peril that will sustain a gift causa mortis." *Id.* at 702. The court explained:

> While it is true that a gift causa mortis is made by the donor with a view to impending death, death is no less impending because of a resolve to commit suicide. Nor does that fixed purpose constitute any lesser or less imminent peril than does a ravaging disease. Indeed, given the despair sufficient to end it all, the peril attendant upon contemplated suicide may reasonably be viewed as even more imminent than that accompanying many illnesses which prove ultimately to be fatal. . . . *Id.* (citations omitted).

Like the . . . New Jersey Supreme Court, we conclude a gift causa mortis can occur in a case where the donor died by suicide as a result of a present mental illness. We therefore reject the Estate's assertion that a gift causa mortis can never be enforced in a case where the donor died by suicide.

In its reply brief, the Estate argues that even if a gift causa mortis can occur in a case where the donor's suicide was caused by a present mental illness, the evidence here did not establish that was the case. We disagree. In support of her summary judgment motion, Stouff submitted evidence that: (1) Oaks was a Vietnam War veteran and was exposed to "Agent Orange" during his military service; (2) Oaks had been diagnosed with post-traumatic stress disorder by a treatment provider and was prescribed an anti-depressant medication on at least one occasion; (3) during the months before his death, Oaks repeatedly complained to Stouff and others of pressure and pain in his head; (4) Oaks was convinced there was a physical problem in his brain that was "causing his various mental health ailments"; (5) Oaks "finally convinced the VA to schedule him an appointment with neurology to get his head scanned and evaluated," but he died before that appointment took place; and (6) Oaks' death certificate listed his cause of death as "SELF INFLICTED GUNSHOT WOUND TO HEAD . . . Due to or as a consequence of 'DEPRESSION.' "

. . . In this case, it is undisputed that Oaks made a gift to Stouff in anticipation of his own death by suicide. In addition, the facts set forth above, if uncontradicted, would establish: (1) that Oaks was suffering from a mental illness at the time of his death—specifically, depression; and (2) that Oaks' mental illness caused his suicide. Accordingly, Stouff established a prima facie case for summary judgment with respect to the second and third requirements for a gift causa mortis.

> **FYI**
>
> On average, 20 veterans die by suicide every day. Stouff's appellate brief noted: "[C]learly there is an alarming correlation between veteran status and death by suicide, indicating much more is at play than a conscious and deliberate choice to end their life, and Oaks is far from the only service member to have lost his last battle with mental illness after returning home."

The Estate did not submit any affidavits or other evidentiary materials in response to Stouff's summary judgment motion, or in support of the Estate's own summary judgment motion. . . . By failing to submit any evidentiary materials that would raise a genuine issue of material fact regarding the second and third requirements for a gift causa mortis, the Estate failed to defeat Stouff's prima facie case for summary judgment with respect to those requirements.

We do not hold that a donor's death by suicide will always be sufficient to establish the second and third requirements for a gift causa mortis. . . . Here, however, Stouff made a prima facie showing that Oaks was suffering from a mental illness at the time of his death and that the mental illness caused his suicide, and the Estate failed to rebut Stouff's prima facie showing. Under these circumstances, the circuit court properly determined, as a matter of law, that Stouff had established the second and third requirements for a gift causa mortis. . . .

Points for Discussion

a. **Suicide**

Many decisions state that a person contemplating suicide cannot make a valid gift *causa mortis*, because upholding such a gift would be contrary to the public policy against suicide. The *Estate of Oaks* court distinguished these cases by attributing Oaks' death to a mental illness that, in turn, caused his suicide. Should a donor's death by suicide *always* be sufficient to uphold a gift *causa mortis*, without proof of mental illness?

b. Death from an Unanticipated Cause

Suppose that after Oaks wrote the notes, he suddenly died from an unanticipated cause—such as a brain injury stemming from his military service. In some jurisdictions, a gift *causa mortis* is still effective even though the donor does not die from the contemplated peril if (1) the death occurs within the same approximate time frame or (2) the cause of death is related to that peril. Other jurisdictions reject this view. Which approach is best?

c. Delivery

On appeal, the Estate also argued that the gift failed because Oaks did not physically deliver the property. Citing Wisconsin case law that "a relaxed rule as to delivery . . . applies when determining whether persons living in the same household have made and received a gift," the court held that Oaks had "delivered his property to Stouff by leaving a note informing her of the gift on a table in their shared residence, which he could be reasonably certain Stouff would find when she came downstairs." *Estate of Oaks*, 944 N.W.2d at 621, 623.

d. Revocation

Estate of Oaks reflects the minority view that a gift *causa mortis* becomes effective only if and when the donor dies. Under the majority approach, such a gift is effective at the time it is made, but may be revoked depending on future circumstances. If the donor recovers, the gift is automatically revoked in many states. In other jurisdictions, the donor who survives must expressly choose to revoke; but delay is dangerous. Restatement (Third) of Property: Wills and Other Donative Transfers § 6.2 cmt. zz provides that the "[f]ailure to revoke within a reasonable time after the donor is no longer in apprehension of imminent death causes the donor's right of revocation to lapse."

e. Judicial Disfavor?

Courts generally disfavor the gift *causa mortis*. The main concern is the potential for fraud: the dead donor is unable to testify about whether any gift was made. Accordingly, many jurisdictions require that a donee establish a gift *causa mortis* by clear and convincing evidence, rather than merely by the usual preponderance of the evidence. *See, e.g., In re Estate of Hansen*, 810 N.W.2d 358 (Wis. Ct. App. 2012). In addition, the delivery requirement is often applied more strictly. Do you agree that the gift *causa mortis* should be disfavored?

f. Aftermath of *Estate of Oaks*

William Bratcher, Stouff's attorney in the case, later became a judge. Reflecting on the decision, he commented:

> The case is important because it is the first time that it has been legally recognized in Wisconsin that death by suicide is not necessarily a conscious choice. Instead, it can be an all-too-deadly symptom of mental illness. In a broader sense, it is also a

recognition that mental illness is just that—an illness, like any other physical ailment. My sincerest hope is that this is a sign that the stigmas associated with mental illness and suicide are breaking down so that we, as a state, country, and society, can better address and treat mental health issues and ultimately prevent suicide, especially among our veterans.

Summary

- **Personal Property.** Tangible personal property consists of movable items such as brooches, paintings, and wallets. Possession of personal property gives the possessor certain rights, depending on how and where possession is obtained.

- **Rule of Capture.** Originally, the rule of capture governed property rights in wild animals; ownership was acquired only by physical possession of the animal. The rule of capture was later used to determine property rights in other natural resources such as water, oil, and natural gas.

- **Finders.** Finders often acquire possession of lost, mislaid, or abandoned items. The nature of the item and the location of the find are important in determining the finder's rights. Generally, lost and abandoned items go to the finder, unless the find is made at an owner-occupied residence. Mislaid items usually belong to the possessor of the place where the item is found. If an employee finds an item in the course of his employment, it belongs to the employer. A finder is a bailee, with a duty to care for the found item.

- **Adverse Possession.** Title to personal property may be obtained by adverse possession. However, the limitations period for the recovery of such property is generally two to six years, shorter than the period for real property. Traditionally, the limitations period begins when the adverse claimant's possession becomes open and notorious. Today, many states apply a discovery rule, which tolls the period until the owner discovers, or reasonably should have discovered, the location of the property. A thief cannot transfer valid title to a good faith purchaser unless the thief gains a new title by adverse possession.

> **Test Your Knowledge**
>
> To assess your understanding of the material in this chapter, click here to take a quiz.

- **Gifts.** Three elements are required for an *inter vivos* gift: donative intent, delivery, and acceptance. The item must be physically handed over to the donee unless such manual delivery is impossible or impracticable, in which event constructive or symbolic delivery may be used. An *inter vivos* gift is irrevocable. Four elements are required for a gift *causa mortis*: the three elements for an *inter vivos* gift, plus a fourth—the donor's anticipation of imminent death.

A gift *causa mortis* is revocable before the donor's death; in most states it is automatically revoked if the donor does not die from the contemplated peril.

> **For More Information**
>
> For more information about the subjects covered in this chapter, please consult these sources:
> - Matt Corriel, Comment, *Up for Grabs: A Workable System for the Unilateral Acquisition of Chattels*, 161 U. Pa. L. Rev. 807 (2013).
> - Carol M. Rose, *Possession as the Origin of Property*, 52 U. Chi. L. Rev. 73 (1985).
> - Lior Jacob Strahilevitz, *The Right to Abandon*, 158 U. Pa. L. Rev. 355 (2010).
> - Symposium, *The Rule of Capture and Its Consequences*, 35 Envtl. L. 647 (2005).

CHAPTER 4

An Introduction to Intellectual Property

Intellectual property protects the creations of the human mind. Suppose that A writes a book and sells a copy to B. B now owns his physical copy of the book. But A, as the copyright holder, owns the intellectual content of the book, including the right to prevent anyone else from selling copies.

Just 100 years ago, intellectual property was relatively unimportant in the United States. Real property, tangible personal property, and intangible property such as shares of stock were the principal sources of societal wealth. Today, however, the value of intellectual property rights in the United States is measured in trillions of dollars. It is estimated that intellectual property comprises up to 80% of the value of many publicly traded corporations. And businesses that rely heavily on intellectual property contribute over $8 trillion to the national economy each year—more than 38% of the gross domestic product.

In this chapter, we will examine four types of intellectual property:

- *Copyrights*: Copyright law protects original works of authorship, such as books, computer programs, plays, sculptures, and songs.
- *Patents*: Patent law protects new inventions, such as cell lines, machines, and medicines.
- *Trademarks*: Trademark law protects words, names, and other symbols which are used by merchants to distinguish their goods and services from those offered by others.
- *Trade secrets*: Trade secret law protects valuable information that is not generally known or readily ascertainable by others, such as customer lists, formulas, manufacturing processes, marketing plans, and new technologies.

Copyrights, patents, trademarks, and trade secrets share certain similarities. All arise under a first-in-time system for allocating entitlements. All provide the owner with essentially the same set of property rights, principally the right to exclude others from using the intellectual property. Finally, all are governed by federal statutes—and are increasingly affected by international law.

A key characteristic of intellectual property is that many people can use it at the same time without interfering with each other's use. In the example above, only one person can read B's copy of the book at a time. But millions of people can simultaneously enjoy the benefits of A's intellectual property by reading different copies of the book. In economic terms, most intellectual property is a *public good*—"a good that can be consumed without reducing any other person's consumption of it." Richard A. Posner, Economic Analysis of Law 402 (9th ed. 2014). But if a public good like a book can be quickly copied by others, what incentive does an author have to write? Or an inventor to invent? Copyright and patent law answer these questions by providing an incentive: a limited monopoly on writings and inventions.

But monopolies on the use of information pose challenges. Without competition, the holder of a copyright or patent may be able to demand an excessive price. Further, as Judge Kozinski observed in *White v. Samsung Electronics America, Inc.* (Chapter 1), an information monopoly that is too broad or too long may stifle creativity, harming all of society.

A. Common Law Approach

Suppose that C develops an idea for a new television series. She communicates the idea to NBC, which later uses it as the basis for a hit show. Or imagine that D, a world-renowned chef, creates a prize-winning recipe for a unique dessert which he shares with his restaurant customers, only to find that a competing restaurant has copied his recipe. Can C and D recover damages?

Broadly speaking, intellectual property rights were *not* recognized at common law. As Justice Brandeis explained in a famous dissent:

> The general rule of law is, that the noblest of human productions—knowledge, truths ascertained, conceptions, and ideas—become, after voluntary communication to others, as free as the air to common use.

International News Service v. Associated Press, 248 U.S. 215, 250 (1918). The types of intellectual property discussed in this chapter—copyrights, patents, trademarks, and trade secrets—are exceptions to this general rule. Another exception is the right of publicity, which you studied in Chapter 1. But the basic rule remains the same: absent some special exception, the law does not recognize intellectual property rights.

What justifies the traditional rule? Please consider this question as you read the following case—a depression-era dispute about "silk [fabric] featuring a polka dot design." *Can Sell Polka Dot Silk*, N.Y. Times, May 8, 1929.

Cheney Brothers v. Doris Silk Corp.

United States Court of Appeals, Second Circuit

35 F.2d 279 (1929), *cert. denied*, 281 U.S. 728 (1930)

LEARNED HAND, CIRCUIT JUDGE.

The plaintiff, a corporation, is a manufacturer of silks, which puts out each season many new patterns, designed to attract purchasers by their novelty and beauty. Most of these fail in that purpose, so that not much more than a fifth catch the public fancy. Moreover, they have only a short life, for the most part no more than a single season of eight or nine months. It is in practice impossible, and it would be very onerous if it were not, to secure design patents upon all of these; it would also be impossible to know in advance which would sell well, and patent only those. Besides, it is probable that for the most part they have no such originality as would support a design patent. Again, it is impossible to copyright them under the Copyright Act (17 USCA § 1 et seq.), or at least so the authorities of the Copyright Office hold. So it is easy for any one to copy such as prove successful, and the plaintiff, which is put to much ingenuity and expense in fabricating them, finds itself without protection of any sort for its pains.

> **What's That?**
>
> The most common type of patent is a *utility patent*—it protects an idea for a useful product or process. However, a *design patent* may be awarded for "any new, original and ornamental design for an article of manufacture." 35 U.S.C. § 171. It appears that the designs at issue in *Cheney Brothers* were not sufficiently original to qualify for this protection.

Taking advantage of this situation, the defendant copied one of the popular designs in the season beginning in October, 1928, and undercut the plaintiff's price. This is the injury of which it complains. The defendant, though it duplicated the design in question, denies that it knew it to be the plaintiff's, and there thus arises an issue which might be an answer to the motion. However, the parties wish a decision upon the equity of the bill, and, since it is within our power to dismiss it, we shall accept its allegation, and charge the defendant with knowledge.

The plaintiff asks for protection only during the season, and needs no more, for the designs are all ephemeral. It seeks in this way to disguise the extent of the proposed innovation, and to persuade us that, if we interfere only a little, the solecism, if there be one, may be pardonable. But the reasoning which would justify any interposition at all demands that it cover the whole extent of the injury. A man whose designs come to harvest in two years, or in five, has prima facie as good right to protection as one who deals only in annuals. Nor could we consistently stop at designs; processes, machines, and secrets have an equal claim. The upshot must be that, whenever any one has contrived any of these, others may be forbidden to copy it. That is not the law.

In the absence of some recognized right at common law, or under the statutes—and the plaintiff claims neither—a man's property is limited to the chattels which embody his invention. Others may imitate these at their pleasure. . . .

Of the cases on which the plaintiff relies, the chief is *International News Service v. Associated Press*, 248 U.S. 215. Although that concerned another subject-matter—printed news dispatches—we agree that, if it meant to lay down a general doctrine, it would cover this case; at least, the language of the majority opinion goes so far. We do not believe that it did. While it is of course true that law ordinarily speaks in general terms, there are cases where the occasion is at once the justification for, and the limit of, what is decided. This appears to us such an instance; we think that no more was covered than situations substantially similar to those then at bar. The difficulties of understanding it otherwise are insuperable. We are to suppose that the court meant to create a sort of common-law patent or copyright for reasons of justice. Either would flagrantly conflict with the scheme which Congress has for more than a century devised to cover the subject-matter.

Cheney Brothers silk fabric
Click here for larger image

. . . It appears to us incredible that the Supreme Court should have had in mind any such consequences. To exclude others from the enjoyment of a chattel is one thing; to prevent any imitation of it, to set up a monopoly in the plan of its structure, gives the author a power over his fellows vastly greater, a power which the Constitution allows only Congress to create. . . .

True, it would seem as though the plaintiff had suffered a grievance for which there should be a remedy, perhaps by an amendment of the Copyright Law, assuming that this does not already cover the case, which is not urged here. It seems a lame answer in such a case to turn the injured party out of court, but there are larger issues at stake than his redress. . . . Whether these would prove paramount we have no means of saying; it is not for us to decide. Our vision is inevitably contracted, and the whole horizon may contain much which will compose a very different picture.

The order is affirmed, and, as the bill cannot in any event succeed, it may be dismissed, if the defendant so desires.

Points for Discussion

a. **Rewarding Theft?**

Should the law allow Doris Silk to steal the results of the Cheney Brothers' creative labor? Suppose that employees of Doris Silk broke into the Cheney Brothers warehouse late at night, removed boxes of silk fabric, and sold them to retail stores. This conduct would clearly be prosecuted as theft. Are the facts in *Cheney Brothers* materially different?

b. **Protecting "Hot News"**

In arguing their case, the attorneys for Cheney Brothers relied heavily on *International News Service v. Associated Press*, 248 U.S. 215 (1918) (*INS*), where the Supreme Court recognized a limited property right in news. Associated Press gathered and published news, which INS then copied and resold to other media outlets. While acknowledging that the factual content of news could not be copyrighted, the Court ruled that Associated Press had a temporary "*quasi* property" right to exclude others from using its news. Why did Learned Hand refuse to follow this precedent? Is a silk pattern analogous to news? Should the *INS* approach apply to anything other than news? For a modern analysis of the INS doctrine, see Shyamkrishna Balganesh, *"Hot News": The Enduring Myth of Property in News*, 111 Colum. L. Rev. 419 (2011).

Perspective and Analysis

In the excerpt below, Professor Douglas Baird reflects on the meaning of *INS*.

> That an individual has a right to reap what he has sown . . . is far from self-evident even as applied to tangible property. . . . We typically can reap only the wheat we sow on our own land. . . . In any event, wheat and information are fundamentally different from one another. It is the nature of wheat or land or any other tangible property that possession by one person precludes possession by anyone else. A court must decide that A should get the wheat or that B should get the wheat. It cannot decide that both of them get it all. Many people, however, can use the same piece of information. . . .
>
> That the analogy between wheat and information does not apply with full force, however, does not mean that it should not apply at all. One can still argue that individuals have the right to enjoy the fruits of their labors, even when the labors are intellectual. But granting individuals exclusive rights to the information they gather conflicts with other rights in a way that granting exclusive rights to tangible property does not.
>
> In a market economy, granting individuals exclusive rights to property is an efficient way of allocating scarce resources. . . . Granting exclusive rights to information does not, however, necessarily promote a market economy.

> Competition depends upon imitation. One person invests labor and money to create a product, such as a food processor, that people will buy. Others may imitate him and take advantage of the new market by selling their own food processors. Their machines may incorporate their own ideas about how such machines should be made. As a result, the quality of the machines may rise and their price may fall. . . .
>
> **Douglas G. Baird, *Common Law Intellectual Property and the Legacy of International News Service v. Associated Press*, 50 U. Chi. L. Rev. 411, 413-14 (1983).**

c. **Monopoly and the Public Interest**

If the law protected the Cheney Brothers' designs, this would give it an incentive to continue production, but might create a monopoly that would allow it to charge a higher price to consumers. On the other hand, without such protection, does Cheney Brothers have any incentive to continue producing new designs? Why? In *Smith v. Chanel, Inc.*, 402 F.2d 562 (9th Cir. 1968), a perfume manufacturer ran advertisements asserting that its inexpensive perfume was as good as the famous fragrance "Chanel No. 5." The Ninth Circuit held that because Chanel No. 5 was unpatented, anyone had a right to copy it. The court reasoned that this outcome served the public good:

> Disapproval of the copyist's opportunism may be an understandable first reaction, "but this initial response to the problem has been curbed in deference to the greater public good." . . . By taking his "free ride," the copyist, albeit unintentionally, serves an important public interest by offering comparable goods at lower prices.

Id. at 568. For a criticism of the common law approach to ideas, see Arthur R. Miller, *Common Law Protection for Products of the Mind: An "Idea" Whose Time Has Come*, 119 Harv. L. Rev. 703 (2006).

d. **The Judicial Role**

Why was Learned Hand concerned about creating "a sort of common-law patent or copyright for reasons of justice"? After all, we can infer that the Supreme Court was not greatly concerned about this issue when it decided *INS*. If Cheney Brothers and similarly situated plaintiffs could obtain new types of intellectual property rights through successful litigation, how would this affect the statutory systems that Congress established for copyrights and patents?

e. **Aftermath of *Cheney Brothers***

Today a fabric design can qualify for copyright protection—as long as it is sufficiently original. However, as a general rule, dress designs are still not recognized as intellectual property in the United States. Accordingly, the new designs worn by stars at the Academy Awards and similar events are promptly copied by "design pirates." A consumer can choose between buying a skirt designed by Prada for over $1,000 or a knockoff version for about $30. Congress has considered many bills that would provide copyright or copyright-like protection for dress designs, but none has succeeded. In contrast, the European Union restricts design piracy. What explains this difference?

B. Copyrights

1. Copyright Basics

A composes an award-winning song; B paints a world-famous watercolor; and C writes a best-selling novel. All of these creative works qualify for protection under copyright law. For example, B may prevent anyone from selling copies of his painting during the copyright term.

The Constitution authorizes Congress to "promote the Progress of Science and the useful Arts, by securing for limited Times to Authors and Inventors the exclusive Right to their respective Writings and Discoveries." U.S. Const. art. I, § 8. Our federal copyright laws arise from the portions of this clause concerning "authors" and "writings." Thus, copyright law exists to serve a specified utilitarian goal: to promote the progress of science and the useful arts. Copyright protection serves this goal by giving authors an incentive to produce works that will benefit the public.

> **FYI**
>
> Copyright law in the United States is primarily governed by federal statutes. When the United States ratified the principal treaties affecting copyright law (the Berne Convention and the Agreement on Trade-Related Aspects of Intellectual Property Rights), the copyright statutes were amended to conform to these treaties.

The owner of a copyright primarily holds a right to exclude. For example, she may prevent any other person from reproducing the work, creating derivative works, distributing copies of the work to the public, publicly performing the work, or publicly displaying the work during the term of the copyright. 17 U.S.C. § 106. In addition, the owner may transfer her copyright to others; she may also effectively destroy the copyright by abandoning it.

How long should copyright protection last? The 1976 Copyright Act extended the basic term for new works to the author's life plus 50 years. By the late 1990s, the copyright terms for a number of famous works were nearing expiration. The song *Happy Birthday to You*, Robert Frost's poems, George Gershwin's music, movies such as the *Wizard of Oz* and *Gone With the Wind*, Disney cartoon characters like Mickey Mouse and Donald Duck, and many other works were about to lose copyright protection and enter the public domain—where they could be freely used by anyone. After extensive lobbying by the Walt Disney Co. and other copyright owners, Congress enacted the Sonny Bono Copyright Term Extension Act (CTEA) in 1998—which critics promptly dubbed the "Mickey Mouse Protection Act." The CTEA extended the terms of all existing and future copyrights by an additional 20 years. Accordingly, the basic copyright term for new works is now equal to the author's life plus 70 years. Other terms apply in special circumstances.

> **What's That?**
>
> In this context, the *public domain* refers to all artistic works, inventions, ideas, and other creations that are not protected by intellectual property law. Any person may use anything in the public domain without payment.

In 1999, Eric Eldred and others filed suit to challenge the CTEA, arguing that it effectively made the copyright term perpetual in violation of the Constitution's mandate that copyrights endure only for "limited Times." Eldred operated a website which made public domain literary works available to everyone; he particularly hoped to interest high school and college students in fine literature. But the CTEA prevented any copyrighted works from entering the public domain for 20 years, frustrating Eldred's hope of adding Frost's poems and other works to his website.

> **FYI**
>
> Eldred explained his motivation for developing the website in this manner: "[W]e feel a responsibility to our public—all human beings on the earth—to preserve our culture of books and art and make it available to as many as we can." *A Virtual Library on the Web*, UNESCO Courier, June 1, 1999.

Eldred v. Ashcroft

Supreme Court of the United States

537 U.S. 186 (2003)

JUSTICE GINSBURG delivered the opinion of the Court.

. . . Text, history, and precedent, we conclude, confirm that the Copyright Clause empowers Congress to prescribe "limited Times" for copyright protection and to secure the same level and duration of protection for all copyright holders, present and future.

The CTEA's baseline term of life plus 70 years, petitioners concede, qualifies as a "limited Tim[e]" as applied to future copyrights. Petitioners contend, however, that existing copyrights extended to endure for that same term are not "limited." Petitioner's argument essentially reads into the text of the Copyright Clause the command that a time prescription, once set, becomes forever "fixed" or "inalterable." The word "limited," however, does not convey a meaning so constricted. At the time of the Framing, that word meant what it means today: "confine[d] within certain bounds," "restrain[ed]," or "circumscribe[d]." S. Johnson, A Dictionary of the English Language (7th ed. 1785). Thus understood, a time span appropriately "limited" as applied to future copyrights does not automatically cease to be "limited" when applied to existing copyrights. . . .

In sum, we find that the CTEA is a rational enactment; we are not at liberty to second-guess congressional determinations and policy judgments of this order, however debatable or arguably unwise they may be. Accordingly, we cannot conclude that the CTEA—which continues the unbroken congressional practice of treating future and existing copyrights in parity for term extension purposes—is an impermissible exercise of Congress' power under the Copyright Clause. . . .

JUSTICE BREYER, dissenting.

The Constitution's Copyright Clause grants Congress the power to "*promote* the *Progress* of Science . . . by securing for *limited* Times to *Authors* . . . the exclusive Right to their respective Writings." Art. I, § 8, cl. 8 (emphasis added). The statute before us . . . extends the term of most existing copyrights to 95 years and that of many new copyrights to 70 years after the author's death. The economic effect of this 20-year extension—the longest blanket extension since the Nation's founding—is to make the copyright term not limited, but virtually perpetual. Its primary legal effect is to grant the extended term not to authors, but to their heirs, estates, or corporate successors. And most importantly, its practical effect is not to promote, but to inhibit, the progress of "Science"—by which word the Framers meant learning or knowledge. . . .

The [Copyright] Clause exists not to "provide a special private benefit" . . . but "to stimulate artistic creativity for the general public good.". . . It does so by "motivat[ing] the creative activities of authors" through "the provision of a special reward.". . . The "reward" is a means, not an end. And that is why the copyright term is limited. It is limited so that its beneficiaries—the public—"will not be permanently deprived of the fruits of an artist's labors.". . .

This statute, like virtually every copyright statute, imposes upon the public certain expression-related costs in the form of (1) royalties that may be higher than necessary to evoke creation of the relevant work, and (2) a requirement that one seeking to reproduce a copyrighted work must obtain the copyright holder's permission. The first of these costs translates into higher prices that will potentially restrict a work's dissemination. The second means search costs that themselves may prevent reproduction even where the author has no objection. Although these costs are, in a sense, inevitable concomitants of copyright protection, there are special reasons for thinking them especially serious here.

. . . [T]he present statute primarily benefits the holders of existing copyrights, *i.e.,* copyrights on works already created. And a Congressional Research Service (CRS) study prepared for Congress indicates that the added royalty-related sum that the law will transfer to existing copyright holders is large. E. Rappaport, CRS Report for Congress, Copyright Term Extension: Estimating the Economic Values (1998) (hereinafter CRS Report). In conjunction with official figures on copyright renewals, the CRS Report indicates that only about 2% of copyrights between 55 and 75 years old retain commercial value—*i.e.,* still generate royalties after that time. But books, songs, and movies of that vintage still earn about $400 million per year in royalties. Hence, (despite declining consumer interest in any given work over time) one might conservatively estimate that 20 extra years of copyright protection will mean the transfer of several billion extra royalty dollars to holders of existing copyrights—copyrights that, together, already will have earned many billions of dollars in royalty "reward." See *id.,* at 16.

The extra royalty payments will not come from thin air. Rather, they ultimately come from those who wish to read or see or hear those classic books or films or recordings that have survived. Even the $500,000 that United Airlines has had to pay for the right to play George Gershwin's 1924 classic Rhapsody in Blue represents a cost of doing business, potentially reflected in the ticket prices of those who fly. See Glanzel, *Copyright or Copywrong?,* 39 Training 36, 42 (Dec. 2002). . . .

What copyright-related benefits might justify the statute's extension of copyright protection? First, no one could reasonably conclude that copyright's traditional economic rationale applies here. The extension will not act as an economic spur encouraging authors to create new works. . . . No potential author can reasonably believe that he has more than a tiny chance of writing a classic that will survive commercially long enough for the copyright extension to matter. After all, if, after 55 to 75 years, only 2% of all copyrights retain commercial value, the percentage surviving after 75 years or more (a typical pre-extension copyright term)—must be far smaller. . . . And any remaining monetary incentive is diminished dramatically by the fact that the relevant royalties will not arrive until 75 years or more into the future, when, not the author, but distant heirs, or shareholders in a successor corporation, will receive them. Using assumptions about the time value of money provided us by a group of economists (including five Nobel prize winners) . . . it seems fair to say that, for example, a 1% likelihood of earning $100 annually for 20 years, starting *75 years into the future,* is worth less than seven cents today.

What potential Shakespeare, Wharton, or Hemingway would be moved by such a sum? What monetarily motivated Melville would not realize that he could do better for his grandchildren by putting a few dollars into an interest-bearing bank account? The Court itself finds no evidence to the contrary. It refers to testimony before Congress (1) that the copyright system's incentives encourage creation, and (2) (referring to Noah Webster) that income earned from one work can help support an artist who "'continue[s] to create.'" But the first of these amounts to no more than a set of undeniably true propositions about the value of incentives *in general*. And the applicability of the second to *this* Act is mysterious. How will extension help today's Noah Webster create new works 50 years after his death? Or is that hypothetical Webster supposed to support himself with the extension's present discounted value, *i.e.,* a few pennies? Or (to change the metaphor) is the argument that Dumas *fils* would have written more books had Dumas *pére*'s Three Musketeers earned more royalties? . . .

> **Food for Thought**
>
> Which branch of government is best able to determine whether the extension of a copyright term provides a meaningful incentive to future authors, Congress or the judiciary? Why?

In any event, the incentive-related numbers are far too small for Congress to have concluded rationally, even with respect to new works, that the extension's economic-incentive effect could justify the serious expression-related harms earlier described. And, of course, in respect to works already created—the source of many of the harms previously described—*the statute creates no economic incentive at all.* . . .

This statute will cause serious expression-related harm. It will likely restrict traditional dissemination of copyrighted works. It will likely inhibit new forms of dissemination through the use of new technology. It threatens to interfere with efforts to preserve our Nation's historical and cultural heritage and efforts to use that heritage, say, to educate our Nation's children. It is easy to understand how the statute might benefit the private financial interests of corporations or heirs who own existing copyrights. But I cannot find any constitutionally legitimate, copyright-related way in which the statute will benefit the public. Indeed, in respect to existing works, the serious public harm and the virtually nonexistent public benefit could not be more clear. . . .

Points for Discussion

a. **"Limited Times"**

Based on the majority's analysis in *Eldred*, does Congress have the power to continue granting extensions of the copyright term every 20 years so that existing copyrights never expire? How can we best reconcile (1) the Framers' intent that the term be limited and (2) the power of Congress to extend the term?

b. **Purpose of Copyright**

Justice Breyer argues that the CTEA does not serve the utilitarian purpose of copyright law. Indeed, he suggests that the act may inhibit creativity. Is Breyer correct? Is the answer relevant given the majority's statement that the Court cannot "second-guess congressional determinations and policy judgments of this order, however debatable or unwise they may be"?

c. Striking the Balance

How much incentive is necessary? Utilitarian theory suggests that the copyright term should be long enough to encourage authors to create new works, but no longer. After all, a copyright provides the holder with monopoly rights that may impair the public good, as Justice Breyer notes. So how long should the copyright term be? Or should we have different terms depending on the nature of the work involved, such as a book, computer program, or song?

Given the incentive justification for copyright, works created by non-humans—such as animals or artificial intelligence technology—should not be protected. For example, in *Naruto v. Slater*, 888 F.3d 418 (9th Cir. 2018), the court reasoned that photos taken by a monkey did not qualify for copyright registration. The Compendium of U.S. Copyright Office Practices § 306 (3d ed. 2021) states that the Office will only register a copyright in a "work [that] was created by a human being." More recently, the Office stressed that "it is well-established that copyright can protect only material that is the product of human creativity." Copyright Registration Guidance: Works Containing Material Generated by Artificial Intelligence, 88 Fed. Reg. 16190–01 (March 16, 2023).

d. International Standards

The Berne Convention requires a minimum copyright term that is equal to the author's life plus 50 years; but it permits countries to provide longer terms. In fact, in most countries the standard term is the author's life plus 70 years—just as the CTEA provides. To what extent is international uniformity in copyright duration desirable?

e. Applying the Law

As a practical matter, it may be difficult to know when a copyright term expires. There is no comprehensive list of U.S. copyrights, because federal registration is not required. Accordingly, it may be impossible to identify the author of a particular work. Even if the author can be identified, a potential user may have trouble determining whether the author is alive or, if not, when she died. How should the law address these problems?

f. Aftermath of *Eldred*

Lawrence Lessig, Eldred's lead attorney in the case, is currently a professor at Harvard Law School. After the decision, Lessig wrote a book entitled Free Culture: How Big Media Uses Technology and the Law to Lock Down Culture and Control Creativity, which he dedicated to Eldred. Reflecting on the Supreme Court argument, Lessig asserts that he made a "clear mistake" in responding to a question from Justice Kennedy. When Kennedy asked whether there was empirical evidence that the copyright term impeded "progress in science and the useful arts," Lessig replied:

"[W]e are not making an empirical claim at all. Nothing in our Copyright Clause claim hangs upon the empirical assertion about impeding progress." In his book, Lessig notes: "The right answer was instead that there was an obvious and profound harm. Any number of briefs had been written about it. . . . This was a softball; my answer was a swing and a miss." *Id.* at 239. Would a different answer have changed the outcome of the case?

> **Hear It**
>
> Click here to hear the portion of the oral argument before the Supreme Court that includes Professor Lessig's "mistaken" response.

The 1976 Copyright Act affords copyright protection to "original works of authorship fixed in any tangible medium of expression." 17 U.S.C. § 102(a). Thus, the three requirements for a valid copyright are (1) originality, (2) work of authorship, and (3) fixation.

- *Originality*: The work must be independently created, not copied from another source. It must also possess at least a minimal degree of creativity.
- *Work of authorship*: Eight categories of "works of authorship" are recognized by statute: (a) literary works (including computer programs); (b) musical works; (c) dramatic works; (d) pantomimes and choreographic works; (e) pictorial, graphic, and sculptural works; (f) motion pictures and other audiovisual works; (g) sound recordings; and (h) architectural works. Because these categories are only illustrative, analogous works may also qualify for protection.
- *Fixation*: The work must be written, recorded, or otherwise embodied in some physical form. Thus, it must be "sufficiently permanent or stable to permit it to be perceived, reproduced, or otherwise communicated for a period of more than transitory duration." 17 U.S.C. § 101. For example, a work could be fixed on a hard drive, a piece of paper, a stone tablet, or even—in the case of a tattoo—on human skin.

It is important to mention two items that are *not* required for a copyright: *registration* and *notice*. A copyright owner may choose to register the copyright with the federal Copyright Office, which provides certain benefits to the owner; but registration is not mandatory. Thus, a copyright arises when the three requirements above are satisfied, without any affirmative action by the government. At one time, the copyright holder was required to give notice, usually by listing his name, the year of creation, and a copyright symbol (©) on the work. The notice requirement was abolished in 1989, in order to align U.S. law with international standards.

The leading decision exploring the originality requirement arose in an unusual context: copying information from a telephone directory. Are telephone directories and other compilations of information such as computer databases sufficiently original to merit copyright protection?

Feist Publications, Inc. v. Rural Telephone Service Co., Inc.

Supreme Court of the United States

499 U.S. 340 (1991)

Justice O'Connor delivered the opinion of the Court.

This case requires us to clarify the extent of copyright protection available to telephone directory white pages.

I.

Rural Telephone Service Company, Inc., is a certified public utility that provides telephone service to several communities in northwest Kansas. It is subject to a state regulation that requires all telephone companies operating in Kansas to issue annually an updated telephone directory. Accordingly, as a condition of its monopoly franchise, Rural publishes a typical telephone directory, consisting of white pages and yellow pages. The white pages list in alphabetical order the names of Rural's subscribers, together with their towns and telephone numbers. The yellow pages list Rural's business subscribers alphabetically by category and feature classified advertisements of various sizes. Rural distributes its directory free of charge to its subscribers, but earns revenue by selling yellow pages advertisements.

Justice Sandra Day O'Connor
Click here for larger image

Feist Publications, Inc., is a publishing company that specializes in area-wide telephone directories. Unlike a typical directory, which covers only a particular calling area, Feist's area-wide directories cover a much larger geographical range, reducing the need to call directory assistance or consult multiple directories. The Feist directory that is the subject of this litigation covers 11 different telephone service areas in 15 counties and contains 46,878 white pages listings—compared to Rural's approximately 7,700 listings. Like Rural's directory, Feist's is distributed free of charge and includes both white pages and yellow pages. Feist and Rural compete vigorously for yellow pages advertising.

As the sole provider of telephone service in its service area, Rural obtains subscriber information quite easily. Persons desiring telephone service must apply to Rural and provide their names and addresses; Rural then assigns them a telephone number. Feist is not a telephone company, let alone one with monopoly status, and therefore lacks independent access to any subscriber information. To obtain white pages listings for its area-wide directory, Feist approached each of the 11 telephone companies operating in northwest Kansas and offered to pay for the right to use its white pages listings.

Of the 11 telephone companies, only Rural refused to license its listings to Feist. Rural's refusal created a problem for Feist, as omitting these listings would have left a gaping hole in its area-wide directory, rendering it less attractive to potential yellow pages advertisers. . . .

Unable to license Rural's white pages listings, Feist used them without Rural's consent. Feist began by removing several thousand listings that fell outside the geographic range of its area-wide directory, then hired personnel to investigate the 4,935 that remained. These employees verified the data reported by Rural and sought to obtain additional information. As a result, a typical Feist listing includes the individual's street address; most of Rural's listings do not. Notwithstanding these additions, however, 1,309 of the 46,878 listings in Feist's 1983 directory were identical to listings in Rural's 1982–1983 white pages. . . . Four of these were fictitious listings that Rural had inserted into its directory to detect copying.

Rural sued for copyright infringement in the District Court for the District of Kansas taking the position that Feist, in compiling its own directory, could not use the information contained in Rural's white pages. . . . [The district court granted summary judgment for Rural, and the Tenth Circuit affirmed.]

II.

This case concerns the interaction of two well-established propositions. The first is that facts are not copyrightable; the other, that compilations of facts generally are. Each of these propositions possesses an impeccable pedigree. That there can be no valid copyright in facts is universally understood. The most fundamental axiom of copyright law is that "[n]o author may copyright his ideas or the facts he narrates." *Harper & Row, Publishers, Inc. v. Nation Enterprises,* 471 U.S. 539, 556 (1985). Rural wisely concedes this point, noting in its brief that

> **Food for Thought**
>
> As the Court observes, it is well-settled that facts cannot be copyrighted. Why not? What are the implications of recognizing a copyright in facts?

"[f]acts and discoveries, of course, are not themselves subject to copyright protection." At the same time, however, it is beyond dispute that compilations of facts are within the subject matter of copyright. . . .

There is an undeniable tension between these two propositions. Many compilations consist of nothing but raw data—*i.e.,* wholly factual information not accompanied by any original written expression. On what basis may one claim a copyright in such a work? Common sense tells us that 100 uncopyrightable facts do not magically change their status when gathered together in one place. Yet copyright law seems to contemplate that compilations that consist exclusively of facts are potentially within its scope.

The key to resolving the tension lies in understanding why facts are not copyrightable. The *sine qua non* of copyright is originality. To qualify for copyright protection, a work must be original to the author. . . . Original, as the term is used in copyright, means only that the work was independently created by the author (as opposed to copied from other works), and that it possesses at least some minimal degree of creativity. . . . To be sure, the requisite level of creativity is extremely low; even a slight amount will suffice. The vast majority of works make the grade quite easily, as they possess some creative spark, "no matter how crude, humble or obvious" it might be. . . . Originality does not signify novelty; a work may be original even though it closely resembles other works so long as the similarity is fortuitous, not the result of copying. To illustrate, assume that two poets, each ignorant of the other, compose identical poems. Neither work is novel, yet both are original and, hence, copyrightable. . . .

> **It's Latin to Me**
>
> *Sine qua non* refers to an indispensable condition—something on which something else must depend.

It is this bedrock principle of copyright that mandates the law's seemingly disparate treatment of facts and factual compilations. "No one may claim originality as to facts.". . . This is because facts do not owe their origin to an act of authorship. The distinction is one between creation and discovery: The first person to find and report a particular fact has not created the fact; he or she has merely discovered its existence. . . .

Factual compilations, on the other hand, may possess the requisite originality. The compilation author typically chooses which facts to include, in what order to place them, and how to arrange the collected data so that they may be used effectively by readers. These choices as to selection and arrangement, so long as they are made independently by the compiler and entail a minimal degree of creativity, are sufficiently original that Congress may protect such compilations through the copyright laws. . . . Thus, even a directory that contains absolutely no protectible written expression, only facts, meets the constitutional minimum for copyright protection if it features an original selection or arrangement. . . .

This protection is subject to an important limitation. The mere fact that a work is copyrighted does not mean that every element of the work may be protected. Originality remains the *sine qua non* of copyright; accordingly, copyright protection may extend only to those components of a work that are original to the author. . . .

This inevitably means that the copyright in a factual compilation is thin. Notwithstanding a valid copyright, a subsequent compiler remains free to use the facts contained in another's publication to aid in preparing a competing work, so long as the competing work does not feature the same selection and arrangement. . . .

It may seem unfair that much of the fruit of the compiler's labor may be used by others without compensation. As Justice Brennan has correctly observed, however, this is not "some unforeseen byproduct of a statutory scheme." *Harper & Row,* 471 U.S., at 589 (dissenting opinion). It is, rather, "the essence of copyright," *ibid.,* and a constitutional requirement. The primary objective of copyright is not to reward the labor of authors, but "[t]o promote the Progress of Science and useful Arts." Art. I, § 8, cl. 8. . . . To this end, copyright assures authors the right to their original expression, but encourages others to build freely upon the ideas and information conveyed by a work. *Harper & Row, supra,* 471 U.S., at 556–557. This principle, known as the idea/expression or fact/expression dichotomy, applies to all works of authorship. As applied to a factual compilation, assuming the absence of original written expression, only the compiler's selection and arrangement may be protected; the raw facts may be copied at will. This result is neither unfair nor unfortunate. It is the means by which copyright advances the progress of science and art. . . .

III.

There is no doubt that Feist took from the white pages of Rural's directory a substantial amount of factual information. At a minimum, Feist copied the names, towns, and telephone numbers of 1,309 of Rural's subscribers. Not all copying, however, is copyright infringement. To establish infringement, two elements must be proven: (1) ownership of a valid copyright, and (2) copying of constituent elements of the work that are original. The first element is not at issue here; Feist appears to concede that Rural's directory, considered as a whole, is subject to a valid copyright because it contains some foreword text, as well as original material in its yellow pages advertisements.

The question is whether Rural has proved the second element. In other words, did Feist, by taking 1,309 names, towns, and telephone numbers from Rural's white pages, copy anything that was "original" to Rural? Certainly, the raw data does not satisfy the originality requirement. Rural may have been the first to discover and report the names, towns, and telephone numbers of its subscribers, but this data does not " 'ow[e] its origin' " to Rural. . . . Rather, these bits of information are uncopyrightable facts; they existed before Rural reported them and would have continued to exist if Rural had never published a telephone directory. . . .

The question that remains is whether Rural selected, coordinated, or arranged these uncopyrightable facts in an original way. As mentioned, originality is not a stringent standard; it does not require that facts be presented in an innovative or surprising way. It is equally true, however, that the selection and arrangement of facts cannot be so mechanical or routine as to require no creativity whatsoever. The standard of originality is low, but it does exist. . . .

The selection, coordination, and arrangement of Rural's white pages do not satisfy the minimum constitutional standards for copyright protection. As mentioned at the outset, Rural's white pages are entirely typical. Persons desiring telephone service in Rural's service area fill out an application and Rural issues them a telephone number. In preparing its white pages, Rural simply takes the data provided by its subscribers and lists it alphabetically by surname. The end product is a garden-variety white pages directory, devoid of even the slightest trace of creativity.

Rural's selection of listings could not be more obvious: It publishes the most basic information—name, town, and telephone number—about each person who applies to it for telephone service. This is "selection" of a sort, but it lacks the modicum of creativity necessary to transform mere selection into copyrightable expression. Rural expended sufficient effort to make the white pages directory useful, but insufficient creativity to make it original. . . .

Nor can Rural claim originality in its coordination and arrangement of facts. The white pages do nothing more than list Rural's subscribers in alphabetical order. This arrangement may, technically speaking, owe its origin to Rural; no one disputes that Rural undertook the task of alphabetizing the names itself. But there is nothing remotely creative about arranging names alphabetically in a white pages directory. It is an age-old practice, firmly rooted in tradition and so commonplace that it has come to be expected as a matter of course. . . . It is not only unoriginal, it is practically inevitable. This time-honored tradition does not possess the minimal creative spark required by the Copyright Act and the Constitution.

We conclude that the names, towns, and telephone numbers copied by Feist were not original to Rural and therefore were not protected by the copyright in Rural's combined white and yellow pages directory. As a constitutional matter, copyright protects only those constituent elements of a work that possess more than a *de minimis* quantum of creativity. Rural's white pages, limited to basic subscriber information and arranged alphabetically, fall short of the mark. As a statutory matter, 17

> **It's Latin to Me**
>
> *De minimis* means trifling or negligible. Thus, a work that reflects an extraordinarily small amount of creativity does not qualify for copyright protection.

U.S.C. § 101 does not afford protection from copying to a collection of facts that are selected, coordinated, and arranged in a way that utterly lacks originality. Given that some works must fail, we cannot imagine a more likely candidate. Indeed, were we to hold that Rural's white pages pass muster, it is hard to believe that any collection of facts could fail. . . .

The judgment of the Court of Appeals is reversed.

Points for Discussion

a. **Idea-Expression Dichotomy**

Copyright law protects the manner in which an idea is expressed—not the idea itself. Thus, concepts, principles, discoveries, facts, systems, procedures, methods of operation, and other ideas are not covered by copyright. This concept is known as the idea-expression dichotomy. So while the precise combination of words used in a book is copyrightable, the ideas in the book are not. Accordingly, the factual information in Rural's directory was not copyrightable, as the *Feist* court notes. So, at best, Rural could argue for a copyright only in the selection and arrangement of these facts.

What about a sequence of yoga poses described in a book? In *Bikram's Yoga College of India, L.P. v. Evolation Yoga, LLC*, 803 F.3d 1032 (9th Cir. 2015), the court held that the sequence was not copyrightable because it was merely an idea. It noted that "courts have routinely held that the copyright for a work describing how to perform a process does not extend to the process itself." *Id.* at 1037–38.

b. **Factual Compilations**

The creation of computer databases and other factual compilations requires substantial investment. Should factual compilations always receive copyright protection, regardless of originality?

c. **How Much Originality?**

What amount of originality should be required in light of the goals of copyright law? Does the *Feist* court set an appropriate standard? In *CDN, Inc. v. Kapes*, 197 F.3d 1256 (9th Cir. 1999), the Ninth Circuit held that published price estimates for collectible coins were sufficiently original to qualify for copyright. The court stated: "CDN does not republish data from another source or apply a set formula or rule to generate prices. The prices CDN creates are compilations of data that represent its best estimate of the value of the coins." *Id.* at 1260. Is *CDN* consistent with *Feist*?

d. **Copyright Problems**

Are the requirements for copyright met in these situations?

> (1) As part of an outdoor competition in Nevada, A carves a large ice sculpture that somewhat resembles the Statue of Liberty.
>
> (2) The copyright term has elapsed for a painting. B takes a photograph of the painting, attempting to copy it as closely as possible.
>
> (3) Using publicly available information, C draws a map of Florida, which shows the locations of interstate highways, county seats, and the state capital.

e. Copyrighting James Bond

Is a movie character protected by copyright? The law is somewhat confused here, because a character may be viewed either as an idea or as the expression of an idea. The modern trend is reflected in *Metro-Goldwyn-Mayer, Inc. v. American Honda Motor Co.*, 900 F. Supp. 1287, 1296 (C.D. Cal. 1995), where the court held that the James Bond character was sufficiently unique to be copyrightable: "Like Rocky, Sherlock Holmes, Tarzan, and Superman, James Bond has certain character traits that have been developed over time through the sixteen films in which he appears."

f. Is Anything Truly New?

In his dissent in *White v. Samsung Electronics America, Inc.* (Chapter 1), Judge Kozinski observed: "Nothing today, likely nothing since we tamed fire, is genuinely new: Culture, like science and technology, grows by accretion, each new creator building on the works of those who came before." How persuasive is this argument? Should it affect the standard for originality?

---

2. Infringement

Suppose you write a book review, quoting short passages from the book to support your analysis. Are you liable for copyright infringement? The most important defense in copyright law is *fair use*. In effect, the fair use doctrine allows minor use of a copyrighted work where the use does not materially affect the rights of the copyright owner. As one court explained, the doctrine avoids "rigid application of the copyright statute when, on occasion, it would stifle the very creativity that law is designed to foster." *Iowa State University Research Foundation, Inc. v. ABC*, 621 F.2d 57, 60 (2d Cir. 1980).

The fair use defense is set forth in 17 U.S.C. § 107:

> ... [T]he fair use of a copyrighted work ... for purposes such as criticism, comment, news reporting, teaching (including multiple copies for classroom use), scholarship, or research, is not an infringement of copyright. In determining whether the use made of a work in any particular case is a fair use the factors to be considered shall include—

> (1) the purpose and character of the use, including whether such use is of a commercial nature or is for nonprofit educational purposes;
>
> (2) the nature of the copyrighted work;
>
> (3) the amount and substantiality of the portion used in relation to the copyrighted work as a whole; and
>
> (4) the effect of the use upon the potential market for or value of the copyrighted work. . . .

Our next case illustrates how the fair use test is applied in practice. It arises out of one of the most famous events in recent American history: the resignation of President Nixon. In the wake of the 1972 Watergate scandal and the discovery of secret tapes of White House conversations, pressure mounted for Nixon to leave office. Facing impeachment and almost certain conviction in the Senate, Nixon resigned in August, 1974. His vice-president, Gerald Ford, was sworn in as president. Ford pardoned Nixon one month later, precluding any criminal prosecution. The pardon was controversial. Some suggested that it was part of a secret deal to obtain Nixon's resignation. But the precise reasons for the pardon remained unclear until Ford decided to publish his memoirs.

FYI

In his proclamation granting the pardon, President Ford noted that during the year or so that it would take to bring Nixon to trial "the tranquility to which this nation has been restored by the events of recent weeks could be irreparably lost by the prospects of bringing to trial a former President of the United States. The prospects of such a trial will cause prolonged and divisive debate over the propriety of exposing to further punishment and degradation a man who has already paid the unprecedented penalty of relinquishing the highest elective office of the United States."

Harper & Row, Publishers, Inc. v. Nation Enterprises

Supreme Court of the United States

471 U.S. 539 (1985)

JUSTICE O'CONNOR delivered the opinion of the Court.

This case requires us to consider to what extent the "fair use" provision of the Copyright Revision Act of 1976, (hereinafter the Copyright Act) 17 U.S.C. § 107, sanctions the unauthorized use of quotations from a public figure's unpublished manuscript. . . .

I.

In February 1977, shortly after leaving the White House, former President Gerald R. Ford contracted with petitioners Harper & Row and Reader's Digest, to publish his as yet unwritten memoirs. The memoirs were to contain "significant hitherto unpublished material" concerning the Watergate crisis, Mr. Ford's pardon of former President Nixon and "Mr. Ford's reflections on this period of history, and the morality and personalities involved." In addition to the right to publish the Ford memoirs in book form, the agreement gave petitioners the exclusive right to license prepublication excerpts, known in the trade as "first serial rights." Two years later, as the memoirs were nearing completion, petitioners negotiated a prepublication licensing agreement with Time, a weekly news magazine. Time agreed to pay $25,000, $12,500 in advance and an additional $12,500 at publication, in exchange for the right to excerpt 7,500 words from Mr. Ford's account of the Nixon pardon. The issue featuring the excerpts was timed to appear approximately one week before shipment of the full length book version to bookstores. Exclusivity was an important consideration; Harper & Row instituted procedures designed to maintain the confidentiality of the manuscript, and Time retained the right to renegotiate the second payment should the material appear in print prior to its release of the excerpts.

President Richard M. Nixon
Click here for larger photo

President Gerald R. Ford
Click here for larger photo

Two to three weeks before the Time article's scheduled release, an unidentified person secretly brought a copy of the Ford manuscript [entitled A Time to Heal: The Autobiography of Gerald R. Ford] to Victor Navasky, editor of The Nation, a political commentary magazine. Mr. Navasky knew that his possession of the manuscript was not authorized and that the manuscript must be returned quickly to his "source" to avoid discovery. He hastily put together what he believed was "a real hot news story" composed of quotes, paraphrases, and facts drawn exclusively from the manuscript. Mr. Navasky attempted no independent commentary, research or criticism, in part because of the need for speed if he was to "make news" by "publish[ing] in advance of publication of the Ford book." The 2,250-word article . . . appeared on April 3, 1979. As a result of The Nation's article, Time canceled its piece and refused to pay the remaining $12,500. [Petitioners brought suit for copyright infringement and prevailed at trial, but the Second Circuit reversed, finding that The Nation's story was a fair use of the Ford manuscript.] . . . .

III.

A.

Fair use was traditionally defined as "a privilege in others than the owner of the copyright to use the copyrighted material in a reasonable manner without his consent." The statutory formulation of the defense of fair use in the Copyright Act reflects the intent of Congress to codify the common-law doctrine. Section 107 requires a case-by-case determination whether a particular use is fair, and the statute notes four nonexclusive factors to be considered. This approach was "intended to restate the [pre-existing] judicial doctrine of fair use, not to change, narrow, or enlarge it in any way." H.R. Rep. No. 94-1476, p. 66 (1976). . . .

B.

Respondents, however, contend that First Amendment values require a different rule under the circumstances of this case. The thrust of the decision below is that "[t]he scope of [fair use] is undoubtedly wider when the information conveyed relates to matters of high public concern." *Consumers Union of the United States, Inc. v. General Signal Corp.*, 724 F.2d 1044, 1050 (CA2 1983). . . . Respondents advance the substantial public import of the subject matter of the Ford memoirs as grounds for excusing a use that would ordinarily not pass muster as a fair use—the piracy of verbatim quotations for the purpose of "scooping" the authorized first serialization. Respondents explain their copying of Mr. Ford's expression as essential to reporting the news story it claims the book itself represents. In respondents' view, not only the facts contained in Mr. Ford's memoirs, but "the precise manner in which [he] expressed himself [were] as newsworthy as what he had to say." Respondents argue that the public's interest in learning this news as fast as possible outweighs the right of the author to control its first publication. . . .

> **Food for Thought**
>
> As we saw in Chapter 1, documents that the President creates during his term in office as part of his official duties are owned by the federal government. Should a former president be entitled to copyright protection for a document describing the performance of these duties which he writes after leaving office?

Respondents' theory, however, would expand fair use to effectively destroy any expectation of copyright protection in the work of a public figure. Absent such protection, there would be little incentive to create or profit in financing such memoirs, and the public would be denied an important source of significant historical information.

The promise of copyright would be an empty one if it could be avoided merely by dubbing the infringement a fair use "news report" of the book. . . .

In view of the First Amendment protections already embodied in the Copyright Act's distinction between copyrightable expression and uncopyrightable facts and ideas, and the latitude for scholarship and comment traditionally afforded by fair use, we see no warrant for expanding the doctrine of fair use to create what amounts to a public figure exception to copyright. Whether verbatim copying from a public figure's manuscript in a given case is or is not fair must be judged according to the traditional equities of fair use.

IV.

. . . The four factors identified by Congress as especially relevant in determining whether the use was fair are: (1) the purpose and character of the use; (2) the nature of the copyrighted work; (3) the substantiality of the portion used in relation to the copyrighted work as a whole; (4) the effect on the potential market for or value of the copyrighted work. We address each one separately.

Purpose of the Use. The Second Circuit correctly identified news reporting as the general purpose of The Nation's use. News reporting is one of the examples enumerated in § 107 to "give some idea of the sort of activities the courts might regard as fair use under the circumstances.". . . This listing was not intended to be exhaustive . . . or to single out any particular use as presumptively a "fair" use. . . . The fact that an article arguably is "news" and therefore a productive use is simply one factor in a fair use analysis. . . .

The fact that a publication was commercial as opposed to nonprofit is a separate factor that tends to weigh against a finding of fair use. "[E]very commercial use of copyrighted material is presumptively an unfair exploitation of the monopoly privilege that belongs to the owner of the copyright." *Sony Corp. of America v. Universal City Studios, Inc.*, 464 U.S. 417, 451 (1984). In arguing that the purpose of news reporting is not purely commercial, The Nation misses the point entirely. The crux of the profit/nonprofit distinction is not whether the sole motive of the use is monetary gain but whether the user stands to profit from exploitation of the copyrighted material without paying the customary price.

In evaluating character and purpose we cannot ignore The Nation's stated purpose of scooping the forthcoming hardcover and Time abstracts. The Nation's use had not merely the incidental effect but the *intended purpose* of supplanting the copyright holder's commercially valuable right of first publication. . . . Also relevant to the "character" of the use is "the propriety of the defendant's conduct." "Fair use presupposes 'good faith' and 'fair dealing.'" *Time Inc. v. Bernard Geis Associates*, 293 F. Supp. 130, 146 (SDNY 1968), The trial court found that The Nation knowingly exploited a purloined manuscript. Unlike the typical claim of fair use, The Nation cannot offer up even the fiction of consent as justification. . . .

Nature of the Copyrighted Work. Second, the Act directs attention to the nature of the copyrighted work. "A Time to Heal" may be characterized as an unpublished historical narrative or autobiography. The law generally recognizes a greater need to disseminate factual works than works of fiction or fantasy. . . . Some of the briefer quotes from the memoirs are arguably necessary adequately to convey the facts; for example, Mr. Ford's characterization of the White House tapes as the "smoking gun" is perhaps so integral to the idea expressed as to be inseparable from it. But The Nation did not stop at isolated phrases and instead excerpted subjective descriptions and portraits of public figures whose power lies in the author's individualized expression. Such use, focusing on the most expressive elements of the work, exceeds that necessary to disseminate the facts. . . .

In the case of Mr. Ford's manuscript, the copyright holders' interest in confidentiality is irrefutable; the copyright holders had entered into a contractual undertaking to "keep the manuscript confidential" and required that all those to whom the manuscript was shown also "sign an agreement to keep the manuscript confidential." While the copyright holders' contract with Time required Time to submit its proposed article seven days before publication, The Nation's clandestine publication afforded no such opportunity for creative or quality control. It was hastily patched together and contained "a number of inaccuracies." A use that so clearly infringes the copyright holder's interests in confidentiality and creative control is difficult to characterize as "fair."

> **FYI**
>
> Between 1971 and 1973, President Nixon arranged for the secret recording of his White House conversations with various aides and staff members. When the existence of the tapes was made public, they were subpoenaed by House and Senate committees investigating the Watergate scandal and ultimately provided the evidence that led to Nixon's resignation.

Amount and Substantiality of the Portion Used. Next, the Act directs us to examine the amount and substantiality of the portion used in relation to the copyrighted work as a whole. In absolute terms, the words actually quoted were an insubstantial portion of "A Time to Heal." The District Court, however, found that "[T]he Nation took what was essentially the heart of the book." 557 F. Supp., at 1072. . . . A Time editor described the chapters on the pardon as "the most interesting and moving parts of the entire manuscript." The portions actually quoted were selected by Mr. Navasky as among the most powerful passages in those chapters. He testified that he used verbatim excerpts because simply reciting the information could not adequately convey the "absolute certainty with which [Ford] expressed himself;" or show that "this comes from President Ford;" or carry the "definitive quality" of the original. In short, he quoted these passages precisely because they qualitatively embodied Ford's distinctive expression. . . .

Stripped to the verbatim quotes, the direct takings from the unpublished manuscript [300 words] constitute at least 13% of the infringing article. The Nation article is structured around the quoted excerpts which serve as its dramatic focal points. In view of the expressive value of the excerpts and their key role in the infringing work, we cannot agree with the Second Circuit that the "magazine took a meager, indeed an infinitesimal amount of Ford's original language."

Effect on the Market. Finally, the Act focuses on "the effect of the use upon the potential market for or value of the copyrighted work." This last factor is undoubtedly the single most important element of fair use. . . . The trial court found not merely a potential but an actual effect on the market. Time's cancellation of its projected serialization and its refusal to pay the $12,500 were the direct effect of the infringement. The Court of Appeals rejected this factfinding as clearly erroneous, noting that the record did not establish a causal relation between Time's nonperformance and respondents' unauthorized publication of Mr. Ford's *expression* as opposed to the facts taken from the memoirs. We disagree. Rarely will a case of copyright infringement present such clear-cut evidence of actual damage. Petitioners assured Time that there would be no other authorized publication of *any* portion of the unpublished manuscript prior to April 23, 1979. *Any* publication of material from chapters 1 and 3 would permit Time to renegotiate its final payment. Time cited The Nation's article, which contained verbatim quotes from the unpublished manuscript, as a reason for its nonperformance. . . . Petitioners established a prima facie case of actual damage that respondents failed to rebut. . . .

It is undisputed that the factual material in the balance of The Nation's article, besides the verbatim quotes at issue here, was drawn exclusively from the chapters on the pardon. The excerpts were employed as featured episodes in a story about the Nixon pardon—precisely the use petitioners had licensed to Time. The borrowing of these verbatim quotes from the unpublished manuscript lent The Nation's piece a special air of authenticity—as Navasky expressed it, the reader would know it was Ford speaking and not The Nation. Thus it directly competed for a share of the market for prepublication excerpts. . . . Placed in a broader perspective, a fair use doctrine that permits extensive prepublication quotations from an unreleased manuscript without the copyright owner's consent poses substantial potential for damage to the marketability of first serialization rights in general. . . .

V.

. . . The Nation conceded that its verbatim copying of some 300 words of direct quotation from the Ford manuscript would constitute an infringement unless excused as a fair use. Because we find that The Nation's use of these verbatim excerpts from the unpublished manuscript was not a fair use, the judgment of the Court of Appeals is reversed, and the case is remanded for further proceedings consistent with this opinion.

JUSTICE BRENNAN . . . dissenting.

The Court holds that The Nation's quotation of 300 words from the unpublished 200,000-word manuscript of President Gerald R. Ford infringed the copyright in that manuscript, even though the quotations related to a historical event of undoubted significance—the resignation and pardon of President Richard M. Nixon. Although the Court pursues the laudable goal of protecting "the economic incentive to create and disseminate ideas," this zealous defense of the copyright owner's prerogative will, I fear, stifle the broad dissemination of ideas and information copyright is intended to nurture. Protection of the copyright owner's economic interest is achieved in this case through an exceedingly narrow definition of the scope of fair use. The progress of arts and sciences and the robust public debate essential to an enlightened citizenry are ill served by this constricted reading of the fair use doctrine. I therefore respectfully dissent. . . .

Points for Discussion

a. **Is News Different?**

The majority recognizes "a greater need to disseminate factual works than works of fiction or fantasy." Take this analysis one step further. Arguably, there is a greater need to disseminate news than other factual works that are not time-sensitive. So should a different fair use test be applied to important news? After all, the decision to pardon Nixon was one of the biggest news stories of the 1970s. Ford's memoir revealed that Alexander Haig (Nixon's chief of staff) had met with Ford *before* Nixon resigned and mentioned the idea of a Nixon pardon if Ford became president. Wasn't this "hot news"?

b. **Bad Faith**

It is sometimes said that "bad facts make bad law." Here, *The Nation* "knowingly exploited a purloined manuscript." How much did *The Nation's* bad faith affect the outcome of the case?

c. **Protecting Parody**

Do skits on *Saturday Night Live* and similar programs infringe various copyrights? No, due to the fair use defense. The leading case to explore when parody constitutes fair use is *Campbell v. Acuff-Rose Music, Inc.*, 510 U.S. 569 (1994). In *Campbell*, the owner of the song *Oh, Pretty Woman* claimed that the

> **Hear It**
>
> Columbia Law School and George Washington University School of Law sponsor the Music Copyright Infringement Resource, which is a website that features clips of songs involved in famous copyright cases. Click here to hear the two songs involved in *Campbell v. Acuff-Rose Music, Inc.*

2 Live Crew song *Pretty Woman* infringed its copyright; 2 Live Crew argued that its song was a parody which qualified for the fair use defense. Although the Court remanded the case for further proceedings, its analysis suggests that many parodies will qualify for fair use protection. It reasoned that the first factor—the purpose and character of the use—turned largely on the extent to which the new work was transformative: "[T]he more transformative the new work, the less will be the significance of other factors, like commercialism, that may weigh against a finding of fair use." *Id.* at 579. It acknowledged that the second factor—the nature of the copyrighted work—was unlikely to be relevant because "parodies almost invariably copy publicly known, expressive works." *Id.* at 586. The Court recognized that parody required copying to some extent—the third factor—because it "must be able to 'conjure up' at least enough of that original to make the object of its critical wit recognizable." *Id.* at 588. Finally, it noted that a parody which harms the potential market for the original work "like a scathing theater review. . . does not produce a harm cognizable under the Copyright Act." *Id.* at 591–92. *See also Dr. Seuss Enterprises, L.P. v. ComicMix LLC,* 983 F.3d 443 (9th Cir. 2020) (*Oh, the Places You'll Boldly Go!,* a Star Trek mashup of Seuss's *Oh, the Places You'll Go!,* was not a parody and did not qualify for the fair use defense).

d. Protecting Art

The Supreme Court seemingly narrowed the *Campbell* approach to the first fair use factor in *Andy Warhol Foundation for the Visual Arts, Inc. v. Goldsmith,* 598 U.S. 508 (2023). The case involved a photo of Prince taken by Lynn Goldsmith, a commercial photographer. In 1984, Goldsmith licensed the photo to *Vanity Fair* magazine as an "artist reference" so that Andy Warhol could create an image of Prince for one of its covers. Warhol later created 15 more artistic works based on the same photo. Warhol died, and his rights in the Prince series passed to the Foundation. In 2016, *Condé Nast* magazine obtained a license from the Foundation to use "Orange Prince," one of the series, on its cover.

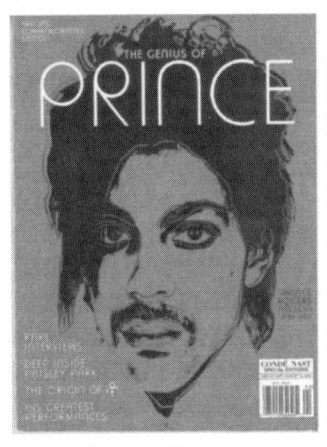

Orange Prince   **Goldsmith photo**

Click here for larger images

When Goldsmith sued for infringement, the district court granted summary judgment for the Foundation based on the fair use defense. But the Second Circuit reversed. Before the Supreme Court, the only issue was whether the first factor favored fair use; the Foundation did not challenge the findings below that the other factors cut against fair use.

The Court applied a balancing test: "[T]he fair use first factor . . . focuses on whether an alleged infringing use has a further purpose or different character, which is a matter of degree, and the degree of difference must be weighed against other considerations, like commercialism." *Id.* at 525. It reasoned that both works shared substantially the same purpose—use as a magazine cover—and that the Foundation's use was commercial in nature. It rejected the Foundation's argument that Orange Prince had a new meaning or message, and was thus sufficiently transformative. Even assuming that Orange Prince portrayed Prince as an " 'iconic, larger-than-life figure,' " whereas Goldsmith's work was "photorealistic," the "degree of difference is not enough for the first factor to favor [the Foundation], given the specific context of the use." *Id.* at 545–46.

In dissent, Justice Kagan observed: "Today, the Court declares that Andy Warhol's eye-popping silkscreen of Prince—a work based on but dramatically altering an existing photograph—is (in copyright lingo) not 'transformative.' " *Id.* at 558. She stressed that in "remaking" the first factor "and thus constricting fair use's boundaries, the majority hampers creative progress and undermines creative freedom." *Id.* at 560.

e. Fair Use in the Digital Era

In *Google LLC v. Oracle America, Inc.*, 141 S. Ct. 1183 (2021), the Supreme Court held that Google's limited copying of Oracle's Java computer code was fair use. It found that the use was transformative because Google utilized this "user interface" code to create new products—to "expand the use and usefulness of Android-based smartphones." *Id.* at 1203. The Court reasoned that the nature of the code "if copyrightable at all, [was] further than are most computer programs . . . from the core of copyright" because it was "inextricably bound together with a general system . . . that no one claims is a proper subject of copyright." *Id.* at 1201–02. It noted that Google had copied only .4% of Oracle's user interface code, a small amount. Finally, it concluded that the fourth factor favored Google because (1) it was unclear that Oracle suffered harm and (2) enforcement of the copyright "would risk harm to the public" by limiting "the future creativity of new programs." *Id.* at 1208. *See also Authors Guild v. Google*, 804 F.3d 202, 207 (2d Cir. 2015) (Google's project to digitize the world's books to create a searchable, on-line database was fair use).

f. Fair Use Problems

Will the fair use defense succeed in these situations?

> (1) Movie star M types his personal diary into a computer each night, never intending it to be published. He inadvertently attaches the diary to an email message that he sends to a reporter at *Time* magazine. One of the 2,000 diary pages describes how he saw S, a well-known singer, die from a drug overdose. Previously, S's death had been attributed to a heart attack. *Time* publishes the diary page concerning S's death.
>
> (2) President P publishes a memoir about her eight-year period in office. The book is initially popular, but sales wane after two years and it goes out of print. Five years later, H, a professional historian, publishes a book about P's presidential years that quotes portions of P's memoir. About 1% of H's book consists of short passages from P's memoir; these include excerpts about the most important decisions of P's presidency.

To win a copyright infringement suit, the plaintiff must prove that: (1) the plaintiff owns a valid copyright; (2) the defendant actually copied the plaintiff's work; and (3) an ordinary observer would conclude that the defendant's work was substantially similar to the plaintiff's work. The defendant's knowledge and intent are irrelevant. Accordingly, a defendant is liable for copyright infringement even if he believed in good faith that he had permission to use the work.

Proving infringement can be comparatively simple. Suppose that A copies the entire text of B's book and sells the book to the public. Assuming B had a valid copyright, A is liable because he copied the work, and his copying was an improper appropriation. But what if the infringing work is a painting, dance, or song that *resembles* an original work, but also has *original* components?

Infringement cases involving songs have been particularly troublesome, because many popular songs are similar. For example, a federal court ruled that George Harrison's 1970 song *My Sweet Lord* infringed the copyright of the 1963 rock and roll classic *He's So Fine* by the Chiffons, apparently due to unconscious plagiarism. *ABKCO Music, Inc. v. Harrisongs Music, Ltd.*, 722 F.2d 988 (2nd Cir. 1983). Harrison later complained in his biography, I Me Mine: "I still don't understand how the courts aren't filled with similar cases—as 99 percent of popular music . . . is reminiscent of something or other."

> **Hear It**
>
> Click here to hear the songs involved in *ABKCO Music, Inc. v. Harrisongs Music, Ltd.*

Selle v. Gibb

United States Court of Appeals, Seventh Circuit

741 F.2d 896 (1984)

CUDAHY, CIRCUIT JUDGE.

The plaintiff, Ronald H. Selle, brought a suit against three brothers, Maurice, Robin and Barry Gibb, known collectively as the popular singing group, the Bee Gees, alleging that the Bee Gees, in their hit tune, "How Deep Is Your Love," had infringed the copyright of his song, "Let It End." The jury returned a verdict in plaintiff's favor on the issue of liability in a bifurcated trial. The district court, Judge George N. Leighton, granted the defendants' motion for judgment notwithstanding the verdict and, in the alternative, for a new trial. . . .

I.

Selle composed his song, "Let It End," in one day in the fall of 1975 and obtained a copyright for it on November 17, 1975. He played his song with his small band two or three times in the Chicago area and sent a tape and lead sheet of the music to eleven music recording and publishing companies. Eight of the companies returned the materials to Selle; three did not respond. This was the extent of the public dissemination of Selle's song. Selle first became aware of the Bee Gees' song, "How Deep Is Your Love," in May 1978 and thought that he recognized the music as his own, although the lyrics were different. He also saw the movie, "Saturday Night Fever," the sound track of which features the song "How Deep Is Your Love," and again recognized the music. He subsequently sued the three Gibb brothers; Paramount Pictures Corporation, which made and distributed the movie; and Phonodisc, Inc., now known as Polygram Distribution, Inc., which made and distributed the cassette tape of "How Deep Is Your Love."

Hear It

Click here to hear the songs involved in *Selle v. Gibb*.

The Bee Gees are internationally known performers and creators of popular music. They have composed more than 160 songs; their sheet music, records and tapes have been distributed worldwide, some of the albums selling more than 30 million copies. The Bee Gees, however, do not themselves read or write music. In composing a song, their practice was to tape a tune, which members of their staff would later transcribe and reduce to a form suitable for copyrighting, sale and performance by both the Bee Gees and others.

In addition to their own testimony at trial, the Bee Gees presented testimony by their manager, Dick Ashby, and two musicians, Albhy Galuten and Blue Weaver, who were on the Bee Gees' staff at the time "How Deep Is Your Love" was composed.

These witnesses described in detail how, in January 1977, the Bee Gees and several members of their staff went to a recording studio in the Chateau d'Herouville about 25 miles northwest of Paris. There the group composed at least six new songs and mixed a live album. Barry Gibb's testimony included a detailed explanation of a work tape which was introduced into evidence and played in court. This tape preserves the actual process of creation during which the brothers, and particularly Barry, created the tune of the accused song while Weaver, a keyboard player, played the tune which was hummed or sung by the brothers. Although the tape does not seem to preserve the very beginning of the process of creation, it does depict the process by which ideas, notes, lyrics and bits of the tune were gradually put together. . . .

The only expert witness to testify at trial was Arrand Parsons, a professor of music at Northwestern University who has had extensive professional experience primarily in classical music. He has been a program annotator for the Chicago Symphony Orchestra and the New Orleans Symphony Orchestra and has authored works about musical theory. Prior to this case, however, he had never made a comparative analysis of two popular songs. Dr. Parsons testified on the basis of several charts comparing the musical notes of each song and a comparative recording prepared under his direction. . . .

Dr. Parsons testified that, in his opinion, "the two songs had such striking similarities that they could not have been written independent of one another." He also testified that he did not know of two songs by different composers "that contain as many striking similarities" as do the two songs at issue here. However, on several occasions, he declined to say that the similarities could only have resulted from copying.

Following presentation of the case, the jury returned a verdict for the plaintiff on the issue of liability, the only question presented to the jury. Judge Leighton, however, granted the defendants' motion for judgment notwithstanding the verdict and, in the alternative, for a new trial. . . .

III.

Selle's primary contention on this appeal is that the district court misunderstood the theory of proof of copyright infringement on which he based his claim. Under this theory, copyright infringement can be demonstrated when, even in the absence of any direct evidence of access, the two pieces in question are so strikingly similar that access can be inferred from such similarity alone. Selle argues that the testimony of his expert witness, Dr. Parsons, was sufficient evidence of such striking similarity that it was permissible for the jury, even in the absence of any other evidence concerning access, to infer that the Bee Gees had access to plaintiff's song and indeed copied it.

In establishing a claim of copyright infringement of a musical composition, the plaintiff must prove (1) ownership of the copyright in the complaining work; (2) originality of the work; (3) copying of the work by the defendant, and (4) a substantial degree of similarity between the two works. *See* Sherman, *Musical Copyright Infringement: The Requirement of Substantial Similarity.* Copyright Law Symposium, Number 92, American Society of Composers, Authors and Publishers 81–82. Columbia University Press (1977) [hereinafter "Sherman, *Musical Copyright Infringement*"]. The only element which is at issue in this appeal is proof of copying; the first two elements are essentially conceded, while the fourth (substantial similarity) is, at least in these circumstances, closely related to the third element under plaintiff's theory of the case.

Proof of copying is crucial to any claim of copyright infringement because no matter how similar the two works may be (even to the point of identity), if the defendant did not copy the accused work, there is no infringement. However, because direct evidence of copying is rarely available, the plaintiff can rely upon circumstantial evidence to prove this essential element, and the most important component of this sort of circumstantial evidence is proof of access. *See generally* 3 Nimmer, *Copyright* § 13.02 at 13–9 (1983) [hereinafter "Nimmer, *Copyright*"]. The plaintiff may be able to introduce direct evidence of access when, for example, the work was sent directly to the defendant (whether a musician or a publishing company) or a close associate of the defendant. On the other hand, the plaintiff may be able to establish a reasonable possibility of access when, for example, the complaining work has been widely disseminated to the public. *See, e.g., Abkco Music, Inc. v. Harrisongs Music, Ltd.,* 722 F.2d 988, 998 (2d Cir. 1983) (finding of access based on wide dissemination).

If, however, the plaintiff does not have direct evidence of access, then an inference of access may still be established circumstantially by proof of similarity which is so striking that the possibilities of independent creation, coincidence and prior common source are, as a practical matter, precluded. If the plaintiff presents evidence of striking similarity sufficient to raise an inference of access, then copying is presumably proved simultaneously, although the fourth element (substantial similarity) still requires proof that the defendant copied a substantial amount of the complaining work. The theory which Selle attempts to apply to this case is based on proof of copying by circumstantial proof of access established by striking similarity between the two works.

One difficulty with plaintiff's theory is that no matter how great the similarity between the two works, it is not their similarity *per se* which establishes access; rather, their similarity tends to prove access in light of the nature of the works, the particular musical genre involved and other circumstantial evidence of access. In other words, striking similarity is just one piece of circumstantial evidence tending to show access and must not be considered in isolation; it must be considered together with other types of circumstantial evidence relating to access.

. . . [A]lthough it has frequently been written that striking similarity *alone* can establish access, the decided cases suggest that this circumstance would be most unusual. The plaintiff must always present sufficient evidence to support a reasonable possibility of access because the jury cannot draw an inference of access based upon speculation and conjecture alone. . . .

The greatest difficulty perhaps arises when the plaintiff cannot demonstrate any direct link between the complaining work and the defendant but the work has been so widely disseminated that it is not unreasonable to infer that the defendant might have had access to it. . . . In *Abkco Music, Inc. v. Harrisongs Music, Ltd.*, 722 F.2d 988, 997–99 (2d Cir. 1983), the court found that there had been a copyright infringement based on a theory of subconscious copying. The complaining work, "He's So Fine," had been the most popular song in the United States for five weeks and among the thirty top hits in England for seven weeks during the year in which George Harrison composed "My Sweet Lord," the infringing song. This evidence, in addition to Harrison's own admission that the two songs were "strikingly similar," supported the finding of infringement. On the other hand, in *Jewel Music Publishing Co. v. Leo Feist, Inc.*, 62 F. Supp. 596, 598 (S.D.N.Y. 1945), almost 10,000 copies of the complaining song had been distributed or sold and the music had also been broadcast on national performances. The court still concluded that the showing of access was insufficient, in combination with the other evidence, to support a reasonable inference of access.

. . . Selle's song certainly did not achieve the extent of public dissemination existing in . . . *Jewel Music Publishing Co.* or *Harrisongs Music,* and there was also no evidence that any of the defendants or their associates were in Chicago on the two or three occasions when the plaintiff played his song publicly. It is not necessary for us, given the facts of this case, to determine the number of copies which must be publicly distributed to raise a reasonable inference of access. Nevertheless, in this case, the availability of Selle's song, as shown by the evidence, was virtually *de minimis*. . . .

Judge Leighton thus based his decision on what he characterized as the plaintiff's inability to raise more than speculation that the Bee Gees had access to his song. The extensive testimony of the defendants and their witnesses describing the creation process went essentially uncontradicted, and there was no attempt even to impeach their credibility. . . . Judge Leighton's conclusions that there was no more than a bare possibility that the defendants could have had access to Selle's song and that this was an insufficient basis from which the jury could have reasonably inferred the existence of access seem correct. . . .

IV.

The grant of the motion for judgment notwithstanding the verdict . . . is also supported by a more traditional analysis of proof of access based only on the proof of "striking similarity" between the two compositions. The plaintiff relies almost exclusively on the testimony of his expert witness, Dr. Parsons, that the two pieces were, in fact, "strikingly similar."[3] Yet formulating a meaningful definition of "striking similarity" is no simple task, and the term is often used in a conclusory or circular fashion. Sherman defines "striking similarity" as a term of art signifying "that degree of similarity as will permit an inference of copying even in the absence of proof of access...." Sherman, *Musical Copyright Infringement*, at 84 n. 15. Nimmer states that, absent proof of access, "the similarities must be so striking as to preclude the possibility that the defendant independently arrived at the same result." Nimmer, *Copyright*, at 13–14....

The judicially formulated definition of "striking similarity" states that "plaintiffs must demonstrate that 'such similarities are of a kind that can only be explained by copying, rather than by coincidence, independent creation, or prior common source.'" *Testa v. Janssen*, 492 F. Supp. 198, 203 (W.D. Pa. 1980).... Sherman adds:

> To prove that certain similarities are "striking," plaintiff must show that they are the sort of similarities that cannot satisfactorily be accounted for by a theory of coincidence, independent creation, prior common source, or any theory other than that of copying. Striking similarity is an extremely technical issue—one with which, understandably, experts are best equipped to deal. Sherman, *Musical Copyright Infringement*, at 96.

Finally, the similarities should appear in a sufficiently unique or complex context as to make it unlikely that both pieces were copied from a prior common source . . . or that the defendant was able to compose the accused work as a matter of independent creation.... With these principles in mind, we turn now to an analysis of the evidence of "striking similarity" presented by the plaintiff.

As noted, the plaintiff relies almost entirely on the testimony of his expert witness, Dr. Arrand Parsons. The defendants did not introduce any expert testimony, apparently because they did not think Parsons' testimony needed to be refuted. Defendants are perhaps to some degree correct in asserting that Parsons, although eminently qualified in the field of classical music theory, was not equally qualified to analyze popular music tunes. More significantly, however, although Parsons used the magic formula, "striking similarity," he only ruled out the possibility of independent creation; he did not state that the similarities could only be the result of copying. In order for proof of "striking similarity" to establish a reasonable inference of access, especially in a case such as this one in which the direct proof of access is so minimal, the plaintiff must show that the similarity is of a type which will preclude any explanation other than that of copying.

In addition, to bolster the expert's conclusion that independent creation was not possible, there should be some testimony or other evidence of the relative complexity or uniqueness of the two compositions. Dr. Parsons' testimony did not refer to this aspect of the compositions and, in a field such as that of popular music in which

---

[3] Plaintiff also relies on the fact that both songs were played on numerous occasions in open court for the jury to hear and on the deposition testimony of one of the Bee Gees, Maurice, who incorrectly identified Theme B of Selle's song as the Bee Gees' composition, "How Deep Is Your Love."

all songs are relatively short and tend to build on or repeat a basic theme, such testimony would seem to be particularly necessary. We agree with the Sixth Circuit which explained that "we do not think the affidavit of [the expert witness], stating in conclusory terms that 'it is extremely unlikely that one set [of architectural plans] could have been prepared without access to the other set,' can fill the gap which is created by the absence of any direct evidence of access." *Scholz Homes, Inc. v. Maddox*, 379 F.2d 84, 86 (6th Cir. 1967).

> **Practice Pointer**
>
> Why didn't the Bee Gees' attorneys use any expert witnesses? According to Melinda Bilyeau et al., The Bee Gees: Tales of the Brothers Gibb 532 (2001), they originally intended to call two experts. But as one of the attorneys later recalled, "[t]he judge gave us indications at least two times during the trial that we should rest our case." *Id*. According to the jury foreman, the jury ruled for Selle because "[t]here was nothing to contradict the plaintiff's evidence. There was no expert for the defense." *Id*. In a copyright infringement case involving popular songs, shouldn't the defendants always use an expert witness?

To illustrate this deficiency more concretely, we refer to a cassette tape, Plaintiff's Exhibit 27, and the accompanying chart, Plaintiff's Exhibit 26. These exhibits were prepared by the defendants but introduced into evidence by the plaintiff. The tape has recorded on it segments of both themes from both the Selle and the Gibb songs interspersed with segments of other compositions as diverse as "Footsteps," "From Me To You" (a Lennon-McCartney piece), Beethoven's 5th Symphony, "Funny Talk," "Play Down," and "I'd Like To Leave If I May" (the last two being earlier compositions by Barry Gibb).[5] There are at least superficial similarities among these segments, when played on the same musical instrument, and the plaintiff failed to elicit any testimony from his expert witness about this exhibit which compared the Selle and the Gibb songs to other pieces of contemporary, popular music. These circumstances indicate that the plaintiff failed to sustain his burden of proof on the issue of "striking similarity" in its legal sense—that is, similarity which reasonably precludes the possibility of any explanation other than that of copying.

The plaintiff's expert witness does not seem to have addressed any issues relating to the possibility of prior common source in both widely disseminated popular songs and the defendants' own compositions. At oral argument, plaintiff's attorney stated that the burden of proving common source should be on the defendant; however, the burden of proving "striking similarity," which, by definition, includes taking steps to minimize the possibility of common source, is on the plaintiff. In essence, the plaintiff failed to prove to the requisite degree that the similarities identified by the expert witness—although perhaps "striking" in a non-legal sense—were of a type which would eliminate any explanation of coincidence, independent creation or

---

[5] The plaintiff, on cross-examination, admitted that there were some similarities, primarily in melody rather than rhythm, between his song and various other popular tunes, including "From Me To You" and several earlier Bee Gee compositions.

common source, including, in this case, the possibility of common source in earlier compositions created by the Bee Gees themselves or by others. In sum, the evidence of striking similarity is not sufficiently compelling to make the case when the proof of access must otherwise depend largely upon speculation and conjecture.

Therefore, because the plaintiff failed both to establish a basis from which the jury could reasonably infer that the Bee Gees had access to his song and to meet his burden of proving "striking similarity" between the two compositions, the grant by the district court of the defendants' motion for judgment notwithstanding the verdict is affirmed. . . .

Points for Discussion

a. **Exploring the Test**

What test does the court use to determine if copying has occurred? Listen to the two songs yourself. Are they so "strikingly similar" that Selle should have won the case? Apparently the jury thought so! Even the Seventh Circuit conceded that the two songs were "perhaps 'striking' in a non-legal sense." Why wasn't this enough?

b. **Toward a New Test**

Many songs sound alike. For example, a key theme from Brahms' First Symphony is quite similar to part of Beethoven's earlier Ninth Symphony. When the similarity was called to the attention of Brahms, he reportedly said: "Any ass knows that." Timothy J. English explored the similarities between 60 pairs of famous popular songs in his book Sounds Like Teen Spirit: Stolen Melodies, Ripped-Off Riffs, and the Secret History of Rock and Roll (2006). What test should be used to determine whether a popular song has infringed an earlier copyright? Should a different test apply to other types of music?

c. **A Commercial Failure**

If Selle's song was "strikingly similar" to the Bee Gees' song *How Deep Is Your Love*, then why was it a commercial failure? One explanation might be that the success of *How Deep Is Your Love* was more attributable to the Bee Gees' fame and reputation than to the song itself. Did this affect the court's decision? Should it?

d. **Contributory Infringement**

Suppose that company X distributes free software that facilitates the sharing of electronic files among computer owners—knowing that the software can be used to illegally download copyrighted songs. Assuming that the computer owners are liable for infringement, is X also liable? In *Metro-Goldwyn-Mayer Studios, Inc. v. Grokster, Ltd.*, 545 U.S. 913, 919 (2005), the Supreme Court held that "one who distributes a device with the object of promoting its use to infringe copyright . . . is liable for the resulting acts of infringement by third parties." The Court found extensive evidence that each defendant "clearly voiced the objective that recipients use it to download copyrighted works, and each took active steps to encourage infringement." *Id.* at 924. What are the implications of this decision?

e. **Infringing Art**

In 1976, artist Saul Steinberg created an iconic poster that presented a New Yorker's view of the world. Almost overnight, it became one of the most famous images of Manhattan. Seeking to promote its new Robin Williams movie, *Moscow on the Hudson*, Columbia Pictures created a movie poster which somewhat resembled the Steinberg work. When Steinberg sued for infringement, access was easily proven: Columbia's art director had instructed the artist to "use Steinberg's poster to achieve a more recognizable New York look." *Steinberg v. Columbia Pictures Industries, Inc.*, 663 F. Supp. 706, 710 (S.D.N.Y. 1987). The test for "substantial similarity" in the Second Circuit was "whether an average lay observer would recognize the alleged copy as having been appropriated from the copyrighted work." *Id.* at 711. Examine both images yourself. Was the test satisfied here? Compare this test to the Seventh Circuit test used in *Selle*. Which one is better?

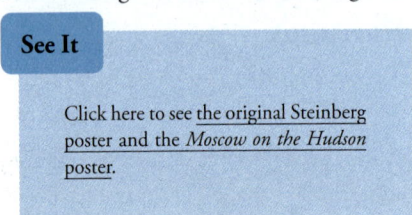

> **See It**
>
> Click here to see the original Steinberg poster and the *Moscow on the Hudson* poster.

f. **Aftermath of *Selle***

After *Selle*, the Bee Gees continued their successful music career. They were inducted into the Songwriters' Hall of Fame and the Rock and Roll Hall of Fame in the 1990s. Over the years, more than 220 million of their records were sold, and they received seven Grammy awards. The soundtrack to *Saturday Night Fever*, including *How Deep Is Your Love*, is one of the most successful movie soundtracks ever.

C. Patents

1. Patent Basics

M invents a new vacuum cleaner; N develops a medicine that cures cancer; and O creates an automobile engine that runs on water. In theory, all of these inventions may qualify for patent protection. If O successfully obtains a patent on her engine, she may exclude others from using this technology without her agreement.

Chapter 4 *An Introduction to Intellectual Property*

Why recognize patents? As the Constitution makes clear, the patent system exists to serve a utilitarian goal: "[t]o promote the Progress of Science and the useful Arts . . . ." U.S. Const. art. I, § 8. The underlying assumption is that patent protection serves as an incentive for inventors to engage in creative effort. The public benefits from this system in two ways. First, it receives new socially-valuable products. Second, because a patent applicant must disclose how her invention is made, others may use this information to create different, non-infringing inventions. Despite this utilitarian mandate, patent law decisions sometimes seem to echo the Lockean concept that the inventor is entitled to the fruits of her labor.

> **FYI**
>
> Patent law arises from federal statutes and interpretative decisions. The United States is a party to the three most important international agreements dealing with patent law: the Paris Convention, the Patent Cooperation Treaty, and the Agreement on Trade-Related Aspects of Intellectual Property Rights. As a result, in some instances the U.S. has amended the patent law statutes to comply with international standards.

The owner of a patent (the *patentee*) holds a key right in the proverbial bundle: the right to exclude. Thus, a patentee may prevent others from making, using, or selling her invention during the patent term. Currently, the patent term is 20 years from the date the application is filed with the U.S. Patent and Trademark Office (PTO). In addition, the patentee may transfer her right to others; and she may effectively destroy the patent by allowing it to lapse. However, a patent does not ensure the right to *use* the patented invention, which may be prohibited or regulated by other laws.

Federal law authorizes the issuance of a patent to anyone who "invents or discovers any new and useful process, machine, manufacture, or composition of matter, or any new and useful improvement thereof." 35 U.S.C. § 101. In *Thaler v. Vidal*, 43 F.4th 1207 (Fed. Cir. 2022), the court held that an artificial intelligence software program could not be listed as the inventor on a patent application: "[T]he Patent Act requires that inventors must be natural persons; that is, human beings." *Id.* at 1210.

An applicant must meet five requirements in order to obtain a patent: (a) patentable subject matter; (b) utility; (c) novelty; (d) nonobviousness; and (e) enablement. If these requirements are satisfied, the PTO will issue a patent. Note that the scope of review by the PTO is limited by time and resources, so the issuance of a patent does not guarantee that it is valid. Many patents are eventually held invalid in litigation.

- *Patentable subject matter*: Four categories of inventions qualify for a patent: "any . . . process, machine, manufacture, or . . . composition of matter." Abstract concepts, mathematical algorithms, scientific principles, and physical phenomena cannot be patented.

- *Utility*: A patent may be issued only for a "useful" invention—one which offers actual benefit to humans. Because virtually any invention provides some sort of minimal benefit, this element is rarely at issue.

- *Novelty*: Only a "new" (or *novel*) invention may be patented. The PTO will examine the *prior art*—all inventions, patents, publications and the like that predated the application—to determine if the invention is novel.

- *Nonobviousness*: An obvious invention does not qualify for protection. If the differences between the invention and the "prior art" before the application date "would have been obvious . . . to a person having ordinary skill" in the area, the PTO will deny the application.

- *Enablement*: The patent application must describe the invention in such detail as to "enable any person skilled in the art to which it pertains . . . to make and use the same."

Recent decades have witnessed a trend toward expanding the scope of patentable subject matter. For example, the PTO has issued a patent for a "method of swallowing a pill," which consists of swallowing a pill together with liquid while the head is in a "downwardly bowed position." U.S. Patent No. 3,418,999 (filed Feb. 12, 1964). But can a living organism be patented?

Diamond v. Chakrabarty

Supreme Court of the United States

447 U.S. 303 (1980)

Mr. Chief Justice Burger delivered the opinion of the Court.

We granted certiorari to determine whether a live, human-made micro-organism is patentable subject matter under 35 U.S.C. § 101.

I.

In 1972, respondent Chakrabarty, a microbiologist, filed a patent application, assigned to the General Electric Co. The application asserted 36 claims related to Chakrabarty's invention of "a bacterium from the genus *Pseudomonas* containing therein at least two stable energy-generating plasmids, each of said plasmids providing a separate hydrocarbon degradative pathway." This human-made, genetically engineered bacterium is capable of breaking down multiple components of crude oil. Because of this property, which is possessed by no naturally occurring bacteria,

Chakrabarty's invention is believed to have significant value for the treatment of oil spills.

Chakrabarty's patent claims were of three types: first, process claims for the method of producing the bacteria; second, claims for an inoculum comprised of a carrier material floating on water, such as straw, and the new bacteria; and third, claims to the bacteria themselves. The patent examiner allowed the claims falling into the first two categories, but rejected claims for the bacteria. His decision rested on two grounds: (1) that microorganisms are "products of nature," and (2) that as living things they are not patentable subject matter under 35 U.S.C. § 101.

Dr. Ananda Chakrabarty
Click here for larger photo

Chakrabarty appealed the rejection of these claims to the Patent Office Board of Appeals, and the Board affirmed the Examiner on the second ground. . . . [The Court of Customs and Patent Appeals reversed this decision, and Diamond, as the Commissioner of Patents and Trademarks, petitioned the Supreme Court for review.]

II.

The Constitution grants Congress broad power to legislate to "promote the Progress of Science and useful Arts, by securing for limited Times to Authors and Inventors the exclusive Right to their respective Writings and Discoveries." Art. I, § 8, cl. 8. The patent laws promote this progress by offering inventors exclusive rights for a limited period as an incentive for their inventiveness and research efforts. *Kewanee Oil Co. v. Bicron Corp.*, 416 U.S. 470, 480–481 (1974). . . . The authority of Congress is exercised in the hope that "[t]he productive effort thereby fostered will have a positive effect on society through the introduction of new products and processes of manufacture into the economy, and the emanations by way of increased employment and better lives for our citizens." *Kewanee, supra,* 416 U.S., at 480.

> **FYI**
>
> The Court of Customs and Patent Appeals was abolished in 1982. Since then, all appeals in patent cases have been heard by the Court of Appeals for the Federal Circuit.

The question before us in this case is a narrow one of statutory interpretation requiring us to construe 35 U.S.C. § 101, which provides:

> Whoever invents or discovers any new and useful process, machine, manufacture, or composition of matter, or any new and useful improvement thereof, may obtain a patent therefor, subject to the conditions and requirements of this title.

Specifically, we must determine whether respondent's micro-organism constitutes a "manufacture" or "composition of matter" within the meaning of the statute.

III.

... [T]his Court has read the term "manufacture" in § 101 in accordance with its dictionary definition to mean "the production of articles for use from raw or prepared materials by giving to these materials new forms, qualities, properties, or combinations, whether by hand-labor or by machinery." *American Fruit Growers, Inc. v. Brogdex Co.*, 283 U.S. 1, 11 (1931). Similarly, "composition of matter" has been construed consistent with its common usage to include "all compositions of two or more substances and ... all composite articles, whether they be the results of chemical union, or of mechanical mixture, or whether they be gases, fluids, powders or solids." *Shell Development Co. v. Watson,* 149 F. Supp. 279, 280 (D.C. 1957). . . . In choosing such expansive terms as "manufacture" and "composition of matter," modified by the comprehensive "any," Congress plainly contemplated that the patent laws would be given wide scope.

The relevant legislative history also supports a broad construction. The Patent Act of 1793, authored by Thomas Jefferson, defined statutory subject matter as "any new and useful art, machine, manufacture, or composition of matter, or any new or useful improvement [thereof]." Act of Feb. 21, 1793, § 1, 1 Stat. 319. . . . Subsequent patent statutes in 1836, 1870, and 1874 employed this same broad language. In 1952, when the patent laws were recodified, Congress replaced the word "art" with "process," but otherwise left Jefferson's language intact. The Committee Reports accompanying the 1952 Act inform us that Congress intended statutory subject matter to "include anything under the sun that is made by man." S. Rep. No. 1979, 82d Cong., 2d Sess., 5 (1952); H.R. Rep. No. 1923, 82d Cong., 2d Sess., 6 (1952).

This is not to suggest that § 101 has no limits or that it embraces every discovery. The laws of nature, physical phenomena, and abstract ideas have been held not patentable. . . . *Funk Brothers Seed Co. v. Kalo Inoculant Co.,* 333 U.S. 127, 130 (1948). . . . Thus, a new mineral discovered in the earth or a new plant found in the wild is not patentable subject matter. Likewise, Einstein could not patent his celebrated law that $E=mc^2$; nor could Newton have patented the law of gravity. Such discoveries are "manifestations of . . . nature, free to all men and reserved exclusively to none." *Funk, supra,* 333 U.S., at 130.

Judged in this light, respondent's micro-organism plainly qualifies as patentable subject matter. His claim is not to a hitherto unknown natural phenomenon, but to a nonnaturally occurring manufacture or composition of matter—a product of human ingenuity "having a distinctive name, character [and] use." *Hartranft v. Wiegmann,* 121 U.S. 609, 615 (1887). . . .

Here . . . the patentee has produced a new bacterium with markedly different characteristics from any found in nature and one having the potential for significant utility. His discovery is not nature's handiwork, but his own; accordingly it is patentable subject matter under § 101.

IV.

... The [petitioner argues] that micro-organisms cannot qualify as patentable subject matter until Congress expressly authorizes such protection. His position rests on the fact that genetic technology was unforeseen when Congress enacted § 101. From this it is argued that resolution of the patentability of inventions such as respondent's should be left to Congress. The legislative process, the petitioner argues, is best equipped to weigh the competing economic, social, and scientific considerations involved, and to determine whether living organisms produced by genetic engineering should receive patent protection. ...

It is, of course, correct that Congress, not the courts, must define the limits of patentability; but it is equally true that once Congress has spoken it is "the province and duty of the judicial department to say what the law is." *Marbury v. Madison*, 1 Cranch 137, 177, 2 L.Ed. 60 (1803). Congress has performed its constitutional role in defining patentable subject matter in § 101; we perform ours in construing the language Congress has employed. In so doing, our obligation is to take statutes as we find them, guided, if ambiguity appears, by the legislative history and statutory purpose. Here, we perceive no ambiguity. The subject-matter provisions of the patent law have been cast in broad terms to fulfill the constitutional and statutory goal of promoting "the Progress of Science and the useful Arts" with all that means for the social and economic benefits envisioned by Jefferson. Broad general language is not necessarily ambiguous when congressional objectives require broad terms.

... This Court frequently has observed that a statute is not to be confined to the "particular application[s] . . . contemplated by the legislators." *Barr v. United States,* 324 U.S. 83, 90 (1945). This is especially true in the field of patent law. A rule that unanticipated inventions are without protection would conflict with the core concept of the patent law that anticipation undermines patentability. Mr. Justice Douglas reminded that the inventions most benefiting mankind are those that "push back the frontiers of chemistry, physics, and the like." *Great A. & P. Tea Co. v. Supermarket Corp.*, 340 U.S. 147, 154 (1950) (concurring opinion). Congress employed broad general language in drafting § 101 precisely because such inventions are often unforeseeable.[10]

To buttress his argument, the petitioner, with the support of *amicus*, points to grave risks that may be generated by research endeavors such as respondent's. The briefs present a gruesome parade of horribles. Scientists, among them Nobel laureates,

---

[10] Even an abbreviated list of patented inventions underscores the point: telegraph (Morse, No. 1,647); telephone (Bell, No. 174,465); electric lamp (Edison, No. 223,898); airplane (the Wrights, No. 821,393); transistor (Bardeen & Brattain, No. 2,524,035); neutronic reactor (Fermi & Szilard, No. 2,708,656); laser (Schawlow & Townes, No. 2,929,922). See generally Revolutionary Ideas, Patents & Progress in America, United States Patent and Trademark Office (1976).

are quoted suggesting that genetic research may pose a serious threat to the human race, or, at the very least, that the dangers are far too substantial to permit such research to proceed apace at this time. We are told that genetic research and related technological developments may spread pollution and disease, that it may result in a loss of genetic diversity, and that its practice may tend to depreciate the value of human life. These arguments are forcefully, even passionately, presented; they remind us that, at times, human ingenuity seems unable to control fully the forces it creates—that with Hamlet, it is sometimes better "to bear those ills we have than fly to others that we know not of."

> **Food for Thought**
>
> The Court brushes aside concerns that patenting genetically-engineered animals "may pose a serious threat to the human race." Why? Judges routinely consider public policy in adjudicating difficult cases, as we saw in *Moore v. Regents of the University of California* (Chapter 1). Should the potential harm that an invention might cause be considered?

It is argued that this Court should weigh these potential hazards in considering whether respondent's invention is patentable subject matter under § 101. We disagree. The grant or denial of patents on micro-organisms is not likely to put an end to genetic research or to its attendant risks. The large amount of research that has already occurred when no researcher had sure knowledge that patent protection would be available suggests that legislative or judicial fiat as to patentability will not deter the scientific mind from probing into the unknown any more than Canute could command the tides. Whether respondent's claims are patentable may determine whether research efforts are accelerated by the hope of reward or slowed by want of incentives, but that is all. . . .

Accordingly, the judgment of the Court of Customs and Patent Appeals is affirmed.

MR. JUSTICE BRENNAN, dissenting.

. . . The only question we need decide is whether Congress, exercising its authority under Art. I, § 8, of the Constitution, intended that [Chakrabarty] be able to secure a monopoly on the living organism itself, no matter how produced or how used. Because I believe the Court has misread the applicable legislation, I dissent.

The patent laws attempt to reconcile this Nation's deep seated antipathy to monopolies with the need to encourage progress. Given the complexity and legislative nature of this delicate task, we must be careful to extend patent protection no further than Congress has provided. In particular, were there an absence of legislative direction, the courts should leave to Congress the decisions whether and how far to extend the patent privilege into areas where the common understanding has been that patents are not available. . . .[1]

The Court protests that its holding today is dictated by the broad language of § 101, which cannot "be confined to the 'particular application[s] . . . contemplated by the legislators,'" quoting *Barr v. United States*, 324 U.S. 83, 90 (1945). But . . . the Court's decision does not follow the unavoidable implications of the statute. Rather, it extends the patent system to cover living material even though Congress plainly has legislated in the belief that § 101 does not encompass living organisms. It is the role of Congress, not this Court, to broaden or narrow the reach of the patent laws. This is especially true where, as here, the composition sought to be patented uniquely implicates matters of public concern.

Points for Discussion

a. Patenting Animals

Should the normal standards for patentability apply to genetically engineered animals? In the wake of *Diamond*, more than 700 animals have been patented. *See, e.g., Ex Parte Allen*, 2 U.S.P.Q.2d 1425 (1987) (genetically developed Pacific oyster was patentable subject matter). Under the Court's test could a human/animal hybrid be patented? Based on *Diamond*, Harvard University obtained a patent on such a hybrid—a mouse with a human immune system. Patents have also been issued for other transgenic animals, including pigs, goats, and sheep. But the PTO rejected an application to patent a "humanzee" (a human/chimpanzee hybrid), apparently because such an animal would be too human. The PTO relied, in part, on the prohibition against slavery in the Thirteenth Amendment; it reasoned that if a human cannot be owned, then a human cannot be patented. Under this approach, the question seems to be: how much human genetic material makes a hybrid "human"?

b. Patenting Human Genes

Should human genes be patentable? The PTO had already issued patents on over 4,000 human genes before the Supreme Court considered the question in *Association for Molecular Pathology v. Myriad Genetics, Inc.*, 569 U.S. 576 (2013). A unanimous Court held that such genes were not patentable subject matter. It acknowledged that respondent Myriad had made a valuable contribution to science by discovering the location and genetic sequence of two genes associated with the risk of developing breast and ovarian cancer. But it stressed that the "location and order" of the genes "existed in nature before Myriad found them." *Id.* at 590. Accordingly, it reasoned that:

---

[1] I read the Court to admit that the popular conception, even among advocates of agricultural patents, was that living organisms were unpatentable.

. . . Myriad did not create anything. To be sure, it found . . . important and useful gene[s], but separating [the genes from the] surrounding genetic material is not an act of invention. . . . Groundbreaking, innovative, or even brilliant discovery does not by itself satisfy the § 101 inquiry. . . . Myriad found the location of the [genes], but that discovery, by itself, does not render the . . . genes "new . . . composition[s] of matter," . . . that are patent eligible. *Id.* at 591.

Is a cloned animal patentable subject matter? Based on *Association for Molecular Pathology*, the Federal Circuit held that Dolly, the famous cloned sheep, was not patentable subject matter. *In re Roslin Institute*, 750 F.3d 1333 (Fed. Cir. 2014). The court reasoned that Dolly and her siblings were "exact genetic copies of patentable ineligible subject matter." *Id.* at 1337.

c. **Novelty**

An invention is novel unless it was patented by someone else, described in a publication, in public use, on sale, or otherwise available to the public *before* the inventor files his patent application. For example, suppose J invents a new type of vacuum cleaner that he offers to sell to the public. K later invents the same device without any knowledge of J's product. K's patent application will be denied due to lack of novelty.

d. **Nonobviousness**

This is usually the most difficult element for an applicant to meet. Even if J's invention is novel, because there are differences between the invention and the prior art, if the differences "would have been obvious . . . to a person of ordinary skill" in the area, it fails to meet this standard. The Supreme Court explained in *Graham v. John Deere Co.*, 383 U.S. 1, 17–18 (1966) that the four most important criteria considered in assessing nonobviousness are: (1) the "scope and content of the prior art;" (2) the "differences between the prior art and the claims at issue;" (3) the "level of ordinary skill in the pertinent art;" and (4) "secondary considerations" such as commercial success or the failure of others. One controversial application sought patent protection for "a large trash bag made of orange plastic and decorated with lines and facial features, allowing the bag, when filled with trash or leaves, to resemble a Halloween-style pumpkin, or jack-o'-lantern." *In re Dembiczak*, 175 F.3d 994, 996 (Fed. Cir. 1999). Although the PTO rejected the application as obvious, the Federal Circuit found nonobviousness and reversed.

e. **Problems in Patentability**

Are the standards for patentability met in the problems below?

> (1) F creates a mold that produces a pizza with three concentric rings of crust, allowing cheese and other pizza fillings to be placed between the rings. F claims that this improves a pizza's flavor and texture.

> (2) G invents a new golfing technique, a method of putting: hold the putter in the right hand, clasp the left hand on the right wrist, and stroke the ball.
>
> (3) S, a surgeon, determines that placing a heart surgery patient on an all-fruit diet for the final two days before an operation shortens the patient's recovery time by 30%.

f. Aftermath of *Diamond*

Reflecting on the decision, Chakrabarty expressed his hope that it would open up new opportunities for biotechnology research, which "has been hindered in the past. The feeling was: Why should I develop something with years of research only to put it on the market and have someone else duplicate it and make money on it?" *Developer of a New Life Form*, N.Y. Times, June 18, 1980. Patent no. 4,259,444 was finally issued on Chakrabarty's invention in March, 1981—about nine years after the application was filed. Ironically, General Electric Co., the owner of the patent, announced that new techniques had surpassed Chakrabarty's method during the intervening years, so the company had no plans to develop his invention.

> **See It**
>
> Click here to see the patent that was issued for Chakrabarty's invention.

2. Infringement

The most important part of a patent application contains the *claims*—the exact content of the invention for which patent protection is sought. Typically, each claim has two or more subparts called *elements*. Once approved by the PTO, the claims are set forth in the patent. Just as the real property description in a deed designates the parcel of land, the claims in the patent delineate the scope of the protected invention.

The owner of a patent may enforce his rights by bringing a lawsuit for infringement. One well-known infringement action arose from a dispute between two competing manufacturers of toy water guns. During the 1980s, Alan Amron and Talk To Me Products, Inc. acquired a patent on a new type of water gun, which they manufactured and sold as the "The Totally Rad Soaker." Larami Corporation sold a competing product called the "Super Soaker." Did the Super Soaker infringe the patent for The Totally Rad Soaker?

Larami Corp. v. Amron

United States District Court, Eastern District of Pennsylvania

1993 WL 69581

REED, J.

This is a patent case concerning toy water guns manufactured by plaintiff Larami Corporation ("Larami"). Currently before me is Larami's motion for partial summary judgment of noninfringement of United States Patent No. 4,239,129 ("the '129 patent") [and for partial summary judgment on defendants' counterclaim for infringement]. . . .

I. BACKGROUND

Larami manufactures a line of toy water guns called "SUPER SOAKERS." This line includes five models: SUPER SOAKER 20, SUPER SOAKER 30, SUPER SOAKER 50, SUPER SOAKER 100, and SUPER SOAKER 200. All use a hand-operated air pump to pressurize water and a "pinch trigger" valve mechanism for controlling the ejection of the pressurized water. All feature detachable water reservoirs prominently situated outside and above the barrel of the gun. The United States Patent and Trademark Office has issued patents covering four of these models. Larami does not claim to have a patent which covers SUPER SOAKER 20.

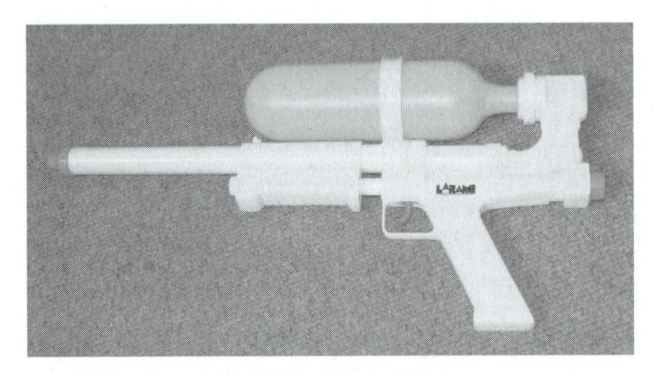

Original Super Soaker
Click here for larger photo

Defendants Alan Amron and Talk To Me Products, Inc. (hereinafter referred to collectively as "TTMP") claim that the SUPER SOAKER guns infringe on the '129 patent which TTMP obtained by assignment from Gary Esposito, the inventor. The '129 patent covers a water gun ["The Totally Rad Soaker"] which, like the SUPER SOAKERS, operates by pressurizing water housed in a tank with an air pump. In the '129 patent, the pressure enables the water to travel out of the tank through a trigger-operated valve into an outlet tube and to squirt through a nozzle. Unlike the

SUPER SOAKERS, the '129 patent also contains various electrical features to illuminate the water stream and create noises. Also, the water tank in the '129 patent is not detachable, but is contained within a housing in the body of the water gun.

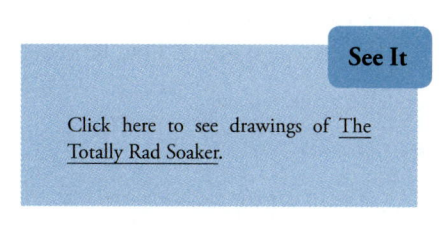

> **See It**
>
> Click here to see drawings of The Totally Rad Soaker.

The "Background of the Invention" contained in the '129 patent reads as follows:

> Children of all ages, especially boys, through the years have exhibited a fascination for water, lights and noise and the subject invention deals with these factors embodied in a toy simulating a pistol.
>
> An appreciable number of U.S. patents have been issued which are directed to water pistols but none appear to disclose a unique assemble of components which can be utilized to simultaneously produce a jet or stream of water, means for illuminating the stream and a noise, or if so desired, one which can be operated without employing the noise and stream illuminating means. A reciprocal pump is employed to obtain sufficient pressure whereby the pistol can eject a stream an appreciable distance in the neighborhood of thirty feet and this stream can be illuminated to more or less simulate a lazer [sic] beam. . . .

II. DISCUSSION

A. *Summary Judgment Standard*

Summary judgment is as appropriate in a patent case as it is in any other. The examination to be undertaken of a summary judgment motion in federal court is set forth in Fed. R. Civ. P. 56. Rule 56(c) states that:

> [t]he judgment sought shall be rendered forthwith if the pleadings, depositions, answers to interrogatories, and admissions on file, together with the affidavits, if any, show that there is no genuine issue as to any material fact and that the moving party is entitled to a judgment as a matter of law. . . .

B. *Infringement and Claim Interpretation*

A patent owner's right to exclude others from making, using or selling the patented invention is defined and limited by the language in that patent's claims. *Corning Glass Works v. Sumitomo Electric U.S.A., Inc.*, 868 F.2d 1251, 1257 (Fed. Cir. 1989). Thus, establishing infringement requires the interpretation of the "elements" or "limitations" of the claim and a comparison of the accused product with those elements as so interpreted. *Key Mfg. Group, Inc. v. Microdot, Inc.*, 925 F.2d 1444, 1448 (Fed. Cir. 1991). Because claim interpretation is a question of law, it is amenable to summary judgment. . . .

A patent holder can seek to establish patent infringement in either of two ways: by demonstrating that every element of a claim (1) is literally infringed or (2) is infringed under the doctrine of equivalents. To put it a different way, because every element of a claim is essential and material to that claim, a patent owner must, to meet the burden of establishing infringement, "show the presence of every element *or* its substantial equivalent in the accused device." *Key Mfg. Group, Inc.*, 925 F.2d at 1447 (emphasis added). If even *one* element of a patent's claim is missing from the accused product, then "[t]here can be no infringement as a matter of law . . . " *London v. Carson Pirie Scott & Co.*, 946 F.2d 1534, 1538–39 (Fed. Cir. 1991).

> **Food for Thought**
>
> Why is the test for patent infringement so narrow? Could a competitor avoid liability for infringement by copying only 99% of another product?

Larami contends, and TTMP does not dispute, that twenty-eight (28) of the thirty-five (35) claims in the '129 patent are directed to the electrical components that create the light and noise. Larami's SUPER SOAKER water guns have no light or noise components. Larami also contends, again with no rebuttal from TTMP, that claim 28 relates to a "poppet valve" mechanism for controlling the flow of water that is entirely different from Larami's "pinch trigger" mechanism. Thus, according to Larami, the six remaining claims (claims 1, 5, 10, 11, 12 and 16) are the only ones in dispute. Larami admits that these six claims address the one thing that the SUPER SOAKERS and the '129 patent have in common—the use of air pressure created by a hand pump to dispense liquid. Larami argues, however, that the SUPER SOAKERS and the '129 patent go about this task in such fundamentally different ways that no claim of patent infringement is sustainable as a matter of law.

In its memorandum of law in opposition to Larami's motion for partial summary judgment, TTMP [only] points to evidence to support its assertion that . . . SUPER SOAKER 20 literally infringes claim 1 and that SUPER SOAKERS 20, 30, 50, 100 and 200 infringe claim 10 under the doctrine of equivalents. TTMP has neither produced nor referred to evidence contradicting facts averred by Larami on all other claims. . . . I conclude, therefore, that TTMP has not met its burden of coming forward with specific evidence showing that there is a genuine issue of material fact as to these claims. Accordingly, this memorandum will address only claims 1 and 10.

1. *Literal Infringement of Claim 1*

TTMP claims that SUPER SOAKER 20 literally infringes claim 1 of the '129 patent. Claim 1 describes the water gun as:

> [a] toy comprising an elongated housing [case] having a chamber therein for a liquid [tank], a pump including a piston having an exposed rod [piston rod] and extending rearwardly of said toy facilitating manual operation for building up an appreciable amount of pressure in said chamber for ejecting a stream of liquid therefrom an appreciable distance substantially forwardly of said toy, and means for controlling the ejection. (bracketed words supplied). . . .

Claim 1 requires, among other things, that the toy gun have "an elongated housing having a chamber therein for a liquid." The SUPER SOAKER 20 water gun, in contrast, has an external water reservoir (chamber) that is detachable from the gun housing, and not contained within the housing. TTMP argues that SUPER SOAKER 20 contains a "chamber therein for a liquid" *as well as* a detachable water reservoir. It is difficult to discern from TTMP's memorandum of law exactly where it contends the "chamber therein" is located in SUPER SOAKER 20. Furthermore, after having examined SUPER SOAKER 20, I find that it is plain that there is no "chamber" for liquid contained within the housing of the water gun. The only element of SUPER SOAKER 20 which could be described as a "chamber" for liquid is the external water reservoir located atop the housing. Indeed, liquid is located within the housing only when the trigger causes the liquid to pass from the external water reservoir through the tubing in the housing and out of the nozzle at the front end of the barrel. SUPER SOAKER 20 itself shows that such a transitory avenue for the release of liquid is clearly not a "chamber therein for liquid." Therefore, because the absence of even one element of a patent's claim from the accused product means there can be no finding of literal infringement, I find that SUPER SOAKER 20 does not infringe claim 1 of the '129 patent as a matter of law. . . .

2. *Infringement by Equivalents of Claim 10*

TTMP claims that all five of the SUPER SOAKER water guns infringe claim 10 of the '129 patent. Claim 10 describes the arrangement of several components of the water gun as follows:

> A toy simulating a pistol comprising wall structure forming an elongated barrel of appreciable cross-section dimensions [case], a tank in the barrel for a liquid [water tank] and a hollow handle, a cylinder disposed axially in said tank and provided with a check valve, a piston mounted in said cylinder for manual reciprocation for pumping air into said tank [air pump], conduit means [discharge tube] connected to said tank and having an outlet located at the front of said barrel [outlet nozzle], valve means interposed in said conduct means, and a trigger operable independently of said piston carried by said handle for operating said valve means [trigger-operated valve] for controlling the forced flow of liquid through said outlet. (bracketed words supplied). . . .

To show infringement under the doctrine of equivalents, the patent owner bears the burden of proving that the accused product has the "substantial equivalent" of *every* limitation or element of a patent claim. . . . Put another way, the patent owner must show that the accused product "performs substantially the same overall function or work, in substantially the same way, to obtain substantially the same overall result as the claimed invention." *Wilson Sporting Goods Co. v. David Geoffrey & Assoc.*, 904 F.2d 677, 683 (Fed. Cir. 1990). . . .

The doctrine of equivalents is used to hinder "the 'unscrupulous copyist' who could otherwise imitate a patented invention as long as [s/he] was careful not to copy every inconsequential detail of the claimed inventions, or to make some 'unimportant and insubstantial' change to the claimed invention." *Lear Siegler, Inc. v. Sealy Mattress Company*, 873 F.2d 1422, 1425 (Fed. Cir. 1989). The doctrine is reserved for the exceptional case. As the U.S. Court of Appeals for the Federal Circuit, recently stated:

> [I]f the public comes to believe (or fear) that the language of patent claims can never be relied on, and that the doctrine of equivalents is simply the second prong of every infringement charge, regularly available to extend protection beyond the scope of the claims, then claims will cease to serve their intended purpose. Competitors will never know whether their actions infringe a granted patent.

London, 946 F.2d at 1538. . . .

[A]t least one . . . element of the '129 patent is absent from the SUPER SOAKER water guns. Claim 10 requires, among other things, "a tank in the barrel for a liquid." As discussed above with regard to claim 1, the SUPER SOAKER water guns have external water reservoirs that are detachable from the gun housing, and not contained within the housing or barrel. No SUPER SOAKER water gun has a "tank in the barrel for a liquid" as described in claim 10 of the '129 patent. To establish that a water tank outside of the housing or barrel is the substantial equivalent of a water tank inside the housing or barrel, TTMP must muster evidence which would create a genuine issue of material fact as to whether the outside tank would have a substantially similar function and use substantially similar means to yield a substantially similar result as the inside tank. *Wilson Sporting Goods*, 904 F.2d at 683.

> **Food for Thought**
>
> Is the court being overly technical here? Why should it matter whether the water tank is inside or outside the barrel?

TTMP claims that the "movement of the water reservoir upwardly simply serves as a cosmetic alteration for the aesthetic looks of the water gun, and does not alter the novel operational characteristics of the water gun [covered by the '129 patent]." The evidence, however, is to the contrary. The SUPER SOAKER design improved on the '129 patent and other prior art by locating the tank outside the housing. First, the external and detachable tank makes manufacturing the device simpler because it is not necessary to make the entire housing pressure tight. Second, this design makes it easier for the consumer to fill the tank because it is detachable. Third, the size and volume of the external water reservoirs are not limited by the size of the housing. Fourth, the external tanks are replaceable if they should become damaged without replacing the entire toy. Finally, users of the SUPER SOAKERS can carry additional, filled tanks on a belt or backpack and replace an empty tank without going back to a source of water. Thus, the external tanks at least function in a very different manner from the '129 patent. . . .

III. CONCLUSION

In patent cases, summary judgment is appropriate where the accused product does not literally infringe the patent and where the patent owner does not muster evidence that is "sufficient to satisfy the legal standard for infringement under the doctrine of equivalents." *London*, 946 F.2d at 1538. Thus, and for the foregoing reasons, Larami's motion for partial summary judgment of noninfringement of the '129 patent will be granted. . . .

Points for Discussion

a. **Infringement in Context**

As you can readily tell from *Larami Corp.*, patent infringement cases are typically complex and technical. Our goal is to provide you with an introduction to patent law, not to make you an instant expert in the field. Although attorneys who handle patent infringement cases are technically adept, the vast majority of federal judges are not. Should patent infringement cases be heard only by judges who have technical backgrounds?

b. **Literal Infringement**

Literal infringement occurs if the accused product includes *every* element of at least one claim for the patented product. Did the *Larami Corp.* court decide this issue correctly? Suppose Claim 1 described the water gun without using the word "therein." Or what if that claim described it as a "toy comprising an elongated housing with a chamber for a liquid . . . ." Would either of these phrasings have changed the outcome?

c. **Doctrine of Equivalents**

If only literal infringement of a patent was prohibited, an unscrupulous person could make minor modifications to a patented invention and avoid prosecution. As the Supreme Court explained in *Graver Tank & Mfg. Co. v. Linde Air Products Co.*, 339 U.S. 605, 607 (1950), this "would place the inventor at the mercy of verbalism and would be subordinating substance to form." The doctrine of equivalents evolved to plug this gap. In *Larami Corp.*, the court quoted the historic three-part test for the doctrine: if the accused product "performs substantially the same overall function or work, in substantially the same way, to obtain substantially the same overall result . . . ." Do you agree with the court's conclusion that infringement by equivalents did not occur? The Supreme Court revisited the "function-way-result" test in *Warner-Jenkinson Co., Inc. v. Hilton Davis Chemical Co.*, 520 U.S. 17 (1997), hinting that an "insubstantial differences" test might be more suitable for analyzing certain inventions.

d. Drafting Claims

How broadly should the claims in a patent application be drafted? Specific claims are more likely to satisfy the requirements of novelty and nonobviousness. But specificity makes it more difficult to win an infringement action, as *Larami Corp.* demonstrates.

e. Fair Use Defense?

Unlike copyright law, there is no fair use defense under patent law. Accordingly, even innocent and minor infringements are deemed to violate the owner's rights. Should the fair use concept be extended to patent law? For a discussion of the issue, see Maureen A. O'Rourke, *Toward a Doctrine of Fair Use in Patent Law*, 100 Colum. L. Rev. 1177 (2000).

f. Aftermath of *Larami Corp.*

The Super Soaker became the best-selling toy in the United States. It is estimated that more than 250 million guns have been sold, generating over one billion dollars in revenue. Larami Corporation was eventually acquired by Hasbro, one of the largest toy companies in the world. Hasbro regularly introduces new models of this popular toy. The Super Soaker was invented by Lonnie Johnson, a former nuclear scientist and spacecraft designer for NASA. Johnson used his Super Soaker royalties to establish an engineering firm that specializes in energy research.

D. Trademarks

1. Trademark Basics

The MGM lion's roar, the name "Rolex," the shape of the Coca-Cola bottle, the name "Microsoft," and the NBC chimes are all examples of trademarks. A *trademark* is any "word, name, symbol, or device" that is used to identify and distinguish the goods sold by one person from those of others. 15 U.S.C. § 1127. A word, name, symbol, or device so used in connection with services is a *service mark*.

The trademark owner has a specialized right to exclude: she may prevent competitors from using the same mark for their goods or services within a particular geographic area. She has the sole right to use that mark for her goods or services in that area; and she may destroy her right to use the mark by abandonment.

While copyright and patent law seek to encourage creative effort, the goals of trademark law are different. One goal is to protect consumers from being deceived into purchasing shoddy goods or services. For example, a watch bearing the trademark "Rolex" is presumably a quality product. A second goal is to provide an incentive for the trademark owner to produce quality goods or services by ensuring that the goodwill behind his mark will be protected.

Historically, trademark protection arose under state common law, which was later supplemented by statutes in some jurisdictions. In 1947, the federal Lanham Act established an additional layer of protection for trademarks and created a national registration system. In general, three elements are required for a valid trademark: (a) distinctiveness; (b) non-functionality; and (c) first use in trade. While federal registration provides certain benefits, it is not required; an unregistered trademark is valid.

- *Distinctiveness*: A mark must distinguish the goods or services of one person from those offered by another person. Some types of marks are considered more distinctive than others.

- *Non-functionality*: Trademark law does not protect a product feature that is functional, because this area is governed by patent law. In general, a feature is functional if it is vital to the use or purpose of the product or if it affects the cost or quality of the product.

- *First use in trade*: As the Supreme Court explained long ago, "[t]he right to a particular mark grows out of its use, not its mere adoption." *United Drug Co. v. Theodore Rectanus Co.*, 248 U.S. 90, 97 (1918). Thus, the first person to use a mark for a good or service in a particular geographic market generally obtains rights to use the mark in that market, unless another person has already registered the mark. Note that the federal Lanham Act requires first use in "commerce," which is narrower than "trade."

Historically, most trademarks were words or symbols. The universe of permissible marks has expanded in recent decades, as demonstrated by the MGM lion's roar—a sound may serve as a trademark. But can a color be a trademark?

Qualitex Co. v. Jacobson Products Co., Inc.

Supreme Court of the United States

514 U.S. 159 (1995)

Justice Breyer delivered the opinion of the Court.

The question in this case is whether the Trademark Act of 1946 (Lanham Act), 15 U.S.C. §§ 1051–1127 permits the registration of a trademark that consists, purely and simply, of a color. We conclude that, sometimes, a color will meet ordinary legal trademark requirements. And, when it does so, no special legal rule prevents color alone from serving as a trademark.

I.

The case before us grows out of petitioner Qualitex Company's use (since the 1950's) of a special shade of green-gold color on the pads that it makes and sells to dry cleaning firms for use on dry cleaning presses. In 1989, respondent Jacobson Products (a Qualitex rival) began to sell its own press pads to dry cleaning firms; and it colored those pads a similar green gold. In 1991, Qualitex registered the special green-gold color on press pads with the Patent and Trademark Office as a trademark. Registration No. 1,633,711 (Feb. 5, 1991). Qualitex subsequently added a trademark infringement count, 15 U.S.C. § 1114(1), to an unfair competition claim, § 1125(a), in a lawsuit it had already filed challenging Jacobson's use of the green-gold color.

> **What's That?**
>
> A *press pad* is part of a machine used to press clothes at dry cleaning plants. In effect, it is the liner for a large industrial pressing machine—the part of the machine that comes into contact with the garment being pressed. The Qualitex website boasts that its press pads "are consistently used by more award-winning dry cleaning plants, by a margin of 8 to 1, than any other press pad on the market." Click here to see the green-gold Qualitex press pad.

Qualitex won the lawsuit in the District Court. But, the Court of Appeals for the Ninth Circuit set aside the judgment in Qualitex's favor on the trademark infringement claim because, in that Circuit's view, the Lanham Act does not permit Qualitex, or anyone else, to register "color alone" as a trademark. . . .

II.

The Lanham Act gives a seller or producer the exclusive right to "register" a trademark, 15 U.S.C. § 1052, and to prevent his or her competitors from using that trademark, § 1114(1). Both the language of the Act and the basic underlying principles of trademark law would seem to include color within the universe of things that can qualify as a trademark. The language of the Lanham Act describes that universe in the broadest of terms. It says that trademarks "includ[e] any word, name, symbol, or device, or any combination thereof." § 1127. Since human beings might use as a "symbol" or "device" almost anything at all that is capable of carrying meaning, this language, read literally, is not restrictive. The courts and the Patent and Trademark Office have authorized for use as a mark a particular shape (of a Coca-Cola bottle), a particular sound (of NBC's three chimes), and even a particular scent (of plumeria blossoms on sewing thread). . . . If a shape, a sound, and a fragrance can act as symbols why, one might ask, can a color not do the same?. . .

True, a product's color is unlike "fanciful," "arbitrary," or "suggestive" words or designs, which almost *automatically* tell a customer that they refer to a brand.

Abercrombie & Fitch Co. v. Hunting World, Inc., 537 F.2d 4, 9–10 (CA2 1976) (Friendly, J.). . . . The imaginary word "Suntost," or the words "Suntost Marmalade," on a jar of orange jam immediately would signal a brand or a product "source;" the jam's orange color does not do so. But, over time, customers may come to treat a particular color on a product or its packaging (say, a color that in context seems unusual, such as pink on a firm's insulating material or red on the head of a large industrial bolt) as signifying a brand. And, if so, that color would have come to identify and distinguish the goods—*i.e.,* "to indicate" their "source"—much in the way that descriptive words on a product (say, "Trim" on nail clippers or "Car-Freshner" on deodorizer) can come to indicate a product's origin. In this circumstance, trademark law says that the word (*e.g.,* "Trim"), although not inherently distinctive, has developed "secondary meaning." *See Inwood Laboratories, Inc. v. Ives Laboratories, Inc.*, 456 U.S. 844, 851, n. 11 (1982) ("[S]econdary meaning" is acquired when "in the minds of the public, the primary significance of a product feature . . . is to identify the source of the product rather than the product itself"). Again, one might ask, if trademark law permits a descriptive word with secondary meaning to act as a mark, why would it not permit a color, under similar circumstances, to do the same?

We cannot find in the basic objectives of trademark law any obvious theoretical objection to the use of color alone as a trademark, where that color has attained "secondary meaning" and therefore identifies and distinguishes a particular brand (and thus indicates its "source"). In principle, trademark law, by preventing others from copying a source-identifying mark, "reduce[s] the customer's costs of shopping and making purchasing decisions," 1 J. McCarthy, McCarthy on Trademarks and Unfair Competition § 2.01[2], p. 2–3 (3d ed. 1994) (hereinafter McCarthy), for it quickly and easily assures a potential customer that *this* item—the item with this mark—is made by the same producer as other similarly marked items that he or she liked (or disliked) in the past. At the same time, the law helps assure a producer that it (and not an imitating competitor) will reap the financial, reputation-related rewards associated with a desirable product. The law thereby "encourage[s] the production of quality products," *ibid.,* and simultaneously discourages those who hope to sell inferior products by capitalizing on a consumer's inability quickly to evaluate the quality of an item offered for sale. It is the source-distinguishing ability of a mark—not its ontological status as color, shape, fragrance, word, or sign—that permits it to serve these basic purposes. And, for that reason, it is difficult to find, in basic trademark objectives, a reason to disqualify absolutely the use of a color as a mark. . . .

> **Food for Thought**
>
> Suppose N begins using orange as a trademark, but before it has developed a secondary meaning, N's competitor O also begins using orange as a trademark. What rights does N now have? How much risk is involved in using a color as a trademark?

It would seem, then, that color alone, at least sometimes, can meet the basic legal requirements for use as a trademark. It can act as a symbol that distinguishes a firm's goods and identifies their source, without serving any other significant function. . . . Indeed, the District Court, in this case, entered findings (accepted by the Ninth Circuit) that show Qualitex's green-gold press pad color has met these requirements. The green-gold color acts as a symbol. Having developed secondary meaning (for customers identified the green-gold color as Qualitex's), it identifies the press pads' source. And, the green-gold color serves no other function. . . . Accordingly, unless there is some special reason that convincingly militates against the use of color alone as a trademark, trademark law would protect Qualitex's use of the green-gold color on its press pads.

III.

Respondent Jacobson Products says that there are . . . special reasons why the law should forbid the use of color alone as a trademark. We shall explain, in turn, why we, ultimately, find them unpersuasive.

First, Jacobson says that, if the law permits the use of color as a trademark, it will produce uncertainty and unresolvable court disputes about what shades of a color a competitor may lawfully use. Because lighting (morning sun, twilight mist) will affect perceptions of protected color, competitors and courts will suffer from "shade confusion" as they try to decide whether use of a similar color on a similar product does, or does not, confuse customers and thereby infringe a trademark. Jacobson adds that the "shade confusion" problem is "more difficult" and "far different from" the "determination of the similarity of words or symbols."

We do not believe, however, that color, in this respect, is special. Courts traditionally decide quite difficult questions about whether two words or phrases or symbols are sufficiently similar, in context, to confuse buyers. They have had to compare, for example, such words as "Bonamine" and "Dramamine" (motion-sickness remedies); "Huggies" and "Dougies" (diapers); "Cheracol" and "Syrocol" (cough syrup); "Cyclone" and "Tornado" (wire fences); and "Mattres" and "1-800-Mattres" (mattress franchisor telephone numbers). Legal standards exist to guide courts in making such comparisons. *See, e.g.,* 2 McCarthy § 15.08; 1 McCarthy §§ 11.24–11.25 ("[S]trong" marks, with greater secondary meaning, receive broader protection than "weak" marks). We do not see why courts could not apply those standards to a color, replicating, if necessary, lighting conditions under which a colored product is normally sold. . . .

Second, Jacobson argues, as have others, that colors are in limited supply. Jacobson claims that, if one of many competitors can appropriate a particular color for use as a trademark, and each competitor then tries to do the same, the supply of colors will soon be depleted. Put in its strongest form, this argument would concede that "[h]undreds of color pigments are manufactured and thousands of colors can be obtained by mixing." L. Cheskin, Colors: What They Can Do For You 47 (1947). But, it would add that, in the context of a particular product, only some colors are usable. By the time one discards colors that, say, for reasons of customer appeal, are not usable, and adds the shades that competitors cannot use lest they risk infringing a similar, registered shade, then one is left with only a handful of possible colors. And, under these circumstances, to permit one, or a few, producers to use colors as trademarks will "deplete" the supply of usable colors to the point where a competitor's inability to find a suitable color will put that competitor at a significant disadvantage.

This argument is unpersuasive, however, largely because it relies on an occasional problem to justify a blanket prohibition. When a color serves as a mark, normally alternative colors will likely be available for similar use by others. *See, e.g., In Re Owens-Corning Fiberglas Corp.*, 774 F.2d 1116, 1121 (CA Fed. 1985) (pink insulation). . . .

[*Finally,*] Jacobson argues that there is no need to permit color alone to function as a trademark because a firm already may use color as part of a trademark, say, as a colored circle or colored letter or colored word, and may rely upon "trade dress" protection, under § 43(a) of the Lanham Act, if a competitor copies its color and thereby causes consumer confusion regarding the overall appearance of the competing products or their packaging, see 15 U.S.C. § 1125(a). The first part of this argument begs the question. One can understand why a firm might find it difficult to place a usable symbol or word on a product (say, a large industrial bolt that customers normally see from a distance); and, in such instances, a firm might want to use color, pure and simple, instead of color as part of a design. Neither is the second portion of the argument convincing. Trademark law helps the holder of a mark in many ways that "trade dress" protection does not. See 15 U.S.C. § 1124 (ability to prevent importation of confusingly similar goods); § 1072 (constructive notice of ownership); § 1065 (incontestible status); § 1057(b) (prima facie evidence of validity and ownership). Thus, one can easily find reasons why the law might provide trademark protection in addition to trade dress protection.

IV.

Having determined that a color may sometimes meet the basic legal requirements for use as a trademark and that respondent Jacobson's arguments do not justify a special legal rule preventing color alone from serving as a trademark (and, in light of the District Court's here undisputed findings that Qualitex's use of the green-gold color on its press pads meets the basic trademark requirements), we conclude that the Ninth Circuit erred in barring Qualitex's use of color as a trademark. . . .

Points for Discussion

a. **Spectrum of Distinctiveness**

Trademarks are conventionally divided into three categories, from strongest to weakest. An *arbitrary* or *fanciful* mark is one that indicates nothing about the good or service; this is the strongest type of mark (e.g., "Exxon"). The next strongest type is the *suggestive* mark, which merely suggests information about the good or service, thus requiring the observer to use her imagination (e.g., "Roach Motel" for an insect trap). Finally, the weakest type is the *descriptive* mark, which merely describes the good or service (e.g., "Coca-Cola," which was originally made with coca leaves and kola nuts). A descriptive mark is not protected unless it has acquired a *secondary meaning*, that is, the public associates the mark with the source of a particular good or service. A term that is frequently used as the name for a certain type of goods or services is *generic*, and thus not eligible for protection. For example, although "yo-yo" was once a protected trademark, it has become generic over the years. *But see U.S. Patent & Trademark Office v. Booking.com B. V.*, 140 S. Ct. 2298, 2301 (2020) ("Booking.com" was not generic because consumers did not perceive it "to signify online hotel-reservation services as a class").

b. Color as a Descriptive Mark

The *Qualitex* court holds that color may be a descriptive mark, entitled to trademark protection if it has acquired a secondary meaning. In fact, "customers identified the green-gold color as Qualitex's," presumably because Qualitex had used it in commerce for many years before registering it as a trademark under federal law. What are the advantages of using color as a mark, compared to using an arbitrary or fanciful mark? The disadvantages?

c. Color Trademarks and the Fashion Industry

Designer Christian Louboutin is famous for the vivid red color on the soles of his fashionable women's shoes, which generate over $130 million in sales annually. The PTO accordingly approved his registration of a trademark for the "Red Sole Mark." When Yves Saint Laurent began marketing shoes with red soles, Louboutin sued YSL for trademark infringement. The district court refused to issue a preliminary injunction because it concluded that recognizing the mark would impermissibly hinder competition among manufacturers of high fashion products, but the Second Circuit reversed this decision in *Christian Louboutin S.A. v. Yves Saint Laurent American Holding, Inc.*, 696 F.3d 206 (2d Cir. 2012). The court explained:

> We see no reason why a single-color mark in the specific context of the fashion industry could not acquire secondary meaning—and therefore serve as a brand or source identifier—if it is used so consistently and prominently by a particular designer that it becomes a symbol [which primarily identifies the source of the product]. *Id*. at 226.

Does this mean that a fashion designer could obtain a trademark for using the color red in other contexts, such as dresses or hats? Do you agree with the outcome in this case?

d. Is There Any Limit?

After *Qualitex*, is there any meaningful limit on what can constitute a trademark? The court suggests that "almost anything at all that is capable of carrying meaning" might qualify. Perhaps more importantly, should there be some limit? In his *White v. Samsung Electronics America, Inc.* dissent (Chapter 1), Judge Kozinski warned that protecting too much as intellectual property would stifle creativity and ultimately restrict culture.

The Lanham Act provides that certain things cannot be registered as trademarks, such as the flag of a foreign country or the name of a living person who has not consented to such use. 15 U.S.C. § 1052. In *Matal v. Tam*, 582 U.S. 218 (2017), the Supreme Court held that the Act's provision which barred registration for trademarks that would "disparage" people or "bring them into contempt... or disrepute" violated the First Amendment, thus allowing an Asian-American band to register its name, *The Slants*. Two years later, in *Iancu v. Brunetti*, 139 S. Ct. 2294 (2019), where the plaintiff sought to register "FUCT" as a trademark for his clothing line, the Court similarly reasoned that the statutory ban on "immoral" and "scandalous" trademarks was unconstitutional.

e. **Trademark Hypotheticals**

Is trademark protection available in these situations?

> (1) Based on public surveys, the law firm of C & D determines that blue is the color most associated with trustworthiness. It begins using blue in all of its television and newspaper advertisements. Some people are beginning to associate the law firm with the color blue.
>
> (2) X, a well-known celebrity, is fond of using the phrase "That's Hot" on television programs and elsewhere. Most people think of X when they hear this phrase.
>
> (3) Y operates a chain of restaurants using the name "Tia Maria." Z later begins selling frozen dinners to supermarkets in the same region, using the name "Aunt Mary's Dinners." Y complains, noting that "Tia Maria" is Spanish for "Aunt Mary."

f. **Trade Dress**

Trademark law also extends to *trade dress*, which the Supreme Court has defined as "the total image of a product." *Two Pesos, Inc. v. Taco Cabana, Inc.*, 505 U.S. 763, 765 (1992). To qualify for protection, "the appearance must be distinctive by reason of the shape or color or texture or other visible or otherwise palpable feature of the product or its packaging," so that the consumer associates it with a particular source. *Publications Int'l, Ltd. v. Landoll, Inc.*, 164 F.3d 337, 338 (7th Cir. 1998). For example, United Parcel Service uses the color brown as trade dress for its delivery service. Consider the design of Apple's iPhone. Is it sufficiently distinctive to qualify for trade dress protection?

2. Infringement and Dilution

The plaintiff in a trademark *infringement* action must prove that: (1) she holds a valid and enforceable trademark with priority over the defendant's claim to the mark; and (2) the defendant used the mark in connection with goods or services in a manner likely to cause confusion or to deceive consumers. For example, suppose winery R uses a seagull logo on its bottle label, which is a famous trademark. If winery T now begins using a similar logo on its bottles, and this is likely to confuse an ordinary consumer about the source of T's wine, T has infringed R's trademark.

Alternatively, T might be liable for trademark *dilution*. In 1996, Congress amended the Lanham Act by adopting the Federal Trademark Dilution Act, which provides protection against the use of a mark that is likely to cause dilution of a famous trademark. Dilution means unauthorized use of a trademark that either (1) weakens its distinctiveness (*blurring*) or (2) harms its reputation (*tarnishment*).

Jack Daniel's Properties, Inc. v. VIP Products LLC

Supreme Court of the United States

599 U.S. 140 (2023)

Justice Kagan delivered the opinion of the Court.

This case is about dog toys and whiskey, two items seldom appearing in the same sentence. Respondent VIP Products makes a squeaky, chewable dog toy designed to look like a bottle of Jack Daniel's whiskey. Though not entirely. On the toy, for example, the words "Jack Daniel's" become "Bad Spaniels." And the descriptive phrase "Old No. 7 Brand Tennessee Sour Mash Whiskey" turns into "The Old No. 2 On Your Tennessee Carpet." The jokes did not impress petitioner Jack Daniel's Properties. It owns trademarks in the distinctive Jack Daniel's bottle and in many of the words and graphics on the label. And it believed Bad Spaniels had both infringed and diluted those trademarks. Bad Spaniels had infringed the marks, the argument ran, by leading consumers to think that Jack Daniel's had created, or was otherwise responsible for, the dog toy. And Bad Spaniels had diluted the marks, the argument went on, by associating the famed whiskey with, well, dog excrement.

Jack Daniel's whiskey   Bad Spaniels dog toy
Click here for larger photos

[Jack Daniel's won at the trial level on both theories. The district court found, based mainly on survey evidence, that consumers were likely to be confused about the source of the toy. It also concluded that the toy created "negative associations" with "canine excrement," which would cause Jack Daniel's reputational harm. On appeal, the Ninth Circuit reversed. *VIP Products LLC v. Jack Daniel's Properties, Inc.*, 953 F.3d 1170 (9th Cir. 2020). First, it concluded that Jack Daniel's infringement claim should be analyzed under the threshold test in *Rogers v. Grimaldi*, 875 F.2d 994, 999 (2d Cir. 1989), which some circuits have adopted to protect "expressive works." Under that test, an infringement lawsuit must be dismissed unless the plaintiff can show either that (1) the challenged use of a mark "has no artistic relevance to the underlying work" or (2) if it has some artistic relevance, unless the use "explicitly misleads as to the source or the content of the work." *Id.* So it remanded the case to the district court to decide if Jack Daniel's could satisfy this test. Second, it awarded judgment on the dilution claim to VIP, holding that the statutory exclusion for "noncommercial use" in 15 U.S.C. § 1125(c)(3)(C) shielded it from liability. The district court found that Jack Daniel's could not satisfy either prong of the *Rogers* test and granted summary judgment for VIP. The Ninth Circuit affirmed.]

Today, we reject both conclusions [of the Ninth Circuit]. The infringement issue is the more substantial. In addressing it, we do not decide whether the threshold inquiry applied in the Court of Appeals is ever warranted. We hold only that it is not appropriate when the accused infringer has used a trademark to designate the source of its own goods—in other words, has used a trademark as a trademark. That kind of use falls within the heartland of trademark law, and does not receive special First Amendment protection. The dilution issue is more simply addressed. The use of a mark does not count as noncommercial just because it parodies, or otherwise comments on, another's products.

> **Hear It**
>
> Click here to hear the oral argument in *Jack Daniel's Properties, Inc. v. VIP Products LLC.*

I

Start at square 1, with what a trademark is and does. The Lanham Act, the core federal trademark statute, defines a trademark as follows: "[A]ny word, name, symbol, or device, or any combination thereof" that a person uses "to identify and distinguish his or her goods . . . from those manufactured or sold by others and to indicate the source of the goods." § 1127. The first part of that definition, identifying the kind of things covered, is broad: It encompasses words (think "Google"), graphic designs (Nike's swoosh), and so-called trade dress, the overall appearance of a product and its packaging (a Hershey's Kiss, in its silver wrapper). The second part of the definition describes every trademark's "primary" function: "to identify the origin or ownership of the article to which it is affixed." *Hanover Star Milling Co. v. Metcalf*, 240 U.S. 403, 412 (1916). Trademarks can of course do other things: catch a consumer's eye, appeal to his fancies, and convey every manner of message. But whatever else it may do, a trademark is not a trademark unless it identifies a product's source (this is a Nike) and distinguishes that source from others (not any other sneaker brand). In other words, a mark tells the public who is responsible for a product.

In serving that function, trademarks benefit consumers and producers alike. A source-identifying mark enables customers to select "the goods and services that they wish to purchase, as well as those they want to avoid." *Matal v. Tam*, 582 U.S. 218, 224 (2017). The mark "quickly and easily assures a potential customer that *this* item—the item with this mark—is made by the same producer as other similarly marked items that he or she liked (or disliked) in the past." *Qualitex Co. v. Jacobson Products Co.*, 514 U.S. 159, 164 (1995). And because that is so, the producer of a quality product may derive significant value from its marks. They ensure that the producer itself—and not some "imitating competitor"—will reap the financial rewards associated with the product's good reputation. . . .

The Lanham Act . . . creates a federal cause of action for trademark infringement. In the typical case, the owner of a mark sues someone using a mark that closely resembles its own. The court must decide whether the defendant's use is "likely to cause confusion, or to cause mistake, or to deceive." §§ 1114(1)(A), 1125(a)(1)(A). . . . And the single type of confusion most commonly in trademark law's sights is confusion "about the source of a product or service." *Moseley v. V Secret Catalogue*, 537 U.S. 418,

428 (2003). Confusion as to source is the bête noire of trademark law—the thing that stands directly opposed to the law's twin goals of facilitating consumers' choice and protecting producers' good will.

Finally, the Lanham Act creates a cause of action for the dilution of famous marks, which can succeed without likelihood of confusion. A famous mark is one "widely recognized" by the public as "designati[ng the] source" of the mark owner's goods. § 1125(c)(2)(A). . . . [But an exclusion] protects a "fair use" of a mark "in connection with . . . parodying, criticizing, or commenting upon the famous mark owner or [its] goods." § 1125(c)(3)(A)(ii). The fair-use exclusion, though, comes with a caveat. A defendant cannot get its benefit—even if engaging in parody, criticism, or commentary—when using the similar-looking mark "as a designation of source for the [defendant's] own goods." § 1125(c)(3)(A). In other words, the exclusion does not apply if the defendant uses the similar mark as a mark. . . .

> **Food for Thought**
>
> Why does the law only protect "famous" marks against dilution? Does this mean that the vast majority of marks—the non-famous marks—may be blurred or tarnished by competitors?

II

Our first and more substantial question concerns Jack Daniel's infringement claim: Should the company have had to satisfy the *Rogers* threshold test before the case could proceed to the Lanham Act's likelihood-of-confusion inquiry? The parties address that issue in the broadest possible way, either attacking or defending *Rogers* in all its possible applications. Today, we choose a narrower path. Without deciding whether *Rogers* has merit in other contexts, we hold that it does not when an alleged infringer uses a trademark in the way the Lanham Act most cares about: as a designation of source for the infringer's own goods. . . .

A

To see why the *Rogers* test does not apply here, first consider the case from which it emerged. The defendants there had produced and distributed a film by Federico Fellini titled "Ginger and Fred" about two fictional Italian cabaret dancers (Pippo and Amelia) who imitated Ginger Rogers and Fred Astaire. When the film was released in the United States, Ginger Rogers objected under the Lanham Act to the use of her name. The Second Circuit rejected the claim. It reasoned that the titles of "artistic works," like the works themselves, have an "expressive element" implicating "First Amendment values." 875 F.2d, at 998. And at the same time, such names posed only a "slight risk" of confusing consumers about either "the source or the content of the work." *Id.*, at 999–1000. So, the court concluded, a threshold filter was appropriate. When a title "with at least some artistic relevance" was not "explicitly misleading as to source or content," the claim could not go forward. *Ibid.* But the court made clear that it was not announcing a general rule. In the typical case, the court thought, the name of a product was more likely to indicate its source, and to be taken by consumers in just that way.

Over the decades, the lower courts adopting *Rogers* have confined it to similar cases, in which a trademark is used not to designate a work's source, but solely to perform some other expressive function. So, for example, when the toymaker Mattel sued a band over the song "Barbie Girl"—with lyrics including "Life in plastic, it's fantastic" and "I'm a blond bimbo girl, in a fantasy world"—the Ninth Circuit applied *Rogers*. *Mattel, Inc. v. MCA Records, Inc.*, 296 F.3d 894, 901 (2002). That was because, the court reasoned, the band's use of the Barbie name was "not [as] a source identifier": The use did not "speak[ ] to [the song's] origin." *Id.*, at 900, 902; see *id.*, at 902 (a consumer would no more think that the song was "produced by Mattel" than would, "upon hearing Janis Joplin croon 'Oh Lord, won't you buy me a Mercedes Benz?,' . . . suspect that she and the carmaker had entered into a joint venture"). . . .

> **FYI**
>
> *Barbie Girl* was rated the "worst song" of the 1990s in a survey. The accompanying story noted that "[m]any people were offended by the portrayal of a woman as a man's plastic doll," which made it an "incredibly polarizing song." *Readers Poll: The Worst Songs of the Nineties*, Rolling Stone, Aug. 31, 2011.

The point is that whatever you make of *Rogers*—and again, we take no position on that issue—it has always been a cabined doctrine. If we put this case to the side, the *Rogers* test has applied only to cases involving "non-trademark uses"—or otherwise said, cases in which "the defendant has used the mark" at issue in a "non-source-identifying way." S. Dogan & M. Lemley, Grounding Trademark Law Through Trademark Use, 92 Iowa L. Rev. 1669, 1684 (2007). . . .

. . . From its definition of "trademark" onward, the Lanham Act views marks as source identifiers—as things that function to "indicate the source" of goods, and so to "distinguish" them from ones "manufactured or sold by others." § 1127. The cardinal sin under the law, as described earlier, is to undermine that function. It is to confuse consumers about source—to make (some of) them think that one producer's products are another's. And that kind of confusion is most likely to arise when someone uses another's trademark as a trademark—meaning, again, as a source identifier—rather than for some other expressive function. . . . So the *Rogers* test—which offers an escape from the likelihood-of-confusion inquiry and a shortcut to dismissal—has no proper application.

Nor does that result change because the use of a mark has other expressive content—*i.e.*, because it conveys some message on top of source. Here is where we most dramatically part ways with the Ninth Circuit, which thought that because Bad Spaniels "communicates a humorous message," it is automatically entitled to *Rogers*' protection. 953 F.3d, at 1175 (internal quotation marks omitted). On that view, *Rogers* might take over much of the world. . . .

The Ninth Circuit was mistaken to believe that the First Amendment demanded such a result. The court thought that trademark law would otherwise "fail[ ] to account for the full weight of the public's interest in free expression." 953 F.3d, at 1174. But as the *Mattel* (*i.e.*, Barbie) court noted, when a challenged trademark use functions as "source-identifying," trademark rights "play well with the First Amendment": "Whatever first amendment rights you may have in calling the brew you make in your bathtub 'Pepsi' " are "outweighed by the buyer's interest in not being fooled into buying it." 296 F.3d, at 900. . . . So for those uses, the First Amendment does not demand a threshold inquiry like the *Rogers* test. When a mark is used as a mark (except, potentially, in rare situations), the likelihood-of-confusion inquiry does enough work to account for the interest in free expression.

B

Here, the District Court correctly held that "VIP uses its Bad Spaniels trademark and trade dress as source identifiers of its dog toy." In fact, VIP conceded that point below. In its complaint, VIP alleged that it both "own[s] and "use[s]" the " 'Bad Spaniels' trademark and trade dress for its durable rubber squeaky novelty dog toy." The company thus represented in this very suit that the mark and dress, although not registered, are used to "identify and distinguish [VIP's] goods" and to "indicate [their] source." § 1127. . . .

Because that is so, the only question in this suit going forward is whether the Bad Spaniels marks are likely to cause confusion. There is no threshold test working to kick out all cases involving "expressive works." But a trademark's expressive message—particularly a parodic one, as VIP asserts—may properly figure in assessing the likelihood of confusion. . . . So although VIP's effort to ridicule Jack Daniel's does not justify use of the *Rogers* test, it may make a difference in the standard trademark analysis. Consistent with our ordinary practice, we remand that issue to the courts below. . . .

III

Our second question, more easily dispatched, concerns Jack Daniel's claim of dilution by tarnishment (for the linkage of its whiskey to less savory substances). Recall that the Ninth Circuit dismissed that claim based on one of the Lanham Act's "[e]xclusions" from dilution liability—for "[a]ny noncommercial use of a mark." § 1125(c)(3)(C). On the court's view, the "use of a mark may be 'noncommercial' even if used to sell a product." 953 F.3d, at 1176 (internal quotation marks omitted). And VIP's use is so, the court continued, because it "parodies" and "convey[s] a humorous message" about Jack Daniel's. *Id.*, at 1175–1176. We need not express a view on the first step of that reasoning because we think the second step wrong. However wide the scope of the "noncommercial use" exclusion, it cannot include, as the Ninth Circuit thought, every parody or humorous commentary.

To begin to see why, consider the scope of another of the Lanham Act's exclusions—this one for "[a]ny fair use." As described earlier, the "fair use" exclusion specifically covers uses "parodying, criticizing, or commenting upon" a famous mark owner. § 1125(c)(3)(A)(ii). But not in every circumstance. Critically, the fair-use exclusion has its own exclusion: It does not apply when the use is "as a designation of source for the person's own goods or services." § 1125(c)(3)(A). In that event, no parody, criticism, or commentary will rescue the alleged dilutor. It will be subject to liability regardless.

The problem with the Ninth Circuit's approach is that it reverses that statutorily directed result, as this case illustrates. Given the fair-use provision's carve-out, parody (and criticism and commentary, humorous or otherwise) is exempt from liability only if *not* used to designate source. Whereas on the Ninth Circuit's view, parody (and so forth) is exempt always—regardless whether it designates source. The expansive view of the "noncommercial use" exclusion effectively nullifies Congress's express limit on the fair-use exclusion for parody, etc. . . .

IV

Today's opinion is narrow. We do not decide whether the *Rogers* test is ever appropriate, or how far the "noncommercial use" exclusion goes. On infringement, we hold only that *Rogers* does not apply when the challenged use of a mark is as a mark. On dilution, we hold only that the noncommercial exclusion does not shield parody or other commentary when its use of a mark is similarly source-identifying. It is no coincidence that both our holdings turn on whether the use of a mark is serving a source-designation function. The Lanham Act makes that fact crucial, in its effort to ensure that consumers can tell where goods come from.

For the reasons stated, we vacate the judgment below and remand for further proceedings consistent with this opinion.

Points for Discussion

a. **Role of the First Amendment**

The Ninth Circuit concluded that "the Bad Spaniels dog toy, although surely not the equivalent of the *Mona Lisa*, is an expressive work. . . . Bad Spaniels comments humorously on precisely those elements which Jack Daniel's seeks to enforce here." *VIP Products*, 953 F.3d at 1175. Do you agree? And, if so, should that matter?

It is often necessary to strike a balance between the free speech protections created by the First Amendment and the protection of intellectual property rights.

Where should the line be drawn? Presumably everyone would agree with the phrase the Supreme Court quotes from *Mattel, Inc. v. MCA Records, Inc.* that "[w]hatever first amendment rights you may have in calling the brew you make in your bathtub 'Pepsi' " are "outweighed by the buyer's interest in not being fooled into buying it." But did anyone buy VIP's dog toy thinking that they were getting whiskey?

b. **Infringement?**

Setting aside the First Amendment issue, did VIP infringe Jack Daniel's trademarks? It is undisputed that Jack Daniel's held valid marks. So the only other issue is whether VIP used the marks in connection with goods in a manner that is likely to confuse consumers. VIP's dog toy was certainly a "good." Were consumers actually confused into believing that the toy was created or authorized by Jack Daniel's? This is what the trial court found. But in her concurrence, Justice Sotomayor was skeptical about this conclusion; she observed that "[s]urvey answers may reflect a mistaken belief among some survey respondents that all parodies require permission from the owner of the parodied mark." *Jack Daniel's*, 599 U.S. at 164. What is your view?

c. **Super Soaker (Again)**

Earlier in this chapter you read about the patent infringement dispute concerning the Super Soaker. Another front in that battle involved alleged trademark infringement. In *Talk to Me Products, Inc. v. Larami Corp.*, 804 F. Supp. 555 (S.D.N.Y. 1992), plaintiff asserted that the trademark for its water gun, "The Totally Rad Soaker," had been infringed by Larami's use of the name "Super Soaker." The trial court granted summary judgment for Larami, among other reasons, because the term "soaker" was merely descriptive and its limited use by plaintiff had not created any secondary meaning.

d. **Trademark Dilution**

Suppose that a manufacturer of cocoa mix started placing the "Rolls Royce" mark on the package. Consumers would probably not be confused, but this might reduce or *blur* the distinctiveness of the mark because the term "Rolls Royce" in ordinary conversation might refer to either automobiles or cocoa mixes. *See Playboy Enterprises, Inc. v. Welles*, 279 F.3d 796, 805 (9th Cir. 2002) (discussing this hypothetical). Similarly, if the owner of a pornographic bookstore called his business "Rolls Royce Books," this might *tarnish* the reputation of the mark. Did VIP's dog toy tarnish Jack Daniel's mark?

e. **Cybersquatting**

In 1999, Congress expanded the Lanham Act to prohibit the practice of *cybersquatting* or *cyberpiracy*—registering the domain name of another person's trademark with the bad faith intent to profit from that mark. *See* 15 U.S.C. § 1125(d). This change was designed to deal with situations like *Panavision, Int'l, L.P. v. Toeppen*, 141 F.3d 1316 (9th Cir. 1998), where the defendant registered plaintiff's trademark as a domain name and then demanded $13,000 to surrender the name. The defendant had obtained domain names for over 100 other famous marks, including Delta Airlines, Neiman Marcus, and Eddie Bauer.

E. Trade Secrets

1. Trade Secret Basics

Trade secret law is the main tool for protecting information in the modern economy. It protects almost every type of secret and valuable information, whether or not it is used in a "trade" or business. The formula for Coca-Cola, the Google search algorithm, and the recipe for KFC chicken are all examples of trade secrets.

Of course, trade secret law overlaps somewhat with patent law. But, depending on the circumstances, it may offer better protection. In particular: (a) trade secret law covers far more information than patent law, because the criteria for patent protection are rigorous; (b) trade secret protection does not require government approval; (c) a trade secret is, by definition, kept secret, while a patentee must disclose her invention to the public; and (d) a trade secret could potentially last forever.

The traditional justification for protecting trade secrets is the need to preserve commercial morality by outlawing unethical behavior. As the Supreme Court noted in *Kewanee Oil Co. v. Bicron Corp.*, 416 U.S. 470, 481 (1974), it helps to ensure the "maintenance of standards of commercial ethics" by penalizing a business that improperly obtains, discloses, or uses a trade secret owned by another. Today courts increasingly stress that trade secret law also encourages innovation—the core policy that underlies patent law.

In general, a trade secret is (a) information that has (b) economic value from (c) not being generally known or readily ascertainable by others, (d) which the owner makes reasonable efforts to keep secret. The law in most states is based on the Uniform Trade Secrets Act. Congress created a civil remedy for trade secret misappropriation for the first time in 2016, with the adoption of the Defend Trade Secrets Act, 18 U.S.C. § 1831 et seq. It closely tracks the Uniform Trade Secrets Act.

- *Information*: Almost any kind of information is eligible for protection under modern law, ranging from new inventions to religious secrets.
- *Economic value*: The information must have actual or potential economic value.

> - *Not generally known or readily ascertainable*: The information must not be generally known by, or readily ascertainable by proper means by, others who can obtain economic value from it.
> - *Efforts to keep secret*: The owner must make reasonable efforts to maintain the secrecy of the information.

2. Misappropriation

To prevail in an action for trade secret *misappropriation*, the plaintiff must prove that: (a) it owns a trade secret; and (b) the defendant wrongfully acquired, disclosed, or used the secret.

For example, liability for wrongful acquisition hinges on whether improper means were used to obtain the secret and the defendant's knowledge of those circumstances. If R obtains S's trade secret by burglarizing S's office, he has knowingly obtained it through improper means, and is accordingly liable for misappropriation. But if R merely finds a document containing the secret while walking down a public sidewalk, he is not liable. Other rules govern liability for wrongful disclosure or use.

Employers often file misappropriation cases against former employees. In the most common situation, an employee learns a trade secret in the course of her work, leaves that job, takes a new job with a competing business, and discloses the trade secret to the new employer. In this situation, the employee is liable for misappropriation because she wrongfully disclosed the secret, even though she acquired it legally. But can an employer get an injunction to stop a former employee from even taking the new job?

PepsiCo, Inc. v. Redmond

United States Court of Appeals, Seventh Circuit

54 F.3d 1262 (1995)

FLAUM, CIRCUIT JUDGE.

Plaintiff PepsiCo, Inc., sought a preliminary injunction against defendants William Redmond and the Quaker Oats Company to prevent Redmond, a former PepsiCo employee, from divulging PepsiCo trade secrets . . . in his new job with Quaker and from assuming any duties with Quaker relating to beverage pricing, marketing, and distribution. The district court agreed with PepsiCo and granted the injunction. We now affirm that decision.

I.

The facts of this case lay against a backdrop of fierce beverage-industry competition between Quaker and PepsiCo, especially in "sports drinks" and "new age drinks." Quaker's sports drink, "Gatorade," is the dominant brand in its market niche. PepsiCo introduced its Gatorade rival, "All Sport," in March and April of 1994, but sales of All Sport lag far behind those of Gatorade. Quaker also has the lead in the new-age-drink category. Although PepsiCo has entered the market through joint ventures with the Thomas J. Lipton Company and Ocean Spray Cranberries, Inc., Quaker purchased Snapple Beverage Corp., a large new-age-drink maker, in late 1994. PepsiCo's products have about half of Snapple's market share. Both companies see 1995 as an important year for their products: PepsiCo has developed extensive plans to increase its market presence, while Quaker is trying to solidify its lead by integrating Gatorade and Snapple distribution. . . .

> **FYI**
>
> In 1965, the head coach for the University of Florida football team—the Gators—wanted a drink to help his players replace the body fluids they lost during games and practices. Scientists at the University's College of Medicine developed a special drink for this purpose, which was later dubbed "Gatorade." Commercial sales of Gatorade began a few years later, and it became the official sports drink of the National Football League.

[Redmond worked in PepsiCo's North American division ("PCNA") for 10 years, eventually becoming the general manager of the Northern California region in 1994. In his employment, he learned various PepsiCo trade secrets, including: (1) PCNA's Strategic Plan, which contained its "plans to compete, its financial goals, and its strategies for manufacturing, production, marketing, packaging, and distribution for the coming three years"; and (2) PCNA's Annual Operating Plan, which specified its "financial goals, marketing plans, promotional event calendars, growth expectations, and operational changes" for 1995. In November, 1994, Redmond accepted Quaker's offer to become the chief operating officer of its Gatorade and Snapple divisions.]

On December 15, 1994, the district court issued an order enjoining Redmond from assuming his position at Quaker through May, 1995, and permanently from using or disclosing any . . . trade secrets. . . .

Gatorade
Click here for larger photo

II.

Both parties agree that the primary issue on appeal is whether the district court correctly concluded that PepsiCo had a reasonable likelihood of success on its . . . claim[ ] for trade secret misappropriation. . . .

The Illinois Trade Secrets Act ("ITSA"), which governs the trade secret issues in this case, provides that a court may enjoin the "actual or threatened misappropriation" of a trade secret. 765 ILCS 1065/3(a). . . . A party seeking an injunction must therefore prove both the existence of a trade secret and the misappropriation. The defendants' appeal focuses solely on misappropriation; although the defendants only reluctantly refer to PepsiCo's marketing and distribution plans as trade secrets, they do not seriously contest that this information falls under the ITSA.[5]

The question of threatened or inevitable misappropriation in this case lies at the heart of a basic tension in trade secret law. Trade secret law serves to protect "standards of commercial morality" and "encourage . . . invention and innovation" while maintaining "the public interest in having free and open competition in the manufacture and sale of unpatented goods." . . . Yet that same law should not prevent workers from pursuing their livelihoods when they leave their current positions. . . .

This tension is particularly exacerbated when a plaintiff sues to prevent not the actual misappropriation of trade secrets but the mere threat that it will occur. While the ITSA plainly permits a court to enjoin the threat of misappropriation of trade secrets, there is little law in Illinois or in this circuit establishing what constitutes threatened or inevitable misappropriation. . . .[6]

The ITSA [and reported decisions] lead to the same conclusion: a plaintiff may prove a claim of trade secret misappropriation by demonstrating that defendant's new employment will inevitably lead him to rely on the plaintiff's trade secrets. . . . Questions remain, however, as to what constitutes inevitable misappropriation and whether PepsiCo's submissions . . . meet that standard. We hold that they do.

---

[5] Under the ITSA, trade secret "means information, including but not limited to, technical or nontechnical data, a formula, pattern, compilation, program, device, method, technique, drawing, process, financial data, or list of actual or potential customers that:

(1) is sufficiently secret to derive economic value, actual or potential, from not generally being known to other persons who can obtain economic value from its disclosure or use; and

(2) is the subject of efforts that are reasonable under the circumstances to maintain its secrecy or confidentiality."

765 ILCS 1065/2(d).

[6] The ITSA definition of misappropriation relevant to this discussion is "the disclosure or use of a trade secret of a person without express or implied consent by another person who . . . at the time of disclosure or use, knew or had reason to know that the knowledge of the trade secret was . . . acquired under circumstances giving rise to a duty to maintain its secrecy. . . ." 765 ILCS 1065/2(b).

PepsiCo presented substantial evidence at the preliminary injunction hearing that Redmond possessed extensive and intimate knowledge about PCNA's strategic goals for 1995 in sports drinks and new age drinks. The district court concluded on the basis of that presentation that unless Redmond possessed an uncanny ability to compartmentalize information, he would necessarily be making decisions about Gatorade and Snapple by relying on his knowledge of PCNA trade secrets. . . .

> **Food for Thought**
>
> Are you convinced that Redmond would have inevitably disclosed or used PepsiCo trade secrets in his work at Quaker?

Admittedly, PepsiCo has not brought a traditional trade secret case, in which a former employee has knowledge of a special manufacturing process or customer list and can give a competitor an unfair advantage by transferring the technology or customers to that competitor. *See, e.g., Glenayre Electronics, Ltd. v. Sandahl*, 830 F.Supp. 1149 (C.D.Ill.1993) (preliminary injunction sought to prevent use of trade secrets regarding pager technology); *Stampede Tool Warehouse, Inc. v. May*, 1995 WL 121439 (Ill.App. 1st Dist. March 22, 1995) (preliminary injunction sought to prevent use of customer lists); *Televation Telecommunication Systems, Inc. v. Saindon*, 169 Ill. App.3d 8, 119 Ill.Dec. 500, 522 N.E.2d 1359 (2d Dist.) (preliminary injunction sought to prevent use of trade secrets regarding analog circuity in a wake-up call device), *appeal denied*, 122 Ill.2d 595, 125 Ill.Dec. 238, 530 N.E.2d 266 (1988). PepsiCo has not contended that Quaker has stolen the All Sport formula or its list of distributors. Rather PepsiCo has asserted that Redmond cannot help but rely on PCNA trade secrets as he helps plot Gatorade and Snapple's new course, and that these secrets will enable Quaker to achieve a substantial advantage by knowing exactly how PCNA will price, distribute, and market its sports drinks and new age drinks and being able to respond strategically. . . .

Quaker and Redmond assert that they have not and do not intend to use whatever confidential information Redmond has by virtue of his former employment. They point out that Redmond has already signed an agreement with Quaker not to disclose any trade secrets . . . gleaned from his earlier employment. . . .

The defendants' arguments fall somewhat short of the mark. . . . PepsiCo believes that Quaker, unfairly armed with knowledge of PCNA's plans, will be able to anticipate its distribution, packaging, pricing, and marketing moves. Redmond and Quaker even concede that Redmond might be faced with a decision that could be influenced by certain confidential information that he obtained while at PepsiCo. In other words, PepsiCo finds itself in the position of a coach, one of whose players has left, playbook in hand, to join the opposing team before the big game. . . .

... [W]e conclude that the district court correctly decided that PepsiCo demonstrated a likelihood of success on its statutory claim of trade secret misappropriation. . . .

Points for Discussion

a. **Conflicting Policies**

Should information such as business strategies be protected by law? As the *PepsiCo* court observed, there is a strong public interest in favor of "free and open competition"; and in our market economy, employees should be free to change jobs if they wish. Treating such broad categories of information as trade secrets undercuts both policies. Do the policies favoring commercial morality and innovation outweigh these concerns?

b. **Misappropriation in General**

Redmond obtained the PepsiCo trade secrets legally, in the ordinary course of his duties for the company. By definition, a corporation or other business entity can only function through employees; as a result, it must disclose trade secrets to employees in order to benefit from their use. But Redmond would be liable for misappropriation if he used any of the secrets on behalf of Quaker or disclosed them to other Quaker employees. Similarly, Quaker itself would be liable for using or disclosing such secrets if other employees knew or had reason to know that Redmond acquired them through PepsiCo.

c. **Inevitable Disclosure**

Should a court prevent an employee from taking a new job because he might disclose a former employer's trade secret? *Inevitable disclosure* is one of the most controversial issues in trade secret law. Many courts reject the doctrine, while others accept it. *See, e.g., Bimbo Bakeries USA, Inc. v. Botticella*, 613 F.3d 102 (3d Cir. 2010) (upholding injunction that prevented former employee who knew the secret recipe for Thomas' English Muffins from working for a competing company). The Defend Trade Secrets Act seems to bar federal courts from using the doctrine; it states that an injunction may not "prevent a person from entering into an employment relationship." 18 U.S.C. § 1836(b)(3)(A)(i)(I).

d. **Aftermath of *PepsiCo***

In 2001, PepsiCo paid $13 billion to purchase Quaker Oats—mainly to acquire the rights to Gatorade. It had to divest All Sport in order to avoid antitrust concerns. Today Gatorade is the leading sports drink in the world, producing over $6 billion in sales revenue each year.

Summary

- **Common Law Approach.** As a general rule, intellectual property rights were not recognized at common law. The main types of intellectual property recognized under federal law (copyrights, patents, trade secrets, and trademarks) are exceptions to this rule.

- **Copyright Basics.** The principal goal of copyright law is to encourage creative effort by giving authors an incentive to produce works that will benefit the public. The requirements for a valid copyright are: (a) originality; (b) work of authorship; and (c) fixation.

- **Fair Use Defense.** The most important defense to liability for copyright infringement is the fair use doctrine, which allows minor use of a copyrighted work where the use does not materially affect the rights of the copyright holder.

- **Copyright Infringement.** To prevail in a copyright infringement action, the plaintiff must prove that: (a) the plaintiff owns a valid copyright; (b) the defendant actually copied the plaintiff's work; and (c) an ordinary observer would conclude that the defendant's work was substantially similar to the plaintiff's work.

- **Patent Basics.** The main goal of patent law is to encourage creative effort by giving inventors an incentive to produce inventions that will benefit the public. The requirements for a valid patent are: (a) patentable subject matter; (b) utility; (c) novelty; (d) nonobviousness; and (e) enablement. The scope of patentable subject matter has been controversial.

- **Patent Infringement.** To prevail in a patent infringement action, the plaintiff must show either literal infringement or infringement under the doctrine of equivalents.

- **Trademark Basics.** The goals of trademark law are: (a) to protect consumers from being deceived about the source of goods and services; and (b) to give trademark owners an incentive to produce quality goods and services. The requirements for a valid trademark are: (a) distinctiveness; (b) non-functionality; and (c) first use in trade.

- **Trademark Infringement.** To prevail in a trademark infringement action, the plaintiff must prove: (a) she holds a valid trademark with priority over the defendant's mark; and (b) the defendant's use of the mark is likely to cause confusion or deceive consumers. Alternatively, a

> **Test Your Knowledge**
>
> To assess your understanding of the material in this chapter, click here to take a quiz.

defendant may be liable for trademark dilution if his conduct blurs or tarnishes the plaintiff's famous mark.

- **Trade Secret Basics.** The goals of trade secret law are: (a) to preserve commercial morality; and (b) to encourage innovation. A trade secret is information that has economic value from not being generally known or ascertainable by others, which the owner makes reasonable efforts to keep secret.

- **Trade Secret Misappropriation.** To prevail in an action for trade secret misappropriation, the plaintiff must prove that: (a) it owns a trade secret; and (b) the defendant wrongfully acquired, disclosed, or used the secret.

For More Information

For more information about the subjects covered in this chapter, please consult these sources:

- Michael Abramowicz & John F. Duffy, *The Inducement Standard of Patentability*, 120 Yale L.J. 1590 (2011).
- Joseph Fishman, *Music as a Matter of Law*, 131 Harv. L. Rev. 1861 (2018).
- Mark A. Lemley, *The Surprising Virtues of Treating Trade Secrets as IP Rights*, 61 Stan. L. Rev. 311 (2008).
- Jessica Litman, *The Public Domain*, 39 Emory L.J. 965 (1990).
- Haochen Sun, *Redesigning Copyright Protection in the Era of Artificial Intelligence*, 107 Iowa L. Rev. 1213 (2022).
- Rebecca Tushnet, *Registering Disagreement: Registration in Modern American Trademark Law*, 130 Harv. L. Rev. 867 (2017).

Chapter 5

Estates and Future Interests

In everyday life, we say that someone "owns" his home. What does this mean? Suppose that B owns Greenacre. An ordinary person would think that B owns a thing—the house and the land it sits on. But as you learned in Chapter 1, B actually owns a bundle of rights concerning the house and land. More precisely, B owns a present possessory *estate*.

Our system of land ownership arose out of the English system of estates and future interests. Accordingly, the forms of ownership that we recognize today are the product of centuries of development. The concept of an estate in land was born in feudal England where all landholders originally held "of" the king, who owned all the land. In that era, each person's economic and social status depended upon the nature of his land holdings. Over centuries, landholders gradually gained increased control over their parcels, and the English law of estates slowly evolved.

The common law of estates is an elaborate system that allows ownership to be split over *time*. An estate is simply one particular temporal slice of ownership rights in relation to a parcel of land. Suppose that O grants his parcel Redacre "to A for life, then to B." A has the right to possess Redacre during her lifetime, and B has the right to possess it once A dies. A and B have legally enforceable rights in Redacre, although their possession occurs at different times. In this example, A has an *estate* (a present possessory interest) and B has a *future interest* (a right to future possession).

> **FYI**
>
> In many civil law countries, title to land cannot be divided into successive interests. Thus, only one person can own a particular parcel at any time. Is this a better approach?

The vocabulary and structure of the feudal system provide the framework for our modern law of estates and future interests. Thus, studying this early history will help you to understand today's property system. As Justice Holmes once remarked, "a page of history is worth a volume of logic." *New York Trust Co. v. Eisner*, 256 U.S. 345, 349 (1921).

A. A Short History

William the Conqueror
Click here for larger image

Our story begins with the Norman Conquest of England in 1066. After invading England and defeating the Saxon army at the Battle of Hastings, William the Conqueror took the throne. He immediately began distributing land to his small band of Norman followers, both to reward their faithful service and to administer the conquered territory. Borrowing from Norman law, William created a feudal system in which the king owned all the land and granted possessory rights to his loyal followers. These *tenants-in-chief* received the right to occupy, possess, and use specific parcels of land owned by the king. In return, each tenant-in-chief was obligated to provide *services* and *incidents* to the king.

The most common form of service was *knight service*—the obligation to provide a set number of knights to fight in the king's army. The obligation to provide these services led most tenants-in-chief to create *subtenures*, by which they distributed possessory rights to their own tenants. For example, a tenant-in-chief who was obligated to provide ten knights to the king might grant a tract of land to a knight in exchange for this service. The knight, in turn, might grant a small portion of that land to another person in exchange for the payment of money or a percentage of the harvest. In effect, the knights who received land from the tenant-in-chief became lords themselves (called *mesne lords*), subinfuedating their land to other tenants in exchange for various services. Thus, an intricate pyramid of feudal tenure was created—each tenant owed services to his lord, and each lord was a tenant to the holder of the tenure above him. Each person's position in the pyramid determined his duties to the lord above him and his rights with respect to the tenants below him.

> **FYI**
>
> William the Conqueror commissioned the Domesday Book, an extensive survey which described every parcel of land in the kingdom. The Book allowed William to determine the services and incidents he could obtain from his subjects. The name "Domesday" arose because there was no appeal from the Book's conclusions about who owned what land. It was written in black and red ink on sheepskin parchment. Click here to see a page from the Book.

In addition to services, each tenant owed his lord obligations known as *incidents*. Incidents included an oath of fealty, monetary payments for the right of the tenant's eldest son to succeed to the tenancy, the return of the land to the lord if the tenant died without heirs (*escheat*), the right to possession of the land until a deceased tenant's heir reached age 21, and special payments in times of financial emergency. As social and economic conditions changed, the feudal services began to lose value. For example, knights were less important during periods of peace and eventually became obsolete. Accordingly, incidents gradually became more valuable than services.

> **See It**
>
> At the Battle of Crécy in 1346, the English longbow proved to be a devastating weapon against a mounted knight, allowing the English army to defeat a much larger French force. Click here to see a painting of the battle. After this point, knight service lost much of its importance.

Over time, tenants grew increasingly unhappy about the payments required by the incidents, especially the payment to transfer lands to their heirs. In fact, many of the provisions of the Magna Carta (1215) address such concerns. Relief finally came in 1290 with the adoption of the Statute Quia Emptores, which gave a tenant the right to transfer his land without permission from the lord. This statute marked the beginning of free alienability—and signaled the impending demise of the feudal system.

Under the feudal system, multiple people could have rights in the same parcel of land at the same time. One person held present possession of the parcel, but his lord and others higher in the feudal pyramid also held rights to take possession of the land in the future. Suppose that tenant A had possession of Greenacre, holding "of" lord B. If A died without heirs, the land would escheat to B. Similarly, if B then died without heirs, Greenacre would escheat to B's lord, C. This concept of recognizing both the right to *present possession* and rights to *future possession* is the foundation of our modern estates system.

> **FYI**
>
> The word *estate* is derived from the Latin word "status," which referred to the feudal connection between a person's ownership of real property and his social status in the community.

With the adoption of Quia Emptores, the forms of land ownership that we now call estates began to evolve. These estates loosely reflected the status that individuals occupied in their relation to the land. As the commercial market in land began to flourish, two types of estates came to be recognized: *freehold estates* and *nonfreehold estates*. There were three basic freehold estates: the *fee simple*, the *life estate*, and the *fee tail*. These estates were mainly held by the nobles and gentry, who were deemed to have *seisin*, a special form of possession; they were created by an elaborate ceremony called *feoffment with livery of seisin*. In contrast, the nonfreehold estates were created informally and held by common people. These estates later evolved into the modern leasehold estates between landlord and tenant, which you will study in Chapter 7.

The English law of estates and future interests that developed over the centuries was extraordinarily complex, reflecting the ebb and flow of divergent economic, political, and social forces. It was a patchwork that accommodated both obsolete feudal concepts and technical mind-numbing rules.

In the newly independent United States, state legislatures incorporated most of the English system into their state property laws. They generally embraced the freehold and nonfreehold estates, and the future interests that accompany them. Over the ensuing decades, states slowly simplified and modernized the traditional English doctrines. However, some technical rules did survive this process. They continue to affect land transactions today, as we will see later in this chapter.

> **What's That?**
>
> In early England, a living person could transfer a freehold estate only through this colorful ceremony. The grantor (feoffor) called upon the grantee (feoffee) to enter the land being transferred. Standing on the land, the feoffor then handed the feoffee a handful of soil or a twig, symbolizing the delivery of possession. Contemporaneously, the feoffor would proclaim: "I give this land to X and his heirs." Some scholars indicate that the ceremony was often witnessed by a young child, someone likely to outlive the parties. The child was apparently slapped during the ritual to ensure that he would remember the transaction. Deeds did not become customary until the Statute of Frauds was enacted in 1677.

B. Modern Freehold Estates

The universe of modern estates and future interests is a limited one. In this chapter, we will examine six freehold estates:

- Fee simple absolute
- Life estate
- Fee tail
- Fee simple determinable
- Fee simple subject to a condition subsequent
- Fee simple subject to an executory limitation

Later in the chapter we will cover the five basic future interests. One of these interests—the remainder—has four variants, making a total of eight future interests.

Today the dominant estate is the fee simple absolute. Over 99% of the land in the United States is held in this estate. The law also recognizes three variants on the fee simple, collectively called fee simple defeasibles. The traditional life estate is rarely seen in modern practice, but the *equitable life estate* is commonly used in the modern *trust*. Finally, the fee tail is almost extinct in the United States.

The rules that determine which estates and future interests are created are few in number and easily memorized. But difficulties may arise if you try to interpret the words of a conveyance using their ordinary or colloquial meanings. Because of the historical context in which estates arose, the actual state of title may be quite different than the words appear to suggest. It is helpful to remember that the terms used in a conveyance have technical and precise meanings.

At this point, you reasonably might ask: *why should we study these antiquated rules?* The simplest response is that these rules still apply in many jurisdictions today. Although the fee simple absolute and the leasehold estates dominate the modern property market, fee simple defeasibles are sometimes used to make gifts for charitable purposes. The life estate and a wide range of future interests are found in many modern trusts. And even though certain rules no longer apply to current transactions, they may still affect the rights that arise from earlier transactions. A title searcher needs to be able to recognize these interests in order to adequately represent her client's interests. Additionally, a solid grounding in estates and future interests will help you to appreciate and understand the current structure of property law.

Before examining the freehold estates in detail, it is useful to discuss terminology. An estate or future interest is usually transferred in one of three ways: deed, will, or intestate succession. Each method involves technical terms.

- *Transfer by deed*: A living person may transfer real property by a deed. The completed transfer is called a *conveyance* or a *grant*. The verbs used to describe the transfer are *convey* or *grant*. The person who makes the transfer is the *grantor*, while the recipient is the *grantee*.

- *Transfer by will*: The property of a decedent may be transferred by a will. The completed transfer of real property is called a *devise*. The verb used to describe this transfer is also *devise*. The person whose will contains the devise is the *testator* if male or *testatrix* if female, while the recipient is the *devisee*. Different terms apply to the transfer of personal property by will.

- *Transfer by intestate succession*: If a person dies without a will, her property will be distributed according to state statutes, usually to her closest living relatives. The completed transfer is called *intestate succession*. The verb used to describe the transfer of real property is *descend*, while the recipient is the *heir*. Thus, we might say that Greenacre descends to an heir. Different terms apply to the transfer of personal property by intestate succession.

How can we distinguish among the six freehold estates? The answer is *duration*. We categorize these estates according to how long they exist. For instance, the fee simple absolute is potentially infinite, while the life estate lasts only for a person's lifetime.

---

1. Fee Simple Absolute

If you own a home, you probably hold a *fee simple absolute* estate, often abbreviated as *fee simple*. The fee simple absolute embodies the largest group of private property rights recognized by our legal system. Thus, the holder has *all* the rights in the metaphorical bundle of sticks. The duration of a fee simple absolute is potentially infinite. It may endure forever, without any limitation or condition. By definition, there is no future interest that accompanies the fee simple absolute. Do you see why?

Traditionally, a fee simple was created by O conveying "to B and his heirs." The words "and his heirs" convey no interest to B's heirs. These are *words of limitation* that describe the estate being granted, rather than *words of purchase* that identify the grantee. The phrase "and his heirs" merely indicates that O is conveying a fee simple. Thus, the grant by O "to B and his heirs" can be more simply read as "O conveys to B in fee simple absolute."

Under the English system, a person could convey a fee simple only if the words "and heirs" were included in the deed. If these words were missing, the law presumed that a life estate was created. Today it is not necessary to use this phrase in order to grant a fee simple. Modern law prizes an active market in real property, and grantors typically intend to convey the most marketable interest, the fee simple. Accordingly, states presume that the grantor intends to convey a fee simple *unless* he uses words of limitation that specifically convey a different estate. Thus, a conveyance "to B" creates a fee simple in B.

The fee simple is freely *alienable* (it can be sold or given away during the owner's lifetime), *devisable* (it can be transferred by will at death), and *descendible* (it can pass by the laws of intestate succession if the owner dies without a will).

Examples

(1) *O conveys "to G and her heirs."* G receives a fee simple estate. The *words of purchase* "to G" denote G as the grantee of the estate. The *words of limitation* "and her heirs" identify the estate as a fee simple. Remember that G's heirs receive no interest by this conveyance.

(2) *O conveys "to G for ever and ever."* G again receives a fee simple. The words "for ever and ever" are not words of limitation, but they reflect O's

> intent to give his entire interest to G. Today, if a conveyance does not contain words that expressly describe the estate, it is presumed the grantor conveyed the largest possible estate, a fee simple.
>
> (3) *O conveys "to Google, Inc., its successors, and assigns."* Google receives a fee simple. The *words of purchase* "to Google, Inc." denote Google as the grantee of the estate. The *words of limitation* "its successors, and assigns" identify the estate as a fee simple. Entities other than persons do not have heirs. Since corporations are not persons, they are followed by successors and assigns.

As you will see throughout this chapter, our property system still uses many of the basic concepts that emerged from English common law. For example, the language of a deed was strictly interpreted under English law; accordingly, it was crucial to use the correct technical wording. As our next case illustrates, mastery of these traditional concepts was a necessity.

Cole v. Steinlauf

Supreme Court of Errors of Connecticut

136 A.2d 744 (1957)

WYNNE, CHIEF JUSTICE.

There is no dispute as to the facts. The case presented a single question of law. It appears from the finding that it was submitted on the pleadings. The only evidence was the deed which was part of the defendant's chain of title. The plaintiffs and the defendant entered into a contract for the sale of real estate situated in Norwalk. The plaintiffs were named as purchasers and the defendant as seller. The contract provided that if the seller was unable to convey title to the premises free and clear of any defect of title, the purchasers had the option of rejecting the seller's deed. In the event of such a rejection, all sums paid on account, together with reasonable fees for the examination of the title, were to be repaid to the purchasers. The

> **Food for Thought**
>
> The alleged defect did not appear in the deed that the defendant received when he acquired title. Rather, plaintiffs attacked the validity of an earlier deed in the defendant's chain of title. Why did it matter if that earlier deed was defective?

plaintiffs paid the defendant $420 as a deposit when the contract was executed. They engaged an attorney to examine the title before the closing date of July 1, 1955. The attorney discovered that a deed had been executed in New York on October 22, 1945, to a predecessor in title of the defendant. It appears from the deed that it ran to the grantee "and assigns forever." No mention was made of "heirs" as would be customary and necessary in a fee simple conveyance made in Connecticut. The plaintiffs refused to accept the defendant's deed on the ground that the 1945 deed did not mention the heirs of the grantee. They made demand upon the defendant for a return of the $420 deposit plus expenses for the search of the title, which it was stipulated amounted to $50. The demand was refused, and the instant suit was thereafter brought.

The trial court found the issues for the defendant, holding that General Statutes § 7087 validated the 1945 deed and that the claimed defect in it did not render the defendant's title unmarketable. This result was reached on the theory that the 1945 conveyance was in law a conveyance of the full fee.

The issue for determination is whether the 1945 deed operated to convey the totality of the fee to the grantee without a flaw or defect which would render the title offered to the plaintiffs unmarketable. To create an estate of inheritance in land by deed, it is necessary to use the word "heirs." *Chappell v. New York, N. H. & H. R. Co.*, 24 A. 997. Where the common-law rule is in effect, as it is in Connecticut, a grant to a grantee "and his assigns forever" vests only a life estate in the grantee. A deed can be reformed to vest a fee in a grantee where the word "heirs" is omitted if it can be determined from the clearly expressed intent of the parties that a fee was intended. *Chamberlain v. Thompson*, 10 Conn. 243, 253. It is impossible to determine the intent of the parties to the 1945 conveyance in this proceeding, for the reason that the necessary parties are not all before the court. . . .

Here, the deed objected to on its face conveyed only a life estate under our law . . . .

There is error, the judgment is set aside and the case is remanded with direction to render judgment for the plaintiffs . . . .

BALDWIN, ASSOCIATE JUSTICE (concurring).

. . . At common law, in order to convey to a natural person a title in fee simple in real property, the document must run from the grantor to the grantee and "his heirs.". . . In the instant case, the deed in the defendant's chain of title runs only to the grantee and his assigns and for that reason is insufficient upon its face to convey a title in fee simple in lands located in this state. . . .

Points for Discussion

a. Who Has an Interest?

Suppose that the seller had a fee simple absolute and transferred title to Cole using a deed that read "to Cole and his heirs." What interest would Cole's children have in the property? If Cole wanted to sell the land, would he need their permission? It is important to remember that the words "and his heirs" would not give the children any interest. These are words of limitation whose sole function is to designate the estate granted—a fee simple. If Cole still owned the property when he died, his heirs might take it by intestate succession, but only at that time and by that manner. Of course, if Cole conveyed the land during his lifetime or devised it to someone else upon death, there would be nothing for the heirs to receive.

b. History of the Fee Simple

A conveyance "to B and his heirs" originally vested inheritance rights in B's eldest son. These terms were words of purchase that designated the son as B's successor in interest. During the early feudal era, a tenant could not transfer his ownership rights either during his lifetime or by will when he died. However, the king could allow a tenant to pass his estate by inheritance to the eldest son. Following the Statute Quia Emptores (1290) and the Statute of Wills (1540), a tenant was able to freely transfer his interest to another person, either by a deed or by a will. Gradually, the words "and his heirs" ceased to be *words of purchase* (designating the grantee) and became *words of limitation* (designating the estate).

c. Presumption in Favor of Fee Simple

If the words of a conveyance or devise are ambiguous, the modern presumption is to favor a fee simple. Thus, courts will construe a grant from O "to B" as creating a fee simple in B. Why? Given the modern need for maintaining an efficient market in land, the law favors free alienation. Therefore, an ambiguity is resolved in favor of finding the most marketable estate, a fee simple. If *Cole* were decided today, how would a court interpret the conveyance?

d. Who Are Heirs?

Suppose X dies. Who gets her farm, Greenacre? If X left a valid will, the answer is simple: Greenacre is distributed as the will directs. But if X dies without such a will, her property will be distributed according to the laws governing *intestate succession* in her state. *Heirs* are the persons who receive real property under the laws of intestate succession. A living person does not have heirs, but only *heirs apparent*. Only individuals who survive the decedent can become her heirs. Persons who receive personal property by intestate succession are called *next of kin*.

If X dies *intestate* (that is, without a valid will), a state will typically distribute her property as follows:

Issue and surviving spouse: *Issue* are lineal descendants—children, grandchildren, and so forth. If the decedent leaves a surviving spouse, the property will be shared among the issue and the spouse. For example, the state might give a one-half share to the spouse and divide the other half among the issue. Where the decedent has no surviving spouse, the property is distributed among the issue.

Parents and their issue: If the decedent does not leave a spouse or issue, the property generally will be distributed first to her parents, and if there are no living parents, to the living issue of the parents.

Ancestors and collaterals: If the decedent does not leave a spouse, issue, parents, or the issue of parents, the property goes (a) to any surviving *ancestors* and/or (b) to any surviving *collaterals* (all other persons related by blood to the decedent other than those already listed above).

Escheat: If the decedent has no living relatives, the property belongs to the state under the doctrine of *escheat*—just like land reverted to the king if a landowner died without heirs in the feudal era. See, e.g., Estate of Ray, 478 P.3d 1126 (Wash. Ct. App. 2020) (decedent's $3,650,000 estate escheated to the state).

e. **Fee Simple Problems**

Which transfers create an estate in fee simple?

> (1) O conveys "to B and his heirs forever."
>
> (2) O devises "to C for life."
>
> (3) O conveys "to D for ten years."
>
> (4) O devises "to E and her heirs provided that E marries."
>
> (5) O conveys "to F, my pet cat."

f. **Aftermath of *Cole***

Four years after *Cole*, the Connecticut Supreme Court (finally) held that use of the word "heirs" was no longer necessary to create a fee simple. The court stated:

> [*Cole*] strongly intimates that in a conveyance the use of the word "heirs" is indispensable to the effective expression of an intention to create a fee simple estate in Connecticut and that the omission of the word necessarily reduces the estate granted to one for life. Such a rule is patently inconsistent with our settled rule that the construction of a conveyance is to be determined by the intention expressed therein.

Dennen v. Searle, 176 A.2d 561, 568 (Conn. 1961). Today every jurisdiction has adopted the modern rule. Most recently, South Carolina amended its code to read:

"Words of inheritance or succession are unnecessary to convey property in fee simple absolute." S.C. Code Ann. § 27–5–130(B).

---

2. Life Estate

The duration of a life estate is measured by the lifetime of a particular person. When that person dies, the estate terminates. Suppose O conveys Greenacre "to B for life." B now holds a life estate for as long as she lives; the holder of a life estate like B is usually called a *life tenant*. You already saw the life estate in *Gruen v. Gruen* (Chapter 3).

In common law England, landowners often used the life estate to provide for future generations. Suppose that O wanted to ensure that his son B and B's son, C, both had a place to live. O could grant Greenacre "to B for life, then to C and his heirs." B's life estate gave him the use and enjoyment of the property during his lifetime, and C obtained possession upon B's death.

A life estate is created by language that clearly indicates this intention, such as "to B for life." The words "for life" are the traditional *words of limitation* creating this estate. But phrases such as "until B dies" or "while B is alive" are commonly accepted as long as they demonstrate the grantor's intent. Thus, a conveyance from O "to B for all of B's life" gives B a life estate in Greenacre that continues until B dies. O retains a future interest (a *reversion*) that becomes possessory upon the end of B's life estate.

A life estate can be measured by the life of a person other than the grantee. If O conveys Greenacre "to B for the life of C," B's estate is measured by the duration of C's life. B's estate is called a life estate *pur autre vie* (for the life of another). The life estate pur autre vie is usually created when the holder of a life estate conveys his interest to someone else. If B holds a life estate measured by his own life and then sells his interest to D, D has a life estate pur autre vie. When B dies, D's estate ends.

Examples

(1) *O conveys "to G for as long as G lives."* The *words of purchase* "to G" denote G as the grantee of the estate. There are no traditional words of limitation in the conveyance; however, the words "for as long as G lives" identify the grantor's intent to create a life estate. Thus, G receives a life estate. Since O carved out a smaller estate from O's larger fee simple, O retains a future interest known as a reversion, which will become possessory when G's life estate ends.

(2) *O conveys "to G for life." G then conveys her estate to M.* The *words of limitation* "for life" identify G's estate as a life estate. When G sells her life

> estate to M, M receives a life estate pur autre vie. M's estate lasts only so long as G lives. But if M dies before G does, M's life estate continues. O retains a reversion, which will become possessory when G dies.
>
> (3) *O conveys "to Google, Inc. for life."* O retains his fee simple. A life estate cannot be created in favor of partnerships, corporations, or similar business entities because they have potentially infinite "lifetimes." Google receives nothing from this conveyance.

An ordinary life estate is alienable, but not devisable or descendible. Because the estate ends at the holder's death, no interest is left to transfer. But the grantee who holds a life estate pur autre vie can devise his estate or allow it to pass by intestate succession to his heirs.

When an owner in fee simple transfers a life estate, a future interest arises automatically. Why? When a person transfers less than his entire estate, there is a gap in our durational timeline that must be filled in for the future. Suppose that O has a fee simple; he grants a life estate to A. Because O has transferred less than he has, he retains a future interest.

The future interest that follows a life estate is usually a reversion or a remainder; the distinction turns on *who* holds the interest. Suppose that O conveys "to A for life." The future interest retained by a grantor in this situation is a reversion. But what if O conveys "to B for life, then to C"? Because the future interest here is held by a third party, it is a remainder.

In medieval England, the life estate was the preferred interest. Unless precise wording was used to show a different intent, the law presumed that a grantor intended to convey a life estate. But today most jurisdictions assume that a fee simple is intended if there is any ambiguity in the conveyance, as our next case demonstrates.

White v. Brown

Supreme Court of Tennessee

559 S.W.2d 938 (1977)

BROCK, JUSTICE.

This is a suit for the construction of a will. The Chancellor held that the will passed a life estate, but not the remainder, in certain realty, leaving the remainder to pass by inheritance to the testatrix's heirs at law. The Court of Appeals affirmed.

Mrs. Jessie Lide died on February 15, 1973, leaving a holographic will which, in its entirety, reads as follows:

April 19, 1972

I, Jessie Lide, being in sound mind declare this to be my last will and testament. I appoint my niece Sandra White Perry to be the executrix of my estate. I wish Evelyn White to have my home to live in and <u>not</u> to be <u>sold</u>.

I also leave my personal property to Sandra White Perry. My house is not to be sold.

Jessie Lide

(Underscoring by testatrix).

Mrs. Lide was a widow and had no children. Although she had nine brothers and sisters, only two sisters residing in Ohio survived her. These two sisters quitclaimed any interest they might have in the residence to Mrs. White. The nieces and nephews of the testatrix, her heirs at law, are defendants in this action.

> **See It**
>
> Click here to see a diagram of the relationships among the *White* parties.

Mrs. White, her husband, who was the testatrix's brother, and her daughter, Sandra White Perry, lived with Mrs. Lide as a family for some twenty-five years. After Sandra married in 1969 and Mrs. White's husband died in 1971, Evelyn White continued to live with Mrs. Lide until Mrs. Lide's death in 1973 at age 88.

Mrs. White, joined by her daughter as executrix, filed this action to obtain construction of the will, alleging that she is vested with a fee simple title to the home. The defendants contend that the will conveyed only a life estate to Mrs. White, leaving the remainder to go to them under our laws of intestate succession. The Chancellor held that the will unambiguously conveyed only a life interest in the home to Mrs. White and refused to consider extrinsic evidence concerning Mrs. Lide's relationship with her surviving relatives. Due to the debilitated condition of the property and in accordance with the desire of all parties, the Chancellor ordered the property sold with the proceeds distributed in designated shares among the beneficiaries.

I.

Our cases have repeatedly acknowledged that the intention of the testator is to be ascertained from the language of the entire instrument when read in the light of surrounding circumstances. *See, e.g, Harris v. Bittikofer,* 541 S.W.2d 372, 384 (Tenn. 1976). . . . But, the practical difficulty in this case, as in so many other cases involving wills drafted by lay persons, is that the words chosen by the testatrix are not specific enough to clearly state her intent. Thus, in our opinion, it is not clear whether Mrs. Lide intended to convey a life estate in the home to Mrs. White, leaving the remainder interest to descend by operation of law, or a fee interest with a restraint on alienation. . . .

In such ambiguous cases it is obvious that rules of construction, always yielding to the cardinal rule of the testator's intent, must be employed as auxiliary aids in the courts' endeavor to ascertain the testator's intent.

In 1851 our General Assembly enacted two such statutes of construction, thereby creating a statutory presumption against partial intestacy.

Chapter 33 of the Public Acts of 1851 (now codified as T.C.A. §§ 64–101 and 64–501) . . . provides:

> Every grant or devise of real estate, or any interest therein, shall pass all the estate or interest of the grantor or devisor, unless the intent to pass a less estate or interest shall appear by express terms, or be necessarily implied in the terms of the instrument.

Chapter 180, Section 2 of the Public Acts of 1851 (now codified as T.C.A. § 32–301) . . . provides:

> A will . . . shall convey all the real estate belonging to (the testator) or in which he had any interest at his decease, unless a contrary intention appear by its words and context.

Thus, under our law, unless the "words and context" of Mrs. Lide's will clearly evidence her intention to convey only a life estate to Mrs. White, the will should be construed as passing the home to Mrs. White in fee. . . .

II.

Thus, if the sole question for our determination were whether the will's conveyance of the home to Mrs. White "to live in" gave her a life interest or a fee in the home, a conclusion favoring the absolute estate would be clearly required. The question, however, is complicated somewhat by the caveat contained in the will that the home is "not to be sold"—a restriction conflicting with the free alienation of property, one of the most significant incidents of fee ownership. We must determine, therefore, whether Mrs. Lide's will, when taken as a whole, clearly evidences her intent to convey only a life estate in her home to Mrs. White. . . .

The intent to create a fee simple or other absolute interest and, at the same time to impose a restraint upon its alienation can be clearly expressed. If the testator specifically declares that he devises land to A "in fee simple" or to A "and his heirs" but that A shall not have the power to alienate the land, there is but one tenable construction, viz., the testator's intent is to impose a restraint upon a fee simple. To construe such language to create a life estate would conflict with the express specification of a fee simple as well as with the pre-

> **FYI**
>
> During the early 1960s, the Chrysler Corporation was trying to purchase all of the properties on Lide's block, apparently in order to expand a factory; it offered $35,000 for her house. Lide adamantly refused. Does this information help to explain the language in Lide's will?

sumption of intent to make a complete testamentary disposition of all of a testator's property. . . .

In our opinion, testatrix's apparent testamentary restraint on the alienation of the home devised to Mrs. White does not evidence such a clear intent to pass only a life estate as is sufficient to overcome the law's strong presumption that a fee simple interest was conveyed.

Accordingly, we conclude that Mrs. Lide's will passed a fee simple absolute in the home to Mrs. White. Her attempted restraint on alienation must be declared void as inconsistent with the incidents and nature of the estate devised and contrary to public policy. . . .

The decrees of the Court of Appeals and the trial court are reversed and the cause is remanded to the chancery court for such further proceedings as may be necessary, consistent with this opinion. . . .

HARBISON, JUSTICE, dissenting.

With deference to the views of the majority, and recognizing the principles of law contained in the majority opinion, I am unable to agree that the language of the will of Mrs. Lide did or was intended to convey a fee simple interest in her residence to her sister-in-law, Mrs. Evelyn White.

The testatrix expressed the wish that Mrs. White was "to have my home to live in and *not* to be *sold*." The emphasis is that of the testatrix, and her desire that Mrs. White was not to have an unlimited estate in the property was reiterated in the last sentence of the will, to wit: "My house is not to be sold.". . .

The will does not seem to me to be particularly ambiguous, and like the Chancellor and the Court of Appeals, I am of the opinion that the testatrix gave Mrs. White a life estate only, and that upon the death of Mrs. White the remainder will pass to the heirs at law of the testatrix. . . .

In the present case the testatrix knew how to make an outright gift, if desired. She left all of her personal property to her niece without restraint or limitation. As to her sister-in-law, however, she merely wished the latter have her house "to live in," and expressly withheld from her any power of sale.

The majority opinion holds that the testatrix violated a rule of law by attempting to restrict the power of the donee to dispose of the real estate. Only by thus striking a portion of the will, and holding it inoperative, is the conclusion reached that an unlimited estate resulted.

In my opinion, this interpretation conflicts more greatly with the apparent intention of the testatrix than did the conclusion of the courts below, limiting the gift to Mrs. White to a life estate. I have serious doubt that the testatrix intended to create any illegal restraint on alienation or to violate any other rules of law. It seems to me that she rather emphatically intended to provide that her sister-in-law was not to be able to sell the house during the lifetime of the latter—a result which is both legal and consistent with the creation of a life estate. . . .

Points for Discussion

a. Lide's Intent

Do you agree with the *White* majority that the language of Lide's will is ambiguous? What ambiguity is contained in the phrase "to have my home to live in"? The dissent argued that Lide intended a life estate because she highlighted the words "not to be sold." Both the Chancellor and the Court of Appeals agreed with this view. Do you?

In *Knopf v. Gray*, 545 S.W.3d 542 (Tex. 2018), the court held that the following devise created a life estate, not a fee simple:

> NOW BOBBY I leave the rest to you, everything, certificates of deposit, land, cattle and machinery. Understand the land is not to be sold but passed on down to your children. . . . TAKE CARE OF IT AND TRY TO BE HAPPY.

The court also rejected the argument that the sale prohibition was an invalid restraint on alienation. Is *Knopf* consistent with *White*?

b. Rules of Construction

If the language of a deed or will is ambiguous, the court will interpret it in accordance with the transferor's intent. But if this intent cannot be determined, the court will apply a rule of construction—in effect, a legal principle that breaks the "tie." In *White*, the court referred to two such rules; each created a presumption that the transferor intends to convey the largest possible estate. Therefore, given what it saw as ambiguous language, the court presumed that Lide intended to devise a fee simple rather than a life estate. What policies support this rule of construction? Did the rule lead to a result that Lide never intended?

c. Valuing a Life Estate

What is the monetary value of a life estate? In *White*, the Chancellor ordered "the property sold with the proceeds distributed in designated shares among the beneficiaries." If White were a life tenant, how much would she have received? To calculate such a figure, courts estimate the amount of income that the property could produce during each year of the life tenant's remaining life, discounted to present value. Suppose a life tenant is statistically expected to live for 20 more years, and the property could be leased today for $10,000 per year for a 20-year term. Assuming a 6% interest rate, the present value of the right to receive $10,000 per year for 20 years is $114,699.

d. Holographic Wills

A *holographic will* is a will written entirely in the handwriting of the decedent and signed by her. In about half of the states, such a will is valid even though it does not comply with the stringent formalities necessary for a regular will (e.g., it is not witnessed). Because they are handwritten by ordinary people without legal training, holographic wills are frequent sources of litigation—as *White* demonstrates. As Lide's attorney, how would you have drafted the will to avoid any ambiguity?

e. Restraints on Alienation

White argued that the "not to be sold" language was an invalid prohibition on sale, not an indication that Lide intended a life estate. The court observed that any attempt to restrict free alienation of the property was "inconsistent with the incidents and nature of the estate devised and contrary to public policy." Why couldn't Lide devise her home to White on the condition that it never be sold?

One of the core policies of our property law system is freedom of alienation. Utilitarian theory holds that transferability is necessary to ensure the productive use of land. A *restraint on alienation* is a provision in a deed or will that prohibits or limits a future transfer of the property. If such a provision expressly prohibits the future transfer of a fee simple, it is void as against public policy. There are three types of restraints: disabling restraints, forfeiture restraints, and promissory restraints.

> - *Disabling restraint*: A restraint that prevents the transferee from transferring her interest; example: O conveys "to B, and any conveyance by B is void."
> - *Forfeiture restraint*: A restraint that leads to a forfeiture of title if the transferee attempts to transfer her interest; example: O conveys "to B, but if B ever tries to sell the estate, then to D."
> - *Promissory restraint*: A restraint that stipulates that the transferee promises not to transfer her interest; example: O conveys "to B, and B promises that she will not sell the estate."

While absolute restraints on a fee simple are void, partial restraints may be valid if they are reasonable as to duration, scope, and purpose. *See* Restatement (Second) of Property: Donative Transfers §§ 4.1, 4.2.

What if a grantor uses language that *indirectly* restrains alienation? In *Winecellar Farm, Inc. v. Hibbard*, 27 A.3d 777 (N.H. 2011) the court held that a lessee's right to harvest hay on the owners' land "in perpetuity" was an invalid restraint because no buyer would be willing to purchase the property subject to that right. *See also Tiner v. Johnson*, 647 S.W.3d 103 (Tex. App. 2022) (100-year option to purchase land at a fixed price was an invalid restraint).

f. Legal and Equitable Life Estates

The ordinary life estate (technically called a *legal life estate*) is rarely created today. Because the life tenant may die at any time and thereby terminate the estate, few people want to buy or lease this estate; and most financial institutions will not make a loan against it.

However, a special type of life estate (called an *equitable life estate*) has continuing importance for the modern trust. The essence of the *trust* is the separation of legal and equitable title. A *trustee* holds legal title to the trust property and manages the assets as a *fiduciary* for the benefit of the trust *beneficiaries*, who hold the equitable title. The interests of the beneficiaries are usually split into present and future interests. The equitable life estate is the most frequent type of present interest. A typical trust might provide: "O conveys Greenacre to T in trust for the use of B for life, then to C." T is a trustee who is given the legal fee simple to Greenacre. B and C are the trust beneficiaries who have, respectively, an equitable life estate and an equitable remainder. B will receive all the income produced by Greenacre during her life, and C will receive the fee simple upon B's death.

g. Life Estate Problems

Which transfers create a life estate?

> (1) O conveys "to B until he dies."
>
> (2) O devises "to C for life, then to X."
>
> (3) O conveys "to D for 200 years."
>
> (4) O devises "to E for life, then to Z for life."
>
> (5) O conveys "to F for life." F then conveys her interest "to Google, Inc."

h. Aftermath of *White*

White died in 1981, and her daughter Sandra White Perry obtained title to the house. Unemployed and in economic distress, she soon sold the property for $10,000, far less than its value. A few years later, the buyer resold the house to the Chrysler Corporation for $40,000—exactly what Lide tried to prevent!

Most people utilize an attorney-drafted *attested will* to transfer their property at death—often combined with a *testamentary trust* (which is effective at death) or a *revocable trust* (which takes effect during the owner's lifetime). In general, an attested will must be in writing, signed by the testator, and signed by at least two witnesses who saw the testator sign the will, thereby *attesting* to the signature. In addition, the testator must have *testamentary intent*—she must intend the document to function as her will. Here is an example of a short attested will in the hypothetical state of Madison.

WILL OF ADAM Z. STONE

I, Adam Z. Stone, a resident of Larchmont, Madison, declare that this is my will, and I expressly revoke all prior wills and codicils that I have previously made. I am single, having never been married, and I have no children.

I give all of my property, both real and personal, to John W. Stone, my father, for life, then to Juanita H. Stone, my sister, and Fred A. Stone, my brother, in equal shares. If any devisee under this will does not survive me by at least 30 days, then I shall be deemed to have survived that person.

I nominate Juanita H. Stone as executor of my will. If she is unable or unwilling to serve, I nominate Fred A. Stone to serve as executor. My executor shall have all powers granted by the applicable laws of Madison, may use any provision for the simplified handling of estates, and shall not be required to post a bond. I direct my executor to pay my debts, funeral expenses, costs of administration, and all taxes which become payable by reason of my death.

In witness whereof, I, Adam Z. Stone, hereby sign this will in the presence of the witnesses hereafter named on this 24th day of December, 2023.

Adam Z. Stone

    Adam Z. Stone

[signatures of witnesses omitted]

Suppose O conveys Redacre "to E for life, and then to F." Life tenant E begins to cut timber and remove minerals from Redacre. Additionally, E neglects the home on the property, failing to fix the deteriorating roof or to remedy a termite infestation. F is concerned that Redacre will be worthless when he finally receives possession. Does F have any remedy?

Property disputes often arise between the life tenant and future interest holders. The life tenant may be motivated to maximize her short-term economic gain, while the future interest holders usually want the property to be maintained in its original condition. The common law doctrine of *waste* developed to resolve such disputes. In general, this doctrine imposes a duty on the life tenant to use the property in a manner that does not significantly injure the rights of the future interest holders.

If the life tenant makes a significant physical change that *increases* the value of the property, is she liable for waste? Our next case explores this question.

Woodrick v. Wood

Court of Appeals of Ohio

1994 WL 236287

Patricia A. Blackmon, Judge.

... Catherine Wood and her husband, George Wood, owned several parcels of land including parcel number 105. George Wood died in 1987. In his will, he made the following bequests with respect to his property:

> I devise and bequeath to my beloved wife, Catherine Dorothy Wood, a life estate in my marital property ... and all my other real estate.
>
> Upon the death of my wife, Catherine Dorothy Wood, I direct that the property ... be bequeathed one-half (50%) to my son, Sheridan George Wood, and one-half (50%) to my daughter, Patricia C. Woodrick.

In 1989, Sheridan Wood conveyed his interest in parcel # 105 to Catherine Wood.

For over 25 years, a barn has been situated on the land. The barn was initially used as a stable but has not housed any horses for many years. Some of the wood in the structure has begun to rot. ...

Catherine Wood and Sheridan Wood sought to raze the barn. ... Woodrick filed a complaint against Catherine and Sheridan Wood seeking to enjoin them from razing the barn. ...

After considering the facts as stipulated by the parties, the trial court ... denied the injunction but ordered Catherine Wood to pay Woodrick the sum of $3200 (the appraised value of the barn) if the barn was torn down. This appeal followed.

The issue raised by this appeal is whether the holder of a remainder interest in a parcel of land may prohibit the life tenant of such property from destroying structures on the land. Woodrick alleges that the destruction of the barn would amount to waste since the barn has a value of $3200. Wood argues that the barn is in a state of disrepair and that the destruction of the barn would enhance the value of the property as residential property. She also claims that, due to changes in local zoning ordinances, the barn could no longer be used for its original purpose (a horse stable).

> **See It**
>
> Click here to see a current photograph of the land involved in *Woodrick*.

An injunction is an available remedy to prevent an act of waste. ...

Waste is defined as an abuse or destructive use of property by one in rightful possession. Blacks' Law Dictionary (5th ed. 1979). Wood was rightfully in possession of the land as a life tenant. . . .

At common law, anything which in any way altered the identity of leased premises was waste, regardless of whether the act happened to be beneficial or detrimental to the remainder interest. However, the common law rule has never been recognized in Ohio. *Crockett et al. v. Crockett et al.* (1853), 2 Ohio St. 180, 185. The Crockett court found that a widow who inherited a dower interest in her husband's undeveloped land should be able to make reasonable use of the land's timber to pay taxes and other things to her benefit and should not be charged with protecting the property for the mere benefit of the reversioner. *Id.* In the case *sub judice*, the life tenant sought to remove the barn in order to improve the value of the property. The preservation of the barn would require the property owner to forego the making of an improvement which would add to the value of the property. The Crockett court held that a life tenant had the right to make beneficial use of the property even though she would be altering the land in order to do so.

In *Bellows Co. v. Covell* (1927), 28 Ohio App. 277, 280, the court stated that acts which would technically constitute waste as defined under the common law would not be enjoined when they resulted in improving rather than injuring the property.

> . . . [F]or actionable waste, substantial pecuniary damage to the reversion should be required and . . . the mere alteration of the demised premises which renders them unfit for their former use without decreasing their general value, is not enough. *Id.* at 281.

Woodrick claims that, since the barn itself has a monetary value of $3200, its destruction would diminish the value of the property by $3200 and would, therefore, constitute waste. This argument is refuted by the evidence submitted by the Woods which indicates that the removal of the barn would actually increase the value of the property. The trial court recognized the value of the barn by ordering the Woods to pay Woodrick $3200 if they destroyed the barn. This order adequately assured that Woodrick would be adequately compensated for the removal of the barn. The removal of the barn would increase the value of the property in which Woodrick had a remainder interest. The destruction of the barn, though objectionable to Woodrick, does not constitute waste to the property.

> **Food for Thought**
>
> If the removal of the barn increased the value of the property, why did Woodrick sue? Should it make a difference in the outcome of the case if Woodrick had a close connection to the barn as a child and was trying to protect a personhood interest?

Woodrick also argues that the trial court's decision to award her the monetary value of the barn authorizes Wood as life tenant to commit waste as long as a proper price is paid. We find this argument unpersuasive. As discussed above, the removal of the barn does not constitute waste to the property since the value of the property will not be diminished by the barn's destruction. Woodrick presented evidence that the barn itself has value and that she has personal property stored there but has not shown that the presence of the barn on the property adds any value to the property. The relevant inquiry is always whether the contemplated act of the life tenant would result in diminution of the value of the property. . . . The trial court's decision to award Woodrick the value of the barn was not a payment to justify waste but was, instead, indicative of the trial court's intent to protect the rights of both parties and to reach a fair resolution of their dispute according to the law. . . .

Points for Discussion

a. **Common Law Approach to Waste**

At common law, a life tenant could not alter the property in any substantial way, even if this increased its value. The *Woodrick* court rejected this approach, holding that in Ohio an action in waste lies only where the alterations reduce the value of the property. The overwhelming majority of jurisdictions follow the *Woodrick* view. Which is the better approach?

b. **Types of Waste**

Traditionally, the common law recognized three kinds of waste:

- *Voluntary waste*: results from an affirmative act that significantly reduces the value of the property (e.g., demolishing a valuable house). This is sometimes called *affirmative waste*.
- *Permissive waste*: results from failure to take reasonable care to protect the estate (e.g., failing to make minor repairs or to pay property taxes).
- *Ameliorative waste*: results from an affirmative act that leads to a substantial change in the property and increases its value (e.g., building a swimming pool).

Which type of waste did Woodrick's complaint involve? In the United States, a future interest holder may obtain damages or injunctive relief if the life tenant commits voluntary or permissive waste. However, most states do not recognize ameliorative waste.

3. Fee Tail

The duration of a *fee tail* is determined by the lives of the lineal descendants of a particular person. It was the most important estate for the landed aristocracy in medieval England. By conveying a fee tail, an owner could keep land within the family for generations, safeguarding the wealth and prestige of his descendants. In its most common form, the estate required that possession move from eldest son to eldest son and so on, continuing as long as the bloodline lasted. England finally abolished the fee tail in 1925.

The fee tail is almost extinct in the United States. Most states rejected it long ago due to concerns that it would both undermine democracy and impair freedom of alienation. Today the fee tail can be created in only four states: Delaware, Maine, Massachusetts, and Rhode Island.

> **Make the Connection**
>
> Thomas Jefferson led the fight to abolish the fee tail in Virginia, fearing that it would lead to a landed aristocracy which would threaten democracy. He explained that his proposal was necessary in order to eradicate "future aristocracy . . . and [create] a foundation for a government truly republican." Thomas Jefferson, Autobiography, 1743–1790. How does Jefferson's argument relate to the civic republican justification for private property that you studied in Chapter 1?

The basic form of fee tail is created by a conveyance to a named person and "the heirs of his body." For example, if O conveys Greenacre "to B and the heirs of his body," B has a fee tail. The words of purchase "to B" designate the grantee. The words of limitation "and the heirs of his body" identify the estate as a fee tail. O retains a reversion, which will become possessory if B's line of lineal descendants expires.

Holding fee tail, B has the right to possession of Greenacre for the duration of his life. Upon his death, the fee tail passes to B's lineal descendants (his children, then grandchildren, etc.). If B's bloodline ever ends, the holder of O's reversion (perhaps O, O's assignee, O's devisee, or O's heir) receives a fee simple in Greenacre.

The holder of a fee tail has only a limited right to transfer the estate. In the example above, B can only alienate his right to possession until his death. When B dies, regardless of who is in possession, the estate passes to B's lineal heir, his son C. Thus, a fee tail is not devisable because it automatically passes to the lineal heir (here, C) upon the holder's death.

> **Examples**
>
> (1) *O conveys "to G and the male heirs of her body."* The words of limitation "and the male heirs of her body" describe the estate as a *fee tail male* (a form of fee tail which passes only to male lineal descendants). Therefore, if G

has two sons and one daughter, upon G's death, the sons receive the fee tail. The estate would then pass only to the males in the sons' lines of descent.

(2) *O conveys "to G and the heirs of her body by R."* The words of limitation "and the heirs of her body by R" identify the estate as a *fee tail special*. A fee tail special is created when the transferor wants to restrict the fee tail only to the descendants of the transferee who are parented by a particular person. The goal of such a conveyance was usually to keep the property within the immediate family bloodline.

Points for Discussion

a. Fee Tail Today

What happens if a person tries to create a fee tail in a state where it has been abolished? The most common result is that a fee simple arises. So if O grants Greenacre "to B and the heirs of his body," B receives a fee simple. A few states preserve the fee tail for the lifetime of the first holder, but then provide that it becomes a fee simple when passed to the holder's children.

In the handful of states that still recognize the fee tail, the holder may easily convert this estate into a fee simple by an inter vivos transfer to another person; this process is called *disentailing the tail*. Suppose that you are practicing law in Delaware, a state that permits the fee tail. Your client X, the holder of a fee tail in Greenacre, wants to devise the land to his spouse. What do you advise?

b. Pride and Prejudice

In Jane Austen's most famous novel, Pride and Prejudice, the Bennets were frantically trying to find suitable husbands for their five daughters. Since Mr. Bennet was wealthy himself, one might suppose that he could easily provide the large doweries which were vital in that era. Can you imagine why the Bennets were concerned? In Chapter 7, Austen writes:

> Mr. Bennet's property consisted almost entirely in an estate of two thousand [pounds] a year, which, unfortunately for his daughters, was entailed, in default of heirs male, on a distant relation. . . .

When Mr. Bennet died, his land would pass in fee tail to his nearest male heir, the dreadful Mr. Collins. For a wonderful essay discussing the connection between property law and personal relationships in nineteenth-century England, see Sandra MacPherson, *Rent to Own: Or, What's Entailed in "Pride and Prejudice,"* Representations, No. 82 (Spring 2003).

Viewers of the PBS series *Downton Abbey* might also note that the Earl of Grantham held his estate in fee tail male. Daughters Mary, Edith, and Sybil could not inherit Downton Abbey; it was destined to go to third cousin Matthew Crawley, the closest male relative. *See* J.B. Ruhl, *The Tale of the Fee Tail In Downton Abbey*, 68 Vand. L. Rev. En Banc 131 (2015).

c. Fee Tail Problems

Which transfers create a fee tail?

> (1) O conveys "to B and the heirs of his body."
>
> (2) O devises "to C and her children."
>
> (3) O conveys "to D and the children of his body."
>
> (4) O conveys "to E and heirs."

4. Fee Simple Defeasible

A landowner might want to control the future of his property long after he transfers title. For example, F may want to sell his family farm, while ensuring that it never becomes a residential subdivision. In response to such concerns, the common law developed the *defeasible* estate: an estate that may end upon the occurrence of some future event.

In this unit, we examine the *fee simple defeasible*—a fee simple that may continue forever *or* may end upon the occurrence of some future event. There are three types: the fee simple determinable, the fee simple subject to a condition subsequent, and the fee simple subject to an executory limitation. Note that it is also possible to create defeasible forms of the other basic estates, such as a life estate determinable or a term of years subject to a condition subsequent.

a. Fee Simple Determinable

A *fee simple determinable* is a fee simple estate that automatically ends when a certain event or condition occurs, giving the right of possession to the transferor. In effect, the potentially infinite duration of the fee simple will be cut short if the event or condition happens. *See, e.g., 1000 Brickell, Ltd. v. City of Miami*, 339 So. 3d 1091 (Fla. Dist. Ct. App. 2022).

The fee simple determinable is characterized by words of duration, such as *so long as, while, until,* and *during*. Suppose that O has a fee simple absolute. If O conveys "to B and his heirs so long as the land is used as a farm," B has a fee simple determinable. The words "and his heirs" are words of limitation that indicate a fee simple; the words of duration "so long as" are words of limitation that indicate the estate is determinable.

The future interest that follows a fee simple determinable is always a *possibility of reverter*. A possibility of reverter can only be retained by the transferor (or his heirs); it cannot be created in a transferee. The possibility of reverter *automatically becomes possessory* upon the happening of the stated condition. In the above example, if the property ceases to be used as a farm, B's estate automatically ends and O immediately receives a fee simple absolute.

> ### Example
>
> *O conveys "to G and her heirs until Alaska secedes from the United States."*
>
> *G*: The words of limitation "and her heirs" identify the estate as a fee simple. However, the additional word "until," which connotes duration, creates a fee simple determinable. The future interest is held by O, the transferor. The estate will automatically end on the occurrence of a specified event—when Alaska secedes.
>
> *O*: O retains a possibility of reverter, which automatically becomes a fee simple absolute when Alaska secedes.

The fee simple determinable is freely alienable, devisable, and descendible. But the durational condition continues to apply to any transferee. In contrast, the possibility of reverter was not devisable or assignable at common law. It could only be transferred by intestate succession. However, today it is alienable, devisable, and descendible in most jurisdictions.

---

b. Fee Simple Subject to a Condition Subsequent

A *fee simple subject to a condition subsequent* is a fee simple estate created in a transferee that may be terminated at the *election* of the transferor when a certain condition or event occurs. If the condition happens, this estate does *not* end automatically; rather, the transferor has the power to terminate the estate by taking action. *See, e.g., In re Northwest Child Dev. Ctrs., Inc.*, 633 B.R. 145 (M.D.N.C. 2021).

The fee simple subject to condition subsequent is characterized by words of condition which expressly allow the estate to be divested upon a specified event. The words that are traditionally used to create this estate include: *provided that*, *but if*, and *on condition that*. In order to avoid ambiguity, it is helpful if the instrument contains a clause stating that "the transferor has the right to re-enter and reclaim the property" or words to that effect. Therefore, if O conveys "to B and his heirs provided that the land is used as a farm, and if it is not, then O may re-enter and reclaim,"

B has a fee simple subject to a condition subsequent. The words "and his heirs" are words of limitation that indicate a fee simple; the words "provided that" are words of limitation that indicate the estate is subject to a condition subsequent.

A *right of entry* (also called a *right of reentry* or *power of termination*) always follows a fee simple subject to condition subsequent. This future interest can only be retained by the transferor (or his heirs); it cannot be created in a transferee. When the condition occurs, the transferor can *elect* to re-enter the property, divesting the transferee of possession. However, unlike the fee simple determinable, the estate is *not* automatically terminated. Thus, B's estate continues in the example above until O exercises his right of entry, despite the breach of the condition. How does a transferor such as O exercise his right of entry? Traditionally, the transferor would physically re-enter the land and retake possession through self-help. Today, many states allow the transferor to end the estate by giving notice to the transferee or by filing a quiet title action.

> **Example**
>
> O conveys "to G and her heirs but if Alaska secedes from the United States, then O has the right to re-enter and reclaim the land."
>
> *G*: The words "but if" connote condition, not duration; and O, the transferor holds the future interest. Accordingly, G has a fee simple subject to a condition subsequent.
>
> *O*: O retains a right of entry. Upon the happening of the stated event, O has the right to re-enter and end the estate if he wishes to do so.

The fee simple subject to a condition subsequent is freely alienable, devisable, and descendible. Of course, any transferee is bound by the condition. At common law, the right of entry could not be assigned or devised; it could only be transferred through intestate succession. Today this future interest is alienable, devisable, and descendible in most jurisdictions.

c. Fee Simple Subject to an Executory Limitation

A *fee simple subject to an executory limitation* (also called a *fee simple on executory limitation*) is a defeasible fee simple estate created in a transferee that is followed by a future interest in another transferee. While the fee simple determinable and fee simple subject to a condition subsequent are followed by future interests retained by the *transferor*, here the future interest is held by a *third party*. The fee simple subject to an executory limitation *automatically ends* when a certain event or condition occurs.

A fee simple subject to an executory limitation is created by the same words of duration or condition that create the other two fee simple defeasible estates: *so long as*, *while*, *during*, *until*, *provided that*, *but if*, and *on condition that*. The distinguishing characteristic is that the future interest is held by a transferee, *not the transferor*. If O conveys "to B and heirs so long as it is used as a farm, then to C," O has granted B a fee simple subject to an executory limitation. The words "and heirs" are words of limitation that indicate a fee simple; the words "so long as" initially signal a determinable estate, but because the future interest is held by C (rather than retained by O), B holds a fee simple subject to an executory limitation.

The future interest that follows the fee simple subject to an executory limitation is an *executory interest*. Accordingly, in the example above C holds an executory interest that will automatically become possessory if the property is no longer used as a farm. You will study executory interests later in this chapter.

> ### Example
>
> O conveys "to G and her heirs so long as Alaska does not secede from the United States, then to M and her heirs."
>
> *G*: The words "so long as" are words of divestment that create a defeasible fee simple in G. Because it is followed by a future interest in a third party (M), G has a fee simple subject to an executory limitation.
>
> *M*: Because M is a transferee and her future interest follows a defeasible fee, it is an *executory interest*. If Alaska secedes, M obtains a fee simple absolute.

The fee simple subject to an executory limitation is alienable, devisable, and descendible; any transferee is also subject to the condition. An executory interest is freely alienable, devisable, and descendible.

Defeasible fee simples are sometimes used to make gifts of land to public entities or charitable institutions. A grantor may want to transfer ownership rights only for a specific purpose, such as a park or a church. If the intended use ends, the grantor wants the property to be returned.

For example, suppose the president of a famous resort hotel company wanted to ensure that the guests could attend religious services nearby. He might use a defeasible fee to grant part of the company land to the local Catholic Diocese so that a church could be built there. This scenario arises in our next case. But did the company convey a fee simple determinable or a fee simple subject to a condition subsequent? As you read the case, consider why this makes a difference.

Paul Smith's College of Arts and Sciences v. Roman Catholic Diocese of Ogdensburg

Supreme Court of New York, Appellate Division

130 N.Y.S.3d 547 (2020)

GARRY, P.J.

In 1896, the president of the Paul Smith's Hotel Company (hereinafter the Hotel Company)—Apollos "Paul" Smith—executed a deed by which the Hotel Company transferred property in Franklin County to the Bishop of Ogdensburg in trust for a Catholic congregation within defendant. The deed stated that the property was to be used "[a]s and for [c]hurch purposes only, . . . and in case the said premises shall be devoted to any other use than for [c]hurch purposes, . . . this conveyance shall be void and the parties of the first part shall have the right to re-enter and take possession of said premises and every part thereof." Shortly thereafter, St. Gabriel the Archangel Catholic Church (hereinafter the church) was erected on the property. The last surviving son of Apollos Smith, Phelps Smith, died in 1937. His will directed the creation of plaintiff as an entity and the transfer of the Hotel Company's assets to plaintiff. The parties stipulated that this transfer included a deed later recorded in 1963, which transferred to plaintiff, as pertinent here, "rights of way, easements, reversionary rights, [and] rights of reentry" held by the Hotel Company.

St. Gabriel the Archangel Catholic Church
Click here for larger image

In 2015, the Bishop of Ogdensburg issued a decree that relegated the property "to profane but not sordid use," and directed the removal of sacred objects. Plaintiff placed no-trespassing signs on the property in 2017, and thereafter commenced this [New York Real Property Actions and Proceedings] article 15 action seeking a determination that it owned the subject property in fee simple. Defendant answered and counterclaimed that it owned the property in fee simple. Upon the parties' joint stipulation of facts, defendant moved for summary judgment dismissing the complaint and seeking judgment upon its counterclaim, and plaintiff cross-moved for summary judgment in its favor. Supreme Court found that the Hotel Company had conveyed to defendant a fee simple subject to a condition subsequent and had reserved a right of reentry, but that right of reentry had been extinguished by the attempted transfer in the 1963 deed. Thus, the court granted defendant's motion in its entirety and denied plaintiff's cross motion, dismissing plaintiff's complaint and holding that defendant was the lawful owner of the property. Plaintiff appeals.

> **What's That?**
>
> In New York, a "Supreme Court" is actually a trial court. Appeals from these courts are heard by the Supreme Court, Appellate Division, an intermediate appellate court, which rendered the decision in this case. The highest court in New York is the Court of Appeals.

The main issue upon appeal is what interest, if any, remains in the Hotel Company as a result of the provision in the 1896 deed limiting defendant's use of the property to "[c]hurch purposes only." Plaintiff contends that, under the 1896 deed, the Hotel Company and its successors retained a possibility of reverter, while defendant, as Supreme Court found, asserts that the conveyance to defendant was subject to a condition subsequent with a right of reentry, which was later extinguished in the attempted transfer to plaintiff in 1963.

At common law, the legal effect of these two interests provided different outcomes. With a fee [simple determinable] subject to a possibility of reverter, "the grantor retain[ed] a right to regain the fee upon the happening of an event; [the grantor] regain[ed] it automatically" (*Fausett v. Guisewhite,* 225 N.Y.S.2d 616 [1962]). Conversely, with fees taken subject to a condition subsequent with a right of reentry, a grantee's failure to perform the condition subsequent did not divest the interest from the grantee, but rather required the grantor to act upon the breach by re-entering the property.

Supreme Court did not find the 1896 conveyance to be ambiguous and focused its analysis on the clause stating that "the parties of the first part shall have the right to re-enter and take possession." However, as plaintiff argues, the court did not address the first part of the provision, which clearly states that the transfer would be "void" should the property be used for purposes other than church purposes. Here, the term "void"—which precedes the right to re-enter language—is distinguishable from the term "voidable." Fees taken subject to a condition subsequent are, by their nature, voidable, as *only* the grantor, upon the grantee's failure to meet the condition, can exercise the option to terminate the grantee's interest, chiefly by re-entering the property; the interest remains with the grantee until this act by the grantor occurs, if ever (*see Nicoll v. New York & Erie R.R. Co.,* 12 N.Y. 121, 131 [1854]). In reading the entire provision to construe the intent of the parties, we instead find that the Hotel Company conveyed a fee [simple determinable] and retained a possibility of reverter, which "automatic[ally] forfeit[ed] . . . the estate" if defendant breached the limitation to use the property for church purposes (*NJCB SPEC-1, LLC v. Budnik,*

77 N.Y.S.3d 92, 94–95 [2018]). This interpretation is further supported by the language in the 1896 deed indicating that the Hotel Company "*shall* have the right to re-enter" (emphasis added) and take possession—a conveyance which does not include permissive language (*compare Fausett v. Guisewhite*, 225 N.Y.S.2d at 620 [indicating that certain language "and also a provision that if the event occurs the conveyor *may* enter and terminate the estate" creates a fee simple subject to a condition subsequent (emphasis added)]; *Allen v. Trustees of Great Neck Free Church*, 269 N.Y.S. 341,

> **FYI**
>
> Apollos "Paul" Smith, a charismatic hunting and fishing guide, founded Paul Smith's Hotel, which became the most fashionable hotel in the Adirondack Mountains in the late 1800s. It was patronized by Mark Twain, Benjamin Harrison, Grover Cleveland, Theodore Roosevelt, Calvin Coolidge, the Vanderbilts, the Rockefellers, and other celebrities of the era.

350 [1934] [citing Restatement provisions, which indicate that a fee simple subject to a condition subsequent is created by certain language and "[a] provision that if the stated event occurs, the conveyor *may* enter and terminate the estate"). Accordingly, we reverse Supreme Court's denial of plaintiff's cross motion for summary judgment and the grant of defendant's motion dismissing plaintiff's complaint.

Similarly, Supreme Court's decision as to the transferability of the interest held by the Hotel Company must also be reversed. A right of reentry, at common law, was "unassignable, undevisable and undescendible before or after breach of condition" (*United Methodist Church in W. Sand Lake v. Dobbins*, 369 N.Y.S.2d 817, 819 [1975]). However, a possibility of reverter has no such restriction and is freely alienable. Here, the 1963 deed "did not invalidate the possibility of reverter" held by the Hotel Company and properly passed the interest to plaintiff (*NJCB SPEC-1, LLC v. Budnik*, 77 N.Y.S.3d at 95).

As plaintiff still held a possibility of reverter, resolution of . . . [this] action hinges upon whether defendant violated the limitation restricting the use of the property to church purposes. The parties' joint stipulation of facts includes the 2015 decree from the Bishop of Ogdensburg that relegated the church "to profane but not sordid use," and indicated that parishioners would be served by a nearby parish. The stained-glass windows and the altar were later removed, leaving only the pews. Under the canon law of the Roman Catholic Church, "if a church cannot be used in any way for divine worship and there is no possibility of repairing it," it can be relegated to profane but not sordid use (*Roman Catholic Bishop of Springfield v. City of Springfield*, 760 F Supp 2d 172, 177 n 2 [2011], *affd in part and vacated in part* 724 F.3d 78 [2013]). "Profane use means use for purposes other than a Roman Catholic worship service," and "sordid" limits that use, prohibiting any use that is disrespectful to the Catholic Church (*id.*). Contrary to defendant's contentions, we find that defendant's use of the property for church purposes ceased pursuant to the 2015 decree, thus violating the limitation in the 1896 deed. Accordingly, it reverted to plaintiff, which now owns the property in fee simple.

As a final matter, defendant claims that, should plaintiff hold a right of reentry as a successor of the Hotel Company, plaintiff should be directed to destroy the church, at its own expense, to avoid unjust enrichment. We find this claim unpersuasive. Unless otherwise stated in a deed, a structure is a fixture that passes with the property. Here, defendant took possession of the property and erected and enjoyed full use of the church for well over a century, fully aware of the limitation contained in the 1896 deed to use the property only for such purpose; upon ceasing to so use it, the property reverted in fee simple to plaintiff, together with the fixtures thereon.

ORDERED that the order is reversed, on the law, with costs, defendant's motion denied, plaintiff's cross motion granted, and it is declared that plaintiff is the owner in fee simple of the subject property.

Points for Discussion

a. Which Estate?

Apollos "Paul" Smith owned and operated Paul Smith's Hotel Company. He clearly intended the Company to convey a fee simple defeasible—but which one? The trial court concluded that the Diocese received a fee simple subject to a condition subsequent because the deed used words of *condition*: "in case" the property was "devoted to any other use than for [c]hurch purposes," then the Company "shall have the right to re-enter and take possession." Accordingly, it found that the Company held a right of reentry. In contrast, the appellate court focused on the deed language relating to *duration*, stressing that the estate would automatically end—"this conveyance shall be void"—if the land was used for a non-church purpose. Under this view, the Diocese received a fee simple determinable, and the Company held a possibility of reverter. Which argument is stronger? Why?

Where a grantor intends to create a fee simple defeasible but uses ambiguous language, courts will generally construe the estate as a fee simple subject to a condition subsequent. The reason is that social policy abhors the forfeiture of estates because this interferes with marketability. Therefore, the fee simple subject to a condition subsequent (which continues the estate, and thus presents only a limited risk of forfeiture) is preferred over the fee simple determinable (which results in automatic forfeiture). Why didn't the court apply this rule?

The Restatement (Third) of Property abandons the distinction among the three defeasible estates and combines all three into one—the *fee simple defeasible*—which is defined as an estate that terminates upon the happening of a stated event. Restatement (Third) of Prop.: Wills & Donative Transfers § 24.3 (2011). A few jurisdictions have already abolished the fee simple determinable and the possibility of reverter. Any language that would be interpreted as creating either under the common law is treated as creating a fee simple subject to a condition subsequent or right of entry. *See, e.g.,* Cal. Civ. Code § 885.020; Ky. Rev. Stat. § 381.218.

b. **What Are "Church Purposes"?**

The Bishop's 2015 decree merely specified that the church could not be used for "worship services." But the deed provided that title would be lost only if the property was used for something other than "[c]hurch purposes." Was there any evidence that the property had actually been *used* for a non-church purpose? Should this matter?

Is "church purposes" a broader term than "worship services?" In *Country Bible Church v. County of Grant*, 2003 WL 21359537 (Minn. Tax Ct.) the court found that a prayer room and a weight room in a church's youth ministry building were being used for "church purposes"—even though neither room was used for worship services—and thus were exempt from property taxes. As the New Hampshire Supreme Court explained in *White v. Auger*, 201 A.3d 670, 674 (N.H. 2019), courts "generally disfavor interpreting deed conditions in such a way that would cause a forfeiture of the property upon breach of such conditions." Accordingly, the term "church purposes" should be broadly interpreted. Could the Diocese have retained title by using the building for church-related purposes such as prayer meetings or religious retreats? Should it have raised this argument in the case?

c. **Transferring Future Interests**

At common law, the possibility of reverter and right of reentry could not be conveyed or devised; they could only be transferred through intestate succession to the holder's heirs. Today in most jurisdictions these interests are freely transferrable; they can be conveyed, devised, and inherited.

But New York used a different approach in 1963, when a deed conveyed the Company's assets to the College. At that time, state law allowed a possibility of reverter to be conveyed to a grantee; but any attempt to convey a right of reentry extinguished it. The main issue in the case was which defeasible estate the Company conveyed to the Diocese in 1896, because this determined the future interest the Company retained. If the Company held a right of reentry, it was extinguished in 1963—and therefore the Diocese obtained a fee simple absolute at that time. On the other hand, if the Company held a possibility of reverter, then it was validly conveyed to the College in 1963; and the College automatically obtained a fee simple absolute when the land was not used for church purposes.

Ironically, in 1967 New York changed its law on the issue, joining the majority view that a right of reentry can be conveyed, devised, and inherited. Did this affect the court's view of the case more than 50 years later?

d. Condemnation Proceeds

Suppose B holds a fee simple determinable in Greenacre, and C has the possibility of reverter. If the city condemns Greenacre, how are the condemnation proceeds distributed? The general rule is that the holder of the fee estate receives all condemnation proceeds, on the theory that such a contingent future interest is highly unlikely to become possessory. *But see El Dorado Land Co., L.P. v. City of McKinney*, 395 S.W.3d 798 (Tex. 2013) (noting that damages would be appropriate if the defeasible event was reasonably certain to occur in the near future).

In *City of Palm Springs v. Living Desert Reserve*, 82 Cal. Rptr. 2d 859 (Ct. App. 1999), the city held a fee simple subject to a condition subsequent to a 30-acre tract; "in the event" that the property was not used as an equestrian center and desert wildlife preserve, then the city's interest would pass to the Living Desert Reserve. When the city condemned the right of entry—in order to build a golf course on the land—the court awarded the Living Desert Reserve the fair market value of fee simple absolute in the land, in part to punish the city for its inequitable behavior. The city eventually paid $1.2 million for the right of entry.

e. Waste and the Fee Simple Defeasible

In many jurisdictions, the doctrine of waste does not apply to a person holding a defeasible fee simple. Suppose O grants Greenacre "to B and her heirs so long as the Red Cross continues in existence, and then to C." Under this approach, if B discovers oil under the property, B can pump and sell all the oil without any liability to C. What explains this rule? The possibility of reverter and right of entry are seen as contingent, speculative interests, too insubstantial to qualify for protection. Does this make sense?

What happens if the holder of a fee simple defeasible remains in possession after the time expires or the condition is breached? Suppose that O conveys Greenacre "to B and her heirs so long as it is used as a hospital." Two years later, a new hospital is built in the region, so the old hospital on Greenacre is closed. For the next ten years, B uses Greenacre as an orphanage. What are B's rights? Would they be different if O's grant had been "to B and her heirs provided that it is used as a hospital"?

Metropolitan Park District v. Unknown Heirs of Rigney

Supreme Court of Washington

399 P.2d 516 (1965)

HAMILTON, JUDGE.

The Metropolitan Park District of Tacoma initiated this action against the known and unknown heirs of one John L. Rigney, seeking to quiet title to a certain parcel of real estate located in the city of Tacoma and originally owned and conveyed by John L. Rigney. The defendant heirs counterclaimed, alleging breach of a condition subsequent specified in the conveyance of John L. Rigney and a resultant forfeiture. All parties moved for summary judgment. The trial court granted the motion of the Metropolitan Park District and entered a decree quieting title in the district. Certain of the heirs appeal.

The essential facts are not in dispute. On August 2, 1884, John L. Rigney and his wife conveyed by deed the property in question to the Tacoma Light and Water Company, a corporation. The deed, in substance, recites that the property is to be used for the purpose of providing a right of way "to conduct fresh water by ditch, canal, flume or other conduit for the supply of the City of Tacoma and its inhabitants," and the grant is made subject to the following provision:

> ... [I]f at any time thereafter said Company, its successors or assigns should ... cease to use said strip of land for the purpose of conducting such water for the supply of the City of Tacoma, that then ... it shall and may be lawful to and for the said party of the first part their heirs, or assigns into and upon the said strip of land hereby granted to re-enter, and the same to have again, repossess and enjoy in his and her first and former Estate. ...

The Tacoma Light and Water Company entered upon and utilized the property for the purpose intended prior to January 1, 1886, and until 1893 when ... it conveyed the property to the city of Tacoma. ... The city continued the water supply usage until sometime prior to February 1, 1905, when such use was discontinued and the property, by ordinance, set aside for park purposes. The Metropolitan Park District was created in 1907, and succeeded the city in the management of the property as a park, with ownership being formalized in the district by deed dated March 13, 1951. In 1920, or thereabouts, tennis courts for public use were constructed and have since been maintained upon the property, although in recent years the courts have fallen in disrepair and are rarely, if ever, used.

All parties and the trial court proceeded upon the basis that the Rigney deed of the property in question conveyed a fee simple estate subject to a condition subsequent; that the condition had been permanently broken prior to 1905; and that neither the Rigneys nor their heirs had claimed a forfeiture or right of re-entry until the counter-claim in the instant suit.

On appeal . . . [t]he only questions presented for our determination are (1) whether the grantee of such an estate may acquire title by adverse possession following a breach of the condition subsequent but prior to a claim of forfeiture, and, if not, (2) whether the lapse of an extensive period of time between a breach and an election of forfeiture waives or otherwise extinguishes the condition.

We answer the first question in the negative and the second in the affirmative.

A fee estate subject to a condition subsequent is the kind of defeasible estate in fee which does not terminate automatically by the breach or happening of the condition or event specified. Title to and enjoyment of the estate following the occurrence remains in the grantee or his successors until affirmative action is taken by the grantor or his heirs to bring about a forfeiture or reversion of the estate. . . . The future interest retained in the grantor under such a grant is termed a "right of entry" or "power of termination," as distinguished from the "possibility of reverter" existing in a fee determinable estate, and

> In terms of legal operation of the two future interests, the principal distinction is clear: the possibility of reverter takes effect in possession immediately and automatically upon the happening of the event named, whereas, on the happening of the event named in a common-law condition subsequent, the possessory estate does not vest immediately in the one having the right of entry for breach of condition. He must first elect to terminate the granted estate before a possessory estate vests in him. Simes & Smith, The Law of Future Interests § 282, p. 330.

Thus, so far as the law of adverse possession be concerned, it is not conceptually logical for the grantee of a fee estate subject to a condition subsequent to acquire an indefeasible estate simply by remaining in possession of the property following breach of the condition. His continued possession and enjoyment of the property does not become adverse to any possessory estate of the grantor until the latter, or his heirs, elect to declare a forfeiture. . . .

In the instant case, it is agreed that no election of forfeiture, on the part of the Rigneys or their heirs, was made prior to initiation of this suit. Accordingly, the estate held by the Metropolitan Park District of Tacoma did not ripen into an indefeasible one by adverse possession.

This is not to say, however, that the holder of a right of entry, following a continuing breach of condition, is entitled to endlessly sit by refusing to declare a forfeiture, and thus control the use of the property indefinitely. An appropriate rule to meet such a contingency, together with the reasons for the rule, is succinctly propounded in Simes & Smith, The Law of Future Interests § 258, p. 310, as follows:

However, the mere fact that the statute of limitations begins to run in favor of the grantee on the grantor's election to forfeit and not on the grantee's breach is no argument for the proposition that the grantor's power to forfeit should last forever. Such a legal club over the grantee would be most undesirable from an economic standpoint, since it would tend to discourage any productive use of the land. From the standpoint of policy, all policy considerations which justify the imposition of statutes of limitation would justify limiting the time within which an election could be made after breach of condition. Courts are naturally reluctant to admit that mere inaction will eventually bar the grantor's power to forfeit, but it is submitted that the sound rule is as follows: *The grantor has a reasonable time after breach within which to declare a forfeiture or to elect not to declare a forfeiture; if he fails to declare a forfeiture within that time, his power to do so has expired.* (Italics ours.)

... The condition in this case has been in continuous breach since sometime prior to 1905. We cannot say that the delay in claiming a forfeiture has been either reasonable or warranted. The time in which the election should have been made has long since passed, and the condition has expired.

The decree quieting title in The Metropolitan Park District is affirmed.

Points for Discussion

a. **Running of the Statute of Limitations**

In *Rigney*, the parties agreed that: (1) the district held a fee simple subject to a condition subsequent; (2) Rigney's heirs held a right of entry; and (3) the condition had been permanently broken since 1905. Why didn't the district have title to the land by adverse possession? As the court points out, a fee simple subject to a condition subsequent continues until the grantor exercises his right of entry; only then does the limitations period begin to run.

On the other hand, the limitations period begins to run as soon as a fee simple determinable ends. For example, assume O conveys "to D and his heirs so long as it is used as a farm." D's estate is cut short and legal title automatically reverts to O when the farm use stops. If D continues in possession, the statute of limitations for adverse possession begins to run. *See, e.g., In re .88 Acres of Property*, 676 A.2d 778 (Vt. 1996).

b. **A "Reasonable Time"**

If the district cannot claim title by adverse possession, shouldn't the Rigney heirs be able to regain title? What is the source of the notion that the grantor has only a "reasonable time after breach" to declare a forfeiture? If a plaintiff's unreasonable delay in asserting an equitable claim causes prejudice to the defendant, it will be barred by the doctrine of laches. Was prejudice proven here?

c. Applying the Law

Suppose that V, a staunch vegetarian, conveys his restaurant "to M so long as only vegetarian meals are sold on the premises, but if not then V may re-enter and reclaim the premises." After several years, M conveys the property to P. Immediately, P begins to offer special "happy hours," during which drinks are served with complimentary fish nuggets. P also offers a boutique Brazilian wine that includes traces of beetle larvae. Six years later, P offers to sell the restaurant to your client, X. What advice would you give X?

d. Problems on Fee Simple Defeasibles

Which transfers create a fee simple defeasible? (Identify both the present possessory estate and the future interest transferred.)

> (1) O conveys "to B and his heirs so long as the land is not used as a nightclub."
>
> (2) O devises "to C and her heirs, but if Boston becomes a state then O's heirs have the right to re-enter and retake the estate."
>
> (3) O conveys "to D for life, then to M and her heirs while the well continues to provide water."
>
> (4) O conveys "to E and her heirs provided that alcohol is never served on the premises."
>
> (5) O conveys "to the First Baptist Church provided that the land is used as a church, then to Google, Inc."

e. Additional Review

Click here to access notes and problems on present possessory estates, taken from Coletta's Workbook on Estates and Future Interests, 3d ed.

The chart below summarizes the rules that govern estates.

Estates

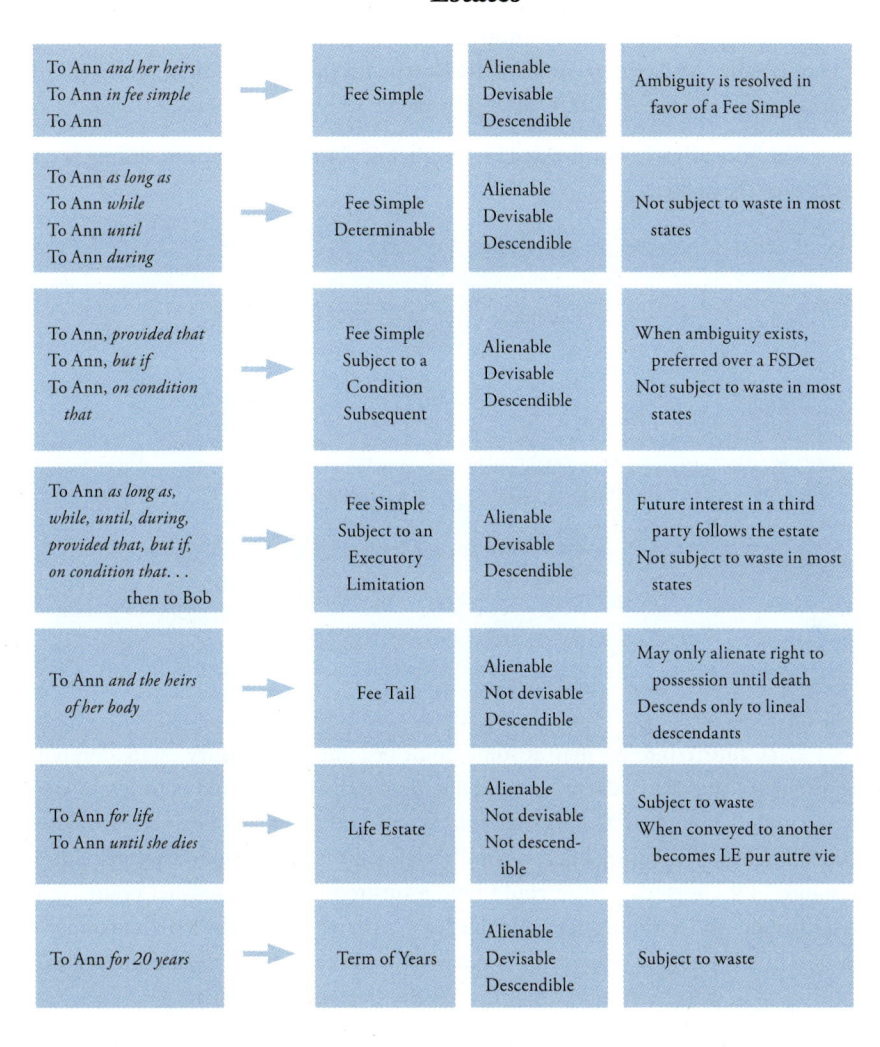

Language	Estate	Characteristics	Notes
To Ann *and her heirs* To Ann *in fee simple* To Ann	Fee Simple	Alienable Devisable Descendible	Ambiguity is resolved in favor of a Fee Simple
To Ann *as long as* To Ann *while* To Ann *until* To Ann *during*	Fee Simple Determinable	Alienable Devisable Descendible	Not subject to waste in most states
To Ann, *provided that* To Ann, *but if* To Ann, *on condition that*	Fee Simple Subject to a Condition Subsequent	Alienable Devisable Descendible	When ambiguity exists, preferred over a FSDet Not subject to waste in most states
To Ann *as long as, while, until, during, provided that, but if, on condition that...* then to Bob	Fee Simple Subject to an Executory Limitation	Alienable Devisable Descendible	Future interest in a third party follows the estate Not subject to waste in most states
To Ann *and the heirs of her body*	Fee Tail	Alienable Not devisable Descendible	May only alienate right to possession until death Descends only to lineal descendants
To Ann *for life* To Ann *until she dies*	Life Estate	Alienable Not devisable Not descendible	Subject to waste When conveyed to another becomes LE pur autre vie
To Ann *for 20 years*	Term of Years	Alienable Devisable Descendible	Subject to waste

C. Modern Future Interests

Let's return to the hypothetical that began this chapter: O conveys Redacre "to A for life, then to B." A, holding the life estate, is entitled to immediate possession of Redacre. B holds a *future interest*—an existing, nonpossessory property right that may become possessory in the future.

The holder of a future interest has a valuable property right. Suppose that Redacre is a prize-winning apple orchard. B will obtain a fee simple absolute in Redacre when A dies. In the interim, B can sell his future interest or use it as security for a loan. He can prevent A from committing waste (e.g., cutting down the apple trees); B may also be entitled to payment if Redacre is taken by condemnation. Upon his death, B can transfer his future interest by devise or by intestate succession.

Traditionally, the law divided future interests into two groups according to the *identity* of the holder:

> *Future interests retained by the transferor*:
> - reversion
> - possibility of reverter
> - right of entry
>
> *Future interests created in a transferee*:
> - indefeasibly vested remainder
> - vested remainder subject to divestment
> - vested remainder subject to open
> - contingent remainder
> - executory interest

Each future interest may at some point become a possessory estate. Suppose again that O conveys Redacre "to A for life, then to B." B now holds a future interest (a remainder), but when A's life estate ends B will have an estate (fee simple absolute). The full name of B's future interest is an "indefeasibly vested remainder in fee simple absolute." Of course, a person could hold a future interest in another estate, such as a life estate, a fee simple determinable, or a term of years. While B's remainder is certain to become possessory, this is not always the case. Many future interests are contingent or uncertain—they may or may not become possessory.

The English laws governing future interests were extraordinarily complex—particularly for future interests held by transferees. These laws evolved over centuries of struggle among three key groups: large landowners, commercial interests, and the Crown. At the risk of oversimplifying a rich and intricate history, large landowners typically wanted the unfettered right to create future interests in order to preserve family wealth and limit taxation. In contrast, commercial interests sought to restrict future interests in order to encourage the productive use of land; and the Crown adopted the same view to facilitate taxation. In this unit, we focus on the legal principles that emerged from this epic conflict, sacrificing history for brevity.

Future Interests

```
                    ┌── Reversion
                    │
    Transferor ─────┼── Possibility
                    │   of Reverter
                    │
                    └── Right
                        of Entry
                                                    ┌── Indefeasibly
                                                    │
                                   ┌── Vested ──────┼── Subject to
                                   │                │   Divestment
                   ┌── Remainder ──┤                │
                   │               │                └── Subject to
                   │               │                    Open
    Transferee ────┤               └── Contingent
                   │
                   │                  ┌── Shifting
                   └── Executory ─────┤
                       Interest       └── Springing
```

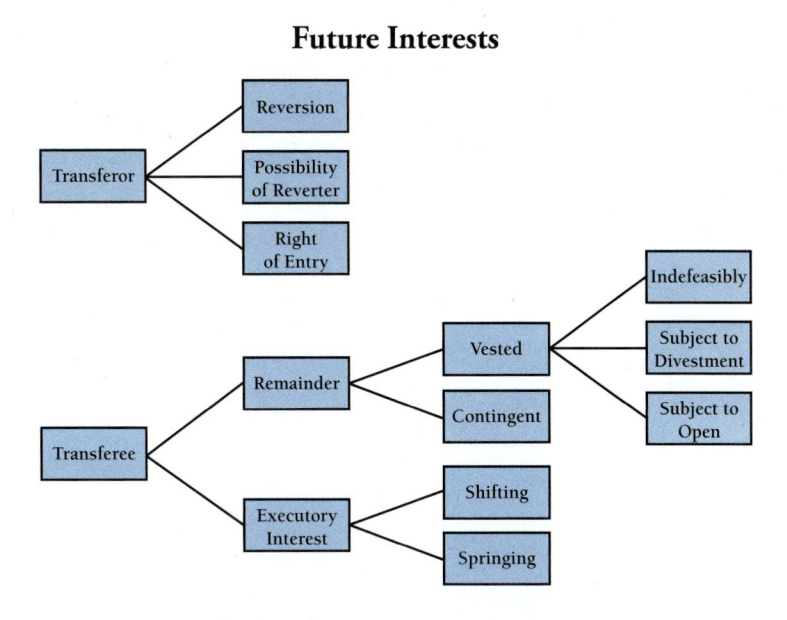

1. Future Interests Retained by the Transferor

The reversion, possibility of reverter, and right of entry can only be held by a transferor. Each one arises when a transferor conveys an estate to a third party that is *smaller* than the estate she holds.

Reversion: A transferor retains a reversion when she conveys a smaller vested estate than the one she has. Technically, a reversion is the future interest remaining in the transferor when she grants a vested estate of lesser quantum (that is, potential duration) than she began with. Suppose O owns a fee simple absolute in Greenacre; she conveys Greenacre "to B for life." O retains a reversion by operation of law. She held a fee simple absolute (an estate with a potentially infinite duration) and conveyed only a life estate (a portion of her whole interest). Thus, when B's life estate ends, O will again have a fee simple absolute in Greenacre. At common law, the four basic possessory estates were ordered by their potential duration, from highest to lowest: fee simple, fee tail, life estate, and leasehold (term of years).

Possibility of reverter: The possibility of reverter is the future interest retained by the transferor who holds a fee simple absolute, but conveys a fee simple determinable. Since there is a possibility that the fee simple determinable *might* end, this future interest gives the transferor the right to possession if that estate terminates. Again, suppose that O holds a fee simple absolute in Greenacre; she conveys Greenacre "to B and her heirs until the land ceases to be used as a farm." If the farm use ends (for example, if the land is developed into an industrial park), B's estate automatically ends, and O's possibility of reverter becomes possessory; O now has a fee simple absolute again.

Right of entry: The right of entry is the future interest retained by the transferor who holds a fee simple absolute, but conveys a fee simple subject to a condition subsequent. Suppose that O conveys Greenacre "to B and her heirs, provided that if B fails to use it as a farm, then O may re-enter and reclaim the property." Of course, B has a fee simple subject to a condition subsequent, so O's future interest must be a right of entry. But the right of entry does *not* become possessory until and unless the holder takes affirmative steps to regain possession. Thus, O must re-enter, give formal notice, or bring legal action in order to terminate B's estate.

Examples

(1) *O conveys "to G for 75 years."* G's estate is a term of years because it has a fixed duration established in advance. Because O carved out a smaller vested estate (a term of years) from his larger estate (a fee simple absolute), he retains a reversion, which will become possessory in 75 years, when the term of years ends.

(2) *O conveys "to G and her heirs so long as alcohol is not sold on the land."* The phrase "so long as" indicates that G's fee simple estate endures only for a period of time and will automatically end upon the occurrence of the specified event: the sale of alcohol. Accordingly, G holds a fee simple determinable. So, by definition, O's future interest is a possibility of reverter.

(3) *O conveys "to G and her heirs, but if alcohol is ever sold on the land, then O shall have the right to re-enter and retake the estate."* The phrase "but if" indicates that G's fee simple estate is subject to a condition subsequent, so G holds a fee simple subject to a condition subsequent. Notice the express words of re-entry in the conveyance that also show O's intent to create this estate. Accordingly, O's future interest is a right of entry.

Suppose that O holds a reversion. His interest is freely alienable, devisable, and descendible. O may convey it to a third party during his lifetime. If O dies, the reversion passes by will to his devisees or by intestate succession to his heirs.

The common law traditionally restricted the transfer of the possibility of reverter and right of entry due to concern that they impaired the marketability of land. These interests could only be transferred by intestate succession. Today the possibility of reverter and right of entry are freely alienable, devisable, and descendible in almost all jurisdictions.

Points for Discussion

Which estates and future interests are created and/or retained by these transfers?

> (1)   O conveys "to A for life, and then to B."
>
> (2)   O devises "to C, but if C ever drinks alcohol, then to D."
>
> (3)   O conveys "to D for six months."
>
> (4)   O conveys "to E for so long as the land is used as a library."
>
> (5)   O conveys "to F for life, and then to G for life."

2. Future Interests Created in a Transferee

Why create a future interest in a transferee? Historically, landowners used these future interests to *control* the destiny of their family lands long after they died, just as the fee tail was utilized to preserve family power and prestige. Suppose that landowner O wanted to provide for his daughters P and R after his death. He might convey Greenacre "to P and R for life, and then to the heirs of P and R." This ensures that P and R have a home during their lifetimes, and then transfers the property to their descendants.

Today, future interests are an important tool in estate planning. Most modern future interests are created in personal property (such as stocks and bonds) that is held in trust, but they are used for the same historic reason: *to provide for the owner's family*. For example, investor J might transfer title to his stocks and bonds "to T, to be held in trust for the benefit of my children K and L for life, and then to the heirs of K and L." K and L have equitable life estates in the assets of the trust. Thus, they are entitled to the income produced by the trust assets during their lifetimes. The heirs of K and L hold future interests (equitable contingent remainders), which will give them complete ownership of the trust assets when K and L die.

A future interest created in a transferee can only be a *remainder* or an *executory interest*. So here's a handy rule: if you encounter a future interest created in a transferee that is not a remainder, it must be an executory interest and vice versa.

a. Remainders

A remainder is a future interest in a transferee that: (1) is capable of becoming possessory immediately upon the expiration of the prior estate; *and* (2) does not divest (or cut short) any interest in a prior transferee. In other words, remainders follow present estates naturally and immediately.

Capable of becoming possessory: Suppose O conveys Greenacre "to A for life, then to B." B will automatically be entitled to possession as soon as A's life estate ends. But guaranteed possession is not required; the *possibility* of possession is enough. Thus, if O conveys "to B for life, then to D if D becomes president," D has a remainder even if he is an 85-year-old high school dropout who has never run for political office. It is still theoretically possible that D *might* become president, so his interest is *capable* of becoming possessory when A's life estate ends.

Does not divest: A remainder "waits patiently" for the preceding estate to expire before it becomes possessory. Suppose O conveys "to B for life, then if D becomes president, to D." D has a remainder because there is no possibility that D can divest B's life estate; his possession begins upon B's death, as shown by the word "then." D must "wait patiently" for B to die before D is entitled to possession. Now consider a quite different grant. O conveys "to B for life, but if D becomes president, to D." The words "but if" show that B holds a defeasible estate (in this case, a life estate subject to an executory limitation). D can gain possession as soon as he becomes president, even if B is still alive, thus cutting short B's estate. In this example, D has an executory interest, not a remainder.

The common law distinguished sharply between two basic types of remainders: the *vested remainder* and the *contingent remainder*. In general, vested remainders were seen as more substantial interests than mere contingent remainders. Over time, three different vested remainders evolved. Accordingly, we will study four remainders:

- Indefeasibly vested remainder
- Vested remainder subject to divestment
- Vested remainder subject to open
- Contingent remainder

Indefeasibly vested remainder: A remainder is vested if (1) it is created in an ascertainable person *and* (2) it is not subject to a condition precedent other than the natural termination of the prior estate. If O conveys Greenacre "to A for life, then to B," B holds an indefeasibly vested remainder (sometimes abbreviated as *vested remainder*)—a remainder in an identifiable person that is certain to become a possessory estate.

Exploring the Vested Remainder

Created in an ascertainable person: Who is an "ascertainable person"? A person who is both alive and identifiable at the time of the transfer. For example, unborn children are not ascertainable. And a person's heirs cannot be ascertained until his death. Suppose that O conveys "to B for life, then to

> D's heirs." If D is alive, then his heirs are not ascertainable, so the remainder in "D's heirs" is not vested.
>
> *No condition precedent*: A condition precedent is a condition that must be met *before* the remainder can become possessory, *other than* the natural termination of the prior estate. Suppose that O conveys "to B for life, then to D if D becomes president." D must meet a special condition (becoming president) before his interest can become possessory; his remainder is not vested. On the other hand, if O conveys "to B for life, then to D" there is no condition precedent that must be satisfied before D is entitled to receive the estate; D's remainder is vested.

Vested remainder subject to divestment: This is a remainder that is vested, but is subject to a *condition subsequent*. Suppose O conveys "to B for life, then to D, but if D does not survive B, then to E." D is an ascertainable person. And his interest is not subject to a condition precedent: his interest is ready to become possessory *unless* a specified event occurs (D dies before B does). But if D dies before B, D's interest will be terminated or *divested*. D has a vested remainder subject to divestment.

Vested remainder subject to open: This is a vested remainder held by one or more living members of a group or *class* that may be enlarged in the future. Suppose O conveys Greenacre "to B for life, then to D's children." At the time, D has two living children, E and F; D might have more children because he is still alive. The remainders in E and F are vested because (1) they are both ascertainable and (2) there is no condition precedent. But E and F may have to *share* the property with later-born children of D, who are not presently ascertainable, so the size of their interests may become proportionately smaller in the future. E and F each have a vested remainder subject to open (sometimes called a *vested remainder subject to partial divestment*). See, e.g., *Folsom v. Rowell*, 640 S.E.2d 5 (Ga. 2007) (testator's daughter received a vested remainder subject to partial divestment when she provided care to her intellectually disabled sister for 13 years).

Contingent remainder: If a remainder is not vested, it is contingent. Thus, a contingent remainder is a remainder that is *either* (1) given to an unascertainable person *or* (2) subject to a condition precedent. For example, suppose O conveys Greenacre "to B for life, then to the heirs of D." Because the heirs of D are not ascertainable, they hold a contingent remainder. Similarly, if O conveys "to B for life, and then to D if D becomes president," D's remainder is subject to the condition precedent of becoming president, so it is a contingent remainder. See, e.g., *Rutledge v. Feher*, 804 S.E.2d 806 (N.C. Ct. App. 2017) (grantees held contingent remainders).

> ### Examples
>
> (1) *O conveys "to G for ten years, then to M and her heirs."* The words "for ten years" identify G's estate as a term of years. M receives a future interest because the word "then" shows that she is entitled to possession only after G's term of years ends. M's future interest is a remainder because (a) it is capable of becoming possessory immediately upon the expiration of G's term of years and (b) it will not divest that estate. It is vested because (a) M is ascertainable at the time of the conveyance *and* (b) there is no condition precedent. The words "and her heirs" identify the estate that M will have when the future interest becomes possessory as a fee simple. M has an indefeasibly vested remainder in fee simple absolute.
>
> (2) *O conveys "to G for life, then if M marries, to M and her heirs."* The words "for life" show that G receives a life estate. M has a remainder because (a) it is capable of becoming possessory immediately upon the expiration of G's life estate and (b) it will not divest that life estate. The remainder is contingent because M must marry *before* she is entitled to take possession. M has a contingent remainder in fee simple absolute. Notice that O retains a reversion in fee simple absolute because the condition in M's remainder may never be satisfied.

Points for Discussion

a. **Significance of the Classification**

At common law, the distinction between vested and contingent remainders was important for four basic reasons.

Transfer: Vested remainders were freely transferable. But contingent remainders could not be conveyed by deed or by will; they were viewed as mere expectancies that might not become possessory. Today both types of remainders are freely alienable, devisable, and descendible in all jurisdictions.

Marketability restrictions: A number of common law restrictions designed to make land more marketable applied only to contingent remainders, such as the Rule in Shelley's Case, the Doctrine of Destructibility of Contingent Remainders, and the Rule Against Perpetuities (*see infra* Section 5D). For example, depending on how a remainder was phrased, it might be subject to the Rule Against Perpetuities and potentially invalid. Does this help you understand the origin of the vested remainder subject to divestment, which arose well *after* the contingent remainder? (Hint: Is there any functional difference between a contingent remainder with a condition precedent *and* a vested remainder subject to divestment?)

Presumption: If the wording of a conveyance was ambiguous, judges presumed that the grantor intended a vested remainder—not a contingent remainder—thereby maximizing the marketability of the land.

Acceleration into possession: A vested remainder gave the holder immediate possession of the land when the prior estate ended.

b. Exercises

Which estates and future interests are created and/or retained by these transfers?

> (1) O conveys "to A for life, then to B."
>
> (2) O conveys "to C for life, then to D and his heirs if D lives to the age of 30."
>
> (3) O conveys "to E for life, then to F's children and their heirs." Assume F has never had children.
>
> (4) O devises "to G for life, then to H, but if H does not survive G, then to I."
>
> (5) O conveys "to J for life, then to K for life, then to L's children." Assume that L is alive and has one child, M.

c. Reading the Instrument

The rules used to classify future interests depend heavily on the *exact language* in the deed or will. When reading an instrument, it is important to evaluate carefully each interest in sequence as it occurs—rather than attempting to find an overall meaning in the conveyance. For example, D has a vested remainder in one of the conveyances below and a contingent remainder in the other, even though the wording is quite similar.

> (1) *O conveys "to B for life, then to D and his heirs, but if E does not survive F, then to me."* D's remainder is *vested* because (a) D is ascertainable at the time of the conveyance and (b) there is no condition precedent. Notice that there is nothing D needs to do to gain possession following B's death. D's right to possession will continue *unless and until* E fails to survive F.
>
> (2) *O conveys "to B for life, then to D and his heirs if E survives F, if not then to me."* Here D has a *contingent* remainder because it is subject to the condition precedent that E survives F. Notice that D can gain possession only *if* at B's death E has outlived F.

b. Executory Interests

An executory interest is a future interest in a transferee that *must divest* another estate or interest to become possessory. This is the exact opposite of the remainder. Thus, if a future interest in a transferee is not a remainder, it is an executory interest.

If an executory interest follows an interest in the transferor, it is a *springing executory interest*; if it follows an interest in a transferee, it is a *shifting executory interest*. There is no substantive legal difference between springing and shifting executory interests. These are only convenient labels.

Suppose that O conveys Greenacre "to B for life, then one year after B's death, to D and his heirs." Once B's life estate ends, O regains a fee simple. One year later, when D's future interest becomes possessory, it will divest O by cutting O's estate short. (Remember that a fee simple is defined as an estate that may potentially endure forever.) Accordingly, D has a springing executory interest, not a remainder. Put another way, D's interest is *not* capable of becoming possessory at the expiration of B's life estate.

Now suppose instead that O conveys Greenacre "to B and her heirs until humans land on Mars, then to D and his heirs." B has a fee simple subject to an executory limitation, but what does D have? The answer is a shifting executory interest. But why? D's possession immediately follows the end of B's estate and D can do nothing to cut B's estate short, so D does *not* divest B. The reason lies in history. The common law provided that a future interest in a transferee following a defeasible fee simple could *only* be an executory interest.

Today an executory interest is alienable, devisable, and descendible in all jurisdictions.

> ### Examples
>
> (1) *O conveys "to G and her heirs so long as the land is used as a hospital, then to M and her heirs."* G has a fee simple subject to an executory limitation. Since M's future interest follows a defeasible fee simple, it is an executory interest. Because it follows an interest in G, another transferee, it is a shifting interest. The words "and her heirs" show that M will receive a fee simple absolute when her interest becomes possessory. So M has a shifting executory interest in fee simple absolute.
>
> (2) *O conveys "to M and her heirs one week from today."* In order to obtain possession, M must divest O's fee simple, which otherwise could endure forever, so M has an executory interest. Because it follows an interest in O, the transferor, it is a springing executory interest. The phrase "and her heirs" shows that M will receive a fee simple, so she has a springing executory interest in fee simple absolute.

Points for Discussion

a. A Bit of History

Executory interests could not be created in early England. At common law, interests in land that divested a grantor (e.g., *O conveys "to B when peace comes to England"*) or shifted title from one grantee to another (e.g., *O conveys "to B, but if D marries E, then to D"*) were invalid. As a way around these inflexible rules, landowners turned to the *use*. In the first example, O would convey "to T *for the use of O*, then *for the use of B* when peace comes to England." T would hold legal title, but O and B would enjoy the beneficial interests in the land. These equitable interests were enforceable in the courts of equity and became the foundation of modern trust law. In 1536, the Statute of Uses authorized springing and shifting interests. The Statute changed (or "executed") these equitable interests into legal interests. Accordingly, they became known as executory interests.

> **See It**
>
> Now that you have completed the unit on future interests, click here to see a flow chart that summarizes the material.

b. Exercises

Which estates and future interests are created and/or retained by these transfers?

> (1) O conveys "to A 15 years from now."
>
> (2) O devises "to B for life, then to C, but if D should return to New York, then to D."
>
> (3) O conveys "to E when E marries."
>
> (4) O devises "to F as long as no alcohol is served on the property and if alcohol is served there, then to Alcoholics Anonymous."
>
> (5) O conveys "to G for life, and then to H if H becomes a lawyer."

c. Restatement (Third) of Property and Future Interests

The Restatement (Third) of Property abandons the traditional distinctions among future interests. Under this approach, a future interest is either a *remainder* (if it is created in a transferee) or a *reversion* (if it is retained by the transferor). The executory interest is classified as a "remainder"; and the right of entry and possibility of reverter are classified as "reversions." For example, if A conveys Greenacre "to B for life, then to C, but if C predeceases B, then to D," C and D would each receive a remainder—rather than C's future interest being a remainder and D's an executory interest. Restatement (Third) of Property: Wills & Other Donative Transfers § 25.2.

d. Additional Review

Click here to access notes and problems on future interests, taken from Coletta's Workbook on Estates and Future Interests, 3d ed.

The chart below shows the relationship between estates and future interests.

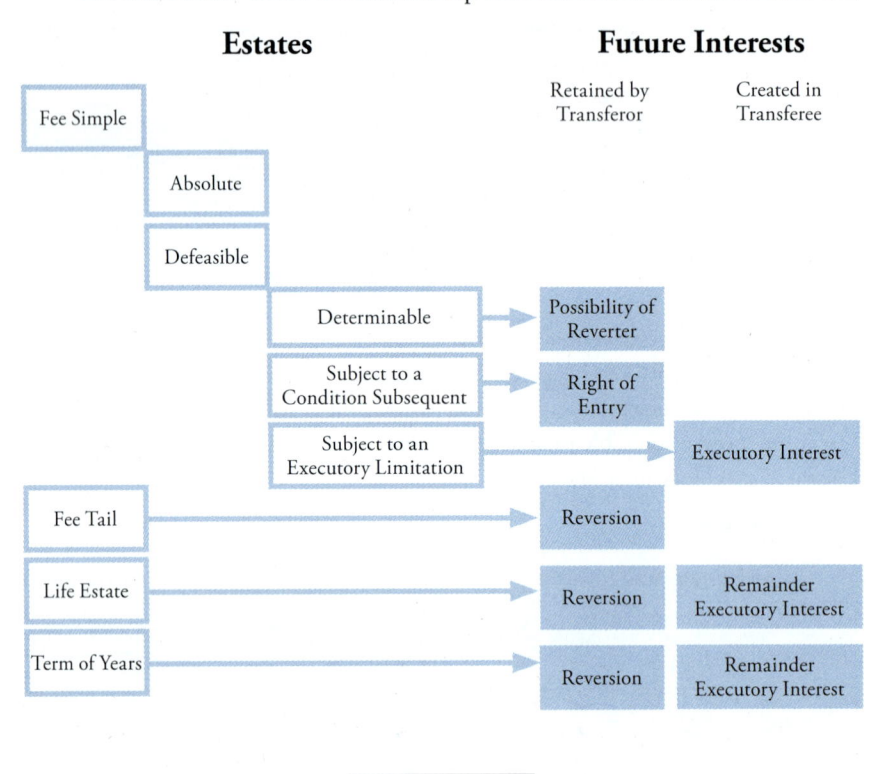

Estates		Future Interests
	Retained by Transferor	Created in Transferee
Fee Simple		
Absolute		
Defeasible		
Determinable	Possibility of Reverter	
Subject to a Condition Subsequent	Right of Entry	
Subject to an Executory Limitation		Executory Interest
Fee Tail	Reversion	
Life Estate	Reversion	Remainder / Executory Interest
Term of Years	Reversion	Remainder / Executory Interest

D. Rules Furthering Marketability

English property law strongly favored the free alienation of land, as you have already seen in earlier sections of this book. For example, the doctrine of restraints on alienation reflects this policy.

Contingent remainders and executory interests harmed the marketability of land. Why? Because of the *uncertainty* they created. For example, one problem was identifying *who* could sell title. Suppose O conveyed Greenacre "to B for life, then to B's heirs." B's heirs held a contingent remainder because they were unascertainable. If X later wanted to purchase a fee simple in Greenacre, he confronted a problem: although B could be found, B's heirs could not be identified. Of course, X could acquire B's life estate. But he was unable to also purchase the future interest simply because the holders were unknown; X had no one with whom to negotiate. This uncertainty impaired the marketability of Greenacre. Buyers like X wanted a fee simple, not a life estate that might end at any time.

In order to make land more marketable, the common law severely restricted contingent remainders and executory interests. Over time, it developed four doctrines for this purpose:

- Rule in Shelley's Case
- Doctrine of Worthier Title
- Doctrine of Destructibility of Contingent Remainders
- Rule Against Perpetuities

The Rule in Shelley's Case and the Doctrine of Worthier Title made land more marketable by placing all interests in the hands of living, ascertainable individuals. The Doctrine of Destructibility of Contingent Remainders and the Rule Against Perpetuities increased marketability by imposing time limits on how long uncertain future interests could continue; in effect, they required that the uncertainty be removed within a set period of time.

Today the first three rules are almost obsolete in the United States. The Rule Against Perpetuities remains in place in most states, but has been eroded by modern reforms.

1. Rule in Shelley's Case

Suppose O conveys Greenacre "to B for life, then to B's heirs." The land would remain unmarketable until B died, because no one could identify his future heirs. The Rule in Shelley's Case addressed this problem by converting the contingent remainder in the *heirs of the grantee* into a vested remainder in that *grantee*.

The rule provides: *If a freehold estate is given to a person and, in the same instrument, a remainder is given to the heirs (or the heirs of the body) of that person, he takes both the freehold estate and the remainder.*

In general, the rule applies if four requirements are satisfied:

(1) *one* instrument
(2) creates a *freehold* estate in a transferee, and
(3) a *remainder* in that transferee's *heirs*, and

> (4) both interests are legal or both equitable.

The contingent remainder in the transferee's heirs (who are unascertainable at the time) becomes a vested remainder in the transferee (who is ascertainable), thereby increasing the marketability of the land. In effect, words of purchase ("to B's heirs") become words of limitation ("to B and his heirs").

> **Food for Thought**
>
> Can you think of a way that the Rule in Shelley's Case can be avoided by using two instruments? Or by more careful drafting?

Consider this example: *O conveys "to B for life, then to B's heirs."* Initially, the conveyance seems to grant B a life estate and B's heirs a contingent remainder in fee simple, leaving a reversion in O. However, under this rule, B holds both the life estate and the remainder. The remainder intended for B's heirs becomes a remainder in fee simple in B. Notice how the *contingent* remainder is transformed into a *vested* remainder. Since B holds both the present possessory interest and the complete future interest, B's two interests *merge* and B now holds a fee simple absolute. B is ascertainable, so any future purchasers can deal directly with B.

In the United States, the rule has been abolished by statute in almost all jurisdictions. Nonetheless, it is still important to understand how the rule operated because it may apply to instruments created before the rule was repealed.

> **Practice Pointer**
>
> The rule is applied even if it is contrary to the transferor's unambiguous intent—even though the grantor expressly states: "I don't want the Rule in Shelley's Case to apply to my conveyance."

Points for Discussion

Which estates and future interests are created in these transfers if we apply the Rule in Shelley's Case?

> (1) O conveys "to B for life, then to M for life, then to M's heirs."
>
> (2) O conveys "to C for life, then to H for life, then to C's heirs."
>
> (3) O conveys "to D for life, then to F's heirs."

2. Doctrine of Worthier Title

Suppose that O conveys Greenacre "to B for life, then to O's heirs." Any potential purchaser of Greenacre faces the impossible task of trying to contract with unascertainable owners, O's heirs.

The Doctrine of Worthier Title was developed to address this marketability problem. At common law, the doctrine applied to any inter vivos conveyance of land by a grantor to a third party in which a future interest was created in the *grantor's own heirs*. The rule provided that a grantor could not create a remainder or executory interest in his heirs. If the grantor attempted to create such an interest, that interest was void and the grantor was deemed to retain a reversion. Because the future interest was now held by the ascertainable grantor, the land was more marketable.

> **FYI**
> Traditionally, the Doctrine of Worthier Title did not apply to wills.

The doctrine is simple: *If a grantor creates a remainder or an executory interest in his own heirs, the grantor retains a future interest in himself rather than creating a future interest in those heirs.*

Thus, the doctrine applies when:

> (1) a conveyance creates a remainder or executory interest
> (2) in the *grantor's heirs*.

The remainder or executory interest becomes a future interest in the grantor, rather than creating a future interest in the grantor's heirs. In effect, the contingent future interest in the heirs (who are unascertainable at the time) becomes a vested future interest in the grantor (who is ascertainable).

Consider this example: *O conveys "to G for life, then to O's heirs."* Initially, the conveyance appears to grant a life estate to G and a contingent remainder to O's heirs, leaving O with a reversion. However, since the conveyance creates a remainder in the *grantor's heirs* (O's heirs), the doctrine applies. The future interest in O's heirs becomes a future interest in O. In effect, the words of purchase ("to O's heirs") become words of limitation ("to O and his heirs"). The contingent future interest in transferees becomes a vested future interest in the grantor.

> **FYI**
> Although originally it was considered a rule of law, Judge Cardozo transformed the doctrine into a rule of construction in *Doctor v. Hughes*, 122 N.E. 221 (1919). This case extended the rule to personal property as well as real property—an important addition because of its applicability to trust law.

The doctrine applies to both remainders and executory interests in the heirs of the *transferor* while the Rule in Shelley's Case applies only to remainders in the heirs of *transferees*. And while the Rule in Shelley's Case is considered a rule of law, the Doctrine of Worthier Title is now viewed merely as a rule of construction in the few states where it survives at all. As such, it *does not* apply if the transferor clearly manifests an intent to create a future interest in his heirs.

Points for Discussion

Which estates and future interests are created in these transfers if we apply the Doctrine of Worthier Title?

> (1) O conveys "to B for life, then to X's heirs."
>
> (2) O conveys "to C for life, then to X for life, then to O's children."
>
> (3) O conveys "to D for life, then to X so long as it is used as a school, then to O's heirs."

3. Doctrine of Destructibility of Contingent Remainders

Suppose that O grants Greenacre "to B for life, then to C if C becomes a lawyer." C's contingent remainder will vest only if C satisfies the condition precedent. Therefore, if C becomes an attorney and then B dies, C obtains a fee simple estate. But what happens if B dies *before* C becomes a lawyer? Or if C *never* becomes a lawyer?

This uncertainty about when a contingent remainder might vest made land less attractive to purchasers. Therefore, the common law developed a rule that required all contingent remainders to vest by the end of the preceding estate.

Notice that this rule is applied on a "wait-and-see" basis. A contingent remainder is valid when created. But if it has not vested by the time the prior estate ends, the contingent remainder is destroyed. In the above example, C continues to hold a contingent remainder throughout B's life even though C has yet to become an attorney. C's contingent remainder is destroyed *only* if he has not become a lawyer by the time of B's death.

The doctrine provides: *Any contingent remainder that has not vested at the termination of the preceding freehold estate is destroyed.*

Thus, the doctrine applies when:

> (1) a contingent remainder

(2) does not vest before the preceding freehold estate (typically a life estate) ends.

If the holder of the remainder cannot take possession at the expiration of the preceding estate, then that contingent remainder is destroyed forever; the right to possession moves to the next vested interest. In other words, if a condition precedent is not fulfilled or the holder of the remainder continues to be unascertained at the expiration of the preceding estate, then the remainder is destroyed. Thus, the doctrine terminates remainders that might vest too far in the future.

> **Food for Thought**
>
> Can you think of a way to avoid the doctrine by careful drafting?

Consider this example: *O conveys "to G for life, then to M and her heirs if M marries."* As a result of this conveyance, G has a life estate and M has a contingent remainder in fee simple, while O holds a reversion. If the property is located in a jurisdiction recognizing the doctrine, then: if M is not married by the time of G's death, M's contingent remainder is "destroyed," and she loses her interest in the estate. O's reversion then becomes possessory. Returning the estate to O promotes marketability, because O now holds the fee and can grant the land to someone else.

> **FYI**
>
> The doctrine does not apply to equitable interests held in trust or to interests in personal property. Because most remainders now are created in trusts, the doctrine has little practical importance today.

Today the doctrine has been abolished in almost every jurisdiction. Under the modern approach, if a contingent remainder does not vest before the prior estate ends, it becomes an executory interest. Do you see why? Return to the above illustration. If M is not married at G's death, then O's reversion becomes possessory. O now holds a fee simple subject to an executory limitation, and M's remainder becomes a springing executory interest.

Points for Discussion

Which estates and future interests are created in these transfers if we apply the Doctrine of Destructibility of Contingent Remainders?

> (1) O conveys "to B for life, then to M's children." Assume M has no children.
>
> (2) O devises "to C for life, but if X marries Y, then to X."

> (3) O conveys "to D for life, then to D's children." Assume D has no children.

4. Rule Against Perpetuities

Suppose O devises Greenacre "to B for life, then to C if a cure for cancer is found." When will C's future interest become possessory? It might become possessory *decades* after O, B, and C die. Or it might *never* become possessory. Title uncertainty like this interfered with the free marketability of land. A buyer was unlikely to purchase Greenacre from B because it was burdened with a contingent future interest. In effect, such a grant allowed an owner like O to control title to land long after his death.

Recall the history that we discussed earlier in the chapter. In general, English landowners wanted unfettered freedom to create contingent future interests in transferees, while commercial interests and the Crown tried to ensure that title to land was freely marketable. The Rule Against Perpetuities reflects a compromise between these two positions.

The rule has been characterized as creating "a fair balance between the desires of members of the present generation, and similar desires of succeeding generations, to do what they wish with the property which they enjoy." Lewis Simes, Public Policy and the Dead Hand 50 (1955). It promotes marketability by limiting an owner's ability to create speculative, contingent future interests. In essence, the rule reflects the view that it is "socially desirable that the wealth of the world be controlled by its living members and not by the dead." *Id.*

Here is the classic statement of the rule: *No interest is good unless it must vest, if at all, no later than 21 years after some life in being at the creation of the interest.*

> **FYI**
> This formulation of the rule was developed by John Chipman Gray, a professor at Harvard Law School and a co-founder of the Boston law firm Ropes & Gray. John C. Gray, The Rule Against Perpetuities 191 (4th ed. 1942).

The rule limits the duration of a contingent interest by providing that it is void unless it *must* vest or forever fail within 21 years of the death of a life in being. Thus, the rule allows a transferor to control title to his property during the lifetimes of persons alive at his death and into the next generation up to age 21, the age of majority. The rule's focus is on *time*—it prohibits an interest from vesting too far into the future.

View the rule as a rule of proof. A contingent interest is valid only if you can logically *prove* that it will either vest or forever fail to vest within the perpetuities period (a life in being plus 21 years). If there is *any possibility* that the interest might vest more than 21 years from the death of the relevant lives in being, the future interest is void when created (*ab initio*). In short, if you can imagine any set of facts under which the interest *might* vest too late, it is void. *See, e.g., Washington State Grange v. Brandt,* 148 P.3d 1069 (Wash. Ct. App. 2006) (invalidating executory interest which provided that land would revert "in event it is no longer used for Grange purposes").

What is "vesting"? This is the point where the title uncertainty is removed. For example, suppose O conveys Greenacre "to B for life, and then to C if C reaches age 21." C holds a contingent remainder because of the condition precedent that C reach age 21; once C lives to 21, the uncertainty is removed, and his contingent remainder becomes a type of vested remainder. But many future interests "vest" only by becoming possessory. For example, if O conveys Greenacre "to B when a human goes to Saturn," the title uncertainty is removed only when a person goes to Saturn; and B is entitled to possession at that time.

Examples

(1) *O conveys "to C if anyone finds a cure for cancer."* C holds a springing executory interest; O retains possession, holding a fee simple subject to an executory limitation. C's executory interest will vest only if a cure is found. This may happen centuries after the conveyance. Because there is no certainty that C's interest will vest or forever fail to vest within 21 years of the last life in being to die (O or C), the interest is void *when created*. Of course, it is possible that a cure may be found tomorrow, and that C's interest would then become possessory. But this does not matter. The rule invalidates contingent interests that *might* vest too late, outside of the perpetuities period.

(2) *O conveys "to C if C finds a cure for cancer."* O and C still have the same interests. When C dies, there are only two logical possibilities. Either he *did* find a cure for cancer, so his interest vested during his lifetime. Or he *did not* find a cure, so his interest forever failed to vest. Therefore, his interest is valid under the rule. Put another way, because C can only find a cure while he is alive, there is no possibility that his interest might vest too late.

Only three interests are subject to the rule: *contingent remainders, executory interests,* and *vested remainders subject to open.* (Even though the vested remainder subject to open is a type of vested remainder, it is considered contingent under the rule because individuals might be added to the class in the future.)

Thus, all present possessory estates (fee simple absolutes; fee simple defeasibles; fee tails; life estates; and leaseholds) and future interests in a grantor (reversions; possibilities of reverter; and rights of entry) are deemed vested for purposes of the rule.

Similarly, indefeasibly vested remainders and vested remainders subject to divestment are exempt from the rule.

Let's examine the rule phrase by phrase.

> *No interest is good...*
>
> *... unless it must vest, if at all*: The rule does not require that an interest actually vest during the perpetuities period. Rather, it is concerned with the possibility that an interest *might vest too late*, after the perpetuities period has expired. Therefore, an interest must be certain to *either* vest *or* forever fail to vest within the perpetuities period.
>
> *... not later than 21 years after some life in being*: The perpetuities period is measured by adding 21 years to the date of death of the last individual who was alive when the interest was created. Remember the rule does not "wait and see" what actually happens (i.e., who dies when); it considers only the possibilities that exist at the moment the interest is created. If an interest is not *logically certain* to vest or forever fail to vest within the perpetuities period, it is void.
>
> *... at the creation of the interest*: This element refers to a single moment in time. In the case of an inter vivos transfer, this is when the deed is delivered; or in the case of a will, when the testator dies. For an inter vivos conveyance, the perpetuities period is 21 years from the death of the last person alive (or conceived) when the grantor delivered the deed. For a devise, the perpetuities period is 21 years from the death of the last person alive (or conceived) when the testator died.

Applying the rule requires *imagination*. It demands that you imagine a world of possibilities that might arise in the future and affect vesting. If you can conceive of just *one situation* where the interest vests outside of the perpetuities period, then the interest is void. This is sometimes called the "what-might-happen?" approach.

When analyzing a deed or will that includes future interests subject to the rule, evaluate the application of the rule separately for each interest. It may be helpful to proceed through the following steps: (a) identify the contingent interest; (b) list the lives in being; (c) consider whether anyone can be born who might affect vesting; (d) kill off the lives in being at some future date and add 21 years; (e) ask yourself, "Is there any possibility that the contingent interest will vest after this point?" If so, it is void; if not, it is valid.

> **More Examples**
>
> (1) *O conveys "to B for life, then to M's first child to reach 30." (Assume M is childless.)* B has a life estate, M's first child to reach 30 has a contingent remainder, and O has a reversion. Because the conveyance created a contingent remainder, the rule must be considered. Might the contingent remainder first vest after the perpetuities period ends, i.e., after the death of the last life in being plus 21 years? Proceed through the suggested steps: (a) The child's contingent remainder must be tested against the rule. (b) O, B, and M are lives in being. (c) M could have a child (P) the next year. (d) One year later, O, B, and M could die in a common disaster; add 21 years from this date. (e) Is there any possibility that the contingent remainder might vest beyond this point? If P lives for another 29 years, he becomes M's first child to reach 30. The contingent remainder would vest at that point (29 years after the death of O, B, and M)—which is *more* than 21 years after the death of the last life in being. The interest is void, so it is stricken from the conveyance. As a result, B receives a life estate and O a reversion.
>
> (2) *O conveys "to B for life, then to M's first child to reach 18." (Assume M is childless.)* M's first child to reach 18 has a contingent remainder. But the interest does not violate the rule. There are only two logical possibilities. First, if M has any children, one of them will reach age 18 within 21 years of the death of M; in this case, the contingent remainder *vests* within the perpetuities period. Second, M may never have any children or all of her children could die before reaching 18; in this case, the remainder *forever fails to vest* within the period. Put another way, there is no possibility that a child of M might first reach age 18 *more than* 21 years after M dies.

The most famous case exploring the rule is *Jee v. Audley*. It involves a seemingly simple bequest of £1000. But first impressions can be deceiving—as is often the case with the rule. In eighteenth-century England, this sum was a veritable fortune, equal to 100 years of wages for a teacher. Was the bequest valid?

Jee v. Audley

Court of Chancery

29 Eng. Rep. 1186 (1787)

Edward Audley, by his will, bequeathed as follows,

Also my will is that £1000 shall be placed out at interest during the life of my wife, which interest I give her during her life, and at her death I give the said £1000 unto my niece Mary Hall and the issue of her body lawfully begotten, and to be begotten, and in default of such issue I give the said £1000 to be equally divided between the daughters then living of my kinsman John Jee and his wife Elizabeth Jee.

It appeared that John Jee and Elizabeth Jee were living at the time of the death of the testator, had four daughters and no son, and were of a very advanced age. Mary Hall was unmarried and of the age of about 40; the wife was dead. The present bill was filed by the four daughters of John and Elizabeth Jee to have the £1000 secured for their benefit upon the event of the said Mary Hall dying without leaving children. And the question was, whether the limitation to the daughters of John and Elizabeth Jee was not void as being too remote; and to prove it so, it was said that this was to take effect on a general failure of issue of Mary Hall; and though it was to the daughters of John and Elizabeth Jee, yet it was not confined to the daughters living at the death of the testator, and consequently it might extend to after-born daughters, in which case it would not be within the limit of a life or lives in being and 21 years afterwards, beyond which time an executory devise is void.

> **FYI**
>
> Even though the language seems to create a fee tail in Hall, she received a type of fee simple. A fee tail could not be created in personal property.

On the other side it was said, that though the late cases had decided that on a gift to children generally, such children as should be living at the time of the distribution of the fund should be let in, yet it would be very hard to adhere to such a rule of construction so rigidly, as to defeat the evident intention of the testator in this case, especially as there was no real possibility of John and Elizabeth Jee having children after the testator's death, they being then 70 years old; that if there were two ways of construing words, that should be adopted which would give effect to the disposition made by the testator; that the cases, which had decided that after-born children should take, proceeded on the implied intention of the testator, and never meant to give an effect to words which would totally defeat such intention.

Master of the Rolls [Sir Lloyd Kenyon]. Several cases . . . have settled that children born after the death of the testator shall take a share in these cases; the difference is, where there is an immediate devise, and where there is an interest in remainder; in the former case the children living at the testator's death only shall take; in the latter those who are living at the time the interest vests in possession; and this being now a settled principle, I shall not strain to serve an intention at the expense of removing the landmarks of the law. . . . The general principles which apply to this case are not disputed: the limitations of personal estate are void, unless they necessarily vest, if at all, within a life or lives in being and 21 years or 9 or 10 months afterwards. This has been sanctioned by the opinion of judges of all times, from the time of the Duke of Norfolk's Case to the present: it is grown reverend by age, and is not now to be broken in upon; I am desired to do in this case something which I do not feel myself at liberty to do, namely to suppose it impossible for persons in so advanced an age as John and Elizabeth Jee to have children; but if this can be done in one case it may in another, and it is a very dangerous experiment, and introductive of the greatest inconvenience to give a latitude to such sort of conjecture. Another thing pressed upon me, is to decide on the events which have happened; but I cannot do this without overturning very many cases. The single question before me is, not whether the limitation is good in the events which have happened, but whether it was good in its creation; and if it were not, I cannot make it so. Then must this limitation, if at all, *necessarily* take place within the limits prescribed by law? The words are "in default of such issue I give the said £1000 to be equally divided between the daughters *then* living of John Jee and Elizabeth his wife." If it had been to "daughters now living," or "who should be living at the time of my death," it would have been very good; but as it stands, this limitation may take in after-born daughters; this point is clearly settled by *Ellison v. Airey*, 1 Ves. 111, and the effect of law on such limitation cannot make any difference in construing such intention. If then this will extended to after-born daughters, is it within the rules of law? Most certainly not, because John and Elizabeth Jee might have children born ten years after the testator's death, and then Mary Hall might die without issue 50 years afterwards; in which case it would evidently transgress the rules prescribed. I am of opinion therefore, though the testator might possibly mean to restrain the limitation to the children who should be living at the time of the death, I cannot, consistently with decided cases, construe it in such restrained sense, but must intend it to take in after-born children. This therefore not being within the rules

Lord Chief Justice Lloyd Kenyon
Click here for larger image

Food for Thought

Kenyon is mistaken here. Can you see why? What difference would it make if Audley's will read "to daughters now living if they are living at the time that Mary dies without issue"?

of law, and as I cannot judge upon subsequent events, I think the limitation void. Therefore dismiss the bill, but without costs.

Points for Discussion

a. Identifying the Interests

Because Audley's wife predeceased him, the will created a fee simple subject to an executory limitation in Hall and an executory interest in the daughters of John and Elizabeth Jee who were alive at the "default" of Hall's issue. Lord Kenyon construed this language to mean a *general failure of issue*—the executory interest would vest only when the last person in Hall's bloodline died. Therefore, the interest would not vest at Hall's death if she still had living descendants. Indeed, it *might* vest only centuries later, when her line of descendants ended.

b. What Might Happen?

The rule considers legal possibilities rather than physical realities. Even the most fantastic and improbable scenario may invalidate a future interest. Lord Kenyon supposed that John and Elizabeth Jee could have additional children even though they were 70 years old, and biologically incapable of producing children. Under the rule, even an infertile couple is deemed able to have children. Of course, today there is the possibility that an adult of any age could adopt a child.

Modern science is stretching our notion of fertility. The creation of sperm and egg banks, and the current reality of *in vitro* conception, produce a range of possibilities unknown to eighteenth-century England. It is now possible for a child to be born long after the death of both donor parents. And new reproductive technologies make it likely that human cloning may become a reality in our lifetimes. How should these developments be handled under the rule? When should a posthumously conceived child be deemed to be "in being" for purposes of the rule? Is the infant properly characterized as a child of the donor parent? For an interesting article reviewing these issues, see Sharona Hoffman & Andrew P. Morriss, *Birth After Death: Perpetuities and the New Reproductive Technologies*, 38 Ga. L. Rev. 575 (2004).

> **Food for Thought**
>
> Kenyon's analysis is given contemporary significance by the 1981 motion picture *Body Heat*. The movie involves a perpetuities dispute over the will of one Edmund Walker. Edmund's sister and daughter received devises under the will; but if their devises were void under the rule, then Edmund would have died intestate and his widow Matty Walker (played by Kathleen Turner) would take his property by intestate succession. Can you guess what the perpetuities problem was in Edmund's will?

c. **Class Gifts**

Audley's will created a gift to a class: the daughters of John and Elizabeth Jee alive when Hall's line of descendants ended. Under the rule, a class gift is void if the interest might vest in any member of the class too remotely. In short, a class gift is not valid as to *any* members of the class unless it is valid for *all* members of the class. Therefore, even though four daughters were living at Audley's death, the gift to the class was invalid if any daughter's interest might vest too remotely. Because the Jees could have *another daughter* in the future (who was not alive at Audley's death and therefore not "a life in being"), this daughter's interest might vest many years after the original four daughters, John and Elizabeth Jee, and Mary Hall had died.

Suppose O conveys Greenacre "to B for life, then to B's children." If B has two children, each receives a vested remainder subject to open. At common law, this future interest was not vested under the rule until the class *closed*, that is, until every member of the class was ascertained. Today, the closing of a class is governed by the *rule of convenience*; it closes when the prior estate ends and identified class members are entitled to possession. Notice that the rule is not violated in this example because all of B's children will be identified (at the latest) by B's death; B is a life in being, so she validates their interests. But what if the conveyance was "to B for life, then to B's children who reach age 30"?

d. **Analyzing *Jee***

Do you understand why the executory interest in the Jee daughters violated the rule? Create a factual scenario under which the interest might first vest too late, after the perpetuities period had expired.

e. **Relevant Lives**

After fixing the perpetuities period at "a life in being plus 21 years," courts determined that any number of lives that were reasonably capable of being tracked could be used as lives in being under the Rule. *See In re Villar*, 1 Ch. 243 (1929) (interest to vest 20 years "from the day of the death of the last survivor of all lineal descendants of Her Late Majesty Queen Victoria who shall be living at the time of my death"). In addition, courts recognized that individuals were "in being" from the time of conception, as long as they were born alive. Therefore, a more exact phrasing of the perpetuities period is: the longest life from any reasonable number of lives in being *plus* 21 years *plus* any periods of gestation. Because corporations, partnerships, and government entities have potentially infinite existence, they are not considered "lives in being" for purposes of the rule.

f. **Classic Snares**

Several notable examples of the rule's complexity have challenged students for generations:

Unborn Widow (Spouse): Suppose O conveys Greenacre "to B for life, then to B's widow for life, then to B's children living at B's widow's death." B has a life estate, B's widow a contingent remainder in a life estate, and B's children a contingent remainder in fee simple. The first contingent remainder does not violate the rule because B's widow will be ascertained (if B has a widow) at B's death; accordingly, there is no possibility of remote vesting. However, what about the contingent remainder in B's children? Remember, think creatively! B could marry D, someone not alive at the time of O's conveyance (and therefore not a life in being). D and B could then have a child F (again, not a life in being). F's interest vests when D dies ("then to B's children living at B's widow's death")—a point *possibly* more than 21 years after O and B die.

Slothful Executor: Suppose O conveys Greenacre "to B for life, then to C when B's will is probated." Although most wills are probated within several months of the testator's death, will contests or administrative problems can extend the period. A very unlikely possibility exists that probate may extend for more than 21 years after all relevant lives in being have died. In the above example, because B's will may be probated more than 21 years after O, B, and C have died, C's executory interest is void.

Fertile Octogenarian: Suppose that O is 80 years old, and has two sons (D and E) and no grandchildren. O conveys Greenacre "to my children for life, then to my grandchildren." The future grandchildren have a contingent remainder because they are unascertainable. Even though O is 80, the rule presumes that O is capable of having another child—as you saw in *Jee*. Therefore, after the conveyance O could have another child, H. O, D, and E (lives in being) could then die, and 40 years later H might have his own child, F. The contingent remainder would vest beyond the perpetuities period; F's interest would vest more than 21 years after the death of the last life in being. Thus, the remainder is void. But what if O made the same transfer in a will? Do you see why the future interest in the grandchildren would then be valid?

> **Food for Thought**
>
> In 1961, the California Supreme Court found the rule to be so complicated that it dismissed a malpractice complaint against an attorney who prepared a will that violated the rule. *Lucas v. Hamm*, 364 P.2d 685 (Cal. 1961). The court quoted one scholar who called the rule a "technicality-ridden legal nightmare" and a "dangerous instrumentality in the hands of most members of the bar." *Id.* at 690. Should an attorney of ordinary competence be expected to apply the rule correctly?

g. Current Applications

Contingent future interests are rarely created in today's real property marketplace. However, options to purchase and rights of first refusal are common, especially in commercial transactions. These interests are usually classified as executory interests and therefore may be subject to the rule. *See, e.g., Caruso v. Young,* 582 S.W.3d 634 (Tex. App. 2019).

Although the rule originated as a device to further the marketability of real property, today it is primarily applied to personal property interests held in trust. Many trusts bifurcate the equitable title held by their beneficiaries into present and future interests. The rule serves to restrict the creation of contingent interests in trust that may remain contingent beyond the perpetuities period.

h. Modern Reforms

All states have reformed the common law rule by statute or judicial decision. What are the advantages and disadvantages of the reforms below?

Wait-and-see: Under this approach, an interest is void if it does not actually vest within "a life in being plus 21 years." The validity of the interest is not determined at creation, but by events that *actually happen* in the future. Remember our example above. O conveys Greenacre "to B for life, then to M's first child to reach 30." Under the common law rule, the first child's contingent remainder is void because there is a possibility of remote vesting. However, under a wait-and-see approach, the contingent remainder is a valid interest *if* it vests within the perpetuities period. Therefore, if M has a son, S, and S reaches 30 (within 21 years of B's or M's death), S's interest is valid under the wait-and-see approach.

Uniform Statutory Rule Against Perpetuities (USRAP): Under this approach, an interest is valid if it satisfies the common law rule *or* if it actually vests within 90 years after its creation. Applying USRAP to the above example, even though the first child's interest does not meet the requirements of the common law approach, it still would be valid if S reached 30 within 90 years of O's conveyance. USRAP also contains reformation provisions that allow courts to rewrite the instrument to allow for vesting within the 90-year period. Most states have adopted USRAP.

Cy pres: Under this approach, courts rewrite the language of the conveyance so that the future interest no longer violates the common law rule in order to honor the transferor's presumed original intent. The rewriting should be "as near as possible" to the transferor's intent. In our example, a court could reform the grant to read, "to B for life, then to M's first child who reaches 21." By reducing the age to 21, there is no possibility of remote vesting under the common law rule. No child of M can reach age 21 *more than* 21 years after M's death.

Future of the rule: Some states have abolished the common law rule. Even where it remains in place, the future of the rule is in doubt. States have increasingly adopted legislation that authorizes the perpetual trust; in effect, this allows contingent interests to endure in perpetuity. *See* Jesse Dukeminier & James E. Krier, *The Rise of the Perpetual Trust*, 50 UCLA L. Rev. 1303 (2003); Stewart E. Sterk, *Jurisdictional Competition to Abolish the Rule Against Perpetuities: R.I.P. for the R.A.P.,* 24 Cardozo L. Rev. 2097 (2003).

i. Savings Clauses

There is a simple way to avoid the rule: insert a *savings clause* in the document. A savings clause prevents any potential violation of the rule by requiring that every interest must vest before the end of the applicable perpetuities period. A savings clause in a trust might provide: "Notwithstanding any other provision in this instrument, any trust created hereunder shall terminate, if it has not previously terminated, 21 years after the death of the survivor of the beneficiaries living at the date this instrument becomes effective." Because the trust ends no later than 21 years after the last beneficiary's death, the rule is not violated.

j. Problems

Which future interests are created and/or retained by these transfers? Are they valid under the common law Rule Against Perpetuities?

> (1) O conveys "to B for life, then to M if M lives to be age 50."
>
> (2) O devises "to City, but if the land is not used as a school, then to H and her heirs."
>
> (3) O conveys "to D provided that if it ceases to be used as a church, then to G if he is living."
>
> (4) O conveys "to E and her heirs so long as the land is used for school purposes, then to S."
>
> (5) O conveys "to F for life, then to F's grandchildren for life, then to K and his heirs."
>
> (6) O devises "to my grandchildren who reach age 21."
>
> (7) O conveys "to my grandchildren who reach age 21."

k. Additional Review

Click here to access notes and problems on the Rule Against Perpetuities, taken from Coletta's Workbook on Estates and Future Interests, 3d ed.

Summary

- **Feudal Foundation.** Our modern property law system is based on the English system of estates and future interests, which evolved from feudal landholding arrangements. A key feature of English feudalism was that multiple people could have rights in the same parcel of land at the same time.

- **Freehold Estates.** There are six basic freehold estates: fee simple absolute; life estate; fee tail; fee simple determinable; fee simple subject to a condition subsequent; and fee simple subject to an executory limitation.

- **Intestate Succession.** If a person dies intestate, his estate is distributed among the surviving spouse, issue, parents, ancestors, and collaterals. If he has no living relatives, it escheats to the state.
- **Restraints on Alienation.** A provision in a deed or will that expressly or effectively prohibits a future transfer of a fee simple is an invalid restraint on alienation.
- **Waste.** An estate owner owes a duty to future interest holders to avoid affirmative waste and permissive waste.
- **Future Interests.** Three future interests may be retained by the transferor: reversion; possibility of reverter; and right of entry. Five future interests may be created in a transferee: indefeasibly vested remainder; vested remainder subject to divestment; vested remainder subject to open; contingent remainder; and executory interest.
- **Protecting Marketability.** The common law restricted contingent remainders and executory interests in order to enhance the marketability of land by four devices: the Rule in Shelley's Case; the Doctrine of Worthier Title; the Doctrine of Destructibility of Contingent Remainders; and the Rule Against Perpetuities.

> **Test Your Knowledge**
>
> To assess your understanding of the material in this chapter, click here to take a quiz.

For More Information

For more information about the subjects covered in this chapter, please consult these sources:

- D. Benjamin Barros, *Toward a Model Law of Estates and Future Interests*, 66 Wash. & Lee L. Rev. 3 (2009).
- Raymond R. Coletta, Workbook on Estates and Future Interests (3d ed. 2013).
- T.P. Gallanis, *The Future of Future Interests*, 60 Wash. & Lee L. Rev. 513 (2003).
- Jessica A. Shoemaker, *Fee Simple Failures: Rural Landscapes and Race*, 119 Mich. L. Rev. 1695 (2021).
- Jay A. Soled & Letha Sgritta McDowell, *Life Estates Reconsidered*, 33 Quinnipiac Prob. L.J. 45 (2019).
- Stewart E. Sterk, *Jurisdictional Competition to Abolish the Rule Against Perpetuities: R.I.P. for the R.A.P.*, 24 Cardozo L. Rev. 2097 (2003).
- Katrina M. Wyman, *In Defense of the Fee Simple*, 93 Notre Dame L. Rev. 1 (2017).

Chapter 6

Concurrent Ownership and Marital Property

A central concept in American property law is that multiple people can hold interests in the same land at the same time. For example, in Chapter 5 we saw that two people can hold the right to possession of land at *different times*. Suppose O conveys Greenacre "to A for life, then to B." A is entitled to possession of Greenacre now, while B has a right to possession in the future.

What if O conveys Greenacre "to A and B"? Now A and B have the right to share possession of Greenacre at the *same time*. The relationship between A and B is a form of concurrent ownership, which gives them equal rights to use and enjoy the entire parcel. The laws governing the property rights of a married—or unmarried—couple create interests akin to concurrent ownership in some jurisdictions. We examine both subjects in this chapter.

A. Concurrent Ownership

The key characteristic of concurrent ownership is that each co-owner or *cotenant* has the right to use and possess the entire property. Suppose that A and B are cotenants in Greenacre, each holding a 50% share. Each has the right to use and possess *all* of Greenacre, not just a particular part of it.

Of course, this shared right of possession may lead to conflicts. What if A, an entrepreneur, wants to build a racetrack on the property, while B, a conservationist, wants to keep the land in its natural condition? Or A wants to live on Greenacre, but B wants to rent it to a third party? As we will see, if cotenants like A and B cannot agree on how the property should be used, their rights and obligations will be governed by a number of common law rules.

1. Modern Concurrent Estates

Today, there are three basic types of concurrent ownership: the tenancy in common, the joint tenancy, and the tenancy by the entirety.

Tenancy in common. If O conveys Greenacre "to A and B," this creates a tenancy in common. Each tenant in common has an undivided, fractional interest in the property. Each may transfer his interest to another person; it is freely alienable, devisable, and descendible. Finally, each has the right to use and possess the whole parcel, even if his fractional interest is smaller than the interests of others. Suppose that O conveys Redacre to "A, B, and C as tenants in common," and B then conveys her interest to A. A and C are tenants in common; A holds a 2/3 interest, and C has the remaining 1/3 interest. C has as much right as A to use and enjoy the entire property. But when the property is sold, the proceeds will be divided according to their proportionate shares. Any conveyance or devise to two or more unmarried persons is presumed to create a tenancy in common, *unless* it contains language showing an intent to create a joint tenancy.

Joint tenancy. Suppose O conveys Greenacre "to A and B as joint tenants with right of survivorship." In most jurisdictions, this creates a joint tenancy. Like tenants in common, joint tenants have an undivided right to use and possess the whole property. But each joint tenant also has a *right of survivorship*. When A dies, A's interest in the estate is removed, and B automatically becomes the sole owner of Greenacre. Because of the right of survivorship, a joint tenancy interest is neither devisable nor descendible.

> **FYI**
>
> Joint tenants are seized *per my et per tout*—by the part and by the whole. A joint tenant owns a distinct share as well as an undivided interest in the whole. Thus, a joint tenant can alienate his particular share during his lifetime.

At common law and in some jurisdictions today, a joint tenancy is created only when the four unities of *time*, *title*, *interest*, and *possession* are present:

- *Time*: All joint tenants must acquire their interests at the same time. If A and B obtain their interests on different days, the unity of time is absent.
- *Title*: They must acquire title by the same instrument. If A and B receive their interests by different deeds, the unity of title is missing.
- *Interest*: They must have the same shares in the estate, equal in size and duration. If A receives an undivided 2/3 interest and B an undivided 1/3 interest, there is no unity of interest.
- *Possession*: They must have an equal right to possess, use, and enjoy the whole property.

If the unity of time, title, or interest is missing, a tenancy in common is created. Suppose O attempts to create a joint tenancy in A, B, and C by conveying a 1/2 interest to A one day, and the next day conveying a 3/8 interest to B and a 1/8 interest to C. The unities of time, title, and interest are missing; A, B, and C are tenants in common.

If one joint tenant transfers her interest, the joint tenancy is *severed*. The transfer breaks the unities of time and title; the right of survivorship is destroyed; and the grantee becomes a tenant in common with the other concurrent owners. Suppose A and B are joint tenants. If B conveys her interest to C, the joint tenancy ends. A and C are now tenants in common, each holding an undivided 1/2 interest in the property.

Tenancy by the entirety. Some states follow the traditional view that any conveyance or devise to a married couple is presumed to create a tenancy by the entirety. However, other states require language showing an intent to create this estate, such as "to A and B as tenants by the entirety." The estate arises only when the four unities of time, title, interest, and possession are present—plus the fifth unity of a valid marriage. Like a joint tenant, each tenant by the entirety has an undivided right to use and possess the whole property and a right of survivorship. But while a joint tenancy can be severed unilaterally by any joint tenant, a tenancy by the entirety can only be ended by death, divorce, or the agreement of both spouses. The common law viewed a husband and a wife as a unity. Because they were viewed as being "one flesh," there were no individual parts to the cotenancy that could be owned separately by either spouse. Thus, in most states that recognize this cotenancy, neither spouse may transfer or encumber his or her interest. The principal benefit of tenancy by the entirety is that in many jurisdictions it allows the holders to partially shield their assets from creditors, as we will discuss later in the chapter.

> **FYI**
>
> Tenants by the entirety are seized *per tout et non per my*—by the whole and not by the part. The husband and wife are a unity. Neither one can individually convey his or her undivided interest to a third party.

Suppose that C wants to create a joint tenancy in A and B. If he conveys Greenacre "to A and B jointly" does this language meet his goal? A similar question arose in our next case. The ambiguous language in the deed defeated the grantor's apparent wish to leave her property only to her *surviving* children.

James v. Taylor

Court of Appeals of Arkansas

969 S.W.2d 672 (1998)

PITTMAN, JUDGE.

The issue in this case is whether a deed from the late Eura Mae Redmon to her three children, W.C. Sewell, Billy Sewell, and appellee Melba Taylor, was a conveyance to them as tenants in common or as joint tenants with the right of survivorship. The chancellor held that Mrs. Redmon intended for her children to take the property as joint tenants with the right of survivorship. We reverse and remand.

The deed in question was executed by Mrs. Redmon on January 14, 1993. The conveyance was made to the three grantees "jointly and severally, and unto their heirs, assigns and successors forever," with the grantor retaining a life estate. W.C. Sewell and Billy Sewell died on November 18, 1993, and May 11, 1995, respectively. Mrs. Redmon died on February 17, 1997. Shortly thereafter, appellee filed a complaint in White County Chancery Court seeking a declaration that her mother had intended to convey the property to the grantees as joint tenants, thereby making appellee, by virtue of her brothers' deaths, sole owner of the property. Appellants, who are descendants of W.C. and Billy Sewell, opposed the complaint on the ground that the deed created a tenancy in common among the grantees.

The case went to trial, and the chancellor, upon hearing extrinsic evidence of Mrs. Redmon's intent, found that she meant to convey the property to her children as joint tenants with the right of survivorship. . . .

Appellants and appellee agree that the term "jointly and severally" as used to describe an estate in property is ambiguous. . . . Appellants contend that, under Arkansas law, a deed to two or more persons presumptively creates a tenancy in common unless the deed expressly creates a joint tenancy. They cite Ark. Code Ann. § 18–12–603 (1987), which reads as follows: "Every interest in real estate granted or devised to two (2) or more persons, other than executors and trustees as such, shall be in tenancy in common unless expressly declared in the grant or devise to be a joint tenancy." According to appellants, the very existence of an ambiguity within the deed means that, under the statute, a tenancy in common has been created. Appellee, on the other hand, points to the well-established rule that, when faced with an ambiguity in a deed, the trial court may determine the intent of the grantor by looking to extraneous circumstances to decide what was really intended by the language in the deed. . . .

The extrinsic evidence considered by the chancellor in this case weighs in favor of appellee. That evidence consisted of appellee's testimony that her mother had informed her attorney that she wanted the deed drafted so that, if one of her children died, the property would belong to the other two children, and so on; that shortly after the death of W.C. Sewell, Mrs. Redmon executed a new will leaving her property to Billy Sewell and appellee and leaving nothing to W.C.'s children; that Mrs. Redmon had set up bank accounts payable upon her death to her children, and, after W.C. and Billy died, deleted their names leaving the name of the surviving child; and that Mrs. Redmon was upset before her death upon learning that there was a problem with the deed. However, we hold that the considerations expressed in Ark. Code Ann. § 18–12–603 override the rule of construction urged by appellee.

Section 18–12–603 is a statute like one of many throughout the country. At common law, joint tenancy was favored and, where possible, that estate was held to exist. . . . However, in Arkansas, and in many other states, statutes have been adopted which presumptively construe an instrument to create a tenancy in common rather than a joint tenancy. . . . These statutes do not prohibit joint tenancies but merely provide for a construction against a joint tenancy if the intention to create it is not clear. . . .

Ordinarily, a statute such as section 18–12–603 does not require the actual use of the words "joint tenancy.". . . Survivorship is the distinctive characteristic of a joint tenancy. 48A C.J.S. *Joint Tenancy* § 3 at 302 (1981). Where, from the four corners of an instrument, a court can interpret the intention of the grantor or testator as creating a survivorship estate, the court will deem the estate to be a joint tenancy with the right of survivorship. . . .

Nothing appears from the four corners of the deed in this case to indicate Mrs. Redmon's intent to convey a survivorship interest, unless that intention is to be found in the term "jointly and severally." Appellants do not cite, nor have we discovered through our own research, any Arkansas case in which a grant of ownership was made to two or more parties "jointly and severally." As the chancellor noted below, "jointly and severally" are words of tort, not property. They have no meaning in the world of estates. . . .

> **FYI**
>
> A "four corners" interpretation of a deed looks at its plain language. Judges consider the ordinary meaning of the document with the view that the party's intent should be evident from the language used.

Appellee argues that, given the deed's ambiguity, our focus should be on the intent of the grantor as gleaned not only from the instrument itself but from the extrinsic evidence presented at trial. However, evidence of the grantor's intention cannot prevail over the statute. To allow that would be to render section 18–12–603 meaningless.

Based upon the foregoing, we hold that the deed in this case did not create a joint tenancy in the grantees. The language of the deed is insufficient to overcome the statutory presumption of a tenancy in common. . . .

Points for Discussion

a. **Grantor's Intent**

Did the extrinsic evidence considered by the chancellor demonstrate Redmon's intention that her children take as joint tenants? If so, why didn't the *James* court consider this evidence? Should the law honor an owner's clear intent?

b. **Resolving Ambiguity**

Historically, the common law favored the joint tenancy because the right of survivorship helped to eliminate fractional interests, thereby concentrating feudal services in a single person. Thus, a deed conveying a concurrent estate was presumed to create a joint tenancy unless the grantor used language clearly showing a different intent. Today, the law presumes that the grantor intends to create a tenancy in common, absent express language to the contrary.

c. **Preferred Language**

In order to avoid ambiguity, attorneys use precise language in drafting conveyances and wills. The following phrases clearly create these estates:

- *Tenancy in common*: "to A and B as tenants in common."
- *Joint tenancy*: "to A and B as joint tenants with right of survivorship."
- *Tenancy by the entirety*: "to A and B as husband and wife as tenants by the entirety."

As *James* reflects, if the wording is unclear, a court may ignore the grantor's actual intent. However, the modern trend is to focus more on the grantor's intent and less on formulaic language. *See Germaine v. Delaine*, 318 So. 2d 681 (Ala. 1975) ("jointly as tenants in common" created a joint tenancy because the deed indicated a clear intent for survivorship).

What if a conveyance reads: "to A and B for life, then to the survivor"? Many courts interpret such language as creating a tenancy in common for life in A and B, followed by a contingent remainder in the survivor. *See Smith v. Cutler*, 623 S.E.2d 644 (S.C. 2005). Do you understand why?

d. **Exercise**

S conveys Greenacre "to A, B, and C as tenants in common." Shortly thereafter, A sells his interest to F; then B dies, devising her interest to G. Who owns what interest in Greenacre? Suppose instead that the grant reads "to A, B, and C as joint tenants with right of survivorship." Would the result change?

e. Use of a Straw Person

Suppose that A, the owner of Greenacre, wants to create a joint tenancy with her sister, B. A executes a deed that conveys the land "to A and B as joint tenants with right of survivorship." Are A and B joint tenants? Surprisingly, the traditional answer is "no." Since A already has title by a prior instrument, the unities of time and title are missing; thus, A and B become tenants in common.

The common law developed a technique to avoid this problem: conveyance to a *straw person*. A could convey Greenacre to C, who would then convey the land "to A and B as joint tenants with right of survivorship." The four unities are now present, and a joint tenancy arises. Today many jurisdictions have eliminated the need for a straw person. The grantor may create a joint tenancy by conveying to herself and another person. See *Littleton v. Plybon*, 395 S.W.3d 505 (Ky. Ct. App. 2012).

f. Will Substitute

The joint tenancy is often used as an inexpensive substitute for a will. If A and B hold Greenacre as joint tenants, B immediately obtains complete title to Greenacre when A dies. Because A's interest is destroyed, there is no asset that needs to go through *probate*—which can save time and expense. It is common for a married couple to hold the family home in joint tenancy for this purpose. Should an attorney encourage her clients to use the joint tenancy as a substitute for a will? What risks does this approach present?

> **FYI**
>
> *Probate* is a judicially-supervised process for administering the estate of a decedent. The court resolves any outstanding claims and orders the distribution of the decedent's assets. Probate can last many months, generating substantial costs and attorney fees. The term "probate" comes from the Latin, *probatus*, meaning "a thing proved."

g. A New Concurrent Estate?

One scholar points out that the three concurrent estates are almost 600 years old; they were "born at a time when the Renaissance was barely gestating, when a flat earth was the center of the universe, and when kings were divine." Peter M. Carrozzo, *Tenancies in Antiquity: A Transformation of Concurrent Ownership for Modern Relationships*, 85 Marq. L. Rev. 423, 423 (2001). He advocates the recognition of a new concurrent estate, which essentially would give a cohabiting couple the protections of a tenancy by the entirety. Do you agree?

---

2. Severance

As you have seen, a joint tenant can end the tenancy simply by conveying her interest to a third party. So if A and B are joint tenants, and A conveys her interest to C, the joint tenancy is severed; B and C are tenants in common. But what if A *leases* her interest to C? Or *mortgages* her interest to D? Does either act sever the joint tenancy? The question arises in our next case.

Tenhet v. Boswell

Supreme Court of California

554 P.2d 330 (1976)

Mosk, Justice.

A joint tenant leases his interest in the joint tenancy property to a third person for a term of years, and dies during that term. We conclude that the lease does not sever the joint tenancy, but expires upon the death of the lessor joint tenant.

Raymond Johnson and plaintiff Hazel Tenhet owned a parcel of property as joint tenants. Assertedly without plaintiff's knowledge or consent, Johnson leased the property to defendant Boswell for a period of 10 years at a rental of $150 per year with a provision granting the lessee an "option to purchase." Johnson died some three months after execution of the lease, and plaintiff sought to establish her sole right to possession of the property as the surviving joint tenant. After an unsuccessful demand upon defendant to vacate the premises, plaintiff brought this action to have the lease declared invalid. The trial court sustained demurrers to the complaint, and plaintiff appealed from the ensuing judgment of dismissal. . . .

II.

An understanding of the nature of a joint interest in this state is fundamental to a determination of the question whether the present lease severed the joint tenancy. Civil Code section 683 provides in part: "A joint interest is one owned by two or more persons in equal shares, by a title created by a single will or transfer, when expressly declared in the will or transfer to be a joint tenancy. . . ." This statute, requiring an express declaration for the creation of joint interests, does not abrogate the common law rule that four unities are essential to an estate in joint tenancy: unity of interest, unity of time, unity of title, and unity of possession. . . .

The requirement of four unities reflects the basic concept that there is but one estate which is taken jointly; if an essential unity is destroyed the joint tenancy is severed and a tenancy in common results. (*Swartzbaugh v. Sampson* (1936) 11 Cal. App.2d 451, 454, 54 P.2d 73; 2 Am. Law of Prop. (1952) § 6.2, p. 9.) Accordingly, one of two joint tenants may unilaterally terminate the joint tenancy by conveying his interest to a third person. (*Delanoy v. Delanoy* (1932) 216 Cal. 23, 26, 13 P.2d 513; *Green v. Skinner* (1921) 185 Cal. 435, 438, 197 P. 60.) Severance of the joint tenancy, of course, extinguishes the principal feature of that estate—the jus accrescendi or right of survivorship. Thus, a joint tenant's right of survivorship is an expectancy that is not irrevocably fixed upon the creation of the estate. . . ; it arises only upon success in the ultimate gamble—survival—and then only if the unity of the estate has not theretofore been destroyed by voluntary conveyance . . . , by partition proceedings . . . or by any other action which operates to sever the joint tenancy.

Our initial inquiry is whether the partial alienation of Johnson's interest in the property effected a severance of the joint tenancy under these principles. It could be argued that a lease destroys the unities of interest and possession because the leasing joint tenant transfers to the lessee his present possessory interest and retains a mere reversion. (*See Alexander v. Boyer* (1969) 253 Md. 511, 253 A.2d 359, 365.) Moreover, the possibility that the term of the lease may continue beyond the lifetime of the lessor is inconsistent with a complete right of survivorship.

> **It's Latin to Me**
>
> The essence of the right of survivorship is summarized in the Latin phrase: *Nihil de re accrescit ei, qui nihil in re quando jus accresceret habet*—"No part of the estate accrues to him who has nothing in the estate when the right accrues."

On the other hand, if the lease entered into here by Johnson and defendant is valid only during Johnson's life, then the conveyance is more a variety of life estate *pur autre vie* than a term of years. Such a result is inconsistent with Johnson's freedom to alienate his interest during his lifetime.

We are mindful that the issue here presented is "an ancient controversy, going back to Coke and Littleton." (2 Am. Law of Prop. (1952) § 6.2, p. 10.) Yet the problem is like a comet in our law: though its existence in theory has been frequently recognized, its observed passages are few. Some authorities support the view that a lease by a joint tenant to a third person effects a complete and final severance of the joint tenancy. . . . Such a view is generally based upon what is thought to be the English common law rule. . . .

Others adopt a position that there is a temporary severance during the term of the lease. If the lessor dies while the lease is in force, under this view the existence of the lease at the moment when the right of survivorship would otherwise take effect operates as a severance, extinguishing the joint tenancy. If, however, the term of the lease expires before the lessor, it is reasoned that the joint tenancy is undisturbed because the joint tenants resume their original relation. . . . The single conclusion that can be drawn from centuries of academic speculation on the question is that its resolution is unclear.

As we shall explain, it is our opinion that a lease is not so inherently inconsistent with joint tenancy as to create a severance, either temporary or permanent. . . .

Under Civil Code sections 683 and 686 a joint tenancy must be expressly declared in the creating instrument, or a tenancy in common results. This is a statutory departure from the common law preference in favor of joint tenancy. . . . Inasmuch as the estate arises only upon express intent, and in many cases such intent will be the intent of the joint tenants themselves, we decline to find a severance in circumstances which do not clearly and unambiguously establish that either of the joint tenants desired to terminate the estate. . . .

If plaintiff and Johnson did not choose to continue the joint tenancy, they might have converted it into a tenancy in common by written mutual agreement. . . . They might also have jointly conveyed the property to a third person and divided the proceeds. Even if they could not agree to act in concert, either plaintiff or Johnson might have severed the joint tenancy, with or without the consent of the other, by an act which was clearly indicative of an intent to terminate, such as a conveyance of her or his entire interest. Either might also have brought an action to partition the property, which, upon judgment, would have effected a severance. Because a joint tenancy may be created only by express intent, and because there are alternative and unambiguous means of altering the nature of that estate, we hold that the lease here in issue did not operate to sever the joint tenancy.

III.

Having concluded that the joint tenancy was not severed by the lease and that sole ownership of the property therefore vested in plaintiff upon her joint tenant's death by operation of her right of survivorship, we turn next to the issue whether she takes the property unencumbered by the lease.

In arguing that plaintiff takes subject to the lease, defendant relies on *Swartzbaugh v. Sampson* (1936) *supra*, 11 Cal.App.2d 451, 54 P.2d 73. In that case, one of two joint tenants entered into lease agreements over the objection of his joint tenant wife, who sought to cancel the leases. The court held in favor of the lessor joint tenant, concluding that the leases were valid.

But the suit to cancel the lease in *Swartzbaugh* was brought during the lifetime of both joint tenants, not as in the present case after the death of the lessor. Significantly, the court concluded that "a lease to all of the joint property by one joint tenant is not a nullity but is a valid and supportable contract *in so far as the interest of the lessor in the joint property is concerned*.". . . During the lifetime of the lessor joint tenant, as the *Swartzbaugh* court perceived, her interest in the joint property was an undivided interest in fee simple that encompassed the right to lease the property.

By the very nature of joint tenancy, however, the interest of the nonsurviving joint tenant extinguishes upon his death. And as the lease is valid only "in so far as the interest of the lessor in the joint property is concerned," it follows that the lease of the joint tenancy property also expires when the lessor dies. . . .

[I]n *People v. Nogarr* (1958) 164 Cal.App.2d 591, 330 P.2d 858, which held that upon the death of a joint tenant who had executed a mortgage on the tenancy property, the surviving joint tenant took the property free of the mortgage. The court reasoned . . . that "as the mortgage lien attached only to such interest as (the deceased joint tenant) had in the real property(,) when his interest ceased to exist the lien of the mortgage expired with it.". . .

As these decisions demonstrate, a joint tenant may, during his lifetime, grant certain rights in the joint property without severing the tenancy. But when such a joint tenant dies his interest dies with him, and any encumbrances placed by him on the property become unenforceable against the surviving joint tenant. For the reasons stated a lease falls within this rule. . . .

Points for Discussion

a. **"Like a Comet"**

Why did the *Tenhet* court hold that the lease did not sever the joint tenancy? In *Alexander v. Boyer*, 253 A.2d 359 (Md. Ct. App. 1969), a Maryland court reached the opposite result. Which is the better approach? Is it relevant that joint tenants are often family members who want their survivorship rights to continue?

The *Tenhet* court also considered whether the lease survived Johnson's death. In other words, did the lease expire when Johnson died or did Tenhet receive a fee simple burdened by the lease? In most jurisdictions, a lease does not survive the cotenant's death. See *Harmon v. Misholy*, 166 N.Y.S.3d 504 (Dist. Ct. 2022). In effect, if a joint tenant leases her interest, the lease ends at the earlier of two events: the end of the lease term or the death of the lessor. What policies support this approach?

b. **Mortgage: Title or Lien?**

Suppose that Johnson mortgaged his interest to Boswell. Would this sever the joint tenancy? In Chapter 9, you will learn that some states follow a *title theory* of mortgages while others use a *lien theory*. Under the title theory, the mortgage is seen as the conveyance of title to the mortgagee; this severs the joint tenancy because it destroys the unities of time and title. Under the lien theory, the mortgage is viewed merely as a lien to secure repayment of the debt; it does not end the joint tenancy because the unities are preserved.

States that follow the lien theory are split as to whether the mortgage survives the death of the joint tenant. In *Smith v. Bank of America*, 957 N.Y.S.2d 705, 709 (App. Div. 2012), the court reasoned that "since a mortgage is only a lien, [the] act of giving a mortgage . . . did not act to sever the joint tenancy" and concluded that "the mortgage ceased to exist" when the debtor joint tenant died. However, many courts hold that a mortgage survives the death of the mortgagor-joint tenant, so the surviving joint tenant takes title subject to the mortgage.

c. **Secret Severance**

Suppose A and B are husband and wife, holding title to their home in joint tenancy. A secretly conveys his interest to himself, transforming the joint tenancy into a tenancy in common. If A dies before B, A can devise his interest to a third party, perhaps his girlfriend C. But if B dies before A, A will destroy the severance deed and claim to be the sole owner. Is it fair to allow A to sever the joint tenancy without telling B? In *Riddle v. Harmon*, 162 Cal. Rptr. 530 (Ct. App. 1980), the court allowed a wife to do exactly that: secretly sever the joint tenancy and then devise her interest to another person. Statutes in a few states require that the deed effecting severance be recorded in order to prevent the severing joint tenant from trying to claim sole title if he outlives the other joint tenant. *See* Minn. Stat. § 500.19(5); Cal. Civ. Code § 683.2. For an interesting article on this subject, see Samuel M. Fetters, *An Invitation to Commit Fraud: Secret Destruction of Joint Tenant Survivorship Rights*, 55 Fordham L. Rev. 173 (1986).

d. **Intent Theory and Severance**

Courts increasingly focus on intent when determining whether a joint tenancy has been created or severed, rather than the traditional four unities. As you have seen, many jurisdictions now allow a grantor to create a joint tenancy by directly conveying to herself and another person, without the formality of a straw person. Similarly, when deciding whether a joint tenancy has been severed, a growing number of courts look beyond whether there has been a break in the four unities—and instead consider whether a party intended to sever the tenancy. *See* R.H. Helmholz, *Realism and Formalism in the Severance of Joint Tenancies*, 77 Neb. L. Rev. 1 (1998); *In re Estate of Johnson*, 739 N.W.2d 493 (Iowa 2007).

---

3. Partition

Conflicts often arise between cotenants. For example, if A and B are co-tenants in a farm, they may disagree about how the farm should be managed. If their dispute cannot be resolved, they might agree to sell the farm and share the proceeds. Or A might purchase B's interest.

But what if A and B cannot agree on how to end the cotenancy? Any tenant in common or joint tenant has the right to sue for *partition* of the property. A partition judgment ends the cotenancy and distributes its assets. In such an action, should the judge physically divide the farm between A and B? Or order the farm to be sold and the proceeds divided?

> **Food for Thought**
>
> A New Jersey court noted in *Mastbaum v. Mastbaum*, 9 A.2d 51, 55 (N.J. Ch. Ct. 1939) that "[t]wo men cannot plow the same furrow." What did the court mean by this comment?

Ark Land Co. v. Harper

Supreme Court of Appeals of West Virginia

599 S.E.2d 754 (2004)

DAVIS, JUSTICE.

I.

This is a dispute involving approximately 75 acres of land situate in Lincoln County, West Virginia. The record indicates that "[t]he Caudill family has owned the land for nearly 100 years." The property "consists of a farmhouse, constructed around 1920, several small barns, and a garden[.]" Prior to 2001, the property was owned exclusively by the Caudill family. However, in 2001 Ark Land acquired a 67.5% undivided interest in the land by purchasing the property interests of several Caudill family members. Ark Land attempted to purchase the remaining property interests held by the Caudill heirs, but they refused to sell. Ark Land sought to purchase all of the property for the express purpose of extracting coal by surface mining.

Caudill family home
Click here for larger photo

After the Caudill heirs refused to sell their interest in the land, Ark Land filed a complaint in the Circuit Court of Lincoln County in October of 2001. Ark Land filed the complaint seeking to have the land partitioned and sold. . . .

The circuit court held a *de novo* review that involved testimony from lay and expert witnesses. On October 30, 2002, the circuit court entered an order directing the partition and sale of the property. . . . From this ruling the Caudill heirs appealed. . . .

III.

The dispositive issue is whether the evidence supported the circuit court's conclusion that the property could not be conveniently partitioned in kind, thus warranting a partition by sale. During the proceeding before the circuit court, the Caudill heirs presented expert testimony by Gary F. Acord, a mining engineer. Mr. Acord testified that the property could be partitioned in kind. Specifically, Mr. Acord testified that lands surrounding the family home did not have coal deposits and could therefore be partitioned from the remaining lands. On the other hand, Ark Land presented expert testimony which indicated that such a partition would entail several million dollars in additional costs in order to mine for coal.

We note at the outset that "[p]artition means the division of the land held in cotenancy into the cotenants' respective fractional shares. If the land cannot be fairly divided, then the entire estate may be sold and the proceeds appropriately divided." 7 Powell on Real Property, § 50.07[1] (2004). It has been observed that, "[i]n the United States, partition was established by statute in each of the individual states. Unlike the partition in kind which existed under early common law, the forced judicial sale was an American innovation.". . .

> **FYI**
>
> Ark Land Company is a subsidiary of Arch Resources, Inc. (formerly known as Arch Coal, Inc.), one of the country's largest coal producers. Arch Coal wanted the Caudill land in order to expand its nearby Hobet 21 "mountaintop removal complex." The Hobet complex was one of the largest surface coal mines in the state, producing over 5 million tons per year until production ceased in 2015.

Partition by sale, when it is not voluntary by all parties, can be a harsh result for the cotenant(s) who opposes the sale. This is because "'[a] particular piece of real estate cannot be replaced by any sum of money, however large; and one who wants a particular estate for a specific use, if deprived of his rights, cannot be said to receive an exact equivalent or complete indemnity by the payment of a sum of money.'" *Wight v. Ingram-Day Lumber Co.*, 195 Miss. 823, 17 So.2d 196, 198 (1944) (quoting *Lynch v. Union Inst. for Savings*, 159 Mass. 306, 34 N.E. 364, 364–365 (1893)). Consequently, "[p]artition in kind . . . is the preferred method of partition because it leaves cotenants holding the same estates as before and does not force a sale on unwilling cotenants." Powell, § 50.07[4][a]. The laws in all jurisdictions "appear to reflect this longstanding principle by providing a presumption of severance of common ownership in real property by partition in-kind[.]" Phyliss Craig-Taylor, *Through a Colored Looking Glass: A View of Judicial Partition, Family Land Loss, and Rule Setting*, 78 Wash. U.L.Q. 737, 753 (2000). "Thus, partitioning sale statutes should be construed narrowly and used sparingly because they interfere with property rights." John G. Casagrande, Jr., Note, *Acquiring Property Through Forced Partitioning Sales: Abuses and Remedies*, 27 B.C. L. Rev. 755, 775 (1986). . . .

In syllabus point 3 of *Consolidated Gas Supply Corp v. Riley,* 161 W.Va. 782, 247 S.E.2d 712 (1978), this Court set out the following standard of proof that must be established to overcome the presumption of partition in kind:

> By virtue of W. Va. Code § 37-4-3, a party desiring to compel partition through sale is required to demonstrate [(1)] that the property cannot be conveniently partitioned in kind, [(2)] that the interests of one or more of the parties will be promoted by the sale, and [(3)] that the interests of the other parties will not be prejudiced by the sale.

In its lengthy order requiring partition and sale, the circuit court addressed each of the three factors . . . as follows:

> (14) That . . . it cannot be conveniently (that is "practically or justly") partitioned, or divided by allotment among its owners . . . . [A]llotting the manor house and the surrounding "bottom land" unto the [Caudill heirs], cannot be affected without undeniably prejudicing [Ark Land's] interests, in violation of the mandatory provisions of Code § 37-4-3; and,
>
> (15) That while its uniform topography superficially suggests a division-in-kind, as proposed by Mr. Acord, the access road, the bottom lands and the relatively flat home site is, in fact, integral to establishing the fair market value of the subject property in its entirety, as its highest and best use as mining property, as shown by the uncontroverted testimony of [Ark Land's] experts Mr. Morgan and Mr. Terry; and,
>
> (16) That . . . [the Caudill heirs] herein, do not wish to sell, or have the Court sell, their interests in the subject property, solely due to their sincere sentiment for it as the family's "home place". Other family members, however, did not feel the same way. Given the equally undisputed testimony of [Ark Land's] experts, it is just and reasonable for the Court to conclude that the interests of all the subject property's owners will not be financially prejudiced, but will be financially promoted, by sale of the subject property and distribution among them of the proceeds, according to their respective interests. The subject property's value as coal mining property, its uncontroverted highest and best use, would be substantially impaired by severing the family's "home place" and allotting it to them separately. . . .

We are troubled by the circuit court's conclusion that partition by sale was necessary because the economic value of the property would be less if partitioned in kind. We have long held that the economic value of property *may* be a factor to consider in determining whether to partition in kind or to force a sale. . . . However, our cases *do not* support the conclusion that economic value of property is the exclusive test for determining whether to partition in kind or to partition by sale. In fact, we explicitly stated in *Hale v. Thacker,* 122 W.Va. 648, 650, 12 S.E.2d 524, 526 (1940), "that many considerations, other than monetary, attach to the ownership of land, and courts should be, and always have been, slow to take away from owners of real estate their common-law right to have the same set aside to them in kind.". . .

Similarly, in *Delfino v. Vealencis,* 181 Conn. 533, 436 A.2d 27 (1980), two plaintiffs owned a 20.5 acre tract of land with the defendant. The defendant used part of the property for her home and a garbage removal business. The plaintiffs filed an action to force a sale of the property so that they could use it to develop residential properties. The trial court concluded that a partition in kind could not be had without great prejudice to the parties, and that the highest and best use of the property was through development as residential property. The trial court therefore ordered that the property be sold at auction. The defendant appealed. The Connecticut Supreme Court reversed for the following reasons:

> The [trial] court's . . . observations relating to the effect of the defendant's business on the probable fair market value of the proposed residential lots . . . are not dispositive of the issue. *It is the interests of all of the tenants in common that the court must consider; and not merely the economic gain of one tenant, or a group of tenants.* The trial court failed to give due consideration to the fact . . . that the [defendant] has made her home on the property; and that she derives her livelihood from the operation of a business on this portion of the property, as her family before her has for many years. A partition by sale would force the defendant to surrender her home and, perhaps, would jeopardize her livelihood. It is under just such circumstances, which include the demonstrated practicability of a physical division of the property, that the wisdom of the law's preference for partition in kind is evident. *Delfino*, 436 A.2d at 32–33 (emphasis added) . . . .

[W]e now make clear and hold that, in a partition proceeding in which a party opposes the sale of property, the economic value of the property is not the exclusive test for deciding whether to partition in kind or by sale. Evidence of longstanding ownership, coupled with sentimental or emotional interests in the property, may also be considered in deciding whether the interests of the party opposing the sale will be prejudiced by the property's sale. This latter factor should ordinarily control when it is shown that the property can be partitioned in kind, though it may entail some economic inconvenience to the party seeking a sale.

In the instant case, the Caudill heirs were not concerned with the monetary value of the property. Their exclusive interest was grounded in the longstanding family ownership of the property and their emotional desire to keep their ancestral family home within the family. It is quite clear that this emotional interest would be prejudiced through a sale of the property.

The expert for the Caudill heirs testified that the ancestral family home could be partitioned from the property in such a way as to not deprive Ark Land of any coal. The circuit court summarily and erroneously dismissed this uncontradicted fact because of the increased costs that Ark Land would incur as a result of a partition in kind. In view of our holding, the additional economic burden that would be imposed on Ark Land, as a result of partitioning in kind, is not determinative under the facts of this case.

. . . The facts in this case reveal that, prior to 2001, Ark Land had no ownership interest in the property. Conversely, for nearly 100 years the Caudill heirs and their ancestors owned the property and used it for residential purposes. In 2001 Ark Land purchased ownership rights in the property from some Caudill family members. When the Caudill heirs refused to sell their ownership rights, Ark Land immediately sought to force a judicial sale of the property. In doing this, Ark Land established that its proposed use of the property, surface coal mining, gave greater value to the property. This showing is self-serving. In most instances, when a commercial entity purchases property because it believes it can make money from a specific use of the property, that property will increase in value based upon the expectations of the commercial entity. This self-created enhancement in the value of property cannot be the determinative factor in forcing a pre-existing co-owner to give up his/her rights in property. To have such a rule would permit commercial entities to always "evict" pre-existing co-owners, because a commercial entity's interest in property will invariably increase its value. . . .

> **FYI**
>
> During oral argument, Phil Melick, representing Ark Land, argued that the court should approve the sale because using the land as a dump site for mining waste "is the highest and best use of the property." Justice McGraw asked: "The highest and best use of the land is dumping?" Melick responded: "That's the reality. The use of land changes over time. . . ."

We are very sensitive to the fact that Ark Land will incur greater costs in conducting its business on the property as a result of partitioning in kind. However, Ark Land voluntarily took an economical gamble that it would be able to get all of the Caudill family members to sell their interests in the property. Ark Land's gamble failed. The Caudill heirs refused to sell their interests. The fact that Ark Land miscalculated on its ability to acquire outright all interests in the property cannot form the basis for depriving the Caudill heirs of their emotional interests in maintaining their ancestral family home. The additional cost to Ark Land that will result from a partitioning in kind simply does not impose the type of injurious inconvenience that would justify stripping the Caudill heirs of the emotional interest they have in preserving their ancestral family home. . . .

IV.

In view of the foregoing, we find that the circuit court erred in determining that the property could not be partitioned in kind. We, therefore, reverse the circuit court's order requiring sale of the property. This case is remanded with directions to the circuit court to enter an order requiring the property to be partitioned in kind, consistent with the report and testimony of the Caudill heirs' mining engineer expert, Gary F. Acord.

Reversed and Remanded.

MAYNARD, CHIEF JUSTICE, concurring, in part, and dissenting, in part.

I concur with the new law created by the majority in this case. That is to say, I agree that evidence of longstanding ownership along with sentimental or emotional attachment to property are factors that should be considered and, in some instances, control the decision of whether to partition in kind or sale jointly-owned property which is the subject of a partition proceeding.

I dissent in this case, however, because I do not believe that evidence to support the application of those factors was presented here. In that regard, the record shows that none of the appellants have resided at the subject property for years. At most, the property has been used for weekend retreats. While this may have been the family "homeplace," a majority of the family has already sold their interests in the property to the appellee. Only a minority of the family members, the appellants, have refused to do so. I believe that the sporadic use of the property by the appellants in this case does not outweigh the economic inconvenience that the appellee will suffer as a result of this property being partitioned in kind.

I am also troubled by the majority's decision that this property should be partitioned in kind instead of being sold because I don't believe that such would have been the case were this property going to be put to some use other than coal mining. For instance, I think the majority's decision would have been different if this property was going to be used in the construction of a four-lane highway. Under those circumstances, I believe the majority would have concluded that such economic activity takes precedence over any long-term use or sentimental attachment to the property on the part of the appellants. In my opinion, coal mining is an equally important economic activity. This decision destroys the value of this land as coal mining property because the appellee would incur several million dollars in additional costs to continue its mining operations. As a result of the majority's decision in this case, many innocent coal miners will be out of work. . . .

Points for Discussion

a. Sentimental Attachments

Should emotion trump economics? Our property law system is founded on the utilitarian belief that society is generally better off if land is devoted to its highest and best economic use. Why should the sentimental attachments of a few cotenants defeat the financial interests of the majority cotenant? Is the personhood perspective (Chapter 1) helpful here? In *Chuck v. Gomes*, 532 P.2d 657, 662 (Hawaii 1975), a dissenting justice of the Hawaii Supreme Court observed:

> [T]here are interests other than financial expediency which I recognize as essential to our Hawaiian way of life. Foremost is the individual's right to retain ancestral land in order to perpetuate the concept of the family homestead. Such right is derived from our proud cultural heritage. . . . [W]e must not lose sight of the cultural traditions which attach fundamental importance to keeping ancestral land in a particular family line.

The Supreme Court of Nebraska took a different approach in *FTR Farms, Inc. v. Rist Farm, Inc.*, 942 N.W.2d 204, 211 (Neb. 2020), noting that the "generally accepted test of whether a partition in kind would result in great prejudice to the owners is whether the value of the share of each in case of a partition would be materially less than the share of the money equivalent that could probably be obtained for the whole." Which approach is better?

b. Balancing the Interests

In his dissent, Chief Justice Maynard reasoned that the level of sentimental attachment was relatively low: most family members had sold their interests, and the appellants only made sporadic visits to the property. In contrast, Ark Land needed the land to continue its socially valuable coal mining operation, which provided jobs for many miners. In deciding whether to order partition by sale, should a judge balance emotional attachments against social utility? How?

c. Efficient Partition

As *Ark Land* reflects, partition in kind is preferred—at least in theory. In practice, partition by sale is used more commonly. Which type is more efficient? Partition in kind tends to fragment property rights, which may lead to the underutilization of land. As Professor Michael Heller notes:

> ... The danger with fragmentation is that it may operate as a one-way ratchet: Because of high transaction costs, strategic behaviors, and cognitive biases, people may find it easier to divide property than to recombine it. If too many people gain rights to use or exclude, then bargaining among owners may break down. With too many owners of property fragments, resources become prone to waste either through overuse in a commons or through underuse in an anticommons.

Michael A. Heller, *The Boundaries of Private Property*, 108 Yale L.J. 1163, 1165–66 (1999). *See also* Thomas W. Mitchell, *Reforming Property Law to Address Devastating Land Loss*, 66 Ala. L. Rev. 1 (2014).

d. Agreements Not to Partition

Suppose that joint tenants A and B agree not to partition their property, but A later seeks partition. Will the court enforce the agreement? Traditionally, such an agreement was viewed as an invalid restraint on alienation. (Recall the discussion of restraints on alienation in Chapter 5 after *White v. Brown*.) Today most jurisdictions allow an agreement against partition if it is reasonable in duration and purpose. *See Pew v. Sayler*, 123 A.3d 522 (Me. 2015).

e. Partition Abuse

Various scholars have explored how forced partition sales can unfairly disadvantage poor and minority communities. For example, Professor Thomas Mitchell highlights case studies that suggest that "black-owned property was sold for prices well below the forced sale prices that white property owners can expect to receive when their properties are sold at forced partition sales." Thomas W. Mitchell et al., *Forced Sale Risk: Class, Race, and The "Double Discount,"* 37 Fla. St. U. L. Rev. 589, 657 (2010). Such unfairness has been a major contributor to land loss for Black Americans. *See* Faith Rivers, *Inequity in Equity: The Tragedy of Tenancy in Common for Heirs' Property Owners Facing Partition in Equity*, 17 Temp. Pol. & Civ. Rts. L. Rev. 1 (2007).

In response to such concerns, many states adopted the Uniform Partition of Heirs Property Act to govern the partition of inherited tenancy-in-common property. Among other things, this act:

- allows any cotenant to purchase the interest of a cotenant who seeks partition by sale;
- requires partition in kind unless this would result in prejudice to the cotenants as a group;
- provides that in assessing prejudice the court must consider sentimental attachment to the property; and
- mandates an open market sale, rather than the customary auction, when partition by sale is used.

f. Aftermath of *Ark Land*

After the decision, Leon Miller, a member of the Caudill family, told a reporter: "I'm on cloud nine. This is going to change the law from now on as far as people taking your property. I think it's about time that somebody stood up to these people." *Court Blocks Sale of Lincoln Family's Land*, Charleston Gazette, May 8, 2004. The Caudills' attorney put it this way: "The decision says that family lands are worthy of protection, and economic interests in land aren't the only kinds of interests our law recognizes. As every West Virginian knows, there are some things that money can't buy." *Id.* By 2011, the Caudill family home was the last house left in the area. A few of the Caudill heirs still visit the property every weekend, and the family holds reunions there every summer as it has for the past 100 years.

---

4. Cotenant Rights and Duties

Suppose that A and B are tenants in common in Greenacre. If B occupies the parcel, must she pay A for her use? If B charges a stranger $5,000 to use Greenacre, must B account to A for $2,500 of this rent? Or if B makes repairs, can she force A to share the cost? If A and B have an agreement on these matters, the answers are easy: the terms of the agreement govern their rights and duties.

It is more likely that A and B have no agreement, like most cotenants. All jurisdictions have developed default rules that establish the rights and duties of cotenants in this situation. In our next case, we examine the New Jersey approach to the issue.

Esteves v. Esteves

Superior Court of New Jersey, Appellate Division

775 A.2d 163 (2001)

LESEMANN, J.A.D.

This appeal deals with the proper division of the proceeds from the sale of a one-family house held by a tenancy in common, with plaintiffs, the parents of defendant owning one-half of the house and defendant owning the other half.

The trial court held that plaintiffs, who had occupied the house by themselves for approximately eighteen years before it was sold, and had paid all of the expenses relating to the house during that period, were entitled to reimbursement from defendant for one-half of the sums they had paid, without any offset for the value of their occupancy. The net effect of that ruling amounted to a determination that plaintiffs were permitted to occupy the premises "rent free" for approximately eighteen years, while they paid one-half of the costs attributable to the house and defendant paid the other half. The trial court found that such a result was compelled by applicable law. We disagree, and conclude that when plaintiffs sought reimbursement from defendant for one-half of the costs of occupying and maintaining the premises, plaintiffs were required to allow defendant credit for the reasonable value of their occupancy of the house. Accordingly we reverse.

Esteves house
Click here for larger photo

The case involves an unhappy family schism. . . . In December 1980, plaintiffs Manuel and Flora Esteves, together with their son Joao Esteves, bought a house. They took title as tenants in common, with Manuel and Flora owning a one-half interest and Joao owning the other one-half. The purchase price was $34,500. Manuel and Flora paid $10,000 in cash as did Joao, and the parties took a mortgage loan for the remaining $14,500. They then moved into the house, and Joao undertook a considerable amount of work involving repairs and improvements while he lived there with his parents for somewhere between three months and eighteen months after closing. Joao then moved out and for approximately the next eighteen years, until the house was sold on February 26, 1998, Manuel and Flora lived there by themselves. . . .

Sale of the house produced net proceeds of $114,453.18. With the parties unable to agree on distribution of the proceeds, they agreed to each take $10,000 and deposit the remaining $94,453.18 in escrow. They then proceeded to trial. . . .

The court found that Manuel and Flora had paid out $17,336 in mortgage payments, including principal and interest; $14,353 for capital expenses; $21,599 for real estate taxes; $3,971 for sewer charges; and $4,633 for homeowners insurance. Those amounts totaled $61,892, and the court found that Joao was obligated to reimburse his parents for one-half that amount. However, the court also found that Joao had supplied labor with a value of $2,000 more than any labor expended by Manuel and Flora, and thus Joao was entitled to a credit for that amount. On the critical issue of credit for the value of plaintiffs' occupancy of the house, the court said this:

> I conclude there being no ouster of the defendant by the plaintiffs that there is no entitlement to the equivalent rent or rental value of the premises. . . . The defendant could have continued to live there if he wanted to; he chose not to. . . . [T]here being no ouster, he's not entitled to anything for the rental value or what the rental could have been to the plaintiffs.

Over the years, there have been varying statements by our courts as to the rights and obligations of tenants in common respecting payment for maintenance of the parties' property and their rights and obligations respecting occupancy thereof. . . . While those decisions may not always have been consistent, in *Baird v. Moore*, 50 N.J. Super. 156, 141 A.2d 324 (App. Div. 1958), this court, in a comprehensive, scholarly opinion by Judge Conford set out what we conceive to be the most appropriate, fair and practical rules to resolve such disputes. . . .

First, as a general proposition, on a sale of commonly owned property, an owner who has paid less than his pro-rata share of operating and maintenance expenses of the property, must account to co-owner who has contributed more than his pro-rata share, and that is true even if the former had been out of possession and the latter in possession of the property.

Second, the fact that one tenant in common occupies the property and the other does not, imposes no obligation on the former to make any contribution to the latter. All tenants in common have a right to occupy all of the property and if one chooses not to do so, that does not give him the right to impose an "occupancy" charge on the other.

Third, notwithstanding those general rules, when on a final accounting following sale, the tenant who had been in sole possession of the property demands contribution toward operating and maintenance expenses from his co-owner, fairness and equity dictate that the one seeking that contribution allow a corresponding credit for the value of his sole occupancy of the premises. To reject such a credit and nonetheless require a contribution to operating and maintenance expenses from someone who (like the defendant here) had enjoyed none of the benefits of occupancy would be patently unfair. . . .

We believe the principles of *Baird* are sound and should be applied here. They support the trial court's conclusions as to defendant's obligation to contribute one-half of the $61,892 expended by his parents respecting the house they all owned. However, against that obligation, the court should offset a credit for the reasonable value of the occupancy enjoyed by the parents over the approximately eighteen years while they, and not their son, occupied the property. The obligation to present evidence of that value, which would normally be represented by rental value of the property, rests on the defendant. Although no such proof was presented at the prior trial, the uncertainty of the law in this area satisfies us that it would be unreasonable to deprive the defendant of the opportunity to do so now. Accordingly, the matter is reversed and remanded to the trial court for further proceedings at which the defendant shall have an opportunity to present evidence related to the value of the plaintiffs' sole occupancy of the property. . . .

Points for Discussion

a. **Right to Occupancy**

Esteves states the prevailing rule: a cotenant *in* possession does not owe any rent to a cotenant *out of* possession, absent an ouster. What is the basis for this rule? Is it a reasonable default position? A few courts take the opposing view. *See e.g., Lerman v. Levine,* 541 A.2d 523 (Conn. App. Ct. 1988). What is the rationale for that approach? For a provocative article on the rental liability of co-owners, see Evelyn Alicia Lewis, *Struggling with Quicksand: The Ins and Outs of Cotenant Possession Value Liability and a Call for Default Rule Reform,* 1994 Wis. L. Rev. 331.

b. **Ouster**

Suppose A occupies Greenacre and prevents her cotenant B from using it. Is A liable? An *ouster* occurs when a cotenant in possession refuses to allow another cotenant to occupy the property. *See Spiller v. Mackereth,* 334 So. 2d 859 (Ala. 1976). Because A ousted B, A is liable to B for B's pro rata share of the rental value of A's occupancy. For example, if the fair rental value of Greenacre is $1,000 per month and both cotenants have equal shares, then A is liable to B for $500 per month. Note that following B's ouster, A is effectively an adverse possessor. B must assert his interest within the statutory period or risk losing it entirely.

c. **Sharing Rents and Profits**

Each cotenant is entitled to his proportionate share of all rents and profits derived from the land. For example, if A rents the cotenancy property to C, she must share those payments with her cotenants on a pro rata basis. Similarly, if A cuts timber or mines coal on the property, the other cotenants share in her net profits. Thus, in *White v. Smyth*, 214 S.W.2d 967 (Tex. 1948), when a cotenant holding a 1/9 interest sold a portion of the rock asphalt on the property, he was required to compensate his cotenants for 8/9 of his net profits. Replying to the claim that he removed less than 1/9 of the rock asphalt and therefore took less than his share, the court reasoned "that a cotenant cannot select and take for himself part of the property jointly owned and thus make a partition." *Id.* at 976. Do you agree with the court?

> **FYI**
>
> An *accounting* is an *equitable* action in which a cotenant seeks to obtain his share of the rents or profits generated by the property. In a *contribution action*, a cotenant seeks reimbursement from her cotenants for expenses she has paid for the operation or maintenance of the property.

d. **Sharing Costs**

In *Esteves,* Manuel and Flora contended that Joao should contribute his one-half share of the operating and maintenance expenses for the home—mortgage payments, capital expenses, real estate taxes, sewer charges, and homeowners insurance. This reflects the general rule that each cotenant must pay his proportionate share of such expenses. If a cotenant fails to pay his share, the other cotenants may seek reimbursement for these expenses in a contribution action. But in most states, there is an exception to the general rule: a cotenant in sole possession of the property cannot recover operating and maintenance payments in a contribution action *unless* these exceed its fair rental value. The *Esteves* court used a similar approach in an accounting action. Does this exception make sense?

What if Manuel and Flora had constructed a pool in the backyard or repaired a leaky roof? Could they obtain reimbursement for these expenses in a contribution action against Joao? The majority rule is "no." Why not? However, a cotenant who pays for needed repairs will receive a credit for these costs in an accounting action or a partition action. And a cotenant who improves the property receives a credit equal to the increased market value produced by the improvement in an accounting action or a partition action.

B. Marital Property

H is an elementary school teacher with few assets. W, an attorney, owns $500,000 in stocks and bonds. Suppose they marry. W later becomes a partner in her law firm; and H leaves teaching to work full-time in the home, caring for their child D. They use W's earnings to buy a large house, two expensive cars, and a collection of modern art. What rights do H and W have in these assets during their marriage? What if they divorce? Or one of them dies?

The answers to these questions turn on the marital property system adopted in their state. The traditional common law approach to marital property is virtually extinct in the United States. Today most jurisdictions use the *separate property* system, while nine states use the *community property* system. We examine both systems below.

1. Common Law Foundation

The historic common law approach reflected profound gender bias. Upon marriage, a woman lost the ability to own, manage, and dispose of her property—except for her clothing and jewelry. The law gave the husband an estate *jure uxoris* in all of the wife's lands. He could use, mortgage, or sell his wife's property; it could also be reached by his creditors. A married woman could not even enter into contracts or execute other legal documents. As Blackstone explained, "[b]y marriage, the husband and wife are one person in law: that is, the very being or legal existence of the woman is suspended during the marriage, or at least incorporated or consolidated into that of the husband: under whose wing, protection, and *cover*, she performs every thing. . . ." William Blackstone, 1 Commentaries on the Laws of England 430 (1766). Accordingly, the husband controlled all the family property. In return, the wife was entitled to her husband's protection and support.

> **It's Latin to Me**
>
> *Jure uxoris* means "by right of the wife." Upon marriage, the wife's status changed from a *feme sole* (a single woman who had the right to own property) to a *feme covert* (a "covered" woman who had no legal rights distinct from those of her husband).

What if the husband died first? In this situation, the common law gave the widow *dower*: a life estate in 1/3 of all the freehold land that was (a) owned by her husband and (b) inheritable by his issue. The wife's dower rights could not be cancelled during the marriage; they remained "attached" to property, even if it was conveyed to a third party, unless she voluntarily released them. Suppose

> **FYI**
>
> Similar to dower, *curtesy* was the right of the *husband* to a life estate in all freehold land that was owned by his wife and that was inheritable by their issue. Curtesy arose only at the birth of a child, not at the time of marriage.

H owned Redacre and Blueacre in fee simple during the marriage; W's dower rights apply to both properties, even though H acquired Redacre before the marriage and sold Blueacre to X during the marriage. What if H received a joint tenancy interest in Orangeacre? W's dower rights would not attach to this interest. Do you understand why?

Over time, the importance of dower declined. Family wealth was increasingly held in cash, stocks, or other forms of personal property to which dower did not apply. Today, most states have other mechanisms for protecting the widow and dower has virtually disappeared. In the few states that still recognize dower, it generally applies to both spouses. *See generally* Ralph C. Brashier, *Disinheritance and the Modern Family*, 45 Case W. Res. L. Rev. 83 (1994).

> **FYI**
>
> Arkansas, Kentucky, and Ohio still recognize dower. Michigan abolished dower rights in 2017.

Legislative reforms in the 1800s granted more property rights to married women. Most states passed *Married Women's Property Acts*, which provided a wife with the same rights as a single woman to own, manage, and dispose of her property. These acts also protected a wife's property from the claims of her husband's creditors. *See* Richard H. Chused, *Married Women's Property Law: 1800–1850*, 71 Geo. L.J. 1359 (1983); Bernie D. Jones, *Revisiting the Married Women's Property Acts: Recapturing Protection in the Face of Equality*, 22 Am. U. J. Gender Soc. Pol'y & L. 91 (2013). In theory, both spouses now had equal property rights. The husband had complete control over his property, and the wife had complete control over her property. But the husband's wages—and assets purchased from them—were considered to be his property. In an era when a wife rarely worked outside of the home, this approach effectively vested control of the family property in the husband.

---

2. Separate Property System

The marital property rights arising under the modern *separate property* system may be divided into three categories: rights during the marriage, at divorce, and at death.

During the marriage. The basic rule is that property is separately owned by the spouse who acquires it. For example, in our hypothetical above, W owned $500,000 in stocks and bonds before she married H; she continues to own this property after the marriage. Similarly, W owns her earnings during the marriage and all property purchased from those earnings; thus, the house, cars, and art collection all belong to W. H presumably owns little or nothing. Under this system, the creditors of a particular spouse can only attach the separate property of that spouse. Thus, H's creditors cannot attach W's property. Of course, a wife and husband could agree to hold property in a concurrent tenancy; or one spouse might make a gift of property to the other.

Divorce. At divorce, most separate property states mandate *equitable distribution* of the property owned by each spouse. This requires a court to divide the property in a just and fair manner, considering factors such as the spouses' incomes, their standard of living, their contributions during marriage, their age and health, any special needs, and the length of the marriage. *See, e.g., Hammond v. Hammond*, 327 So. 3d 173 (Miss. Ct. App. 2021) (trial court erred in failing to consider husband's adultery as a factor in equitable distribution). The "property" subject to equitable distribution is usually defined as any property acquired with the earnings of either spouse during the marriage, although a few states also include property acquired before the marriage. Some states presume that equal distribution is appropriate, absent special concerns. But as a general matter, the trial judge has broad discretion to decide how the property should be divided. Suppose that H and W now divorce. In most jurisdictions, the property subject to distribution consists of the house, cars, and art collection—all acquired with W's earning during the marriage and now worth $2,000,000. The stock and bond portfolio that W owned before the marriage remains her separate property.

Death. At death, most states offer the surviving spouse a *forced share* (or *elective share*) of the decedent's estate. This means that the survivor has a choice: (a) take under the decedent's will or (b) receive a defined portion of the decedent's estate, usually a 1/3 or 1/2 share. Suppose that W dies, devising all of her property to her daughter, D. In this situation, H can claim his forced share of W's property. For example, if W's assets are valued at $3,000,000, H will receive $1,000,000 in many jurisdictions. Can a dying spouse intentionally avoid the forced share by giving her property away *before* she dies? In many states, the forced share applies to gifts made for this purpose. *See* Martin D. Begleiter, *Grim Fairy Tales: Studies of Wicked Stepmothers, Poisoned Apples, and the Elective Share*, 78 Alb. L. Rev. 521 (2014–2015).

---

3. Community Property System

The *community property* system is used today in nine states: Arizona, California, Idaho, Louisiana, Nevada, New Mexico, Texas, Washington, and Wisconsin.

During the marriage. All earnings during the marriage—and all assets acquired from those earnings—are owned by both spouses equally. Growing out of the French and Spanish civil law traditions, this system is based on the concept that the husband and wife contribute equally to the marriage. Marriage is seen as a partnership: the spouse who works inside the home contributes as much as the spouse who works outside the home. Now assume W earns $300,000 each year as an attorney, while H works only inside the home. W's earnings are community property, owned by both

H and W. Suppose W uses her earnings to purchase a vacation cabin, taking title in her name only. The vacation cabin is community property, owned by both spouses. Each spouse holds an equal, undivided share in the community property, although neither can transfer that share to a third party. Unlike a joint tenancy or tenancy by the entirety, neither spouse has a right of survivorship. Property acquired before marriage or after marriage by gift or inheritance remains the separate property of the individual spouse.

> **FYI**
>
> We might arguably add Alaska, Florida, Kentucky, South Dakota, and Tennessee to the list of community property states. They give married couples the *option* of holding their assets as community property, most commonly through a trust.

Divorce. At divorce, all community property is divided between the spouses. In some states, each receives an equal share; in others, the assets are allocated using equitable distribution factors. So suppose that H and W divorce. If they own $3,000,000 in community property, each will receive $1,500,000 in many states. W retains the stock and bond portfolio she acquired before the marriage as her separate property.

Death. At death, the decedent may devise her half of the community property and all her separate property as she desires. The other half of the community property belongs to the surviving spouse. Accordingly, community property states do not provide a forced share to the survivor. Suppose that H and W own $3,000,000 in community property assets when H dies. H may devise his $1,500,000 share, together with any separate property, as he wishes. But suppose H and W retire to a community property state after living for 30 years in a separate property state; what happens when W dies?

---

4. Tenancy by the Entirety

At common law, every conveyance to a married couple was presumed to create a tenancy by the entirety. Today, only half of the states recognize this cotenancy. In states where it is still permitted, the tenancy by the entirety may offer significant protection from creditors.

Suppose that H negligently injures two pedestrians while driving his car. The pedestrians bring a personal injury action. H's only asset is the family home, which he and his wife hold as tenants by the entirety. Shortly before judgment is entered, H and his wife convey the home to their sons as a gift. Is this a *fraudulent conveyance*—one made for the purpose of avoiding a judgment—which the judgment creditors can set aside?

Sawada v. Endo

Supreme Court of Hawai'i

561 P.2d 1291 (1977)

MENOR, JUSTICE.

This is a civil action brought by the plaintiffs-appellants, Masako Sawada and Helen Sawada, in aid of execution of money judgments in their favor, seeking to set aside a conveyance of real property from judgment debtor Kokichi Endo to Samuel H. Endo and Toru Endo, defendants-appellees herein, on the ground that the conveyance as to the Sawadas was fraudulent.

On November 30, 1968, the Sawadas were injured when struck by a motor vehicle operated by Kokichi Endo. On June 17, 1969, Helen Sawada filed her complaint for damages against Kokichi Endo. Masako Sawada filed her suit against him on August 13, 1969. The complaint and summons in each case was served on Kokichi Endo on October 29, 1969.

On the date of the accident, Kokichi Endo was the owner, as a tenant by the entirety with his wife, Ume Endo, of a parcel of real property situate at Wahiawa, Oahu, Hawaii. By deed, dated July 26, 1969, Kokichi Endo and his wife conveyed the property to their sons, Samuel H. Endo and Toru Endo. This document was recorded in the Bureau of Conveyances on December 17, 1969. No consideration was paid by the grantees for the conveyance. Both were aware at the time of the conveyance that their father had been involved in an accident, and that he carried no liability insurance. Kokichi Endo and Ume Endo, while reserving no life interests therein, continued to reside on the premises.

> **FYI**
>
> A short time later, the Endos transferred all the funds in their bank accounts to their sons and another person. Patricia A. Cain, *Two Sisters vs. A Father and Two Sons: The Story of* Sawada v. Endo, in Property Stories (Gerald Korngold & Andrew P. Morriss eds., 2d ed. 2009).

On January 19, 1971, after a consolidated trial on the merits, judgment was entered in favor of Helen Sawada and against Kokichi Endo in the sum of $8,846.46. At the same time, Masako Sawada was awarded judgment on her complaint in the amount of $16,199.28. Ume Endo, wife of Kokichi Endo, died on January 29, 1971. She was survived by her husband, Kokichi. Subsequently, after being frustrated in their attempts to obtain satisfaction of judgment from the personal property of Kokichi Endo, the Sawadas brought suit to set aside the conveyance which is the subject matter of this controversy. The trial court refused to set aside the conveyance, and the Sawadas appeal.

The determinative question in this case is, whether the interest of one spouse in real property, held in tenancy by the entireties, is subject to levy and execution by his or her individual creditors. This issue is one of first impression in this jurisdiction.

A brief review of the present state of the tenancy by the entirety might be helpful. Dean Phipps, writing in 1951, pointed out that only nineteen states and the District of Columbia continued to recognize it as a valid and subsisting institution in the field of property law. Phipps, *Tenancy by Entireties,* 25 Temple L.Q. 24 (1951). Phipps divided these jurisdictions into four groups. He made no mention of Alaska and Hawaii, both of which were then territories of the United States.

> **Food for Thought**
>
> In community property states, the tenancy by the entirety is not available. Why not?

In the Group I states (Massachusetts, Michigan, and North Carolina) the estate is essentially the common law tenancy by the entireties, unaffected by the Married Women's Property Acts. As at common law, the possession and profits of the estate are subject to the husband's exclusive dominion and control. . . . In all three states, as at common law, the husband may convey the entire estate subject only to the possibility that the wife may become entitled to the whole estate upon surviving him. . . . As at common law, the obverse as to the wife does not hold true. Only in Massachusetts, however, is the estate in its entirety subject to levy by the husband's creditors. . . . In both Michigan and North Carolina, the use and income from the estate is not subject to levy during the marriage for the separate debts of either spouse. . . .

> **FYI**
>
> In 1925, the Law of Property Act abolished the tenancy by the entirety in England, where the estate originated. This converted all tenancies by the entirety into joint tenancies. An interesting history of this cotenancy is provided in John V. Orth's *Tenancy by the Entirety: The Strange Career of the Common-Law Marital Estate,* 1997 BYU L. Rev. 35.

In the Group II states (Alaska, Arkansas, New Jersey, New York, and Oregon) the interest of the debtor spouse in the estate may be sold or levied upon for his or her separate debts, subject to the other spouse's contingent right of survivorship. . . . Alaska, which has been added to this group, has provided by statute that the interest of a debtor spouse in any type of estate, except a homestead as defined and held in tenancy by the entirety, shall be subject to his or her separate debts. . . .

In the Group III jurisdictions (Delaware, District of Columbia, Florida, Indiana, Maryland, Missouri, Pennsylvania, Rhode Island, Vermont, Virginia, and Wyoming) an attempted conveyance by either spouse is wholly void, and the estate may not be subjected to the separate debts of one spouse only. . . .

In Group IV, the two states of Kentucky and Tennessee hold that the contingent right of survivorship appertaining to either spouse is separately alienable by him and attachable by his creditors during the marriage.... The use and profits, however, may neither be alienated nor attached during coverture.

It appears, therefore, that Hawaii is the only jurisdiction still to be heard from on the question. Today we join that group of states and the District of Columbia which hold that under the Married Women's Property Acts the interest of a husband or a wife in an estate by the entireties is not subject to the claims of his or her individual creditors during the joint lives of the spouses. In so doing, we are placing our stamp of approval upon what is apparently the prevailing view of the lower courts of this jurisdiction.

Hawaii has long recognized and continues to recognize the tenancy in common, the joint tenancy, and the tenancy by the entirety, as separate and distinct estates. *See Paahana v. Bila*, 3 Haw. 725 (1876). That the Married Women's Property Act of 1888 was not intended to abolish the tenancy by the entirety was made clear by the language of Act 19 of the Session Laws of Hawaii, 1903 (now HRS § 509-1).... The tenancy by the entirety is predicated upon the legal unity of husband and wife, and the estate is held by them in single ownership. They do not take by moieties, but both and each are seized of the whole estate....

A joint tenant has a specific, albeit undivided, interest in the property, and if he survives his cotenant he becomes the owner of a larger interest than he had prior to the death of the other joint tenant. But tenants by the entirety are each deemed to be seized of the entirety from the time of the creation of the estate. At common law, this taking of the "whole estate" did not have the real significance that it does today, insofar as the rights of the wife in the property were concerned. For all practical purposes, the wife had no right during coverture to the use and enjoyment and exercise of ownership in the marital estate. All she possessed was her contingent right of survivorship.

The effect of the Married Women's Property Acts was to abrogate the husband's common law dominance over the marital estate and to place the wife on a level of equality with him as regards the exercise of ownership over the whole estate. The

> **FYI**
>
> Before 1820, when missionaries arrived in Hawaii, social rank was more important than gender in determining a person's rights. Married and unmarried *alii* (high-ranking) women could freely inherit and sell land, and own personal property that they did not have to share with their husbands. These rights disappeared as Christianity was introduced to the islands. While Hawaii's Married Women's Property Act of 1888 was a step toward aligning the rights of Hawaiian women with those of women in the United States, it was still more restrictive than the prior custom. *See* Judith R. Gething, *Christianity and Coverture: Impact on the Legal Status of Women in Hawaii, 1820-1920*, 11 Haw. J. Hist. 188 (1977).

tenancy was and still is predicated upon the legal unity of husband and wife, but the Acts converted it into a unity of equals and not of unequals as at common law. . . . No longer could the husband convey, lease, mortgage or otherwise encumber the property without her consent. The Acts confirmed her right to the use and enjoyment of the whole estate, and all the privileges that ownership of property confers, including the right to convey the property in its entirety, jointly with her husband, during the marriage relation. . . . They also had the effect of insulating the wife's interest in the estate from the separate debts of her husband. . . .

Neither husband nor wife has a separate divisible interest in the property held by the entirety that can be conveyed or reached by execution. *Fairclaw v. Forrest*, 76 U.S. App. D.C. 197, 130 F.2d 829 (1942). A joint tenancy may be destroyed by voluntary alienation, or by levy and execution, or by compulsory partition, but a tenancy by the entirety may not. The indivisibility of the estate, except by joint action of the spouses, is an indispensable feature of the tenancy by the entirety. . . .

We are not persuaded by the argument that it would be unfair to the creditors of either spouse to hold that the estate by the entirety may not, without the consent of both spouses, be levied upon for the separate debts of either spouse. No unfairness to the creditor is involved here. We agree with the court in *Hurd v. Hughes*, 12 Del. Ch. 188, 109 A. 418 (1920):

> But creditors are not entitled to special consideration. If the debt arose prior to the creation of the estate, the property was not a basis of credit, and if the debt arose subsequently the creditor presumably had notice of the characteristics of the estate which limited his right to reach the property. 109 A. at 420.

We might also add that there is obviously nothing to prevent the creditor from insisting upon the subjection of property held in tenancy by the entirety as a condition precedent to the extension of credit. Further, the creation of a tenancy by the entirety may not be used as a device to defraud existing creditors. *In re Estate of Wall*, 142 U.S. App. D.C. 187, 440 F.2d 215 (1971).

Were we to view the matter strictly from the standpoint of public policy, we would still be constrained to hold as we have done here today. In *Fairclaw v. Forrest, supra*, the court makes this observation:

> The interest in family solidarity retains some influence upon the institution [of tenancy by the entirety]. It is available only to husband and wife. It is a convenient mode of protecting a surviving spouse from inconvenient administration of the decedent's estate and from the other's improvident debts. It is in that protection the estate finds its peculiar and justifiable function. 130 F.2d at 833.

It is a matter of common knowledge that the demand for single-family residential lots has increased rapidly in recent years, and the magnitude of the problem is emphasized by the concentration of the bulk of fee simple land in the hands of a few. The shortage of single-family residential fee simple property is critical and government has seen fit to attempt to alleviate the problem through legislation. When a family can afford to own real property, it becomes their single most important asset. Encumbered as it usually is by a first mortgage, the fact remains that so long as it remains whole during the joint lives of the spouses, it is always available in its entirety for the benefit and use of the entire family. Loans for education and other emergency expenses, for example, may be obtained on the security of the marital estate. This would not be possible where a third party has become a tenant in common or a joint tenant with one of the spouses, or where the ownership of the contingent right of survivorship of one of the spouses in a third party has cast a cloud upon the title of the marital estate, making it virtually impossible to utilize the estate for these purposes.

> **Food for Thought**
>
> Does the policy argument in favor of protecting family property make sense on the facts of this case? By the time of this decision, Kokichi Endo (the negligent driver) had been a widower for six years. And does the nature of the property matter? Suppose the Endos' property was a beachfront estate worth $10 million.

If we were to select between a public policy favoring the creditors of one of the spouses and one favoring the interests of the family unit, we would not hesitate to choose the latter. But we need not make this choice for, as we pointed out earlier, by the very nature of the estate by the entirety as we view it, and as other courts of our sister jurisdictions have viewed it, "[a] unilaterally indestructible right of survivorship, an inability of one spouse to alienate his interest, and, importantly for this case, a broad immunity from claims of separate creditors remain among its vital incidents." *In re Estate of Wall, supra*, 440 F.2d at 218.

Having determined that an estate by the entirety is not subject to the claims of the creditors of one of the spouses during their joint lives, we now hold that the conveyance of the marital property by Kokichi Endo and Ume Endo, husband and wife, to their sons, Samuel H. Endo and Toru Endo, was not in fraud of Kokichi Endo's judgment creditors. . . .

Affirmed.

KIDWELL, JUSTICE, dissenting.

. . . The majority reaches its conclusion by holding that the effect of the Married Women's Act was to equalize the positions of the spouses by taking from the husband his common law right to transfer his interest, rather than by elevating the wife's right of alienation of her interest to place it on a position of equality with the husband's. I disagree. I believe that a better interpretation of the Married Women's Acts is that offered by the Supreme Court of New Jersey in *King v. Greene*, 30 N.J. 395, 412, 153 A.2d 49, 60 (1959):

> It is clear that the Married Women's Act created an equality between the spouses in New Jersey, insofar as tenancies by the entirety are concerned. If, as we have previously

concluded, the husband could alienate his right of survivorship at common law, the wife, by virtue of the act, can alienate her right of survivorship. And it follows, that if the wife takes equal rights with the husband in the estate, she must take equal disabilities. Such are the dictates of common equality. Thus, the judgment creditors of either spouse may levy and execute upon their separate rights of survivorship.

One may speculate whether the courts which first chose the path to equality now followed by the majority might have felt an unexpressed aversion to entrusting a wife with as much control over her interest as had previously been granted to the husband with respect to his interest. Whatever may be the historical explanation for these decisions, I feel that the resultant restriction upon the freedom of the spouses to deal independently with their respective interests is both illogical and unnecessarily at odds with present policy trends. Accordingly, I would hold that the separate interest of the husband in entireties property, at least to the extent of his right of survivorship, is alienable by him and subject to attachment by his separate creditors, so that a voluntary conveyance of the husband's interest should be set aside where it is fraudulent as to such creditors, under applicable principles of the law of fraudulent conveyances.

Points for Discussion

a. Avoiding Creditors

Shouldn't the guilty Endo be compelled to make the innocent Sawadas whole? Endo's home was a valuable asset that could have been used to satisfy the Sawadas' judgments. Why should the law allow Endo to convey his home for the purpose of defeating these judgments?

b. Three Approaches

Today there is still a split of authority on whether creditors can reach property held in tenancy by the entirety:

- *No rights*: Most states follow the *Sawada* view that creditors cannot reach property held in tenancy by the entirety (Group III approach).

- *Full interest*: Some states allow creditors to attach the full interest of the debtor spouse, but subject to the innocent spouse's interest (Group II approach).

- *Survivorship interest*: In Kentucky and Tennessee, creditors can only attach the survivorship interest of the debtor spouse (Group IV approach).

Which of the three approaches is best? If Hawaii followed New Jersey's view, would the Sawadas have had a remedy? What would the result be in Kentucky? One interesting consequence of these distinctions arises in the fight against drug trafficking operations, where property purchased with proceeds from the illegal sale of drugs may be seized by government agencies. Could a drug kingpin insulate his property from seizure by holding it in tenancy by the entirety? In *United States v. Parcel of Real Property Known as 1500 Lincoln Avenue*, 949 F.2d 73 (3d Cir. 1991), the court held that the federal government could only seize the survivorship interest of the guilty spouse in tenancy by the entirety property. How would a court rule in Hawaii?

c. **Protecting the Family**

The *Sawada* court stressed that public policy favors the interests of the family unit over the interests of creditors. What did the court mean by this? Is there some special relationship between Hawaiians and their lands that justifies the court's ruling? (Recall the Hawaii Supreme Court dissent in *Chuck v. Gomes*, appearing in the notes after *Ark Land*.) Why should married couples have this protection against creditors, when unmarried people do not? Note that if the Endos held title to the home as joint tenants or as tenants in common, it would be subject to creditors' claims.

d. **Voluntary v. Involuntary Creditors**

The Sawadas argued that allowing Endo to escape liability would be unfair to them as creditors. In response, the court pointed out that a creditor normally has the ability to investigate a person's financial status before extending credit. How would the costs of such investigation affect the price of goods and services? Perhaps *voluntary* creditors can protect themselves. But Sawadas were *involuntary* creditors who could not have foreseen the accident. Should tort victims receive more protection than voluntary creditors?

e. **Death and Taxes**

It is said that only two things in life are inevitable: death and taxes. But can a tenancy by the entirety be used to avoid a lien for unpaid federal taxes? In *United States v. Craft*, 535 U.S. 274 (2002), the Supreme Court held that the interest of a spouse in tenancy by entirety property did constitute "property" or a "right to property" within the meaning of the legislation authorizing a federal tax lien. Should the federal government have greater rights than other creditors?

5. Defining Marital Property

Suppose that W works outside the home to support H while he attends law school. H graduates, passes the bar examination, gets a job at a prestigious law firm—and then files for divorce. Should H's law degree be viewed as marital property, which is subject to equitable distribution? Is a professional degree "property" at all?

Guy v. Guy

Supreme Court of Mississippi

736 So. 2d 1042 (1999)

PITTMAN, PRESIDING JUSTICE, for the Court:

STATEMENT OF THE CASE

Robert Sidney Guy, Jr. (hereinafter Rob) and Audra Marian Guy (hereinafter Audra) were married May 14, 1994. They were separated on April 12, 1997. No children were born to the couple. The couple was awarded a divorce on the grounds of irreconcilable differences on November 20, 1997.

In the final judgment of divorce, the chancellor attempted to distribute equitably the couple's marital assets. In doing so, he valued Audra's nursing degree, which she had obtained during the marriage, at $35,000. The chancellor credited that $35,000 value amount to Audra's portion of the marital assets.

The chancellor assigned the value of $35,000 to Audra's nursing degree as a result of Rob testifying that this was the amount he spent on Audra's expenses and support while she pursued and completed her nursing degree during the couple's brief marriage.

Audra filed a Motion to Alter or Amend Judgment, or, alternatively, for Relief from Judgment which the chancellor denied on February 2, 1998. Thereafter, Audra timely perfected this appeal. . . .

DISCUSSION OF THE LAW

. . . The novel question presented in this appeal is whether a professional degree is marital property. This is a question of first impression before this Court. This is a question of law which will be reviewed de novo by this Court. . . .

Although there is no Mississippi case directly on point, the seminal Mississippi case regarding equitable division of marital property is *Ferguson v. Ferguson*, 639 So. 2d 921, 928 (Miss. 1994). . . .While *Ferguson* certainly did not list a professional degree as marital property to be equitably divided, it did list the contribution made by the supporting spouse to the attainment of that degree by the other spouse to be at least considered when equitably dividing the marital assets.

We also look to our sister states whose courts have specifically addressed this issue. As with most legal issues, the jurisdictions are split. Nevertheless, there is a clear majority and minority position as to whether professional degrees are to be considered marital property. Eighteen jurisdictions have held that a spouse's degree was not a marital asset. The minority approach, followed by some courts in three jurisdictions (most notably New York) is that a professional degree is marital property.

> **What About Your State?**
>
> Click here to learn whether your state treats a professional degree as a marital asset.

The reason that most states have determined that professional degrees are not marital property is best articulated by the Colorado Supreme Court in *In re Marriage of Graham*, 194 Colo. 429, 574 P.2d 75 (1978), where that Court stated:

> An educational degree, such as an M.B.A., is simply not encompassed even by the broad views of the concept of "property." It does not have an exchange value or any objective transferable value on an open market. It is personal to the holder. It terminates on death of the holder and is not inheritable. It cannot be assigned, sold, transferred, conveyed, or pledged. An advanced degree is a cumulative product of many years of previous education, combined with diligence and hard work. It may not be acquired by the mere expenditure of money. It is simply an intellectual achievement that may potentially assist in the future acquisition of property. In our view, it has none of the attributes of property in the usual sense of that term. 574 P.2d at 77.

We join the majority of states and hold that professional degrees are not marital property. In the present case, Audra's nursing degree is not marital property. Her nursing license is not a chattel which can be divided or assigned. Rob may not share in it. The nursing degree and license may only be issued to a qualified holder. We do not intend "property" in the sense of "marital property" to include intellectual or technical mental enhancement gained during the course of a marriage. However, the analysis does not end here because

> [T]here is . . . clear agreement that the contributing spouse should be entitled to some form of compensation for the financial efforts and support provided to the student spouse in the expectation that the marital unit would prosper in the future as a direct result of the couple's previous sacrifices.

In re Marriage of Weinstein, 128 Ill.App.3d 324, 470 N.E.2d 551, 557 (1 Dist. 1984).

We recognize the potential inequity of a situation such as the present one, where one spouse works full-time to put the other spouse through school where they obtain a college degree. After obtaining this degree at the expense and sacrifice of the supporting spouse, the supported spouse leaves the supporting spouse with nothing more than the knowledge that they aided their now ex-spouse in increasing his/her future earning capacity. This sentiment is echoed by the New Jersey Supreme Court in *Mahoney v. Mahoney*, 91 N.J. 488, 453 A.2d 527 (1982). There the New Jersey Supreme Court stated:

> . . . [A] supporting spouse has contributed more than mere earnings to her husband with the mutual expectation that both of them—she has well as he—will realize and enjoy material improvements in their marriage as a result of his increased earning capacity. Also, the wife has presumably made personal sacrifices, resulting in a reduced or lowered standard of living. Additionally, her husband, by pursuing preparations for a future career, has foregone gainful employment and financial contributions to the marriage that would have been forthcoming had he been employed. He thereby has further reduced the level of support his wife might otherwise have received, as well as the standard of living both of them would have otherwise enjoyed. In effect, through her contributions, the supporting spouse has consented to live at a lower material level while her husband has prepared for another career. She has postponed, as it were, present consumption and a higher standard of living, for the future prospect of greater support and material benefits. The supporting spouse's sacrifices would have been rewarded had the marriage endured and mutual expectations of both of them been fulfilled. The unredressed sacrifices—loss of support and reduction of the standard of living—coupled with the unfairness attendant upon the defeat of the supporting spouse's shared expectation of future advantages, further justify a remedial reward. In this sense, an award that is referable to the spouse's monetary contribution to her partner's education significantly implicates basic considerations of marital support and standard of living—factors that are clearly relevant in the determination and award of conventional alimony. *Id.* at 533–34. . . .

We return to the words of the Supreme Court of New Jersey on this issue,

> *Marriage should not be a free ticket to professional education* and training without subsequent obligations. . . . One spouse ought not to receive a divorce complaint when the other receives a diploma. Those spouses supported through professional school should recognize that they may be called upon to reimburse the supporting spouses for the financial contributions they received in pursuit of their professional training. And they cannot deny the basic fairness of this result. *Mahoney*, 453 A.2d at 535 (emphasis added & footnotes omitted).

In the present case we adopt the majority approach in recognizing the need for equitable reimbursement of the supporting spouse. Rob may be entitled to lump sum alimony to replace any investment by him in the degree. As this Court has noted, ". . . the chancellor may divide marital assets, real and personal, as well as *award periodic and/or lump sum alimony, as equity demands.*" *Ferguson*, 639 So.2d at 929 (emphasis added.)

The next question is how should chancellors go about doing this? The Supreme Court of Appeals of West Virginia allows reimbursement alimony. In *Hoak v. Hoak*, 179 W.Va. 509, 370 S.E.2d 473, 477–78 (1988), the Supreme Court of Appeals of West Virginia stated,

> As the name indicates, reimbursement alimony is designed to repay or reimburse the supporting spouse for his or her financial contributions to the professional education of the student spouse. Unlike an award based on the value of a professional degree, reimbursement alimony is based on the actual amount of contributions, and does

not require a judge to guess about future earnings, inflation, the relative values of the spouses' contributions, etc. . . .

We therefore conclude that the trial judge in a divorce proceeding may in an appropriate case award reimbursement alimony to a working spouse who contributed financially to the professional education of a student spouse, where the contribution was made with the expectation of achieving a higher standard of living for the family unit, and the couple did not realize that expectation due to divorce.

We adopt a similar approach, allowing the supporting spouse to be reimbursed for putting the student spouse through school where the supported spouse obtained a degree and then leaves the supporting spouse. Audra's argument that the $35,000 consisted of housing, food, and clothing expenses in addition to books and tuition is irrelevant. We recognize that it takes more than books and tuition money to attend school and obtain a higher education. Housing, clothing, and food must also be paid for in order to attend a university.

> **FYI**
>
> *Reimbursement alimony* is unlike other forms of alimony because it is not intended to support a former spouse, but rather to provide restitution. It is generally awarded only after short marriages of young couples, because they have little property to divide and neither spouse has an income large enough to support the other. Some states limit reimbursement alimony to marriages shorter than five years.

Here, the simple facts are that Rob worked while Audra studied. Within a month of Audra's receiving her nursing degree, she left Rob who had paid the majority of the bills for the couple during the entire marriage during which Audra was a student including many of her school fees and expenses. Audra's degree is not marital property and on that point, the chancellor is reversed. However, it would be inequitable for Rob to have paid for Audra's education only to have her leave the marriage. . . .

Rob's proof that he invested $35,000 in Audra's nursing education was insufficient. We require greater proof than was introduced here—Rob's estimate that he spent $35,000 in aiding Audra in obtaining her nursing degree.

CONCLUSION

A professional degree obtained by a student spouse during a marriage is not marital property. Nevertheless, we recognize that the supporting spouse has a right to be compensated or reimbursed, upon proper proof, for his or her financial contributions to the professional education of the student spouse.

For these reasons, we reverse the judgment below in part to the extent that it divided marital property including a $35,000 value to Audra's nursing degree, and we remand this case for (1) a determination, upon appropriate proof, of the amount of lump-sum alimony, if any, which would adequately reimburse Rob for his expenditures towards Audra's attaining her nursing degree and (2) a recalculation of the division of marital property. . . .

WALLER, JUSTICE, dissenting.

Historically we have divided marital assets based on the composition of the estate at the time of separation. We require chancellors to review the makeup of the marital estate and equitably divide the parties' assets based on our decision in *Ferguson v. Ferguson,* 639 So.2d 921 (Miss. 1994), and its progeny.

Today's majority sets a dangerous precedent by allowing reimbursement alimony to be paid to one spouse for contributions by that spouse to the costs of the other spouse's professional degree. Contributions to the educational costs of a spouse should be considered only as part of a *Ferguson* equitable distribution analysis. Today's decision in effect creates a separate category for contributions made by one spouse to the other spouse's education. Today's decision also ignores the fact that *both* parties contributed to the marriage. Just because Rob worked while Audra went to school does not mean Audra made less significant contributions to the marriage. *See Hemsley v. Hemsley,* 639 So.2d 909, 915 (Miss. 1994) ("We assume for divorce purposes that the contributions and efforts of the marital partners, whether economic, domestic or otherwise are of equal value.").

To be sure, Rob is entitled to consideration of his payments toward Audra's education in the context of an equitable distribution of the couple's property. He is not, however, entitled to a dollar-for-dollar reimbursement of those costs as alimony. . . .

Points for Discussion

a. **Defining "Property"**

Why did the *Guy* court hold that a professional degree is not marital property? What policy reasons support this view? Re-examine the excerpt from *In re Marriage of Graham* that the *Guy* court relies on. How would you respond to each item on that list? For example, must something have value to be "property"? What about old love letters? And is transferability required? Many forms of property are not transferable (e.g., certain pensions).

b. **The Problem of Valuation**

One practical problem is how to assign a monetary value to the degree. How would you value Audra's degree for equitable distribution? Is it the present value of her increased earning potential measured by the highest available salary? Audra might decide to work in a neighborhood clinic which pays a low salary; or she might become disabled and unable to work at all. How should factors like this be weighed in the balance? On the other hand, in a wrongful death action the court must determine the present value of the decedent's future earnings. Is valuing a professional degree more difficult?

c. Equitable Distribution

As *Guy* notes, the clear majority rule is that a professional degree is not marital property. However, in many jurisdictions a spouse's contributions to the education of the other spouse will be considered as a factor in the equitable distribution of marital property at divorce. Yet this remedy is meaningless in a situation like *Guy,* where the couple has not accumulated much marital property before the divorce.

d. Reimbursement Alimony

While refusing to characterize a professional degree as marital property, the *Guy* court held that Rob should receive *reimbursement alimony* for the contributions he made to Audra's education. Which contributions should be included? In *Mahoney v. Mahoney,* 453 A.2d 527, 534 (N.J. 1982), the New Jersey Supreme Court stated that reimbursement "should cover *all* financial contributions towards the former spouse's education, including household expenses, educational costs, school travel expenses and any other contributions used by the supported spouse in obtaining his or her degree or license." Do you agree? Should any value be assigned to the emotional support provided to the student spouse?

e. Premarital Agreements

Can an engaged couple avoid the marital property system by contract? The answer is generally "yes." Most states adopted the 1983 Uniform Premarital Agreement Act, which provides that such an agreement is enforceable unless *either*:

- the objecting party did not execute it voluntarily *or*
- the agreement was unconscionable, and the objecting party (a) did not receive "fair and reasonable" financial disclosure from the other party, (b) did not "voluntarily and expressly waive" any right to additional financial disclosure, and (c) could not obtain "adequate knowledge" of the other party's financial condition.

See, e.g., Marriage of Porter, 381 P.3d 873 (Or. Ct. App. 2016) (agreement was invalid because wife did not sign voluntarily). The 2012 Uniform Premarital and Marital Agreements Act, which is intended to supersede the prior act, would make it easier for a complaining spouse to invalidate such an agreement, but only a handful of states have adopted it. As an attorney, would you advise your client to enter into a premarital agreement with his future wife?

f. Aftermath of *Guy*

Suppose W works to put H through medical school, and then stays home to raise their child. When they divorce, W claims that H's medical practice is a marital asset. Shouldn't the result in Mississippi be the same as in *Guy*? In *Mace v. Mace*, 818 So. 2d 1130, 1132 (Miss. 2002), the Mississippi Supreme Court reasoned that these facts posed a different issue: should a spouse be awarded an equitable percentage of the *income-producing enterprise* that the other spouse's professional degree made possible? The court held that although an individual's right to practice medicine is not a property right, the value of the practice as a business is subject to division. Do you agree with this distinction?

6. Unmarried Couples

Today millions of couples live together without marriage. They share their lives, their friends, and their assets. But if their relationship ends, two cohabitants will not receive the same rights as a married couple. For example, neither cohabitant can obtain equitable distribution, and the surviving cohabitant is not entitled to a forced share.

Suppose B and S live together for many years, but never marry. B starts two small businesses and acquires other assets as well, taking title in his own name. S helps to build the businesses, cares for their child, and runs their household. Several times B tells S that the assets belong to both of them. If S leaves B, does she have any property rights?

Gazvoda v. Wright

Court of Appeals of Indiana

2007 WL 2284722

FRIEDLANDER, JUDGE.

Bruce Gazvoda appeals the trial court's judgment ordering him to pay $250,000 to Sabrina Wright, with whom he cohabitated for sixteen years and had a child. The sole issue for our review is whether there is sufficient evidence to support the trial court's order. . . .

Bruce and Sabrina began living together in August 1988. Sabrina had just turned seventeen and was still in high school, and Bruce was twenty-eight and earning $9.00 per hour working at an electric company. At the time, the parties lived in a small rental home and their combined net worth was less than $2,000.00.

One year later, Bruce obtained his electrician's license. Sabrina dropped out of high school when Bruce asked her to accompany him to job sites to learn the electric business so they could start a business of their own in the future. Bruce and Sabrina worked together every day, sometimes for up to twelve hours.

Between 1989 and 1993, Bruce and Sabrina built up an electrical business. Bruce performed the licensed electrical work, and Sabrina wired boxes and stuffed plugs. She also trained electrical helpers, handled the company's billing and payroll, and oversaw job sites when Bruce was not available to do so. During this time, Sabrina neither requested nor received hourly compensation for her work. Also, during this time, she maintained the parties' home and was responsible for the cooking and cleaning.

In September 1993, Sabrina gave birth to the parties' daughter, J. Thereafter, Sabrina ceased most of the work she did for the electrical business and devoted her time to taking care of J. Shortly after J. was born, the parties opened a joint checking account in the name of Bruce and Sabrina Gazvoda. Bruce deposited the business's income into the account, and Sabrina paid the bills.

Two years later, in 1995, Bruce incorporated the electrical services business as Bruce's Electric Services, Inc. The following year, Bruce started a limited liability company, Bruce's Investment Properties, which included several rental properties that Bruce built. Sabrina had significant responsibilities for the rental properties, including managing and maintaining them.

During the course of their relationship, Bruce and Sabrina discussed marriage on several occasions. During these discussions, Bruce told Sabrina that the businesses and assets belonged to both of them and that marriage was just a piece of paper.

> **Make the Connection**
>
> Could Sabrina have successfully argued that Bruce made her an *inter vivos* gift of half of these assets? Consider the material on these gifts in Chapter 3.

In January 2004, Sabrina left Bruce. In March 2004, Bruce filed a Declaratory Action for Determination of Interests in Property. Sabrina responded with a counter-complaint against Bruce and his companies seeking recovery under the theories of implied contract and unjust enrichment. At the time of the action the couple's combined net worth was over one million dollars.

At trial, vocational specialist, Tom Roundtree testified that he had analyzed the services that Sabrina performed over the course of the parties' relationship, applying values to her work at the electrical company, the rental properties, and at home. Roundtree valued Sabrina's services from 1989 to 2003 at $471,628. Sabrina sought recovery of $720,336.19 based on an amortization of Roundtree's figure as well as prejudgment interest.

Following the hearing, the trial court issued an order that provides in part as follows:

> 8. In addition to her contributions to the family, Sabrina's work for [Bruce's Electric and Bruce's Investments] went beyond the traditional family arrangement of one person maintaining a household and raising the parties' child in exchange for the other person providing home and living expenses. Sabrina worked in the field as

an electrician's helper, handled paperwork, served as a receptionist, and provided significant services for the rental properties all without direct compensation and all in lieu of independent work that may have provided her with a separate salary, allowing her to accumulate assets in her own name, and allowing her to contribute toward Social Security. While there was no specific agreement between the parties that Sabrina would receive any type of hourly wage for her services, the court finds there was an expectation that Sabrina would be compensated by benefiting from and sharing in the profits of the businesses.

9. In addition, Bruce's representations to Sabrina that the assets and businesses were "ours," combined with the parties['] actions, create a legitimate expectation that Sabrina would share in the assets titled only in Bruce's name.

10. . . . [T]he court finds that Bruce would be unjustly enriched were he to retain the full value of the assets accumulated through the joint efforts of the parties during the parties' cohabitation.

11. Consequently, the court finds Sabrina is entitled to share in the accumulated assets. . . .

12. However, the court finds that Sabrina is not entitled to one-half of the value of the accumulated assets. The parties' joint efforts, their lifestyle, and Bruce's representations that the assets and businesses were "ours" created an expectation that both parties had access to the assets while they remained together and that both parties had an interest in the assets. However, the efforts and comments were insufficient to create an expectation of an equal division of property upon any separation of the parties. Bruce contributed more to the businesses than Sabrina. The presumption of an equal division of assets that would apply in a dissolution of marriage does not apply here. . . .

13. Considering all of the evidence, the court finds that Sabrina is entitled to an award in the sum of $250,000.00. . . .

Bruce argues that the trial court erred in ordering him to pay Sabrina $250,000.00. Specifically, he contends that he fully compensated her for all her benefits conferred while they were cohabitating and that an award under the theory of unjust enrichment was unwarranted.

A party who cohabitates with another person without subsequent marriage is entitled to relief upon a showing of an express contract or a viable equitable theory such as an implied contract or unjust enrichment. Here, the trial court found that Sabrina had presented evidence to support recovery under a theory of unjust enrichment. In order to prevail on a claim for unjust enrichment, Sabrina needed to show that a measurable benefit had been conferred on Bruce under such circumstances that Bruce's retention of the benefit without payment would be unjust. Principles of equity prohibit unjust enrichment of a party who accepts the unrequested benefits another person provides despite having the opportunity to decline those benefits.

In *Turner*, Danny Turner and Angela Freed lived together for ten years. During that time, Freed took care of their child. In addition, Freed regularly maintained the home and contributed financially by performing one of Turner's daily newspaper delivery routes. While Freed took care of the children and the home, Turner had the time to develop his water softener business. From the income generated through his employment, Turner purchased a home and furnishings. The parties referred to the property acquired during their cohabitation as "ours." When the parties separated, Freed filed a Petition for Palimony. The value of the assets accumulated during the parties' cohabitation, including Turner's interest in his water softener business, was approximately $108,000.00. After a hearing, the trial court ordered Turner to pay Freed $18,000.00 under a theory of unjust enrichment. Turner appealed.

> **Food for Thought**
>
> Should the court have awarded Sabrina an amount equal to half of the couple's assets, based on an express or implied contract theory?

This court agreed with the trial court that Turner substantially benefited from the services that Freed provided and that Turner would be unjustly enriched if Freed were awarded no part of the value of the assets Turner acquired in his name alone during their cohabitation. *Turner v. Freed*, 792 N.E.2d 947 [Ind. Ct. App. 2003]. We therefore found sufficient evidence to support the trial court's finding that Turner had been unjustly enriched.

Here, Bruce and Sabrina lived together for sixteen years. During that time, Sabrina helped Bruce build up his electrical business and managed his rental properties. In addition, Sabrina took care of the parties' daughter and home, allowing Bruce the time to develop his businesses. As in *Turner*, Bruce and Sabrina referred to the property acquired during their cohabitation as "ours."

The value of the assets acquired during the parties' cohabitation was over one million dollars. Following a hearing, the trial court ordered Bruce to pay Sabrina $250,000.00 under a theory of unjust enrichment. We agree with the trial court that Bruce substantially benefited from the services that Sabrina provided and that Bruce would be unjustly enriched if Sabrina were awarded no part of the assets that Bruce acquired in his name during the cohabitation. As we did in *Turner*, we find sufficient evidence to support the trial court's judgment. . . .

Points for Discussion

a. **Cohabiting Couples**

Sabrina and Bruce were a cohabiting couple—they lived together as a family in an intimate relationship without being married. Millions of couples are cohabiting in the United States, usually without much thought about property rights.

States traditionally recognized common law marriage—where a cohabiting couple had the intent to be married and held themselves out as married, but did not obtain a license or have a ceremonial marriage. In the handful of states which still cling to this approach, the parties have the same marital property rights as a conventionally-married couple.

Over time, most states rejected this approach, refusing to recognize any property rights between cohabitants, on the basis that sexual relationships outside of marriage were contrary to public policy. Yet today many states follow the *Gazvoda* approach of recognizing property rights based on an express contract or an equitable theory such as implied contract or unjust enrichment. Oregon and Washington even apply the rules governing property distribution at divorce to cohabitants, by analogy. *See, e.g., Ross v. Hamilton*, 2011 WL 1376767, *7 (Wash. Ct. App.) ("Property acquired during a committed intimate relationship creates a rebuttable presumption that it belongs to both parties."). By contrast, some states still follow the traditional view. *See, e.g., Long v. Marino*, 441 S.E.2d 475, 476 (Ga. Ct. App. 1994) ("Meretricious sexual relationships are by nature repugnant to social stability, and our courts have on sound public policy declined to reward them by allowing a money recovery therefor."). What is the best approach?

b. Origin of Palimony

The term *palimony* was popularized in media reports following the landmark decision of the California Supreme Court in *Marvin v. Marvin*, 557 P.2d 106 (Cal. 1976), a case involving the actor Lee Marvin. *Marvin* held that a cohabitant could have enforceable rights in the property of the other cotenant even without an express contract—an implied contract or a "tacit understanding" might suffice. It reasoned that "[t]he mores of the society have indeed changed so radically in regard to cohabitation that we cannot impose a standard based on alleged moral considerations that have apparently been so widely abandoned by so many." *Id.* at 122. *See* Emily J. Stolzenberg, *Properties of Intimacy*, 80 Md. L. Rev. 627 (2021).

> **FYI**
>
> Lee Marvin won the Academy Award for Best Actor based on his 1965 performance in *Cat Ballou*, the same year that his relationship with Michelle Triola (aka Michelle Marvin) began. Triola originally sued for half of the $3.6 million that Marvin earned during their six years of cohabitation. A trial court eventually awarded her $140,000, but this decision was reversed on appeal; Triola received nothing from the case.

Suppose you are an attorney in a jurisdiction like California that imposes liability for palimony based on an implied contract or tacit understanding. Your wealthy client X is about to start living with her penniless boyfriend Z. X wants to avoid any future palimony claim by Z. What advice would you give her?

c. Which Contributions Matter?

Although the couple's net worth was over $1,000,000, the trial court in *Gazvoda* awarded Sabrina only $250,000. It reasoned that "Bruce contributed more to the businesses than Sabrina," so the parties could not have expected an equal division of the property. The court apparently placed no value on Sabrina's household services, which included maintaining the home, cooking and cleaning, and caring for their child. Should the court have given her credit for this labor?

In *Turner v. Freed*, 792 N.E.2d 947 (Ind. Ct. App. 2003), cited in *Gazvoda*, the court awarded $18,000 to Angela Freed based on the value of her "homemaking and housekeeping" services, rather than her contributions to the family business. Is *Gazvoda* consistent with *Turner*?

---

7. Same-Sex Marriage

Imagine that Robert and Alice fall in love and marry. The law offers a wide variety of benefits to married couples like Robert and Alice—including the marital property rights explored in this chapter and much more. But what if it was Roberta who fell in love with Alice?

Marriage in the United States was traditionally limited to heterosexual unions. Same-sex intimacy was generally viewed as immoral and deemed to be a criminal offense. In this environment, gays and lesbians experienced widespread discrimination. Among other things, they were barred from government employment, rejected for military service, and denied immigration rights. Over time, gays and lesbians gradually gained important new legal protections. But states continued to ban same-sex marriage. In 1996, the Defense of Marriage Act (DOMA) became federal law. DOMA restricted marriage for federal purposes to male-female unions and allowed states to refuse to recognize same-sex marriages performed in other states.

In 2003, Massachusetts became the first state to legalize same-sex marriage, through the decision in *Goodridge v. Department of Public Health*, 798 N.E.2d 941 (Mass. 2003). The reaction to *Goodridge* was swift: voters in over twenty states approved state constitutional amendments defining marriage as the union of a man and a woman. But the movement for equal marriage rights continued to advance elsewhere, and national public opinion began to shift. In 2013, the Supreme Court overturned the DOMA definition of marriage in *United States v. Windsor*, 570 U.S. 744 (2013). As a result, same-sex couples gained federal benefits, and same-sex marriages received federal recognition. Subsequently, a number of lower courts ruled that same-sex marriage bans violated constitutional guarantees. When the Sixth Circuit reached the opposite result in a 2014 decision, the Supreme Court agreed to hear the case—which led to a landmark decision in favor of equal marriage rights.

Obergefell v. Hodges

Supreme Court of the United States

576 U.S. 644 (2015)

Justice Kennedy delivered the opinion of the Court.

The Constitution promises liberty to all within its reach, a liberty that includes certain specific rights that allow persons, within a lawful realm, to define and express their identity. The petitioners in these cases seek to find that liberty by marrying someone of the same sex and having their marriages deemed lawful on the same terms and conditions as marriages between persons of the opposite sex.

I.

These cases come from Michigan, Kentucky, Ohio, and Tennessee, States that define marriage as a union between one man and one woman. See, *e.g.,* Mich. Const., Art. I, § 25; Ky. Const. § 233A; Ohio Rev. Code Ann. § 3101.01 (Lexis 2008); Tenn. Const., Art. XI, § 18. The petitioners are 14 same-sex couples and two men whose same-sex partners are deceased. The respondents are state officials responsible for enforcing the laws in question. The petitioners claim the respondents violate the Fourteenth Amendment by denying them the right to marry or to have their marriages, lawfully performed in another State, given full recognition. . . .

Justice Anthony M. Kennedy
Click here for larger photo

II.

. . . Petitioner James Obergefell, a plaintiff in the Ohio case, met John Arthur over two decades ago. They fell in love and started a life together, establishing a lasting, committed relation. In 2011, however, Arthur was diagnosed with amyotrophic lateral sclerosis, or ALS. This debilitating disease is progressive, with no known cure. Two years ago, Obergefell and Arthur decided to commit to one another, resolving to marry before Arthur died. To fulfill their mutual promise, they traveled from Ohio to Maryland, where same-sex marriage was legal. It was difficult for Arthur to move, and so the couple were wed inside a medical transport plane as it remained on the tarmac in Baltimore. Three months later, Arthur died. Ohio law does not permit Obergefell to be listed as the surviving spouse on Arthur's death certificate. By statute, they must remain strangers even in death, a state-imposed separation Obergefell deems "hurtful for the rest of time.". . .

The cases now before the Court involve other petitioners as well, each with their own experiences. Their stories reveal that they seek not to denigrate marriage but rather to live their lives, or honor their spouses' memory, joined by its bond. . . .

III.

Under the Due Process Clause of the Fourteenth Amendment, no State shall "deprive any person of life, liberty, or property, without due process of law." The fundamental liberties protected by this Clause include most of the rights enumerated in the Bill of Rights. *See Duncan v. Louisiana*, 391 U.S. 145, 147–149 (1968). In addition these liberties extend to certain personal choices central to individual dignity and autonomy, including intimate choices that define personal identity and beliefs. See, *e.g., Eisenstadt v. Baird*, 405 U.S. 438, 453 (1972); *Griswold v. Connecticut*, 381 U.S. 479, 484–486 (1965).

The identification and protection of fundamental rights is an enduring part of the judicial duty to interpret the Constitution. That responsibility, however, "has not been reduced to any formula." *Poe v. Ullman*, 367 U.S. 497, 542 (1961) (Harlan, J., dissenting). Rather, it requires courts to exercise reasoned judgment in identifying interests of the person so fundamental that the State must accord them its respect. . . .

> **Hear It**
>
> Click here to hear the oral argument in *Obergefell v. Hodges*.

The nature of injustice is that we may not always see it in our own times. The generations that wrote and ratified the Bill of Rights and the Fourteenth Amendment did not presume to know the extent of freedom in all of its dimensions, and so they entrusted to future generations a charter protecting the right of all persons to enjoy liberty as we learn its meaning. When new insight reveals discord between the Constitution's central protections and a received legal stricture, a claim to liberty must be addressed. . . .

. . . [T]he Court has long held the right to marry is protected by the Constitution. In *Loving v. Virginia*, 388 U.S. 1, 12 (1967), which invalidated bans on interracial unions, a unanimous Court held marriage is "one of the vital personal rights essential to the orderly pursuit of happiness by free men." The Court reaffirmed that holding in *Zablocki v. Redhail*, 434 U.S. 374, 384 (1978), which held the right to marry was burdened by a law prohibiting fathers who were behind on child support from marrying. The Court again applied this principle in *Turner v. Safley*, 482 U.S. 78 (1987), which held the right to marry was abridged by regulations limiting the privilege of prison inmates to marry. Over time and in other contexts, the Court has reiterated that the right to marry is fundamental under the Due Process Clause. . . .

. . . In defining the right to marry these cases have identified essential attributes of that right based in history, tradition, and other constitutional liberties inherent in this intimate bond. . . . And in assessing whether the force and rationale of its cases apply to same-sex couples, the Court must respect the basic reasons why the right to marry has been long protected. . . .

This analysis compels the conclusion that same-sex couples may exercise the right to marry. The four principles and traditions to be discussed demonstrate that the reasons marriage is fundamental under the Constitution apply with equal force to same-sex couples.

A first premise of the Court's relevant precedents is that the right to personal choice regarding marriage is inherent in the concept of individual autonomy. This abiding connection between marriage and liberty is why *Loving* invalidated interracial marriage bans under the Due Process Clause. . . . Like choices concerning contraception, family relationships, procreation, and childrearing, all of which are protected by the Constitution, decisions concerning marriage are among the most intimate that an individual can make. . . .

A second principle in this Court's jurisprudence is that the right to marry is fundamental because it supports a two-person union unlike any other in its importance to the committed individuals. This point was central to *Griswold v. Connecticut*, which held the Constitution protects the right of married couples to use contraception. 381 U.S., at 485. Suggesting that marriage is a right "older than the Bill of Rights," *Griswold* described marriage this way:

> Marriage is a coming together for better or for worse, hopefully enduring, and intimate to the degree of being sacred. It is an association that promotes a way of life, not causes; a harmony in living, not political faiths; a bilateral loyalty, not commercial or social projects. Yet it is an association for as noble a purpose as any involved in our prior decisions. *Id.*, at 486. . . .

A third basis for protecting the right to marry is that it safeguards children and families and thus draws meaning from related rights of childrearing, procreation, and education. See *Pierce v. Society of Sisters,* 268 U.S. 510 (1925); *Meyer v. Nebraska,* 262 U.S. 390, 399 (1923). The Court has recognized these connections by describing the varied rights as a unified whole: "[T]he right to 'marry, establish a home and bring up children' is a central part of the liberty protected by the Due Process Clause." *Zablocki,* 434 U.S., at 384 (quoting *Meyer, supra,* at 399).

As all parties agree, many same-sex couples provide loving and nurturing homes to their children, whether biological or adopted. And hundreds of thousands of children are presently being raised by such couples. . . . Most States have allowed gays and lesbians to adopt, either as individuals or as couples, and many adopted and foster children have same-sex parents. . . . This provides powerful confirmation from the law itself that gays and lesbians can create loving, supportive families.

Fourth and finally, this Court's cases and the Nation's traditions make clear that marriage is a keystone of our social order. . . .

. . . [J]ust as a couple vows to support each other, so does society pledge to support the couple, offering symbolic recognition and material benefits to protect and nourish the union. Indeed, while the States are in general free to vary the benefits they confer on all married couples, they have throughout our history made marriage the basis for an expanding list of governmental rights, benefits, and responsibilities. These aspects of marital status include: taxation; inheritance and property rights; rules of intestate succession; spousal privilege in the law of evidence; hospital access; medical decisionmaking authority; adoption rights; the rights and benefits of survivors; birth and death certificates; professional ethics rules; campaign finance restrictions; workers' compensation benefits; health insurance; and child custody, support, and visitation rules. . . . Valid marriage under state law is also a significant status for over a thousand provisions of federal law. . . .

The limitation of marriage to opposite-sex couples may long have seemed natural and just, but its inconsistency with the central meaning of the fundamental right to marry is now manifest. With that knowledge must come the recognition that laws excluding same-sex couples from the marriage right impose stigma and injury of the kind prohibited by our basic charter. . . .

. . . If rights were defined by who exercised them in the past, then received practices could serve as their own continued justification and new groups could not invoke rights once denied. This Court has rejected that approach, both with respect to the right to marry and the rights of gays and lesbians. See *Loving*, 388 U.S., at 12; *Lawrence* [*v. Texas,*] 539 U.S. [539,] 566-567 [(2003)].

. . . Many who deem same-sex marriage to be wrong reach that conclusion based on decent and honorable religious or philosophical premises, and neither they nor their beliefs are disparaged here. But when that sincere, personal opposition becomes enacted law and public policy, the necessary consequence is to put the imprimatur of the State itself on an exclusion that soon demeans or stigmatizes those whose own liberty is then denied. Under the Constitution, same-sex couples seek in marriage the same legal treatment as opposite-sex couples, and it would disparage their choices and diminish their personhood to deny them this right.

The right of same-sex couples to marry that is part of the liberty promised by the Fourteenth Amendment is derived, too, from that Amendment's guarantee of the equal protection of the laws. . . .

. . . It is now clear that the challenged laws burden the liberty of same-sex couples, and it must be further acknowledged that they abridge central precepts of equality. Here the marriage laws enforced by the respondents are in essence unequal: same-sex couples are denied all the benefits afforded to opposite-sex couples and are barred from exercising a fundamental right. Especially against a long history of disapproval of their relationships, this denial to same-sex couples of the right to marry works a grave and continuing harm. The imposition of this disability on gays and lesbians serves to disrespect and subordinate them. And the Equal Protection

Clause, like the Due Process Clause, prohibits this unjustified infringement of the fundamental right to marry. . . .

> **FYI**
>
> As he heard supporters sing the national anthem outside the Supreme Court after the ruling, Jim Obergefell remarked: "It was beautiful to hear that on a day when, inside that courtroom, I felt more like an equal American than I had in a very long time."

These considerations lead to the conclusion that the right to marry is a fundamental right inherent in the liberty of the person, and under the Due Process and Equal Protection Clauses of the Fourteenth Amendment couples of the same-sex may not be deprived of that right and that liberty. The Court now holds that same-sex couples may exercise the fundamental right to marry. No longer may this liberty be denied to them. . . .

IV.

The dynamic of our constitutional system is that individuals need not await legislative action before asserting a fundamental right. The Nation's courts are open to injured individuals who come to them to vindicate their own direct, personal stake in our basic charter. An individual can invoke a right to constitutional protection when he or she is harmed, even if the broader public disagrees and even if the legislature refuses to act. . . .

No union is more profound than marriage, for it embodies the highest ideals of love, fidelity, devotion, sacrifice, and family. In forming a marital union, two people become something greater than once they were. As some of the petitioners in these cases demonstrate, marriage embodies a love that may endure even past death. It would misunderstand these men and women to say they disrespect the idea of marriage. Their plea is that they do respect it, respect it so deeply that they seek to find its fulfillment for themselves. Their hope is not to be condemned to live in loneliness, excluded from one of civilization's oldest institutions. They ask for equal dignity in the eyes of the law. The Constitution grants them that right.

> **FYI**
>
> The Court also ruled that the Constitution requires all states to recognize same-sex marriages validly performed in another state.

The judgment of the Court of Appeals for the Sixth Circuit is reversed.

[The dissenting opinions of Chief Justice Roberts and Justices Alito, Scalia, and Thomas are omitted.]

Points for Discussion

a. **Equal Marriage Rights**

In their briefs, the petitioners emphasized that they were not seeking a constitutional right to same-sex marriage, but rather an equal right to enter the existing institution of marriage. Reflecting this emphasis, Justice Kennedy wrote: "It is now clear that the challenged laws burden the liberty of same-sex couples, and it must be further acknowledged that they abridge central precepts of equality. Here the marriage laws enforced by the respondents are in essence unequal: same-sex couples are denied all the benefits afforded to opposite-sex couples and are barred from exercising a fundamental right." *Obergefell*, 576 U.S. at 675.

b. **Judicial Overreach?**

Each dissenting Justice expressed concern about judicial overreach. For example, noting the homogeneous backgrounds of the members of the Court, Justice Scalia stressed that "to allow the policy question of same-sex marriage to be considered and resolved by a select, patrician, highly unrepresentative panel of nine is to violate a principle even more fundamental than no taxation without representation: no social transformation without representation." *Id.* at 718.

Should momentous social changes such as recognition of same-sex marriage be decided by the democratic process rather than by a few judges whose life experiences are vastly different from those of most Americans? For an ardent response to the *Obergefell* dissents, see Christopher R. Leslie, *Dissenting from History: The False Narratives of the* Obergefell *Dissents,* 92 Ind. L.J. 1007 (2017).

c. **Procreation and Marriage**

A common argument against same-sex marriage was the fear that it would sever the link between procreation and marriage. Historically, procreation required sex between a man and woman. When a child is conceived, its prospects generally are considered better if the parents remain together as a couple. Therefore, by limiting marriage to heterosexual couples, as the argument goes, procreation is encouraged and the social fabric enhanced. Adopting this rationale in his dissent, Chief Justice Roberts concluded, "for the good of children and society, sexual relations that can lead to procreation should occur only between a man and a woman committed to a lasting bond." *Obergefell*, 576 U.S. at 689. What is your response to this argument?

d. **Property Rights After *Obergefell***

Today same-sex spouses enjoy the same property rights that all married couples possess, in areas ranging from inheritance to divorce. Yet with these new rights come new questions. For example, in a community property jurisdiction, the creditor of one spouse may attach all the community assets, including wages of the non-debtor spouse. As two scholars observe, "gay spouses themselves might be surprised to find that the legal sanctioning of their unions has inured, in large part, to the benefit of their creditors." *See* Andrea B. Carroll & Christopher K. Odinet, *Gay Marriage and the Problem of Property*, 93 Wash. U. L. Rev. 847, 848 (2016).

Does the logic of *Obergefell* apply to other groups who may wish to marry? And, if so, how should an attorney advise her clients about entering into property transactions with members of such groups? For instance, most states allow first cousins to marry, but a few do not. Is such a ban constitutional? Or if a man wants to marry two women, but the state prohibits polygamy, would this violate the *Obergefell* holding?

e. **Aftermath of *Obergefell***

Same-sex marriage is now legal in all states, Washington, D.C., and all U.S. territories, except American Samoa. *Obergefell* does not apply to Native American lands since the federal courts have no legal authority over them. Tribes have the right to adopt their own marriage laws, and same-sex marriage is recognized in over 30 tribal jurisdictions.

Summary

- **Tenancy in Common.** Each cotenant has an undivided, fractional interest in the property, and the right to use and possess the whole parcel. A cotenant's interest is freely alienable, devisable, and descendible.

- **Joint Tenancy.** Each cotenant has an equal fractional share in the property, the right to possess and use the whole parcel, *and* the right of survivorship. Traditionally, four unities are needed to create a joint tenancy: time, title, interest, and possession. Any joint tenant can sever the joint tenancy, destroying the right of survivorship and converting his interest into a tenancy in common.

- **Tenancy by the Entirety.** The spouses hold the property as *one person*. In most states that recognize tenancies by the entirety, neither spouse can alienate his or her interest, and the creditors of one spouse cannot reach the property.

- **Separate Property Systems.** Earnings during marriage belong to the wage earner. Upon divorce, most states apply the principle of equitable distribution to assets acquired during marriage, minimizing some of the inequities that historically grew out of the common law system. The surviving spouse is entitled to a forced share in the decedent spouse's estate.

> **Test Your Knowledge**
>
> To assess your understanding of the material in this chapter, click here to take a quiz.

- **Community Property Systems.** Earnings during marriage belong to the community. Community property is based on the idea that each spouse contributes equally to the success of the marriage and that both should share equally in the assets acquired during marriage.

- **Unmarried Couples.** Many states enforce both express and implied agreements between unmarried cohabitants about how their property will be divided on separation or death.
- **Same-Sex Marriage.** The Due Process and Equal Protection Clauses of the U.S. Constitution guarantee same-sex couples the right to marry in all states and require all states to recognize same-sex marriages performed in other states.

For More Information

For more information about the subjects covered in this chapter, please consult these sources:

- Albertina Antognini, *The Law of Nonmarriage*, 58 B.C. L. Rev. 1 (2017).
- Naomi Cahn, *What's Wrong About the Elective Share "Right"?*, 53 U.C. Davis L. Rev. 2087 (2020).
- Debbie Cenziper & Jim Obergefell, Love Wins: The Lovers and the Lawyers Who Fought the Landmark Case for Marriage Equality (2016).
- Ruth Colker, *The Freedom to Choose to Marry*, 30 Colum. J. Gender & L. 383 (2015).
- Katherine Wells Meighan, *For Better or For Worse: A Corporate Finance Approach to Valuing Educational Degrees at Divorce*, 5 Geo. Mason L. Rev. 193 (1997).
- Allison Anna Tait, *Divorce Equality*, 90 Wash. L. Rev. 1245 (2015).

Chapter 7

Leasing Real Property

Suppose that you lease an apartment from landlord L. What are your rights? And what duties do you owe to L? Your landlord-tenant relationship with L is governed by a complex body of property law and contract law.

Traditionally, a leasehold was seen as an estate in land—a *nonfreehold estate*—akin to the freehold estates that you studied in Chapter 5. Under this model, the landlord (or *lessor*) transferred the exclusive right to possession of the premises to the tenant (or *lessee*), and retained a future interest (usually a *reversion*). Thus, the lease was governed by property law concepts.

In the 1960s, courts began using contract law to redefine the landlord-tenant relationship for residential leases. This shift reflected a practical reality: landlords and tenants usually think of the lease as a contract, not as an instrument conveying an estate in land. Today most jurisdictions view the lease as a hybrid, governed by *both* property law and contract law.

> **Perspective and Analysis**
>
> In the last two decades we have witnessed a revolution in residential landlord-tenant law. The residential tenant, long the stepchild of the law, has now become its ward and darling. Tenants' rights have increased dramatically; landlords' rights have decreased dramatically. . . .
>
> Traditionally, courts considered the landlord's rights to determine the amount of rent, to gain possession at the end of the term, and to choose tenants, and the right of the parties to decide on the extent of landlord services as basic rights that rested on fundamental legal principles. Yet lawmakers have significantly modified these basic rights as well as a large number of less central doctrines. . . .
>
> Edward H. Rabin, *The Revolution in Residential Landlord-Tenant Law: Causes and Consequences*, 69 Cornell L. Rev. 517, 519, 521 (1984).

As a result of the landlord-tenant revolution, the rights of a residential tenant today are much greater than they were 60 years ago. But this revolution has only produced minor changes in the principles governing commercial leases. Courts reason that a commercial tenant is sophisticated enough to protect its interests by negotiating an appropriate lease.

Bear in mind that landlord-tenant principles may serve different functions. Some rules can be seen as *immutable rules*; that is, they supersede any contrary provisions in the lease, usually in order to protect vulnerable residential tenants. But *default rules* play quite a different role: they fill in the gaps that the parties did not address in the lease. Thus, the parties are free to ignore a default rule in lease negotiations, but they cannot evade an immutable rule. As you read the materials in this chapter, consider which rules serve each function.

A. Creating the Tenancy

1. Selecting the Tenant

Suppose that L owns a five-unit apartment building. She places an ad in the local paper seeking a tenant for a vacant unit. T answers the ad, inspects the unit, and offers to lease it. Must L lease to T?

As we saw in Chapter 1, a landowner has a broad right to exclude any other person from her property. Consistent with this approach, the law traditionally permitted a landlord to refuse to rent to anyone for any reason. But modern federal and state statutes which prohibit discrimination have limited this rule. Thus, for example, L may not refuse to rent to T because of T's race, gender, or national origin.

The federal Fair Housing Act of 1968, 42 U.S.C. § 3601 et seq., is the most important statute regulating the landlord's right to exclude. The Supreme Court explained the genesis of the Act in our next case.

Texas Department of Housing and Community Affairs v. Inclusive Communities Project, Inc.

Supreme Court of the United States

576 U.S. 519 (2015)

KENNEDY, J., delivered the opinion of the Court. . . .

De jure residential segregation by race was declared unconstitutional almost a century ago, *Buchanan v. Warley,* 245 U.S. 60, 38 S.Ct. 16, 62 L.Ed. 149 (1917), but its vestiges remain today, intertwined with the country's economic and social life. Some segregated housing patterns can be traced to conditions that arose in the mid-

20th century. Rapid urbanization, concomitant with the rise of suburban developments accessible by car, led many white families to leave the inner cities. This often left minority families concentrated in the center of the Nation's cities. During this time, various practices were followed, sometimes with governmental support, to encourage and maintain the separation of the races: Racially restrictive covenants prevented the conveyance of property to minorities, see *Shelley v. Kraemer*, 334 U.S. 1, 68 S.Ct. 836, 92 L.Ed. 1161 (1948); steering by real-estate agents led potential buyers to consider homes in racially homogenous areas; and discriminatory lending practices, often referred to as redlining, precluded minority families from purchasing homes in affluent areas. . . . By the 1960's, these policies, practices, and prejudices had created many predominantly black inner cities surrounded by mostly white suburbs.

> **Make the Connection**
>
> You will study *Shelley v. Kraemer* in Chapter 10 and exclusionary zoning in Chapter 11.

The mid-1960's was a period of considerable social unrest; and, in response, President Lyndon Johnson established the National Advisory Commission on Civil Disorders, commonly known as the Kerner Commission. . . . After extensive fact-finding the Commission identified residential segregation and unequal housing and economic conditions in the inner cities as significant, underlying causes of the social unrest. The Commission found that "[n]early two-thirds of all nonwhite families living in the central cities today live in neighborhoods marked by substandard housing and general urban blight." The Commission further found that both open and covert racial discrimination prevented black families from obtaining better housing and moving to integrated communities. The Commission concluded that "[o]ur Nation is moving toward two societies, one black, one white—separate and unequal." To reverse "[t]his deepening racial division," it recommended enactment of "a comprehensive and enforceable open-occupancy law making it an offense to discriminate in the sale or rental of any housing . . . on the basis of race, creed, color, or national origin."

In April 1968, Dr. Martin Luther King, Jr., was assassinated in Memphis, Tennessee, and the Nation faced a new urgency to resolve the social unrest in the inner cities. Congress responded by adopting the Kerner Commission's recommendation and passing the Fair Housing Act. . . .

The most important provision of the Act is 42 U.S.C. § 3604, which states:

> As made applicable by section 3603 of this title and except as exempted by sections 3606(b) and 3607 of this title, it shall be unlawful—
>
> (a) To refuse to sell or rent after the making of a bona fide offer, or to refuse to negotiate for the sale or rental of, or otherwise make unavailable or

deny, a dwelling to any person because of race, color, religion, sex, familial status, or national origin.

(b) To discriminate against any person in the terms, conditions, or privileges of sale or rental of a dwelling, or in the provision of services or facilities in connection therewith, because of race, color, religion, sex, familial status, or national origin.

(c) To make, print, or publish, or cause to be made, printed, or published any notice, statement, or advertisement, with respect to the sale or rental of a dwelling that indicates any preference, limitation, or discrimination based on race, color, religion, sex, handicap, familial status, or national origin, or an intention to make any such preference, limitation, or discrimination. . . .

(f)(1) To discriminate in the sale or rental, or to otherwise make unavailable or deny, a dwelling to any buyer or renter because of a handicap of—

(A) that buyer or renter. . . .

(2) To discriminate against any person in the terms, conditions, or privileges of sale or rental of a dwelling, or in the provision of services or facilities in connection with such a dwelling, because of a handicap of—

(A) that person. . . .

(3) For the purposes of this subsection, discrimination includes—

(A) a refusal to permit, at the expense of the handicapped person, reasonable modifications of existing premises occupied or to be occupied by such person if such modifications may be necessary to afford such person full enjoyment of the premises except that, in the case of a rental, the landlord may . . . condition permission for a modification on the renter agreeing to restore the interior of the premises to the condition that existed before the modification, reasonable wear and tear excepted;

(B) a refusal to make reasonable accomodations in rules, policies, practices or services, when such accomodations may be necessary to afford such person equal opportunity to use and enjoy a dwelling. . . .

The phrase "familial status" can be confusing. It refers to discrimination against (a) families with minor children or (b) pregnant women.

Suppose that O, the owner of a large apartment building, refuses to rent to applicant P. P strongly suspects that the reason for O's refusal is racial discrimination, in violation of section 3604(a). But to win his case, P must show O's discriminatory intent—that O refused to rent to him "because of race." How can P prove this? As our next case illustrates, federal courts have developed a solution to the problem of proving intent in Fair Housing Act cases.

Neithamer v. Brenneman Property Services, Inc.

United States District Court, District of Columbia

81 F. Supp. 2d 1 (1999)

KESSLER, DISTRICT JUDGE.

Plaintiff William Neithamer, who is gay and HIV positive, brings this action against Brenneman Property Services, Inc. and several of its agents under the Fair Housing Act ("FHA"), 42 U.S.C. § 3601 *et seq.,* and the D.C. Human Rights Act ("DCHRA"), D.C. Code § 1–2515. Plaintiff alleges that Defendants discriminated against him when he applied for housing because of his sexual orientation and his medical disability. This matter comes before the Court on Defendants' Motion for Summary Judgment. . . . Upon consideration of the pleadings and the entire record herein, for the reasons stated below, Defendants' Motion for Summary Judgment is denied. . . .

I. Background

In September 1997, in his search for new rental housing, Plaintiff contacted Defendant Brenneman Property Services, Inc. ("Brenneman Property") in response to an advertisement for a townhouse on the Northwest side of the District of Columbia. Plaintiff viewed the property, and upon finding it to his liking, filed an application with Brenneman Property for rental of the property.

Plaintiff provided Defendant Padraig A. Wholihan, the agent of Brenneman Property who handled the transaction, with bank statements and credit references in addition to the application. He also informed Wholihan that his credit report would show that he failed to make payments to some of his creditors a few years earlier. He explained that the reason for this was that several years ago, he had devoted his financial resources to paying the medical bills of his lover, who died in 1994 of AIDS. Plaintiff assured Wholihan that since 1994, he had maintained good credit, and that the bank statements and credit references would confirm this.

After Wholihan presented Plaintiff's application to Alida Stephens, the owner of the property, Stephens rejected Plaintiff's application. Upon being informed of this, Plaintiff offered to pay a second month's rent as additional security to rent the property. Wholihan informed Plaintiff that Stephens had rejected this offer too. Plaintiff was then able to obtain a co-signor for the lease, Reverend Louise Lusignan, who completed a co-signor form on Plaintiff's behalf. Wholihan, however, did not run a credit report on Reverend Lusignan's application. Stephens also rejected Plaintiff's offer of a co-signor. At that point, Plaintiff made his final offer to pre-pay one year's rent. Wholihan informed Plaintiff that Mrs. Stephens had rejected this offer as well.

Upon learning of the rejection of his final offer, Plaintiff called Brenneman Property to inquire why his offer was rejected, and spoke with Defendant George Brenneman, the owner of Brenneman Property, as well as Wholihan. When Plaintiff stated he felt he was a victim of discrimination, Plaintiff alleges that Brenneman became angry and shouted, "if you try to sue me, I have a pack of bloodsucking lawyers who will place countersuits against you for libel and drive you into the ground." . . .

> **Practice Pointer**
>
> ABA Model Rule of Professional Conduct 4.4(a) provides that "[i]n representing a client, a lawyer shall not use means that have no substantial purpose other than to embarrass, delay, or burden a third person. . . ."

III. Analysis

Defendants bring their Motion for Summary Judgment, arguing that there is no basis in fact for either of Plaintiff's claims: discrimination under the FHA and the DCHRA, and intimidation and coercion under those same statutes. . . .

Although the D.C. Circuit Court of Appeals has not yet addressed the issue, a number of other Circuit Courts have already ruled that when a plaintiff offers no direct evidence of discrimination, his claim of discrimination under the FHA is to be examined under the burden-shifting framework of *McDonnell Douglas Corp. v. Green*, 411 U.S. 792, 802–05 (1973), established in Title VII cases. *Gamble v. City of Escondido,* 104 F.3d 300, 305 (9th Cir. 1997); *Mountain Side Mobile Estates Partnership v. Secretary of Hous. and Urban Dev.*, 56 F.3d 1243, 1250–51 (10th Cir. 1995). . . .

Under this framework, Plaintiff must establish a prima facie case of discrimination by showing: (1) that he is a member of a protected class and Defendants knew or suspected that he was; (2) that he applied for and was qualified to rent the property in question; (3) that Defendants rejected his application; and (4) that the property remained available thereafter. Plaintiff must provide sufficient evidence to show that he was "rejected under circumstances which give rise to an inference of unlawful discrimination." *Texas Dep't of Community Affairs v. Burdine*, 450 U.S. 248, 253 (1981). Once Plaintiff establishes a prima facie case, the burden shifts to Defendants to articulate some legitimate, nondiscriminatory reason for their rejection of Plaintiff's application. If Defendants satisfy this burden, Plaintiff must show either that Defendants' reasons are pretext or that material facts are disputed, precluding summary judgment.

Of the four elements of a prima facie case, the last two are undisputed in this case (that Defendants rejected Plaintiff's application, and that the property remained available thereafter). Whether Plaintiff has established the first two elements, however, is very much in dispute.

As to the first element, it is clear that Plaintiff has established a prima facie case as to his sexual orientation. Plaintiff is gay, and Defendants knew or suspected that he was. Although the DCHRA prohibits discrimination based on sexual orientation, the FHA does not. Thus, in order to make a prima facie case under the FHA, Plaintiff must also establish that he is disabled, as that word is used in the FHA, and that Defendants knew or suspected he was.

It is undisputed that Plaintiff is HIV positive and that being HIV positive constitutes a handicap under the FHA. *See, e.g., Hogar Agua y Vida en el Desierto, Inc. v. Suarez-Medina*, 36 F.3d 177, 179 (1st Cir. 1994). Plaintiff alleges that he is handicapped within the meaning of § 3602(h)(3) of the FHA, that is, Defendants regarded or perceived him as being handicapped, while Defendants deny that they ever knew or suspected that Plaintiff was HIV positive. The question is whether Plaintiff has provided enough evidence to give rise to an inference that Defendants perceived he was HIV positive.

> **FYI**
>
> The Fair Housing Act defines a "handicap" as: "(1) a physical or mental impairment which substantially limits one or more of [the person's] major life activities, (2) a record of having such an impairment, or (3) being regarded as having such an impairment, but . . . does not include current, illegal use of or addiction to a controlled substance." 42 U.S.C. § 3602(h).

Plaintiff provides the following evidence in support of this inference. Plaintiff told Wholihan that his lover had died of AIDS; because of the pernicious stereotyping surrounding those infected with AIDS, Defendants likely suspected that Plaintiff had had sexual relations with his lover, and thus became exposed to the AIDS virus; there is no other explanation for the way that Plaintiff was treated by Defendants, especially given their failure to make exceptions to their rules for him, which they had done for others, and their failure to relay to the owner of the property all of Plaintiff's counteroffers. Plaintiff argues that these facts are sufficient to state a prima facie case that Defendants suspected he had AIDS. Plaintiff also argues that Defendants' denial of any such suspicions makes this issue a question for the jury, because it involves critical questions of credibility, and cannot be decided as a matter of law.

There are no cases which address the question of the plaintiff's burden of proving a prima facie case of perceived disability in a housing discrimination case. There are, however, two cases which address the question of whether the plaintiff can establish a prima facie case when the defendant denies knowledge of the plaintiff's protected-class status. In both *Sanders v. Dorris*, 873 F.2d 938, 942 (6th Cir. 1989) and *Bullen v. Thanasouras*, 1994 WL 6868, *3–*4 (N.D. Ill. 1994), the defendants denied knowing that the plaintiffs were black, and thus argued that plaintiffs had failed to establish a prima facie case of racial discrimination. Both cases found, however, considering all the facts in the light most favorable to the plaintiffs, that the defendants must have suspected that plaintiffs were black, because the defendants were presented with sufficient "clues" to have supported such suspicions, especially in light of their subsequent behavior towards the plaintiffs.

That reasoning is especially compelling here. First, HIV status is not easily identifiable as race usually is. Second, dismissing a case at the summary judgment stage because a plaintiff cannot prove a defendant's suspicions would subject HIV-positive individuals to the very discrimination that Congress sought to prevent, by denying them a remedy even when such discrimination existed. The very fact that this case is brought under the *perceived* disability section of the FHA informs how the question of the plaintiff's burden of proof at the prima facie stage must be approached. Given the difficulty of identifying a person's HIV status, rarely will another's perceptions of that status be obvious. Even if someone had suspicions of another's HIV status, such perceptions could easily be denied. Therefore, requiring a plaintiff to show definitive proof of a defendant's perceptions at the summary judgment stage creates an impossible burden of proof, one that is inappropriate at the prima facie stage. It is sufficient for a plaintiff to demonstrate that there is a material dispute as to the defendant's perception of him as an individual with HIV or AIDS. Defendant's credibility regarding denials of such perceptions is for the jury to decide.

Considering all the facts in this case most favorably to the Plaintiff, the non-moving party, there are enough "clues" to allow a reasonable jury to conclude that Defendants suspected that Plaintiff was infected with HIV or AIDS: Plaintiff immediately informed Defendants that his lover had died of AIDS. It is no leap of logic to assume that he had had sexual relations with this lover, and was probably exposed to the AIDS virus. Whether Defendants actually made assumptions and had suspicions based on these clues is, however, a material disputed fact, which Plaintiff will have to prove at trial by a preponderance of the evidence.

The second element of a prima facie case, that Plaintiff applied for and was qualified for the property in question, is hotly disputed. Defendants argue that Plaintiff's dismal credit record clearly shows that he was not qualified to rent the property.

It is undisputed that at the time he applied for the apartment in question, Plaintiff's credit report was, indeed, dismal. If his credit report were the only factor Defendants had to evaluate, it would be simple to conclude that Plaintiff was unqualified for the rental. That is not, however, all the information Defendants had at their disposal regarding his application. Specifically, Defendants also knew that Plaintiff's bad credit history was due to a one-time medical catastrophe; that he had significant assets in his bank accounts; that he had credit references and a co-signor; and that he offered to prepay one year's rent on the property. Looking at the record as a whole, Plaintiff has established that he was qualified to rent the property, and thus he has established a prima facie case of discrimination.

Defendants have proffered the following nondiscriminatory reasons for rejecting Plaintiff's application: (1) Plaintiff's credit was so extremely poor that any reasonable real estate agent examining his application would have likewise rejected it; and (2) the decisions to reject Plaintiff's application and subsequent offers were all made by Stephens, for whom Defendants were merely acting as agents.

Plaintiff has provided more than sufficient evidence to call into question Defendants' proffered reasons. Plaintiff has provided evidence indicating that Defendants did not consistently follow their own policy regarding rejecting applicants with poor credit. Additionally, Plaintiff has provided evidence that Defendants did not present Stephens with all of Plaintiff's offers, or all the relevant information about those offers. . . .

Plaintiff has advanced evidence suggesting that Defendants' proffered reasons are pretext, and has also established that material disputed facts exist which cannot be resolved on summary judgment. Consequently, Defendants' motion shall be denied as to the discrimination claims. . . .

Points for Discussion

a. **Proving Discriminatory Intent**

Did Neithamer produce any evidence that the defendants in fact intended to discriminate against him? Why not? *Neithamer* illustrates the three-step approach that federal courts use to establish discriminatory intent under the Fair Housing Act: (1) the plaintiff establishes a prima facie case of discrimination; (2) the burden then shifts to the defendant to prove a legitimate, nondiscriminatory reason for his conduct; and (3) if the defendant meets that burden, then the plaintiff must show that the reason is a mere pretext. Neithamer relied on a *disparate treatment* approach to make the required prima facie showing: he was a member of a class protected by the Act, he was qualified and applied to rent, he was rejected, and the unit remained open thereafter. For other examples of this approach, see *Jancik v. Department of Housing & Urban Development*, 44 F.3d 553 (7th Cir. 1995) (discrimination based on race and family status) and *Sullivan v. Hernandez*, 215 F. Supp. 2d 635 (D. Md. 2002) (discrimination based on race and disability). In some cases, plaintiffs can establish a prima facie case with statistical evidence which shows that a defendant's conduct has a *disparate impact* on a group of people in a protected class. The Supreme Court endorsed this approach—which had long been used by lower courts—in *Texas Department of Housing and Community Affairs v. Inclusive Communities Project, Inc.*, 576 U.S. 519 (2015).

b. **Scope of "Handicap"**

Why does the definition of "handicap" include a person who does not suffer from an impairment, but who is *perceived* as having such an impairment? Why was the evidence in *Neithamer* about the defendants' perception enough to avoid summary judgment? Suppose that landlord X refuses to rent an apartment unit to Z because Z is a recovering alcoholic. Has X violated the Fair Housing Act? What if Z has extremely poor eyesight, but is not legally blind?

c. **Exemptions from the Fair Housing Act**

The anti-discrimination provisions of the Fair Housing Act (42 U.S.C. § 3604(a), (b), (f)) do not apply to two types of property: (1) "rooms or units in dwellings containing living quarters occupied . . . by no more than four families living independently of each other, if the owner . . . occupies one of such living quarters as his residence"; and (2) any single-family house sold or rented by an owner if he does not own more than three houses *and* does not use a real estate broker or agent in the sale or rental. 42 U.S.C. § 3603(b). Why did Congress adopt these exemptions? Suppose that Neithamer had applied to rent an apartment in a duplex where the other unit was occupied by Stephens, the duplex owner. Would this have affected the outcome of *Neithamer*?

d. **Civil Rights Act of 1866**

42 U.S.C. § 1982, part of the Civil Rights Act of 1866, provides additional protection against racial discrimination:

> All citizens of the United States shall have the same right, in every State and Territory, as is enjoyed by white citizens thereof to inherit, purchase, lease, sell, hold, and convey real and personal property.

Compare this provision to the Fair Housing Act. How are they similar? How do they differ?

e. **Hypotheticals on Discrimination**

Have the Fair Housing Act or the Civil Rights Act of 1866 been violated in these situations?

> (1) A posts this notice on a website: "For rent. 1-bedroom apartment in 10-unit building. Prefer tenant who can speak French or German."
>
> (2) B, a Black woman, applies to rent a single-family residence owned by C. C tells B: "I won't rent to you for two reasons. You are Black and female."
>
> (3) D, a mother with four minor children, applies to rent a two-bedroom apartment in a large complex. E, the building manager, tells her: "You have too many children for an apartment that small."
>
> (4) F, who owns a duplex, places this ad in a local newspaper to find a tenant for her vacant unit: "Female tenant wanted for apartment near university." F lives in the other unit.
>
> (5) G, a confirmed vegetarian, applies to rent a studio apartment in a 5-unit complex owned by H. H refuses to rent to G because she is a vegetarian.
>
> (6) J, a Latino man in good financial standing, applies to rent a one-bedroom unit in a 200-unit apartment tower owned by K. K refuses to rent to J, giving no reason. The unit is still vacant.

f. Discrimination by Tenants

Is the landlord liable under the Fair Housing Act for tenant-on-tenant harassment? In *Francis v. King Park Manor, Inc.*, 992 F.3d 67 (2d Cir. 2021), the court held that the landlord was not liable for failing to take steps to prevent one tenant from repeatedly insulting another tenant with a racial epithet. *But see Wetzel v. Glen St. Andrew Living Cmty., LLC*, 901 F.3d 856 (7th Cir. 2018) (landlord was liable for failing to take reasonable steps to prevent tenant-on-tenant harassment based on sex). Which result is correct?

g. State Statutes Barring Discrimination

State statutes may provide greater protection against discrimination than federal law affords. For example, state law may prevent a landlord from refusing to rent to an unmarried opposite-sex couple. But what if the landlord's refusal is based on a religious belief that such cohabitation is sinful? *Compare Smith v. Fair Employment & Housing Commission*, 913 P.2d 909 (Cal. 1996) (landlord cannot refuse) *with North Dakota Fair Hous. Council, Inc. v. Peterson*, 625 N.W.2d 551 (N.D. 2001) (landlord can refuse). Suppose that a landlord refuses to rent to a tenant whose monthly income is less than three times the monthly rent. Is this illegal discrimination based on the tenant's economic status? *See Harris v. Capital Growth Investors XIV*, 805 P.2d 873 (Cal. 1991) (no).

h. Aftermath of *Neithamer*

When Neithamer read the decision, he knew that it would set an important precedent for the rights of people living with HIV and AIDS. "I cried when I read it," he said. Neithamer eventually settled the case in return for a payment of $19,500.

Today the Fair Housing Act covers discrimination based on sexual orientation. In *Bostock v. Clayton County*, 140 S. Ct. 1731 (2020), the Supreme Court held that the portion of the Civil Rights Act of 1964 which prohibits an employer from discriminating "because of . . . sex" covers "homosexual or transgender" employees. *Id.* at 1741. The Court's interpretation of this text is equally applicable to the parallel language in the Fair Housing Act. *See* Rigel C. Oliveri, *Sexual Orientation and Gender Identity Claims under the Fair Housing Act after* Bostock v. Clayton County, 69 U. Kan. L. Rev. 409 (2021).

Suppose G has rented a two-bedroom apartment and now seeks a roommate who will help her pay the rent. Can G run an ad that includes the phrase "female preferred"? And if H, a man, applies to share the apartment, must G agree?

Fair Housing Council of San Fernando Valley v. Roommate.com, LLC

United States Court of Appeals, Ninth Circuit

666 F.3d 1216 (2012)

KOZINSKI, CHIEF JUDGE:

There's no place like home. In the privacy of your own home, you can take off your coat, kick off your shoes, let your guard down and be completely yourself. While we usually share our homes only with friends and family, sometimes we need to take in a stranger to help pay the rent. When that happens, can the government limit whom we choose? Specifically, do the anti-discrimination provisions of the Fair Housing Act ("FHA") extend to the selection of roommates?

FACTS

Roommate.com, LLC ("Roommate") operates an internet-based business that helps roommates find each other. Roommate's website receives over 40,000 visits a day and roughly a million new postings for roommates are created each year. When users sign up, they must create a profile by answering a series of questions about their sex, sexual orientation and whether children will be living with them. . . . Users are asked to list their preferences for roommate characteristics, including sex, sexual orientation and familial status. Based on the profiles and preferences, Roommate matches users and provides them a list of housing-seekers or available rooms meeting their criteria. Users can also search available listings based on roommate characteristics, including sex, sexual orientation and familial status.

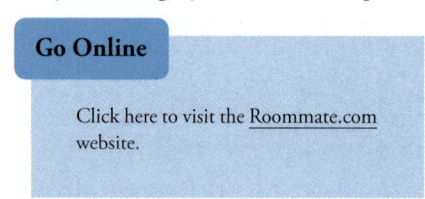

The Fair Housing Councils of San Fernando Valley and San Diego ("FHCs") sued Roommate in federal court, alleging that the website's questions requiring disclosure of sex, sexual orientation and familial status, and its sorting, steering and matching of users based on those characteristics, violate the Fair Housing Act ("FHA"), 42 U.S.C. § 3601 et seq. . . . [T]he district court held that Roommate's prompting of discriminatory preferences from users, matching users based on that information and publishing these preferences violated the FHA . . . and enjoined Roommate from those activities. Roommate appeals the grant of summary judgment and permanent injunction. . . .

ANALYSIS

If the FHA extends to shared living situations, it's quite clear that what Roommate does amounts to a violation. The pivotal question is whether the FHA applies to roommates.

I

The FHA prohibits discrimination on the basis of "race, color, religion, sex, familial status, or national origin" in the "sale or rental *of a dwelling*." 42 U.S.C. § 3604(b) (emphasis added). The FHA also makes it illegal to

> make, print, or publish, or cause to be made, printed, or published any notice, statement, or advertisement, with respect to the sale or rental *of a dwelling* that indicates any preference, limitation, or discrimination based on race, color, religion, sex, handicap, familial status, or national origin, or an intention to make any such preference, limitation, or discrimination.

Id. § 3604(c) (emphasis added). The reach of the statute turns on the meaning of "dwelling."

The FHA defines "dwelling" as "any building, structure, or portion thereof which is occupied as, or designed or intended for occupancy as, a residence by one or more families." *Id.* § 3602(b). A dwelling is thus a living unit designed or intended for occupancy by a family, meaning that it ordinarily has the elements generally associated with a family residence: sleeping spaces, bathroom and kitchen facilities, and common areas, such as living rooms, dens and hallways.

It would be difficult, though not impossible, to divide a single-family house or apartment into separate "dwellings" for purposes of the statute. Is a "dwelling" a bedroom plus a right to access common areas? What if roommates share a bedroom? Could a "dwelling" be a bottom bunk and half an armoire? It makes practical sense to interpret "dwelling" as an independent living unit and stop the FHA at the front door.

There's no indication that Congress intended to interfere with personal relationships *inside* the home. Congress wanted to address the problem of landlords discriminating in the sale and rental of housing, which deprived protected classes of housing opportunities. But a business transaction between a tenant and landlord is quite different from an arrangement between two people sharing the same living space. We seriously doubt Congress meant the FHA to apply to the latter. Consider, for example, the FHA's prohibition against sex discrimination. Could Congress, in the 1960s, really have meant that women must accept men as roommates? Telling women they may not lawfully exclude men from the list of acceptable roommates would be controversial today; it would have been scandalous in the 1960s. . . .

II

The Supreme Court has recognized that "the freedom to enter into and carry on certain intimate or private relationships is a fundamental element of liberty protected by the Bill of Rights." *Bd. of Dirs. of Rotary Int'l v. Rotary Club of Duarte*, 481 U.S. 537, 545 (1987). "[C]hoices to enter into and maintain certain intimate human relationships must be secured against undue intrusion by the State because of the role of such relationships in safeguarding the individual freedom that is central to our constitutional scheme." *Roberts v. U.S. Jaycees*, 468 U.S. 609, 617–18 (1984). Courts have extended the right of intimate association to marriage, child bearing, child rearing and cohabitation with relatives. *Id.* While the right protects only "highly personal relationships," *IDK, Inc. v. Clark Cnty.*, 836 F.2d 1185, 1193 (9th Cir. 1988) (quoting *Roberts*, 468 U.S. at 618), the right isn't restricted exclusively to family. The right to association also implies a right *not* to associate.

> **Food for Thought**
>
> What does Kozinski mean when he states that "[t]he right to association also implies a right *not* to associate"? What are the implications of this approach?

To determine whether a particular relationship is protected by the right to intimate association we look to "size, purpose, selectivity, and whether others are excluded from critical aspects of the relationship." *Bd. of Dirs. of Rotary Int'l*, 481 U.S. at 546. The roommate relationship easily qualifies: People generally have very few roommates; they are selective in choosing roommates; and non-roommates are excluded from the critical aspects of the relationship, such as using the living spaces. Aside from immediate family or a romantic partner, it's hard to imagine a relationship more intimate than that between roommates, who share living rooms, dining rooms, kitchens, bathrooms, even bedrooms.

Because of a roommate's unfettered access to the home, choosing a roommate implicates significant privacy and safety considerations. The home is the center of our private lives. Roommates note our comings and goings, observe whom we bring back at night, hear what songs we sing in the shower, see us in various stages of undress and learn intimate details most of us prefer to keep private. Roommates also have access to our physical belongings and to our person.... Taking on a roommate means giving him full access to the space where we are most vulnerable.

Equally important, we are fully exposed to a roommate's belongings, activities, habits, proclivities, and way of life. This could include matter we find offensive (pornography, religious materials, political propaganda); dangerous (tobacco, drugs, firearms); annoying (jazz, perfume, frequent overnight visitors, furry pets); [and] habits that are incompatible with our lifestyle (early risers, messy cooks, bathroom hogs, clothing borrowers)....

Government regulation of an individual's ability to pick a roommate thus intrudes into the home, which "is entitled to special protection as the center of the private lives of our people." *Minnesota v. Carter*, 525 U.S. 83, 99 (1998) (Kennedy, J., concurring). "Liberty protects the person from unwarranted government intrusions into a dwelling or other private places. In our tradition the State is not omnipresent in the home." *Lawrence v. Texas*, 539 U.S. 558, 562 (2003). Holding that the FHA applies inside a home or apartment would allow the government to restrict our ability to choose roommates compatible with our lifestyles. This would be a serious invasion of privacy, autonomy and security.

For example, women will often look for female roommates because of modesty or security concerns. As roommates often share bathrooms and common areas, a girl may not want to walk around in her towel in front of a boy. She might also worry about unwanted sexual advances or becoming romantically involved with someone she must count on to pay the rent.

An orthodox Jew may want a roommate with similar beliefs and dietary restrictions, so he won't have to worry about finding honey-baked ham in the refrigerator next to the potato latkes. Non-Jewish roommates may not understand or faithfully follow all of the culinary rules, like the use of different silverware for dairy and meat products, or the prohibition against warming non-kosher food in a kosher microwave. . . .

It's a "well-established principle that statutes will be interpreted to avoid constitutional difficulties." *Frisby v. Schultz*, 487 U.S. 474, 483 (1988). "[W]here an otherwise acceptable construction of a statute would raise serious constitutional problems, the Court will construe the statute to avoid such problems unless such construction is plainly contrary to the intent of Congress." *Pub. Citizen v. U.S. Dep't of Justice*, 491 U.S. 440, 466 (1989). Because the FHA can reasonably be read either to include or exclude shared living arrangements, we can and must choose the construction that avoids raising constitutional concerns. . . . Reading "dwelling" to mean an independent housing unit is a fair interpretation of the text and consistent with congressional intent. Because the construction of "dwelling" to include shared living units raises substantial constitutional concerns, we adopt the narrower construction that excludes roommate selection from the reach of the FHA. . . . Because we find that the FHA doesn't apply to the sharing of living units, it follows that it's not unlawful to discriminate in selecting a roommate. . . .

> **Take Note**
>
> Notice that Kozinski does not directly assert that applying the anti-discrimination provisions of the FHA to the selection of roommates would be unconstitutional. Instead, he merely says that this would raise "constitutional concerns." What is the difference between these approaches?

Because precluding individuals from selecting roommates based on their sex, sexual orientation and familial status raises substantial constitutional concerns, we interpret the FHA . . . as not applying to the sharing of living units. Therefore, we hold that Roommate's prompting, sorting and publishing of information to facilitate roommate selection is not forbidden by the FHA. . . .

Points for Discussion

a. **Defining a "Dwelling"**

The Fair Housing Act defines a "dwelling" as "any *building*, structure, *or portion thereof* which is occupied as, or designed or *intended for occupancy as, a residence* by one *or more families*." 42 U.S.C. § 3602(b) (emphasis added). "Family" includes a single person. 42 U.S.C. § 3602(c). Does the plain language of the statute cover the rental of any portion of a building intended for occupancy as a residence by one or more people, such as an apartment shared by roommates? Or can the statute be read "either to include or exclude shared living arrangements"? Why?

b. **Discrimination in Selecting Roommates**

Most people would agree that there are legitimate reasons for gender discrimination in selecting roommates, as Kozinski notes. But the scope of *Fair Housing Council* extends far beyond this situation. The court flatly holds that "it's not unlawful to discriminate in selecting a roommate." Would this allow someone to reject a potential roommate because of race, color, or national origin? Are there any legitimate reasons for such a result? Notice that the court explains that its holding allows people to "choose roommates compatible with our lifestyles." What does this mean?

Fair Housing Council is the first decision that arguably extends the right of intimate association to roommates. As the court notes, prior cases have recognized the right only among family members or between people involved in sexual relationships. Is the relationship among roommates comparable to these situations?

c. **Discrimination in Advertising**

Remember that certain dwellings, such as owner-occupied duplexes, are exempt from the anti-discrimination provisions of the Fair Housing Act. But the Act's prohibition on discriminatory advertising in 42 U.S.C. § 3604(c) applies to all dwellings. In effect, the Act permits discrimination in renting under certain circumstances, but not discrimination in advertising. What explains this difference?

Before the case was filed, the listings on the defendant's website contained discriminatory statements such as: "I prefer a Christian male;" "I am not looking for black Muslims;" and "I am seeking a single Asian Male or Female student." The plaintiffs in *Fair Housing Council* sued to prevent such discriminatory advertising. In light of the decision, would it be lawful for a person seeking a roommate to run an ad that specifies "No Jews"? What about an ad that states "Whites only"?

> ### Homelessness and Property Law
>
> Over 500,000 Americans are homeless. On any given night, about 40% are unsheltered, meaning that their primary residence is a park, sidewalk, vacant lot, vehicle, or other place which is not suitable for human habitation. The lack of affordable housing is a major cause of homelessness, although drug addiction, mental illness, and other factors contribute to the problem. As you study landlord-tenant law and other doctrines, consider how property law affects homelessness.
>
> In *Lindsey v. Normet*, 405 U.S. 56 (1972), the Supreme Court held that the Constitution does not create a right to housing. It rejected the claim that the "need for decent shelter" was a "fundamental interest," noting that "the Constitution does not provide judicial remedies for every social and economic ill." *Id*. at 73. However, in *Martin v. City of Boise*, 920 F.3d 584 (9th Cir. 2019), the court ruled that people experiencing homelessness at least had the right to sleep outside. It reasoned that the Cruel and Unusual Punishment Clause of the Eighth Amendment barred the "enforcement of a statute prohibiting sleeping outside against homeless individuals with no access to alternative shelter." *Id*. at 615.
>
> Should the law recognize a right to shelter? The United States is a party to the International Covenant on Economic, Social, and Cultural Rights, which protects "the right of everyone to an adequate standard of living . . . including adequate . . . housing." *Id*. art. 11(1). But most state and local governments do not recognize this right. The notable exception is New York City, where the consent decree in *Callahan v. Carey*, No. 42582/79 (N.Y. Sup. Ct., Aug. 1981) and its progeny have created a broad right to shelter. *Callahan* is based on New York State Constitution art. 17, § 1, which provides: "The aid, care and support of the needy are public concerns and shall be provided by the state and by such of its subdivisions, and in such a manner and by such means, as the legislature may from time to time determine."

2. Selecting the Estate

As you saw in Chapter 5, the estates system arose in feudal England. The nobles and gentry held freehold estates, while the common people who worked the land were virtual slaves. Over time, the custom developed that the lord would permit a peasant to farm a particular parcel of land, and this relationship eventually evolved into the nonfreehold estate. From the beginning, the nonfreehold estate was seen as less important and less prestigious than the freehold estate. The noble who owned a freehold estate was literally the "lord" of the land, with broad power to control the daily lives of his tenants. Our modern system of landlord-tenant estates is based on these early nonfreehold estates.

The common law developed four nonfreehold estates:

- Term of years tenancy
- Periodic tenancy
- Tenancy at will
- Tenancy at sufferance

Suppose that L and T are ready to enter into a landlord-tenant relationship today. Which estate should they select?

a. Term of Years Tenancy

The *term of years tenancy* has a fixed duration that is agreed upon in advance (such as six months, two years, or 100 years). Once the term ends, the tenant's possessory right automatically expires, and the landlord may retake possession of the premises. For example, suppose L leases Greenacre to T "from July 1, 2018 until June 30, 2028," a fixed term of ten years. T's estate terminates at midnight on June 30, 2028. The term of years tenancy is commonly used in commercial leases and often seen in residential leases.

b. Periodic Tenancy

The *periodic tenancy* is automatically renewed for successive periods unless the landlord or tenant terminates the tenancy by giving advance notice. Suppose that L leases Greenacre "to T from month to month, beginning July 1, 2024." In order to end this tenancy, either L or T must give one month's advance notice to the other. Thus, if T gives his notice of termination to L on May 31, 2027, the tenancy will end at midnight on June 30. Month-to-month periodic tenancies are frequently used in residential leases. Of course, the basic period could be longer than a month, which will increase the period for giving notice. For example, notice must be given six months in advance to terminate a year-to-year tenancy.

c. Tenancy at Will

The *tenancy at will* has no fixed ending point. Rather, it continues "only so long as both the landlord and the tenant desire." Restatement (Second) of Property: Landlord and Tenant § 1.6. If L leases Greenacre to T "for as long as both of us wish," this creates a tenancy at will. But often the tenancy at will arises by implication, without an express agreement. At common law, either the landlord or the tenant could end the tenancy without any advance notice to the other. Today, most states require advance notice to end this tenancy, usually equal to the period of time between rent payments. The tenancy terminates automatically if either party dies, the tenant abandons possession, or the landlord sells the property—unlike the term of years tenancy and the periodic tenancy.

d. Tenancy at Sufferance

The so-called *tenancy at sufferance* is created when a person who rightfully took possession of land continues in possession after that right ends. It arises from the occupant's improper conduct, not from an agreement. Accordingly, it is more a convenient label for a type of wrongful occupancy than a true estate. Suppose that L and T enter into a 12-year term of years tenancy for Greenacre on January 1, 2015. The tenancy ends at midnight on December 31, 2026, but T wrongfully continues in possession, becoming a *holdover tenant*. The common law gave the landlord two options in this situation: (1) treat T as a trespasser and evict him; or (2) renew T's tenancy for another term. Today most states have abolished or limited the second option, in order to avoid unfairness to the tenant. For example, some states require the payment of double rent during the holdover period, while others limit the length of the renewed tenancy to no more than one year.

Points for Discussion

a. Term of Years or Periodic Tenancy?

It is vital to know when the tenancy ends. Until that point, the tenant is entitled to the use and enjoyment of the premises, is liable for rent, and is owed various duties by the landlord. Suppose T and L enter into a lease agreement that does not describe the term, but merely says that the rent is "$12,000 per year, payable $1,000 each month." Is this a periodic tenancy or a term of years tenancy? And if it is a periodic tenancy, is the basic term one year or one month? Suppose the lease simply provides that the rent "is $1,000 every month." What estate does this create?

b. Tenancy at Will or Tenancy at Sufferance?

In *City of New York v. Utsey*, 714 N.Y.S.2d 410 (Sup. Ct. 2000), squatters occupied a city-owned house for eight years. The city made a "conscious decision to allow the occupants to remain in the premises for an indefinite term" because the funding was not yet available for the urban renewal project planned for the region. *Id.* at 413. When the city then tried to retake possession, the squatters claimed that they were either tenants at sufferance or tenants at will, and hence entitled to advance notice of termination. The court held that a tenancy at will had arisen by implication, which required the city to serve a 30-day notice of termination. Why weren't the squatters deemed tenants at sufferance?

c. **Lease or License?**

Suppose you purchase a ticket to see a movie, pick a seat in the theater, and sit down. Your arrangement with the theater is a *license*, not a lease. A license is a personal privilege to use the land of another for some specific purpose; in contrast, a lease transfers the exclusive right of possession to the tenant. As you would expect, a licensee's rights are minimal, while a tenant's rights are extensive. Should a student's rights in a college dormitory room be viewed as a license or a lease? In *Cook v. University Plaza*, 427 N.E.2d 405, 407 (Ill. App. Ct. 1981), the court held that a dormitory contract at Northern Illinois University created a license, in part because the contract permitted the university "to require the resident to move from one room to another." *But see Burch v. University of Kansas*, 756 P.2d 431 (Kan. 1988) (holding that students living in dormitories were tenants).

What about cohabitation? In *Drost v. Hookey*, 881 N.Y.S.2d 839 (Dist. Ct. 2009), the court reasoned that the homeowner's live-in girlfriend was a licensee, not a tenant, because she did not have exclusive dominion and control over a particular part of the home.

Can new types of nonfreehold estates be created today? Suppose A wants to lease her property to B for the duration of B's life—a *tenancy for life*. If A and B agree to this arrangement, should the state abide by their wishes?

Effel v. Rosberg

Court of Appeals of Texas

360 S.W.3d 626 (2012)

JUSTICE MORRIS.

This is an appeal from the trial court's judgment awarding Robert G. Rosberg possession of property in a forcible detainer action. Appellant Lena Effel [contends that] the trial court . . . erred in concluding Rosberg was entitled to possession of the property. After examining the record on appeal and reviewing the applicable law, we conclude appellant's arguments are without merit. We affirm the trial court's judgment.

I.

On March 1, 2006, Robert G. Rosberg filed suit against Henry Effel and Jack Effel in district court asserting various claims. . . . The parties settled the dispute and signed a settlement agreement and release of claims. As part of the settlement, Rosberg purchased residential property in Dallas County owned by Henry and Jack Effel. The settlement agreement stated that the current resident of the property, appellant, "shall continue to occupy the property for the remainder of her natural life, or until such time as she voluntarily chooses to vacate the premises." The settlement agreement further stated that a lease agreement incorporating the terms of the settlement agreement would be prepared before the closing date of the purchase. Appellant was neither a party nor a signatory to the settlement agreement.

The property in question was deeded to Rosberg with no reservation of a life estate. A lease for appellant was prepared by the Effels' attorney. The term of the lease was "for a term equal to the remainder of the Lessee's life, or until such time that she voluntarily vacates the premises." The lease also contained various covenants relating to payment of rent and charges for utilities as well as the use and maintenance of the grounds. The lease provided that if there was any default in the payment of rent or in the performance of any of the covenants, the lease could be terminated at the option of the lessor. The lease was signed by Rosberg as lessor and by Henry Effel on behalf of appellant under a power of attorney as lessee.

> **FYI**
>
> The home in dispute had been in the Effel family for 40 years, and Lena Effel had lived there for many years with her twin brother (the father of Henry and Jack) before his death. When the case was filed, Lena was 97 years old and incapable of managing her own affairs; this is why Henry signed the lease on her behalf using a power of attorney. The lease provided that the rent would be the real estate taxes in the property—an amount far below its market rental value—because it was part of a settlement agreement.

Three years later, on February 24, 2010, Rosberg, through his attorney, sent a letter to appellant both by regular mail and certified mail stating that he was terminating her lease effective immediately. The reason for the termination, according to the letter, was Rosberg's discovery that appellant had installed a wrought iron fence in the front yard of the property in violation of two covenants of the lease. The letter stated that appellant was required to leave and surrender the premises within ten days and, if she did not vacate the premises, Rosberg would commence eviction proceedings. Appellant did not vacate the property.

In April 29, 2010, Rosberg filed this forcible detainer action in the justice court. The justice court awarded possession of the property to Rosberg, and appellant appealed the decision to the county court at law. The county court held a trial de novo without a jury and, again, awarded the property to Rosberg. The court concluded the lease created a tenancy at will terminable at any time by either party. The court further concluded that Rosberg was authorized to terminate the lease. . . . Appellant now appeals the county court's judgment.

II.

. . . Although appellant asserted in her pleadings that she had a life estate in the property at issue, she introduced no evidence at trial to support this allegation or create a question of fact on the issue. The evidence in the record shows that appellant had a lease on the property, the stated term of which was "equal to the remainder of her life or until such time that she voluntarily vacates the premises." The warranty deed transferring the property from Henry and Jack Effel to Rosberg does not reserve a life estate in favor of appellant, and appellant does not challenge the validity of the deed. All of the evidence, therefore, demonstrates that appellant's legal status in connection with the property is solely that of a tenant. . . .

In appellant's . . . tenth issue, appellant challenges the county court's first conclusion of law in which it stated "[t]he lease, which purported to be for the rest of Lena Effel's life, created only a tenancy at will terminable at any time by either party." Appellant argues that the lease must be read together with the settlement agreement and the court must give effect to the intent of the parties. Appellant was not a party to the settlement agreement, however. Appellant was a party only to the lease. It is the lease, and not the settlement agreement, that forms the basis of this forcible detainer action. Accordingly, we look solely to the lease to determine appellant's rights in this matter.

The lease states that appellant was a lessee of the property "for a term equal to the remainder of Lessee's life, or until such time as she voluntarily vacates the premises." It is the long-standing rule in Texas that a lease must be for a certain period of time or it will be considered a tenancy at will. *See Holcombe v. Lorino*, 124 Tex. 446, 79 S.W.2d 307, 310 (1935). Courts that have applied this rule to leases that state they are for the term of the lessee's life have concluded that the uncertainty of the date of the lessee's death rendered the lease terminable at will by either party. *See Nitschke v. Doggett*, 489 S.W.2d 335, 337 (Tex. Civ. App.-Austin 1972), *vacated on other grounds*, 498 S.W.2d 339 (Tex.1973); see also, *Kajo Church Square, Inc. v. Walker*, No. 12–02–00131–CV, 2003 WL 1848555, at *5 (Tex.App.-Tyler April 9, 2003, no pet.) (mem. op.).

Appellant argues the current trend in court decisions is away from finding a lease such as hers to be terminable at will. Appellant relies on the 1982 decision of *Philpot v. Fields*, 633 S.W.2d 546 (Tex.App.-Texarkana 1982, no writ). In *Philpot*, the court stated that the trend in law was away from requiring a lease to be of a definite and certain duration. *Id. at* 548. In reviewing the law since *Philpot*, however, we discern no such trend. *See Kajo*, 2003 WL 1848555 at *5. The rule continues to be that a lease for an indefinite and uncertain length of time is an estate at will. *See Providence*

Land Servs., L.L.C. v. Jones, 353 S.W.3d 538, 542 (Tex. App.-Eastland 2011, no pet. h.). In this case, not only was the term of the lease stated to be for the uncertain length of appellant's life, but her tenancy was also "until such time that she voluntarily vacates the premises." If a lease can be terminated at the will of the lessee, it may also be terminated at the will of the lessor. *See Holcombe*, 79 S.W.2d at 310. Because the lease at issue was terminable at will by either party, the trial court's first conclusion of law was correct. We resolve appellant's tenth issue against her. . . .

> **Take Note**
>
> *Philpot v. Fields* held that a lease with no definite ending term was enforceable. The court noted: "Common sense, logic and the trend in the law support this decision. It appears that the parties intended to create a perpetual right to lease the land. When the parties' intent is made clear, courts should enforce the agreement as written. . . ."

We affirm the trial court's judgment.

Points for Discussion

a. Freedom of Choice

As we saw in Chapter 1, the law generally respects an owner's right to transfer her property as she wishes. Why didn't the *Effel* court enforce the "leasehold for life"? Put another way, why should the law recognize only four nonfreehold estates?

b. Life Estate

In *Garner v. Gerrish*, 473 N.E.2d 223 (N.Y. 1984), the New York Court of Appeals considered a lease which described its duration in these words: "for and during the term of *quiet enjoyment* from the *first* day of *May*, 1977 which term will end—*Lou Garrish has the privilege of termination [sic] this agreement at a date of his own choice*." The court found that this phrase created a life estate terminable at the will of the tenant, Lou Gerrish, not a tenancy at will. In light of *Garner*, was *Effel* wrongly decided?

c. Advising the Effels

The "leasehold for life" was part of a larger transaction between Rosberg, on the one hand, and Henry and Jack Effel, on the other. The lease was prepared by the Effels' attorney. Should the attorney have anticipated that it might be construed as a tenancy at will? (Notice that Rosberg's attorney also seemed to assume that the lease was valid, since the original basis for the eviction was that Lena Effel had allegedly breached the lease by installing a fence.) Suppose you represented the Effel family in the original negotiations with Rosberg. How could you have structured the transaction in order to meet the family's goals and comply with the law?

d. Fifth Nonfreehold Estate?

In a few states, a residential landlord may evict a periodic tenant only for *good cause*, as you will see later in this chapter. Typical examples of good cause are failure to pay rent, engaging in criminal activity, or harassing other tenants. Some scholars suggest that this standard effectively creates a fifth nonfreehold estate. Do you agree?

e. Aftermath of *Effel*

Rosberg later sued Lena Effel for post-eviction damages, in part on the basis that she had *removed* the wrought iron fence—even though he had sued for eviction on the theory that she had wrongfully *installed* the fence. Two years after being evicted from her home, Effel died at age 102.

---

3. Negotiating the Lease

Three aspects of lease negotiations merit special attention:

Statute of Frauds: Virtually all states have adopted a Statute of Frauds which mandates that a lease of real property for a term of more than one year cannot be enforced unless it is in writing. For example, a term of years tenancy for two years is subject to the Statute of Frauds, while a month-to-month periodic tenancy is exempt. In order to meet this standard, the lease or another document must contain the key lease terms (parties, property, duration, and rent) and be signed by the party against whom enforcement is sought.

> **See It**
>
> Click here to see (1) a sample apartment lease and (2) a sample shopping center store lease.

Standard forms: The landlord and tenant usually negotiate the key terms of a residential lease: the amount of rent and the duration of the tenancy. But the typical tenant is then asked to sign a pre-printed standard lease form, without any meaningful opportunity to negotiate the other terms. Predictably, the form will favor the landlord's position. How should the law react to this reality? *See* Curtis J. Berger, *Hard Leases Make Bad Law*, 74 Colum. L. Rev. 791 (1974) (concluding that judges try to circumvent unfair terms through interpretation and other techniques). In contrast, extensive bargaining often precedes the execution of a commercial lease.

Rent control: In a few states, local ordinances may limit the amount of rent that a residential landlord can charge, especially in large cities. A typical rent control ordinance establishes a "base rent" for each unit, and then allows landlords an automatic increase for all units each year. Individual landlords may also seek discretionary increases for particular units based on special circumstances. Rent control is controversial. Proponents argue that it protects tenants from being forced out of their homes by exorbitant rent increases, while opponents assert that it discourages construction of new housing units. *See* Edgar O. Olsen, *Is Rent Control Good Social Policy?*, 67 Chi.-Kent L. Rev. 931 (1991).

4. Delivering Possession

Suppose that T and L enter into an apartment lease that creates a one-year tenancy beginning on July 1. When T's moving van pulls up to the apartment building at 8:00 a.m. on July 1, T learns that the unit is still occupied by X, the prior tenant whose lease expired on June 15. Assume that the lease says nothing about L's duty to deliver possession. What are T's rights?

During the 1960s, Technology Square—a complex of three commercial office buildings—was the heart of the computer industry in Cambridge, Massachusetts. Located near MIT, it was occupied by tenants such as IBM, NASA, and Keydata Corporation. Keydata was one of the first companies to lease computer time to other users on a network basis, through its mainframe UNIVAC computer. By 1968, Keydata was so successful that it needed to move its operations to a larger space in another complex. At the same time, NASA needed more room for its computer equipment to facilitate work on the Apollo program, with the goal of landing the first human on the moon. NASA accordingly arranged to lease Keydata's premises. The resulting dispute produced an important precedent about the landlord's duty to deliver possession.

Keydata Corp. v. United States

United States Court of Claims

504 F.2d 1115 (1974)

DAVIS, JUDGE.

In 1968, Keydata Corporation and the National Aeronautics and Space Administration (NASA) were both leasing space at 575 Technology Square, Cambridge, Massachusetts, an office building owned by the Wyman Street Trust. Early in that year NASA decided to expand its footage in the structure, and at the same time Keydata was seeking to move to larger quarters in another

> **FYI**
>
> The leased space at issue in the case was intended to be part of NASA's Electronics Research Center, which conducted research on space guidance systems, space optics, microwave radiation, laser communication, photovoltaic energy conversion and other subjects.

location. After negotiations in which NASA was represented by the General Services Administration (GSA), an agreement was reached as to NASA's rental of Keydata's 2,093 square foot computer room on the first floor. . . . The agreement was embodied in two lease amendments, one between Keydata and Wyman, the other between the Government and Wyman. These modifications provided that Keydata would surrender possession of the computer room [to Wyman], and the Government would lease it [from Wyman], either on October 1, 1968 or on a date mutually agreeable to Keydata and the Government. . . .

The amendments also provided separately for the sale of certain fixtures. The Government promised to pay Wyman $39,000 for air conditioning equipment which Keydata had installed in the computer room, and Wyman obliged itself in the same amount in payment to Keydata. These improvements had been installed by Keydata with Wyman's consent, and the tenant retained the right to remove the equipment so long as the premises were returned to their original condition.

The two lease amendments summarized above were executed on March 11, 1968. Keydata and the Government later selected the January 1, 1969 move-in date, by using the mechanism set up in the lease . . . amendments. . . . [B]oth parties agree that Keydata had not vacated by January 1, 1969, and that on the next day GSA sent Keydata a letter informing it

> that the Government hereby cancels the proposed acquisition of 2093 square feet on the first floor at 575 Technology Square. . . . This action is necessary because of the fact that the space above referred to was not available for Government occupancy on January 1, 1969. . . .

The Government did not pay the $39,000 due under the agreements for the computer room improvements.

[Keydata later vacated the space and wanted to recover the $39,000 payment for its equipment. It sued Wyman for this amount. The judge resolved that case by ordering Wyman to assign its rights to collect the $39,000 payment from the Government, if any, to Keydata. Keydata then brought this second lawsuit against the Government, in the place of Wyman. Keydata's theory was that Wyman fully performed it obligations as a landlord by delivering the *legal right to possession* of the premises to the Government on January 1, 1969, so that (1) the Government's cancellation of the lease amendment was illegal and, accordingly, (2) Wyman was entitled to the $39,000 payment. In response, the Government alleged that Wyman was obli-

> **Practice Pointer**
>
> In general, a cause of action may be assigned to another person or entity. Thus, if A has a claim against B, A may assign that claim to C. But note the irony in this case. Keydata, which wrongfully remained in possession, ends up suing NASA, the incoming tenant which was unable to take possession due to Keydata's fault! Did this affect the outcome of the case?

gated to deliver *physical possession* of the leased premises, in addition to the legal right to possession, which it failed to do. Keydata and the Government both filed motions for summary judgment on this claim.]

. . . Keydata's motion for summary judgment asserts that the Government had no legal right to rescind its lease agreement with Wyman, despite plaintiff's holding-over. The argument is that the lease amendment obligated Wyman to do no more than convey to the Government the right to take possession of the computer room, that Wyman did not explicitly promise to deliver actual possession, and that no such promise can be implied.

Keydata's description of the lack of obligation of a landlord to secure his tenant in possession (in the absence of an express undertaking) is an accurate reflection of the present Massachusetts law. But there is a clear split among the states between the "American" and "English" rules on the liability of a landlord when the demised premises are occupied by a third party at the commencement of the lease term. Under the so-called "American" rule, the landlord merely covenants that possession will not be withheld by himself or by one having paramount title. This is the current rule in Massachusetts. *Snider v. Deban*, 249 Mass. 59, 144 N.E. 69 (1924). It is sometimes justified on the ground that, since the lessor has conveyed the sole and exclusive right of possession to the new lessee, he cannot maintain an action for possession in his own name.

The other doctrine, called the "English" rule, requires that, when the lease is silent on the point, the landlord deliver actual possession of the premises at the beginning of the term. The lessee's rights are based on breach of the lessor's implied covenant that he has a right to lease the premises, or of the implied undertaking that the lessor will deliver possession to the lessee. 2 R. Powell, Real Property (Rohan ed. 1966) § 225 [1]. If the lessee cannot take possession because of a holdover tenant, or some other obstructing third person, the landlord is in breach of his obligation.

This division in view compels us to face the problems of whether we are bound to follow the Massachusetts rule because the real property is located there—and, if not, what standard to apply. It will prove simpler to reverse these questions and first take up the issue of what rule to adopt if we are free to choose on the merits of the competing principles. In such an area of free choice, we "should take account of the best in modern decision and discussion." *Padbloc Co. v. United States*, 161 Ct. Cl. 369, 377 (1963). . . .

The American Law Institute's most recent formulation, accepting the "English" rule, seems to us to represent "the best in modern decision and discussion." The Institute's phrasing (Restatement of the Law, Second, Property, Landlord and Tenant, § 6.2, p. 137 (Tent. Draft No. 2, 1974)) is this:

> Except to the extent the parties to the lease validly agree otherwise, there is a breach of the landlord's obligations if a third person is improperly in possession of the leased property on the date the tenant is entitled to possession and the landlord does not act

promptly to remove such person and does not in fact remove him within a reasonable period of time. For such breach, the tenant may (1) terminate the lease. . . .

The Restatement gives persuasive reasons in support of this choice (Restatement of the Law, Second, Property, Landlord and Tenant, § 6.2, Comment a, p. 139 (Tent. Draft No. 2, 1974)):

> (1) The landlord knows, or should know, the status of the possession of the leased property better than the tenant in the period prior to the date the tenant is entitled to possession.
>
> (2) The landlord knows, or should know, better than the tenant whether a person in possession of the leased property prior to the date the tenant is entitled to possession is properly or improperly on the leased property.
>
> (3) Prior to the date the tenant is entitled to possession of the leased property, the landlord is the only one of the two who can evict a person improperly in possession of the leased property.
>
> (4) In the situation where the person in possession of the leased property is entitled to be there until the date the tenant is entitled to possession, the case of the possible holdover prior tenant, the landlord is the only one of the two who had an opportunity to get some assurance that the prior tenant would not hold over.
>
> (5) The tenant will have received less than he bargained for if he must go forward with the lease and bear the cost of legal proceedings to clear the way for his entry on the leased property.

This "English" rule conforms to the commonsense notion of what a lease is. The tenant is buying space—in a building or in the open—and not merely the right to bring a lawsuit to try to get the space. The "American" (or Massachusetts) rule, on the other hand, . . . represents an unfortunate example of mechanical jurisprudence, grinding out a result without any regard for the true interests or policies involved.

Plaintiff objects that adoption for federal leases of the rule requiring the landlord to deliver actual possession places a Massachusetts lessor in a dilemma—he must deliver possession but cannot evict a third party or holdover tenant after the lease term has begun. *See Snider v. Deban*, supra, 249 Mass. at 66, 144 N.E. at 72. As the ALI comment suggests this difficulty is not insuperable. First, a landlord is able to protect himself in the lease document by expressly limiting or disclaiming his obligation to deliver possession, or else by requiring security of a prior tenant in possession that he will not hold over. Second, the landlord may have a remedy in damages against a holdover tenant; such at least is the majority American rule. Third, the landlord is still in a better position to appraise, anticipate and bear the risk of this loss than a prospective tenant not yet in possession. The risk ought to be upon the owner, unless the prospective tenant expressly agrees to shoulder it.

Are we, however, free to elect the "English" rule as a uniform federal standard applicable to government leases in all domestic jurisdictions, including Massachusetts? The states have a considerable interest in the definition of the property interests within their borders, and some aspects of federal law do defer to that concern. But though a lease may concern and convey a property interest, it is also very much a contract—and it is settled that the contracts of the Federal Government are normally governed, not by the particular law of the states where they are made or performed, but by a uniform federal law. *Padbloc Co. v. United States*, 161 Ct. Cl. 369, 377 (1963). . . . Leases are not sufficiently different from other federal procurement contracts to call for a different policy across-the-board in the construction of their terms. At least in this case in which there is no question as to the content of the property interest transferred, but merely a delineation of one of the landlord's collateral obligations, there is no adequate reason to subordinate federal to state law. . . .

> **Food for Thought**
>
> How convincing is the court's reasoning that a lease should be governed by federal law because it is a contract? Isn't it also a type of property right, traditionally governed by state law?

The Federal Government's need for a uniform rule is strong. It ought to know in advance what its rights are if the premises are not available on the due date. But there are many jurisdictions in which it is not yet firmly established whether the "American" or the "English" rule controls, and the Government would either have to litigate or take a substantial chance on its position. On the other hand, as we have already indicated, the interest of the state in the landlord's obligation if the premises are unavailable seems to us minor, and relatively unconnected with its concern with the definition of property interests within its jurisdiction.

We hold, therefore, that we are free to disregard the Massachusetts rule, and we do so—for the reasons we have given—in favor of the "English" rule as set forth in the Restatement, as the appropriate standard for government leases. Accordingly, we deny the plaintiff's motion for summary judgment, grant on this ground the defendant's motion as to the first cause of action, and dismiss that portion of the petition. . . .

Points for Discussion

a. **Expectations and Bargaining**

The Wyman Street Trust, as lessor, and NASA, as lessee, were presumably represented by attorneys in the lease negotiations. Can we assume that the attorneys for both sides (1) knew that existing Massachusetts law followed the American rule, (2) did not try to modify that rule by negotiation, and (3) therefore expected that it would apply to this lease? If so, how could NASA argue for the English rule?

b. The Best Rule?

Which policies favor the English rule? The American rule? On balance, which is the better view? In formulating your answer, consider how each rule affects (1) the availability of rental space and (2) the rent charged for that space. Today most states follow the English rule.

c. The Problem of Remedies

In an American rule jurisdiction, the incoming tenant may sue the holdover tenant to recover possession and damages; but she has no claim against the landlord. In an English rule jurisdiction, the tenant may terminate the lease and sue the landlord for damages. Alternatively, she may affirm the lease, pay no rent until the premises are vacant, and collect damages from the landlord.

d. Legal Right to Possession

Despite the split of authority about whether the landlord must deliver *physical possession*, all states agree that he is required to deliver the *legal right to possession* when the lease term begins. Suppose L leases a single-family house to T for a term of five years starting in 2024, but later leases the same house to X for a term that begins in 2026. Because L previously leased to T, he cannot deliver the legal right to possession to X; L is liable to X for damages.

e. Special Rule for the Federal Government

What are the consequences of allowing the federal government to ignore the state laws that normally govern leases? Note that after *Keydata*, the law in Massachusetts is complex: the American rule governs most leases, but the English rule applies to any lease where the federal government is a party. How will this affect the behavior of landlords, tenants, and attorneys?

B. Condition of the Premises

1. The Challenge of Substandard Housing

The revolution in landlord-tenant law was ignited by a stark truth: many poor urban tenants were living in abysmal conditions. The problem was not new. As urbanization accelerated during the early 1900s, housing conditions worsened and slums developed. Disease, overcrowding, vermin, and filth threatened the health and safety of tenants.

One response to this crisis was the development of zoning ordinances during the 1920s, which you will study in Chapter 11. Another response was the adoption of housing codes which require that each dwelling meet certain minimum living standards, e.g., hot and cold running water, heating, plumbing facilities, safe wiring, watertight walls and roofs, and no infestation by vermin.

But many urban landlords concluded that they could maximize profits by ignoring the housing codes. They spent little or no money on repair and maintenance. As a result, conditions in rental housing were often appalling. The case excerpt below illustrates the problem.

In re Clark

United States Bankruptcy Court, Eastern District of Pennsylvania

96 B.R. 569 (1989)

DAVID A. SCHOLL, JUDGE.

[Clark, the debtor in this bankruptcy proceeding, owned a 24-unit apartment building in Philadelphia. Five of Clark's former tenants filed a complaint against him seeking damages based on the condition of their apartments.]

. . . The Claimants here were subject to extensive discomfort and annoyance as a result of the condition of their respective rental units. Williams had crumbling walls in her bathroom and holes in her kitchen walls. Her toilet failed to work for months and, when it did, it ran over into the bathtub. Williams testified that her apartment was infested with mice. She testified graphically about finding the mice in her child's crib. She slept at night with the lights on to keep the mice away, but, even so, she stated that she could feel them eating away at her bed's box spring at night. In the morning, she was greeted by the sight of mice coming into the apartment through a hole in the wall from the bathroom. Furthermore, one of her children was injured by eating debris from the apartment's walls that turned out to be infested with lead paint.

The other Claimants' testimony duplicated that of Williams. Robbins testified that the sound of mice chewing through the wall kept her awake at night. Robbins' kitchen ceiling had fallen in as a result of leaks, her sink was broken, and the kitchen floor had sunk, preventing her from using most of her kitchen. The Palmers and Nelson presented similar testimony regarding their leaky ceilings, crumbling walls, and warped and sloping floors.

Most notable and egregious among the problems that the claimants experienced are the fact that they lived without *any* heat or hot water since early spring, 1987. As a result, they attempted to obtain some heat by use of electric and kerosene heaters and the warmth generated from their gas stoves. Reliance on these alternate sources to heat an apartment, of course, presents additional dangers of fire and other detriments to the health and safety of tenants. As a result of the lack of heat and hot water, the

Palmers and Williams were compelled to place their minor children with relatives during the cold winter months. . . .

Points for Discussion

a. **Why Did the Market Fail?**

The law traditionally assumed that a tenant could protect his interests by negotiating an appropriate lease. Why didn't the tenants in *Clark* negotiate leases which required the landlord to repair their apartments? The answer is that Clark and many other residential landlords insisted on the use of standard form leases and refused to bargain for any changes. These forms typically placed the repair burden on the tenant, who lacked the knowledge, skills, and resources to fix defects. If the form contained no provision about repairs, the tenant was still responsible for making repairs under the common law doctrine of *permissive waste*. Finally, even a lease that did assign the burden to the landlord often provided no benefits to the tenant, because the promises in a lease were seen as *independent covenants* at common law. In other words, even if the landlord breached his promise to repair, the tenant could not terminate the lease for this reason. Instead, the tenant was entitled to file a lawsuit against the landlord for damages—and was required to continue paying the rent each month during the litigation. For most tenants, this theoretical remedy was meaningless.

b. **Why Did Regulation Fail?**

Why didn't the housing code prevent the conditions in *Clark*? The housing codes were weakly enforced in Philadelphia and most urban areas. Tenants were reluctant to report problems, fearing a rent increase or even eviction. When a violation was proven, the penalty imposed on the landlord was typically a small fine—often less than the cost of repairs. In fact, Clark was cited for 43 separate violations of the housing code between 1985 and 1988; but he did not fix the problems. In part because of situations like *Clark*, there is a modern trend toward imposing higher penalties. For example, in *City & County of San Francisco v. Sainez*, 92 Cal. Rptr. 2d 418 (Ct. App. 2000), the landlord was required to pay a fine of $663,000 for housing code violations.

c. **Aftermath of *Clark***

The bankruptcy court commented that Clark's testimony was "disjointed, and occasionally loud and belligerent." Clark complained bitterly that his tenants had caused the problems. But the court found no evidence to support these claims, calling them "irrational attempts by the Debtor to blame his shortcomings as a landlord on others." The court awarded $9,350 in damages to the tenants, although it is unclear if they were able to collect. Clark was later murdered by a former tenant.

2. Constructive Eviction

Tenant A enters into a five-year lease for a unit in landlord B's apartment complex. One month after taking possession, A returns home during a rainstorm to discover that water is leaking from the roof into her apartment. She puts buckets under the many leaks and calls B to complain. B explains that the roof "always leaks when it rains"; he refuses to fix the problem. What should A do?

The common law offered one special protection for the tenant in defective leased premises: the doctrine of *constructive eviction*. Wrongful conduct by the landlord that substantially interfered with the tenant's beneficial use and enjoyment of leased premises was deemed a constructive eviction. Under these circumstances, the tenant could vacate the premises and end the lease, thus avoiding liability for future rent.

How did the doctrine evolve? The common law acknowledged that each lease included an *implied covenant of quiet enjoyment*—a promise by the landlord that he would not wrongfully interfere with the tenant's possession. As noted above, the promises in a lease were originally seen as independent covenants, so the landlord's breach of this covenant did not excuse the tenant's continued performance. There was one exception to this rule: *actual eviction*. If the landlord physically evicted the tenant, this breached the covenant of quiet enjoyment and ended the lease. Over time, creative attorneys successfully argued that conduct other than actual eviction might so substantially interfere with the tenant's possession that it was the *functional equivalent* of actual eviction. This concept was dubbed "constructive" eviction.

The cases below consider constructive eviction in two different contexts: abortion protestors and stereo store noise. But they share the key questions found in every constructive eviction case. What constitutes "wrongful conduct"? Which conduct is "by the landlord"? And what conduct "substantially interferes" with the tenant's rights?

Fidelity Mutual Life Insurance Co. v. Kaminsky

Court of Appeals of Texas

768 S.W.2d 818 (1989)

MURPHY, JUSTICE.

The issue in this landlord-tenant case is whether sufficient evidence supports the jury's findings that the landlord and appellant, Fidelity Mutual Life Insurance Company ["Fidelity"], constructively evicted the tenant, Robert P. Kaminsky, M.D., P.A. ["Dr. Kaminsky"], by breaching the express covenant of quiet enjoyment contained in the parties' lease. We affirm.

Dr. Kaminsky is a gynecologist whose practice includes performing elective abortions. In May 1983, he executed a lease contract for the rental of approximately 2,861 square feet in the Red Oak Atrium Building for a two year term which began on June 1, 1983. The terms of the lease required Dr. Kaminsky to use the rented space solely as "an office for the practice of medicine." Fidelity owns the building and hires local companies to manage it. At some time during the lease term, Shelter Commercial Properties ["Shelter"] replaced the Horne Company as managing agents. Fidelity has not disputed either management company's capacity to act as its agent.

The parties agree that: they executed a valid lease agreement; Paragraph 35 of the lease contains an express covenant of quiet enjoyment conditioned on Dr. Kaminsky's paying rent when due, as he did through November 1984; Dr. Kaminsky abandoned the leased premises on or about December 3, 1984 and refused to pay additional rent; anti-abortion protestors began picketing at the building in June of 1984 and repeated and increased their demonstrations outside and inside the building until Dr. Kaminsky abandoned the premises.

When Fidelity sued for the balance due under the lease contract following Dr. Kaminsky's abandonment of the premises, he claimed that Fidelity constructively evicted him by breaching Paragraph 35 of the lease. Fidelity apparently conceded during trial that sufficient proof of the constructive eviction of Dr. Kaminsky would relieve him of his contractual liability for any remaining rent payments. Accordingly, he assumed the burden of proof and the sole issue submitted to the jury was whether Fidelity breached Paragraph 35 of the lease, which reads as follows:

> *Quiet Enjoyment.*
>
> Lessee, on paying the said Rent, and any Additional Rental, shall and may peaceably and quietly have, hold and enjoy the Leased Premises for the said term.

A constructive eviction occurs when the tenant leaves the leased premises due to conduct by the landlord which materially interferes with the tenant's beneficial use of the premises. *See Downtown Realty, Inc. v. 509 Tremont Bldg.*, 748 S.W.2d 309, 313 (Tex. App.-Houston [14th Dist.] 1988, n.w.h.). Texas law relieves the tenant of contractual liability for any remaining rentals due under the lease if he can establish a constructive eviction by the landlord.

In order to prevail on his claim that Fidelity constructively evicted him and thereby relieved him of his rent obligation, Dr. Kaminsky had to show the following: 1) Fidelity intended that he no longer enjoy the premises, which intent the trier of fact could infer from the circumstances; 2) Fidelity, or those acting for Fidelity or with its permission, committed a material act or omission which substantially interfered with use and enjoyment of the premises for their leased purpose, here an office for the practice of medicine; 3) Fidelity's act or omission permanently deprived Dr. Kaminsky of the use and enjoyment of the premises; and 4) Dr. Kaminsky abandoned the premises within a reasonable period of time after the act or omission. *E.g., Downtown Realty, Inc.*, 748 S.W.2d at 311. . . .

[T]he jury found that Dr. Kaminsky had established each element of his constructive eviction defense. The trial court entered judgment that Fidelity take nothing on its suit for delinquent rent. . . .

Fidelity's first point of error relies on *Angelo v. Deutser*, 30 S.W.2d 707 (Tex. Civ. App.-Beaumont 1930, no writ), *Thomas v. Brin*, 38 Tex. Civ. App. 180, 85 S.W. 842 (1905, no writ) and *Sedberry v. Verplanck*, 31 S.W. 242 (Tex. Civ. App. 1895, no writ). These cases all state the general proposition that a tenant cannot complain that the landlord constructively evicted him and breached a covenant of quiet enjoyment, express or implied, when the eviction results from the actions of third parties acting without the landlord's authority or permission. Fidelity insists the evidence conclusively establishes: a) that it did nothing to encourage or sponsor the protestors and; b) that the protestors, rather than Fidelity or its agents, caused Dr. Kaminsky to abandon the premises. . . .

Although this point of error appears to challenge both the legal and factual sufficiency of the evidence, we have construed it as raising only a "no evidence" or legal sufficiency challenge for two reasons. First, Fidelity relies on record references to "undisputed" evidence and bases its arguments on "established" rules of law. After reviewing Fidelity's oral and written arguments and its references to the record, we conclude that Fidelity essentially disputes the legal sufficiency of the evidence to show that *its own* conduct constructively evicted Dr. Kaminsky. . . .

The protests took place chiefly on Saturdays, the day Dr. Kaminsky generally scheduled abortions. During the protests, the singing and chanting demonstrators picketed in the building's parking lot and inner lobby and atrium area. They approached patients to speak to them, distributed literature, discouraged patients from entering the building and often accused Dr. Kaminsky of "killing babies." As the protests increased, the demonstrators often occupied the stairs leading to Dr. Kaminsky's office and prevented patients from entering the office by blocking the doorway. Occasionally they succeeded in gaining access to the office waiting room area.

Dr. Kaminsky complained to Fidelity through its managing agents and asked for help in keeping the protestors away, but became increasingly frustrated by a lack of response to his requests. The record shows that no security personnel were present on Saturdays to exclude protestors from the building, although the lease required Fidelity to provide security service on Saturdays. The record also shows that Fidelity's attorneys prepared a written statement to be handed to the protestors soon after Fidelity hired Shelter as its managing agent. The statement tracked Tex. Penal Code Ann. § 30.05 (Vernon Supp. 1989) and generally served to inform trespassers that they risked criminal prosecution

> **Food for Thought**
>
> As an attorney, what other advice would you have given to Fidelity about how to deal with the protestors?

by failing to leave if asked to do so. Fidelity's attorneys instructed Shelter's representative to "have several of these letters printed up and be ready to distribute them and verbally demand that these people move on and off the property." The same representative conceded at trial that she did not distribute these notices. Yet when Dr. Kaminsky enlisted the aid of the Sheriff's office, officers refused to ask the protestors to leave without a directive from Fidelity or its agent. Indeed, an attorney had instructed the protestors to remain *unless* the landlord or its representative ordered them to leave. It appears that Fidelity's only response to the demonstrators was to state, through its agents, that it was aware of Dr. Kaminsky's problems.

Both action and lack of action can constitute "conduct" by the landlord which amounts to a constructive eviction. *E.g., Downtown Realty Inc.*, 748 S.W.2d at 311. In *Steinberg v. Medical Equip. Rental Serv., Inc.*, 505 S.W.2d 692 (Tex. Civ. App.-Dallas 1974, no writ) accordingly, the court upheld a jury's determination that the landlord's failure to act amounted to a constructive eviction and breach of the covenant of quiet enjoyment. Like Dr. Kaminsky, the tenant in *Steinberg* abandoned the leased premises and refused to pay additional rent after repeatedly complaining to the landlord. The *Steinberg* tenant complained that Steinberg placed trash bins near the entrance to the business and allowed trucks to park and block customers' access to the tenant's medical equipment rental business. The tenant's repeated complaints to Steinberg yielded only a request "to be patient." *Id*. Fidelity responded to Dr. Kaminsky's complaints in a similar manner: although it acknowledged his problems with the protestors, Fidelity, like Steinberg, effectively did nothing to prevent the problems.

This case shows ample instances of Fidelity's failure to act in the fact of repeated requests for assistance despite its having expressly covenanted Dr. Kaminsky's quiet enjoyment of the premises. These instances provided a legally sufficient basis for the jury to conclude that Dr. Kaminsky abandoned the leased premises, not because of the trespassing protestors, but because of Fidelity's lack of response to his complaints about the protestors. Under the circumstances, while it is undisputed that Fidelity did not "encourage" the demonstrators, its conduct essentially allowed them to continue to trespass. The general rule of the *Angelo, Thomas* and *Sedberry* cases, that a landlord is not responsible for the actions of third parties, applies only when the landlord does not permit the third party to act. *See e.g., Angelo*, 30 S.W.2d at 710 ["the act or omission complained of must be that of the landlord and not merely of a third person *acting without his authority or permission*" (emphasis added)]. We see no distinction between Fidelity's lack of action here, which the record shows resulted in preventing patients' access to Dr. Kaminsky's medical office, and the *Steinberg* case where the landlord's inaction resulted in trucks blocking customer access to the tenant's business. We overrule the first point of error. . . .

In its fourth point of error, Fidelity maintains the evidence is factually insufficient to support the jury's finding that its conduct permanently deprived Dr. Kaminsky of use and enjoyment of the premises. Fidelity essentially questions the permanency of Dr. Kaminsky's being deprived of the use and enjoyment of the leased premises. To support its contentions, Fidelity points to testimony by Dr. Kaminsky in which he concedes that none of his patients were ever harmed and that protests and demonstrations continued despite his leaving the Red Oak Atrium building. Fidelity also disputes whether Dr. Kaminsky actually lost patients due to the protests.

The evidence shows that the protestors, whose entry into the building Fidelity failed to prohibit, often succeeded in blocking Dr. Kaminsky's patients' access to his medical office. Under the reasoning of the *Steinberg* case, omissions by a landlord which result in patients' lack of access to the office of a practicing physician would suffice to establish a permanent deprivation of the use and enjoyment of the premises for their leased purpose, here "an office for the *practice* of medicine." *Steinberg*, 505 S.W.2d at 697; *accord, Downtown Realty, Inc.*, 748 S.W.2d at 312 (noting jury's finding that a constructive eviction resulted from the commercial landlord's failure to repair a heating and air conditioning system in a rooming house).

Texas law has long recited the requirement, first stated in *Stillman [v. Youmans]*, 266 S.W.2d 913, 916 (Tex. Civ. App.-Galveston 1954, no writ)], that the landlord commit a "material and permanent" act or omission in order for his tenant to claim a constructive eviction. However, as the *Steinberg* and *Downtown Realty, Inc.* cases illustrate, the extent to which a landlord's acts or omissions permanently and materially deprive a tenant of the use and enjoyment of the premises often involves a question of degree. Having reviewed all the evidence before the jury in this case, we cannot say that its finding that Fidelity's conduct permanently deprived Dr. Kaminsky of the use and enjoyment of his medical office space was so against the great weight and preponderance of the evidence as to be manifestly unjust. We overrule the fourth point of error.

> **Food for Thought**
>
> How convincing is the court's conclusion that Kaminsky was "permanently" deprived of the use and enjoyment of the premises? Based on this interpretation, how "permanent" must a problem be to establish constructive eviction in Texas?

We affirm the judgment of the trial court.

JMB Properties Urban Co. v. Paolucci

Appellate Court of Illinois

604 N.E.2d 967 (1992)

JUSTICE SLATER delivered the opinion of the court:

Plaintiffs, JMB Properties Urban Company (JMB) and Carlyle Real Estate Limited Partnership XIV (Carlyle), sued defendant, Alfred Paolucci, for recovery of unpaid rent and other damages resulting from defendant's breach of a commercial lease. The trial court found that defendant had been constructively evicted, and plaintiffs appeal. Because we find that defendant waived any claim of constructive eviction, we reverse and remand.

> **See It**
>
> Click here to see photographs of the Louis Joliet Mall.

Defendant opened a jewelry store in the Louis Joliet Mall in Joliet, Illinois, in 1978. Barretts Audio and Video Store (Barretts) moved in next door to defendant in November of 1984. Defendant and Barretts shared a common wall. In December of 1984, defendant began complaining to then-landlord Homart Development Company about the high level of noise emanating from Barretts. Defendant continued to lodge such complaints periodically until Barretts vacated the mall in February of 1990.

Carlyle purchased the mall in September of 1985 and took an assignment of all outstanding leases from Homart. Carlyle hired JMB to manage the mall, negotiate new leases and collect rent from mall tenants.

In August of 1986, defendant entered into a new six year lease with Carlyle which required that defendant operate the jewelry store during the entire term of the lease and refrain from operating any similar business within a five mile radius of the mall. Defendant failed to pay rent for July, 1990, and vacated the premises in August, 1990, two years prior to the end of the lease. Defendant moved to a new location within a five mile radius of the mall.

Carlyle and JMB (collectively Carlyle) filed actions against defendant seeking recovery of past due rent and penalties for violating the lease. Defendant filed a counterclaim seeking declaratory relief, alleging that he had been constructively evicted as a result of Carlyle's failure to control the excessive noise generated by Barretts. . . .

A bench trial was held on October 18, November 22, and December 20, 1991. Several witnesses testified on behalf of defendant concerning the noise emanating from Barretts during their five year tenancy. Defendant and his employees testified that when Barretts' employees conducted demonstrations of their stereo equipment the walls of the jewelry store literally shook causing pictures to rattle on the jewelry store walls. The vibrations caused merchandise in display cases to move or topple over so that the display cases had to be reset almost daily. Defendant testified that Barretts' employees refused numerous requests to lower the volume.

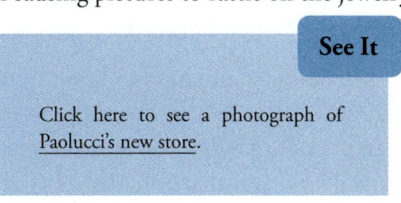

> **See It**
>
> Click here to see a photograph of Paolucci's new store.

One of defendant's employees testified that the noise was so loud that at one point she resorted to wearing ear plugs at work. Customers occasionally complained of the noise and at times were unwilling to conduct business in the jewelry store because of the nuisance.

At Carlyle's direction, Barretts insulated the common wall in an attempt to sound proof it in 1985, but this failed to alleviate the problem. Evidence was presented to show that defendant lost at least some profits as a result of the noise because he was unable to perform intricate repair work on watches and jewelry. Defendant lodged approximately 500 complaints with the mall management during the course of Barretts' five and one-half year tenancy. Despite the defendant's numerous complaints, and despite the fact that each call was responded to by Carlyle, the excessive noise problem continued throughout Barretts' tenancy. . . .

After hearing the evidence and the arguments of counsel, the court held that defendant had been constructively evicted, and awarded back rent to Carlyle only for the two months during which defendant remained in possession of the premises without paying rent. . . .

On appeal, Carlyle contends that the trial court erred in finding that the noise emanating from Barretts was sufficient to amount to a constructive eviction. A constructive eviction results from a landlord's failure to keep the premises in a tenantable condition. (*RNR Realty, Inc. v. Burlington Coat Factory Warehouse of Cicero, Inc.* (1988), 168 Ill. App. 3d 210, 522 N.E.2d 679). Unable to perform intricate repair Untenantability exists when the interference with occupancy is of such a nature that the property cannot be used for the purpose for which it was rented. *RNR Realty*, 168 Ill.App.3d at 218, 522 N.E.2d at 685.

We need not address the question of whether the noise was sufficient to render the premises untenantable because we find that defendant waived any claim of constructive eviction by remaining on the premises for an unreasonable length of time after the rise of the untenantable condition. Constructive eviction cannot exist where the tenant does not surrender the property. (*First National Bank v. Sousanes*, (1981), 96 Ill. App. 3d 1047, 422 N.E.2d 188.) Following a constructive eviction, the tenant is not required to vacate the premises immediately, but is entitled to a reasonable time to do so. The tenant bears the burden of proving that he did abandon the premises within a reasonable time after the untenantable condition occurred. If the tenant fails to vacate within a reasonable time, the tenant is considered to have waived the landlord's breach of covenant. . . .

The untenantable condition in this case first arose in December of 1985. Defendant remained on the leasehold premises until of August of 1990, nearly five years after the condition arose and six months after Barretts moved out of the mall. Defendant claims that he remained on the premises for six months after Barretts left because his new store was still under construction. We realize that one factor to be considered in determining the reasonableness of the delay is the time required to find a new location. Even if the last six months of defendant's occupancy could be excused on this basis, defendant fails to explain why he tolerated the alleged untenantable condition for more than four years. Defendant cites no case, and our research reveals none, where a delay of this length was excused. . . .

We also note that defendant entered into a new six year lease with Carlyle in 1986, nearly two years after Barretts moved in and after defendant threatened to sue Barretts in March of 1985. While defendant claims that he received assurances from Carlyle before he signed the new lease that the noise problem would be taken care of, we believe the fact that defendant had an opportunity to leave the mall in 1986 but instead chose to remain and enter into a new six year lease is a factor to be considered in our determination of the reasonableness of the delay in this case. In light of the above facts we find the trial court's determination that defendant did not waive his claim of constructive eviction to be against the manifest weight of the evidence. . . .

Points for Discussion

a. **"Wrongful Conduct . . ."**

The "wrongful conduct" requirement may be satisfied by an act or omission. Examples of wrongful *acts* by landlords include: (1) blocking access to the tenant's premises; (2) creating a nuisance that affects the tenant; (3) harassing the tenant's customers; and (4) repeatedly trespassing on the tenant's premises.

When is an *omission* wrongful? Cases have found that this standard is met where the landlord: (1) fails to perform an obligation in the lease; (2) fails to adequately maintain and control the common area; (3) breaches a statutory duty owed to the tenant; (4) fails to perform promised repairs; or (5) allows nuisance-like behavior. Did the landlords in *Kaminsky* or *Paolucci* commit a wrongful omission?

Constructive eviction encompasses many types of wrongful conduct, as these examples indicate:

- *Allergies*: In *Cohen v. Clark*, 945 N.W.2d 792 (Iowa 2020), a tenant who was allergic to dogs moved into an apartment with a "no pets" policy; she was constructively evicted when the landlord leased another unit to a tenant with an emotional support dog.

- *Leaks*: In *Village Commons, LLC v. Marion County Prosecutor's Office*, 882 N.E.2d 210 (Ind. Ct. App. 2008) repeated water leaks into the prosecutor's leased office that damaged boxes of evidence and caused microbiological contamination constituted constructive eviction.

- *Prejudice*: The tenant in *Gray v. Oxford Worldwide Group*, 139 P.3d 267 (Utah Ct. App. 2006) leased the property to operate a language training school for Latino members of the LDS Church; the property manager "exhibited her prejudice against Latinos by yelling, swearing, and using ethnic epithets," which constituted constructive eviction. *Id.* at 268.

b. **". . . By the Landlord . . ."**

There was no evidence in *Kaminsky* that the landlord participated in the protests or requested that they occur. Similarly, the landlord in *Paolucci* did not create the loud stereo noise. As a general rule, a tenant cannot assert constructive eviction due to the acts of third parties. But many courts—and Restatement (Second) of Property: Landlord and Tenant § 6.1 cmt. d—recognize an exception to this principle if the landlord has a legal right to control the third party conduct. Did the landlords have that right in *Kaminsky* or *Paolucci*?

c. **". . . That Substantially Interferes" with the Tenant's Use and Enjoyment**

How would you explain to a client what "substantial interference" means? In *Kaminsky* and *Paolucci*, the third party conduct did interfere with the tenants' businesses. But why was the interference "substantial"? After all, presumably Kaminsky was able to practice medicine six days each week without any problems; and he could have tried to perform abortions on a weekday, when protestors might have been working and unable to appear. Similarly, there is little evidence that Paolucci actually lost any business due to the noise; customers only complained occasionally. And he could have performed the delicate repair work at night when the stereo store was closed.

d. **Procedural Steps**

In general, a tenant seeking to rely on constructive eviction must notify the landlord about the problem, give the landlord a reasonable period to fix the problem, and then vacate the premises. What facts show that the tenant in *Kaminsky* satisfied these requirements? Why might a tenant be concerned about vacating the premises? Some states allow the tenant to remain in possession and recover damages on a constructive eviction theory. Restatement (Second) of Property: Landlord and Tenant § 6.1(2) endorses this approach. Which is the better view?

e. Too Soon or Too Late?

A tenant who wants to use constructive eviction cannot vacate too soon—and he also cannot vacate too late. Why did the court find that Paolucci waived his constructive eviction claim? After all, he complained approximately 500 times before leaving the premises. Was it reasonable for Paolucci to believe that the landlord would fix the noise problem, as it promised before he signed the 1986 lease? As an attorney, what factors would you consider in determining how long a tenant claiming constructive eviction should remain in possession?

f. Constructive Eviction Problems

Can the tenants below vacate the premises and successfully assert the defense of constructive eviction?

> (1) A enters into a ten-year term of years tenancy in B's commercial office building in a southwestern state, where she plans to open an accounting firm. The lease states that "B will provide air conditioning," but it says nothing about the required temperature. When A takes occupancy, she learns that B's building policy is to ensure that the office temperature never exceeds 78°F; B explains this is an energy conservation measure. As a result, A's employees are frequently hot, sweaty, and short-tempered; an expert consultant finds that their productivity is 4% lower than it would be at 72°F. B refuses to change his policy.
>
> (2) C enters into a year-to-year periodic tenancy for a retail store space in D's shopping center. D is aware that C plans to use the premises to operate a Christian bookstore. Two days after C takes possession D leases the adjacent store space to E, who immediately opens a pornographic bookstore. C's business is doing poorly, and some customers have complained about E's adjacent store. D refuses to do anything about E's bookstore.

g. Residential Tenants and Constructive Eviction

The constructive eviction doctrine applies to both residential and commercial tenancies. But as *Kaminsky* and *Paolucci* illustrate, it is most commonly used by commercial tenants. Why didn't the tenants in *Clark* use the constructive eviction remedy? Housing in Philadelphia was in short supply, so they could not find affordable apartments to rent. Because many poor urban tenants found themselves in the same situation, the constructive eviction doctrine did little to improve housing conditions. But the real answer is that the *Clark* tenants had a better theory, which we will see in the next case: the implied warranty of habitability.

In addition, an increasing number of states provide a remedy akin to constructive eviction for residential tenants who are victims of domestic violence, stalking, or sexual assault. A victim who has a reasonable fear that this abuse may continue if she remains in the unit can terminate her lease and avoid future rent liability, without obtaining the landlord's consent. Section 1102 of the Revised Uniform Residential Landlord and Tenant Act (2015) endorses this approach.

h. Aftermath of *Kaminsky* and *Paolucci*

Kaminsky and others later obtained an injunction preventing anti-abortion protestors from demonstrating too closely to their offices and homes, together with a punitive damages award of over $1,000,000. *Operation Rescue-National v. Planned Parenthood*, 975 S.W.2d 546 (Tex. 1998). Paolucci continues to sell diamonds and other jewelry at his new store, located about one mile south of the Louis Joliet Mall.

---

3. The Implied Warranty of Habitability

The most significant accomplishment of the landlord-tenant revolution was a new doctrine to protect residential tenants from defective housing conditions: the *implied warranty of habitability*. The Utah Supreme Court adopted this doctrine in the decision below.

Wade v. Jobe

Supreme Court of Utah

818 P.2d 1006 (1991)

DURHAM, JUSTICE:

In June 1988, defendant Lynda Jobe (the tenant) rented a house in Ogden, Utah, from plaintiff Clyde Wade (the landlord). Jobe had three young children. Shortly after she took occupancy, the tenant discovered numerous defects in the dwelling, and within a few days, she had no hot water. Investigation revealed that the flame of the water heater had been extinguished by accumulated sewage and water in the basement which also produced a foul odor throughout the house. The tenant notified the landlord, who came to the premises a number of times, each time pumping the sewage and water from the basement onto the sidewalk and relighting the water heater. These and other problems persisted from July through October 1988.

In November 1988, the tenant notified the landlord that she would withhold rent until the sewage problem was solved permanently. The situation did not improve, and an inspection by the Ogden City Inspection Division (the division) in December 1988 revealed that the premises were unsafe for human occupancy due to the lack of a sewer connection and other problems. Within a few weeks, the division made another inspection, finding numerous code violations which were a substantial hazard to the health and safety of the occupants. The division issued a notice that the property would be condemned if the violations were not remedied.

Jobe's house
Click here for larger photo

After the tenant moved out of the house, the landlord brought suit in the second circuit court to recover the unpaid rent. The tenant filed a counterclaim, seeking an offset against rent owed because of the uninhabitable condition of the premises and seeking damages. . . .

At trial, the landlord was awarded judgment of unpaid rent of $770, the full rent due under the parties' original agreement. The tenant was denied any offsets, and her counterclaim was dismissed. . . . This appeal followed, raising two issues: First, may a tenant recover at common law for breach of a warranty of habitability? . . .

I. WARRANTY OF HABITABILITY

At common law, the leasing of real property was viewed primarily as a conveyance of land for a term, and the law of property was applied to landlord/tenant transactions. At a time when the typical lease was for agricultural purposes, it was assumed that the land, rather than any improvements, was the most important part of the leasehold. *See generally Javins v. First Nat'l Realty Corp.*, 428 F.2d 1071, 1077 (D.C. Cir.), cert. denied, 400 U.S. 925 (1970). Under the rule of caveat emptor, a tenant had a duty to inspect the premises to determine their safety and suitability for the purposes for which they were leased before entering a lease. Moreover, absent deceit or fraud on the part of the landlord or an express warranty to the contrary, the landlord had

> **It's Latin to Me**
>
> *Caveat emptor* means "let the buyer beware" in Latin. This maxim reflects the common law view that the tenant took leased premises in "as is condition," without any obligation on the part of the landlord to make repairs.

no duty to make repairs during the course of the tenancy. Under the law of waste, it was the tenant's implied duty to make most repairs.

Unlike tenants in feudal England, most modern tenants bargain for the use of structures on the land rather than the land itself. Modern tenants generally lack the necessary skills or means to inspect the property effectively or to make repairs. *Javins*, 428 F.2d at 1078–79. Moreover, the rule of caveat emptor assumes an equal bargaining position between landlord and tenant. Modern tenants, like consumers of goods, however, frequently have no choice but to rely on the landlord to provide a habitable dwelling. See *Javins*, 428 F.2d at 1079. Where they exist, housing shortages, standardized leases, and racial and class discrimination place today's tenants, as consumers of housing, in a poor position to bargain effectively for express warranties and covenants requiring landlords to lease and maintain safe and sanitary housing. *Javins*, 428 F.2d at 1079.

In consumer law, implied warranties are designed to protect ordinary consumers who do not have the knowledge, capacity, or opportunity to ensure that goods which they are buying are in safe condition. See *Henningsen v. Bloomfield Motors, Inc.*, 32 N.J. 358, 161 A.2d 69, 78 (1960); Utah Code Ann. §§ 70A–2–314 to –316 (implied warranties contained in Uniform Commercial Code). The implied warranty of habitability has been adopted in other jurisdictions to protect the tenant as the party in the less advantageous bargaining position.

The concept of a warranty of habitability is in harmony with the widespread enactment of housing and building codes which reflect a legislative desire to ensure decent housing. It is based on the theory that the residential landlord warrants that the leased premises are habitable at the outset of the lease term and will remain so during the course of the tenancy. The warranty applies to written and oral leases . . . and to single-family as well as to multiple-unit dwellings. The warranty of habitability has been adopted, either legislatively or judicially, in over forty states and the District of Columbia.

In recent years, this court has conformed the common law in this state to contemporary conditions by rejecting the strict application of traditional property law to residential leases, recognizing that it is often more appropriate to apply contract law. See *Reid v. Mutual of Omaha Ins. Co.*, 776 P.2d 896, 902 n. 3 (Utah 1989). . . . Similarly, we have expanded landlord liability in tort. See *Stephenson v. Warner*, 581 P.2d 567 (Utah 1978) (landlord must use ordinary care to ensure leased premises are reasonably safe). Consistent with prevailing trends in consumer law, products liability law, and the law of torts, we reject the rule of caveat emptor and recognize the common law implied warranty of habitability in residential leases.

The determination of whether a dwelling is habitable depends on the individual facts of each case. To guide the trial court in determining whether there is a breach of the warranty of habitability, we describe some general standards that the landlord is required to satisfy. We note initially that the warranty of habitability does not require the landlord to maintain the premises in perfect condition at all times, nor does it preclude minor housing code violations or other defects. Moreover, the landlord will not be liable for defects caused by the tenant. *See Javins*, 428 F.2d at 1082 n. 62. Further, the landlord must have a reasonable time to repair material defects before a breach can be established.

As a general rule, the warranty of habitability requires that the landlord maintain "bare living requirements," *see Academy Spires, Inc. v. Brown*, 111 N.J. Super. 477, 268 A.2d 556, 559 (1970), and that the premises are fit for human occupation. *See Hilder v. St. Peter*, 144 Vt. 150, 478 A.2d 202, 208 (1984). Failure to supply heat or hot water, for example, breaches the warranty. A breach is not shown, however, by evidence of minor deficiencies such as the malfunction of venetian blinds, minor water leaks or wall cracks, or a need for paint.

Substantial compliance with building and housing code standards will generally serve as evidence of the fulfillment of a landlord's duty to provide habitable premises. Evidence of violations involving health or safety, by contrast, will often sustain a tenant's claim for relief. At the same time, just because the housing code provides a basis for implication of the warranty, a code violation is not necessary to establish a breach so long as the claimed defect has an impact on the health or safety of the tenant. *Hilder v. St. Peter,* 478 A.2d at 209.

In the instant case, in support of her claim that the premises were not in habitable condition, the tenant presented two city housing inspection reports detailing numerous code violations which were, in the words of the trial judge, "a substantial hazard to the health and safety of the occupants." Those violations included the presence of raw sewage on the sidewalks and stagnant water in the basement, creating a foul odor. At trial, the tenant testified that she had repeatedly informed the landlord of the problem with the sewer connection and the resulting lack of hot water, but the landlord never did any more than temporarily alleviate the problem. The landlord did not controvert the evidence of substantial problems. At trial, the court granted judgment for the landlord, concluding that Utah law did not recognize an implied warranty of habitability for residential rental premises. As discussed above, we have now recognized the warranty. We therefore remand this case to the trial court to determine whether the landlord has breached the implied warranty of habitability as defined in this opinion. If the trial court finds a breach of the warranty of habitability, it must then determine damages.

> **Food for Thought**
>
> Based on the standards contained in the court's opinion, did Wade breach the implied warranty of habitability?

A. Remedies

Under traditional property law, a lessee's covenant to pay rent was viewed as independent of any covenants on the part of the landlord. Even when a lessor expressly covenanted to make repairs, the lessor's breach did not justify the lessee's withholding rent. Under the prevailing contemporary view of the residential lease as a contractual transaction, however, the tenant's obligation to pay rent is conditioned upon the landlord's fulfilling his part of the bargain. The payment of rent by the tenant and the landlord's duty to provide habitable premises are, as a result, dependent covenants.

Once the landlord has breached his duty to provide habitable conditions, there are at least two ways the tenant can treat the duty to pay rent. The tenant may continue to pay rent to the landlord or withhold the rent.[3] If the tenant continues to pay full rent to the landlord during the period of uninhabitability, the tenant can bring an affirmative action to establish the breach and receive a reimbursement for excess rents paid. Rent withholding, on the other hand, deprives the landlord of the rent due during the default, thereby motivating the landlord to repair the premises. *See* 2 R. Powell, *The Law of Real Property* ¶ 228[6][d], at 16A-51 (1990). . . .

B. Damages

In general, courts have applied contract remedies when a breach of the warranty of habitability has been shown. One available remedy, therefore, is damages. Special damages may be recovered when, as a foreseeable result of the landlord's breach, the tenant suffers personal injury, property damage, relocation expenses, or other similar injuries. General damages recoverable in the form of rent abatement or reimbursement to the tenant are more difficult to calculate.

Several different measures for determining the amount of rent abatement to which a tenant is entitled have been used by the courts. The first of these is the fair rental value of the premises as warranted less their fair rental value in the unrepaired condition. Under this approach, the contract rent may be considered as evidence of the value of the premises as warranted. Another measure is the contract rent less the fair rental value of the premises in the unrepaired condition. Methodological difficulties inherent in both of these measures, combined with the practical difficulties of producing evidence on fair market value, however, limit the efficacy of those measures for dealing with residential leases. For this reason, a number of courts have adopted what is called the "percentage diminution" (or percentage reduction in use) approach which places more discretion with the trier of fact.

Under the percentage diminution approach, the tenant's recovery reflects the percentage by which the tenant's use and enjoyment of the premises has been reduced by the uninhabitable conditions. In applying this approach, the trial court must carefully review the materiality of the particular defects and the length of time such defects have existed. *See Academy Spires, Inc. v. Brown*, 268 A.2d at 562. It is true that the percentage diminution approach requires the trier of fact to exercise broad discretion and some subjective judgment to determine the degree to which the

---

[3] In addition, some jurisdictions recognize rent application, also known as "repair and deduct," allowing the tenant to use the rent money to repair the premises. Because this remedy has not been relied on or sought in the instant case, we do not at this time make a ruling on its availability in Utah.

defective conditions have diminished the habitability of the premises. It should be noted, however, that despite their theoretical appeal, the other approaches are not objectively precise either. Furthermore, they involve the use of an expert witness's subjective opinion of the "worth" of habitable and uninhabitable premises.

As the foregoing discussion demonstrates, the determination of appropriate damages in cases of a breach of the warranty of habitability will often be a difficult task. None of the approaches described above is inherently illegitimate, but we think that the percentage diminution approach has a practical advantage in that it will generally obviate the need for expert testimony and reduce the cost and complexity of enforcing the warranty of habitability. . . .

Teller v. McCoy

Supreme Court of Appeals of West Virginia

253 S.E.2d 114 (1978)

[The majority opinion adopted the implied warranty of habitability for reasons similar to those set forth in *Wade v. Jobe*.]

NEELY, JUSTICE, concurring in part, dissenting in part:

. . . I do not dispute for a moment that it would be wonderful if everyone could inhabit housing meeting both his taste and his budget but, unfortunately, the majority opinion cannot build houses, lower rents, or in any other way create more housing than already exists. Many people live in quarters which are less than luxurious because they cannot afford to pay more than what they already pay for rent. Ritz Hotel type housing cannot be provided where none otherwise exists unless someone pays for it. In our economy that means either (1) the landlord, (2) the tenant, or (3) the government. The government is trying to do its share, but its resources are limited. The landlord cannot make substantial renovations without passing his costs on to the tenant, and the tenant may then find that he has been given more luxury than he can afford. It is very much as if one were to write an opinion which implied that everyone had a natural law right to a Rolls Royce and that an action in warranty would lie against all other automobile manufacturers if they provided anything less elegant. Many damage awards might follow, but eventually all other automobile

> **FYI**
>
> The Ritz Hotel in London—nicknamed "the Ritz"—is one of the most expensive and famous hotels in the world. It inspired the 1929 hit song by Irving Berlin, *Puttin' on the Ritz*. Is Justice Neely suggesting that the implied warranty of habitability requires the same level of luxury as the Ritz?

manufacturers would be out of business, notwithstanding that very few Rolls Royces had come into the hands of those whom the opinion was intended to help. . . .

Points for Discussion

a. **Adoption of the Implied Warranty**

The implied warranty of habitability is now recognized in almost every state. The warranty first gained prominence in the landmark case of *Javins v. First National Realty Corp.*, 428 F.2d 1071 (D.C. Cir. 1970). Influenced by *Javins*, many courts adopted the warranty through case law. In other states, the warranty arose through legislation. These statutes are most commonly based on Uniform Residential Landlord and Tenant Act § 2.104, which generally requires the landlord to "do whatever is necessary to put and keep the premises in a fit and habitable condition" and imposes specific duties as well, such as providing running water (including hot water); adequate heating, lighting, and plumbing; trash facilities; and safe and clean common areas. The Revised Uniform Residential Landlord and Tenant Act (2015) extends this list to include: effective waterproofing; control of rodents, bedbugs, and vermin; prevention of exposure to hazardous substances such as lead paint, mold, and radon gas; floors, doors, stairways, etc. in good repair; locks and other security devices in good repair; and provision of safety equipment required by law. For an overview of the implied warranty doctrine, see Donald E. Campbell, *Forty (Plus) Years After the Revolution: Observations on the Implied Warranty of Habitability*, 35 U. Ark. Little Rock L. Rev. 793 (2013).

b. **Rationale for the Implied Warranty**

How persuasive are the policy arguments in *Wade*? For example, the court states that "housing shortages, standardized leases, and racial and class discrimination place today's tenants . . . in a poor position to bargain effectively" for protection against defective conditions. Is this true for all tenants? Should it matter if the court relies on generalizations that are overbroad? And how would the *Wade* court respond to the concerns raised in Justice Neely's *Teller* dissent?

c. **Defining Habitability**

States vary in their standards for habitability. Many define the scope of the warranty by the building and housing codes, the yardstick endorsed by *Javins*. Other states endorse more general tests, such as "clean, safe, and fit for human habitation." *Hilder v. St. Peter*, 478 A.2d 202, 208 (Vt. 1984). *Wade* follows the modern trend by blending these two approaches. Based on *Wade*, what is the standard for habitability in Utah? Could a condition in a Utah apartment that complies with the local building and housing codes ever violate the implied warranty?

A wide range of problems may render a home uninhabitable, as evidenced by these examples:

- *Leaks*: The landlord's failure to repair a clogged downspout which caused water leaks in the tenant's unit breached the warranty in *Parham v. CIH Properties, Inc.*, 208 F. Supp. 3d 116 (D.D.C. 2016).

- *Mold*: In *Wiesel v. 310 East 46 LLC*, 880 N.Y.S.2d 10 (App Div. 2009), the court found that the tenant adequately stated a claim by alleging that the warranty was breached due to mold in her apartment.

- *Rodents*: The court in *Landis & Landis Construction, LLC v. Nation*, 286 P.3d 979 (Wash. Ct. App. 2012) held that rodent infestation made the rented house uninhabitable.

- *Smoke*: In *Poyck v. Bryant*, 820 N.Y.S.2d 774, 777–78 (Civ. Ct. 2006), the court suggested that secondhand smoke in an apartment building might violate the warranty because it is "just as insidious and invasive" as more common problems like odors or noise.

d. Waiver?

Suppose that A, a sophisticated building contractor, wants to lease a single-family house in Utah from B, an elderly widow. The market rent would normally be $1,000 per month, but they negotiate a lease by which A "waives all of his rights under the implied warranty of habitability" in exchange for a rent reduction of $100 per month. Should a Utah court permit this waiver? Following the *Javins* approach, most courts hold that any waiver of the warranty is invalid as against public policy. Why not allow a waiver in situations like the A-B hypothetical?

e. Procedural Requirements

In order to use the implied warranty of habitability, the tenant must notify the landlord about the defects and allow a reasonable time for the landlord to make repairs. But the tenant is not required to vacate the premises. In fact, one of the tenant's remedies is to remain in possession and withhold rent until the landlord cures the habitability problem. In this light, compare the implied warranty of habitability to constructive eviction. Which doctrine best meets the needs of poor urban tenants?

f. Remedies for Breach

If the implied warranty is breached, most jurisdictions allow the tenant to select one of four different remedies:

> *Withhold rent*: This is usually the most effective remedy because, as the *Wade* court observes, it gives the landlord an incentive to repair the premises. In most jurisdictions, the tenant may withhold all rent, even for a partial breach of the warranty. Some courts recommend that rent be paid into an escrow fund under judicial control. Why wouldn't the landlord just evict the tenant

for nonpayment of rent? The answer is simple: breach of the implied warranty is a defense to an eviction action.

Repair and deduct: In many states, the tenant may withhold rent and use these funds to repair the defects.

Sue for damages: The tenant may sue for damages while remaining in possession or after vacating the premises. Courts differ widely on the appropriate measure of damages. For example, in *Hilder* the Vermont Supreme Court used "the difference between the value of the dwelling as warranted and the value of the dwelling as it exists in its defective condition." Using this standard, the tenant was awarded *all* of the rent she had paid during the tenancy. Compare this standard to the "percentage diminution" test adopted in *Wade*. Which approach is better?

Terminate the lease: In most states, the tenant may terminate the lease and vacate the premises, thus avoiding liability for future rent.

g. Does the Implied Warranty Work?

Justice Neely asserted in his *Teller* dissent that the implied warranty of habitability might harm poor tenants. Is he correct? *Compare* Charles J. Meyers, *The Covenant of Habitability and the American Law Institute*, 27 Stan. L. Rev. 879 (1975) (arguing that tenants will be harmed) *with* Duncan Kennedy, *The Effect of the Warranty of Habitability on Low Income Housing: "Milking" and Class Violence*, 15 Fla. St. U. L. Rev. 485 (1987) (arguing that tenants will be benefited). What is the relationship among the quality, quantity, and price of rental housing?

h. Implied Warranty Hypotheticals

Using the *Wade* standard, has the implied warranty of habitability been breached in these situations?

(1) Due to a city-wide strike, no one picked up the garbage at the apartment building where A lives for four weeks. This attracted cockroaches and other vermin to the building, where they infested A's unit.

(2) B's ground-floor apartment unit is located in a high-crime area. There is no deadbolt on the front door; there are no bars on the windows. Four of the 52 units in the complex have been burglarized over the last year.

(3) C's unit is located on the fifth floor of an apartment building. One of the tenants on the fourth floor regularly smokes cigarettes inside his unit. C smells this smoke every day because it travels through the building's ventilation system. The odor of smoke is quite strong about seven days each month, but is barely noticeable the rest of the time.

(4) The dishwasher inside D's rented house is broken. D's landlord has tried to fix it on three occasions, but is unable to do so because the needed part is no longer sold.

> (5) The painted walls inside E's duplex unit are cracked and scratched, and some of the lead paint is falling off.

i. Aftermath of *Wade*

Five years after *Wade*, the Utah Supreme Court extended its holding to commercial leases in *Richard Barton Enterprises, Inc. v. Tsern*, 928 P.2d 368 (Utah 1996). Thus, a commercial tenant in Utah may withhold rent if the landlord breaches a covenant that was a "significant inducement to the consummation of the lease or to the purpose for which the lessee entered the lease." *Id.* at 378. This is distinctly a minority view; in most states, the implied warranty does not apply to commercial leases.

C. Transferring the Tenant's Interest

Suppose T leases retail space in L's shopping mall for a 20-year term in order to open an upscale shoe store. Eight years later, T's store is so successful that she plans to move her business to a much larger space at a different mall. T now wants to transfer her interest to a replacement tenant, so that she can avoid liability to L for future rent. Can T transfer her interest?

As a general rule, the tenant and the landlord are both entitled to transfer their interests to third parties. After all, a core policy underlying property law is freedom of alienation. A tenant may transfer her rights by either an *assignment* or a *sublease*. The method which is chosen will affect the rights and duties of all three parties—landlord, tenant, and transferee—after the transfer occurs. How can we tell if a particular transfer is an assignment or a sublease? This question is explored in the case below.

At this point, consider the technical legal relationships between T and L in the shoe store lease. Because the lease is a type of contract, T and L have the relationship of *privity of contract*; they both have rights and duties under contract law. But because the lease is also seen as the conveyance of an estate in land, T and L have a relationship arising under property law which is called *privity of estate*. Accordingly, T and L *also* have rights and duties arising from privity of estate, *regardless* of contract law. It is helpful to think of privity of estate as a feudal holdover, reflecting the idea that a person who occupies land owned by another has certain rights and duties based simply on that possession. But what happens to these relationships when the tenant transfers her interest to another person?

Ernst v. Conditt

Court of Appeals of Tennessee

390 S.W.2d 703 (1964)

CHATTIN, JUDGE.

Complainants, B. Walter Ernst and wife, Emily Ernst, leased a certain tract of land in Davidson County, Tennessee, to Frank D. Rogers on June 18, 1960, for a term of one year and seven days, commencing on June 23, 1960.

Rogers went into possession of the property and constructed an asphalt race track and enclosed the premises with a fence. He also constructed other improvements thereon such as floodlights for use in the operation of a Go-Cart track.

We quote those paragraphs of the lease pertinent to the question for consideration in this controversy:

> 3. Lessee covenants to pay as rent for said leased premises the sum of $4,200 per annum, payable at the rate of $350 per month or 15% of all gross receipts, whether from sales or services occurring on the leased premises, whichever is the larger amount. . . . All payments shall be payable to the office of Lessors' agent, Guaranty Mortgage Company, at 316 Union Street, Nashville, Tennessee, on the first day of each month in advance. Lessee shall have the first right of refusal in the event Lessors desire to lease said premises for a period of time commencing immediately after the termination date hereof. . . .

> 5. Lessee shall have no right to assign or sublet the leased premises without prior written approval of Lessors. In the event of any assignment or sublease, Lessee is still liable to perform the covenants of this lease, including the covenant to pay rent, and nothing herein shall be construed as releasing Lessee from his liabilities and obligations hereunder. . . .

> 9. Lessee agrees that upon termination of this contract, or any extensions or renewals thereof, that all improvements above the ground will be moved at Lessee's expense and the property cleared. This shall not be construed as removing or digging up any surface paving; but if any pits or holes are dug, they shall be leveled at Lessors' request.

Rogers operated the business for a short time. In July, 1960, he entered into negotiations with the defendant, A. K. Conditt, for the sale of the business to him. During these negotiations, the question of the term of the lease arose. Defendant desired a two-year lease of the property. He and Rogers went to the home of complainants and negotiated an extension of the term of the lease which resulted in the following amendment to the lease, and the sublease or assignment of the lease as amended to Conditt by Rogers:

By mutual consent of the parties, the lease executed the 18th day of June 1960, between B. Walter Ernst and wife, Emily H. Ernst, as Lessors, and Frank G. Rogers as Lessee, is amended as follows:

1. Paragraph 2 of said lease is amended so as to provide that the term will end July 31, 1962 and not June 30, 1961.

2. The minimum rent of $350 per month called for in paragraph 3 of said lease shall be payable by the month and the percentage rental called for by said lease shall be payable on the first day of the month following the month for which the percentage is computed. . . .

5. Lessor hereby consents to the subletting of the premises to A. K. Conditt, but upon the express condition and understanding that the original Lessee, Frank K. Rogers, will remain personally liable for the faithful performance of all the terms and conditions of the original lease and of this amendment to the original lease.

Except as modified by this amendment, all terms and conditions of the original lease dated the 18th day of June, 1960, by and between the parties shall remain in full force and effect.

In witness whereof the parties have executed this amendment to lease on this the 4 day of August, 1960.

B. Walter Ernst
Emily H. Ernst
Lessors
Frank D. Rogers
Lessee

For value received and in consideration of the promise to faithfully perform all conditions of the within lease as amended, I hereby sublet the premises to A. K. Conditt upon the understanding that I will individually remain liable for the performance of the lease.

This 4 day of Aug, 1960.

Frank D. Rogers
Frank D. Rogers

The foregoing subletting of the premises is accepted, this the 4 day of Aug, 1960.

A. K. Conditt
A. K. Conditt

Conditt operated the Go-Cart track from August until November, 1960. He paid the rent for the months of August, September and October, 1960, directly to complainants. In December, 1960, complainants contacted defendant with reference to the November rent and at that time defendant stated he had been advised he was not liable to them for rent. However, defendant paid the basic monthly rental of $350.00 to complainants in June, 1961. This was the final payment received by complainants during the term of the lease as amended. The record is not clear whether defendant continued to operate the business after the last payment of rent or abandoned it. Defendant, however, remained in possession of the property until the expiration of the leasehold.

On July 10, 1962, complainants, through their Attorneys, notified Conditt by letter the lease would expire as of midnight July 31, 1962; and they were demanding a settlement of the past due rent and unless the improvements on the property were removed by him as provided in paragraph 9 of the original lease, then, in that event, they would have same removed at his expense. Defendant did not reply to this demand.

On August 1, 1962, complainants filed their bill in this cause seeking a recovery of $2,404.58 which they alleged was the balance due on the basic rent of $350.00 per month for the first year of the lease and the sum of $4,200.00, the basic rent for the second year, and the further sum necessary for the removal of the improvements constructed on the property.

> **See It**
> Click here to see a photo of a sample go-cart track like the one at issue in *Ernst*.

The theory of the bill is that the agreement between Rogers, the original lessee, and the defendant, Conditt, is an assignment of the lease; and, therefore, defendant is directly and primarily liable to complainants.

The defendant by his answer insists the agreement between Rogers and himself is a sublease and therefore Rogers is directly and primarily liable to complainants.

The Chancellor heard the matter on the depositions of both complainants and three other witnesses offered in behalf of complainants and documentary evidence filed in the record. The defendant did not testify nor did he offer any evidence in his behalf.

The Chancellor found the instrument to be an assignment. A decree was entered sustaining the bill and entering judgment for complainants in the sum of $6,904.58 against defendant.

Defendant has appealed to this Court and has assigned errors insisting the Chancellor erred in failing to hold the instrument to be a sublease rather than an assignment.

To support his theory the instrument is a sublease, the defendant insists the amendment to the lease entered into between Rogers and complainants was for the express purpose of extending the term of the lease and obtaining the consent of the lessors to a "subletting" of the premises to defendant. That by the use of the words "sublet" and "subletting" no other construction can be placed on the amendment and the agreement of Rogers and the acceptance of defendant attached thereto.

Further, since complainants agreed to the subletting of the premises to defendant "upon the express condition and understanding that the original lessee, Frank D. Rogers, will remain personally liable for the faithful performance of all the terms and conditions of the original lease and this amendment to the original lease," no construction can be placed upon this language other than it was the intention of complainants to hold Rogers primarily liable for the performance of the original lease and the amendment thereto. And, therefore, Rogers, for his own protection, would have the implied right to re-enter and perform the lease in the event of a default on the part of the defendant. This being true, Rogers retained a reversionary interest in the property sufficient to satisfy the legal distinction between a sublease and an assignment of a lease.

It is then urged the following rules of construction of written instruments support the above argument:

> Where words or terms having a definite legal meaning and effect are knowingly used in a written instrument the parties thereto will be presumed to have intended such words or terms to have their proper legal meaning and effect, in the absence of any contrary intention appearing in the instrument. 12 Am. Jur., Contracts, Section 238.

> Technical terms or words of art will be given their technical meaning unless the context, or local usage shows a contrary intention. 3 Williston on Contracts, Section 68, Sub. S. 2.

As stated in complainants' brief, the liability of defendant to complainants depends upon whether the transfer of the leasehold interest in the premises from Rogers is an assignment of the lease or a sublease. If the transfer is a sublease, no privity of [estate] exists between complainants and defendant; and, therefore, defendant could not be liable to complainants on the covenant to pay rent and the expense of the removal of the improvements. But, if the transfer is an assignment of the lease, privity of [estate] does exist between complainants and defendant; and defendant would be liable directly and primarily for the amount of the judgment. *Brummitt Tire Company v. Sinclair Refining Company*, 18 Tenn. App. 270, 75 S.W.2d 1022.

> **Food for Thought**
>
> In the original case, the court used the phrase "privity of contract" twice in this paragraph, when it should have said "privity of estate." Do you understand why the court's phrasing was incorrect?

The general rule as to the distinction between an assignment of a lease and a sublease is an assignment conveys the whole term, leaving no interest nor reversionary interest in the grantor or assignor. Whereas, a sublease may be generally defined as a transaction whereby a tenant grants an interest in the leased premises less than his own, or reserves to himself a reversionary interest in the term.

The common law distinction between an assignment of a lease and a sublease is succinctly stated in the case of *Jaber v. Miller,* 219 Ark. 59, 239 S.W.2d 760:

If the instrument purports to transfer the lessee's estate for the entire remainder of his term it is an assignment, regardless of its form or of the parties' intention. Conversely, if the instrument purports to transfer the lessee's estate for less than the entire term—even for a day less—it is a sublease, regardless of its form or of the parties' intention.

The modern rule which has been adopted in this State for construing written instruments is stated in the case of *City of Nashville v. Lawrence*, 153 Tenn. 606, 284 S.W. 882: "The cardinal rule to be followed in this state, in construing deeds and other written instruments, is to ascertain the intention of the parties."

In *Williams v. Williams*, 84 Tenn. 164, 171, it was said:

We have most wisely abandoned technical rules in the construction of conveyances in this State, and look to the intention of the instrument alone for our guide, that intention to be arrived at from the language of the instrument read in the light of the surrounding circumstances. . . .

It is our opinion under either the common law or modern rule of construction the agreement between Rogers and defendant is an assignment of the lease.

The fact that Rogers expressly agreed to remain liable to complainants for the performance of the lease did not create a reversion nor a right to re-enter in Rogers either express or implied. The obligations and liabilities of a lessee to a lessor, under the express covenants of a lease, are not in anywise affected by an assignment or a subletting to a third party, in the absence of an express or implied agreement or some action on his part which amounts to a waiver or estops him from insisting upon compliance with the covenants. This is true even though the assignment or sublease is made with the consent of the lessor. By an assignment of a lease the privity of estate between the lessor and lessee is terminated, but the privity of contract between them still remains and is unaffected. Neither the privity of estate or contract between the lessor and lessee are affected by a sublease.

> **FYI**
>
> After an assignment or sublease, the original tenant remains liable to the landlord for the full performance of the obligations in the lease because privity of contract still exists between them. Of course, the landlord could expressly release the tenant from future liability; such a release is called a *novation*.

Thus, the express agreement of Rogers to remain personally liable for the performance of the covenants of the lease created no greater obligation on his part or interest in the leasehold, other than as set forth in the original lease.

The argument that since the agreement between Rogers and defendant contains the words, "sublet" and "subletting" is conclusive the instrument is to be construed as a sublease is, we think, unsound.

A consent to sublet has been held to include the consent to assign or mortgage the lease; and a consent to assign has been held to authorize a subletting. 51 C.J.S. Landlord and Tenant § 36, page 552.

Prior to the consummation of the sale of the Go-Cart business to defendant, he insisted upon the execution of the amendment to the lease extending the term of the original lease. For value received and on the promise of the defendant to perform all of the conditions of the lease as amended, Rogers parted with his entire interest in the property. Defendant went into possession of the property and paid the rent to complainants. He remained in possession of the property for the entire term. By virtue of the sale of the business, defendant became the owner of the improvements with the right to their removal at the expiration of the lease.

Rogers reserved no part or interest in the lease; nor did he reserve a right of re-entry in event of a breach of any of the conditions or covenants of the lease on the part of defendant.

It is our opinion the defendant, under the terms of the agreement with Rogers, had a right to the possession of the property for the entire term of the lease as amended, including the right to remove the improvements after the expiration of the lease. Rogers merely agreed to become personally liable for the rent and the expense of the removal of the improvements upon the default of defendant. He neither expressly, nor by implication, reserved the right to re-enter for a condition broken by defendant.

Thus, we are of the opinion the use of the words, "sublet" and "subletting" is not conclusive of the construction to be placed on the instrument in this case; it plainly appearing from the context of the instrument and the facts and circumstances surrounding the execution of it the parties thereto intended an assignment rather than a sublease.

It results [that] the assignments are overruled and the decree of the Chancellor is affirmed with costs.

Points for Discussion

a. **Assignment/Sublease Distinction**

The Ernsts argued that Conditt was an assignee, while Conditt maintained he was a sublessee. Why did this matter? Why didn't the Ernsts sue Rogers?

b. **Objective Test**

Under the majority approach, the test for distinguishing between an assignment and a sublease is deceptively simple: did the tenant transfer his right of possession for all of the remaining lease term (assignment) or not (sublease)? For example, suppose that X transfers the entire remaining 25-year term of her agricultural lease to Z—except that X holds the right to possession on the final two days of the term.

This is a sublease under the majority approach. *See American Comm. Stores Corp. v. Newman*, 441 N.W.2d 154 (Neb. 1989). What if X held the right to possession for only the last minute of the term?

Suppose that Rogers had retained an express right to re-enter the premises and retake possession if Conditt violated any provision of the original lease. In most jurisdictions, a transfer that reserves a contingent right of re-entry is still considered to be an assignment. In *Ernst*, of course, Conditt claimed that Rogers held an *implied* right of re-entry—an argument that the court rejected.

c. Subjective Test

In some jurisdictions, the distinction between assignment and sublease turns on the intent of the parties. Under this approach, it would be possible to have a sublease for the entire remaining term of the original lease. The leading case advocating the subjective test is *Jaber v. Miller*, 239 S.W.2d 760, 763–64 (Ark. 1951), where the court explained:

> . . . [W]e do not feel compelled to adhere to an unjust rule which was logical only in the days of feudalism. The execution of leases is a very practical matter that occurs a hundred times a day without legal assistance. The layman appreciates the common sense distinction between a sublease and an assignment, but he would not even suspect the existence of the common law distinction. . . .
>
> A lawyer trained in common law technicalities can prepare either instrument without fear that it will be construed to be the other. But for the less skilled lawyer or the layman the common law rule is simply a trap that leads to hardship and injustice by refusing to permit the parties to accomplish the result they seek. . . .

The *Ernst* court used this intent-based approach, together with the majority test. The various documents signed by the *Ernst* parties all contained sublease terminology. But the court held that "the parties . . . intended an assignment rather than a sublease." Compare the *Ernst* analysis to *Abernathy v. Adous*, 149 S.W.3d 884, 889 (Ark. Ct. App. 2004), where the court found the parties intended a sublease because they "consistently referred to their arrangement as a sublease." Was *Ernst* wrongly decided? Which is the better standard: the objective test or the subjective test?

d. Assignment: A Triangular Relationship

In an assignment, the tenant (the *assignor*) transfers (*assigns*) her entire interest in the leased premises to a third party (the *assignee*). Suppose that T assigns her rights in the shoe store space to U. This creates a triangular relationship among T, L, and U. Privity of contract continues between T and L; it also arises between T and U, because their agreement is a contract. But privity of estate now exists *only* between L and U; in effect, U has taken T's place. T no longer has a property right in the leased premises. L and U now have mutual rights and duties as a matter of property law as long as U remains in possession, even though there is no contract between them. For example, U has a duty to pay rent to L.

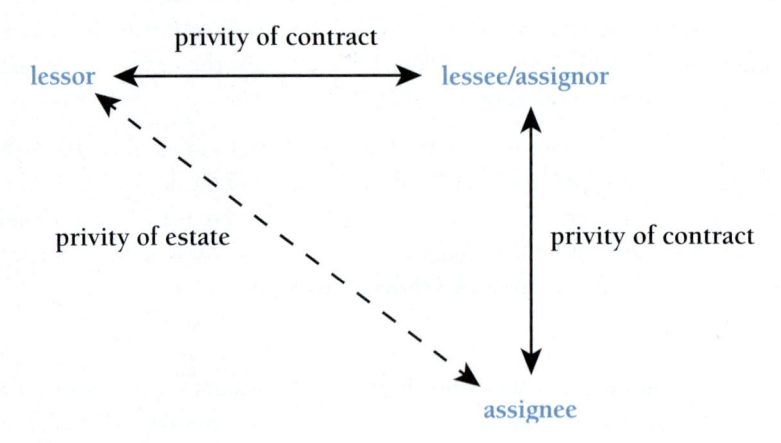

```
                    privity of contract
    lessor  ◄──────────────────────►  lessee/assignor
        ▲                                    ▲
         ╲                                   │
          ╲                                  │
           ╲                                 │
     privity of estate              privity of contract
             ╲                               │
              ╲                              │
               ╲                             ▼
                ╲──────────────────►      assignee
```

What are the mutual rights and duties that arise from privity of estate? As a general matter, L and U are obligated to perform all of the covenants in the original lease that "run with the land." This is a complex subject which you will study in more depth in Chapter 10. Almost all lease covenants do "run with the land" because they relate to use or occupancy of the premises, such as the duties to repair, to pay rent, to provide heat, or to use the premises for specified purposes. But a covenant which has no connection to the use or occupancy of the premises does not bind either party. For example, a clause in the lease about who pays attorneys fees if litigation occurs does not "run with the land."

e. **Sublease: Two Separate Relationships**

A sublease essentially involves two separate landlord-tenant relationships. The tenant (the *sublessor*) transfers (*subleases*) part of her interest in the leased premises to a third party (the *sublessee*). Suppose that T has 12 years left on her shoe store lease. She subleases the space to U for a period of 10 years; thus, T retains the right to possession for the final 2 years of the lease.

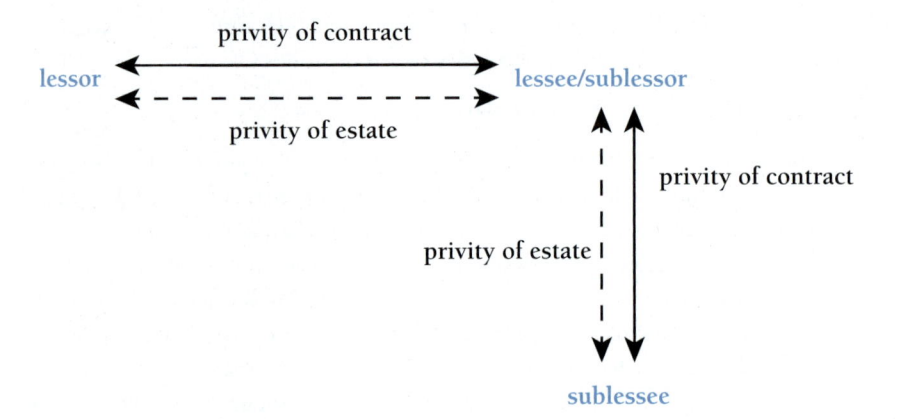

```
                   privity of contract
    lessor  ◄──────────────────────►  lessee/sublessor
            ◄─ ─ ─ ─ ─ ─ ─ ─ ─ ─ ─►           ▲
                privity of estate             │
                                              │
                                              │ privity of contract
                                    privity of estate
                                              │
                                              ▼
                                          sublessee
```

In this situation, L and T still have privity of contract and privity of estate, which continues their mutual rights and duties; their original landlord-tenant relationship remains intact. But a new landlord-tenant relationship arises between sublessor T and sublessee U. Accordingly, T and U *also* have privity of contract and privity of estate, which creates rights and duties between them. But L and U have no legal relationship. Thus, for example, U has no duty to pay rent to L. Of course, if T fails to pay rent to L, then L can evict U from the premises. Why might an attorney want to structure a transfer as a sublease rather than an assignment?

f.   Third-Party Beneficiary?

Even if the court found that the Rogers-Conditt transfer was a sublease, Conditt might have been liable to the Ernsts under a third-party beneficiary theory. A fundamental principle of contract law is that if A makes a promise in a contract with B in order to benefit C, then C may enforce the promise against A. Re-read the transfer documents quoted in *Ernst*. Did Conditt make a promise to Rogers for the benefit of the Ernsts?

g.   Transfer Problems

Who owes rent to L in the problems below? Assume that L leased to T for a term of 12 years, beginning in 2018.

> (1)   In 2019, T assigns to B; in 2021, B assigns to C; in 2023, C subleases to D.
>
> (2)   In 2023, T "assigns, subleases, and transfers all my interest in the lease" to A.
>
> (3)   In 2023, T transfers all of his rights in the leased premises to E "for a period of four years."

Even though leasehold interests may be freely transferred at common law, the parties to a lease may alter this rule. Most modern leases expressly restrict the tenant's right to transfer. For example, a lease may simply prohibit any transfer. Or it may permit a transfer only if the landlord consents, like the lease in *Ernst*.

Suppose that T and L enter into a lease that requires L's consent to any transfer by T. T now wishes to transfer her rights to Z. What standard governs L's decision? There are three basic possibilities:

> - *Sole discretion clause*: The lease might provide that L may refuse consent for any reason whatsoever in his "sole discretion."
> - *Reasonableness clause*: The lease might provide that L may refuse consent only on a commercially reasonable basis. For example, L might deny consent if Z has a bad credit record.

> - *No standard in lease*: The lease might require L's consent, but contain no standard to guide L's decision; such a provision is called a *silent consent clause*.

Suppose that the T-L lease contains a silent consent clause. Is L's decision governed by the sole discretion test, the reasonableness test, or some other test?

The most famous modern decision about the silent consent clause arose near California's Silicon Valley—perhaps the leading high-tech research and development center in the world. One of the best ways for businessmen to travel to Silicon Valley during the 1980s was by private plane or jet. Most of these aircraft came through the nearby San Jose Airport. As a result, airplane-related businesses at the airport became quite successful. In this environment, the owner of an airplane maintenance business operating in a subleased hangar decided to sell the business. But he needed the sublessor's consent in order to transfer his rights in the hangar, and the sublease contained a silent consent clause.

Kendall v. Ernest Pestana, Inc.

Supreme Court of California

709 P.2d 837 (1985)

BROUSSARD, JUSTICE.

This case concerns the effect of a provision in a commercial lease that the lessee may not assign the lease or sublet the premises without the lessor's prior written consent. The question we address is whether, in the absence of a provision that such consent will not be unreasonably withheld, a lessor may unreasonably and arbitrarily withhold his or her consent to an assignment.[3] This is a question of first impression in this court.

I.

. . . The allegations of the complaint may be summarized as follows. The lease at issue is for 14,400 square feet of hangar space at the San Jose Municipal Airport. The City of San Jose, as owner of the property, leased it to Irving and Janice Perlitch, who in turn assigned their interest to respondent Ernest Pestana, Inc. Prior to assigning their interest to respondent, the Perlitches entered into a 25-year sublease with one Robert Bixler commencing on January 1, 1970. The sublease covered an original five-year term plus four 5-year options to renew. The rental rate was to be increased every 10 years in the same proportion as rents increased on the master lease from the

---
[3] Since the present case involves an assignment rather than a sublease, we will speak primarily in terms of assignments. However, our holding applies equally to subleases. . . .

City of San Jose. The premises were to be used by Bixler for the purpose of conducting an airplane maintenance business.

Bixler conducted such a business under the name "Flight Services" until, in 1981, he agreed to sell the business to appellants Jack Kendall, Grady O'Hara and Vicki O'Hara. The proposed sale included the business and the equipment, inventory and improvements on the property, together with the existing lease. The proposed assignees had a stronger financial statement and greater net worth than the current lessee, Bixler, and they were willing to be bound by the terms of the lease

> **See It**
>
> Click here to see a diagram of the relationships among the *Kendall* parties.

The [Perlitch-Bixler sublease] provided that written consent of the [sub]lessor was required before the [sub]lessee could assign his interest, and that failure to obtain such consent rendered the [sub]lease voidable at the option of the [sub]lessor.[5] Accordingly, Bixler requested consent from the Perlitches' successor-in-interest, respondent Ernest Pestana, Inc. Respondent refused to consent to the assignment and maintained that it had an absolute right arbitrarily to refuse any such request. The complaint recites that respondent demanded "increased rent and other more onerous terms" as a condition of consenting to Bixler's transfer of interest.

The proposed assignees brought suit for declaratory and injunctive relief and damages seeking, inter alia, a declaration "that the refusal of Ernest Pestana, Inc. to consent to the assignment of the lease is unreasonable and is an unlawful restraint on the freedom of alienation. . . ." The trial court sustained a demurrer to the complaint without leave to amend and this appeal followed.

II.

The law generally favors free alienability of property, and California follows the common law rule that a leasehold interest is freely alienable. Contractual restrictions on the alienability of leasehold interests are, however, permitted. "Such restrictions are justified as reasonable protection of the interests of the lessor as to who shall possess and manage property in which he has a reversionary interest and from which he is deriving income." (Schoshinski, American Law of Landlord and Tenant (1980) § 8:15, at pp. 578-579.)

The common law's hostility toward restraints on alienation has caused such restraints on leasehold interests to be strictly construed against the lessor. . . . This is particularly true where the restraint in question is a "forfeiture restraint," under which

---

[5] Paragraph 13 of the sublease between the Perlitches and Bixler provides: "Lessee shall not assign this lease, or any interest therein, and shall not sublet the said premises or any part thereof, or any right or privilege appurtenant thereto, or suffer any other person (the agents and servants of Lessee excepted) to occupy or use said premises, or any portion thereof, without written consent of Lessor first had and obtained. . . . Any such assignment or subletting without this consent shall be void, and shall, at the option of Lessor, terminate this lease. . . ."

the lessor has the option to terminate the lease if an assignment is made without his or her consent. . . .

Nevertheless, a majority of jurisdictions have long adhered to the rule that where a lease contains an approval clause (a clause stating that the lease cannot be assigned without the prior consent of the lessor), the lessor may arbitrarily refuse to approve a proposed assignee no matter how suitable the assignee appears to be and no matter how unreasonable the lessor's objection. The harsh consequences of this rule have often been avoided through application of the doctrines of waiver and estoppel, under which the lessor may be found to have waived (or be estopped from asserting) the right to refuse consent to assignment.

The traditional majority rule has come under steady attack in recent years. A growing minority of jurisdictions now hold that where a lease provides for assignment only with the prior consent of the lessor, such consent may be withheld *only where the lessor has a commercially reasonable objection to the assignment*, even in the absence of a provision in the lease stating that consent to assignment will not be unreasonably withheld.

For the reasons discussed below, we conclude that the minority rule is the preferable position. . . .

III.

The impetus for change in the majority rule has come from two directions, reflecting the dual nature of a lease as a conveyance of a leasehold interest and a contract. The policy against restraints on alienation pertains to leases in their nature as *conveyances*. Numerous courts and commentators have recognized that "[i]n recent times the necessity of permitting reasonable alienation of commercial space has become paramount in our increasingly urban society." (*Schweiso v. Williams* (1984) 150 Cal.App.3d 883, 887, 198 Cal. Rptr. 238. . . .)

Civil Code section 711 provides: "Conditions restraining alienation, when repugnant to the interest created, are void." It is well settled that this rule is not absolute in its application, but forbids only *unreasonable* restraints on alienation. Reasonableness is determined by comparing the justification for a particular restraint on alienation with the quantum of restraint actually imposed by it. "[T]he greater the quantum of restraint that results from enforcement of a given clause, the greater must be the justification for that enforcement." (*Wellencamp v. Bank of America* (1978) 21 Cal.3d 943, 949, 582 P.2d 970.) In *Cohen v. Ratinoff* (1983) 147 Cal.App.3d 321, 195 Cal. Rptr. 84, the court examined the reasonableness of the restraint created by an approval clause in a lease:

> Because the lessor has an interest in the character of the proposed commercial assignee, we cannot say that an assignment provision requiring the lessor's consent to an assignment is inherently repugnant to the leasehold interest created. We do conclude, however, that *if such an assignment provision is implemented in such a manner that its*

underlying purpose is perverted by the arbitrary or unreasonable withholding of consent, an unreasonable restraint on alienation is established.

(*Id.,* 147 Cal.App.3d at p. 329, 195 Cal.Rptr. 84, italics added.). . . .

The Restatement Second of Property adopts the minority rule on the validity of approval clauses in leases: "A restraint on alienation without the consent of the landlord of a tenant's interest in leased property is valid, *but the landlord's consent to an alienation by the tenant cannot be withheld unreasonably,* unless a freely negotiated provision in the lease gives the landlord an absolute right to withhold consent." (Rest. 2d Property, § 15.2(2) (1977), italics added.). . . .[14] Under the Restatement rule, the lessor's interest in the character of his or her tenant is protected by the lessor's right to object to a proposed assignee on reasonable commercial grounds. The lessor's interests are also protected by the fact that the original lessee remains liable to the lessor as a surety even if the lessor consents to the assignment and the assignee expressly assumes the obligations of the lease.

The second impetus for change in the majority rule comes from the nature of a lease as a *contract.* As the Court of Appeal observed in *Cohen v. Ratinoff, supra,* "[s]ince *Richard v. Degan & Brody, Inc.* [espousing the majority rule] was decided, . . . there has been an increased recognition of and emphasis on the duty of good faith and fair dealing inherent in every contract." (*Id.,* 147 Cal.App.3d at p. 329, 195 Cal. Rptr. 84.) Thus, "[i]n every contract there is an implied covenant that neither party shall do anything which will have the effect of destroying or injuring the right of the other party to receive the fruits of the contract. . . ." (*Universal Sales Corp. v. Cal. etc. Mfg. Co.* (1942) 20 Cal.2d 751, 771, 128 P.2d 665). "[W]here a contract confers on one party a discretionary power affecting the rights of the other, a duty is imposed to exercise that discretion in good faith and in accordance with fair dealing." (*Cal. Lettuce Growers v. Union Sugar Co.* (1955) 45 Cal.2d 474, 484, 289 P.2d 785). Here the lessor retains the discretionary power to approve or disapprove an assignee proposed by the other party to the contract; this discretionary power should therefore be exercised in accordance with commercially reasonable standards. . . .

Under the minority rule, the determination whether a lessor's refusal to consent was reasonable is a question of fact. Some of the factors that the trier of fact may properly consider in applying the standards of good faith and commercial reasonableness are: financial responsibility of the proposed assignee; suitability of the use for the particular

> **Food for Thought**
>
> As the court notes, these are examples of factors that may be considered in determining commercial reasonableness. What other factors are relevant?

---

[14] This case does not present the question of the validity of a clause absolutely prohibiting assignment, or granting absolute discretion over assignment to the lessor. We note that under the Restatement rule such a provision would be valid if freely negotiated.

property; legality of the proposed use; need for alteration of the premises; and nature of the occupancy, i.e., office, factory, clinic, etc.

Denying consent solely on the basis of personal taste, convenience or sensibility is not commercially reasonable. Nor is it reasonable to deny consent "in order that the landlord may charge a higher rent than originally contracted for." (*Schweiso v. Williams, supra,* 150 Cal.App.3d at p. 886, 198 Cal.Rptr. 238). This is because the lessor's desire for a better bargain than contracted for has nothing to do with the permissible purposes of the restraint on alienation—to protect the lessor's interest in the preservation of the property and the performance of the lease covenants. " '[T]he clause is for the protection of the landlord *in its ownership and operation of the particular property*—not for its general economic protection.' " (*Ringwood Associates v. Jack's of Route 23, Inc.* (1977) 153 N.J. Super. 294, 379 A.2d 508, 512).

In contrast to the policy reasons advanced in favor of the minority rule, the majority rule has traditionally been justified on three grounds. Respondent raises a fourth argument in its favor as well. None of these do we find compelling.

First, it is said that a lease is a conveyance of an interest in real property, and that the lessor, having exercised a personal choice in the selection of a tenant and provided that no substitute shall be acceptable without prior consent, is under no obligation to look to anyone but the lessee for the rent. This argument is based on traditional rules of conveyancing and on concepts of freedom of ownership and control over one's property.

A lessor's freedom at common law to look to no one but the lessee for the rent has, however, been undermined by the adoption in California of a rule that lessors—like all other contracting parties—have a duty to mitigate damages upon the lessee's abandonment of the property by seeking a substitute lessee. Furthermore, the values that go into the personal selection of a lessee are preserved under the minority rule in the lessor's right to refuse consent to assignment on any commercially reasonable grounds. Such grounds include not only the obvious objections to an assignee's financial stability or proposed use of the premises, but a variety of other commercially reasonable objections as well. (*See, e.g., Arrington v. Walter E. Heller Int'l Corp.* (1975) 30 Ill.App.3d 631, 333 N.E.2d 50 [desire to have only one "lead tenant" in order to preserve "image of the building" as tenant's international headquarters]; *Warmack v. Merchants Nat'l Bank of Fort Smith* (Ark. 1981) 612 S.W.2d 733 [desire for good "tenant mix" in shopping center]; *List v. Dahnke* (Col. App. 1981) 638 P.2d 824 [lessor's refusal to consent to assignment of lease by one restaurateur to another was reasonable where lessor believed proposed specialty restaurant would not succeed at that location].) The lessor's interests are further protected by the fact that the original lessee remains a guarantor of the performance of the assignee.

The second justification advanced in support of the majority rule is that an approval clause is an unambiguous reservation of absolute discretion in the lessor over assignments of the lease. The lessee could have bargained for the addition of a reasonableness clause to the lease (i.e., "consent to assignment will not be unreasonably withheld"). The lessee having failed to do so, the law should not rewrite the parties' contract for them.

Numerous authorities have taken a different view of the meaning and effect of an approval clause in a lease, indicating that the clause is not "clear and unambiguous," as respondent suggests. As early as 1940, the court in *Granite Trust Bldg. Corp. v. Great Atlantic & Pacific Tea Co.*, 36 F. Supp. 77 (D. Mass. 1940), examined a standard approval clause and stated: "It would seem to be the better law that when a lease restricts a lessee's rights by requiring consent before these rights can be exercised, *it must have been in the contemplation of the parties that the lessor be required to give some reason for withholding consent.*" (*Id.*, at p. 78, italics added.). . . .

In light of the interpretations given to approval clauses in the cases cited above, and in light of the increasing number of jurisdictions that have adopted the minority rule in the last 15 years, the assertion that an approval clause "clearly and unambiguously" grants the lessor absolute discretion over assignments is untenable. It is not a rewriting of a contract, as respondent suggests, to recognize the obligations imposed by the duty of good faith and fair dealing, which duty is implied by law in every contract.

The third justification advanced in support of the majority rule is essentially based on the doctrine of stare decisis. . . . As pointed out above, however, the majority viewpoint has been far from universally held and has never been adopted by this court. Moreover, the trend in favor of the minority rule should come as no surprise to observers of the changing state of real property law in the 20th century. . . .

A final argument in favor of the majority rule is advanced by respondent and stated as follows: "Both tradition and sound public policy dictate that the lessor has a right, under circumstances such as these, to realize the increased value of his property." Respondent essentially argues that any increase in the market value of real property during the term of a lease properly belongs to the lessor, not the lessee. We reject this assertion. . . .

Respondent here is trying to get *more* than it bargained for in the lease. A lessor is free to build periodic rent increases into a lease, as the lessor did here. Any increased value of the property beyond this "belongs" to the lessor only in the sense, as explained above, that the lessor's reversionary estate will benefit from it upon the expiration of the lease. . . .

IV.

In conclusion, both the policy against restraints on alienation and the implied contractual duty of good faith and fair dealing militate in favor of adoption of the rule that where a commercial lease provides for assignment only with the prior consent of the lessor, such consent may be withheld only where the lessor has a commercially reasonable objection to the assignee or the proposed use. Under this rule, appellants have stated a cause of action against respondent Ernest Pestana, Inc. . . .

Points for Discussion

a. **Evaluating *Kendall***

How persuasive is the court's analysis? Is it fair for a landlord to insist on a rent increase in exchange for consent to a transfer? In *Schweiso v. Williams*, 198 Cal. Rptr. 238 (Ct. App. 1984), the court described such a demand as "blood money." On the other hand, Bixler could have protected his position by negotiating for a reasonableness clause in the sublease. Why should the court intervene to help a commercial lessee who failed to negotiate for adequate protection?

b. **Status of the *Kendall* Approach**

The *Kendall* standard is still a minority rule, but it seems to be the modern trend for commercial leases. *See, e.g., Pantry, Inc. v. Mosley*, 126 So. 3d 152 (Ala. 2013). In *Slavin v. Rent Control Board*, 548 N.E.2d 1226 (Mass. 1990), the court refused to apply the reasonableness approach to a residential lease. Do you agree with the *Slavin* court?

c. **Commercially Reasonable Objections**

The *Kendall* court lists examples of commercially reasonable objections that a landlord might have to a potential transferee. One application of the reasonableness standard is found in *Van Sloun v. Agans Brothers, Inc.*, 778 N.W.2d 174 (Iowa 2010), where the tenant proposed to sublease his office space to a grocery store. The Iowa Supreme Court found that the landlord's refusal was commercially reasonable because: (1) the sublessee would compete with another tenant, an existing grocery store; (2) the sublessee planned to install kitchen equipment which would require alterations in the building structure; (3) food odors could travel from the sublessee's store through the ventilation system to spaces occupied by other tenants; and (4) deliveries to the sublessee could interfere with deliveries to the landlord's own business in the same building.

When the Idaho Supreme Court adopted the reasonableness approach in *Funk v. Funk*, 633 P.2d 586 (Idaho 1981), a dissenting justice observed "that the effect of the decision is to potentially subject every denial of consent to litigation and approval by a judge." *Id.* at 591. Does the *Kendall* standard encourage litigation?

d. **Restraints on Alienation**

Suppose that the Perlitch-Bixler sublease required the sublessor's consent for any transfer and stated that the sublessor could "deny consent for any reason whatsoever in his sole discretion." Under the logic of *Kendall*, would this clause be valid? After *Kendall* was decided, the state legislature adopted California Civil Code § 1995.230, which provides that "[a] restriction on transfer of a tenant's interest [in a commercial lease] may absolutely prohibit transfer." Why was this statute necessary?

e. Landlord Consent Problems

L and T enter into a 25-year lease for a space in L's shopping mall that T will use as a furniture store; the lease contains a silent consent clause. Under the *Kendall* standard, must L consent if T wants to transfer his interest to U, V, or X below?

> (1) U plans to open a wine store. The store will include a "wine bar" where customers may sample various wines. L believes that drinking alcohol is morally wrong; he is also concerned that customers at the wine bar may become drunk, causing problems for other businesses in the mall.
>
> (2) V will open a greeting card store. G, another tenant in the same shopping mall, already operates a greeting card store. L is convinced that V's store will adversely affect G's store.
>
> (3) X wants to start a comic book store. X is 24 years old and has no business experience, but her wealthy father will co-sign the lease and ensure that all rent payments are made. L has met X and does not like her.

f. Aftermath of *Kendall*

The state legislature later "codified" *Kendall* by adopting California Civil Code § 1995.260. It provides that if a commercial lease "requires the landlord's consent for transfer but provides no standard for giving or withholding consent, the restriction on transfer shall be construed to include an implied standard that the landlord's consent may not be unreasonably withheld. . . ." The tenant has the burden of proof on unreasonableness, which is a question of fact. An official comment to the statute notes that "in some circumstances, it may be commercially reasonable for the landlord to require . . . that the premium received by the tenant for the assignment be paid to the landlord." Is this comment consistent with *Kendall*?

D. Ending the Tenancy

Most tenancies end without controversy. Assume that tenant T has a one-year term of years tenancy, ending on May 31. It is likely that T will simply vacate the premises when the term ends, and landlord L will retake possession. Of course, T and L could mutually agree to terminate the lease early; this is called a *surrender*.

But suppose that T vacates the premises in January, before the lease term expires, and stops paying rent. What are the rights of T and L when such an *abandonment* occurs? Alternatively, what if T stops paying rent in January, but remains in the premises? In this situation, L may seek to retake possession of the premises by *eviction*.

1. Abandonment

What is abandonment? Restatement (Second) of Property: Landlord and Tenant § 12.1 cmt. i explains it this way:

> An abandonment of the leased property by the tenant occurs when he vacates the leased property without justification and without any present intention of returning and he defaults in the payment of the rent.

Notice that if a tenant vacates the premises with justification—for example, due to a constructive eviction—no abandonment occurs.

Suppose that tenant T abandons the leased premises before the lease term ends. Traditionally, landlord L could choose among three options in this situation:

- *Sue for all rent*: L could keep the premises vacant until the lease term expired, and then sue T for all the accrued rent.

- *Terminate the lease*: L could treat T's abandonment as an implied offer of surrender and terminate the lease.

- *Mitigate damages and then sue for rent*: L could mitigate his damages by reletting the premises to another tenant, retaining that rent, and then suing T for the balance.

James Kridel, a New Jersey student, was about to be married. He entered into a two-year lease for an apartment unit where he and his future wife would live. But the wedding never occurred, and Kridel never moved in. After the lease term expired, the landlord sued Kridel for two full years of rent. In the ensuing litigation, the New Jersey Supreme Court reexamined the landlord's rights when the tenant abandons.

Sommer v. Kridel

Supreme Court of New Jersey

378 A.2d 767 (1977)

PASHMAN, J.

We granted certification in these cases [*Sommer v. Kridel* and *Riverview Realty Co. v. Perosio*] to consider whether a landlord seeking damages from a defaulting tenant is under a duty to mitigate damages by making reasonable efforts to re-let an apartment wrongfully vacated by the tenant. Separate parts of the Appellate Division held that, in accordance with their respective leases, the landlords in both cases could recover rents due under the leases regardless of whether they had attempted to re-let the vacated apartments. Although they were of different minds as to the fairness of this result, both parts agreed that it was dictated by *Joyce v. Bauman*, 113 N.J.L. 438, 174 A. 693 (E. & A. 1934).... We now reverse and hold that a landlord does have an obligation to make a reasonable effort to mitigate damages in such a situation. We therefore overrule *Joyce v. Bauman* to the extent that it is inconsistent with our decision today. [Only the case of *Sommer v. Kridel* is discussed below.]

I.

This case was tried on stipulated facts. On March 10, 1972 the defendant, James Kridel, entered into a lease with the plaintiff, Abraham Sommer, owner of the "Pierre Apartments" in Hackensack, to rent apartment 6-L in that building.[1] The term of the lease was from May 1, 1972 until April 30, 1974, with a rent concession for the first six weeks, so that the first month's rent was not due until June 15, 1972.

One week after signing the agreement, Kridel paid Sommer $690. Half of that sum was used to satisfy the first month's rent. The remainder was paid under the lease provision requiring a security deposit of $345. Although defendant had expected to begin occupancy around May 1, his plans were changed. He wrote to Sommer on May 19, 1972, explaining

> I was to be married on June 3, 1972. Unhappily the engagement was broken and the wedding plans cancelled. Both parents were to assume responsibility for the rent after our marriage. I was discharged from the U.S. Army in October 1971 and am now a student. I have no funds of my own, and am supported by my stepfather.
>
> In view of the above, I cannot take possession of the apartment and am surrendering all rights to it. Never having received a key, I cannot return same to you.
>
> I beg your understanding and compassion in releasing me from the lease, and will of course, in consideration thereof, forfeit the 2 month's rent already paid.
>
> Please notify me at your earliest convenience.

Plaintiff did not answer the letter.

Subsequently, a third party went to the apartment house and inquired about renting apartment 6-L. Although the parties agreed that she was ready, willing and able to rent the apartment, the person in charge told her that the apartment was not being shown since it was already rented to Kridel. In fact, the landlord did not re-enter the apartment or exhibit it to anyone until August 1, 1973. At that time it was rented to a new tenant for a term beginning on September 1, 1973. The new rental was for $345 per month with a six week concession similar to that granted Kridel.

Prior to re-letting the new premises, plaintiff sued Kridel in August 1972, demanding $7,590, the total amount due for the full two-year term of the lease. Fol-

---

[1] Among other provisions, the lease prohibited the tenant from assigning or transferring the lease without the consent of the landlord. If the tenant defaulted, the lease gave the landlord the option of re-entering or re-letting, but stipulated that failure to re-let or to recover the full rental would not discharge the tenant's liability for rent.

lowing a mistrial, plaintiff filed an amended complaint asking for $5,865, the amount due between May 1, 1972 and September 1, 1973. The amended complaint included no reduction in the claim to reflect the six week concession provided for in the lease or the $690 payment made to plaintiff after signing the agreement. Defendant filed an amended answer to the complaint, alleging that plaintiff breached the contract, failed to mitigate damages and accepted defendant's surrender of the premises. He also counterclaimed to demand repayment of the $345 paid as a security deposit.

The trial judge ruled in favor of defendant. Despite his conclusion that the lease had been drawn to reflect "the 'settled law' of this state," he found that "justice and fair dealing" imposed upon the landlord the duty to attempt to re-let the premises and thereby mitigate damages. He also held that plaintiff's failure to make any response to defendant's unequivocal offer of surrender was tantamount to an acceptance, thereby terminating the tenancy and any obligation to pay rent. As a result, he dismissed both the complaint and the counterclaim. The Appellate Division reversed in a per curiam opinion, 153 N.J. Super. 1 (1976), and we granted certification. . . .

Pierre Apartments
Click here for larger photo

II.

As the lower courts in both appeals found, the weight of authority in this State supports the rule that a landlord is under no duty to mitigate damages caused by a defaulting tenant. See *Joyce v. Bauman, supra*. . . . This rule has been followed in a majority of states . . . and has been tentatively adopted in the American Law Institute's Restatement of Property. Restatement (Second) of Property, § 11.1(3) (Tent. Draft No. 3, 1975).

Nevertheless, while there is still a split of authority over this question, the trend among recent cases appears to be in favor of a mitigation requirement. . . .

The majority rule is based on principles of property law which equate a lease with a transfer of a property interest in the owner's estate. Under this rationale the lease conveys to a tenant an interest in the property which forecloses any control by the landlord; thus, it would be anomalous to require the landlord to concern himself with the tenant's abandonment of his own property. *Wright v. Baumann*, 239 Or. 410, 398 P.2d 119, 120–21 (1965).

For instance, in *Muller v. Beck*, [94 N.J.L. 311, 110 A. 831 (Sup. Ct. 1920)] where essentially the same issue was posed, the court clearly treated the lease as governed by property, as opposed to contract, precepts.[3] The court there observed that the "tenant had an estate for years, but it was an estate qualified by this right of the landlord to prevent its transfer," 94 N.J.L. at 313, 110 A. at 832, and that "the tenant has an estate with which the landlord may not interfere." Id. at 314, 110 A. at 832. Similarly, in *Heckel v. Griese*, [12 N.J. Misc. 211, 171 A. 148 (Sup. Ct. 1934)], the court noted the absolute nature of the tenant's interest in the property while the lease was in effect, stating that "when the tenant vacated, . . . no one, in the circumstances, had any right to interfere with the defendant's possession of the premises." 12 N.J. Misc. at 213, 171 A. 148, 149. Other cases simply cite the rule announced in *Muller v. Beck*, *supra*, without discussing the underlying rationale. See *Joyce v. Bauman*, *supra*, 113 N.J.L. at 440, 174 A. 693. . . .

Yet the distinction between a lease for ordinary residential purposes and an ordinary contract can no longer be considered viable. As Professor Powell observed, evolving "social factors have exerted increasing influence on the law of estates for years." 2 Powell on Real Property (1977 ed.), § 221[1] at 180–81. The result has been that

> [t]he complexities of city life, and the proliferated problems of modern society in general, have created new problems for lessors and lessees and these have been commonly handled by specific clauses in leases. This growth in the number and detail of specific lease covenants has reintroduced into the law of estates for years a predominantly contractual ingredient. [Id. at 181]. . . .

Application of the contract rule requiring mitigation of damages to a residential lease may be justified as a matter of basic fairness. Professor McCormick first commented upon the inequity under the majority rule when he predicted in 1925 that eventually

> the logic, inescapable according to the standards of a "jurisprudence of conceptions" which permits the landlord to stand idly by the vacant, abandoned premises and treat them as the property of the tenant and recover full rent, while yield to the more realistic notions of social advantage which in other fields of the law have forbidden a recovery for damages which the plaintiff by reasonable efforts could have avoided. (McCormick, *The Rights of the Landlord Upon Abandonment of the Premises by the Tenant*, 23 Mich. L. Rev. 211, 221–22 (1925)).

Various courts have adopted this position. . . .

The pre-existing rule cannot be predicated upon the possibility that a landlord may lose the opportunity to rent another empty apartment because he must first rent the apartment vacated by the defaulting tenant. Even where the breach occurs in a multi-dwelling building, each apartment may have unique qualities which make it

---

[3] It is well settled that a party claiming damages for a breach of contract has a duty to mitigate his loss. . . .

attractive to certain individuals. Significantly, in *Sommer v. Kridel*, there was a specific request to rent the apartment vacated by the defendant; there is no reason to believe that absent this vacancy the landlord could have succeeded in renting a different apartment to this individual.

> **Food for Thought**
>
> Exactly what are the "more modern notions of fairness and equity" that underpin the court's decision? What is the court's rationale for changing the law?

We therefore hold that antiquated real property concepts which served as the basis for the pre-existing rule, shall no longer be controlling where there is a claim for damages under a residential lease. Such claims must be governed by more modern notions of fairness and equity. A landlord has a duty to mitigate damages where he seeks to recover rents due from a defaulting tenant.

If the landlord has other vacant apartments besides the one which the tenant has abandoned, the landlord's duty to mitigate consists of making reasonable efforts to re-let the apartment. In such cases he must treat the apartment in question as if it was one of his vacant stock.

As part of his cause of action, the landlord shall be required to carry the burden of proving that he used reasonable diligence in attempting to re-let the premises. We note that there has been a divergence of opinion concerning the allocation of the burden of proof on this issue. While generally in contract actions the breaching party has the burden of proving that damages are capable of mitigation, here the landlord will be in a better position to demonstrate whether he exercised reasonable diligence in attempting to re-let the premises.

III.

The *Sommer v. Kridel* case presents a classic example of the unfairness which occurs when a landlord has no responsibility to minimize damages. Sommer waited 15 months and allowed $4658.50 in damages to accrue before attempting to re-let the apartment. Despite the availability of a tenant who was ready, willing and able to rent the apartment, the landlord needlessly increased the damages by turning her away. While a tenant will not necessarily be excused from his obligations under a lease simply by finding another person who is willing to rent the vacated premises, *see, e.g., Reget v. Dempsey-Tegler & Co.,* 70 Ill. App. 2d 32, 216 N.E.2d 500 (Ill. App. 1966) (new tenant insisted on leasing the premises under different terms); *Edmands v. Rust & Richardson Drug Co.,* 191 Mass. 123, 77 N.E. 713 (1906) (landlord need not accept insolvent tenant), here there has been no showing that the new tenant would not have been suitable. We therefore find that plaintiff could have avoided the damages which eventually accrued, and that the defendant was relieved of his duty to continue paying rent. Ordinarily we would require the tenant to bear the cost of any reasonable expenses incurred by a landlord in attempting to re-let the premises, but no such expenses were incurred in this case. . . .

In assessing whether the landlord has satisfactorily carried his burden, the trial court shall consider, among other factors, whether the landlord, either personally or through an agency, offered or showed the apartment to any prospective tenants, or advertised it in local newspapers. Additionally, the tenant may attempt to rebut such evidence by showing that he proffered suitable tenants who were rejected. However, there is no standard formula for measuring whether the landlord has utilized satisfactory efforts in attempting to mitigate damages, and each case must be judged upon its own facts. Compare *Hershorin v. La Vista, Inc.*, 110 Ga. App. 435, 138 S.E.2d 703 (App. 1964) ("reasonable effort" of landlord by showing the apartment to all prospective tenants); *Carpenter v. Wisniewski*, 139 Ind. App. 325, 215 N.E.2d 882 (App. 1966) (duty satisfied where landlord advertised the premises through a newspaper, placed a sign in the window, and employed a realtor); *Re Garment Center Capitol, Inc.*, 93 F.2d 667 (2 Cir. 1938) (landlord's duty not breached where higher rental was asked since it was known that this was merely a basis for negotiations); *Foggia v. Dix,* 265 Or. 315, 509 P.2d 412, 414 (1973) (in mitigating damages, landlord need not accept less than fair market value or "substantially alter his obligations as established in the pre-existing lease"); with *Anderson v. Andy Darling Pontiac, Inc.*, 257 Wis. 371, 43 N.W.2d 362 (1950) (reasonable diligence not established where newspaper advertisement placed in one issue of local paper by a broker). . . .

Points for Discussion

a. **Rationale for Mitigation**

After *Sommer*, a New Jersey landlord has only two options when the tenant abandons: mitigate damages or terminate the lease. How convincing is the court's rationale for changing New Jersey law? Notice that the lease allowed Kridel to assign his interest with the landlord's consent, so Kridel could have minimized or avoided any loss by finding a replacement tenant himself. Should the burden of finding a replacement tenant be placed upon the abandoning tenant who breached the lease?

b. **The "Lost Sale"?**

Suppose landlord L owns a two-unit building in New Jersey today; unit 1 is rented to D, and unit 2 is empty. D abandons the premises; L tries to mitigate damages by advertising both units for rent; and E decides to rent unit 1. Has L now "lost" the opportunity to rent unit 2 to E, and thus suffered a net loss? How persuasive is the *Sommer* court's response to this concern?

c. **The Mitigation Majority**

Today almost all states follow the *Sommer* approach: after abandonment, the landlord must either terminate the lease or mitigate damages. Although *Kridel* involves a residential tenancy, the doctrine generally applies to commercial tenancies as well.

But Restatement (Second) of Property: Landlord and Tenant § 12.1(3) continues to endorse the traditional no-mitigation rule, reasoning that it discourages abandonment and prevents vandalism. For an evaluation of the majority approach, see David Crump, *Should the Commercial Landlord Have a Duty to Mitigate Damages After the Tenant Abandons? A Legal and Economic Analysis*, 49 Wake Forest L. Rev. 187 (2014).

d. Mitigation Problems

Tenant T enters into a two-year lease with landlord L for a studio apartment on the fourth floor of L's 20-unit complex, agreeing to pay rent of $1,000 each month. One year later, T abandons the apartment. Under the *Sommer* standard, has landlord L acted properly to mitigate her damages in the following situations?

> (1)   L places an ad in the local newspaper to rent her vacant studio apartments. When U visits in response to the ad, L first shows U the other vacant studios in the complex, leaving T's unit for last.
>
> (2)   L puts a sign in the window of T's unit. The sign is 2 feet tall and 3 feet wide; it reads: "For rent. Call 851-0341." No one comes to look at T's unit.
>
> (3)   L hires a real estate broker to find tenants for all of her vacant apartments, including T's unit. The broker finds V, who wants to rent T's apartment; V offers to pay rent of $900 per month. L refuses.

e. Aftermath of *Sommer*

Kridel was a first-year student at Rutgers Law School when he wrote the letter to Sommer. After graduating from Rutgers with honors in 1974, he represented himself in this case, all the way up to the New Jersey Supreme Court. He later received an LL.M. degree in taxation from New York University Law School. Today he practices law in New Jersey and New York.

---

2. Security Deposits

Most states have adopted legislation that regulates the security deposits provided by residential tenants. One example is California Civil Code § 1950.5:

> (a)   This section applies to security for a rental agreement for residential property that is used as the dwelling of the tenant.
>
> (b)   As used in this section, "security" means any payment, fee, deposit, or charge . . . used or to be used for any purpose, including, but not limited to, any of the following:
>
> > (1)   The compensation of a landlord for a tenant's default in the payment of rent.

(2) The repair of damages to the premises, exclusive of ordinary wear and tear, caused by the tenant or by a guest or licensee of the tenant.

(3) The cleaning of the premises upon termination of the tenancy necessary to return the unit to the same level of cleanliness it was in at the inception of the tenancy. . . .

(4) To remedy future defaults by the tenant in any obligation under the rental agreement to restore, replace, or return personal property or appurtenances, exclusive of ordinary wear and tear. . . .

(c)(1) . . . [A] landlord may not demand or receive security, however denominated, in an amount or value in excess of an amount equal to one month's rent, in addition to any rent for the first month paid on or before initial occupancy. . . .

(e) The landlord may claim of the security only those amounts as are reasonably necessary for the purposes specified in subdivision (b). The landlord may not assert a claim against the tenant or the security for damages to the premises or any defective conditions that preexisted the tenancy, for ordinary wear and tear . . . or for the cumulative effects of ordinary wear and tear occurring during any one or more tenancies. . . .

(g)(1) No later than 21 calendar days after the tenant has vacated the premises . . . the landlord shall furnish the tenant, by personal delivery or by first-class mail, postage prepaid, a copy of an itemized statement indicating the basis for, and the amount of, any security received and the disposition of the security, and shall return any remaining portion of the security to the tenant. . . .

(*l*) The bad faith claim or retention by a landlord . . . of the security or any portion thereof . . . may subject the landlord . . . to statutory damages of up to twice the amount of the security, in addition to actual damages. The court may award damages for bad faith whenever the facts warrant that award, regardless of whether the injured party has specifically requested relief. In any action under this section, the landlord . . . shall have the burden of proof as to the reasonableness of the amounts claimed or the authority pursuant to this section to demand additional security deposits.

(m) No lease or rental agreement may contain any provision characterizing any security as "nonrefundable."

Points for Discussion

a. **Why Regulate?**

As a general rule, states do not restrict the amount of rent that a landlord may charge, leaving this issue to the market. Why should government regulate the amount of security deposits or the conditions under which they are refunded?

b. Lack of Statement

What is the tenant's remedy under Cal. Civil Code § 1950.5 if the landlord fails to provide the required statement within 21 days? In *Garcia v. Thong*, 895 P.2d 226 (N.M. 1995), the New Mexico Supreme Court held that the landlord forfeited any claim to the security deposit under these circumstances. Would a California court do the same?

---

3. Eviction

Traditionally, a landlord was free to terminate a periodic tenancy for any reason—or for no reason at all. This power reflected the broad scope of the right to exclude, which you studied in Chapter 1. Over time, however, the law has increasingly restricted the landlord's right to terminate a tenancy. For example, a landlord may not terminate a periodic tenancy in violation of the Fair Housing Act of 1968. Section 3604(a) of that Act provides that it is illegal to "make unavailable or deny, a dwelling to any person" for a discriminatory reason.

Suppose that tenant A rents an apartment on a month-to-month basis from landlord B. A complains to B that her apartment has lacked heat for three days. The next day, B notifies A that her tenancy will end in 30 days. A refuses to move, and B sues to evict her. Does A have any defense to this action?

Elk Creek Management Co. v. Gilbert

Supreme Court of Oregon

303 P.3d 929 (2013)

WALTERS, J.

ORS 90.385 prohibits a landlord from "retaliat[ing] by" serving notice to terminate a tenancy after the tenant has made a complaint that is in good faith and related to the tenancy. In this case, we conclude that, to prove retaliation under ORS 90.385, a tenant must establish that the landlord served the notice of termination *because of* the tenant's complaint. The tenant need not prove, in addition, that the complaint caused the landlord actual or perceived injury or that the landlord intended to cause the tenant equivalent injury in return. . . .

This case concerns a month-to-month tenancy [in a single-family home] pursuant to a written rental agreement. . . . At some time before May 19, 2009, the tenants [Harold Gilbert and Melissa Strittmatter] "made some sort of general complaint(s) to [the owner] about the electrical system on the property." . . . On May 19, [Elk

Creek Management Company, the property manager] . . . gave the tenants written notice that the owner wanted to do a "walk-through" of the premises. . . . After the initial walk-through, [Elk Creek] advised the tenants that [the owner] wanted to do another walk-through on June 16. A licensed electrician accompanied the owner and [an Elk Creek employee] on that second walk-through, and, at its conclusion, the electrician recommended that the owner make repairs to the electrical system. It was apparent "to everyone" that those repairs would "involve a cost to the owner." [The Elk Creek employee] . . . called the tenants the next afternoon and informed them that the owner had decided to terminate their lease. The following day, the tenants received a 30-day no-cause termination notice and a note from the [Elk Creek employee], which stated:

> I am sorry that I have to give you the thirty days notice. [The owner] has several repairs including updating the electrical. If there is anything I can do please let me know.

> **See It**
>
> Click here to see the termination notice. The home in this case was over 100 years old. At trial, the electrician testified that the needed repairs would cost between $3,500 and $4,000; he also said that the work could be done without having the tenants vacate the house. Are these facts relevant to the tenants' retaliatory eviction defense?

[The tenants refused to vacate, and Elk Creek filed an eviction lawsuit on behalf of the owner. The tenants asserted the defense of retaliatory eviction, but the trial judge rejected this claim on the basis that termination of the tenancy was not "retaliation" by the landlord. The judge stated: "The concept of *retaliation (lex talionis)* has ancient foundations and in common language is easily understood in metaphors such as 'an eye for an eye' or a 'tooth for a tooth.' The essence of the concept is that when one suffers a real or perceived wrong, a like injury will be inflicted upon the one who did the initial real or perceived harm." The judge concluded that this standard was not met on the facts of the case, because the tenants did not cause any injury to the landlord, so the landlord could not have been motivated by retaliation in terminating the tenancy. The Court of Appeals affirmed.]

> **What's That?**
>
> The *lex talionis* concept dates back at least to the Code of Hammurabi in 1750 B.C., one of the first known statutes: "If a man destroys the eye of another man, they shall destroy his eye. If one breaks a man's bone, they shall break his bone." An early version of the code carved into a black basalt pillar is on display at the Louvre Museum in Paris.

. . . We allowed the tenants' petition for review to consider the tenants' argument that the Court of Appeals incorrectly interpreted ORS 90.385 when it declared that "[t]he concept of retaliation as the term is used in ORS 90.385 involves an intention on the part of the landlord to cause some sort of disadvantage to the tenant, motivated by an injury (or perceived injury) that the tenant has caused the landlord." The tenants contend that, to prove retaliation under ORS 90.385, a tenant must prove only that a landlord took one of the actions specified in ORS 90.385 because a tenant engaged in a statutorily protected activity; no additional proof of injury or intent to harm is required. . . .

ORS 90.385(1) prohibits a landlord from "retaliat[ing] by" taking certain described acts "after" a tenant has engaged in certain described activities. A landlord may not retaliate by (1) "increasing rent or decreasing services"; (2) "serving a notice to terminate the tenancy"; or (3) "bringing or threatening to bring an action for possession," after a tenant has (1) made or expressed an intent to make specified complaints, including a complaint that is "in good faith and related to the tenancy"; (2) "organized or become a member of a tenants' union or similar organization"; (3) "testified against the landlord in any judicial, administrative or legislative proceeding"; (4) with certain exceptions, "successfully defended an action for possession brought by the landlord within the previous six months"; or (5) "performed or expressed intent to perform any other act for the purpose of asserting, protecting or invoking the protection of any right secured to tenants under any federal, state or local law."

> **Make the Connection**
>
> In most states, retaliatory eviction laws were adopted *after* the implied warranty of habitability was recognized. Do you understand why the retaliatory eviction doctrine became necessary? What parts of the Oregon statute protect a tenant against retaliatory eviction after he complains that his residence is not habitable?

. . . In describing the relationship between the prohibited landlord acts and the protected tenant acts, ORS 90.385 states that a landlord may not "retaliate by" taking one of the prohibited acts "after" the tenant has taken one of the protected acts. ORS 90.385 does not expressly require that a tenant demonstrate that the tenant's protected acts caused injury to the landlord or that the landlord perceived the tenant's acts as causing injury. ORS 90.385 also does not expressly require that a tenant demonstrate that a landlord took one of the prohibited acts with an intent to cause injury to the tenant. Thus, the question before us is whether the legislature nevertheless intended to impose those requirements, and, if not, what requirement or requirements the legislature did intend to impose. . . .

[To determine t]he correct construction of ORS 90.385, [we must consider] the context in which the legislature used the word "retaliate" and other indicators of the legislature's intent. When we do so, we conclude, for the reasons that follow, that the legislature did not intend to require that a tenant prove that the tenant's protected act caused the landlord actual or perceived injury or that the landlord intended to cause the tenant injury in return; rather, the statute is satisfied if the landlord made the decision to act *because of* the tenant's protected activity.

First, as explained, a tenant who takes one of the actions referenced in ORS 90.385(1) takes an action that the tenant has a right to take and that the legislature intends to protect. . . . It would be inconsistent with those interests for the legislature to impose a requirement that the tenant prove that his or her exercise of those rights caused the landlord injury.

Second, the enactment history of ORS 90.385 demonstrates that the legislature did not intend to require proof of injury or intent to harm. The Oregon Residential Landlord and Tenant Act (ORLTA), which includes ORS 90.385, was enacted in 1973. The ORLTA was modeled on the Uniform Residential Landlord and Tenant Act (1972) (URLTA) . . . and, as originally enacted, ORS 90.385 mirrored section 5–101 of that Uniform Act. Both acts prohibited a landlord from "retaliat[ing] by" taking specified actions after a tenant had engaged in protected activities, including complaining of a landlord's violation of statutory habitability requirements. . . .

[The] drafters of the Uniform Act deliberately chose not to include a requirement. . . . that the landlord intend its action as a penalty for the tenant's conduct. Instead, the drafters chose to require proof that the landlord had "retaliate[d] by" taking action after a tenant engaged in protected activity. . . . If the URLTA framers had wanted to include . . . a requirement [that the landlord's conduct was motivated by "malice or hostility"], it is likely that they would have done so explicitly or used an alternative formulation that more clearly incorporated that concept. . . .

A question remains, however, about the height of the causal bar that the Oregon Legislature requires Oregon tenants to clear. Did the Oregon Legislature intend to require tenants to prove that a tenant's protected activity was the sole reason for the landlord's action, or did it intend to impose some other causal standard? . . . [T]he drafters of both the URLTA and the ORLTA . . . declined to expressly require . . . that the tenant prove that the tenant's protected activity was the "sole" or "dominant" reason for the landlord's prohibited action. It is therefore likely that the drafters did not intend to impose either of those more strictly stated causal requirements. . . .

We conclude that ORS 90.385 requires a tenant to prove that, "but for" the tenant's protected activity, the landlord would not have made the decision that it did. In the circumstance in which . . . two causes concur, but either operating alone would have been sufficient to cause the result, a tenant also may prevail by proving that the tenant's protected activity was a "material and substantial factor" in the landlord's decision. The tenant need not prove that the tenant's protected activity was the "sole" or "dominant" reason for the landlord's decision. . . .

Although the trial court decided that the tenants' complaints were one of the reasons that the owner decided to conduct the initial walk-through, the court did not explicitly decide whether the tenants' complaints were also one of the reasons that the owner decided to serve the notice of termination; the trial court speculated that the owner may have given that notice for other "valid business reasons." Without explicitly elaborating on what those "valid business reasons" may have been, the trial court discussed whether the tenants had inflicted harm on the owner and whether the owner had attempted to harm the tenants by terminating their tenancy. . . . However, as we have explained, whether the owner was thankful, threatened, or neutral when the tenants notified her of electrical problems, and whether the owner considered the costs of improving the electrical system injurious or simply necessary, ORS 90.385 prohibited the owner from serving the tenants with notice of termination because of the tenants' complaints. . . .

That does not mean, of course, that a landlord must continue to lease that property it owns or that a landlord is always prohibited from evicting a tenant after the tenant complains about the condition of a dwelling. For example, if the landlord offers evidence that it made the decision to serve a notice of termination for some reason unrelated to the tenant's complaint, such as that the tenant failed to pay rent or violated other terms of the lease, or that it made its decision to evict before the tenant complained, a factfinder may conclude that the tenant's complaint was not a factor that made a difference in the landlord's decision.

In this case, the trial court could have inferred, from the temporal connection between the tenants' complaint and the owner's decision to evict them, that the tenants' complaints made a difference in the owner's decision. However, the trial court did not do so and instead speculated that the owner may have had other "valid business reasons" for her action. Although the record does not reveal any such reasons, we hesitate to decide what conclusion the trial court would have reached had it applied the correct legal standard. We therefore reverse and remand for further proceedings consistent with this decision. . . .

Points for Discussion

a. Right to Exclude

What policy reasons support the Oregon statute involved in this case? Does this statute go too far in restricting the landlord's right to exclude? Should a landlord have more freedom in selecting a tenant than in terminating a tenancy?

b. Scope of the Doctrine

Today most states protect tenants from retaliatory eviction, often by statutes similar to the one in *Elk Creek Management*. See, e.g., *Central Hous. Assocs., LP v. Olson*, 929 N.W.2d 398 (Minn. 2019). But the scope of this protection varies widely. States disagree on issues such as: which tenant conduct is covered; whether the doctrine applies to the refusal to renew a term of years tenancy; whether it applies to commercial tenancies; and whether the doctrine also covers increases in rent and/or decreases in services. What is your opinion on these issues?

c. Proving Intent

When it was originally enacted in 1973, the Oregon retaliatory eviction statute provided that "evidence of a complaint within one year before the alleged act of retaliation creates a presumption that the landlord's conduct was in retaliation." Under this approach, retaliatory intent was presumed if the eviction occurred within a year of the tenant's protected conduct, but the landlord could rebut this presumption with evidence; conversely, if the eviction occurred more than a year after the protected conduct, the tenant had the burden of proving intent. Many state statutes—and the Uniform Residential Landlord and Tenant Act—also presume retaliatory intent for a specified period. But the Oregon legislature later eliminated the presumption, thus always requiring the tenant to prove retaliatory intent. Which approach is better? Why?

The *Elk Creek Management* court suggests that in this case the trial judge could have inferred a "temporal connection between the tenants' complaint and the owner's decision." Is this a sensible approach? Is it consistent with the Oregon legislature's decision to abolish the presumption?

d. Good Faith Eviction?

A few jurisdictions go beyond the retaliatory eviction doctrine by providing that a landlord may evict a tenant only for a good faith reason. *See, e.g., AIMCO Properties, LLC v. Dziewisz*, 883 A.2d 310 (N.H. 2005) (holding that the New Hampshire good faith eviction statute applies to the failure to renew a term of years tenancy). This approach is akin to the commercial reasonableness standard that you studied in *Kendall v. Ernest Pestana, Inc.* Should a landlord be able to evict a tenant for no reason at all? Is the good faith eviction standard an appropriate protection for the tenant or an improper restriction on the landlord's right to exclude?

e. Aftermath of *Elk Creek Management*

Ed Johnson of the Oregon Law Center, the attorney who represented the tenants, later commented that the decision "restored the right of tenants in Oregon to complain about the condition of their housing without the fear of being evicted. This right makes it easier for the 40% of Oregonians who rent their housing to live in habitable conditions."

Suppose that landlord L is entitled to evict tenant T. What procedure must L follow? Traditionally, L could evict T in either of two ways:

- *Use self-help*: L could retake possession through self-help by physically entering the premises and causing T to leave, as long as L used only a reasonable amount of force.
- *Sue the tenant*: L could sue T, secure a judgment ordering T's eviction, and have the judgment enforced by a law enforcement officer.

Which is the better approach? Why? The Minnesota Supreme Court addressed these questions in our next case.

Berg v. Wiley

Supreme Court of Minnesota

264 N.W.2d 145 (1978)

ROGOSHESKE, JUSTICE.

Defendant landlord, Wiley Enterprises, Inc., and defendant Rodney A. Wiley (hereafter collectively referred to as Wiley) appeal from a judgment upon a jury verdict awarding plaintiff tenant, A Family Affair Restaurant, Inc., damages for wrongful eviction from its leased premises. The issues for review are whether the evidence was sufficient to support the jury's finding that the tenant did not abandon or surrender the premises and whether the trial court erred in finding Wiley's reentry forcible and wrongful as a matter of law. We hold that the jury's verdict is supported by sufficient evidence and that the trial court's determination of unlawful entry was correct as a matter of law, and affirm the judgment.

On November 11, 1970, Wiley, as lessor and tenant's predecessor in interest as lessee, executed a written lease agreement letting land and a building in Osseo, Minnesota, for use as a restaurant. The lease provided a 5-year term beginning December 1, 1970, and specified that the tenant agreed to bear all costs of repairs and remodeling, to "make no changes in the building structure" without prior written authorization from Wiley, and to "operate the restaurant in a lawful and prudent manner." Wiley also reserved the right "at [his] option [to] retake possession" of the premises "[s]hould the Lessee fail to meet the conditions of this Lease."[1] In early 1971, plaintiff Kathleen Berg took assignment of the lease from the prior lessee, and on May 1, 1971, she opened "A Family Affair Restaurant" on the premises. In January 1973, Berg incorporated the restaurant and assigned her interest in the lease to "A Family Affair Restaurant, Inc." As sole shareholder of the corporation, she alone continued to act for the tenant.

---

[1] The provisions of the lease pertinent to this case provide:

Item #5 The Lessee will make no changes to the building structure without first receiving written authorization from the Lessor. The Lessor will promptly reply in writing to each request and will cooperate with the Lessee on any reasonable request.

Item #6 The Lessee agrees to operate the restaurant in a lawful and prudent manner during the lease period.

Item #7 Should the Lessee fail to meet the conditions of this Lease the Lessor may at their [sic] option retake possession of said premises. In any such event such act will not relieve Lessee from liability for payment [of] the rental herein provided or from the conditions or obligations of this lease.

Site of Berg's restaurant
Click here for larger photo

    The present dispute has arisen out of Wiley's objection to Berg's continued remodeling of the restaurant without procuring written permission and her consequent operation of the restaurant in a state of disrepair with alleged health code violations. Strained relations between the parties came to a head in June and July 1973. In a letter dated June 29, 1973, Wiley's attorney charged Berg with having breached lease items 5 and 6 by making changes in the building structure without written authorization and by operating an unclean kitchen in violation of health regulations. The letter demanded that a list of eight remodeling items be completed within 2 weeks from the date of the letter, by Friday, July 13, 1973, or Wiley would retake possession of the premises under lease item 7. Also, a June 13 inspection of the restaurant by the Minnesota Department of Health had produced an order that certain listed changes be completed within specified time limits in order to comply with the health code. The major items on the inspector's list, similar to those listed by Wiley's attorney, were to be completed by July 15, 1973.

    During the 2-week deadline set by both Wiley and the health department, Berg continued to operate the restaurant without closing to complete the required items of remodeling. The evidence is in dispute as to whether she intended to permanently close the restaurant and vacate the premises at the end of the 2 weeks or simply close for about 1 month in order to remodel to comply with the health code. At the close of business on Friday, July 13, 1973, the last day of the 2-week period, Berg dismissed her employees, closed the restaurant, and placed a sign in the window saying "Closed for Remodeling." Earlier that day, Berg testified, Wiley came to the premises in her absence and attempted to change the locks. When she returned and asserted her right to continue in possession, he complied with her request to leave the locks unchanged. Berg also testified that at about 9:30 p.m. that evening, while she and four of her friends were in the restaurant, she observed Wiley hanging from the awning peering into the window. Shortly thereafter, she heard Wiley pounding on the back door demanding admittance. Berg called the county sheriff to come and preserve order. Wiley testified that he observed Berg and a group of her friends in the restaurant removing paneling from a wall. Allegedly fearing destruction of his property, Wiley called the city police, who, with the sheriff, mediated an agreement between the parties to preserve the status quo until each could consult with legal counsel on Monday, July 16, 1973.

Wiley testified that his then attorney advised him to take possession of the premises and lock the tenant out. Accompanied by a police officer and a locksmith, Wiley entered the premises in Berg's absence and without her knowledge on Monday, July 16, 1973, and changed the locks. Later in the day, Berg found herself locked out. The lease term was not due to expire until December 1, 1975. The premises were re-let to another tenant on or about August 1, 1973. Berg brought this damage action against Wiley and three other named defendants, including the new tenant, on July 27, 1973. A second amended complaint sought damages for lost profits, damage to chattels, intentional infliction of emotional distress, and other tort damages based upon claims in wrongful eviction, contract, and tort. Wiley answered with an affirmative defense of abandonment and surrender and counterclaimed for damage to the premises. . . . At the close of Berg's case, all defendants other than Rodney A. Wiley and Wiley Enterprises, Inc., were dismissed from the action. Only Berg's action for wrongful eviction and intentional infliction of emotional distress and Wiley's affirmative defense of abandonment and his counterclaim for damage to the premises were submitted by special verdict to the jury. With respect to the wrongful eviction claim, the trial court found as a matter of law that Wiley did in fact lock the tenant out, and that the lockout was wrongful.

The jury, by answers to the questions submitted, found no liability on Berg's claim for intentional infliction of emotional distress and no liability on Wiley's counterclaim for damages to the premises, but awarded Berg $31,000 for lost profits and $3,540 for loss of chattels resulting from the wrongful lockout. . . .

On this appeal, Wiley seeks an outright reversal of the damages award for wrongful eviction, claiming insufficient evidence to support the jury's finding of no abandonment or surrender and claiming error in the trial court's finding of wrongful eviction as a matter of law.

The first issue before us concerns the sufficiency of evidence to support the jury's finding that Berg had not abandoned or surrendered the leasehold before being locked out by Wiley. Viewing the evidence to support the jury's special verdict in the light most favorable to Berg, as we must, we hold it amply supports the jury's finding of no abandonment or surrender of the premises. While the evidence bearing upon Berg's intent was strongly contradictory, the jury could reasonably have concluded, based on

Berg's testimony and supporting circumstantial evidence, that she intended to retain possession, closing temporarily to remodel. Thus, the lockout cannot be excused on ground that Berg abandoned or surrendered the leasehold.

The second and more difficult issue is whether Wiley's self-help repossession of the premises by locking out Berg was correctly held wrongful as a matter of law.

Minnesota has historically followed the common-law rule that a landlord may rightfully use self-help to retake leased premises from a tenant in possession without incurring liability for wrongful eviction provided two conditions are met: (1) The landlord is legally entitled to possession, such as where a tenant holds over after the lease term or where a tenant breaches a lease containing a reentry clause; and (2) the landlord's means of reentry are peaceable. *Mercil v. Broulette*, 66 Minn. 416, 69 N.W. 218 (1896). Under the common-law rule, a tenant who is evicted by his landlord may recover damages for wrongful eviction where the landlord either had no right to possession or where the means used to remove the tenant were forcible, or both.

Wiley contends that Berg had breached the provisions of the lease, thereby entitling Wiley, under the terms of the lease, to retake possession, and that his repossession by changing the locks in Berg's absence was accomplished in a peaceful manner. In a memorandum accompanying the post-trial order, the trial court stated two grounds for finding the lockout wrongful as a matter of law: (1) It was not accomplished in a peaceable manner and therefore could not be justified under the common-law rule, and (2) any self-help reentry against a tenant in possession is wrongful under the growing modern doctrine that a landlord must always resort to the judicial process to enforce his statutory remedy against a tenant wrongfully in possession. Whether Berg had in fact breached the lease and whether Wiley was hence entitled to possession was not judicially determined. . . .

In applying the common-law rule, we have not before had occasion to decide what means of self-help used to dispossess a tenant in his absence will constitute a nonpeaceable entry, giving a right to damages without regard to who holds the legal right to possession. Wiley argues that only actual or threatened violence used against a tenant should give rise to damages where the landlord had the right to possession. We cannot agree.

It has long been the policy of our law to discourage landlords from taking the law into their own hands, and our decisions and statutory law have looked with disfavor upon any use of self-help to dispossess a tenant in circumstances which are likely to result in breaches of the peace. We gave early recognition to this policy in *Lobdell v. Keene*, 85 Minn. 90, 101, 88 N.W. 426, 430 (1901), where we said:

> The object and purpose of the legislature in the enactment of the forcible entry and unlawful detainer statute was to prevent those claiming a right of entry or possession of lands from redressing their own wrongs by entering into possession in a violent and forcible manner. All such acts tend to a breach of the peace, and encourage high-handed oppression. The law does not permit the owner of land, be his title ever

so good, to be the judge of his own rights with respect to a possession adversely held, but puts him to his remedy under the statutes.

To facilitate a resort to judicial process, the legislature has provided a summary procedure in Minn. St. 566.02 to 566.17 whereby a landlord may recover possession of leased premises upon proper notice and showing in court in as little as 3 to 10 days. As we recognized in *Mutual Trust Life Ins. Co. v. Berg*, 187 Minn. 503, 505, 246 N.W. 9, 10 (1932), "[t]he forcible entry and unlawful detainer statutes were intended to prevent parties from taking the law into their own hands when going into possession of lands and tenements. . . ." To further discourage self-help, our legislature has provided treble damages for forcible evictions, § 557.08 and 557.09, and has provided additional criminal penalties for intentional and unlawful exclusion of a tenant. In *Sweeney v. Meyers*, [199 Minn. 21, 270 N.W. 906 (1937)], we allowed a business tenant not only damages for lost profits but also punitive damages against a landlord who, like Wiley, entered in the tenant's absence and locked the tenant out.

In the present case, as in *Sweeney*, the tenant was in possession, claiming a right to continue in possession adverse to the landlord's claim of breach of the lease, and had neither abandoned nor surrendered the premises. Wiley, well aware that Berg was asserting her right to possession, retook possession in her absence by picking the locks and locking her out. The record shows a history of vigorous dispute and keen animosity between the parties. Upon this record, we can only conclude that the singular reason why actual violence did not erupt at the moment of Wiley's changing of the locks was Berg's absence and her subsequent self-restraint and resort to judicial process. Upon these facts, we cannot find Wiley's means of reentry peaceable under the common-law rule. Our long-standing policy to discourage self-help which tends to cause a breach of the peace compels us to disapprove the means used to dispossess Berg. To approve this lockout, as urged by Wiley, merely because in Berg's absence no actual violence erupted while the locks were being changed, would be to encourage all future tenants, in order to protect their possession, to be vigilant and thereby set the stage for the very kind of public disturbance which it must be our policy to discourage. . . .

We recognize that the growing modern trend departs completely from the common-law rule to hold that self-help is never available to dispossess a tenant who is in possession and has not abandoned or voluntarily surrendered the premises. This growing rule is founded on the recognition that the potential for violent breach of peace inheres in any situation where a landlord attempts by his own means to remove a tenant who is claiming possession adversely to the landlord. Courts adopting the rule reason that there is no cause to sanction such potentially disruptive self-help where adequate and speedy means are provided for removing a tenant peacefully through judicial process. At least 16 states have adopted this modern rule, holding that judicial proceedings, including the summary procedures provided in those states' unlawful detainer statutes, are the exclusive remedy by which a landlord may remove a tenant claiming possession. . . .

While we would be compelled to disapprove the lockout of Berg in her absence under the common-law rule as stated, we approve the trial court's reasoning and adopt as preferable the modern view represented by the cited cases. To make clear our departure from the common-law rule for the benefit of future landlords and tenants, we hold that, subsequent to our decision in this case, the only lawful means to dispossess a tenant who has not abandoned nor voluntarily surrendered but who claims possession adversely to a landlord's claim of breach of a written lease is by resort to judicial process. . . .

Points for Discussion

a. **Peaceable Self-Help**

Why wasn't Wiley's entry deemed "peaceable"? No violence erupted; no one was hurt; no property was damaged. As the *Berg* court interprets the common law standard, when would self-help ever be peaceable?

b. **What Did Wiley Do Wrong?**

Notice that Wiley was represented by an attorney in this dispute. It is fair to assume that he sought and received his attorney's advice about how to retake possession in a peaceable manner, consistent with Minnesota law. But consider the result. Wiley, the innocent party who presumably relied in good faith on his attorney's advice, ends up owing almost $34,000 to Berg, who clearly breached the lease. What did Wiley do wrong?

c. **Prohibiting Self-Help**

Berg reflects the national trend. In the vast majority of states, the landlord's only remedy is to evict a residential tenant through judicial process. However, a number of states allow peaceable self-help to evict a commercial tenant. *See, e.g., Fronczak v. Town of Ocean Park,* 106 N.Y.S.3d 771 (Sup. Ct. 2019). How convincing is the *Berg* court's rationale for abolishing self-help eviction? In framing your answer, consider the justifications for property discussed in Chapter 1. For a policy analysis of self-help eviction, see Adam B. Badawi, *Self-Help and the Rules of Engagement,* 29 Yale J. on Reg. 1 (2012).

Like Minnesota, most states use expedited procedures for eviction lawsuits. But the *Berg* court's observation that a judicially-supervised eviction may be complete in "as little as 3 to 10 days" applies to evictions that tenants do not contest; contested evictions take longer. For example, one study showed that the judicial eviction process required an average of 108 days in Los Angeles. Randy G. Gerchick, Comment, *No Easy Way Out: Making the Summary Eviction Process a Fairer and More Efficient Alternative to Landlord Self-Help*, 41 UCLA L. Rev. 759, 809 (1994).

> **See It**
>
> A summary eviction proceeding is a form of accelerated, simplified litigation. Typically the tenant is given only a few days to respond to the complaint, and the trial occurs quickly. Some states streamline the process by using standardized pleadings. Click here to see the preprinted (1) complaint and (2) answer forms that are used in California.

d. **Impact on Rents**

Self-help eviction is quick and cheap; eviction by judicial process is slower and more costly. Will the Minnesota prohibition on self-help increase rents? If so, should the court have considered this impact?

e. **Waiver?**

Suppose that L and T enter into a commercial lease for 10,000 square feet of retail space in Minnesota, where T plans to operate a clothing store. One of the lease clauses provides:

> 35. *Rent Reduction*. T, being fully advised by counsel, hereby forever waives and releases any right which T would otherwise have under *Berg v. Wiley*. T expressly agrees that L may use self-help to retake possession of the premises if T ever defaults in his lease obligations. In consideration of this special agreement, T acknowledges that the rent for the premises has been reduced by $200 per month.

Would a Minnesota court enforce this clause? Would it make any difference if the clause was in a residential lease? *See Rucker v. Wynn*, 441 S.E.2d 417 (Ga. Ct. App. 1994) (noting that similar clause would be enforceable in a commercial lease, but not in a residential lease).

Summary

- **Landlord-Tenant "Revolution."** A leasehold was traditionally viewed as an estate in land, governed by property law. In the 1960s, courts began to use contract law to redefine the rights of residential tenants. Today the residential lease is governed by both property law and contract law.

- **Discrimination.** In general, a landlord may refuse to rent to any prospective tenant. But federal and state statutes prohibit the landlord from discrimination based on race, religion, sex, or other factors.

- **Nonfreehold Estates.** The law recognizes four nonfreehold estates: the term of years tenancy; the periodic tenancy; the tenancy at will; and the tenancy at sufferance. New types of nonfreehold estates cannot be created.

- **Delivery of Possession.** The landlord is obligated to deliver the legal right to possession when the lease term begins. Under the majority view, he is also required to deliver physical possession of the premises at the same time.

- **Condition of Premises.** At common law, the duty to repair the premises was placed on the tenant. However, if the landlord engages in wrongful conduct that substantially interferes with the tenant's use and enjoyment of the premises, the tenant may vacate the premises and terminate the lease under the doctrine of constructive eviction. The modern implied warranty of habitability requires a residential landlord to maintain the premises in habitable condition.

- **Assignment v. Sublease.** The transfer of a tenant's entire remaining lease term to a third person is an assignment under the majority test; the transfer of less than the entire term is a sublease. If the lease requires the landlord's consent to any transfer by the tenant, but fails to specify a standard for granting consent, the modern trend is that the landlord may withhold consent only if he has a commercially reasonable objection.

> **Test Your Knowledge**
>
> To assess your understanding of the material in this chapter, click here to take a quiz.

- **Abandonment.** If the tenant abandons the premises, modern law provides that the landlord may either (a) terminate the lease or (b) attempt to mitigate damages and then sue the tenant for any unpaid balance.

- **Defenses to Eviction.** In general, the landlord may terminate a periodic tenancy for any reason, other than discrimination. But most states protect tenants from retaliatory eviction. In a few states the landlord may evict a tenant only for good cause.

- **Method of Eviction.** In most states, the landlord can evict the tenant only by using judicial process. Some states still follow the traditional view that the landlord can retake possession by self-help.

For More Information

For more information about the subjects covered in this chapter, please consult these sources:

- Paula A. Franzese & Stephanie J. Beach, *Promises Still to Keep: The Fair Housing Act Fifty Years Later*, 40 Cardozo L. Rev. 1207 (2019).
- Gerald Korngold, *Whatever Happened to Landlord-Tenant Law?*, 77 Neb. L. Rev. 703 (1998).
- Florence Wagman Roisman, *The Right to Remain: Common Law Protections for Security of Tenure*, 86 N.C. L. Rev. 817 (2008).
- Nadav Shoked, *American Courts' Image of a Tenant*, 117 Nw. U. L. Rev. 251 (2022).
- Nicole Summers, *The Limits of Good Law: A Study of Housing Court Outcomes*, 87 U. Chi. L. Rev. 145 (2020).
- Dale A. Whitman, *Fifty Years of Landlord-Tenant Law: A Perspective*, 35 U. Ark. Little Rock L. Rev. 785 (2013).

Chapter 8

Selling Real Property

Thousands of parcels of real property are sold every day in the United States. Most of these sales involve *residential property*, such as single-family homes or condominium units. But sales of factories, farms, office buildings, ranches, shopping malls, and undeveloped land—collectively called *commercial property*—are also common.

Owning a home is the American dream. As one scholar explained: "[O]wning one's own home is . . . an empowering act, giving people a stake in society and a sense of control over their lives. Put differently, homeownership strengthens the social fabric." Joan Williams, *The Rhetoric of Property*, 83 Iowa L. Rev. 277, 327 (1998). The purchase of a home is a major life event for the average person—and probably the biggest single investment that she will ever make.

Suppose Wendy and Henry Baker, a married couple, find their ideal home: a detached single-family residence that owner Adam Stone wants to sell. They verbally agree on a sales price of $300,000. What happens next? What concerns should each keep in mind?

This chapter explores a key right in the metaphorical bundle of sticks: the right to transfer. We will examine the three major steps in a typical real property sales transaction:

- *Purchase contract*: The parties negotiate and sign a written purchase contract, and prepare to consummate the transaction.
- *Closing*: The contract is fully performed at the closing: the buyer pays the purchase price, the lender advances the loan funds, and the seller transfers title.
- *Title protection*: The buyer protects her title through title covenants, a title opinion based on a search of public land records, and/or a title insurance policy.

Our focus in this chapter is on the most basic transaction: the sale of a home. While the sale of commercial property is more intricate than this simple model, it is largely governed by the same principles.

The role of attorneys in real property sales has evolved over time. Many years ago, the average home sale was handled by an attorney. Today brokers, escrow agents, and title insurance companies—advised by their own attorneys—collectively perform this function in most regions. Of course, the buyer and seller will typically retain attorneys if a dispute develops between them. In contrast, the attorney is still the main professional involved in the sale of commercial property.

The typical sales transaction is governed by state common law principles which vary among jurisdictions. These principles are somewhat different from the modern Uniform Commercial Code provisions that apply to the sale of goods. And despite the rapid development of electronic commerce, the transaction is usually based on paper documents—though this is slowly changing.

Finally—as we are focused on the sale of a home—it is important to recall from Chapter 7 that the Fair Housing Act (FHA) and the Civil Rights Act of 1866 provide protection against unlawful discrimination in the purchase and sale of real property. In particular, the FHA prohibits discrimination based on race, color, religion, sex (including sexual orientation), familial status, national origin, or handicap. Illegal discrimination includes refusing to sell a dwelling, falsely denying that a dwelling is available for sale, or demanding different prices for the sale of a dwelling.

A. The Purchase Contract

The contract used in the purchase of a house is usually a standard, preprinted form supplied by a real estate broker. The parties fill in the blanks on the form to customize it for their transaction. The contract will set forth the price, method of payment, time for performance, various conditions, and other terms.

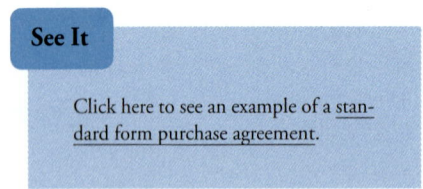

> **See It**
>
> Click here to see an example of a standard form purchase agreement.

Once the contract is signed, the parties prepare for the closing. During this stage of the transaction: (1) the seller's title is examined; (2) the condition of the property is evaluated; (3) the buyer obtains financing from a bank or other lender; (4) an escrow is opened to consummate the transaction; and (5) various documents are prepared, including the deed, mortgage, promissory note, and escrow instructions.

A wide variety of legal problems can arise during this period. In the materials below, we examine four of the most common issues: the Statute of Frauds, marketable title, equitable conversion, and the seller's duty to disclose.

1. Statute of Frauds

Let's return to our hypothetical transaction, where the Bakers and Stone orally agreed that the Bakers would buy Stone's house. With Stone's consent, the Bakers immediately begin repainting the inside of the house. One week later, Curtis offers a higher price for the house, and Stone accepts this offer. Can the Bakers enforce their agreement against Stone?

As a general rule, an oral agreement for the sale of an interest in real property is not enforceable. Every state has adopted a Statute of Frauds—modeled on the original English Statute of Frauds of 1677—which requires that such a contract must meet these requirements:

> **FYI**
>
> The Statue of Frauds was adopted by Parliament as "An Act for the Prevention of Frauds and Perjuries." It provided, in part: "[N]o action shall be brought . . . upon any contract or sale of lands . . . or any interest in or concerning them . . . unless the agreement upon which such action shall be brought, or some memorandum or note thereof, shall be in writing, and signed by the party to be charged therewith, or some other person thereunto by him lawfully authorized." Click here to see an original version of the text and an original copy of the Statute.

- *Essential terms*: the essential terms of the contract (usually the identity of the parties, the price, and the property description) must be set forth in a writing.
- *Writing*: the writing can be a formal contract or an informal memorandum.
- *Signature*: the writing must be signed by the party sought to be bound.

Note that failure to comply with the Statute does *not* make the contract void; it simply prevents the contract from being enforced.

Why is an oral contract unenforceable? The original purposes of the Statute of Frauds were to prevent fraud and discourage perjury. But any rigid rule may sometimes produce injustice. *Hickey v. Green*, our next case, is a typical dispute about an oral purchase contract, presenting facts that are similar to the hypothetical Baker-Stone dispute above. As you read the decision, consider how the court balances the Hickeys' request for relief against the requirements of the Statute of Frauds.

Hickey v. Green

Appeals Court of Massachusetts

442 N.E.2d 37 (1982)

CUTTER, JUSTICE.

This case is before us on a stipulation of facts (with various attached documents). A Superior Court judge has adopted the agreed facts as "findings." We are in the same position as was the trial judge (who received no evidence and saw and heard no witnesses).

Mrs. Gladys Green owns a lot (Lot S) in the Manomet section of Plymouth. In July, 1980, she advertised it for sale. On July 11 and 12, Hickey and his wife discussed with Mrs. Green purchasing Lot S and "orally agreed to a sale" for $15,000. Mrs. Green on July 12 accepted a deposit check of $500, marked by Hickey on the back, "Deposit on Lot . . . Massasoit Ave. Manomet . . . Subject to Variance from Town of Plymouth." Mrs. Green's brother and agent "was under the impression that a zoning variance was needed and [had] advised . . . Hickey to write" the quoted language on the deposit check. It turned out, however, by July 16 that no variance would be required. Hickey had left the payee line of the deposit check blank, because of uncertainty whether Mrs. Green or her brother was to receive the check and asked "Mrs. Green to fill in the appropriate name." Mrs. Green held the check, did not fill in the payee's name, and neither cashed nor endorsed it. Hickey "stated to Mrs. Green that his intention was to sell his home and build on Mrs. Green's lot."

"Relying upon the arrangements . . . with Mrs. Green," the Hickeys advertised their house on Sachem Road in newspapers on three days in July, 1980, and agreed with a purchaser for its sale and took from him a deposit check for $500 which they deposited in their own account.[3] On July 24, Mrs. Green told Hickey that she "no longer intended to sell her property to him" but had decided to sell to another for $16,000. Hickey told Mrs. Green that he had already sold his house and offered her $16,000 for Lot S. Mrs. Green refused this offer.

The Hickeys filed this complaint seeking specific performance. Mrs. Green asserts that relief is barred by the Statute of Frauds contained in G.C. c. 259 § 1. The trial judge granted specific performance. Mrs. Green has appealed.

---

[3] On the back of the check was noted above the Hickeys' signatures endorsing the check "Deposit on Purchase of property at Sachem Rd. and First St., Manomet, Ma. Sale price, $44,000."

The present rule applicable in most jurisdictions in the United States is succinctly set forth in Restatement (Second) of Contracts, § 129 (1981). The section reads, "A contract for the transfer of an interest in land may be specifically enforced notwithstanding failure to comply with the Statute of Frauds if it is established that the party seeking enforcement, *in reasonable reliance on the contract* and on the continuing assent of the party against whom enforcement is sought, *has so changed his position that injustice can be avoided only by specific enforcement*" (emphasis supplied).[6] The earlier Massachusetts decisions laid down somewhat strict requirements for an estoppel precluding the assertion of the Statute of Frauds. . . . Frequently there has been an actual change of possession and improvement of the transferred property, as well as full payment of the full purchase price, or one or more of these elements. . . .

> **Make the Connection**
>
> As you will learn in contracts, the Statute of Frauds also generally applies to contracts: (a) for the sale of goods totaling $500 or more; (b) that cannot be performed within one year; (c) in which a person guarantees the debts of another; or (d) in consideration of marriage.

The present facts reveal a simple case of a proposed purchase of a residential vacant lot, where the vendor, Mrs. Green, knew that the Hickeys were planning to sell their former home (possibly to obtain funds to pay her) and build on Lot S. The Hickeys, relying on Mrs. Green's oral promise, moved rapidly to make their sale without obtaining any adequate memorandum of the terms of what appears to have been intended to be a quick cash sale of Lot S. So rapid was action by the Hickeys that, by July 21, less than ten days after giving their deposit to Mrs. Green, they had accepted a deposit check for the sale of their house, endorsed the check, and placed it in their bank account. Above their signatures endorsing the check was a memorandum probably sufficient to satisfy the Statute of Frauds. . . . At the very least, the Hickeys had bound themselves in a manner in which, to avoid a transfer of their own house,

---

[6] Comments *a* and *b* to § 129, read (in part):

"*a* . . . This section restates what is widely known as the 'part performance doctrine.' Part performance is not an accurate designation of such acts as taking possession and making improvements when the contract does not provide for such acts, but such acts regularly bring the doctrine into play. The doctrine is contrary to the words of the Statute of Frauds, but it was established by English courts of equity soon after the enactment of the Statute. Payment of purchase-money, without more, was once thought sufficient to justify specific enforcement, but a contrary view now prevails, since in such cases restitution is an adequate remedy. . . . Enforcement has . . . been justified on the ground that repudiation after 'part performance' amounts to a 'virtual fraud.' A more accurate statement is that courts with equitable powers are vested by tradition with what in substance is a dispensing power based on the promisee's reliance, *a discretion to be exercised with caution* in the light of all the circumstances. . . ." [emphasis supplied].

"*b* . . . Two distinct elements enter into the application of the rule of this Section: first, the extent to which the evidentiary function of the statutory formalities is fulfilled by the conduct of the parties; second, the reliance of the promisee, providing a compelling substantive basis for relief in addition to the expectations created by the promise."

they might have had to engage in expensive litigation. No attorney has been shown to have been used either in the transaction between Mrs. Green and the Hickeys or in that between the Hickeys and their purchaser.

There is no denial by Mrs. Green of the oral contract between her and the Hickeys. This, under § 129 of the Restatement, is of some significance.[9] There can be no doubt (a) that Mrs. Green made the promise on which the Hickeys so promptly relied, and also (b) she, nearly as promptly, but not promptly enough, repudiated it because she had a better opportunity. The stipulated facts require the conclusion that in equity Mrs. Green's conduct cannot be condoned. This is not a case where either party is shown to have contemplated the negotiation of a purchase and sale agreement. If a written agreement had been expected, even by only one party, or would have been natural (because of the participation by lawyers or otherwise), a different situation might have existed. . . .

> **Food for Thought**
>
> Would the court have reached the same result if Green denied that any contract existed? How would she explain the check?

No public interest . . . will be violated if Mrs. Green fairly is held to her precise bargain by principles of equitable estoppel. . . .

Over two years have passed since July, 1980, and over a year since the trial judge's findings were filed on July 6, 1981. At that time, the principal agreed facts of record bearing upon the extent of the injury to the Hickeys (because of their reliance on Mrs. Green's promise to convey Lot S) were those based on the Hickeys' new obligation to convey their house to a purchaser. Performance of that agreement had been extended to May 1, 1981. If that agreement has been abrogated or modified since the trial, the case may take on a different posture. If enforcement of that agreement still will be sought, or if that agreement has been carried out, the conveyance of Lot S by Mrs. Green should be required now.

The case, in any event, must be remanded to the trial judge for the purpose of amending the judgment to require conveyance of Lot S by Mrs. Green only upon payment to her in cash within a stated period of the balance of the agreed price of $15,000. The trial judge, however, in her discretion and upon proper offers of proof by counsel, may reopen the record to receive, in addition to the presently stipulated

---

[9] Comment *d* of Restatement (Second) of Contracts, § 129, reads "*d* . . . Where specific enforcement is rested on a transfer of possession plus either part payment of the price or the making of improvements, it is commonly said that the action taken by the purchaser must be unequivocally referable to the oral agreement. But this requirement is not insisted on *if the making of the promise is admitted or is clearly proved.* The promisee *must act in reasonable reliance on the promise, before the promisor has repudiated* it, and the action must be such that the remedy of restitution is inadequate. If these requirements are met, *neither taking of possession nor payment of money nor the making of improvements is essential.* . . ." (emphasis supplied).

facts, a stipulation or evidence concerning the present status of the Hickeys' apparent obligation to sell their house. If the circumstances have changed, it will be open to the trial judge to require of Mrs. Green, instead of specific performance, only full restitution to the Hickeys of all costs reasonably caused to them in respect of these transactions (including advertising costs, deposits, and their reasonable costs for this litigation) with interest. The case is remanded to the Superior Court Department for further action consistent with this opinion. The Hickeys are to have costs of this appeal.

Points for Discussion

a. **A Writing**

Why didn't the deposit check that the Hickeys gave to Green serve as a writing to satisfy the Statute of Frauds? What about the check that the Hickeys received from their buyer? Even an informal document such as a letter or a check may suffice as the required writing.

Of course, the writing must contain the essential terms of the transaction. But even here courts are somewhat flexible. For example, many courts accept a formula for calculating the purchase price in place of a precise dollar amount. And an informal description of the property may be adequate. *See Lafayette Place Assocs. v. Boston Redevelopment Auth.*, 694 N.E.2d 820 (Mass. 1998) (reference to the "Hayward Parcel" was sufficient even though the exact boundaries were unclear); *but see Halbert v. Forney*, 945 P.2d 1137 (Wash. Ct. App. 1997) (street address was insufficient property description).

b. **Describing the Property**

Three types of property descriptions are used most commonly:

Government survey: Most property in the United States can be described by referring to the government's Public Land Survey System (PLSS). This system divides land into six-mile-square *townships*. Townships are subdivided into 36 one-square-mile *sections*, each containing 640 acres. Sections themselves are typically subdivided into quarter sections. A permanent marker or monument is normally placed at each section corner. Each PLSS survey begins at an initial point called the *Principal Meridian*; there are 37 Principal Meridians throughout the continental United States, each a line running north-south. The east-west line that runs through an initial point perpendicular to the Principal Meridian is called the *base line*. Every township

> **See It**
>
> Click here to see (a) a map showing the Principal Meridians and Base Lines of the PLSS and (b) a diagram illustrating the PLSS.

is identified with a township and range designation. *Township designations* indicate the property's location north or south of the base line. *Range designations* indicate the property's location east or west of the Principal Meridian. A land description includes the State, Principal Meridian, township and range designations, and the section number. A typical description might read: "Kansas, Sixth Principal Meridian, T2S, R3W, sec. 14".

Metes and bounds: Starting at an identifiable geographic point, this system describes the parcel using distances and directions. The system is based largely on visible topographic features, such as ridge lines, streams, and trees. A metes and bounds description might read: "100 feet north from the large oak tree, thence 200 feet east, thence 150 feet south," and so forth. One problem with the metes and bounds system is that local landmarks may change over time. For example, streams may alter course, and trees may die.

Subdivision map: When a tract of land is subdivided into smaller parcels, a map shows where each lot is located. For example, "Lot 10, as set forth on the map recorded in Book 332, Page 17, Alameda County Records, California" refers to one particular lot.

c. Signed by the Party to Be Bound

Even if a writing contains the essential terms, it must still be signed by the party against whom enforcement is sought. Accordingly, even if the Hickeys' check was a sufficient writing, the purchase contract could not be enforced against Green because she did not sign the check. But Green could have enforced the contract against the Hickeys. Is this fair?

Can another person sign the writing on behalf of the buyer or seller? The Statute of Frauds provides that an agent's authority to bind a party to a contract for the purchase of real property must be set forth in a writing duly signed by that party; this is called the *equal dignities rule*. The rule also applies to signatures on other documents subject to the Statute of Frauds, such as deeds and mortgages.

d. Conveyance by Deed

The Statute of Frauds also applies to an instrument used to transfer an interest in real property. Suppose that M delivers a signed deed to her son S, conveying her house to S as a birthday present. A few years later, M becomes bankrupt and asks S to return the house so that she can have a place to live. S hands his deed back to M, saying: "Mom, the house is yours again." M destroys the deed. Who owns the house?

e. Part Performance

The doctrine of *part performance* is a major exception to the Statute of Frauds. An oral contract for the sale of real property may be enforced if the buyer: (1) takes possession; (2) pays at least part of the purchase price; and (3) makes improvements to the property. Many jurisdictions require that the buyer take possession *and* either pay the purchase price *or* make improvements. Some require payment *and* either possession *or* improvements. Why? Courts reason that the buyer would perform these actions only if a contract existed; so this conduct serves as a substitute for the writing. Should the court have enforced the oral contract in *Hickey* based on part performance?

> **FYI**
>
> Justice Holmes famously stated that the acts of part performance must be "unequivocally referable to a contract for the sale of land." *Burns v. McCormick*, 135 N.E. 273, 274 (N.Y. 1922). What did he mean by this?

f. Estoppel

Estoppel is another exception to the Statute of Frauds. An oral contract may be enforced if: (1) one party acts to his detriment in reasonable reliance on another's oral promise; and (2) serious injury would result if enforcement is refused. In the context of real property sales, courts usually apply the doctrine if the complaining party has relied on the oral agreement by selling another property or by refusing other offers for the property in dispute. However, some courts require a high degree of hardship. In *Brown v. Branch*, 758 N.E.2d 48, 53 (Ind. 2001), the court ruled that a boyfriend's oral promise to convey his house to his girlfriend did not inflict an "unjust and unconscionable injury and loss," even though she quit her job, dropped out of school, and moved back to Indiana in reliance on his promise.

Courts sometimes blur the distinction between part performance and estoppel, observing that acts of part performance evidence both reasonable reliance on a contract and a change of position that necessitates its enforcement. The *Hickey* court cited the Restatement (Second) of Contracts § 129, which discusses both doctrines. What was the basis of the court's decision in *Hickey*, part performance or estoppel? Could Green have enforced her oral agreement against the Hickeys under one of these exceptions?

g. Statute of Frauds in the Computer Era

Every state has adopted a version of the Uniform Electronic Transactions Act (UETA). Under the UETA, an electronic document can be used to satisfy the Statute of Frauds. In addition, Congress enacted the Electronic Signatures in Global and National Commerce Act (the "E-Sign Act") in 2000, which authorizes the use of electronic signatures in any transaction affecting interstate commerce. Consequently, a contract for the sale of real estate can be valid even though it is in electronic form with an e-signature. For example, in *Shattuck v. Klotzbach,* 2001 WL 1839720 (Mass. Super. Ct.), the court held that three emails could constitute an enforceable contract for the sale of property valued at $1,825,000.

> ### Perspective and Analysis
>
> Scholars debate whether the Statute of Frauds achieves its goals of preventing fraud and perjury. (In fact, might it facilitate deceptive conduct?) But there are other reasons to require that real property contracts be in writing:
>
>> (1) Written agreements are more certain than oral ones; (2) they are not as open to misinterpretation; (3) only written agreements can take advantage of certain other statutes and legal rules, such as the parole evidence rule and the recordation and registry laws; (4) the discipline of a writing requires the parties to think through their agreement in more detail than they might otherwise; and (5) the ceremony of a writing encourages the parties to take their undertaking seriously, thus increasing the likelihood of voluntary performance. These reasons are compelling enough that parties likely would use written agreements even if no statute of frauds existed.
>
> **Michael Braunstein, *Remedy, Reason, and the Statute of Frauds: A Critical Economic Analysis*, 1989 Utah L. Rev. 383, 385–86.** Do you agree with Professor Braunstein? Does an electronic document created by an exchange of email messages serve these functions? *See, e.g., Brantley v. Wilson*, 2006 WL 436121 (W.D. Ark.).

2. Marketable Title

Suppose Stone believes that he obtained title to his home by adverse possession. While he is in the process of selling the home to the Bakers, the original owner of the property brings suit claiming that she still owns the land. Under these circumstances, Stone may not have marketable title.

In every contract for the sale of real property, the seller expressly or impliedly promises that she will deliver *marketable title* (also known as *merchantable title*), unless the contract specifies otherwise. Generally, marketable title is defined as title reasonably free from doubt as to its validity. The basic principle is that a buyer should be able to purchase property without fear of litigation about her title. Of course, title need not be perfect to be marketable; almost every property has a few minor title blemishes. If a reasonable and prudent purchaser would pay fair market value for the property, then title is considered to be marketable.

The most common title defects are *encumbrances*. An encumbrance is a right or interest in land—other than a freehold estate—that reduces the value or use of that land. CC&Rs, easements, leases, liens, mortgages, options, and water rights are all examples of encumbrances.

Generally, title is unmarketable if:

> (1) the seller's property interest is less than the one she purports to sell;
> (2) the seller's title is subject to an encumbrance; or
> (3) there is reasonable doubt about either (1) or (2).

For example, if the seller promises to convey a fee simple absolute but only has a life estate, title is unmarketable. Similarly, if the title is subject to a right of way that allows neighbors to cross the land, title is not free from encumbrances and consequently is unmarketable.

In our next case, the Bowers owned a house in Emporia, Kansas. They entered into a contract to sell it to Lohmeyer. But the buyer discovered title problems before the closing and sought rescission. As you read the decision, pay special attention to the factors that led the court to conclude title was unmarketable.

Lohmeyer v. Bower

Supreme Court of Kansas

227 P.2d 102 (1951)

PARKER, JUSTICE.

This action originated in the district court of Lyon County when plaintiff filed a petition seeking to rescind a contract in which he had agreed to purchase certain real estate on the ground title tendered by the defendants was unmerchantable. The defendants Bower and Bower, husband and wife, answered contesting plaintiff's right to rescind and by cross-petition asked specific performance of the contract. . . . The case was tried upon the pleadings and stipulated facts by the trial court which rendered judgment for the defendants generally and decreed specific performance of the contract. The plaintiff appeals from that judgment. . . .

Plaintiff's petition alleges execution of the contract whereby he agreed to purchase Lot 37 in Berkley Hills Addition in the city of Emporia. . . . It avers that after execution of the agreement it came to his attention that the house on the real estate therein described had been placed there in violation of Section 5–224 of the Ordinances of the city of Emporia in that the house was located

> **Food for Thought**
>
> The contract provided that the Bowers would convey "good merchantable title . . . free and clear of all encumbrances . . . subject, however, to all restrictions and easements of record. . . ." Was this provision more beneficial to the sellers or to the buyer?

within approximately 18 inches of the north line of such lot in violation of the ordinance providing that no frame building should be erected within 3 feet of a side or rear lot line. It further avers that after execution of the agreement it came to plaintiff's knowledge the dedication of the Berkley Hills Addition requires that only a two story house should be erected on the lot described in the contract whereas the house located thereon is a one story house. . . . It next alleges that after becoming aware of such violations plaintiff notified the defendants in writing thereof, demanded that he be released from his contract and that defendants refused such demand. Finally it charges that such violations made the title unmerchantable and asks that the agreement be cancelled and set aside and that all moneys paid by plaintiff under its terms be refunded. . . .

[S]ince resort to the contract makes it clear appellees agreed to convey the involved property with an abstract of title showing good merchantable title, free and clear of all encumbrances, it becomes apparent the all decisive issue presented by the pleadings and the stipulation is whether such property is subject to encumbrances or other burdens making the title unmerchantable and if so whether they are such as are excepted by the provision of the contract which reads "subject, however, to all restrictions and easements of record applying to this property."

Decision of the foregoing issue can be simplified by directing attention early to the appellant's position. Conceding he purchased the property, subject to all restrictions of record he makes no complaint of the restrictions contained in the declaration forming a part of the dedication of Berkley Hills Addition nor of the ordinance restricting the building location on the lot but bases his right to rescission of the contract solely upon presently existing violations thereof. . . . [A]lthough it must be conceded there are some decisions to the contrary, the rule supported by the better reasoned decisions, indeed if not by the great weight of authority, is that municipal restrictions of such character, existing at the time of the execution of a contract for the sale of real estate, are not such encumbrances or burdens on title as may be availed of by a vendee to avoid his agreement to purchase on the ground they render his title unmerchantable. For authorities upholding this conclusion see *Hall v. Risley,* 188 Or. 69 213 P.2d 818; *Miller v. Milwaukee Odd Fellows Temple,* 206 Wis. 547, 240 N.W. 193; *Wheeler v. Sullivan,* 90 Fla. 711, 106 So. 876; *Lincoln Trust Co. v. Williams Bldg. Corp.,* 229 N.Y. 313, 128 N.E. 209. . . .

On the other hand there can be no question the rule respecting restrictions upon the use of land or the location and type of buildings that may be erected thereon fixed by covenants or other private restrictive agreements, including those contained in the declaration forming a part of the dedication of Berkley Hills Addition, is directly contrary to the one to which we have just referred. Such restrictions, under all the authorities, constitute encumbrances rendering the title to land unmerchantable. . . .

Bowers house
Click here for larger photo

There can be no doubt regarding what constitutes a marketable or merchantable title in this jurisdiction. This court has been called on to pass upon that question on numerous occasions. See our recent decision in *Peatling v. Baird*, 168 Kan. 528, 213 P.2d 1015, 1016, and cases there cited, wherein we held:

> A marketable title to real estate is one which is free from reasonable doubt, and a title is doubtful and unmarketable if it exposes the party holding it to the hazard of litigation.

> To render the title to real estate unmarketable, the defect of which the purchaser complains must be of a substantial character and one from which he may suffer injury. Mere immaterial defects which do not diminish in quantity, quality or value the property contracted for, constitute no ground upon which the purchaser may reject the title. Facts must be known at the time which fairly raise a reasonable doubt as to the title; a mere possibility or conjecture that such a state of facts may be developed at some future time is not sufficient.

Under the rule just stated, and in the face of facts such as are here involved, we have little difficulty in concluding that the violation of section 5–224 of the ordinances of the city of Emporia as well as the violation of the restrictions imposed by the dedication declaration so encumber the title to Lot 37 as to expose the party holding it to the hazard of litigation and make such title doubtful and unmarketable. It follows, since, as we have indicated, the appellees had contracted to convey such real estate to appellant by warranty deed with an abstract of title showing good merchantable title, free and clear of all encumbrances, that they cannot convey the title contracted for and that the trial court should have rendered judgment rescinding the contract. This, we may add is so, notwithstanding the contract provides the conveyance was to be made subject to all restrictions and easements of record, for, as we have seen, it is the violation of the restrictions imposed by both the ordinance and the dedication declaration, not the existence of those restrictions, that renders the title unmarketable. . . .

Finally appellees point to the contract which, it must be conceded, provides they shall have time to correct imperfections in the title and contend that even if it be held the restrictions and the ordinance have been violated they are entitled to time in which to correct those imperfections. Assuming, without deciding, they might remedy the violation of the ordinance by buying additional ground the short and simple answer to their contention with respect to the violation of the restrictions imposed by the dedication declaration is that any changes in the house would compel the purchaser to take something that he did not contract to buy.

Conclusions heretofore announced require reversal of the judgment with directions to the trial court to cancel and set aside the contract and render such judgment as may be equitable and proper under the issues raised by the pleadings.

Points for Discussion

a. Factors Affecting Marketability

In *Lohmeyer*, the court focused on two problems: the house (1) had only one story and (2) was located within 18 inches of the lot line. Why did these problems make title unmarketable?

Almost any private encumbrance causes title to be unmarketable. A buyer normally does not expect to purchase title that is clouded by a mortgage, mechanic's lien, easement, or another defect. Why didn't the existence of the private restriction which required a two-story house render the Bowers' title unmarketable?

Conversely, statutes, ordinances, and other public restrictions do not make title unmarketable—even if they severely restrict the use of the property. Accordingly, Lohmeyer could not argue that the mere existence of the three-foot setback requirement was a title defect. So what was the basis for his complaint on this point? Why should public restrictions be treated differently from private encumbrances?

b. Drafting Title Provisions

Marketable title is a default standard. The buyer and seller may agree to any title standard that they wish. But if the contract does not specify a standard, the law requires marketable title. In addition, parties often select marketable title as an express title standard. The *Lohmeyer* contract called for good merchantable title "subject . . . to all restrictions and easements of record." Lohmeyer therefore agreed to accept any and all encumbrances that were shown in the public land records. As his attorney, would you have advised him to accept this provision? What concerns should the seller's attorney have when drafting a title provision?

c. **Physical Condition of the Property**

Marketable title concerns the *title* to property, not the *physical condition* of that property. As the California Supreme Court explained: "One can hold perfect title to land that is valueless; one can have marketable title to land while the land itself is unmarketable." *Hocking v. Title Ins. & Trust Co.,* 234 P.2d 625, 629 (Cal. 1951). Accordingly, the presence of hazardous waste on property does not make title unmarketable. *See* Pamela A. Harbeson, Comment, *Toxic Clouds on Titles: Hazardous Waste and the Doctrine of Marketable Title,* 19 B.C. Envtl. Aff. L. Rev. 355 (1991). Some courts reason that title to landlocked property is unmarketable (*Myerberg, Sawyer & Rue, P.A. v. Agee,* 446 A.2d 69 (Md. Ct. Spec. App. 1982)), while others hold that this problem affects value, not title (*Sinks v. Karleskint,* 474 N.E.2d 767 (Ill. App. Ct. 1985)).

d. **Buyer's Knowledge**

What if Lohmeyer had noticed a large sewer line crossing the property *before* he signed the purchase agreement? In some jurisdictions, if property is burdened by a visible encumbrance or the buyer actually knows about an encumbrance, it is presumed that he impliedly agreed to accept title burdened by that encumbrance—and took this into account in setting the purchase price. However, in other jurisdictions title is unmarketable if any encumbrance exists, whether or not the buyer knows or reasonably should know about it.

e. **Hypotheticals on Marketable Title**

Is title marketable in the situations below?

> (1) S has title to only 25 of the 40 acres he agreed to sell to B.
>
> (2) After signing the contract, B learns that the property is worth less than the purchase price because it is located in a flood zone.
>
> (3) Before signing the contract, B sees electric lines crossing part of the land. After signing, B learns that the local electric company has an easement across the property for these lines.
>
> (4) S claims title to the land by adverse possession. P, the original owner, brings a quiet title action against S. S tells B: "Don't worry! There's no chance that I will lose this case. Go ahead and close the deal."

f. **Insurable Title and Record Title**

Insurable title and record title are different from marketable title. An *insurable title* is one that a title insurance company would be willing to insure at normal rates. Since title insurers evaluate risk (and may therefore ignore minor title defects), an insurable title standard may provide less protection than a marketable title standard. *See, e.g., 111-38 Mgmt. Corp. v. Benitez*, 895 N.Y.S.2d 468 (App. Div. 2010) (appellant not required to convey marketable title because contract provided for conveying title that reputable title company would be willing to insure). *Record title* refers to the title that appears in the public land records. Even if a seller has record title, her title may be invalid; for example, title obtained through a forged deed is void. The record title standard also does not protect against title defects that are not reflected in the public record—such as adverse possession. Did the Bowers have insurable title? Record title? Why wouldn't a buyer always demand *insurable*, *record*, and *marketable title*? Or should a buyer insist on "perfect" title?

g. **When Is Marketable Title Required?**

Suppose that the Bakers and Stone sign a sales contract, but one day later the Bakers discover that the property is encumbered by an easement. Can the Bakers rescind? Most courts hold that the seller is not required to produce a marketable title until the closing. Thus, the seller can use the time before the closing to cure any defects. For example, he might pay off a mortgage or remedy a zoning violation. But if it becomes clear in advance that the seller will not be able to convey marketable title, the buyer may rescind before the closing. *See Bethurem v. Hammett*, 736 P.2d 1128 (Wyo. 1987). If a title problem is discovered shortly before closing, the seller has a reasonable time to cure it unless the contract stipulates that *time is of the essence*.

> **FYI**
>
> When a contract specifies that "time is of the essence," the failure to act within the required time is a breach. Any delay, whether reasonable or not, is a basis for terminating the contract. The general rule is that time is not of the essence unless the contract expressly so indicates.

Once a buyer accepts the deed at closing, she can no longer sue to enforce the seller's promise to deliver marketable title. Unless the parties agree otherwise, all rights under the purchase agreement are extinguished or "merged" into the deed. Thereafter, the rights of the parties are governed by the title covenants in the deed, if any.

> **Make the Connection**
>
> You will study the *doctrine of merger* later in this chapter in connection with title covenants.

3. Equitable Conversion

Suppose that Stone and the Bakers sign an agreement for the sale of Stone's house. A few days later, lightning strikes—and the house burns down. Can Stone still enforce the contract against the Bakers?

Surprisingly, the answer may be "yes." During the period between the contract signing and the closing (known as the *executory period*), the property might be damaged or destroyed. The contract may contain a provision that specifies who bears this risk. Absent such a provision, many states place the risk on the buyer through the doctrine of *equitable conversion*. Under this approach, the buyer is seen as the equitable owner of the property once the contract is signed, while the seller is viewed as the equitable owner of the purchase price. Thus, the buyer is still obligated to pay the purchase price even if the property is destroyed.

For example, suppose the property is damaged by hail during the executory period. Hailstones can range up to six inches in diameter and over one pound in weight. Unsurprisingly, they regularly damage buildings, crops, and equipment. The risk of hail damage is particularly high in the region where Colorado, Nebraska, and Wyoming meet—a triangle of land known as "Hail Alley." This area, which averages more than ten dangerous hailstorms every year, provides the setting for our next case.

Brush Grocery Kart, Inc. v. Sure Fine Market, Inc.

Supreme Court of Colorado

47 P.3d 680 (2002)

JUSTICE COATS delivered the Opinion of the Court.

. . . In October 1992 Brush Grocery Kart, Inc. and Sure Fine Market, Inc. entered into a five-year "Lease with Renewal Provisions and Option to Purchase" for real property, including a building to be operated by Brush as a grocery store. Under the contract's purchase option provision, any time during the last six months of the lease, Brush could elect to purchase the property at a price equal to the average of the appraisals of an expert designated by each party.

Shortly before expiration of the lease, Brush notified Sure Fine of its desire to purchase the property and begin the process of determining a sale price. Although each party offered an appraisal, the parties were unable to agree on a final price by the time the lease expired. Brush then vacated the premises, returned all keys to Sure Fine, and advised Sure Fine that it would discontinue its casualty insurance covering the property during the lease. Brush also filed suit, alleging that Sure Fine failed to negotiate the price term in good faith and asking for the appointment of a special master to determine the purchase price. Sure Fine agreed to the appointment of a special master and counterclaimed, alleging that Brush negotiated the price term in bad faith and was therefore the breaching party.

During litigation over the price term, the property was substantially damaged during a hail storm. With neither party carrying casualty insurance, each asserted that the other was liable for the damage. The issue was added to the litigation at a stipulated amount of $60,000. . . . The court . . . found that under the doctrine of equitable conversion, Brush was the equitable owner of the property and bore the risk of loss. It therefore declined to abate the purchase price or award damages to Brush for the loss.

> **See It**
>
> Click here to see photographs of the original building and the current store.

Brush appealed the loss allocation and the court of appeals affirmed on similar grounds. . . .

In the absence of statutory authority, the rights, powers, duties, and liabilities arising out of a contract for the sale of land have frequently been derived by reference to the theory of equitable conversion. *People v. Alexander*, 663 P.2d 1024, 1030 n. 6 (Colo. 1983) (quoting III *American Law of Property* § 11.22, at 62–63 (A. Casner ed. 1974)). This theory or doctrine, which has been described as a legal fiction . . . is based on equitable principles that permit the vendee to be considered the equitable owner of the land and debtor for the purchase money and the vendor to be regarded as a secured creditor. *Alexander*, 663 P.2d at 1030 n. 6. The changes in rights and liabilities that occur upon the making of the contract result from the equitable right to specific performance. *Id*. Even with regard to third parties, the theory has been relied on to determine, for example, the devolution, upon death, of the rights and liabilities of each party with respect to the land, *see Chain O'Mines*, 101 Colo. at 234–35, 72 P.2d at 266, and to ascertain the powers of creditors of each party to reach the land in payment of their claims. *Alexander*, 663 P.2d at 1030 n. 6.

The assignment of the risk of casualty loss in the executory period of contracts for the sale of real property varies greatly throughout the jurisdictions of this country. What appears to yet be a slim majority of states . . . places the risk of loss on the vendee from the moment of contracting, on the rationale that once an equitable conversion takes place, the vendee must be treated as owner for all purposes. *See Skelly Oil v. Ashmore*, 365 S.W.2d 582, 588 (Mo. 1963) (criticizing this approach). Once the vendee becomes the equitable owner, he therefore becomes responsible for the condition of the property, despite not having a present right of occupancy or control. In sharp contrast, a handful of other states reject the allocation of casualty loss risk as a consequence of the theory of equitable conversion and follow the equally rigid "Massachusetts Rule," under which the seller continues to bear the risk until actual transfer of the title, absent an express agreement to the contrary. *See, e.g., Skelly Oil*, 365 S.W.2d at 588–89. A substantial and growing number of jurisdictions, however, base the legal consequences of no-fault casualty loss on the right to possession of the property at the time the loss occurs. . . . This view has found expression in the Uniform Vendor and Purchaser Risk Act, and while a number of states have adopted some variation of the Uniform Act, others have arrived at a similar position through the interpretations of their courts. . . .

In *Wiley v. Lininger*, 119 Colo. 497, 204 P.2d 1083, where fire destroyed improvements on land occupied by the vendee during the multi-year executory period of an installment land contract, we held, according to the generally accepted rule, that neither the buyer nor the seller, each of whom had an insurable interest in the property, had an obligation to insure the property for the benefit of the other. *Id.* at 502, 204 P.2d at 1085–86. We also adopted a rule, which we characterized as "the majority rule," that "the vendee under a contract for the sale of land, being regarded as the equitable owner, assumes the risk of destruction of or injury to the property *where he is in possession*, and the destruction or loss is not proximately caused by the negligence of the vendor." *Id.* (emphasis added). The vendee in possession was therefore not relieved of his obligation to continue making payments according to the terms of the contract, despite material loss by fire to some of the improvements on the property. . . .

Those jurisdictions that indiscriminately include the risk of casualty loss among the incidents or "attributes" of equitable ownership do so largely in reliance on ancient authority or by considering it necessary for consistent application of the theory of equitable conversion. . . . Under virtually any accepted understanding of the theory, however, equitable conversion is not viewed as entitling the purchaser to every significant right of ownership, and particularly not the right of possession. As a matter of both logic and equity, the obligation to maintain property in its physical condition follows the right to have actual possession and control rather than a legal right to force conveyance of the property through specific performance at some future date. . . .

The equitable conversion theory is literally stood on its head by imposing on a vendee, solely because of his right to specific performance, the risk that the vendor will be unable to specifically perform when the time comes because of an accidental casualty loss. It is counterintuitive, at the very least, that merely contracting for the sale of real property should not only relieve the vendor of his responsibility to maintain the property until execution but also impose a duty on the vendee to perform despite the intervention of a material, no-fault casualty loss preventing him from ever receiving the benefit of his bargain. Such an extension of the theory of equitable conversion to casualty loss has never been recognized by this jurisdiction, and it is neither necessary nor justified solely for the sake of consistency.

By contrast, there is substantial justification, both as a matter of law and policy, for not relieving a vendee who is entitled to possession before transfer of title, like the vendee in *Wiley*, of his duty to pay the full contract price, notwithstanding an accidental loss. In addition to having control over the property and being entitled to the benefits of its use, an equitable owner who also has the right of possession has already acquired virtually all of the rights of ownership and almost invariably will have already paid at least some portion of the contract price to exercise those rights. By expressly including in the contract for sale the right of possession, which otherwise generally accompanies transfer of title . . . the vendor has for all practical purposes already transferred the property as promised, and the parties have in effect expressed their joint intention that the vendee pay the purchase price as promised. . . .

In the absence of a right of possession, a vendee of real property that suffers a material casualty loss during the executory period of the contract, through no fault of his own, must be permitted to rescind and recover any payments he had already made. *Cf.* Uniform Vendor and Purchaser Risk Act § 1. . . .

Here, Brush was clearly not in possession of the property as the equitable owner. Even if the doctrine of equitable conversion applies to the option contract between Brush and Sure Fine and could be said to have converted Brush's interest to an equitable ownership of the property at the time Brush exercised its option to purchase . . . neither party considered the contract for sale to entitle Brush to possession. Brush was, in fact, not in possession of the property, and the record indicates that Sure Fine considered itself to hold the right of use and occupancy and gave notice that it would consider Brush a holdover tenant if it continued to occupy the premises other than by continuing to lease the property. . . . Both the court of appeals and the district court therefore erred in finding that the doctrine of equitable conversion required Brush to bear the loss caused by hail damage. . . .

> **FYI**
>
> Brush Grocery Kart has quadrupled in size—adding a pharmacy, liquor department, and gas station—since moving across the street from the property at issue in this case.

Points for Discussion

a. Equitable Conversion in Context

Why should the risk of loss shift to the buyer when the contract is signed? The equitable conversion doctrine evolved in an agrarian era, when the purpose of a purchase contract was to acquire land for farming. In that era, accidental destruction of a building on the property did not interfere with the buyer's primary purpose; he could still farm the land. Does this justification make sense today? What expectations did Brush Grocery

> **FYI**
>
> Arguing that the equitable conversion doctrine is obsolete, one treatise stated: "Only the hoary age and frequent repetition of the maxim prevents a general recognition of its absurdity." 4 Williston, Contracts, § 929, at 2607.

Kart have when it signed the contract? When deciding who should bear the risk of loss today, should it matter whether the contract concerns rural land or urban land? Or whether the destruction is caused by the fault of the seller, the fault of the buyer, or the forces of nature?

b. Alternative Approaches

The *Brush Grocery Kart* court identifies three approaches: (1) the buyer bears the risk as the equitable owner; (2) the seller bears the risk as the legal owner; and (3) the party entitled to possession bears the risk. What are the advantages and disadvantages of each approach? What policies did the court rely on to justify its position? Wouldn't an efficient rule minimize social cost by assigning the risk to the party best positioned to prevent any loss? Of course, a careful attorney will avoid any later dispute by including an express *risk of loss provision* in the contract.

c. A Curious Consequence

Suppose that Sure Fine insured the premises before the storm and then won its case before the Colorado Supreme Court. Could it demand specific performance, obtain the full purchase price, *and* keep all the insurance proceeds? Incredibly, in some states the answer is "yes." *See, e.g., In re Gay*, 213 B.R. 500 (E.D. Ky. 1997). Today, many courts mitigate the harshness of this approach by imposing a constructive trust on the insurance proceeds and applying them to the purchase price.

d. Inheritance

What if the buyer or the seller dies before the closing? Under the doctrine of equitable conversion, the contract is still valid; it can be enforced by the heirs and devisees of either party. Suppose that S and B contract for the sale of S's house, but both die before closing. S devises his real property to X and bequeaths his personal property to Y. B devises her real property to R and bequeaths her personal property to Q. At closing, who is entitled to the house? And who receives the purchase price? Under equitable conversion, S's interest in the house is treated as personal property, so Y receives the purchase price; B's interest is treated as real property and passes to R, who receives the house. Surprisingly, in some jurisdictions, any amount still owed on the purchase price will be paid out of the personal assets of B's estate, thereby reducing what Q receives. *See In re Estate of Wyatt*, 2002 WL 1332485 (Tenn. Ct. App. June 17, 2002), app. denied (Tenn. 2002).

---

4. Duty to Disclose

Stone knows that his house has a leaky roof. He contracts to sell the property to the Bakers without mentioning the problem. Two weeks before the closing, the Bakers visit the house during a minor rainstorm; they discover water dripping from the ceiling in 25 different locations. Can the Bakers rescind the contract?

Under the common law doctrine of *caveat emptor* (Latin for "buyer beware"), the seller of real property had no duty to disclose defects to the buyer. In effect, the buyer had the complete responsibility to assess the condition of the premises. The seller was liable only if he (a) affirmatively misrepresented the condition of the property, (b) actively concealed its defects, or (c) owed a fiduciary duty to the buyer. Today this approach lingers in only a few states. In such jurisdictions, as one commentator remarked, "the law offers more protection to a person buying a dog leash than it does to the purchaser of a house." John H. Scheid, Jr., Note, *Mandatory Disclosure Law: A Statute for Illinois*, 27 J. Marshall L. Rev. 155, 160 (1993).

> **Make the Connection**
>
> *Caveat venditor*, "let the seller beware," is the opposite of caveat emptor. One of the landmark cases using the doctrine is *MacPherson v. Buick Motor Co.*, 111 N.E. 1050 (N.Y. 1916), which established that direct privity between a product user and the product manufacturer is not required for tort liability.

In most jurisdictions, the seller of residential real property is obligated to disclose defects he knows about that (a) materially affect the value of the property and (b) are not known to or readily discoverable by a buyer. *See Johnson v. Davis*, 480 So. 2d 625 (Fla. 1985). Many states impose the same duty on real estate brokers involved in the transaction. Notice that *actual knowledge* of the defect is generally required; whether the seller or realtor *should have known* about it is inconsequential. *See Eiman v. Sullivan*, 173 So. 3d 994 (Fla. Dist. Ct. App. 2015). As you would expect, litigation often arises over whether a particular defect is "material" or "readily observable." For instance, would you want to know if the house you were about to purchase was "occupied" by ghosts? How would you discover their presence? Who are you going to call? As the following case points out, the answer is "Ghostbusters"!

Stambovsky v. Ackley

Supreme Court of New York, Appellate Division

572 N.Y.S.2d 672 (1991)

RUBIN, JUSTICE.

Plaintiff, to his horror, discovered that the house he had recently contracted to purchase was widely reputed to be possessed by poltergeists, reportedly seen by defendant seller and members of her family on numerous occasions over the last nine years. Plaintiff promptly commenced this action seeking rescission of the contract of sale. Supreme Court reluctantly dismissed the complaint, holding that plaintiff has no remedy at law in this jurisdiction.

The unusual facts of this case, as disclosed by the record, clearly warrant a grant of equitable relief to the buyer who, as a resident of New York City, cannot be expected to have any familiarity with the folklore of the Village of Nyack. Not being a "local", plaintiff could not readily learn that the home he had contracted to purchase is haunted. Whether the source of the spectral apparitions seen by defendant seller are parapsychic or psychogenic, having reported their presence in both a national publication (Readers' Digest) and the local press (in 1977 and 1982, respectively), defendant is estopped to deny their existence and, as a matter of law, the house is haunted. More to the point, however, no divination is required to conclude that it is defendant's promotional efforts in publicizing her close encounters with these spirits which fostered the home's reputation in the community. In 1989, the house was included in five-home walking tour of Nyack and described in a November 27th newspaper article as "a riverfront Victorian (with ghost)." The impact of the reputation thus created goes to the very essence of the bargain between the parties, greatly impairing both the value of the property and its potential for resale. The extent of this impairment may be presumed for the purpose of reviewing the disposition of this motion to dismiss the cause of action for rescission (*Harris v City of New York*, 147 AD2d 186, 188–189) and represents merely an issue of fact for resolution at trial.

> **FYI**
>
> In her 1977 *Reader's Digest* article, Ackley described one of the poltergeists as a "cheerful apple-cheeked man" who resembled Santa Claus; five years later, she told a local reporter that the spirits were "dressed in Revolutionary period clothing, perhaps frozen in a time warp." Ackley later commented: "I feel [the ghosts] are very good friends. It's very comforting to have them around when you are by yourself." *Court Rules that House in N.Y. Is Haunted*, S.F. Chron., July 20, 1991.

Stambovsky house
Click here for larger photo

While I agree with Supreme Court that the real estate broker, as agent for the seller, is under no duty to disclose to a potential buyer the phantasmal reputation of the premises and that, in his pursuit of a legal remedy for fraudulent misrepresentation against the seller, plaintiff hasn't a ghost of a chance, I am nevertheless moved by the spirit of equity to allow the buyer to seek rescission of the contract of sale and recovery of his down payment. New York law fails to recognize any remedy for damages incurred as a result of the seller's mere silence, applying instead the strict rule of caveat emptor. Therefore, the theoretical basis for granting relief, even under the extraordinary facts of this case, is elusive if not ephemeral. . . .

From the perspective of a person in the position of plaintiff herein, a very practical problem arises with respect to the discovery of a paranormal phenomenon: "Who you gonna' call?" as a title song to the movie "Ghostbusters" asks. Applying the strict rule of caveat emptor to a contract involving a house possessed by poltergeists conjures up visions of a psychic or medium routinely accompanying the structural engineer and Terminix man on an inspection of every home subject to a contract of sale. It portends that the prudent attorney will establish an escrow account lest the subject of the transaction come back to haunt him and his client—or pray that his malpractice insurance coverage extends to supernatural disasters. In the interest of avoiding such untenable consequences, the notion that a haunting is a condition which can and should be ascertained upon reasonable inspection of the premises is a hobgoblin which should be exorcised from the body of legal precedent and laid quietly to rest.

> **FYI**
>
> Starring Bill Murray and Dan Aykroyd, *Ghostbusters* was an immediate hit when it was released in 1984. It was followed by *Ghostbusters II* in 1989, and became the basis for two television series. The American Film Institute has ranked *Ghostbusters* as the 28th best comedy film of all time.

It has been suggested by a leading authority that the ancient rule which holds that mere nondisclosure does not constitute actionable misrepresentation "finds proper application in cases where the fact undisclosed is patent, or the plaintiff has equal opportunities for obtaining information which he may be expected to utilize, or the defendant has no reason to think that he is acting under any misapprehension" (Prosser, Law of Torts § 106, at 696 [4th ed 1971]). However, with respect to transactions in real estate, New York adheres to the doctrine of caveat emptor and imposes no duty upon the vendor to disclose any information concerning the premises (*London v Courduff*, 141 AD2d 803) unless there is a confidential or fiduciary relationship between the parties (*Moser v Spizzirro*, 31 AD2d 537, affd 25 N.Y.2d 941; *IBM Credit Fin. Corp. v Mazda Motor Mfg.* [USA] Corp., 152 AD2d 451) or some conduct on the part of the seller which constitutes "active concealment" (*see, 17 E. 80th Realty Corp. v 68th Assocs.*, 173 AD2d 245, 269 [dummy ventilation system constructed by seller]; *Haberman v Greenspan*, 82 Misc 2d 263 [foundation cracks covered by seller]). Normally, some affirmative misrepresentation . . . or partial disclosure . . . is required to impose upon the seller a duty to communicate undisclosed conditions affecting the premises. . . .

The doctrine of caveat emptor requires that a buyer act prudently to assess the fitness and value of his purchase and operates to bar the purchaser who fails to exercise due care from seeking the equitable remedy of rescission (*see, e.g., Rodas v Manitaras*, 159 AD2d 341). . . . It should be apparent, however, that the most meticulous inspection and the search would not reveal the presence of poltergeists at the premises or unearth the property's ghoulish reputation in the community. Therefore, there is no sound policy reason to deny plaintiff relief for failing to discover a state of affairs which the most prudent purchaser would not be expected to even contemplate. . . .

> **FYI**
>
> Two paranormal researchers wrote the book Sir George: The Ghost of Nyack (1995) about the *Stambovsky* house. Sir George and his supernatural housekeeper, Margaret, allegedly told the researchers that haunting the house was more fun when Ackley lived there.

The case law in this jurisdiction dealing with the duty of a vendor of real property to disclose information to the buyer is distinguishable from the matter under review. The most salient distinction is that existing cases invariably deal with the physical condition of the premises . . . and other factors affecting its operation. No case has been brought to this court's attention in which the property value was impaired as the result of the reputation created by information disseminated to the public by the seller (or, for that matter, as a result of possession by poltergeists).

Where a condition which has been created by the seller materially impairs the value of the contract and is peculiarly within the knowledge of the seller or unlikely to be discovered by a prudent purchaser exercising due care with respect to the subject transaction, nondisclosure constitutes a basis for rescission as a matter of equity. Any other outcome places upon the buyer not merely the obligation to exercise care in his purchase but rather to be omniscient with respect to any fact which may affect the bargain. No practical purpose is served by imposing such a burden upon a purchaser. To the contrary, it encourages predatory business practice and offends the principle that equity will suffer no wrong to be without a remedy. . . .

> **Make the Connection**
>
> In Chapter 7, you examined the shift from caveat lessee to the modern implied warranty of habitability in residential leases. How does that shift compare to the movement away from caveat emptor toward the seller's duty to disclose?

In the case at bar, defendant seller deliberately fostered the public belief that her home was possessed. Having undertaken to inform the public-at-large, to whom she has no legal relationship, about the supernatural occurrences on her property, she may be said to owe no less a duty to her contract vendee. It has been remarked that the occasional modern cases which permit a seller to take unfair advantage of a buyer's ignorance so long as he is not actively misled are "singularly unappetizing" (Prosser, Law of Torts § 106, at 696 [4th ed 1971]). Where, as here, the seller not only takes unfair advantage of the buyer's ignorance but has created and perpetuated a condition about which he is unlikely to even inquire, enforcement of the contract (in whole or in part) is offensive to the court's sense of equity. Application of the remedy of rescission, within the bounds of the narrow exception to the doctrine of caveat emptor set forth herein, is entirely appropriate to relieve the unwitting purchaser from the consequences of a most unnatural bargain....

SMITH, JUSTICE. (dissenting)

... "It is settled law in New York State that the seller of real property is under no duty to speak when the parties deal at arm's length. The mere silence of the seller, without some act or conduct which deceived the purchaser, does not amount to a concealment that is actionable as a fraud (*see, Perin v Mardine Realty Co.,* 5 AD2d 685, affd 6 N.Y.2d 920; *Moser v Spizzirro,* 31 AD2d 537, affd 25 N.Y.2d 941). The buyer has the duty to satisfy himself as to the quality of his bargain pursuant to the doctrine of caveat emptor, which in New York State still applies to real estate transactions."...

The parties herein were represented by counsel and dealt at arm's length.... There is no allegation that defendants, by some specific act, other than the failure to speak, deceived the plaintiff. Nevertheless, a cause of action may be sufficiently stated where there is a confidential or fiduciary relationship creating a duty to disclose and there was a failure to disclose a material fact, calculated to induce a false belief.... However, plaintiff herein has not alleged and there is no basis for concluding that a confidential or fiduciary relationship existed between these parties to an arm's length transaction such as to give rise to a duty to disclose. In addition, there is no allegation that defendants thwarted plaintiff's efforts to fulfill his responsibilities fixed by the doctrine of caveat emptor....

[I]f the doctrine of caveat emptor is to be discarded, it should be for a reason more substantive than a poltergeist. The existence of a poltergeist is no more binding upon the defendants than it is upon this court....

Points for Discussion

a. **Caveat Emptor in New York**

Before *Stambovsky*, New York strictly adhered to the caveat emptor approach. Why did the court allow Stambovsky to rescind? What policies justify imposing a disclosure requirement on the seller of residential real property? Do you agree with the dissent that a seller should have no duty to disclose when the parties are each represented by counsel, deal at arm's length, and have no fiduciary relationship?

b. Proving Material Impairment

The effect of the *Stambovsky* decision was to remand the case for trial. How would plaintiffs prove that the presence of poltergeists "materially impairs the value of the contract"? About 70% of Americans do not believe in ghosts. Does this mean that most buyers would be willing to purchase the house? One survey showed that 38% of home buyers in the U.S. would not purchase a house that was allegedly haunted, while 75% of those willing to buy would expect a price reduction. But 12% would pay full value or more for a haunted house. Sanette Tanaka, *"Haunted" House? A Tough Sell*, Wall Street Journal, Oct. 17, 2013. Is this case about the presence of ghosts or the reputation of the home?

c. Disclosure Hypotheticals

In the following hypotheticals, does S have a duty to disclose under the majority approach? Under the *Stambovsky* approach?

> (1) S strongly suspects that the prior owner of his house used lead paint when she repainted the living room, but S has never done any testing to confirm this suspicion. S knows that B has a five-year-old son.
>
> (2) S knows that the electric wiring in the house is old and brittle. Twenty years ago, while S owned the house, there was a small fire caused by a frayed wire in a light switch. B is an experienced electrician.
>
> (3) After S purchased the house, she accidentally discovered that it rests on a thin layer of rock perched over a vast cavern, which was produced by underground streams; a geologist advised her that it might fall into the cavern at any moment. There is no indication in the house or on the grounds that the cavern exists, so B did not find it when he inspected.
>
> (4) S is selling a condominium unit to B. S knows that T, his former tenant, was raped while T lived in the unit, even though it has a state-of-the-art security system. B informs S that she is buying the unit because two burglaries occurred at her prior house.

d. Statutory Reforms

Statutes in many jurisdictions require the seller of residential property to provide a written disclosure statement to the buyer. Although the precise requirements vary from state to state, problems such as building code violations, zoning violations, structural defects, and drainage issues must typically be disclosed.

> **See It**
>
> Click here to see the disclosure checklist required by California Civil Code § 1102.6.

Conversely, statutes in many states specify conditions that the seller *does not have to disclose*. Why do you think such legislation was passed? Many of these statutes deal with conditions that may have a psychological impact on some buyers—for example, that the property was the site of a mass murder or that the seller has HIV/AIDS. Should a seller be allowed to conceal such information? *See* Ronald B. Brown & Thomas H. Thurlow III, *Buyers Beware: Statutes Shield Real Estate Brokers and Sellers Who Do Not Disclose that Properties Are Psychologically Tainted*, 49 Okla. L. Rev. 625 (1996). *See also Milliken v. Jacono*, 103 A.3d 806 (Pa. 2014) (psychological stigmas such as a murder/suicide are not material defects and do not need to be disclosed).

e. **"As Is" Clauses**

Suppose that a purchase contract includes the following clause:

> Buyer agrees that the Property is being sold "as is" and that Seller makes no representations or warranties about its condition. Buyer understands that it is Buyer's responsibility to fully examine and inspect the Property and to determine whether it is sufficient for Buyer's intended purposes. Buyer may rescind this contract at any time before the closing if, in Buyer's sole discretion, he has any concern about the condition of the Property.

Should this provision relieve the seller from the duty to disclose? Should it matter whether the property is residential or commercial?

f. **Buyer's Duty to Disclose**

Suppose S is willing to sell his farm to B at the fair market price for agricultural land. B knows that there are substantial oil reserves under the farm, but S does not. Should B disclose this information? In other words, if the seller has a duty to disclose, should the buyer have the same duty? *See Zaschak v. Traverse Corp.*, 333 N.W.2d 191 (Mich. Ct. App. 1983) (prospective buyer has no duty to disclose facts which materially affect the value of the property).

g. **Implied Warranty of Quality**

Another exception to the caveat emptor doctrine in many states is the *implied warranty of quality*. Under this approach, the developer of newly-constructed residential property—like houses in a subdivision—impliedly warrants that the property is fit for its intended use. Thus, the developer may be liable even if he has no actual knowledge of defects in the houses he sells. *See Zambrano v. M & RC II LLC*, 517 P.3d 1168 (Ariz. 2022). What if the original owner resells the house? In most jurisdictions, the warranty runs to subsequent buyers of the property.

h. **Disclosure of Off-Site Conditions**

So far, we have examined the seller's duty to disclose conditions *on the property* being sold. Must the seller also disclose *off-site* conditions? The answer for the most part is "no." But in *Strawn v. Canuso*, 657 A.2d 420 (N.J. 1995) the builder-developer of a housing tract was held liable for failing to disclose the presence of a nearby landfill contaminated with toxic waste. The court limited liability to professional sellers of housing and the brokers representing them. It explained that the seller was "liable for nondisclosure of off-site physical conditions known to it and unknown and not readily observable by the buyer if the existence of those conditions is of sufficient materiality to affect the habitability, use, or enjoyment of the property and, therefore, render the property substantially less desirable or valuable to the objectively reasonable buyer." *Id*. at 431. How difficult will it be to meet this standard? Should the duty to disclose off-site problems be extended to all sellers?

i. Aftermath of *Stambovsky*

Ackley later sold the house to another buyer and moved to Florida. She told a local reporter: "I guess [the ghosts] decided to stay where they are. They did seem pretty put out when we left." *Follow-Up: Haunted House Owner*, Orlando Sentinel, Sept. 30, 1992. Subsequent owners have not reported seeing any ghosts, and a local paranormal investigator stated she was "unimpressed" with the house. Bill Batson, *1 Poltergeist Place, Nyack, NY?*, Nyack News & Views, Oct. 30, 2012. In 2002, the state legislature enacted the New York Property Condition Disclosure Act, N.Y. Real Prop. Law § 462, which requires that the seller of residential property provide a written disclosure statement to the buyer that lists any defects in the property.

B. The Closing

The closing is the point when the purchase contract is performed. In many states, the closing is supervised by an *escrow agent*. The escrow agent is a neutral third party who receives the purchase price, the deed, the mortgage, the promissory note, and any other documents needed to consummate the transaction. When all the conditions in the contract have been satisfied, the escrow agent distributes the funds and documents as directed by written *escrow instructions* signed by the parties. In other states, the custom is to have a "table" closing where the buyer and seller meet under the supervision of an attorney or other professional to sign and exchange the documents needed to close the transaction.

> **FYI**
>
> In 1974, Congress enacted the Real Estate Settlement Procedures Act (RESPA), 12 U.S.C. § 2601 et seq. This Act seeks to provide the consumer with detailed information about the nature and costs of the closing process in order to prevent abuses such as secret kickbacks.

At a typical closing: (1) the buyer pays the purchase price to the seller, and executes a mortgage and promissory note for the lender; (2) the lender advances the loan funds; and (3) the seller transfers title to the buyer by delivering a deed. The deed and mortgage are then recorded in the public land records. Title insurance policies are later issued to insure the lender's mortgage and the buyer's title.

In this section, we first examine the law governing the key document used in the closing: the deed. We then consider the remedies available if the contract is breached. You will study the mortgage and other financing devices in Chapter 9.

---

1. The Deed

Suppose that F signs a deed conveying Greenacre to his daughter, D. F hands the deed to D saying, "Keep this safe, and record it when I die." F continues living on the property, making repairs and paying the mortgage. Who owns Greenacre?

A deed is only effective when it is *delivered*. Thus, an undelivered deed—even if signed by the grantor—conveys nothing. While the requirements for delivery vary from state to state, in general the grantor must manifest an intention to immediately transfer title to the grantee. In the F-D hypothetical above, F still owns Greenacre because his words and actions show that he intends to transfer title only in the future.

Delivery is not a problem in the ordinary sales transaction: the seller physically hands the deed to the buyer or her agent under circumstances showing his intent to immediately convey title. But problems sometimes arise when a grantor attempts to transfer title to a family member as a gift, as our next case demonstrates.

Rosengrant v. Rosengrant

Court of Appeals of Oklahoma

629 P.2d 800 (1981)

BOYDSTON, JUDGE.

This is an appeal by J. W. (Jay) Rosengrant from the trial court's decision to cancel and set aside a warranty deed which attempted to vest title in him to certain property owned by his aunt and uncle, Mildred and Harold Rosengrant. The trial court held the deed was invalid for want of legal delivery. We affirm that decision.

Harold and Mildred were a retired couple living on a farm southeast of Tecumseh, Oklahoma. They had no children of their own but had six nieces and nephews through Harold's deceased brother. One of these nephews was Jay Rosengrant. He and his wife lived a short distance from Harold and Mildred and helped the elderly couple from time to time with their chores.

In 1971, it was discovered that Mildred had cancer. In July, 1972 Mildred and Harold went to Mexico to obtain laetrile treatments accompanied by Jay's wife. Jay remained behind to care for the farm.

Shortly before this trip, on June 23, 1972, Mildred had called Jay and asked him to meet her and Harold at Farmers and Merchants Bank in Tecumseh. Upon arriving at the bank, Harold introduced Jay to his banker J. E. Vanlandengham who presented Harold and Mildred with a deed to their farm which he had prepared according to their instructions. Both Harold and Mildred signed the deed and informed Jay that they were going to give him "the place," but that they wanted Jay to leave the deed at the bank with Mr. Vanlandengham and when "something happened" to them, he was to take it to Shawnee and record it and "it" would be theirs. Harold personally handed the deed to Jay to "make this legal." Jay accepted the deed and then handed it back to the banker who told him he would put it in an envelope and keep it in the vault until he called for it.

In July, 1974, when Mildred's death was imminent, Jay and Harold conferred with an attorney concerning the legality of the transaction. The attorney advised them it should be sufficient but if Harold anticipated problems he should draw up a will.

In 1976, Harold discovered he had lung cancer. In August and December 1977, Harold put $10,000 into two certificates of deposit in joint tenancy with Jay.

Harold died January 28, 1978. On February 2, Jay and his wife went to the bank to inventory the contents of the safety deposit box. They also requested the envelope containing the deed which was retrieved from the collection file of the bank.

Jay went to Shawnee the next day and recorded the deed.

The petition to cancel and set aside the deed was filed February 22, 1978, alleging that the deed was void in that it was never legally delivered and alternatively that since it was to be operative only upon recordation after the death of the grantors it was a testamentary instrument and was void for failure to comply with the Statute of Wills.

The trial court found the deed was null and void for failure of legal delivery. The dispositive issue raised on appeal is whether the trial court erred in so ruling. We hold it did not and affirm the judgment. . . .

In cases involving attempted transfers such as this, it is the grantor's intent *at the time the deed is delivered* which is of primary and controlling importance. It is the function of this court to weigh the evidence presented at trial as to grantor's intent and unless the trial court's decision is clearly against the weight of the evidence, to uphold that finding.

The grantor and banker were both dead at the time of trial. Consequently, the only testimony regarding the transaction was supplied by the grantee, Jay. The pertinent part of his testimony is as follows:

A. [A]nd was going to hand it back to Mr. Vanlandingham [*sic*], and he wouldn't take it.

Q. What did Mr. Vanlandingham [*sic*] say?

A. Well, he laughed then and said that "We got to make this legal," or something like that. And said, "You'll have to give it to Jay and let Jay give it back to me."

Q. And what did Harold do with the document?

A. He gave it to me.

Q. Did you hold it?

A. Yes.

Q. Then what did you do with it?

A. Mr. Vanlandingham [*sic*], I believe, told me I ought to look at it.

Q. And you looked at it?

A. Yes.

Q. And then what did you do with it?

A. I handed it to Mr. Vanlandingham [*sic*].

Q. And what did he do with the document?

A. He had it in his hand, I believe, when we left.

Q. Do you recall seeing the envelope at any time during this transaction?

A. I never saw the envelope. But Mr. Vanlandingham [*sic*] told me when I handed it to him, said, "Jay, I'll put this in an envelope and keep it in a vault for you until you call for it."

A. Well, Harold told me while Mildred was signing the deed that they were going to deed me the farm, but they wanted me to leave the deed at the bank with Van, and that *when something happened to them* that I would go to the bank and pick it up and take it to Shawnee to the court house and record it, and *it would be mine*. (emphasis added)

> **Food for Thought**
>
> Did Vanlandengham engage in the unauthorized practice of law? Recall that he instructed the parties how to "make this legal." Should he have played a more passive role? Professionals such as bankers, accountants, and notaries may end up practicing law by giving their clients advice or helping them fill out standard forms. Could Jay have sued Vanlandengham for malpractice?

When the deed was retrieved, it was contained in an envelope on which was typed: "J. W. Rosengrant- or Harold H. Rosengrant."

The import of the writing on the envelope is clear. It creates an inescapable conclusion that the deed was, in fact, retrievable at any time by Harold before his death. The bank teller's testimony as to the custom and usage of the bank leaves no other conclusion but that at any time Harold was free to retrieve the deed. There was, if not an expressed, an implied agreement between the banker and Harold that the grant was not to take effect until two conditions occurred: the death of both grantors and the recordation of the deed.

In support of this conclusion conduct relative to the property is significant and was correctly considered by the court. Evidence was presented to show that after the deed was filed Harold continued to farm, use and control the property. Further, he continued to pay taxes on it until his death and claimed it as his homestead.

Grantee confuses the issues involved herein by relying upon grantors' goodwill toward him and his wife as if it were a controlling factor. From a fair review of the record it is apparent Jay and his wife were very attentive, kind and helpful to this elderly couple. The donative intent on the part of grantors is undeniable. We believe they fully intended to reward Jay and his wife for their kindness. Nevertheless, where a grantor delivers a deed under which he reserves a right of retrieval and attaches to that delivery the condition that the deed is to become operative only after the death of grantors and further continues to use the property as if no transfer had occurred grantor's actions are nothing more than an attempt to employ the deed as if it were a will. Under Oklahoma law this cannot be done. The ritualistic "delivery of the deed" to the grantee and his redelivery of it to the third party for safe keeping created under these circumstances only a symbolic delivery. It amounted to a pro forma attempt to comply with the legal aspects of delivery. Based on all the facts and circumstances the true intent of the parties is expressed by the notation on the envelope and by the later conduct of the parties in relation to the land. Legal delivery is not just a symbolic gesture. It necessarily carries all the force and consequence of absolute, outright ownership at the time of delivery or it is no delivery at all.

> **Make the Connection**
>
> Did Harold and Mildred intend to make a present transfer of a future interest or a future transfer of a present interest? How does their intent compare to that of Victor Gruen in *Gruen v. Gruen* (Chapter 3)?

The trial court interpreted the envelope literally. The clear implication is that grantor intended to continue to exercise control and that the grant was not to take effect until such time as both he and his wife had died and the deed had been recorded. From a complete review of the record and weighing of the evidence we find the trial court's judgment is not clearly against the weight of the evidence. Costs of appeal are taxed to appellant.

BRIGHTMIRE, JUDGE, concurring specially.

. . . A valid in praesenti conveyance requires two things: (1) actual or constructive delivery of the deed to the grantee or to a third party; and (2) an intention by the grantor to divest himself of the conveyed interest. Here the trial judge found there was no delivery despite the testimony of Jay Rosengrant to the contrary that one of the grantors handed the deed to him at the suggestion of banker J. E. Vanlandengham.

So the question is, was the trial court bound to find the fact to be as Rosengrant stated? In my opinion he was not for several reasons. Of the four persons present at the bank meeting in question only Rosengrant survives which, when coupled with the self-serving nature of the nephew's statements, served to cast a suspicious cloud over his testimony. And this, when considered along with other circumstances detailed in the majority opinion, would have justified the fact finder in disbelieving it. I personally have trouble with the delivery testimony in spite of the apparent "corroboration" of the lawyer, Jeff Diamond. The only reason I can see for Vanlandengham suggesting such a physical delivery would be to assure the accomplishment of a valid conveyance of the property at that time. But if the grantors intended that then why did[n't] they simply give it to the named grantee and tell him to record it? Why did they go through the delivery motion in the presence of Vanlandengham and then give the deed to the banker? Why did the banker write on the envelope containing the deed that it was to be given to either the grantee "or" a grantor? The fact that the grantors continued to occupy the land, paid taxes on it, offered to sell it once and otherwise treated it as their own justifies an inference that they did not make an actual delivery of the deed to the named grantee. Or, if they did, they directed that it be left in the custody of the banker with the intent of reserving a *de facto* life estate or of retaining a power of revocation by instructing the banker to return it to them if they requested it during their lifetimes or to give it to the named grantee upon their deaths. In either case, the deed failed as a valid conveyance. . . .

Points for Discussion

a. Delivery as Intent

Harold physically handed the deed to Jay. Why wasn't this effective delivery? Delivery is a matter of intention. The question is whether the grantor demonstrated his intent that the grantee receive an immediate interest in the property. As one court explained: "Delivery is essential to make a deed operative, but no particular ceremony is necessary. It may be by acts without words or words without acts, or both. No particular form or ceremony is necessary. . . . Intention is the controlling element. . . . " *Phenneger v. Kendrick*, 133 N.E. 637, 638 (Ill. 1921); see also *Hoefer v. Musser*, 417 S.W.3d 330 (Mo. Ct. App. 2013).

> **FYI**
>
> Sir Edward Coke famously stated: "As a deed may be delivered to the party without words, so may a deed be delivered by words without any act of delivery." 1 Co. Litt. 36a.

The Uniform Simplification of Land Transfers Act § 1–201(3) defines delivery as "an act manifesting an intent to make a present transfer of real estate," while the

Restatement (Second) of Property: Donative Transfers § 32.1 indicates that delivery is accomplished when "the donor manifests that the document is to be legally operative while the donor is alive." What facts suggest that Harold and Mildred did not intend to immediately transfer title? But remember Jay's testimony: (1) the banker told him: "Jay, I'll put this in an envelope and keep it in a vault for *you* until *you* call for it" (emphasis added); and (2) Jay never saw what was written on the envelope.

b.   Physical Delivery?

The delivery requirement dates back to the ceremony of feoffment with livery of seisin. In pre-literate England, the grantor evidenced his clear intent to transfer title by placing a clod of dirt or another object in the grantee's hands as part of a memorable ceremony. But this form of physical delivery is no longer required by modern courts.

> **What's That?**
>
> Feoffment with livery of seisin was the principal method for transferring title to land in medieval England (recall the child-slapping ceremony discussed in Chapter 5). Feoffment is from the Old French, meaning "gift." The term "livery of seisin" means "transfer of possession" and comes from the Old French *livrer* (delivery) and *seisin* (possession).

Many jurisdictions use rebuttable presumptions to help resolve delivery disputes. For example, in most states the manual transfer of the deed to the grantee creates a presumption that the deed has been delivered. Delivery is also presumed if the deed is recorded. And in some states, the absence of a manual transfer creates a presumption of nondelivery. See LeMehaute v. LeMehaute, 585 S.W.2d 276 (Mo. Ct. App. 1979); *In re Estate of Hardy*, 910 So. 2d 1052 (Miss. 2005).

c.   Applying *Rosengrant*

S executes a deed that, on its face, conveys Greenacre to Y. As S hands the deed to Y, S makes one of the statements below. Has delivery occurred?

> (1) "I have now transferred Greenacre to you. Give the deed back to me, and I will keep it in my bedside drawer until you graduate from law school."
>
> (2) "I want you to have Greenacre, but I want to live there until I die."
>
> (3) "Here's my deed to you. Please hold it safe until I talk with my wife, and then you can record it when I say it's OK."
>
> (4) "Place the deed in our safety deposit box, and when I die Greenacre will be yours."

d.   Brightmire's Concurrence

In his concurrence, Judge Brightmire seemed suspicious of Jay's statement that Harold handed him the deed "to make it legal." If you were Jay's attorney, how would you respond to Judge Brightmire's concern? Does *Gruen v. Gruen* (Chapter 3) provide a suggestion?

e.   Statute of Frauds

To satisfy the Statute of Frauds, a deed must (1) be in writing, (2) contain the essential terms (identity of the grantor and grantee; description of the property; and words showing an intent to convey title), and (3) be signed by the grantor. Under the Uniform Electronic Transactions Act, an electronic deed satisfies the Statute of Frauds if it contains the essential terms and the grantor's e-signature.

f.   Acceptance

A deed is effective only if it is delivered *and* accepted. Usually acceptance is presumed even if the grantee is unaware of the gift. But a grantee might refuse to accept a deed. For example, suppose your friend K wants to give you a lot that is contaminated by toxic waste. Would you accept that deed? Can you think of other examples where a grantee would not accept a deed?

g.   Aftermath of *Rosengrant*

After the deed was set aside, the farm passed by intestate succession to Harold and Mildred's six nieces and nephews, including Jay and the plaintiff in the case, Jay's brother Walter. Jay purchased the tenancy in common interests held by his siblings and lived on the farm until his death. Three years after the case was decided, Oklahoma banking authorities shut down the Farmers and Merchants Bank when it suffered major losses. A state banking official commented that there was "mismanagement and very imprudent lending all the way around." *Concealed Loan Loss at Failed Oklahoma Bank*, Amer. Banker, Oct. 10, 1984. Might this mismanagement have affected the outcome of the case?

In *Rosengrant*, Harold and Mildred gave the deed to their banker with instructions to allow Jay to retrieve it when they died; the court held this deed was not delivered. The facts in our next case, *Vasquez v. Vasquez*, are similar: the grantor gave the deed to her lawyer with instructions to hand it to the grantee when she died. But the *Vasquez* court ruled that the deed was delivered. What explains this difference?

Vasquez v. Vasquez

Court of Appeals of Texas

973 S.W.2d 330 (1998)

SEERDEN, CHIEF JUSTICE.

. . . The facts of this case are undisputed. On July 29, 1992, Juanita Vasquez Carr, the unquestioned owner of the property at issue, executed a will naming Ignacio Vasquez as her independent executor, and Ignacio and Jose Vasquez, appellants, sole beneficiaries. Thereafter, on February 6, 1993, Juanita Vasquez Carr executed a quitclaim deed granting the same property to Brigido D. Vasquez, appellee. Juanita left the quitclaim deed in the custody of her attorney with instructions not to file it and not to tell anybody about it, including appellee, until after her death. Juanita continued with the uninterrupted possession, use, and benefit of the subject property until her death on September 29, 1993.

Upon her death, Juanita's attorney, Michael George, mailed the quitclaim deed to the appropriate county clerk for filing. The deed was recorded on October 6, 1993, and soon thereafter, appellee was notified as to the existence of the deed.

On January 13, 1994, Juanita's last will and testament was filed and admitted to probate. On February 21, 1994, under the terms of the will, appellant Ignacio Vasquez, as the duly appointed and qualified independent executor of Juanita's estate, executed a special warranty deed conveying the property in question to appellants.

The question soon arose: who is the rightful owner of the property in question? The case was submitted to the trial court on stipulated facts as recited above. The trial court, after hearing the evidence and arguments of counsel, found that the deed from Juanita Vasquez Carr was delivered when it was tendered to Juanita's attorney, thus transferring the real property to appellee as of February 6, 1993. This finding was set out in the trial court's conclusions of law. Appellants bring this appeal. . . .

It is elementary that a deed must be delivered, as that term is legally interpreted, in order to be an effective transfer of the ownership of land. In determining whether a deed has been effectively delivered when said deed is placed in the control of a third person, the question is whether the grantor parted with all dominion and control over the instrument at the time she delivered it to the third person with the intent that it take effect as a conveyance at the very time of delivery. *Ragland v. Kelner*, 148 Tex. 132, 221 S.W.2d 357, 359 (1949); *Stout v. Clayton*, 674 S.W.2d 821, 825 (Tex. App.-San Antonio 1984, writ ref'd n.r.e.). Thus, the issue before us in this case is whether the evidence supports a finding that Juanita intended to relinquish all dominion and control over the quitclaim deed at the time she delivered it to her attorney. . . .

It is undisputed that Juanita signed the quitclaim deed and gave the deed to her attorney with specific instructions. According to her attorney, those instructions were to keep the existence of the deed a secret, to keep it in his custody, and to file and deliver the deed to the named grantee after Juanita's death. There was no mention in those instructions of Juanita's power to recall the deed. In fact, when questioned by appellants' attorney as to whether Juanita instructed her attorney to "keep that until I die *or until I give you instructions otherwise*," Juanita's attorney responded, "Well, no. I keep the deed, and then I'm not to tell anybody or file it or do anything until after they've spewed her ashes." . . .

> **Practice Pointer**
>
> Suppose that Vasquez changed her mind and demanded that her attorney return the deed to her. Wouldn't the attorney be ethically obligated to comply? ABA Model Rule of Professional Conduct 1.2(a) provides that "a lawyer shall abide by a client's decisions concerning the objectives of representation. . . ."

It is true that Juanita retained possession of the subject property until her death. However, possession is not determinative. Where the grantor delivers a deed to a third person with the intent to part with all control, the legal effect of the transaction is tantamount to a delivery of the deed to the grantee, conveying him the fee while reserving for the grantor the use and enjoyment of the land during his natural life. *See Ragland*, 221 S.W.2d at 360 (present transfer with right of possession, use, and enjoyment of the property remaining in grantor during her lifetime); *Stout*, 674 S.W.2d at 825 (valid delivery found despite evidence that grantor claimed ownership and occupied the property until her death). . . .

The only evidence in the record bearing directly on Juanita's intent to deliver the deed in question shows that Juanita executed the deed, and handed it over to her attorney with specific instructions to deliver the deed to appellee on her death without reserving a right to recall the deed. When a grantor delivers a deed to a third person without a reservation of a right to recall it, and instructs the third person to deliver it to the grantee on the grantor's death, he thereby makes an effective delivery as a matter of law. *Ragland*, 221 S.W.2d at 360.

Accordingly, we agree with the trial court's conclusion that the deed was effectively delivered by Juanita when she tendered the deed to her attorney on February 6, 1993. Accordingly, we overrule all points of error and affirm the judgment of the trial court.

Points for Discussion

a. **Explaining *Vasquez***

Why did the *Vasquez* court conclude that Juanita could not recall the deed? In order to make an effective delivery, the grantor must relinquish dominion and control of the deed. Did this occur in *Vasquez*? In *Rosengrant*? *See Johnson v. Johnson*, 760 S.E.2d 618 (Ga. Ct. App. 2014).

b. **Death Escrow**

In the normal escrow, the grantor deposits the deed with a neutral third party, who is instructed to deliver the deed to the grantee at the closing. But suppose the grantor gives a deed to an escrow company and then directs it to deliver the deed to the grantee *only when the grantor dies*. Is this an effective delivery? Or an invalid attempt to transfer title in the future? Most jurisdictions find an effective delivery on these facts if the grantor is unable to retrieve the deed. In *Rosengrant,* how significant was it that under the bank's customary practice Harold could retrieve the deed whenever he wanted? The *Vasquez* court found that Juanita delivered her deed "without reserving a right to recall." But what facts suggest that she did *not* make an irrevocable delivery?

c. **Transfer on Death Deed**

A majority of states now authorize a novel type of deed: the *transfer on death deed* (also called the *beneficiary deed*). This deed allows an owner of real property to designate the beneficiaries she wants to receive the property upon her death; it is revocable by the grantor during her lifetime. By signing and recording such a deed, the owner causes her interest to be automatically conveyed to the listed beneficiaries upon her death. Because the deed is not legally operative until the grantor's death, delivery is not required. The property is not part of the decedent's estate and therefore does not go through probate, avoiding those costs and delays. Would this type of deed accomplish the goals of Vasquez and the Rosengrants? For a comprehensive explanation of the transfer on death deed, see Michael A. Kirtland & Catherine Anne Seal, *Beneficiary Deeds and Estate Planning*, 66 Ala. Law. 118 (2005) and Dennis M. Horn & Susan N. Gary, *Death Without Probate: TOD Deeds—The Latest Tool in the Toolbox*, 24 Prob. & Prop. 12 (2010).

> **See It**
>
> Click here to see an example of a transfer on death deed.

d. **Revocable Deeds**

Suppose Juanita hands Brigido a deed that expressly provides that Juanita can revoke the grant at any time in the future. Is this a valid transfer? In many jurisdictions, the answer is "yes." In *St. Louis County National Bank v. Fielder*, 260

> **Food for Thought**
>
> When land was transferred in medieval England by feoffment, the grantor could not reserve a power of revocation. Since the ceremony itself provided the sole evidence of the conveyance, any reserved power that could retransfer the land would be difficult to prove. Do the same concerns exist today? If not, should we allow revocable deeds?

S.W.2d 483 (Mo. 1953), a grantor reserved a life estate with the power to sell the property during his lifetime. Noting that this condition was the equivalent of a power of revocation, the Missouri Supreme Court endorsed the "modern trend" of upholding revocable deeds. Some courts hold that a revocable deed does not satisfy the delivery requirement because the grantor has not relinquished control. Still others view the conveyance as valid, but conclude that the power to revoke is void.

2. Remedies for Breach

At the time set for closing the Baker-Stone contract, Stone suddenly declares: "I've changed my mind about selling you the house. But don't worry. I'll pay you the difference between its fair market value and our contract price." Can the Bakers compel Stone to convey title to them?

Specific performance is an equitable remedy that requires the breaching party to perform the contract, as you saw in *Hickey v. Green* earlier in this chapter. In general, it is more difficult for the buyer to compel specific performance than to obtain damages. Why? This remedy arose in England's equity courts, like the injunction. While damages were readily available in the law courts, the equity courts imposed special restrictions on equitable remedies in the interest of fairness. One important limit was that specific performance would be granted only if monetary damages were *inadequate*. As a general matter, land is considered to be *unique*, unlike most chattels. Thus, if the seller refused to perform a contract for the purchase of real property, courts traditionally reasoned that damages would not adequately compensate the buyer.

But is every piece of real property really unique? What about a unit in a large condominium complex?

Giannini v. First Nat'l Bank of Des Plaines

Appellate Court of Illinois

483 N.E.2d 924 (1985)

JIGANTI, PRESIDING JUSTICE.

John Giannini d/b/a J.G. Sewer Contractors (Giannini) executed an agreement to purchase a condominium unit in the Castilian Courts Condominium Complex to be constructed in Glenview, Illinois and paid $62,330 in earnest money on the property. Although the building in which his unit was located was subsequently constructed, it was never formally declared a condominium and as a result the terms of the agreement were never fulfilled.

Castilian Courts Condominium building
Click here for larger photo

Giannini filed a two-count complaint against First National Bank of Des Plaines (Des Plaines Bank), the record title holder of the complex pursuant to a land trust agreement; Frank R. Stape Builders, Inc. (Stape Builders), the developer of the project and signer of Giannini's purchase agreement as agent of the beneficiary of the trust in which title to the complex was held; and Unity Savings Association (Unity), a mortgage holder on the property. His complaint requested specific performance of the purchase agreement by Unity, Stape Builder and Des Plaines Bank (count I) and money damages from Stape Builders and Des Plaines Bank (count II). . . .

Giannini filed his complaint on October 19, 1981. In the count for specific performance, he alleged in pertinent part that on or about March 27, 1980, he entered into a written agreement with Stape Builders as agent for the beneficiaries of the land trust to purchase a specified condominium unit for the sum of $79,515. He stated that although construction of the premises had been completed, Stape Builders and Des Plaines Bank refused to perform their obligations under the terms of the purchase agreement. He also alleged that Unity had or purported to have an interest in the unit. Giannini claimed that he was ready, willing, and able to fulfill his obligations under the agreement and requested specific performance of the contract because he had no adequate legal remedy.

Giannini attached a copy of the purchase agreement to his pleadings and incorporated it therein by reference. . . . The contract specified the particular unit which Giannini was to receive (unit B-70), set forth its common and legal description, stated a total purchase price of $79,515, and required Giannini to pay $62,330 as earnest money. . . .

Unity apparently obtained title to the complex in lieu of foreclosure of its mortgage on the property. . . .

[T]he entire condominium project consisted of five buildings (A, B, C, D, and E) with a total of 256 units. . . . [A]lthough all buildings were originally intended to be condominiums only buildings D and E had been so recorded; buildings A, B (in which Giannini's unit was located) and C were instead rental buildings. . . . [T]he buildings had not been declared as condominium buildings because of the poor economy and in particular the "unsaleable real estate and condominium market." . . .

> **FYI**
>
> To avoid foreclosure, the trust simply conveyed title to the complex to Unity. Thus, Unity received a *deed in lieu of foreclosure*. This means that Unity took title subject to all existing encumbrances, including Giannini's contract.

Upon consideration of the parties' pleadings, documents, and written and oral argument, the trial court granted Unity's motion to dismiss count I of the complaint as to Unity. In its oral pronouncement, the court concluded that specific performance was improper because: 1) there was no condominium "in existence" which Unity could be ordered to convey to Giannini; 2) the remedy would be economically disadvantageous to Unity; and 3) the remedy would be cumbersome and time-consuming because it would obligate the court to supervise conversion. . . .

We first consider the trial court's dismissal of count I of the original complaint which sought specific performance of the purchase agreement. . . .

Unity first claimed that dismissal of the specific performance claim was appropriate because the condominium unit was not in existence. It argued that the unit was non-existent because the building in which it was located had not been declared a condominium building.

Generally, "[w]here it is out of the power of the defendant to perform the agreement, such fact necessarily constitutes a sufficient reason why the court should refuse to decree specific performance, that is, to enter a decree which would be nugatory, because of the impossibility of enforcing its execution." (*Saur v. Ferris* (1893), 145 Ill. 115, 118–19, 34 N.E. 52). . . . Thus, "specific performance cannot be decreed of an agreement to convey property which has no existence or to which the defendant has no title. . . ." (*Sellers v. Greer* (1898), 172 Ill. 549, 558, 50 N.E. 246. . . .)

Unity argues that Giannini's unit does not "exist" because the building in which it is located has not been declared a condominium. Thus Unity claims that it is impossible for it to perform the obligations of the purchase agreement. We find this reasoning unpersuasive. The record demonstrates that the unit in question does indeed exist in a literal, physical sense of the term. The "non-existence" to which Unity refers, in contrast, is of a figurative, legal nature: in order to come into "existence," the unit need simply be declared a condominium pursuant to the legal requirements of the Illinois Condominium Property Act (Ill. Rev. Stat. 1981, ch. 30, par. 325.) As a result any form of "non-existence" of the unit is nothing more than a direct result of Unity's refusal to declare the building as a condominium. Consequently we are unconvinced that specific performance was properly denied here on the ground that the unit was "non-existent" and any conveyance thereof thus impossible. . . .

> **Practice Pointer**
>
> As a general rule, a multi-unit building becomes a condominium only when the owner executes and records a special instrument—usually called a *declaration*—pursuant to state law. In *Giannini*, such a declaration was never made for building B, where Giannini's unit B-70 was located. Thus, unit B-70 never became a legal parcel that could be conveyed separately from the rest of the building.

The second reason stated by Unity for dismissal of Giannini's claim is that specific performance was not imperative because a condominium is not so unique as to require such relief. Thus, Unity seeks to distinguish condominium units from other types of real property. . . .

Illinois courts have long held that where the parties have fairly and understandingly entered into a valid contract for the sale of real property, specific performance of the contract is a matter of right and equity will enforce it, absent circumstances of oppression and fraud. . . . "Contracts to devise or convey real estate are enforced by specific performance on the ground that the law cannot do perfect justice." (*Hagen v. Anderson* (1925), 317 Ill. 173, 177, 147 N.E. 791.) Thus "[w]here land, or any estate therein, is the subject matter of the agreement, the inadequacy of the legal remedy is well settled, and the equitable jurisdiction is firmly established. . . ." 4 J. Pomeroy, Equity Jurisprudence sec. 1402, at 1034 (5th ed. S. Symons 1941).

Unity argues that these rules should not obtain here because "exactly the same condominium units are available to Plaintiff in the two other buildings which have been converted to condominium in the same development." To support this claim, Unity notes that Buildings D and E of the Complex are already condominium buildings.

We find this argument insufficient ground to avoid application of the rules set forth above pertaining to specific performance of real estate purchase agreements in general. We observe that Unity has not attempted to claim that a condominium unit is not a type of realty. Furthermore, even if we assume that similarity between Giannini's unit and those of other buildings in the Complex would be sufficient ground to deny specific performance in certain circumstances, we note that there is nothing in the record to indicate the degree of similarity, if any, between the unit which Giannini contracted to purchase and those which have been declared condominium and are for sale as such. There is moreover no evidence to establish the price, terms, or conditions under which such units have been sold or are likely to be for sale. As a result there is no adequate basis for comparison of the sale of these units and the purchase agreement which Giannini stands ready to perform. Under these circumstances we find unpersuasive Unity's contention that a condominium unit should be treated differently than other forms of realty with regard to specific performance of an agreement to purchase the property. . . .

As a third basis for dismissal, Unity argues that specific performance was properly denied because it would be uneconomical to it. Generally the decision to grant specific performance rests within the sound discretion of the trial court to be determined by the facts and circumstances of each individual case. . . . In this regard the court should balance the equities between the parties. . . . Accordingly a court using its equitable powers may refuse to grant specific performance where the remedy would cause a peculiar hardship or an inequitable result. (*Geist v. Lehmann* (1974), 19 Ill.App.3d 557, 561, 312 N.E.2d 42.)

Nevertheless "[t]here is no hardship in compelling the seller to do what he agreed to do when he thought it was to his advantage." (*Smith v. Farmer's State Bank* (1945), 390 Ill. 374, 380, 61 N.E.2d 557.) Thus the fact that the contract cannot be performed without great or unanticipated expense is not such an impossibility that will usually excuse performance. . . .

Based upon this precedent, Unity's claim that declaration of the building as a condominium would be uneconomical to it was insufficient to establish a peculiar hardship which amounted to an oppressive or inequitable result which totally defeated or negated Giannini's claim. The record establishes the Unity had previously represented in its foreclosure proceeding that it would abide by Stape Builders' plans for the project. In other words, the evidence shows that Unity agreed to honor Giannini's contract when this was to its advantage to do so. Accordingly it cannot now seek to avoid the agreement because of financial hardship. . . .

Points for Discussion

a. **Obtaining Specific Performance**

Why did the *Giannini* court conclude that monetary damages were inadequate? Courts have traditionally held that damages are an inadequate remedy for the seller's breach of a contract to sell real property. This rule evolved in early England, where each parcel of farm land was truly unique—the soil quality, drainage, access, location, topography, water availability, and other factors varied widely. Does this rule make sense today?

b. **Unique?**

The *Giannini* court suggested that each unit in the condominium complex was unique. Do you agree? In *Centex Homes Corp. v. Boag*, 320 A.2d 194, 198 (N.J. Sup. Ct. Ch. Div. 1974), the court observed:

> Here the subject matter of the real estate transaction—a condominium apartment unit—has no unique quality but is one of hundreds of virtually identical units being offered by a developer for sale to the public. . . . The sales prices for the units are fixed in accordance with [a] schedule filed by Centex as part of its offering plan, and the only variance as between apartments having the same floor plan (of which six plans are available) is the floor level or the building location within the project. In actuality, the condominium apartment units, regardless of their realty label, share the same characteristics as personal property.

See also Nancy Perkins Spyke, *What's Land Got to Do With It? Rhetoric and Indeterminacy in Land's Favored Legal Status*, 52 Buff. L. Rev. 387 (2004). Is it fair to assume that Unity offered Giannini the right to purchase one of the condominium units in the other buildings—which he refused? What should we infer from his refusal?

c. **Seller's Remedy**

Under the traditional rationale, should the seller be entitled to specific performance if the buyer breaches? Perhaps illogically, most courts say "yes." *See, e.g., Davis v. Harmony Development, LLC*, 460 P.3d 230 (Wyo. 2020). *But see Centex Homes Corp. v. Boag*, supra (denying specific performance because damages sustained by condominium seller were "readily measurable").

d. **Role of Hardship**

As an equitable remedy, specific performance is subject to the court's discretion. Accordingly, the court may deny this remedy if it would impose an undue hardship on the defendant. As one example, a New Jersey court denied specific performance when the seller became disabled with a progressive neurological condition and her physician expressed concern that moving might "precipitate respiratory failure and hasten [her] demise." *Kilarjian v. Vastola*, 877 A.2d 372, 375 (N.J. Super. Ct. Ch. Div. 2005). Should the *Giannini* court have been more concerned that specific performance would cause hardship to Unity? Note that the court seems to equate hardship with "impossibility"—but these are actually separate standards.

e. Other Remedies

Damages: The non-breaching party can obtain damages, usually calculated as the difference between the contract price and the fair market value on the date of the breach. In determining whether to award "benefit of the bargain" damages, some courts consider whether the seller acted in good faith. *See BGW Development Corp. v. Mt. Kisco Lodge No. 1552*, 669 N.Y.S.2d 56 (App. Div. 1998). What happens if the fair market value at breach is the same as the contract price? Given the depressed market for condominium units in *Giannini*, is it likely that Giannini would be entitled to any damages?

Rescission: Alternatively, the innocent party may rescind the contract and receive restitution. Rescission restores the parties to their original positions. For example, the buyer who seeks restitution damages recovers her deposit.

C. Title Assurance

Suppose again that the Bakers enter into a contract to purchase the home from Stone for $300,000. Exactly what are they buying? Under our definition of "property," they are not purchasing the home itself. Rather, they are buying a bundle of legal rights—fee simple absolute in the home. The sale of real property is actually a *sale of title*. After all, if Stone has no title, then the Bakers will pay $300,000 for nothing.

What title risks should buyers like the Bakers be concerned about? Of course, they want to ensure that Stone is legally able to convey the promised estate, fee simple absolute. But even if Stone holds this estate, his title may be burdened with *encumbrances*—rights or interests held by third parties that affect the value or use of the land—as you saw in *Lohmeyer v. Bower*. For example, the title might be subject to an easement, a lease, and two mortgages. Accordingly, the Bakers will want to ensure that Stone can convey title without significant encumbrances.

Three methods of title assurance are widely used in the United States:

- *Title covenants*: the grantor promises in the deed that he has good title to convey.

- *Title opinion based on search of public records*: an attorney or other professional renders an opinion about the state of title after searching the public land records.

- *Title insurance*: a title insurance company issues a policy that insures the grantee's title.

None of these methods provides complete protection. Accordingly, the prudent buyer will normally use two methods—for example, title covenants plus a title insurance policy.

We examine all three methods in this chapter. As you read these materials, evaluate the strengths and weaknesses of each approach. Are more effective forms of title protection needed? Or does the present system strike the right balance between protecting the buyer against loss and respecting the seller's right to transfer?

---

1. Title Covenants

After the closing occurs on the Stone-Baker contract, the Bakers learn that the house is encumbered by an easement. Do the Bakers have any claim against Stone? A deed usually contains *title covenants*—express promises by the grantor about the state of title. Here, the Bakers' rights will depend on (a) the type of deed they received and (b) the scope of any promises that Stone made in that deed.

At common law, the promises that the parties made in the contract ended at the closing *unless* they were restated in the deed. The *doctrine of merger* provided that once the grantee accepted the deed all prior promises were extinguished; the contract was "merged" into the deed. Accordingly, grantees began to demand that grantors provide assurances of title in the deed.

Three types of deeds are commonly used today. They differ according to the amount of protection that each provides:

> - *General warranty deed*: the grantor warrants title against all defects, whether they arose *before or after* he obtained title.
> - *Special warranty deed*: the grantor warrants title against all defects that arose *after* he obtained title.
> - *Quitclaim deed*: the grantor makes no warranties about title, so the grantee receives only what the grantor has, if anything.

The general warranty deed offers the best protection, because the grantor promises that title is free from all defects at the closing, regardless of when they were created. In contrast, the special warranty deed limits the grantor's assurances only to any title defects that arose during his ownership; they do not cover any problems created before he obtained title. Of course, the quitclaim deed provides no assurances at all.

For example, in the Stone-Baker hypothetical above, suppose that Stone obtained title from Paulson; during the period that Paulson owned the land, she granted an easement to her neighbor Norris. If the Bakers have a general warranty deed, Stone is liable for this encumbrance. But if the Bakers have a special warranty deed, Stone is not liable because the easement arose before he obtained title. And if the Bakers merely have a quitclaim deed, Stone is not liable for any title defects.

The general warranty deed and special warranty deed both contain specific title covenants. There are six standard covenants:

- *Covenant of seisin*: a promise that the grantor owns the estate he purports to convey; for example, this covenant is breached if the grantor purports to convey a fee simple but only owns a life estate. (*Seisin* is pronounced like "season.")
- *Covenant of right to convey*: a promise that the grantor has the right to convey title; for example, this covenant is breached if the grantor is a trustee who lacks the authority to transfer title to the trust property.
- *Covenant against encumbrances*: a promise that there are no encumbrances on the title, other than those expressly listed in the deed; for example, this covenant is breached if there is a prior mortgage on the property.
- *Covenant of warranty*: a promise that the grantor will defend the grantee against any claim of superior title; for example, if a third party holds better title than the grantee does, the grantor must defend the grantee's title.
- *Covenant of quiet enjoyment*: a promise that the grantee's possession of the property will not be disturbed by anyone holding superior title; for example, this covenant is breached if the grantee is evicted because of a defect in her title.
- *Covenant of further assurances*: a promise that the grantor will take all future steps reasonably necessary to cure title defects that existed at closing.

The first three covenants (seisin, right to convey, and against encumbrances) are called *present covenants*. They are breached, if at all, at the moment the deed is delivered. At that instant the grantor either has the estate he claims to convey or he does not. Taken together, these three covenants provide much the same assurance as the implied covenant of marketable title. So what is the difference between these concepts? The marketable title doctrine applies to defects discovered *before* the closing, while title covenants protect against defects discovered *after* the closing.

See It

Click here to view examples of the general warranty deed, special warranty deed, and quitclaim deed.

The last three covenants (warranty, quiet enjoyment, and further assurances) are known as *future covenants*. They are breached, if at all, after the closing—most commonly when the grantee is actually or constructively evicted by a third party holding superior title.

Here is a sample general warranty deed in the hypothetical state of Madison:

> **GENERAL WARRANTY DEED**
>
> Adam Z. Stone ("Grantor"), in consideration of $300,000 and other valuable consideration, hereby grants to Wendy A. Baker and Henry O. Baker ("Grantees"), as joint tenants with right of survivorship, the real property located in Larchmont, Plata County, Madison, described as "Lot 6, as shown on the subdivision map of Larchmont Estates, recorded in Map Book 47, Page 118, Plata County Records, on June 23, 1983" ("Property").
>
> Grantor, for himself and his heirs, successors, and assigns, hereby covenants with Grantees, and their heirs, successors, and assigns, that: (1) Grantor is lawfully seized in fee simple absolute of the Property; (2) Grantor has the right to convey the same; (3) the estate is free from all encumbrances; (4) Grantor warrants and will defend the title to the Property against the lawful claims of all persons; (5) Grantor will guarantee the quiet enjoyment of the Property against the lawful claims of all persons; and (6) Grantor will do any acts reasonably necessary for the further assurance of the title to the Property.
>
> *Adam Z. Stone*   January 1, 2024
> Adam Z. Stone
>
> [Acknowledgment by notary public]

Suppose instead that your client Adam Stone wanted to use a special warranty deed in the transaction. What changes would be needed? What changes would be needed if he wanted to use a quitclaim deed?

Suppose that the Stone home is located on a ten-acre parcel. The Stone-Baker transaction closes, and the Bakers later learn that they hold title to only eight of those acres; the other two acres are owned by a neighbor, Norris. Is Stone liable under any title covenants?

Our next case involves a similar situation: grantees who received only 1/3 of the mineral rights they expected to acquire. As you read the decision, consider why none of the title covenants provided any relief.

Brown v. Lober

Supreme Court of Illinois

389 N.E.2d 1188 (1979)

UNDERWOOD, JUSTICE.

Plaintiffs instituted this action in the Montgomery County circuit court based on an alleged breach of the covenant of seisin in their warranty deed. The trial court held that although there had been a breach of the covenant of seisin, the suit was barred by the 10-year statute of limitations in section 16 of the Limitations Act (Ill. Rev. Stat. 1975, ch. 38, par. 17.) Plaintiffs' post-trial motion, which was based on an alleged breach of the covenant of quiet enjoyment, was also denied. A divided Fifth District Appellate Court reversed and remanded. (63 Ill.App.3d 727, 20 Ill.Dec. 286, 379 N.E.2d 1354.) We allowed the defendant's petition for leave to appeal.

> **See It**
>
> Click here to see a contemporary photograph of the land involved in *Brown*.

... Plaintiffs purchased 80 acres of Montgomery County real estate from William and Faith Bost and received a statutory warranty deed (Ill. Rev. Stat. 1957, ch. 30, par. 8), containing no exceptions, dated December 21, 1957. Subsequently, plaintiffs took possession of the land and recorded their deed.

On May 8, 1974, plaintiffs granted a coal option to Consolidated Coal Company (Consolidated) for the coal rights on the 80-acre tract for the sum of $6,000. Approximately two years later, however, plaintiffs "discovered" that they, in fact, owned only a one-third interest in the subsurface coal rights. It is a matter of public record that, in 1947, a prior grantor had reserved a two-thirds interest in the mineral rights on the property. Although plaintiffs had their abstract of title examined in 1958 and 1968 for loan purposes, they contend that until May 4, 1976, they believed that they were the sole owners of the surface and subsurface rights on the 80-acre tract. Upon discovering that a prior grantor had reserved a two-thirds interest in the coal rights, plaintiffs and Consolidated renegotiated their agreement to provide for payment of $2,000 in exchange for a one-third interest

> **FYI**
>
> The "statutory warranty deed" that the Browns received was a general warranty deed.

in the subsurface coal rights. On May 25, 1976, plaintiffs filed this action against the executor of the estate of Faith Bost, seeking damages in the amount of $4,000. . . .

Subsection 1 [of the warranty deed] contains the covenant of seisin and the covenant of good right to convey. These covenants, which are considered synonymous . . . assure the grantee that the grantor is, at the time of the conveyance, lawfully seized and has the power to convey an estate of the quality and quantity which he professes to convey. . . .

Subsection 3 sets forth the covenant of quiet enjoyment, which is synonymous with the covenant of warranty in Illinois. . . . By this covenant, "the grantor warrants to the grantee, his heirs and assigns, the possession of the premises and that he will defend the title granted by the terms of the deed against persons who may lawfully claim the same, and that such covenant shall be obligatory upon the grantor, his heirs, personal representatives, and assigns." *Biwer v. Martin* (1920), 294 Ill. 488, 497, 128 N.E. 518, 522.

Plaintiffs' complaint is premised upon the fact that "William Roy Bost and Faith Bost covenanted that they were the owners in fee simple of the above described property at the time of the conveyance to the plaintiffs." While the complaint could be more explicit, it appears that plaintiffs were alleging a cause of action for breach of the covenant of seisin. This court has stated repeatedly that the covenant of seisin is a covenant *in praesenti* and, therefore, if broken at all, is broken at the time of delivery of the deed. *Tone v. Wilson* (1876), 81 Ill. 529.

Since the deed was delivered to the plaintiffs on December 21, 1957, any cause of action for breach of the covenant of seisin would have accrued on that date. The trial court held that this cause of action was barred by the statute of limitations. No question is raised as to the applicability of the 10-year statute of limitations. We conclude, therefore, that the cause of action for breach of the covenant of seisin was properly determined by the trial court to be barred by the statute of limitations since plaintiffs did not file their complaint until May 25, 1976, nearly 20 years after their alleged cause of action accrued.

> **Food for Thought**
>
> Why didn't the Browns claim that they owned the 2/3 interest in the mineral rights as adverse possessors? Recall the discussion of adverse possession in Chapter 2. What elements are missing?

In their post-trial motion, plaintiffs set forth as an additional theory of recovery an alleged breach of the covenant of quiet enjoyment. The trial court, without explanation, denied the motion. The appellate court reversed, holding that the cause of action on the covenant of quiet enjoyment was not barred by the statute of limitations. The appellate court theorized that plaintiffs' cause of action did not accrue until 1976, when plaintiffs discovered that they only had a one-third interest in the subsurface coal rights and renegotiated their contract with the coal company for one-third of the previous contract price. The primary issue before us, therefore, is when, if at all, the plaintiffs' cause of action for breach of the covenant of quiet enjoyment is deemed to have accrued.

This court has stated on numerous occasions that, in contrast to the covenant of seisin, the covenant of warranty or quiet enjoyment is prospective in nature and is breached only when there is an actual or constructive eviction of the covenantee by the paramount titleholder. . . .

The question is whether plaintiffs have alleged facts sufficient to constitute a constructive eviction. They argue that if a covenantee fails in his effort to sell an interest in land because he discovers that he does not own what his warranty deed purported to convey, he has suffered a constructive eviction and is thereby entitled to bring an action against his grantor for breach of the covenant of quiet enjoyment. We think that the decision of this court in *Scott v. Kirkendall* (1878), 88 Ill. 465, is controlling on this issue and compels us to reject plaintiffs' argument.

In *Scott*, an action was brought for breach of the covenant of warranty by a grantee who discovered that other parties had paramount title to the land in question. The land was vacant and unoccupied at all relevant times. This court, in rejecting the grantee's claim that there was a breach of the covenant of quiet enjoyment, quoted the earlier decision in *Moore v. Vail* (1855), 17 Ill. 185, 191:

> Until that time, (the taking possession by the owner of the paramount title,) he might peaceably have entered upon and enjoyed the premises, without resistance or molestation, which was all his grantors covenanted he should do. They did not guarantee to him a perfect title, but the possession and enjoyment of the premises. 88 Ill. 465, 468.

Relying on this language in *Moore*, the *Scott* court concluded:

> We do not see but what this fully decides the present case against the appellant. It holds that the mere existence of a paramount title does not constitute a breach of the covenant. That is all there is here. There has been no assertion of the adverse title. The land has always been vacant. Appellant could at any time have taken peaceable possession of it. He has in no way been prevented or hindered from the enjoyment of the possession by any one having a better right. It was but the possession and enjoyment of the premises which was assured to him, and there has been no disturbance or interference in that respect. True, there is a superior title in another, but appellant has never felt "its pressure upon him." 88 Ill. 465, 468–69.

Admittedly, *Scott* dealt with surface rights while the case before us concerns subsurface mineral rights. We are, nevertheless, convinced that the reasoning employed in *Scott* is applicable to the present case. While plaintiffs went into possession of the surface area, they cannot be said to have possessed the subsurface minerals. "Possession of the surface does not carry possession of the minerals. . . . To possess the mineral estate, one must undertake the actual removal thereof from the ground or do such other act as will apprise the community that such interest is in the exclusive use and enjoyment of the claiming party." *Failoni v. Chicago & North Western Ry. Co.* (1964), 30 Ill.2d 258, 262, 195 N.E.2d 619, 622.

Since no one has, as yet, undertaken to remove the coal or otherwise manifested a clear intent to exclusively "possess" the mineral estate, it must be concluded that the subsurface estate is "vacant." As in *Scott*, plaintiffs "could at any time have taken peaceable possession of it. [They have] in no way been prevented or hindered from the enjoyment of the possession by any one having a better right." Accordingly, until such time as one holding paramount title interferes with plaintiffs' right of possession (*e.g.*, by beginning to mine the coal), there can be no constructive eviction and, therefore, no breach of the covenant of quiet enjoyment. . . .

As this court stated in *Scott v. Kirkendall* (1878), 88 Ill. 465, 469:

> **What's That?**
>
> A *mineral estate* is the right to search for, develop, and remove minerals from the land. Most commonly, such minerals are located underneath the land surface. In this context, minerals include coal, gold, iron, natural gas, oil, and other chemical substances with commercial value. Ownership of the surface estate and the mineral estate can be separate, as in *Brown v. Lober*.

> To sustain the present action would be to confound all distinction between the covenant of warranty and that of seizin, or of right to convey. They are not equivalent covenants. An action will lie upon the latter, though there be no disturbance of possession. A defect of title will suffice. Not so with the covenant of warranty, or for quiet enjoyment, as has always been held by the prevailing authority.

The covenant of seisin, unquestionably, was breached when the Bosts delivered the deed to plaintiffs, and plaintiffs then had a cause of action. However, despite the fact that it was a matter of public record that there was a reservation of a two-thirds interest in the mineral rights in the earlier deed, plaintiffs failed to bring an action for breach of the covenant of seisin within the 10-year period following delivery of the deed. The likely explanation is that plaintiffs had not secured a title opinion at the time they purchased the property, and the subsequent examiners for the lenders were not concerned with the mineral rights. Plaintiffs' oversight, however, does not justify us in overruling earlier decisions in order to recognize an otherwise premature cause of action. The mere fact that plaintiffs' original contract with Consolidated had to be modified due to their discovery that paramount title to two-thirds of the subsurface minerals belonged to another is not sufficient to constitute the constructive eviction necessary to a breach of the covenant of quiet enjoyment. . . .

Accordingly, the judgment of the appellate court is reversed, and the judgment of the circuit court of Montgomery County is affirmed.

Points for Discussion

a. **Breaching a Present Covenant**

How was the covenant of seisin breached in *Brown*? And why wasn't Bost's estate liable for the breach? Remember that a present covenant is breached when the deed is delivered, so the statute of limitations begins running at that time. The measure of damages for breach of a title covenant is normally determined by the purchase price paid by the grantee plus interest. However, the standard for breach of the covenant against encumbrances is the lesser of (1) the amount necessary to remove the encumbrance or (2) the amount by which it reduces property value.

When is the violation of a statute, ordinance, or other public restriction an "encumbrance"? In *Galvan v. Poon*, 2023 WL 4496998 (Mich.), the Michigan Supreme Court held that a building code violation—which was not subject to any enforcement action when the deed was delivered—was not an encumbrance. It explained that "an encumbrance has traditionally related to rights to or interests in the land itself rather than the condition of the property." *Id.* at *4. The court distinguished cases holding that zoning code violations are encumbrances, explaining that those violations are more easily discoverable and pose the same problems as traditional encumbrances. Does this draw a sufficiently clear line between what is and what is not an encumbrance?

b. Breaching a Future Covenant

The *Brown* court recognized that the Browns received only 1/3 of the promised mineral rights. Why wasn't Bost's estate liable for breaching the covenant of quiet enjoyment? A future covenant is breached when the grantee is actually or constructively evicted by someone holding superior title. Why wasn't Consolidated Coal's demand that the Browns modify the contract enough interference to constitute constructive eviction?

c. Discovering Title Defects

The Browns failed to have a title search conducted before they purchased the land. As the court acknowledged, the reservation of 2/3 of the mineral rights was a matter of public record—which would have been discovered by a standard title search. Should the Browns' failure to search for title defects insulate the sellers from liability for breach of title covenants? No! Even if a defect could have been found by a search, this does not defeat a title covenant claim.

d. Advise the Browns

Assume that *Brown* has just been decided, and you are an attorney in private practice in Illinois. Unhappy with their prior attorney, the Browns come to you for advice about their rights. Their goal is to recover damages from Bost's estate for breach of the covenant of quiet enjoyment. What would you advise them to do? What ethical concerns might arise?

e. Rights of Remote Grantees

Do title covenants "run" to remote grantees? Suppose that P conveys Greenacre to S by a general warranty deed. S then conveys Greenacre to B by a special warranty deed. Months later, B discovers that P never had title to the land; it is actually owned by X. Because S gave B a special warranty deed, B cannot successfully sue S; the defect arose before S received title. But can B sue P for breach of the covenants in the P-S deed?

Traditionally, only future covenants ran with the land to remote grantees. Because a present covenant was breached when made, if at all, the breach created a *cause of action*—which could not be assigned at common law. Today, a cause of action is usually transferable. But the law in many states still provides that present covenants do not run to remote grantees. For an example of a contrary view, see *Rockafellor v. Gray*, 191 N.W. 107 (Iowa 1922).

f. Selecting the Deed

Which type of deed would a seller prefer? What about a buyer? Custom and market conditions usually dictate the type of deed that is used. In many states, the custom is for the seller to provide a special warranty deed; the buyer usually obtains additional protection by buying title insurance.

Today title covenants are less important than in the past. When they first arose, the public land record system was in its infancy, so the buyer needed to rely on the seller's guarantees. The modern buyer places more emphasis on a search of the public records to determine the state of title, as reflected in a title opinion or (indirectly) in a title insurance policy.

g. Statutory Deeds

Statutes in many states set forth approved types of short form deeds, which simplify the drafting process. For example, in Maine every short form warranty deed is *deemed* to include the covenants of seisin, right to convey, against encumbrances, warranty, and quiet enjoyment, even though they are not expressly set forth in the form.

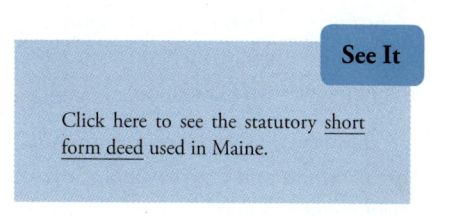

> **See It**
>
> Click here to see the statutory short form deed used in Maine.

h. Estoppel by Deed

Suppose A purports to convey title to Greenacre to B, using a warranty deed. But A does not hold title to the land. If A later acquires title, it automatically passes to B under the doctrine of *estoppel by deed*.

i. Aftermath of *Brown*

Today the property involved in *Brown* is fertile farm land, growing wheat and other seasonal crops. Despite Consolidated Coal's efforts to secure the coal rights, coal has never been discovered on the property. For more information about the decision, see Peter Salsich, *A Short Course in Land Transactions: Protecting Title to Land*—Brown v. Lober, in Property Stories 221 (Gerald Korngold & Andrew P. Morriss eds., 2d ed. 2009).

2. Title Opinion Based on Search of Public Records

The second method of title assurance is a *title opinion* based on a search of public land records. In our Stone-Baker transaction, it is possible that the Bakers might search the record themselves. But it is more likely that they will retain an attorney or other professional to conduct the search and give them a written opinion on the state of title. Suppose the Bakers retain an attorney for this purpose. The attorney will inspect the land records to determine (a) if Stone holds a fee simple absolute in the house and (b) if so, whether his title is subject to any encumbrances or other defects.

a. The Recording System

In early England, there was no system of public land records. Title to land was transferred through the ceremony of feoffment with livery of seisin, without using a deed. Transactions were usually between neighbors; most people were illiterate; and land seldom changed hands—so public records were unnecessary.

What happened when title disputes arose? Suppose K transferred Castleacre to L, and one day later transferred the same land to M. If two parties had competing claims to the same property during this era, the person who received his interest *first* prevailed. The common law reasoned that a grantor could only convey title once. Under this mindset, a later conveyance was ineffective because the grantor had nothing left to transfer. Thus, in the above hypothetical, L owned Castleacre because he was first in time.

> **It's Latin to Me**
>
> This legal rule was summed up in the Latin phrase "*Nemo dat quod non habet*"—No one can give what he does not have.

However, as social and economic conditions changed, conveyances became more common and less personal. Buyers increasingly demanded certainty that they would receive good title. To meet these concerns, a public system of land records was developed in the United States. Anyone holding an estate or interest in land may record a deed or other instrument to give notice of his rights to the world. In essence, the system is a "library" of documents that an attorney or buyer can inspect to determine whether anyone other than the seller claims any interest in the land.

In our modern Stone-Baker transaction, assume that the attorney inspects the land records. She discovers a recorded deed by which Stone conveyed a fee simple absolute to Dorn one week ago. She will inform the Bakers that Stone does not hold title to the property, and the Bakers will not complete the purchase.

What if the Bakers never retain anyone to search the land records and simply complete the purchase? They are charged with notice of the recorded Stone-Dorn deed because it would have been found in a title search. Accordingly, as between the Bakers and Dorn, Dorn owns the house.

But what if the Stone-Dorn deed was never recorded? The attorney's inspection of the land records will not reveal any adverse title claims, so she will advise the Bakers that Stone has good title. Suppose that the Bakers complete the purchase and record their deed from Stone. One year later, Dorn visits the property, produces his unrecorded deed, and demands that the Bakers leave. Who owns the house? As between the Bakers and Dorn, the Bakers own the house. Dorn's interest was created first, so he would have prevailed in early England. But the modern recording statutes give special protection to a *subsequent bona fide purchaser* who acquires title without notice of an adverse claim and pays valuable consideration.

b. How to Search Title

In order to determine the state of title, the searcher must (1) *locate* the recorded documents that affect title to the parcel and then (2) *evaluate* their legal significance.

In the United States, land records are typically filed at a county agency, often called the "recorder's office." State law determines both the types of documents that can be recorded and how they are organized. For example, a recorded deed might be inserted into a volume filled with other deeds, which is stored on shelves containing hundreds of similar volumes. Or a photograph of the deed might be placed on microfiche or microfilm, along with thousands of others. Or the deed might exist only in electronic form. Accordingly, a single recorder's office might contain millions of documents.

> **Make the Connection**
>
> A title searcher who fails to carefully examine the chain of title may be liable for negligence. Expert testimony is often needed to determine whether the searcher acted as a reasonable member of the profession would under similar circumstances. For example, if a title searcher fails to follow the grantor-grantee index back as needed, he may be found liable. *Southwind Exploration, LLC v. Street Abstract Co.*, 209 P.3d 728 (Kan. Ct. App. 2009).

How can a title searcher locate the relevant documents? Every state has a method for indexing deeds, mortgages, and other documents that affect title. The recorder's office will use one of two systems: (1) the *grantor-grantee index*, which is organized by the names of the parties to the transaction; or (2) the *tract index*, which is organized by the parcel involved.

Grantor-Grantee Index. The most commonly used method is the grantor-grantee index. Under this system, every recorded document is indexed in two places: the grantee index and the grantor index. In the grantee index, each entry is organized alphabetically by the grantee's last name; the grantor index is organized by the grantor's last name. Along with the parties' names, an index entry will contain the type of instrument, the time of recordation, the location of the recorded document (for example, a volume and page number), and a brief description of the property involved. Here is a simplified entry:

Grantee	Grantor	Instrument	Recorded	Book & Page	Description
Chen, Eric	Perez, Alex	Deed	9:05 a.m., 12/5/1997	515–378	Lot 7 on map filed in B. 499, P. 116

The first step in the process is to establish a *chain of title* for the parcel. As you will recall from Chapter 1, a chain of title is the history of ownership backward through time. It is built link by link, starting from a known grantee (the current owner) and tracing ownership back deed by deed in the grantee index until the searcher reaches the point where the land was owned by a sovereign such as the federal government. Alternatively, the local custom may be to perform a less intensive search, e.g., back for only 40 years.

In the typical home purchase, the buyer's seller is the first link in the chain. To find the seller's grantor, a searcher looks up the seller's name in the grantee index and finds the name of the person he purchased from, where that deed can be found, and when it was recorded. The searcher then repeats the process, deed by deed, with each grantee's name until he reaches a sovereign or other ending point.

> **FYI**
>
> A rural Georgia lawyer once remarked: "Son, I never began searching a title unless I was starving to death, and I never finished one without wishing I had." C. Dent Bostick, *Land Title Registration: An English Solution to an American Problem*, 63 Ind. L J. 55, 62 (1988).

At this point, the searcher moves over to the grantor index. Beginning with the first grantor in the chain, the searcher moves forward in time, looking under each grantor's name, deed by deed, to see if he conveyed an interest to anyone who is not in the known chain of title. Typically, the searcher examines all entries in the grantor index under each grantor's name from (1) *the date he received his interest* until (2) *the date the deed conveying his interest to a grantee was recorded*.

In this manner, the searcher can locate all the recorded documents that affect title. He will then read these documents, evaluate their legal significance, and determine the state of title.

Tract Index. In a jurisdiction with a tract index, the search process is simple. Each parcel of land is assigned a unique identifier, sometimes called a *parcel identification number*. Every document affecting that parcel is typically filed in a folder under its unique number. A title searcher can simply examine the documents in the folder to assess the state of title.

c. Operation of the Recording System

You should now understand the basic operation of the recording system. Deeds, mortgages, and other documents affecting land title are filed in the public records where they can be located and evaluated. A title searcher can review these records to determine if the seller is able to convey good title. Note that some title problems—such as adverse possession—may not be found in the public records, so additional investigation is required to guard against these risks, as discussed later in this chapter.

The recording system also protects the current owner from losing title to a later buyer. If the Bakers purchase the home from Stone, they will immediately record their deed. Suppose Stone attempts to sell the home again. Anyone who searches the records will find the Stone-Baker deed and thus cannot qualify for protection as a bona fide purchaser.

In practice, the traditional recording system using the grantor-grantee index is complex and cumbersome. As our next case illustrates, *even if a document is recorded it may not give constructive notice* to a searcher.

Luthi v. Evans

Supreme Court of Kansas

576 P.2d 1064 (1978)

PRAGER, JUSTICE.

. . . On February 1, 1971, Grace V. Owens was the owner of interests in a number of oil and gas leases located in Coffey County. On that date Owens, by a written instrument designated "Assignment of Interest in Oil and Gas Leases," assigned to defendant International Tours, Inc. (hereinafter Tours) all of such oil and gas interests. This assignment provided as follows:

> **See It**
>
> Click here to see (a) a photograph of the land involved in *Luthi* and (b) a map of the leases that Owens assigned to International Tours.

ASSIGNMENT OF INTEREST IN OIL AND GAS LEASES
KNOW ALL MEN BY THESE PRESENTS:

That the undersigned Grace Vannocker Owens, . . . Connie Sue Vannocker, . . . Larry R. Vannocker, . . . individually and also doing business as Glacier Petroleum Company and Vannocker Oil Company, hereinafter called Assignors, for and in consideration of $100.00 and other valuable consideration, the receipt whereof is hereby acknowledged, do hereby sell, assign, transfer and set over unto International Tours, Inc., a Delaware Corporation, hereinafter called Assignee, all their right, title, and interest (which includes all overriding royalty interest and working interest) in and to the following Oil and Gas Leases located in Coffey County, Kansas, more particularly specified as follows, to-wit: [lease descriptions and recording data on 7 oil and gas leases not involved in the case are stated here] together with the rights incident thereto and the personal property thereon, appurtenant thereto or used or obtained in connection therewith.

And for the same consideration the *Assignors . . . intend to convey, and by this instrument convey, to the Assignee all interest of whatsoever nature in all working interests and overriding royalty interest in all Oil and Gas Leases in Coffey County, Kansas, owned by them whether or not the same are specifically enumerated above with all oil field and oil and gas lease equipment owned by them in said County whether or not located on the leases above described*, or elsewhere in storage in said County, but title is warranted only to the specific interests above specified, and assignors retain their title to all minerals in place and the corresponding royalty (commonly referred to as land owners royalty) attributable thereto.

The effective date of this Assignment is February 1, 1971, at 7:00 o'clock a.m.

/s/ Grace Vannocker Owens

Connie Sue Vannocker

Larry R. Vannocker

(Acknowledgment by Grace Vannocker Owens before notary public with seal impressed thereon dated Feb. 5, 1971, appears here.) (Emphasis supplied.)

This assignment was filed for record in the office of the register of deeds of Coffey County on February 16, 1971.

It is important to note that in the first paragraph of the assignment, seven oil and gas leases were specifically described. Those leases are not involved on this appeal. In addition to the seven leases specifically described in the first paragraph, Owens was also the owner of a working interest in an oil and gas lease known as the Kufahl lease which was located on land in Coffey County. The Kufahl lease was not one of the leases specifically described in the assignment. . . .

See It

Click here to view the assignment signed by Owens.

On January 30, 1975, the same Grace V. Owens executed and delivered a second assignment of her working interest in the Kufahl lease to the defendant, J. R. Burris. Prior to the date of that assignment, Burris personally checked the records in the office of the register of deeds and, following the date of the assignment to him, Burris secured an abstract [of] title to the real estate in question. Neither his personal inspection nor the abstract of title reflected the prior assignment to Tours.

> **What's That?**
>
> An *abstract of title* is a summary of all conveyances and encumbrances of public record that affect title to a parcel. In a number of jurisdictions, it is prepared by an attorney and often used as the basis for issuing a policy of title insurance.

The controversy on this appeal is between Tours and Burris over ownership of what had previously been Owens's interest in the Kufahl lease. It is the position of Tours that the assignment dated February 1, 1971, effectively conveyed from Owens to Tours, Owens's working interest in the Kufahl lease by virtue of the general description contained in paragraph two of that assignment. Tours then contends that the recording of that assignment in the office of the register of deeds of Coffey County gave constructive notice of such conveyance to subsequent purchasers, including Burris. Hence, Tours reasons, it is the owner of Owens's working interest in the Kufahl lease.

Burris admits that the general description and language used in the second paragraph of Owens's assignment to Tours was sufficient to effect a valid transfer of the Owens interest in the Kufahl lease to Tours *as between the parties to that instrument*. Burris contends, however, that the general language contained in the second paragraph of the assignment to Tours, as recorded, which failed to state with specificity the names of the lessor and lessee, the date of the lease, any legal description, and the recording data, was not sufficient to give constructive notice to a subsequent innocent purchaser for value without actual notice of the prior assignment. Burris argues that as a result of those omissions in the assignment to Tours, it was impossible for the register of deeds of Coffey County to identify the real estate involved and to make the proper entries in the numerical index. Accordingly, even though he checked the records at the courthouse, Burris was unaware of the assignment of the Kufahl lease to Tours and he did not learn of the prior conveyance until after he had purchased the rights from Grace V. Owens. The abstract of title also failed to reflect the prior assignment to Tours. Burris maintains that as a result of the omissions and the inadequate description of the interest in real estate to be assigned under the second paragraph of the assignment to Tours, the Tours assignment, as recorded, was not sufficient to give constructive notice to a subsequent innocent purchaser for value. It is upon this point that Burris prevailed before the district court. On appeal, the Court of Appeals held the general description contained in the assignment to Tours to be sufficient, when recorded, to give constructive notice to a subsequent purchaser for value, including Burris.

At the outset, it should be noted that a deed or other instrument in writing which is intended to convey an interest in real estate and which describes the property to be conveyed as "all of the grantor's property in a certain county," is commonly referred to as a "Mother Hubbard" instrument. The language used in the second paragraph of the assignment from Owens to Tours in which the assignor conveyed to the assignee "all interest of whatsoever nature in all working interests . . . in all Oil and Gas Leases in Coffey County, Kansas," is an example of a "Mother Hubbard" clause. . . . The so-called "Mother Hubbard" clauses . . . are seldom used in this state, but in the past have been found to be convenient for death bed transfers and in situations where time is of the essence and specific information concerning the legal description of the property to be conveyed is not available. . . .

> **FYI**
>
> In a *Mother Hubbard clause*, property interests are conveyed in general terms (typically "all interests within the county"), rather than each interest being separately described. Just as Mother Hubbard in the old nursery rhyme had nothing more to give her dog, a Mother Hubbard clause leaves the grantor with no remaining property interest to convey.

The parties in this case agree, and the Court of Appeals held, that the second paragraph of the assignment from Owens to Tours, providing that the assignors convey to the assignee all interests in all oil and gas leases in Coffey County, Kansas, owned by them, constituted a valid transfer of the Owens interest in the Kufahl lease to Tours *as between the parties to that instrument*. We agree. We also agree with the parties and the Court of Appeals that a single instrument, properly executed, acknowledged, and delivered, may convey separate tracts by specific description and by general description capable of being made specific, where the clear intent of the language used is to do so. We agree that a subsequent purchaser, who has *actual* notice or knowledge of such an instrument, is bound thereby and takes subject to the rights of the assignee or grantor.

This case involves a legal question which is one of first impression in this court. As noted above, the issue presented is whether or not the recording of an instrument of conveyance which uses a "Mother Hubbard" clause to describe the property conveyed, constitutes *constructive notice to a subsequent purchaser*. The determination of this issue requires us to examine the pertinent Kansas statutes covering the conveyance of interests in land and the statutory provisions for recording the same. . . .

It is the position of Tours that . . . the assignment from Owens to Tours was properly executed and acknowledged as required by the statutes and constituted a valid transfer of the Owens interest in the Kufahl lease to Tours. This instrument, when filed for record in full compliance with the provisions of K.S.A. 58–2221, imparted constructive notice to all subsequent purchasers, including Burris, who are deemed to purchase with notice under K.S.A. 58–2222. This was the position taken by the Court of Appeals.

Burris maintains that our examination must extend beyond the statutes set forth above. It is his position that we must also consider the Kansas statutes which govern the custody and the recordation of instruments of conveyance, and the duties of the register of deeds in regard thereto, as contained at K.S.A. 19–1201 through K.S.A. 19–1219. We will discuss only those statutes which we deem pertinent in the present controversy. K.S.A. 19–1204 makes it the duty of the register of deeds in each county to take custody of and preserve all of the records in his office and to record all instruments authorized by law to be recorded. K.S.A. 19–1205 requires the register of deeds to keep a general index, direct and inverted, in his office. The register is required to record in the general index under the appropriate heading the names of grantors and grantees, the nature of the instrument, the volume and page where recorded, and, where appropriate, *a description of the tract.* . . .

At this point we should refer back to K.S.A. 58–2221. . . . That statute makes it the duty of the register of deeds in those counties where a numerical index is maintained to compare any instrument offered for recordation, before copying the same in the record, with the last record of transfer in his office of *the property described*; if the register of deeds finds that such instrument contains apparent errors, he shall not record the same until he shall have notified the grantee where such notice is reasonably possible. The second paragraph of K.S.A. 58–2221 requires either the grantor or grantee, upon recording the instrument in the office of the register of deeds, to furnish the register of deeds the full name and last known post-office address of the person to whom the property is conveyed. The register of deeds is required to forward the necessary information to the county clerk who shall make any necessary changes in address records for mailing tax statements. These two provisions in K.S.A. 58–2221 show a legislative intent that instruments of conveyance should describe the land conveyed with sufficient specificity to enable the register of deeds to determine the correctness of the description from the numerical index and also to make it possible to make any necessary changes in address records for mailing tax statements. . . .

It also seems obvious to us that the purpose of the statutes authorizing the recording of instruments of conveyance is to impart to a subsequent purchaser notice of instruments which affect the title to a *specific tract of land* in which the subsequent purchaser is interested at the time. From a reading of all of the statutory provisions together, we have concluded that the legislature intended that recorded instruments of conveyance, to impart constructive notice to a subsequent purchaser or mortgagee, should describe the land conveyed with sufficient specificity so that the specific land conveyed can be identified. . . .

Again, we wish to emphasize that an instrument which contains a "Mother Hubbard" clause, describing the property conveyed in the general language involved here, is valid, enforceable, and effectively transfers the entire property interest as between the parties to the instrument. Such a transfer is not effective as to subsequent purchasers and mortgagees unless they have *actual* knowledge of the transfer. If, because of emergency, it becomes necessary to use a "Mother Hubbard" clause in an instrument of conveyance, the grantee may take steps to protect his title against subsequent purchasers. He may take possession of the property. Also, as soon as a specific description can be obtained, the grantee may identify the specific property covered by the conveyance by filing an affidavit or other appropriate instrument or document with the register of deeds.

We also wish to make it clear that in situations where an instrument of conveyance containing a sufficient description of the property conveyed is duly recorded but not properly indexed, the fact that it was not properly indexed by the register of deeds will not prevent constructive notice. . . .

From what we have said above, it follows that the recording of the assignment from Owens to Tours, which did not describe with sufficient specificity the property covered by the conveyance, was not sufficient to impart constructive notice to a subsequent purchaser such as J. R. Burris in the present case. Since Burris had no *actual* knowledge of the prior assignment from Owens to Tours, the later assignment to Burris prevails over the assignment from Owens to Tours.

The judgment of the Court of Appeals is reversed and the judgment of the district court is affirmed.

Points for Discussion

a. **Role of Recordation**

An unrecorded deed is perfectly valid. However, recordation is important to protect the grantee from title claims made by third parties. If Tours' assignment was properly recorded, why didn't it provide notice to Burris? How could Burris contend both that (1) the assignment validly transferred the Kufahl lease from Owens to Tours and (2) Burris' later interest in the Kufahl lease had priority over Tours' prior interest?

b. **Advise Tours**

Do you think that Owens intended to assign the Kufahl lease to Tours? On the day the assignment was signed, did Tours believe that it covered the Kufahl lease? The *Luthi* court notes that the Mother Hubbard clause is used in unusual situations, such as death bed transfers where time is of the essence—not in ordinary commercial transactions. Suppose that you are an attorney representing Tours in the transaction, your client intends that the assignment cover the Kufahl lease, and the assignment must be finalized within five minutes; there is no time to obtain the property description for that lease. What would you advise Tours to do?

c. **Establishing Priority by Possession**

Once Tours received its assignment with the Mother Hubbard clause, how could it have protected its interest in the Kufahl lease? As the court noted, one option was for Tours to take possession of the leased property. Why would this have helped?

d. **What Did Burris See?**

At the time, the grantor-grantee index for Coffey County included a property description. When Burris reviewed the index, he would have seen the entry for the assignment from Owens to Tours, with this handwritten information under "Description of Property:" "Entire 7/8 W.I. in W^2NE^4 less 10a. 12-23-14 & 10a. E^2NE^4 12-23-14. NE^4; SW^4SE^4; SE^4SE^4 & N^2SE^4 in 14-23-14; E^1SE^4 in 1-23-14; N^2NW^4 & S^2NW^4 in 13–23." This describes the land affected by the seven leases specifically identified in the assignment, by reference to the government survey system—but it does not include the Kufahl property. For example, "12-23-14" refers to part of Section 12, Township 23, Range 14. The Kufahl lease was located in part of Section 11, Township 23, Range 13. Remember that a section is a square mile, so the Kufahl property was in a different square mile from the other parcels. Also note that there is no reference to the "Mother Hubbard" clause in the entry.

e. **Improper Indexing**

Towards the end of its opinion, the *Luthi* court stated that even if a deed or other document is incorrectly indexed or lost by the indexing clerk, it still provides constructive notice. Does this make sense? Which party is best situated to deal with such an error—the grantee of the improperly indexed deed or a later prospective buyer?

f. **How Far Back?**

A search often traces the chain of title back to the original patent from a sovereign. However, many states limit the length of the search to 30 or 40 years, hoping

> **FYI**
>
> In a famous exchange, a Louisiana attorney purportedly stated: "I am in receipt of your favor of the fifth inst. inquiring as to the state of the title of this property prior to the year 1803. Please be advised that in the year 1803 the United States of America acquired the territory of Louisiana from the Republic of France by purchase; the Republic of France had in turn acquired title from the Spanish Crown by conquest, the Spanish Crown having originally acquired title by virtue of the discoveries of one Christopher Columbus, a Genoese sailor, who had been duly authorized to embark upon his voyage of discovery by Isabella, Queen of Spain; Isabella, before granting such authority, had obtained the sanction of his Holiness, the Pope; the Pope is the Vicar on earth of Jesus Christ; Jesus Christ is the son and heir apparent of God; God made Louisiana."

to increase the efficiency of the process. Under these *marketable title acts*, title defects that exist before the statutorily-determined *root of title* are extinguished. For example, in North Carolina a person who holds record title to real property for 30 years or more "with nothing appearing of record . . . purporting to divest such claimant of the estate claimed . . . [has] marketable record title . . . free and clear of all rights, estates, interests, claims, or charges whatsoever, the existence of which depends upon any act, title transaction, event or omission that occurred prior to such 30-year period." N.C. Gen. Stat. § 47B–2(b), (c).

g.   Electronic Records

The computer era has ushered in new possibilities for storing and retrieving title information. Most states adopted the Uniform Real Property Electronic Recording Act, which authorizes local recorder's offices to record documents in electronic form, including deeds, mortgages, and other instruments. Today over half of these offices accept electronic documents, at least to some extent.

Scholars have promoted the advantages of moving to electronic records to simplify real estate transactions for many years. *See, e.g.,* Arthur R. Gaudio, *Electronic Real Estate Records: A Model for Action*, 24 W. New Eng. L. Rev. 271 (2002); *see also* Jessica Kopplin Kranz, Note, *Expedition E-Recording, First Stop URPERA: How Universal E-Recording Under URPERA Could Revolutionize Real Estate Recording in the United States and Why It Should*, 13 Minn. J.L. Sci. & Tech. 383 (2012).

In recent decades, some recorder's offices have created computerized indexes for *new* recordings. By entering the name of a grantor or grantee, the searcher can locate recordings relating to that person, regardless of their chronological sequence. In certain offices, it is also possible to search by property description, usually by street address or lot number.

Go Online

Click here to see a sample computerized index maintained by the Clerk of Travis County, Texas.

But few offices have developed such indexes for *past* recordings, because the cost is prohibitive. Accordingly, a title searcher must usually navigate through the traditional grantor-grantee index. Ironically, private companies that issue title insurance policies have used their own computerized title systems for decades.

h.   Aftermath of *Luthi*

Oil is still produced on the Kufahl property; between 1,700 and 2,100 barrels are extracted each year. Several members of the Luthi family hold oil leases on nearby parcels. Today the Kufahl property and most of the Luthi properties are operated by the Evans Oil Company.

d. The Recording Acts

Suppose Stone conveys the home to the Bakers for $300,000 on January 1, but they fail to record their deed. On February 1, a forgetful Stone conveys the home to Curtis, who pays $350,000; Curtis has no notice of the earlier Stone-Baker deed. The Bakers record their deed on March 1, and Curtis records his deed a few days later. Who owns the home?

In order to answer questions like this, all states begin with the common law principle of *first-in-time*. As a general rule, the person whose interest was created first prevails. But virtually all states recognize a major exception to this principle: the *bona fide purchaser* doctrine. The recording acts create special protection for the subsequent bona fide purchaser, which supersedes the first-in-time rule.

Why protect the bona fide purchaser? A vibrant property market demands that buyers have confidence they will receive good title. Accordingly, a primary goal of the recording system is to protect buyers from unknown adverse claims. In general, the diligent buyer who conducts a careful search of the public records and finds no title defects will be protected against existing unrecorded interests.

So who is a protected bona fide purchaser? Each state has a recording act which establishes the method for determining priority between adverse claimants. There are three basic types of acts:

- *Race*: the purchaser *who records first* has priority.
- *Notice*: the subsequent *bona fide purchaser* has priority.
- *Race-notice*: the subsequent *bona fide purchaser who records first* has priority.

Race jurisdictions: Under a race statute, a subsequent purchaser has priority over a previously created interest if she records first—even if she actually knows about that interest. Priority is given to the person who wins the "race" to the recorder's office. Most of the early recording acts in the United States were race statutes. However, the inherent unfairness of this method led most states to adopt the notice or race-notice approaches. Today only Delaware, Louisiana, and North Carolina still have race statutes that apply to all deeds and other instruments. A few states use race statutes only for mortgages and deeds of trust.

Notice jurisdictions: A notice statute provides that a subsequent purchaser for value prevails if he takes without notice of a prior interest. The purchaser does not have to record in order to gain priority. However, even in a notice jurisdiction the purchaser is motivated to record quickly. If he fails to do so, he may lose his interest to a subsequent bona fide purchaser. About half of the states use notice statutes.

Race-notice jurisdictions: A race-notice statute protects the subsequent purchaser for value who *both* takes without notice *and* records first. Roughly half of the states have race-notice statutes.

What are the advantages and disadvantages of each approach? *See* B. Taylor Mattis, *Recording Acts: Anachronistic Reliance,* 25 Real Prop. Prob. & Tr. J. 17 (1990). Remember that the first-in-time rule governs any title dispute unless the subsequent purchaser qualifies for protection under the state's recording act.

> **Take Note**
>
> Notice and race-notice statutes require that in order to gain the protection of the recording act the subsequent purchaser must take her interest without notice of an outstanding earlier interest. In this section, we focus on one type of notice: *record notice* (notice provided by a reasonable search of the public records). There are two other types of notice: *actual* and *inquiry*. We will examine these later in this chapter.

Let's return to the problem at the beginning of this section. Under each type of recording act, who prevails, the Bakers or Curtis? In a race jurisdiction, the Bakers win because they recorded first. In a notice jurisdiction, Curtis prevails. When Curtis received his deed, he had no notice of the Bakers' interest because their deed was not yet recorded. Finally, in a race-notice jurisdiction, the Bakers win. Although Curtis had no notice of the Bakers' interest, Curtis failed to record before the Bakers recorded.

When a grantee records her deed, a later grantee is deemed to have *record notice* of that deed—and thus cannot qualify for protection as a bona fide purchaser. But what constitutes an effective recording? In general, a deed or other document affecting title must be *acknowledged* in order to qualify for recordation. This means that the grantor must certify to a notary public that her signature on the document is genuine; the normal requirement is that the grantor must sign the document in the presence of the notary. The notary will affix a notary seal or stamp to the document to confirm the acknowledgment. A county official will then accept the document for recordation and add it to the public land records, where it can be found by anyone searching title. But what if the acknowledgment is invalid?

In our next case, Harold, the first grantee, argued that his sister Deborah, the second grantee, was not protected as a bona fide purchaser because his deed was recorded first—and thus she had record notice of his deed. But there was a hidden defect in the acknowledgment of Harold's deed—which a later grantee like Deborah could not have discovered from looking at the document. Does this mean that Deborah was a bona fide purchaser because Harold's deed was not properly "recorded"? As you read this decision, consider whether the court's reasoning advances the polices that underly the recording acts.

Allen v. Allen

Appeals Court of Massachusetts

16 N.E.3d 1078 (2014)

KATZMANN, J.

    This case concerns competing claims between adult siblings for the ownership of the house formerly owned by their now-deceased parents. Harold Allen, Jr. (Harold) traces his ownership to a July, 2001, deed (July deed) from the siblings' mother, Ethel Allen (Ethel). Harold's sister Deborah Allen (Deborah) claims ownership by virtue of a November, 2001, deed (November deed) from Ethel to the Allen Realty Trust (Trust), of which Deborah was a cotrustee along with Ethel.

    Deborah brought an action alleging that the July deed was forged and claiming that the property was rightfully hers.[2] Following a jury-waived trial, a judge of the Land Court determined that, because the acknowledgment of the July deed was defective, its recording did not give constructive notice to Deborah of the conveyance and the deed was not enforceable against her. This is an issue of first impression, not yet addressed by our appellate courts.

    . . . We summarize the relevant facts as found by the judge in his memorandum of decision and postjudgment order, supplemented as necessary with undisputed facts from the record. We reserve certain details for discussion with the specific issues raised.

    Deborah and Harold are two of the six children of Ethel and Harold Allen, Sr. (Harold, Sr.). Harold, Sr. and Ethel owned a house at 257 Marrett Road, in Lexington, and lived in that home for many years. Over the course of their marriage, Harold, Sr. and Ethel created numerous estate plans, which consistently excluded their two sons, Harold and Lawrence, because Harold, Sr., and Ethel had provided for them through lifetime gifts.[3] After Harold, Sr., died, Ethel continued this pattern.[4]

---

[2] The rights of other siblings, who, along with Deborah, are beneficiaries of the Trust, are also affected by the determination as to which deed is valid. Deborah's complaint does not purport to divest the other siblings of their interest in the property.

[3] In 1987, Harold, Sr., transferred a one-third ownership stake in the family home heating oil business, Sherwood Oil Co., Inc., to Harold and a one-third ownership stake in the business to Lawrence.

[4] Ethel's final will, executed on February 28, 2008, stated:

    "I have intentionally and not as the result of any accident or mistake, made no specific provision for my sons, LARRY ALLEN and HAROLD J. ALLEN, Jr., and their issue, not for lack of love or affection, but rather because my sons have been provided for by my late Husband and myself."

Allen family home
Click here for larger photo

The events at the center of this dispute occurred during 2001. In late April, 2001, Ethel began the process of moving from her Lexington home to live with one of her daughters, Nancy Oldro, in Nashua, New Hampshire. After evaluating conflicting testimony, the judge concluded that Ethel had fully moved in by mid-July, 2001.

Harold traces his claim to a deed Ethel executed on July 23, 2001, conveying the house to Harold and to Ethel as joint tenants with a right of survivorship. This deed is the subject of the present dispute. Attorney Paul Maloy prepared the deed and signed a certificate of acknowledgment, dated July 23, 2001, which reads: "Then personally appeared the above named Ethel M. Allen and acknowledged the foregoing instrument to be her free act and deed, before me, [/s] Paul F. Maloy—Notary Public." Maloy recorded the deed on August 10, 2001. . . .

On November 30, 2001, Ethel established the Allen Realty Trust and executed a deed conveying the Lexington property to herself and to Deborah as cotrustees of the Trust, reserving a life estate for herself. She specified that the property would be sold upon her death and the proceeds divided among several of her descendants, including Deborah.[5] This deed was recorded on February 8, 2002.

See It

Click here to see a diagram of the relationships among the Allen parties.

Only after Ethel died on December 20, 2009, did Harold reveal the July 23, 2001 deed. Neither Deborah nor her sister Nancy nor the attorney who prepared the November deed had discovered the July conveyance. In January, 2010, Deborah commenced the present action, disputing Harold's claim to the property. After a trial that included forensic testimony regarding the July deed, the judge found that Ethel's signature on the July deed was authentic. But he determined that, contrary to the certificate of acknowledgment on the deed, Ethel never appeared before Attorney

---

[5] Once again, she did not include Harold or Lawrence as a beneficiary.

Maloy to acknowledge the deed. The judge found that, instead, she had signed the deed in front of Harold, who then brought it to Maloy for his signature. Harold appeals from the judgment . . . .

"[O]rdinarily an acknowledgment is not an essential part of a deed; but if it is desired to record the deed in order to charge the world with notice of the conveyance, then it is necessary that the deed be acknowledged and that a certificate reciting this fact be attached to the deed. Doubtless, that is the principal function of a certificate of acknowledgment." *McOuatt v. McOuatt,* 69 N.E.2d 806, 809 (Mass. 1946) (*McOuatt*). See G.L. c. 183, § 4, as appearing in St. 1973, c. 205 ("A conveyance . . . shall not be valid as against any person, except the grantor or lessor, his heirs and devisees and persons having actual notice of it, unless it . . . is recorded in the registry of deeds for the county or district in which the land to which it relates lies"); *Gordon v. Gordon,* 398 N.E.2d 497, 499 (Mass. App. Ct. 1979) ("[T]itle to real estate may be transferred by a deed which has not been acknowledged, and such deed is good against the grantor and his heirs and those having actual notice").

> **FYI**
>
> Massachusetts is a *notice jurisdiction*, as shown by General Laws c. 183, § 4: a deed is not valid as against another person—except for (a) the grantor (and his heirs and devisees) and (b) persons with *actual notice*—unless it is recorded, which provides *record notice*.

The certificate of acknowledgment "furnishes formal proof of the authenticity of the execution of the instrument when presented for recording." *Id.*, citing *McOuatt,* 69 N.E.2d at 809. "The certificate of acknowledgment is of evidentiary character, and the taking of the acknowledgment has always been regarded in this Commonwealth as a ministerial and not as a judicial act and the recitals contained in the certificate may be contradicted." *McOuatt, supra* at 809.

In *McOuatt,* the Supreme Judicial Court held that where an acknowledgment had not actually occurred, a facially correct certificate of acknowledgment failed to satisfy the statutory requirement that in order for a deed conveying property between spouses to be valid, it must be acknowledged and recorded. Here, as in *McOuatt,* the deed included a facially correct certificate of acknowledgment, with the required signature and recitals, and was recorded. Also, as in *McOuatt,* the judge here concluded that the acknowledgment never actually occurred.

Notwithstanding the facially correct certificate of acknowledgment, because the July deed was never actually acknowledged, it was not entitled to be recorded. See G.L. c. 183, § 29 ("No deed shall be recorded unless a certificate of its acknowledgment or of the proof of its due execution, made as hereinafter provided, is endorsed upon or annexed to it"); *Dole v. Thurlow,* 53 Mass. 157, 163 (1846) ("[A]s a prerequisite to recording, acknowledgment, or proof by one or more subscribing witnesses, was necessary. Actual recording, without one of these prerequisites, would not give effect to the deed").

An improvidently recorded deed cannot give constructive notice of the conveyance. See *Graves v. Graves,* 72 Mass. 391, 392–393 (1856) (where assignment was recorded notwithstanding fact that it had not been acknowledged, court held that the assignment was improvidently recorded, the recorded document did "not operate as constructive notice of the execution of the assignment . . . as against [a] . . . creditor . . . ; and therefore the title of the . . . creditor, though subsequent in time, takes precedence").

As in *McOuatt,* the facially correct certificate of acknowledgment does not remedy the absence of a proper acknowledgment. Indeed, as the judge here observed, to determine otherwise would reward a grantee who records a deed that falsely purports to be acknowledged. And, pursuant to *Graves,* an improvidently recorded deed cannot provide constructive notice to subsequent grantees. We therefore conclude that the latent defect in the certificate of acknowledgment of the July deed prevented it from giving constructive notice to Deborah of the prior conveyance. . . .

Judgment affirmed.

Points for Discussion

a. **Transforming "No Title" into "Good Title"**

The deed from Ethel to Harold and herself as joint tenants was valid, regardless of the acknowledgment defect. So you might logically conclude that Ethel had no title to convey to herself and Deborah, as trustees, because she had previously conveyed all of her interest. Isn't this a simple case with an obvious outcome? No!

For policy reasons, the recording acts protect the bona fide purchaser. Any grantee can protect his title by properly recording his deed; but if he fails to do so, he runs the risk that a later buyer will qualify for bona fide purchaser protection. In effect, the law may allow a grantor to convey an interest that she no longer owns. Do you understand why it is necessary to allow a person who has "no title" to be able to transfer "good title"?

b. **Invalid Acknowledgments**

As a general rule, when an unacknowledged deed is entered in the public land records, it is not deemed to be "recorded" and thus it does not provide record notice. Where the acknowledgement appears to be valid on the face of the deed—but is defective due to a *hidden flaw*—most states treat the deed as validly recorded.

Exactly what was the problem with the acknowledgment on Harold's deed? If Deborah had searched the land records before obtaining her deed, she would have found the deed to Harold and have no reason to believe that the acknowledgment was defective. If you were the judge, would you hold that Deborah had constructive knowledge of Harold's deed?

c. **Protecting "Purchasers"**

The recording acts seek to protect the reasonable expectations of *purchasers*—people who make economic investments in good faith reliance on the state of record title, not those who merely receive gifts. Accordingly, donees, devisees, and heirs are not purchasers for value. As a general rule, the grantee need not pay full fair market value, but almost all courts agree that she must pay more than mere nominal value. *See, e.g., Holmquist v. King Cnty.*, 328 P.3d 1000, 1007 (Wash. Ct. App. 2014) ($10 payment was a "nominal amount" and thus inadequate).

Massachusetts courts have recognized that the key statute at issue in the case—General Laws ch. 183, § 4—only protects purchasers, though its text is silent on the issue. *See, e.g., Gomes v. Harrison*, 150 N.E.3d 815, 822 (Mass. App. Ct. 2020). The trial judge noted that Ethel's conveyance to Deborah and herself as trustees was for "nominal consideration" because it was made "in the estate planning context." Should Deborah have won the case?

d. **Lack of Delivery, Forgery, and Fraud**

An *undelivered* deed or a *forged* deed is *void*, transferring no interest to the grantee. Thus, any subsequent grantees in that chain of title, including bona fide purchasers, receive nothing. *See Brock v. Yale Mortgage Corp.*, 700 S.E.2d 583 (Ga. 2010).

In contrast, a deed that is induced by *fraud* is *voidable* by the grantor; but if the grantee conveys title to a bona fide purchaser, the subsequent purchaser prevails. Do you understand why? Recall the discussion of voidable title in *O'Keeffe v. Snyder* (Chapter 3). As between two innocent parties, who could most easily have avoided the loss? There was no evidence in *Allen* that Harold's deed was procured by fraud.

e. **Effective Recording Revisited**

Suppose S conveys title to B, and later also conveys title to C. B and C do not record. C conveys to D, and D records. If D does not know about the S-B deed, should D prevail in a race-notice jurisdiction? The answer is "no" if the jurisdiction follows the *Zimmer* rule: a subsequent purchaser is deemed to have "recorded" his conveyance only if all prior conveyances in his chain of title are properly recorded. *Zimmer v. Sundell*, 296 N.W. 589 (Wis. 1941). This minority rule is controversial. But should a purchaser rely on a deed from a grantor who is a stranger to title according to the public records?

f. The Shelter Rule

Suppose that S conveys Greenacre to B, who fails to record her deed. S conveys Greenacre to C, who immediately records. C then conveys Greenacre to D, who records. D knew about the S-B deed when his deed was delivered. Who owns Greenacre, D or B? Because D knew about B's interest, D cannot be a subsequent bona fide purchaser. But a special doctrine protects buyers in D's situation. Under the *shelter rule*, a bona fide purchaser is allowed to transfer his protection to a later grantee. Why is this rule necessary for an effective market?

g. Problems

In the following situations, who owns Greenacre (1) under the first-in-time rule, (2) in a race jurisdiction, (3) in a notice jurisdiction, and (4) in a race-notice jurisdiction? Assume that all grantees pay valuable consideration unless otherwise indicated.

> (1) S conveys to B, who does not record.
> S conveys to C.
> C records.
> B records.
>
> (2) S conveys to B, who does not record.
> S conveys to C as a gift.
> C records.
> B records.
>
> (3) S conveys to B, who does not record.
> S conveys to C, who does not record.
> S conveys to D, who does not record.
> C records.
>
> (4) S conveys to B, who does not record.
> S conveys to C, who does not record.
> C conveys to D, who knows about the S-B deed.
> C records.
> B records.
> D records.

h. An Alternative Approach: Title Registration

Recording systems suffer from two major defects: (1) they do not conclusively establish title; and (2) even purchasers who scrupulously search the records may lose title due to unrecorded interests that are outside the scope of the recording acts.

Title registration provides an alternative approach: the government assumes the role of title assurer by maintaining an authoritative registry of title. To determine the state of title, a purchaser simply examines the registered title. She need not delve into historical title records that stretch back for decades. A few jurisdictions in the United States utilize a type of title registration called the *Torrens system*. This system was devised by Sir Robert Torrens in 1858 in South Australia and is used throughout the British Commonwealth.

Under the Torrens system, title is passed by registration in a government agency. In order to set up such a system, the ownership of each parcel of real property must be determined by litigation. Once the court determines the state of title, the property is registered with the government agency, which issues a certificate of title to the owner.

> **See It**
>
> Click here to view a copy of a Torrens certificate of title.

The owner can transfer his interest only by registering title in the name of the buyer. Unregistered interests are invalid, except for a few exceptions (e.g., short-term leaseholds).

Although originally enacted in over 20 states, the Torrens system has lost favor in the United States. Currently, only a handful of states maintain any sort of Torrens system, and fewer still utilize them extensively. In theory, the Torrens system is more efficient than a traditional recording system and provides better title assurance as well. However, several factors contributed to its demise in the United States: (1) it was not mandatory; (2) the initial judicial determination of title was expensive; and (3) statutory and judicial exceptions undermined its effectiveness.

> **FYI**
>
> Three states have active Torrens systems in a number of counties: Hawaii, Minnesota, and Massachusetts. Hawaii has the largest Torrens registration, with over 40 percent of its land registered.

e. Chain of Title Problems

If a recorded document cannot be found in a standard title search, it is considered to be *outside* the chain of title and provides no notice to subsequent buyers. Because the public land records are voluminous, it would be extraordinarily difficult for a searcher to review every recorded document. In some counties, this would literally require years of searching.

There are four classic situations where a recorded document is outside the chain of title:

> *Wild deed*
>
> S conveys to B, who does not record.
>
> B conveys to C.
>
> C records.
>
> S conveys to D.
>
> D records.

In a normal title search, D will trace title back through S to a sovereign or other ending point. D will then follow this chain forward, looking under S's name *from the time S received title until the present*. D will not discover C's interest because B (C's predecessor) failed to record the S-B deed. The B-C deed is a *wild deed*, unable to be captured by the reasonable searcher. Certainly, C's interest is discoverable—but only if the searcher wades through every instrument in the recorder's office, an unreasonable burden. Although the B-C deed is recorded, it is not *properly* recorded and therefore does not provide notice. D owns the property.

> *Deed recorded too late*
>
> S conveys to B, who does not record.
>
> S conveys to C, who has actual knowledge of B.
>
> C records.
>
> B records.
>
> C conveys to D.
>
> D records.

Once D establishes his chain of title, he will follow it forward, looking under S's name *from the time S received title until the date the S-C deed was recorded*. D will then look under C's name, *from the time C received title until the present*. D will not discover B's interest because the S-B deed was recorded at a point when D is no longer searching under S's name. The deed was recorded too late and does not provide notice. D owns the property.

However, some jurisdictions mandate a more extensive search. They require the title searcher to look under each grantor's name from the time the grantor received title *until the present*. In this case, the searcher would find the S-B deed. D is thus on record notice of B's interest, and cannot be a subsequent bona fide purchaser. Accordingly, B has priority over D as first-in-time. This approach is less efficient because it increases the burden of searching title.

> *Deed recorded too early*
>
> S owns Greenacre.
>
> B conveys to C.
>
> C records.
>
> S conveys to B.
>
> B records.
>
> B conveys to D.
>
> D records.

In following his chain of title forward, D will look under S's name *from the time S received title until the date the S-B deed was recorded*. D will then check under B's name *from the time B received title until the present*. D will not discover C's interest because the B-C deed was recorded at a point when D is not looking under B's name. The deed was recorded too early, so D owns the property.

In a few jurisdictions, the title searcher is required to search under each grantor's name *for every year the grantor is alive*. The searcher would therefore look under B's name not simply from the time B received title, but from the time of B's birth. In such a jurisdiction, she would find the B-C deed, and thus D is on record notice of B's prior interest. Since D is no longer a subsequent bona fide purchaser, B has priority as first-in-time.

> *Deed from a common grantor*
>
> S owns Greenacre and Forestacre.
>
> S conveys Greenacre to B, granting an easement to cross Forestacre for the purpose of accessing Greenacre.
>
> B records.
>
> S conveys Forestacre to C, who is not aware of the easement.
>
> C records.

In following his chain of title forward, C will look under S's name *from the time S received title until the present*. But because C is purchasing Forestacre, C only will look at those conveyances *relating to Forestacre* (since C is not interested in the state of title of other properties that S owns). Thus, C would not discover the easement since it is part of B's deed relating to Greenacre.

However, about half of the states require that C expand his search to include all properties deeded out by a common grantor. *See Guillette v. Daly Dry Wall, Inc.*,

325 N.E.2d 572 (Mass. 1975) (subsequent purchasers are bound by restrictions contained in deeds their neighbors received from a common grantor). In this case, C would examine all deeds from S—including B's recorded deed—and have notice of the easement. Earlier in this chapter, *Luthi v. Evans* acknowledged that Mother Hubbard clauses may not impart constructive notice to subsequent purchasers. Would *Luthi* have been decided differently if the jurisdiction followed the *Guillette* approach?

Our next case provides an example of a chain of title problem. Although all the deeds were recorded and indexed, Hughes, a subsequent purchaser, argued that a reasonable search would not have revealed the Board of Education's prior deed. While it was technically recorded, the Board's deed was not *properly* recorded and therefore it did not provide notice to Hughes.

Board of Education of Minneapolis v. Hughes

Supreme Court of Minnesota

136 N.W. 1095 (1912)

BUNN, J.

Action to determine adverse claims to a lot in Minneapolis. The complaint alleged that plaintiff owned the lot, and the answer denied this, and alleged title in defendant L. A. Hughes. The trial resulted in a decision in favor of plaintiff, and defendants appealed from an order denying a new trial.

The facts are not in controversy and are as follows: On May 16, 1906, Carrie B. Hoerger, a resident of Faribault, owned the lot in question, which was vacant and subject to unpaid delinquent taxes. Defendant L. A. Hughes offered to pay $25 for this lot. His offer was accepted, and he sent his check for the purchase price of this and two other lots bought at the same time to Ed. Hoerger, husband of the owner, together with a deed to be executed and returned. The name of the grantee in the deed was not inserted; the space for the same being left blank. It was executed and acknowledged by Carrie B. Hoerger and her husband on May 17, 1906, and delivered to defendant Hughes by mail. The check was retained and cashed. Hughes filled in the name of the grantee, but not until

> **Food for Thought**
>
> Minn. Stat. Ann. § 507.34 provides: "Every conveyance of real estate shall be recorded in the office of the county recorder of the county where such real estate is situated; and every such conveyance not so recorded shall be void as against any subsequent purchaser in good faith and for a valuable consideration . . . whose conveyance is first duly recorded. . . ." What type of recording act does Minnesota have?

shortly prior to the date when the deed was recorded, which was December 11, 1910. On April 27, 1909, Duryea & Wilson, real estate dealers, paid Mrs. Hoerger $25 for a quitclaim deed to the lot, which was executed and delivered to them, but which was not recorded until December 21, 1910. On November 19, 1909, Duryea & Wilson executed and delivered to plaintiff a warranty deed to the lot, which deed was filed for record January 27, 1910. It thus appears that the deed to Hughes was recorded before the deed to Duryea & Wilson, though the deed from them to plaintiff was recorded before the deed to defendant.

The questions for our consideration may be thus stated: (1) Did the deed from Hoerger to Hughes ever become operative? (2) If so, is he a subsequent purchaser whose deed was first duly recorded, within the language of the recording act?

> **See It**
>
> Click here to see a diagram of the relationships among the *Hughes* parties.

The decision of the first question involves a consideration of the effect of the delivery of a deed by the grantor to the grantee with the name of the latter omitted from the space provided for it, without express authority to the grantee to insert his own or another name in the blank space. It is settled that a deed that does not name a grantee is a nullity, and wholly inoperative as a conveyance, until the name of the grantee is legally inserted. *Allen v. Allen*, 48 Minn. 462, 51 N. W. 473. . . . It is clear, therefore, and this is conceded, that the deed to defendant Hughes was not operative as a conveyance until his name was inserted as grantee.

Defendant, however, contends that Hughes had implied authority from the grantor to fill the blank with his own name as grantee, and that when he did so the deed became operative. This contention must, we think, be sustained. Whatever the rule may have been in the past, or may be now in some jurisdictions, we are satisfied that at the present day, and in this state, a deed which is a nullity when delivered because the name of the grantee is omitted becomes operative without a new execution or acknowledgment if the grantee, with either express or implied authority from the grantor, inserts his name in the blank space left for the name of the grantee. . . .

[W]e hold that Hughes, when he received the deed from Mrs. Hoerger, had implied authority to insert his name as grantee, in the absence of evidence showing the want of such authority. The delay in filling up the blank has no bearing on the question of the validity of the instrument when the blank was filled. . . .

Our conclusion is, therefore, that the deed to Hughes became operative as a conveyance when he inserted his name as grantee.

When the Hughes deed was recorded, there was of record a deed to the lot from Duryea & Wilson to plaintiff, but no record showing that Duryea & Wilson had any title to convey. The deed to them from the common grantor had not been recorded.

We hold that this record of a deed from an apparent stranger to the title was not notice to Hughes of the prior unrecorded conveyance by his grantor. He was a subsequent purchaser in good faith for a valuable consideration, whose conveyance was first duly recorded; that is, Hughes' conveyance dates from the time when he filled the blank space, which was after the deed from his grantor to Duryea & Wilson. He was, therefore, a "subsequent purchaser," and is protected by the recording of his deed before the prior deed was recorded. The statute cannot be construed so as to give priority to a deed recorded before, which shows no conveyance from a record owner. It was necessary, not only that the deed to plaintiff should be recorded before the deed to Hughes, but also that the deed to plaintiff's grantor should be first recorded. . . . *Losey v. Simpson,* 11 N. J. Eq. 246.

> **Take Note**
>
> Hughes became a "purchaser" shortly before December 11. This is key to the court's decision. Do you understand why?

Our conclusion is that the learned trial court should have held on the evidence that defendant L. A. Hughes was the owner of the lot.

Order reversed, and new trial granted.

Points for Discussion

a. **Adequate Notice**

The recording acts seek to protect the subsequent purchaser who has no notice of prior adverse interests. In *Hughes*, the Board of Education paid valuable consideration, had no notice of any adverse interests, and recorded its deed. Shouldn't the recording act protect the Board? Why must Hughes win for the recording acts to function properly?

b. **Defining "Recorded"**

Minnesota is a race-notice jurisdiction. In order to qualify for protection Hughes needed to prove that he was a subsequent bona fide purchaser who recorded his deed before the Board did. The Board recorded its deed on January 27, 1910, and Hughes recorded his deed more than ten months later. Why did Hughes win? If a deed is not properly recorded, it is not considered "recorded" either (1) for providing notice to a subsequent purchaser or (2) for being "first-recorded." Therefore, Hughes is viewed as having recorded his deed before the Board.

c. **Chain of Title**

In the following sequence of events, assume that all grantees pay valuable consideration and all deeds are validly created:

(1) Hoerger conveys to Hughes, who does not record.
(2) Hoerger conveys to D&W, who does not record.
(3) D&W conveys to the Board.
(4) Board records.
(5) Hughes records.
(6) D&W record.

Assuming that Hughes received his interest *immediately* when Hoerger handed him the deed, who holds title, Hughes or the Board? What if this jurisdiction applies the *Zimmer* rule? Would the result be different in a notice jurisdiction?

d. Effect of Computerized Index

Would Hughes have won if the recorder's office had a computerized index that covered 1910 recordings? Most chain of title problems arise from the burden of searching the traditional grantor-grantee index. If recorder's offices continue to develop computerized indexes—which seems inevitable—what will eventually happen to the wild deed doctrine? What about the other special chain of title doctrines: the deed recorded too early, the deed recorded too late, and the deed from a common grantor? *See* Emily Bayer-Pacht, Note, *The Computerization of Land Records: How Advances in Recording Systems Affect the Rationale Behind Some Existing Chain of Title Doctrine,* 32 Cardozo L. Rev. 337 (2010).

e. Problems

In the following situations, who owns Greenacre under (1) a notice statute, and (2) a race-notice statute? Assume that all grantees pay valuable consideration. As these problems demonstrate, the question is not who has *perfect* title, but rather who has *better* title.

(1) S conveys to B, who does not record.
S conveys to C, who knows about the S-B deed.
B records.
C records.
C conveys to D.
D records.

(2) S conveys to B, who does not record.
S conveys to C, who knows about the S-B deed.
C records.
B records.
C conveys to D.
D records.

(3) S conveys to B, who does not record.
B conveys to C.
C records.
S conveys to D.
D records.
B records.

(4) S conveys to B, who does not record.
S conveys to C, who does not record
B records.
C records.

(5) S conveys to B, who does not record.
S conveys to C.
C records.
B records.
C conveys to D, who knows about the S-B deed.
D records.

f. What Constitutes "Notice"?

In notice and race-notice jurisdictions, a subsequent purchaser gains priority only if she takes her interest *without notice* of any adverse title claims. But when is a purchaser "without notice"? Three primary forms of notice exist:

- *Actual notice*: knowledge of a prior interest.
- *Record notice*: notice of any prior interest that would be discovered by a standard search of the public land records.
- *Inquiry notice*: notice of any prior interest that would have been obtained by investigating suspicious circumstances.

Record notice and inquiry notice are forms of *constructive notice*. The subsequent purchaser is deemed to know the information that she could have learned by examining the public land records or making an appropriate investigation, even if she fails to do so.

Suppose that Stone contracts to sell his home to the Bakers, but Curtis is living on the property at the time. Is Curtis' possession a suspicious circumstance that should lead the Bakers to make further inquiries? And if the Bakers do inquire, what will they learn? It is often said that possession of real property is constructive notice to the entire world of whatever rights the possessor has in the property. Accordingly, a prudent buyer will carefully inspect the land she is buying in order to discover any adverse claims.

In our next case, General Income fraudulently acquired title to Raub's home. It then mortgaged the property to two banks. Did Raub's continued occupancy give notice of her rights in the home?

Raub v. General Income Sponsors of Iowa, Inc.

Supreme Court of Iowa

176 N.W.2d 216 (1970)

LeGrand, Justice.

This de novo appeal of two consolidated cases involves an attempt by Jessie O. Raub to set aside a deed to her homestead allegedly obtained from her by fraud and to declare invalid two mortgages which the grantee of that deed later placed on the property. The trial court entered a decree declaring the deed void and providing that neither mortgage was a lien on her property.

This appeal is by First National Bank of Fort Dodge, Iowa, holder of the first mortgage, and by Manson State Bank of Manson, Iowa, holder of the second mortgage. General Income Sponsors of Iowa, Inc., the grantee in the controversial deed, does not appeal. . . .

As already mentioned, General Income Sponsors of Iowa, Inc. does not appeal. The decree holding that its warranty deed was obtained from plaintiff by fraud is therefore a finality. Indeed the evidence is overwhelming that plaintiff was the unfortunate victim of gross fraud practiced upon her by Clark Barczewski and Joseph Huffman, officers and agents of General Income Sponsors of Iowa, Inc., over a period of more than three years during which they bilked her of some $33,000.00 for which she now has nothing. These unscrupulous men, having once ingratiated themselves with plaintiff, did not rest until they had taken virtually all she had saved. She testified she is now "financially drained." . . .

Plaintiff was interested in providing for her eventual retirement. She was then 58 years old and expected to work only a few more years. She talked with Barczewski about her plans, and he advised her concerning what course her investments should take. Within a short time he had her complete trust and confidence. . . . Little by little he prevailed upon her to place all her money in stock of General Income Sponsors of Iowa, Inc., about which she knew nothing. He told her this was a company he and Mr. Huffman were starting and she should "get it all in General Income Sponsors." By a series of transactions from February to October (1965) she gave Barczewski $10,000.00 for stock in that corporation. On December 2, 1965, plaintiff executed and delivered to General Income Sponsors of Iowa, Inc. a warranty deed to her homestead, which by then had been cleared of its existing mortgage, in return for which she was to receive an additional $14,000.00 in company stock. Although she asked for the stock certificate several times, apparently she never received it. The warranty deed was recorded December 20, 1965. Thereafter plaintiff remained in possession of the real estate as a tenant, paying $70.00 a month rent from December, 1965, through August, 1966. The rent was paid to Mr. Barczewski on behalf of General Income Sponsors of Iowa, Inc.

On September 17, 1966, the defendant, First National Bank of Fort Dodge, took a mortgage on this property from General Income Sponsors in the amount of $6000.00. The mortgage was promptly recorded. On October 25, 1966, the Manson State Bank placed a second mortgage on the real estate to secure payment of $10,350.00. This mortgage was recorded on November 7, 1966. . . .

As we understand defendants' argument, they concede plaintiff's warranty deed of December 2, 1965, was obtained by fraud and was properly set aside by the trial court. However, they assert they are nevertheless entitled to enforce the liens of their mortgages because they qualify as bona fide purchasers.

A bona fide purchaser is one who takes a conveyance of real estate in good faith from the holder of legal title, paying a valuable consideration for it without notice of outstanding equities. . . .

We have held a mortgagee is regarded the same as a purchaser for this purpose. . . .

In considering the status of defendants, no serious dispute exists except as to good faith and notice of outstanding equities. The evidence clearly establishes both mortgages were taken from the legal title holder, General Income Sponsors of Iowa, Inc., and each defendant paid valuable consideration for its mortgage.

The critical question is: did defendants have notice, either actual or constructive, that their mortgagor's title had been obtained by fraud? The trial court found, and we agree, that the defendant banks, as well as plaintiff, were the victims of Barczewski's fraud. However, this does not answer the question. There may still be notice to defendants if circumstances are shown which would lead a reasonably prudent person to investigate the possible existence of outstanding rights hostile to the grantor's title. If such circumstances do exist, and if such investigation is not made, then one who claims to be a bona fide purchaser is nevertheless charged with all knowledge which that investigation would probably have disclosed. . . .

A consideration of this problem requires us to determine, first, if plaintiff's possession of the property after she had conveyed it away imparted notice of her present claim; and, second, apart from that, were there any other circumstances which should have put a reasonably prudent person on notice to investigate concerning outstanding equities. We discuss these in reverse order.

> **Food for Thought**
>
> Raub and the banks are all innocent victims of fraud. What is the fairest solution to their dispute? Should they share the value of the home?

One who asserts he is a bona fide purchaser must prove his good faith; and good faith is lacking if he knew or, as a reasonably prudent person, should have known others made claims hostile to his grantor's title.

In 55 Am. Jur., Vendor and Purchaser, section 697, page 1075, we find this:

> It is a well settled general rule, in determining whether a purchaser had notice of outstanding equities or unrecorded interests so as to preclude him from being entitled to protection as a bona fide purchaser, that if he has knowledge of circumstances which, in the exercise of common reason and prudence, ought to put a man upon particular inquiry, he will be presumed to have made inquiry, and will be charged with notice of every fact which such suggested investigation would in all probability have disclosed had it been properly pursued. The purchaser may not act in contravention to the dictates of reasonable prudence, or refuse to inquire when the propriety of the inquiry is naturally suggested by circumstances known to him. . . .

Although the trial court found the defendants, too, had been victimized by the fraud of Barczewski and Huffman, it also found the defendants should have known of the fraud by which plaintiff had been induced to transfer her property to General Income Sponsors.

> **FYI**
>
> Raub was one of at least 50 people who were defrauded by Barczewski and Huffman. The victims were clients of a legitimate securities firm where the two had previously worked. They took the firm's client contact information, quit their jobs, formed three corporations, and sold stock in those corporations for $10 a share. Most of the money went into a $2 million resort development in Twin Lakes, Iowa that never came to fruition.

We have searched the record carefully and can find no evidence to charge defendants with such knowledge or to put them on notice to make inquiry.

There was nothing about the mortgage transactions to arouse defendants' suspicions as to the conditions under which the mortgagor's title had been obtained. They were dealing with the holder of legal title, whose deed had been recorded. The record showed payment of adequate consideration. . . .

We are here concerned with circumstances which would impute to defendants "knowledge of such facts as would put a reasonably prudent man upon inquiry" to determine if the title of General Income Sponsors of Iowa, Inc. had been obtained by fraud.

There is no such evidence in this record.

Even if this is true, however, plaintiff asserts that, since she was the occupant of the real estate at the time of the mortgages, the banks were obliged to investigate her occupancy. Having failed to do so, she argues, they are now charged with notice that the deed to her property had been obtained by fraud.

To put it another way: Did the plaintiff's possession of the real estate in question after the execution and delivery of the warranty deed in question import notice to defendants of her present claim? . . .

We follow the rule that possession of land by one other than the grantor is ordinarily sufficient to put parties on inquiry as to the rights of the party in possession. *Clark v. Chapman*, 213 Iowa 737, 744, 239 N.W. 797, 802. . . .

However, there is a general exception to this rule which we also observe: possession by the grantor of a recorded deed does not impart such notice. This is because occupancy, to impart notice, must be hostile to or inconsistent with that of the holder of legal title. . . . We have held the occupancy by one who has conveyed his title, at least for a reasonable period, is not inconsistent with the rights of the person to whom he has conveyed. . . .

We are forced to the conclusion that plaintiff's possession of the property following her warranty deed did not impart notice to defendants that she claimed any right or interest therein.

Perhaps we could stop our discussion here, but we desire to comment briefly to show it would be of no benefit to plaintiff even if we had held defendants were obligated to investigate her occupancy of the premises. . . .

At the time the mortgages were given plaintiff was paying rent as a tenant and made no claim to the property. She did not then know the deed had been obtained from her by fraud. She was still completely convinced of Barczewski's loyalty, so much so that she had named him as her executor shortly before that time. She testified she trusted both men "beyond September or October of 1966."

If an investigation had been made, it would have disclosed simply that plaintiff had conveyed her property by warranty deed to General Income Sponsors of Iowa, Inc.; that she continued to occupy the property as a tenant; that she was paying $70.00 a month rent; and that she claimed no ownership interest in the property. . . .

We fully recognize plaintiff has lost her life savings through fraud of Barczewski and Huffman. We futher recognize she is probably without redress against them.

The corporation is now apparently defunct. Huffman has plead guilty to a charge of obtaining money under false pretenses. Barczewski has been indicted on a similar charge. At the time this case was tried, he had not been apprehended to stand trial.

Raub's house
Click here for larger photo

These are tragic circumstances brought about by the trust and confidence which plaintiff mistakenly reposed in Barczewski and Huffman. We agree with the trial court that this was an outrageous scheme unscrupulously carried out until plaintiff was completely improverished. While we would like to rescue her from the consequences of her own folly, we cannot do so by improperly shifting the loss to defendants simply because they are better able to stand it.

The decree of the trial court is accordingly affirmed in part and reversed in part.

Points for Discussion

a. **Inquiry Notice Based on Possession**

Raub's possession was inconsistent with record title. Why didn't this fact defeat the banks' claim of priority? Didn't the banks have a duty to inquire? Iowa takes the view that possession by a *grantor*, at least for a reasonable period of time after a conveyance, does not put a subsequent buyer on notice. Do you agree with this position?

Even if the banks had inquired, what would they have learned? When Raub answered the door, what would she have said? Remember, inquiry notice only imputes information that would have been discovered by reasonable investigation. *See In re Clare House Bungalow Homes, L.L.C.*, 447 B.R. 617 (E.D. Wash. 2011).

b. **Inquiry Notice Based on the Record**

Sometimes information in a recorded instrument may prompt the title searcher to make further inquiries. For example, if an instrument *within* the chain of title refers to a document *outside* of the chain, most courts require further investigation. Thus, if a recorded deed within the chain refers to a "lost" deed or an unrecorded lease, the searcher must locate and review these documents. *See Harper v. Paradise*, 210 S.E.2d 710 (Ga. 1974); *Mister Donut of America, Inc. v. Kemp*, 330 N.E.2d 810 (Mass. 1975).

c. **Multi-Unit Developments and the Duty of Inquiry**

Suppose that S owns a 200-unit condominium development. S sells Unit 111 to B, who moves in but fails to record her deed. A few weeks later, S executes a mortgage on the entire development to C as security for a loan. C records its mortgage. Several of the condominium units are occupied by individuals who were invited by S to occupy them as part of its marketing campaign; these individuals have no legal interest in the units. Local developers frequently use such marketing techniques in order to increase sales. If C forecloses on its mortgage, who has title to Unit 111, C or B? *See Waldorff Ins. & Bonding, Inc. v. Eglin Nat'l Bank*, 453 So. 2d 1383 (Fla. Dist. Ct. App. 1984).

d. **Efficiency v. Fairness**

Inquiry notice potentially expands a buyer's search to off-record matters, which raises costs, imposes delays, and increases litigation risks. On the other hand, inquiry notice may prevent an unfair result. In many jurisdictions, Raub would have prevailed. What is the appropriate balance between efficiency and fairness? Should inquiry notice be abolished?

---

3. Title Insurance

Today title insurance is the main method of title protection in the United States. The typical buyer will purchase a title insurance policy to supplement the title covenants in his deed. The basic concept is simple: if the buyer suffers a loss from a title defect that existed on the effective date of the policy, he receives compensation from the title company.

In general, title insurance offers better protection than a title opinion based on a search of the public land records. For example, title insurance covers certain off-record defects such as a forged deed in the chain of title, unlike a title opinion. Similarly, title insurance is usually provided by state-regulated insurance companies which have substantial assets to cover losses, far exceeding the recoverable assets of an attorney who prepares a title opinion. Finally, a title insurance company is contractually obligated to pay claims under the policy, while negligence must be proven to recover damages for a faulty title opinion.

Most title insurance companies use standard policy forms prepared by the American Land Title Association (ALTA). As a result, title policies are remarkably similar across the country. There are two basic types of ALTA policies: the owner's policy and the lender's policy. As their names suggest, each is designed for a different holder. If the buyer is borrowing money to purchase the property, the lender will require its own policy to guarantee that the mortgage is a first-priority lien on the property. The discussion below focuses on the owner's policy.

The basic ALTA owner's policy has five sections:

- *Cover page*: setting forth the scope of coverage provided.
- *Exclusions*: listing specific items that are excluded from coverage for all properties.
- *Schedule A*: stating the name of the insured party, the maximum amount insured by the policy, and the estate that is insured.
- *Schedule B*: listing specific items that are excepted from coverage for this property.
- *Conditions*: specifying procedural requirements, such as the time and manner for making claims.

As the policy provisions quoted in our next case demonstrate, the *coverage* provided by a title insurance policy is quite broad. But this coverage is limited by standard exclusions and property-specific exceptions. An *exclusion* is a potential risk that the company is unwilling to cover in *any* policy, such as encumbrances created or agreed to by the insured party. An *exception* is a problem that concerns the *particular* parcel, which the title company discovers by searching its computerized version of the public land records. For example, the parcel might be burdened by an easement which cannot be removed. A title insurance company will not insure against this known defect, so it will be excepted from coverage. After all, the purpose of title insurance is to protect the buyer against unknown risks, not known title problems.

> **See It**
>
> Click here to see a sample ALTA owner's policy.

A title insurance policy imposes two obligations on the insurance company: the *duty to defend* and the *duty to indemnify*. The first duty requires the company to pay the attorneys fees and costs necessary to protect the owner's title as guaranteed by the policy, while the second obligates the insurer to compensate the owner if a loss occurs. The duty to defend is generally broader than the duty to indemnify. This means that a title insurance company may be required to defend the owner's title even if it is not completely clear that the potential defect is covered by the policy.

Suppose that B purchases a large tract of mountain land. He buys a title insurance policy in order to safeguard his investment. B then discovers that he does not have a legal right to reach the land in a vehicle; he can only reach it on foot or on horseback. B's policy guarantees that he will have a "right of access to and from the land." Is B entitled to compensation under his policy?

Riordan v. Lawyers Title Insurance Corp.

United States District Court, District of New Mexico

393 F. Supp. 2d 1100 (2005)

BRACK, DISTRICT JUDGE.

This matter came before the Court on Defendant's Motion for Summary Judgment filed on September 28, 2004. . . . Having considered the submissions of the parties, relevant law, and being otherwise fully advised, I find that this motion should be granted.

I. Background

Plaintiffs were owners of 160 acres of real property (hereinafter "Property") located in an "in-holding"[1] in the middle of the Sandia Mountain Wilderness of the Cibola National Forest near Albuquerque, New Mexico. Defendant issued an insurance policy (hereinafter "Policy") insuring Plaintiffs' title to the Property. Plaintiffs allege that they sustained a loss, covered by the Policy, as a result of lawsuit that they filed against the United States of America to declare a vehicular right of way to the Property. *See Riordan, et al. v. United States, et al.,* CIV 01-0092 DJS/WWD (hereinafter "Primary Action"). . . .

> **See It**
>
> The land in question is located at an elevation of 8,000 feet in the middle of the Sandia Mountain Wilderness, east of Albuquerque, New Mexico. The region is sacred to the Sandia Pueblo, whose members regularly visit the mountain for ceremonial purposes. Click here to see a map showing the land at issue in the case.

II. Facts

At all relevant times, the Property has been accessed by the Piedra Lisa Trail, which is a hiking and horse trail maintained by the United States Forest Service ("USFS"). The Property is located two and a half miles from the nearest paved road. The Piedra Lisa Trail was and is unsuitable for vehicular access. Mr. Riordan testified at his deposition that, at the time he purchased the Property in 1995, there were several former roads that had been used to access the Property, including roads that were

---

[1] In-holdings are lands surrounded by federally owned lands. *See* 16 U.S.C. § 3210(a).

accessible by jeep. Before Plaintiffs purchased the Property, the prior owner represented that he had accessed the Property by jeep over an access route other than the Piedra Lisa Trail. Mr. Riordan testified that a USFS employee informed Mr. Riordan that the Property had vehicular access and suggested the access route was near the original homestead on the Property.

Sandia Mountain Wilderness
Click here for larger photo

On May 5, 1995, Riordan signed a Vacant-Land Purchase Agreement to purchase the property for $225,000. Prior to closing, Riordan visited the Property by walking and riding his horse on the Piedra Lisa Trail. Plaintiffs closed on the Property on July 6, 1995.

Defendant issued the owner's policy of title insurance, effective September 11, 1995. The Policy provides in pertinent part:

SUBJECT TO THE EXCLUSIONS FROM COVERAGE, THE EXCEPTIONS FROM COVERAGE CONTAINED IN SCHEDULE B AND THE CONDITIONS AND STIPULATIONS, LAWYERS TITLE INSURANCE CORPORATION . . . Insures . . . against loss or damage, not exceeding the Amount of Insurance stated in Schedule A, sustained or incurred by the insured by reason of:

    1. Title to the estate or interest described in Schedule A being vested other than as stated therein;

    2. Any defect and /or lien or encumbrance on the title;

    3. Unmarketability of the title;

    4. Lack of a right of access to and from the land.

The Policy contains the following exclusion from coverage:

The following matters are expressly excluded from the coverage of this policy and the Company will not pay loss or damage, costs, attorneys' fees or expenses which arise by reason of:

> 1(a) Any law, ordinance or government regulation . . . restricting, regulating, prohibiting or relating to (i) the occupancy, use, or enjoyment of the land. . . .

The Plaintiffs brought the Primary Action to declare a vehicular right of way to the Property. The United States raised affirmative defenses in the primary action, but did not assert counterclaims against Plaintiffs. Defendant hired attorney Joseph Werntz to represent Plaintiffs in the Primary Action. In September 2002, the property appraised for $2.8 million. Thereafter, Plaintiffs sold the property to Sandia Pueblo for $1.3 million and a tax deduction for a $1.5 million charitable donation to the Pueblo. The Primary Action was dismissed as moot by stipulation on December 18, 2002. Plaintiffs made three demands for payment under the policy. The demands were rejected. . . .

IV. Discussion

Plaintiffs assert that the Policy insured against a lack of vehicular access to the Property. Defendant argues that the Policy covers a lack of a right of access, and does not insure the quality of that access. . . .

The Policy insures against loss caused by a "lack of right of access." Plaintiffs argue that this language should be construed to cover a lack of vehicular access based on their reasonable expectations. "An insurance contract should be construed as a complete and harmonious instrument designed to accomplish a reasonable end." *Knowles v. United Services Auto. Ass'n*, 113 N.M. 703, 705, 832 P.2d 394, 396 (1992). The doctrine of reasonable expectations only applies where the policy terms are ambiguous. . . . "Absent ambiguity, provisions of [an insurance] contract need only be applied, rather than construed or interpreted." *Richardson v. Farmers Ins. Co. of Ariz.*, 112 N.M. 73, 74, 811 P.2d 571, 572 (1991). Clear and unambiguous contract terms must be enforced as written. . . . The Policy insures against loss or damage sustained or incurred by the insured by reason of a lack of a right of access to and from the land. This language is clear and unambiguous. For this reason, the policy language controls and the doctrine of reasonable expectations is inapplicable.

> **Practice Pointer**
>
> Do you understand why Lawyers Title hired Werntz to represent Riordan and the other insured parties in the "Primary Action"? The United States refused to allow vehicular access over the wilderness land surrounding the plaintiffs' land. If Lawyers Title had insured a right of vehicular access, then it had the duty to defend that right by financing litigation to enforce it.

Unambiguous insurance contracts must be construed in their usual and ordinary sense. . . . When the language in the policy is unambiguous, the New Mexico courts "will not strain the words to encompass meanings they do not clearly express."

Gonzales v. Allstate Ins. Co., 122 N.M. 137, 140–141, 921 P.2d 944, 947–948 (1996). The Policy insures against a lack of right of access; it does not insure that the Property has vehicular or any other type of access.

Although no New Mexico cases have addressed this point, courts in other jurisdictions have found that coverage for a "lack of right of access" to the insured property is not triggered where access is merely impractical or difficult as long as the right to access exists. . . . Plaintiffs admit that they had, and were never denied, a right to pedestrian access to and from the property over the Piedra Lisa Trail. Indeed, their right of access was mandated by federal law. *See* 16 U.S.C. § 3210(a). Accordingly, there was no lack of right of access to the property that would trigger coverage under the policy.

Plaintiffs rely on *Marriott Financial Services, Inc. v. Capitol Funds, Inc.*, 288 N.C. 122, 217 S.E.2d 551, 565 (1975) in support of their claim of coverage. In *Marriott*, the court construed "right of access" to mean "without unreasonable restriction" and stated in dicta that pedestrian access was unreasonable in that case. *Id.* This dicta in *Marriott* has been roundly criticized. . . . Moreover, *Marriott* is inapposite to Plaintiffs' case. In *Marriott*, the subject property was adjacent to a heavily traveled city street in a commercial area. *Marriott*, 217 S.E.2d at 565. The Property in this case is located in the middle of a wilderness area, two and a half miles from the nearest paved road. Thus, even if the *Marriott* dicta were applied to this case, pedestrian access to the Property was without unreasonable restriction.

Finally, the holding in *Marriott* does not support Plaintiffs' position. In *Marriott*, the court held that the claim was barred by the government action exclusion of the title insurance policy. The insured in that case was required to apply for a driveway permit with the city, but had never actually filed the application because of the city's stated intention not to approve the application if it were filed. *Marriott*, 217 S.E.2d at 565. The *Marriott* court held that because the insured had not applied, access had not been denied, and even if the application had been submitted and rejected, coverage would still be excluded under the government action exclusion. *Id.*

The Policy in the instant case contains a similar government action exclusion. The Policy, excludes any claim that arises by reasons of "any law, ordinance or governmental regulation . . . restricting, regulating, prohibiting or relating to . . . the occupancy, use, or enjoyment of the land." Plaintiffs complain that they were deprived of a right of access because the United States allegedly intended to reject any application for a special use authorization for vehicular access to the Property. However, Plaintiffs never applied for a special use permit, and they sold the property before obtaining a final determination in the Primary Action. Thus, *Marriott* does not support Plaintiffs' claim of coverage based on the government action exclusion.

Plaintiffs' claim that the property was unmarketable is similarly unavailing. Defects in the physical condition of the property do not constitute unmarketability of title. *See Chicago Title Ins. Co. v. Kumar*, 24 Mass.App.Ct. 53, 506 N.E.2d 154,

156 (1987); *Hocking v. Title Ins. & Trust Co.*, 37 Cal.2d 644, 652, 234 P.2d 625, 629 (1951). A difference exists between economic lack of marketability, which relates to physical conditions affecting the use of the property, and title marketability, which relates to defects affecting legally recognized rights and incidents of ownership. *See Kumar*, 506 N.E.2d at 157. Here, Plaintiffs had a right of access to the property at all relevant times. The fact that Plaintiffs were able to sell the property at a substantial profit militates against a determination that the title was unmarketable. Under these circumstances, the title was marketable. . . .

Points for Discussion

a. **Right of Access**

Was it reasonable for the plaintiffs to conclude that the "right of access" covered by their policy was for vehicular access? The phrase "right of access" was not defined in the policy. As a general rule, an ambiguity in a title policy is interpreted in favor of the insured party. *White v. Western Title Insurance Co.*, 710 P.2d 309 (Cal. 1985). Should the court have used that principle here? Note that Lawyers Title hired an attorney to sue the United States on plaintiffs' behalf to obtain vehicular access. Does this suggest that Lawyers Title thought its policy might guarantee such access?

b. **Marketability of Title**

If the value of plaintiffs' property without a right of vehicular access was zero, would title be unmarketable? No! A title policy insures the quality of the owner's title, not the market value of the land. *Hocking v. Title Insurance & Trust Co.*, 234 P.2d 625, 629 (Cal. 1951).

c. **Toxic Contamination**

Four days after buying a tract of land, X discovers that it is contaminated with toxic wastes. Can he recover under his title insurance policy? Courts uniformly reject such claims, holding that the presence of contamination is not an encumbrance and does not render title unmarketable. *Chicago Title Ins. Co. v. Kumar*, 506 N.E.2d 154 (Mass. App. Ct. 1987). *See also Bear Fritz Land Co. v. Kachemak Bay Title Agency, Inc.*, 920 P.2d 759 (Alaska 1996) (holding that owner of federally regulated wetlands could not recover damages under title insurance policy on theories that regulations were an encumbrance or rendered title unmarketable).

d. **Exclusions**

An adage of title insurance is that "the big print giveth and the small print taketh away." In other words, the standard ALTA policy provides broad coverage, but the exclusions set forth in small print erode much of that protection. For example, the effect of any law or regulation relating to the occupancy or use of land is typically excluded from coverage, as you see in *Riordan*. Thus, even if plaintiffs had been able to prove that vehicular access was within the general *coverage* of the policy, they might have lost because the effect of laws restricting access were specifically *excluded*.

Matters that could be discovered through an inspection or survey of the land, such as adverse possession or boundary line disputes, are also often excluded. *See Walker Rogge, Inc. v. Chelsea Title & Guaranty Co.*, 562 A.2d 208 (N.J. 1989) (refusing recovery where parcel contained 12 acres instead of the promised 19 acres because this problem could have been found by a survey).

e. **Title Covenants**

Does title insurance provide more protection than title covenants? Or less? For an enlightening article comparing the two, see Jerome J. Curtis, Jr., *Title Assurance in Sales of California Residential Realty: A Critique of Title Insurance and Title Covenants with Suggested Reforms,* 7 Pac. L.J. 1 (1976).

f. **Negligence Liability**

Suppose that title insurance company T issues a policy to buyer B that mistakenly does not exclude a recorded set of CC&Rs (covenants, conditions, and restrictions) from coverage. T is clearly liable in contract on the policy because the CC&Rs are an encumbrance. But can B instead sue T for negligently searching title? Courts are split on the issue. As one court explained, the insured has a "reasonable expectation that the title company will search the title." *Walker Rogge, Inc. v. Chelsea Title & Guaranty Co.*, 562 A.2d 208, 218 (N.J. 1989). But if an insured party like B can sue in tort, he can avoid the agreed-upon limitations in the policy, such as the exclusions from coverage and the policy ceiling on the amount of recoverable damages. If a title company can be sued for negligence, how will this affect the price of title insurance?

g. **Aftermath of *Riordan***

After selling the land, Riordan told a reporter: "I'm happy for the public. I think it's going to be in good hands with Sandia Pueblo." *Pueblo Buys 160 Acres*, Albuquerque Jour., Sept. 11, 2002. In 2014, the Pueblo transferred the land to the United States to be held in trust, subject to the restriction that it be preserved in its natural state, and in return received a 700-acre parcel on the western edge of the Sandia Mountain Wilderness.

Summary

- **Statute of Frauds.** To be enforceable, a contract for the sale of land must be in writing, contain the essential terms, and be signed by the party sought to be bound. An oral contract for the sale of land is unenforceable, unless part performance or estoppel can be proven.

- **Marketable Title.** Every purchase contract contains an implied covenant that the seller will deliver marketable title at the closing, unless the parties agree to a different title standard. Marketable title is title reasonably free from doubt: the seller owns the estate he is selling and there are no encumbrances on the property. As a general rule, private encumbrances make title unmarketable; governmental restrictions do not.

- **Equitable Conversion.** Traditionally, the law placed the risk of loss during the executory period on the buyer. The modern trend is to assign this risk to the party who is entitled to possession.

- **Duty to Disclose.** In most jurisdictions, the seller of a single-family home is obligated to disclose known defects that materially affect the value of the property and are not known to or readily discoverable by the buyer. A few states extend the disclosure duty to off-site conditions.

- **Delivery.** A deed is effective only when delivered. Delivery requires a manifestation of the grantor's intent to immediately convey an interest in the property.

- **Deed Types.** A general warranty deed provides that the grantor is liable for title defects occurring before and during the grantor's ownership. A special warranty deed imposes liability only for defects arising during the grantor's ownership. A quitclaim deed provides no warranties.

- **Deed Warranties.** Present covenants are breached, if at all, when the deed is delivered and traditionally did not run with the land to successors. Future covenants are breached only when the grantee is actually or constructively evicted, and do run to successors.

- **Recording System.** The recording statutes seek to protect the subsequent bona fide purchaser and thereby create a reliable property market. The common law principle of first-in-time controls unless the subsequent purchaser qualifies for protection under the state's recording statute.

- **Types of Recording Acts.** There are three types of recording acts: race (first to record gains priority); notice (subsequent bona fide purchaser gains priority); race-notice (subsequent bona fide purchaser who records first gains priority). In notice and race-notice states, the purchaser must have no actual, record, or inquiry notice of the prior interest.

- **Chain of Title Problems.** Under some circumstances, a recorded deed may not provide record notice. Wild deeds, late-recorded deeds, and early-recorded deeds do not provide notice in jurisdictions that require a normal title search. However, in jurisdictions that mandate a more extensive search, late-recorded

> **Test Your Knowledge**
>
> To assess your understanding of the material in this chapter, click here to take a quiz.

deeds, early-recorded deeds, and deeds from a common grantor may provide notice.

- **Title Insurance.** A title insurance policy provides coverage against title defects. However, the policy will contain exclusions and exceptions which reduce the scope of protection.

For More Information

For more information about the subjects covered in this chapter, please consult the following sources:

- Ann M. Burkhart, *Real Estate Practice in the Twenty-First Century*, 72 Mo. L. Rev. 1031 (2007).
- Tom Hayden & Jordan Kelner, *The Value of Title Insurance*, 15 J. Bus. & Tech. L. 305 (2020).
- Donald J. Kochan, *Certainty of Title: Perspectives After the Mortgage Foreclosure Crisis on the Essential Role of Effective Recording Systems*, 66 Ark. L. Rev. 267 (2013).
- Katherine A. Pancak et al., *Residential Disclosure Laws: The Further Demise of Caveat Emptor*, 24 Real Est. L.J. 291 (1996).
- Gregory L. Pierson, *Striking Down the Impervious Shields: Why Caveat Emptor Must Be Abandoned in Commercial Real Property Sales and Leases*, 47 Stetson L. Rev. 111 (2017).

Chapter 9

Financing Real Property

Our national economy depends on the availability of credit. In particular, almost all real property transactions are financed by borrowed money. Suppose that a married couple, Wendy and Henry Baker, is planning to purchase a new home for $300,000. They have saved $30,000 to use as a down payment, but will need to borrow the remaining $270,000 from a bank or another lender. What happens next? Which laws govern their rights and duties?

In this chapter, we will explore the four key parts of a real property finance transaction:

- *Obligation*: The borrower's duty to repay a loan evidenced by a written *promissory note* or to perform other duties is called the *obligation*.
- *Security*: The borrower will provide *security* to the lender through a *mortgage*, a *deed of trust*, or a similar encumbrance on the property.
- *Foreclosure*: If the borrower defaults on the obligation, the lender will have the property sold at a *judicial foreclosure sale* or a *nonjudicial foreclosure sale* and use the sales proceeds to satisfy the loan.
- *Rights after foreclosure*: The borrower and the lender may have additional rights after the foreclosure sale occurs.

Let's explore the Baker loan hypothetical above. If a lender agrees to make the loan, it will require that the Bakers sign a promissory note—a contract by which they promise to pay the debt. The lender will also require that the Bakers provide security for the loan. Why? If a lender makes a loan without any security—an *unsecured loan*—it may never be repaid. For example, the borrower might sell the property, lose all of his money gambling in Las Vegas, and then file bankruptcy. In this situation, the lender would probably collect nothing.

Suppose that the lender loans $270,000 to the Bakers and receives a mortgage that encumbers the house they are buying; this is called a *secured loan*. The loan will end when the Bakers make their final payment. But if they fail to make the required payments, the lender can foreclose on its mortgage, sell the house, and use the sales proceeds to repay the loan.

The concept of a secured loan is both ancient and simple: *when the loan is made, the lender requires the borrower to provide collateral—something of value.* That way, if the borrower defaults, the lender can sell the item and pay off the loan with the sales proceeds. Almost anything can be used as security. For instance, if O owns a diamond ring, she could get a loan from a pawnshop on the security of the ring; she would hand it over to the pawnbroker, who would be entitled to sell it if O failed to repay the loan.

The most common form of *security* for a large loan is an interest in real property. But real property is immovable. It cannot be physically handed over to a lender, unlike a ring. The mortgage and other types of security instruments were developed to solve this problem. They allow the lender to hold a security interest in real property—that is, the right to sell the property to repay the debt—even though the borrowers are in possession of the land.

This chapter focuses on the most basic loan transaction: the purchase of a home. But the same principles apply to more complex transactions, such as the construction of a condominium project or the purchase of a shopping center.

The law in this area seeks to strike the right balance between two competing goals: (1) ensuring an adequate supply of affordable credit and (2) protecting borrowers against unfair treatment. Lenders typically have more bargaining power than borrowers. Accordingly, if their relationship were governed exclusively by freedom of contract, borrowers might be forced to accept inequitable terms on a "take it or leave it" basis. At the same time, laws intended to protect borrowers may inadvertently go too far, making loans less available and more expensive.

> **Food for Thought**
>
> Lenders always seek to minimize the risk that the loan will not be repaid. If you were an attorney asked to draft loan documents on behalf of a lender, what kinds of provisions would you include to deal with this risk?

A. Creating the Obligation

The most common obligation is the borrower's duty to repay a loan, as evidenced by a written *promissory note*. A promissory note is a specialized type of contract between the borrower and the lender by which the borrower agrees to repay the loan on certain terms and conditions. A note has intrinsic value; it is a negotiable instrument that can be sold to another person.

By contrast, a mortgage or other security instrument has no intrinsic value. It essentially provides a *remedy* which the lender can use to satisfy the obligation if the borrower defaults. When the obligation is satisfied, the mortgage has no legal force or effect, even if it still appears in the public land records. Although people sometimes talk informally about getting a "mortgage" from a lender, technically a borrower receives a *loan secured by a mortgage*.

Assume that the Bakers apply to Madison State Bank for a $270,000 loan to finance their home purchase. The Bank will evaluate their creditworthiness and financial condition to ensure that they can make the loan payments. The Bank will also appraise the home to be certain that it provides adequate security for the loan. Ultimately, the Bank agrees to make the loan to the Bakers, at a fixed interest rate of 4% per year. This will be a *fully amortized loan*, meaning that if the Bakers pay $1,289 each month for 30 years, they will fully repay the loan with interest. As part of the transaction, the Bakers will sign a promissory note like the one below.

> **What's That?**
>
> With a *fully amortized loan*, the equal installment payments the borrower makes will completely repay all principal and interest by the end of the loan term. Many loans are not fully amortized; this means that the borrower must make a large final payment (a *balloon payment*) to repay the loan.

PROMISSORY NOTE

For value received, Wendy A. Baker and Henry O. Baker ("Borrowers") promise to pay Madison State Bank ("Lender") the sum of TWO HUNDRED SEVENTY THOUSAND dollars ($270,000), with interest from January 1, 2024 on unpaid principal at the rate of 4% per annum, with principal and interest payable in installments of ONE THOUSAND TWO HUNDRED EIGHTY-NINE dollars ($1,289) on the 1st day of each month beginning on the 1st day of February, 2024 through and including the 1st day of January, 2054.

Should default be made in payment of any installment when due, the entire sum of principal and interest shall immediately become due at the option of Lender. If any action is instituted on this note, Borrowers promise to pay such sum as the Court may fix as reasonable attorney's fees. This note is secured by a Mortgage executed on the same date.

If Borrowers ever sell, convey or alienate the property encumbered by the Mortgage, or any part thereof, voluntarily or involuntarily, then Lender shall have the right, at its option, to declare any indebtedness or obligations secured thereby immediately due and payable.

Wendy A. Baker   January 1, 2024
Wendy A. Baker

Henry O. Baker
Henry O. Baker

Points for Discussion

a. Acceleration Clause

Notice that the note allows the lender to demand payment of the entire loan if the borrowers miss even one monthly payment. Most notes contain such an *acceleration clause*, which is valid in all states. Acceleration of the loan after default is a preliminary step in the foreclosure process.

b. Due-on-Sale Clause

The final paragraph in the note is called a *due-on-sale clause*. It gives the lender the option to demand full payment of the loan if the borrowers sell the property or any part of it. Why? The main purpose of a due-on-sale clause is to allow the lender to force repayment of a lower-than-market rate loan during an era when interest rates are rising. In effect, it requires the buyer to obtain a new, higher-interest rate loan rather than take over the seller's existing loan. In general, a due-on-sale clause is fully enforceable, pursuant to federal law that preempts any conflicting state laws.

c. Nonmonetary Obligations

There is always a risk that the price paid at a foreclosure sale may not be high enough to fully repay the debt, particularly if the property is damaged. Accordingly, the lender has an incentive to make sure that the property is preserved in good condition. For this reason, a mortgage usually provides that the lender can *also* foreclose if the borrower fails to satisfy certain nonmonetary obligations, such as (1) keeping the property in good repair, (2) avoiding waste, (3) maintaining adequate property insurance, and (4) defending his title to the property in litigation with third parties.

d. Liability of Successor Owners

Suppose the Bakers sell the house to the Changs five years later. Usually, an existing loan is paid off when the property is resold. But assume that the parties choose to keep the loan in place. Further assume that the Bank knows about the sale and decides not to enforce the due-on-sale clause. Who is obligated to pay the loan? The Bakers are still personally liable for the debt—simply because they signed the promissory note and the Bank has not released them from their obligation. But are the Changs *also* personally liable for the debt? This depends on the agreement that the Bakers made with the Changs.

> ### Assuming v. Taking Subject To
>
> - *Assuming*: If the agreement provides that the buyer will *assume* the loan, then he is personally liable to repay it, together with the borrowers. If the loan goes into default, the lender can sue the buyer for breach of contract and collect the resulting judgment from the buyer's other assets—unless the buyer has a defense under one of the rules discussed in Section D below.
>
> - *Taking subject to*: If the agreement provides that the buyer will take title *subject to* the loan, then he is not personally liable. Of course, if payments are not made, the lender may foreclose and eliminate the buyer's estate in the home. Thus, while the buyer has an economic incentive to make sure that someone makes the payments due on the loan, his other assets are not at risk.

e. **Subprime Lending**

Between 2000 and 2006, the use of *subprime loans* exploded. These risky loans were made to borrowers with poor credit, uncertain income prospects, and often little or no down payment. Most of these loans involved *adjustable-rate mortgages* (ARMs). Typically, such a loan would begin with a low, fixed interest rate for the first few years (called a *teaser rate*) and then would reset to an adjustable rate for the duration of the loan. Because interest rates rose during the mid-2000s, the required monthly payments increased for most borrowers once the adjustable rates took effect. Borrowers who counted on being able to refinance their loans when the initial rate expired had a rude awakening when the housing bubble burst in 2006, causing home values to fall and making refinancing difficult or impossible. Without the ability to make the higher payments, borrowers defaulted and lenders foreclosed. Millions of families lost their homes during this crisis.

Another disturbing aspect of the subprime loan crisis was the exploitation of minorities. Black and Latino borrowers were more likely to receive subprime loans. For example, 53% of Black borrowers received subprime loans in 2006, compared to only 17% of Caucasian borrowers. Even when credit risks were equal, Caucasians were given lower interest rates almost 70% of the time. *See* Monique W. Morris, Discrimination and Mortgage Lending in America: A Summary of the Disparate Impact of Subprime Mortgage Lending on African Americans (2009).

B. Providing the Security

In this chapter, we will consider four methods to provide security for an obligation:

> - Mortgage
> - Deed of trust
> - Installment land contract
> - Equitable mortgage (or absolute deed as security)

1. Mortgage

The *mortgage* is the traditional security instrument. The borrower (the *mortgagor*) conveys an interest in real property to the lender (the *mortgagee*) as security for the performance of an obligation, usually payment of a promissory note. Once the borrower repays the loan in full, the mortgage is automatically extinguished. But if the borrower defaults, the property will be sold at foreclosure and the sales proceeds will be used to pay off the loan. Broadly speaking, the mortgage is governed by property law. Because the mortgage transfers an interest in real property, it must comply with the Statute of Frauds.

> **Mortgage Theories**
>
> Although it may seem strange, the states are split on a fundamental question: what rights does the lender receive?
> - *Title theory*: Some states follow the common law view that the mortgage is a transfer of title from the borrower to the lender. In theory, the lender has the right to possession of the property before default, but in practice this right is rarely exercised.
> - *Intermediate theory*: In a few states, the lender holds title, but does not hold the right to possession until the borrower defaults.
> - *Lien theory*: In most states, the mortgage is seen as a creating a *lien* or security interest, not conveying title. Accordingly, the lender does not have the right to possession until foreclosure occurs.

When the mortgage evolved in fourteenth-century England, it took the form of a fee simple subject to a condition subsequent. In other words, borrower B would convey a fee simple to lender L, but B retained the right to regain title if he repaid the loan by a specified date. If B failed to do so, L obtained a fee simple absolute.

But this arrangement often produced harsh results. If the borrower was unable to repay the loan on the stated day for any reason, he lost all rights to the property—even if it was worth more than the loan amount. Suppose that B owned land worth 10 pounds and borrowed 5 pounds from L secured by a mortgage, but was unable to pay the debt; L would receive property worth 10 pounds for a 5 pound debt.

Over time, the English equity courts intervened to protect the borrower by allowing him to repay the debt and thus *redeem* the land long after the designated payment day. This right was called the borrower's *equity of redemption*. But the recognition of this right created a problem for the lender: how could he know when the equity of redemption ended, so that he held a fee simple absolute? The equity courts responded by allowing the lender to bring a lawsuit to *foreclose* or terminate the equity of redemption if the loan was not repaid. This procedure evolved into the modern foreclosure sale, which technically ends the borrower's equity of redemption.

In some states, the only way to foreclose a mortgage is through a specialized type of lawsuit, which is called *judicial foreclosure*. But many states allow *nonjudicial foreclosure* (also called *power of sale foreclosure*)—that is, a sale conducted without any judicial involvement—if the mortgage expressly provides such a power. This is called a *mortgage with power of sale*.

Let's return to the loan that the Bakers are obtaining from Madison State Bank. Assume that the Bank requires the Bakers to execute a mortgage with power of sale to secure the $270,000 promissory note. It might look like this:

MORTGAGE WITH POWER OF SALE

Wendy A. Baker and Henry O. Baker ("Mortgagors") hereby mortgage to Madison State Bank ("Mortgagee") the real property located in Larchmont, Plata County, Madison, described as "Lot 6, as shown on that certain subdivision map of Larchmont Estates, recorded in Map Book 47, Page 118, Plata County Records on June 23, 1983" ("Property"), together with the rents and profits therefrom, for the purpose of securing: (1) payment of the sum of $270,000 with interest thereon according to the terms of a promissory note of even date made payable by Mortgagors to Mortgagee; (2) the performance of each agreement contained in this Mortgage; and (3) the payment of additional sums and interest thereon which may be loaned to Mortgagors by Mortgagee in the future, when evidenced by another promissory note reciting that it is secured by this Mortgage.

> To protect the security of this Mortgage, Mortgagors agree: [Here the typical mortgage sets forth standard provisions that are mainly designed to (1) protect the security (requiring the mortgagors to maintain adequate property insurance payable to the mortgagee, to avoid waste, etc.) and (2) establish the procedure for power of sale foreclosure. A sample power of sale provision is set forth below.]
>
> 14. Power of Sale Foreclosure: As an alternative to judicial foreclosure, upon default Mortgagee may declare all sums secured by this Mortgage immediately due and payable. After all notices required by law have been given, and the required time period has elapsed, Mortgagee may sell the Property at the time and place set forth in the notice of sale at public auction to the highest bidder for cash in lawful money of the United States, payable at the time of sale. After deducting all costs of foreclosure, Mortgagee shall apply the proceeds of the sale (a) to payment of all sums secured by this Mortgage with accrued interest and (b) the remainder, if any, to the persons legally entitled to such proceeds.
>
> *Wendy A. Baker*   January 1, 2024
>   Wendy A. Baker
>
> *Henry O. Baker*
>   Henry O. Baker
>
> [Acknowledgment by notary public]

Points for Discussion

a. **Recording the Mortgage**

An unrecorded mortgage is valid. But the standard practice is to record a mortgage as soon as possible—just like a deed—in order to avoid any claim that a third party is a subsequent bona fide purchaser or encumbrancer of the property.

b. **Purchase Money Mortgage**

A *purchase money mortgage* arises when the buyer of real property finances her purchase by giving the seller a promissory note secured by a mortgage on the property. Where the buyer obtains a loan from a third party (such as Madison State Bank in our hypothetical transaction) that is used to pay the seller and secured by a mortgage on the property, most states also view the mortgage as a purchase money mortgage.

c. **Multiple Mortgages?**

It is common for a property to be encumbered by multiple mortgages. This creates a risk that the sale of the property may not generate enough money to pay off all the secured debts. In this situation, it is important to determine the relative *priority* of each mortgage. Consider a basic situation: the unrecorded mortgage. Assume S borrows $100,000 from B, secured by a mortgage on S's home; but B fails to record its mortgage. S then borrows $50,000 from C, also secured by a mortgage on the home, and C promptly records. Assuming C had no notice of B's mortgage, C is a bona fide encumbrancer. Thus, C's mortgage has first priority and B's mortgage has second priority. Can you see why this might be a problem?

> **Make the Connection**
>
> The laws governing mortgage priority are based on the principles that you studied in Chapter 8, though there are some specialized rules that you will study later in this chapter. A subsequent lender who qualifies for protection under the recording acts is usually called a *subsequent bona fide encumbrancer*, rather than a subsequent bona fide purchaser.

d. **Rents and Profits Clause**

Notice that the security for the sample mortgage above is both (1) the real property and (2) the *rents and profits* that the property produces. Suppose, for example, that the security is an apartment building. This clause authorizes the lender to collect the rents directly from the tenants (usually through a court-appointed *receiver*) during the period after default and before the foreclosure sale.

e. **Future Advance Clause**

The sample mortgage also secures repayment of *future advances*—that is, loans that the lender may make to the borrowers in the future—if the parties so agree. A mortgage with such a clause is called a *future advance mortgage*. Such future loans may create questions about mortgage priority, as discussed later in this chapter.

f. **Clogging the Equity of Redemption**

Finally, consider what is missing from the sample mortgage. Given the unequal power relationship between borrowers and lenders, you might expect to find a boilerplate clause by which the borrowers waive their equity of redemption, and thus allow the lender to obtain title without foreclosure. But such a clause would be ineffective. As Restatement (Third) of Property: Mortgages § 3.1 provides, "any agreement in or created contemporaneously with [the] mortgage" to waive the right to be foreclosed upon is unenforceable. It is a fundamental principle that courts will not allow *clogging of the equity of redemption*. Do you understand why this helps to protect borrowers?

2. Deed of Trust

The most common mortgage substitute is the *deed of trust*. In fact, today it is the main security instrument used in many states. The deed of trust is a three-party relationship. In form, the borrower (the *trustor*) conveys real property "in trust" to a third party (the *trustee*) for the benefit of the lender (the *beneficiary*). The text creates an express *power of sale*. If the borrower defaults on her obligation, the lender may instruct the trustee to sell the property at foreclosure; the trustee will then distribute the sales proceeds to the lender as necessary to repay the loan.

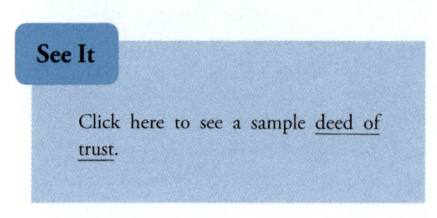

See It

Click here to see a sample deed of trust.

In form, the deed of trust closely resembles the sample mortgage shown above, except for the involvement of the trustee. For example, if a deed of trust were used in the Baker-Madison State Bank loan transaction, it might begin as follows: "Wendy A. Baker and Henry O. Baker ("Trustors") hereby grant to Trustee Services, Inc. ("Trustee") in trust, with power of sale, for the benefit of Madison State Bank ("Beneficiary") the real property . . . ."

The deed of trust was a twentieth-century invention intended to allow lenders to circumvent laws that protect borrowers. Lenders argued that these laws did not apply because the deed of trust was not a "mortgage"—even though it served exactly the same function as a mortgage. Over time, courts and legislatures rejected this formalistic assertion. Today the law in most states treats the deed of trust just like a mortgage with power of sale. In general, the trustor has the same rights and duties as a mortgagor; and the beneficiary has the same rights and duties as a mortgagee. Thus, despite the rather confusing name, the deed of trust is not a type of "trust." Given the functional similarity between the mortgage and the deed of trust, we will use the term "mortgage" in the discussion below, with the understanding that the same rules also generally apply to the deed of trust.

3. Installment Land Contract

The *installment land contract* (also known as a *land sale contract* or *contract for deed*) is another alternative to the mortgage. In this type of contract, the buyer (the *vendee*) promises to pay the purchase price to the seller (the *vendor*) in installments over a fixed period of time, for example, 15 years. The buyer is allowed to take possession of the property, but the seller retains title until all payments are made. The installment land contract is often used when the buyer lacks a down payment or the credit rating necessary to obtain a traditional loan secured by a mortgage. It may also be helpful for a seller because she can reach a larger pool of prospective buyers and thus potentially obtain a higher price.

Traditionally, the installment land contract includes a clause that provides for forfeiture of the land and all payments made if the buyer misses even *one* payment. Suppose that G enters into an installment land contract to purchase a home from H for $120,000, with interest to accrue at the rate of 9.5% per year, payable in monthly installments over 15 years. G makes all the required payments for 10 years, but then loses her job and misses a payment. Pursuant to the contract, H declares that G has forfeited her interest in the home. This allows H to (a) retake possession of the home, now worth $200,000, without going through foreclosure and (b) keep the $150,360 in payments that G has made. Does this seem fair? Should the law supersede the contract and provide a remedy for G?

Slone v. Calhoun

Court of Appeals of Kentucky

386 S.W.3d 745 (2012)

Taylor, Judge.

Rosa Lea Slone brings this appeal from a March 10, 2011, judgment of the Knott Circuit Court, dismissing her complaint for damages under a land contract. For the reasons stated, we reverse.

In August 2005, Slone entered into a land contract with Michael Calhoun for the purchase of a lot and a mobile home. Under the agreement, Slone was to pay $313 per month, as well as the taxes and insurance for the property. Slone claims that in January 2009, without her knowledge or approval, Calhoun executed a land contract with Jerry Sumner for the same lot and mobile home. In May 2009, Slone informed Calhoun that she was unable to continue making the monthly payment and moved from the property. In November 2009, Slone filed a lawsuit against Calhoun and Sumner seeking damages for breach of contract. She alleged that Calhoun and Sumner had forced her to move out. However, sometime between May and November, Calhoun and Sumner discovered that their land contract erroneously described its subject matter as the property that was contained in Slone's contract. Upon finding the error, they executed a corrected contract for other real property adjacent to Slone's lot.

The Knott Circuit Court conducted a bench trial on March 7, 2011. Slone, Calhoun, Sumner, Sumner's wife, and attorney Bobby Williams, who drafted the land agreements for Calhoun, testified. The trial court found that the 2009 Calhoun/Sumner land agreement actually pertained to land behind or adjacent to Slone's lot. The trial court further found that Slone had voluntarily terminated her 2005 land contract with Calhoun by vacating the premises in May of 2009. Under the land contract forfeiture provisions, the trial court ruled that Slone forfeited her interest in the property, including any payments made during the terms of the land contract. This appeal follows. . . .

Upon conducting a bench trial in this action, the trial court held as a matter of law that the parties had entered into a land contract in August of 2005 for the purchase of a lot and trailer thereon. The trial court further found that during the term of this land contract, Slone was to make monthly payments thereon until the entire purchase price was paid in full, whereupon the deed would be delivered. As a matter of law, the trial court has concluded that an installment land sale contract was entered into between the parties. . . . The trial court went on to conclude that the forfeiture provision in the land contract precluded any claims by Slone and thus dismissed the case.

> **See It**
>
> Click here to see a sample installment land contract.

Based upon the trial court's legal ruling that the parties had entered into an installment land contract, this case is controlled exclusively by *Sebastian v. Floyd*, 585 S.W.2d 381 (Ky. 1979) and its progeny. In *Sebastian*, the Kentucky Supreme Court held that the forfeiture provision in an installment land sale contract that provided for the forfeiture of the buyers' payments upon the buyers' default was invalid and otherwise not enforceable in Kentucky. The Supreme Court noted that there was no practical distinction between a land sale contract and a purchase money mortgage. The Court made the following observation regarding this issue:

> There is no practical distinction between the land sale contract and a purchase money mortgage, in which the seller conveys legal title to the buyer but retains a lien on the property to secure payment. The significant feature of each device is the seller's financing the buyer's purchase of the property, using the property as collateral for the loan.
>
> Where the purchaser of property has given a mortgage and subsequently defaults on his payments, his entire interest in the property is not forfeited. The mortgagor has the right to redeem the property by paying the full debt plus interest and expenses incurred by the creditor due to default. In order to cut off the mortgagor's right to redeem, the mortgagee must request a court to sell the property at public auction. . . . From the proceeds of the sale, the mortgagee recovers the amount owed him on the mortgage, as well as the expenses of bringing suit; the mortgagor is entitled to the balance, if any.

Sebastian, 585 S.W.2d at 383.

The Supreme Court in *Sebastian* also made the following observation regarding the legal status of this type of land contract:

> When a typical installment land contract is used as the means of financing the purchase of property, legal title to the property remains in the seller until the buyer has paid the entire contract price or some agreed-upon portion thereof, at which time the seller tenders a deed to the buyer. However, equitable title passes to the buyer when

the contract is entered. The seller holds nothing but the bare legal title, as security for the payment of the purchase price.

Sebastian, 585 S.W.2d at 382.

Although neither party cited *Sebastian* as authority to this Court in this appeal, it nonetheless is controlling as concerns the legal issues raised in this case. Our Courts have a duty to address issues not properly raised when the facts reveal a fundamental basis for a decision not presented by the parties to avoid a misleading application of the law. *Mitchell v. Hadl*, 816 S.W.2d 183 (Ky. 1991). The trial court erred as a matter of law in forfeiting Slone's interest in this property. Not only does Slone have an equitable ownership interest in the property to the extent of the monthly payments that were made thereon over a period of approximately four years, Slone also has redemption rights in the property under applicable Kentucky law. Kentucky Revised Statutes 426.530. . . .

As required by the Kentucky Supreme Court in *Sebastian*, the only judicial remedy to resolve the alleged breach of the land contract between the parties is a judicial sale of the property. See *Sebastian*, 585 S.W.2d 381. The forfeiture provisions set forth in the agreement are invalid as a matter of law and are otherwise not enforceable. Regardless of who defaulted under the terms of the land contract, which is an issue we do not reach, the only recourse for the parties in this case is to seek a judicial sale, which will result in a judgment that will quiet title as well as determine the parties' respective rights to the proceeds therefrom.

> **FYI**
>
> After foreclosure, the sales proceeds would be divided as follows: (1) Calhoun receives full payment of all sums Slone owes under the installment land contract; and (2) Slone receives the remainder. Notice that Slone has an additional right under Ky. Rev. Stat. 426.530, called a *statutory right of redemption*. This section allows her to buy the property back after the foreclosure sale under certain conditions.

For the foregoing reasons, the judgment in the Knott Circuit Court is reversed for further proceedings consistent with *Sebastian v. Floyd*, 585 S.W.2d 381.

COMBS, JUDGE, Dissenting.

I file this dissent because this case is highly distinguishable from *Sebastian*. Unlike the situation in *Sebastian,* the case before us invokes abandonment of the contested property and a voluntary termination of the underlying contract. . . .

Points for Discussion

a. **Forfeiture Clauses**

A typical forfeiture clause in an installment land contract might read:

> Time is of the essence in this contract. If vendee fails to pay any installment payment on or before its due date, then after giving 10 days written notice of such default, (1) vendor may retain all prior payments made by vendee as liquidated damages, which shall not be construed as a penalty, (2) this contract shall be null and void, and (3) vendee shall have no further right, title, or interest in the property.

> **What's That?**
>
> *Liquidated damages* are damages that are agreed to in advance by the parties to a contract as compensation for a future breach.

Such a clause permits the seller to regain possession of the property (without going through foreclosure) and keep all the payments made by the buyer as *liquidated damages* for the breach. For decades, courts routinely enforced forfeiture clauses, even when this produced harsh results.

b. **"A Predatory Agreement"**

For decades, the Federal Housing Administration refused to insure loans secured by mortgages on property in predominantly Black neighborhoods, which were labeled in red on its maps. Due to this *redlining*, many Black buyers ended up purchasing homes through risky installment land contracts. *See* Mehrsa Baradaran, *Jim Crow Credit,* 9 U.C. Irvine L. Rev. 887 (2019). Reflecting on this era, one author characterized the installment land contract as "a predatory agreement that combined all the responsibilities of homeownership with all the disadvantages of renting—while offering the benefits of neither." Ta-Nehisi Coates, *The Case for Reparations*, The Atlantic, Oct. 31, 2016.

In recent years, investors seeking to resell foreclosed properties have often targeted low-income Black and Latino buyers—using installment land contracts to sell dilapidated homes at inflated prices. For example, in *Horne v. Harbour Portfolio VI, LP,* 304 F. Supp. 3d 1332 (N.D. Ga. 2018), plaintiffs alleged that the defendants (1) purchased homes in poor condition, (2) sold them to predominantly Black buyers using installment land contracts, (3) marked up the sales price four or five times their purchase price, and (4) charged 10% per year in interest. The district court held that the plaintiffs had alleged a prima facie violation of the Fair Housing Act, in the form of *reverse redlining*—"extending credit on unfair terms because of the plaintiff's race and geographic area." *Id.* at 1339.

c. Remedies for Breach

Modern courts increasingly scrutinize forfeiture clauses, particularly where the buyer has paid a substantial portion of the purchase price. As *Slone* suggests, concern for fairness and equity has led most courts to protect the defaulting buyer. A number of courts now view the installment land contract merely as a mortgage substitute and thus extend many of the traditional borrower protections to the buyer. For example, Restatement (Third) of Property: Mortgages § 3.4(b) provides that an installment land contract "creates a mortgage." Some states follow the *Slone* approach, declaring the forfeiture clause invalid and calling for judicial foreclosure upon default. In a second group of states, mortgage protections apply only to certain installment land contracts, especially where the buyer has paid a large portion of the purchase price and lived in the property for a long time. Finally, some courts enforce forfeiture clauses as written, but provide the buyer with partial reimbursement if her payments so greatly exceed the seller's actual damages as to constitute a penalty.

d. Character of the "Default"

In his *Slone* dissent, Judge Combs characterized Slone's abandonment as a "voluntary termination" of the contract. If the buyer abandons the property (rather than merely failing to make payments), should the forfeiture clause be strictly enforced? *See Bean v. Walker*, 464 N.Y.S.2d 895, 899 (App. Div. 1983) ("If the vendee abandons the property and absconds, logic compels that the forfeiture provisions of the contract may be enforced.") Should a buyer who abandons the property be treated differently from one who fails to pay because of special hardship?

---

4. Equitable Mortgage

Suppose that C delivers a deed that transfers fee simple title to her home to L, as part of what appears to be a sales transaction by which L purchases the home for $200,000. But the parties have an oral agreement that L will convey title back to C if C pays L $250,000 within a year. Is this a true sale? Or do the parties actually intend the deed to function as a mortgage? Although the transaction is a sale in form, a court would probably conclude that it is a mortgage in substance and thus provide the "seller" with the normal rights of a borrower. This is called an *equitable mortgage* or an *absolute deed as security*. If we view this as a loan, C is charging an interest rate of 25%—a rate which is illegal in most states.

How can we determine whether a transaction is a true sale or an equitable mortgage? This issue arose in our next case.

Zaman v. Felton

Supreme Court of New Jersey

98 A.3d 503 (2014)

JUSTICE PATTERSON delivered the opinion of the Court.

This appeal requires the Court to analyze an agreement for the sale of a residential property and a subsequent lease and repurchase agreement, and to determine whether the transactions collectively gave rise to an equitable mortgage. . . .

We reverse the portion of the Appellate Division's opinion that affirmed the trial court's dismissal of [Barbara] Felton's claim that the parties' agreements constituted a single transaction that gave rise to an equitable mortgage. We adopt the eight-factor standard for the determination of an equitable mortgage set forth by the United States Bankruptcy Court in *O'Brien v. Cleveland*, 423 B.R. 477, 491 (Bankr. D.N.J. 2010). We remand to the trial court for application of that standard to this case. . . .

I.

. . . Felton was an experienced buyer and seller of real estate, who had participated in prior land sales and financing transactions that involved significant sums of money. . . . Felton purchased the property at issue in this case, consisting of approximately fifteen acres of land in Plumsted Township, and commenced construction of a residence on the property. . . . As of 2007, a construction mortgage in the amount of $105,000 obtained by Felton was in default, and Felton confronted the imminent foreclosure of her unfinished home. . . .

> **What's That?**
>
> The court's reference to a "construction mortgage" is shorthand for a *construction loan*—a loan used to build a home or other structure, which is secured by a mortgage on the property.

Felton was introduced to [Tahir] Zaman by a mutual acquaintance, Joseph Richardson. . . . Zaman disclosed to Felton that he had a real estate license. On June 16, 2007, Felton, Zaman, and Richardson met at the Plumsted Township property to discuss its potential sale. . . . Felton requested a price of $250,000 for the property, and Zaman made a $200,000 counteroffer. According to the testimony of Zaman, Felton said that she wanted to keep the property. In response, Zaman told Felton that if she accepted his offer of $200,000, he would agree to a buy-back option and would allow her to remain on the property as a tenant.

During the June 16, 2007 meeting, Felton and Zaman executed a written land sale agreement, and Richardson signed the agreement as a witness. The agreement, a standard form obtained by Zaman from the real estate office with which he was associated, identified Zaman as the buyer and Felton as the seller. It described the location of the property and set forth a sale price of $200,000. . . . The agreement contained no reference to a buy-back or lease provision. . . .

The closing took place on June 23, 2007. . . . On the day of the closing, Felton and Zaman executed documents in two stages. First, at a Bordentown diner, they signed the lease and a seller's residency certification. . . . After a brief dispute over the terms of the lease and buy-back agreements, Felton and Zaman agreed that Felton would pay Zaman $1,000 per month in rent. They also agreed that Felton would have an option to repurchase her property within three months for $237,000. . . . Later, at the local branch of a bank, Felton signed the deed, an affidavit of title, and the buy-back agreement. Zaman gave Felton a cashier's check in the amount of $85,960, which was calculated by subtracting from the $200,000 purchase price the amount that Zaman needed to pay off the existing mortgage, satisfy outstanding property tax obligations, and pay other expenses related to the sale. . . . The parties did not execute any mortgage documents.

Felton house
Click here for larger photo

At trial, Zaman maintained that he did not offer a mortgage to Felton, and that he has never offered a mortgage to anyone. Felton, in contrast, testified that she understood the parties' transaction to be a mortgage. By Felton's account, she thought that Zaman was loaning her $200,000. She also construed the $85,960 check issued to her to be the down payment on the loan, and understood that she would satisfy the terms of the mortgage loan if she paid Zaman $237,000 within three months of closing. Felton admitted that she never inquired about the interest rate applied to the purported mortgage, and that the parties never discussed any such interest rate.

[After the closing, Zaman repaid the construction loan. Felton] attempted to rescind the sale agreement by sending a check in the amount of $85,983.65 to Zaman, but Zaman refused to cash the check. . . . For the next seventeen months, Felton continued to occupy the property. She did not pay rent in accordance with the lease agreement, or exercise her contractual right to repurchase the property.

II.

In December 2008, Zaman filed a complaint against Felton in [which he] sought possession of real property and damages derived from Felton's allegedly illegal use and occupancy of the property. Felton filed a counterclaim, asserting [inter alia, that Zaman committed fraud and that the transaction created an equitable mortgage.]. . . .

[The trial court conducted a bifurcated trial. In the first phase, the jury determined that Zaman had not committed fraud and that "Felton knowingly agreed to sell her property to him." In the second phase, the judge considered Felton's other claims, including her equitable mortgage claim.]. . . . [T]he trial court held that no equitable mortgage was created by the parties' agreements. In that regard, the trial court cited the jury's finding that Felton intended to sell her property, as well as evidence that Felton understood that a sale of her property was her only alternative to foreclosure. The court held that the subsequent lease and buy-back provisions were separate agreements that were intended to protect the seller after closing and permit her to remain on the property, and that those agreements were not components of the original sale. . . . [Felton appealed and the lower appellate court affirmed the trial court's decision.]

IV.

. . . We first consider the trial court's rejection of Felton's claim that the parties entered into an equitable mortgage. Felton claims that although her initial agreement with Zaman was structured as a sale, the parties' agreements should be construed as a single transaction, which was effectively a high interest loan secured by the deed to her property.

> **See It**
>
> When the case reached the New Jersey Supreme Court, Felton's counsel began his oral argument as follows: "There are so many wrongs to Mrs. Felton . . . presented by this case. Fortunately, there are strong laws available to right those wrongs and allow a widow in poor health to finally have the chance to live in the house that she and her husband worked so long and hard to build." Click here to see his oral argument.

The doctrine of equitable mortgages "is founded upon that cardinal maxim in equity which regards as done that which has been agreed to be, and ought to have been, done." *Rutherford Nat'l Bank v. H.R. Bogle & Co.*, 114 N.J. Eq. 571, 573–74, 169 A. 180 (N.J. Ch. 1933). . . . As an Appellate Division panel observed,

"[i]f a transaction resolves itself into a security, whatever may be its form and whatever name the parties may choose to give it, it is, in equity, a mortgage. If a deed or contract, lacking the characteristics of a common law mortgage, is used for the purpose of pledging real property, or some interest therein, as security for a debt or obligation, and with the intention that it shall have effect as a mortgage, equity will give effect to the intention of the parties. Such is an equitable mortgage."

[*Welsh v. Griffith-Prideaux, Inc.*, 60 N.J. Super. 199, 208,158 A.2d 529 (App. Div. 1960) (quoting *J.W. Pierson Co. v. Freeman*, 113 N.J. Eq. 268, 270–71, 166 A. 121 (E. & A. 1933)).]

> **Practice Pointer**
>
> Felton essentially argued that Zaman loaned her $200,000 for three months in return for $37,000 in interest—an interest rate of 74% per year. *Usury laws* in New Jersey and most states impose a ceiling on the amount of interest that a lender may charge. In many states, the penalty for making a usurious loan is that the lender forfeits all interest. Note, however, that certain categories of lenders—typically the lenders most likely to make secured loans, such as banks and savings and loan associations—are often exempt from these laws.

. . . Ordinarily, the conveyance of a property accompanied or followed by a leaseback transaction is precisely what it purports to be: a sale in which the parties separately agree that the seller will become the tenant, and the buyer will become the landlord, in accordance with the terms of a lease. However, "New Jersey courts have repeatedly found that sale-leaseback arrangements made to avoid foreclosure are in fact equitable mortgages." *Johnson* [*v. NovaStar Mortg., Inc.*, 698 F. Supp. 2d 463, 469 (D.N.J. 2010)]. . . . It is the trial court's task to discern whether the transaction has been labeled as a land sale in order to mask its actual objective: a mortgage loan secured by a deed to the property at issue.

In *Johnson*, *supra*, the United States District Court for the District of New Jersey adopted a standard articulated by the United States Bankruptcy Court for the District of New Jersey in *O'Brien, supra,* 423 B.R. at 491. In *O'Brien, supra,* the Bankruptcy Court scrutinized a residential sale that was conducted under the threat of imminent foreclosure, in which the parties agreed that the seller would remain in his home and buy the home back from the buyer in a series of payments over time. It identified eight factors to assist trial judges in determining whether a given transaction gives rise to an equitable mortgage:

> (1) Statements by the homeowner or representations by the purchaser indicating an intention that the homeowner continue ownership; (2) A substantial disparity between the value received by the homeowner and the actual value of the property; (3) Existence of an option to repurchase; (4) The homeowner's continued possession of the property; (5) The homeowner's continuing duty to bear ownership responsibilities, such as paying real estate taxes or performing property maintenance; (6) Disparity in bargaining power and sophistication, including the homeowner's lack of representation by counsel; (7) Evidence showing an irregular purchase process, including the fact that the property was not listed for sale or that the parties did not conduct an appraisal or investigate title; (8) Financial distress of the homeowner, including the imminence of foreclosure and prior unsuccessful attempts to obtain loans.

Under the *O'Brien* framework, the court considers not only the form of the transaction itself but circumstances that can motivate a party to disguise a mortgage secured by a property as a sale of land and indications that both parties intend the seller to retain the land notwithstanding the purported sale. . . . We adopt the *O'Brien* factors as a comprehensive and practical standard to guide trial courts as they determine whether a particular transaction, or series of transactions, gives rise to an equitable mortgage.

We remand the matter to permit the trial court to make findings addressing each of the eight factors that comprise the *O'Brien* test. Because the parties presented extensive evidence at trial regarding Felton's financial situation, the parties' respective experiences with land sale transactions, their negotiations, their statements about their intent to enter into the transactions, the terms of each agreement, and the conduct of each party following closing, the trial court's findings on remand may be based upon the existing record, without the need for further testimony.

> **FYI**
>
> The *O'Brien* court held that a transaction structured as a home sale, lease, and repurchase option was in fact an equitable mortgage where, among other things: a foreclosure was pending at the time; the owners were in financial distress and not represented by counsel; the home was worth over $800,000 but "sold" for $555,000, with an option to repurchase for $650,000; and the owners testified that their intent was to obtain a loan.

We note that in ruling that the parties' transactions did not give rise to an equitable mortgage, the trial court relied in part on the jury's determination that Felton intended to sell her property, and the absence of any indication in the parties' agreements that they contemplated a mortgage loan. Consistent with the limitation of its inquiry to the issue of fraud, the jury was not instructed on the question of whether the parties intended to create an equitable mortgage. The jury's determination that Felton knowingly sold her property does not itself resolve the question of whether the parties created an equitable mortgage. Its finding that Zaman had proven by a preponderance of the evidence that Felton knowingly entered into a land sale may, however, be relevant to one or more of the *O'Brien* factors in the trial court's inquiry on remand. Other considerations cited by the trial court, such as the imminent foreclosure proceedings, Felton's inability to obtain a new mortgage or meet her obligations under her existing loan, and Felton's failure to exercise her right of repurchase, may also be relevant to the trial court's application of the *O'Brien* factors on remand. . . .

Points for Discussion

a. Role of Equity

If Zaman and Felton chose to structure their transaction as a sale, why should a court intervene? Both were sophisticated parties: Felton was an "experienced buyer and seller of real estate," while Zaman was a licensed real estate agent. Does the equitable mortgage doctrine undercut the traditional concern for stability of land title?

b. Structuring the Transaction

If Zaman and Felton intended the transaction to be a loan, they could have used standard documents. Felton would have executed (1) a promissory note payable to Zaman and (2) a mortgage encumbering the property. What incentive did they have to disguise the transaction as a sale? This arrangement provides several potential advantages for the lender. First, it permits the lender to avoid various disclosure requirements and rescission rights mandated by federal and state law. Second, it may allow the lender to covertly obtain an interest rate that violates state *usury laws*. Finally, it permits the lender to circumvent the protections that the law extends to a defaulting borrower; for example, it enables the lender to eliminate the borrower's equity of redemption without foreclosure. Assuming that Felton's version is correct, she was desperate to avoid a pending foreclosure and thus willing to agree to disguise the true nature of the deal.

c. Equitable Mortgage?

On remand, the trial judge decided (again) that the transaction was a sale, not an equitable mortgage. Felton then moved for an order vacating this decision and designating a new judge to hear the case, arguing that the trial judge had "demonstrated that his mind is so firmly made up . . . that he cannot fairly try the issues." But the court denied her motion. Did the judge properly apply the *O'Brien* factors?

d. Aftermath of *Zaman*

Five years after the *Zaman* transaction, New Jersey adopted the Foreclosure Rescue Fraud Prevention Act, N.J. Stat. § 46:10B–53 et seq., to protect homeowners. Among other things, it prohibits the consensual sale of an owner-occupied residence while foreclosure proceedings are pending if (1) the owner fails to receive at least 82% of fair market value or (2) the owner receives an option to repurchase or lease containing terms which are "unfair or commercially unreasonable."

C. Foreclosing on the Security

1. Borrower's Rights Before the Foreclosure Sale

Suppose that the Bakers miss a monthly payment, and the Bank threatens foreclosure. What can the Bakers do to avoid losing their home?

> - *Reinstatement*: As a general rule, a borrower can avoid foreclosure by paying the missed payments before the lender accelerates the loan. Some states also allow the borrower to reinstate for a limited period after acceleration occurs.
> - *Equitable redemption*: All states allow the borrower to avoid foreclosure by paying the loan in full (plus any incurred costs) after default but before the sale occurs.

But if the Bakers fail to use one of these remedies, their home may be sold at a foreclosure sale.

2. Judicial Foreclosure

Judicial foreclosure is the traditional remedy for collecting on a secured loan after the borrower's default. It is still the exclusive or dominant method in about one third of the states. Judicial foreclosure is simply a specialized form of litigation. The lender begins the process by filing a complaint against the *necessary parties*: the borrower, any junior lienors, and anyone else holding interests in the property that are junior in priority to the mortgage. If a junior interest holder is not named as a defendant, its interest is not affected by the foreclosure. After service of process, the defendants may file answers that raise any potential objections to foreclosure; and this may ultimately lead to a hearing to determine whether foreclosure is appropriate. But in most cases, no answer is filed and the lender obtains a default judgment.

Armed with its judgment authorizing foreclosure, the lender now gives notice of the time and place of the foreclosure sale. The auction is typically conducted in a public location, such as the steps of the local courthouse. The lender's auctioneer reads the notice of sale aloud, calls for bids, and sells the property to the highest bidder. The lender usually bids the amount of the remaining loan balance (a *credit bid*) and is not required to bid with cash. Do you understand why? Other bidders are usually required to bid with cash or the equivalent of cash (e.g., cashier's checks). In many cases, the lender is the only bidder.

The final step is judicial *confirmation* of the sale. The court may refuse to confirm the sale in its discretion, in order to protect the borrower's interests. But confirmation is almost always granted. Once confirmation occurs, an official delivers a quitclaim deed to the successful bidder and the borrower's equity of redemption terminates.

3. Nonjudicial Foreclosure

In most states, *nonjudicial foreclosure* is the dominant method for collecting on a secured loan after the borrower's default. Why? Lenders generally prefer nonjudicial foreclosure because it is quicker and cheaper than judicial foreclosure. But this type of foreclosure may present greater risks for the borrower due to the lack of judicial supervision.

A nonjudicial foreclosure is similar to a judicial foreclosure except it takes place with no judicial involvement. Once a default occurs, the lender or trustee gives notice of the time and place of the foreclosure sale to the borrower, junior lienors, and all others holding junior interests; the sale must occur in a public location. The sale is conducted by an auctioneer, and the property is sold to the highest bidder. All bidders must generally bid with cash or a cash equivalent, except for the lender, who can use a credit bid. Once the property is sold and the purchase price is paid, the auctioneer executes and delivers a quitclaim deed to the successful bidder; this terminates the borrower's equity of redemption. The proceeds from the sale are distributed in the same manner as proceeds from a judicial sale. Again, a junior interest holder without notice of the sale is not affected by it.

What if the lender starts nonjudicial sale proceedings when it is not entitled to foreclose? Here the borrower's remedy is to file a lawsuit seeking an injunction to prevent the sale.

4. Results of the Foreclosure Sale

Two basic principles govern foreclosure sales. Both are based on the *priority* of the mortgage being foreclosed. The rules that you studied in Chapter 8 about priority generally also apply to mortgage priority: the lender whose mortgage was created first has priority under the first-in-time rule unless a subsequent purchaser or lender is protected under the state's recording act. Remember that (a) a subsequent *bona fide purchaser or encumbrancer* may be protected against prior interests and (b) the *shelter rule* may also protect a subsequent party.

- *Principle 1*: *Foreclosure eliminates or "wipes out" the mortgage being foreclosed and all junior interests, but does not affect senior interests.*

Why? The lender accepts a certain risk of nonpayment, measured by facts that exist when the loan is made. But the borrower cannot be allowed to *increase* the lender's risk by transactions that occur *after* the loan is made. Thus, foreclosure also wipes out all interests that are junior in priority to the mortgage which is foreclosed. This includes junior mortgages and any other junior interests, such as easements, leases, and covenants. See, e.g., CFS 915, LLC v. Unetixs Vascular, Inc., 226 A.3d 1058 (R.I. 2020).

> *Example*: Suppose that O's home is encumbered by three mortgages: (1) a first priority mortgage (*first mortgage*) held by L1 securing a $270,000 loan; (2) a second priority mortgage (*second mortgage*) held by L2 securing a $30,000 loan; and (3) a third priority mortgage (*third mortgage*) held by L3 securing a $20,000 loan. If L1 forecloses, this eliminates its mortgage and all junior mortgages (L2 and L3). The buyer takes title free and clear of all mortgages.
>
> *Example*: Suppose instead that L2 forecloses. The sale eliminates L2's mortgage and L3's mortgage, but does not affect L1's mortgage. The buyer takes title subject to L1's mortgage.

- *Principle 2: Foreclosure sales proceeds are distributed first to the foreclosing lender, and then to junior interests in order of priority; any surplus proceeds go to the borrower.*

The reason for this principle is the same: it protects the lender's ability to recover on its loan based on the risk it knowingly accepted. Notice that excess sales proceeds do not go to senior lienors because their liens are not affected by the sale. Rather, these proceeds are first used to compensate junior lienors; any remaining surplus then goes to the borrower for the loss of her property.

> *Example*: Let's return to the hypothetical above. Suppose again that L1 forecloses; the high bidder at the sale pays $305,000. The first $270,000 pays off L1's loan; the next $30,000 pays off L2's loan; and the remaining $5,000 partially pays L3's loan. Again, the buyer takes title free and clear of all mortgages.
>
> *Example*: Suppose instead that L2 forecloses, and the buyer pays $60,000. The first $30,000 pays off L2's loan; the next $20,000 pays off L3's loan; and the $10,000 surplus goes to O. L1 does not receive any of the proceeds because the sale has no effect on its senior mortgage. The buyer takes title subject to L1's mortgage.

Points for Discussion

What is the state of title after foreclosure in the problems below? Who gets the sales proceeds? Assume there are no disputes about the priority of the mortgages.

> (1) O's farm is encumbered by three mortgages. L1 holds a first mortgage for $100,000; L2 holds a second mortgage for $50,000; and L3 holds a third mortgage for $75,000. L1 forecloses, and B buys the land for $110,000.
>
> (2) O's house is encumbered by two mortgages. L1 holds a first mortgage for $300,000; L2 holds a second mortgage for $150,000. L2 forecloses, and B buys the house for $200,000.

> (3) O's factory is encumbered by two mortgages and an easement. L1 holds a first mortgage for $500,000; L2 holds a second mortgage for $700,000; and N holds an easement over O's factory land which is junior to both mortgages. L1 forecloses, and B buys the factory for $500,000.

5. Special Mortgage Priority Rules

Special rules govern mortgage priority in three situations:

> - Purchase money mortgage
> - Future advance mortgage
> - Deed in lieu of foreclosure

A *purchase money mortgage* has priority over any other lien or interest that attaches to the property purchased through the buyer, such as a judgment lien, dower, or community property. For example, if H purchases a home from S in a community property jurisdiction, making a down payment from community funds and giving S a promissory note secured by a mortgage for the balance, S's mortgage takes priority over the community property interest of H's spouse.

As discussed above, the *future advance mortgage* has a clause which provides that the mortgage will serve as security for future loans to the borrower. In most states, if the mortgage *obligates* the lender to make such an additional loan, the new loan takes priority from the date of the mortgage. But if making such a loan is merely *optional* and the lender has *notice* that a third party has acquired an interest in the property after its original loan was made, then the new loan takes priority only as of the day it is made.

After default, the lender may be willing to accept a *deed in lieu of foreclosure*, which allows the borrower to avoid foreclosure by conveying title to the property to the lender. One drawback of a deed in lieu of foreclosure is that it does not wipe out junior interests. Thus, the lender takes title subject to these interests. A second potential concern is that the mortgage itself might be extinguished under the *merger* doctrine, though this turns on the intent of the parties. Notice that such an arrangement does not clog the equity of redemption because it comes *after* the loan has been made.

Points for Discussion

Consider these more advanced priority problems.

(1) C has a recorded judgment lien against O for $50,000. O now purchases a home from S for $180,000, giving S $20,000 in cash and a promissory note for $160,000, secured by a recorded mortgage on the home. Six months later, O defaults on the loan, and S forecloses. X buys the home at the sale for $180,000. Who gets the sale proceeds? What is the state of title?

(2) O borrows $500,000 from L1, planning to use the money to build a home; the mortgage securing the loan provides that L1 may make future advances secured by the mortgage, but is not obligated to do so. O has trouble finishing the home and borrows $25,000 from L2, secured by a mortgage on the property, to continue the work. O later obtains $100,000 in additional loan funds from L1, secured by the original mortgage; L1 knows about the mortgage that O gave to L2. A year later, O defaults on his loan from L2, and L2 forecloses. At the sale, Z buys the property for $530,000. Who gets the sale proceeds? What is the state of title?

(3) O borrows $100,000 from L1 which is secured by a first mortgage, $50,000 from L2 secured by a second mortgage, and $200,000 from L3 secured by a third mortgage. O defaults. L1 accepts a deed in lieu of foreclosure from O. What is the state of title?

D. Exercising Rights After Foreclosure

1. Protecting the Borrower

There is an obvious risk that the borrower may be treated unfairly during the foreclosure process. Suppose that the Bakers lose their home when the Bank forecloses on its mortgage. What rights do the Bakers have at this point?

- *Statutory right of redemption*: In about half of the states, a borrower may regain title by redeeming the property from the successful bidder within a set period of time, such as a year. In some states, the right only applies if the property is a home or farm. To exercise this right, the borrower must pay the sales price (plus interest and costs) to the bidder.

- *Setting aside the sale*: The borrower may be able to set aside the foreclosure sale. In most jurisdictions, a nonjudicial sale will be set aside if the sales price is so inadequate as to "shock the conscience" of the court or is "grossly inadequate." The case law varies on this point. For example, a sale for 20% or less of market value will usu-

> ally meet this standard, but not always. In addition, a nonjudicial sale may be set aside where a significant procedural irregularity has occurred, such as where the lender fails to give the notice required by law or tries to suppress bidding. More commonly, a nonjudicial sale is set aside when both factors are present: the sales price is substantially below fair market value and a procedural irregularity occurred. *See, e.g., Matter of George*, 856 S.E.2d 483 (N.C. 2021). The same objections may be raised by the borrower in a judicial foreclosure proceeding when the lender asks the court to confirm the sale. Finally, it should be noted that a few jurisdictions impose a higher duty on the lender conducting a nonjudicial sale, requiring it to use reasonable efforts to attract bidders and obtain a fair price. *See, e.g., Property Acquisition Group, LLC v. Ivester*, 122 N.E.3d 10 (Mass. App. Ct. 2019).

2. Protecting the Lender

The lender may also have special rights after the foreclosure sale. Suppose that the Bakers owe $270,000 to the Bank, secured by a mortgage on their home. Due to a recession, home values plummet across the nation. The Bakers lose their jobs and default on their loan payments. When the foreclosure sale occurs, the home is worth only $200,000; the Bank bids this amount at the sale and obtains title. But the Bakers still owe $70,000 ($270,000 minus $200,000). How does the Bank collect this money?

When the foreclosure sale proceeds do not fully repay the loan, the lender can usually sue the borrower for breach of contract—failure to pay the promissory note. In this lawsuit, it can obtain a *deficiency judgment* for the unpaid amount. In the hypothetical above, the Bank can obtain a deficiency judgment against the Bakers for $70,000. Of course, in many situations a deficiency judgment is worthless because the defaulting borrower has no assets that a creditor can reach.

In turn, the lender's right to obtain a deficiency judgment may be unfair to the borrower. Suppose now that the Bakers default on their $270,000 loan when their home is worth $280,000. At the nonjudicial foreclosure sale, the Bank is the only bidder and purchases the home for $50,000. The Bank then sues the Bakers and obtains a deficiency judgment for $220,000 ($270,000 minus $50,000) which it collects from their other assets. In this manner, the Bank receives $500,000 ($280,000 home value plus $220,000 judgment) in payment for a $270,000 loan.

Given this potential for unfairness, many states restrict deficiency judgments through *anti-deficiency legislation* or judicial action, especially where the property is a home.

- *Fair value*: Most states restrict the size of a deficiency judgment by limiting it to the amount by which the unpaid loan balance *exceeds* the fair market value of the property as of the foreclosure sale date. See, e.g., *HawaiiUSA Federal Credit Union v. Monalim*, 464 P.3d 821 (Haw. 2020) (adopting fair value test). In the hypothetical above, no deficiency judgment would be allowed because the loan balance ($270,000) is *less* than the property value ($280,000).

- *Prohibition*: Legislation in some states prohibits deficiency judgments altogether in certain situations, most commonly after non-judicial foreclosure or foreclosure on a purchase money mortgage.

- *Other approaches*: A number of courts will invalidate deficiency judgments based on inadequacy of the sales price or unfairness in the foreclosure process.

Our next case arises from the foreclosure of two deeds of trust used to secure agricultural loans. Farmers often take out seasonal loans to cover their expenses in producing crops, planning to repay the loans in full when the crops are sold. But farming is a risky business. When crops fail or crop prices fall, farmers may be unable to repay their loans, leading to foreclosure.

Wansley v. First Nat'l Bank of Vicksburg

Supreme Court of Mississippi

566 So. 2d 1218 (1990)

ROBERTSON, JUSTICE.

I.

First National Bank of Vicksburg has petitioned that we reconsider our April 5, 1989, decision holding invalid two foreclosure sales and setting aside deficiency judgments the Bank had obtained in the lower court. In our original opinion we held that the Bank's failure to appoint a disinterested trustee rendered the sales voidable. Upon rehearing we consider other stratagems deeply embedded in our law more likely effective in protecting mortgage debtors from overreaching at foreclosure. . . .

We grant the petition for rehearing, withdraw our earlier opinion, and reinstate and affirm the judgment below.

II.

Tom D. Wansley and Julian E. Wansley are brothers and farmers. Heretofore, the Wansleys have held as co-tenants some 4,200 acres of farm land in rural Sharkey

County, Mississippi. They divided their farming operations, each independently working half of the land.

For some fifteen years the Wansleys have obtained annual crop production loans through First National Bank of Vicksburg. In later years the Wansleys were unable to repay these loans in full and began renewing their unpaid debts with each new production loan. As their indebtedness mounted, the Bank required additional security—the Wansleys' land.

On February 25, 1982, Tom Wansley and his wife, Mary Ann Wansley, executed and delivered a deed of trust conveying their interest in the land to John C. Wheeless, Jr., as trustee. The instrument reflected a conveyance in trust to secure Tom's indebtedness to the Bank of $620,000.00. On April 22, 1983, Julian Wansley and his wife, Mary Frances Wansley, executed a like deed of trust, conveying their interest in the land to Wheeless, as trustee, to secure Julian's indebtedness to the Bank of $850,000.00. Each deed of trust secured future advances, and each stood as security for the Wansleys' farm-related financing through the 1984 crop year.

When their 1984 crops were harvested and sold, the Wansleys were unable to pay even a substantial portion of what each owed. The Bank declared their debts in default and directed Wheeless, as trustee, to foreclose. On March 29, 1985, Trustee Wheeless offered the Wansleys' lands at public auction. The Bank was the lone bidder, offering $500,000.00 for each brother's interest. Wheeless accepted these bids. On April 1, 1985, Wheeless executed trustee's deeds and delivered these to the Bank.

On March 8, 1986, the Wansleys filed a complaint in the Chancery Court of Sharkey County to cancel and set aside the trustee's deeds. The Bank counterclaimed, seeking to confirm its title in the foreclosed lands, plus entry of deficiency judgments against the Wansleys for the amounts of each of the indebtedness over and above $500,000.00.

> **FYI**
>
> Why did the Wansleys have trouble repaying their loans? During the 1980s, American farmers endured their worst financial crisis since the Great Depression. Low interest rates in the 1970s led many farmers to go into debt on the assumption that crop prices would increase. But interest rates rose sharply: the prime lending rate soared from 6.25% in 1976 to 21.5% by 1980, before dipping to 12% in 1984. During the same era, crop prices fell. For example, between 1981 and 1983 crop prices dropped by 21%. Squeezed between higher costs and lower income, thousands of farmers lost their lands in foreclosure.

At trial the Wansleys argued that the Court should void the foreclosure because Trustee Wheeless was personally financially interested in the Bank and hence was not an impartial and disinterested trustee. The proof developed that Wheeless was general counsel for the Bank and served on its board of directors. Although his stock ownership was not shown of record, Wheeless freely acknowledges that he was "one of the [Bank's] largest" shareholders. . . .

On October 17, 1986, the Chancery Court confirmed the Bank's fee simple title to the foreclosed lands as against the claims of the Wansleys. The Court dismissed the Wansleys' complaint, but found for the Bank on its counterclaim, entering deficiency judgments against Tom and Mary Ann Wansley for $493,294.00, plus interest, and against Julian and Mary Frances Wansley for $230,030.00, plus interest.

On December 31, 1987, the Bank sold the lands to L.G. Willis, Jr. and John T. Pitts. The sales price was substantially lower than $1,000,000.00, the aggregate amount credited the Wansleys upon foreclosure, creating a substantial loss for the Bank. . . .

III.

A.

The field of secured credit transactions has generated some of our law's great triumphs. Sitting in his office, the lawyer as architect has created a variety of legal structures that have enabled both debtor and creditor to do much that each desires but, without law, may not do. These privately made structures have enriched our society beyond the realm of the economic. Mississippi's crop economy would have no existence without them.

The common law mortgage and its progeny may work their way only because we enforce them. As one leading authority has put it,

> The law of mortgages today has been forged between the hammer of practice and the anvil of equity. The extent to which a creditor is willing to lend money upon security is determined in part upon the interest received and in part upon the ease with which the creditor can realize upon the security to satisfy a defaulted debt.

9 Thompson on Real Property § 4650, at 2 (1958). We once thought a lawsuit necessary upon default that a creditor may realize upon his collateral. Attendant cost and inefficiency reduced the mortgage's utility. The deed of trust and the power of sale foreclosure were more perfect forms of real property secured transactions and our lawyers developed and their clients accepted these because they circumvented the trouble and expense of judicial foreclosure. . . .

Still we have learned better than to allow complete freedom of contract. Experience found the economic power of creditors concentrated in the hands of a

> **Food for Thought**
>
> Why not allow "complete freedom of contract" in loan transactions? For example, the Wansley brothers were sophisticated businessmen who owned over 6 square miles of farm land. And presumably they were worried about the deficiency judgments only because they had other assets that the bank could reach. Why should the law limit deficiency judgments at all?

few while that of debtors was diffuse. There has always been a problem of protection of debtors from unfairness and overreaching. . . .

B.

In today's context, our focus has been—and is—upon assuring that the debtor is given credit toward his obligations in an amount fairly reflecting the market value of the collateral, all to the end that he may not be saddled with an inequitable deficiency judgment.

The theory of our original opinion was that holding the trustee to a strict standard of independence would promote that policy. Upon reflection, we find that (a) the independent trustee rule is practically unworkable, particularly in our smaller and more rural communities and, (b) even if we could refine and clarify that rule, by its nature it is not capable of affording the debtor the protections he may need.

The independent trustee rule without more will little aid beleaguered debtors. The trustee's independence is little consolation where the debtor winds up stuck with a large deficiency judgment. If the sale is conducted in a commercially reasonable manner, the debtor has no legitimate interest served by insisting that the trustee have no prior connection with the secured creditor. . . .

C.

. . . The deed of trust and the power of sale foreclosure arose in the all too familiar fashion. Lawyers had clients in need, and, where there is a client's will, there is a lawyer's way. Lawyers found a vehicle from another area of the law and forced it to fit, a square peg into a round hole, if you will. The trust was a recognized and ready facility.

The problem is that the typical secured land transaction bears at best a superficial analogy to a trust. The underlying reality is that the deed of trust under our law is little more than a common law mortgage with a power to convey in the event of default. The trustee is little more than an agent, albeit for both parties, and the writing prescribes his duties.

> **FYI**
>
> "Just as a panda is not an ordinary bear, a trustee of a deed of trust is not an ordinary trustee. A trustee under a deed of trust has neither the powers nor the obligations of a strict trustee. . . ." *Stephens, Partain & Cunningham v. Hollis*, 242 Cal. Rptr. 251, 255 (Ct. App. 1987). As the court explained in a footnote, the panda is actually a member of the raccoon family.

As so often happens, we are asked to take seriously the (borrowed) form and to forget the substance. We are urged to treat the trustee in a deed of trust as we would any other trustee. The problem becomes acute if we start implying onto the deed of trust all of the common law rules and responsibilities regulating trusts and trustees, e.g., the trustee's duty of prudence in management and reasonable maximization of profits from the trust assets. In the deed of trust, legal title is vested in the trustee. We doubt debtors would be very happy if the trustee/titleholders sought to assume control of their land and manage it.

We sensed the point in *Smith v. Beard,* 128 Miss. 1, 8, 90 So. 592, 593 (1922). Courts of California have been more explicit. *Lancaster Security Investment Corporation v. Kessler,* 159 Cal. App. 2d 649, 656, 324 P.2d 634, 638 (1958) correctly observes that

> A trustee under a deed of trust does not assume the important obligations which in some instances are cast upon a trustee by operation of law. [citation omitted] The trustee of a trust deed is not a trustee in the strict sense of the word. The role of such a trustee is more nearly that of a common agent of the parties to the instrument. . . .

D.

The price obtained at foreclosure formerly fixed the value of the collateral for purposes of computing a possible deficiency. If the independent trustee rule may be seen as one necessary and requisite to assuring a fair price at foreclosure, we should enforce it. A series of decisions over the past ten years make clear that the proffered rule may not be so seen, that it is, at best, superfluous!

Mississippi Valley Title Insurance Co. v. Horne Construction Co., Inc., 372 So. 2d 1270, 1272 (Miss. 1979) holds that the creditor has no right to a deficiency judgment until he satisfies the court that it would be equitable, in the light of the sales price, to authorize a deficiency judgment.

We added to that idea in *Lake Hillsdale Estates, Inc. v. Galloway,* 473 So. 2d 461, 465 (Miss. 1985). There we gave lip service to the idea that mere inadequacy of price will not operate to set the sale aside, unless the consideration is so grossly inadequate as to shock the conscience of the Court. On the separate question raised by the creditor's suit for a deficiency, however, *Lake Hillsdale* held that

> something more than a difference between the price paid at the foreclosure and the amount of the indebtedness must be demonstrated before the mortgagee is entitled to a deficiency judgment. . . . Though we have concluded above that the price paid at the foreclosure sale was not so inadequate as to require setting aside the sale, we cannot conclude that the value of the property thereby obtained is insufficient to satisfy the indebtedness of the mortgagor.

Lake Hillsdale, 473 So. 2d at 466. . . . This is but another way of saying that, before we will respect them for deficiency purposes, terms of a foreclosure sale must be commercially reasonable. . . .

In this view the Wansleys' insistence upon independence of the trustee is seen as something of an anachronism. . . . Commercial reasonableness has become our touchstone.

E.

There is no need to modify or dispatch the old rule to the effect that a foreclosure sale may not be set aside unless the sales price is so inadequate as to shock the conscience of the Court "or to amount to fraud." *Haygood v. First National Bank of New Albany*, 517 So. 2d 553 (Miss. 1987). This rule concerns only the legality of the foreclosure sale for purposes of vesting title to the collateral in the creditor or other purchaser at foreclosure. It has nothing whatsoever to do with the separate and distinct question of what, if any, deficiency judgment may be allowed.

. . . Subject to our otherwise governing statutes, we declare that, if the secured creditor is authorized to foreclose by power of sale, after the debtor's default and upon compliance with the deed of trust or other instrument, the secured creditor may sell any or all of the real estate that is subject to the security interest in its then condition or after any reasonable rehabilitation or preparation for sale. *Every aspect of the sale, including the method, advertising, time, place and terms, must be commercially reasonable.* This is an objective standard.

We apply these premises to the case at bar. We find that the Bank bid in the auctioned interest at each sale. Thereafter, the Bank credited Julian Wansley and Tom Wansley each with $500,000.00 following foreclosure, even though at that time the Bank had not realized so much as a penny out of the property. We find nothing in the proceedings before us suggesting that these sums did not fairly reflect the value of each Wansley's interest at the time, nor are we told of any other inadequacy in the foreclosure process. In sum, the Bank's behavior has been commercially reasonable, notwithstanding Wheeless' interests. . . .

> **Make the Connection**
>
> In *Kendall v. Ernest Pestana, Inc.* (Chapter 7), you learned that the modern trend is to apply the commercial reasonableness standard to a silent consent clause concerning assignment and sublease in a commercial lease. How does the rationale for that trend compare to the rationale for the applying the commercial reasonableness standard to deficiency judgments?

PETITION FOR REHEARING GRANTED; AFFIRMED.

Points for Discussion

a. A Disinterested Trustee?

Notice that the *Wansley* opinion followed a rehearing of the case. In its first opinion, the Mississippi Supreme Court invalidated the nonjudicial foreclosure sales and the deficiency judgments because Wheeless—who conducted the sales—was not a disinterested trustee. Why did the court reject this approach in its second opinion? How effective is a disinterested trustee in protecting borrowers from unfairness?

b. **Deed of Trust as Mortgage**

The *Wansley* court characterized the deed of trust as "little more than a common law mortgage with a power to convey in the event of default." This reflects the modern approach which equates the deed of trust with the mortgage with power of sale.

c. **Setting Aside the Sales**

The average value of Mississippi farm land reached a new historic high of $981 per acre in 1982, but then fell sharply to $685 per acre by 1987—a 30% decline. The Wansley land sold for only $238 per acre at the 1986 foreclosure sales, and the bank resold the land in late 1987 for "substantially" less than this amount. Assuming that the Wansley land was worth about $750 per acre when the sales occurred, should the court have set them aside based on inadequacy of the sales prices? Notice that the plaintiffs failed to present evidence that the sales prices "did not fairly reflect the value of each Wansley's interest at the time. . . ."

d. **Commercial Reasonableness**

What does a Mississippi lender have to do in order to conduct a commercially reasonable sale and thus obtain a deficiency judgment? For example, when the *Wansley* court states that the "terms" of the sale must be commercially reasonable, does this mean that the property must be sold for fair market value? If not, is the "fair value" approach a better method to protect the borrower? Notice that on the facts of *Wansley* there was only one bidder present at the sale—the foreclosing lender. Is it commercially reasonable to conduct a foreclosure sale when no outside bidders are present? Does the lack of outside bidders suggest that the advertising was insufficient? Or that the loan amount exceeded the value of the land?

e. **Limits on Deficiency Judgments**

As *Wansley* indicates, in many states the test for obtaining a deficiency judgment is *higher* than the test for conducting a valid foreclosure sale. Thus, even if the borrower cannot set aside the sale, she still may be able to avoid a deficiency judgment. What is the basis for this distinction?

f. **Problems**

In the problems below, should the sale be set aside? Should the lender obtain a deficiency judgment?

> (1) O borrows $250,000 from L, secured by a recorded mortgage on O's home. After O defaults, L issues a notice that sets a nonjudicial foreclosure sale for 9:00 a.m. on May 1. But at the time set for the sale, only three outside bidders are present, fewer than expected. L concludes that other bidders might

have been delayed due to overnight rains which flooded some roads, and he decides to delay the sale until 9:30 a.m. By that time, one of the outside bidders has left, and no new bidders have arrived. An outside bidder purchases the home for $200,000. Assume that the home is worth $200,000 on the sale date, because home values in the region have fallen.

(2) O borrows $2,000,000 from L, secured by a recorded mortgage on O's office building. After O defaults, L schedules a nonjudicial foreclosure sale. A few minutes before the sale begins, O watches as C (one of the outside bidders) hands small amounts of cash to the other four outside bidders, who immediately depart. L and C are the only bidders at the sale. L bids $2,000,000; C then bids $2,001,000 and obtains title. Assume the building is worth $6,000,000 on the sale date.

(3) O borrows $500,000 from L, secured by a recorded mortgage on O's factory. O sells the factory to D, who takes title subject to L's mortgage. D then borrows $100,000 from E, secured by a recorded mortgage on the factory. No one makes payments on L's loan, so L begins nonjudicial foreclosure proceedings. L notifies O and D about the sale, but fails to notify E. L is the only bidder at the sale and purchases the factory for $500,000. Assume that the factory is worth $1,500,000 on the sale date.

Summary

- **Obligation.** The most common obligation is the borrower's duty to repay a loan evidenced by a written promissory note. The borrower's successor is personally liable for repayment if he "assumes" the loan, but not if he takes title "subject to" the loan.

- **Security.** The borrower will provide security to the lender in the form of a mortgage, a deed of trust, or similar encumbrance on real property. The security is a remedy which the lender can use to repay the loan if the borrower defaults.

- **Mortgage.** The mortgage is the traditional security instrument. There are three theories on the nature of the mortgage: the title theory; the intermediate theory; and the lien theory.

- **Deed of Trust.** Despite its name, a deed of trust does not create a trust. Today most states treat the deed of trust like a mortgage with power of sale.

- **Installment Land Contract.** The modern trend is to provide equitable remedies for the defaulting vendee under an installment land contract, regardless of its express terms, due to its use as a mortgage substitute.

- **Equitable Mortgage.** If the parties disguise a mortgage transaction as a sale, the court will construe it as an equitable mortgage and provide the "seller" with the rights of a borrower.

- **Borrower's Rights re Foreclosure.** Before foreclosure, the borrower has two core rights: reinstatement and equitable redemption. After foreclosure, the borrower also has two core rights: the statutory right of redemption and, perhaps, the right to set aside the sale.

> **Test Your Knowledge**
>
> To assess your understanding of the material in this chapter, click here to take a quiz.

- **Foreclosure.** Judicial foreclosure is the traditional remedy for collecting on a secured loan in default; it is a specialized form of litigation. Foreclosure eliminates the mortgage being foreclosed and all junior interests, but does not affect senior interests. Foreclosure sale proceeds are distributed first to the foreclosing lender, then to junior lenders in order of priority, and then to the borrower. The general rules about deed priority also apply to mortgage priority except for three special situations: the purchase money mortgage; the future advance mortgage; and the deed in lieu of foreclosure. Nonjudicial foreclosure is similar to judicial foreclosure except that it occurs with no judicial supervision, which may present greater risks for the borrower.

- **Deficiency Judgment.** If the foreclosure sale proceeds do not fully repay the loan, the lender can usually sue the borrower for breach of contract and obtain a deficiency judgment for the remaining balance. However, many states have restricted deficiency judgments through legislation or judicial action.

> **For More Information**
>
> For more information about the subjects covered in this chapter, please consult the following sources:
>
> - Mehrsa Baradaran, *Jim Crow Credit*, 9 U.C. Irvine L. Rev. 887 (2019).
> - Grant S. Nelson & Dale A. Whitman, *Reforming Foreclosure: The Uniform Nonjudicial Foreclosure Act*, 53 Duke L.J. 1399 (2004).
> - Christopher K. Odinet, *Modernizing Mortgage Law*, 100 N.C. L. Rev. 89 (2021).
> - Michael H. Schill, *An Economic Analysis of Mortgagor Protection Laws*, 77 Va. L. Rev. 489 (1991).
> - Alan M. Weinberger, *Tools of Ignorance: An Appraisal of Deficiency Judgments*, 72 Wash. & Lee L. Rev. 829 (2015).
> - Alan M. White, *The Case for Banning Subprime Mortgages*, 77 U. Cin. L. Rev. 617 (2008).

Chapter 10

Private Land Use Planning

Imagine that D owns Redacre, a 1,000-acre tract of vacant land that is suitable for a wide range of purposes: factory, shopping center, farm, toxic waste dump, ranch, golf course, or houses. How much discretion does D have to choose among these options? And how can he utilize private land use planning to maximize the value of his property?

In this chapter, we examine the traditional building blocks of land use planning: easements, real covenants, and equitable servitudes. Today over 75 million Americans live in privately planned communities: single-family housing tracts, townhouse developments, condominium projects, and entire private towns. These communities are regulated by land use restrictions known as *covenants, conditions, and restrictions* (*CC&Rs*). In this manner, private land use planning has fundamentally changed the nature of home ownership. Similar techniques are often used to develop commercial and industrial projects.

Historically, land use was viewed primarily as a private matter, not as a public concern. Accordingly, a landowner like D was generally free to do what he wished with his property. But under some circumstances, an owner's plan might conflict with a core policy underlying American property law: encouraging the productive use of land. Common law principles evolved to deal with such conflicts:

- *Easements*: Land cannot be used unless the owner has adequate access to it, which may require an easement across land owned by another. Although most easements are the product of agreement, courts will sometimes impose an easement without the consent of the burdened owner.

- *Land use restrictions*: An owner might agree to restrict the use of his land by creating a *real covenant* or an *equitable servitude*. Courts were traditionally hostile to these restrictions due to fear they would impair productive use, but modern law recognizes their value in private land use planning, notably their use in enforcing CC&Rs.

As a general matter—subject to some exceptions—there is a basic difference between (1) an easement and (2) a real covenant or equitable servitude. Almost always, an easement authorizes A to do something on land owned by B; for example, it could allow A to cross B's land to reach A's own land. On the other hand, a covenant or servitude, compels B to do or not to do something on B's own land. For example, it might bar B from using B's land for business purposes; A could sue B for an injunction or damages if B violates this restriction.

The principles that governed easements, real covenants, and equitable servitudes were intricate and inconsistent. In the 1980s, the new importance of private land use planning led scholars to reexamine this area. This effort culminated in the publication of the Restatement (Third) of Property: Servitudes in 2000, which we will simply call the "Restatement." Characterizing the common law approach as "one of the most complex and archaic bodies of 20th century American law," the Restatement seeks to simply and clarify the law.

The Restatement merges the easement, the real covenant, and the equitable servitude into one doctrine: the *servitude*. It then provides a streamlined set of principles for creating, enforcing, modifying, or terminating a servitude. The Restatement reflects the view that "servitudes are useful devices that people ought to be able to use without artificial constraints." Restatement, ch. 2, intro. note. Thus, it rejects the historic approach that "emphasized the free use of land, sometimes at the expense of frustrating intent." *Id.* at ch. 4, intro. note.

As a result, the law of easements, real covenants, and equitable servitudes is in transition. Yet the pace of change is slow. Based on a study of reported decisions, one scholar concludes that the Restatement has not led to significant reforms in the law of any state, though its overall impact has been "mildly positive." Ronald H. Rosenberg, *Fixing a Broken Common Law—Has the Property Law of Easements and Covenants Been Reformed by a Restatement?*, 44 Fla. St. U. L. Rev. 143, 191 (2016). In the materials below, we examine both the traditional rules and the Restatement approach.

A. Easements

Suppose that A owns a remote 500-acre tract of forest land called Greenacre. Because the access road to her land is impassible during the winter, A wants the right to travel across B's land to reach Greenacre. A needs an *easement*—a nonpossessory right to use the land of another person.

The easement is a vital tool for the productive use of land. Easements are most commonly created to allow an owner such as A to travel to her land. But they are also used in a variety of other situations. For example, A may need to run a cable television line, an electric line, a telephone line, a gas pipe, a sewage pipe, or a water pipe across B's land in order to effectively use Greenacre.

In this chapter, you will study the basic easements recognized under modern law:

- Express easement
- Implied easement by prior existing use
- Easement by necessity
- Prescriptive easement
- Easement by estoppel (or irrevocable license)

The express easement arises only with the agreement of the owner whose land is burdened. But the remaining four types are imposed as a matter of law, *without* the owner's agreement.

Easement law uses special terminology. Let's examine these terms using the A-B hypothetical above. Assume that B grants A an easement over his land.

- *Property*: Greenacre, the land benefited by the easement, is called the *dominant tenement* or *dominant land*. B's land, which is burdened by the easement, is the *servient tenement* or *servient land*.
- *Parties*: A, the easement holder, is called the *dominant owner*. B, the owner of the servient tenement, is the *servient owner*.
- *Appurtenant or in gross*: An *appurtenant easement* benefits the holder in her use of a specific parcel of land, the dominant tenement. A's easement is appurtenant because it benefits A in her use of Greenacre. An *easement in gross* is not connected to the holder's use of any particular land; rather, it is personal to the holder. Most easements are appurtenant.
- *Affirmative or negative*: An *affirmative easement* allows the holder to perform an act on the servient land. A's easement is affirmative because it allows her to cross B's property. A *negative easement* allows the holder to prevent the servient owner from performing an act on the servient land. Most easements are affirmative.

1. Creating Easements

The most common type of easement is the *express easement*. This is simply an easement which is voluntarily created by the servient owner, usually in a deed. In the hypothetical above, the access easement which B conveyed to A was an express easement. This easement may arise by either *grant* or *reservation*:

- *Express easement by grant*: This arises when the servient owner grants an easement to the dominant owner, as in the A-B example above.

> - *Express easement by reservation*: This arises when the dominant owner grants the servient land to the servient owner, but retains or *reserves* an easement over that property.

An express easement may be created only in a writing that satisfies the Statute of Frauds. A well-drafted easement will: (a) identify the parties; (b) describe the servient land and the dominant land (if any); (c) describe the exact location of the easement on the servient land; and (d) state the purposes for which the easement may be used.

Here is a sample express easement by grant in the hypothetical state of Madison:

> **EASEMENT DEED**
>
> For a valuable consideration, receipt of which is hereby acknowledged, Simon G. Appleby hereby grants to Bethany H. Moreno a non-exclusive perpetual easement for vehicular and pedestrian ingress and egress over the real property located in Larchmont, Plata County, Madison, described as "the westerly 12 feet of Lot 23, as shown on the subdivision map of Larchmont Estates, recorded in Map Book 47, Page 118, Plata County Records on June 23, 1983."
>
> This easement is appurtenant to and for the benefit of the real property located in Larchmont, Plata County, Madison, described as "Lot 51, as shown on the subdivision map of Larchmont Estates, recorded in Map Book 47, Page 118, Plata County Records on June 23, 1983."
>
> *Simon G. Appleby*   May 1, 2024
>   Simon G. Appleby
>
> [Acknowledgment by notary public]

Traditionally, an express easement by reservation could only be reserved in favor of the dominant owner. However, most modern decisions allow this easement to be reserved in favor of a third party. *See Willard v. First Church of Christ, Scientist*, 498 P.2d 987 (Cal. 1972). Thus, assume X conveys his land to Y; in the deed, X could reserve an easement over the land in favor of Z, a third party.

Points for Discussion

a. Easement or License?

A *license* is an informal permission that allows the holder to use the land of another for a particular purpose. But it is not classified as an interest in land and, accordingly, can be revoked at any time. Licenses are common in everyday life. If you buy a movie ticket or receive an invitation to a party at a friend's house, you hold a license. In some situations, however, it is hard to determine whether a particular right is a license or an easement. This turns on the intent of the parties. For example, in *Markstein v. Countryside I, L.L.C.*, 77 P.3d 389 (Wyo. 2003), the court concluded that the parties intended to create an easement for fishing, even though their agreement referred to it as a "license." In reaching this conclusion, the court considered "the manner in which the right was created, the nature of the right created, the duration of the right, the amount of consideration given for the right, and whether there is a reservation of power to revoke the right." *Id*. at 399. *See also Millbrook Hunt, Inc. v. Smith*, 670 N.Y.S.2d 907 (App. Div. 1998) (agreement created an easement to hunt foxes, not a license).

b. Easement or Profit?

A *profit* (or *profit à prendre*) is a right to enter the land of another to remove game, gravel, minerals, timber, or other natural resources. The fishing right in *Markstein*, for example, might be viewed as a profit in some states. Although the legal principles governing profits and easements were somewhat different in the past, today most courts apply the same rules to both. In fact, Restatement § 1.2 defines the profit as a specialized form of easement.

c. Easements and Conveyances

What happens to an easement when the servient land is conveyed to a new owner? The easement remains attached to the land like any other encumbrance, unless the grantee is a bona fide purchaser. Suppose A holds a recorded easement to reach her home by crossing B's land, and B sells his land to C. C is bound by A's easement.

When can an easement be transferred to a new holder? Because an appurtenant easement is seen as attached to land, the transfer of the dominant land automatically transfers the benefit of the easement to the grantee. In the example above, A has an appurtenant easement. Thus, if A sells her home to D, D now holds the easement. On the other hand, in some states an easement in gross is transferable only if it serves a commercial purpose. The modern trend is to allow the transfer of an easement in gross unless the parties had a contrary intent. *See* Restatement § 4.6(1)(c) (generally, "[a] benefit in gross is freely transferable").

The recognition of express easements is noncontroversial—and perhaps boring. We generally expect our legal system to enforce property rights that are created by agreement. But when should the law impose an easement on an owner *without* his consent? And why? We now turn to easements that arise by operation of law, without an express agreement.

Suppose that C owns two adjacent residential lots. He builds his home on the western lot, and installs a pipeline underneath the eastern lot to connect his plumbing system to the nearest sewer main. C sells the eastern lot to D, without reserving an express easement. D now demands that C remove the pipeline. In this situation, C may be entitled to an *implied easement by prior existing use*.

Emanuel v. Hernandez

Appellate Court of Illinois

728 N.E.2d 1249 (2000)

JUSTICE BOWMAN delivered the opinion of the court:

Defendants and third-party plaintiffs, Jose and Lisa Hernandez, appeal an order granting plaintiffs, Wayne and Katherine Emanuel, summary judgment . . . on one count of a complaint for declaratory judgment. The trial court ruled that plaintiffs have an easement . . . over defendants' property. Defendants argue that the judgment cannot stand because plaintiffs failed to prove all the elements of . . . an easement by prior existing use. We agree with defendants and reverse.

Plaintiffs own the property at 920 Pearl Street in Belvidere and defendants own the property immediately north of them at 914 Pearl Street. Pearl Street is on the west side of the properties. Other residential property is to the east. The property line bisects a driveway, but most of the driveway is on defendants' land. Plaintiffs' . . . complaint alleged in part that defendants had blocked the driveway with railroad ties and had begun constructing a fence on the property line so that plaintiffs could not use the driveway. [The complaint] sought an easement by implication over the driveway.

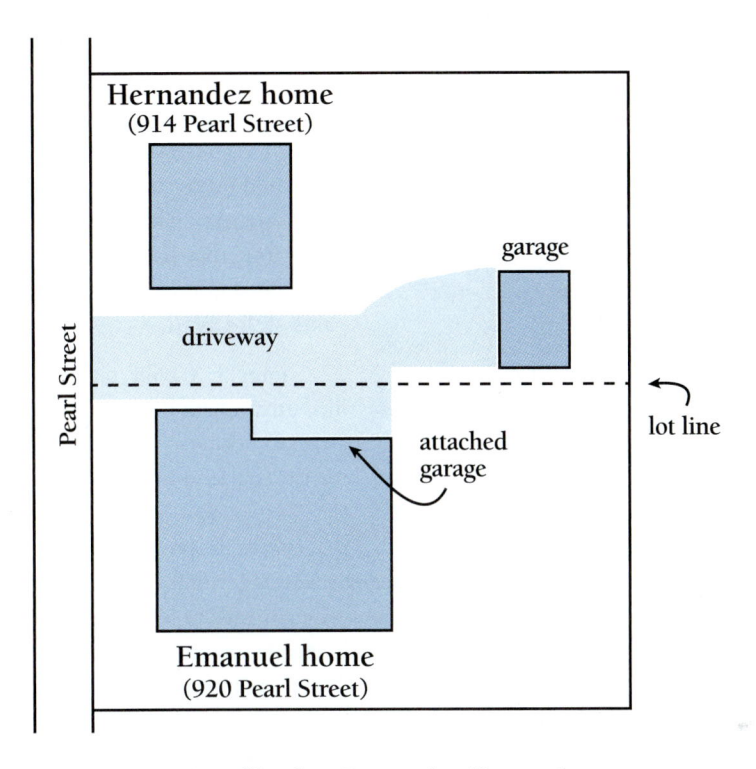

Map of land in *Emanuel v. Hernandez*

. . . The complaint alleged the following. Plaintiffs had owned the property at 920 Pearl since December 1965. Defendants had recently acquired the property at 914 Pearl. Originally, one person owned both properties. Before title was separated, the use of the driveway to gain access to the garage was so long continued, open, and obvious as to show that it was intended to be permanent. The use of the driveway is essential to the enjoyment of the property at 920 Pearl, as the driveway is the only way a car can get to the garage. . . .

Plaintiffs moved for summary judgment . . . attaching affidavits from Wayne Emanuel, Ruth Garrigan, and John H. Maville. Wayne Emanuel's affidavit stated the following. When plaintiffs took possession of the property in 1965, there was a driveway on the north side of the property. The driveway served both 920 Pearl and 914 Pearl and an attached garage at the rear of his property. The garage could be reached only via the driveway. Since moving in, plaintiffs had several times shared the costs of improving or repairing the driveway with their neighbors at 914 Pearl Street. Emanuel no longer lived at 920 Pearl, but his tenants continued to use the driveway to get to the garage until early 1996, when defendants started to block the driveway. Whoever lived at 920 Pearl could not get to the garage without using the driveway and, for much of the year, could not park on Pearl Street itself. Therefore, without the use of the driveway, the property could not be used without disproportionate expense or effort. . . .

Ruth Garrigan's affidavit stated that she and her husband purchased the property at 920 Pearl Street in 1953. At that time, at the rear of the house was an attached garage that could be reached via the driveway. The Garrigans used the driveway the whole time they lived at 920 Pearl, and they shared upkeep costs with the occupants of 914 Pearl.

> **Food for Thought**
>
> Should the defendants be allowed to deprive the plaintiffs of access to their garage, considering that this access had been continually used for decades? Is it fair to assume that the defendants knew about the shared driveway before they purchased the home?

John H. Maville, plaintiffs' lawyer, filed an affidavit describing a variety of attached exhibits, primarily deeds showing the chains of title to the two properties. As pertinent here, these deeds show that title to the properties was severed in 1890, when Benjamin Brock, who owned the west eight rods of lots 1, 2, and 3 in block 5 of Allen's Addition, conveyed the west eight rods of block 3—what is now plaintiffs' property—to Arthur E. Bassett. (Defendants' property is the west eight rods of block 2.) The affidavit also included a 1922 map prepared by the Belvidere public works department showing the locations of residences and garages on what are now plaintiffs' and defendants' properties.

> **What's That?**
>
> A *rod* is a unit of measurement, traditionally used by surveyors, which is 16½ feet long.

In seeking summary judgment . . . , plaintiffs asserted that the undisputed facts demonstrated that they had an "easement by implication." Relying on *Deem v. Cheeseman*, 113 Ill. App.3d 876, 446 N.E.2d 904 (1983), plaintiffs argued that all they had to prove to establish such an easement was that (1) title to the properties had been severed at some point; and (2) at the present time, the easement was necessary so that plaintiffs' property could be used without disproportionate effort or expense. Defendants countered that plaintiffs could not prevail because they had not shown a third element of such an easement—that, at the time of the severance of title, there was an existing use of the property that was of such a character that it would have survived as an easement by implication. . . .

The trial court agreed with plaintiffs and held that, under *Deem*, it was not fatal to the claim of an easement that plaintiffs had not shown either that their property was landlocked or "that the easement was created prior to the severance of the common ownership." The court considered it sufficient that there had been a severance of title and that, at present, the easement was highly beneficial because, without it, plaintiffs could not use their garage. . . . Defendants timely appealed. . . .

An easement may be implied when the owner of property conveys or otherwise surrenders title to part of the property. There are two types of implied easement—the easement by necessity and the easement implied from a preexisting use. *Granite Properties Ltd. Partnership v. Manns*, 117 Ill.2d 425, 435, 512 N.E.2d 1230 (1987). . . . An easement from a prior existing use will be implied when the owner of a tract or of two parcels conveys part of the property after having used the land so that one part of the parcel derives from another a benefit that is apparent, continuous, and permanent. . . .

> **Make the Connection**
>
> Should the plaintiffs have claimed a *prescriptive* easement? A prescriptive easement arises from long-term use of another person's land based on factors similar to adverse possession. You will study prescriptive easements later in this chapter.

It is crucial to recognize that an implied easement is the product of the intention of the parties to the conveyance. *Manns*, 117 Ill.2d at 437, 512 N.E.2d 1230; Restatement of Property § 476, Comment a, at 2978 (1944). The easement is "implied" in that courts attempt to ascribe an intention to parties who themselves did not put any such intention into words at the time of the conveyance. . . . Because the intention of the parties to the conveyance that severs title is the crucial consideration, whether an easement exists depends wholly on the circumstances at the time of the severance of title. *Manns*, 117 Ill.2d at 437, 512 N.E.2d 1230. . . . Thus, if an easement by implication does not arise at the moment of severance, a change in circumstances since the severance, no matter how great, cannot create any such easement.

We . . . conclude that the evidence does not support plaintiffs' claim of an easement by preexisting use. The elements of this easement are (1) common ownership of the dominant and servient parcels and a conveyance or other transfer separating that ownership; (2) before the conveyance or transfer severing the unity of title, the common owner used part of the united parcel for the benefit of another part, and this use was apparent and obvious, continuous, and permanent; and (3) the claimed easement is necessary and beneficial to the enjoyment of the parcel conveyed or retained by the grantor or transferor. *Manns*, 117 Ill.2d at 437, 512 N.E.2d 1230. . . . Here, plaintiffs plainly failed to establish, either by direct evidence or by inference, the second of these elements—the preexisting use.

Plaintiffs introduced no evidence that the driveway or anything comparable even existed when Brock conveyed the property in 1890 or that Brock ever used what is now the driveway. *A fortiori*, plaintiffs did not prove that, before the conveyance, Brock made an apparent, obvious, and continuous use of the part of the property he retained for the benefit of the part that he conveyed. Indeed, insofar as the historical evidence tells us anything, it tends to refute any claim of a preexisting use. Plaintiffs assert that the driveway is necessary for access to the garage, yet they concede that there is no evidence that the garage even existed before the 1920s. It is a reasonably safe guess that, in 1890, no easement was necessary for automobile travel to and from what is now plaintiffs' property. In short, there is simply nothing to suggest that, when Brock divided his property in 1890, he intended to give Bassett an easement across what remained of Brock's land.

With no evidence to prove that the parties to the 1890 conveyance intended an easement, there is clearly no basis to award one to plaintiffs, even if present-day circumstances may make it desirable. Plaintiffs failed to prove at least one element of an easement by preexisting use—the preexisting use.

> **FYI**
>
> Historians agree that the first American car was manufactured in 1893 by the Duryea Motor Wagon Company—three years *after* Brock sold to Bassett.

However, plaintiffs maintain, and the trial court apparently agreed, that they did not need to prove a preexisting use as long as they proved that, as of the time of the suit, the claimed easement was reasonably necessary to the enjoyment of their property. Apparently, the trial court concluded that plaintiffs needed only to prove (1) a severance of the unity of title and (2) some degree of present-day necessity for the claimed easement. This conclusion is simply erroneous and cannot be squared with the long-standing law that an easement by preexisting use requires the proof of three elements—severance, use prior to severance, and necessity. The trial court's decision is also irreconcilable with the logic behind these requirements: that an easement by implication depends on the intent of the parties at the time of the severance, and the claimant's proof must therefore relate to the circumstances at that time.

The trial court's error appears to have resulted from its reliance on *Deem v. Cheeseman*, 113 Ill.App.3d 876, 446 N.E.2d 904 (1983), which does seem to lend support to plaintiffs' recasting of the established requirements for an easement by implication. We hold that, insofar as *Deem* supports plaintiffs' position, Deem is unsound and should not be followed. . . .

Apparently, the *Deem* court simply dropped one element out of the three-part test for an easement by preexisting use. This element was the preexisting use itself. . . . In so doing, the court ignored established case law and improperly removed its focus from the intention of the parties to the conveyance as shown by the circumstances at the time of the conveyance. The court's apparent willingness to create an implied easement based on only the first and third elements of an easement by preexisting use was inconsistent with long-standing law. . . .

. . . Plaintiffs' entire discussion is based on the circumstances as they existed at or near the time of their lawsuit, not on the circumstances in 1890, when the severance of title occurred. Plaintiffs adduced insufficient evidence that the parties to the 1890 conveyance intended to create the easement that plaintiffs now claim. Therefore, the trial court erred in granting them summary judgment. . . .

Points for Discussion

a. Why Did the Plaintiffs Lose?

Why did the plaintiffs lose, exactly? The court notes that they failed to present any evidence that the driveway existed in 1890 when Brock conveyed to Bassett. How could they have obtained such evidence 110 years after that conveyance, when Brock and Bassett were long dead? The plaintiffs did present evidence that the driveway had been used by their predecessors in title since 1953. Why wasn't this enough? Did plaintiffs lose merely because the key witnesses were dead?

b. Why Recognize This Easement?

What policies justify the implied easement by prior existing use? The court implies that it is justified by owner autonomy. In other words, if the parties to the 1890 conveyance intended to create an easement, the court should honor that intent—even if the parties failed to create an express easement. But another potential policy underlying this easement is promoting the productive use of land. After all, if the plaintiffs cannot access their garage via the shared driveway, this impairs the full utilization of their home. Why shouldn't the plaintiffs obtain an easement if it was "reasonably necessary to the enjoyment of their property" as they asserted?

c. Required Elements

Three elements are usually required for an implied easement by prior existing use:

- severance of title to land held in common ownership;
- an existing, apparent, and continuous use of one parcel for the benefit of another at the time of severance; and
- reasonable necessity for that use at the time of severance.

Bird v. Bidwell, 209 P.3d 647 (Idaho 2009). The three elements used by the *Emanuel* court are similar to this general standard. The first element is satisfied here: Brock owned both lots, but severed title in 1890 when he sold one (now 920 Pearl) to Bassett. The second element was a problem for the plaintiffs. Before that sale, did Brock use one lot (now 914 Pearl) for the benefit of the other lot (now 920 Pearl)? It is certainly possible that Brock used a driveway across 914 Pearl before 1890 in order to access a barn, stable, or home on 920 Pearl—but there is no evidence to prove this. Finally, note that there must be "reasonable necessity" for the existing use to continue at the time title is severed, here 1890; again, there was no evidence of this.

d. Defining Reasonable Necessity

What is *reasonable necessity*? The easement must be beneficial or convenient for the use of the dominant tenement, but need not be essential. For example, in *Russakoff v. Scruggs*, 400 S.E.2d 529 (Va. 1991), the court found that homeowners in a subdivision that included an artificial lake had reasonable necessity to access the lake for recreation. Restatement § 2.12 cmt. e explains: "Reasonable necessity usually means that alternative access or utilities cannot be obtained without a substantial expenditure of money or labor."

e. By Grant or by Reservation

An implied easement by prior existing use may arise either by *grant* or by *reservation*. In this case, the plaintiffs argued that Bassett received an implied easement by grant. Should the requirements be the same for both?

f. Exercise

Suppose D owns a mansion located on 50 forested acres; a public highway adjoins the east side of her land. A gravel road goes across D's land from the highway to the mansion on the west side of the property; a thin black telephone cable runs from a pole next to the highway, through the trees, and then connects to the mansion's telephone system. The line is almost entirely concealed in the foliage, but could be spotted by a very diligent observer. D conveys the west half of her land to E. The D-E deed expressly gives E an access easement along the gravel road, but says nothing about telephone service. D now plans to cut the telephone line. Does E have an implied easement by prior existing use?

g. Implied Easement from Plat

Another type of implied easement arises when a developer conveys a lot in a subdivision by reference to a plat or subdivision map, such as "Lot 10, as set forth on the map recorded in Book 332, Page 17, Alameda County Records, California." In this situation, the grantee receives an implied easement over the streets and other common areas shown on the plat—unless the parties have an actual intent to the contrary. *See, e.g., Read's Landscape Constr., Inc. v. Town of West Warwick*, 252 A.3d 713 (R.I. 2021).

Suppose that E owns a 100-acre tract of rural land that adjoins a public highway on its west side. She splits her land in half and conveys the eastern portion to F. The E-F deed does not mention any access rights. F's property is now *landlocked*—meaning that F does not have a legal right to access it from a public road. How can F get to his land? The answer to this dilemma is the *easement by necessity*.

Berge v. State of Vermont

Supreme Court of Vermont

915 A.2d 189 (2006)

Dooley, J.

Plaintiff David Berge appeals from a summary judgment of the Washington Superior Court rejecting his claim to an easement by necessity on the ground that his property was accessible by navigable water. For the reasons set forth below, we disagree with the trial court ruling, and accordingly reverse and remand for further proceedings.

The material facts are not in dispute. In 1959, Florence Davis subdivided her estate, conveying 7,001 acres to the State of Vermont. That conveyance comprises the majority of the acreage of what is now the Bill Sladyk Wildlife Management Area (WMA). The 7,001 acres did not represent all of Davis's holdings in the area; she reserved, among other parcels, a lot of approximately thirty-eight acres on the western shore of Norton Pond, known as the Norton Pond Exclusion. The 1959 deed reserved no express easement for access to the Norton Pond Exclusion across the land conveyed to the State.

In 1961, Davis conveyed the Norton Pond Exclusion to George McDonald and Bruce Washburn. The 1961 deed again contained no reference to any easement across the WMA. McDonald and Washburn subdivided the Norton Pond Exclusion into eighteen lots, reserving a right of way for each lot over every other lot in the subdivision. In 1997, plaintiff purchased two of the lots from a successor in title to McDonald and Washburn. Since then, plaintiff has regularly accessed the property by car over a gravel road that begins on Route 114 . . . and then [runs] across the WMA to his property. Although plaintiff owns a fishing boat which he launches in the spring from a public boat-access on the opposite shore, he stated without contradiction that he does not use the boat to access the property.

> **FYI**
>
> Berge's property is located on the northwest side of the pond, about a half mile north of the pond's public boat ramp. Click here to see the gravel road that Berge used to reach his land before the dispute arose.

The instant controversy arose when the State placed a gate across the Route 114 access road, depriving plaintiff of overland access to his property. Plaintiff filed a complaint in superior court, seeking to enjoin the State's obstruction. He asserted, among other claims, that the 1959 deed had created an easement by necessity for the benefit of his property over the land conveyed to the State. The State moved for summary judgment, maintaining that plaintiff's ability to access his property by water, across Norton Pond, defeated a finding of necessity. The trial court agreed, and accordingly granted the motion and entered judgment in favor of the State. This appeal followed. . . .

Our common law has long recognized that "when, as a result of the division and sale of commonly owned land, one parcel is left entirely without access to a public road, the grantee of the landlocked parcel is entitled to a way of necessity over the remaining lands of the common grantor or his successors in title." *Traders, Inc. v. Bartholomew*, 142 Vt. 486, 491, 459 A.2d 974, 978 (1983). . . . In *Okemo Mountain, Inc. v. Town of Ludlow*, we outlined the basic requirements for an easement by necessity as: "(1) there was a division of commonly owned land, and (2) the division resulted in creating a landlocked parcel." 171 Vt. 201, 206, 762 A.2d 1219, 1224 (2000). The easement is said to remain in effect so long as the necessity exists. *Traders*, 142 Vt. at 493, 459 A.2d at 979.

Although plaintiff opposed the State's motion here on the ground that his property—having originated from a division of commonly owned land that resulted in a parcel lacking access to a public road—satisfied the fundamental requirements for an easement by necessity, the trial court did not address these criteria. Instead, the court concluded that plaintiff's claim was defeated solely by virtue of the fact that he could reach the property by water. In so holding, the court stated that " 'necessity' is the operative term in the doctrine," and explained that it could not recognize an easement "merely because water access is not as desirable as the road access that is sought." The court relied on a few early Vermont decisions characterizing the requisite standard as one of "strict necessity," as well as several out-of-state decisions adhering to the view that water access, unless completely useless, bars a finding of necessity.

While the court's conclusion is understandable given the relatively little attention accorded the easement-by-necessity doctrine in recent years, it is nevertheless erroneous in several respects. The term "strict necessity" first appeared in our law in *Howley v. Chaffee*, 88 Vt. 468, 474, 93 A. 120, 122 (1915). The issue there, however, was not whether the Court should apply a rule of "strict" or "loose" necessity in easement-by-necessity cases. Indeed, there was no dispute that the plaintiff could not show necessity because his parcel "front[ed] on one of the principal streets of the city." *Id.* at 473, 93 A. at 122. The issue instead was whether a reservation of an easement by implication, a separate doctrine, required the element of necessity as defined for an easement by necessity, or some other standard easier to meet. The answer was that the implied reservation required necessity as defined in the easement by necessity cases, particularly in *Dee v. King*, 73 Vt. 375, 50 A. 1109 (1901). To the extent the Court used the word "strict," it was to compare the elements in the different theories; that is, the plaintiff strictly had to show necessity and nothing less. See *Poronto v. Sinnott*, 89 Vt. 479, 481–82, 95 A. 647, 648 (1915) (summarizing holding in *Howley* that "strict necessity" is required in a case of easement by implied reservation).

In *Dee,* the plaintiff also was able to access his property, but only over a hill that could not "be crossed without making several turns, and then only with very light loads." 73 Vt. at 377, 50 A. at 1110. The Court drew a fundamental distinction—to which we have repeatedly returned—between "extreme inconvenience," which would not justify an easement by necessity, and "necessity, and not convenience, that gives the right." 73 Vt. at 378, 50 A. at 1110. . . . As *Dee* explained, the plaintiff's access to his property was "inconvenient and expensive" but not "impracticable," and therefore was not so deficient as to invoke the doctrine. 73 Vt. at 378, 50 A. at 1110. . . .

Therefore, if there is a distinction to be drawn from our prior decisions, it is between mere inconvenience and necessity, with a lack of reasonably practical access required to find an easement by necessity. Thus understood, the record here leaves no doubt that without use of the road across State land, plaintiff would have no reasonably consistent, *practical* means of reaching his property; rather, he would be subject to the constant vicissitudes of motor boats, weather, and water conditions. In addition, he would have virtually no access for those periods of the year when the pond could not be safely traversed because of ice or snow.[2]

> **Food for Thought**
>
> What other factual situations would meet the court's test? How predictable are the results from this test?

The real lesson of these cases, however, lies in the nature of the property interest protected. On this point, the holding of *Traders* is significant. As we there explained, "since the easement is based on social considerations encouraging land use, its scope ought to be sufficient for the dominant owner to have the reasonable enjoyment of his land for all lawful purposes." 142 Vt. at 494, 459 A.2d at 979–80. . . .

Plainly, without use of the road, plaintiff would lack any practical means of access for the "reasonable enjoyment of his land." While the property may be accessible by water for part of the year, the State made no real claim—and the trial court here made no finding—that this represents access adequate for reasonable enjoyment of the property. We depend on roads and automobiles for transporting not only our family and friends, but all our basic necessities to and from our homes, and it is a quaint but ultimately pointless fiction to pretend that water—much less ice—represents a sufficient substitute. . . .

[T]he question remains whether our . . . precedents or sound policy support the navigable-water exception. The trial court concluded that we must apply the exception because it was the law in 1959, at the time of the original conveyance in this case. We disagree for two reasons. First, as noted, our case law has long made practical

---

[2] On this point, the dissent states that plaintiff conceded that the road "is not generally passable between late November and the time 'the Access Road becomes passable in the spring,' " and that year-round access by car "is not available to him now." That is not an accurate statement of plaintiff's discovery response. He described the Berge property as his "principal residence." He explained that he uses the access road "very frequently" from the time the road becomes passable in the spring and stated: "I also use the Access Road to get to the Berge property in the winter."

access to a *public road* the linchpin of the easement-by-necessity doctrine. This was the law at the time of the original conveyance in 1959, and it remains so today. . . .

Second, we are not, in fact, persuaded that we must apply different versions of the common law based on when interests in land arise, and act as if we were judges at that time. The issue here is about use. As the Restatement (Third) of Property (Servitudes) § 2.15 cmt. d (2000) states:

> What is necessary depends on the nature and location of the property, and may change over time. Access by water, while adequate at one time, is generally not sufficient to make reasonably effective use of property today. Land access will almost always be necessary, even though water access is available. . . .

> Until recently, access for foot and vehicular traffic tended to be the only rights regarded as necessary for the enjoyment of surface possessory estates. However, the increasing dependence in recent years on electricity and telephone service, delivered through overland cables, justify the conclusion that implied servitudes by necessity will be recognized for those purposes. . . .

We should not freeze the common law in time, holding that for some landowners water access is sufficient, and for others it is not, or that some landowners can have electricity but others cannot. Today's standards compel the conclusion that access to navigable water is generally not legally sufficient, standing alone, to defeat a finding of necessity.

Because its holding was based solely on the erroneous conclusion that water access defeated plaintiff's easement-by-necessity claim, the trial court failed to address or make findings related to the essential elements of the claim, the location of the easement if those elements are satisfied, and any related defenses to be raised by the State. Accordingly, the matter must be remanded for further proceedings.

REIBER, C.J., dissenting.

. . . I . . . take issue with the bright line the majority would draw between water access (no matter how convenient, practical or longstanding) on the one hand, and land access (no matter how inconvenient or impractical) on the other. . . .

[T]he bright line between water and land access, seductive though it is, gives only the shortest shrift to the countervailing policy concerns that have historically animated our reluctance to so easily grant easements by necessity. The public's interest in access to landlocked property must be balanced against the serious consequences inherent in granting one landowner an uncompensated interest in the property of a neighbor. See *Hyde v. Town of Jamaica*, 27 Vt. 443, 460 (1855) (affirming preeminent legal and constitutional standing of real property); see also *Burling v. Leiter*, 272 Mich. 448, 262 N.W. 388, 391 (1935) ("If we adopt any other rule than that of strict necessity, we open the door to doubt and uncertainty, to the disturbance and questioning of titles, and to controversies as to matters of fact outside the language of the deed.") . . .

Points for Discussion

a. **Why Recognize This Easement?**

Two justifications are suggested for the easement by necessity: (1) the implied intent of the parties; and (2) the public policy favoring the productive use of land. Do these justifications make sense today? *See Hurlocker v. Medina,* 878 P.2d 348 (N.M. Ct. App. 1994) (discussing policy bases for easement by necessity); *see also* Stewart E. Sterk, *Neighbors in American Land Law,* 87 Colum. L. Rev. 55 (1987). The law is clear that an easement by necessity will not arise if this would contradict the actual intent of the parties. Why not? The *Berge* dissent cautioned against "the serious consequences inherent in granting one landowner an uncompensated interest in the property of a neighbor." Should the law recognize an easement by necessity only on condition that the dominant owner compensate the servient owner?

b. **Required Elements**

Courts generally require two elements for an easement by necessity:

- severance of title to land held in common ownership; and
- necessity for the easement at the time of severance.

How do the elements required for an easement by necessity compare to those needed for an implied easement by prior existing use? What explains the differences?

c. **How Much Necessity?**

Under the traditional approach *strict necessity* is required; this is found only when the owner has no legal right of access to her land. Thus, the parcel must be surrounded by privately owned land, and the owner must not have a right to cross that land to reach a public road. Suppose that owner A has a legal right of access to his land, but it would be extremely inconvenient or expensive to use it. Strict necessity does not exist on these facts. *See, e.g., Thompson v. Whinnery,* 895 P.2d 537 (Colo. 1995) (denying easement by necessity because owner had legal access to land by foot and on horseback).

The modern trend—endorsed by the Restatement—is to require less "necessity" than the traditional view. Under this approach, an easement is "necessary" if the property "cannot otherwise be used without disproportionate effort or expense." *See* § 2.15 cmt. d. For example, in *Bartkowski v. Ramondo,* 219 A.3d 1083, 1094 (Pa. 2019) the court recognized that an easement by necessity was appropriate where it was "manifestly impracticable, even though theoretically possible, to create ingress and egress across one's own property." The *Berge* court adopted a somewhat similar position: the "lack of reasonably practical access." What does this mean? The unusual twist in *Berge* was that the plaintiff's property could still be reached by boat. Should water access prevent Berge from receiving an easement for road access?

d. **Exercise**

Suppose that R owns two adjacent parcels, Redacre and Greenacre. She sells Greenacre to S for $200,000. Greenacre is divided by a deep canyon which could be bridged at a cost of $75,000. The portion of Greenacre that adjoins Redacre has no access to a public road; the other part of Greenacre adjoins a public road. A public road runs through Redacre. Is S entitled to an easement by necessity across Redacre to reach his land?

e. **Scope and Duration**

Traditionally, the easement by necessity doctrine applied in only one situation: road access to a landlocked parcel. Suppose that Berge's house is not connected to electric and telephone lines. Should an easement by necessity also be recognized for these utilities, as the Restatement advocates? In this era of solar panels, portable generators, and cell phones, is it necessary to have electric and telephone lines? *See, e.g., Francini v. Goodspeed Airport, LLC*, 174 A.3d 779 (Conn. 2018) (approving easement by necessity for utilities where owner held express easement for access).

Turning to duration, it is well-settled that an easement by necessity lasts only so long as the necessity continues. For example, if the state built a public road next to Berge's property, his easement by necessity would end.

f. **Aftermath of** *Berge*

On remand, the main issue was the location of the easement. In general, the owner of the servient land is entitled to select the route for an easement by necessity, as long as it is reasonable. *Griffeth v. Eid*, 573 N.W.2d 829, 834 (N.D. 1998). Suppose the state insists that the easement follow an old road which has become so degraded over time that it can no longer be used unless Berge spends thousands of dollars to improve it; the state prefers that Berge use this road because it is outside the "core" of the management area, thus minimizing any impact on wildlife. Berge prefers another road, already in good condition, which runs closer to the center of the management area. Is the state's choice reasonable?

Suppose that G crosses H's property in an open and notorious manner in order to reach his own land. If G continues this conduct for a sufficient period, he may obtain a *prescriptive easement*. Just as title to land may be acquired by adverse possession, an easement may be acquired by similar conduct. Remember that Lutz mistakenly sought such a prescriptive easement in his first lawsuit, which preceded *Van Valkenburgh v. Lutz* (Chapter 2).

O'Dell v. Stegall

Supreme Court of Appeals of West Virginia

703 S.E.2d 561 (2010)

KETCHUM, JUSTICE:

Two-and-a-half centuries ago . . . the doctrine of prescriptive easements took root in our common law. When estates were so large that the boundaries were unknown, and vast tracts were owned by individuals who never set foot on the land, it was reasonable and economical for the law to reward a diligent user of the land with an easement by prescription at the expense of the absentee owner. . . .

But in today's world, our law on the doctrine of prescriptive easements is a tangled mass of weeds. The doctrine essentially rewards a trespasser, and grants the trespasser the right to use another's land without compensation. Such a significant imposition on the rights of modern landowners discourages neighborly conduct, and does not square with the modern ideal that we live in a congested but sophisticated, peaceful society.

In this appeal from the Circuit Court of Jefferson County, we are asked to examine a jury's verdict finding that a plaintiff had acquired a prescriptive easement to use a gravel lane. . . . After a thorough examination of the record, we believe that the plaintiff wholly failed to establish that he had a prescriptive easement. . . .

I.

Facts and Background

In 2006, plaintiff (and appellee) Michael J. O'Dell bought land and a home on the Old Leetown Pike—now Route 15—in Jefferson County, West Virginia. The plaintiff's home was originally built and used as the German Baptist Brethren Church starting sometime around 1898, and was converted into a residence sometime after 1999. The plaintiff's lot abuts the Leetown Pike/Route 15, and the plaintiff has a driveway that connects directly to this public road.

Directly behind and adjacent to the plaintiff's property, defendants (and appellants) Robert and Virginia Stegall own land and a home. The defendants' property is "landlocked" and surrounded on all sides by land owned by other individuals.

This case concerns a private, 25-foot-wide gravel lane that borders on the northern edges of both the defendants' property and the plaintiff's property. The defendants do not own the gravel lane, but it is their only access to a public highway (the Leetown Pike/Route 15).

The central question is whether the plaintiff has a legal right to use the gravel lane for ingress to and egress from the *north* side of his home. The plaintiff already

> **See It**
>
> Click here to see (a) a photo of O'Dell's house and (b) a letter from defendant Stegall objecting to O'Dell's use of the gravel lane.

has access to the Leetown Pike/Route 15 by way of his own driveway across his property on the *south* side of his home. The plaintiff does not know who owns the land beneath the gravel lane, but he insists that he has a prescriptive easement to use the lane as an additional access to his property from the Leetown Pike. The defendants retort that the plaintiff does not have a prescriptive easement, and assert that the plaintiff's use will cause wear and tear to the gravel lane which the defendants are contractually obligated to repair.

. . . This case demonstrates that there is nothing more vicious than a fight over a piece of land between two neighbors. The parties' briefs and the record from the trial court reveal more ridiculing than reasoning, more finger-pointing than fact-finding. . . .

In 2008, numerous disagreements arose between plaintiff O'Dell and the defendant Stegalls. Essentially, the plaintiff claimed that he had the right to use the gravel lane to access a horseshoe-shaped driveway on the northern edge of his land. This horseshoe-shaped driveway appears to have been partially constructed and connected to the gravel lane sometime after 1999. The defendants objected to the plaintiff's use of the gravel lane to access the horseshoe-shaped driveway, called the police two times, and threatened to have the plaintiff prosecuted for trespassing. . . .

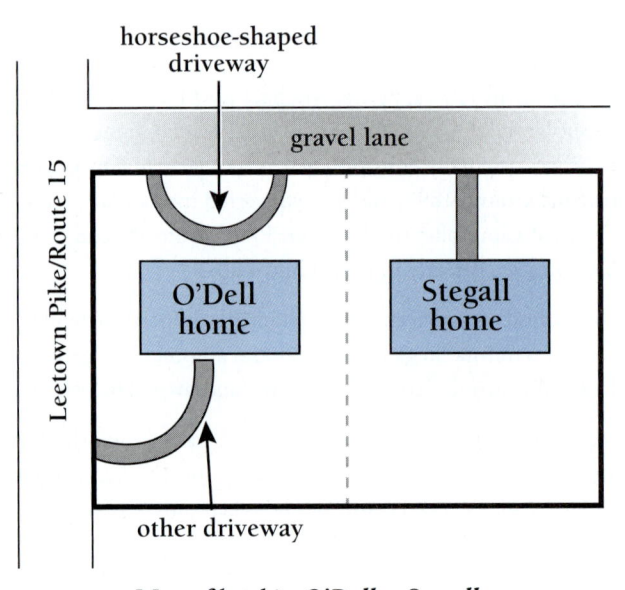

Map of land in *O'Dell v. Stegall*

In response to the defendants' objections, plaintiff Michael O'Dell filed the instant lawsuit in September 2008 against all of his neighbors who border the gravel lane.... The primary count in the plaintiff's complaint sought to "quiet title by way of a prescriptive easement" allowing the plaintiff to use the gravel lane. The plaintiff claimed that the gravel lane had, "by its nature and duration of its open, continuous, notorious and adverse use, as to any owner of the parcel" become a "community driveway servicing as an ingress and egress easement" to the plaintiff's property. [Plaintiff settled his claims against everyone but the Stegalls.]

... A jury trial against the defendant Stegalls was held in June 2009, wherein the plaintiff asserted that he had a prescriptive easement to use the gravel lane. To support this assertion, he introduced the testimony of several individuals who stated that there used to be a parking lot behind the church that now serves as the plaintiff's home. These individuals said that, for several decades prior to 1999, visitors to the church had continuously used the gravel lane to access the parking lot....

After a three-day trial, on June 11, 2009, the jury concluded that the plaintiff had established a prescriptive easement to use the gravel lane as an "ordinary access to his residence." The jury also awarded the plaintiff $5,300.00 in compensatory damages and $4,700.00 in punitive damages against the defendant Stegalls.... The defendants now appeal the circuit court's judgment entered on the jury's verdict, and refusal to set aside the judgment....

III.

A.

The Law of Prescriptive Easements

... A prescriptive easement arises through the adverse use of another person's land. "There is a similarity between the elements which must be shown to establish a prescriptive easement and those necessary for adverse possession." *Veach v. Day*, 172 W.Va. 276, 278, 304 S.E.2d 860, 863 (1983) (*per curiam*). The main distinction between adverse possession and a prescriptive easement "is that an adverse possession claimant occupies or possesses the disputed land, whereas one seeking a prescriptive easement makes some easement-like limited use of the disputed land." *Newman v. Michel*, 224 W.Va. 735, 743, 688 S.E.2d 610, 618 (2009)....

> Prescription doctrine rewards the long-time user of property and penalizes the property owner who sleeps on his or her rights. In its positive aspect, the rationale for prescription is that it rewards the person who has made productive use of the land, it fulfills expectations fostered by long use, and it conforms titles to actual use of the property. The doctrine protects the expectations of purchasers and creditors who act on the basis of the apparent ownerships suggested by the actual uses of the land.

Restatement (Third) of Property (Servitudes), § 2.17, cmt. c. "[I]ts underlying philosophy is basically that land use has historically been favored over disuse, and that therefore he who uses land is preferred in the law to he who does not, even though the latter is the rightful owner." *Finley v. Yuba County Water Dist.*, 99 Cal.App.3d 691, 696, 160 Cal.Rptr. 423, 427 (3d. Dist. 1979). . . .

Our examination of our prior cases applying the doctrine of prescriptive easements reveals a lack of any clear enunciation of the meanings of the concepts underlying the doctrine. . . . [W]e will now attempt to set out definitions of the elements necessary to establish a prescriptive easement, definitions intended to guide a finder of fact. . . .

(1) Elements of the Prescriptive Easement Doctrine

. . . [A] person claiming a prescriptive easement must prove each of the following elements: (1) the adverse use of another's land; (2) that the adverse use was continuous and uninterrupted for at least ten years; (3) that the adverse use was actually known to the owner of the land, or so open, notorious and visible that a reasonable owner of the land would have noticed the use; and (4) the reasonably identified starting point, ending point, line, and width of the land that was adversely used, and the manner or purpose for which the land was adversely used. . . .

(2) "Adverse Use" of Another's Land Defined

A person claiming a prescriptive easement must first show that his or her use of the servient estate was "adverse" to the rights of the true owner. . . .

But what does "adverse" truly mean? . . . Our cases discussing prescriptive easements have lobbed around the words "adverse" and "hostile," but have never attempted to posit a forthright definition to guide a finder of fact. . . .

Moreover, instead of defining "adverse use," in many of our early cases this Court simply presumed that a claimant's use of another's property was adverse, if the claimant had otherwise proven the remaining elements of the prescriptive easement doctrine. In doing so, the Court shifted the burden of proof from the claimant to the landowner, who had to prove that the servient estate *had not* been used adversely (*e.g.,* the land had been used with permission). . . . This Court has never—until this case—addressed or attempted to explain this incongruity in our law.

The term "adverse use" does not imply that the person claiming a prescriptive easement has animosity, personal hostility, or ill will toward the landowner; the uncommunicated mental state of the person is irrelevant. Instead, adverse use is measured by the observable actions and statements of the person claiming a prescriptive easement and the owner of the land. *Kellison v. McIsaac*, 131 N.H. 675, 680, 559 A.2d 834, 837 (1989) (subjective intent of adverse claimant does not determine validity of prescriptive claim). . . .

"Adverse use" generally means the "use of property as the owner himself would exercise, entirely disregarding the claims of others, asking permission from no one[.]" *Malnati v. Ramstead*, 50 Wash.2d 105, 108, 309 P.2d 754 (1957). Use of a servient estate is adverse "when a party . . . has received no permission from the owner of the soil, and uses the way as the owner would use it, disregarding his claims entirely, using it as though he owned the property himself." *Blanchard v. Moulton*, 63 Me. 434, 437 (1873). . . .

We hold that in the context of prescriptive easements, an "adverse use" of land is a wrongful use, made without the express or implied permission of the owner of the land. An "adverse use" is one that creates a cause of action by the owner against the person claiming the prescriptive easement; no prescriptive easement may be created unless the person claiming the easement proves that the owner could have prevented the wrongful use by resorting to the law. A use of another's land that began as permissive will not become adverse unless the license (created by the granting of permission) is repudiated.

We now turn to the incongruity with our prior case law, namely that our cases allow a finder of fact to conclusively presume that a use was adverse if the other elements of the prescriptive easement doctrine are established.

Easements by prescription are not favored in the law, because they essentially reward a trespasser and allow the taking of another's property without compensation. In this modern age, it does little to encourage civility between neighbors to have a rule whereby a landowner, who allows his neighbor to use some part of his land, runs the risk that the use may transmogrify into a legally-binding prescriptive use merely by the passage of time. Such a rule, as this case demonstrates, encourages expensive litigation between neighbors to either obtain some legal injunction to stop the use of the land, or obtain a legal ruling definitively establishing an easement. Worse, such a rule might impel neighbors to resort to aggressive, extra-legal acts in defense of their property.

We therefore hold that the burden of proving adverse use is upon the party who is claiming a prescriptive easement against the interests of the true owner of the land. To the extent our prior cases suggest that proof of adverse use is not required, or that the continuous and uninterrupted use of another's land for ten years is presumed to be adverse, they are hereby overruled. . . .

B.

The Lack of Evidence at Trial of a Prescriptive Easement

. . . As we have previously related, the plaintiff introduced the testimony of several individuals who stated that the front part of the gravel lane had, for many decades prior to 1999, been regularly used by churchgoers approximately twice a week to access a parking lot at the rear of the church. . . . [O]n the basis of this testimony, the jury concluded that the plaintiff had a prescriptive easement. . . .

First and foremost, the plaintiff failed to show that his use of the gravel lane was adverse, that is, that it was wrongful and made without the express or implied permission of the rightful owner of the land. In part, this is because the plaintiff wholly failed to show that the defendants *owned the land* upon which the gravel lane rests. "The essence of an adverse use is that such use be made of the land of another." *Keller v. Hartman*, 175 W.Va. 418, 424, 333 S.E.2d 89, 95 (1985). . . .

Furthermore, the plaintiff failed to show that the prior use of the gravel lane, by himself and his predecessors, was in any way wrongful toward, or without the express or implied permission of, the owner of the servient estate. The plaintiff was required to prove that his actions (and the actions of his predecessors) amounted to trespassing, and that the owner—whoever it might be—would have wanted to prevent the plaintiff's use, or the churchgoers' use, by resorting to the law. . . . Nothing in the record suggests that the churchgoers' use of the gravel lane was anything more than a neighborly accommodation by the owner of the gravel lane. . . .

> **Practice Pointer**
>
> Notice that O'Dell failed to name the owner of the road as a defendant, an omission which proved fatal to his case. In an action to establish a prescriptive easement, the owner of the servient land is an indispensable party defendant. But what if the owner's identity is unknown? Statutes in most states allow a plaintiff who seeks to establish rights in real property to sue any and all unknown defendants who might claim any right, title, or interest in the property and to serve process on such defendants by posting and publication.

In sum, we conclude that the plaintiff failed to establish, by clear and convincing evidence, that a prescriptive easement was created to use the gravel lane to access a horseshoe driveway at the north side of his home for routine ingress and egress. . . .

Points for Discussion

a. **Why Recognize This Easement?**

Most commentators agree that the prescriptive easement promotes the efficient use of land by allowing access to parcels that otherwise might remain idle. Are you convinced by the *O'Dell* court's argument that the doctrine is increasingly obsolete in modern society? Does this doctrine penalize an owner who graciously allows others to use her land? Should the law require the adverse claimant to pay for the easement? See *Warsaw v. Chicago Metallic Ceilings, Inc.*, 676 P.2d 584 (Cal. 1984) (holding no payment was required).

b. **Required Elements**

Although the prescriptive easement elements are similar to those required for adverse possession, the precise formula differs somewhat from state to state. One common approach requires that the claimant's use be:

- open and notorious;
- adverse and hostile;
- continuous;
- for the statutory period.

In most states, the statutory period is the same as the period required for adverse possession. Tacking may be used to satisfy the prescriptive period if there is privity between the successive users. The Restatement follows the traditional approach. Section 2.17 provides that a prescriptive easement will arise if the claimant's use is: (1) adverse, (2) "open or notorious," and (3) "continued without interruption for the prescriptive period." *See* John A. Lovett, *Restating the Law of Prescriptive Easements*, 104 Marq. L. Rev. 939 (2021).

c. **Adverse or Permissive Use?**

In the typical case, there is little or no evidence about whether the claimant's use was adverse or permissive; the facts simply show that the owner did not object. Under these circumstances, should the law presume adversity or consent? Most states presume adversity, which was the law in West Virginia before *O'Dell* was decided. Would O'Dell have won the case under this standard? Some states presume consent, especially where the land is wild and unenclosed. How persuasive are the *O'Dell* court's arguments for adopting the minority view?

d. **A Trap for the Unwary?**

Golfers routinely hit golf balls off the course and onto neighboring properties. Might this create a prescriptive easement for golf balls? Suppose that a group of neighbors living next to a golf course asks your advice about how to prevent this from happening. What would you suggest? In *Beers v. Brown*, 129 P.3d 756 (Or. Ct. App. 2006), the court held that the defendant golf course had not obtained a prescriptive easement for golf balls to enter plaintiff's property because the use was not open and notorious. Plaintiff conceded that balls "occasionally" came onto her property during the ten-year prescriptive period, but there was no evidence as to the number of balls or their frequency. *But see MacDonald Properties, Inc. v. Bel-Air Country Club*, 140 Cal. Rptr. 367 (App. 1977) (finding prescriptive easement where "several balls per day" were hit onto neighbor's property and retrieved by golfers).

e. **Public Prescriptive Easements**

The traditional view was that the public could not acquire a prescriptive easement. However, many modern courts recognize public prescriptive easements. *See, e.g., Clickner v. Magothy River Ass'n, Inc.*, 35 A.3d 464 (Md. 2012). Is this good policy? Under what circumstances should a public prescriptive easement be recognized?

f. Beach Access and the Public Trust Doctrine

The *public trust doctrine* provides that navigable waters and certain related lands belong to the government as a trustee for the benefit of the public. Thus, if the government sells such property to a private owner, his title is subject to the public's right to use the land for fishing, navigation, swimming, and similar activities. For example, in *Raleigh Avenue Beach Assn. v. Atlantis Beach Club, Inc.*, 879 A.2d 112 (N.J. 2005), the New Jersey Supreme Court held that a private beach club could not unreasonably interfere with the public use of the club's dry sand beach on the Atlantic Ocean. You will learn more about the public trust doctrine in Chapter 12.

Suppose that J owns an unimproved landlocked lot—but is not entitled to an easement by necessity. He asks his neighbor K for permission to cross K's land to access his lot, and K agrees. J arranges to have a contractor build a house on the lot. For ten months, the contractor and his workers travel across K's land, bringing building materials and equipment to J's lot, until the house is finally complete. One day later, K says to J: "Sorry, but you can't use my road in the future." Under these circumstances, J is entitled to an *easement by estoppel* (or an *irrevocable license*) in most states.

Kienzle v. Myers

Court of Appeals of Ohio

853 N.E.2d 1203 (2006)

SINGER, PRESIDING JUDGE.

This is an appeal from a summary judgment issued by the Wood County Court of Common Pleas in a property dispute. Because we conclude that a property owner's reasonable reliance on an adjacent owner's permission for use ripened into an easement by estoppel, we reverse in part and affirm in part.

Jo An Van Duyne . . . and Ruth Bauer were friends and neighbors on adjoining property on West River Road in Perrysburg. In 1981, following construction of a public sewer line along West River Road, both Van Duyne and Bauer were required by law to connect to the public system.

For Bauer, a direct connection to the River Road sewer line meant that her driveway would have to be excavated, at substantial cost and inconvenience. The two women talked and reached an accommodation. They agreed that Bauer would install her sewer through a 96-foot-long trench from her home to Van Duyne's property, where it would share a 207-foot trench with Van Duyne's connector line to the street. Because of the hilly topography of the area, the pipes were buried at a depth of five and one-half feet. Each party bore her own tap and assessment fees. It is not clear

CHAPTER 10 *Private Land Use Planning*

from the record as to whether there was any sharing of excavation or installation costs for the sewer line.

In 1982, Jo An Van Duyne's daughter and son-in-law, Susan S. and David W. Kienzle, moved into her River Road property. In 1987, appellee, Susan S. Kienzle Trust, acquired the property. In 1989, appellants, Michael P. and Joan Myers, acquired the Bauer property.

On November 5, 2003, counsel for the Kienzles sent a letter to appellants advising them that the Kienzles had "decided to terminate the revocable license" by which appellants' sewer pipe crossed the Kienzle property. The letter directed appellants to "make other arrangements" within 30 days. Subsequent letters from David Kienzle threatened to "cap" the sewer line absent certain concessions.

> **See It**
>
> Click here to see a photograph of the Van Duyne land where the sewer pipe was buried. As the map shows, there was a creek in a deep ravine between Bauer's house and the road; the driveway crossed the creek on a bridge. It would have been expensive for Bauer to construct a similar bridge for her sewer pipe or to route the pipe underneath the creek.

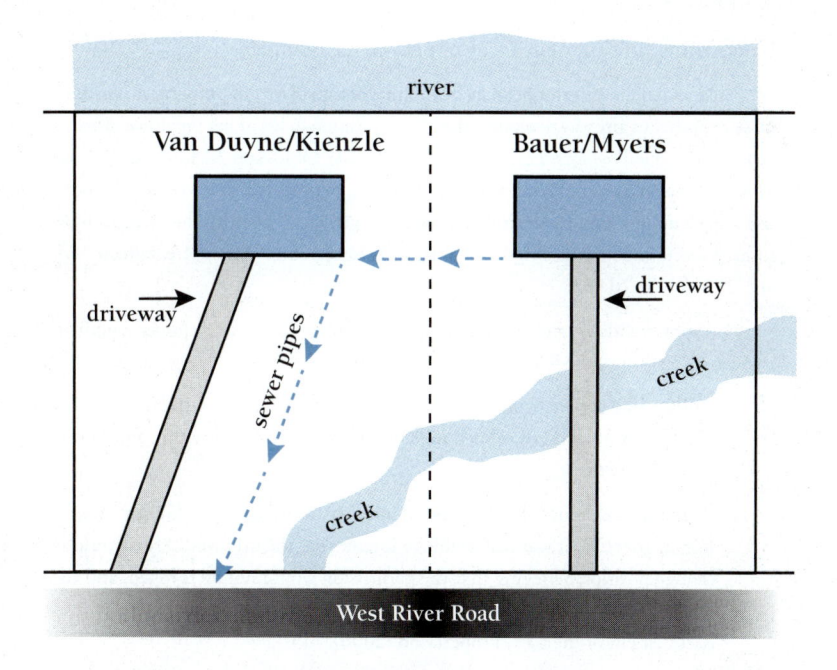

Map of land in *Kienzle v. Myers*

On March 26, 2004, appellee sued appellants, seeking to quiet title with respect to appellants' "encroachment" across appellee's property and to enjoin further trespass, as well as damages. Appellants answered, denying an encroachment on appellee's property, maintaining that they possessed an easement, an easement by estoppel, or a prescriptive easement for the sewer line. Appellants also filed a counterclaim, seeking a declaration of easement, an injunction barring appellee from interfering with the sewer line, and damages from the Kienzles for cutting vegetation on appellants' property.

> **Food for Thought**
>
> How could the appellants claim both an easement by estoppel and a prescriptive easement? One requires permission; the other requires hostility.

Following discovery, appellee was granted partial summary judgment. The trial court rejected appellants' assertion that their use of appellee's property was by easement. The matter then proceeded to a trial on the issue of appellants' counterclaim and for damages.

Following trial, the court awarded appellee $14,000 for the "cost of capping the sewer line" and rejected appellants' counterclaim. Appellants now bring this appeal. . . .

Easements may be created by express grant, by implication, by prescription, or by estoppel. *Schmiehausen v. Zimmerman*, 6th Dist. No. OT-03-027, 2004 WL 1367278, at ¶ 20. . . .

> Concerning an easement by estoppel, we have stated:
>
> > An easement by estoppel may be found when an owner of property misleads or causes another in any way to change the other's position to his or her prejudice. *Monroe Bowling Lanes v. Woodsfield Livestock Sales* (1969), 17 Ohio App.2d 146, 244 N.E.2d 762. "Where an owner of land, without objection, permits another to expend money in reliance upon a supposed easement, when in justice and equity the former ought to have disclaimed his conflicting rights, he is estopped to deny the easement." *Id.* at 151, 244 N.E.2d 762.
>
> > A more modern, and slightly broader, statement of the doctrine is contained in Section 2.10(1) of the Restatement of Property:
>
> > "If injustice can be avoided only by establishment of a servitude, the owner or occupier of land is estopped to deny the existence of a servitude burdening the land when:
>
> > (1) the owner or occupier permitted another to use that land under circumstances in which it was reasonable to foresee that the user would substantially change position believing that the permission would not be revoked, and the user did substantially change position in reasonable reliance on that belief. . . ." Restatement of the Law, Property 3d (2000), 143.
>
> > According to the commentary accompanying Section 2.10(1), the rule . . . "covers the situation where a land owner or occupier gives permission to another to use the land, but does not characterize the permission as an easement or profit, and does not expressly state the duration of the permission."
>
> > A servitude is established if the permission is given under such circumstances that the person who gives it should reasonably foresee that the recipient will substan-

tially change position on the basis of that permission, believing that the permission is not revocable. *Id.* at 145, 244 N.E.2d 762.

Schmiehausen, 2004 WL 1367278 at ¶ 21–26.

In *Schmiehausen,* a couple purchased a 28-acre parcel with the intention to subdivide. After the purchase, the couple discovered that the land was diagonally bisected by a 900-foot long, 12-inch diameter drainage pipe belonging to a neighboring farmer. Discovery of the pipe resulted in the need to redesign the site plan at some expense. The couple sued the seller, asserting a violation of general warranty covenants.

There was evidence in the trial court that the neighboring farmer and the seller's predecessor in interest reached a gentleman's agreement for installation of the pipe. The farmer then hired a contractor to install it. The trial court found an easement and awarded damages on the breach of warranty. We affirmed, noting that installation of a 12-inch diameter pipe, 900-feet long, involved a substantial cost by the farmer in reliance on the predecessor in interest's agreement to permit its installation. We concluded that "[a]pplying either Restatement Section 2.10(1) or Ohio case law, an easement by estoppel was created by the transaction between [the farmer] and [the sellers'] predecessor in interest." *Schmiehausen*, 2004 WL 1367278 at ¶ 54.

In this matter, the trial court distinguished *Schmiehausen* as follows. . . .

> The Court . . . finds that Defendants cannot establish all the elements necessary to prove estoppel either under common law or the broader Restatement standard. Under common law, an easement claimant must establish reasonable reliance upon a representation, resulting in actual prejudice. In this case, it is undisputed that the construction of the sewer pipe was with Van Duyne's permission. There is no evidence of misrepresentation. There is also no evidence of prejudice. . . .
>
> The Court also finds that Defendants cannot establish easement by estoppel under the Restatement standard. The rule under the Restatement is prefaced by the phrase "[i]f injustice can be avoided only by establishment of a servitude." It is apparent to the Court that the broader Restatement approach was crafted to cover fact situations where otherwise justice cannot be accomplished. . . . [T]here is no allegation of concealment or personal substantial expenditure related to the creation of the easement. Therefore, the facts in the present case are not sufficient to fulfill the particular requirement that injustice can be avoided only by establishment of easement by estoppel.

We disagree with the trial court's analysis. There is no requirement for an easement by estoppel in the common law that a property owner must mislead or misrepresent. The rule simply states that if an owner misleads *or causes another in any way* to change his or her position to that party's prejudice, the owner is estopped from denying the existence of an easement. *Schmiehausen*, 2004 WL 1367278 at ¶ 21, citing *Monroe Bowling Lanes*, 17 Ohio App.2d at 149, 244 N.E.2d 762. While permissive use may prevent an easement by prescription from arising, in another context an owner's grant of permission for land use may act as an inducement for another to act, especially when the permission granted is for an act not easily undone.

In *Schmiehausen*, for example, it was permission from the original property owner that induced the neighboring farmer to install 900 feet of large-diameter drainage tile. Moreover, from the scope of the act for which permission was granted it may be reasonably inferred that neither party expected the project to be transient or temporary. Thus, when the farmer expended money to complete the project, the owner was estopped from denying existence of an easement.

In the present matter, Jo An Van Duyne gave Ruth Bauer permission to install her sewer line in the same trench as Van Duyne's. There was testimony in the damage phase that plastic sewer lines have a 50-year expected lifespan. It can be reasonably inferred that neither party anticipated that burying a sewer pipe in a five and one-half foot deep trench would be a transient or temporary event. Thus, Van Duyne's permission reasonably induced appellants' predecessor in interest to change her position.

The trial court also refused to find prejudice in that Bauer would have had to pay for the construction of the sewer pipe even had she located it on her own property. Again, we disagree with this analysis. "Prejudice," in this context, is used as a synonym for "detriment." That is, Bauer relied upon Van Duyne's permission to her prejudice or detriment. This may be shown not only by the expenditures of funds but by the forbearance of some right to which one might otherwise be entitled. *G.M. Sader Excavating & Paving, Inc. v. R.G. Zachrich Constr., Inc.* (Dec. 12, 1980), 6th Dist. No. WD-80-37, 1980 WL 351645.

While it is true that, in any event, Bauer would have had to spend money to connect to the public sewer, it is also true that but for Van Duyne's acquiescence to Bauer's use of her property, Bauer would have linked to the sewer wholly on her own property. Thus, Bauer's decision to cross Van Duyne's land constituted a change in position which placed her access to the public sewer out of her control. As the present lawsuit suggests, this decision disadvantaged Bauer.

> **Food for Thought**
>
> How much reliance is needed to constitute a "substantial" change in position? Why was this conduct enough?

With respect to the Restatement formulation, which is nothing more than a reformulated recitation of the executed parol license doctrine, Restatement, supra, at 145, which has long been accepted in Ohio, see *Wilson v. Chalfant* (1846), 15 Ohio 248, 1846 WL 98, syllabus, we find the trial court's attempt to distinguish unpersuasive. It would seem that the equities would favor not disturbing a 25-year-old arrangement which seems to have only recently concerned anyone. . . .

Points for Discussion

a. Easement by Estoppel or Irrevocable License?

The easement by estoppel discussed in *Kienzle* is called an *irrevocable license* by many courts. *Kienzle* relied on the Restatement, which provides that "[a]n irrevocable license is a license that becomes an easement by estoppel under the circumstances set forth in § 2.10. . . ." Restatement § 1.2 cmt. g. Most authorities agree that there is no functional difference between an easement by estoppel and an irrevocable license. However, some jurisdictions do not recognize either doctrine.

b. Why Recognize This Easement?

An oral agreement to create an easement is unenforceable under the Statute of Frauds. So what explains the easement by estoppel? The main rationale is simple fairness: it would be unjust to allow a landowner to revoke his permission after the user has relied on it in good faith by substantially changing his position. Do you agree with this justification? Does the doctrine penalize a landowner who politely allows a neighbor to use his land?

c. Irrevocable License Elements

In jurisdictions that recognize the doctrine, an irrevocable license arises when these elements are met:

- a landowner allows another to use his land, thus creating a license;
- the licensee relies in good faith on the license, usually by making physical improvements or by incurring significant costs; and
- the licensor knows or reasonably should expect such reliance will occur.

See Van Horn v. Harmony Sand & Gravel, Inc., 122 A.3d 1021 (N.J. Super. Ct. App. Div. 2015). How do these elements compare to the standards used in *Kienzle*? Note that a license may arise by implication, even without any express agreement. Given the policy basis for the irrevocable license, how long should it last?

d. Reasonable Reliance?

In *Kienzle*, was it reasonable for Bauer to rely on her informal arrangement with Van Duyne? Do most people understand that some type of writing is needed to acquire a property right? Should a court take into account the knowledge and sophistication of the person claiming an easement by estoppel?

e. Licensor's Knowledge

In *Harber v. Jensen*, 97 P.3d 57 (Wyo. 2004), plaintiffs claimed an irrevocable license to cross their neighbors' ranch. Although the neighbors had consented to the use, they were unaware the plaintiffs had built sheds, corrals, and other improvements in reliance on this access. The Wyoming Supreme Court rejected plaintiffs' claim:

> . . . [C]oncluding, as the district court did, that the [plaintiffs] had an irrevocable license to use the access road, essentially granted them a prescriptive easement, which they could not establish because the use was permissive, even though they failed to give the landowners any notice of their intent to expend money in reliance upon their continued use of the road. We believe that result is unwise. . . . The policy of promoting neighborliness runs throughout both our prescriptive easement and license precedent. The aid of both is to support permissive use without subjecting landowners to unintended consequences by their mere cooperation with a neighbor.

Id. at 64. Should the law require that the licensor have actual knowledge of the licensee's reliance? Or is it enough that reliance is foreseeable?

f. Exercise

P owned a large parcel of rural land that adjoined a lake. He developed a vacation home subdivision on the property and sold all the lots. But he retained title to the 100-foot-wide strip of land between the houses and the lake. H and other homeowners in the subdivision often crossed the strip in P's presence to swim in the lake, and he never objected. Without asking P's permission, H spends $5,000 for lumber to build a dock at the water line (partly on P's land and partly onto the lakebed). As H begins construction, P walks past and smiles pleasantly. After the dock is finished, P fences off the 100-foot strip, posts "no trespassing" signs, and begins to use the new dock himself. Does H have an easement by estoppel or an irrevocable license?

2. Interpreting Easements

Are there any limits on how an easement may be used? Conflict may arise between the easement holder and owner of the servient land about the manner, frequency, and intensity of use. One problem is technological change. Does the scope of an easement evolve to accommodate new technology or should it be determined by the original intent of the parties? For example, suppose that L grants an express easement to M in the 1930s for "an electric transmission line." Does the easement now allow M to install a cable television line?

Marcus Cable Associates, L.P. v. Krohn

Supreme Court of Texas

90 S.W.3d 697 (2002)

JUSTICE O'NEILL delivered the opinion of the Court. . . .

In this case, we must decide whether an easement that permits its holder to use private property for the purpose of constructing and maintaining "an electric transmission or distribution line or system" allows the easement to be used for cable-television lines. We hold that it does not. . . . Accordingly, we affirm the court of appeals' judgment reversing summary judgment in the cable company's favor.

I. Background

This case centers around the scope of a property interest granted over sixty years ago. In 1939, Alan and Myrna Krohn's predecessors in interest granted to the Hill County Electric Cooperative an easement that allows the cooperative to use their property for the purpose of constructing and maintaining "an electric transmission or distribution line or system." . . .

In 1991, Hill County Electric entered into a "Joint Use Agreement" with a cable-television provider, which later assigned its rights under the agreement to Marcus Cable Associates, L.P. Under the agreement, Marcus Cable obtained permission from Hill County Electric to attach its cable lines to the cooperative's poles. The agreement permitted Marcus Cable to "furnish television antenna service" to area residents, and allowed the cable wires to be attached only "to the extent [the cooperative] may lawfully do so." The agreement further provided that the electric cooperative did not warrant or assure any "right-of-way privileges or easements," and that Marcus Cable "shall be responsible for obtaining its own easements and rights-of-way."

Seven years later, the Krohns sued Marcus Cable, alleging that the company did not have a valid easement and had placed its wires over their property without their knowledge or consent. The Krohns asserted a trespass claim, and alleged that Marcus Cable was negligent in failing to obtain their consent before installing the cable lines. The Krohns sought an injunction ordering the cable wires' removal, as well as actual and exemplary damages. In defense, Marcus Cable asserted a right to use Hill County Electric's poles under the cooperative's easement. [The trial court granted summary judgment in favor of Marcus Cable, but the court of appeals reversed.] . . .

II. Common Law

A property owner's right to exclude others from his or her property is recognized as " 'one of the most essential sticks in the bundle of rights that are commonly characterized as property.' " *Dolan v. City of Tigard*, 512 U.S. 374, 384 (1994). A landowner may choose to relinquish a portion of the right to exclude by granting an easement, but such a relinquishment is limited in nature. . . .

Marcus Cable claims rights under Hill County Electric's express easement, that is, an easement conveyed by an express grant. While the common law recognizes that certain easements may be assigned or apportioned to a third party, the third party's use cannot exceed the rights expressly conveyed to the original easement holder. Marcus Cable's rights, therefore, turn on whether the cooperative's easement permits the Krohns' property to be used for the purpose of installing cable-television lines. . . .

A. Express Easements

We apply basic principles of contract construction and interpretation when considering an express easement's terms. *Armstrong v. Skelly Oil, Co.*, 81 S.W.2d 735, 736 (Tex. Civ. App.-Amarillo 1935, writ ref'd). The contracting parties' intentions, as expressed in the grant, determine the scope of the conveyed interest. . . .

When the grant's terms are not specifically defined, they should be given their plain, ordinary, and generally accepted meaning. An easement's express terms, interpreted according to their generally accepted meaning, therefore delineate the purposes for which the easement holder may use the property. Thus, if a particular purpose is not provided for in the grant, a use pursuing that purpose is not allowed. . . .

The common law does allow some flexibility in determining an easement holder's rights. In particular, the manner, frequency, and intensity of an easement's use may change over time to accommodate technological development. Restatement (Third) of Property (Servitudes) § 4.10. But such changes must fall within the purposes for which the easement was created, as determined by the grant's terms. *See id* § 1.2 cmt. d ("The holder of the easement . . . is entitled to make only the uses reasonably necessary for the specified purpose."); § 4.10 & cmt. a (noting that manner, frequency, and intensity of easement may change to take advantage of technological advances, but only for purposes for which easement was created); *see, e.g., Edgcomb v. Lower Valley Power & Light, Inc.*, 922 P.2d 850, 854–55, 858 (Wyo. 1996) (holding that, under easement granted for an electric or telephone line, the easement holder could increase the electricity-carrying capacity and replace the static-telephone line with fiber-optics line as a matter of "normal development of the respective rights and use"). . . . Thus, contrary to Marcus Cable's argument, an express easement encompasses only those technological developments that further the particular purpose for which the easement was granted. . . .

The emphasis our law places upon an easement's express terms serves important public policies by promoting certainty in land transactions. In order to evaluate the burdens placed upon real property, a potential purchaser must be able to safely rely upon granting language. Similarly, those who grant easements should be assured that their conveyances will not be construed to undermine private-property rights—like the rights to "exclude others" or to "obtain a profit"—any more than what was intended in the grant.

Marcus Cable suggests that we should give greater weight to the public benefit that results from the wide distribution of cable-television services, arguing that technological advancement in Texas will be substantially impeded if the cooperative's easement is not read to encompass cable-television use. But even if that were so, we may not circumvent the contracting parties' intent by disregarding the easement's express terms and the specific purpose for which it was granted. *See* Restatement (Third) of Property (Servitudes) § 4.1 & cmt. d (indicating that a court may not adopt an easement interpretation based on public policy unless that interpretation is supported by the grant's terms). Adhering to basic easement principles, we must decide not what is most convenient to the public or profitable to Marcus Cable, but what purpose the contracting parties intended the easement to serve. . . .

> **FYI**
>
> Restatement § 4.1 cmt. j provides: "[I]f there is more than one reasonable interpretation of the servitude, that which is more consonant with public policy should generally be preferred." Was there more than one reasonable interpretation here?

Finally, Marcus Cable contends that its use should be allowed because attaching cable-television wires to Hill County Electric's utility poles does not materially increase the burden to the servient estate. But again, if a use does not serve the easement's express purpose, it becomes an unauthorized presence on the land whether or not it results in any noticeable burden to the servient estate. *See McDaniel Bros. v. Wilson*, 70 S.W.2d 618, 621 (Tex. Civ. App.-Beaumont 1934, writ ref'd) ("[E]very unauthorized entry upon land of another is a trespass even if no damage is done or the injury is slight. . . ."). . . . Thus, the threshold inquiry is not whether the proposed use results in a material burden, but whether the grant's terms authorize the proposed use. With these principles in mind, we turn to the easement at issue in this case.

B. Hill County Electric's Easement

Both parties urge us to determine Marcus Cable's easement rights as a matter of law. When an easement is susceptible to only one reasonable, definite interpretation after applying established rules of contract construction, we are obligated to construe it as a matter of law even if the parties offer different interpretations of the easement's terms. Because the easement here can be given a definite meaning, we interpret it as a matter of law.

The easement granted Hill County Electric the right to use the Krohns' property for the purpose of constructing and maintaining an "electric transmission or distribution line or system." The terms "electric transmission" and "electric distribution" are commonly and ordinarily associated with power companies conveying electricity to the public. *See, e.g., Texas Power & Light Co. v. Cole*, 158 Tex. 495, 313 S.W.2d 524, 526–27, 530 (1958). Texas cases decided around the time the cooperative's easement was granted strongly suggest that this was the commonly understood meaning of those terms.

Marcus Cable does not argue that the generally prevailing meaning of the easement's grant encompasses cable-television services. Instead, it claims that, for reasons of public policy, we should construe the easement to embrace modern developments, without regard to the easement's language. In support of that position, Marcus Cable cites a number of decisions in other jurisdictions that have allowed the use of easements predating cable technology to allow installation of cable transmission lines.

The cases Marcus Cable cites, however, involve different granting language and do not support the proposition that we may disregard the parties' expressed intentions or expand the purposes for which an easement may be used. To the contrary, those cases involve easements containing much broader granting language than the easement before us. Most of them involved easements granted for communications media, such as telegraph and telephone, in addition to electric utility easements. In concluding that the easements were broad enough to encompass cable, the reviewing courts examined the purpose for which the easement was granted and essentially concluded that the questioned use was a more technologically advanced means of accomplishing the same communicative purpose.

For example, in *Salvaty v. Falcon Cable Television*, the 1926 easement permitted its holder to maintain both electric wires *and* telephone wires. 165 Cal. App. 3d 798, 212 Cal. Rptr. 31, 32, 35 (1985). The court held that cable-television lines were within the easement's scope, observing that cable television is "part of the natural evolution of *communications* technology." *Id.* at 34–35 (emphasis added); *accord Witteman v. Jack Barry Cable TV*, 228 Cal. Rptr. 584, 589 (Cal. Ct. App. 1986) (same). Similarly, the Fourth Circuit held that an easement allowing its holder to use the land for the purpose of maintaining pole lines for "electrical and telephone service" was sufficiently broad to encompass cable-television lines. *C/R TV, Inc. v. Shannondale, Inc.*, 27 F.3d 104, 106, 109–10 (4th Cir. 1994) (applying West Virginia law). In reaching its conclusion, the court relied on the similar communicative aspects of both "telephone services" and cable-television services. *Id.* at 109–10. Other cases Marcus Cable cites also involved easements granted for communications-transmission purposes. . . .

We express no opinion about whether the cases Marcus Cable relies upon were correctly decided. But, unlike the cases Marcus Cable cites, Hill County Electric's easement does not convey the right to use the property for purposes of transmitting communications. While cable television may utilize electrical impulses to transmit communications, as Marcus Cable claims, television transmission is not a more technologically advanced method of delivering electricity. Thus, the above-referenced cases do not support Marcus Cable's argument that the easement here encompasses the additional purpose of transmitting television content to the public. . . .

Justice Hecht, dissenting.

The electric television (not its short-lived electro-mechanical predecessor) was conceived in 1921 by fourteen-year-old Philo Farnsworth, who made a working model in 1927, twelve years before RCA's National Broadcasting Company first began regular telecasts from the World's Fair in New York City, and H.W. and Ruth Curtis granted Hill County Electric Cooperative an easement on their land north of Sardis, Texas, "to place, construct, operate, repair, maintain, relocate and replace . . . an electric transmission and distribution line or system." After 1939, television took off. Cable television is said to have originated in 1948 when John Walson of Mahanoy City, Pennsylvania, used a twin-lead wire to transmit an electric signal from a remote antenna to his store to demonstrate to his customers how reception could be improved and thereby increase his sales of the newfangled television sets. The Curtises no doubt intended that by granting the Co-op an easement, wires strung on poles erected on their property would be used to transmit electric current to power lights and appliances. They probably did not envision that one such appliance in the Sardis area would be a television set. And they could not possibly have imagined that televisions powered by the electric current carried by lines over their easement would have better reception if supplied with an electric signal transmitted over another look-alike line hung on the same poles, even if the Curtises had been as precocious as Philo Farnsworth himself.

> **FYI**
>
> Philo Farnsworth sold his television patents to RCA Victor for $1,000,000 in 1939, and RCA began selling television sets to the public. In the same year, the first major league baseball game and the first college football game were televised.

So if the question is, what were the Curtises thinking in 1939 when they gave the Co-op an easement for "an electric transmission and distribution line or system," the answer is easy: they were thinking about electric power, not an electric cable television signal, even though both are electric. But that's not the question because, as the Court correctly holds, the scope of an easement is measured by the parties' intent as expressed in the words used, broadened by changes in the manner, frequency, and intensity of the intended use that are due to technological advances and do not unreasonably burden the servient estate. . . . [A] use that is within the language of an easement as it has come to be understood with changes in technology is not prohibited simply because it was not part of the parties' original thinking. So the question in this case is whether a cable carrying an electric television signal to various users is "an electric transmission and distribution line or system" as we have come to understand more of what those words entail.

Now if one were to stick just to the words, the answer would clearly be yes. A television cable is a "line". A television signal is "electric", assuming, as the Court does, that the cable is not fiber optic (although even if the cable were fiber optic, the signal would still start out electric at the transmitter and end up electric at the receiver). Sending the signal is "an electric transmission." Transmitting it among a number of users is "an electric distribution." Thus, a television cable is "an electric transmission and distribution line." Looking at a pole carrying lines transmitting electric power and a line transmitting television signals, a person unfamiliar with differences in the physics of the transmissions could not tell which was which. . . .

> **Food for Thought**
>
> Should the court have interpreted the easement strictly, as the dissent suggests? Sending a cable television program along wires is literally an "electric transmission."

I would hold that the easement in the present case can be shared with a cable television provider if the servient estate is not additionally burdened. . . .

Points for Discussion

a. Technological Change v. Property Rights

Marcus Cable echoes the Restatement view that the "manner, frequency, and intensity of an easement's use may change over time to accommodate technological development." Why didn't the court hold that the easement could be used for cable television lines? Is it more important for courts to facilitate technological change or to protect traditional property rights? Notice that the cable television lines were attached to existing utility poles, so they did not "materially increase the burden on the servient estate." Why bar them?

b. Rethinking *Marcus Cable*

West v. Louisville Gas & Electric Co., 951 F.3d 827, 830 (7th Cir. 2020) involved a 1938 easement for "a line or lines of poles . . . and all necessary . . . wires . . . in connection therewith, for the transmission, distribution and delivery of electrical energy to the Grantee and other persons and concerns and to the public in general for light, heat, power, telephone and/or other purposes." The court reasoned that this language also allowed the grantee, Louisville Gas, to install fiber optic cables, despite the opposition of West, the servient owner:

> In 2000, [Louisville Gas] concluded that the existing easement allows the installation of wires that carry photons (that is, fiber-optic cables) along with the [existing] wires that carry electrons. . . . *Id.* at 828.
>
> [I]nformation passes across West's land constantly: over-the-air radio and TV signals, cell phone communications (voice and data), microwaves, and more. None of that differs from laser light traveling through glass fiber. . . . *Id.* at 831.

[Indiana law] treats easements as permitting new uses compatible with the original grant. *See Howard v. United States,* 964 N.E.2d 779, 783 (Ind. 2012) ("a new use that is compatible with the original *purpose* is within the scope of the easement") (emphasis in original). . . . [A] telecom cable is "compatible" with electric transmission. Both photons and electrons are in the electromagnetic spectrum. . . . *Id.* at 832.

In light of *West,* was *Marcus Cable* wrongly decided?

c. **Hypotheticals**

Consider these hypotheticals on the scope of express easements:

> (1) C's land is benefited by an 1880 easement providing "access for wagons" across D's servient land. Can C drive a car along the easement?
>
> (2) E's land is benefited by an easement providing a "right of way" across F's servient land. Can E install underground electric lines in the right of way?

d. **Intensifying a Permitted Use**

Suppose X has an express easement to reach his 50-acre farm by traveling over Z's ranch. X now wants to build a 25-house subdivision on his farm, which is close to an expanding city. Will the homeowners be able to use the easement? The answer is probably "yes." Restatement § 4.10 provides that the "manner, frequency, and intensity of the use may change over time . . . to accommodate the normal development of the dominant estate. . . ." *See Shooting Point, LLC v. Wescoat,* 576 S.E.2d 497 (Va. 2003) (approving continued use of easement after dominant land was converted from agricultural use to 18-lot subdivision).

e. **Relocating an Easement**

Now suppose that ranch owner Z wants to change the route of X's easement in order to minimize the impact of traffic from X's planned subdivision. May he? The traditional rule is that the location of an easement can be changed only if both the servient and dominant owners agree. But Restatement § 4.8 provides that the servient owner may relocate an easement as long as this does not significantly lessen the utility of the easement, increase the burdens on the easement holder, or frustrate the purpose of the easement. *See M.P.M. Builders, LLC v. Dwyer,* 809 N.E.2d 1053 (Mass. 2004) (adopting Restatement approach).

f. **Using an Easement to Benefit Other Land**

Finally, suppose that X owns a separate 150-acre parcel which he wants to include in his subdivision. Will those homeowners be able to use the easement across Z's ranch even though the 150-acre parcel is not part of the dominant land? The general rule is "no," unless Z consents. Restatement § 4.11. An interesting variant on this rule appeared in *Brown v. Voss,* 715 P.2d 514 (Wash. 1986), where the owners of the dominant land planned to build a single-family residence that straddled the boundary line between that land (Parcel B) and another parcel they also owned (Parcel C); the access road planned to reach the home would cross both Parcels B and C. The Washington Supreme Court agreed that this was a "misuse" of the easement, but upheld the trial court's decision which refused to enjoin use of the easement and awarded only $1 in damages to the owner of the servient land. Does this outcome effectively nullify the rule?

3. Terminating Easements

Suppose that N holds an express easement to operate a railroad over land owned by O. If N ceases railroad operations, will his easement be terminated by *abandonment*?

In our next case, the Rutland-Canadian Railroad Company opened its "Island Line" in 1901, connecting Boston and Quebec. Part of the line traveled along Lake Champlain near the border between New York and Vermont, providing passengers with spectacular views. The line became less profitable over time, and service stopped in 1970. In 1983, Congress enacted the Rails-to-Trails Act, 16 U.S.C. § 1247(d), which facilitated the conversion of unused rail lines into recreational trails. Three years later, a scenic portion of the old Island Line was converted into a 7.5-mile public hiking and biking trail, running along the east shore of Lake Champlain through Burlington, Vermont. Two of the servient owners claimed that the railroad's easement had been abandoned and sued for damages on a takings theory.

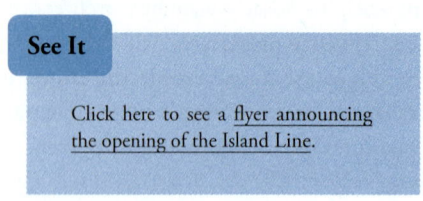

> **See It**
>
> Click here to see a flyer announcing the opening of the Island Line.

Preseault v. United States

United States Court of Appeals, Federal Circuit

100 F.3d 1525 (1996)

PLAGER, CIRCUIT JUDGE.

In this Takings case, the United States denies liability under the Fifth Amendment of the Constitution for actions it took pursuant to the Federal legislation known as the Rails-to-Trails Act. The original parties to the case were the property owners, J. Paul and Patricia Preseault, plaintiffs, and the United States (the "Government"), defendant. The State of Vermont (the "State"), claiming an interest in the properties involved, intervened . . . as a co-defendant. The Court of Federal Claims, on summary judgment after hearings and argument, concluded that the law was on the Government's side, and rendered judgment against the complaining property owners. *Preseault v. United States*, 27 Fed. Cl. 69 (1992). The property owners appeal. . . .

A. Introduction and Summary

In brief, the issue in this case is whether the conversion, under the authority of the Rails-to-Trails Act . . . of a long unused railroad right-of-way to a public recreational hiking and biking trail constitutes a taking of the property of the owners of the underlying fee simple estate. . . .

B. Factual Background

The Preseaults own a fee simple interest in a tract of land near the shore of Lake Champlain in Burlington, Vermont, on which they have a home. This tract of land is made up of several previously separate properties, the identities of which date back to before the turn of the century. The dispute centers on three parcels within this tract, areas over which the original railroad right-of-way ran. The areas are designated by the trial court as Parcels A, B, and C. . . .

The Rutland-Canadian Railroad Company, a corporation organized under the laws of Vermont, acquired in 1899 the rights-of-way at issue on Parcels A, B, and C, over which it laid its rails and operated its railroad. . . . [The State of Vermont later acquired title to the assets of Rutland-Canadian, and leased them to the Vermont Railway, which operated the railroad. Vermont Railway stopped service in 1970; the tracks and other railroad equipment were removed in 1975. In 1985, the State leased the railroad rights-of-way to the City of Burlington pursuant to the Rails-to-Trails Act, for use as a public hiking and biking trail; the Interstate Commerce Commission approved this transfer, pursuant to its authority under the Act. The trail opened in 1986.]

Meanwhile, ownership of the properties over which the rights-of-way ran passed through the hands of successors in interest, eventually arriving in the hands of the Preseaults. A map of the Preseault tract, showing the various parcels and the areas subject to the railroad's rights-of-way, appears in 27 Fed.Cl. at 72. . . . [The trail "is used regularly by members of the public for walking, skating, and bicycle riding. On warm weekends up to two hundred people an hour go through the Preseaults' Property."]

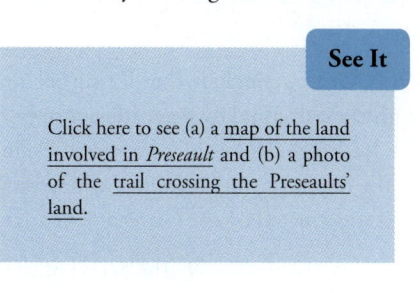

See It

Click here to see (a) a map of the land involved in *Preseault* and (b) a photo of the trail crossing the Preseaults' land.

C. The Property Interests

. . . The determinative issues in the case . . . are three: (1) . . . did the Railroad by the 1899 transfers acquire only easements, or did it obtain fee simple estates; (2) if the Railroad acquired only easements, were the terms of the easements limited to use for railroad purposes, or did they include future use as public recreational trails; and (3) even if the grants of the Railroad's easements were broad enough to encompass recreational trails, had those easements terminated prior to the alleged taking so that the property owners at that time held fee simples unencumbered by the easements. . . .

. . . With regard to the two parcels, A and B, derived from the Barker estate, the . . . Commissioner's Award . . . is the only document that memorializes the event. . . . [It] is unlike a deed in that it does not contain the usual . . . habendum clause (defining the extent of the ownership interest conveyed). . . . Vermont cases are consistent in holding that, practically without regard to the documentation and manner of acquisition, when a railroad for its purposes acquires an estate in land for laying track and operating railroad equipment thereon, the estate acquired is no more than that needed for the purpose, and that typically means an easement, not a fee simple estate. . . .

> **FYI**
>
> The Takings Clause provides that private property shall not be taken for public use, without just compensation. For an analysis of the takings issue in *Preseault* and similar decisions, see Danaya C. Wright, *Eminent Domain, Exactions, and Railbanking: Can Recreational Trails Survive the Court's Fifth Amendment Takings Jurisprudence?*, 26 Colum. J. Envtl. L. 399 (2001).

Determining the provenance of the third parcel, C, derived from the Manwell tract, tests the above stated proposition even further. The operative instrument is a warranty deed . . . [that] appears to be the standard form used to convey a fee simple title from a grantor to a grantee. . . . At trial, the Preseaults argued that . . . the deed was given following survey and location of the right-of-way and therefore it should be construed as conveying only an easement in accordance with Vermont railroad law. . . . On balance it would seem that . . . the proceeding retained its eminent domain flavor, and the railroad acquired only that which it needed, an easement for its roadway. . . .

We . . . conclude that fee simple title to all three parcels in dispute remained with their original owners, subject only to the burden of the easements in favor of the Railroad. Those titles passed through various hands, coming to rest eventually in the hands of the Preseaults, where they lay in 1986 when the public recreational trail was created by the Government's action. . . .

D. The Scope of the Railroad's Easement

We turn then to the question of whether the easements granted to the Railroad, to which the Preseaults' title was subject, are sufficiently broad in their scope so that the use of the easements for a public recreational trail is not a violation of the Preseaults' rights as owners of the underlying fee estate. . . .

When the easements here were granted to the Preseaults' predecessors in title at the turn of the century, specifically for transportation of goods and persons via railroad, could it be said that the parties contemplated that a century later the easements would be used for recreational hiking and biking trails, or that it was necessary to so construe them in order to give the grantee railroad that for which it bargained? We think not. Although a public recreational trail could be described as a roadway for the transportation of persons, the nature of the usage is clearly different. In the one case, the grantee is a commercial enterprise using the easement in its business, the transport of goods and people for compensation. In the other, the easement belongs to the public, and is open for use for recreational purposes, which happens to involve people engaged in exercise or recreation on foot or on bicycles. It is difficult to imagine that either party to the original transfers had anything remotely in mind that would resemble a public recreational trail. . . .

E. Abandonment

. . . The Preseaults contend that under Vermont law the original easements were abandoned, and thus extinguished, in 1975. If that is so, the State could not, over ten years later in 1986, have re-established the easement even for the narrow purposes provided in the original conveyances without payment of the just compensation required by the Constitution. . . .

Typically the grant under which such rights-of-way are created does not specify a termination date. The usual way in which such an easement ends is by abandonment, which causes the easement to be extinguished by operation of law. *See generally* Restatement of Property § 504. Upon an act of abandonment, the then owner of the fee estate, the "burdened" estate, is relieved of the burden of the easement. In most jurisdictions, including Vermont, this happens automatically when abandonment of the easement occurs. . . .

Vermont law recognizes the well-established proposition that easements, like other property interests, are not extinguished by simple non-use. As was said in *Nelson v. Bacon*, 113 Vt. 161, 32 A.2d 140, 146 (1943), "[o]ne who acquires title to an easement in this manner [by deed in that case] has the same right of property therein as an owner of the fee and it is not necessary that he should make use of his right in order to maintain his title." . . .

Something more is needed. The Vermont Supreme Court in *Nelson* summarized the rule in this way: "In order to establish an abandonment there must be in addition to nonuser, acts by the owner of the dominant tenement conclusively and unequivocally manifesting *either* a present intent to relinquish the easement *or* a purpose inconsistent with its future existence." *Nelson*, 32 A.2d at 146 (emphasis added). . . . The record here establishes that these easements, along with the other assets of the railroad, came into the hands of the State of Vermont in the 1960s. The State then leased them to an entity called the Vermont Railway, which operated trains over them. In 1970, the Vermont Railway ceased active transport operations on the line which included the right-of-way over the parcels at issue, and used the line only to store railroad cars. In 1975 the Railroad removed all of the railroad equipment, including switches and tracks, from the portion of the right-of-way running over the three parcels of land now owned by the Preseaults. In light of these facts, the trial court concluded that under Vermont law this amounted to an abandonment of the easements, and adjudged that the easements were extinguished as a matter of law in 1975. . . .

The Government and the State argue that there are facts inconsistent with that determination, but we are not persuaded that any of them significantly undercut the trial court's conclusion. For example, when the Vermont Railway removed its tracks in 1975, it did not remove the two bridges or any of the culverts on the line, all of which remained "substantially intact." That is not surprising. The Railroad was under no obligation to restore the former easement to its original condition. Tearing out existing structures would simply add to its costs, whereas the rails that were taken up could be used for repairs of defective rails elsewhere on the line. It is further argued that, since the rail line continues to operate to a point approximately one and one-third miles south of the Preseaults' property, it is possible to restore the line to full operation. The fact that restoration of the northern portion of the line would be technically feasible tells us little. The question is not what is technically possible to do in the future, but what was done in the past.

Almost immediately after the tracks were removed, members of the public began crossing over the easement. Perhaps illustrating the difficulty in getting government paperwork to catch up with reality, or perhaps indicating that revenue collectors do not give up easily, the State of Vermont and Vermont Railway, as they had done before the removal of the tracks, continued to collect fees under various license and crossing agreements from persons wishing to establish fixed crossings. In January 1976, the Preseaults executed a crossing agreement with the Vermont Railway which gave the Preseaults permission to cross the right-of-way. In March 1976, the Preseaults entered into a license agreement with the State and the Vermont Railway to locate a driveway and underground utility service across the railroad right-of-way. As late as 1991, 985 Associates (through Paul Preseault) paid a $10 license fee to "Vermont Railroad" (sic), presumably pursuant to one of the 1976 agreements. The Preseaults paid "under protest." Much of this activity suggests that, initially at least, the adjacent property owners decided it was cheaper to pay a nominal license fee to the State than to litigate the question of whether the State had the right to extract the fee. In view of all the contrary evidence of physical abandonment, we find this behavior by the State's

> **Food for Thought**
>
> If the Railway continued to collect license fees from the Preseaults and other landowners, did it really intend to abandon the easement?

revenue collectors unconvincing as persuasive evidence of a purpose or intent not to abandon the use of the right-of-way for actual railroad purposes.

One uncontrovertible piece of evidence in favor of abandonment is that, in the years following the shutting down of the line in 1970 and the 1975 removal of the tracks, no move has been made by the State or by the Railroad to reinstitute service over the line, or to undertake replacement of the removed tracks and other infrastructure necessary to return the line to service. The declarations in the 1985 lease between the State of Vermont, Vermont Railway, and the City of Burlington, which refer to the possible resumption of railroad operations at some undefined time in the future are of course self-serving and not indicative of the facts and circumstances in 1975. Other events occurring after 1975 are also of little probative value. . . .

The trial judge in this case . . . concluded that as a fact the Railroad had effected in 1975 an abandonment of the easement running over parcels A, B, and C. . . . [O]ur review of the facts and circumstances leading up to the events of 1975 persuades us that the trial judge is correct. . . . That determination provides an alternative ground for concluding that a governmental taking occurred. . . .

Points for Discussion

a. **Rethinking Abandonment**

Do you agree that the railroad abandoned its easement? What facts suggest that the railroad did not intend to relinquish the easement or manifest "a purpose inconsistent with its future existence"? In *Washington Wildlife Preservation, Inc. v. State of Minnesota*, 329 N.W.2d 543 (Minn. 1983), the court found that a railroad did not abandon its easement when the right-of-way was converted into a public recreational trail. As *Preseault* reflects, most jurisdictions agree that mere nonuse of an easement is not abandonment. *See, e.g., Graves v. Dennis*, 691 N.W.2d 315 (S.D. 2004) (nonuse of road easement did not constitute abandonment).

b. **Advising the Railroad**

Suppose that you are the general counsel for the railroad in 1975. The railroad intends to remove the tracks, but wants to preserve its easement from being terminated through abandonment—if it can do so at little or no expense. The railroad president asks you to develop a cost-effective strategy to minimize the risk of abandonment. What would you advise? How likely is it that your strategy will succeed?

c. **Scope of the Easement**

In *Chevy Chase Land Co. v. United States*, 733 A.2d 1055 (Md. Ct. App. 1999), the court rejected a takings claim on facts similar to those in *Preseault*. It concluded that recreational biking and hiking were forms of transportation, and thus within the scope of the easement: "The fact that the right-of-way may be used for recreational as well as transportation purposes has no bearing on our analysis, since the 'recreation' involved . . . consists of the enjoyment one may have in transporting oneself." *Id.* at 1078. Which court is correct?

d. **Prescription**

An easement may be terminated by *prescription*, using essentially the same standard for acquiring a prescriptive easement. Thus, if the servient owner blocks use of the easement in an open and notorious, adverse and hostile, and continuous manner for the prescriptive period, the easement ends. Could the Preseaults have built a fence across the trail in order to terminate the easement?

e. **Other Methods of Termination**

An express easement may terminate by its own terms. For example, an easement created to "continue for 50 years" ends after that period. In addition, an easement may be terminated by:

> - *Condemnation*: Condemnation of the servient land also terminates the easement. In this event, the easement holder is entitled to just compensation.
> - *Estoppel*: An easement ends if the servient owner substantially changes his position in reasonable reliance on the holder's statement that the easement will not be used in the future.
> - *Merger*: If one person obtains title to both the easement and the servient land, then the easement terminates under the doctrine of merger.
> - *Misuse*: In some jurisdictions, if the holder seriously misuses the easement, it may be ended through forfeiture.
> - *Release*: The easement holder may release the easement to the servient owner by executing and delivering a writing that complies with the Statute of Frauds.

f. **Aftermath of *Preseault***

The trial court later limited the easement to a width of 12 feet (an 8-foot paved path and 2-foot shoulders), plus the right to access adjacent land to maintain the path. Since the trail segment in question is less than 500 feet long, approximately 6,000 square feet of the Preseaults' land was taken. They eventually recovered a judgment of over $1.4 million for this taking. Paul Preseault commented: "No amount of money can make up for the invasion of our privacy by a paved and heavily-trafficked bicycle and roller-blade path next to our front door. . . . " *Government to Pay Landowners for "Trail Taking,"* PR Newswire, May 23, 2001.

The Supreme Court subsequently held that rights of way through public lands granted to railroads under the General Railroad Right-of-Way Act of 1875 were easements, not fee simple estates, and therefore were terminated by abandonment when railroad use stopped. *Marvin M. Brandt Revocable Trust v. United States*, 572 U.S. 93 (2014). Justice Sotomayor dissented, expressing concern that the decision would threaten the Rails-to-Trails program: "By changing course today, the Court undermines the legality of thousands of miles of former rights of way that the public now enjoys as means of transportation and recreation." *Id.* at 117.

4. Negative Easements

Suppose that P holds an easement which allows her to prevent Q from building any structure on Q's land in order to preserve the view from P's home. This is a *negative easement*—an easement that entitles the dominant owner to prevent the servient owner from performing an act on the servient land.

English common law traditionally disfavored the negative easement due to concern that it would interfere with the productive use of land. For example, P's easement means that Q's land is effectively restricted to agricultural use; Q could not build a factory or a school. Accordingly, the common law accepted only a few types of negative easements. For example, an owner like P could hold an easement that prevented Q from interfering with water flowing in a defined channel through Q's land to reach P's property.

Today courts recognize that private restrictions may encourage productive land use. These modern restrictions usually take the form of real covenants or equitable servitudes—doctrines that you will study later in this chapter—rather than negative easements. Only a few types of negative easements are recognized in modern law, such as express view easements or special easements that are authorized by statute.

The most common negative easement is the *conservation easement*, which is authorized by legislation in nearly all jurisdictions. A conservation easement restricts the development and use of the servient land in order to preserve open space, farm land, historical sites, or wild and undeveloped land. The servient owner usually conveys the easement to a land trust or other conservation group—often receiving income tax and property tax benefits—and may continue to use the land as permitted by the easement. For example, owner R might convey a conservation easement on a 2,000-acre tract of forest land to the Nature Conservancy, preventing any development of the land in perpetuity. After the conveyance, R and his successors may use the land for hiking, fishing, birdwatching, hunting, and other nondevelopmental purposes.

To date, only a handful of decisions have explored the legal issues surrounding the conservation easement. For example, *Bjork v. Draper*, 886 N.E.2d 563 (Ill. App. Ct. 2008) involved an easement that required the grounds of the Kerrigan House (one of the oldest homes in Lake Forest, Illinois) to be "retained forever predominantly in . . . scenic and open space condition." The Drapers owned both the Kerrigan House and the servient land. They entered into two agreements with the easement holder to amend the easement; the plan was to *remove* 800 square feet of land from the easement property, and *replace* it with another parcel of equal size and quality. When the neighbors sued, the appellate court invalidated the amendments:

> . . . Although section 23(d) provided that the easement could be amended, that section must be interpreted in harmony with the other provisions of the easement. That is accomplished by interpreting section 23(d) to mean that, although the easement allows amendments, no amendment is permissible if it conflicts with other parts of the easement. Section 3 expressly prohibits improvements of any kind to the easement property. However, that is what the first and second amendments specifically authorize, allowing the Drapers to construct a driveway that encroaches onto the easement property.

Id. at 574. Does the *Bjork* holding make sense? Are there circumstances where a court should allow the parties to amend—or even terminate—a conservation easement? For an overview of conservation easements, see Frederico Cheever & Nancy A. McLaughlin, *An Introduction to Conservation Easements in the United States: A Simple Concept and a Complicated Mosaic of Law*, 1 J.L. Prop. & Soc'y 107 (2015).

Points for Discussion

a. Merits of Private Preservation

Over 40 million acres in the United States are now protected by conservation easements—an area roughly the size of Florida. This easement is an important device for private preservation of sensitive areas. In most cases, it is cheaper to purchase a conservation easement than a fee simple title, so it is cost-effective for a nonprofit group like the Nature Conservancy to buy an easement.

b. Rethinking the Conservation Easement

Does it make sense to allow a private owner to prohibit development of her land in perpetuity? How might this affect the development of other lands? How can the conservation easement be made flexible enough to adjust to changing conditions without eliminating its benefits? For more discussion of these issues, see Jessica Owley, *Changing Property in a Changing World: A Call for the End of Perpetual Conservation Easements*, 30 Stan. Envtl. L.J. 121 (2011).

B. Land Use Restrictions

Suppose that D wants to subdivide his 40-acre tract into residential lots. Private land use restrictions—for example, a ban on non-residential uses—can make his development more attractive to buyers. These restrictions are usually created through a simple process authorized by statute. D will record a declaration containing covenants, conditions, and restrictions (CC&Rs) against all the lots before any of them are sold. If buyer B later tries to violate the residential-only restriction—for example, by building a gas station—the other owners can enforce the restriction against B.

Traditionally, it was difficult to create a restriction that would bind and benefit future landowners. A group of owners could enter into a contract to restrict their properties—but at common law this contract would not bind their successors. Somewhat grudgingly, the English law courts eventually recognized the *real covenant*, which allowed the benefits and burdens of a restriction to "run with the land" to successive owners. But they imposed a complex set of requirements that curtailed its use. A similar device—the *equitable servitude*—evolved in the equity courts, with less stringent requirements.

We first examine the traditional approach to *creation* of real covenants and equitable servitudes, and then contrast this with the Restatement view. We devote the balance of the chapter to defenses against *enforcement*, starting with the landmark decision of *Shelley v. Kraemer*—which held that judicial enforcement of discriminatory covenants was unconstitutional. Today enforcement issues arise most commonly in planned residential communities, where CC&Rs are sought to be enforced as real covenants or equitable servitudes.

1. Traditional Approach

a. Real Covenants

A *real covenant* is a promise concerning the use of land that benefits and burdens both the *original parties* to the promise and their *successors*. It is sometimes called a *covenant running at law*. The traditional remedy for breach of a real covenant is money damages.

The common law rules governing the creation of the real covenant are often confusing. As one scholar explained: "The intrepid soul who ventures into this formidable wilderness never emerges unscarred. Some, the smarter ones, quickly turn back. . . . Others, having lost their way, plunge on and after weeks of effort emerge not far from where they began, clearly the worse for wear." Edward H. Rabin, Fundamentals of Modern Property Law 489 (1974). The materials below provide an overview of this complex subject.

Every real covenant has two *sides*: the burden and the benefit. The duty to perform the promise is called the *burden*; the right to enforce the promise is the *benefit*.

Traditionally, six elements must be proven for the *burden* of the promise to bind the promisor's successors; but only four of those elements are generally required for the *benefit* to run to the promisee's successors. The elements are:

(1) *Compliance with Statute of Frauds*: The covenant must be contained in a document that satisfies the Statute of Frauds.

(2) *Intent to bind successors*: The original parties must intend to bind their successors. The needed intent is usually found in the express language of the document, but it may also be inferred from circumstances.

(3) *"Touch and concern"*: The covenant must "touch and concern" land. In other words, it must relate to the enjoyment, occupation, or use of the property. A *negative covenant*—one that restricts the use of land—almost always satisfies this requirement. For example, covenants prohibiting certain uses or limiting the height of buildings do touch and concern the land. *See, e.g., Kosciusko County Cmty. Fair, Inc. v. Clemens*, 116 N.E.3d 1131 (Ind. Ct. App. 2018) (covenant not to conduct motorized races at fairground did touch and concern). Most of the controversy about the touch and concern requirement concerns the *affirmative covenant*—one that requires the promisor to perform an affirmative act, usually the payment of money. Modern courts agree that monetary covenants which are closely tied to the occupancy of land, such as a tenant's obligation to pay rent or an owner's obligation to pay dues to a homeowners association, do touch and concern. But a purely monetary obligation does not touch and concern. *See, e.g., Equestrian Ridge Homeowners Ass'n v. Equestrian Ridge Ests. II Homeowners Ass'n*, 953 N.W.2d 16 (Neb. 2021) (covenant to pay maintenance costs for private street connecting subdivision to public roads did touch and concern).

(4) *Notice*: The promisor's successor must have notice of the covenant. This requirement is satisfied by actual notice, record notice, or inquiry notice.

(5) *Horizontal privity*: Horizonal privity concerns the relationship between the *original parties* to the promise. It requires the transfer of an interest in land *other than the covenant itself*, as discussed below. In England, horizontal privity was deemed to exist only between a landlord and a tenant, so real covenants were only possible in leases. In the United States, there is a split of authority on the point:

- *Mutual interests*: In most states, the horizontal privity requirement is met where the original parties have mutual simultaneous interests in the affected land (e.g., landlord and tenant; cotenants; or owners of the dominant and servient lands for an easement).

- *Successive interests*: In almost all states that require horizontal privity, this element can also be satisfied by a grantor-grantee relationship between the original parties, so that they have successive interests in the affected land.

- *No requirement*: An increasing number of states have abandoned the requirement; this is the modern trend. *But see* Michael Lewyn,

The Puzzling Persistence of Horizontal Privity, 27 Prob. & Prop. 32 (2013).

(6) *Vertical privity*: Vertical privity concerns the relationship between an *original party* to the promise and his *successor*. Some states no longer require vertical privity. The states that retain this element usually distinguish between the burden and the benefit:

- *Burden*: Vertical privity exists only if the successor receives the *entire* estate that the original promisor held. If promisor A holds a fee simple absolute and conveys it to B, this requirement is met.

- *Benefit*: On the benefit side, a less demanding test is used. Vertical privity is found if the successor receives either the original promisee's entire estate or a *smaller* estate. If promisee C holds a fee simple absolute and transfers a term of years tenancy to D, vertical privity exists.

The diagram below shows the relationship between horizontal privity and vertical privity.

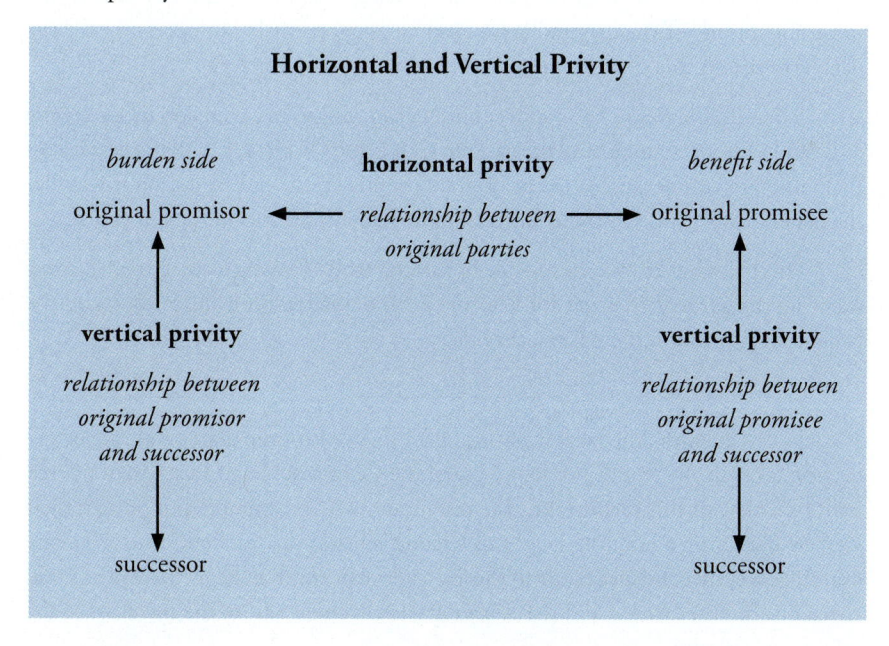

Horizontal and Vertical Privity

burden side	**horizontal privity**	*benefit side*
original promisor ←	*relationship between original parties*	→ original promisee
vertical privity		**vertical privity**
relationship between original promisor and successor		*relationship between original promisee and successor*
successor		successor

The chart below lists the elements that are *traditionally* required for the burden and the benefit to run to successors. But remember that many courts have modified or abandoned the horizontal and vertical privity elements, as discussed above.

Real Covenant Requirements		
	For the burden to run	*For the benefit to run*
Statute of Frauds	yes	yes
Intent to bind successors	yes	yes
Touch and concern	yes	yes
Notice	yes	no
Horizontal privity	yes	no
Vertical privity	yes	yes (lower standard)

Suppose N leases Greenacre to O for a term of 20 years; the lease provides that it is intended to benefit the successors and assigns of the parties. One clause requires that O maintain a large garden on part of the property. The lease is recorded. A year later, O assigns the lease to P. P stops watering the garden, and N sues P. Under these circumstances, the burden of the promise to maintain the garden runs to P—all six elements are met. Remember the materials on assignment in Chapter 7? This is why most obligations of the original lease bind an assignee. It is not necessary for the benefit to run in this situation because N is the original promisee.

What if N leases to O as above, but N then assigns his reversion in Greenacre to R, and O stops maintaining the garden. Can R sue O? Here, it is not necessary for the burden to run because O is the original promisor. The only question is whether the benefit runs to R. On these facts, all four elements are met, so R can sue O.

Finally, what if N leases to O, N assigns to R, O assigns to P, and P stops watering the garden? In order for R to sue P for damages, both the burden and the benefit must run. On these facts, they do.

Lake Chelan is the largest natural lake in Washington state, and one of the deepest lakes in the world. For many years, the Cosina del Lago Restaurant offered patrons a view of this scenic lake. The restaurant owners attempted to protect their view by obtaining a building height restriction on the adjacent land. Our next case examines whether the successors to those owners can enforce the restriction as a real covenant. In other words, did the *benefit* of the covenant run to the *successors* of the original promisees?

Deep Water Brewing, LLC v. Fairway Resources Ltd.

Court of Appeals of Washington

215 P.3d 990 (2009)

SWEENEY, J.

This suit follows a dispute between a developer and a restaurant owner. The restaurant owner's predecessor in interest granted the developer a right-of-way in exchange for money and the developer's promise to restrict the height of houses in the development so as not to impair the view of Lake Chelan from the restaurant building. The trial court concluded that the developer ultimately breached that agreement.... The court awarded the restaurant owner damages and attorney fees. We conclude that the restaurant owner was entitled to enforce the height restriction covenant as one that runs with the land....

FACTS

Cindy Smith and Robert Ahlquist (Ahlquist) are siblings. They owned and operated the Cosina del Lago Restaurant overlooking Lake Chelan in Washington state. The dining room was on the second floor of the building and the lounge was on the first floor. The land between the restaurant building and the lake was a mature apple orchard.

Jack Johnson is the sole shareholder and president of Key Development Corporation.... [Johnson and Key Development] wanted to develop the property between the restaurant and the lake for single family housing. But any development required access over Ahlquist's property....

[In 1995, Ahlquist, Key Development, and Johnson entered into two related agreements (the "easement agreement" and the "right-of-way agreement") by which: (a) Ahlquist agreed to grant a right-of-way (an easement) to allow the planned subdivision and (b) Key Development and Johnson agreed that the new houses would not interfere with the view of the lake from the restaurant or its lounge. Ahlquist conveyed the right-of-way to Key Development in April, 1996. Johnson then formed the Key Bay Homeowners Association and recorded restrictive covenants that burdened the subdivision land. The covenants imposed a maximum building height of 16 feet, which prevented any structure from interfering with the lake view from the restaurant and lounge.]

Meanwhile Robert and Roberta Kenagy purchased the restaurant from Ahlquist in 1998.... [The Kenagys knew about the easement agreement and the right-of-way agreement before they purchased.] Mr. Kenagy leased the building to his business, Deep Water Brewing, LLC. Deep Water operated the restaurant as a brew pub....

[In 2000, an addendum to the restrictive covenants was recorded by Johnson, as president of the Homeowners Association, which allowed maximum building heights of up to 26 feet. In 2002, Deep Water sued Johnson, Key Development, Fairway Resources Ltd., and others seeking injunctive relief to prevent any interference with the restaurant and lounge views. The complaint was later amended to include the Kenagys as plaintiffs and to add claims for damages. By the time the trial began in 2006, several two-story houses had been built in the subdivision; these houses violated the original 16-foot building limit and interfered with the view of the lake from the restaurant lounge. The trial court awarded the Kenagys $245,000 in damages against Johnson and Key Development. . . . On appeal, the defendants asserted that the Kenagys had no right to sue for breach of the agreements. The Kenagys argued, inter alia, that they could enforce the agreements as real covenants because they were successors to Ahlquist, the original promisees.]

Lake view from restaurant lounge
Click here for larger photo

LIABILITY

. . . The elements of a running real covenant are:

(1) the covenants must have been enforceable between the original parties, such enforceability being a question of contract law except insofar as the covenant must satisfy the statute of frauds; (2) the covenant must "touch and concern" both the land to be benefited and the land to be burdened; (3) the covenanting parties must have intended to bind their successors in interest; (4) there must be vertical privity of estate, *i.e.*, privity between the original parties to the covenant and the present disputants; and (5) there must be horizontal privity of estate, or privity between the original parties.

Leighton v. Leonard, 22 Wash.App. 136, 139, 589 P.2d 279 (1978) (footnote omitted) (citing William B. Stoebuck, *Running Covenants: An Analytical Primer*, 52 Wash. L. Rev. 861 (1977)).

> Professor Stoebuck explains in *Washington Practice: Real Estate: Property Law:*
>
> Enforcement between the original parties is a matter of the law of contract. . . . But the doctrine with which we are concerned here is the doctrine, generally regarded as part of the law of real property, under which the covenant by the original parties may be enforced by or against persons who succeed to interests they held in the burdened or benefited land. The doctrine of "running" is analogous to the contract doctrines of assignment of rights and delegation of duties; it is a doctrine whereby remote parties are bound or benefited by contractual covenants made by the original parties. *However, while a party must consensually undertake assignment or delegation, the law of running covenants imposes a duty or confers a benefit upon remote parties, not because they consensually agree, but because the covenant bore a certain relationship to parcels of land and because they stepped into a certain relationship with the same parcels.* The essence of the law of running covenants has to do with what these relationships must be for the remote parties to be bound or benefited.

17 William B. Stoebuck & John W. Weaver, Washington Practice: Real Estate: Property Law § 3.2, at 126 (2d ed. 2004) (emphasis added).

Here, the first *Leighton* element is met. The agreements between Ahlquist, Key Development, and Jack Johnson required protection of a view by covenants restricting heights. It was a condition of the right-of-way being granted. And Key Development acknowledged as much and met that obligation when it first recorded covenants that restricted the height of buildings in its development to 16 feet.

The trial judge also concluded that the parties knew what land was benefited by and what land was burdened with the restriction despite the absence of a formal legal description. The street address of the restaurant building was included in the easement agreement. That conclusion is not challenged here on appeal.

The second element required by *Leighton* requires a showing that the burden touches and concerns the land, or more accurately the benefit and burden must "touch and concern" estates in the land with which they run. A covenant touches and concerns the land if it is connected with the use and enjoyment of the land. *Rodruck v. Sand Point Maint. Comm'n*, 48 Wash.2d 565, 574–76, 295 P.2d 714 (1956) (promise to pay assessment for maintenance was a running covenant). The covenant must be so related to the land as to enhance its value and confer a benefit upon it. *Id.* at 575, 295 P.2d 714; *see also City of Seattle v. Fender*, 42 Wash.2d 213, 218, 254 P.2d 470 (1953). A covenant touches and concerns the land when, by restricting the use of one parcel, it enhances the value of another. *Mountain Park Homeowners Ass'n v. Tydings*, 72 Wash.App. 139, 145, 864 P.2d 392 (1993), *aff'd*, 125 Wash.2d 337, 883 P.2d 1383 (1994); *see also* 17 Stoebuck & Weaver, *supra*, § 3.3, at 136. A promise to do or refrain from doing a physical act upon the land, such as restricting the height, size, or location of structures is an example of a covenant that touches and concerns the land.

Here, the 16-foot height restriction in the 1996 covenants would have made Key Development lots . . . less desirable. And the height restrictions would have enhanced the value of the restaurant and lounge by protecting the view. The view was critical to the restaurant owners. We conclude, then, that the restriction here touched and concerned land.

The third *Leighton* element is intent to bind successors in interest. And generally that would require some expression of intent to assign or bind successors but:

> No American decision has been found in which a court has held that the word "assigns" must be used. The most that can be said, from the little American authority on the point, is that, in some general way, there must be an intent that a running covenant bind successors. Intent may be drawn from all the language, including the nature of the covenant. In fact, it seems if a covenant is found to touch and concern, this alone may often be enough to show an intent that it should bind successors. When that is the case, of course, intent is subsumed in touch and concern and loses significance as an independent element.

17 Stoebuck & Weaver, *supra*, § 3.4, at 137. . . .

The covenant here touched and concerned land, and we conclude it therefore reached beyond those obligations that are generally limited to the contracting parties only. To conclude otherwise would mean that the parties to these agreements intended that the view of the lake was to be preserved only so long as Ahlquist owned the building. The import of the agreements is otherwise. Indeed, the right-of-way agreement required Key Development to establish the Homeowners Association to implement the agreements and through that Association to assure compliance with the negotiated height restrictions. This included creating covenants to ensure compliance with those provisions of the agreements that there "shall not be any homes or structures in the development that interfere with the view of the lake from the restaurant or its lounge." Key Development through its Homeowners Association recorded complying covenants in 1996 and thereby gave notice to the world of the contents of the covenants. *Strong v. Clark*, 56 Wash.2d 230, 232, 352 P.2d 183 (1960). The evidence then supports Finding of Fact 1.29 that the parties "intended to require that there shall not be any homes or structures in the Key Bay Development that interfere or affect the sight or views of Lake Chelan from any portion of either the upstairs or the downstairs of the Premises."

Moreover, the very existence of the Key Bay development is due, in part, to Ahlquist's grant of a right-of-way subject to view protections that would burden Key Bay lots with the height restrictions. The intent then to confer a benefit to one property and impose a burden on another is clear. We conclude that both parties to the original agreements intended for the covenants to benefit and bind successors in interest.

Finally, requirements for both vertical and horizontal privity are met here. Vertical privity requires that the original parties' successors be in privity with them. The Kenagys purchased from Ahlquist. And Key Development was an original party to both the agreements. Horizontal privity requires "the transfer of some interest in land, other than the covenant itself, between covenantor and covenantee in connection with the making of the covenant." 17 Stoebuck & Weaver, *supra*, § 3.6, at 138; *see Bremmeyer Excavating, Inc. v. McKenna*, 44 Wash.App. 267, 721 P.2d 567 (1986) (disputed contract to provide fill material did not pass in conjunction with estate in land); *Feider v. Feider*, 40 Wash.App. 589, 593, 699 P.2d 801 (1985) (no horizontal privity because personal right of first refusal did not pass with estate in land). Here, the height restriction was made as a requirement of the agreements and ultimately in the right-of-way deeded to Key Development and for Key Development's benefit....

... All the elements necessary for a running covenant have been satisfied.... We affirm the judgment....

Points for Discussion

a. **Changing Theories**

Notice that plaintiff Deep Water Brewing initially sued for an injunction to prevent any interference with the view; this was an attempt to enforce the height restriction promise as an *equitable servitude*, a topic which we discuss later in this chapter. When the complaint was amended to seek damages, this reflected the plaintiff's decision to enforce the promise as a *real covenant*, which was ultimately successful. Why did Deep Water Brewing decide to seek damages? And why was it prudent to add the Kenagys as plaintiffs when this occurred?

b. **The Benefit**

The *Deep Water Brewing* court seemed to have no difficulty in holding that the *benefit* of the height restriction promise ran to the Kenagys, as the successors to Ahlquist. So what was the basis for the defendants' appeal on this point? Which element or elements of a real covenant do you think they contested? Notice that there could have been no doubt that the promise met the "touch and concern" requirement because it restricted the defendants' ability to perform a physical action on their land; in fact, a height restriction is one of the classic examples that meets this requirement. Moreover, the Statute of Frauds was satisfied; and the Kenagys were in vertical privity because they purchased the entire interest of Ahlquist. So were the defendants hoping to show there was a lack of intent to bind successors? How convincing is the court's analysis on this point? (Notice that Washington law seems to require both notice and horizontal privity for the *benefit* to run to successors, *unlike the law in most jurisdictions*. Both elements are met here.)

c. The Burden

Defendant Key Development ultimately sold the lots in the subdivision to various buyers, including several who later built homes that impaired the view from the restaurant lounge. Did the *burden* of the height restriction promise run to these buyers as successors to Key Development? If so, why didn't the plaintiffs sue them?

d. Aftermath of *Deep Water Brewing*

The Cosina del Lago had been closed for over a year before the Kenagys purchased the property. They leased the building to their wholly-owned corporation, Deep Water Brewing, LLC, which operated the Deep Water Brewery & Saloon there for several years. By the time the lawsuit reached the Washington Court of Appeals, however, the brew pub had ceased operations—apparently due to lack of business. With this hindsight, did the view blockage justify $245,000 in damages?

---

b. Equitable Servitudes

Today the *equitable servitude* is the principal tool for enforcing private land use restrictions. It emerged as a response to the shortcomings of the real covenant, which was difficult to use in practice because the required elements were often hard to prove. In contrast, it was generally easier to enforce a restriction as an equitable servitude because horizontal and vertical privity were not required. The traditional remedy for breach of an equitable servitude is an injunction.

Gambrell v. Nivens

Court of Appeals of Tennessee

275 S.W.3d 429 (2008)

DAVID R. FARMER, J.

This case involves the enforcement of restrictive covenants in equity. After subdividing their property, imposing restrictions on the three lots they sold, and retaining the remaining land, vendors brought suit against remote grantees to enforce the restrictive covenants and to enjoin them from operating a wedding chapel, for commercial use, on the land. . . . Following a trial on the matter, the trial court permanently enjoined the commercial activity because the remote grantees took title with actual notice of the restrictions. Finding ample support for the imposition of an equitable servitude, we concur in the trial court's judgment. . . .

In 1991, Joe and Jeri Gambrell . . . purchased approximately 69 acres in Fayette County and subdivided the parcel into four (4) lots, selling three (3) of them, and retaining one (1) twenty-one acre lot for themselves. In September of 1992, they sold the subject lot to Mr. Frank Foshee. . . . In the deed to Mr. Foshee, the Gambrells left blank the space reserved for reciting encumbrances on the property. Instead, they attached to the deed an untitled, undated, and unsigned page listing the restrictions and recorded it along with the deed. The deed made no mention of the attachment, nor did the text of the attachment refer to the deed. The attachment set forth, in pertinent part, the following:

> 1. THESE COVENANTS ARE TO RUN WITH THE LAND AND SHALL BE BINDING ON ALL PARTIES AND ALL PERSONS CLAIMING UNDER THEM FOR A PERIOD OF THIRTY YEARS FROM THE DATE THESE COVENANTS ARE RECORDED. . . .
>
> 2. ENFORCEMENT—ENFORCEMENT SHALL BE BY A PROCEEDING AT LAW OR IN EQUITY AGAINST ANY PERSON OR PERSONS VIOLATING OR ATTEMPTING TO VIOLATE ANY COVENANT, EITHER TO RESTRAIN VIOLATION OR TO RECOVER DAMAGES. . . .
>
> 4. LAND USE AND BUILDING TYPE—NO LOT SHALL BE USED EXCEPT FOR RESIDENTIAL PURPOSES. NO MOBILE, MODULAR, OR PREFAB HOMES SHALL BE PERMITTED. . . .

The Gambrells . . . placed the same restrictions, verbatim, upon all three lots. . . . Mr. Foshee conveyed his lot to Sonny and Carrie Nivens . . . by warranty deed in May of 1996. . . . [The real estate agent for the Nivenses] provided them a copy of the covenants prior to the purchase. . . .

The Nivenses had begun to build a large wedding chapel and facility, known as Carahills Estate, when the Gambrells filed suit on February 18, 1998, to enforce the purported restrictions and enjoin the Nivenses from completing the chapel's construction and using it for commercial purposes. . . . The matter proceeded to a bench trial on April 4, 2003, after which the trial court concluded that the Gambrells were entitled to enforce the restrictions. . . . [T]he trial court issued a permanent injunction prohibiting the Nivenses from operating the chapel or any other commercial enterprise on their property. . . . [On appeal, the Nivenses argued that the covenants were not enforceable as equitable servitudes.]

> **FYI**
>
> The Nivens parcel at issue is about 20 acres in size and located in a rural area east of Memphis, Tennessee. The wedding chapel was built to hold up to 150 people, with an adjacent parking lot that provided space for 50 cars. During the year before the trial, over 100 weddings occurred in the chapel, producing more than $500,000 in income.

An owner of land may sell portions of it and make restrictions as to its use for the benefit of himself as well as for the benefit of those to whom he sells. Even though Tennessee law does not favor private restrictions upon the use and enjoyment of land, our courts will enforce the covenants as they would contracts, according to the clearly expressed intention of the parties. Covenants that fail the more exacting requirements for real covenants at law may still be enforced in equity as an equitable servitude. An equitable servitude is a "covenant respecting the use of land enforceable against successor owners or possessors in equity regardless of its enforceability at law." 2 *American Law of Property* § 9.31 (A.J. Casner ed. 1952). This Court has noted that

> [w]here an owner of land enters into a contract that he will use or abstain from using his land in a particular way or manner, equity will enforce the agreement against any purchaser or possessor with notice who attempts to use the land in violation of its terms, irrespective of whether the agreement creates a valid covenant running with the land at law or not.

Tennsco Corp. v. Attea, No. M2001–01378–COA–R3–CV, 2002 WL 1298808, at *2 (Tenn. Ct. App. June 13, 2002) (*no perm. app. filed*) (quoting 2 *American Law of Property* § 9.24 (A.J. Casner ed. 1952)). For a covenant to bind remote grantees in equity, (1) it must "touch and concern" the land; (2) the original parties to the covenant must intend that it run with the land and bind remote grantees; and (3) the remote grantee must have had notice of the covenant. *Id.* at *1–*2 (quoting 5 Richard R. Powell & Patrick J. Rohan, *The Law of Real Property* § 673 (1991)). To have binding effect, valid restrictions on property need not be in the chain of title if the purchaser had actual notice of them. Nonetheless, even where the remote grantee takes title with actual notice, the first two requirements—that the covenant "touch and concern" the land and that the original parties intend the covenant to run—must still be established.

> **Make the Connection**
>
> Although the *Gambrell* court listed only three requirements for an equitable servitude to bind remote grantees, it is generally agreed that a fourth element is also needed: the covenant must be in writing or implied from a "common plan." Presumably the court did not mention this fourth element because it was met on the facts of the case. At the end of the decision, the court observed that the Gambrells were "suing upon written covenants."

The instant facts satisfy each element with ease. First, and most fundamental, is the covenant itself, as the equitable servitude arises out of a promise. The record reveals that a central element of the Gambrell-Foshee conveyance was Mr. Foshee's covenant to restrict the use of his property. We agree with the Nivenses' assertion that the attachment creating the restrictions is not part of the deed itself. Under Tennessee law, undated and unsigned writings located below the signatures and the certificate of acknowledgment in a deed do not constitute part of that deed. *Anderson v. Howard*, 18 Tenn. App. 169, 74 S.W.2d 387, 390 (1934). To conclude otherwise would "open wide the door to the perpetration of fraud." *Id.* But there is no dispute regarding the agreement between the Gambrells and Mr. Foshee at the time of the conveyance. The record makes clear that the language of the deed itself did not express the true intention of the parties. In his deposition, Mr. Foshee unequivocally stated that the terms of their contract included the restrictions, that he understood the restrictions would run with the land for thirty years, and that the list was attached to the deed and duly recorded. Despite the omission of encumbrances on the face of the Gambrell-Foshee deed, Mr. Foshee never believed his property to be unencumbered. Certainly, the undated, unsigned, and unacknowledged written covenants fail in form; however, the original covenanting parties confirmed their substance.

Additionally, the language in the attachment clearly expresses an intent that the covenants run with the land and bind remote grantees. The first paragraph of the attached restrictions leaves little doubt in this regard. . . .

Further, the restrictions "touch and concern" the land. Although there is some dispute among authorities as to the test for this requirement, there is little question that building restrictions embodied in a covenant between owners in fee satisfy this test, both as to the benefit and the burden. *Tennsco Corp.*, 2002 WL 1298808, at *2. And, finally, . . . the Nivenses do not dispute . . . that they had actual notice of the covenants well before accepting the deed from Mr. Foshee.

Indeed, the case at bar is strikingly similar to the landmark English case of *Tulk v. Moxhay*, in which the court enforced restrictions on equitable principles even though the covenants did not meet the requirements for enforcement at law. There, the owner of property conveyed to his purchaser the area known as Leicester Square and included in the deed the covenant that the grantee, his heirs, and assigns, would keep the area as a garden for the benefit of the residents in the area. The grantor, still owning land adjacent to the square, sued a remote grantee, whose deed did not contain the restriction, but who admitted he took title with notice of it. The court stated:

> **See It**
>
> Click here to see an early picture of Leicester Square in the 1800s; notice the equestrian statue in the middle of the square.

> Here there is no question about the contract: the owner of certain houses in the square sells land adjoining, with a covenant from the purchaser. . . . And it is now contended, not that the vendee could violate the contract, but that he might sell the piece of land, and that the purchaser from him may violate it without this Court having any power to interfere. If that were so, it would be impossible for an owner of land to sell part of it without incurring the risk of rendering what he retains worthless. It is said that, the covenant being one which does not run with the land, this Court cannot enforce it; but the question is, not whether the covenant runs with the land, but whether a party shall be permitted to use the land in a manner inconsistent with the contract entered into by his vendor, and with notice of which he purchased. . . .
>
> That the question does not depend upon whether the covenant runs with the land is evident from this, that if there was a mere agreement and no covenant, this Court would enforce it against a party purchasing with notice of it; for if an equity is attached to the property by the owner, no one purchasing with notice of that equity can stand in a different situation from the party from whom he purchased.

Tulk v. Moxhay, 2 Phillips 774, 41 Eng. Rep. 1143 (1848). Like the plaintiff grantor in *Tulk v. Moxhay,* the Gambrells are similarly suing upon written covenants of which the defendant took title with actual notice. Additionally, the language of the covenants in this case, like that in Tulk, establishes that the restrictions "touch and concern" the land and that the covenanting parties intended to bind the successors and assigns of the grantee. . . .

For the foregoing reasons, we affirm the judgment of the trial court. . . .

Points for Discussion

a. ***Gambrell* in Context**

Suppose that you were the attorney for the Gambrells before the litigation began. Why might you advise your clients to enforce the covenant as an equitable servitude rather than a real covenant? On the facts of this case, could the Gambrells have prevailed on either theory? Notice that the court found the Gambrells had proven all of the equitable servitude elements "with ease."

b. **Common Plan Exception**

Because the equitable servitude was recognized as a matter of equity, case law developed a special exception to the Statute of Frauds. Where a developer has manifested a *common plan* to impose uniform restrictions on a subdivision, all lots are burdened and benefited by the restrictions even if they do not appear in the chain of title to every lot. For instance, in *Sanborn v. McLean*, 206 N.W. 496 (Mich. 1925), the court held that all 91 lots in a Detroit subdivision were limited to residential use even though this restriction was contained in deeds for only 53 lots. Sales literature, statements by the developer and—most importantly—the percentage of deeds containing restrictions are used to determine whether a common plan exists. *See also Riverview Comm. Group v. Spencer & Livingston*, 337 P.3d 1076 (Wash. 2014) (common plan may arise from developer's representations and project map even if restriction does not appear in any deeds).

c. **Creating an Equitable Servitude**

It is easier to create an equitable servitude than a real covenant. The chart on the next page lists the elements that are *usually* required for the burden and the benefit to run to successors.

Equitable Servitude Requirements		
	For the burden to run	*For the benefit to run*
Statute of Frauds	yes, or common plan	yes, or common plan
Intent to bind successors	yes	yes
Touch and concern	yes	yes
Notice	yes	no
Horizontal privity	no	no
Vertical privity	no	no

d. Exercises

Can these restrictions be enforced as equitable servitudes? As real covenants?

(1) A and B own adjacent vacant lots in a residential subdivision. They enter into a written agreement promising "on behalf of ourselves and our successors" that no structure higher than 30 feet may be built on either lot; they sign and record the agreement. B sells her lot to C, who now plans to build a house that will be 35 feet high. A sues C.

(2) D and E purchase homes in a 20-lot subdivision. D's property and 16 of the other lots contain express restrictions in their chain of title that all houses in the subdivision must be painted in "earth tones, such as beige or brown." The restriction is not in E's chain of title. All houses in the subdivision are painted beige or brown. E now leases her property to F for a 99-year term, without telling her about the restriction. F plans to paint the house bright blue. D sues F.

e. Real Covenant v. Equitable Servitude

The real covenant and the equitable servitude are remarkably similar. Like the real covenant, the equitable servitude is a promise concerning the use of land that benefits and burdens both the original parties to the promise and their successors. One difference lies in the available remedy. The traditional remedy for breach of a real covenant is damages, while the equitable servitude is enforced by an injunction. But modern courts often blur this distinction. *See Sloan v. Johnson*, 491 S.E.2d 725 (Va. 1997) (granting injunction for breach of real covenant). The other distinction between the two is that the standard equitable defenses are available against an equitable servitude claim.

Should the real covenant and the equitable servitude be merged into one doctrine? The reason that we have two doctrines is an accident of history: one arose in the law courts, the other in the equity courts. Most scholars agree that the two doctrines should be combined. *See, e.g.,* Susan F. French, *Toward a Modern Law of Servitudes: Reweaving the Ancient Threads*, 55 S. Cal. L. Rev. 1261 (1982).

f. Aftermath of *Gambrell*

Although the Gambrells won on appeal, the Carahills Estate wedding chapel is still operating today. Its website explains that the chapel provides a beautiful, stress-free wedding, with all-inclusive packages for 100 guests beginning at $11,500. Presumably, the parties settled the case in a manner that allowed the chapel to remain in business.

Carahills Estate wedding chapel
Click here for larger photo

2. Restatement Approach

The Restatement combines the real covenant and the equitable servitude into one doctrine: the *covenant that runs at law*. It explains that the distinctions between the two "were gradually reduced to the point where they made little difference in the world of land development, but confounded students and occasionally trapped the poorly represented.... [T]he 19th century complexity is irrelevant and unnecessary." Restatement § 1.4 cmt. a.

Under the Restatement approach, a covenant that runs at law is a type of *servitude*. A servitude arises when:

- the owner of the property to be burdened intends to create a servitude;
- he enters into a contract or conveyance to this effect that satisfies the Statute of Frauds; and
- the servitude is not arbitrary, unconstitutional, unconscionable, or violative of certain public policies (e.g., it cannot unreasonably restrain alienation).

Restatement §§ 2.1, 3.1. Notice that this standard abandons the requirements of touch and concern and horizontal privity. The Restatement provides that vertical privity is never required for a negative covenant and is required for an affirmative covenant only in certain situations. Restatement § 5.2. Notice to successors is not required to create a valid servitude, but lack of notice is a defense to enforcement.

Scholars broadly endorse the Restatement approach to real covenants and equitable servitudes. But it has not yet not been adopted by any court. Why not? What are the costs and benefits of this approach?

---

3. Discriminatory Covenants

Racially restrictive covenants still exist in the chains of title to millions of homes across the United States. These covenants purport to restrict who can buy, rent, or live in a property according to race or ethnicity. In our next case, the Supreme Court held that judicial enforcement of such covenants violated the Fourteenth Amendment.

Shelley v. Kraemer

Supreme Court of the United States

334 U.S. 1 (1948)

CHIEF JUSTICE VINSON delivered the opinion of the Court.

> **FYI**
>
> This decision resolved two cases with similar facts that were argued at the same time, *Shelley v. Kraemer* and *McGhee v. Sipes*. Thurgood Marshall, Chief Counsel for the NAACP Legal Defense and Educational Fund, represented the petitioners in *McGhee*. He was later appointed to the Supreme Court.

These cases present for our consideration questions relating to the validity of court enforcement of private agreements, generally described as restrictive covenants, which have as their purpose the exclusion of persons of designated race or color from the ownership or occupancy of real property. Basic constitutional issues of obvious importance have been raised.

The first of these cases comes to this Court on certiorari to the Supreme Court of Missouri. On February 16, 1911, thirty out of a total of thirty-nine owners of property fronting both sides of Labadie Avenue between Taylor Avenue and Cora Avenue in the city of St. Louis, signed an agreement, which was subsequently recorded, providing in part:

> * * * the said property is hereby restricted to the use and occupancy for the term of Fifty (50) years from this date, so that it shall be a condition all the time and whether recited and referred to as [sic] not in subsequent conveyances and shall attach to the land, as a condition precedent to the sale of the same, that hereafter no part of said property or any portion thereof shall be, for said term of Fifty-years, occupied by

any person not of the Caucasian race, it being intended hereby to restrict the use of said property for said period of time against the occupancy as owners or tenants of any portion of said property for resident or other purpose by people of the Negro or Mongolian Race.

. . . On August 11, 1945, pursuant to a contract of sale, petitioners Shelley, who are Negroes, for valuable consideration received from one Fitzgerald a warranty deed to the parcel in question. The trial court found that petitioners had no actual knowledge of the restrictive agreement at the time of the purchase.

On October 9, 1945, respondents, as owners of other property subject to the terms of the restrictive covenant, brought suit in Circuit Court of the city of St. Louis praying that petitioners Shelley be restrained from taking possession of the property and that judgment be entered divesting title out of petitioners Shelley and revesting title in the immediate grantor or in such other person as the court should direct. The trial court denied the requested relief. . . .

The Supreme Court of Missouri sitting en banc reversed and directed the trial court to grant the relief for which respondents had prayed. That court held the agreement effective and concluded that enforcement of its provisions violated no rights guaranteed to petitioners by the Federal Constitution. At the time the court rendered its decision, petitioners were occupying the property in question. . . .

[The facts in the second case, *McGhee v. Sipes*, are omitted.]

Petitioners have placed primary reliance on their contentions, first raised in the state courts, that judicial enforcement of the restrictive agreements in these cases has violated rights guaranteed to petitioners by the Fourteenth Amendment of the Federal Constitution and Acts of Congress passed pursuant to that Amendment. Specifically, petitioners urge that they have been denied the equal protection of the laws, deprived of property without due process of law, and have been denied privileges and immunities of citizens of the United States.

> **FYI**
>
> The Fourteenth Amendment provides, in part: "No State shall make or enforce any law which shall abridge the privileges or immunities of citizens of the United States; nor shall any State deprive any person of life, liberty, or property, without due process of law; nor deny to any person within its jurisdiction the equal protection of the laws."

I.

Whether the equal protection clause of the Fourteenth Amendment inhibits judicial enforcement by state courts of restrictive covenants based on race or color is a question which this Court has not heretofore been called upon to consider. . . .

It cannot be doubted that among the civil rights intended to be protected from discriminatory state action by the Fourteenth Amendment are the rights to acquire, enjoy, own and dispose of property. Equality in the enjoyment of property rights was regarded by the framers of that Amendment as an essential pre-condition to the realization of other basic civil rights and liberties which the Amendment was intended to guarantee. Thus, § 1978 of the Revised Statutes, derived from § 1 of the Civil Rights Act of 1866 which was enacted by Congress while the Fourteenth Amendment was also under consideration, provides:

> All citizens of the United States shall have the same right, in every State and Territory, as is enjoyed by white citizens thereof to inherit, purchase, lease, sell, hold, and convey real and personal property.

This Court has given specific recognition to the same principle. *Buchanan v. Warley*, 1917, 245 U.S. 60.

. . . [T]he present cases . . . do not involve action by state legislatures or city councils. Here the particular patterns of discrimination and the areas in which the restrictions are to operate, are determined, in the first instance, by the terms of agreements among private individuals. Participation of the State consists in the enforcement of the restrictions so defined. The crucial issue with which we are here confronted is whether this distinction removes these cases from the operation of the prohibitory provisions of the Fourteenth Amendment. . . .

II.

. . . [F]rom the time of the adoption of the Fourteenth Amendment until the present, it has been the consistent ruling of this Court that the action of the States to which the Amendment has reference, includes action of state courts and state judicial officials. Although, in construing the terms of the Fourteenth Amendment, differences have from time to time been expressed as to whether particular types of state action may be said to offend the Amendment's prohibitory provisions, it has never been suggested that state court action is immunized from the operation of those provisions simply because the act is that of the judicial branch of the state government.

III.

Against this background of judicial construction, extending over a period of some three-quarters of a century, we are called upon to consider whether enforcement by state courts of the restrictive agreements in these cases may be deemed to be the acts of those States; and, if so, whether that action has denied these petitioners the equal protection of the laws which the Amendment was intended to insure.

We have no doubt that there has been state action in these cases in the full and complete sense of the phrase. The undisputed facts disclose that petitioners were willing purchasers of properties upon which they desired to establish homes. The owners of the properties were willing sellers; and contracts of sale were accordingly consummated. It is clear that but for the active intervention of the state courts, supported by the full panoply of state power, petitioners would have been free to occupy the properties in question without restraint.

Shelley property
Click here for larger photo

These are not cases, as has been suggested, in which the States have merely abstained from action, leaving private individuals free to impose such discriminations as they see fit. Rather, these are cases in which the States have made available to such individuals the full coercive power of government to deny to petitioners, on the grounds of race or color, the enjoyment of property rights in premises which petitioners are willing and financially able to acquire and which the grantors are willing to sell. The difference between judicial enforcement and nonenforcement of the restrictive covenants is the difference to petitioners between being denied rights of property available to other members of the community and being accorded full enjoyment of those rights on an equal footing.

The enforcement of the restrictive agreements by the state courts in these cases was directed pursuant to the common-law policy of the States as formulated by those courts in earlier decisions. In the Missouri case, enforcement of the covenant was directed in the first instance by the highest court of the State after the trial court had determined the agreement to be invalid. . . . The judicial action in each case bears the clear and unmistakable imprimatur of the State. We have noted that previous decisions of this Court have established the proposition that judicial action is not immunized from the operation of the Fourteenth Amendment simply because it is taken pursuant to the state's common-law policy. Nor is the Amendment ineffective simply because the particular pattern of discrimination, which the State has enforced, was defined initially by the terms of a private agreement. State action, as that phrase is understood for the purposes of the Fourteenth Amendment, refers to exertions of state power in all forms. And when the effect of that action is to deny rights subject to the protection of the Fourteenth Amendment, it is the obligation of this Court to enforce the constitutional commands.

We hold that in granting judicial enforcement of the restrictive agreements in these cases, the States have denied petitioners the equal protection of the laws and that, therefore, the action of the state courts cannot stand. . . .[26]

Points for Discussion

a. **Racial Exclusion**

The widespread use of racially restrictive covenants started in the early twentieth century, an era when many Black Americans were migrating to cities. Beginning in the 1930s, the Federal Housing Administration actively promoted such covenants in connection with its mortgage insurance program. For instance, one FHA manual recommended the use of "[r]ecorded deed restrictions" which included "[p]rohibition of the occupancy of properties except by the race for which they are intended." FHA Underwriting Manual § 284 (1936).

When *Shelley* was argued in 1948, these discriminatory covenants were so common that three Supreme Court justices decided to disqualify themselves from hearing the case—presumably to avoid the appearance of a conflict of interest. It is believed that their District of Columbia houses were encumbered by such covenants. The case was ultimately decided by a 6–0 vote.

b. **Non-Constitutional Theories**

Under the traditional approach you studied earlier in this chapter, could the *Shelley* restriction be enforced as a covenant running at law? Which element or elements would be at issue? Could it be enforced as an equitable servitude?

Alternatively, would the covenant be an invalid restraint on alienation of a fee simple, which you studied in Chapter 5? We would view it as a partial restraint because it did not prohibit alienation, but instead limited the pool of potential transferees.

---

[26] Restrictive agreements of the sort involved in these cases have been used to exclude other than Negroes from the ownership or occupancy of real property. We are informed that such agreements have been directed against Indians, Jews, Chinese, Japanese, Mexicans, Hawaiians, Puerto Ricans, and Filipinos, among others.

c. State Action

The Fourteenth Amendment only applies to actions taken by a state, not to purely private conduct. Thus, the issue in *Shelley* was whether judicial enforcement of the covenant should be viewed as *state action*. Are you convinced by the Court's rationale? And should the logic of this case extend to judicial enforcement of any covenant? For example, consider a covenant that bans political signs in a subdivision. Owner A erects a sign in her front yard that supports a candidate running for Congress. If other owners seek an injunction against the sign, can A successfully argue that enforcement of the covenant deprives her of "liberty . . . without due process of law"?

d. Aftermath of *Shelley*

The Fair Housing Act of 1968 supplemented *Shelley* by providing that it is "unlawful . . . [t]o make, print, or publish . . . any . . . notice [or] statement . . . with respect to the sale or rental of a dwelling that indicates any preference, limitation, or discrimination based on race. . . ." 42 U.S.C. § 3604(c). Accordingly, it is illegal to create a racially restrictive covenant. *See also* Stevie J. Swanson, *Indignity Perpetuated: Race-Based Housing Post-Reconstruction to the Fair Housing Act's Impact on the Digital Age: Where Do We Go from Here?*, 22 Conn. Pub. Int. L.J. 126 (2023) (arguing that county recorders violate the FHA by "publishing" discriminatory covenants when they upload deeds containing such covenants to their online searchable databases).

Today any racially restrictive covenant—whenever created—has no legal force or effect. In addition to *Shelley*, both the Fair Housing Act and the Civil Rights Act of 1866 (as now interpreted) bar judicial enforcement of such a covenant.

> **Expunging Discriminatory Covenants**
>
> Discriminatory covenants still exist in deeds and other documents in the public land records. Many feel that their presence is offensive and hurtful. Can these covenants be expunged?
>
> A number of states permit an owner to record a modification document which declares that a discriminatory covenant in the chain of title to his home is "removed," "discharged," or void. *See, e.g.,* Minn. Stat. Ann. § 507.18; Nev. Rev. Stat. § 111.237. The problem with this approach is that it does not physically remove the covenant from the records. In contrast, California adopted Government Code § 12956.3 in 2021, which requires county recorders to "redact" discriminatory covenants from public land records by rerecording these documents without the covenants—a process that will take years to complete.
>
> In *Mason v. Adams County Recorder*, 901 F.3d 753 (6th Cir. 2018), a Black plaintiff sued to compel all county recorders in Ohio to remove these covenants from land records. He argued that their continued existence violated

> the Fair Housing Act's prohibition on making statements concerning the "sale or rental of a dwelling that indicates any preference, limitation, or discrimination based on race. . . ." 42 U.S.C. § 3604(c). He alleged that such covenants discouraged people from buying property "by creating a feeling that they are unwelcome or do not belong in certain neighborhoods." *Mason*, 901 F.3d at 757. The Sixth Circuit rejected his claim based on lack of standing, since he did not allege that these covenants affected his personal decision to buy or rent property. It observed: "A feeling cannot be unfelt. But Mason's discomfort at the expression of historical language does not create particularized injury." *Id*. Would a plaintiff with standing win such a case?

4. Termination of Covenants

Today disputes rarely arise about whether particular restrictions were validly created as real covenants or equitable servitudes. The law has evolved to the point where it is comparatively simple for a developer or other party to create legally binding restrictions. The more difficult question is whether the affected owner has a defense to enforcement.

E purchases a home in a subdivision, aware that the CC&Rs require wood shingle roofs. In the years since the CC&Rs were created, the national forest that adjoins the subdivision has become a greater fire danger. Trees are dying due to insect infestation, and the undergrowth is extremely dry due to global climate change. In recent years, burning embers from nearby forest fires have sparked fires on the wood shingle roofs of 10 of the 50 homes in the development. E now wants to install a metal roof for fire safety. Is the wood shingle requirement unenforceable due to *changed conditions*?

Vernon Township Volunteer Fire Department, Inc. v. Connor

Supreme Court of Pennsylvania

855 A.2d 873 (2004)

JUSTICE NEWMAN.

In these consolidated cases . . . William E. Connor [and others] (collectively, Appellants), landowners within the Culbertson Subdivision, a tract of land in Vernon Township, Crawford County, appeal from an Order of the Superior Court reversing an Order of the Court of Common Pleas of Crawford County (trial court). The trial court had granted Judgment in favor of Appellants and against the Vernon Township Volunteer Fire Department, Inc. (Fire Department), a non-profit Pennsylvania Corporation, in an action to quiet title and for declaratory relief. For the reasons discussed herein, we reverse the Order of the Superior Court. . . .

Facts and Procedural History

In a document dated May 15, 1946 entitled "Restrictions" (Agreement), all of the property owners of the Culbertson Subdivision signed a restrictive covenant prohibiting the sale of alcoholic beverages on their land. The Agreement provides in relevant part that:

> [I]n consideration of the premises and intending to be legally bound hereby, we, the undersigned owners of the legal and/or equitable title of certain lots, pieces or parcels of land situate, lying and being in Vernon Township, Crawford County, Pennsylvania . . . do hereby mutually covenant and agree with each other that from and after the date hereof, *no vinous, spirituous, malt or brewed liquors, or any admixture thereof, shall be sold, or kept for sale,* on any of said lots, pieces or parcels of land, or on any part thereof, or in any building, or any part thereof, now or hereafter erected thereon.
>
> This agreement shall be binding upon our respective heirs, executors, administrators, successors, assigns, lessees, tenants and the occupiers of any of said lots, pieces or parcels of land, and is hereby specifically declared to be a covenant running with the lots, pieces or parcels of land held by the respective signers thereof, or in which we, or any of us, have an interest.

(emphasis added). The intent of the original signatories, as set forth in the Agreement, is "to protect each for himself and for the common advantage of all, our health, peace, safety and welfare and that of our successors in title . . . ." *Id.* The Agreement was duly recorded in Crawford County Agreement Book 26, page 9, on June 10, 1946.

On July 3, 1997, the Fire Department purchased a 3.25-acre parcel of land within the Culbertson Subdivision for the purpose of building a new truck room and social hall that would sell alcohol to its patrons.[4] This newly acquired parcel is located approximately 2,000 feet from the Fire Department's existing truck room and social hall in Vernon Township. At the time of purchase, the Fire Department did not have actual notice of the restrictive covenant banning the sale of alcoholic beverages on the land. However, the Fire Department did have constructive notice of the restrictive covenant from a title search that its attorney conducted. Nevertheless, the alcohol restriction was not brought to the attention of the Fire Depart-

> **See It**
>
> Click here to see the "truck room" and "social hall" at issue in *Vernon Township*.

---

[4] The social hall is not open to the general public and limits the sale of alcohol to only club members. According to the Fire Department, the social hall is the "economic engine" that funds the operations of the Fire Department. The Fire Department insists that it is not self-sustaining without the critical funds it raises through the sale of alcohol and small games of chance at the social hall.

ment until November of 1999, well after it had already commenced building the new social hall. . . .[6]

Presently, there are no establishments within the Culbertson Subdivision that possess liquor licenses. The closest alcohol-serving establishment is the Fire Department's current social hall, which is located in Vernon Township, approximately one-half mile from the restricted lots. In addition, there are two bars located within two miles of the restricted tract. One bar is situated approximately one and one-half miles away in Vernon Township, and the other is approximately two miles away in the City of Meadville.

Upon learning of the restrictive covenant, the Fire Department stopped construction of the new social hall and sought to have all of the property owners within the restricted tract sign a Limited Release of Restrictions. The owners of sixty-eight of the seventy-seven parcels within the Culbertson Subdivision signed the Limited Release of Restrictions and agreed to waive enforcement of the restrictive covenant as to the 3.25-acre parcel purchased by the Fire Department. The owners of three parcels neither signed the release nor sought to enforce the restrictive covenant. The remaining six parcel owners, now Appellants in this matter, refused to sign the Limited Release of Restrictions. As a result, the Fire Department brought the instant action at law seeking to quiet title to its parcel. In particular, the Fire Department sought to have the restrictive covenant prohibiting the sale of alcoholic beverages invalidated because changed conditions in the immediate neighborhood effectively rendered the restriction obsolete.

> **Make the Connection**
>
> Why didn't the fire department eliminate the restriction by using *eminent domain*? Usually a fire department is part of a city, county, or other government entity. Here, however, the fire department was a private, non-profit corporation which contracted to provide its services to the township. Accordingly, it did not have the power of eminent domain. You will study eminent domain in Chapter 13.

On August 29, 2001 . . . the trial court granted Judgment in favor of Appellants. The trial court determined that the restrictive covenant prohibiting the sale of alcoholic beverages was valid and enforceable. . . .

[T]he Superior Court reversed the Judgment of the trial court in a Memorandum Opinion dated December 23, 2002. . . . [T]he court found that conditions in the neighborhood had changed, such that the restrictive covenant no longer had significant value to Appellants. In reaching this conclusion, the Superior Court relied upon the existence of other alcohol-serving establishments within the immediate neighborhood. Moreover, the court noted that sixty-eight of the seventy-seven owners within the Culbertson Subdivision signed the Limited Release of Restrictions. The

---

[6] By the time that the Fire Department halted construction of the new social hall, it had already invested approximately $790,000.00 in the project.

Superior Court also explained that all of the property owners who testified stated that they did not rely upon the alcohol restriction when purchasing the property. . . .

Discussion

. . . As a general matter, restrictive covenants on the use of land interfere with an owner's free use and enjoyment of real property and, therefore, are not favored by the law. *Mishkin v. Temple Beth El of Lancaster*, 429 Pa. 73, 239 A.2d 800, 803 (1968). Because land use restrictions are not favored in the law, they are to be strictly construed, and "nothing will be deemed a violation of such a restriction that is not in plain disregard of its express words. . . ." *Jones v. Park Lane for Convalescents, Inc.*, 384 Pa. 268, 120 A.2d 535, 537 (1956). Although the law may disfavor restrictions on an owner's free use and enjoyment of real property, restrictive covenants are legally enforceable. . . .

In order to discharge the covenant, the burden of proof is on the Fire Department to show that the original purpose of the restriction has been materially altered or destroyed by changed conditions, and that a substantial benefit no longer extends to Appellants by enforcement of the restriction. *Daniels v. Notor*, 389 Pa. 510, 133 A.2d 520, 523 (1957). As a general rule, a restrictive covenant may be discharged if there has been acquiescence in its breach by others, or an abandonment of the restriction. *Kajowski v. Null*, 405 Pa. 589, 177 A.2d 101, 106 (1962). In addition, changes in the character of a neighborhood may result in the discharge of a restrictive covenant. *Deitch v. Bier*, 460 Pa. 394, 333 A.2d 784, 785 (1975). Where changed or altered conditions in a neighborhood render the strict adherence to the terms of a restrictive covenant useless to the dominant lots, we will refrain from enforcing such restrictions. This is based on the general rule that "land shall not be burdened with permanent or long-continued restrictions which have ceased to be of any advantage. . . ." *Daniels*, 133 A.2d at 524-25. In considering changed conditions in a neighborhood, the word "neighborhood" is a relative term, and only the immediate, and not the remote, neighborhood should be measured.

When deciding whether the character of the immediate neighborhood has changed to warrant non-enforcement of a restriction, the court must consider adjoining tracts, as well as the restricted tract. . . . [W]hile changes in the immediate neighborhood do not automatically invalidate a restrictive covenant, such changes are material and relevant in determining whether a restrictive covenant should be enforced. . . .

As such, the relevant inquiry concerning changes to the immediate neighborhood is whether such changes alter or eliminate the benefit that the restriction was intended to achieve. In determining whether changed circumstances rendered enforcement of the present alcohol restriction useless, we find guidance in *Benner v. Tacony Athletic Association*, 328 Pa. 577, 196 A. 390 (1938). In *Benner*, property owners sought to enjoin several liquor-serving establishments from selling alcohol in violation of a restrictive covenant contained in their deeds. . . . The alcohol-serving establishments . . . challenged the restrictive covenant, arguing that neighborhood conditions had changed to the extent that the restriction should not be enforced. Nonetheless, the Court explained that "while it is true that some of the tract has become commercial or industrial in character, the larger part remains almost exclusively residential." *Id.* at 392. The Court noted that "the fact that commercial establishments have crept in here and there does not impair the utility of the restriction against the sale of beer or liquor; that restriction, to the residents of the neighborhood, has a desirability and an object unaffected by the encroachments of business." *Id.* In upholding the enforceability of the restrictive covenant, the Court stated that "[i]t is only when violations are permitted to such an extent as to indicate that the entire restrictive plan has been abandoned that objection to further violations is barred." *Id.* at 393.

Contrary to the argument of the Fire Department and the holding of the Superior Court, the existence of three other liquor-serving establishments located outside of the Culbertson Subdivision does not warrant a finding of changed circumstances to invalidate the restrictive covenant. . . . As *Benner* recognized, changed conditions outside of the restricted tract do not necessarily impair the value of an alcohol restriction to the residents of the restricted tract. The stated purpose of the restrictive covenant was to protect the "health, peace, safety and welfare" of the occupants of the land by preventing the sale of alcoholic beverages within the tract. The original signatories clearly intended to protect themselves and their heirs from the vices of alcohol consumption by restricting the sale of alcohol within the Culbertson Subdivision. As the trial court noted, "[i]f people are not drinking at establishments in the neighborhood, they are not exhibiting objectionable behavior which accompanies overdrinking, like public drunkenness and driving under the influence." Thus, Appellants will continue to benefit from the restriction as long as alcohol is not sold within the restricted tract.

> **FYI**
>
> The "Limited Release of Restrictions" signed by most owners provided: "The following owners of certain lots or parcels of land hereinafter mentioned in Vernon Township, Crawford County, Pennsylvania and for the mutual considerations contained hereafter and for the sum of $1.00 . . . do hereby release, abandon and extinguish any and all restrictions [contained in the May 15, 1946 Agreement] insofar as said restrictions relate to . . . [the] lots . . . owned by the Vernon Township Fire Department. . . ." Should the department have offered more than $1.00 to the holdouts?

In determining that the restrictive covenant no longer had substantial value to Appellants, the Superior Court found it significant that a majority of the property owners within the restricted tract agreed to release the alcohol restriction. Moreover, the Superior Court noted that Appellants testified that they did not rely upon the restrictive covenant when purchasing their property. However, the restriction clearly benefits Appellants by hindering the nuisances that inherently result from the sale and consumption of alcoholic beverages. . . . Accordingly, the Superior Court erred by substituting its factual determinations for those of the trial court. . . .

Justice Castille, Dissenting.

. . . [I]n an appropriate case, our courts will invalidate restrictive covenants that have outlived their usefulness, which is what I believe the record demonstrates has occurred in this case. I agree with the Superior Court that the existence of three alcohol-serving establishments in close proximity to the Culbertson Subdivision constitutes a material alteration or change of the original purpose of the restrictive covenant. That 71 of the 77 purportedly affected owners find no value to the covenant and the other six did not rely upon the covenant in purchasing their properties is a clear signal that the covenant lacks significant value to the subdivision owners at this time. Anachronisms need not persist for their own sake. Accordingly, I would affirm the Superior Court's decision discharging the restrictive covenant in this case. . . .

Points for Discussion

a. **Preserving an Anachronism?**

Why did the fire department lose this case? In *El Di, Inc. v. Town of Bethany Beach*, 477 A.2d 1066 (Del. 1984), the Delaware Supreme Court invalidated an alcohol ban due to changed conditions. The restricted tract was originally developed as a church-affiliated residential area, but had evolved into a tourist resort over the years. Is *Vernon Township* consistent with *El Di*?

b. **The Border Lot**

The changed conditions doctrine is most commonly asserted in cases where a vacant lot on the edge of a subdivision is restricted to residential use, but is no longer suitable for this purpose—typically because it now fronts on a busy commercial street. *See, e.g., River Heights Assos. L.P. v. Batten*, 591 S.E.2d 683 (Va. 2004). Finding that the residential-only restriction still benefits the lots *inside* the subdivision, courts tend to reject such claims. Note that the *Vernon Township* court appears to consider conditions both *inside* and *outside* of the subdivision. Is this appropriate?

c. **Burden v. Benefit**

Should a court invalidate a restriction if its burden outweighs its benefit, regardless of changed conditions? Private land use restrictions on the sale of alcohol were more common during the early twentieth century, when Prohibition was in force. At the time, many viewed the sale of alcohol as immoral. But the vast majority of landowners in *Vernon Township* agreed to release the restriction—clear evidence that they felt its burden was greater than its benefit. In a modern common interest community, the CC&Rs almost always provide that they can be amended by a vote of the owners. But the older type of agreement at issue in *Vernon Township* did not provide for amendment. Should this matter?

d.   Law and Economics

Law and economics theory posits that humans are rational maximizers. As expressed in the Coase Theorem, the logical implication of this view is that the initial allocation of a property right is irrelevant because competing parties will bargain their way to an efficient resolution, assuming no transaction costs. But here 6 of 77 homeowners refused to release their rights. Why? Is the right to hold out an inherent part of the fee simple absolute? Professor Richard Epstein observes: "Ownership is meant to be a bulwark against the collective preferences of others; it allows one, rich or poor, to stand alone against the world no matter how insistent or intense its collective preferences." Richard A. Epstein, *Notice and Freedom of Contract in the Law of Servitudes,* 55 S. Cal. L. Rev. 1353, 1366–67 (1982).

The Restatement suggests that a court should be more willing to invalidate a restriction based on changed conditions where there are serious obstacles to bargaining: "Where transaction costs are likely to be high because large numbers of people are involved . . . a court should be more ready to intervene than where transaction costs are likely to be low." Restatement § 7.10 cmt. a. How would this principle apply to *Vernon Township*?

e.   An Efficient Solution?

Alternatively, should the *Vernon Township* court have resolved the dispute by imposing an economically efficient solution on the parties? It could have (1) invalidated the restriction and (2) compensated the objecting owners with damages. Restatement § 8.3(1) provides that a servitude may be enforced by "any appropriate remedy . . . which may include . . . compensatory damages." It notes that monetary relief may be more appropriate than an injunction where "a servitude has little continuing utility because the purpose it was designed to serve is less important . . . than when the servitude was created. . . ." *Id.* cmt. e.

f.   Other Methods of Termination

A covenant might end by its own terms. For example, in *Gambrell v. Nivens*, the covenants lasted only for "a period of thirty years." Or the benefited party might voluntarily *release* the covenant. And the defenses of *laches* and *unclean hands* are available when equitable relief is sought. In addition, a covenant may be terminated due to:

> - *Abandonment*: Abandonment occurs "when the average person . . . upon inspection . . . will readily observe sufficient violations that he or she will logically infer that the property owners neither adhere to nor enforce the restriction." *Fink v. Miller*, 896 P.2d 649, 653 (Utah Ct. App. 1995). In *Fink*, the court found abandonment where 23

of the 81 homes in the subdivision did not comply with a covenant that required wood shingle roofs.

- *Acquiescence*: Acquiescence occurs where the plaintiff has failed to enforce the covenant against other breaching owners but then tries to enforce it against the defendant.

- *Condemnation*: Condemnation of the servient land terminates the covenant.

- *Estoppel*: When it is inequitable to enforce the covenant because the defendant has substantially changed his position in reliance on the plaintiff's conduct, the covenant will be terminated by estoppel.

- *Merger*: If one person owns all the land benefited and burdened by the covenant, it ends due to merger.

- *Prescription*: A covenant can be ended by prescription, using essentially the same standard for acquiring a prescriptive easement.

- *Public policy*: Based in part on *Shelley v. Kraemer*, it is now generally accepted that a restriction which contravenes an important public policy is unenforceable. In *Taylor v. Northam*, 862 S.E.2d 458, 461 (Va. 2021), for example, the court held that restrictive covenants which required the state to maintain a monument to Robert E. Lee were unenforceable due to the state's strong policy against racial discrimination.

5. Common Interest Communities

A *common interest community* (CIC) is a planned residential development (a) where all properties are subject to comprehensive private land use restrictions and (b) which is regulated by a homeowners association. Today millions of Americans live in CICs—and this number continues to increase. In many regions, the overwhelming majority of new single-family housing tracts, townhouse developments, and condominium projects are CICs.

The CIC is typically created by a written instrument called a *declaration*. The declaration usually has four basic parts:

- *Homeowners association*: It establishes the association that will administer the CIC, specifies the association's powers, and provides for an elected board of directors or similar group.

- *CC&Rs*: It imposes CC&Rs or similar restrictions on all land within the CIC. These restrictions may be enforced as real covenants or equitable servitudes.

> - *Assessments*: It requires all unit owners to pay monetary assessments which finance the operation of the association.
> - *Ownership rights*: It generally provides that each unit owner holds fee simple absolute in his particular unit, an undivided interest in *common area* of the CIC (for example, a swimming pool, tennis courts, and meeting rooms), and a membership interest in the association. Alternatively, title to the common area may be held by the association on behalf of the unit owners.

In some ways, the CIC can be viewed as a private government—and this raises questions which our legal system has not yet fully addressed. For example, are CC&Rs more like a constitution or a contract? And is the homeowners association more like a public entity or a private corporation? Consider these issues as you read the materials below.

a. Enforcing Restrictions

Suppose that the CC&Rs for New Village, a condominium development, ban almost all pets. Is this restriction *unreasonable* and thus unenforceable? In our next case, Natore Nahrstedt purchased a condominium unit and moved in with her three beloved cats, Boo-Boo, Dockers, and Tulip. The homeowners association later demanded that she remove the cats, pointing out that the CC&Rs prohibited all pets except for domestic fish and birds. Nahrstedt refused: "I will not get rid of these cats. They're my babies. I chose to have cats instead of babies. . . . " *Cat Fight*, L.A. Times, Dec. 24, 1992.

Nahrstedt v. Lakeside Village Condominium Association, Inc.

Supreme Court of California

878 P.2d 1275 (1994)

KENNARD, JUSTICE.

A homeowner in a 530-unit condominium complex sued to prevent the homeowners association from enforcing a restriction against keeping cats, dogs, and other animals in the condominium development. The owner asserted that the restriction, which was contained in the project's declaration recorded by the condominium project's developer, was "unreasonable" as applied to her because she kept her three cats indoors and because her cats were "noiseless" and "created no nuisance." Agreeing with the premise underlying the owner's complaint, the Court of Appeal concluded that the homeowners association could enforce the restriction only upon proof that plaintiff's cats would be likely to interfere with the right of other homeowners "to the peaceful and quiet enjoyment of their property."

Those of us who have cats or dogs can attest to their wonderful companionship and affection.... But the issue before us is not whether in the abstract pets can have a beneficial effect on humans. Rather, the narrow issue here is whether a pet restriction that is contained in the recorded declaration of a condominium complex is enforceable against the challenge of a homeowner. As we shall explain, the Legislature, in Civil Code section 1354, has required that courts enforce the covenants, conditions and restrictions contained in the recorded declaration of a common interest development "unless unreasonable."

... Under [the] standard established by the Legislature, enforcement of a restriction does not depend upon the conduct of a particular condominium owner. Rather, the restriction must be uniformly enforced in the condominium development to which it was intended to apply unless the plaintiff owner can show that the burdens it imposes on affected properties so substantially outweigh the benefits of the restriction that it should not be enforced against any owner. Here, the Court of Appeal did not apply this standard in deciding that plaintiff had stated a claim for declaratory relief. Accordingly, we reverse the judgment of the Court of Appeal and remand for further proceedings consistent with the views expressed in this opinion.

I.

Lakeside Village is a large condominium development in Culver City, Los Angeles County. It consists of 530 units spread throughout 12 separate 3-story buildings. The residents share common lobbies and hallways, in addition to laundry and trash facilities.

The Lakeside Village project is subject to certain covenants, conditions and restrictions (hereafter CC & R's) that were included in the developer's declaration recorded with the Los Angeles County Recorder on April 17, 1978, at the inception of the development project. Ownership of a unit includes membership in the project's homeowners association, the Lakeside Village Condominium Association (hereafter Association), the body that enforces the project's CC & R's, including the pet restriction, which provides in relevant part: "No animals (which shall mean dogs and cats), livestock, reptiles or poultry shall be kept in any unit."[3]

In January 1988, plaintiff Natore Nahrstedt purchased a Lakeside Village condominium and moved in with her three cats. When the Association learned of the cats' presence, it demanded their removal and assessed fines against Nahrstedt for each successive month that she remained in violation of the condominium project's pet restriction.

---

[3] The CC & R's permit residents to keep "domestic fish and birds."

Nahrstedt's condominium building
Click here for larger photo

Nahrstedt then brought this lawsuit against the Association, its officers, and two of its employees, asking the trial court to invalidate the assessments, to enjoin future assessments, to award damages for violation of her privacy when the Association "peered" into her condominium unit, to award damages for infliction of emotional distress, and to declare the pet restriction "unreasonable" as applied to indoor cats (such as hers) that are not allowed free run of the project's common areas. Nahrstedt also alleged she did not know of the pet restriction when she bought her condominium. . . .

The Association demurred to the complaint. . . . The trial court sustained the demurrer as to each cause of action and dismissed Nahrstedt's complaint. Nahrstedt appealed.

A divided Court of Appeal reversed the trial court's judgment of dismissal. In the majority's view, the complaint stated a claim for declaratory relief based on its allegations that Nahrstedt's three cats are kept inside her condominium unit and do not bother her neighbors. According to the majority, whether a condominium use restriction is "unreasonable," as that term is used in section 1354, hinges on the facts of a particular homeowner's case. Thus, the majority reasoned, Nahrstedt would be entitled to declaratory relief if application of the pet restriction in her case would not be reasonable. . . .

II.

Today, condominiums, cooperatives, and planned-unit developments with homeowners associations have become a widely accepted form of real property ownership. These ownership arrangements are known as "common interest" developments. The owner not only enjoys many of the traditional advantages associated with individual ownership of real property, but also acquires an interest in common with others in the amenities and facilities included in the project. It is this hybrid nature of property rights that largely accounts for the popularity of these new and innovative forms of ownership in the 20th century. . . .

[S]ubordination of individual property rights to the collective judgment of the owners association together with restrictions on the use of real property comprise the chief attributes of owning property in a common interest development. As the Florida District Court of Appeal observed in *Hidden Harbour Estates, Inc. v. Norman* (Fla. Dist. Ct. App. 1975) 309 So. 2d 180, a decision frequently cited in condominium cases:

> . . . [I]nherent in the condominium concept is the principle that to promote the health, happiness, and peace of mind of the majority of the unit owners since they are living in such close proximity and using facilities in common, each unit owner must give up a certain degree of freedom of choice which he [or she] might otherwise enjoy in separate, privately owned property. Condominium unit owners comprise a little democratic sub-society of necessity more restrictive as it pertains to use of condominium property than may be existent outside the condominium organization. (*Id.* at pp. 181-182).

. . . One significant factor in the continued popularity of the common interest form of property ownership is the ability of homeowners to enforce restrictive CC & R's against other owners (including future purchasers) of project units. Generally, however, such enforcement is possible only if the restriction that is sought to be enforced meets the requirements of equitable servitudes or of covenants running with the land. . . .

When restrictions limiting the use of property within a common interest development satisfy the requirements of covenants running with the land or of equitable servitudes, what standard or test governs their enforceability? In California, as we explained at the outset, our Legislature has made common interest development use restrictions contained in a project's recorded declaration "enforceable . . . *unless unreasonable.*" (§ 1354, subd. (a), italics added.). . . .

In *Hidden Harbour Estates v. Basso* (Fla. Dist. Ct. App.1981) 393 So. 2d 637, the Florida court distinguished two categories of use restrictions: use restrictions set forth in the declaration or master deed of the condominium project itself, and rules promulgated by the governing board of the condominium owners association or the board's interpretation of a rule. (*Id.* at p. 639.) The latter category of use restrictions, the court said, should be subject to a "reasonableness" test, so as to "somewhat fetter the discretion of the board of directors." (*Id.* at p. 640.). . . .

By contrast, restrictions contained in the declaration or master deed of the condominium complex, the Florida court concluded, should not be evaluated under a "reasonableness" standard. (*Hidden Harbour Estates v. Basso, supra,* 393 So. 2d at pp. 639-640.) Rather, such use restrictions are "clothed with a very strong presumption of validity" and should be upheld even if they exhibit some degree of unreasonableness. (*Id.* at pp. 639, 640.) Nonenforcement would be proper only if such restrictions were arbitrary or in violation of public policy or some fundamental constitutional right. (*Id.* at pp. 639–640.). . . .

To what extent are these general principles reflected in California's statutory scheme governing condominiums and other common interest developments? We shall explore that in the next section.

III.

. . . [W]hen enforcing equitable servitudes, courts are generally disinclined to question the wisdom of agreed-to restrictions. This rule does not apply, however, when the restriction does not comport with public policy. Equity will not enforce any restrictive covenant that violates public policy. (*See Shelley v. Kraemer* (1948) 334 U.S. 1 [racial restriction unenforceable].) Nor will courts enforce as equitable servitudes those restrictions that are arbitrary, that is, bearing no rational relationship to the protection, preservation, operation or purpose of the affected land. (*See Laguna Royale Owners Assn. v. Darger* (1981) 119 Cal. App .3d 670, 684, 174 Cal. Rptr. 136.)

These limitations on the equitable enforcement of restrictive servitudes that are either arbitrary or violate fundamental public policy are specific applications of the general rule that courts will not enforce a restrictive covenant when "the harm caused by the restriction is so disproportionate to the benefit produced" by its enforcement that the restriction "ought not to be enforced." (Rest., Property, § 539, com. *f,* pp. 3229–3230). When a use restriction bears no relationship to the land it burdens, or violates a fundamental policy inuring to the public at large, the resulting harm will always be disproportionate to any benefit. . . .

> **Food for Thought**
>
> When *Nahrstedt* was decided, California Civil Code § 1354 provided that CC&Rs were enforceable "unless unreasonable." This section was later replaced by California Civil Code § 6856 which contains the same language. Does this mean that CC&Rs are enforceable only if they are *reasonable*?

With these principles of equitable servitude law to guide us, we now turn to section 1354. As mentioned earlier, under subdivision (a) of section 1354 the use restrictions for a common interest development that are set forth in the recorded declaration are "enforceable equitable servitudes, unless unreasonable." In other words, such restrictions should be enforced unless they are wholly arbitrary, violate a fundamental public policy, or impose a burden on the use of affected land that far outweighs any benefit. . . .

When courts accord a presumption of validity to all such recorded use restrictions and measure them against deferential standards of equitable servitude law, it discourages lawsuits by owners of individual units seeking personal exemptions from the restrictions. This also promotes stability and predictability in two ways. It provides substantial assurance to prospective condominium purchasers that they may rely with confidence on the promises embodied in the project's recorded CC & R's. And it protects all owners in the planned development from unanticipated increases in association fees to fund the defense of legal challenges to recorded restrictions.

How courts enforce recorded use restrictions affects not only those who have made their homes in planned developments, but also the owners associations charged with the fiduciary obligation to enforce those restrictions. When courts treat recorded use restrictions as presumptively valid, and place on the challenger the burden of proving the restriction "unreasonable" under the deferential standards applicable to equitable servitudes, associations can proceed to enforce reasonable restrictive covenants without fear that their actions will embroil them in costly and prolonged legal proceedings. . . .

Contrary to the dissent's accusations that the majority's decision "fray[s]" the "social fabric" we are of the view that our social fabric is best preserved if courts uphold and enforce solemn written instruments that embody the expectations of the parties rather than treat them as "worthless paper" as the dissent would. Our social fabric is founded on the stability of expectation and obligation that arises from the consistent enforcement of the terms of deeds, contracts, wills, statutes, and other writings. To allow one person to escape obligations under a written instrument upsets the expectations of all the other parties governed by that instrument (here, the owners of the other 529 units) that the instrument will be uniformly and predictably enforced. . . .

V.

Under the holding we adopt today, the reasonableness or unreasonableness of a condominium use restriction that the Legislature has made subject to section 1354 is to be determined *not* by reference to facts that are specific to the objecting homeowner, but by reference to the common interest development as a whole. As we have explained, when, as here, a restriction is contained in the declaration of the common interest development and is recorded with the county recorder, the restriction is presumed to be reasonable and will be enforced uniformly against all residents of the common interest development *unless* the restriction is arbitrary, imposes burdens on the use of lands it affects that substantially outweigh the restriction's benefits to the development's residents, or violates a fundamental public policy. . . .

We conclude, as a matter of law, that the recorded pet restriction of the Lakeside Village condominium development prohibiting cats or dogs but allowing some other pets is not arbitrary, but is rationally related to health, sanitation and noise concerns legitimately held by residents of a high-density condominium project such as Lakeside Village, which includes 530 units in 12 separate 3-story buildings.

Nahrstedt's complaint alleges no facts that could possibly support a finding that the burden of the restriction on the affected property is so disproportionate to its benefit that the restriction is unreasonable and should not be enforced. . . .

[W]e discern no fundamental public policy that would favor the keeping of pets in a condominium project. There is no federal or state constitutional provision or any California statute that confers a general right to keep household pets in condominiums or other common interest developments. . . .

ARABIAN, JUSTICE, dissenting.

"There are two means of refuge from the misery of life: music and cats."[1]

I respectfully dissent. While technical merit may commend the majority's analysis, its application to the facts presented reflects a narrow, indeed chary, view of the law that eschews the human spirit in favor of arbitrary efficiency. In my view, the resolution of this case well illustrates the conventional wisdom, and fundamental truth, of the Spanish proverb, "It is better to be a mouse in a cat's mouth than a man in a lawyer's hands." . . .

I find the provision known as the "pet restriction" contained in the covenants, conditions, and restrictions (CC & R's) governing the Lakeside Village project patently arbitrary and unreasonable within the meaning of Civil Code section 1354. Beyond dispute, human beings have long enjoyed an abiding and cherished association with their household animals. Given the substantial benefits derived from pet ownership, the undue burden on the use of property imposed on condominium owners who can maintain pets within the confines of their units without creating a nuisance or disturbing the quiet enjoyment of others substantially outweighs whatever meager utility the restriction may serve in the abstract. It certainly does not promote "health, happiness [or] peace of mind" commensurate with its tariff on the quality of life for those who value the companionship of animals. Worse, it contributes to the fraying of our social fabric. . . .

[T]he value of pets in daily life is a matter of common knowledge and understanding as well as extensive documentation. People of all ages, but particularly the elderly and the young, enjoy their companionship. Those who suffer from serious disease or injury and are confined to their home or bed experience a therapeutic, even spiritual, benefit from their presence. Animals provide comfort at the death of a family member or dear friend, and for the lonely can offer a reason for living when life seems to have lost its meaning. . . . While pet ownership may not be a fundamental right as such, unquestionably it is an integral aspect of our daily existence, which cannot be lightly dismissed and should not suffer unwarranted intrusion into its circle of privacy. . . .

---

[1] Albert Schweitzer.

From the statement of the facts through the conclusion, the majority's analysis gives scant acknowledgment to any of the foregoing considerations but simply takes refuge behind the "presumption of validity" now accorded *all* CC & R's irrespective of subject matter. They never objectively scrutinize defendants' blandishments of protecting "health and happiness" or realistically assess the substantial impact on affected unit owners and *their* use of *their* property. . . .

Here, such inquiry should start with an evaluation of the interest that will suffer upon enforcement of the pet restriction. In determining the "burden on the use of land," due recognition must be given to the fact that this particular "use" transcends the impersonal and mundane matters typically regulated by condominium CC & R's, such as whether someone can place a doormat in the hallway or hang a towel on the patio rail or have food in the pool area, and reaches the very quality of life of hundreds of owners and residents. Nonetheless, the majority accept uncritically the proffered justification of preserving "health and happiness" and essentially consider only one criterion to determine enforceability: was the restriction recorded in the original declaration? If so, it is "presumptively valid," unless in violation of public policy. Given the application of the law to the facts alleged and by an inversion of relative interests, it is difficult to hypothesize any CC & R's that would not pass muster. Such sanctity has not been afforded any writing save the commandments delivered to Moses on Mount Sinai, and they were set in stone, not upon worthless paper.

Moreover, unlike most conduct controlled by CC & R's, the activity at issue here is strictly confined to the owner's interior space; it does not in any manner invade other units or the common areas. Owning a home of one's own has always epitomized the American dream. More than simply embodying the notion of having "one's castle," it represents the sense of freedom and self-determination emblematic of our national character. Granted, those who live in multi-unit developments cannot exercise this freedom to the same extent possible on a large estate. But owning pets that do not disturb the quiet enjoyment of others does not reasonably come within this compromise. Nevertheless, with no demonstrated or discernible benefit, the majority arbitrarily sacrifice the dream to the tyranny of the "commonality." . . .

In contravention, the majority's failure to consider the real burden imposed by the pet restriction unfortunately belittles and trivializes the interest at stake here. Pet ownership substantially enhances the quality of life for those who desire it. When others are not only undisturbed by, but *completely unaware of,* the presence of pets being enjoyed by their neighbors, the balance of benefit and burden is rendered disproportionate and unreasonable, rebutting any presumption of validity. Their view, shorn of grace and guiding philosophy, is devoid of the

> **FYI**
>
> Justice Arabian later wrote a law review article expanding upon the themes in his dissent. *See* Armand Arabian, *Condos, Cats, and CC&Rs: Invasions of the Castle Common,* 23 Pepp. L. Rev. 1 (1995).

humanity that must temper the interpretation and application of all laws, for in a civilized society that is the source of their authority. As judicial architects of the rules of life, we better serve when we construct halls of harmony rather than walls of wrath.

I would affirm the judgment of the Court of Appeal.

Points for Discussion

a. The *Nahrstedt* Test

Does this test strike the right balance between enforcing CC&Rs and protecting individual freedom? Notice that the court is interpreting a statute which provides that CC&Rs are enforceable unless they are "unreasonable." The dissent suggests that the majority's test is meaningless: "[I]t is difficult to hypothesize any CC&Rs that would not pass muster." Do you agree? Consider the standard adopted by Restatement § 3.1: a servitude is valid unless it is "illegal or unconstitutional or violates public policy." Under this approach, a servitude violates public policy if it: (1) is arbitrary, spiteful, or capricious; (2) unreasonably burdens a fundamental constitutional right; (3) imposes an unreasonable restraint on alienation; (4) imposes an unreasonable restraint on trade or competition; or (5) is unconscionable. Do you prefer the *Nahrstedt* test or the Restatement approach? Why?

b. Home as Castle?

In his dissent, Justice Arabian invokes the familiar adage that "a person's home is her castle." Should CC&Rs be allowed to control what a person does inside the privacy of her own condominium? Conversely, why should a condominium owner ever be allowed to challenge the validity of CC&Rs? As a prudent buyer, Nahrstedt should have read the CC&Rs before she purchased. And she can certainly try to convince the other owners to amend the CC&Rs to allow pets.

c. CC&R Problems

Suppose the New Village CC&Rs contain the following provisions. Are they valid under the *Nahrstedt* test? Under the Restatement test?

> (1) "Only college graduates may live at New Village."
>
> (2) "While on the New Village property, all residents must wear clothing made from natural fibers in order to help preserve our environment."
>
> (3) "No one may watch television at New Village."
>
> (4) "No animals shall be kept at New Village." Unit owner X has become blind and needs a guide dog.

d. Validity of Specific Restrictions

Commercial uses: Courts routinely enforce covenants that prohibit commercial uses. But what about short-term rentals like Airbnb? Most courts reason that this is a residential use, not a commercial use. *See, e.g., JBrice Holdings, LLC v. Wilcrest Walk Townhomes Ass'n, Inc.*, 644 S.W.3d 179 (Tex. 2022); *Forshee v. Neuschwander*, 914 N.W.2d 643 (Wis. 2018).

Leases and sales: Courts generally enforce CC&Rs that restrict or prohibit leasing units. Restrictions on the sale of units—such as requiring the association to approve any sale or giving the association a preemptive right to purchase—are upheld if reasonable. *Laguna Royale Association v. Darger*, 174 Cal. Rptr. 136 (Ct. App. 1981).

Sex offenders: In *Mulligan v. Panther Valley Property Owners Assn.*, 766 A.2d 1186 (N.J. Sup. Ct. App. Div. 2001), the residents of a gated residential community voted to amend the declaration to prohibit anyone who was registered as a Tier 3 sex offender from living there. The court upheld the amendment without reaching the merits, because the plaintiff had not met her burden of providing an adequate record. But the court expressed concern that "large segments of the State could entirely close their doors to such individuals, confining them to a narrow corridor and thus perhaps exposing those within that remaining corridor to a greater risk of harm. . . ." *Id.* at 1193. Would such an amendment be valid under the *Nahrstedt* test?

e. Interpreting CC&Rs

Restrictive covenants were narrowly construed at common law because they interfered with the free use of land. As Restatement § 4.1 cmt. a explains, today we recognize that these covenants "are widely used in modern land development and ordinarily play a valuable role in utilization of land resources." Accordingly, the modern view is that a CC&R provision "should be interpreted to give effect to the intention of the parties ascertained from the language used in the instrument, or the circumstances surrounding the creation of the servitude, and to carry out the purpose for which it was created." Restatement § 4.1(1). *See, e.g., Fountain Valley Chateau Blanc Homeowners Ass'n v. Dept. of Veterans Affairs*, 79 Cal. Rptr. 2d 248, 256 (App. 1998) (covenant requiring owners to maintain the inside of their units in "attractive condition" did not require defendant to "clean up his own bedroom").

f. Aftermath of *Nahrstedt*

In response to the ruling, Nahrstedt commented: "I'm disappointed in their decision, but that doesn't mean that I'm going to campaign to have it overturned by the Legislature." *Condo Cat Fight*, L.A. Times, Sept. 4, 1994. She later moved out of Lakeside Village with her three cats—having spent over $50,000 on legal fees.

Under pressure from pet owners, the state legislature partially overturned the *Nahrstedt* decision by enacting California Civil Code § 4715. It provides that each owner of a unit in a common interest community may keep at least "one pet," regardless of any contrary CC&R provision. "Pet" is defined to mean "any domesticated bird, cat, dog, aquatic animal kept within an aquarium, or other animal as agreed to between the association and the homeowner."

b. Governing the Development

Today there are more than 300,000 homeowners associations in the United States. The typical CIC declaration provides that the association will:

- maintain the common area of the CIC;
- enforce the CC&Rs;
- adopt and enforce rules to supplement the CC&Rs;
- collect assessments from the unit owners; and
- take such other actions as are necessary to administer the CIC.

These powers are usually exercised by a board of directors elected by the owners. Suppose that an owner disagrees with a discretionary decision made by the board. Can the owner successfully challenge the decision in litigation?

States disagree about the appropriate scope of judicial review in this situation. Some courts reason that a homeowners association is akin to a corporation, and accordingly use the *business judgment rule* from corporate law. Under this approach, the association is not liable if the board made the decision in good faith and rationally believed that it was appropriate. However, most courts review these decisions using a *reasonableness standard*. Adopting this approach, Restatement § 6.13(1)(c) requires an association to "act reasonably in the exercise of its discretionary powers."

Suppose that G purchased her home in New Village because of its excellent golf course. The developer advertised New Village to prospective buyers as a "golfer's paradise," and the course is part of the development's common area. The board of directors of the New Village Homeowners Association now votes to close the golf course because (1) it is expensive to maintain and (2) many owners no longer use it. Will G win her lawsuit challenging this decision?

Schaefer v. Eastman Community Association

Supreme Court of New Hampshire

836 A.2d 752 (2003)

DUGGAN, J.

This case involves a dispute between the plaintiffs, certain homeowners in the planned, private community of Eastman, and the defendant, Eastman Community Association (ECA or association), a non-profit corporation that governs Eastman. ECA appeals a decision by the Superior Court (Mangones, J.) finding that ECA did not have authority under its Declaration of Covenants and Restrictions (declaration) to close Snow Hill ski area. We reverse.

Eastman is a planned, private, four seasons, recreational community located primarily within the town of Grantham.... The amenities include a golf course, tennis courts, an indoor pool, cross country skiing, hiking, and a lake with beaches and facilities for boating and swimming. Until September 1999, Eastman also offered downhill skiing at its own ski area known as Snow Hill. While the association owns and maintains the recreational amenities, the residents of Eastman own their homes and also own indivisible, equal interests in the common property.

> **FYI**
>
> Click here to visit the Eastman Community Association website, which contains pictures of the development.

The Articles of Agreement (articles) establish ECA as a non-profit corporation organized under RSA chapter 292. The articles provide that ECA's affairs shall be managed by a board of directors, subject to the powers and limitations set forth in the declaration. The declaration is the governing document for the Eastman community and sets forth the residents' rights and privileges and the terms of the association's operation. All property within Eastman is subject to the declaration....

The ECA Board of Directors (board) is comprised of nine directors who are elected by the property owners for three-year terms. The board has numerous powers enumerated in the declaration and has the ultimate responsibility for making decisions regarding policies, finances and administration at Eastman.

As early as 1984, the residents and the governing bodies debated whether the Snow Hill ski area should remain open. In 1994, the results of the Eastman Long Range Planning Committee's survey of Eastman residents indicated that Snow Hill ski area was of little importance to the families and the community. In 1998, Cilley & Associates conducted a survey that found that of 695 respondents, sixty-eight percent had never used Snow Hill....

On September 17, 1999, the board voted eight to one to close Snow Hill and sell the chairlift. . . .

The plaintiffs subsequently filed an action in superior court seeking: (1) to enjoin ECA from closing Snow Hill and selling the chairlift; and (2) damages based on trespass, deceit, negligent misrepresentation, violation of RSA chapter 358-A and *ultra vires*. . . . [T]he plaintiffs argued, and the superior court agreed, that ECA acted *ultra vires* in closing the Snow Hill ski area because the declaration did not provide for the closing of an amenity. . . .

[On appeal,] ECA first argues that the trial court erred in finding that the board's September 17, 1999 vote to close Snow Hill ski area was *ultra vires*. Because we hold that the board acted within its authority under the declaration when it voted to close Snow Hill ski area on September 17, 1999, we need not address the other issues raised by ECA.

"When a court is called upon to assess the validity of [an action taken] by a board of directors, it first determines whether the board acted within its scope of authority and, second, whether the [action] reflects reasoned or arbitrary and capricious decision making." *Beachwood Villas Condo. v. Poor*, 448 So.2d 1143, 1144 (Fla. Dist. Ct. App. 1984); *accord Lamden v. La Jolla Shores Clubdominium Homeowners Ass'n.*, 21 Cal.4th 249, 980 P.2d 940, 944 (1999). Because the reasonableness of the board's decision to close Snow Hill ski area was not questioned below or on appeal, we are only concerned with the scope of the board's authority.

> **It's Latin to Me**
>
> An act is *ultra vires* when it is beyond the scope of power granted by the declaration, corporate charter, or other instrument.

Inquiry into this area begins with a review of the association's legal documents. The association's legal documents are "a contract that governs the legal rights between the [a]ssociation and [property] owners." *Lacy v. Sutton Place Condo. Ass'n. Inc.*, 684 A.2d 390, 393 (D.C. 1996). Because the association is a corporation, it may not act in any way not authorized by the articles or the declaration. "[A]cts beyond the scope of the powers so [authorized] are *ultra vires*." *Seabrook Island Prop. Owners Ass'n. v. Pelzer*, 292 S.C. 343, 356 S.E.2d 411, 414 (App. 1987). Accordingly, whether the association's action was within its authority requires us to interpret the articles and declaration. This is a question of law that we review *de novo*.

In determining whether the declaration provides the board with the authority to close Snow Hill ski area, we should be mindful that the declaration is the association's "constitution." *See Beachwood Villas Condo.*, 448 So.2d at 1145. Generally, declarations and other governing documents contain "broad statements of general policy with due notice that the board of directors is empowered to implement these policies and address day-to-day problems in the [association's] operation." *Id*. Thus, the declaration should not be so narrowly construed so as to eviscerate the association's intended role as the governing body of the community. Rather, a broad view of the powers delegated to the association "is justified by the important role these communities play in maintaining property values and providing municipal-like services. . . . If unable to act, the common property may fall into disrepair. . . ." Restatement (Third) of Property § 6.4 comment a at 90 (2000); *cf. Joslin v. Pine River Dev. Corp.,* 116 N.H. 814, 817, 367 A.2d 599 (1976) ("[P]rivate land use restrictions 'have been particularly important in the twentieth century when the value of property often depends in large measure upon maintaining the character of the neighborhood in which it is situated.' ").

Because an association's power should be interpreted broadly, the association, through its appropriate governing body, is "entitled to exercise all powers of the community except those reserved to the members." Restatement (Third) of Property § 6.16. Accordingly, "provided that a [board's action] does not contravene either an express provision of the declaration or a right reasonably inferable therefrom, it will be found valid, within the scope of the board's authority." *Beachwood Villas Condo.*, 448 So.2d at 1145. This rule preserves the concept of delegated management and carries out the expectations of property owners who purchased property subject to, and with notice of, the association's governing instruments. Moreover, the rights of property owners are safeguarded by the terms of the governing instruments and through their power to remove or replace the board members through the election process. *See* Restatement (Third) of Property § 6.16 comment b at 289; *see also Beachwood Villas Condo.*, 448 So.2d at 1145.

In the present case, the decision to close Snow Hill ski area does not contravene an express provision of the declaration; nor is it a decision reserved to the members. Rather, the defendant relies upon three provisions of Article 7.6 of the declaration that affirmatively provide the association with authority to close the Snow Hill ski area. These provisions provide that:

> The Board shall take all such measures as may be necessary to: . . .
>
> (h) take steps necessary to protect the Association's assets and insure its financial stability[;] . . . .
>
> (j) buy and sell property when deemed in the best interests of the Association; . . . .
>
> (n) take such other action as it may deem necessary to further the purposes of this Declaration or to be in the best interests of this Association.

Because the decision to close the ski area or any other amenity may be necessary to insure financial stability or be in the best interests of the association, it is a decision that is reserved in Article 7.6 for the association to make, through the board, and thus within the board's authority.

The plaintiffs argue that, pursuant to the declaration, ECA lacked authority to close the ski area because it was neither "necessary to insure ECA's financial stability," nor "in the best interests of Eastman." This argument is misplaced. Whether the association's decision was in fact either necessary to ECA's financial stability or in the best interests of Eastman is a question of the reasonableness of the association's action. So long as ECA's action "does not contravene either an express provision of the declaration or a right reasonably inferable therefrom, it will be found valid, within the scope of the board's authority." *Beachwood Villas Condo.,* 448 So.2d at 1145. The plaintiffs, both in their brief and at oral argument, argued that the "reasonableness of ECA's decision is not relevant here because the Board did not act within its authority. . . ."

The plaintiffs also argue that, because the declaration does not expressly authorize ECA to close an amenity, such authority cannot "reasonably be inferred from the [d]eclaration in light of ECA's express purpose to preserve and maintain the recreational amenities, as set forth in the preamble, and in light of the fact that ECA from its inception has promoted the availability of downhill skiing at Eastman." Essentially, the plaintiffs are asking that we narrowly construe the board's powers enumerated in the declaration because of the general purposes of the ECA and Eastman's promotional materials.

> **See It**
>
> Click here to see pictures of the Snow Hill ski lift taken shortly after it was closed.

The plaintiffs argue that the board's powers must be narrowly construed to deny the board the authority to close the ski area because such an interpretation is consistent with the general purposes of the community. The plaintiffs assert that the general purposes of the community are found in the preamble of the declaration and ECA's statement of purpose. The preamble states that Eastman is to be "a planned residential and recreational community with permanent parks, open spaces and other common facilities for the benefit of such community and the health, safety, and social welfare of the Owners . . . within such community." In addition, the preamble further states that ECA is to "provide for the preservation, maintenance and improvement of said parks, open spaces and common facilities." ECA's statement of purpose states that ECA "was established in order to hold, maintain, and administer the Community's facilities and Open Spaces within Eastman."

In addition, the plaintiffs argue that a narrow interpretation of the board's powers would be consistent with promotional materials distributed by Eastman. The plaintiffs point to a number of materials that specifically promote the Snow Hill ski area, which they relied upon in deciding to purchase a home at Eastman. For example, a Community Services Guide that was published shortly before ECA closed the ski area promoted Eastman as:

> [A] recreational community for all seasons offering residents the best of all worlds in its 3500 acres of protected natural environment . . . a 325-acre lake for swimming, boating, fishing and other water sports . . . a championship 18-hole golf course, tennis courts, and indoor pool . . . miles of nature trails, 30 kilometers of cross-country ski trails . . . its own downhill ski run, softball diamond, volleyball and basketball courts.

(Emphasis omitted.). . . . Many brochures directly promoted the ski area by describing Snow Hill as "skiing past evergreens glistening with snow" and as "the perfect 'Special Place' for active, young families who will enjoy skiing from their front doors, down the slope to the lift facilities in winter." Finally, the "Prospective Buyer's Guide to Eastman," which was prepared and distributed by ECA, emphasized Eastman's recreational amenities, including its own downhill ski area and double chairlift.

Accordingly, the plaintiffs argue, that "[w]hen considered in the overall scheme of Eastman and the purposes of ECA set forth in the [d]eclaration, discontinuance of downhill skiing at Snow Hill is not authorized by the [d]eclaration." We disagree. While the plaintiffs may have relied upon the assertions contained in Eastman's promotional materials and the overall general purposes of the ECA, neither limit the broad authority granted to ECA and its governing bodies in the declaration. Because the decision to close Snow Hill ski area does not contravene an express provision of the declaration and there are several provisions of the declaration that reserve such decision-making to the board, the board had the authority, under the declaration, to close the ski area despite the promotional materials or the stated general purposes. Moreover, the plaintiffs purchased their properties subject to, and on notice of, the terms of the declaration, not the promotional materials provided by Eastman.

We should note that, while the board had the authority to act as it did, the plaintiffs or other similarly situated homeowners are not without recourse. The plaintiffs and other homeowners have the power under the declaration to remove or replace [the board members] through the election process. . . .

Points for Discussion

a. Scope of Authority

Because Eastman was planned and marketed as a "four season" resort community, the Snow Hill ski area was an attractive feature to many buyers—a core component of the community. And the declaration did not expressly authorize the association to close it. Under these circumstances, should the court have found that the board lacked the authority to make this decision? *See, e.g., Sainani v. Belmont Glen Homeowners Ass'n, Inc.* 831 S.E.2d 662 (Va. 2019) (board lacked authority to regulate owners' holiday decorations and lighting). The *Schaefer* court implies that it is appropriate to take a broad view of the association's powers in order to maintain property values. Does that rationale apply here? If we envision the declaration as a "constitution," shouldn't it protect owners holding a minority view from unfair treatment by the majority? Could the board also close the golf course, tennis courts, and other recreational facilities?

b. **Reasonableness Standard**

As a general matter, discretionary decisions by a homeowners association in New Hampshire are reviewed under a reasonableness standard. Why didn't the plaintiffs challenge the reasonableness of the board's decision? Alternatively, should the court have utilized a more searching standard of review here since its decision concerned a "core" feature of the development? The precedents cited in *Schaefer* involve relatively minor decisions. For example, *Beachwood Villas Condominium v. Poor*, 448 So. 2d 1143 (Fla. Dist. Ct. App. 1984) concerns rules regulating the rental of units, while *Lamden v. La Jolla Shores Clubdominium Homeowners Ass'n*, 980 P.2d 940 (Cal. 1999) examines a decision about the appropriate method to eradicate termites.

c. **Validity of Rules**

Suppose that the board of directors of a homeowners association adopts a new *rule*: it bans satellite dishes. Should the validity of this rule be governed by the same standard applied to the original CC&Rs or by a different standard? As the *Nahrstedt* majority notes, most courts uphold such rules as long as they are reasonable—a less deferential standard. *Neuman v. Grandview at Emerald Hills, Inc.*, 861 So. 2d 494 (Fla. Dist. Ct. App. 2003).

d. **Architectural Review Committees**

CC&Rs often include architectural review provisions. In effect, these provisions allow a neighborhood committee to regulate the appearance and design of new homes. What are the benefits and costs of this approach? Predictably, the discretionary decisions of architectural review committees are often attacked in litigation. Courts tend to uphold such decisions as long as they are reasonable. *See, e.g., Smith v. Butler Mountain Estates Property Owners Ass'n*, 367 S.E.2d 401 (N.C. Ct. App. 1988) (committee's refusal to allow geodesic dome house in conventional subdivision was reasonable).

Summary

- **Types of Easements.** The law recognizes five basic types of easements: express easement; implied easement by prior existing use; easement by necessity; prescriptive easement; and easement by estoppel (or irrevocable license).

- **Scope of Easements.** In general, the scope of an express easement depends on the intention of the parties. The manner, frequency, and intensity of the use of an easement may change over time as technology evolves.

- **Termination of Easements.** An easement may be terminated by abandonment, prescription, and other methods. Abandonment requires both nonuse of the easement and words or conduct manifesting an intention to relinquish it.

- **Real Covenants.** A real covenant is a promise concerning the use of land that benefits and burdens the original parties to the promise and their successors; the remedy for breach is damages.

- **Equitable Servitudes.** An equitable servitude is also a promise concerning the use of land that benefits and burdens the original parties to the promise and their successors; the remedy for breach is an injunction.

- **Common Interest Communities.** A common interest community is a private residential development (a) where all properties are subject to comprehensive land use restrictions known as CC&Rs and (b) which is governed by a homeowners association.

- **Enforcement of CC&Rs.** CC&Rs may be enforced as real covenants or equitable servitudes. Three key defenses to enforcement are unreasonableness, abandonment, and changed conditions.

- **Governing the Community.** The powers of a homeowners association are exercised by an elected board of directors. Most courts use a standard of reasonableness in reviewing board decisions; some courts apply the more deferential business judgment rule.

> **Test Your Knowledge**
>
> To assess your understanding of the material in this chapter, click here to take a quiz.

> **For More Information**
>
> For more information about the subjects covered in this chapter, please consult these sources:
>
> - Alfred L. Brophy, *Contemplating When Equitable Servitudes Run with the Land*, 46 St. Louis U. L.J. 691 (2002).
> - Robert C. Ellickson, *Stale Real Estate Covenants*, 63 Wm. & Mary L. Rev. 1831 (2022).
> - Susan F. French, *Highlights of the New Restatement (Third) of Property: Servitudes*, 35 Real Prop. Prob. & Tr. J. 225 (2000).
> - Michael V. Hernandez, *Restating Implied, Prescriptive, and Statutory Easements*, 40 Real Prop. Prob. & Tr. J. 75 (2005).
> - Ronald H. Rosenberg, *Fixing a Broken Common Law—Has the Property Law of Easements and Covenants Been Reformed by a Restatement?*, 44 Fla. St. U. L. Rev. 143 (2016).

CHAPTER 11

Land Use Regulation

Suppose that B owns fee simple absolute in Greenacre, which is not encumbered by any privately created restrictions. In other words, there are no conditions, covenants, easements, equitable servitudes, or similar constraints that limit B's conduct. Does B have the right to build a shopping mall on the land? Perhaps not. Under modern law, B's ability to use Greenacre is restricted by a complex network of ordinances and statutes. Virtually every parcel of land in the United States is subject to comprehensive regulation that limits how it may be used.

Traditionally, an owner like B had complete discretion to decide how to use her land, subject only to private restrictions and nuisance law. A few large cities did adopt ordinances attacking specific problems, such as slaughterhouses or livery stables. But these were isolated exceptions to the prevailing view that land use was a private matter, not a public concern.

In this chapter, we explore four aspects of land use regulation:

- *Nuisance law*: This is the traditional tool used to resolve land use conflicts.

- *Basics of zoning*: In *Village of Euclid v. Ambler Realty Co.*, 272 U.S. 365 (1926), the Supreme Court upheld the constitutionality of Euclid's zoning ordinance—which became the model for ordinances across the nation.

- *Zoning flexibility*: The main flexibility tools are zoning amendments, variances, and conditional uses.

- *Outer limits*: How far can land use regulation go? Modern controversies include aesthetic regulation, "family" zoning, and exclusionary zoning.

A. Nuisance Law

Suppose that A's high roof casts a shadow on B's adjacent solar collector, which impairs its operation. What are B's rights? In *Prah v. Maretti*, which you studied in Chapter 1, the Wisconsin Supreme Court held that A's conduct might be a *nuisance*.

In this chapter, we examine nuisance law in more depth. Before the widespread adoption of zoning ordinances in the early twentieth century, nuisance law was the main tool to reconcile conflicting land uses—and it is still useful today in some situations. The early zoning ordinances were upheld, in part, on the basis that they were effective methods of preventing nuisances. In addition, nuisance law played a role in the evolution of regulatory takings jurisprudence, which you will study in Chapter 14.

Restatement (Second) of Torts § 821D defines the *private nuisance* as "a nontrespassory invasion of another's interest in the private use and enjoyment of land." Almost all nuisances (such as the shadow from A's house) are private nuisances. In contrast, a *public nuisance* is an improper interference with a right common to the public.

The plaintiff in a private nuisance case must establish that the defendant's conduct resulted in an intentional, nontrespassory, unreasonable, and substantial interference with the use and enjoyment of the plaintiff's land.

- *Intentional*: The defendant's conduct is intentional if he acts for the purpose of causing the harm *or* he knows that the harm is resulting or is substantially certain to result from his conduct.

- *Nontrespassory*: The interference must not involve any physical entry onto the land of another. For example, noise, vibration, light, and odors are all viewed as nontrespassory invasions.

- *Unreasonable*: Jurisdictions differ about the meaning of this element. Some states follow the *gravity of the harm* test: the defendant's conduct is unreasonable if it causes substantial harm, regardless of the social utility of the conduct. Many states use the Restatement standard: conduct is unreasonable if the *gravity of the harm* outweighs the *utility of the conduct*. Restatement (Second) of Torts § 826(a). A number of states use multi-factor tests that fall somewhere between these two approaches.

- *Substantial interference*: There must be a "real and appreciable invasion of the plaintiff's interests," involving "more than slight inconvenience or petty annoyance." Restatement (Second) of Torts § 821F cmt. c.

- *Use and enjoyment of land*: The defendant's conduct must interfere with the use and enjoyment of land, e.g., causing physical damage to the property or personal injury to occupants.

Perhaps the most famous nuisance case in the United States arose near Albany, New York, where a plant operated by the Atlantic Cement Company produced dust and vibration that injured its neighbors. Cement dust coated the cars at Oscar and June Boomer's adjacent junkyard, which damaged the paint and made the auto parts harder to sell. Vibrations from blasting at the plant's nearby quarry created large cracks in the walls and ceiling of the home owned by Floyd and Barbara Millious. The Boomers, Milliouses, and other neighbors brought suit seeking an injunction to close the plant.

Boomer v. Atlantic Cement Co., Inc.

Court of Appeals of New York

257 N.E.2d 870 (1970)

BERGAN, JUDGE.

Defendant operates a large cement plant near Albany. These are actions for injunction and damages by neighboring land owners alleging injury to property from dirt, smoke and vibration emanating from the plant. A nuisance has been found after trial, temporary damages have been allowed; but an injunction has been denied.

The public concern with air pollution arising from many sources in industry and in transportation is currently accorded ever wider recognition accompanied by a growing sense of responsibility in State and Federal Governments to control it. Cement plants are obvious sources of air pollution in the neighborhoods where they operate.

Atlantic Cement Co. plant
Click here for larger photo

But there is now before the court private litigation in which individual property owners have sought specific relief from a single plant operation. The threshold question raised by the division of view on this appeal is whether the court should resolve the litigation between the parties now before it as equitably as seems possible; or whether, seeking promotion of the general public welfare, it should channel private litigation into broad public objectives.

A court performs its essential function when it decides the rights of parties before it. Its decision of private controversies may sometimes greatly affect public issues. Large questions of law are often resolved by the manner in which private litigation is decided. But this is normally an incident to the court's main function to settle controversy. It is a rare exercise of judicial power to use a decision in private litigation as a purposeful mechanism to achieve direct public objectives greatly beyond the rights and interests before the court. . . .

It seems apparent that the amelioration of air pollution will depend on technical research in great depth; on a carefully balanced consideration of the economic impact of close regulation; and of the actual effect on public health. It is likely to require massive public expenditure and to demand more than any local community can accomplish and to depend on regional and interstate controls.

A court should not try to do this on its own as a by-product of private litigation and it seems manifest that the judicial establishment is neither equipped in the limited nature of any judgment it can pronounce nor prepared to lay down and implement an effective policy for the elimination of air pollution. This is an area beyond the circumference of one private lawsuit. It is a direct responsibility for government and should not thus be undertaken as an incident to solving a dispute between property owners and a single cement plant—one of many—in the Hudson River valley.

The cement making operations of defendant have been found by the court of Special Term to have damaged the nearby properties of plaintiffs in these two actions. That court, as it has been noted, accordingly found defendant maintained a nuisance and this has been affirmed at the Appellate Division. The total damage to plaintiffs' properties is, however, relatively small in comparison with the value of defendant's operation and with the consequences of the injunction which plaintiffs seek.

The ground for the denial of injunction, notwithstanding the finding both that there is a nuisance and that plaintiffs have been damaged substantially, is the large disparity in economic consequences of the nuisance and of the injunction. This theory cannot, however, be sustained without overruling a doctrine which has been consistently reaffirmed in several leading cases in this court and which has never been disavowed here, namely that where a nuisance has been found and where there has been any substantial damage shown by the party complaining an injunction will be granted.

The rule in New York has been that such a nuisance will be enjoined although marked disparity be shown in economic consequence between the effect of the injunction and the effect of the nuisance. . . .

Although the court at Special Term and the Appellate Division held that injunction should be denied, it was found that plaintiffs had been damaged in various specific amounts up to the time of the trial and damages to the respective plaintiffs were awarded for those amounts. The effect of this was, injunction having been denied, plaintiffs could maintain successive actions at law for damages thereafter as further damage was incurred.

The court at Special Term also found the amount of permanent damage attributable to each plaintiff, for the guidance of the parties in the event both sides stipulated to the payment and acceptance of such permanent damage as a settlement of all the controversies among the parties. The total of permanent damages to all plaintiffs thus found was $185,000. This basis of adjustment has not resulted in any stipulation by the parties.

This result at Special Term and at the Appellate Division is a departure from a rule that has become settled; but to follow the rule literally in these cases would be to close down the plant at once. This court is fully agreed to avoid that immediately drastic remedy; the difference in view is how best to avoid it.[1]

One alternative is to grant the injunction but postpone its effect to a specified future date to give opportunity for technical advances to permit defendant to eliminate the nuisance; another is to grant the injunction conditioned on the payment of permanent damages to plaintiffs which would compensate them for the total economic loss to their property present and future caused by defendant's operations. For reasons which will be developed the court chooses the latter alternative.

If the injunction were to be granted unless within a short period—e.g., 18 months—the nuisance be abated by improved methods, there would be no assurance that any significant technical improvement would occur.

The parties could settle this private litigation at any time if defendant paid enough money and the imminent threat of closing the plant would build up the pressure on defendant. If there were no improved techniques found, there would inevitably be applications to the court at Special Term for extensions of time to perform on showing of good faith efforts to find such techniques.

> **Food for Thought**
>
> Is the court correct that the case could be settled "at any time if defendant paid enough money"? Why is this relevant?

Moreover, techniques to eliminate dust and other annoying by-products of cement making are unlikely to be developed by any research the defendant can undertake within any short period, but will depend on the total resources of the cement industry nationwide and throughout the world. The problem is universal wherever cement is made.

---

[1] Respondent's investment in the plant is in excess of $45,000,000. There are over 300 people employed there.

For obvious reasons the rate of the research is beyond control of defendant. If at the end of 18 months the whole industry has not found a technical solution a court would be hard put to close down this one cement plant if due regard be given to equitable principles.

On the other hand, to grant the injunction unless defendant pays plaintiffs such permanent damages as may be fixed by the court seems to do justice between the contending parties. All of the attributions of economic loss to the properties on which plaintiffs' complaints are based will have been redressed. . . .

It seems reasonable to think that the risk of being required to pay permanent damages to injured property owners by cement plant owners would itself be a reasonable effective spur to research for improved techniques to minimize nuisance. . . .

The damage base here suggested is consistent with the general rule in those nuisance cases where damages are allowed. "Where a nuisance is of such a permanent and unabatable character that a single recovery can be had, including the whole damage past and future resulting therefrom, there can be but one recovery" (66 C.J.S. Nuisances § 140, p. 947). It has been said that permanent damages are allowed where the loss recoverable would obviously be small as compared with the cost of removal of the nuisance (*Kentucky-Ohio Gas Co. v. Bowling*, 264 Ky. 470, 477, 95 S.W.2d 1). . . .

Thus it seems fair to both sides to grant permanent damages to plaintiffs which will terminate this private litigation. The theory of damage is the "servitude on land" of plaintiffs imposed by defendant's nuisance. (*See United States v. Causby*, 328 U.S. 256, 261, where the term "servitude" addressed to the land was used by Justice Douglas relating to the effect of airplane noise on property near an airport.)

Food for Thought

Does the decision effectively force plaintiffs to sell Atlantic a right to pollute their properties—a servitude? Should the law protect their right to exclude Atlantic's pollution? Note that the court cites *United States v. Causby*, which you studied in Chapter 2. In *Causby*, the defendant United States had the power of eminent domain. Here, Atlantic is a private company. Is this difference relevant?

The judgment, by allowance of permanent damages imposing a servitude on land, which is the basis of the actions, would preclude future recovery by plaintiffs or their grantees.

This should be placed beyond debate by a provision of the judgment that the payment by defendant and the acceptance by plaintiffs of permanent damages found by the court shall be in compensation for a servitude on the land. . . .

The orders should be reversed, without costs, and the cases remitted to Supreme Court, Albany County to grant an injunction which shall be vacated upon payment by defendant of such amounts of permanent damage to the respective plaintiffs as shall for this purpose be determined by the court.

JASEN, JUDGE (dissenting).

I agree with the majority that a reversal is required here, but I do not subscribe to the newly enunciated doctrine of assessment of permanent damages, in lieu of an injunction, where substantial property rights have been impaired by the creation of a nuisance.

It has long been the rule in this State, as the majority acknowledges, that a nuisance which results in substantial continuing damage to neighbors must be enjoined. To now change the rule to permit the cement company to continue polluting the air indefinitely upon the payment of permanent damages is, in my opinion, compounding the magnitude of a very serious problem in our State and Nation today. . . .

The specific problem faced here is known as particulate contamination because of the fine dust particles emanating from defendant's cement plant. . . . This type of pollution, wherein very small particles escape and stay in the atmosphere, has been denominated as the type of air pollution which produces the greatest hazard to human health. We have thus a nuisance which not only is damaging to the plaintiffs, but also is decidedly harmful to the general public.

> **FYI**
>
> Particulate matter—such as fine cement dust—can cause asthma, lung cancer, heart problems, and premature death. Each year more than 50,000 Americans die from exposure to particulate matter.

I see grave dangers in overruling our long-established rule of granting an injunction where a nuisance results in substantial continuing damage. In permitting the injunction to become inoperative upon the payment of permanent damages, the majority is, in effect, licensing a continuing wrong. It is the same as saying to the cement company, you may continue to do harm to your neighbors so long as you pay a fee for it. Furthermore, once such permanent damages are assessed and paid, the incentive to alleviate the wrong would be eliminated, thereby continuing air pollution of an area without abatement. . . .

I would enjoin the defendant cement company from continuing the discharge of dust particles upon its neighbors' properties unless, within 18 months, the cement company abated this nuisance. . . .

Points for Discussion

a. Gravity of the Harm

Notice that the *Boomer* court did not apply the Restatement standard. It simply notes that "plaintiffs had been damaged" in the amount of $185,000, a conclusion which is seemingly based on the gravity of the harm test. How do we measure the gravity of the harm? In relationship to what? For perspectives on *Boomer*, see Daniel A. Farber, *The Story of* Boomer: *Pollution and the Common Law*, 32 Ecology L.Q. 113 (2005) and *Symposium on Nuisance Law: Twenty Years After* Boomer v. Atlantic Cement Co., 54 Alb. L. Rev. 171 (1990).

b. Nuisance v. Trespass

Why was the dust seen as a nontrespassory interference? If Atlantic's employees threw dirt clods onto the Boomers' land, this would be a trespass. Dust particles consist of tangible matter, just like dirt clods. The answer lies in history. The distinction between nuisance and trespass originated when scientific knowledge was primitive. Dust, fumes, and smoke were seen as more akin to noise or vibration than to physical matter. Today some courts impose trespass liability for entries by microscopic particles, such as dust or fumes. But most courts continue to follow the traditional approach. *See, e.g., Babb v. Lee County Landfill SC, LLC*, 747 S.E.2d 468, 480 (S.C. 2013) ("only intrusions by physical, tangible things [are] capable of constituting a trespass").

c. The Appropriate Remedy

Before *Boomer*, the remedy for a continuing nuisance in New York was an injunction. Why did the court refuse an injunction? On the other hand, suppose that the court had issued an injunction that effectively closed the plant. What negotiations would have followed? *See* Richard A. Posner, Economic Analysis of Law 72 (9th ed. 2014).

Is there a more equitable solution to *Boomer*? Should the court have denied the injunction on condition that Atlantic purchase the plaintiffs' properties for fair market value, assuming no nuisance existed? Or could the court have enjoined the plant on condition that the plaintiffs compensate Atlantic for its loss? *See Spur Industries, Inc. v. Del E. Webb Development Co.*, 494 P.2d 700 (Ariz. 1972) (enjoining feed lot operation, but requiring plaintiff to indemnify defendant).

d. Nonmonetary Harm

In selecting the appropriate remedy, should the court have considered nonmonetary damage: the risks that the plant presented to human health and the natural environment? The dissent points out that the dust particles the plant emitted were "the greatest hazard to human health." But the majority views this as a case about $185,000 in property damage. *See* Michael C. Blumm, *A Dozen Landmark Nuisance Cases and Their Environmental Significance*, 62 Ariz. L. Rev. 403 (2020).

e. Anticipatory Nuisance

In most states, a plaintiff can obtain an injunction against conduct which will be a nuisance in the future. Recall that in *Prah v. Maretti* (Chapter 1), Prah sought to enjoin the construction of Maretti's house because it would create a harmful shadow. But the threshold for enjoining an anticipatory nuisance is high. For example, as the court explained in *Krueger v. AllEnergy Hixton, LLC,* 918 N.W.2d 458, 467 (Wis. Ct. App. 2018), to obtain such an injunction in Wisconsin the plaintiff must show that the proposed conduct will "necessarily" or "certainly" create a nuisance which will cause "inevitable and undoubted" harm.

f. Aftermath of *Boomer*

Atlantic eventually installed air pollution control technology at the plant in order to comply with the federal Clean Air Act. This system captured so much dust that the company had trouble storing it. Testing revealed that the dust contained high levels of calcium oxide and potash, two key ingredients in fertilizer. Accordingly, the company began selling the dust (dubbed "NewLime") to farmers to enhance crop production. Jack Gordon, the president of Atlantic, remarked: "It wasn't a waste product; we were just wasting it." Steve Geimann, *New York Business Feature*, UPI, Dec. 21, 1983.

Our next case presents a situation somewhat similar to *Boomer*, but on a smaller scale. Plaintiffs argue that the smoke emitted from their neighbors' chimney is a nuisance and seek an injunction to remedy the problem. In deciding the case, the appellate court follows the Restatement approach—comparing the gravity of the harm and the utility of the actor's conduct.

Thomsen v. Greve

Court of Appeals of Nebraska

550 N.W.2d 49 (1996)

HANNON, JUDGE.

This is a nuisance action brought by the plaintiffs, Elmer Thomsen and Phyllis Thomsen, to enjoin the defendants, Ron Greve and Nancy Greve, from using a wood-burning stove to heat their home and for damages resulting from the smoke originating from the stove. . . .

I. FACTS

. . . The evidence produced at that trial may be summarized as follows: The parties own and live in adjacent homes in Pender, Nebraska. The Greves have lived in their home since 1973. In 1990, the Thomsens moved into the house situated 15 feet west of the Greves' home. For approximately the first 2 years, the Thomsens and the Greves had a friendly relationship. Phyllis Thomsen and Nancy Greve visited in each other's homes on a frequent and regular basis. The parties have had some disputes, such as the location of their boundary line west of the Greves' fence and the Greves' practice of raising rabbits, which led to the demise of their friendship. Nancy Greve testified she has not spoken to the Thomsens since August 1992.

In August 1992, the Thomsens complained to the Greves about the odor and smoke from the wood-burning stove, claiming that it smelled dirty. The Greves both testified that in the 6 years in which they had been operating the stove, this was the first time anyone complained about the smoke. The Greves both testified that Phyllis Thomsen told them that the smoke made the Thomsens' house smell dirty, but that Elmer Thomsen stated that it only had happened once and that it was not that bad. The Thomsens agree that in August they complained to the Greves about the smoke, but they deny that Elmer Thomsen stated it happened only once. They testified that Nancy Greve told them to just keep their windows and doors shut.

Ron Greve is a licensed electrician who owned his own business. In 1986, the Greves put an addition on their home, at which time they installed a wood-burning stove. Since 1986, the wood-burning stove has been the primary source of heat in the Greves' home; prior to that time they had a gas furnace and then electrical baseboard heat. The Greves claim to have burned only "dry, hard wood" in their stove and that Ron has cleaned the chimney once a month to prevent the buildup of creosote. The Greves supplement the wood-burning stove with electrical heat only on days when the temperature is below zero. They claim to never have burned garbage or railroad ties or anything else containing creosote. . . .

The Greves also testified that the smoke was not malodorous and that they burn nothing but clean, dry wood, usually ash, in their stove. . . .

Phyllis Thomsen testified that during the previous 4 years, the smoke entered her house about 140 times in total and that the smoke entered under certain weather conditions. The air has to be "moist" and the wind either still or from the northeast in order for the smoke to get into the Thomsens' home. The Thomsens described the smoke as "unbearable." They claimed that it was a creosote smell, which was a "rotten smell." They both testified that when the weather was right, the smoke would surround their house and creep inside. The smell made them physically ill. Phyllis Thomsen testified that besides making her distraught, the smoke gets in her throat and nose, causing a burning and scratchy sensation. She

> **See It**
>
> Click here to see (a) a 1992 photograph of the Greves' smoke drifting toward the Thomsens' house and (b) a modern photograph of the houses after the Greves' chimney was extended upward.

testified that at times the odor is so bad she would be forced to leave her home to escape it, and at times it causes them to not be able to sleep at night. Elmer Thomsen testified that he gets a bad cough as a result of the smoke, which forces him to leave his house on occasion to clear it up. The smoke and odor have prevented the Thomsens from having family get-togethers and visitors over to their home. They testified that the smoke and odor infiltrate their home to such a degree that even their clothes dryer fills with the smoky odor.

Frank Appleton, chairman of the Pender Village Board, went to the Thomsens' home on two separate occasions, and he testified that the smoke smelled like wood burning. The Pender chief of police also visited the Thomsens, as did another board member, and both testified that the smoke smelled like wood burning, and it was not an offensive odor. On cross-examination, it was revealed that Ron Greve served on the village board for some time prior to the filing of the petition in this case.

The Thomsens called family members and a neighbor to testify on their behalf. The Greves also called several neighbors who testified that the smoke from the Greves' chimney did not smell like creosote. The witnesses for both sides were impeached to a degree by a showing of friendship or other reasons for their partiality to the party calling them.

After the trial, the court found the smoke to be a nuisance and ordered the Greves to raise the height of the chimney by 3 feet and to burn only "clean dry firewood." The court also found that the Thomsens failed to prove with specificity the actual monetary loss or damage, and thus awarded no damages. [The Thomsens appealed and the Greves cross-appealed.]. . . .

III. STANDARD OF REVIEW

This is an appeal of a nuisance action for both an injunction and damages, and as such, the Supreme Court has stated the following standard of review applies:

> An action for an injunction sounds in equity. . . . In an appeal of an equity action, an appellate court tries factual questions de novo on the record and reaches a conclusion independent of the findings of the trial court, provided, when credible evidence is in conflict on a material issue of fact, the appellate court considers and may give weight to the fact that the trial judge heard and observed the witnesses and accepted one version of the facts rather than another. . . .

Goeke v. National Farms, Inc., 245 Neb. 262, 264, 512 N.W.2d 626, 629 (1994).

IV. DISCUSSION

The Greves argue that the Thomsens failed to meet their burden to show the wood-burning stove was a nuisance. Since this issue is an issue of fact, we will consider the Greves' arguments on the weight of the evidence in a de novo trial of the factual issue later in this opinion. The Greves also argue that their conduct did not create a nuisance as a matter of law. They argue that they are unable to find any case where a court has been asked to determine that using a wood-burning stove created a nuisance, and they argue that under the principles set forth in §§ 826 through 828 of the Restatement (Second) of Torts (1979), the trial court should have determined their activity did not create a nuisance as a matter of law. . . .

Could Greves' Conduct Create Nuisance?

A private nuisance is a nontrespassory invasion of another's interest in the private use and enjoyment of land. *Hall v. Phillips*, 231 Neb. 269, 436 N.W.2d 139 (1989). The Nebraska Supreme Court has expressly adopted the Restatement (Second) of Torts (1979) as the law of private nuisance actions in Nebraska, specifically citing § 822 as expressing a " 'suitable standard to determine when one may be subject to liability. . . .' " *Kopecky v. National Farms, Inc.*, 244 Neb. 846, 851, 510 N.W.2d 41, 47 (1994) (quoting *Hall v. Phillips, supra*). . . .

Section 822 provides in significant part: "One is subject to liability for a private nuisance if, but only if, his conduct is a legal cause of an invasion of another's interest in the private use and enjoyment of land, and the invasion is . . . intentional and unreasonable. . . ."

The Supreme Court has recognized that the principles stated in the Restatement . . . are to be used by judges as a guide to determine whether an intentional interference is unreasonable as a matter of law. *Kopecky v. National Farms, Inc., supra*. Section 826 defines what constitutes an unreasonable invasion and provides in significant part: "An intentional invasion of another's interest in the use and enjoyment of land is unreasonable if . . . the gravity of the harm outweighs the utility of the actor's conduct. . . ."

The following sections further refine the definition of "unreasonable" and assist in determining whether the gravity of the harm suffered by the Thomsens is outweighed by the utility of the Greves' conduct. Section 827 provides:

> In determining the gravity of the harm from an intentional invasion of another's interest in the use and enjoyment of land, the following factors are important:
>
> (a) the extent of the harm involved;
>
> (b) the character of the harm involved;
>
> (c) the social value that the law attaches to the type of use or enjoyment invaded;
>
> (d) the suitability of the particular use or enjoyment invaded to the character of the locality; and
>
> (e) the burden on the person harmed of avoiding the harm.

Section 828 provides:

> In determining the utility of conduct that causes an intentional invasion of another's interest in the use and enjoyment of land, the following factors are important:
>
> (a) the social value that the law attaches to the primary purpose of the conduct;

(b) the suitability of the conduct to the character of the locality; and

(c) the impracticability of preventing or avoiding the invasion.

. . . In applying these principles to the instant case to determine whether or not the Greves' conduct could create a nuisance, we must necessarily assume that the Greves' conduct on their land interferes with Thomsens' enjoyment of their land in the manner that the Thomsens claim. Whether as a matter of fact the Thomsens have suffered the damages they claim is an issue of fact that need only be determined if the Greves' conduct under the Thomsens' version of the facts could be a nuisance.

The evidence shows that the parties live in a residential neighborhood in a small Nebraska town. Both their homes appear to be small one-story homes of a type that has been built since the 1950's. Pictures in evidence show both parties' homes to be attractive and in an attractive setting insofar as grass, trees, bushes, flowers, and other amenities.

The Thomsens testified that in a 4-year period the smoke entered their home approximately 140 times, which has made their house smell of creosote, a "rotten smell." It affected their use of their home and affected them physically. We have no trouble concluding that, at least in our society, to have the use and enjoyment of one's home interfered with by smoke, odor, and similar attacks upon one's senses is a serious harm. The social value of allowing people to enjoy their homes is great, and persons subjected to odor or smoke from a neighbor cannot avoid such harm except by moving. One should not be required to close windows to avoid such harm.

On the other hand, aside from the simple right to use their property as they wish, it is difficult to assign any particular social value to the Greves' wood-burning stove. This method of heating does save on fossil fuels, but assuming that the stove used by the Greves emits foul-smelling smoke, society is certainly blessed if only a few people avail themselves of the opportunity to save fuel by using such stoves. The Greves could avoid invading the Thomsens' property by using other means of heating.

Under the Restatement (Second) of Torts § 822 (1979), we therefore conclude that if the Thomsens' evidence is true, the Greves' invasion of the Thomsens' land in the manner claimed by the Thomsens is unreasonable. . . .

Did Greves' Conduct Create Nuisance?

The facts adduced by both parties are in direct conflict on the issue of whether the Greves have actually created a nuisance. The trial court heard and observed the witnesses and their manner of testifying, and it necessarily accepted the Thomsens' version of the facts to the extent necessary to find that a nuisance existed. In concluding that the Greves have created a nuisance by their conduct, we rely heavily upon the trial court's determination, but not entirely.

The fact that the chairman of the village board smelled smoke in the Thomsens' house on two occasions, when there was no source other than the Greves' wood-burning stove for that smell, is significant. The Pender chief of police was called as a witness by the Greves. He testified to seeing smoke down between the parties' homes and to similar observations about smoke from another home in Pender that burns wood. On one occasion, the police chief was called to the Thomsens' residence in regard to the smoke. He reported smelling the strong odor of smoke in the Thomsens' home, but said that it smelled like wood burning. When the judge asked him if he found the odor in the Thomsens' home offensive, he said, "Well, it was just a heavy wood-burning," but he stated it did not smell of creosote. Another member of the village board went to the Thomsens' home, and he testified, "It smelled to me like they had a wood-burning stove in their house." He also testified "it stunk" outside of the house. He took the complaint seriously enough to contact the State Fire Marshal and others in an attempt to solve the problem. These witnesses characterized the Thomsens' smoke problem differently than the Thomsens and their witnesses, yet they support the Thomsens' claim to the extent that the Thomsens had a significant smoke odor in their house, and the source of that odor had to be outside. . . .

> **Food for Thought**
>
> According to the non-party witnesses, how severe was the smoke problem inside the Thomsens' house? Was it a substantial interference with their use and enjoyment of the property?

We conclude that the Greves have created a nuisance which the Thomsens are entitled to have abated. . . . [The court directed that the trial court's decree be amended to provide (a) a damages award to the Thomsens in the amount of $4,000 and (b) that "the Greves are ordered to abate the nuisance of smoke and odor emanating from their home."]

Points for Discussion

a. Gravity v. Utility

How can smoke from a neighbor's chimney be a nuisance? Notice that the appellate court was not bound by the factual findings of the trial court; rather, it conducted an independent, de novo review based on the Restatement standard. How effectively did the *Thomsen* court apply the Restatement criteria to the facts of the case? Five criteria concern gravity, and three deal with utility. Consider the evidence relevant to each criterion and then do your own analysis. Do you agree with the *Thomsen* court?

b. Nuisance Examples

Bird feeding: The plaintiff in *Simpkins v. Speck*, 443 P.3d 428 (Mont. 2019) complained that the manner in which his neighbor fed wild birds in her backyard was a nuisance. The court agreed, citing the plaintiff's testimony that "there are bird droppings on his property, driveway, and vehicles, that there is noise from dawn to dusk, and that there are feathers, dead birds, and dismembered birds in his yard." *Id.* at 431.

Concerts: In *Shore v. Maple Lane Farms*, 411 S.W.3d 405 (Tenn. 2013), the court found that the plaintiff had presented a prima facie case for nuisance liability based on testimony that her neighbor hosted a series of loud open-air concerts featuring amplified music. It concluded that the plaintiff "was forced out of her home during daytime concerts, and . . . was a hostage to the noise at night." *Id.* at 425

Radiation: *Page County Appliance Center, Inc. v. Honeywell, Inc.*, 347 N.W.2d 171 (Iowa 1984), involved a computer which emitted radiation, interfering with the television reception in plaintiff's appliance store and thus harming sales. The appellate court agreed that a reasonable jury could find a nuisance under the Restatement standard on these facts, but remanded the case to determine whether the appliance store was an unusually sensitive use.

Wind turbine: In *Sowers v. Forest Hills Subdivision*, 294 P.3d 427 (Nev. 2013), the court held that a wind turbine in a residential subdivision was a nuisance. It reasoned that the turbine would produce noise comparable to the "hum" of a freeway, generate shadow flicker, and lower nearby property values, all of which far outweighed the benefits of the proposed turbine—saving energy and reducing electricity bills.

c. Aesthetic Nuisance

Suppose C erects a grotesque sculpture in his front yard. Can his neighbors successfully argue that the sculpture is a nuisance? In most states, the mere appearance of a thing does not make it a nuisance. For example, in *Myrick v. Peck Electric Co.*, 164 A.3d 658 (Vt. 2017), the Vermont Supreme Court rejected the plaintiffs' claim that the unsightliness of a commercial solar panel installation near their homes made it a nuisance. It explained that an "unattractive sight" is not a "substantial interference as a matter of law" because it does not affect a person's ability to use and enjoy her lands. *Id.* at 661. The court also commented that "[t]he judicial branch is ill-suited to be an arbiter of style or taste." *Id.* at 662. *But see* Raymond R. Coletta, *The Case for Aesthetic Nuisance: Rethinking Traditional Judicial Attitudes*, 48 Ohio St. L.J. 141 (1987).

d. Choice of Remedy

The *Boomer* court refused to enjoin Atlantic from emitting cement dust—a serious threat to human health—thus endangering the general public. In contrast, the *Thomsen* court enjoined the Greves from emitting smoke which occasionally caused one neighbor to get a "bad cough" and another to have a "burning and scratching sensation" in her throat and nose. These conditions were unpleasant but not life-threatening. What explains the difference? Should the *Thomsen* court have chosen a different remedy?

e. **Nuisance Exercises**

Does a nuisance exist in either situation below under the gravity of the harm test? Under the Restatement standard? If so, what remedy is most appropriate?

> (1) Two months ago, Church A opened a shelter for the homeless on its church property, which is surrounded by single-family homes. About 15 homeless people eat and sleep there each day. Since the shelter opened, many neighbors have found litter in their yards; burglaries have occurred at five homes; inebriated shelter residents have scared small children on three occasions; and everyone in the neighborhood is worried. An appraiser estimates that the shelter has lowered the value of adjacent properties by 2%.
>
> (2) S and T, a married couple, purchased a house in an industrial area next to a large wholesale bakery. Trucks from the bakery routinely deliver bread, rolls, muffins, and other products to grocery stores between midnight and 7:00 a.m., in order to ensure that the products are fresh; they have made such night deliveries for years. The loud and frequent truck noise makes it very difficult for S and T to sleep; they are often nervous and tired.

B. Basics of Zoning

By the early twentieth century, living conditions in many American cities were truly horrible. Industrial development and increased urbanization had produced slums where the impoverished residents lived in damp, dark, and unhealthy conditions. The density levels were among the highest in the world, with up to 1,700 people per acre in some areas. Fire and crime were ever-present dangers, while diseases such as cholera, diphtheria, and scarlet fever were common. The existing land use tools—nuisance law, covenants, and servitudes—could not effectively respond to these new problems.

> ### Perspective and Analysis
>
> Jacob Riis, a muckraking journalist who devoted his life to improving housing conditions, generated public support for reform legislation with his classic book How the Other Half Lives: Studies Among the Tenements of New York:
>
>> . . . To-day three-fourths of [New York City residents] live in the tenements, and the nineteenth century drift of the population to the cities is sending ever-increasing multitudes to crowd them. . . . We now know that there is no way out; that the "system" that was the evil offspring of public

> neglect and private greed has come to stay, a storm-centre forever of our civilization. . . .
>
> . . . The story is dark enough . . . to send a chill to any heart. If it shall appear that the sufferings and the sins of the "other half," and the evil they breed, are but as a just punishment upon the community that gave it no other choice, it will be because that is the truth. The boundary line lies there because, while the forces for good on one side vastly outweigh the bad . . . in the tenements all the influences make for evil; because they are the hot-beds of the epidemics that carry death to rich and poor alike; the nurseries of pauperism and crime that fill our jails and police courts; that throw off a scum of forty thousand human wrecks to the island asylums and workhouses year by year; that turned out in the last eight years a round half million beggars to prey upon our charities; that they maintain a standing army of ten thousand tramps with all that that implies; because, above all, they touch the family life with deadly moral contagion. This is their worst crime. . . .
>
> **Jacob A. Riis, How the Other Half Lives: Studies Among the Tenements of New York 1–3 (1890).**

Idealistic reformers—influenced by the "garden city" movement in England—argued that these urban evils could be eliminated by developing new, low-density towns in the countryside. Each single-family home would stand in the center of its own garden, far from the nuisance-like impacts of commercial or industrial uses. The centerpiece of this plan was comprehensive regulation of land use. The reformers reasoned that government had the inherent *police power* to protect the public health, safety, morals and welfare through zoning laws. Each city would be divided into geographical areas or *zones* where different uses were permitted, with limits on the size and location of buildings in each zone.

The nation's first comprehensive zoning ordinance was adopted by New York City in 1916. It was sparked in part by construction of the Equitable Building—then the world's largest office building—which cast a shadow over seven acres of Manhattan. New Yorkers were already concerned about both slum conditions and the movement of garment factories into residential and retail areas. The risk that large portions of the city would be cast into darkness by future skyscrapers was unacceptable.

> **See It**
>
> The reason the Equitable Building cast such a huge shadow is that it occupied an entire city block, with no setback from the sidewalk. Click here to see an early picture of the building. The 1916 New York City zoning law sought to allow sunlight to reach street level by imposing setback requirements and other restrictions on new buildings. The lasting influence of the setback requirements can be seen in the Empire State Building and other post-1916 structures.

The 1920s produced a tidal wave of zoning ordinances in the United States. This process was facilitated by the Department of Commerce, which drafted a standardized zoning law in 1922. The resulting *Standard State Zoning Enabling Act* was a model law that states could adopt if they wished, and many did. The Act both (1) empowered local governments to adopt zoning ordinances and (2) specified the key provisions for an effective ordinance. Given this heritage, zoning ordinances in cities and counties across the nation are often remarkably similar.

1. Constitutionality of Zoning

Many landowners argued that zoning laws were an unconstitutional interference with traditional private property rights. It was widely believed that the conservative Supreme Court would endorse this view. Accordingly, Ambler Realty Company and fourteen other property owners banded together to finance a test case against the new zoning ordinance in Euclid, Ohio. But they lost—and the resulting opinion is the foundation of American zoning law.

The events leading up to *Village of Euclid v. Ambler Realty Co.*, 272 U.S. 365 (1926) seem almost like the plot of a novel. The attorney for plaintiff Ambler Realty was Newton D. Baker, who had previously served both as Secretary of War under Woodrow Wilson and as mayor of Cleveland. The Village of Euclid was defended by James Metzenbaum, a Euclid resident who later became the foremost scholar on American zoning law. The case was tried before Judge D.C. Westenhaver, who President Wilson had appointed to the federal bench at Baker's urging. Westenhaver found the Euclid ordinance unconstitutional, but opined that the case was "obviously destined to go higher."

Baker and Metzenbaum argued the case before the Supreme Court in January, 1926. On the train back to Cleveland that night, Metzenbaum worried that Baker's arguments had convinced the Court; he resolved to seek permission to file a reply brief.

Perspective and Analysis

> Unable to telephone from the train, Metzenbaum drafted a telegram to [Chief Justice] Taft: . . . *Because of the importance of the cause and not for any mere purpose of winning, am compelled by conscientious duty to request permission to file short Reply Brief.* As the train slowed along a siding where freight cars were being shoveled out of the snow, Metzenbaum shouted to a workman, tossed the telegram form wrapped with money, and saw it land in a bank of snow. Only after reaching Cleveland did he learn that the telegram had been sent.

Timothy Alan Fluck, Euclid v. Ambler: *A Retrospective*, **52 J. Am. Planning Ass'n 31 (1986).**

Metzenbaum was given permission to file his brief. This led the Court to order that the case be re-argued in October, 1926—and Euclid won.

Village of Euclid v. Ambler Realty Co.

Supreme Court of the United States

272 U.S. 365 (1926)

Justice Sutherland delivered the opinion of the Court.

The Village of Euclid is an Ohio municipal corporation. It adjoins and practically is a suburb of the City of Cleveland. Its estimated population is between 5,000 and 10,000, and its area from 12 to 14 square miles, the greater part of which is farm lands or unimproved acreage. It lies, roughly, in the form of a parallelogram measuring approximately 3½ miles each way. East and west it is traversed by three principal highways: Euclid Avenue, through the southerly border, St. Clair Avenue, through the central portion, and Lake Shore Boulevard, through the northerly border, in close proximity to the shore of Lake Erie. The Nickel Plate Railroad lies from 1,500 to 1,800 feet north of Euclid Avenue, and the Lake Shore Railroad 1,600 feet farther to the north. The three highways and the two railroads are substantially parallel.

Appellee is the owner of a tract of land containing 68 acres, situated in the westerly end of the village, abutting on Euclid Avenue to the south and the Nickel Plate Railroad to the north. . . .

On November 13, 1922, an ordinance was adopted by the village council, establishing a comprehensive zoning plan for regulating and restricting the location of trades, industries, apartment houses, two-family houses, single family houses, etc., the lot area to be built upon, the size and height of buildings, etc.

The entire area of the village is divided by the ordinance into six classes of use districts, denominated U-1 to U-6, inclusive; three classes of height districts, denominated H-1 to H-3, inclusive; and four classes of area districts, denominated A-1 to A-4, inclusive. The use districts are classified in respect of the buildings which may be erected within their respective limits, as follows: U-1 is restricted to single family dwellings . . . ; U-2 is extended to include two-family dwellings; U-3 is further extended to include apartment houses, hotels, churches, schools, public libraries, [and other public buildings]; U-4 is further extended to include banks, offices, studios, telephone exchanges, fire and police stations, restaurants, theaters, [and other "retail stores and shops"]; U-5 is further extended to include ["light industrial" uses]; U-6 is further extended to include [general "manufacturing and industrial operations"]. There is a seventh class of uses which is prohibited altogether.

Class U-1 is the only district in which buildings are restricted to those enumerated. In the other classes the uses are cumulative; that is to say, uses in class U-2 include those enumerated in the preceding class U-1; class U-3 includes uses enumerated in the preceding classes, U-2, and U-1; and so on. . . .

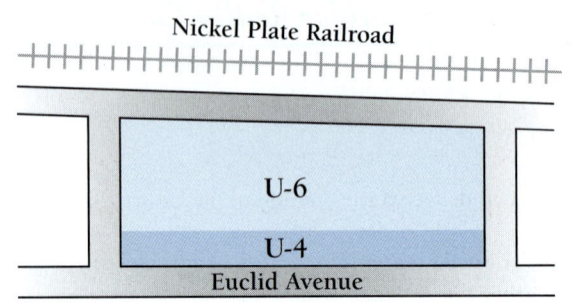

"Normal and reasonably to be expected use and development" of Ambler Realty Co. land

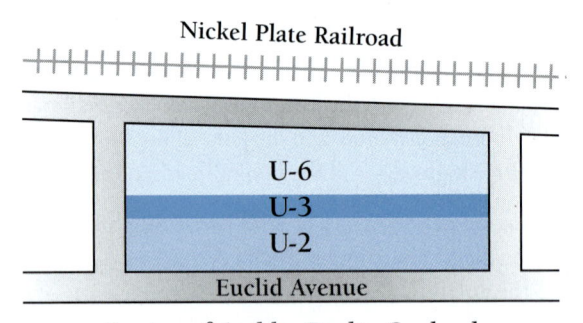

Zoning of Ambler Realty Co. land

Appellee's tract of land comes under U-2, U-3 and U-6. The first strip of 620 feet immediately north of Euclid Avenue falls in class U-2, the next 130 feet to the north, in U-3, and the remainder in U-6. The uses of the first 620 feet, therefore, do not include apartment houses, hotels, churches, schools, or other public and semipublic buildings, or other uses enumerated in respect of U-3 to U-6, inclusive. The uses of the next 130 feet include all of these, but exclude industries, theaters, banks, shops, and the various other uses set forth in respect of U-4 to U-6, inclusive. . . .

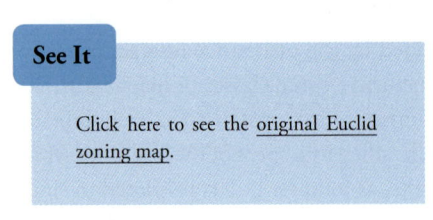

See It

Click here to see the original Euclid zoning map.

The lands lying between the two railroads for the entire length of the village area and extending some distance on either side to the north and south, having an average width of about 1,600 feet, are left open, with slight exceptions, for industrial and all other uses. This includes the larger part of appellee's tract. Approximately one-sixth of the area of the entire village is included in U-5 and U-6 use districts. . . .

The enforcement of the ordinance is intrusted to the inspector of buildings, under rules and regulations of the board of zoning appeals. Meetings of the board are public, and minutes of its proceedings are kept. It is authorized to adopt rules and regulations to carry into effect provisions of the ordinance. Decisions of the inspector of buildings may be appealed to the board by any person claiming to be adversely affected by any such decision. The board is given power in specific cases of practical difficulty or unnecessary hardship to interpret the ordinance in harmony with its general purpose and intent, so that the public health, safety and general welfare may be secure and substantial justice done. Penalties are prescribed for violations. . . .

The ordinance is assailed on the grounds that it is in derogation of § 1 of the Fourteenth Amendment to the federal Constitution in that it deprives appellee of liberty and property without due process of law and denies it the equal protection of the law, and that it offends against certain provisions of the Constitution of the State of Ohio. The prayer of the bill is for an injunction restraining the enforcement of the ordinance and all attempts to impose or maintain as to appellee's property any of the restrictions, limitations or conditions. The court below held the ordinance to be unconstitutional and void, and enjoined its enforcement, 297 F. 307.

Before proceeding to a consideration of the case, it is necessary to determine the scope of the inquiry. The bill alleges that the tract of land in question is vacant and has been held for years for the purpose of selling and developing it for industrial uses, for which it is especially adapted, being immediately in the path or progressive industrial development; that for such uses it has a market value of about $10,000 per acre, but if the use be limited to residential purposes the market value is not in excess of $2,500 per acre; that the first 200 feet of the parcel back from Euclid Avenue, if unrestricted in respect of use, has a value of $150 per front foot, but if limited to residential uses, and ordinary mercantile business be excluded therefrom, its value is not in excess of $50 per front foot.

> **Make the Connection**
>
> The Fifth Amendment to the Constitution provides, in part: "[N]or shall private property be taken for public use, without just compensation." Did Euclid "take" part of the property owned by Ambler Realty? You will study the Takings Clause in Chapter 14.

It is specifically averred that the ordinance attempts to restrict and control the lawful uses of appellee's land, so as to confiscate and destroy a great part of its value. . . .

The record goes no farther than to show, as the lower court found, that the normal and reasonably to be expected use and development of that part of appellee's land adjoining Euclid Avenue is for general trade and commercial purposes, particularly retail stores and like establishments, and that the normal and reasonably to be expected use and development of the residue of the land is for industrial and trade purposes. Whatever injury is inflicted by the mere existence and threatened enforcement of the ordinance is due to restrictions in respect of these and similar uses; to which perhaps should be added—if not included in the foregoing—restrictions in respect of apartment houses. . . .

It is not necessary to set forth the provisions of the Ohio Constitution which are thought to be infringed. The question is the same under both Constitutions, namely, as stated by appellee: Is the ordinance invalid, in that it violates the constitutional protection "to the right of property in the appellee by attempted regulations under the guise of the police power, which are unreasonable and confiscatory"?

Building zone laws are of modern origin. They began in this country about 25 years ago. Until recent years, urban life was comparatively simple; but, with the great increase and concentration of population, problems have developed, and constantly are developing, which require, and will continue to require, additional restrictions in respect of the use and occupation of private lands in urban communities. Regulations, the wisdom, necessity, and validity of which, as applied to existing conditions, are so apparent that they are now uniformly sustained, a century ago, or even half a century ago, probably would have been rejected as arbitrary and oppressive. Such regulations are sustained, under the complex conditions of our day, for reasons analogous to those which justify traffic regulations, which, before the advent of automobiles and rapid transit street railways, would have been condemned as fatally arbitrary and unreasonable. And in this there is no inconsistency, for, while the meaning of constitutional guaranties never varies, the scope of their application must expand or contract to meet the new and different conditions which are constantly coming within the field of their operation. In a changing world it is impossible that it should be otherwise. . . .

The ordinance now under review, and all similar laws and regulations, must find their justification in some aspect of the police power, asserted for the public welfare. The line which in this field separates the legitimate from the illegitimate assumption of power is not capable of precise delimitation. It varies with circumstances and conditions. A regulatory zoning ordinance, which would be clearly valid as applied to the great cities, might be clearly invalid as applied to rural communities. In solving doubts, the maxim *sic utere tuo ut alienum non laedas*, which lies at the foundation of so much of the common law of nuisances, ordinarily will furnish a fairly helpful clew. And the law of nuisances, likewise, may be consulted, not for the purpose of controlling, but for the helpful aid of its analogies in the process of ascertaining the scope of, the power. Thus the question whether the power exists to forbid the erection of a building of a particular kind or for a particular use, like the question whether a particular thing is a nuisance, is to be determined, not by an abstract consideration of the building or of the thing considered apart, but by considering it in connection with the circumstances and the locality. . . . A nuisance may be merely a right thing in the wrong place, like a pig in the parlor instead of the barnyard. If the validity of the legislative classification for zoning purposes be fairly debatable, the legislative judgment must be allowed to control. . . .

There is no serious difference of opinion in respect of the validity of laws and regulations fixing the height of buildings within reasonable limits, the character of materials and methods of construction, and the adjoining area which must be left open, in order to minimize the danger of fire or collapse, the evils of overcrowding and the like, and excluding from residential sections offensive trades, industries and structures likely to create nuisances. . . .

Here, however, the exclusion is in general terms of all industrial establishments, and it may thereby happen that not only offensive or dangerous industries will be excluded, but those which are neither offensive nor dangerous will share the same fate. But this is no more than happens in respect of many practice-forbidding laws which this court has upheld, although drawn in general terms so as to include individual cases that may turn out to be innocuous in themselves. . . . The inclusion of a reasonable margin, to insure effective enforcement, will not put upon a law, otherwise valid, the stamp of invalidity. Such laws may also find their justification in the fact that, in some fields, the bad fades into the good by such insensible degrees that the two are not capable of being readily distinguished and separated in terms of legislation. In the light of these considerations, we are not prepared to say that the end in view was not sufficient to justify the general rule of the ordinance, although some industries of an innocent character might fall within the proscribed class. It cannot be said that the ordinance in this respect "passes the bounds of reason and assumes the character of a merely arbitrary fiat." *Purity Extract Co. v. Lynch*, 226 U.S. 192, 204. Moreover, the restrictive provisions of the ordinance in this particular may be sustained upon the principles applicable to the broader exclusion from residential districts of all business and trade structures, presently to be discussed.

. . . [T]he village, though physically a suburb of Cleveland, is politically a separate municipality, with powers of its own and authority to govern itself as it sees fit. . . . Its governing authorities, presumably representing a majority of its inhabitants and voicing their will, have determined, not that industrial development shall cease at its boundaries, but that the course of such development shall proceed within definitely fixed lines. . . .

We find no difficulty in sustaining restrictions of the kind thus far reviewed. The serious question in the case arises over the provisions of the ordinance excluding from residential districts apartment houses, business houses, retail stores and shops, and other like establishments. This question involves the validity of what is really the crux of the more recent zoning legislation, namely, the creation and maintenance of residential districts, from which business and trade of every sort, including hotels and apartment houses, are excluded. Upon that question this court has not thus far spoken. The decisions of the state courts are numerous and conflicting; but those which broadly sustain the power greatly outnumber those which deny it altogether or narrowly limit it, and it is very apparent that there is a constantly increasing tendency in the direction of the broader view. . . .

The decisions [adopting the broader view] . . . agree that the exclusion of buildings devoted to business, trade, etc., from residential districts, bears a rational relation to the health and safety of the community. Some of the grounds for this conclusion are promotion of the health and security from injury of children and others by separating dwelling houses from territory devoted to trade and industry; suppression and prevention of disorder; facilitating the extinguishment of fires, and the enforcement of street traffic regulations and other general welfare ordinances; aiding the health and safety of the community, by excluding from residential areas the confusion and danger of fire, contagion, and disorder, which in greater or less degree attach to the location of stores, shops, and factories. . . .

The matter of zoning has received much attention at the hands of commissions and experts, and the results of their investigations have been set forth in comprehensive reports. These reports which bear every evidence of painstaking consideration, concur in the view that the segregation of residential, business and industrial buildings will make it easier to provide fire apparatus suitable for the character and intensity of the development in each section; that it will increase the safety and security of home life, greatly tend to prevent street accidents, especially to children, by reducing the traffic and resulting confusion in residential sections; decrease noise and other conditions which produce or intensify nervous disorders; preserve a more favorable environment in which to rear children, etc. With particular reference to apartment houses, it is pointed out that the development of detached house sections is greatly retarded by the coming of apartment houses, which has sometimes resulted in destroying the entire section for private house purposes; that in such sections very often the apartment house is a mere parasite, constructed in order to take advantage of the open spaces and attractive surroundings created by the residential character of the district. Moreover, the coming of one apartment house is followed by others, interfering by their height and bulk with the free circulation of air and monopolizing the rays of the sun which otherwise would fall upon the smaller homes, and bringing, as their necessary accompaniments, the disturbing noises incident to increased traffic and business, and the occupation, by means of moving and parked automobiles, of larger portions of the streets, thus detracting from their safety and depriving children of the privilege of quiet and open spaces for play, enjoyed by those in more favored localities—until, finally, the residential character of the neighborhood and its desirability as a place of detached residences are utterly destroyed. Under these circumstances, apartment houses, which in a different environment would be not only entirely unobjectionable but highly desirable, come very near to being nuisances.

If these reasons, thus summarized, do not demonstrate the wisdom or sound policy in all respects of those restrictions which we have indicated as pertinent to the inquiry, at least, the reasons are sufficiently cogent to preclude us from saying, as it must be said before the ordinance can be declared unconstitutional, that such provisions are clearly arbitrary and unreasonable, having no substantial relation to the public health, safety, morals, or general welfare. . . .

Under these circumstances, therefore, it is enough for us to determine, as we do, that the ordinance in its general scope and dominant features, so far as its provisions are here involved, is a valid exercise of authority, leaving other provisions to be dealt with as cases arise directly involving them. . . .

Decree reversed.

JUSTICES VAN DEVANTER, MCREYNOLDS, and BUTLER dissent.

Points for Discussion

a. **Identifying the *Euclid* Test**

Ambler Realty attacked the Euclid ordinance as a violation of its right to substantive due process and equal protection under the Fourteenth Amendment. In deciding the case, the Supreme Court used a standard that is now known as the *rational basis test*: a law is unconstitutional only if it is "clearly arbitrary and unreasonable, having no substantial relation to the public health, safety, morals, or general welfare." Under this test, how likely is it that a zoning ordinance will be invalidated? Why? *Compare Schefer v. City Council of City of Falls Church*, 691 S.E.2d 778 (Va. 2010) (upholding ordinance that established different height limits on single-family dwellings in the same zone) *with Town of Rhine v. Bizzell*, 751 N.W.2d 780 (Wis. 2008) (invalidating ordinance that required issuance of a discretionary permit for any use in the zone).

Modern courts still use the rational basis test to evaluate the constitutionality of a land use regulation unless the law discriminates against a *suspect class* (such as one based on race) or impairs a *fundamental right* (such as freedom of religion), when the *strict scrutiny test* is used instead. Under the strict scrutiny test, a law is constitutional only if it is narrowly tailored to accomplish a "compelling state interest"—a higher standard than a mere "rational basis."

b. **"As Applied" Challenges to Zoning**

In *Nectow v. City of Cambridge*, 277 U.S. 183 (1928), the Supreme Court recognized that a zoning law could be unconstitutional *as applied* to an individual property. Because the facts demonstrated that "no practical use" could be made of plaintiff's property for residential purposes—the only permitted use—the Court held that the zoning did not *in fact* promote the public health, safety, or welfare. In practice, however, modern courts are reluctant to invalidate zoning ordinances on this basis. *See, e.g., Board of County Commissioners of Teton County v. Crow*, 65 P.3d 720 (Wyo. 2003) (rejecting "as applied" attack on ordinance that limited new homes in the Teton Valley to 8,000 square feet of habitable space).

c. **Applying the *Euclid* Test**

Would the following ordinances be constitutional under the *Euclid* test?

> (1) City A's ordinance provides that each residential lot must be at least 20 acres in size.
>
> (2) County B's ordinance creates a "felon-free" zone where no convicted felons may reside.
>
> (3) City C's ordinance requires each landlord to allow a cable television company to install equipment on the landlord's premises in order to provide cable service for the landlord's tenants.
>
> (4) County D's ordinance mandates that every residence have a swimming pool.
>
> (5) City E's ordinance provides that any parcels in the "Wetland Zone" may not be developed, but must be left in natural condition.

d. **The Nuisance Analogy**

How persuasive is the *Euclid* Court's analogy to nuisance law? Not every industrial use in a single-family residential zone is a nuisance. So what is the basis for upholding the ordinance? The Court states that the "serious question" in the case is whether apartment houses, retail stores, and similar establishments may be excluded from single-family residential zones. Are you convinced by the Court's rationale?

e. ***Euclid* and the Single-Family Home**

The most favored use under the Euclid plan was the traditional single-family home: a free-standing residence accommodating one family. Thus, the ordinance created large U-1 zones where only single-family homes were permitted. It also effectively required that each house stand in the middle of the lot, by mandating "setbacks" from the front, side, and rear lot lines. Euclid's brief before the Supreme Court stressed the value of protecting the home:

> [W]e wish to avert to the question of that so-called "greater public welfare" about which the Supreme Court of the United States itself has spoken. We refer to the question of the American Home. . . . It is generally conceded that the home owner who has the opportunity to have his little garden and to rear his family in a house and to raise his children with a greater freedom of fresh air and abundance of light, is one of the most important factors in the sustaining of the American People. . . .

Compare the Court's attitude toward the single-family home with its apparent attitude toward apartments. What accounts for the difference? Does *Euclid* facilitate discrimination based on race, wealth, or other factors? Note that nine years before *Euclid*, the Supreme Court struck down a city ordinance that expressly barred Black Americans from living on blocks predominantly occupied by white residents, finding it to be an improper exercise of the police power. *Buchanan v. Warley*, 245 U.S. 60 (1917).

f. Impact of *Euclid*

Euclid is the foundation of modern land use regulation in the United States. Assured that Euclid-style zoning was constitutional, cities and counties across the nation enacted zoning ordinances, many of them patterned on the Euclid model. The key assumption underlying that Euclid ordinance—that separation of uses is desirable—ultimately led to the rapid expansion of single-family subdivisions after World War II and to modern concerns about suburban sprawl. Today virtually every city and county in the nation has a zoning ordinance in place. The major exception is Houston, Texas; but it generally resembles any other big city. So should zoning be abolished? *See* Bernard H. Siegan, *Non-Zoning in Houston*, 13 J.L. & Econ. 71 (1970). For academic perspectives on *Euclid*, see *Symposium on the Seventy-Fifth Anniversary of* Village of Euclid v. Ambler Realty Co., 51 Case W. Res. L. Rev. 593 (2001).

g. Aftermath of *Euclid*

Ironically, most of the land at issue in *Euclid* was eventually rezoned for industrial use as Ambler Realty wanted. A defense plant was built on the property during World War II. General Motors later purchased the facility for an auto parts factory, which closed in the 1990s. Today, about 5% of the site is devoted to light industrial use; the balance is covered with empty buildings and weed-filled parking lots.

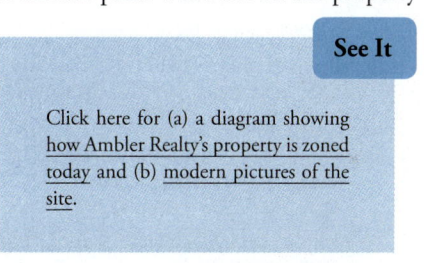

> **See It**
>
> Click here for (a) a diagram showing how Ambler Realty's property is zoned today and (b) modern pictures of the site.

2. Typical Zoning Ordinance

The typical zoning ordinance is adopted by a city or county as a legislative act. It has two basic components: (a) the text of the ordinance; and (b) maps that implement the ordinance.

The ordinance text creates different types of zones where particular uses are allowed. For example, an ordinance might establish a zone where only detached single-family residences are permitted; or the uses in a zone might be limited to agriculture. The zoning map shows where each zone is located.

Suppose that you represent A, a new client who hopes to open a bakery in City C; A needs to know where the bakery can be located. You would first consult the text of the City C zoning ordinance to determine the zones where bakeries are allowed; you would then review the zoning maps to locate those zones and advise A accordingly.

The ordinance text will also impose height, bulk, and related restrictions, either on all structures in a particular zone or on structures devoted to a particular use. For example, if your client B wants to build a single-family home in City C, the ordinance will probably mandate: (a) a minimum lot size (e.g., 12,000 square feet); (b) a height limit (e.g., 30 feet); (c) a lot coverage requirement (e.g., no more than 40% of the lot may be covered by a structure); and (d) setback requirements (e.g., the home must be located at least 40 feet away from the front and rear lot lines, and 8 feet away from each side lot line).

The drafters of the Standard State Zoning Enabling Act contemplated that zoning would be a two-step process. First, the city or county would adopt a *comprehensive plan* that sets forth its general planning goals. Second, it would enact a specific ordinance to implement that plan. In the minority of states that follow this approach, a zoning ordinance is valid only if it is "consistent" with the preexisting plan. But in most states it is not necessary for the city or county to adopt such a separate plan before adopting a zoning ordinance; in effect, the ordinance itself is also the plan. *See, e.g., Apple Group, Ltd. v. Granger Twp. Bd. of Zoning Appeals*, 41 N.E.3d 1185 (Ohio 2015). Today the comprehensive plan is usually called the *general plan*.

> **For More Information**
>
> Click here to see the Standard State Zoning Enabling Act.

3. Nonconforming Uses

Suppose that X is lawfully operating a junkyard in a city that adopts a new zoning ordinance. If the ordinance restricts X's land to single-family residential use only, what happens to the junkyard? Almost always, a new zoning ordinance will provide that it does not apply to lawful uses that already exist. These prior *nonconforming uses*—like X's junkyard—are allowed to continue. Thus, zoning regulates future development, not existing uses.

Why protect nonconforming uses? The early advocates of zoning assumed that such uses would wither away over time. They also realized that any frontal attack on existing uses might be unconstitutional, particularly as a "taking" of property without compensation in violation of the Fifth Amendment. In fact, nonconforming uses "tend to continue and prosper because of the artificial monopoly accorded them by the law." *Board of Supervisors of Cerro Gordo County v. Miller*, 170 N.W.2d 358, 362 (Iowa 1969). And because the owner of a nonconforming use has the right to pass on that protected status to a buyer, it may continue for many years.

Zoning ordinances typically restrict the nonconforming use in order to hasten its demise. Generally, a nonconforming use cannot be expanded. And while ordinary repairs are allowed, major repairs that would extend the duration of the use are barred.

Chapter 11 Land Use Regulation

Trip Associates, Inc. v. Mayor and City Council of Baltimore

Court of Appeals of Maryland

898 A.2d 449 (2006)

BELL, CHIEF JUDGE.

The question this case presents is whether the Board of Municipal and Zoning Appeals ("the Board") erred when it restricted the number of days per week the appellants could operate a valid nonconforming use. The appellants' property, located in the B-5-1 Zoning District in Baltimore City, is being used for the operation of "Club Choices," a nightclub and after-hours establishment that sometimes features adult entertainment. The Club is owned by the appellant, Anthony Dwight Triplin ("Triplin"), who also is the owner of Trip Associates, Inc., the other appellant.

Triplin purchased 1815–17 North Charles Street, the property at issue, in 1983. Prior to his purchase, the property had been a nightclub featuring adult entertainment, including male and female exotic dancing. The adult entertainment had been presented up to five nights a week since 1979. When Triplin purchased the property, the applicable zoning ordinance did not prohibit the use of the property as an adult entertainment facility. Nevertheless, Triplin reduced the number of nights of nude or exotic dancing from five to two nights per week, featuring music and comedy on the other nights. . . .

> **FYI**
>
> Club Choices has a "smoky and dimly lit interior [that] creates an atmosphere that will make 'shaking-off' to Baltimore club music seem second nature. . . . While every other club is closing its doors at 2 a.m. on Saturday nights, Club Choices kicks the fun into another gear and keeps the music pumping until dawn. . . . The dark dance floor and heart-pounding beats of club music make standing around with your arms folded virtually impossible." Ashlie Baylor, *The Skinny on the Local Clubs*, Baltimore Sun, March 8, 2007.

On December 15, 1994, Ordinance No. 443 was enacted. That ordinance . . . provided that "[a]ny adult entertainment business existing on September 10, 1993 [and located in the B-5 Central Commercial District] is considered a nonconforming use. . . ." After this Ordinance was passed, Triplin continued to use the facility as a club that provided adult entertainment after hours. That use was unchallenged until April 14, 2000, when a Baltimore City zoning inspector issued a "Code Violation Notice and Order" . . . [that directed Triplin to stop using the premises for adult entertainment].

Triplin appealed to the Board. On appeal, Triplin testified that Club Choices featured exotic dancing and adult entertainment two times a week, Wednesdays and

Fridays, for two hours each night. That testimony was confirmed by employees, who offered further that such dancing with partial nudity has been presented two nights per week since 1983. [The Board ruled that Triplin was entitled to provide adult entertainment two nights each week. Triplin then sued, challenging "the Board's power temporally to restrict the nonconforming use," because he wanted the ability to offer nude dancing more frequently than two nights per week. He lost before the trial court and the Court of Special Appeals.]. . . .

A.

. . . [A] "nonconforming use" is defined as "any lawfully existing use of a structure or of land that does not conform to the applicable use regulations of the district in which it is located." Baltimore City Zoning Code § 13–101(c). A valid and lawful nonconforming use is established if a property owner can demonstrate that before, and at the time of, the adoption of a new zoning ordinance, the property was being used in a then-lawful manner for a use that, by later legislation, became non-permitted.

. . . [N]onconforming uses are not favored. *County Council v. Gardner, Inc.,* 443 A.2d 114, 119 (Md. 1982) ("These local ordinances must be strictly construed in order to effectuate the purpose of eliminating nonconforming uses."); *Grant v. Mayor and City Council of Baltimore,* 129 A.2d 363, 365 (Md. 1957) ("[T]here is general agreement that the fundamental problem facing zoning is the inability to eliminate the nonconforming use"). . . .

Nevertheless, a "nonconforming use is a vested right entitled to constitutional protection." *Amereihn v. Kotras,* 71 A.2d 865, 869 (Md. 1950). . . . A nonconforming use may be . . . eliminated in two ways: by "amortization," that is, requiring its termination over a reasonable period of time, and by "abandonment," *i.e.* non-use for a specific period of time. Thus, in *Grant*, the Court held that an amortization period of five years to remove nonconforming billboards was valid, and that a five-year period was not an arbitrary time period. So long as it provides for a reasonable relationship between the amortization and the nature of the nonconforming use, an ordinance prescribing such amortization is not unconstitutional. . . .

The Baltimore City ordinance takes the "abandonment" approach. Section 13–406 . . . prohibits the expansion of any nonconforming use, except as authorized by the Board. Under § 13–407, "Discontinuance or abandonment," the failure actively and continuously to operate the nonconforming use results in its abandonment. That section provides:

(a) *Discontinuance* or *abandonment*

(1) Except as specified in this section, whenever the active and continuous operation of any . . . nonconforming use, or any part of that use, has been discontinued for 12 consecutive months:

(i) the discontinuance constitutes an abandonment of the discontinued nonconforming use . . . regardless of any reservation of an intent to resume active operations or otherwise not abandon the use . . . .

There is no issue with regard to Club Choices' status; it is a valid . . . nonconforming use property under . . . the Zoning Code. It is an adult-entertainment business, presently existing, that was also operating as such on September 10, 1993. . . . As to that status, there is no contention that Triplin has abandoned or discontinued it, at least in whole. The issue is . . . whether using the valid nonconforming use more frequently than it was being used when the use became nonconforming—presenting adult entertainment more than two nights per week—would be a prohibited expansion of the use or a mere intensification of the use.

B.

Despite Maryland's well settled policy against nonconforming uses . . . and the Baltimore City Zoning Code's explicit prohibition against expansion of those uses, Maryland recognizes, and our cases have held, that an intensification of a nonconforming use is permissible, so long as the nature and character of that use is unchanged and is substantially the same. See *Jahnigen v. Staley*, 225 A.2d 277, 281 (Md. 1967); *Green v. Garrett*, 63 A.2d 326, 339 (Md. 1949); [other cases omitted].

> **FYI**
>
> At the time of this case, Baltimore City Zoning Code § 13–406 provided that a "nonconforming use may not be expanded in any manner" without approval by the Board.

In *Green, supra*, citizens of Baltimore City sought to enjoin the Department of Recreation and Parks of Baltimore City . . . from allowing professional baseball to be played at Baltimore Stadium. . . . Baltimore Stadium was constructed prior to 1931, when the district in which it was located was rezoned residential, after which it was used infrequently for football games, track meets and civic events. It was used more frequently after 1939, when lights were installed, a speaker system having been installed earlier. That increased use consisted mainly of football games and other events, not baseball games. In 1944, however, a fire destroyed the baseball stadium, then known as Oriole Park. This resulted in more baseball games being played at Baltimore Stadium. . . .

When that occurred, neighboring citizens contended that the use of the Stadium for baseball games for a considerable portion of the year was an enlargement of the valid nonconforming use of the Stadium and, therefore, contravened the zoning ordinance. . . . This Court disagreed. Acknowledging that the "spirit of the zoning ordinance is against the extension of non-conforming uses and that such uses should not be perpetuated any longer than necessary," we observed:

> We have never held that the more frequent use of a property for a purpose which does not conform to the ordinary restrictions of the neighborhood is an extension of an infrequent use of the same building for a similar purpose. We do not think such a contention is tenable. Nor does it seem to us that a different use is made of the Stadium when the players of games there are paid. The use of the property remains the same.

63 A.2d at 330. . . .

In these cases, we have consistently held that merely increasing the frequency of a nonconforming use did not constitute an unlawful extension; rather, it was but an intensification of the use. . . . To be sure, as the intermediate appellate court noted, the cases, with the exception of *Green*, do not address the situation *sub judice*. On the other hand, *Green* did not draw, expressly or otherwise, the distinction that the Court of Special Appeals draws; we did not, in *Green*, say, or signal in any way, that any increase in the nonconforming use, except temporally, by adding days or hours of operation, would be an intensification, but that the temporal modification would be an unlawful expansion of the use. We do not read the cases so narrowly. In each of the cases, the frequency of the use of the subject property in the nonconforming manner was increased, often significantly so, without regard to the hours of operation. Their focus was, as it should be, on the actual use made of the property, not the times when that use occurs. . . .

> **It's Latin to Me**
>
> *Sub judice* merely refers to the case in which the phrase appears. As Black's Law Dictionary notes, "[l]egal writers sometimes use *case sub judice* when the *present case* would be more comprehensible."

If the intermediate appellate court is correct, *Green* is no longer good law and our definition of "intensification" is misleading, if not largely meaningless. Indeed, the concept of intensification would have no meaning at all in the nightclub context, or in any other where there are discrete hours of operation, such as retail. In *Feldstein v. LaVale Zoning Board*, we distinguished an "intensification" of a nonconforming use from an "extension" of such use, noting that the former is "the more frequent present use of property for the same or a similar use than that for which it had been used less frequently theretofore." *Feldstein v. LaVale Zoning Board*, 227 A.2d 731, 734 (Md. 1967). Increasing the number of nights on which adult entertainment is presented at Club Choices from two to five, for example, would fit within the definition of "intensification"—it would be a "more frequent present use of property for the same or a similar use than that for which it had been used less frequently theretofore." In fact, that was the rationale for *Green*; going from infrequent baseball games to their presentation for much of the year seems a similar, if not identical, scenario. . . .

Nor are we persuaded by the out-of-state cases upon which the appellees and the Court of Special Appeals relied. . . . These [cases] would prohibit the distinction between intensification and expansion that is, and long has been, recognized in Maryland. . . .

JUDGMENT OF THE COURT OF SPECIAL APPEALS REVERSED. . . .

Points for Discussion

a. **Adult Entertainment**

The ordinance that made adult entertainment at Club Choices a nonconforming use applied to all properties in the traditional downtown commercial core of Baltimore. Why do you suppose the City Council wanted to ban adult entertainment in this area? Is opposition to adult entertainment primarily a question of morality or is it based on adverse impacts such as traffic problems, noise, and crowd control issues?

b. **Expansion v. Intensification**

Does the *Trip Associates* distinction between expansion and intensification make sense to you? Suppose that a Baltimore bakery is deemed a nonconforming use because it generates noise and fumes in a residential neighborhood. If the bakery owner wanted to construct a new building to house the business, this type of physical expansion would not be permitted—because this would allow the noise and fumes to continue for a longer period of time. But if the owner wanted to expand his production periods from two hours per day to 20 hours per day, this would seemingly be permitted under *Trip Associates*—even though this also allows the noise and fumes to continue for a longer period. For a contrary approach, see *Williston Park v. 280 Hillside Ave. Rest. Corp.*, 390 N.Y.S.2d 637 (App. Div. 1977) (nonconforming bar could not extend its operating hours).

c. **Termination**

In addition to abandonment/discontinuance and amortization, which the *Trip Associates* court mentions, a nonconforming use can also be terminated: (1) by destruction of the structure housing the use; (2) if the use is a nuisance; and (3) by eminent domain—that is, by government action which takes private property for public use upon payment of just compensation to the owner. You will study eminent domain in Chapter 13. The Baltimore Development Corporation, the city's quasi-public economic development entity, expressed interest in buying Club Choices on several occasions—in response to complaints from neighbors and local activists—but was unwilling to pay the $20 million that Triplin wanted for the property.

d. **Amortization**

Most jurisdictions allow the use of amortization to terminate a nonconforming use as long as a reasonable period is allowed. In general, courts do not require mathematical certainty that the amortization period is long enough for the landowner to recover his investment. For example, in *AVR, Inc. v. City of St. Louis Park*, 585 N.W.2d 411 (Minn. App. 1998), the court considered eight factors—including the benefit to the public and the burden on the owner—in determining an appropriate period. In a controversial decision, the *AVR* court held that two years was a sufficient period to amortize a nonconforming "ready-mix" plant that made cement for construction projects. In contrast, *Trip Associates* cites a Maryland case that upheld the amortization of a less intensive use (billboards) over a longer period (five years). What would be an appropriate period for terminating adult entertainment at Club Choices?

e. **Abandonment v. Discontinuation**

Abandonment generally terminates a nonconforming use. Abandonment occurs if the landowner both (1) intends to relinquish his right to the use and (2) voluntarily ceases the use for a set period of time, varying by jurisdiction from 30 days to two years. As you would expect, this standard has generated extensive litigation. Alternatively, in Maryland and certain other jurisdictions, mere discontinuance of the use is sufficient for termination, regardless of the owner's intent. *See, e.g., Rodehorst Brothers v. City of Norfolk Board of Adjustment*, 844 N.W.2d 755 (Neb. 2014) (owner of four-unit apartment building in area zoned for single-family homes and duplexes lost right to nonconforming use by leaving two units vacant for many years). Which approach is better?

f. **Vested Rights**

What happens if the zoning changes before a new project is completed? In most jurisdictions, the landowner in this situation acquires *vested rights* in the current zoning—and is protected under the nonconforming use doctrine—if she has already (1) acquired the necessary permits and (2) spent a substantial amount of money in good faith reliance. In some jurisdictions, vested rights arise from substantial expenditures on the project, regardless of whether permits are actually obtained. *See, e.g., Carson v. Brown*, 856 S.E.2d 5 (Ga. Ct. App. 2021) (developer who spent $83,000 on plans, appraisals, and studies for subdivision had vested rights).

C. Rigid Zoning or Flexible Zoning?

The pioneering zoners assumed that there would be little need for changes after a zoning plan was adopted. And they worried that piecemeal changes would threaten the integrity of comprehensive zoning. Thus, the Standard State Zoning

Enabling Act provided only three ways for an owner to escape a zoning ordinance: (1) the *amendment*; (2) the *variance*; and (3) the *conditional use* (or *special exception*). In recent decades, however, new tools for zoning flexibility have emerged.

1. Zoning Amendments

Like any other law, a zoning ordinance may be amended. For example, if A's land is zoned for agricultural use only, it could be rezoned for single-family residences by an *amendment* to the ordinance.

But rezoning presents special dangers. First, it threatens the goal of comprehensive land use planning. If many individual parcels are rezoned for different uses, the zoning plan may become meaningless. Second, it creates a heightened risk of governmental corruption. If the value of A's land is $5,000 per acre for farm use, but $50,000 per acre for single-family use, A has an economic incentive to influence the outcome through bribery or other improper influence.

Most jurisdictions review the constitutionality of rezoning under the same general standard normally applied to a new zoning ordinance: a rezoning decision is valid unless it is "clearly arbitrary and unreasonable, having no substantial relation to the public health, safety, morals, or general welfare." *Village of Euclid v. Ambler Realty Co.*, 272 U.S. 365, 395 (1926). A handful of states use the *change or mistake approach*, under which rezoning is valid only (a) if conditions in the zone have significantly changed or (b) a mistake was made in the original zoning ordinance. *See, e.g., Edwards v. Harrison County Board of Supervisors*, 22 So. 3d 268 (Miss. 2009) (rezoning was proper in light of neighborhood changes produced by Hurricane Katrina).

Smith v. City of Little Rock

Supreme Court of Arkansas

648 S.W.2d 454 (1983)

HOLT, JUSTICE.

The Little Rock City Board of Directors voted unanimously to change the zoning classification of property located at 4908–4932 West Markham, between Monroe and Jackson Streets, from a single family and quiet office classification to "C-3", a general commercial classification as requested by the property owners. A Wendy's restaurant is to be constructed on that site if rezoned.

> **FYI**
>
> Wendy's is a national chain of fast-food restaurants that specializes in serving square hamburgers. In 1983, the year *Smith* was decided, Wendy's opened its 2,500th branch.

The appellants, who are property owners in that vicinity, filed suit in chancery court to have the rezoning set aside. The chancellor held there is a presumption the Board had acted in a reasonable manner and the appellants had failed to meet their burden of proof which requires them to demonstrate the arbitrariness of its action, so he denied the petition. We affirm. . . .

The standard of review applicable here is well settled. The decision of the chancellor will be affirmed unless it is clearly erroneous (clearly against the preponderance of the evidence). ARCP, Rule 52(a); *City of Little Rock v. Breeding*, 619 S.W.2d 664 (Ark. 1981). There we also said there is a presumption that the City Board acted in a fair, just, and reasonable manner when it rezones or refuses to rezone property and the burden is on the persons attacking the rezoning or refusal to show otherwise. The courts do not have the authority to review zoning legislation *de novo*. *City of Conway v. Conway Housing Authority*, 584 S.W.2d 10 (Ark. 1979). There we said:

> [W]hen a municipality, pursuant to authority granted by the General Assembly, takes action in zoning classifications, it is exercising a legislative function and is not subject to review by the courts of its wisdom in so doing. . . . The judiciary has no right or authority to substitute its judgment for that of the legislative branch of government. In zoning matters the General Assembly has delegated legislative power to the cities in matters relating to zoning property. The role of the courts is, therefore, simply to determine whether or not the action of the municipality is arbitrary. Arbitrary has been defined as "arising from unrestrained exercise of will, caprice, or personal preference, based on random or convenient choice, rather than on reason or nature." Courts are not super zoning commissions and have no authority to classify property according to zones. . . .

The appellants argue, *inter alia*, that the rezoning here is inconsistent with the Heights/Hillcrest Plan, a guide for land use decisions adopted in an ordinance on March 17, 1981. This plan, of course, serves only as an advisory or guide and is not binding. *Taylor v. City of LR*, 583 S.W.2d 72 (Ark. 1979). Here, eight property owners in the area testified that the rezoning to allow a Wendy's restaurant to be built would have detrimental effects on the largely residential neighborhood; e.g., there would be increased traffic problems and hazards, noise, litter, unpleasant odors, vandalism, lights shining into windows at night, and rodents. One was of the view it would be spot zoning. Most of the witnesses were longtime residents in the area. None of the property owners testified they had relied upon the recent Heights/Hillcrest Plan, but some did testify they had chosen to live in the area because of the type of neighborhood it was.

The property in question is, as indicated, located between Monroe and Jackson Streets on the north side of the Markham Street corridor. On the south side of Markham are located the State Hospital, the University of Arkansas Medical Center, War Memorial Park (directly across from the subject property), the State Health Department, and War Memorial Stadium. Jerry Speece, Zoning Administrator for the City of Little Rock, testified in detail with respect to the character of the area on the north side of Markham Street. To the east on the same block are located a single family home and an establishment which sells and rents scuba diving equipment. On the six blocks east of Monroe are located a savings and loan, a branch bank, Peck's Drive-In, a liquor store, a drug store, and other businesses. In the three blocks west of the rezoned property are situated a McDonald's restaurant, an Exxon station, the Black Angus restaurant, a Kentucky Fried Chicken restaurant, Rob's restaurant, and a motel. Speece also testified that the volume of traffic on Markham is 6,000 to 8,000 vehicles per day below its capacity. He said the Heights/Hillcrest Plan is merely a general guide for city planning and, furthermore, the rezoning in this case is not inconsistent with that plan. He stated the rezoning did not constitute spot zoning, because spot zoning involves zoning one lot in a manner entirely different from the surrounding area, which was not done here.... In his opinion, as a professional planner, the rezoning from single family and quiet business to commercial use is a reasonable classification.

> **See It**
>
> Click here for (a) a map of the area involved in this case and (b) pictures of the neighborhood near the proposed Wendy's site. Note that the War Memorial Stadium (the secondary home of the University of Arkansas "Razorback" football team) is across the street from the site.

We cannot say that the decision of the chancellor holding that the rezoning by the City Board of Directors was not arbitrary and capricious is clearly erroneous....

Affirmed.

HICKMAN, JUSTICE, dissenting.

The majority has taken a rather passive role in this case and decided to uphold a decision by the Little Rock City Board of Directors which rezones five residential lots to a high commercial use, thereby permitting the construction of a fast-food outlet, Wendy's, in the middle of a residential area. The only justification for the city's action can be that the lots are located not far from a commercial area on West Markham Street, which includes a McDonald's restaurant, an Exxon station and several other similar types of commercial enterprises. In my judgment this case represents a retreat to the city development approach approved in *City of Little Rock v. Pfeifer*, 277 S.W. 883 (Ark. 1925).

In my opinion the city's action was arbitrary for two reasons: First, this is clearly a case of spot zoning and therefore arbitrary; second, it is a flagrant breach of faith with the history of the area, the city's plan, and a decision this court made regarding this very property in 1966. *City of Little Rock v. Faith Evangelical [Lutheran] Church*, 406 S.W.2d 875 (Ark. 1966). Furthermore, the only justification I can find for permitting the fast-food restaurant to be built is that the landowners want to make money and the enterprise will benefit the city economically by jobs. Neither is a legal justification for rezoning these lots. . . .

There is a serious disagreement about the facts and their relative value in this case. But more important than that, and even this case itself, is the purpose of city planning, and our role, which is to keep the city honest. By and large the city of Little Rock has had good plans for the entire city. When the city has defended those plans against commercial assaults we have, by and large, upheld them as we should have. . . . Now we have the same City Board of Directors deciding to place a fast-food restaurant in the middle of a residential area in violation of its own plan. . . . In *Faith Evangelical Lutheran Church*, we upheld the city's decision to protect this part of Markham Street used primarily as a residential area, and we upheld the city's refusal to allow any more commercial intrusions into this neighborhood. Actually the area allows a use for quiet business purposes but there was no objection voiced by any of the landowners of such a use; it was the prospect of a fast-food restaurant that raised their ire, as it should have. Who would want such a place next to their home? At best, they are intolerable; at worst, they are noisy, unsanitary, unsightly, bright at night, odorous, and attract large amounts of traffic. Such an enterprise is totally incompatible with single family residences. Such places do not close down at 5:00 p.m.; in fact, that is when they begin to reach one of their busiest periods, just when the next-door neighbors will arrive home to their haven from the noise, hustle and bustle of city life.

> **Make the Connection**
>
> Is the dissent suggesting that a Wendy's in this location would be a common law nuisance? Consider this question in light of the nuisance materials that you studied earlier in this chapter.

The majority does not address the question of whether this was spot zoning. It simply says Jerry Speece, Zoning Administrator for the city of Little Rock, testified that in his opinion this was not spot zoning and not an incompatible use. He was wrong in both instances. (He conceded he did not participate in preparing the Hillcrest/Pulaski Heights Plan.) It is undisputed that the five lots are surrounded on three sides by residences. On the other side is Markham Street. It is a busy street, one of the avenues used to funnel traffic to and from downtown Little Rock. But that alone cannot be a factor justifying rezoning. More importantly, West Markham is the southern boundary of Pulaski Heights/Hillcrest area, a residential area of uncommon beauty and serenity. There have been no changes in the area since 1966. It is an old residential area, improving in quality, not declining. . . . This part of Markham Street is a boundary that has to remain inviolate if the integrity of the Pulaski Heights/Hillcrest area is to be maintained. Several residents testified they had improved their residences next to this property, after our decision in 1966, relying on that decision that the area would not go commercial, but would remain primarily residential.

It is incredible that the zoning administrator said this was not spot zoning:

Spot zoning amendments are those which by their terms single out a particular lot or parcel of land, usually small in relative size, and place it in an area, the land use pattern of which is inconsistent with the small lot or parcel so placed, thus projecting an inharmonious land use pattern. 1 E. Yokley, Zoning Law and Practice § 8–3 (1968).

Spot Zoning . . . singles out a small parcel of land for use in a manner inconsistent with the other predominant land uses in the area. R. Wright, *Zoning Law in Arkansas: A Comparative Analysis*, 3 Ark. L. Rev. 421, 442 (1980).

These are perfect descriptions of what happened in this case. Why do cities spot zone property? "Such amendments are usually triggered by efforts to secure special benefits for particular property owners, without proper regard for the rights of adjacent owners." 1 E. Yokley, § 8–3. And that is what happened in this case. It is universally agreed that spot zoning is arbitrary. . . . In *Riddell v. City of Brinkley*, 612 S.W.2d 116 (Ark. 1981), we said:

> Spot zoning, by definition, is invalid because it amounts to an arbitrary, capricious and unreasonable treatment of a limited area within a particular district. As such, it departs from the comprehensive treatment or privileges not in harmony with the other use classifications in the area and without any apparent circumstances which call for different treatment. Spot zoning almost invariably involves a single parcel or at least a limited area. R. Wright and S. Webber, Land Use (1978).

. . . I do not suggest we substitute our judgment for that of a city in a zoning matter. . . . But that does not mean we should go to the other extreme and meekly accept whatever the city does as right in zoning cases, because there is always strong pressure on city boards to make exceptions. There is money to be made and such motives have no social conscience. . . . In this case, Wendy's can be built somewhere else in an authorized commercial zone, and no damage will be done to commercial or residential interests. . . .

Points for Discussion

a. **Arbitrary Rezoning in *Smith*?**

Why wasn't the rezoning in *Smith* "arbitrary" as defined by Arkansas law? The project opponents demonstrated that the rezoning (1) was contrary to the land use plan and (2) would generate traffic, noise, litter, odors, and so forth. What evidence before the court supported the view that the rezoning was appropriate? Is it enough that "the landowners want to make money and the enterprise will benefit the city economically by jobs"?

b. Spot Zoning Confusion

The law governing spot zoning is confusing. The factors listed in the dissenting opinion in *Smith* are typical of those most courts consider. Thus, spot zoning exists when a zoning amendment:

> (1) singles out a small parcel of land for different treatment;
>
> (2) primarily for the benefit of the private owner, rather than the public;
>
> (3) in a manner inconsistent with the general plan for the community.

See, e.g., Beard v. City of Ridgeland, 245 So. 3d 380 (Miss. 2018) (amendment to allow Costco store was spot zoning). However, spot zoning may be found even if one or more of these criteria are absent, depending on the jurisdiction. *See, e.g., Gaida v. Planning & Zoning Commission*, 947 A.2d 361 (Conn. App. Ct. 2008) (finding spot zoning based on first and third criteria). Accordingly, the case law on spot zoning is often inconsistent. But why should the law prohibit spot zoning at all? As cities grow, change is inevitable. Is the spot zoning doctrine an obstacle to progress that should be abolished? Note that reverse spot zoning is also possible; this can occur when the first and third elements are met, but the amendment changes the zone to a less intensive use, thus harming the owner. *See, e.g., Helena Sand & Gravel, Inc. v. Lewis & Clark Cty. Planning & Zoning Comm'n*, 290 P.3d 691 (Mont. 2012).

c. Spot Zoning in *Smith*?

Was this spot zoning? Note that the majority opinion barely mentions the issue, while the dissent is almost impassioned on the point. Does the majority give too much deference to the opinion of the Zoning Administrator? On the other hand, the property in question is located on a busy street, across from a football stadium and close to a McDonald's—hardly a pristine residential zone.

d. Rezoning Exercises

Evaluate the legality of these rezoning decisions under both (1) the *Euclid* test and (2) spot zoning law.

> (1) City A rezones a vacant 20-acre tract in the middle of a 500-house subdivision from R-1 (single-family residential only) to I-4 (light industrial use). The permitted uses in the I-4 zone include scientific laboratories engaged in research and development. O, the non-profit corporation that owns the tract, plans to build a laboratory facility to study infectious disease and thereby improve medical care for the public. There is a 1 in 1,000,000 chance that infectious disease germs will escape from the lab over a 20-year period. The City's general plan notes the need for "more economic development."
>
> (2) County B rezones a 100-acre ranch in a remote rural area from A-2 (general agricultural use) to R-5 (condominiums, with an average of 10 units per acre). This change increases the value of the land from $200,000 to

$4,000,000. The County's comprehensive plan stresses the "importance of preserving our agricultural heritage," but also observes that "increased housing opportunities would be desirable." Neighboring ranchers complain about the impacts of a condominium development: much greater traffic and noise; risk that new residents will raise nuisance claims; and increased property taxes for nearby ranches.

e. **Alternative Approaches to Rezoning**

In *Fasano v. Board of County Commissioners*, 507 P.2d 23 (Or. 1973), the Oregon Supreme Court endorsed a new approach to the problem: treating rezoning as quasi-judicial action. It reasoned that a zoning amendment affecting one parcel is more akin to a judicial decision than to legislation, because it essentially applies a general rule to a factual situation affecting only one owner. Thus, the rezoning decision should be subject to a more rigorous standard of review, like other judicial action. To what extent does this approach mitigate rezoning abuse?

Alternatively, should all rezoning decisions be approved by the voters? In *City of Eastlake v. Forest City Enterprises, Inc.*, 426 U.S. 668 (1976), the Supreme Court upheld a city charter provision that required all zoning amendments and other land use decisions to be approved by the electorate. What are the strengths and weaknesses of this approach?

f. **Aftermath of *Smith***

After the Arkansas Supreme Court upheld the rezoning decision, a Wendy's restaurant was constructed on the site. The restaurant is still in operation today.

Wendy's restaurant built on site
Click here for larger photo

2. Variances

The zoning pioneers recognized that strict enforcement of a zoning ordinance might cause hardship in particular situations. Accordingly, the Standard State Zoning Enabling Act offered a special safety valve: the *variance*. It authorized local zoning officials to approve:

> in specific cases such variance from the terms of the ordinance as will not be contrary to the public interest, where, owing to special conditions, a literal enforcement of the provisions of the ordinance will result in unnecessary hardship, and so that the spirit of the ordinance shall be observed and substantial justice done.

Today, most jurisdictions use a similar test, as reflected in the Pennsylvania statute involved in the next case, 53 Pa. Stat. § 10910.2(a):

> . . . The board may grant a variance [to avoid unnecessary hardship to the owner], provided that all of the following findings are made where relevant in a given case:
>
> (1) That there are unique physical circumstances or conditions, including irregularity, narrowness, or shallowness of lot size or shape, or exceptional topographical or other physical conditions peculiar to the particular property and that the unnecessary hardship is due to such conditions. . . .
>
> (2) That because of such physical circumstances or conditions, there is no possibility that the property can be developed in strict conformity with the provisions of the zoning ordinance and that the authorization of a variance is therefore necessary to enable the reasonable use of the property.
>
> (3) That such unnecessary hardship has not been created by the applicant.
>
> (4) That the variance . . . will not alter the essential character of the neighborhood or district in which the property is located, nor substantially or permanently impair the appropriate use or development of adjacent property, nor be detrimental to the public welfare. . . .
>
> (5) That the variance . . . will represent the minimum variance that will afford relief. . . .

Detwiler v. Zoning Hearing Board of Lower Salford Township

Commonwealth Court of Pennsylvania

596 A.2d 1156 (1991)

BARBIERI, SENIOR JUDGE.

Philip and Babette Detwiler (Appellants) appeal an order of the Court of Common Pleas of Montgomery County which affirmed the decision of the Zoning Hearing Board of Lower Salford Township (Board), granting Donald and Mary Miller (Millers) a variance for the construction of a house.

The Millers own a lot, consisting of approximately 2.8 acres, in Lower Salford Township and would like to construct a house thereon. The lot is located in an R-1A Residence District. According to the Township's zoning ordinance, single-family detached dwellings are permitted in R-1A Residence Districts, as long as the premises, with the dwelling, complies with the area, width, and yard regulations of Article VI, Section 164-28 of the Lower Salford Township Code (Code), which provides, *inter alia*, that both the front and rear yards must be at least seventy-five feet deep and that the side yards must be at least forty feet wide.

On March 28, 1989, the Millers filed an application with the Board in which they requested a variance from the seventy-five foot rear yard requirement so that they could build a house on their lot. It is the Millers' position that the imposition of the minimum front and rear yard setback provisions, as applied to their lot,[2] completely negates any practical residential development because of the absence of any appreciable "building envelope"[3] within which a house of even the leanest proportions might be built.[4] As such, the Millers requested a variance for a reduction of the rear yard requirement from seventy-five feet to forty feet.

> **See It**
>
> Without a variance, the setback requirements would require the Millers to build their house within a narrow triangle of land about 560 feet long but only 10 feet wide at its widest point. Click here to see a diagram of the lot.

---

[2] The Board found that the Millers' lot "is a somewhat irregularly shaped lot, rectangular and narrow in appearance. . . ."

[3] The "building envelope" is determined by subtracting the setback requirements from the actual boundary of the premises.

[4] The front, rear, and side boundary lines of the Millers' lot measure 643.25 feet, 638.00 feet, 190.00 feet and 199.70 feet, respectively. In addition to the yard regulations found in Section 164–28 of the Code, the Millers' lot is also subject to a forty foot setback from the road on which it borders. . . . With all of the setbacks, the lot, absent a variance, would not permit any dwelling at all or, even if placed in the widest area of the lot, would only permit a dwelling of less than ten feet deep.

Appellants live directly across the street from the Millers' lot. Appellants' house, a restored Mennonite dwelling, is listed on the National Register of Historic Places. Appellants challenged the Millers' request for a variance on the ground that it would adversely impact their property, which, they contend, "serves as an asset to the community because of its historic value."

> **FYI**
>
> The Detwiler house was built in about 1717 by a German immigrant who developed a 150-acre farm, which originally included the Miller lot.

Despite Appellants' opposition, the Board granted the Millers' request for a variance, concluding that without the grant of a variance, the Millers' lot "could quite easily suffer the fate of terminal sterility." The Board further concluded that, in granting the Millers a variance, "there would appear to be no discernible adverse impact or consequence upon neighboring properties."

On appeal, the trial court, without taking any additional evidence, affirmed the decision of the Board. In its opinion, the trial court discussed each of the five requirements that must be satisfied in order to grant a variance under Section 910.2 of the Pennsylvania Municipalities Planning Code (MPC), Act of July 31, 1968, P.L. 805, *as amended*, added by Section 89 of the Act of December 21, 1988, P.L. 1329, 53 P.S. § 10910.2, and then concluded that the Millers' request satisfied each requirement. This appeal followed.

Detwiler house
Click here for larger photo

Pursuant to Section 910.2 of the MPC, five requirements must be met before a variance may be granted. To establish a right to a variance, a landowner must show that the effect of a zoning ordinance is to burden property with an unnecessary hardship that is unique to the property; that the hardship was not self-inflicted; that the granting of the variance will not have an adverse impact on the public health, safety and welfare; and that the variance sought is the minimum variance that will afford relief. *Cope v. Zoning Hearing Board of South Whitehall Township*, 134 Pa. Commonwealth Ct. 236, 578 A.2d 1002 (1990).

Appellants do not dispute that the unique configuration of the Millers' lot makes the lot unusable as a building lot, absent a variance. They do contend, however, that the fact that the lot is unusable as a building lot is not an unnecessary hardship for the Millers. It is Appellants' position that since the Millers' lot can be and, in fact, is currently being used for agricultural uses, which are permitted in R-1A Residence Districts as a matter of right, the variance should have been denied. We disagree.

According to Section 910.2(a)(2) of the MPC, 53 P.S. § 10910.2(a)(2), a board may grant a variance where, *inter alia*, it is necessary to enable a reasonable use of the property. In this case, the permitted uses for property located within an R-1A Residence District are single-family detached dwellings and agricultural. Section 164–27 of the Code. Although the Code fails to provide a description of what uses are considered to be "agricultural," it does provide a definition of the term "agriculture." That word is used in the Code to mean "[t]he cultivating of the soil and the raising and harvesting of the products of the soil, including, but not by way of limitation, nursery, horticulture and forestry." Section 164-5 of the Code.

At the hearing before the Board, the following testimony was elicited from Mr. Miller regarding the uses and characteristics of his lot:

Q. What is the current use of the property?

A. One of the local farmers takes the hay off it and I use it for some farm animals. I guess he sells it to other farms. . . .

Initially, we note that it could be argued that the activities which are currently occurring on the Millers' lot do not pertain to "agriculture" as that word is defined by the Code. In any event, even if the lot is currently being used for some limited agricultural uses, it would be unreasonable to force the Millers to continue that use. The size of the Millers' lot as well as its physical characteristics are such that, to limit its use to agricultural purposes, would, for all intents and purposes, render the lot practically valueless. That fact, in and of itself, constitutes "unnecessary hardship." *See Canter v. Township of Abington Zoning Hearing Board*, 43 Pa. Commonwealth Ct. 132, 401 A.2d 1240 (1979).

Additionally, in evaluating hardship, the use of adjacent and surrounding land is unquestionably relevant. *Valley View Civic Association v. Zoning Board of Adjustment*, 501 Pa. 550, 462 A.2d 637 (1983). As noted by the trial court, the district in which the Millers' lot is situated is zoned *residential*. Indeed, from the record, it appears that the majority of the neighborhood surrounding the Millers' lot is residential, rather than agricultural. As such, it would not have been unreasonable for the Board to infer that the Millers' lot, so situated, would be undesirable and, hence, unmarketable for agricultural uses, thereby causing the lot to suffer the fate of terminal sterility.

Finally, we wish to emphasize that the use which the Millers desire for their lot, a single-family dwelling, is a permitted use within an R-1A Residence District. They are not seeking a use variance for their property, only a dimensional one. With regards to dimensional variances, we have held on numerous occasions that where, as here,[8] the yard requirements make the construction of a residence impossible, an unnecessary hardship results to the landowner. . . .

Appellants next argue that the Millers' asserted hardship is self-inflicted because they had advance knowledge of the zoning district in which their lot is located before they purchased it. Again, we must disagree.

A landowner's knowledge of zoning requirements prior to the purchase of property is not sufficient, in and of itself, to bar the grant of a variance. *Franklin Towne Realty, Inc. v. Zoning Hearing Board of the Borough of Franklin Park*, 37 Pa. Commonwealth Ct. 632, 391 A.2d 63 (1978). Hardship is self-inflicted only where a landowner has paid a high price for the property because he assumed that a variance which he anticipated would justify that price. *Gro Appeal*, 440 Pa. 552, 269 A.2d 876 (1970). Here, Appellants do not allege that the Millers paid a high price for their lot in anticipation of a dimensional variance. Indeed, the fact that the lot has been in the Miller family for some time suggests otherwise. . . .

Finally, Appellants argue that granting the Millers a variance will have an adverse impact on the public health, safety and welfare in that it will cause a house to be built directly across the street from their property, which is on the National Register of Historic Places. From our reading of the record, however, Appellants submitted no evidence to support their bald statement. It appears that Appellants simply do not want a house built across the street from their property. Specifically, the record reflects the following. . . .

> MR. GIFFORD: How exactly is this proposal going to adversely impact you since the front yard, which separates the house from your house, is going to comply?
>
> MR. DETWILER: I think the location of the house on that ground will adversely impact the property that I own.
>
> MR. GIFFORD: I'm saying how?
>
> MR. DETWILER: By being there.
>
> MR. GIFFORD: What will it do to your property is my question?
>
> MR. DETWILER: It will place a structure across the street from my property which since the early seventeen hundreds as far as I know has been located fifty feet from the road. If my property were one hundred fifty feet from the road I don't think I would have that problem. But I bought that property and it's been there long before any of the circumstances involved in this application. . . .

---

[8] Here we find, as a matter of law, that the cumulative impact of the setback requirements make the construction of a residence so unreasonable as to be impossible. *See* n. 4.

From the above-quoted testimony, it is evident that the interest which Appellants seek to protect in this suit is their own, rather than the public's.

Moreover, like the trial court, we cannot see how there would be an injury to the historic status of Appellants' house if the Millers constructed their house in accordance with the variance as granted. This is especially true in light of the fact that the Millers sought a variance with regard to their rear yard setback and Appellants' property is located across the street from the *front* of the Millers' lot.

Having determined that the Board did not abuse its discretion or commit an error of law in granting the Millers a variance, the decision of the trial court is hereby affirmed.

Points for Discussion

a. **Invalid Variances**

Scholars suggest that up to 90% of all variances granted by local zoning boards would be found invalid if challenged through litigation. Why are the standards for a variance so stringent? Why do zoning boards often ignore the standards? Note that the issuance of a variance is a quasi-judicial process—unlike a zoning amendment—so most courts give little deference to a local government's decision. For a modern analysis of the variance, see David W. Owens, *The Zoning Variance: Reappraisal and Recommendations for Reform of a Much-Maligned Tool,* 29 Colum. J. Envtl. L. 279 (2004).

b. **What Constitutes "Hardship"?**

The lot involved in *Detwiler* is located in a rural area where the predominant use is agriculture; there are only four residences within 500 feet of the property. Couldn't the Millers have continued the existing agricultural use? If so, where is the hardship that justifies a variance? Like Pennsylvania, most states follow the view that hardship exists only if no reasonable use of the land is permitted under the existing zoning. *See, e.g., Krummenacher v. City of Minnetonka,* 783 N.W.2d 721, 728 (Minn. 2010) (hardship exists only if applicant shows "the property in question cannot be put to a reasonable use" without the variance). On the other hand, should a person have a right to build a home on any land that he owns?

c. **Physical Condition of the Land**

The "unique physical circumstances" requirement was satisfied in *Detwiler* by the shallowness of the lot. The setback requirements would permit a house "less than ten feet deep" at the widest. (Try to design such a house!) What other physical conditions would meet the standard for a variance? *But see Martin v. City of Alexandria,* 743 S.E.2d 139 (Va. 2013) (shallow and wide residential lot did not qualify for setback variances because owners could build house without them).

d. Impact on the Public

How much discretion does a zoning board have in determining whether a variance would be "detrimental to the public welfare"? What would happen if the Detwilers submitted expert testimony that having a house on the Miller lot would reduce the value of other parcels in the neighborhood, including their own? Or if the evidence showed that allowing any structure on the Miller lot would greatly impair the experience of tourists who came to view the Detwilers' historic home? In some jurisdictions, a variance will be denied if it would lower the value of surrounding properties or adversely affect the "visual environment" of the area. *See Commons v. Westwood Zoning Board of Adjustment*, 410 A.2d 1138 (N.J. 1980). Note that the rear border of the Miller lot adjoins a large tract of open farm land, so as a practical matter the variance had no adverse impact on the owner of that tract.

e. Two Types of Variances

Most jurisdictions recognize two types of variances. An *area variance* permits a modification of lot size, setback, height, frontage, density, or similar requirements, like the setback requirement at issue in *Detwiler*. A *use variance* authorizes a type of use that is otherwise prohibited by the zoning ordinance. Because there is a risk that a use variance will circumvent the uniformity of the zoning plan—without the procedural safeguards built into the amendment process—some states impose higher standards on this type of variance. In these states, a use variance usually requires a showing of strict hardship, while an area variance may be granted under the less-demanding *practical difficulties test*. This test simply requires that the land cannot practically be used given the existing zoning, even if a permitted use is theoretically possible. Notice that the *Detwiler* court also distinguishes between the two types of variances, stressing that the Millers "are not seeking a use variance for their property, but only a dimensional one."

f. Variance Problems

Would the following variances be valid under the Pennsylvania statute involved in *Detwiler*?

> (1) O's single-family home is built on a lot that drops off steeply to a river in a deep ravine, so most of the back yard is unusable. O wants to add a wooden deck behind the house to provide a level play area for her two-year-old child. The zoning ordinance requires a 30-foot setback from the rear lot line. O seeks a variance to reduce the rear setback to 12 feet so that she can build the deck. One neighbor objects that this will impair his view of the river.
>
> (2) P buys a single-family home, aware that it is located in an R-2 Residential District where the permitted uses are residences, home occupations, agriculture, golf courses, and the like. The home fronts on a busy street, where cars travel over 50 miles per hour. Because of the traffic volume and noise, P concludes the property is not suitable as a residence. He seeks a variance that would allow him to operate an accounting business. Some nearby parcels on

> the street are used for businesses, including a tavern, an auto body shop, a bank, a church, and a day care facility; others are used as residences.

3. Conditional Uses

A *conditional use (or special exception)* is a use that is permitted in the zone if certain conditions specified in the zoning ordinance are met. It is typically utilized to regulate uses that might cause aesthetic, noise, traffic, or other problems in a neighborhood, such as airports, junkyards, landfills, and office buildings. Unlike a variance, the conditional use is a use authorized by the ordinance—but one that must be regulated on a case-by-case basis to avoid injury to existing nearby uses.

A landowner seeking a conditional use will apply to the local zoning authorities for a permit to implement the use. Some zoning ordinances require that the applicant meet specific, detailed criteria in order to qualify for the permit. But others broadly authorize a conditional use if the zoning authorities find that it is consistent with the general public welfare—a standard that provides broad discretion to local decision-makers; in such jurisdictions, the zoning board is typically given the power to impose conditions on the project in order to minimize its impact on the neighborhood. Because the approval of a conditional use is viewed as quasi-judicial action, it is subject to more intensive judicial review than a zoning amendment.

4. New Approaches to Land Use Regulation

The rigid universe of Euclidean zoning is slowly collapsing. Most local governments have adopted newer, more flexible techniques to regulate land use, and this trend will continue. All of the following tools vest greater discretion in government officials, so that regulation can be individually tailored to the needs of the particular situation:

> - *Conditional zoning*: Rezoning a particular parcel when the owner satisfies conditions imposed by the city or county, in order to mitigate the impact of the zoning change.
> - *Floating zone*: A zoning district with detailed provisions (usually to accommodate large-scale developments such as shopping centers) which does not have a specific location until an owner applies to have the zone applied to her property.
> - *Cluster zone*: A residential zone that restricts the number of homes, but allows the developer choice about where the homes will be

located; this permits the "clustering" of residences and encourages preservation of open space.
- *Planned unit development*: Zoning that allows a developer to plan an entire community (with homes, businesses, and public services), subject to guidelines for density and other concerns; this is essentially cluster zoning extended to all uses.

In a larger sense, modern land use planners increasingly reject the assumptions of Euclidean zoning: (a) separation of uses; (b) low-density development; (c) auto-dependency; and (d) lot-by-lot regulation. For instance, the "Smart Growth" movement advocates development that: (a) mixes land uses; (b) creates high-density neighborhoods to preserve open space; (c) is transit and pedestrian-oriented; and (d) is planned on a regional basis. The New Urbanist approach to architecture, as discussed in the article below, is closely related to the Smart Growth perspective.

Perspective and Analysis

For most of the twentieth century, American land use regulation sought to segregate land uses and to reduce population density, while American parking and street design regulation sought to facilitate driving by mandating wide streets and forcing landlords and businesses to build parking lots for their tenants and customers.

These policies have combined to create a pattern of land use often described as "sprawl": low-density, automobile-oriented development. Where "single-use zoning" separates housing from commerce, and residential zones cover large amounts of thinly populated land, few people can live within walking distance of commercial zones. Where wide streets speed up motor vehicle traffic, walking is unpleasant and perhaps even dangerous. . . .

Over the past two decades, a group of architects generally known as the "New Urbanist" movement has sought to design more pedestrianfriendly neighborhoods. New Urbanists argue that:

- Automobile-dependent sprawl reduces individual freedom by immobilizing Americans too young or too old to drive.
- Sprawling development increases driving, which in turn has led to increased traffic congestion and pollution.
- "Sprawl is ugly, produc[ing] nothing in the public realm worthy of aesthetic contemplation."
- Pedestrian-friendly communities might improve public health by allowing their residents to get more exercise.

> - Pedestrian-friendly neighborhoods, unlike sprawling subdivisions, foster community by encouraging chance meetings between their residents.
>
> - Sprawling development consumes more land than more compact development, thus reducing the supply of farmland, open space, and wildlife habitat.
>
> The New Urbanist remedy is to build Traditional Neighborhood Developments (TNDs)—neighborhoods with streets narrow enough for pedestrians to safely cross and with housing within walking distance of schools, workplaces, shops, and other human activities.
>
> TNDs often conflict with conventional zoning and street design regulations. While New Urbanists seek to build mixed-use, compact neighborhoods, conventional land use regulation favors single-use, low-density sprawl. Developers have occasionally been able to build TNDs by obtaining exemptions from zoning codes—but nevertheless, conventional, automobile-oriented subdivisions are far easier to build than TNDs under existing land use law. Because existing zoning is so hostile to New Urbanism, New Urbanists have begun to develop alternative zoning codes codifying New Urbanist principles.
>
> **Michael Lewyn, *New Urbanist Zoning for Dummies*, 58 Ala. L. Rev. 257, 257-60 (2006).**

Points for Discussion

a. **Rethinking Euclidean Zoning**

Do you agree with the New Urbanist critique of Euclidean zoning? What changes in our zoning laws would be necessary to implement the New Urbanist vision? The first New Urbanist town in the United States was Seaside, Florida, founded in 1981; it served as the setting for the Jim Carrey movie *The Truman Show*. Other well-known examples of New Urbanism are Celebration, Florida (developed by the Walt Disney Company) and Playa Vista in Los Angeles, California (the largest modern in-fill project in Los Angeles).

b. **American Dreaming**

The classic American dream is a single-family detached home in the suburbs—exactly what Euclidean zoning has produced on a large scale. In fact, one could argue that sprawl is the inevitable product of the post-World War II boom that brought prosperity to the middle class. Do Americans want to live in high-density, condominium-like residences? If so, why do developers continue to build detached single-family homes? *See* Clint Bolick, *Subverting the American Dream: Government Dictated "Smart Growth" Is Unwise and Unconstitutional,* 148 U. Pa. L. Rev. 859 (2000). Should government mandate that future housing projects comply with New Urbanist principles?

c. A Better Approach?

In many cities, more than 75% of the land is zoned exclusively for single-family detached homes. Economists agree that this increases the price of housing; land and construction costs are higher for a detached home than for a unit of multi-family housing. One solution is rezoning single-family districts to allow more intense development. For example, Oregon adopted a law requiring cities with at least 25,000 residents—covering half of the state's population—to *also* permit duplexes, triplexes, quadplexes, "cottage clusters," and townhouses in single-family zones. Or. Rev. Stat. § 197.758. Do you agree with the Oregon approach? What concerns arise when state law supersedes local zoning ordinances?

D. How Far Can Land Use Regulation Go?

As you saw in *Euclid*, the early zoning ordinances were justified largely as tools to control nuisance-like conduct. Over the last century, however, the purposes of land use regulation have expanded dramatically—and this regulation has accordingly become much more intensive. In fact, one text concludes that "[l]and use regulation is probably the area of law that most affects the quality of life in the United States." Daniel P. Selmi et al., Land Use Regulation: Cases and Materials 3 (5th ed. 2017).

So what are the outer limits of land use regulation? The materials below explore three controversial issues: (1) aesthetic regulation; (2) "family" zoning; and (3) zoning that excludes newcomers.

1. Aesthetic Regulation

Ladue is a wealthy suburb of St. Louis, Missouri, with a population of about 9,000 residents. Its citizens are the best-educated and the highest-paid in the state; 82% of adults have a college degree, and the median household income is $190,000. Almost all of the city is zoned for single-family residences only; the median house price is about $950,000. The city's website states:

> Established in 1936, the City of Ladue is a residential community that prides itself on preserving its unique character and way of life by adhering to the City's Master Plan and Zoning Ordinance. The City strives to provide its citizens with the finest community services in the most tranquil and serene environment it can possibly maintain. . . .

The citizens of Ladue are quite concerned about preserving the visual appearance of their community. Fortunately for students of property law, Ladue's litigation has generated a landmark case about aesthetic regulation. Can Ladue bar construction of a house with a "pyramid shape" because is different from the designs of the other houses in the area?

> **FYI**
>
> The community of Ladue was originally designed in the 1930s by Harland Bartholomew, one of the pioneers of urban planning in the United States. A close friend of President Truman, Bartholomew later served as the chair of the National Capital Planning Commission, which coordinates city planning in the District of Columbia region.

State ex rel. Stoyanoff v. Berkeley

Supreme Court of Missouri

458 S.W.2d 305 (1970)

PRITCHARD, COMMISSIONER.

Upon summary judgment the trial court issued a peremptory writ of mandamus to compel appellant to issue a residential building permit to respondents. The trial court's judgment is that the below-mentioned ordinances are violative of Section 10, Article I of the Constitution of Missouri, 1945, V.A.M.S., in that restrictions placed by the ordinances on the use of property deprive the owners of their property without due process of law. Relators' petition pleads that they applied to appellant Building Commissioner for a building permit to allow them to construct a single family residence in the City of Ladue, and that plans and specifications were submitted for the proposed residence, which was unusual in design, "but complied with all existing building and zoning regulations and ordinances of the City of Ladue, Missouri."

It is further pleaded that relators were refused a building permit for the construction of their proposed residence upon the ground that the permit was not approved by the Architectural Board of the City of Ladue. Ordinance 131, as amended by Ordinance 281 of that city, purports to set up an Architectural Board to approve plans and specifications for buildings and structures erected within the city and in a preamble to

> conform to certain minimum architectural standards of appearance and conformity with surrounding structures, and that unsightly, grotesque and unsuitable structures, detrimental to the stability of value and the welfare of surrounding property, structures and residents, and to the general welfare and happiness of the community, be

avoided, and that appropriate standards of beauty and conformity be fostered and encouraged.

It is asserted in the petition that the ordinances are invalid, illegal and void, "are unconstitutional in that they are vague and provide no standard nor uniform rule by which to guide the architectural board," that the city acted in excess of statutory powers (§ 89.020, RS Mo 1959, V.A.M.S.) in enacting the ordinance, which "attempt to allow respondent to impose aesthetic standards for buildings in the City of Ladue, and are in excess of the powers granted the City of Ladue by said statute."

> **Make the Connection**
>
> If a statute is so vague that people "of common intelligence must necessarily guess at its meaning and differ as to its application," it is unconstitutional. *FCC v. Fox Television Stations, Inc.*, 567 U.S. 239, 253 (2012). You will study this *void for vagueness* doctrine in Constitutional Law.

Relators filed a motion for summary judgment and affidavits were filed in opposition thereto. Richard D. Shelton, Mayor of the City of Ladue, deposed that the facts in appellant's answer were true and correct, as here pertinent: that the City of Ladue constitutes one of the finer suburban residential areas of Metropolitan St. Louis, the homes therein are considerably more expensive than in cities of comparable size, being homes on lots from three fourths of an acre to three or more acres each; that a zoning ordinance was enacted by the city regulating the height, number of stories, size of buildings, percentage of lot occupancy, yard sizes, and the location and use of buildings and land for trade, industry, residence and other purposes; that the zoning regulations were made in accordance with a comprehensive plan "designed to promote the health and general welfare of the residents of the City of Ladue," which in furtherance of said objectives duly enacted said Ordinances numbered 131 and 281. Appellant also asserted in his answer that these ordinances were a reasonable exercise of the city's governmental, legislative and police powers, as determined by its legislative body, and as stated in the above-quoted preamble to the ordinances. It is then pleaded that relators' description of their proposed residence as " 'unusual in design' is the understatement of the year. It is in fact a monstrosity of grotesque design, which would seriously impair the value of property in the neighborhood."

The affidavit of Harold C. Simon, a developer of residential subdivisions in St. Louis County, is that he is familiar with relators' lot upon which they seek to build a house, and with the surrounding houses in the neighborhood; that the houses therein existent are virtually all two-story houses of conventional architectural design, such as Colonial, French Provincial or English; and that the house which relators propose to construct is of ultramodern design which would clash with and not be in conformity with any other house in the entire neighborhood. It is Mr. Simon's opinion that the design and appearance of relators' proposed residence would have a substantial adverse effect upon the market values of other residential property in the neighborhood, such average market value ranging from $60,000 to $85,000 each.

As a part of the affidavit of Russell H. Riley, consultant for the city planning and engineering firm of Harland Bartholomew & Associates, photographic exhibits of homes surrounding relators' lot were attached. To the south is the conventional frame residence of Mrs. T. R. Collins. To the west is the Colonial two-story frame house of the Lewis family. To the northeast is the large brick English Tudor home of Mrs. Elmer Hubbs. Immediately to the north are the large Colonial homes of Mr. Alex Cornwall and Mr. L. Peter Wetzel. In substance Mr. Riley went on to say that the City of Ladue is one of the finer residential suburbs in the St. Louis area with a minimum of commercial or industrial usage. The development of residences in the city has been primarily by private subdivisions, usually with one main lane or drive leading therein (such as Lorenzo Road Subdivision which runs north off of Ladue Road in which relators' lot is located). The homes are considerably more expensive than average homes found in a city of comparable size. The ordinance which has been adopted by the City of Ladue is typical of those which have been adopted by a number of suburban cities in St. Louis County and in similar cities throughout the United States, the need therefor being based upon the protection of existing property values by preventing the construction of houses that are in complete conflict with the general type of houses in a given area. The intrusion into this neighborhood of relators' unusual, grotesque and nonconforming structure would have a substantial adverse effect on market values of other homes in the immediate area. According to Mr. Riley the standards of Ordinance 131, as amended by Ordinance 281, are usually and customarily applied in city planning work and are:

> (1) whether the proposed house meets the customary architectural requirements in appearance and design for a house of the particular type which is proposed (whether it be Colonial, Tudor English, French Provincial, or Modern), (2) whether the proposed house is in general conformity with the style and design of surrounding structures, and (3) whether the proposed house lends itself to the proper architectural development of the City; and that in applying said standards the Architectural Board and its Chairman are to determine whether the proposed house will have an adverse affect on the stability of values in the surrounding area.

Photographic exhibits of relators' proposed residence were also attached to Mr. Riley's affidavit. They show the residence to be of a pyramid shape, with a flat top, and with triangular shaped windows or doors at one or more corners. . . .

. . . [R]elators' position is that "the creation by the City of Ladue of an architectural board for the purpose of promoting and maintaining 'general conformity with the style and design of surrounding structures' is totally unauthorized by our Enabling Statute." (§§ 89.020, 89.040, RS Mo 1959, V.A.M.S.) It is further contended by relators that Ordinances 131 and 281 are invalid and unconstitutional as being an

---

See It

Click here to see the homes owned at the time by Cornwall, Hubbs, Lewis, and Wetzel, four of the complaining neighbors.

unreasonable and arbitrary exercise of the police power (as based entirely on aesthetic values); and that the same are invalid as an unlawful delegation of legislative powers (to the Architectural Board).

Section 89.020 provides [for the regulation of the height, location and size of buildings; lot size; population density; historic preservation; etc. in order to promote the] "health, safety, morals [and] the general welfare of the community. . . ." Section 89.040 provides:

> Such regulations shall be made in accordance with a comprehensive plan and designed to . . . promote health *and the general welfare*; to provide adequate light and air; to prevent the overcrowding of land; . . . *Such regulations shall be made with reasonable consideration, among other things, to the character of the district and its peculiar suitability for particular uses, and with a view to conserving the values of buildings and encouraging the most appropriate use of land throughout such municipality.* (Italics added.)

Relators say that "Neither Sections 89.020 or 89.040 nor any other provision of Chapter 89 mentions or gives a city the authority to regulate architectural design and appearance. There exists no provision providing for an architectural board and no entity even remotely resembling such a board is mentioned under the enabling legislation." Relators conclude that the City of Ladue lacked any power to adopt Ordinance 131 as amended by Ordinance 281 "and its intrusion into this area is wholly unwarranted and without sanction in the law." As to this aspect of the appeal relators rely upon the 1961 decision of *State ex rel. Magidson v. Henze*, Mo. App., 342 S.W.2d 261. That case had the identical question presented. . . . The court held that § 89.020, RS Mo 1949, V.A.M.S., does not grant to the city the right to impose upon the landowner aesthetic standards for the buildings he chooses to erect.

As is clear from the affidavits and attached exhibits, the City of Ladue is an area composed principally of residences of the general types of Colonial, French Provincial and English Tudor. The city has a comprehensive plan of zoning to maintain the general character of buildings therein. The Magidson case . . . did not consider the effect of § 89.040 . . . and the italicized portion relating to the character of the district, its suitability for particular uses, and the conservation of the values of buildings therein. These considerations, sanctioned by statute, are directly related to the general welfare of the community. . . . In *Marrs v. City of Oxford* (D.C.D. Kan.) 24 F.2d 541, 548, it was said, "The stabilizing of property values, and giving some assurance to the public that, if property is purchased in a residential district, its value as such will be preserved, is probably the most cogent reason back of zoning ordinances." The preamble to Ordinance 131, quoted above in part, demonstrates that its purpose is to conform to the dictates of § 89.040, with reference to preserving values of property by zoning procedure and restrictions on the use of property. This is an illustration of what was referred to in *Deimeke v. State Highway Commission*, Mo., 444 S.W.2d

480, 484, as a growing number of cases recognizing a change in the scope of the term "general welfare." In the *Deimeke* case on the same page it is said, "Property use which offends sensibilities and debases property values affects not only the adjoining property owners in that vicinity but the general public as well because when such property values are destroyed or seriously impaired, the tax base of the community is affected and the public suffers economically as a result."

> **Food for Thought**
>
> In *Euclid*, the Supreme Court suggested that the goal of zoning ordinances was to control nuisance-like uses. Here the Missouri Supreme Court seems to endorse the view that the most important reason for zoning is to preserve property values. What are the implications of this view?

Relators say further that Ordinances 131 and 281 are invalid and unconstitutional as being an unreasonable and arbitrary exercise of the police power. It is argued that a mere reading of these ordinances shows that they are based entirely on aesthetic factors in that the stated purpose of the Architectural Board is to maintain "conformity with surrounding structures" and to assure that structures "conform to certain minimum architectural standards of appearance." The argument ignores the further provisos in the ordinance: ". . . and that unsightly, grotesque and unsuitable structures, *detrimental to the stability of value and the welfare of surrounding property, structures, and residents, and to the general welfare and happiness of the community*, be avoided, and that appropriate standards of beauty and conformity be fostered and encouraged." (Italics added.) Relators' proposed residence does not descend to the "patently offensive character of vehicle graveyards in close proximity to such highways" referred to in the *Deimke* case, supra (444 S.W.2d 484). Nevertheless, the aesthetic factor to be taken into account by the Architectural Board is not to be considered alone. Along with that inherent factor is the effect that the proposed residence would have upon the property values in the area. In this time of burgeoning urban areas, congested with people and structures, it is certainly in keeping with the ultimate ideal of general welfare that the Architectural Board, in its function, preserve and protect existing areas in which structures of a general conformity of architecture have been erected. The area under consideration is clearly, from the record, a fashionable one. In *State ex rel. Civello v. City of New Orleans*, 154 La. 271, 97 So. 440, 444, the court said, "If by the term 'aesthetic considerations' is meant a regard merely for outward appearances, for good taste in the matter of the beauty of the neighborhood itself, we do not observe any substantial reason for saying that such a consideration is not a matter of general welfare. The beauty of a fashionable residence neighborhood in a city is for the comfort and happiness of the residents, and it sustains in a general way the value of property in the neighborhood."

In the matter of enacting zoning ordinances and the procedures for determining whether any certain proposed structure or use is in compliance with or offends the basic ordinance, it is well settled that courts will not substitute their judgments for the city's legislative body, if the result is not oppressive, arbitrary or unreasonable and does not infringe upon a valid preexisting nonconforming use. . . . The denial by appellant of a building permit for relators' highly modernistic residence in this area where traditional Colonial, French Provincial and English Tudor styles of architecture are erected does not appear to be arbitrary and unreasonable when the basic purpose to be served is that of the general welfare of persons in the entire community.

In addition to the above-stated purpose in the preamble to Ordinance 131, it establishes an Architectural Board of three members, all of whom must be architects. Meetings of the Board are to be open to the public, and every application for a building permit, except those not affecting the outward appearance of a building, shall be submitted to the Board along with plans, elevations, detail drawings and specifications, before being approved by the Building Commissioner. . . . The Board shall disapprove the application if it determines the proposed structure will constitute an unsightly, grotesque or unsuitable structure in appearance, detrimental to the welfare of surrounding property or residents. . . . If the Board's disapproval is given and the applicant refuses to comply with recommendations, the Building Commissioner shall refuse the permit. Thereafter provisions are made for an appeal to the Council of the city for review of the decision of the Architectural Board. . . .

Relators claim that the above provisions of the ordinance amount to an unconstitutional delegation of power by the city to the Architectural Board. It is argued that the Board cannot be given the power to determine what is unsightly and grotesque and that the standards . . . are inadequate. . . . Ordinances 131 and 281 are sufficient in their general standards calling for a factual determination of the suitability of any proposed structure with reference to the character of the surrounding neighborhood and to the determination of any adverse effect on the general welfare and preservation of property values of the community. . . .

The judgment is reversed.

Points for Discussion

a. **Legislating Beauty**

An old adage says that "beauty is in the eye of the beholder." What are the "appropriate standards of beauty and conformity" that govern residential architecture in Ladue? What design advice would you provide to a client who hoped to build a home there? It is now well-settled that a city or county has the inherent police power to regulate aesthetics. As the Supreme Court observed in *Berman v. Parker*, 348 U.S. 26, 33 (1954), "[i]t is within the power of the legislature to determine that the community should be beautiful as well as healthy . . . ."

b. The *Stoyanoff* Holding

What is the basis for the court's holding? Test your understanding by considering how the *Stoyanoff* court would resolve these hypotheticals.

> (1) O wants to build the same pyramid house on the same Ladue lot, except that the evidence shows the house would increase property values in the area. Must Ladue issue a building permit to O?
>
> (2) Ladue adopts an ordinance that requires all homes to be painted green, in order to "preserve our desirable visual environment." Assuming that the ordinance has no impact on property values, is it constitutional?
>
> (3) X owns a run-down office building in Ladue. Z plans to construct a modern office building next door; X worries that her tenants will move to Z's building, lowering the value of her building. Can Ladue enact a zoning ordinance that requires each new office building to have an old-looking, run-down façade?
>
> (4) A member of the Ladue City Council asks you, the city attorney: "Are there any meaningful limits on the city's ability to regulate the appearance of houses? Or can we do just about anything we want?" How would you reply?

c. Traditional Private Property Rights

The Supreme Court has recognized that "[t]he State's interest in protecting the well-being, tranquility, and privacy of the home is certainly of the highest order in a free and civilized society." *Carey v. Brown*, 447 U.S. 455, 471 (1980). How important was it to the outcome in *Stoyanoff* that the proposed house would adversely affect homes, rather than stores or factories? Conversely, should a landowner have the right to build whatever type of house he wishes on his own land, so long as it is not a nuisance?

d. Architecture as Art

What impact does a Ladue-like ordinance have on artistic expression? Novel architecture—like most great art—is rarely appreciated in its time. Presumably, Frank Lloyd Wright would have been unable to build his celebrated houses in a city like Ladue. Should the *Stoyanoff* court have considered this in its decision? (Of course, Wright himself once commented that "[t]he physician can bury his mistakes, but the architect can only advise his clients to plant vines.")

e. Architecture as Speech

The First Amendment restricts government from making any law "abridging the freedom of speech." Does this protection extend to architecture? Suppose, for example, that the plaintiffs in *Stoyanoff* wanted to build a pyramid-style house in order to advocate that the United States improve its relationship with Egypt. Should this motive make a difference? *See* Janet Elizabeth Haws, Comment, *Architecture as Art? Not in My Neocolonial Backyard: A Case for Providing First Amendment Protection to Expressive Residential Architecture*, 2005 BYU L. Rev. 1625 (2005).

In *Burns v. Town of Palm Beach*, 999 F.3d 1317 (11th Cir. 2021), plaintiff appealed from the town's refusal to issue a building permit for his proposed "mid-century modern style" mansion on the basis that it violated his right to free speech. *Id.* at 1322. He argued that the design "communicated that the new home was clean, fresh, independent, and modern—a reflection of his evolved philosophy of simplicity in lifestyle and living . . . ." *Id.* at 1325. But the court noted that the planned landscaping would prevent potential viewers off the property from seeing the house and reasoned that, even if they could, they would probably not "understand that it conveyed some sort of message." *Id.* at 1343. Without deciding whether residential architecture could ever be protected by the First Amendment, the court held that the house would not be expressive conduct: "[B]urn's proposed new mansion is not Monticello or Versailles . . . It's just a really big beachfront house that can't be seen, located on a quiet residential street . . . ." *Id.* at 1349.

f. Signs as Speech

Controls on signs pose obvious First Amendment concerns. For example, in *City of Ladue v. Gilleo*, 512 U.S. 43 (1994), Gilleo posted a sign in a window of her home during the Gulf War era which stated: "For Peace in the Gulf." When the city asserted that the sign violated a local ordinance, she challenged the law as a violation of her right to free speech. The Supreme Court unanimously struck down the ordinance because it entirely foreclosed a traditional medium of expression: residential signs. It stressed that displaying a sign at one's home is cheap, convenient, and uniquely identifies the speaker, features that alternative methods do not possess. *See also Brown v. Town of Cary*, 706 F.3d 294 (4th Cir. 2013) (upholding ordinance that town used to challenge large fluorescent orange sign that resident painted on his house reading "Screwed by the Town of Cary"); *Willson v. City of Bel-Nor*, 924 F.3d 995 (8th Cir. 2019) (owner who displayed a "Black Lives Matter" sign and two signs endorsing political candidates on his property was entitled to an injunction against enforcement of an ordinance that allowed only one sign).

---

2. "Family" Zoning

Can the government decide who lives in your house? In recent years, many municipalities have adopted ordinances providing that only members of a "family" may occupy a single-family residence.

In *Village of Belle Terre v. Boraas*, 416 U.S. 1 (1974), the Supreme Court upheld such a "family" zoning ordinance against due process and equal protection attacks. The Belle Terre ordinance—apparently aimed at preventing local college students from living together—defined "family" as "[o]ne or more persons related by blood, adoption, or marriage" or up to two unrelated persons. Six unrelated students who had rented a house together challenged the ordinance. Echoing

Euclid's rational basis test, the Court held that the ordinance was reasonable and not arbitrary, bearing a reasonable relationship to the legitimate state objective of regulating noise, parking, traffic, and other density-related problems. Justice Marshall's dissent argued that the strict scrutiny test should be used instead, because the ordinance abridged the rights of association and privacy. He observed that "[t]he choice of household companions . . . involves deeply personal considerations as to the kind and quality of intimate relationships within the home." *Id.* at 16.

Fifty years have elapsed since *Belle Terre* was decided—and American society has changed greatly in the interval. Is the *Belle Terre* rationale now obsolete?

Moore v. City of East Cleveland

Supreme Court of the United States

431 U.S. 494 (1977)

JUSTICE POWELL announced the judgment of the Court. . . .

East Cleveland's housing ordinance, like many throughout the country, limits occupancy of a dwelling unit to members of a single family. § 1351.02. But the ordinance contains an unusual and complicated definitional section that recognizes as a "family" only a few categories of related individuals, § 1341.08.[2] Because her family, living together in her home, fits none of those categories, appellant stands convicted of a criminal offense. The question in this case is whether the ordinance violates the Due Process Clause of the Fourteenth Amendment.

I.

Appellant, Mrs. Inez Moore, lives in her East Cleveland home together with her son, Dale Moore Sr., and her two grandsons, Dale, Jr., and John Moore, Jr. The two

---

[2] Section 1341.08 . . . provides:

"Family" means a number of individuals related to the nominal head of the household or to the spouse of the nominal head of the household living as a single housekeeping unit in a single dwelling unit, but limited to the following:

(a) Husband or wife of the nominal head of the household.

(b) Unmarried children of the nominal head of the household or of the spouse of the nominal head of the household, provided, however, that such unmarried children have no children residing with them.

(c) Father or mother of the nominal head of the household or of the spouse of the nominal head of the household.

(d) Notwithstanding the provisions of subsection (b) hereof, a family may include not more than one dependent married or unmarried child of the nominal head of the household or of the spouse of the nominal head of the household and the spouse and dependent children of such dependent child. For the purpose of this subsection, a dependent person is one who has more than fifty percent of his total support furnished for him by the nominal head of the household and the spouse of the nominal head of the household.

(e) A family may consist of one individual.

boys are first cousins rather than brothers; we are told that John came to live with his grandmother and with the elder and younger Dale Moores after his mother's death.

In early 1973, Mrs. Moore received a notice of violation from the city, stating that John was an "illegal occupant" and directing her to comply with the ordinance. When she failed to remove him from her home, the city filed a criminal charge. Mrs. Moore moved to dismiss, claiming that the ordinance was constitutionally invalid on its face. Her motion was overruled, and upon conviction she was sentenced to five days in jail and a $25 fine. The Ohio Court of Appeals affirmed after giving full consideration to her constitutional claims and the Ohio Supreme Court denied review. . . .

> **See It**
>
> East Cleveland is a suburb of Cleveland, Ohio, with a population of 13,000 residents. Click here to see photographs of typical homes in the city.

II.

The city argues that our decision in *Village of Belle Terre v. Boraas*, 416 U.S. 1 (1974), requires us to sustain the ordinance attacked here. Belle Terre, like East Cleveland, imposed limits on the types of groups that could occupy a single dwelling unit. Applying the constitutional standard announced in this Court's leading land-use case, *Euclid v. Ambler Realty Co.*, 272 U.S. 365 (1926), we sustained the Belle Terre ordinance on the ground that it bore a rational relationship to permissible state objectives.

But one overriding factor sets this case apart from *Belle Terre*. The ordinance there affected only *unrelated* individuals. It expressly allowed all who were related by "blood, adoption, or marriage" to live together, and in sustaining the ordinance we were careful to note that it promoted "family needs" and "family values." 416 U.S., at 9. East Cleveland, in contrast, has chosen to regulate the occupancy of its housing by slicing deeply into the family itself. This is no mere incidental result of the ordinance. On its face it selects certain categories of relatives who may live together and declares that others may not. In particular, it makes a crime of a grandmother's choice to live with her grandson in circumstances like those presented here.

When a city undertakes such intrusive regulation of the family, neither *Belle Terre* nor *Euclid* governs; the usual judicial deference to the legislature is inappropriate. . . . [W]hen the government intrudes on choices concerning family living arrangements, this Court must examine carefully the importance of the governmental interests advanced and the extent to which they are served by the challenged regulation. . . .

When thus examined, this ordinance cannot survive. The city seeks to justify it as a means of preventing overcrowding, minimizing traffic and parking congestion, and avoiding an undue financial burden on East Cleveland's school system. Although these are legitimate goals, the ordinance before us serves them marginally, at best. For example, the ordinance permits any family consisting only of husband, wife, and unmarried children to live together, even if the family contains a half dozen licensed drivers, each with his or her own car. At the same time it forbids an adult brother and sister to share a household, even if both faithfully use public transportation. The ordinance would permit a grandmother to live with a single dependent son and children, even if his school-age children number a dozen, yet it forces Mrs. Moore to find another dwelling for her grandson John, simply because of the presence of his uncle and cousin in the same household. We need not labor the point. Section 1341.08 has but a tenuous relation to alleviation of the conditions mentioned by the city. . . .

> **Food for Thought**
>
> Dissenting in this case, Justices Rehnquist and Stewart stated: "To suggest that the biological fact of common ancestry necessarily gives related persons constitutional rights of association superior to those of unrelated persons is to misunderstand the nature of the associational freedoms that the Constitution has been understood to protect." Who has the stronger argument on this point, the majority or the dissent?

III.

Our decisions establish that the Constitution protects the sanctity of the family precisely because the institution of the family is deeply rooted in this Nation's history and tradition. It is through the family that we inculcate and pass down many of our most cherished values, moral and cultural. . . .

Ours is by no means a tradition limited to respect for the bonds uniting the members of the nuclear family. The tradition of uncles, aunts, cousins, and especially grandparents sharing a household along with parents and children has roots equally venerable and equally deserving of constitutional recognition. . . .

Reversed.

MR. JUSTICE BRENNAN, with whom MR. JUSTICE MARSHALL joins, concurring.

I join the plurality's opinion. . . . I do not question that a municipality may constitutionally zone to alleviate noise and traffic congestion and to prevent overcrowded and unsafe living conditions, in short to enact reasonable land-use restrictions in furtherance of the legitimate objectives East Cleveland claims for its ordinance. But the zoning power is not a license for local communities to enact senseless and arbitrary restrictions which cut deeply into private areas of protected family life. . . .

In today's America, the "nuclear family" is the pattern so often found in much of white suburbia. . . . The Constitution cannot be interpreted, however, to tolerate the imposition by government upon the rest of us of white suburbia's preference in patterns of family living. The "extended family" that provided generations of early

Americans with social services and economic and emotional support in times of hardship, and was the beachhead for successive waves of immigrants who populated our cities, remains not merely still a pervasive living pattern, but under the goad of brutal economic necessity, a prominent pattern virtually a means of survival for large numbers of the poor and deprived minorities of our society. For them compelled pooling of scant resources requires compelled sharing of a household.

The "extended" form is especially familiar among black families. We may suppose that this reflects the truism that black citizens, like generations of white immigrants before them, have been victims of economic and other disadvantages that would worsen if they were compelled to abandon extended, for nuclear, living patterns. Even in husband and wife households, 13% of black families compared with 3% of white families include relatives under 18 years old, in addition to the couple's own children. In black households whose head is an elderly woman, as in this case, the contrast is even more striking: 48% of such black households, compared with 10% of counterpart white households, include related minor children not offspring of the head of the household.

I do not wish to be understood as implying that East Cleveland's enforcement of its ordinance is motivated by a racially discriminatory purpose: The record of this case would not support that implication. But the prominence of other than nuclear families among ethnic and racial minority groups, including our black citizens, surely demonstrates that the "extended family" pattern remains a vital tenet of our society. . . .

Points for Discussion

a. *Moore* and *Belle Terre*

How convincingly does the *Moore* Court distinguish *Belle Terre*? Which standard does the Court use: the rational basis test, the strict scrutiny test, or a different test? What is the justification for heightened judicial review of ordinances that regulate family living arrangements?

b. **Modern Families**

The nature of the American family has changed since *Belle Terre* was decided. The "traditional" family model of a married, heterosexual couple living with their children is no longer the norm, if indeed it ever was. Should a non-traditional family be entitled to the protected status of a "family" under the logic of *Moore*? How does the right of intimate association discussed in *Fair Housing Council v. Roommate. com* (Chapter 7) bear on this question? *See generally* Rigel C. Oliveri, *Single-Family Zoning, Intimate Association, and the Right to Choose Household Companions*, 67 Fla. L. Rev. 1401 (2015); *but see Fed. Hill Cap., LLC v. City of Providence*, 227 A.3d 980

(R.I. 2020) (upholding ordinance which provided that no more than three college students could live in a home).

c. **The (Very) Extended Family**

Does *Moore* stand for the proposition that a city must allow all family members to live together, including distant cousins? DNA research suggests that "all living beings are related to a single woman who lived roughly 150,000 years ago in Africa, a 'mitochondrial Eve.' " James Shreeve, *The Greatest Journey*, National Geographic 60, Mar. 1, 2006. How would the *Moore* majority respond to this argument?

d. **Legal and Religious Barriers**

Suppose that a "single-family" zoning ordinance defines "family" to mean "two or more people related by blood or marriage." What about groups that wish to live together but who cannot for legal or religious reasons meet this definition of "family," such as a group of Catholic priests? *See Missionaries of Our Lady of La Salette v. Village of Whitefish Bay*, 66 N.W.2d 627 (Wis. 1954) (holding that six priests and two lay brothers were a "family" for purposes of the "single-family" zoning ordinance).

e. **Zoning Exercises**

Under the standards of review used in *Euclid* and *Belle Terre*, would it be constitutional for a city to prohibit the following persons from living in a particular neighborhood?

> (1) Musicians
> (2) Lawyers
> (3) Members of the Nazi party
> (4) Truck drivers

f. **Group Homes**

Zoning ordinances are sometimes adopted to exclude group homes from "single-family" districts. A "group home" is a non-profit facility, usually located in a residential neighborhood, that provides treatment or temporary housing for mentally-ill persons, battered women, recovering addicts, or other persons who require special care. In *City of Cleburne v. Cleburne Living Center*, 473 U.S. 432 (1985), the Supreme Court struck down a "family" zoning ordinance that

> **Make the Connection**
>
> The federal Fair Housing Act, which you studied in Chapter 7, also restricts the enforcement of "family" zoning ordinances against group homes for the handicapped. *See Association for Advancement of the Mentally Handicapped, Inc. v. City of Elizabeth*, 876 F. Supp. 614 (D.N.J. 1994) (invalidating ordinance).

excluded a group home for people with intellectual disabilities because it violated the Equal Protection Clause.

---

3. Growth Controls and Exclusion

Can a city prohibit all residential construction and thereby close its borders to new residents? Or can it adopt zoning policies that effectively exclude certain groups—such as low-income people—while permitting others to enter? Both questions share a common theme: can a community exclude newcomers? In practice, the law has distinguished between the two concepts.

The first question addresses *growth control ordinances*, which make it more difficult for residents to move into a community by restricting the number of housing units that may be built. Courts generally uphold such ordinances when adopted for legitimate, non-discriminatory reasons.

The second question concerns *exclusionary zoning*—land use regulation that has the effect of excluding minority groups from a community. For example, suppose that City C zones all of its residential areas for large single-family detached homes, thus prohibiting apartments, duplexes, and other forms of multi-family housing. As a practical matter, this tends to exclude racial and ethnic minorities, who are less likely to afford such homes.

In 1969, Ethel Lawrence and others hoped to build an affordable housing project in Mount Laurel, New Jersey. Working with a local contractor, they applied for permission to build a complex of two-story townhouse buildings, each containing three or four units. (A *townhouse* is a single-family residence that shares one or more walls with another unit.) But the township denied their application because its ordinance did not allow townhouses in any zone. Together with the NAACP, Lawrence and others filed a lawsuit that resulted in a leading decision on exclusionary zoning.

Southern Burlington County NAACP v. Township of Mount Laurel

Supreme Court of New Jersey

336 A.2d 713 (1975)

HALL, J.

This case attacks the system of land use regulation by defendant Township of Mount Laurel on the ground that low and moderate income families are thereby unlawfully excluded from the municipality. . . .

Plaintiffs represent the minority group poor (black and Hispanic) seeking such quarters. But they are not the only category of persons barred from so many municipalities by reason of restrictive land use regulations. We have reference to young and elderly couples, single persons and large, growing families not in the poverty class, but who still cannot afford the only kinds of housing realistically permitted in most places—relatively high-priced, single-family detached dwellings on sizeable lots and, in some municipalities, expensive apartments. We will, therefore, consider the case from the wider viewpoint that the effect of Mount Laurel's land use regulation has been to prevent various categories of persons from living in the township because of the limited extent of their income and resources. In this connection, we accept the representation of the municipality's counsel at oral argument that the regulatory scheme was not adopted with any desire or intent to exclude prospective residents on the obviously illegal bases of race, origin or believed social incompatibility. . . .

I.

Mount Laurel is a flat, sprawling township, 22 square miles, or about 14,000 acres, in area, on the west central edge of Burlington County. . . .

[29.2% of the township (4,121 acres) was zoned only for industrial use. But only 100 acres were actually being used for this purpose, and the rest of the area was undeveloped.] . . . [I]t appears that . . . much more land has been so zoned than the reasonable potential for industrial . . . expansion warrants. . . .

The amount of land zoned for retail business use under the general ordinance is relatively small—169 acres, or 1.2% of the total. . . .

The balance of the land area, almost 10,000 acres, has been developed until recently in the conventional form of major subdivisions. The general ordinance provides for four residential zones, designated R-1, R-1D, R-2 and R-3. All permit only single-family, detached dwellings, one house per lot—the usual form of grid development. Attached townhouses, apartments (except on farms for agricultural workers) and mobile homes are not allowed anywhere in the township under the general ordinance. . . .

The general ordinance requirements . . . realistically allow only homes within the financial reach of persons of at least middle income. The R-1 zone requires a minimum lot area of 9,375 square feet, a minimum lot width of 75 feet at the building line, and a minimum dwelling floor area of 1,100 square feet if a one-story building. . . . Originally this zone comprised about 2,500 acres. Most of the subdivisions have been constructed within it so that only a few hundred acres remain. . . . The R-2 zone, comprising a single district of 141 acres in the northeasterly corner, has been completely developed. While it only required a minimum floor area of 900 square feet for a one-story dwelling, the minimum lot size was 11,000 square feet; otherwise the requisites were the same as in the R-1 zone.

The general ordinance places [almost all of] the remainder of the township . . . in the R-3 zone. This zone comprises over 7,000 acres. . . . The testimony was that about 4,600 acres of it then remained available for housing development. Ordinance requirements are substantially higher, however, in that the minimum lot size is increased to about one-half acre (20,000 square feet). . . . Lot width at the building line must be 100 feet. Minimum dwelling floor area is as in the R-1 zone. Presently this section is primarily in agricultural use. . . .

The record thoroughly substantiates the findings of the trial court that over the years Mount Laurel "has acted affirmatively to control development and to attract a selective type of growth" and that "through its zoning ordinances has exhibited economic discrimination in that the poor have been deprived of adequate housing and the opportunity to secure the construction of subsidized housing, and has used federal, state, county and local finances and resources solely for the betterment of middle and upper-income persons." . . .

This pattern of land use regulation has been adopted for the same purpose in developing municipality after developing municipality. Almost every one acts solely in its own selfish and parochial interest and in effect builds a wall around itself to keep out those people or entities not adding favorably to the tax base, despite the location of the municipality or the demand for varied kinds of housing. . . .

II.

The legal question before us . . . is whether a developing municipality like Mount Laurel may validly, by a system of land use regulation, make it physically and economically impossible to provide low and moderate income housing in the municipality for the various categories of persons who need and want it and thereby, as Mount Laurel has, exclude such people from living within its confines because of the limited extent of their income and resources. . . .

We conclude that every such municipality must, by its land use regulations, presumptively make realistically possible an appropriate variety and choice of housing. More specifically, presumptively it cannot foreclose the opportunity of the classes of people mentioned for low and moderate income housing and in its regulations must affirmatively afford that opportunity, at least to the extent of the municipality's fair share of the present and prospective regional need therefor. These obligations must be met unless the particular municipality can sustain the heavy burden of demonstrating peculiar circumstances which dictate that it should not be required so to do.

We reach this conclusion under state law and so do not find it necessary to consider federal constitutional grounds urged by plaintiffs. We begin with some fundamental principles as applied to the scene before us. . . . .

It is elementary theory that all police power enactments, no matter at what level of government, must conform to the basic state constitutional requirements of substantive due process and equal protection of the laws. These are inherent in art. I, par. 1 of our Constitution, the requirements of which may be more demanding than those of the federal Constitution. It is required that, affirmatively, a zoning regulation, like any police power enactment, must promote public health, safety, morals or the general welfare. . . .

[Prior decisions have raised the issue] of *whose* general welfare must be served or not violated in the field of land use regulation. Frequently the decisions in this state . . . have spoken only in terms of the interest of the enacting municipality, so that it has been thought, at least in some quarters, that such was the only welfare requiring consideration. . . . However, it is fundamental and not to be forgotten that the zoning power is a police power of the state and the local authority is acting only as a delegate of that power and is restricted in the same manner as is the state. So, when regulation does have a substantial external impact, the welfare of the state's citizens beyond the borders of the particular municipality cannot be disregarded and must be recognized and served. . . .

> **Make the Connection**
>
> How does the test for evaluating a zoning regulation under the New Jersey state constitution differ from the *Euclid* approach?

It is plain beyond dispute that proper provision for adequate housing of all categories of people is certainly an absolute essential in promotion of the general welfare required in all local land use regulation. Further the universal and constant need for such housing is so important and of such broad public interest that the general welfare which developing municipalities like Mount Laurel must consider extends beyond their boundaries and cannot be parochially confined to the claimed good of the particular municipality. It has to follow that, broadly speaking, the presumptive obligation arises for each such municipality affirmatively to plan and provide, by its land use regulations, the reasonable opportunity for an appropriate variety and choice of housing, including, of course, low and moderate cost housing, to meet the needs, desires and resources of all categories of people who may desire to live within its boundaries. Negatively, it may not adopt regulations or policies which thwart or preclude that opportunity. . . .

Mount Laurel's zoning ordinance is . . . so restrictive in its minimum lot area, lot frontage and building size requirements, earlier detailed, as to preclude single-family housing for even moderate income families. Required lot area of at least 9,375 square feet in one remaining regular residential zone and 20,000 square feet (almost half an acre) in the other, with required frontage of 75 and 100 feet, respectively, cannot be called small lots and amounts to low density zoning, very definitely increasing the cost of purchasing and improving land and so affecting the cost of housing. As to building size, the township's general requirements of a minimum dwelling floor area of 1,100 square feet for all one-story houses and 1,300 square feet for all of one and one-half stories or higher is without regard to required minimum lot size or frontage or the number of occupants.... Again it is evident these requirements increase the size and so the cost of housing. The conclusion is irresistible that Mount Laurel permits only such middle and upper income housing as it believes will have sufficient taxable value to come close to paying its own governmental way.

Akin to large lot, single-family zoning restricting the population is the zoning of very large amounts of land for industrial and related uses. Mount Laurel has set aside almost 30% of its area, over 4,100 acres, for that purpose; the only residential use allowed is for farm dwellings. In almost a decade only about 100 acres have been developed industrially.... [I]t seems plain that the likelihood of anywhere near the whole of the zoned area being used for the intended purpose in the foreseeable future is remote indeed and that an unreasonable amount of land has thereby been removed from possible residential development, again seemingly for local fiscal reasons.

Without further elaboration at this point, our opinion is that Mount Laurel's zoning ordinance is presumptively contrary to the general welfare and outside the intended scope of the zoning power in the particulars mentioned. A facial showing of invalidity is thus established, shifting to the municipality the burden of establishing valid superseding reasons for its action and non-action. We now examine the reasons it advances.

The township's principal reason in support of its zoning plan and ordinance housing provisions, advanced especially strongly at oral argument, is the fiscal one previously adverted to, *i.e.*, that by reason of New Jersey's tax structure which substantially finances municipal governmental and educational costs from taxes on local real property, every municipality may, by the exercise of the zoning power, allow only such uses and to such extent as will be beneficial to the local tax rate. In other words, the position is that any municipality may zone extensively to seek and encourage the "good" tax ratables of industry and commerce and limit the permissible types of housing to those having the fewest school children or to those providing sufficient value to attain or approach paying their own way taxwise.

> **Food for Thought**
>
> What "valid superseding reasons" would allow a New Jersey city to avoid the *Mount Laurel* mandate?

... We have no hesitancy in now saying, and do so emphatically, that, considering the basic importance of the opportunity for appropriate housing for all classes of our citizenry, no municipality may exclude or limit categories of housing for that reason or purpose....

By way of summary, what we have said comes down to this. As a developing municipality, Mount Laurel must, by its land use regulations, make realistically possible the opportunity for an appropriate variety and choice of housing for all categories of people who may desire to live there, of course including those of low and moderate income. It must permit multifamily housing, without bedroom or similar restrictions, as well as small dwellings on very small lots, low cost housing of other types and, in general, high density zoning, without artificial and unjustifiable minimum requirements as to lot size, building size and the like, to meet the full panoply of these needs. . . .

III.

. . . [T]he trial court invalidated the zoning ordinance in *toto* and ordered the township to make certain studies and investigations and to present to the court a plan of affirmative public action designed "to enable and encourage the satisfaction of the indicated needs" for township related low and moderate income housing. . . .

We are not at all sure what the trial judge had in mind as ultimate action with reference to the approval of a plan for affirmative public action concerning the satisfaction of indicated housing needs and the entry of a final order requiring implementation thereof. Courts do not build housing nor do municipalities. . . . It is not appropriate at this time . . . to deal with the matter of the further extent of judicial power in the field or to exercise any such power. The municipality should first have full opportunity to itself act without judicial supervision. We trust it will do so in the spirit we have suggested. . . .

> **Food for Thought**
>
> How small can a "small dwelling" be? Must a New Jersey municipality allow "tiny homes," which usually range from 100 to 400 square feet? *See* Lisa T. Alexander, *Community in Property: Lessons from Tiny Homes Villages*, 104 Minn. L. Rev. 385 (2019).

Points for Discussion

a. Intent v. Effect

A zoning ordinance enacted with the *intent* to exclude racial or ethnic minorities would violate the Equal Protection Clause of the Fourteenth Amendment to the Constitution. But the *Mount Laurel* court accepted the township's representation that its ordinance was not adopted "with any desire or intent" to exclude minority groups.

In *Village of Arlington Heights v. Metropolitan Housing Development Corp.*, 429 U.S. 252 (1977), the Supreme Court ruled that a zoning ordinance with a discriminatory *effect* did not violate the Equal Protection Clause. Notice that the *Mount Laurel* court based its decision on the New Jersey state constitution. A number of jurisdictions have endorsed the *Mount Laurel* approach.

But an ordinance with a discriminatory *effect* may violate the Fair Housing Act. For example, in *United States v. City of Black Jack*, 508 F.2d 1179 (8th Cir. 1974), the court ruled that a "virtually all white" city violated the Act by adopting an ordinance that prohibited construction of any new multi-family dwellings and thereby prevented "85 percent of the blacks living in the metropolitan area from obtaining housing in Black Jack." *Id.* at 1183, 1186. *See also Martinez v. City of Clovis,* 307 Cal. Rptr. 3d 64, 106 (App. 2023) (plaintiff adequately pleaded a claim under the Act where "City failed to accommodate and provide opportunities to develop lower income housing" which had a disparate impact on people of color); John G. Sprankling, *The Constitutional Right to "Establish A Home,"* 90 Geo. Wash. L. Rev. 632 (2022) (arguing that the Due Process Clause of the Fourteenth Amendment bars governments from unduly interfering with a person's ability to rent or own a home).

b. **Defining the Doctrine**

How would you explain the *Mount Laurel* doctrine to a client? What is a "developing" municipality? And what does the decision require such a municipality to do, exactly? Suppose that City D changes its land use regulations to comply with *Mount Laurel,* but no one builds affordable housing there. Is the city obligated to do something more? If so, what?

c. **Other Approaches?**

As the *Mount Laurel* court summarized: "Almost every [municipality] acts solely in its own selfish and parochial interest and in effect builds a wall around itself to keep out those people or entities not adding favorably to the tax base . . . ." Is *Mount Laurel* the best approach to this problem? What other approaches might be considered? Would you have dissented from the decision and, if so, why?

Unlike Mount Laurel, some jurisdictions have adopted *inclusionary zoning* ordinances, which require developers to sell a certain percentage of their new housing units at prices that low and moderate income families can afford. *See, e.g., California Building Industry Ass'n v. City of San Jose,* 351 P.3d 974 (Cal. 2015) (upholding ordinance which mandates that at least 15% of units in new housing projects be sold on this basis).

d. **Democratic Values**

Do residents have the right to decide the future of their city? In *Mount Laurel,* the zoning ordinance was adopted by the duly-elected members of the township council. Should a court intervene in this democratic process? How can candidates for a city council effectively campaign for office if their future actions as council members are circumscribed by obligations to non-residents?

e. **Land Use Feudalism?**

Land use in the United States has been criticized as a "feudal system under which the entire pattern of land development [is] controlled by thousands of individual local governments, each seeking to maximize its tax base and minimize its social problems, and caring less about what happens to all the others." Fred Bosselman & David Callies, The Quiet Revolution in Land Use Control 1 (1971). True, Oregon has a state-wide land use planning system, and a number of states (including Florida and Vermont) have some form of regional land use management. But most land use decisions are still made by local governments, mainly cities and counties—and this situation raises the concerns discussed in *Mount Laurel*. What are the benefits and costs of this approach?

f.   Aftermath of *Mount Laurel*

The New Jersey Supreme Court's hope that Mount Laurel would act "in the spirit we have suggested" proved to be futile. Only 20 acres of land were rezoned for multi-family housing, and these areas were not suitable for residential development. In the successor case of *Southern Burlington County NAACP v. Township of Mount Laurel*, 456 A.2d 390, 410 (N.J. 1983), the court lamented: "We have learned from experience . . . that unless a strong judicial hand is used, *Mount Laurel* will not result in housing, but in paper, process, witnesses, trials, and appeals." It accordingly held that the *Mount Laurel* test would be satisfied only "if the municipality has *in fact* provided a realistic opportunity for the construction of its fair share of low and moderate income housing." *Id.* at 421. State legislation and more litigation ensued.

In 1997, the township finally approved plans for the housing project that sparked the litigation. When the development was completed in 2000, it was named "Ethel R. Lawrence Homes" in honor of the activist who had died six years earlier.

Ethel R. Lawrence Homes
Click here for larger photo

Summary

- **Nuisance Liability.** An intentional, nontrespassory, unreasonable, and substantial interference with the use and enjoyment of land is a private nuisance.

- **Remedies for Nuisance.** The traditional remedy for a nuisance was an injunction. Today courts usually balance the equities to determine if the appropriate remedy is an injunction or damages.

- **Origins of Zoning.** Zoning began as a utilitarian response to rapid industrialization and urbanization during the early twentieth century. Government has the inherent police power to protect the public health, safety, morals, and welfare through land use regulation.

- **Constitutionality of Zoning.** The Supreme Court upheld the constitutionality of zoning in *Village of Euclid v. Ambler Realty Co.* Under the *Euclid* standard, zoning is valid unless it is arbitrary and unreasonable, having no substantial relation to the public health, safety, morals, or welfare. This standard reflects judicial deference to legislative decisions.

- **From Rigidity to Flexibility.** Euclidean zoning is dying a slow death, as local governments increasingly move toward more flexible forms of land use regulation. While this increased flexibility should improve the quality of land use decisions, it necessarily vests more discretion in local officials, which creates an increased risk of improper influence.

- **Nonconforming Uses.** Prior nonconforming uses are exempt from new zoning ordinances, but may be terminated by abandonment, destruction, eminent domain, nuisance law, or, in most jurisdictions, amortization.

- **Zoning Amendments.** The constitutionality of a zoning amendment is generally determined under the deferential *Euclid* standard, which raises the risk of government corruption. The spot zoning doctrine is the most important tool used to combat this problem.

- **Variances.** A variance is an authorized deviation from the literal terms of the zoning ordinance in order to avoid special hardship arising from physical conditions on a particular tract of land.

- **Conditional Uses.** A conditional use is a use that is permitted under certain conditions specified in the zoning ordinance.

- **Expanded Goals of Land Use Regulation.** Land use regulation has evolved to serve new goals, such as protecting property values, preserving the environment, and expanding the property tax base. Given the deferential *Euclid* standard, it is likely that the scope of land use regulation will continue to expand over time.

- **Aesthetic Regulation.** Despite extensive controversy, aesthetic regulation is now widely accepted in the United States; the most common justification

> **Test Your Knowledge**
>
> To assess your understanding of the material in this chapter, click here to take a quiz.

is that it protects property values. However, the First Amendment restricts the scope of such regulation.

- **Family Zoning.** Courts generally uphold zoning ordinances which provide that only members of a "family" may occupy a single-family residence. However, a zoning ordinance that prevents family members from living together is subject to a more searching scope of review.

- **Growth Controls and Exclusion.** A temporary moratorium on development will be upheld when supported by a rational basis. Increasingly, courts are limiting the ability of local governments to adopt land use regulations which have the effect of excluding minorities or the poor.

For More Information

For more information about land use regulation, please consult these sources:

- Steve P. Calandrillo et al., *Making "Smart Growth" Smarter*, 83 Geo. Wash. L. Rev. 829 (2015).
- Patricia E. Salkin, *From* Euclid *to Growing Smart: The Transformation of the American Local Land Use Ethic into Land Use and Environmental Controls*, 20 Pace Envtl. L. Rev. 109 (2002).
- Christopher Serkin, *A Case for Zoning*, 96 Notre Dame L. Rev. 749 (2020).
- Michael Allan Wolf, *A Common Law of Zoning*, 61 Ariz. L. Rev. 771 (2019).
- Michael Allan Wolf, The Zoning of America: *Euclid v. Ambler* (2008).

CHAPTER 12

An Introduction to Environmental Law

The boundary line between property law and environmental law is imprecise—and perhaps nonexistent. Many environmental law doctrines affect how property can be used; and property law concepts are sometimes applied to solve environmental problems. In this chapter, we examine the common ground shared by these two bodies of law.

Environmental law began to develop in the United States during the 1960s, sparked by Rachel Carson's book Silent Spring which exposed the dangers of the pesticide DDT. A series of federal environmental statutes followed, each aimed at a different problem: pesticides, air, water, toxics, endangered species, wilderness areas, and so forth. Taken together, they create a comprehensive federal regulatory framework that sometimes intersects with state laws governing property.

A. Property and Ecology

Is land different from other types of property? The dominant view underlying American property law is that land is a commodity, much like apples or wheat. We now turn to a different perspective—an ecological view of property. As you read the materials below, consider the implications of this approach.

Does an owner have a right to transform his land for beneficial economic use? Or could the law require that land remain in its natural condition? These questions arise in our first case, set on the shoreline of Lake Noquebay in Wisconsin.

Just v. Marinette County

Supreme Court of Wisconsin

201 N.W.2d 761 (1972)

HALLOWS, CHIEF JUSTICE.

[The Justs owned land fronting on Lake Noquebay in Marinette County; it was designated as "swamps or marshes" by the U.S. Geological Survey. In 1967, the County adopted an ordinance which rezoned the Justs' land and other shoreline properties into the "conservancy district," where only a few uses were permitted as a matter of right, such as harvesting wild crops, hunting, and fishing. However, an owner could apply for a conditional use permit to bring fill material onto his property, to farm, or to engage in certain other uses. The Justs violated the ordinance by placing fill material on their property without a permit. They sued the County, arguing that the ordinance was a taking of their land in violation of the Fifth Amendment.]. . . .

This case causes us to reexamine the concepts of public benefit in contrast to public harm and the scope of an owner's right to use of his property. In the instant case we have a restriction on the use of a citizen's property, not to secure a benefit for the public, but to prevent a harm from the change in the natural character of the citizen's property. We start with the premise that lakes and rivers in their natural state are unpolluted and the pollution which now exists is man made. The state of Wisconsin under the trust doctrine has a duty to eradicate the present pollution and to prevent further pollution in its navigable waters. This is not, in a legal sense, a gain or a securing of a benefit by the maintaining of the natural *status quo* of the environment. What makes this case different from most condemnation or police power zoning cases is the interrelationship of the wetlands, the swamps and the natural environment of shorelands to the purity of the water and to such natural resources as navigation, fishing, and scenic beauty. Swamps and wetlands were once considered wasteland, undesirable, and not picturesque. But as the people became more sophisticated, an appreciation was acquired that swamps and wetlands serve a vital role in nature, are part of the balance of nature and are essential to the purity of the water in our lakes and streams. Swamps and wetlands are a necessary part of the ecological creation and now, even to the uninitiated, possess their own beauty in nature.

> **See It**
>
> Click here to see a photograph of the south shore of Lake Noquebay, close to the location of the Justs' property.

Is the ownership of a parcel of land so absolute that man can change its nature to suit any of his purposes? The great forests of our state were stripped on the theory man's ownership was unlimited. But in forestry, the land at least was used naturally, only the natural fruit of the land (the trees) were taken. The despoilage was in the failure to look to the future and provide for the reforestation of the land. An owner of land has no absolute and unlimited right to change the essential natural character of his land so as to use it for a purpose for which it was unsuited in its natural state and which injures the rights of others. The exercise of the police power in zoning must be reasonable and we think it is not an unreasonable exercise of that power to prevent harm to public rights by limiting the use of private property to its natural uses.

This is not a case where an owner is prevented from using his land for natural and indigenous uses. The uses consistent with the nature of the land are allowed and other uses recognized and still others permitted by special permit. The shoreland zoning ordinance prevents to some extent the changing of the natural character of the land within 1,000 feet of a navigable lake and 300 feet of a navigable river because of such land's interrelation to the contiguous water. The changing of wetlands and swamps to the damage of the general public by upsetting the natural environment and the natural relationship is not a reasonable use of that land which is protected from police power regulation. Changes and filling to some extent are permitted because the extent of such changes and fillings does not cause harm. We realize no case in Wisconsin has yet dealt with shoreland regulations and there are several cases in other states which seem to hold such regulations unconstitutional; but nothing this court has said or held in prior cases indicate that destroying the natural character of a swamp or a wetland so as to make that location available for human habitation is a reasonable use of that land when the new use, although of a more economical value to the owner, causes a harm to the general public. . . .

Perspective and Analysis

Professor Joseph Sax explores the ecological view of property in his article excerpted below. How does his perspective compare to the court's analysis in *Just*?

> There are two fundamentally different views of property rights to which I shall refer as land in the "transformative economy" and land in the "economy of nature." The conventional perspective of private property, the transformative economy, builds on the image of property as a discrete entity that can be made one's own by working it and transforming it into a human artifact. A piece of iron becomes an anvil, a tree becomes lumber, and a forest becomes a farm. Traditional property law treats undeveloped land as essentially inert. The land is there, it may have things on or in it (e.g., timber or coal), but it is in a passive state, waiting to be put to use. . . .
>
> An ecological view of property, the economy of nature, is fundamentally different. Land is not a passive entity waiting to be transformed by its

> landowner. Nor is the world comprised of distinct tracts of land, separate pieces independent of each other. Rather, an ecological perspective views land as consisting of systems defined by their function, not by man-made boundaries. Land is already at work, performing important services in its unaltered state. For example, forests regulate the global climate, marshes sustain marine fisheries, and prairie grass holds the soil in place. Transformation diminishes the functioning of this economy and, in fact, is at odds with it. . . .
>
> Viewing land through the lens of nature's economy reduces the significance of property lines. Thus a wetland would be an adjunct of a river, in service to the river as a natural resource. Beach dune land would be the frontal region of a coastal ecosystem extending far beyond the beach itself. A forest would be a habitat for birds and wildlife, rather than simply a discrete tract of land containing the commodity timber. Under such a view the landowner cannot justify development by simply internalizing the effect of such development on other properties. Rather, the landowner's desire to do anything at all creates a problem, because any development affects the delicate ecosystem which the untouched land supports. In an economy of nature the landowner's role is perforce custodial at the outset, before the owner ever transforms the land. Moreover, the object of the custody generally extends beyond the owner's legally defined dominion. The notion that land is solely the owner's property, to develop as the owner pleases, is unacceptable. . . .
>
> **Joseph L. Sax, *Property Rights and the Economy of Nature: Understanding Lucas v. South Carolina Coastal Council*, 45 Stan. L. Rev. 1433, 1442, 1444–45 (1993).**

Points for Discussion

a. **Rethinking *Just***

Should an owner have the right to change the natural character of his land in order to use it for a productive purpose? Under the Marinette County ordinance, the Justs could not even build a home on their land. Why not? Would it be a nuisance? In Chapter 1, we studied the scope of the right to destroy property. Is that concept relevant here?

b. **An Ecological Perspective**

What is your reaction to the ecological view of property advanced by Professor Sax? He criticizes the "notion that land is solely the owner's property, to develop as the owner pleases. . . ." Under traditional utilitarian theory, should there be any limits on an owner's ability to develop his land as he chooses? If so, what? For more discussion of these issues, see Eric T. Freyfogle, *The Owning and Taking of Sensitive Lands,* 43 UCLA L. Rev. 77 (1995).

c. A Green Theory of Property?

Professor Peter Byrne argued that property law should be reformulated to implement the "ecological land ethic, as formulated by such thinkers as Aldo Leopold, which emphasize the moral duty of humanity to act as a steward of natural life." J. Peter Byrne, *Green Property*, 7 Const. Comment. 239, 243 (1990). He suggested these standards:

> (1) Any change in the character of land that impairs its natural value would require a permit.
>
> (2) No permit would be granted unless the development served a compelling human need.
>
> (3) If the development appears to cause some specific harm to the environment not directly forbidden by positive regulations . . . it can be permitted only if:
>
>> (a) it will be accomplished with the minimum of environmental damage,
>>
>> (b) the developer will pay in dollars the costs of environmental damage, and
>>
>> (c) the human gains from development substantially exceed the environmental harm from the project.

What is your view of this proposal? What impact would it have on the national economy? On traditional concepts of land ownership?

B. Water and Wetlands

As *Just* reflects, water and wetlands were traditionally subject to more governmental oversight than other types of property. As the young United States developed, the ability to freely transport goods on rivers, lakes, and other navigable waters was vital for commerce. Fishing was a major sector of the economy, so the protection of fisheries was also important. Accordingly, navigable waters and their shorelines have long been protected by various legal doctrines. These doctrines were developed to support what Professor Sax calls the "transformative economy." But over time, their focus has enlarged to serve environmental goals as well.

Our next case explores the *public trust doctrine*, which you encountered in Chapter 10. Los Angeles is a sprawling city built in a semi-arid region, without adequate drinking water for its population. For decades, the city has held legal rights to water that it imports from the Sierra Nevadas in Northern California. But can the city exercise those rights in a manner that damages the environment?

National Audubon Society v. Superior Court

Supreme Court of California

658 P.2d 709 (1983), *cert. denied*, 464 U.S. 977 (1983)

BROUSSARD, JUSTICE.

    Mono Lake, the second largest lake in California, sits at the base of the Sierra Nevada escarpment near the eastern entrance to Yosemite National Park. The lake is saline; it contains no fish but supports a large population of brine shrimp which feed vast numbers of nesting and migratory birds. Islands in the lake protect a large breeding colony of California gulls, and the lake itself serves as a haven on the migration route for thousands of Northern Phalarope, Wilson's Phalarope, and Eared Greve. Towers and spires of tufa on the north and south shores are matters of geological interest and a tourist attraction.

    Although Mono Lake receives some water from rain and snow on the lake surface, historically most of its supply came from snowmelt in the Sierra Nevada. Five freshwater streams—Mill, Lee Vining, Walker, Parker and Rush Creeks—arise near the crest of the range and carry the annual runoff to the west shore of the lake. In 1940, however, the Division of Water Resources, the predecessor to the present California Water Resources Board, granted the Department of Water and Power of the City of Los Angeles (hereafter DWP) a permit to appropriate virtually the entire flow of four of the five streams flowing into the lake. DWP promptly constructed facilities to divert about half the flow of these streams into DWP's Owens Valley aqueduct. In 1970 DWP completed a second diversion tunnel, and since that time has taken virtually the entire flow of these streams.

    As a result of these diversions, the level of the lake has dropped; the surface area has diminished by one-third; one of the two principal islands in the lake has become a peninsula, exposing the gull rookery there to coyotes and other predators and causing the gulls to abandon the former island. The ultimate effect of continued diversions is a matter of intense dispute, but there seems little doubt that both the scenic beauty and the ecological values of Mono Lake are imperiled.

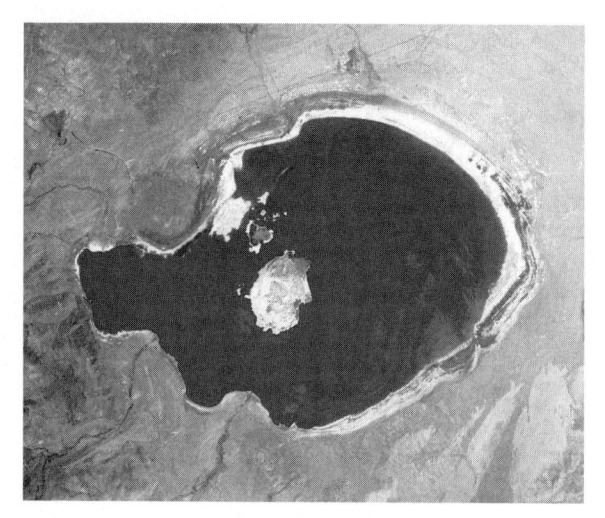

Aerial photo of Mono Lake
Click here for larger photo

Plaintiffs filed suit in superior court to enjoin the DWP diversions on the theory that the shores, bed and waters of Mono Lake are protected by a public trust. . . .

This case brings together for the first time two systems of legal thought: the appropriative water rights system which since the days of the gold rush has dominated California water law, and the public trust doctrine which, after evolving as a shield for the protection of tidelands, now extends its protective scope to navigable lakes. Ever since we first recognized that the public trust protects environmental and recreational values (*Marks v. Whitney* (1971) 6 Cal.3d 251, 98 Cal.Rptr. 790, 491 P.2d 374), the two systems of legal thought have been on a collision course. They meet in a unique and dramatic setting which highlights the clash of values. Mono Lake is a scenic and ecological treasure of national significance, imperiled by continued diversions of water; yet, the need of Los Angeles for water is apparent, its reliance on rights granted by the board evident, the cost of curtailing diversions substantial. . . .

2. *The Public Trust Doctrine in California.*

"By the law of nature these things are common to mankind—the air, running water, the sea and consequently the shores of the sea." (Institutes of Justinian 2.1.1.) From this origin in Roman law, the English common law evolved the concept of the public trust, under which the sovereign owns "all of its navigable waterways and the lands lying beneath them 'as trustee of a public trust for the benefit of the people.'" (*Colberg, Inc. v. State of California ex rel. Dept. Pub. Works* (1967) 67 Cal.2d 408, 416, 62 Cal.Rptr. 401, 432 P.2d 3.) The State of California acquired title as trustee to such lands and waterways upon its admission to the union; from the earliest days its judicial decisions have recognized and enforced the trust obligation.

Three aspects of the public trust doctrine require consideration in this opinion: the purpose of the trust; the scope of the trust, particularly as it applies to the non-navigable tributaries of a navigable lake; and the powers and duties of the state as trustee of the public trust. We discuss these questions in the order listed.

(a) *The purpose of the public trust.*

The objective of the public trust has evolved in tandem with the changing public perception of the values and uses of waterways. As we observed in *Marks v. Whitney, supra,* 6 Cal.3d 251, 98 Cal.Rptr. 790, 491 P.2d 374, "[p]ublic trust easements [were] traditionally defined in terms of navigation, commerce and fisheries. They have been held to include the right to fish, hunt, bathe, swim, to use for boating and general recreation purposes the navigable waters of the state, and to use the bottom of the navigable waters for anchoring, standing, or other purposes." (P. 259, 98 Cal. Rptr. 790, 491 P.2d 374.) We went on, however, to hold that the traditional triad of uses . . . did not limit the public interest in the trust res. In language of special importance to the present setting, we stated that

> [t]he public uses to which tidelands are subject are sufficiently flexible to encompass changing public needs. In administering the trust the state is not burdened with an outmoded classification favoring one mode of utilization over another. . . . There is a growing public recognition that one of the most important public uses of the tidelands—a use encompassed within the tidelands trust—is the preservation of those lands in their natural state, so that they may serve as ecological units for scientific study, as open space, and as environments which provide food and habitat for birds and marine life, and which favorably affect the scenery and climate of the area.

(Pp. 259–260, 98 Cal.Rptr. 790, 491 P.2d 374.)

Mono Lake is a navigable waterway. It supports a small local industry which harvests brine shrimp for sale as fish food, which endeavor probably qualifies the lake as a "fishery" under the traditional public trust cases. The principal values plaintiffs seek to protect, however, are recreational and ecological—the scenic views of the lake and its shore, the purity of the air, and the use of the lake for nesting and feeding by birds. Under *Marks v. Whitney, supra,* 6 Cal.3d 251, 98 Cal.Rptr. 790, 491 P.2d 374, it is clear that protection of these values is among the purposes of the public trust.

(b) *The scope of the public trust.*

. . . It is . . . well settled in the United States generally and in California that the public trust is not limited by the reach of the tides, but encompasses all navigable lakes and streams.

Mono Lake is, as we have said, a navigable waterway. The beds, shores and waters of the lake are without question protected by the public trust. The streams diverted by DWP, however, are not themselves navigable. Accordingly, we must address in this case a question not discussed in any recent public trust case—whether the public trust limits conduct affecting nonnavigable tributaries to navigable waterways.

This question was considered in ... *People v. Gold Run D. & M. Co.* (1884) 66 Cal. 138, 4 P. 1152,... one of the epochal decisions of California history, a signpost which marked the transition from a mining economy to one predominately commercial and agricultural. The Gold Run Ditch and Mining Company and other mining operators used huge water cannon to wash gold-bearing gravel from hillsides; in the process they dumped 600,000 cubic yards of sand and gravel annually into the north fork of the American River. The debris, washed downstream, raised the beds of the American and Sacramento Rivers, impairing navigation, polluting the waters, and creating the danger that in time of flood the rivers would turn from their channels and inundate nearby lands.

> **See It**
>
> Click here to see water cannon being used in hydraulic mining during the 1860s in California's gold country.

Although recognizing that its decision might destroy the remains of the state's gold mining industry, the court affirmed an injunction barring the dumping.... Rejecting the argument that dumping was sanctioned by custom and legislative acquiescence, the opinion asserted that

> the rights of the people in the navigable rivers of the State are paramount and controlling. The State holds the absolute right to all navigable waters and the soils under them.... The soil she holds as trustee of a public trust for the benefit of the people; and she may, by her legislature, grant it to an individual; but she cannot grant the rights of the people to the use of the navigable waters flowing over it....

(Pp. 151–152, 4 P. 1152.)....

We conclude that the public trust doctrine, as recognized and developed in California decisions, protects navigable waters from harm caused by diversion of nonnavigable tributaries.

(c) *Duties and powers of the state as trustee.*

In the following review of the authority and obligations of the state as administrator of the public trust, the dominant theme is the state's sovereign power and duty to exercise continued supervision over the trust. One consequence, of importance to this and many other cases, is that parties acquiring rights in trust property generally hold those rights subject to the trust, and can assert no vested right to use those rights in a manner harmful to the trust....

Thus, the public trust is more than an affirmation of state power to use public property for public purposes. It is an affirmation of the duty of the state to protect the people's common heritage of streams, lakes, marshlands and tidelands, surrendering that right of protection only in rare cases when the abandonment of that right is consistent with the purposes of the trust....

4. *The relationship between the Public Trust Doctrine and the California Water Rights System.*

As we have seen, the public trust doctrine and the appropriative water rights system administered by the Water Board developed independently of each other. Each developed comprehensive rules and principles which, if applied to the full extent of their scope, would occupy the field of allocation of stream waters to the exclusion of any competing system of legal thought. . . .

We are unable to accept either position. . . . Therefore, seeking an accommodation which will make use of the pertinent principles of both the public trust doctrine and the appropriative water rights system, and drawing upon the history of the public trust and the water rights system, the body of judicial precedent, and the views of expert commentators, we reach the following conclusions:

a. The state as sovereign retains continuing supervisory control over its navigable waters and the lands beneath those waters. This principle, fundamental to the concept of the public trust, applies to rights in flowing waters as well as to rights in tidelands and lakeshores; it prevents any party from acquiring a vested right to appropriate water in a manner harmful to the interests protected by the public trust. . . .

b. As a matter of current and historical necessity, the Legislature, acting directly or through an authorized agency such as the Water Board, has the power to grant usufructuary licenses that will permit an appropriator to take water from flowing streams and use that water in a distant part of the state, even though this taking does not promote, and may unavoidably harm, the trust uses at the source stream. The population and economy of this state depend upon the appropriation of vast quantities of water for uses unrelated to in-stream trust values. . . .

c. The state has an affirmative duty to take the public trust into account in the planning and allocation of water resources, and to protect public trust uses whenever feasible. Just as the history of this state shows that appropriation may be necessary for efficient use of water despite unavoidable harm to public trust values, it demonstrates that an appropriative water rights system administered without consideration of the public trust may cause unnecessary and unjustified harm to trust interests. . . .

Once the state has approved an appropriation, the public trust imposes a duty of continuing supervision over the taking and use of the appropriated water. In exercising its sovereign power to allocate water resources in the public interest, the state is not confined by past allocation decisions which may be incorrect in light of current knowledge or inconsistent with current needs. . . .

It is clear that some responsible body ought to reconsider the allocation of the waters of the Mono Basin. No vested rights bar such reconsideration. We recognize the substantial concerns voiced by Los Angeles—the city's need for water, its reliance upon the 1940 board decision, the cost both in terms of money and environmental impact of obtaining water elsewhere. Such concerns must enter into any allocation decision.

We hold only that they do not preclude a reconsideration and reallocation which also takes into account the impact of water diversion on the Mono Lake environment. . . .

Points for Discussion

a. **Public Trust Doctrine**

Under this doctrine, navigable waters and related lands are deemed to be owned in trust by the sovereign for the benefit of the public. In the landmark case of *Illinois Central R.R. Co. v. Illinois*, 146 U.S. 387, 452 (1892), the Supreme Court explained that it was "a title held in trust for the people of the State that they may enjoy the navigation of the waters, carry on commerce over them, and have liberty of fishing therein." *See* Joseph L. Sax, *The Public Trust Doctrine in Natural Resource Law: Effective Judicial Intervention*, 68 Mich. L. Rev. 471 (1970); Gerald Torres & Nathan Bellinger, *The Public Trust: The Law's DNA*, 4 Wake Forest J. L. & Pol'y 281 (2014). How did the *National Audubon Society* court define the purpose of the trust?

b. **Bundle of Rights**

If a private owner obtains title to public trust land, his ability to use the land is restricted by the trust. Suppose D purchases coastal land that is subject to the ebb and flow of the ocean; it is only above water at low tide. Does D have the right to build a home on the land? No, because this would conflict with the historic purposes of the trust: navigation and fishing. The theory is that when D acquired title, the bundle of rights he received did not include the right to violate the public trust. *See Marks v. Whitney*, 491 P.2d 374 (Cal. 1971). In *National Audubon Society*, the court had to strike a balance between two arguably inconsistent bodies of law: the public trust doctrine and the principles governing water rights. In the vast majority of cases, such a conflict does not exist. How would the *National Audubon Society* court decide *Just*?

c. **Defining the Trust**

What property is protected by the trust? States differ on the scope of the trust. For example, in California it applies to ocean waters, tidal wetlands, the wet-sand ocean beach, navigable bodies of water, and to certain fresh water wetlands. *National Audubon Society* seems to expand the trust to encompass nonnavigable tributaries of navigable waters. If the scope of the public trust expands over time, how does this affect private owners of land subject to the trust? Are their property rights correspondingly reduced? For an analysis of how the public trust doctrine is defined in different jurisdictions, see Robin Kundis Craig, *A Comparative Guide to the Western States' Public Trust Doctrines: Public Values, Private Rights, and the Evolution Toward an Ecological Public Trust*, 37 Ecology L.Q. 53 (2010).

Is groundwater extraction limited by the public trust doctrine? Conflicts over groundwater are increasing in the United States. For example, in *White Bear Lake Restoration Association v. Minnesota Department of Natural Resources*, 946 N.W.2d 373 (Minn. 2020), non-profit organizations alleged that groundwater pumping pursuant to state-issued permits had caused the lake's water level to drop; they argued that this violated the common-law public trust doctrine. On appeal, the Minnesota Supreme Court refused to extend the doctrine to cover this situation, holding that plaintiffs' claims were exclusively governed by the statutory framework addressing water use. *But see Environmental Law Found. v. State Water Resources Control Bd.*, 237 Cal. Rptr. 3d 393 (App. 2018) (public trust doctrine applied to groundwater extraction that lowered water level in a hydrologically connected river).

d. **Exercises**

Are the following government actions justified by the public trust doctrine?

> (1) In 1950, L purchased an oceanfront lot in State S that had been flooded every day at high tide for decades. Over time, the natural contours of the beach in front of the lot changed to the point where the lot was never inundated by seawater except during unusually strong storms. In order to protect lives and property from storm damage, State S adopts a statute that bars L from building any structure on the lot.
>
> (2) A navigable mountain lake in State C is renowned for the clarity of its waters. A nonnavigable stream flows into the lake. Scientists discover that silt brought in by the stream is reducing the lake's clarity. The silt is produced when construction occurs on the hillsides surrounding the lake. Once the natural land surface is disturbed, rainwater gradually washes silt downhill into the stream and then into the lake. State C adopts a statute that prohibits any construction within 1,000 feet of the stream.

e. **Aftermath of *National Audubon Society***

Litigation over Mono Lake continued for ten years after the Supreme Court decision. In 1993, Los Angeles decided to construct a $50 million plant to reclaim waste water, reducing its need for Mono Lake water by half. In 1994, the State Water Resources Control Board finally reached a decision. It reduced the amount of water the city could remove from the Mono Basin from 91,000 to 12,100 acre feet per year—a reduction of 87%—until the water level in the lake rises by 16 feet. An Audubon Society representative called the decision "an environmental victory of lifetime proportions." *Environmentalists Hail Ruling on Mono Lake Water*, S.F. Examiner, Sept. 28, 1994.

Swamps, marshes, and other wetlands serve important ecological functions. They provide habitat for fish, birds, and other wildlife; filter contaminants from water; absorb storm water; and help recharge groundwater basins. Unfortunately, about half of the wetlands that once existed in the nation have been lost. In the late 1960s, scientific and environmental groups became increasingly concerned about the need to protect the wetlands that remained.

The U.S. Army Corps of Engineers is the federal agency charged with ensuring that navigable waters remain open to navigation and commerce. In 1972, the federal Clean Water Act, 33 U.S.C. § 1251 et seq., assigned a new responsibility to the Corps: regulating the discharge of pollutants into navigable waters, including adjacent wetlands.

Suppose F purchases a vacant lot which is 300 feet from a navigable lake. The lot is situated behind a row of lakefront houses, and a road borders the rear side of the lot. On the other side of the road is a fen—a type of peat-accumulating wetland. F cannot build a home without filling in some areas on the lot that are periodically inundated with water. Should F be concerned about the Clean Water Act?

Sackett v. Environmental Protection Agency

Supreme Court of the United States

598 U.S. 651 (2023)

JUSTICE ALITO delivered the opinion of the Court.

This case concerns a nagging question about the outer reaches of the Clean Water Act (CWA), the principal federal law regulating water pollution in the United States. . . .

The Act applies to "the waters of the United States," but what does that phrase mean? Does the term encompass any backyard that is soggy enough for some minimum period of time? Does it reach "mudflats, sandflats, wetlands, sloughs, prairie potholes, wet meadows, [or] playa lakes?" How about ditches, swimming pools, and puddles?

For more than a half century, the agencies responsible for enforcing the Act have wrestled with the problem and adopted varying interpretations. On three prior occasions, this Court has tried to clarify the meaning of "the waters of the United States." But the problem persists. When we last addressed the question 17 years ago, we were unable to agree on an opinion of the Court. Today, we return to the problem and attempt to identify with greater clarity what the Act means by "the waters of the United States."

I

A

For most of this Nation's history, the regulation of water pollution was left almost entirely to the States and their subdivisions. . . .

Congress's early efforts at directly regulating water pollution were tepid. Although the Federal Water Pollution Control Act of 1948 allowed federal officials to seek judicial abatement of pollution in interstate waters, it imposed high hurdles, such as requiring the consent of the State where the pollution originated. . . .

Congress eventually replaced this scheme in 1972 with the CWA. The Act prohibits "the discharge of any pollutant" into "navigable waters." 33 U.S.C. §§ 1311(a), 1362(12)(A). It broadly defines the term " 'pollutant' " to include not only contaminants like "chemical wastes," but also more mundane materials like "rock, sand," and "cellar dirt." § 1362(6). . . .

> **Make the Connection**
>
> All federal laws must rely on an enumerated power granted in the U.S. Constitution. Often environmental laws are supported by the Commerce Clause, Article I, Section 8, clause 3. You will study the doctrine of enumerated powers in Constitutional Law.

The Environmental Protection Agency (EPA) and the Army Corps of Engineers (Corps) jointly enforce the CWA. . . . On the front end, both agencies are empowered to issue permits exempting activity that would otherwise be unlawful under the Act. Relevant here, the Corps controls permits for the discharge of dredged or fill material into covered waters. The costs of obtaining such a permit are "significant," and both agencies have admitted that "the permitting process can be arduous, expensive, and long." . . . Success is also far from guaranteed, as the Corps has asserted discretion to grant or deny permits based on a long, nonexclusive list of factors that ends with a catchall mandate to consider "in general, the needs and welfare of the people." . . .

Due to the CWA's capacious definition of "pollutant," its low *mens rea*, and its severe penalties, regulated parties have focused particular attention on the Act's geographic scope. . . . [T]he CWA prohibits the discharge of pollutants into only "navigable waters," which it defines as "the waters of the United States, including the territorial seas," 33 U.S.C. §§ 1311(a), 1362(7), (12)(A) (2018 ed.). . . .

B

Michael and Chantell Sackett have spent well over a decade navigating the CWA. . . . In 2004, they purchased a small lot near Priest Lake, in Bonner County, Idaho. In preparation for building a modest home, they began backfilling their property with dirt and rocks. A few months later, the EPA sent the Sacketts a compliance order informing them that their backfilling violated the CWA because their property contained protected wetlands. The EPA demanded that the Sacketts immediately " 'undertake activities to restore the Site' ". . . . The order threatened the Sacketts with penalties of over $40,000 per day if they did not comply.

At the time, the EPA interpreted "the waters of the United States" to include "[a]ll . . . waters" that "could affect interstate or foreign commerce," as well as "[w]etlands adjacent" to those waters. . . . "[A]djacent" was defined to mean not just "bordering" or "contiguous," but also "neighboring." . . . Agency guidance instructed officials to assert jurisdiction over wetlands "adjacent" to non-navigable tributaries when those wetlands had "a significant nexus to a traditional navigable water." A "significant nexus" was said to exist when " 'wetlands, either alone or in combination with *similarly situated lands* in the region, *significantly affect* the chemical, physical, and biological integrity' " of those waters. . . . In looking for evidence of a "significant nexus," field agents were told to consider a wide range of open-ended hydrological and ecological factors. . . .

According to the EPA, the "wetlands" on the Sacketts' lot are "adjacent to" (in the sense that they are in the same neighborhood as) what it described as an "unnamed tributary" on the other side of a 30-foot road. . . . That tributary feeds into a non-navigable creek, which, in turn, feeds into Priest Lake, an intrastate body of water that the EPA designated as traditionally navigable. To establish a significant nexus, the EPA lumped the Sacketts' lot together with the Kalispell Bay Fen, a large nearby wetland complex that the Agency regarded as "similarly situated." According to the EPA, these properties, taken together, "significantly affect" the ecology of Priest Lake. Therefore, the EPA concluded, the Sacketts had illegally dumped soil and gravel onto "the waters of the United States."

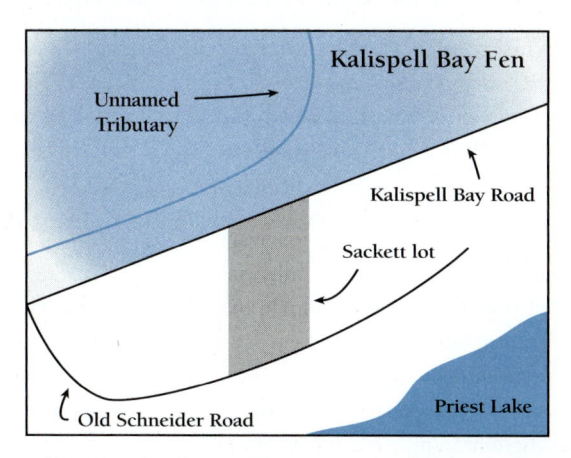

Map of land in *Sackett v. Environmental Protection Agency*

The Sacketts filed suit under the Administrative Procedure Act . . . alleging that the EPA lacked jurisdiction because any wetlands on their property were not "waters of the United States." . . . After seven years of additional proceedings on remand, the District Court entered summary judgment for the EPA. . . . The Ninth Circuit affirmed, holding that the CWA covers adjacent wetlands with a significant nexus to traditional navigable waters and that the Sacketts' lot satisfied that standard.

We granted certiorari to decide the proper test for determining whether wetlands are "waters of the United States."

II

A

In defining the meaning of "the waters of the United States," we revisit what has been "a contentious and difficult task." . . .

Eventually the EPA and Corps settled on materially identical definitions. . . . These broad definitions encompassed "[a]ll . . . waters" that "could affect interstate or foreign commerce." So long as the potential for an interstate effect was present, the regulation extended the CWA to, for example, "intrastate lakes, rivers, streams (including intermittent streams), mudflats, sandflats, wetlands, sloughs, prairie potholes, wet meadows, playa lakes, or natural ponds." The agencies likewise took an expansive view of the CWA's coverage of wetlands "adjacent" to covered waters. As noted, they defined "adjacent" to mean "bordering, contiguous, or neighboring" and clarified that "adjacent" wetlands include those that are separated from covered waters "by man-made dikes or barriers, natural river berms, beach dunes and the like." They also specified that "wetlands" is a technical term encompassing "those areas that are inundated or saturated by surface or ground water at a frequency and duration sufficient to support, and that under normal conditions do support, a prevalence of vegetation typically adapted for life in saturated soil conditions." . . .

This Court first construed the meaning of "the waters of the United States" in *United States v. Riverside Bayview Homes, Inc.*, 474 U.S. 121 (1985). There, we were confronted with the Corps' assertion of authority under the CWA over wetlands that "actually abut[ted] on a navigable waterway." Although we expressed concern that wetlands seemed to fall outside "traditional notions of 'waters,' " we nonetheless deferred to the Corps, reasoning that "the transition from water to solid ground is not necessarily or even typically an abrupt one." . . .

The agencies responded to *Riverside Bayview* by expanding their interpretations even further. Most notably, they issued the "migratory bird rule," which extended jurisdiction to any waters or wetlands that "are or would be used as [a] habitat" by migratory birds or endangered species. As the Corps would later admit, "nearly all waters were jurisdictional under the migratory bird rule."

In *Solid Waste Agency of Northern Cook Cty. v. Army Corps of Engineers*, 531 U.S. 159 (2001) (*SWANCC*), this Court rejected the migratory bird rule, which the Corps had used to assert jurisdiction over several isolated ponds located wholly within the State of Illinois. . . .

Days after our decision, the agencies issued guidance that sought to minimize *SWANCC*'s impact. They took the view that this Court's holding was "strictly limited to waters that are 'nonnavigable, isolated, and intrastate' " and that "field staff should continue to exercise CWA jurisdiction to the full extent of their authority" for "any waters that fall outside of that category." The agencies never defined exactly what they regarded as the "full extent of their authority." They instead encouraged local field agents to make decisions on a case-by-case basis. . . .

It was against this backdrop that we granted review in *Rapanos v. United States* [547 U.S. 715 (2006)]. The lower court in the principal case before us had held that the CWA covered wetlands near ditches and drains that eventually emptied into navigable waters at least 11 miles away, a theory that had supported the petitioner's conviction in a related prosecution. Although we vacated that decision, no position commanded a majority of the Court. Four Justices concluded that the CWA's coverage did not extend beyond two categories: first, certain relatively permanent bodies of water connected to traditional interstate navigable waters and, second, wetlands with such a close physical connection to those waters that they were "as a practical matter indistinguishable from waters of the United States." . . . Four Justices would have deferred to the Government's determination that the wetlands at issue were covered under the CWA. . . . [O]ne Justice concluded that jurisdiction under the CWA requires a "significant nexus" between wetlands and navigable waters and that such a nexus exists where "the wetlands, either alone or in combination with similarly situated lands in the region, significantly affect the chemical, physical, and biological integrity" of those waters. . . .

In the decade following *Rapanos*, the EPA and the Corps issued guidance documents that "recognized larger grey areas and called for more fact-intensive individualized determinations in those grey areas.". . .

The agencies recently promulgated yet another rule attempting to define waters of the United States. Under that broader rule, traditional navigable waters, interstate waters, and the territorial seas, as well as their tributaries and adjacent wetlands, are waters of the United States. . . . So are any "[i]ntrastate lakes and ponds, streams, or wetlands" that either have a continuous surface connection to categorically included waters or have a significant nexus to interstate or traditional navigable waters. Like the post-*Rapanos* guidance, the rule states that a significant nexus requires consideration of a list of open-ended factors. Finally, the rule returns to the broad pre-2020 definition of "adjacent." . . .

B

With the benefit of a half century of practice under the CWA, it is worth taking stock of where things stand. The agencies maintain that the significant-nexus test has been and remains sufficient to establish jurisdiction over "adjacent" wetlands. And by the EPA's own admission, "almost all waters and wetlands" are potentially susceptible to regulation under that test. . . . This puts many property owners in a precarious position because it is "often difficult to determine whether a particular piece of property contains waters of the United States." . . . And because the CWA can sweep broadly enough to criminalize mundane activities like moving dirt, this unchecked definition of "the waters of the United States" means that a staggering array of landowners are at risk of criminal prosecution or onerous civil penalties.

What are landowners to do if they want to build on their property? The EPA recommends asking the Corps for a jurisdictional determination, which is a written decision on whether a particular site contains covered waters. . . .

If the landowner is among the vast majority who receive adverse jurisdictional determinations, what then? It would be foolish to go ahead and build since the jurisdictional determination might form evidence of culpability in a prosecution or civil action. The jurisdictional determination could be challenged in court, but only after the delay and expense required to exhaust the administrative appeals process. And once in court, the landowner would face an uphill battle under the deferential standards of review that the agencies enjoy. Another alternative would be simply to acquiesce and seek a permit from the Corps. But that process can take years and cost an exorbitant amount of money. Many landowners faced with this unappetizing menu of options would simply choose to build nothing.

III

With this history in mind, we now consider the extent of the CWA's geographical reach.

A

We start, as we always do, with the text of the CWA. As noted, the Act applies to "navigable waters," which had a well-established meaning at the time of the CWA's enactment. But the CWA complicates matters by proceeding to define "navigable waters" as "the waters of the United States," § 1362(7), which was decidedly not a well-known term of art. . . . [F]or the reasons explained below, we conclude that the *Rapanos* plurality was correct: the CWA's use of "waters" encompasses "only those relatively permanent, standing or continuously flowing bodies of water 'forming geographic[al] features' that are described in ordinary parlance as 'streams, oceans, rivers, and lakes.' "

> **Hear It**
>
> The Justices were grappling with a difficult line-drawing problem in this case. Click here to listen to the oral argument before the Court.

This reading follows from the CWA's deliberate use of the plural term "waters." That term typically refers to bodies of water like those listed above. See, *e.g.*, Webster's [New International Dictionary] 2882 [(2d ed. 1954)]; Black's Law Dictionary 1426 (5th ed. 1979) ("especially in the plural, [water] may designate a body of water, such as a river, a lake, or an ocean, or an aggregate of such bodies of water, as in the phrases 'foreign waters,' *waters of the United States,*' and the like" (emphasis added)); Random House Dictionary of the English Language 2146 (2d ed. 1987) (Random House Dictionary) (defining "waters" as "a. flowing water, or water moving in waves: The river's mighty waters. b. the sea or seas bordering a particular country or continent or located in a particular part of the world" (emphasis deleted)). This meaning is hard to reconcile with classifying "lands," wet or otherwise, as "waters."

This reading also helps to align the meaning of "the waters of the United States" with the term it is defining: "navigable waters." . . . Although we have acknowledged that the CWA extends to more than traditional navigable waters, we have refused to read "navigable" out of the statute, holding that it at least shows that Congress was focused on "its traditional jurisdiction over waters that were or had been navigable in fact or which could reasonably be so made." . . .

More broadly, this reading accords with how Congress has employed the term "waters" elsewhere in the CWA and in other laws. The CWA repeatedly uses "waters" in contexts that confirm the term refers to bodies of open water. See 33 U.S.C. § 1267(i)(2)(D) ("the waters of the Chesapeake Bay"); § 1268(a)(3)(I) ("the open waters of each of the Great Lakes"); § 1324(d)(4)(B)(ii) ("lakes and other surface waters"); § 1330(g)(4)(C)(vii) ("estuarine waters"); § 1343(c)(1) ("the waters of the territorial seas, the contiguous zone, and the oceans"); §§ 1346(a)(1), 1375a(a) ("coastal recreation waters"); § 1370 (state "boundary waters"). The use of "waters" elsewhere in the U. S. Code likewise correlates to rivers, lakes, and oceans.

. . . The EPA argues that "waters" is "naturally read to encompass wetlands" because the "presence of water is 'universally regarded as the most basic feature of wetlands.' " But that reading proves too much. Consider puddles, which are also defined by the ordinary presence of water even though few would describe them as "waters." . . . Finally, it is also instructive that the CWA expressly "protect[s] the primary responsibilities and rights of States to prevent, reduce, and eliminate pollution" and "to plan the development and use . . . of land and water resources." It is hard to see how the States' role in regulating water resources would remain "primary" if the EPA had jurisdiction over anything defined by the presence of water.

B

. . . In *Rapanos*, the plurality spelled out clearly when adjacent wetlands are part of covered waters. It explained that "waters" may fairly be read to include only those wetlands that are "as a practical matter indistinguishable from waters of the United States," such that it is "difficult to determine where the 'water' ends and the 'wetland' begins." That occurs when wetlands have "a continuous surface connection to bodies that are 'waters of the United States' in their own right, so that there is no clear demarcation between 'waters' and wetlands." We agree with this formulation of when wetlands are part of "the waters of the United States." We also acknowledge that temporary interruptions in surface connection may sometimes occur because of phenomena like low tides or dry spells.

In sum, we hold that the CWA extends to only those wetlands that are "as a practical matter indistinguishable from waters of the United States." This requires the party asserting jurisdiction over adjacent wetlands to establish "first, that the adjacent [body of water constitutes] . . . 'water[s] of the United States,' (*i.e.*, a relatively permanent body of water connected to traditional interstate navigable waters); and second, that the wetland has a continuous surface connection with that water, making it difficult to determine where the 'water' ends and the 'wetland' begins.". . .

. . . This holding compels reversal here. The wetlands on the Sacketts' property are distinguishable from any possibly covered waters. . . .

JUSTICE KAVANAUGH, with whom JUSTICE SOTOMAYOR, JUSTICE KAGAN, and JUSTICE JACKSON join, concurring in the judgment.

. . . I agree with the Court's reversal of the Ninth Circuit. In particular, I agree with the Court's decision not to adopt the "significant nexus" test for determining whether a wetland is covered under the Act. And I agree with the Court's bottom-line judgment that the wetlands on the Sacketts' property are not covered by the Act and are therefore not subject to permitting requirements.

I write separately because I respectfully disagree with the Court's new test for assessing when wetlands are covered by the Clean Water Act. The Court concludes that wetlands are covered by the Act only when the wetlands have a "continuous surface connection" to waters of the United States—that is, when the wetlands are "adjoining" covered waters. In my view, the Court's "continuous surface connection" test departs from the statutory text, from 45 years of consistent agency practice, and from this Court's precedents. The Court's test narrows the Clean Water Act's coverage of "adjacent" wetlands to mean only "adjoining" wetlands. But "adjacent" and "adjoining" have distinct meanings: Adjoining wetlands are contiguous to or bordering a covered water, whereas adjacent wetlands include both (i) those wetlands contiguous to or bordering a covered water, *and* (ii) wetlands separated from a covered water only by a man-made dike or barrier, natural river berm, beach dune, or the like. By narrowing the Act's coverage of wetlands to only adjoining wetlands, the Court's new test will leave some long-regulated adjacent wetlands no longer covered by the Clean Water Act, with significant repercussions for water quality and flood control throughout the United States. Therefore, I respectfully concur only in the Court's judgment. . . .

Points for Discussion

a. **Scope of Federal Jurisdiction**

How did the Court determine that the wetlands on the Sackett property were not covered by the Clean Water Act? Why is it important for landowners to know whether they have wetlands on their property that are protected by the Act?

Sackett clarified that only wetlands with a continuous surface connection to bodies of water which are "waters of the United States" in their own right are regulated. But uncertainty over the scope of federal jurisdiction continues. For instance, it is not clear whether small tributaries which are not navigable-in-fact qualify as covered waters under the Court's formulation. Moreover, at one point in the case the Court seems to require that a water of the United States be a traditional *interstate* navigable water. This would further narrow the scope of protected wetlands.

Federal agencies published a new rule in response to the *Sackett* holding. Revised Definition of "Waters of the United States," 88 Fed. Reg. 61964 (Sept. 8, 2023). This rule eliminates the significant nexus test and uses the continuous surface connection test for determining when wetlands are covered.

b. **An Alternative Approach**

Justice Kavanaugh expressed concern that the majority's test is too narrow because it excludes protection for wetlands which are *nearby* covered waters of the United States, but separated from them by man-made dikes, natural river berms or beach dunes.

For example, suppose F buys a lot containing wetlands which is near the ocean. A large beach dune separates the ocean from the lot. F does not need a Clean Water Act permit to develop the lot into a condominium complex under the majority view, but would under Kavanaugh's concurrence. Alternatively, imagine that G inherits a large undeveloped wetland parcel near a navigable river. A thin strip of land covered with vegetation that naturally developed over time separates G's parcel from the river. G intends to develop the property into a restaurant, destroying the wetlands. Under the majority opinion G does not need a permit, but under Kavanaugh's approach a permit would be required.

c. **Discharge of a Pollutant**

The Clean Water Act prohibits the "discharge" of a "pollutant" into the "waters of the United States." "Discharge" is the addition of pollutant to jurisdictional waters. What was the "pollutant" that the Sacketts were accused of discharging? Given the broad definitions of "discharge" and "pollutant," can you see why the scope of jurisdiction is such an important issue?

d. Permit Process

As the Court discussed, the agencies have authority to exempt activity that would otherwise be unlawful under the Act. Why didn't the Sacketts apply for a permit? In many cases, it is difficult or impossible to qualify for a permit to fill wetlands. In reviewing a permit application, the Corps performs a "public interest" analysis that considers a range of economic, environmental, and social factors. *See, e.g., City of Olmsted Falls v. U.S. Environmental Protection Agency*, 435 F.3d 632 (6th Cir. 2006).

The Corps has a streamlined authorization process—the Nationwide Permits Program—for projects with no more than minimal individual and cumulative adverse effects. In particular, Nationwide Permit 29 (Residential Developments) authorizes construction of building foundations and pads and attendant features necessary for the use of a residence.

e. Applying *Sackett*

Under the *Sackett* standard, are the following wetlands "waters of the United States"?

> (1) After heavy rains that occur primarily in the spring months, the wetlands on D's property flow over land into Marigold Lake, a navigable body of water.
>
> (2) F's property contains wetlands that continuously exchange water through a subsurface connection with Belle River, a navigable river.

C. Land Surface

For decades, American businesses disposed of hazardous wastes in the cheapest possible manner, with little regard for human health or the environment. But in 1978, the Love Canal tragedy pushed the issue into the national spotlight. Investigators discovered that this residential community near Niagara Falls, New York had been built on top of a toxic waste dump. The chemicals caused residents to suffer miscarriages, birth defects, epilepsy, and other illnesses. Haunted by the fear of future Love Canals, millions of Americans demanded action.

As a result, Congress enacted the Comprehensive Environmental Response, Compensation, and Liability Act of 1980, 42 U.S.C. § 9601 et seq. (CERCLA), the main federal statute governing the cleanup of sites contaminated with hazardous wastes. The goal of CERCLA was to protect the public and the environment by forcing the prompt cleanup of hazardous waste sites.

Suppose that G is planning to purchase a 100-acre parcel that was once the site of a toy factory. The factory was demolished years ago, and the land is now a meadow full of wildflowers. Should G be concerned about CERCLA?

United States v. Monsanto Co.

United States Court of Appeals, Fourth Circuit

858 F.2d 160 (1988), *cert. denied,* 490 U.S. 1106 (1989)

SPROUSE, CIRCUIT JUDGE:

Oscar Seidenberg and Harvey Hutchinson (the site-owners) and Allied Corporation, Monsanto Company, and EM Industries, Inc. (the generator defendants), appeal from the district court's entry of summary judgment holding them liable to the United States and the State of South Carolina (the governments) under section 107(a) of the Comprehensive Environmental Response, Compensation, and Liability Act of 1980 (CERLCA). 42 U.S.C.A. § 9607(a) (West Supp. 1987). The court determined that the defendants were liable jointly and severally for $1,813,624 in response costs accrued from the partial removal of hazardous waste from a disposal facility located near Columbia, South Carolina. . . . We affirm the district court's liability holdings. . . .

I.

In 1972, Seidenberg and Hutchinson leased a four-acre tract of land they owned to the Columbia Organic Chemical Company (COCC), a South Carolina chemical manufacturing corporation. The property, located along Bluff Road near Columbia, South Carolina, consisted of a small warehouse and surrounding areas. The lease was verbal, on a month-to-month basis, and according to the site-owners' deposition testimony, was executed for the sole purpose of allowing COCC to store raw materials and finished products in the warehouse. Seidenberg and Hutchinson received monthly lease payments of $200, which increased to $350 by 1980.

In the mid-1970s, COCC expanded its business to include the brokering and recycling of chemical waste generated by third parties. It used the Bluff Road site as a waste storage and disposal facility for its new operations. In 1976, COCC's principals incorporated South Carolina Recycling and Disposal Inc. (SCRDI), for the purpose of assuming COCC's waste-handling business, and the site-owners began accepting lease payments from SCRDI.

SCRDI contracted with numerous off-site waste producers for the transport, recycling, and disposal of chemical and other waste. Among these producers were agencies of the federal government and South Carolina, and various private entities including the three generator defendants in this litigation. Although SCRDI operated other disposal sites, it deposited much of the waste it received at the Bluff Road facility.

The waste stored at Bluff Road contained many chemical substances that federal law defines as "hazardous."

Between 1976 and 1980, SCRDI haphazardly deposited more than 7,000 fifty-five gallon drums of chemical waste on the four-acre Bluff Road site. It placed waste laden drums and containers wherever there was space, often without pallets to protect them from the damp ground. It stacked drums on top of one another without regard to the chemical compatibility of their contents. It maintained no documented safety procedures and kept no inventory of the stored chemicals. Over time many of the drums rusted, rotted, and otherwise deteriorated. Hazardous substances leaked from the decaying drums and oozed into the ground. The substances commingled with incompatible chemicals that had escaped from other containers, generating noxious fumes, fires, and explosions.

On October 26, 1977, a toxic cloud formed when chemicals leaking from rusted drums reacted with rainwater. Twelve responding firemen were hospitalized. Again, on July 24, 1979, an explosion and fire resulted when chemicals stored in glass jars leaked onto drums containing incompatible substances. SCRDI's site manager could not identify the substances that caused the explosion, making the fire difficult to extinguish.

In 1980, the Environmental Protection Agency (EPA) inspected the Bluff Road site. Its investigation revealed that the facility was filled well beyond its capacity with chemical waste. The number of drums and the reckless manner in which they were stacked precluded access to various areas in the site. Many of the drums observed were unlabeled, or their labels had become unreadable from exposure, rendering it impossible to identify their contents. The EPA concluded that the site posed "a major fire hazard."

Later that year, the United States filed suit under section 7003 of the Resource Conservation and Recovery Act, 42 U.S.C. § 6973, against SCRDI, COCC, and Oscar Seidenberg. The complaint was filed before the December 11, 1980, effective date of CERCLA, and it sought only injunctive relief. Thereafter, the State of South Carolina intervened as a plaintiff in the pending action.

> **What's That?**
>
> The Resource Conservation and Recovery Act (RCRA) is the main federal statute that governs the generation, storage, and disposal of newly created hazardous wastes.

In the course of discovery, the governments identified a number of waste generators, including the generator defendants in this appeal, that had contracted with SCRDI for waste disposal. The governments notified the generators that they were potentially responsible for the costs of cleanup at Bluff Road under section 107(a) of the newly-enacted CERCLA. As a result of these contacts, the governments executed individual settlement agreements with twelve of the identified off-site producers.

The generator defendants, however, declined to settle. [Using funds from the settlements and other monies, the governments proceeded to clean up the site.]. . . .

In 1982, the governments filed an amended complaint, adding the three generator defendants and site-owner Harvey Hutchinson, and including claims under section 107(a) of CERCLA against all of the nonsettling defendants. The governments alleged that the generator defendants and site-owners were jointly and severally liable under section 107(a) for the costs expended completing the surface cleanup at Bluff Road.

In response, the site-owners contended that they were innocent absentee landlords unaware of and unconnected to the waste disposal activities that took place on their land. They maintained that their lease with COCC did not allow COCC (or SCRDI) to store chemical waste on the premises, but they admitted that they became aware of waste storage in 1977 and accepted lease payments until 1980.

The generator defendants likewise denied liability for the governments' response costs. Among other defenses, they claimed that none of their specific waste materials contributed to the hazardous conditions at Bluff Road, and that retroactive imposition of CERCLA liability on them was unconstitutional. They also asserted that they could establish an affirmative defense to CERCLA liability under section 107(b)(3), 42 U.S.C. § 9607(b)(3), by showing that the harm at the site was caused solely through the conduct of unrelated third parties. All parties thereafter moved for summary judgment.

After an evidentiary hearing, the district court granted the governments' summary judgment motion on CERCLA liability. The court found that all of the defendants were responsible parties under section 107(a), and that none of them had presented sufficient evidence to support an affirmative defense under section 107(b). The court further concluded that the environmental harm at Bluff Road was "indivisible," and it held all of the defendants jointly and severally liable for the governments' response costs. *United States v. South Carolina Recycling & Disposal, Inc.*, 653 F. Supp. 984 (D.S.C. 1984).

As to the site-owners' liability, the court found it sufficient that they owned the Bluff Road site at the time hazardous substances were deposited there. It rejected their contentions that Congress did not intend to subject "innocent" landowners to CERCLA liability. The court similarly found summary judgment appropriate against the generator defendants because it was undisputed that (1) they shipped hazardous substances to the Bluff Road facility; (2) hazardous substances "like" those present in the generator defendants' waste were found at the facility; and (3) there had been a release of hazardous substances at the site. In this context, the court rejected the generator defendants' arguments that the governments had to prove that their specific waste contributed to the harm at the site, and it found their constitutional contentions to be "without force." Finally, since none of the defendants challenged the governments' itemized accounting of response costs, the court ordered them to pay the full $1,813,624 that had been requested. . . .

II.

... In CERCLA, Congress established "an array of mechanisms to combat the increasingly serious problem of hazardous substance releases." *Dedham Water Co. v. Cumberland Farms Dairy, Inc.*, 805 F.2d 1074, 1078 (1st Cir. 1986). Section 107(a) of the statute sets forth the principal mechanism for recovery of costs expended in the cleanup of waste disposal facilities. At the time the district court entered judgment, section 107(a) provided in pertinent part:

(a) Covered persons; scope

Notwithstanding any other provision or rule of law, and subject only to the defenses set forth in subsection (b) of this section. . . .

(2) any person who at the time of disposal of any hazardous substance owned or operated any facility at which such hazardous substances were disposed of, [and]

(3) any person who by contract, agreement, or otherwise arranged for disposal or treatment, or arranged with a transporter for transport for disposal or treatment, of hazardous substances owned or possessed by such person, by any other party or entity, at any facility owned or operated by another party or entity and containing such hazardous substances, and

(4) . . . from which there is a release, or a threatened release which causes the incurrence of response costs, of a hazardous substance, shall be liable for—

> (A) all costs of removal or remedial action incurred by the United States Government or a State not inconsistent with the national contingency plan.

42 U.S.C.A. § 9607(a) (West Supp. 1987).

In our view, the plain language of section 107(a) clearly defines the scope of intended liability under the statute and the elements of proof necessary to establish it. We agree with the overwhelming body of precedent that has interpreted section 107(a) as establishing a strict liability scheme. Further, in light of the evidence presented here, we are persuaded that the district court correctly held that the governments satisfied all the elements of section 107(a) liability as to both the site-owners and the generator defendants.

In light of the strict liability imposed by section 107(a), we cannot agree with the site-owners contention that they are not within the class of owners Congress intended to hold liable. The traditional elements of tort culpability on which the site-owners rely simply are absent from the statute. The plain language of section 107(a)(2) extends liability to owners of waste facilities regardless of their degree of participation in the subsequent disposal of hazardous waste.

Under section 107(a)(2), *any* person who owned a facility at a time when hazardous substances were deposited there may be held liable for all costs of removal or remedial action if a release or threatened release of a hazardous substance occurs. The site-owners do not dispute their ownership of the Bluff Road facility, or the fact that releases occurred there during their period of ownership. Under these circumstances, all the prerequisites to section 107(a) liability have been satisfied.[14]

The site-owners nonetheless contend that the district court's grant of summary judgment improperly denied them the opportunity to present an affirmative defense under section 107(b)(3). Section 107(b)(3) sets forth a limited affirmative defense based on the complete absence of causation. It requires proof that the release or threatened release of hazardous substances and resulting damages were caused solely by "a third party other than . . . one whose act or omission occurs in connection with a contractual relationship, existing directly or indirectly, with the defendant. . . ." 42 U.S.C. § 9607(b)(3). A second element of the defense requires proof that the defendant "took precautions against foreseeable acts or omissions of any such third party and the consequences that could foreseeably result from such acts or omissions." *Id.* We agree with the district court that under no view of the evidence could the site-owners satisfy either of these proof requirements.

First, the site-owners could not establish the absence of a direct or indirect contractual relationship necessary to maintain the affirmative defense. They concede they entered into a lease agreement with COCC. They accepted rent from COCC, and after SCRDI was incorporated, they accepted rent from SCRDI. Second, the site-owners presented no evidence that they took precautionary action against the foreseeable conduct of COCC or SCRDI. They argued to the trial court that, although they were aware COCC was a chemical manufacturing company, they were completely ignorant of all waste disposal activities at Bluff Road before 1977. They maintained that they never inspected the site prior to that time. In our view, the statute does not sanction such willful or negligent blindness on the part of absentee owners. The district court committed no error in entering summary judgment against the site-owners. . . .

III.

The appellants next challenge the district court's imposition of joint and several liability for the governments' response costs. The court concluded that joint and several liability was appropriate because the environmental harm at Bluff Road was "indivisible" and the appellants had "failed to meet their burden of proving otherwise." We agree with its conclusion.

While CERCLA does not mandate the imposition of joint and several liability, it permits it in cases of indivisible harm. In each case, the court must consider traditional and evolving principles of federal common law, which Congress has left to the courts to supply interstitially.

---

[14] Congress . . . acknowledged that landowners may affirmatively avoid liability if they can prove they did not know and had no reason to know that hazardous substances were disposed of on their land at the time they acquired title or possession. 42 U.S.C.A. § 9601(35) (West Supp. 1987). This explicitly drafted exception further signals Congress' intent to impose liability on landowners who cannot satisfy its express requirements.

Under common law rules, when two or more persons act independently to cause a single harm for which there is a reasonable basis of apportionment according to the contribution of each, each is held liable only for the portion of harm that he causes. When such persons cause a single and indivisible harm, however, they are held liable jointly and severally for the entire harm. We think these principles, as reflected in the Restatement (Second) of Torts, represent the correct and uniform federal rules applicable to CERCLA cases.

Section 433A of the Restatement provides:

(1) Damages for harm are to be apportioned among two or more causes where

   (a) there are distinct harms, or

   (b) there is a reasonable basis for determining the contribution of each cause to a single harm.

(2) Damages for any other harm cannot be apportioned among two or more causes.

Restatement (Second) of Torts § 433A (1965).

Placing their argument into the Restatement framework, the generator defendants concede that the environmental damage at Bluff Road constituted a "single harm," but contend that there was a reasonable basis for apportioning the harm. They observe that each of the off-site generators with whom SCRDI contracted sent a potentially identifiable volume of waste to the Bluff Road site, and they maintain that liability should have been apportioned according to the volume they deposited as compared to the total volume disposed of there by all parties. In light of the conditions at Bluff Road, we cannot accept this method as a basis for apportionment. . . .

IV.

The generator defendants raise numerous constitutional challenges to the district court's interpretation and application of CERCLA. They contend that the imposition of "disproportionate" liability without proof of causation violated constitutional limitations on retroactive statutory application and that it converted CERCLA into a bill of attainder and an *ex post facto* law. They further assert, along with the site-owners, that the trial court's construction of CERCLA infringed their substantive due process rights.

> **What's That?**
>
> A *bill of attainder* is a legislative act that imposes punishment on a person for a crime without any trial; the Constitution forbids bills of attainder. An *ex post facto* law is one that retroactively changes the legal consequences of conduct that occurred before the law took effect.

The district court held that CERCLA does not create retroactive liability, but imposes a prospective obligation for the post-enactment environmental consequences of the defendants' past acts. Alternatively, the court held that even if CERCLA is understood to operate retroactively, it nonetheless satisfies the dictates of due process because its liability scheme is rationally related to a valid legislative purpose. We agree with the court's latter holding, and we find no merit to the generator defendants' bill of attainder and *ex post facto* arguments. . . .

While the generator defendants profited from inexpensive waste disposal methods that may have been technically "legal" prior to CERCLA's enactment, it was certainly foreseeable at the time that improper disposal could cause enormous damage to the environment. CERCLA operates remedially to spread the costs of responding to improper waste disposal among all parties that played a role in creating the hazardous conditions. Where those conditions are indivisible, joint and several liability is logical, and it works to ensure complete cost recovery. We do not think these consequences are "particularly harsh and oppressive," *United States Trust Co. v. New Jersey*, 431 U.S. 1, 17 n. 13 (1977) (retrospective civil liability not unconstitutional unless it is particularly harsh and oppressive), and we agree with the Eighth Circuit that retroactive application of CERCLA does not violate due process. *United States v. Northeastern Pharmaceutical & Chemical Co., Inc.*, 810 F.2d 726, 734 (8th Cir. 1986), *cert. denied*, 484 U.S. 848 (1987). . . .

VI.

In view of the above, the judgment of the district court as to the CERCLA liability of the site-owners and generator defendants is affirmed. . . .

Points for Discussion

a. **CERCLA Liability**

Owners Seidenberg and Hutchinson claimed to be "innocent absentee landlords unaware of and unconnected to the waste disposal activities." Why were they held liable under CERCLA? How does the CERCLA liability standard compare to the traditional tort principles? 42 U.S.C. § 9607(a) imposes liability on four categories of *potentially responsible parties* or *PRP*s:

- current owners and operators;
- owners and operators at time of disposal;
- persons who arrange for the disposal or treatment of wastes; and
- waste transporters who select the disposal or treatment site.

However, a person holding a nonpossessory interest in land such as an easement is not deemed an owner under the statute. *See Long Beach Unified School Dist. v. Dorothy B. Godwin California Living Trust*, 32 F.3d 1364 (9th Cir. 1994).

b. Third Party Defense

Why didn't Seidenberg and Hutchison qualify for the *third party defense* set forth in 42 U.S.C. § 9607(b)(3)? Should an ordinary lease be viewed as a "contractual relationship" that precludes an owner from using this defense, as *Monsanto* indicates? *See Westwood Pharmaceuticals, Inc. v. National Fuel Gas Distribution Corp.*, 964 F.2d 85 (2d Cir. 1992) (holding that the defense is available unless the contract relates to handling hazardous substances or gives the owner control over the third party's conduct).

c. Innocent Buyer Defense

If a person acquires title to a contaminated site, she becomes strictly liable under CERCLA as a *current owner*—unless she qualifies for the *innocent buyer defense*. Consider our hypothetical buyer G who is planning to purchase a former factory site. To successfully assert this defense, she must (1) acquire the land after disposal of any hazardous substance, (2) have "no reason to know that any hazardous substance" was disposed of at the property, and (3) fully cooperate with government officials. 42 U.S.C. § 9601(35). The second requirement—have "no reason to know"—is explained in detail by regulations which require extensive pre-purchase investigation, often including soil and groundwater tests. What if G qualifies for the innocent buyer defense, and then sells the land to H without telling him about the contamination? G loses the protection of this defense; she is now strictly liable.

d. Contractual Protection

The risk of CERCLA liability has affected the substance of land purchase negotiations. In many commercial transactions, the buyer will require the seller to warrant that no hazardous substances are present on or under the land. The buyer will also demand that the seller agree to indemnify him for any future cleanup costs that arise under CERCLA or related statutes. These warranty and indemnity provisions tend to be quite detailed; in some instances, they may occupy 10 pages in a 20-page purchase contract. Such agreements are enforceable as between the parties, but not against the government. *Smith Land & Improvement Corp. v. Celotex Corp.*, 851 F.2d 86 (3d Cir. 1988). For a useful overview of this subject, see Eva M. Fromm et al., *Allocating Environmental Liabilities in Acquisitions*, 22 J. Corp. L. 429 (1997). *See also* Garry A. Gabison, *The Problems with the Private Enforcement of CERCLA: An Empirical Analysis*, 7 Geo. Wash. J. Energy & Envtl. L. 189 (2016).

e. **Aftermath of *Monsanto***

Cleanup of the contaminated soil at the Bluff Road site was completed in 1998, at a cost of $2.7 million. Once this work was finished, treatment of groundwater began. The groundwater is being removed by extraction wells, treated to remove the contaminants, and reinjected into the ground. Over 800 million gallons of groundwater have been treated to date.

> **Go Online**
>
> The EPA maintains a searchable database of CERCLA cleanups on its "Cleanups in My Community" website. Click here to find information about hazardous waste cleanups across the United States by selecting a state or territory or searching by zip code area or city.

The Endangered Species Act, 16 U.S.C. § 1531 et seq., was uncontroversial when it was adopted in 1973. But it quickly became apparent that the Act would have a significant effect on private property rights. The Act protects species that are officially determined to be endangered or threatened. First, it requires each federal agency to ensure that its activities do not "jeopardize the continued existence" of any protected species "or result in the destruction or adverse modification of habitat of such species which is determined . . . to be critical. . . ." 16 U.S.C. § 1536(a)(2). For example, the U.S. Forest Service could not lease national forest land to a ski resort if this would imperil an endangered species. Second, the Act makes it illegal to "take any such species within the United States. . . ." 16 U.S.C. § 1538(a)(1). *See generally* Daniel J. Rohlf, *The Endangered Species Act at Forty: The Good, the Bad, and the Ugly*, 20 Animal L. 251 (2014).

What does it mean to "take" an animal? For example, suppose L owns a large tract of forest which is part of the habitat for an endangered bird species. If L cuts the trees on his land in order to build a new shopping center, is this an illegal "taking"?

Babbitt v. Sweet Home Chapter of Communities for a Greater Oregon

Supreme Court of the United States

515 U.S. 687 (1995)

JUSTICE STEVENS delivered the opinion of the Court.

The Endangered Species Act of 1973 (ESA or Act), 16 U.S.C. § 1531, contains a variety of protections designed to save from extinction species that the Secretary of the Interior designates as endangered or threatened. Section 9 of the Act makes it unlawful for any person to "take" any endangered or threatened species. The Secretary has promulgated a regulation that defines the statute's prohibition on takings to include "significant habitat modification or degradation where it actually kills or injures wildlife." This case presents the question whether the Secretary exceeded his authority under the Act by promulgating that regulation.

I.

. . . Section 3(19) of the Act defines the statutory term "take":

> The term "take" means to harass, harm, pursue, hunt, shoot, wound, kill, trap, capture, or collect, or to attempt to engage in any such conduct. 16 U.S.C. § 1532(19).

The Act does not further define the terms it uses to define "take." Interior Department regulations that implement the statute, however, define the statutory term "harm":

> *Harm* in the definition of "take" in the Act means an act which actually kills or injures wildlife. Such act may include significant habitat modification or degradation where it actually kills or injures wildlife by significantly impairing essential behavioral patterns, including breeding, feeding, or sheltering. 50 CFR § 17.3 (1994). . . .

Respondents in this action are small landowners, logging companies, and families dependent on the forest products industries in the Pacific Northwest and in the Southeast, and organizations that represent their interests. They brought this declaratory judgment action against petitioners, the Secretary of the Interior and the Director of the Fish and Wildlife Service, in the United States District Court for the District of Columbia to challenge the statutory validity of the Secretary's regulation defining "harm," particularly the inclusion of habitat modification and degradation in the definition. Respondents challenged the regulation on its face. Their complaint alleged that application of the "harm" regulation to the red-cockaded woodpecker, an endangered species, and the northern spotted owl, a threatened species, had injured them economically. . . .

II.

. . . The text of the Act provides three reasons for concluding that the Secretary's interpretation is reasonable. First, an ordinary understanding of the word "harm" supports it. The dictionary definition of the verb form of "harm" is "to cause hurt or damage to: injure." Webster's Third New International Dictionary 1034 (1966). In the context of the ESA, that definition naturally encompasses habitat modification that results in actual injury or death to members of an endangered or threatened species.

Respondents argue that the Secretary should have limited the purview of "harm" to direct applications of force against protected species, but the dictionary definition does not include the word "directly" or suggest in any way that only direct or willful action that leads to injury constitutes "harm." Moreover, unless the statutory term "harm" encompasses indirect as well as direct injuries, the word has no meaning that does not duplicate the meaning of other words that § 3 uses to define "take." A reluctance to treat statutory terms as surplusage supports the reasonableness of the Secretary's interpretation.

Second, the broad purpose of the ESA supports the Secretary's decision to extend protection against activities that cause the precise harms Congress enacted the statute to avoid. In *TVA v. Hill*, 437 U.S. 153 (1978), we described the Act as "the most comprehensive legislation for the preservation of endangered species ever enacted by any nation." *Id.,* at 180. Whereas predecessor statutes enacted in 1966 and 1969 had not contained any sweeping prohibition against the taking of endangered species except on federal lands, the 1973 Act applied to all land in the United States and to the Nation's territorial seas. As stated in § 2 of the Act, among its central purposes is "to provide a means whereby the ecosystems upon which endangered species and threatened species depend may be conserved. . . ." 16 U.S.C. § 1531(b). . . .

Northern spotted owl
Click here for larger photo

Third, the fact that Congress in 1982 authorized the Secretary to issue permits for takings that § 9(a)(1)(B) would otherwise prohibit, "if such taking is incidental to, and not the purpose of, the carrying out of an otherwise lawful activity," 16 U.S.C. § 1539(a)(1)(B), strongly suggests that Congress understood § 9(a)(1)(B) to prohibit indirect as well as deliberate takings. The permit process requires the applicant to prepare a "conservation plan" that specifies how he intends to "minimize and mitigate" the "impact" of his activity on endangered and threatened species, 16 U.S.C. § 1539(a)(2)(A), making clear that Congress had in mind foreseeable rather than merely accidental effects on listed species. No one could seriously request an "incidental" take permit to avert § 9 liability for direct, deliberate action against a member of an endangered or threatened species, but respondents would read "harm" so narrowly that the permit procedure would have little more than that absurd purpose. "When Congress acts to amend a statute, we presume it intends its amendment to have real and substantial effect." *Stone v. INS*, 514 U.S. 386, 397 (1995). Congress' addition of the § 10 permit provision supports the Secretary's conclusion that activities not intended to harm an endangered species, such as habitat modification, may constitute unlawful takings under the ESA unless the Secretary permits them. . . .

IV.

When it enacted the ESA, Congress delegated broad administrative and interpretive power to the Secretary. See 16 U.S.C. §§ 1533, 1540(f). The task of defining and listing endangered and threatened species requires an expertise and attention to detail that exceeds the normal province of Congress. Fashioning appropriate standards for issuing permits under § 10 for takings that would otherwise violate § 9 necessarily requires the exercise of broad discretion. The proper interpretation of a term such as "harm" involves a complex policy choice. When Congress has entrusted the Secretary with broad discretion, we are especially reluctant to substitute our views of wise policy for his. In this case, that reluctance accords with our conclusion, based on the text, structure, and legislative history of the ESA, that the Secretary reasonably construed the intent of Congress when he defined "harm" to include "significant habitat modification or degradation that actually kills or injures wildlife."

In the elaboration and enforcement of the ESA, the Secretary and all persons who must comply with the law will confront difficult questions of proximity and degree; for, as all recognize, the Act encompasses a vast range of economic and social enterprises and endeavors. These questions must be addressed in the usual course of the law, through case-by-case resolution and adjudication.

The judgment of the Court of Appeals is reversed. . . .

JUSTICE O'CONNOR, concurring.

. . . In my view, the regulation is limited by its terms to actions that actually kill or injure individual animals. Justice Scalia disagrees, arguing that the harm regulation "encompasses injury inflicted, not only upon individual animals, but upon populations of the protected species." At one level, I could not reasonably quarrel with this observation; death to an individual animal always reduces the size of the population in which it lives, and in that sense, "injures" that population. But by its insight, the dissent means something else. Building upon the regulation's use of the word "breeding," Justice Scalia suggests that the regulation facially bars significant habitat modification that actually kills or injures *hypothetical* animals (or, perhaps more aptly, causes potential additions to the population not to come into being). Because "[i]mpairment of breeding does not 'injure' living creatures," Justice Scalia reasons, the regulation *must* contemplate application to "*a population* of animals which would otherwise have maintained or increased its numbers."

I disagree. As an initial matter, I do not find it as easy as Justice Scalia does to dismiss the notion that significant impairment of breeding injures living creatures. To raze the last remaining ground on which the piping plover currently breeds, thereby making it impossible for any piping plovers to reproduce, would obviously injure the population (causing the species' extinction in a generation). But by completely preventing breeding, it would also injure the individual living bird, in the same way that sterilizing the creature injures the individual living bird. To "injure" is, among other things, "to impair." Webster's Ninth New Collegiate Dictionary 623 (1983). One need not subscribe to theories of "psychic harm" to recognize that to make it impossible for an animal to reproduce is to impair its most essential physical functions and to render that animal, and its genetic material, biologically obsolete. This, in my view, is actual injury.

In any event, even if impairing an animal's ability to breed were not, *in and of itself,* an injury to that animal, interference with breeding can cause an animal to suffer other, perhaps more obvious, kinds of injury. The regulation has clear application, for example, to significant habitat modification that kills or physically injures animals which, because they are in a vulnerable breeding state, do not or cannot flee or defend themselves, or to environmental pollutants that cause an animal to suffer physical complications during gestation. Breeding, feeding, and sheltering are what animals do. If significant habitat modification, by interfering with these essential behaviors, actually kills or injures an animal protected by the Act, it causes "harm" within the meaning of the regulation. . . .

JUSTICE SCALIA, with whom THE CHIEF JUSTICE and JUSTICE THOMAS join, dissenting.

I think it unmistakably clear that the legislation at issue here (1) forbade the hunting and killing of endangered animals, and (2) provided federal lands and federal funds *for the acquisition of private lands,* to preserve the habitat of endangered animals. The Court's holding that the hunting and killing prohibition incidentally preserves habitat on private lands imposes unfairness to the point of financial ruin—not just upon the rich, but upon the simplest farmer who finds his land conscripted to national zoological use. I respectfully dissent. . . .

> **Make the Connection**
>
> If private land is "taken" for public use, the owner is entitled to compensation under the Takings Clause of the Fifth Amendment. You will study the Takings Clause in Chapters 13 and 14.

The regulation has three features which . . . do not comport with the statute. First, it interprets the statute to prohibit habitat modification that is no more than the cause-in-fact of death or injury to wildlife. *Any* "significant habitat modification" that in fact produces that result by "impairing essential behavioral patterns" is made unlawful, regardless of whether that result is intended or even foreseeable, and no matter how long the chain of causality between modification and injury. . . .

Second, the regulation does not require an "act": The Secretary's officially stated position is that an *omission* will do. The previous version of the regulation made this explicit. When the regulation was modified in 1981 the phrase "or omission" was taken out, but only because (as the final publication of the rule advised) "the [Fish and Wildlife] Service feels that 'act' is inclusive of either commissions or omissions which would be prohibited by section [1538(a)(1)(B)]."

The third and most important unlawful feature of the regulation is that it encompasses injury inflicted, not only upon individual animals, but upon populations of the protected species. "Injury" in the regulation includes "significantly impairing essential behavioral patterns, including *breeding*," 50 CFR § 17.3 (1994) (emphasis added). Impairment of breeding does not "injure" living creatures; it prevents them from propagating, thus "injuring" *a population* of animals which would otherwise have maintained or increased its numbers. What the face of the regulation shows, the Secretary's official pronouncements confirm. The Final Redefinition of "Harm" accompanying publication of the regulation said that "harm" is not limited to "direct physical injury to an individual member of the wildlife species," and refers to "injury *to a population*" (emphasis added). . . .

The Endangered Species Act is a carefully considered piece of legislation that forbids all persons to hunt or harm endangered animals, but places upon the public at large, rather than upon fortuitously accountable individual landowners, the cost of preserving the habitat of endangered species. There is neither textual support for, nor even evidence of congressional consideration of, the radically different disposition contained in the regulation that the Court sustains. For these reasons, I respectfully dissent.

Points for Discussion

a. Defining "Take"

A federal agency has broad discretion in adopting regulations to implement a statute enacted by Congress; but a regulation cannot be inconsistent with the statute. Are you persuaded that the agency's definition of "harm" is a reasonable interpretation of the statutory term "take"? Did Congress intend "take" to include habitat modification? In the wake of *Sweet Home*, the Endangered Species Act has been applied to a wide variety of land development activities. For example, in *Rancho Viejo, LLC v. Norton*, 323 F.3d 1062 (D.C. Cir. 2003), the court upheld the determination of the U.S. Fish and Wildlife Service that a proposed 202-acre housing project would adversely affect the habitat of the endangered arroyo southwestern toad, thereby blocking the project. For more discussion of this question, see Paul Boudreaux, *Understanding "Take" in the Endangered Species Act*, 34 Ariz. St. L.J. 733 (2002).

b. Why Save Endangered Species?

Should humans preserve non-human species? Some scholars defend the Endangered Species Act on moral grounds. Another theme might be called environmentally-conscious utilitarianism—the concept that we should preserve species because they might provide future benefits to humans, for example, as a source of new medicines. Less than 1% of known species have been studied in depth. One author suggests that the Act provides a mechanism for preserving all species within an ecosystem, endangered or not. *See* Oliver A. Houck, *Why Do We Protect Endangered Species, and What Does That Say About Whether Restrictions on Private Property to Protect Them Constitute "Takings"?*, 80 Iowa L. Rev. 297 (1995).

c. Habitat Conservation Plans

Partly in response to *Sweet Home*, the use of habitat conservation plans (HCPs) has increased over time. As the Court noted, the Act authorizes the U.S. Fish and Wildlife Service (FWS) to allow the "incidental take" of an endangered species; this is defined as a "take" that is "incidental to, and not the purpose of, the carrying out of a lawful activity." 16 U.S.C. § 1539(a)(1)(B). In order to obtain this permission, a landowner must provide a conservation plan that will "minimize and mitigate" the impact on the protected species. In effect, an HCP allows a landowner to modify the habitat of a protected species as long as the FWS determines that adequate mitigation has occurred. This is typically accomplished by purchasing land which is permanently dedicated as replacement habitat. Today over 50 million acres are subject to HCPs.

For example, in *National Wildlife Federation v. Norton*, 306 F. Supp. 2d 920 (E.D. Cal. 2004), the court upheld an HCP which allowed development of almost 2,000 acres of habitat for the Giant Garter Snake and the Swainson's Hawk. The plan provided that for every acre of land that was developed, one half-acre of habitat would be protected.

d.   Aftermath of *Sweet Home*

The Clinton administration negotiated a compromise between logging interests and environmental groups, the Northwest Forest Plan. It designated almost seven million acres of old-growth forest as "critical habitat" for the northern spotted owl, where logging was either prohibited or restricted. The U.S. Fish and Wildlife Service approved a recovery plan for the owl in 2008, but environmental groups brought suit claiming that the plan was legally insufficient. In 2011, the Service adopted a revised recovery plan with the goal of removing the owl from protected status within 30 years. The revised plan is estimated to cost over $127 million. Today, the owl is in a worse situation than when it was initially listed. It faces a new threat—the invasive barred owl, which outcompetes native species. In addition to working to preserve remaining habitat for the northern spotted owl, authorities are also taking actions to try to control barred owl populations.

D. Atmosphere

Global climate change is a reality. As the U.S. Global Change Research Program—a task force composed of scientists from different federal agencies—has reported to Congress: "Observations show that the warming of the climate is unequivocal. The climate change observed over the past 50 years is due primarily to human-induced emissions of heat-trapping gases." Scientists predict that climate change will produce a variety of harmful effects, including rising sea levels, more extreme weather events, fresh water scarcity, and reductions in agricultural production.

How should the law react to this challenge? And what implications does global climate change have for property law? One obvious impact of rising sea levels is the risk of flooding to coastal properties. In *Massachusetts v. Environmental Protection Agency*, 549 U.S. 497 (2007), Massachusetts and other plaintiffs sued the U.S.

Environmental Protection Agency; they asserted that EPA had the authority to regulate emissions of carbon dioxide and other greenhouse gases under the Clean Air Act, but that it had improperly refused to do so. One of the issues before the Court was whether the plaintiffs had *standing* to sue—whether they had a sufficient "personal stake in the outcome of the controversy." *Id*. at 517. Based on the plaintiffs' uncontested affidavits, the court held, *inter alia*, that Massachusetts had demonstrated standing because the "rising seas have already begun to swallow Massachusetts' coastal land." *Id*. at 522. The Court ultimately ruled that (1) EPA did have the authority to regulate greenhouse gases and (2) its refusal to regulate was unjustified.

> **See It**
>
> Click here to see a photograph of a Massachusetts beach being affected by the global rise in sea level.

Can private litigation be used to combat climate change? In recent years, plaintiffs have brought a variety of lawsuits against entities whose greenhouse gas emissions are warming the planet—largely without success. *See, e.g., American Electric Power Co., Inc. v. Connecticut*, 564 U.S. 410 (2011) (rejecting common law public nuisance claims against power companies). Lawsuits brought by states and local governments based on state public nuisance and other tort-law doctrines against energy companies are now beginning to gain traction. *See* Tracy D. Hester, *A New Front Blowing in: State Law and the Future of Climate Change Public Nuisance Litigation*, 31 Stan. Envtl. L.J. 49 (2012). But is there a constitutional right to a stable climate system? And is our climate system protected by the public trust doctrine?

Juliana v. United States

United States District Court, District of Oregon

217 F. Supp. 3d 1224 (2016)

AIKEN, JUDGE.

BACKGROUND

This is no ordinary lawsuit. Plaintiffs challenge the policies, acts, and omissions of the President of the United States [and many federal agencies]. This lawsuit challenges decisions defendants have made across a vast set of topics—decisions like whether and to what extent to regulate CO_2 emissions from power plants and vehicles, whether to permit fossil fuel extraction and development to take place on federal lands, how much to charge for use of those lands, whether to give tax breaks to the fossil fuel industry, whether to subsidize or directly fund that industry, whether to fund the construction of fossil fuel infrastructure such as natural gas pipelines at home and abroad, whether to permit the export and import of fossil fuels from and to the

United States, and whether to authorize new marine coal terminal projects. Plaintiffs assert defendants' decisions on these topics have substantially caused the planet to warm and the oceans to rise. They draw a direct causal line between defendants' policy choices and floods, food shortages, destruction of property, species extinction, and a host of other harms.

This lawsuit is not about proving that climate change is happening or that human activity is driving it. For the purposes of this motion, those facts are undisputed. The questions before the Court are whether defendants are responsible for some of the harm caused by climate change, whether plaintiffs may challenge defendants' climate change policy in court, and whether this Court can direct defendants to change their policy. . . . [Plaintiffs sought several forms of declaratory relief and an injunction ordering defendants to phase out fossil fuel emissions and reduce atmospheric carbon dioxide. The defendants moved to dismiss the complaint, inter alia, for failure to state a claim. The district court denied the motion.]

DISCUSSION

III. Due Process Claims

The Due Process Clause of the Fifth Amendment to the United States Constitution bars the federal government from depriving a person of "life, liberty, or property" without "due process of law." Plaintiffs allege defendants have violated their due process rights by "directly caus[ing] atmospheric CO_2 to rise to levels that dangerously interfere with a stable climate system required alike by our nation and Plaintiffs[,]"; "knowingly endanger[ing] Plaintiffs' health and welfare by approving and promoting fossil fuel development, including exploration, extraction, production, transportation, importation, exportation, and combustion,"; and, "[a]fter knowingly creating this dangerous situation for Plaintiffs, . . . continu[ing] to knowingly enhance that danger by allowing fossil fuel production, consumption, and combustion at dangerous levels."

> **See It**
>
> Click here to see a sample coal-fired power plant emitting carbon dioxide into the atmosphere.

When a plaintiff challenges affirmative government action under the due process clause, the threshold inquiry is the applicable level of judicial scrutiny. The default level of scrutiny is rational basis, which requires a reviewing court to uphold the challenged governmental action so long as it "implements a rational means of achieving a legitimate governmental end[.]" *Kim v. United States*, 121 F.3d 1269, 1273 (9th Cir. 1997). When the government infringes a "fundamental right," however, a reviewing court applies strict scrutiny. Substantive due process "forbids the government to infringe certain 'fundamental' liberty interests *at all*, no matter what process is provided, unless the infringement is narrowly tailored to serve a compelling state interest." *Reno v. Flores*, 507 U.S. 292, 302, 113 S.Ct. 1439, 123 L.Ed.2d 1 (1993) (emphasis in original). It appears undisputed by plaintiffs, and in any event is clear to this Court, that defendants' affirmative actions would survive rational basis review. Resolution of this part of the motions to dismiss therefore hinges on whether plaintiffs have alleged infringement of a fundamental right.

Fundamental liberty rights include both rights enumerated elsewhere in the Constitution and rights and liberties which are either (1) "deeply rooted in this Nation's history and tradition" or (2) "fundamental to our scheme of ordered liberty[.]" *McDonald v. City of Chicago, Ill.*, 561 U.S. 742, 767, 130 S.Ct. 3020, 177 L.Ed.2d 894 (2010). The Supreme Court has cautioned that federal courts must "exercise the utmost care whenever we are asked to break new ground in this field, lest the liberty protected by the Due Process Clause be subtly transformed into" judicial policy preferences. *Washington v. Glucksberg*, 521 U.S. 702, 720, 117 S.Ct. 2258, 138 L.Ed.2d 772 (1997).

This does not mean that "new" fundamental rights are out of bounds, though. When the Supreme Court broke new legal ground by recognizing a constitutional right to same-sex marriage, Justice Kennedy wrote that

> The nature of injustice is that we may not always see it in our own times. The generations that wrote and ratified the Bill of Rights . . . did not presume to know the extent of freedom in all its dimensions, and so they entrusted to future generations a charter protecting the right of all persons to enjoy liberty as we learn its meaning. When new insight reveals discord between the Constitution's central protections and a received legal stricture, a claim to liberty must be addressed.

Obergefell v. Hodges, ___ U.S. ___, 135 S.Ct. 2584, 2598, 192 L.Ed.2d 609 (2015). Thus, "[t]he identification and protection of fundamental rights is an enduring part of the judicial duty to interpret the Constitution . . . [that] has not been reduced to any formula." *Id.* In determining whether a right is fundamental, courts must exercise "reasoned judgment," keeping in mind that "[h]istory and tradition guide and discipline this inquiry but do not set its outer boundaries." *Id.* The genius of the Constitution is that its text allows "future generations [to] protect . . . the right of all persons to enjoy liberty as we learn its meaning." *Id.*

Make the Connection

You studied *Obergefell v. Hodges* in Chapter 6. To what extent does it support the court's analysis here?

. . . Exercising my "reasoned judgment," I have no doubt that the right to a climate system capable of sustaining human life is fundamental to a free and ordered society. Just as marriage is the "foundation of the family," a stable climate system is quite literally the foundation "of society, without which there would be neither civilization nor progress." *Id.* (quoting *Maynard v. Hill*, 125 U.S. 190, 211, 8 S.Ct.

723, 31 L.Ed. 654 (1888)); *cf. Minors Oposa v. Sec'y of the Dep't of Envt'l & Natural Res.*, G.R. No. 101083, 33 I.L.M. 173, 187–88 (S.C., Jul. 30, 1993) (Phil.) (without "a balanced and healthful ecology," future generations "stand to inherit nothing but parched earth incapable of sustaining life."). . . .

. . . In this opinion, this Court simply holds that where a complaint alleges governmental action is affirmatively and substantially damaging the climate system in a way that will cause human deaths, shorten human lifespans, result in widespread damage to property, threaten human food sources, and dramatically alter the planet's ecosystem, it states a claim for a due process violation, To hold otherwise would be to say that the Constitution affords no protection against a government's knowing decision to poison the air its citizens breathe or the water its citizens drink. Plaintiffs have adequately alleged infringement of a fundamental right. . . .

> **Take Note**
>
> *Juliana* was brought on behalf of 21 young plaintiffs, represented by the nonprofit law firm Our Children's Trust. Here the court cites the *Minors Oposa* case, which determined that a class of minor plaintiffs could sue on behalf of themselves and future generations to enforce their constitutional right to a balanced and healthful ecology in the Philippines. That case is fundamental in international environmental law, as the court recognized the plaintiffs' capacity to sue based on the concept of *intergenerational responsibility* in relation to the right to a balanced and healthful ecology.

IV. Public Trust Claims

In its broadest sense, the term "public trust" refers to the fundamental understanding that no government can legitimately abdicate its core sovereign powers. . . . The doctrine conceives of certain powers and obligations—for example, the police power—as inherent aspects of sovereignty. Permitting the government to permanently give one of these powers to another entity runs afoul of the public trust doctrine because it diminishes the power of future legislatures to promote the general welfare.

Plaintiffs' public trust claims arise from the particular application of the public trust doctrine to essential natural resources. With respect to these core resources, the sovereign's public trust obligations prevent it from "depriving a future legislature of the natural resources necessary to provide for the well-being and survival of its citizens.". . . Application of the public trust doctrine to natural resources predates the United States of America. Its roots are in the Institutes of Justinian, part of the Corpus Juris Civilis, the body of Roman law that is the "foundation for modern civil law systems." . . . The Institutes of Justinian declared "the following things are by natural law common to all—the air, running water, the sea, and consequently the seashore." J. Inst. 2.1.1 (J.B. Moyle trans.). The doctrine made its way to the United States through the English common law. . . .

The natural resources trust operates according to basic trust principles, which impose upon the trustee a fiduciary duty to "protect the trust property against damage or destruction." George G. Bogert et al., *Bogert's Trusts and Trustees*, § 582 (2016). The trustee owes this duty equally to both current and future beneficiaries of the trust. . . . In natural resources cases, the trust property consists of a set of resources important enough to the people to warrant public trust protection. . . . The government, as trustee, has a fiduciary duty to protect the trust assets from damage so that current and future trust beneficiaries will be able to enjoy the benefits of the trust. The public trust doctrine is generally thought to impose three types of restrictions on governmental authority:

> [F]irst, the property subject to the trust must not only be used for a public purpose, but it must be held available for use by the general public; second, the property may not be sold, even for a fair cash equivalent; and third, the property must be maintained for particular types of uses.

Joseph L. Sax, *The Public Trust Doctrine in Natural Resource Law: Effective Judicial Intervention*, 68 Mich. L. Rev. 471, 477 (1970).

This lawsuit is part of a wave of recent environmental cases asserting state and national governments have abdicated their responsibilities under the public trust doctrine. . . . These lawsuits depart from the "traditional" public trust litigation model, which generally centers on the second restriction, the prohibition against alienation of a public trust asset. Instead, plaintiffs assert defendants have violated their duties as trustees by nominally retaining control over trust assets while actually allowing their depletion and destruction, effectively violating the first and third restrictions by excluding the public from use and enjoyment of public resources. . . .

The complaint alleges defendants violated their duties as trustees by failing to protect the atmosphere, water, seas, seashores, and wildlife. Defendants and intervenors argue plaintiffs' public trust claims fail because the complaint focuses on harm to the atmosphere, which is not a public trust asset. I conclude that it is not necessary at this stage to determine whether the atmosphere is a public trust asset because plaintiffs have alleged violations of the public trust doctrine in connection with the territorial sea.[10]

The federal government holds title to the submerged lands between three and five miles from the coastlines of the United States. . . . Time and again, the Supreme Court has held that the public trust doctrine applies to "lands beneath tidal waters."

---

[10] To be clear, today's opinion should not be taken to suggest that the atmosphere is not a public trust asset. The Institutes of Justinian included the air in the list of assets "by natural law common to all." J. Inst. 2.1.1 (J.B. Moyle trans.). . . . Even Supreme Court case law suggests the atmosphere may properly be deemed part of the public trust res. See *United States v. Causby*, 328 U.S. 256, 261, 66 S.Ct. 1062, 90 L.Ed. 1206 (1946) (holding that private rights to airspace have "no place in the modern world" because recognition of such claims would "transfer into private ownership that to which only the public has a just claim.") The dearth of litigation focusing on atmosphere may reflect the limited state of scientific knowledge rather than signal a determination that the air is outside the scope of the public trust.

See Phillips Petroleum Co., 484 U.S. at 474, 108 S.Ct. 791 (discussing *Shively*, 152 U.S. at 57, 14 S.Ct. 548 and *Knight v. U.S. Land Ass'n*, 142 U.S. 161, 183, 12 S.Ct. 258, 35 L.Ed. 974 (1891)); *Alabama v. Texas*, 347 U.S. 272, 278, 74 S.Ct. 481, 98 L.Ed. 689 (1954) (Black, J., dissenting) ("In ocean waters bordering our country, if nowhere else, day-to-day national power—complete, undivided, flexible, and immediately available—is an essential attribute of federal sovereignty."); *id.* at 282, 74 S.Ct. 481 (Douglas, J., dissenting) ("Thus we are dealing here with incidents of national sovereignty. . . . The authority over [the sea] can no more be abdicated than any of the other great powers of the Federal Government. It is to be exercised for the benefit of the whole."); *see also* Joseph L. Sax, *The Public Trust Doctrine in Natural Resource Law; Effective Judicial Intervention*, 68 Mich. L. Rev. 471, 556 (1970) (public trust law covers "that aspect of the public domain below the low-water mark on the margin of the sea and the great lakes, the waters over those lands, and the waters within rivers and streams of any consequence"). Because a number of plaintiffs' injuries relate to the effects of ocean acidification and rising ocean temperatures, they have adequately alleged harm to public trust assets. . . .

CONCLUSION

. . . This action is of a different order than the typical environmental case. It alleges that defendants' actions and inactions—whether or not they violate any specific statutory duty—have so profoundly damaged our home planet that they threaten plaintiffs' fundamental constitutional rights to life and liberty.

A deep resistance to change runs through defendants' and intervenors' arguments for dismissal: they contend a decision recognizing plaintiffs' standing to sue, deeming the controversy justiciable, and recognizing a federal public trust and a fundamental right to climate system capable of sustaining human life would be unprecedented, as though that alone requires its dismissal. This lawsuit may be groundbreaking, but that fact does not alter the legal standards governing the motions to dismiss. . . .

. . . Defendants' Motion to Dismiss . . . [is] DENIED.

Points for Discussion

a. **Evaluating *Juliana***

Is there a constitutional right to a stable climate system? In a few situations, the Supreme Court has recognized a right not specifically enumerated in the Constitution as a fundamental right, through interpreting the term "liberty" in the Due Process Clause. But these are all highly personal rights, such as the right to have an abortion and the right to marry. Is a right to a stable climate system similarly fundamental? *See* Mia Hammersley, *The Right to a Healthy and Stable Climate System: Fundamental or Unfounded?*, 7 Ariz. J. Envtl. L. & Pol'y 117 (2017). *See also In re Maui Electric Co., Ltd.*, 408 P.3d 1, 13 (Haw. 2017) (holding that "the right to a clean and healthful environment" in the state constitution is "a property interest protected by due process").

Moreover, traditionally the public trust doctrine applies only to bodies of water, watercourses, wetlands, beaches, and certain other lands directly affected by water. Should this doctrine be extended to include the atmosphere? *See Sanders-Reed v. Martinez*, 350 P.3d 1221, 1227 (N.M. Ct. App. 2015) ("[C]ourts cannot independently intervene to impose a common law public trust duty upon the State to regulate greenhouse gases in the atmosphere.").

b.   Global Climate Change and Property Law

Among other impacts, climate change will presumably increase coastal flooding; reduce rain and snow in some regions; reduce soil moisture; change the crops, trees, and other vegetation that can grow in particular areas; change animal migration patterns; and endanger some animal and plant species. How will these impacts, in turn, affect the evolution of American property law? Are there economic reasons to combat climate change? Or is it a moral duty?

c.   Land Use Regulation

Can global climate change be mitigated at the state level? California—one of the largest emitters of greenhouse gases in the world—has established the goals of (1) reducing its statewide emissions to 40% of 1990 levels by 2030 and (2) achieving net zero greenhouse gas emissions by 2045. Cal. Health & Safety Code §§ 38566, 38562.2. One of the techniques used to reach this goal will be land use regulation. For example, the California Environmental Quality Act, Cal. Pub. Res. Code § 21000 et seq., effectively requires the preparation of an environmental impact report for any new development project that may have a significant effect on the environment. Adverse impacts must be eliminated or mitigated in order for the project to gain approval. In the past, the potential climate change impacts of a project—usually carbon dioxide emissions caused by increased traffic—were ignored. State and local regulators are beginning to consider the global impacts of local projects. *See* Dave Owen, *Climate Change and Environmental Assessment Law*, 33 Colum. J. Envtl. L. 57 (2008). How might this process affect the design and location of future housing projects?

d.   Emissions Trading Systems

Can a property rights system in greenhouse gas emissions help to stop climate change? The United States insisted that such an emissions trading arrangement be included in the Kyoto Protocol, the principal treaty that mandates international reductions in greenhouse gas emissions. A number of states already have active cap-and-trade systems in place. Do you understand why this approach may be an efficient method to reduce emissions?

e. **Coastal Flooding**

Suppose that rising sea levels eventually flood O's oceanfront property; it is underwater every day at high tide. Is it now subject to the public trust doctrine, such that O cannot build anything on the land? Alternatively, could O install a dike around his land to fend off the incoming ocean? Of course, this would divert ocean water onto the lands of other owners, worsening their problems. Would O's dike be a private nuisance?

f. **Landmark Climate Change Case**

In *Held v. Montana*, 2023 WL 5229257 (Mont. Dist. Ct.), youth plaintiffs successfully challenged laws adopted by the state legislature that required no consideration of greenhouse gas emissions and climate change impacts of energy development as violating the Montana State Constitution's protection of a constitutional right to a healthy environment. *Held* was the first youth-led constitutional climate change lawsuit to actually go to trial. David Gelles and Mike Baker, *Judge Rules in Favor of Montana Youths in a Landmark Climate Case*, N.Y. Times, Aug. 14, 2023. What distinct interests do youth plaintiffs represent in their lawsuits seeking protection of the environment?

g. **Aftermath of *Juliana***

After extensive appellate litigation, the Ninth Circuit "[r]eluctantly" ordered that the case be dismissed because granting relief "is beyond our constitutional power." *Juliana v. United States*, 947 F.3d 1159, 1165 (9th Cir. 2020). However, on June 1, 2023 Judge Aiken granted the *Juliana* plaintiffs' motion to amend their complaint to seek a more limited form of declaratory relief, including a declaration that the current United States' national energy system violates the plaintiffs' rights to substantive due process and equal protection of the law. Accordingly, she ruled that the case could proceed to trial. Her order stated:

> It is a foundational doctrine that when government conduct catastrophically harms American citizens, the judiciary is constitutionally required to perform its independent role and determine whether the challenged conduct, not exclusively committed to any branch by the Constitution, is unconstitutional.

Juliana v. United States, 2023 WL 3750334 at *8 (D. Or.).

Summary

- **Ecological Perspective.** Under the ecological perspective, the right of an owner to change the natural character of his land is not absolute.
- **Public Trust.** Navigable waters and related lands are held in trust by federal and state governments for the benefit of the public. The traditional uses of public

trust lands are navigation, commerce, and fisheries. Some states have expanded the public trust doctrine to serve new purposes.

- **Clean Water Act.** The discharge of a pollutant into "navigable waters" without a permit is a violation of the Act. Adjacent wetlands are included within the meaning of navigable waters.

- **CERCLA.** This Act imposes strict liability for the cleanup of a hazardous waste site on four categories of parties who are linked to the site: current owners and operators; past owners and operators at time of disposal; generators; and transporters.

> **Test Your Knowledge**
>
> To assess your understanding of the material in this chapter, click here to take a quiz.

- **Endangered Species Act.** Modifying the habitat of a protected species may be an illegal "take" under the Act. Habitat conservation plans are used to avoid this problem.

- **Climate Change.** Climate change will affect the evolution of American property law. In turn, property concepts may help to combat climate change.

> **For More Information**
>
> For more information about the subjects covered in this chapter, please consult these sources:
>
> - Harrison Beck, *Locating Liability for Climate Change: A Comparative Analysis of Recent Trends in Climate Jurisprudence*, 50 Envtl. L. 885 (2020).
> - J. Peter Byrne, *The Cathedral Engulfed: Sea-Level Rise, Property Rights, and Time*, 73 La. L. Rev. 69 (2012).
> - Eric T. Freyfogle, *The Owning and Taking of Sensitive Lands*, 43 UCLA L. Rev. 77 (1995).
> - Stephen M. Meyer, *The Economic Impact of the Endangered Species Act on the Housing and Real Estate Markets*, 6 N.Y.U. Envtl. L.J. 450 (1998).
> - Eric A. Posner & Cass R. Sunstein, *Climate Change Justice*, 96 Geo. L.J. 1565 (2008).
> - Jedediah Purdy, *Our Place in the World: A New Relationship for Environmental Ethics and Law*, 62 Duke L.J. 857 (2013).

Chapter 13

Eminent Domain

Suppose that the federal government plans to build a new interstate highway through land owned by A. What if A is unwilling to sell her land? The government may take the property over A's objection by using its power of *eminent domain*. The process of using eminent domain to take property is called *condemnation*.

Eminent domain allows federal, state, and local governments to take property from a private owner who refuses to sell voluntarily. Government entities often need to acquire property that is owned by private citizens. For example, the federal government might need land for a military installation; a state might require a site for a university; or a city might want property for a park. If government did not have the eminent domain power, an owner like A could flatly refuse to convey property that is needed for the general welfare of society. Or she could demand an exorbitant purchase price, far above the fair market value of the property.

The Framers of our Constitution viewed the eminent domain power as an *inherent* attribute of sovereignty. But they recognized the tension between a citizen's right to own property and the government's interest in acquiring it for the public good. Accordingly, the Constitution *limits* the government's eminent domain power. These limits are contained in the *Takings Clause* of the Fifth Amendment, which provides: "[N]or shall private property be taken for public use, without just compensation." Thus, the Constitution places two restrictions on eminent domain: (1) the government may take property only for a "public use;" and (2) the private owner must receive "just compensation."

> **FYI**
>
> Originally, the Fifth Amendment only restricted the conduct of the federal government. However, the Fourteenth Amendment extended the provisions of the Fifth Amendment to state and local governments. In addition, virtually every state constitution contains a provision similar to the federal Takings Clause.

What is the purpose of the Takings Clause? In *Tyler v. Hennepin County*, 598 U.S. 631, 647 (2023)—a unanimous opinion—the Court reiterated that the Clause "was designed to bar Government from forcing some people alone to bear public burdens which, in all fairness and justice, should be borne by the public as a whole" (quoting *Armstrong v. United States*, 364 U.S. 40, 49 (1960)).

A. Defining Public Use

What is a *public use*? Most of this chapter is devoted to answering that question. Of course, the standard is easily satisfied when government takes land that will physically be used by the public (such as a highway) or by government employees (such as a military installation).

But suppose that a city evicts low-income residents from their homes and turns the properties over to private developers who intend to build office buildings, shopping centers, and tourist facilities in order to revive the city's deteriorating downtown core. Is this a taking for public use or a taking for private benefit? Increasingly, local governments use eminent domain to clear slums, redistribute land, attract businesses, create jobs, and revitalize distressed urban centers. In effect, such a city is forcing one private owner to transfer her land to another private owner. Whether this transfer meets the public use test is an issue of considerable importance—and complexity.

> ### Perspective and Analysis
>
> Colonial and early American uses of eminent domain were confined mainly to the building of roads, schools, and other public buildings. In some cases eminent domain furthered economic development, but generally, while the eminent domain power was established and accepted, little discussion about the meaning of public use occurred. Moreover, the Fifth Amendment Takings Clause did not apply to the states until 1897; thus, unless local state constitutions had a public use stipulation, states were not limited by federal constitutional standards. . . .
>
> From the 1840s on the broad public benefit construction of public use seemed to be eclipsed by the narrow "use by the public" standard. . . . Despite the fact that the narrow doctrine was influential in the latter half of the nineteenth century, its use did not go unquestioned. . . . [T]he narrow construction was mostly given lip service during the nineteenth century and by the beginning of the twentieth century it was all but dead. The narrow doctrine, declaring void any transfer of land from one private party to another regardless of the ultimate public purpose, did not really halt many state eminent domain projects. . . .
>
> [T]hroughout the nineteenth century the scope of legislative power to take property was tied to its authority to define "public use," but that authority was not always clear or consistent. There was debate over which branch of government had the right to make public use decisions and authorize the taking of private property. It was not until after World War II that the debate over the construction of this term was resolved in favor of legislatures.
>
> **David A. Schultz, Property, Power, and American Democracy 75–78 (1992).**

In the 1960s, most private land in Hawaii was owned by a handful of individuals, often descendants of Hawaiian royal families. Due to this concentrated ownership, land prices were extremely high, beyond the reach of most residents. This small group of landowners generally refused to sell fee simple titles; instead, they preferred to lease their properties. The Hawaii Legislature adopted a statute that allowed a state agency to use eminent domain to take fee titles from the lessors for resale to the lessees. Our next case examines whether such takings meet the public use requirement.

Hawaii Housing Authority v. Midkiff

Supreme Court of the United States

467 U.S. 229 (1984)

JUSTICE O'CONNOR delivered the opinion of the Court.

The Fifth Amendment of the United States Constitution provides, in pertinent part, that "private property [shall not] be taken for public use, without just compensation." These cases present the question whether the Public Use Clause of that Amendment, made applicable to the States through the Fourteenth Amendment, prohibits the State of Hawaii from taking, with just compensation, title in real property from lessors and transferring it to lessees in order to reduce the concentration of ownership of fees simple in the State. We conclude that it does not. . . .

> **FYI**
>
> Plaintiff Frank Midkiff was a trustee of the Bishop Estate, one of the largest landowners in Hawaii; he and the other trustees sued in this case on behalf of the Estate. At the time, the Estate owned 9% of all the land in the state, including 22% of all privately owned land on the island of Oahu. One of the richest private charities in the world, the Estate was funded by the will of Princess Bernice Pauahi Bishop, the great-granddaughter of King Kamehameha. Click here to see a photograph of Princess Bishop. The Estate used the revenue from its extensive lands to support the Kamehameha Schools, which provided education to thousands of underprivileged Hawaiian children.

I.

. . . Beginning in the early 1800's, Hawaiian leaders and American settlers repeatedly attempted to divide the lands of the kingdom among the crown, the chiefs, and the common people. These efforts proved largely unsuccessful, however, and the land remained in the hands of a few. In the mid-1960's, after extensive hearings, the Hawaii Legislature discovered that, while the State and Federal Governments owned almost 49% of the State's land, another 47% was in the hands of only 72 private landowners. . . . The legislature further found that 18 landholders, with tracts of 21,000 acres or more, owned more than 40% of this land and that on Oahu, the most urbanized of the islands, 22 landowners owned 72.5% of the fee simple titles. . . . The legislature concluded that concentrated land ownership was responsible for skewing the State's residential fee simple market, inflating land prices, and injuring the public tranquility and welfare.

To redress these problems, the legislature . . . considered requiring large landowners to sell lands which they were leasing to homeowners. However, the landowners strongly resisted this scheme, pointing out the significant federal tax liabilities they would incur. Indeed, the landowners claimed that the federal tax laws were the primary reason they previously had chosen to lease, and not sell, their lands. Therefore, to accommodate the needs of both lessors and lessees, the Hawaii Legislature enacted the Land Reform Act of 1967 (Act), Haw. Rev. Stat., ch. 516, which created a mechanism for condemning residential tracts and for transferring ownership of the condemned fees simple to existing lessees. By condemning the land in question, the Hawaii Legislature intended to make the land sales involuntary, thereby making the federal tax consequences less severe while still facilitating the redistribution of fees simple. . . .

Under the Act's condemnation scheme, tenants living on single-family residential lots within developmental tracts at least five acres in size are entitled to ask the Hawaii Housing Authority (HHA) to condemn the property on which they live. Haw. Rev. Stat. §§ 516–1(2), (11), 516–22 (1977). When 25 eligible tenants, or tenants on half the lots in the tract, whichever is less, file appropriate applications, the Act authorizes HHA to hold a public hearing to determine whether acquisition by the State of all or part of the tract will "effectuate the public purposes" of the Act. . . . If HHA finds that these public purposes will be served, it is authorized to designate some or all of the lots in the tract for acquisition. It then acquires, at prices set either by condemnation trial or by negotiation between lessors and lessees, the former fee owners' full "right, title, and interest" in the land. . . .

> **Practice Pointer**
>
> *Condemnation* is a multistage process. Usually, the government begins the process by contacting the owner and attempting to negotiate a voluntary sale of the property. If the parties cannot come to an agreement, the government will file an eminent domain lawsuit against the unwilling owner. If the government is successful in demonstrating that its taking is for a public use and that it has met all other requirements of the jurisdiction, the court will determine the fair market value of the property and render a judgment that mandates the transfer of title to the government.

[A]ppellees filed suit, in February 1979, in United States District Court, asking that the Act be declared unconstitutional and that its enforcement be enjoined. . . . The District Court found that the Act's goals were within the bounds of the State's police powers and that the means the legislature had chosen to serve those goals were not arbitrary, capricious, or selected in bad faith.

The Court of Appeals for the Ninth Circuit reversed. 702 F.2d 788 (CA9 1983).... [T]he Court of Appeals determined that the Act could not pass the requisite judicial scrutiny of the Public Use Clause. It found that the transfers contemplated by the Act were unlike those of takings previously held to constitute "public uses" by this Court. The court further determined that the public purposes offered by the Hawaii Legislature were not deserving of judicial deference. The court concluded that the Act was simply "a naked attempt on the part of the state of Hawaii to take the private property of A and transfer it to B solely for B's private use and benefit." *Id.*, at 798. . . . We now reverse. . . .

III.

The starting point for our analysis of the Act's constitutionality is the Court's decision in *Berman v. Parker*, 348 U.S. 26 (1954). In *Berman*, the Court held constitutional the District of Columbia Redevelopment Act of 1945. That Act provided both for the comprehensive use of the eminent domain power to redevelop slum areas and for the possible sale or lease of the condemned lands to private interests. In discussing whether the takings authorized by that Act were for a "public use," the Court stated:

> We deal, in other words, with what traditionally has been known as the police power. An attempt to define its reach or trace its outer limits is fruitless, for each case must turn on its own facts. The definition is essentially the product of legislative determinations addressed to the purposes of government, purposes neither abstractly nor historically capable of complete definition. Subject to specific constitutional limitations, when the legislature has spoken, the public interest has been declared in terms well-nigh conclusive. In such cases the legislature, not the judiciary, is the main guardian of the public needs to be served by social legislation, whether it be Congress legislating concerning the District of Columbia ... or the States legislating concerning local affairs.... This principle admits of no exception merely because the power of eminent domain is involved.... *Id.*, at 32 (citations omitted).

... The "public use" requirement is thus coterminous with the scope of a sovereign's police powers.

There is, of course, a role for courts to play in reviewing a legislature's judgment of what constitutes a public use, even when the eminent domain power is equated with the police power....

But where the exercise of the eminent domain power is rationally related to a conceivable public purpose, the Court has never held a compensated taking to be proscribed by the Public Use Clause....

On this basis, we have no trouble concluding that the Hawaii Act is constitutional. The people of Hawaii have attempted, much as the settlers of the original 13 Colonies did, to reduce the perceived social and economic evils of a land oligopoly traceable to their monarchs. The land oligopoly has, according to the Hawaii Legislature, created artificial deterrents to the normal functioning of the State's residential land market and forced thousands of individual homeowners to lease, rather than buy, the land underneath their homes. Regulating oligopoly and the evils associated with it is a classic exercise of a State's police powers. . . .

> **Practice Pointer**
>
> An attorney can shape a court's understanding of a case by how she frames the issue. In *Midkiff*, the attorney representing the Hawaiian Housing Authority was Laurence Tribe, a professor at Harvard Law School and a nationally renowned expert on constitutional law. Tribe argued in his brief that the "issue in this case is whether the United States Constitution freezes the fiftieth state into its feudal past." What is your reaction to this statement of the issue?

Of course, this Act, like any other, may not be successful in achieving its intended goals. But "whether in fact the provision will accomplish its objectives is not the question: the [constitutional requirement] is satisfied if . . . the . . . [state] Legislature *rationally could have believed* that the [Act] would promote its objective." *Western & Southern Life Ins. Co. v. State Bd. of Equalization*, 451 U.S. 648, 671–672 (1981). . . . When the legislature's purpose is legitimate and its means are not irrational, our cases make clear that empirical debates over the wisdom of takings—no less than debates over the wisdom of other kinds of socioeconomic legislation—are not to be carried out in the federal courts. Redistribution of fees simple to correct deficiencies in the market determined by the state legislature to be attributable to land oligopoly is a rational exercise of the eminent domain power. Therefore, the Hawaii statute must pass the scrutiny of the Public Use Clause. . . .

The mere fact that property taken outright by eminent domain is transferred in the first instance to private beneficiaries does not condemn that taking as having only a private purpose. The Court long ago rejected any literal requirement that condemned property be put into use for the general public. . . . As the unique way titles were held in Hawaii skewed the land market, exercise of the power of eminent domain was justified. . . . In such cases, government does not itself have to use property to legitimate the taking; it is only the taking's purpose, and not its mechanics, that must pass scrutiny under the Public Use Clause. . . .

IV.

The State of Hawaii has never denied that the Constitution forbids even a compensated taking of property when executed for no reason other than to confer a private benefit on a particular private party. A purely private taking could not withstand the scrutiny of the public use requirement; it would serve no legitimate purpose of government and would thus be void. But no purely private taking is involved in these cases. The Hawaii Legislature enacted its Land Reform Act not to benefit a particular class of identifiable individuals but to attack certain perceived evils of concentrated property ownership in Hawaii—a legitimate public purpose. Use of the condemnation power to achieve this purpose is not irrational. Since we assume for purposes of these appeals that the weighty demand of just compensation has been met, the requirements of the Fifth and Fourteenth Amendments have been satisfied. Accordingly, we reverse the judgment of the Court of Appeals, and remand these cases for further proceedings in conformity with this opinion.

Points for Discussion

a. **Who Should Bear the Burden?**

Justice O'Connor's opinion noted that state and federal governments owned almost 49% of the land in Hawaii. Why couldn't the state have accomplished its twin goals of (1) reducing the concentration of land ownership and (2) deflating land prices by selling some of these lands? Why should private owners bear the burden of this social reordering?

b. **Public Use Limitation**

At a minimum, the public use limitation prevents government from using its eminent domain power to take property for a purely private use, *even if* it is willing to pay fair market value to the owner. But beyond this point, the precise meaning of "public use" is less than clear. Under a *narrow* definition, "public use" could be taken quite literally to mean physical use by members of the public, as mentioned in the Schultz excerpt above. Under this definition, government could exercise its eminent domain power to take land for purposes such as public highways, parks, and universities (which could be used by the public), but not for private hotels, office buildings, or shopping centers (from which the public could be excluded). Using a *broad* construction, "public use" would simply require that the project provide some public benefit, regardless of who physically uses the land. Under this definition, government could use eminent domain to clear slums or redevelop struggling inner-city economies by forcing individual owners to sell to private developers. Which definition did the Court employ in *Midkiff*? Which is the better view?

c. **Understanding Public Use**

Which of the following examples of eminent domain satisfy the public use test as defined in *Midkiff*?

(1) City A acquires older homes and sells them to X, an internationally renowned architect, who plans to convert them into ultra-modern, luxury houses for sale to the wealthy.

> (2) Township B takes title to a historic house owned by grandmother G, and transfers it to Z, a billionaire who owns a famous software company, as an incentive to keep his company in the community.
>
> (3) City C acquires a professional football team to keep it from moving to another state, and thereby maintain the viability of the city's arena, restaurants, and stores, all of which depend on business generated by the team's presence.

d. **Legislative Deference**

How much deference should a court give to the decision of a local legislature (like a city council) that a particular exercise of eminent domain is for a public use? Courts generally give great deference to such decisions. Indeed, the *Midkiff* Court noted that it had *never* held a compensated taking to be barred by the Takings Clause if the condemnation was rationally related to a conceivable public purpose. In one of the most cited passages from the opinion, Justice O'Connor stated, "[t]he 'public use' requirement is . . . coterminous with the scope of a sovereign's police powers." Does this authorize the use of eminent domain whenever a reasonable person could believe that it relates to a permissible government goal? Should a court's review be limited to assuring that the condemnation is rationally related to the health, safety, or general welfare of the community? Or is a higher standard of review appropriate?

e. **Rationale for Eminent Domain**

Eminent domain is a vital government power. Without it, government would be placed at the mercy of monopoly control. Suppose that a state needs to acquire 100 separate pieces of land in order to build a new university. If the state lacked eminent domain power, any *one* landowner could refuse to sell (or "hold out"), thus dooming the *entire* project. Alternatively, the owner might agree to sell, but only for an exorbitant purchase price; he might demand $1,000,000 for a parcel worth $50,000. As one early court noted, "[a] railway cannot run around unreasonable land-owners." *Ryerson v. Brown*, 35 Mich. 333, 340 (1877). Armed with eminent domain power, however, the government can ensure that no single owner will block important projects that benefit all citizens. Interestingly, in *Midkiff* the state used eminent domain to *disperse* the concentration of land ownership, not to *aggregate* parcels. Is such a use supported by the rationale for eminent domain?

f. **Just Compensation**

An important limit on eminent domain is the requirement that government pay *just compensation*. Just compensation is often equated with fair market value. But the determination of fair market value is less precise than most people would expect. Theoretically, *fair market value* is the price that a willing seller would accept and a willing buyer would pay for a particular property on the open market. By definition, however, the owner whose property is taken by eminent domain is *not* a willing seller. So how can fair market value be computed? By analyzing the recent sales prices for nearby, comparable parcels, an appraiser can generally estimate the price that a willing buyer would have paid for the parcel. But this process may not accurately reflect the value of the property to the unwilling seller.

> **What About Your State?**
>
> Click here to learn how your state determines "just compensation" for properties taken by eminent domain.

Other issues arise as well. For example, does the owner receive consequential damages, such as moving expenses and carrying charges? (generally not) Does fair market value include the owner's subjective or emotional attachments to the property? (no) Is greater compensation required when dealing with an elderly or poor owner, who may have fewer options to find replacement shelter? (no) If an ongoing business with an established customer base is condemned, do damages include the loss of goodwill? (generally not) If only a portion of the land is condemned, is the owner entitled to compensation for the "severance damage" to his remaining land? (yes)

g. Aftermath of *Midkiff*

In *Midkiff*, the Court conceded that the state's program might not be successful in achieving its goals of (1) creating a more robust housing market and (2) thereby reducing the cost of housing. In fact, land prices skyrocketed in Hawaii after *Midkiff*, spurred on by investors who purchased the newly available fee simple estates. These investors often tore down the existing houses and built large, expensive homes which they marketed as vacation residences. As a result, housing in Hawaii became less available and more expensive.

B. Scope of Public Use

In 1998, Pfizer Inc.—a major pharmaceuticals company—announced that it would build a research facility in the economically depressed city of New London, Connecticut. The city prepared a plan to redevelop 90 acres near the Pfizer site in order to create jobs, increase tax revenues, and revitalize the local economy. Under its plan, the city would acquire title to the privately owned parcels in the redevelopment area, and then transfer title to various private developers who would construct new homes, offices, restaurants, shops, and other improvements. When a group of homeowners refused to sell, the city decided it would take their properties by eminent domain. But can a city take private property from one owner in order to transfer it to a new owner who will use it more productively?

Kelo v. City of New London

Supreme Court of the United States

545 U.S. 469 (2005)

JUSTICE STEVENS delivered the opinion of the Court.

In 2000, the city of New London approved a development plan that, in the words of the Supreme Court of Connecticut, was "projected to create in excess of 1,000 jobs, to increase tax and other revenues, and to revitalize an economically distressed city, including its downtown and waterfront areas." In assembling the land needed for this project, the city's development agent has purchased property from willing sellers and proposes to use the power of eminent domain to acquire the remainder of the property from unwilling owners in exchange for just compensation. The question presented is whether the city's proposed disposition of this property qualifies as a "public use" within the meaning of the Takings Clause of the Fifth Amendment to the Constitution.

> **See It**
>
> Click here to view a map of the planned development.

I.

The city of New London (hereinafter City) sits at the junction of the Thames River and the Long Island Sound in southeastern Connecticut. Decades of economic decline led a state agency in 1990 to designate the City as a "distressed municipality." In 1996, the Federal Government closed the Naval Undersea Warfare Center, which had been located in the Fort Trumbull area of the City and had employed over 1,500 people. In 1998, the City's unemployment rate was nearly double that of the State, and its population of just under 24,000 residents was at its lowest since 1920.

These conditions prompted state and local officials to target New London, and particularly its Fort Trumbull area, for economic revitalization. To this end, respondent New London Development Corporation (NLDC), a private non-profit entity established some years earlier to assist the City in planning economic development, was reactivated. In January 1998, the State authorized a $5.35 million bond issue to support the NLDC's planning activities and a $10 million bond issue toward the creation of a Fort Trumbull State Park. In February, the

> **FYI**
>
> Click here to view the economic impact report on the redevelopment project for the Fort Trumbull region that was prepared by the Connecticut Center for Economic Analysis.

pharmaceutical company Pfizer Inc. announced that it would build a $300 million research facility on a site immediately adjacent to Fort Trumbull; local planners hoped that Pfizer would draw new business to the area, thereby serving as a catalyst to the area's rejuvenation. . . .

The Fort Trumbull area is situated on a peninsula that juts into the Thames River. The area comprises approximately 115 privately owned properties, as well as the 32 acres of land formerly occupied by the naval facility (Trumbull State Park now occupies 18 of those 32 acres). The development plan encompasses seven parcels. Parcel 1 is designated for a waterfront conference hotel at the center of a "small urban village" that will include restaurants and shopping. This parcel will also have marinas for both recreational and commercial uses. A pedestrian "riverwalk"

Kelo's house (moved to new location)
Click here for larger photo

will originate here and continue down the coast, connecting the waterfront areas of the development. Parcel 2 will be the site of approximately 80 new residences organized into an urban neighborhood and linked by public walkway to the remainder of the development, including the state park. This parcel also includes space reserved for a new U.S. Coast Guard Museum. Parcel 3, which is located immediately north of the Pfizer facility, will contain at least 90,000 square feet of research and development office space. Parcel 4A is a 2.4-acre site that will be used either to support the adjacent state park, by providing parking or retail services for visitors, or to support the nearby marina. Parcel 4B will include a renovated marina, as well as the final stretch of the riverwalk. Parcels 5, 6, and 7 will provide land for office and retail space, parking, and water-dependent commercial uses. . . .

The NLDC intended the development plan to capitalize on the arrival of the Pfizer facility and the new commerce it was expected to attract. In addition to creating jobs, generating tax revenue, and helping to "build momentum for the revitalization of downtown New London," the plan was also designed to make the City more attractive and to create leisure and recreational opportunities on the waterfront and in the park. . . .

II.

Petitioner Susette Kelo has lived in the Fort Trumbull area since 1997. She has made extensive improvements to her house, which she prizes for its water view. Petitioner Wilhelmina Dery was born in her Fort Trumbull house in 1918 and has lived there her entire life. Her husband Charles (also a petitioner) has lived in the house since they married some 60 years ago. In all, the nine petitioners own 15 properties in Fort Trumbull—4 in parcel 3 of the development plan and 11 in parcel 4A. Ten of the parcels are occupied by the owner or a family member; the other five are held as investment properties. There is no allegation that any of these properties is blighted or otherwise in poor condition; rather, they were condemned only because they happen to be located in the development area.

In December 2000, petitioners brought this action in the New London Superior Court. They claimed, among other things, that the taking of their properties would violate the "public use" restriction in the Fifth Amendment. After a 7-day bench trial, the Superior Court granted a permanent restraining order prohibiting the taking of the properties located in parcel 4A (park or marina support). It, however, denied petitioners relief as to the properties located in parcel 3 (office space)....

After the Superior Court ruled, both sides took appeals to the Supreme Court of Connecticut. That court held, over a dissent, that all of the City's proposed takings were valid. It began by upholding the lower court's determination that the takings were authorized by chapter 132, the State's municipal development statute. See Conn. Gen. Stat. § 8–186 *et seq.* (2005). That statute expresses a legislative determination that the taking of land, even developed land, as part of an economic development project is a "public use" and in the "public interest." Next, relying on cases such as *Hawaii Housing Authority v. Midkiff,* 467 U.S. 229 (1984), and *Berman v. Parker,* 348 U.S. 26 (1954), the court held that such economic development qualified as a valid public use under both the Federal and State Constitutions....

We granted certiorari to determine whether a city's decision to take property for the purpose of economic development satisfies the "public use" requirement of the Fifth Amendment....

III.

Two polar propositions are perfectly clear. On the one hand, it has long been accepted that the sovereign may not take the property of *A* for the sole purpose of transferring it to another private party *B,* even though *A* is paid just compensation. On the other hand, it is equally clear that a State may transfer property from one private party to another if future "use by the public" is the purpose of the taking; the condemnation of land for a railroad with common-carrier duties is a familiar example....

As for the first proposition, the City would no doubt be forbidden from taking petitioners' land for the purpose of conferring a private benefit on a particular private party. . . . Nor would the City be allowed to take property under the mere pretext of a public purpose, when its actual purpose was to bestow a private benefit. The takings before us, however, would be executed pursuant to a "carefully considered" development plan. The trial judge and all the members of the Supreme Court of Connecticut agreed that there was no evidence of an illegitimate purpose in this case. Therefore . . . the City's development plan was not adopted "to benefit a particular class of identifiable individuals."

On the other hand, this is not a case in which the City is planning to open the condemned land—at least not in its entirety—to use by the general public. . . . But although such a projected use would be sufficient to satisfy the public use requirement, this "Court long ago rejected any literal requirement that condemned property be put into use for the general public." . . .

The disposition of this case therefore turns on the question whether the City's development plan serves a "public purpose." Without exception, our cases have defined that concept broadly, reflecting our longstanding policy of deference to legislative judgments in this field.

In *Berman v. Parker*, 348 U.S. 26 (1954), this Court upheld a redevelopment plan targeting a blighted area of Washington, D. C., in which most of the housing for the area's 5,000 inhabitants was beyond repair. Under the plan, the area would be condemned and part of it utilized for the construction of streets, schools, and other public facilities. The

> **Hear It**
>
> Wesley Horton represented the City of New London before the Supreme Court. Click here to hear part of Horton's oral argument, where several justices question him about the propriety of "taking from private citizen A and giving to private citizen B."

remainder of the land would be leased or sold to private parties for the purpose of redevelopment, including the construction of low-cost housing.

The owner of a department store located in the area challenged the condemnation, pointing out that his store was not itself blighted and arguing that the creation of a "better balanced, more attractive community" was not a valid public use. . . . Writing for a unanimous Court, Justice Douglas refused to evaluate this claim in isolation, deferring instead to the legislative and agency judgment that the area "must be planned as a whole" for the plan to be successful. . . . The Court explained that "community redevelopment programs need not, by force of the Constitution, be on a piecemeal basis-lot by lot, building by building." . . . The public use underlying the taking was unequivocally affirmed:

> We do not sit to determine whether a particular housing project is or is not desirable. The concept of the public welfare is broad and inclusive. . . . The values it represents are spiritual as well as physical, aesthetic as well as monetary. It is within the power of the legislature to determine that the community should be beautiful as well as healthy, spacious as well as clean, well-balanced as well as carefully patrolled. In the

present case, the Congress and its authorized agencies have made determinations that take into account a wide variety of values. It is not for us to reappraise them. If those who govern the District of Columbia decide that the Nation's Capital should be beautiful as well as sanitary, there is nothing in the Fifth Amendment that stands in the way. *Id.,* at 33.

In *Hawaii Housing Authority v. Midkiff,* 467 U.S. 229, 244 (1984), the Court considered a Hawaii statute whereby fee title was taken from lessors and transferred to lessees (for just compensation) in order to reduce the concentration of land ownership. We unanimously upheld the statute and rejected the Ninth Circuit's view that it was "a naked attempt on the part of the state of Hawaii to take the property of A and transfer it to B solely for B's private use and benefit." . . . Reaffirming *Berman's* deferential approach to legislative judgments in this field, we concluded that the State's purpose of eliminating the "social and economic evils of a land oligopoly" qualified as a valid public use. . . . Our opinion also rejected the contention that the mere fact that the State immediately transferred the properties to private individuals upon condemnation somehow diminished the public character of the taking. "[I]t is only the taking's purpose, and not its mechanics," we explained, that matters in determining public use. . . .

IV.

. . . Those who govern the City were not confronted with the need to remove blight in the Fort Trumbull area, but their determination that the area was sufficiently distressed to justify a program of economic rejuvenation is entitled to our deference. The City has carefully formulated an economic development plan that it believes will provide appreciable benefits to the community, including—but by no means limited to—new jobs and increased tax revenue. As with other exercises in urban planning and development, the City is endeavoring to coordinate a variety of commercial, residential, and recreational uses of land, with the hope that they will form a whole greater than the sum of its parts. To effectuate this plan, the City has invoked a state statute that specifically authorizes the use of eminent domain to promote economic development. Given the comprehensive character of the plan, the thorough deliberation that preceded its adoption, and the limited scope of our review, it is appropriate for us, as it was in *Berman,* to resolve the challenges of the individual owners, not on a piecemeal basis, but rather in light of the entire plan. Because that plan unquestionably serves a public purpose, the takings challenged here satisfy the public use requirement of the Fifth Amendment.

To avoid this result, petitioners urge us to adopt a new bright-line rule that economic development does not qualify as a public use. Putting aside the unpersuasive suggestion that the City's plan will provide only purely economic benefits, neither precedent nor logic supports petitioners' proposal. Promoting economic development is a traditional and long accepted function of government. There is, moreover, no principled way of distinguishing economic development from the other public purposes that we have recognized. In our cases upholding takings that facilitated agriculture and mining, for example, we emphasized the importance of those industries to the welfare of the States in question, see, *e.g., Strickley* [*v. Highland Boy Gold Mining Co.,*] 200 U.S. 527 [(1906)]; in *Berman,* we endorsed the purpose of transforming a blighted area into a "well-balanced" community through redevelopment, 348 U.S., at 33; in *Midkiff,* we upheld the interest in breaking up a land oligopoly that "created artificial deterrents to the normal functioning of the State's residential land market," 467 U.S., at 242; and in *Monsanto,* we accepted Congress' purpose of eliminating a "significant barrier to entry in the pesticide market," [*Ruckelshaus v. Monsanto Co.,*] 467 U.S. [986], at 1014–1015 [(1984)]. It would be incongruous to hold that the City's interest in the economic benefits to be derived from the development of the Fort Trumbull area has less of a public character than any of those other interests. Clearly, there is no basis for exempting economic development from our traditionally broad understanding of public purpose. . . .

In affirming the City's authority to take petitioners' properties, we do not minimize the hardship that condemnations may entail, notwithstanding the payment of just compensation. We emphasize that nothing in our opinion precludes any State from placing further restrictions on its exercise of the takings power. Indeed, many States already impose "public use" requirements that are stricter than the federal baseline. Some of these requirements have been established as a matter of state constitutional law, while others are expressed in state eminent domain statutes that carefully limit the grounds upon which takings may be exercised.[23] As the submissions of the parties and their *amici* make clear, the necessity and wisdom of using eminent domain to promote economic development are certainly matters of legitimate public debate. This Court's authority, however, extends only to determining whether the City's proposed condemnations are for a "public use" within the meaning of the Fifth Amendment to the Federal Constitution. Because over a century of our case law interpreting that provision dictates an affirmative answer to that question, we may not grant petitioners the relief that they seek.

The judgment of the Supreme Court of Connecticut is affirmed. . . .

JUSTICE KENNEDY, concurring.

. . . This Court has declared that a taking should be upheld as consistent with the Public Use Clause, U.S. Const., Amdt. 5, as long as it is "rationally related to a conceivable public purpose." *Hawaii Housing Authority v. Midkiff,* 467 U.S. 229, 241 (1984). . . . The determination that a rational-basis standard of review is appropriate does not, however, alter the fact that transfers intended to confer benefits on particular, favored private entities, and with only incidental or pretextual public benefits, are forbidden by the Public Use Clause. . . .

---

[23] Under California law, for instance, a city may only take land for economic development purposes in blighted areas. Cal. Health & Safety Code Ann. §§ 33030–33037. . . .

The trial court concluded . . . that benefiting Pfizer was not "the primary motivation or effect of this development plan"; instead, "the primary motivation for [respondents] was to take advantage of Pfizer's presence." . . . Likewise, the trial court concluded that "[t]here is nothing in the record to indicate that . . . [respondents] were motivated by a desire to aid [other] particular private entities." . . . Even the dissenting justices on the Connecticut Supreme Court agreed that respondents' development plan was intended to revitalize the local economy, not to serve the interests of Pfizer . . . or any other private party. . . .

This is not the occasion for conjecture as to what sort of cases might justify a more demanding standard, but it is appropriate to underscore aspects of the instant case that convince me no departure from *Berman* and *Midkiff* is appropriate here. This taking occurred in the context of a comprehensive development plan meant to address a serious citywide depression, and the projected economic benefits of the project cannot be characterized as *de minimis*. The identities of most of the private beneficiaries were unknown at the time the city formulated its plans. The city complied with elaborate procedural requirements that facilitate review of the record and inquiry into the city's purposes. In sum, while there may be categories of cases in which the transfers are so suspicious, or the procedures employed so prone to abuse, or the purported benefits are so trivial or implausible, that courts should presume an impermissible private purpose, no such circumstances are present in this case. . . .

JUSTICE O'CONNOR, with whom THE CHIEF JUSTICE, JUSTICE SCALIA, and JUSTICE THOMAS join, dissenting.

. . . Today the Court abandons [a] long-held, basic limitation on government power. Under the banner of economic development, all private property is now vulnerable to being taken and transferred to another private owner, so long as it might be upgraded—*i.e.,* given to an owner who will use it in a way that the legislature deems more beneficial to the public—in the process. To reason, as the Court does, that the incidental public benefits resulting from the subsequent ordinary use of private property render economic development takings "for public use" is to wash out any distinction between private and public use of property—and thereby effectively to delete the words "for public use" from the Takings Clause of the Fifth Amendment. Accordingly I respectfully dissent. . . .

Where is the line between "public" and "private" property use? We give considerable deference to legislatures' determinations about what governmental activities will advantage the public. But were the political branches the sole arbiters of the public-private distinction, the Public Use Clause would amount to little more than hortatory fluff. An external, judicial check on how the public use requirement is interpreted, however limited, is necessary if this constraint on government power is to retain any meaning. . . .

The Court's holdings in *Berman* and *Midkiff* were true to the principle underlying the Public Use Clause. In both those cases, the extraordinary, precondemnation use of the targeted property inflicted affirmative harm on society—in *Berman* through blight resulting from extreme poverty and in *Midkiff* through oligopoly resulting from extreme wealth. And in both cases, the relevant legislative body had found that eliminating the existing property use was necessary to remedy the harm. *Berman, supra,* at 28–29; *Midkiff, supra,* at 232. Thus a public purpose was realized when the harmful use was eliminated. Because each taking *directly* achieved a public benefit, it did not matter that the property was turned over to private use. Here, in contrast, New London does not claim that Susette Kelo's and Wilhelmina Dery's well-maintained homes are the source of any social harm. Indeed, it could not so claim without adopting the absurd argument that any single-family home that might be razed to make way for an apartment building, or any church that might be replaced with a retail store, or any small business that might be more lucrative if it were instead part of a national franchise, is inherently harmful to society and thus within the government's power to condemn.

> **Food for Thought**
>
> Did Justice O'Connor convincingly distinguish her majority opinion in *Midkiff*? If Kelo and the other owners refused to sell, wouldn't their decisions harm the city?

In moving away from our decisions sanctioning the condemnation of harmful property use, the Court today significantly expands the meaning of public use. It holds that the sovereign may take private property currently put to ordinary private use, and give it over for new, ordinary private use, so long as the new use is predicted to generate some secondary benefit for the public—such as increased tax revenue, more jobs, maybe even esthetic pleasure. But nearly any lawful use of real private property can be said to generate some incidental benefit to the public. Thus, if predicted (or even guaranteed) positive side-effects are enough to render transfer from one private party to another constitutional, then the words "for public use" do not realistically exclude *any* takings, and thus do not exert any constraint on the eminent domain power. . . .

The specter of condemnation hangs over all property. Nothing is to prevent the State from replacing any Motel 6 with a Ritz-Carlton, any home with a shopping mall, or any farm with a factory. . . .

Any property may now be taken for the benefit of another private party, but the fallout from this decision will not be random. The beneficiaries are likely to be those citizens with disproportionate influence and power in the political process, including large corporations and development firms. As for the victims, the government now has license to transfer property from those with fewer resources to those with more. The Founders cannot have intended this perverse result. "[T]hat alone is a *just* government," wrote James Madison, "which *impartially* secures to every man, whatever is his *own*." For the National Gazette, Property (Mar. 27, 1792), reprinted in 14 Papers of James Madison 266 (R. Rutland et al. eds. 1983). . . .

JUSTICE THOMAS, dissenting.

. . . Today's decision is simply the latest in a string of our cases construing the Public Use Clause to be a virtual nullity, without the slightest nod to its original meaning. . . . Our cases have strayed from the Clause's original meaning, and I would reconsider them. . . .

The most natural reading of the Clause is that it allows the government to take property only if the government owns, or the public has a legal right to use, the property, as opposed to taking it for any public purpose or necessity whatsoever. . . .

Tellingly, the phrase "public use" contrasts with the very different phrase "general Welfare" used elsewhere in the Constitution. See [Article I, § 8] ("Congress shall have Power To . . . provide for the common Defence and general Welfare of the United States"); preamble (Constitution established "to promote the general Welfare"). The Framers would have used some such broader term if they had meant the Public Use Clause to have a similarly sweeping scope. Other founding-era documents made the contrast between these two usages still more explicit. . . . The Constitution's text, in short, suggests that the Takings Clause authorizes the taking of property only if the public has a right to employ it, not if the public realizes any conceivable benefit from the taking. . . .

The consequences of today's decision are not difficult to predict, and promise to be harmful. So-called "urban renewal" programs provide some compensation for the properties they take, but no compensation is possible for the subjective value of these lands to the individuals displaced and the indignity inflicted by uprooting them from their homes. Allowing the government to take property solely for public purposes is bad enough, but extending the concept of public purpose to encompass any economically beneficial goal guarantees that these losses will fall disproportionately on poor communities. Those communities are not only systematically less likely to put their lands to the highest and best social use, but are also the least politically powerful. . . . The deferential standard this Court has adopted for the Public Use Clause is therefore deeply perverse. It encourages "those citizens with disproportionate influence and power in the political process, including large corporations and development firms," to victimize the weak. *Ante*, at 505 (O'CONNOR, J., dissenting).

Those incentives have made the legacy of this Court's "public purpose" test an unhappy one. In the 1950's, no doubt emboldened in part by the expansive understanding of "public use" this Court adopted in *Berman*, cities "rushed to draw plans" for downtown development. B. Frieden & L. Sagalyn, Downtown, Inc. How America Rebuilds Cities 17 (1989). "Of all the families displaced by urban renewal from 1949 through 1963, 63 percent of those whose race was known were nonwhite, and of these families, 56 percent of nonwhites and 38 percent of whites had incomes low enough to qualify for public housing, which, however, was seldom available to them." *Id.*, at 28. Public works projects in the 1950's and 1960's destroyed predominantly minority communities in St. Paul, Minnesota, and Baltimore, Maryland. *Id.*, at 28–29. . . . Urban renewal projects have long been associated with the displacement of blacks; "[i]n cities across the country, urban renewal came to be known as 'Negro removal.'" Pritchett, The "Public Menace" of Blight: Urban Renewal and the Private Uses of Eminent Domain, 21 Yale L. & Pol'y Rev. 1, 47 (2003). Over 97 percent of the individuals forcibly removed from their homes by the "slum-clearance" project upheld by this Court in *Berman* were black. 348 U.S., at 30. Regrettably, the predictable consequence of the Court's decision will be to exacerbate these effects. . . .

Points for Discussion

a. **Future of Public Use**

Does *Kelo* mean that the Takings Clause has now been shortened to read: "[N]or shall private property be taken ~~for public use~~, without just compensation"? Can government now take private property *for private use* whenever (1) any conceivable public benefit results and (2) just compensation is paid? Some scholars suggest that the public use requirement is no longer a meaningful limit on the eminent domain power. On the other hand, isn't the *Kelo* holding consistent with the Court's approach in *Midkiff*? If New London could not use eminent domain, would this allow Kelo to stop the entire redevelopment project—thereby eliminating more than 1,000 new jobs?

b. **Potential Abuses**

In her dissent, Justice O'Connor argued that the majority's holding would allow the state to replace "any Motel 6 with a Ritz Carlton, any home with a shopping mall, or any farm with a factory." She predicted that large corporations and development firms who hold "disproportionate influence and power in the political process" will be the "beneficiaries" of *Kelo*, while ordinary people with fewer resources will be the "victims." Do you agree? Will the decision harm people of color, as Justice Thomas fears? How concerned should we be about potential abuse of the eminent domain power? Note that Justice Kennedy—who provided the crucial fifth vote for the majority opinion—concurred separately to suggest that a taking would not meet the public use test if its purpose was "to confer benefits on particular, favored private entities . . . with only incidental or pretextual public benefits. . . ."

c. **Means v. Ends**

Midkiff and *Kelo* focus on the purpose for the government's exercise of eminent domain. Under this view, as long as government is pursuing a legitimate *end*, it has broad discretion to determine the *means* used to accomplish that end.

> **Perspective and Analysis**
>
> Professor Thomas Merrill argues that a better approach is to ask whether eminent domain is an appropriate means to achieve a particular end.
>
> > . . . The ends question asks what the government plans to do once the property is obtained. This inquiry, in turn, requires a clear conception of the legitimate functions or purposes of the state. May the state promote employment by subsidizing the construction of a privately owned factory? May it own a professional football team or undertake land reform? The answers to such questions demand an exercise in high political theory that most courts today are unwilling (or unable) to undertake. The means question, by contrast, is narrower. It asks where and how the government should get property, not what it may do with it. For example, the means approach accepts that a state may own a professional football team. It then asks: how should the state acquire the team? Must it purchase the team through voluntary negotiations? Or may the state coerce a transfer by condemning the team? Or may it simply commandeer the team under its police power? The means approach, of course, is also "political" in that it concerns state actions that will advance or retard conflicting interests. Nevertheless, the means approach demands a more narrowly focused and judicially manageable inquiry than the ends approach.
>
> **Thomas W. Merrill, *The Economics of Public Use*, 72 Cornell L. Rev. 61, 66–67 (1986).**

If the public use limitation is recast in this light, it could serve as an important restriction on eminent domain. Presumably a court would have a more active role in reviewing a means-based exercise of eminent domain, because the focus would be on whether the power of eminent domain was a necessary (rather than convenient) method for achieving the legislative end. What advantages does a means-test hold over an ends-test? Which is the better approach? How would *Midkiff* be decided under a means-based test? How would *Kelo* be decided?

d. Psychological Damage

The condemnation of property may cause serious psychological damage to the displaced owners. A home is much more than a house. When people are uprooted from a home where they have lived all their lives, they often are affected less by the razing of the physical structure than by the destruction of the emotional ties that it represents. Should we apply a narrower public use standard when an owner-occupied residence is condemned? In this regard, consider the personhood theory of property that you studied in Chapter 1. Doesn't the average homeowner believe that her "bundle of sticks" includes the right to decide when and to whom she sells her property?

Several years after *Kelo* was decided, Justice Stevens observed that "the opinion . . . is the most unpopular opinion that I wrote during my thirty-four year tenure on the Supreme Court. Indeed, I think it is the most unpopular opinion that any member of the Court wrote during that period." Justice John Paul Stevens, Kelo, *Popularity, and Substantive Due Process*, 63 Ala. L. Rev. 941, 941 (2012). Should Justice Stevens reconsider his analysis in the face of such extreme public reaction?

e. The Scope of Public Use

Which of the following examples of eminent domain satisfy the public use test as defined in *Kelo*?

> (1) T, a billionaire developer, wants to add a limousine parking lot to his Atlantic City hotel and casino. When the owners of two adjacent parcels refuse to sell, he asks State Agency A to condemn their properties.
>
> (2) County B plans to acquire ten owner-occupied homes by eminent domain. It intends to immediately convey these parcels to X, the owner of a Major League Soccer franchise, who will build a new arena on the land. County B hopes that the new arena will revitalize the area. However, its decision to condemn the parcels is not part of a comprehensive development plan, nor is it intended to address a county-wide economic downturn.
>
> (3) General Motors threatens to leave City D unless it can build a new assembly plant at a site of its choosing. If GM leaves, thousands of jobs will be lost, with severe economic consequences to the community. City D now plans to condemn 200 owner-occupied homes in order to convey them to GM.

f. Aftermath of *Kelo*

The public outcry following *Kelo* was widespread and bitter. Protests erupted across the nation. Newspaper editorials decried the invasion of private property rights. The U.S. House of Representatives passed a resolution noting its "grave disapproval" of the decision. In the year after the decision, 26 states adopted legislation to curb the perceived abuse of condemning property for a "private use."

In the years following *Kelo*, the promised revitalization of downtown New London failed to occur. The city's redevelopment plan was abandoned when the developer could not obtain sufficient financing; thus, the anticipated jobs and tax revenues never materialized. In 2010, Pfizer announced that it was closing its $350 million research center in New London, and relocating over 1,400 jobs to another town. Ultimately, Kelo's lot and most of the surrounding properties became "a barren wasteland of weeds, litter, and rubble." Jeff Benedict, Little Pink House: A True Story of Defiance and Courage 377 (2009). However, a $40 million community recreation center is now being built on the site, and the city has also authorized the construction of 600 apartment units, a 100-room hotel, and a 1,200-space parking garage.

g. State Legislative Responses

As the *Kelo* majority noted, states may choose to adopt a more narrow definition of public use. While states must provide at least *as much* protection for property owners as the federal Takings Clause requires, they can (and often do) provide *more* protection. Accordingly, almost all states did adopt new legislation in the wake of *Kelo*, both to limit the exercise of the eminent domain power as a general matter, and to restrict or prohibit its use for economic development purposes. Most commonly, these statutes reflect one or more of the following approaches: (1) defining "public use" as possession or enjoyment of the property by the public; (2) restricting eminent domain to blighted properties that harm the public health or safety; (3) requiring compensation greater than fair market value for condemnation of a primary residence; or (4) placing a moratorium on the use of eminent domain for economic development. As one example, Alaska adopted a statute that provides in part:

> (b) The power of eminent domain may not be exercised to acquire private property from a private person for the purpose of transferring title to the property to another private person for economic development. . . .

Alaska Stat. § 29.35.030. If you were amending your state constitution in order to limit the effect of *Kelo*, what approach would you take?

Summary

- **Fifth Amendment.** The Fifth Amendment imposes two restrictions on government's power to take private property by eminent domain: (a) property may be taken only for a public use; and (b) just compensation must be paid to the owner.

- **Public Use.** The public use requirement is clearly satisfied when government takes land so that it may be physically used by the public or by government employees. More broadly, the Supreme Court has held that the requirement is satisfied if a taking serves a public purpose.

- **Economic Development.** The Supreme Court has held that taking private property for the primary purpose of economic redevelopment pursuant to a comprehensive plan satisfies the public use requirement.

- **State Laws.** A state may interpret its state constitution as requiring a more narrow definition of public use than is used to interpret the federal Takings Clause. Accordingly, some states do not allow the condemnation of private land for economic redevelopment. Similarly, a state may enact legislation that provides property owners with more protection against condemnation than the Takings Clause requires.

> **Test Your Knowledge**
>
> To assess your understanding of the material in this chapter, click here to take a quiz.

- **Just Compensation.** Just compensation is generally defined to mean fair market value—the amount that a willing buyer would pay a willing seller on the open market. An inherent problem in calculating fair market value in a condemnation action is that the government seeks to buy from an unwilling seller.

> **For More Information**
>
> For more information about eminent domain, please consult these sources:
> - Abraham Bell & Gideon Parchomovsky, *The Uselessness of Public Use*, 106 Colum. L. Rev. 1412 (2006).
> - Mark Kelman, *The Conceptual Conundrum at the Core of the* Kelo *Dissent*, 16 Duke J. Const. L. & Pub. Pol'y 121 (2021).
> - Susan Lourne, Comment, Hawaii Housing Authority v. Midkiff: *A New Slant on Social Legislation: Taking from the Rich to Give to the Well-to-Do*, 25 Nat. Resources J. 773 (1985).
> - Marc Mihaly & Turner Smith, *Kelo's Trail: A Survey of State and Federal Legislative and Judicial Activity Five Years Later*, 38 Ecology L.Q. 703 (2011).
> - *Symposium on* Kelo v. City of New London, 23 Geo. Mason L. Rev. 253 (2016).

Chapter 14

Takings

Suppose B owns a beachfront lot in a residential zone in City C where she plans to build her dream home. The City wants to protect oceanfront land from development in order to preserve open space and encourage tourism. Of course, it could acquire B's lot through eminent domain by paying just compensation. But can the City effectively obtain the same benefits by regulation? Assume that the City rezones B's land into the newly created "Beachfront Preservation" zone, where the only permitted uses are camping, picnicking, and nature study. Is B entitled to compensation?

The Takings Clause of the Fifth Amendment mandates compensation when private property is "taken" for public use. As you saw in Chapter 13, the government must pay just compensation when it *seizes* possession of land for a public purpose; we might call this conduct a *physical taking*. But a regulation might restrict an owner's rights so much that it becomes the functional *equivalent* of a seizure—a *regulatory taking*. So where is the line between an appropriate regulation and a regulatory taking? There is no easy answer to this question. In fact, it is the most challenging issue in modern property law.

A. Foundation Era

Traditionally, a landowner such as B was not entitled to compensation. The conventional wisdom was that the Takings Clause applied only when the government physically seized private property. If it merely regulated the use of property under the police power to prevent harm to the public, no "taking" occurred.

The first lawsuits challenging the validity of regulations under the Takings Clause appeared in the late nineteenth century. For example, *Mugler v. Kansas*, 123 U.S. 623 (1887), involved a state statute which prohibited the manufacture of alcohol; this law forced Mugler's brewery out of business, leaving his property with "little value" for any other purpose. Reasoning that an owner was not entitled to "inflict injury" upon the public by "a noxious use" of his property, the Supreme Court held that the statute was not a taking: "A prohibition simply upon the use of property for purposes . . . injurious to the health, morals, or safety of the community, cannot . . . be deemed a taking . . . ." *Id.* at 668–69.

The Court followed the same approach in *Hadacheck v. Sebastian*, 239 U.S. 394 (1915), where a Los Angeles ordinance prohibited the manufacture of bricks within the city limits. As a result, the value of Hadacheck's profitable brick factory fell from $800,000 to about $60,000. In operation, the factory emitted fumes, smoke, and soot which sickened nearby residents. Noting that the police power was "one of the most essential powers of government—one that is the least limitable," the Court upheld the ordinance as an appropriate measure to protect the public. *Id.* at 410.

The *Mugler-Hadacheck* approach later became known as the *noxious use* or *nuisance test*: a regulation adopted under the police power to protect the public health, safety, or welfare was not a "taking" as defined by the Fifth Amendment—even if it reduced the value of property.

B. A New Doctrine

The regulatory takings doctrine was first recognized in the landmark case of *Pennsylvania Coal Co. v. Mahon* in 1922. The legal standard followed in *Pennsylvania Coal* has been superseded by more modern tests, as you will see later in the chapter. But the case is an important step in the evolution of regulatory takings jurisprudence—and is frequently cited in contemporary decisions.

Pennsylvania Coal Co. v. Mahon

Supreme Court of the United States

260 U.S. 393 (1922)

MR. JUSTICE HOLMES delivered the opinion of the Court.

This is a bill in equity brought by the defendants in error to prevent the Pennsylvania Coal Company from mining under their property in such way as to remove the supports and cause a subsidence of the surface and of their house. The bill sets out a deed executed by the Coal Company in 1878, under which the plaintiffs claim. The deed conveys the surface but in express terms reserves the right to remove all the coal under the same and the grantee takes the premises with the risk and waives all claim for damages that may arise from mining out the coal. But the plaintiffs say that whatever may have been the Coal Company's rights, they were taken away by an Act of Pennsylvania, approved May 27, 1921 (P.L. 1198), commonly known there as the Kohler Act. The Court of Common Pleas found that if not restrained the defendant would cause the damage to prevent which the bill was brought but denied an injunction, holding that the statute if applied to this case would be unconstitutional. On appeal the Supreme Court of the State agreed that the defendant had contract and property rights protected by the Constitution of the United States, but held that the statute was a legitimate exercise of the police power and directed a decree for the plaintiffs, a writ of error was granted bringing the case to this Court.

> **FYI**
>
> The Pennsylvania Coal Company granted the land to Alexander Craig, Mahon's future father-in-law, in 1878. The deed conveyed title to Craig:
>
> "Excepting and reserving to the said Pennsylvania Coal Company . . . all the coal and other minerals under, in or upon said lot of land. . . . [T]he said Pennsylvania Coal Company . . . to be at liberty to mine and remove the same and to make and drive tunnels, passages and ways under said surface of said lot . . . and not to be liable to the said Alexander Craig, his heirs or assigns to or for any injury or damages that may occur. . . . "

Mahon house
Click here for larger photo

The statute forbids the mining of anthracite coal in such way as to cause the subsidence of, among other things, any structure used as a human habitation, with certain exceptions, including among them land where the surface is owned by the owner of the underlying coal and is distant more than one hundred and fifty feet from any improved property belonging to any other person. As applied to this case the statute is admitted to destroy previously existing rights of property and contract. The question is whether the police power can be stretched so far.

Government hardly could go on if to some extent values incident to property could not be diminished without paying for every such change in the general law. As long recognized some values are enjoyed under an implied limitation and must yield to the police power. But obviously the implied limitation must have its limits or the contract and due process clauses are gone. One fact for consideration in determining such limits is the extent of the diminution. When it reaches a certain magnitude, in most if not in all cases there must be an exercise of eminent domain and compensation to sustain the act. So the question depends upon the particular facts. The greatest weight is given to the judgment of the legislature but it always is open to interested parties to contend that the legislature has gone beyond its constitutional power.

> **Food for Thought**
>
> Does the case concern only the risk of subsidence damage to *this* particular house? How important is this characterization to the majority's ruling?

This is the case of a single private house. No doubt there is a public interest even in this, as there is in every purchase and sale and in all that happens within the commonwealth. Some existing rights may be modified even in such a case. *Rideout v. Knox*, 19 N.E. 390. But usually in ordinary private affairs the public interest does not warrant much of this kind of interference. A source of damage to such a house is not a public nuisance even if similar damage is inflicted on others in different places. The damage is not common or public. *Wesson v. Washburn Iron Co.*, 13 Allen (Mass.) 96, 103. The extent of the public interest is shown by the statute to be limited, since the statute ordinarily does not apply to land when the surface is owned by the owner of the coal. Furthermore, it is not justified as a protection of personal safety. That could be provided for by notice. Indeed the very foundation of this bill is that the defendant gave timely notice of its intent to mine under the house. On the other hand the extent of the taking is great. It purports to abolish what is recognized in Pennsylvania as an estate in land—a very valuable estate—and what is declared by the Court below to be a contract hitherto binding the plaintiffs. If we were called upon to deal with the plaintiffs' position alone we should think it clear that the statute does not disclose a public interest sufficient to warrant so extensive a destruction of the defendant's constitutionally protected rights. . . .

> **FYI**
>
> Pennsylvania recognized three distinct estates in land: the surface estate, the mineral estate, and the support estate. In practice, mining companies often reserved the support estate when they sold the surface rights.

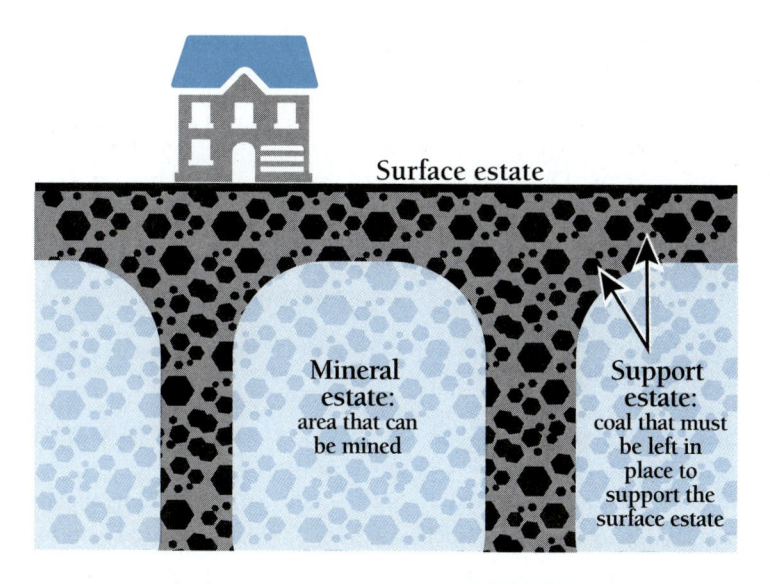

Estates in *Pennsylvania Coal Co. v. Mahon*

It is our opinion that the act cannot be sustained as an exercise of the police power, so far as it affects the mining of coal under streets or cities in places where the right to mine such coal has been reserved. As said in a Pennsylvania case, "For practical purposes, the right to coal consists in the right to mine it." *Commonwealth v. Clearview Coal Co.*, 100 Atl. 820. What makes the right to mine coal valuable is that it can be exercised with profit. To make it commercially impracticable to mine certain coal has very nearly the same effect for constitutional purposes as appropriating or destroying it. This we think that we are warranted in assuming that the statute does.

It is true that in *Plymouth Coal Co. v. Pennsylvania,* 232 U.S. 531, it was held competent for the legislature to require a pillar of coal to the left along the line of adjoining property, that with the pillar on the other side of the line would be a barrier sufficient for the safety of the employees of either mine in case the other should be abandoned and allowed to fill with water. But that was a requirement for the safety of employees invited into the mine, and secured an average reciprocity of advantage that has been recognized as a justification of various laws. . . .

The general rule at least is that while property may be regulated to a certain extent, if regulation goes too far it will be recognized as a taking. It may be doubted how far exceptional cases, like the blowing up of a house to stop a conflagration, go—and if they go beyond the general rule, whether they do not stand as much upon tradition as upon principle. *Bowditch v. Boston*, 101 U.S. 16. In general it is not plain that a man's misfortunes or necessities will justify his shifting the damages to his neighbor's shoulders. *Spade v. Lynn & Boston Ry. Co.*, 52 N.E. 747. We are in danger of forgetting that a strong public desire to improve the public condition is not enough to warrant achieving the desire by a shorter cut than the constitutional way of paying for the change. As we already have said this is a question of degree—and therefore cannot be disposed of by general propositions. . . .

We assume, of course, that the statute was passed upon the conviction that an exigency existed that would warrant it, and we assume that an exigency exists that would warrant the exercise of eminent domain. But the question at bottom is upon whom the loss of the changes desired should fall. So far as private persons or communities have seen fit to take the risk of acquiring only surface rights, we cannot see that the fact that their risk has become a danger warrants the giving to them greater rights than they bought.

Decree reversed.

MR. JUSTICE BRANDEIS dissenting.

The Kohler Act prohibits, under certain conditions, the mining of anthracite coal within the limits of a city in such a manner or to such an extent "as to cause the subsidence of any dwelling or other structure used as a human habitation, or any factory, store, or other industrial or mercantile establishment in which human labor is employed." . . . Coal in place is land, and the right of the owner to use his land is not absolute. He may not so use it as to create a public nuisance, and uses, once harmless, may, owing to changed conditions, seriously threaten the public welfare. Whenever they do, the Legislature has power to prohibit such uses without paying compensation; and the power to prohibit extends alike to the manner, the character and the purpose of the use. Are we justified in declaring that the Legislature of Pennsylvania has, in restricting the right to mine anthracite, exercised this power so arbitrarily as to violate the Fourteenth Amendment?

> **FYI**
>
> Subsidence caused major problems across the state. As the City of Scranton complained in its brief in support of Mahon: "Our once level streets are in humps and sags, our gas mains have broken, our water mains threaten to fail us in time of conflagration, our sewers spread their pestilential contents into the soil, our buildings have collapsed under their occupants or fallen into the streets, our people have been swallowed up in sudden yawning chasms, blown up by gas explosions or asphyxiated in their sleep, our cemeteries have opened and the bodies of our dead have been torn from their caskets."

Every restriction upon the use of property imposed in the exercise of the police power deprives the owner of some right theretofore enjoyed, and is, in that sense, an abridgment by the state of rights in property without making compensation. But restriction imposed to protect the public health, safety or morals from dangers threatened is not a taking. The restriction here in question is merely the prohibition of a noxious use. The property so restricted remains in the possession of its owner. The state does not appropriate it or make any use of it. The state merely prevents the owner from making a use which interferes with paramount rights of the public. Whenever the use prohibited ceases to be noxious—as it may because of further change in local or social conditions—the restriction will have to be removed and the owner will again be free to enjoy his property as heretofore.

The restriction upon the use of this property cannot, of course, be lawfully imposed, unless its purpose is to protect the public. But the purpose of a restriction does not cease to be public, because incidentally some private persons may thereby receive gratuitously valuable special benefits. . . . If by mining anthracite coal the owner would necessarily unloose poisonous gases, I suppose no one would doubt the power of the state to prevent the mining, without buying his coal fields. And why may not the state, likewise, without paying compensation, prohibit one from digging so deep or excavating so near the surface, as to expose the community to like dangers? In the latter case, as in the former, carrying on the business would be a public nuisance.

It is said that one fact for consideration in determining whether the limits of the police power have been exceeded is the extent of the resulting diminution in value, and that here the restriction destroys existing rights of property and contract. But values are relative. If we are to consider the value of the coal kept in place by the restriction, we should compare it with the value of all other parts of the land. That is, with the value not of the coal alone, but with the value of the whole property. . . . For aught that appears the value of the coal kept in place by the restriction may be negligible as compared with the value of the whole property, or even as compared with that part of it which is represented by the coal remaining in place and which may be extracted despite the statute. . . .

It is said that this is a case of a single dwelling house, that the restriction upon mining abolishes a valuable estate hitherto secured by a contract with the plaintiffs, and that the restriction upon mining cannot be justified as a protection of personal safety, since that could be provided for by notice. . . . May we say that notice would afford adequate protection of the public safety where the Legislature and the highest court of the state, with greater knowledge of local conditions, have declared, in effect, that it would not? If the public safety is imperiled, surely neither grant, nor contract, can prevail against the exercise of the police power. . . .

This case involves only mining which causes subsidence of a dwelling house. But the Kohler Act contains provisions in addition to that quoted above; and as to these, also, an opinion is expressed. These provisions deal with mining under cities to such an extent as to cause subsidence of—

> (a) Any public building or any structure customarily used by the public as a place of resort, assemblage, or amusement, including, but not limited to, churches, schools, hospitals, theaters, hotels, and railroad stations.
>
> (b) Any street, road, bridge, or other public passageway, dedicated to public use or habitually used by the public.

(c) Any track, roadbed, right of way, pipe, conduit, wire, or other facility, used in the service of the public by any municipal corporation or public service company as defined by the Public Service Law, section 1.

A prohibition of mining which causes subsidence of such structures and facilities is obviously enacted for a public purpose; and it seems, likewise, clear that mere notice of intention to mine would not in this connection secure the public safety. Yet it is said that these provisions of the act cannot be sustained as an exercise of the police power where the right to mine such coal has been reserved. The conclusion seems to rest upon the assumption that in order to justify such exercise of the police power there must be "an average reciprocity of advantage" as between the owner of the property restricted and the rest of the community; and that here such reciprocity is absent. . . . But where the police power is exercised, not to confer benefits upon property owners but to protect the public from detriment and danger, there is in my opinion, no room for considering reciprocity of advantage . . . unless it be the advantage of living and doing business in a civilized community. That reciprocal advantage is given by the act to the coal operators.

Points for Discussion

a. **"Too Far"**

Justice Holmes' statement that a regulation will be recognized as a taking if it goes "too far" is the most famous phrase in takings jurisprudence. How far is "too far"? The majority opinion in *Pennsylvania Coal* clearly recognized that a regulatory taking *could* exist—in fact, it is the birthplace of the regulatory takings doctrine. But the opinion failed to provide a clear standard for deciding whether a taking *did* exist. What factors should a court consider in determining whether regulation goes too far?

b. **Diminution-in-Value Test**

Holmes stressed that "one fact for consideration in determining whether the limits of the police power have been exceeded" was "the extent of the resulting diminution in value." This approach—often called the *diminution-in-value test*—considers the financial impact of the regulation on the value of the property. How did Holmes apply this test in *Pennsylvania Coal*? What was Brandeis' response? Did Holmes consider other factors as well? Or does any substantial loss of value require compensation?

c. **What Property?**

How should we define the "property" when applying the diminution-in-value test? What approach did Holmes take? What about Brandeis? Did it make any difference that Pennsylvania considered the "right to support" to be a separate estate in land? Although the Holmes view prevailed in *Pennsylvania Coal*, modern law generally follows the Brandeis approach.

d. Nuisance Exception

The *Mugler-Hadacheck* line of cases had previously held that a regulation enacted to prevent a nuisance or other harm to the public was not a taking. Brandeis relied on these precedents to assert that the Kohler Act was designed to prevent a "noxious" use of land—excavation that would cause the surface to collapse—and hence was not a taking. Was he right? Or was Holmes correct because the facts of the case did not involve a nuisance? Did the nuisance test survive *Pennsylvania Coal*?

e. Key Facts

How important was each of these facts to the majority's decision in *Pennsylvania Coal*? (1) Mahon's predecessor expressly contracted to accept the risk of subsidence; (2) there was no nuisance; (3) the coal lost its commercial value if left in place; (4) the case involved a single parcel owned by a single individual; and (5) the state did not appropriate or make any use of the property.

f. Average Reciprocity of Advantage

Holmes approvingly referred to *Plymouth Coal Co. v. Pennsylvania*, 232 U.S. 531 (1914), an earlier decision upholding a statute that required pillars of coal to be left in place along adjoining property lines. Did this statute have the same impact on property rights as the Kohler Act? How could Holmes reconcile that opinion with his decision in *Pennsylvania Coal*? Holmes pointed out that the statute in *Plymouth Coal* "secured an average reciprocity of advantage that has been recognized as a justification of various laws." The classic example of reciprocity of advantage is a zoning ordinance. Suppose that owner O's land is restricted to residential use only. While the ordinance burdens O (by restricting the use of his land) it also benefits O (because all other parcels are similarly restricted). In short, the benefit mitigates the burden.

Does the existence of "average reciprocity of advantage" make it less likely that a court will find a taking? Did the Kohler Act provide any reciprocity of advantage to the Pennsylvania Coal Company? *See* Raymond R. Coletta, *Reciprocity of Advantage and Regulatory Takings: Toward a New Theory of Takings Jurisprudence*, 40 Am. U. L. Rev. 297 (1990).

g. Applying *Pennsylvania Coal*

Under the *Pennsylvania Coal* standard, has a taking occurred in either of these situations?

> (1) J owns a grove of cedar trees that adds significant value to his single-family home in State C. The trees host a bacteria called red cedar rust. The rust is benign to the cedar trees, but can cause serious damage to any nearby apple orchards. To protect the apple industry, State C adopts a statute that requires state employees to destroy cedar trees which host this rust. All of J's cedar trees are cut down, lowering the value of J's home from $200,000 to $180,000.

> (2) The land in City D is rich in silica quartz. When the land surface is disturbed in any manner (e.g., by plowing, mining, or excavating foundations for new houses), dust laden with silica pollutes the air. Because silica is known to cause cancer, the dust is quite dangerous to humans. City D adopts an ordinance which prevents all landowners from disturbing the land surface in any way. The ordinance reduces the value of undeveloped land within the City by 90%.

h. **Historical Perspectives**

Professor William Fischel explains that Mahon was an attorney who had purchased the house from his father-in-law, an executive with the Pennsylvania Coal Company. William Fischel, Regulatory Takings (1995). Mahon apparently sued at the request of Pennsylvania Coal, so that the constitutionality of the Kohler Act could be litigated in a favorable jurisdiction. Is it ethical for an attorney to bring a collusive lawsuit?

Fischel points out that most Pennsylvania mining companies routinely compensated the surface owner when a dwelling was damaged by subsidence. So why did Pennsylvania Coal sue? It objected to a provision in a companion statute, the Fowler Act, which required solvent coal companies to pay for subsidence damage caused by insolvent companies.

i. **Scholarly Perspectives**

Pennsylvania Coal has been analyzed in hundreds of books and articles over the years. For more information about the case, see Richard A. Epstein, Takings: Private Property and the Power of Eminent Domain (1985); Lawrence M. Friedman, *A Search for Seizure:* Pennsylvania Coal Co. v. Mahon *in Context*, 4 Law & Hist. Rev. 1 (1986); and Carol M. Rose, Mahon *Reconstructed: Why the Takings Issue Is Still a Muddle*, 57 S. Cal. L. Rev. 561 (1984). *See also* J. Peter Byrne, *Ten Arguments for the Abolition of the Regulatory Takings Doctrine*, 22 Ecology L.Q. 89 (1995).

j. **Aftermath of *Pennsylvania Coal***

In 1966, Pennsylvania adopted the Bituminous Mine Subsidence and Land Conservation Act to protect against surface subsidence. It allowed a coal mining company to remove only 50% of the coal underneath any building on the surface so that the remaining coal would prevent collapse. In *Keystone Bituminous Coal Ass'n v. DeBenedictis*, 480 U.S. 470 (1987), the Supreme Court held that this statute did not effect a regulatory taking. Although the statute was remarkably similar to the Kohler Act, the Court took pains to distinguish *Pennsylvania Coal*, rather than to overrule it. Writing for the 5-4 majority, Justice Stevens stressed that the 1966 Act (1) had only a minor economic impact on the coal company and (2) removed a significant threat to the general welfare. Are these arguments consistent with *Pennsylvania Coal*?

Perspective and Analysis

Professor William Treanor argues that the Framers understood the Takings Clause to require compensation only when the government physically seized private property—it did not apply to regulation at all. In the excerpt below, Treanor explores Justice Holmes' approach to the Takings Clause.

Pennsylvania Coal represented the culmination of Justice Holmes's career-long critique of a physicalist view of property and the attendant view of the Takings Clause. As a young lawyer, Holmes criticized the use of the police power doctrine to justify governmental actions that affected property values without providing compensation. In an 1872 book review, he suggested that the term police power was "invented to cover certain acts of the legislature which are seen to be unconstitutional, but which are believed to be necessary." On the Massachusetts Supreme Judicial Court, he wrote one of the first opinions to suggest that a governmental regulation that undermined the value of property too greatly could be a taking. In *Rideout v. Knox*, the court upheld a statute that barred property owners from building fences more than six feet in height. Holmes stated that the statute did not give rise to an obligation to compensate, but that a greater restriction might have done so:

> It may be said that the difference is only one of degree. Most differences are, when nicely analyzed. At any rate, difference of degree is one of the distinctions by which the right of the legislature to exercise the police power is determined. Some small limitations of previously existing rights incident to property may be imposed for the sake of preventing manifest evil; larger ones could not be, except by exercise of the right of eminent domain. . . .

That an overwhelmingly conservative Supreme Court would reach the *Pennsylvania Coal* result is not surprising. By extending the Takings Clause beyond physical takings, *Pennsylvania Coal* enabled the judiciary to review the full range of majoritarian decisionmaking concerning property rights. The use of a balancing test—a regulation is invalid if it "goes too far"—paralleled the earlier rise of similar tests in the context of substantive due process, which also permitted the judiciary to scrutinize a broad range of majoritarian decisions.

Given his strong support of active government intervention in the economy, it is similarly unsurprising that Justice Brandeis dissented. His opinion reflects the narrow reading of the Takings Clause established by precedent: "[R]estriction imposed to protect the public health, safety or morals from dangers threatened is not a taking. The restriction here in question is merely the prohibition of a noxious use." In contrast, Holmes's decision puzzled contemporary commentators and has provoked extensive academic commentary since then. As one Holmes biographer has observed, Holmes's approach in *Pennsylvania Coal* is "almost exactly the reverse" of his approach in his due process dissents, in which the police power took precedence over individual rights. But his views in the takings area were consistent. Both

> *Pennsylvania Coal* and *Rideout* reflect a belief that property is properly viewed as value, not physical possession, and that the Takings Clause should therefore protect more than physical possession. Holmes's position seems to be the product not of his larger jurisprudential concerns, but of his embrace of a syllogism: The Takings Clause protects property. Property is value. Therefore, the Takings Clause protects value.
>
> **William Michael Treanor,** *The Original Understanding of the Takings Clause and the Political Process,* **95 Colum. L. Rev. 782, 798–802 (1995).**
> Do you agree with the Holmes view? Should the Takings Clause protect value?

C. The *Penn Central* Standard

After *Pennsylvania Coal*, more than 50 years elapsed before the next major Supreme Court decision on regulatory takings. During this period, it was clear that a regulatory taking could exist in theory. But *Pennsylvania Coal* provided little guidance to state courts and lower federal courts that struggled to determine when regulation went "too far" and thereby became an unconstitutional taking.

Based mainly on the *Mugler-Hadacheck* approach, many scholars reasoned that regulation to protect the public from harm was not a taking. But what if a law was adopted to benefit the public? Logically, a benefit-conferring regulation might be a taking. This *harm-benefit distinction* became an important concept in takings jurisprudence.

The Supreme Court revisited the regulatory takings doctrine in *Penn Central Transportation Co. v. City of New York*. The case involved Grand Central Terminal, a spectacular 1913 building which served as the main transportation hub for New York City. The *Penn Central* Court created a new three-factor balancing test for determining if a regulatory taking had occurred. This is the basic standard used in most regulatory takings decisions today.

Penn Central Transportation Co. v. City of New York

Supreme Court of the United States

438 U.S. 104 (1978)

MR. JUSTICE BRENNAN delivered the opinion of the Court.

I.

A.

... Over the past 50 years, all 50 States and over 500 municipalities have enacted laws to encourage or require the preservation of buildings and areas with historic or aesthetic importance. These nationwide legislative efforts have been precipitated by two concerns. The first is recognition that, in recent years, large numbers of historic structures, landmarks, and areas have been destroyed without adequate consideration of either the values represented therein or the possibility of preserving the destroyed properties for use in economically productive ways. The second is a widely shared belief that structures with special historic, cultural, or architectural significance enhance the quality of life for all. Not only do these buildings and their workmanship represent the lessons of the past and embody precious features of our heritage, they serve as examples of quality for today. . . .

New York City, responding to similar concerns and acting pursuant to a New York State enabling Act, adopted its Landmarks Preservation Law in 1965. See N.Y.C. Admin. Code, ch. 8-A, § 205–1.0 *et seq.* (1976). The city acted from the conviction that "the standing of [New York City] as a world-wide tourist center and world capital of business, culture and government" would be threatened if legislation were not enacted to protect historic landmarks and neighborhoods from precipitate decisions to destroy or fundamentally alter their character. The city believed that comprehensive measures to safeguard desirable features of the existing urban fabric would benefit its citizens in a variety of ways: *e.g.*, fostering "civic pride in the beauty and noble accomplishments of the past"; protecting and enhancing "the city's attractions to tourists and visitors"; "support[ing] and stimul[ating] business and industry"; "strengthen[ing] the economy of the city"; and promoting "the use of historic districts, landmarks, interior landmarks and scenic landmarks for the education, pleasure and welfare of the people of the city." . . .

The operation of the law can be briefly summarized. The primary responsibility for administering the law is vested in the Landmarks Preservation Commission (Commission), a broad based, 11-member agency assisted by a technical staff. The Commission first performs the function, critical to any landmark preservation effort, of identifying properties and areas that have "a special character or special historical or aesthetic interest or value as part of the development, heritage or cultural characteristics of the city, state or nation." If the Commission determines, after giving all interested parties an opportunity to be heard, that a building or area satisfies the ordinance's criteria, it will designate a building to be a "landmark," situated on a particular "landmark site," or will designate an area to be a "historic district." After the Commission makes a designation, New York City's Board of Estimate, after considering the relationship of the designated property "to the master plan, the zoning resolution, projected public improvements and any plans for the renewal of the area involved," may modify or disapprove the designation, and the owner may seek judicial review of the final designation decision. Thus far, 31 historic districts and over 400 individual landmarks have been finally designated, and the process is a continuing one.

> **FYI**
>
> The Landmarks Preservation Commission is the country's largest historic preservation agency. It was created in response to the 1963 razing of Pennsylvania Station, which was designed in the same beaux-arts style as Grand Central Terminal. The Commission has designated 156 historic districts and more than 37,000 individual landmark properties across all five boroughs.

Final designation as a landmark results in restrictions upon the property owner's options concerning use of the landmark site. First, the law imposes a duty upon the owner to keep the exterior features of the building "in good repair" to assure that the law's objectives not be defeated by the landmark's falling into a state of irremediable disrepair. Second, the Commission must approve in advance any proposal to alter the exterior architectural features of the landmark or to construct any exterior improvement on the landmark site, thus ensuring that decisions concerning construction on the landmark site are made with due consideration of both the public interest in the maintenance of the structure and the landowner's interest in use of the property. . . .

Although the designation of a landmark and landmark site restricts the owner's control over the parcel, designation also enhances the economic position of the landmark owner in one significant respect. Under New York City's zoning laws, owners of real property who have not developed their property to the full extent permitted by the applicable zoning laws are allowed to transfer development rights to contiguous parcels on the same city block. . . .

B.

This case involves the application of New York City's Landmarks Preservation Law to Grand Central Terminal (Terminal). The Terminal, which is owned by the Penn Central Transportation Co. and its affiliates (Penn Central), is one of New York City's most famous buildings. Opened in 1913, it is regarded not only as providing an ingenious engineering solution to the problems presented by urban railroad stations, but also as a magnificent example of the French beaux-arts style. . . .

Grand Central Terminal
Click here for larger photo

On August 2, 1967, following a public hearing, the Commission designated the Terminal a "landmark" and designated the "city tax block" it occupies a "landmark site." The Board of Estimate confirmed this action on September 21, 1967. Although appellant Penn Central had opposed the designation before the Commission, it did not seek judicial review of the final designation decision.

On January 22, 1968, appellant Penn Central, to increase its income, entered into a renewable 50-year lease and sublease agreement with appellant UGP Properties, Inc. (UGP), a wholly owned subsidiary of Union General Properties, Ltd., a United Kingdom corporation. Under the terms of the agreement, UGP was to construct a multistory office building above the Terminal. UGP promised to pay Penn Central $1 million annually during construction and at least $3 million annually thereafter. The rentals would be offset in part by a loss of some $700,000 to $1 million in net rentals presently received from concessionaires displaced by the new building.

Appellants UGP and Penn Central then applied to the Commission for permission to construct an office building atop the Terminal. Two separate plans, both designed by architect Marcel Breuer and both apparently satisfying the terms of the applicable zoning ordinance, were submitted to the Commission for approval. The first, Breuer I, provided for the construction of a 55-story office building, to be cantilevered above the existing facade and to rest on the roof of the Terminal. The second, Breuer II Revised, called for tearing down a portion of the Terminal that included the 42d Street facade, stripping off some of the remaining features of the Terminal's facade, and constructing a 53-story office building. The Commission denied a certificate of no exterior effect on September 20, 1968. Appellants then applied for a certificate of "appropriateness" as to both proposals. After four days of hearings at which over 80 witnesses testified, the Commission denied this application as to both proposals.

The Commission's reasons for rejecting certificates respecting Breuer II Revised are summarized in the following statement: "To protect a Landmark, one does not tear it down. To perpetuate its architectural features, one does not strip them off." . . . Breuer I, which would have preserved the existing vertical facades of the present structure, received more sympathetic consideration. The Commission first focused on the effect that the proposed tower would have on one desirable feature created by the present structure and its surroundings: the dramatic view of the Terminal from Park Avenue South. Although appellants had contended that the Pan-American Building had already destroyed the silhouette of the south facade and that one additional tower could do no further damage and might even provide a better background for the facade, the Commission disagreed, stating that it found the majestic approach from the south to be still unique in the city and that a 55-story tower atop the Terminal would be far more detrimental to its south facade than the Pan-American Building 375 feet away. . . .

Breuer I   **Breuer II**

Appellants did not seek judicial review of the denial of either certificate. . . . Instead, appellants filed suit in New York Supreme Court, Trial Term, claiming, *inter alia*, that the application of the Landmarks Preservation Law had "taken" their property without just compensation in violation of the Fifth and Fourteenth Amendments and arbitrarily deprived them of their property without due process of law in violation of the Fourteenth Amendment. Appellants sought a declaratory judgment, injunctive relief barring the city from using the Landmarks Law to impede the construction of any structure that might otherwise lawfully be constructed on the Terminal site, and damages for the "temporary taking" that occurred between August 2, 1967, the designation date, and the date when the restrictions arising from the Landmarks Law would be lifted. The trial court granted the injunctive and declaratory relief, but severed the question of damages for a "temporary taking."

Appellees appealed, and the New York Supreme Court, Appellate Division, reversed. 50 A.D.2d 265 (1975). The Appellate Division held that the restrictions on the development of the Terminal site were necessary to promote the legitimate public purpose of protecting landmarks and therefore that appellants could sustain their constitutional claims only by proof that the regulation deprived them of all reasonable beneficial use of the property.... The Appellate Division concluded that all appellants had succeeded in showing was that they had been deprived of the property's most profitable use, and that this showing did not establish that appellants had been unconstitutionally deprived of their property.

The New York Court of Appeals affirmed. 366 N.E.2d 1271 (1977)....

II.

The issues presented by appellants are (1) whether the restrictions imposed by New York City's law upon appellants' exploitation of the Terminal site effect a "taking" of appellants' property for a public use within the meaning of the Fifth Amendment, which of course is made applicable to the States through the Fourteenth Amendment, *see Chicago, B. & Q. R. Co. v. Chicago*, 166 U.S. 226, 239 (1897), and, (2), if so, whether the transferable development rights afforded appellants constitute "just compensation" within the meaning of the Fifth Amendment. We need only address the question whether a "taking" has occurred....

> **FYI**
>
> *Transferable development rights* are a simple mechanism for government to ameliorate the effects of land use restrictions. TDRs have been an effective tool for directing development away from "sensitive" areas. They are widely used to preserve agricultural lands, historic buildings, open space, and natural habitats.

A.

... The question of what constitutes a "taking" for purposes of the Fifth Amendment has proved to be a problem of considerable difficulty. While this Court has recognized that the "Fifth Amendment's guarantee ... [is] designed to bar Government from forcing some people alone to bear public burdens which, in all fairness and justice, should be borne by the public as a whole," *Armstrong v. United States*, 364 U.S. 40, 49 (1960), this Court, quite simply, has been unable to develop any "set formula" for determining when "justice and fairness" require that economic injuries caused by public action be compensated by the government, rather than remain disproportionately concentrated on a few persons. . . .

In engaging in these essentially ad hoc, factual inquiries, the Court's decisions have identified several factors that have particular significance. The economic impact of the regulation on the claimant and, particularly, the extent to which the regulation has interfered with distinct investment-backed expectations are, of course, relevant considerations. . . . So, too, is the character of the governmental action. A "taking" may more readily be found when the interference with property can be characterized as a physical invasion by government . . . than when interference arises from some public program adjusting the benefits and burdens of economic life to promote the common good. . . .

B.

. . . [Appellants] first observe that the airspace above the Terminal is a valuable property interest. . . . They urge that the Landmarks Law has deprived them of any gainful use of their "air rights" above the Terminal and that, irrespective of the value of the remainder of their parcel, the city has "taken" their right to this superadjacent airspace, thus entitling them to "just compensation" measured by the fair market value of these air rights.

Apart from our own disagreement with appellants' characterization of the effect of the New York City law, the submission that appellants may establish a "taking" simply by showing that they have been denied the ability to exploit a property interest that they heretofore had believed was available for development is quite simply untenable. . . . "Taking" jurisprudence does not divide a single parcel into discrete segments and attempt to determine whether rights in a particular segment have been entirely abrogated. In deciding whether a particular governmental action has affected a taking, this Court focuses rather both on the character of the action and on the nature and extent of the interference with rights in the parcel as a whole—here, the city tax block designated as the "landmark site."

> **FYI**
>
> At the time of this case, New York City zoning laws used a *floor area ratio,* or *FAR*, to determine the maximum square footage that a structure could contain in relation to the size of the lot. Using the FAR standard, over 96% of the site's potential development was lost because of the landmark restriction.

Secondly, appellants, focusing on the character and impact of the New York City law, argue that it effects a "taking" because its operation has significantly diminished the value of the Terminal site. Appellants concede that the decisions sustaining other land-use regulations, which, like the New York City law, are reasonably related to the promotion of the general welfare, uniformly reject the proposition that diminution in property value, standing alone, can establish a "taking," see *Euclid v. Ambler Realty Co.*, 272 U.S. 365 (1926) (75% diminution in value caused by zoning law); *Hadacheck v. Sebastian*, 239 U.S. 394 (1915) (87½% diminution in value)....

Next, appellants observe that New York City's law differs from zoning laws and historic-district ordinances in that the Landmarks Law does not impose identical or similar restrictions on all structures located in particular physical communities. It follows, they argue, that New York City's law is inherently incapable of producing the fair and equitable distribution of benefits and burdens of governmental action which is characteristic of zoning laws and historic-district legislation and which they maintain is a constitutional requirement if "just compensation" is not to be afforded. It is, of course, true that the Landmarks Law has a more severe impact on some landowners than on others, but that in itself does not mean that the law effects a "taking." Legislation designed to promote the general welfare commonly burdens some more than others. The owners of the brickyard in *Hadacheck*, of the cedar trees in *Miller v. Schoene*, and of the gravel and sand mine in *Goldblatt v. Hempstead*, were uniquely burdened by the legislation sustained in those cases.[30] Similarly, zoning laws often affect some property owners more severely than others but have not been held to be invalid on that account. For example, the property owner in *Euclid* who wished to use its property for industrial purposes was affected far more severely by the ordinance than its neighbors who wished to use their land for residences....

C.

... [T]he New York City law does not interfere in any way with the present uses of the Terminal. Its designation as a landmark not only permits but contemplates that appellants may continue to use the property precisely as it has been used for the past 65 years: as a railroad terminal containing office space and concessions. So the law does not interfere with what must be regarded as Penn Central's primary expectation concerning the use of the parcel. More importantly, on this record, we must regard the New York City law as permitting Penn Central not only to profit from the Terminal but also to obtain a "reasonable return" on its investment.

Appellants, moreover, exaggerate the effect of the law on their ability to make use of the air rights above the Terminal in two respects. First, it simply cannot be

---

[30] Appellants attempt to distinguish these cases on the ground that, in each, government was prohibiting a "noxious" use of land and that in the present case, in contrast, appellants' proposed construction above the Terminal would be beneficial. We observe that the uses in issue in *Hadacheck, Miller*, and *Goldblatt* were perfectly lawful in themselves. They involved no "blameworthiness,... moral wrongdoing or conscious act of dangerous risk-taking which induce[d society] to shift the cost to a pa[rt]icular individual." Sax, *Takings and the Police Power*, 74 Yale L.J. 36, 50 (1964). These cases are better understood as resting not on any supposed "noxious" quality of the prohibited uses but rather on the ground that the restrictions were reasonably related to the implementation of a policy—not unlike historic preservation—expected to produce a widespread public benefit and applicable to all similarly situated property....

Nor, correlatively, can it be asserted that the destruction or fundamental alteration of a historic landmark is not harmful....

maintained, on this record, that appellants have been prohibited from occupying *any* portion of the airspace above the Terminal. While the Commission's actions in denying applications to construct an office building in excess of 50 stories above the Terminal may indicate that it will refuse to issue a certificate of appropriateness for any comparably sized structure, nothing the Commission has said or done suggests an intention to prohibit *any* construction above the Terminal. . . .

Second, to the extent appellants have been denied the right to build above the Terminal, it is not literally accurate to say that they have been denied *all* use of even those pre-existing air rights. Their ability to use these rights has not been abrogated; they are made transferable to at least eight parcels in the vicinity of the Terminal, one or two of which have been found suitable for the construction of new office buildings. Although appellants and others have argued that New York City's transferable development-rights program is far from ideal, the New York courts here supportably found that, at least in the case of the Terminal, the rights afforded are valuable. While these rights may well not have constituted "just compensation" if a "taking" had occurred, the rights nevertheless undoubtedly mitigate whatever financial burdens the law has imposed on appellants and, for that reason, are to be taken into account in considering the impact of regulation. . . .

How transferable development rights work

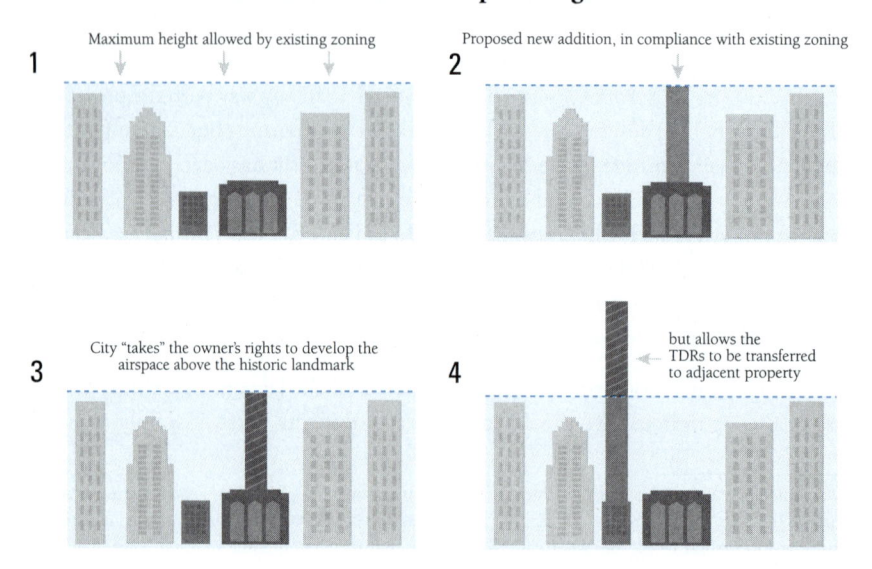

1 — Maximum height allowed by existing zoning

2 — Proposed new addition, in compliance with existing zoning

3 — City "takes" the owner's rights to develop the airspace above the historic landmark

4 — but allows the TDRs to be transferred to adjacent property

On this record, we conclude that the application of New York City's Landmarks Law has not effected a "taking" of appellants' property. The restrictions imposed are substantially related to the promotion of the general welfare and not only permit reasonable beneficial use of the landmark site but also afford appellants opportunities further to enhance not only the Terminal site proper but also other properties.

Affirmed.

MR. JUSTICE REHNQUIST, with whom THE CHIEF JUSTICE and MR. JUSTICE STEVENS join, dissenting.

. . . The question in this case is whether the cost associated with the city of New York's desire to preserve a limited number of "landmarks" within its borders must be borne by all of its taxpayers or whether it can instead be imposed entirely on the owners of the individual properties. . . .

> **Hear It**
>
> Oral argument before the Supreme Court can have its lighter moments. Click here to hear Justice Marshall's questions in *Penn Central* about whether New York is the "greatest" city.

I.

The Fifth Amendment provides in part: "nor shall private property be taken for public use, without just compensation." In a very literal sense, the actions of appellees violated this constitutional prohibition. Before the city of New York declared Grand Central Terminal to be a landmark, Penn Central could have used its "air rights" over the Terminal to build a multistory office building, at an apparent value of several million dollars per year. Today, the Terminal cannot be modified in *any* form, including the erection of additional stories, without the permission of the Landmark Preservation Commission, a permission which appellants, despite good-faith attempts, have so far been unable to obtain. . . .

Appellees are not prohibiting a nuisance. The record is clear that the proposed addition to the Grand Central Terminal would be in full compliance with zoning, height limitations, and other health and safety requirements. Instead, appellees are seeking to preserve what they believe to be an outstanding example of beaux-arts architecture. Penn Central is prevented from further developing its property basically because *too good* a job was done in designing and building it. The city of New York, because of its unadorned admiration for the design, has decided that the owners of the building must preserve it unchanged for the benefit of sightseeing New Yorkers and tourists. . . .

Even where the government prohibits a noninjurious use, the Court has ruled that a taking does not take place if the prohibition applies over a broad cross section of land and thereby "secure[s] an average reciprocity of advantage." *Pennsylvania Coal Co. v. Mahon*, 260 U.S., at 415. It is for this reason that zoning does not constitute a "taking." While zoning at times reduces *individual* property values, the burden is shared relatively evenly and it is reasonable to conclude that on the whole an individual who is harmed by one aspect of the zoning will be benefited by another.

Here, however, a multimillion dollar loss has been imposed on appellants; it is uniquely felt and is not offset by any benefits flowing from the preservation of some 400 other "landmarks" in New York City. Appellees have imposed a substantial cost on less than one one-tenth of one percent of the buildings in New York City for the general benefit of all its people. It is exactly this imposition of general costs on a few individuals at which the "taking" protection is directed. . . .

As Mr. Justice Holmes pointed out in *Pennsylvania Coal Co. v. Mahon*, "the question at bottom" in an eminent domain case "is upon whom the loss of the changes desired should fall." 260 U.S., at 416. The benefits that appellees believe will flow from preservation of the Grand Central Terminal will accrue to all the citizens of New York City. There is no reason to believe that appellants will enjoy a substantially greater share of these benefits. If the cost of preserving Grand Central Terminal were spread evenly across the entire population of the city of New York, the burden per person would be in cents per year—a minor cost appellees would surely concede for the benefit accrued. Instead, however, appellees would impose the entire cost of several million dollars per year on Penn Central. But it is precisely this sort of discrimination that the Fifth Amendment prohibits. . . .

Appellees contend that, even if they have "taken" appellants' property, TDR's constitute "just compensation." Appellants, of course, argue that TDR's are highly imperfect compensation. Because the lower courts held that there was no "taking," they did not have to reach the question of whether or not just compensation has already been awarded. . . . And in other cases the Court of Appeals has noted that TDR's have an "uncertain and contingent market value" and do "not adequately preserve" the value lost when a building is declared to be a landmark. . . . Because the record on appeal is relatively slim, I would remand to the Court of Appeals for a determination of whether TDR's constitute a "full and perfect equivalent for the property taken."

II.

Over 50 years ago, Mr. Justice Holmes, speaking for the Court, warned that the courts were "in danger of forgetting that a strong public desire to improve the public condition is not enough to warrant achieving the desire by a shorter cut than the constitutional way of paying for the change." *Pennsylvania Coal Co. v. Mahon*, 260 U.S., at 416. The Court's opinion in this case demonstrates that the danger thus foreseen has not abated. The city of New York is in a precarious financial state, and some may believe that the costs of landmark preservation will be more easily borne by corporations such as Penn Central than the overburdened individual taxpayers of New York. But these concerns do not allow us to ignore past precedents construing the Eminent Domain Clause to the end that the desire to improve the public condition is, indeed, achieved by a shorter cut than the constitutional way of paying for the change.

Points for Discussion

a. Ad Hoc Inquiries?

Justice Brennan explained that prior takings decisions involved "essentially ad hoc, factual inquiries." What does this mean? Is it better to establish a clear test for regulatory takings or to decide disputes on a case-by-case basis?

b. The Balancing Test

The balancing test developed in *Penn Central* is the *general test* for determining whether a regulatory taking exists. As we will see later in the chapter, the Court also has developed three *categorical tests* that apply in certain situations. The *Penn Central* factors are:

> - The economic impact of the regulation on the claimant.
> - The extent to which the regulation has interfered with distinct investment-backed expectations.
> - The character of the governmental action.

Note that all three factors supported the Court's conclusion in *Penn Central* that no taking had occurred. How do these factors differ from those used in *Pennsylvania Coal*? How would *Pennsylvania Coal* be decided under the *Penn Central* test? For scholarly analysis of the *Penn Central* approach, see Eric R. Claeys, *The* Penn Central *Test and Tensions in Liberal Property Theory*, 30 Harv. Envtl. L. Rev. 339 (2006) and John D. Echeverria, *Making Sense of* Penn Central, 23 UCLA J. Envtl. L. & Pol'y 171 (2005).

c. Examining the *Penn Central* Factors

Economic impact. This factor considers the extent of the economic loss suffered by the landowner as a result of the regulation, usually measured by diminution in market value. But the *Penn Central* court suggests that "diminution in property value" caused by a land use regulation that is "reasonably related to the promotion of the general welfare" is not a taking. For example, it notes that the 87½% diminution in value in *Hadacheck* did not result in a taking. What was the economic impact on Penn Central's property interest? Will it ever be able to use the airspace above the terminal?

Investment-backed expectations. The focus here is on the owner's reasonable expectations when he invested in the property. What were Penn Central's expectations when it purchased the terminal? To what extent did the landmarks preservation law interfere with these plans? Suppose that the law had been in place when Penn Central bought the terminal. Would this be relevant? *See Palazzolo v. Rhode Island*, 533 U.S. 606 (2001) (suggesting that notice of an existing restriction would not necessarily bar a takings claim). How does this factor apply to donees, such as heirs and devisees?

Character of governmental action. The decision notes that a taking will more readily be found when the interference stems from a physical invasion by the government, rather than from a government program that promotes the common good. How does the nuisance test relate to this factor? If a regulation is enacted to protect the public from harm, does this cut against finding a taking? Note how the *Penn Central* court handles the harm-benefit distinction in footnote 30. Are you convinced by its rationale? For a detailed analysis of the phrase "the character of the governmental action," see Thomas W. Merrill, *The Character of the Governmental Action*, 36 Vt. L. Rev. 649 (2012). The scope of this factor is less clear after *Cedar Point Nursery v. Hassid*, 141 S. Ct. 2063 (2021), which you will study later in this chapter. It held that many government-authorized physical invasions are categorical takings, and thus not subject to the *Penn Central* test.

d. Factoring in Government Benefit

Is the market value of land partly attributable to government programs? For example, publicly financed highways, schools, fire stations, police departments, and other services are vital for many types of land uses, such as residential subdivisions. Should government's contribution to land value be considered in the takings analysis? In *Penn Central*, much of the economic value of the terminal was arguably created by government. For instance, the railroad received large public subsidies for decades, and the terminal building was exempt from property taxes. For a discussion of this issue, see Jed Rubenfeld, *Usings*, 102 Yale L.J. 1077 (1993).

e. Transferable Development Rights

Justices Brennan and Rehnquist both discuss how transferable development rights (TDRs) should be handled. How do their positions differ? Is the availability of TDRs relevant to (1) whether a taking has occurred or (2) whether government has provided fair compensation for the taking? In *Suitum v. Tahoe Regional Planning Agency*, 520 U.S. 725, 747–48 (1997), Justice Scalia addressed this question:

> . . . Just as a cash payment from the government would not relate to whether the regulation "goes too far" (*i.e.*, restricts use of the land so severely as to constitute a taking), but rather to whether there has been adequate compensation for the taking; and just as a chit or coupon from the government, redeemable by and hence marketable to third parties, would relate not to the question of taking but to the question of compensation; so also the marketable TDR, a peculiar type of chit which enables a third party not to get cash from the government but to use his land in ways the government would otherwise not permit, relates not to taking but to compensation. . . .
>
> Putting TDRs on the taking rather than the just compensation side of the equation . . . is a clever, albeit transparent, device that seeks to take advantage of a peculiarity of our Takings Clause jurisprudence: Whereas once there *is* a taking, the Constitution requires just (*i.e.*, full) compensation, . . . a regulatory taking generally does not *occur* so long as the land retains substantial (albeit not its full) value. . . . If money that the government-regulator gives to the landowner can be counted on the question of whether there *is* a taking (causing the courts to say that the land retains

substantial value, and has thus not been taken) . . . the government can get away with paying much less. . . .

Should TDRs be used to determine if a taking exists under the *Penn Central* test? Is this relevant to the economic impact on the owner?

f.   Applying the *Penn Central* Test

Under the *Penn Central* standard, has a taking occurred in any of these situations?

> (1)   The American bald eagle is the official bird of State F. The number of bald eagles in the state has been declining rapidly. The state adopts a statute that makes it illegal to sell or purchase any part of a bald eagle, including feathers. B owns a costume business that specializes in renting and selling lavish feathered costumes for Mardi Gras and similar events. The new statute threatens to bankrupt B.
>
> (2)   City G rezones all undeveloped land in its downtown district into the new "Open Space Recreation Zone," where the only permitted use is recreation. This measure is a response to community concern that too many children are overweight and have no place to exercise. Before the rezoning, C purchased a vacant lot in the heart of the downtown district for $10 million; he planned to build the nation's most luxurious McDonald's restaurant, which was allowed under the previous zoning. Under the ordinance, a landowner may charge a fee of $5.00 per year to anyone who wants to enter his land for recreation.

g.   Role of Aesthetics

The police power may be used to protect aesthetic values, as we saw in Chapter 11. How much weight should be given to a community's aesthetic preferences when balancing the *Penn Central* factors? Did Penn Central lose this case because a handful of highly-sophisticated New Yorkers were enamored of the French beaux-arts style? Conversely, does *Penn Central* encourage a developer to adopt an unimaginative design and thereby avoid the risk that his building will someday be declared a landmark?

h.   Determining the Relevant "Parcel"

How did the majority define the "parcel" that was subject to its balancing test? How does this compare to the approaches Holmes and Brandeis used in *Pennsylvania Coal*?

Determining the property unit against which an owner's loss of value should be measured is a challenging issue. Commonly referred to as the *denominator issue or conceptual severance*, it often becomes a threshold question in takings cases. For example, if regulation destroys all value in 5 acres of a 50-acre parcel, is this (1) a 100% taking of the 5 acres or (2) a 10% taking of the 50 acres? The Supreme Court offered some guidance on this subject in *Murr v. Wisconsin*, 582 U.S. 383 (2017), when it adopted a multi-factor test to assess when an owner's properties should be treated as one parcel or multiple parcels for the takings analysis. For further discussion of this issue, you may want to jump ahead to the notes after *Lucas v. South Carolina Coastal Council*.

i. **Aftermath of *Penn Central***

Penn Central's TDRs remained largely unused for over 40 years. In 2006, a consortium purchased the Terminal, together with the TDRs. Later, the consortium hoped to sell up to 600,000 square feet of its TDRs for $475 million to a developer who planned to build a 67-floor skyscraper called One Vanderbilt on an adjacent parcel. But the city rezoned the skyscraper site in 2015, which allowed the developer to build without TDRs. The consortium then sued the city, asserting that the rezoning had "taken" its TDRs. The case was settled for a token amount. For more information, see Christopher Serkin, Penn Central *Take Two*, 92 Notre Dame L. Rev. 913 (2016).

> **Perspective and Analysis**
>
> Professor Joseph Sax argues that *Penn Central* signals a transformation in our understanding of private property—redefining the bundle of sticks to focus less on rights and more on responsibilities:
>
>> . . . We have endowed individuals and enterprises with property because we assume that the private ownership system will allocate and reallocate the property resource to socially desirable uses. Any such allocational system will, of course, fail from time to time. But when the system regularly fails to allocate property to "correct" uses, we begin to lose faith in the system itself. Just as older systems of property, like feudal tenures, declined as they became nonfunctional, so our own system is declining to the extent it is perceived as a functional failure. Since such failures are becoming increasingly common, the property rights that lead to such failures are increasingly ceasing to be recognized. Thus, the interesting question in the *Penn Central* case is not why the owner failed to receive compensation, but why private ownership of Grand Central Station did not lead to the correct allocation, that is, to maintaining the property as an unobstructed, architecturally distinctive railroad station. . . .
>>
>> Movement away from the nuisance justification for zoning in favor of concern about neighborhood character, seeing the community as a common, reflects a shift from primary concern with exclusive consumption (with its connotations of individualization and privatization) to nonexclusive consumption (with its connotations of community and shared values). . . . As one begins to see urban and suburban land use less through the lens of individuals who have bought isolated tracts that need protection against intrusions from outside, and more as situations in which one has acquired a package of common amenities—such as quality schools, quietude, low

levels of crime and the like—the values of nonexclusive consumption and of commonly enjoyed benefits come to the fore.

To be sure, none of this is entirely new, and it could be argued that even the most traditional zoning of a half-century ago was always more community-oriented than its nuisance-type justification implied. It may be that we are only now seeing the final result of a situation in which belief in free-wheeling development and individualism on the one hand, and the interest in community and what I have called nonexclusive consumption benefits on the other, are finally reaching an unresolvable tension. With this change the importance of protection and preservation becomes greater, relatively speaking, than that of development. Historic preservation looms larger than an additional high-rise; the coastline as a public amenity becomes more significant than the coastline as a commodity to be divided up and given over to exclusive housing development. . . .

What all this suggests is a transition in which an ever greater proportion of our well-being is realized in the form of shared wealth, or things that are nonexclusively consumed, rather than in the form of privatized or exclusive-consumption wealth. It seems a paradox that such changes should be occurring simultaneously with the blossoming of the "me" generation and the highly privatized gratification that goes with it. Perhaps the simultaneous rise of community-based nonexclusive benefits is a compensating substitute for the loss of more traditional social values focused around one's work and the more tightly-knit family.

Joseph L. Sax, *Some Thoughts on the Decline of Private Property*, 58 Wash. L. Rev. 481, 484, 491–93 (1983). What is your reaction to Professor Sax's perspective? Is our definition of property shifting toward greater focus on the responsibilities of owners? If so, how would this trend affect takings jurisprudence?

D. Three Categorical Tests

The *Penn Central* majority declared that there was "no set formula" for determining when a regulation constituted a taking. Rather, this issue would be resolved by using the Court's multi-factor balancing test.

Over time, the Court developed new tests to supplement the general *Penn Central* test in three specific situations. Each of these categorical tests provides a formula-like rule for deciding if a taking exists under certain conditions. But great uncertainty remains about what these tests mean and how they apply to specific situations. Broadly speaking, a taking will be found under these tests if a government entity:

> - Adopts a regulation that causes the *loss of all economically beneficial or productive use of land*, unless justified by *background principles of property or nuisance law*; or
> - Demands an *exaction* that has no *essential nexus* to a legitimate state interest or lacks *rough proportionality* to the impacts of the particular project; or
> - Adopts a regulation that results in a *physical appropriation of property*, unless a *special exception* applies.

1. Loss of All Economically Beneficial or Productive Use

Suppose K owns 100 acres of prairie grassland in State M that is zoned for residential development, but is currently used for cattle grazing. The state adopts a new statute that restricts the use of K's property and other privately owned grasslands, in order "to preserve our wild grassland heritage for the benefit of all citizens." Under the statute, K may only use her land for hiking and camping. The new law lowers the value of her property from $100,000 to zero. Has a taking occurred?

A similar question arose in our next case, *Lucas v. South Carolina Coastal Council*. Some scholars argued that the Court should expand its regulatory takings doctrine based on renewed concern for the sanctity of traditional private property rights. *See, e.g.,* Richard A. Epstein, Takings: Private Property and the Power of Eminent Domain (1985). When *Lucas* reached the Supreme Court, property rights advocates anticipated that the conservative majority would impose new limits on the government's regulatory power.

Lucas v. South Carolina Coastal Council

Supreme Court of the United States

505 U.S. 1003 (1992)

JUSTICE SCALIA delivered the opinion of the Court.

In 1986, petitioner David H. Lucas paid $975,000 for two residential lots on the Isle of Palms in Charleston County, South Carolina, on which he intended to build single-family homes. In 1988, however, the South Carolina Legislature enacted the Beachfront Management Act . . . which had the direct effect of barring petitioner from erecting any permanent habitable structures on his two parcels. A state trial court found that this prohibition rendered Lucas's parcels "valueless." This case requires us to decide whether the Act's dramatic effect on the economic value of Lucas's lots accomplished a taking of private property under the Fifth and Fourteenth Amendments requiring the payment of "just compensation."

I.

A.

South Carolina's expressed interest in intensively managing development activities in the so-called "coastal zone" dates from 1977 when, in the aftermath of Congress's passage of the federal Coastal Zone Management Act of 1972, . . . the legislature enacted a Coastal Zone Management Act of its own. *See* S.C. Code Ann. § 48–39–10 *et seq.* (1987). In its original form, the South Carolina Act required owners of coastal zone land that qualified as a "critical area" (defined in the legislation to include beaches and immediately adjacent sand dunes), to obtain a permit from the newly created South Carolina Coastal Council (Council) prior to committing the land to a "use other than the use the critical area was devoted to on [September 28, 1977]." § 48–39–130(A).

> **FYI**
>
> Why did the state restrict development? One reason is that construction in sensitive coastal areas may threaten human safety. For example, development on a barrier island reduces its ability to slow the waves and tidal surges produced by hurricanes, which increases storm dangers for mainland residents. One year after the state barred construction on the *Lucas* lots, Hurricane Hugo hit the South Carolina coast, killing 56 people and causing $10 billion in property damage.

In the late 1970's, Lucas and others began extensive residential development of the Isle of Palms, a barrier island situated eastward of the city of Charleston. Toward the close of the development cycle for one residential subdivision known as "Beachwood East," Lucas in 1986 purchased the two lots at issue in this litigation for his own account. No portion of the lots, which were located approximately 300 feet from the beach, qualified as a "critical area" under the 1977 Act; accordingly, at the time Lucas acquired these parcels, he was not legally obliged to obtain a permit from the Council in advance of any development activity. His intention with respect to the lots was to do what the owners of the immediately adjacent parcels had already done: erect single-family residences. He commissioned architectural drawings for this purpose.

> **See It**
>
> Click here to see a diagram of the shifting nature of the shoreline adjoining the *Lucas* lots.

The Beachfront Management Act brought Lucas's plans to an abrupt end. Under that 1988 legislation, the Council was directed to establish a "baseline" connecting the landward-most "point[s] of erosion . . . during the past forty years" in the region of the Isle of Palms that includes Lucas's lots. . . . In action not challenged here, the Council fixed this baseline landward of Lucas's parcels. That was significant, for under the Act construction of occupiable improvements was flatly prohibited seaward of a line drawn 20 feet landward of, and parallel to, the baseline. . . . The Act provided no exceptions.

Lucas lots (on right and left sides of center house)
Click here for larger photo

B.

Lucas promptly filed suit in the South Carolina Court of Common Pleas, contending that the Beachfront Management Act's construction bar effected a taking of his property without just compensation. Lucas did not take issue with the validity of the Act as a lawful exercise of South Carolina's police power, but contended that the Act's complete extinguishment of his property's value entitled him to compensation regardless of whether the legislature had acted in furtherance of legitimate police power objectives. Following a bench trial, the court agreed. Among its factual determinations was the finding that "at the time Lucas purchased the two lots, both were zoned for single-family residential construction and . . . there were no restrictions imposed upon such use of the property by either the State of South Carolina, the County of Charleston, or the Town of the Isle of Palms." The trial court further found that the Beachfront Management Act decreed a permanent ban on construction insofar as Lucas's lots were concerned, and that this prohibition "deprive[d] Lucas of any reasonable economic use of the lots, . . . eliminated the unrestricted right of use, and render[ed] them valueless." The court thus concluded that Lucas's properties had been "taken" by operation of the Act, and it ordered respondent to pay "just compensation" in the amount of $1,232,387.50.

The Supreme Court of South Carolina reversed. It found dispositive what it described as Lucas's concession "that the Beachfront Management Act [was] properly and validly designed to preserve . . . South Carolina's beaches." 404 S.E.2d 895, 896 (1991). . . . The court ruled that when a regulation respecting the use of property is designed "to prevent serious public harm," . . . no compensation is owing under the Takings Clause regardless of the regulation's effect on the property's value. . . .

We granted certiorari. . . .

III.

A.

Prior to Justice Holmes's exposition in *Pennsylvania Coal Co. v. Mahon*, 260 U.S. 393 (1922), it was generally thought that the Takings Clause reached only a "direct appropriation" of property, *Legal Tender Cases*, 12 Wall. 457, 551, (1871), or the functional equivalent of a "practical ouster of [the owner's] possession," *Transportation Co. v. Chicago*, 99 U.S. 635, 642 (1879). . . . Justice Holmes recognized in *Mahon*, however, that if the protection against physical appropriations of private property was to be meaningfully enforced, the government's power to redefine the range of interests included in the ownership of property was necessarily constrained by constitutional limits. 260 U.S., at 414–415. If, instead, the uses of private property were subject to unbridled, uncompensated qualification under the police power, "the natural tendency of human nature [would be] to extend the qualification more and more until at last private property disappear[ed]." . . . These considerations gave birth in that case to the oft-cited maxim that, "while property may be regulated to a certain extent, if regulation goes too far it will be recognized as a taking." . . .

Nevertheless, our decision in *Mahon* offered little insight into when, and under what circumstances, a given regulation would be seen as going "too far" for purposes of the Fifth Amendment. In 70-odd years of succeeding "regulatory takings" jurisprudence, we have generally eschewed any "'set formula'" for determining how far is too far, preferring to "engag[e] in . . . essentially ad hoc, factual inquiries." *Penn Central Transportation Co. v. New York City*, 438 U.S. 104, 124 (1978) (quoting *Goldblatt v. Hempstead*, 369 U.S. 590, 594 (1962)). . . . We have, however, described at least two discrete categories of regulatory action as compensable without case-specific inquiry into the public interest advanced in support of the restraint. The first encompasses regulations that compel the property owner to suffer a physical

> **Practice Pointer**
>
> When a short form of a case name is used in legal writing, only one party's name is referenced. If one of the parties is a government, geographical area, or common litigant, the other party's name is commonly used. Although this book and many scholars refer to *Pennsylvania Coal*, Justice Scalia used the name *Mahon* to differentiate the famous takings case from the other approximately 50 reported actions in which the Pennsylvania Coal Company was a party.

"invasion" of his property. In general (at least with regard to permanent invasions), no matter how minute the intrusion, and no matter how weighty the public purpose behind it, we have required compensation. For example, in *Loretto v. Teleprompter Manhattan CATV Corp.*, 458 U.S. 419 (1982), we determined that New York's law requiring landlords to allow television cable companies to emplace cable facilities in their apartment buildings constituted a taking... even though the facilities occupied at most only 1½ cubic feet of the landlord's property. ...

The second situation in which we have found categorical treatment appropriate is where regulation denies all economically beneficial or productive use of land. ... As we have said on numerous occasions, the Fifth Amendment is violated when land-use regulation "does not substantially advance legitimate state interests *or denies an owner economically viable use of his land.*" *Agins v. City of Tiburon*, 447 U.S. 255, 260 (1980) (emphasis added).[7]

We have never set forth the justification for this rule. Perhaps it is simply, as Justice Brennan suggested, that total deprivation of beneficial use is, from the landowner's point of view, the equivalent of a physical appropriation. See *San Diego Gas & Electric Co. v. San Diego*, 450 U.S., at 652 (dissenting opinion). "[F]or what is the land but the profits thereof[?]" 1 E. Coke, Institutes, ch. 1, § 1 (1st Am. ed. 1812).

> **Food for Thought**
>
> Do owners have the same expectations about personal property? The state traditionally has greater control over personal property. Would a prohibition on the sale of an eagle feather collection be a taking if it renders the property economically worthless? *See Andrus v. Allard*, 444 U.S. 51 (1979).

Surely, at least, in the extraordinary circumstance when *no* productive or economically beneficial use of land is permitted, it is less realistic to indulge our usual assumption that the legislature is simply "adjusting the benefits and burdens of economic life," *Penn Central Transportation Co.*, 438 U.S., at 124, in a manner that secures an "average reciprocity of advantage" to everyone concerned, *Pennsylvania Coal Co. v. Mahon*, 260 U.S., at 415. And the *functional* basis for permitting the government, by regulation, to affect property values without compensation—that "Government hardly could go on if to some extent values incident to property could not be diminished without paying for every such change

---

[7] Regrettably, the rhetorical force of our "deprivation of all economically feasible use" rule is greater than its precision, since the rule does not make clear the "property interest" against which the loss of value is to be measured. When, for example, a regulation requires a developer to leave 90% of a rural tract in its natural state, it is unclear whether we would analyze the situation as one in which the owner has been deprived of all economically beneficial use of the burdened portion of the tract, or as one in which the owner has suffered a mere diminution in value of the tract as a whole. (For an extreme—and, we think, unsupportable—view of the relevant calculus, *see Penn Central Transportation Co. v. New York City*, 42 N.Y.2d 324, 333–334 (1977), *aff'd*, 438 U.S. 104 (1978), where the state court examined the diminution in a particular parcel's value produced by a municipal ordinance in light of total value of the takings claimant's other holdings in the vicinity.) ...

in the general law,"—does not apply to the relatively rare situations where the government has deprived a landowner of all economically beneficial uses.

On the other side of the balance, affirmatively supporting a compensation requirement, is the fact that regulations that leave the owner of land without economically beneficial or productive options for its use—typically, as here, by requiring land to be left substantially in its natural state—carry with them a heightened risk that private property is being pressed into some form of public service under the guise of mitigating serious public harm. . . . As Justice Brennan explained: "From the government's point of view, the benefits flowing to the public from preservation of open space through regulation may be equally great as from creating a wildlife refuge through formal condemnation or increasing electricity production through a dam project that floods private property." *San Diego Gas & Elec. Co., supra*, 450 U.S., at 652 (dissenting opinion). . . .

We think, in short, that there are good reasons for our frequently expressed belief that when the owner of real property has been called upon to sacrifice *all* economically beneficial uses in the name of the common good, that is, to leave his property economically idle, he has suffered a taking.[8] . . .

B.

. . . It is correct that many of our prior opinions have suggested that "harmful or noxious uses" of property may be proscribed by government regulation without the requirement of compensation. For a number of reasons, however, we think the South Carolina Supreme Court was too quick to conclude that that principle decides the present case. The "harmful or noxious uses" principle was the Court's early attempt to describe in theoretical terms why government may, consistent with the Takings Clause, affect property values by regulation without incurring an obligation to compensate—a reality we nowadays acknowledge explicitly with respect to the full scope of the State's police power. . . .

The transition from our early focus on control of "noxious" uses to our contemporary understanding of the broad realm within which government may regulate without compensation was an easy one, since the distinction between

---

[8] Justice Stevens criticizes the "deprivation of all economically beneficial use" rule as "wholly arbitrary," in that "[the] landowner whose property is diminished in value 95% recovers nothing," while the landowner who suffers a complete elimination of value "recovers the land's full value." . . . This analysis errs in its assumption that the landowner whose deprivation is one step short of complete is not entitled to compensation. Such an owner might not be able to claim the benefit of our categorical formulation, but, as we have acknowledged time and again, "[t]he economic impact of the regulation on the claimant and . . . the extent to which the regulation has interfered with distinct investment-backed expectations" are keenly relevant to takings analysis generally. *Penn Central Transportation Co. v. New York City*, 438 U.S. 104, 124 (1978). It is true that in at least some cases the landowner with 95% loss will get nothing, while the landowner with total loss will recover in full. But that occasional result is no more strange than the gross disparity between the landowner whose premises are taken for a highway (who recovers in full) and the landowner whose property is reduced to 5% of its former value by the highway (who recovers nothing). Takings law is full of these "all-or-nothing" situations. . . .

"harm-preventing" and "benefit-conferring" regulation is often in the eye of the beholder. It is quite possible, for example, to describe in *either* fashion the ecological, economic, and esthetic concerns that inspired the South Carolina Legislature in the present case. One could say that imposing a servitude on Lucas's land is necessary in order to prevent his use of it from "harming" South Carolina's ecological resources; or, instead, in order to achieve the "benefits" of an ecological preserve. . . . Whether one or the other of the competing characterizations will come to one's lips in a particular case depends primarily upon one's evaluation of the worth of competing uses of real estate. . . . A given restraint will be seen as mitigating "harm" to the adjacent parcels or securing a "benefit" for them, depending upon the observer's evaluation of the relative importance of the use that the restraint favors. . . .

When it is understood that "prevention of harmful use" was merely our early formulation of the police power justification necessary to sustain (without compensation) *any* regulatory diminution in value; and that the distinction between regulation that "prevents harmful use" and that which "confers benefits" is difficult, if not impossible, to discern on an objective, value-free basis; it becomes self-evident that noxious-use logic cannot serve as a touchstone to distinguish regulatory "takings"—which require compensation—from regulatory deprivations that do not require compensation. . . .

Where the State seeks to sustain regulation that deprives land of all economically beneficial use, we think it may resist compensation only if the logically antecedent inquiry into the nature of the owner's estate shows that the proscribed use interests were not part of his title to begin with. This accords, we think, with our "takings" jurisprudence, which has traditionally been guided by the understandings of our citizens regarding the content of, and the State's power over, the "bundle of rights" that they acquire when they obtain title to property. It seems to us that the property owner necessarily expects the uses of his property to be restricted, from time to time, by various measures newly enacted by the State in legitimate exercise of its police powers; "[a]s long recognized, some values are enjoyed under an implied limitation and must yield to the police power." *Pennsylvania Coal Co. v. Mahon*, 260 U.S., at 413. . . .

Where "permanent physical occupation" of land is concerned, we have refused to allow the government to decree it anew (without compensation), no matter how weighty the asserted "public interests" involved, *Loretto v. Teleprompter Manhattan CATV Corp.*, 458 U.S., at 426—though we assuredly *would* permit the government to assert a permanent easement that was a pre-existing limitation upon the land owner's title. . . . We believe similar treatment must be accorded confiscatory regulations, *i.e.,* regulations that prohibit all economically beneficial use of land: Any limitation so severe cannot be newly legislated or decreed (without compensation), but must inhere in the title itself, in the restrictions that background principles of the State's law of property and nuisance already place upon land ownership. A law or decree with such an effect must, in other words, do no more than duplicate the result that could have been achieved in the courts—by adjacent landowners (or other uniquely affected persons) under the State's law of private nuisance, or by the State under its complementary power to abate nuisances that affect the public generally, or otherwise.[16]

On this analysis, the owner of a lake-bed, for example, would not be entitled to compensation when he is denied the requisite permit to engage in a landfilling operation that would have the effect of flooding others' land. Nor the corporate owner of a nuclear generating plant, when it is directed to remove all improvements from its land upon discovery that the plant sits astride an earthquake fault. Such regulatory action may well have the effect of eliminating the land's only economically productive use, but it does not proscribe a productive use that was previously permissible under relevant property and nuisance principles. The use of these properties for what are now expressly prohibited purposes was *always* unlawful, and (subject to other constitutional limitations) it was open to the State at any point to make the implication of those background principles of nuisance and property law explicit. . . . When, however, a regulation that declares "off-limits" all economically productive or beneficial uses of land goes beyond what the relevant background principles would dictate, compensation must be paid to sustain it. . . .

It seems unlikely that common-law principles would have prevented the erection of any habitable or productive improvements on petitioner's land; they rarely support prohibition of the "essential use" of land. . . . The question, however, is one of state law to be dealt with on remand. We emphasize that to win its case South Carolina must do more than proffer the legislature's declaration that the uses Lucas desires are inconsistent with the public interest, or the conclusory assertion that they violate a common-law maxim such as *sic utere tuo ut alienum non laedas*. . . . Instead, as it would be required to do if it sought to restrain Lucas in a common-law action for public nuisance, South Carolina must identify background principles of nuisance and property law that prohibit the uses he now intends in the circumstances in which the property is presently found. Only on this showing can the State fairly claim that, in proscribing all such beneficial uses, the Beachfront Management Act is taking nothing.[18]

The judgment is reversed, and the case is remanded for proceedings not inconsistent with this opinion. . . .

---

[16] The principal "otherwise" that we have in mind is litigation absolving the State (or private parties) of liability for the destruction of "real and personal property, in cases of actual necessity, to prevent the spreading of a fire" or to forestall other grave threats to the lives and property of others. *Bowditch v. Boston*, 101 U.S. 16, 18–19, 25 L.Ed. 980 (1880).

[18] Justice Blackmun decries our reliance on background nuisance principles at least in part because he believes those principles to be as manipulable as we find the "harm prevention"/"benefit conferral" dichotomy. There is no doubt some leeway in a court's interpretation of what existing state law permits—but not remotely as much, we think, as in a legislative crafting of the reasons for its confiscatory regulation. We stress that an affirmative decree eliminating all economically beneficial uses may be defended only if an objectively reasonable application of relevant precedents would exclude those beneficial uses in the circumstances in which the land is presently found.

JUSTICE BLACKMUN, dissenting.

Today the Court launches a missile to kill a mouse.

The State of South Carolina prohibited petitioner Lucas from building a permanent structure on his property from 1988 to 1990. Relying on an unreviewed (and implausible) state trial court finding that this restriction left Lucas' property valueless, this Court granted review to determine whether compensation must be paid in cases where the State prohibits all economic use of real estate. According to the Court, such an occasion never has arisen in any of our prior cases, and the Court imagines that it will arise "relatively rarely" or only in "extraordinary circumstances." Almost certainly it did not happen in this case.

Nonetheless, the Court presses on to decide the issue, and as it does, it ignores its jurisdictional limits, remakes its traditional rules of review, and creates simultaneously a new categorical rule and an exception (neither of which is rooted in our prior case law, common

> **Food for Thought**
>
> Why would the Supreme Court be interested in addressing a regulatory takings issue that rarely, if ever, arises?

law, or common sense). I protest not only the Court's decision, but each step taken to reach it. More fundamentally, I question the Court's wisdom in issuing sweeping new rules to decide such a narrow case. . . .

The South Carolina Supreme Court found that the Beachfront Management Act did not take petitioner's property without compensation. The decision rested on two premises that until today were unassailable—that the State has the power to prevent any use of property it finds to be harmful to its citizens, and that a state statute is entitled to a presumption of constitutionality. . . .

If the state legislature is correct that the prohibition on building in front of the setback line prevents serious harm, then, under this Court's prior cases, the Act is constitutional. "Long ago it was recognized that all property in this country is held under the implied obligation that the owners use of it shall not be injurious to the community, and the Takings Clause did not transform that principle to one that requires compensation whenever the State asserts its power to enforce it." *Keystone Bituminous Coal Assn. v. DeBenedictis*, 480 U.S. 470, 491–492 (1987). . . . The Court consistently has upheld regulations imposed to arrest a significant threat to the common welfare, whatever their economic effect on the owner. *See, e.g., Goldblatt v. Hempstead*, 369 U.S. 590, 592–593 (1962); *Euclid v. Ambler Realty Co.*, 272 U.S. 365 (1926); *Mugler v. Kansas*, 123 U.S. 623 (1887).

Petitioner never challenged the legislature's findings that a building ban was necessary to protect property and life. Nor did he contend that the threatened harm was not sufficiently serious to make building a house in a particular location a "harmful" use, that the legislature had not made sufficient findings, or that the legislature was motivated by anything other than a desire to minimize damage to coastal areas. . . .

Ultimately even the Court cannot embrace the full implications of its *per se* rule: It eventually agrees that there cannot be a categorical rule for a taking based on economic value that wholly disregards the public need asserted. Instead, the Court decides that it will permit a State to regulate all economic value only if the State prohibits uses that would not be permitted under "background principles of nuisance and property law." . . .

The threshold inquiry for imposition of the Court's new rule, "deprivation of all economically valuable use," itself cannot be determined objectively. As the Court admits, whether the owner has been deprived of all economic value of his property will depend on how "property" is defined. The "composition of the denominator in our 'deprivation' fraction," is the dispositive inquiry. Yet there is no "objective" way to define what that denominator should be. "We have long understood that any land-use regulation can be characterized as the 'total' deprivation of an aptly defined entitlement. . . . Alternatively, the same regulation can always be characterized as a mere 'partial' withdrawal from full, unencumbered ownership of the landholding affected by the regulation. . . ." Michelman, *Takings*, 1987, 88 Colum. L. Rev. 1600, 1614 (1988). . . .

Even more perplexing, however, is the Court's reliance on common-law principles of nuisance in its quest for a value-free takings jurisprudence. In determining what is a nuisance at common law, state courts make exactly the decision that the Court finds so troubling when made by the South Carolina General Assembly today: They determine whether the use is harmful. Common-law public and private nuisance law is simply a determination whether a particular use causes harm. . . . There is nothing magical in the reasoning of judges long dead. They determined a harm in the same way as state judges and legislatures do today. If judges in the 18th and 19th centuries can distinguish a harm from a benefit, why not judges in the 20th century, and if judges can, why not legislators? There simply is no reason to believe that new interpretations of the hoary common-law nuisance doctrine will be particularly "objective" or "value free." Once one abandons the level of generality of *sic utere tuo ut alienum non laedas*, one searches in vain, I think, for anything resembling a principle in the common law of nuisance. . . .

Justice Stevens, dissenting.

. . . In addition to lacking support in past decisions, the Court's new rule is wholly arbitrary. A landowner whose property is diminished in value 95% recovers nothing, while an owner whose property is diminished 100% recovers the land's full value. . . .

Moreover, because of the elastic nature of property rights, the Court's new rule will also prove unsound in practice. In response to the rule, courts may define "property" broadly and only rarely find regulations to effect total takings. . . .

On the other hand, developers and investors may market specialized estates to take advantage of the Court's new rule. The smaller the estate, the more likely that a regulatory change will effect a total taking. Thus, an investor may, for example, purchase the right to build a multifamily home on a specific lot, with the result that a zoning regulation that allows only single-family homes would render the investor's property interest "valueless." In short, the categorical rule will likely have one of two effects: Either courts will alter the definition of the "denominator" in the takings "fraction," rendering the Court's categorical rule meaningless, or investors will manipulate the relevant property interests, giving the Court's rule sweeping effect. To my mind, neither of these results is desirable or appropriate, and both are distortions of our takings jurisprudence. . . .

> **FYI**
>
> Professor Radin refers to the practice of dividing the fee into a patchwork of specialized estates as *conceptual severance*. Under this strategy, an owner hypothetically or conceptually severs from the whole bundle of rights merely those strands that are affected by the regulation, and then claims that that particular "whole" has been permanently taken. *See* Margaret Jane Radin, *The Liberal Conception of Property: Cross Currents in the Jurisprudence of Takings*, 88 Colum. L. Rev. 1667, 1676 (1988).

Like many bright-line rules, the categorical rule established in this case is only "categorical" for a page or two in the U.S. Reports. No sooner does the Court state that "total regulatory takings must be compensated," than it quickly establishes an exception to that rule.

The exception provides that a regulation that renders property valueless is not a taking if it prohibits uses of property that were not "previously permissible under relevant property and nuisance principles." . . .

The Court's holding today effectively freezes the State's common law, denying the legislature much of its traditional power to revise the law governing the rights and uses of property. Until today, I had thought that we had long abandoned this approach to constitutional law. More than a century ago we recognized that "the great office of statutes is to remedy defects in the common law as they are developed, and to adapt it to the changes of time and circumstances." *Munn v. Illinois*, 94 U.S. 113, 134 (1877). . . .

Arresting the development of the common law is not only a departure from our prior decisions; it is also profoundly unwise. The human condition is one of constant learning and evolution—both moral and practical. Legislatures implement that new learning; in doing so they must often revise the definition of property and the rights of property owners. Thus, when the Nation came to understand that slavery was morally wrong and mandated the emancipation of all slaves, it, in effect, redefined "property." On a lesser scale, our ongoing self-education produces similar changes in the rights of property owners: New appreciation of the significance of endangered species, *see, e.g., Andrus v. Allard*, 444 U.S. 51 (1979); the importance of wetlands, *see, e.g.,* 16 U.S.C. § 3801 *et seq.*; and the vulnerability of coastal lands, *see, e.g.,* 16 U.S.C. § 1451 *et seq.,* shapes our evolving understandings of property rights. . . .

The Court's categorical approach rule will, I fear, greatly hamper the efforts of local officials and planners who must deal with increasingly complex problems in land-use and environmental regulation. As this case—in which the claims of an *individual* property owner exceed $1 million—well demonstrates, these officials face both substantial uncertainty because of the ad hoc nature of takings law and unacceptable penalties if they guess incorrectly about that law. . . .

Points for Discussion

a. Economically Beneficial Use

Lucas established a new categorical rule: a regulation that deprives land of all economically beneficial use is a *per se* taking, no matter how weighty the public interests involved. Unfortunately, the Court failed to define clearly what it meant by "economically beneficial use." Is there a difference between deprivation of all "economically beneficial use" and deprivation of all "economic value"? What use could Lucas make of his lots if he could not build on them? Is this situation similar to the coal pillars in *Pennsylvania Coal*?

b. The Denominator Issue Returns

In *Penn Central*, Justice Brennan stated that takings jurisprudence "does not divide a single parcel into discrete segments and attempt to determine whether rights in a particular segment have been entirely abrogated." *Id.* at 130. Thus, the "property" at issue in *Penn Central* was the entire city block, including the airspace rights and the subsurface rights. But in *Lucas,* Justice Scalia indicated that the denominator issue was still unresolved.

The denominator issue is pivotal: if regulation eliminates all economically beneficial use of a "parcel," *Lucas* applies; if not, *Penn Central* applies. In *Murr v. Wisconsin,* 582 U.S. 383 (2017), the Court provided guidance on how to identify the relevant "parcel." The case involved two adjacent lots that the Murrs owned as tenants in common; one was improved with a cabin, and the other was unimproved. Under the local zoning ordinance, these commonly owned lots were effectively "merged" and treated as one parcel for the purpose of development. As a result, the ordinance barred the Murrs from building a cabin on the unimproved lot, which they claimed was a taking.

Delivering the opinion of the Court, Justice Kennedy reasoned that courts should consider a number of factors to determine the denominator, including (1) the treatment of the land under state and local law, (2) the physical characteristics of the land, and (3) the prospective value of the regulated land. He explained that this process "should determine whether reasonable expectations about property ownership would lead a landowner to anticipate that his holdings would be treated as one parcel, or, instead, as separate tracts." *Id.* at 397. Applying these guidelines, the Court held that the Murrs' two lots should be treated as one parcel and, accordingly, that no taking had occurred. For more information about *Murr*, see Daniel A. Farber, Murr v. Wisconsin *and the Future of Takings Law*, 2017 Sup. Ct. Rev. 115.

Does inserting an additional multifactor test into *Penn Central's* multifactor test create too much uncertainty? Would a bright-line test—such as presuming that the formal lot lines define the relevant parcel—be a better approach?

c. Background Principles of Law

Even if a regulation deprived land of all economically viable use, Justice Scalia explained that it would not be a taking under *Lucas* if the restriction stemmed from "background principles" in state property or nuisance law. How are these background principles defined? For example, do they vary from owner to owner (based on when title was acquired) or from state to state? Scalia seems to suggest that these principles are found in historic common law, not in legislation. Does this restrict the power of legislators to enact new laws in response to new technology or other changing conditions? *See* Louise A. Halper, *Why the Nuisance Knot Can't Undo the Takings Muddle*, 28 Ind. L. Rev. 329 (1995). However, in *Palazzolo v. Rhode Island*, 533 U.S. 606, 629 (2001), the Court implied that legislation might be a background principle under some circumstances.

In the wake of *Lucas*, lower courts have identified a limited set of background principles, including the public trust doctrine; the navigational servitude; customary beach access rights; access to burial grounds; public necessity; nuisance law; certain setback requirements; public ownership of wildlife; public ownership of water; and some zoning restrictions. *See* Michael C. Blumm & Rachael G. Wolfard, *Revisiting Background Principles in Takings Litigation*, 71 Fla. L. Rev. 1165 (2019).

d. Applying *Lucas*

Under the *Lucas* standard, has a taking occurred in any of these situations?

> (1) N applies ZZ fertilizer to his 1,000 acres of farm land in State P for three years. A team of university researchers concludes that any exposure to ZZ increases a person's risk of brain cancer by 3%, but the weight of scientific opinion is that ZZ is safe. To protect its citizens, the state adopts a law which prohibits any person from entering land where ZZ was ever used. This law reduces the value of N's property by 99%.

> (2)   R applies to State S for a building permit to construct a seawall on the dry-sand portion of her oceanfront property. The state denies the permit, explaining that the state's "common law custom" since the 1940s has been that private owners cannot prevent the public from using the dry-sand portions of beaches. R's seawall would indeed prevent public access. But without the seawall, the rising ocean level will eventually cover R's property, eliminating all of its value.
>
> (3)   While building his house in State T, U discovers that the lot he purchased for $75,000 is located on the site of an eighteenth-century Native American burial ground. State law prohibits any owner from disturbing Native American remains. As a result, U cannot build his house or any other structure on the lot, which is zoned for residential use only. But because the local ordinance allows an owner to hold "garage sales" in this zone, U can use the land for this purpose.
>
> (4)   V owns a small restaurant in City X. When a highly contagious virus sweeps the nation, the city adopts an ordinance requiring all restaurants (and most other businesses) to close temporarily in order to protect the public. During the closure, the restaurant produces no income, but V is still obligated to pay the rent, insurance, and other expenses needed to preserve the business. Six months later, V's unpaid debts exceed the value of the restaurant, and he files for bankruptcy.

e. Temporary Takings

Is the *Lucas* standard violated if a city places a moratorium on all new construction for a year? Suppose X owns ten lots in a residential zone; he cannot obtain any income from those lots until the moratorium ends. If we view his property in temporal terms, he has lost 100% of the income from those lots during the moratorium period. Has he been deprived of all economically beneficial use? In *Tahoe-Sierra Preservation Council, Inc. v. Tahoe Regional Planning Agency*, 535 U.S. 302 (2002), the Court answered "no." It observed: "Petitioners' 'conceptual severance' argument is unavailing because it ignores *Penn Central*'s admonition that in regulatory takings cases we must focus on the 'parcel as a whole.' . . . Logically, a fee simple estate cannot be rendered valueless by a temporary prohibition on economic use, because the property will recover value as soon as the prohibition is lifted." *Id.* at 331–32. But might a moratorium be a taking under *Penn Central*?

What if government action causes temporary flooding? In *Arkansas Game and Fish Commission v. United States*, 568 U.S. 23 (2012), a unanimous Court rejected the argument that compensation was due only when government-induced flooding was a permanent or recurring condition. Writing for the Court, Justice Ginsburg stressed that the duration of the flooding was only one factor to be considered in the temporary takings analysis. She noted that other relevant factors included (1) the degree to which the invasion was an intended or "foreseeable result of authorized government action,"

(2) the character of the land, (3) the severity of the interference, and (4) the owner's "reasonable investment-backed expectations regarding the land's use." *Id.* at 38–39.

f. Pre-Existing Use Restrictions

If Lucas had purchased his lots *after* the Beachfront Management Act was passed, would he be able to bring a takings claim? In *Palazzolo v. Rhode Island*, 533 U.S. 606 (2001), the Supreme Court held that an owner could challenge a regulation that already existed when he obtained title. It reasoned that any other rule would allow states "to put an expiration date on the Takings Clause. . . . Future generations, too, have a right to challenge unreasonable limitations on the use and value of land." *Id.* at 627. But why should a later buyer be able to contest such a regulation? Did he receive an implied assignment of the prior owner's cause of action?

g. Zero Value?

Does *Lucas* apply only if regulation reduces the value of the land to zero? If so, can a state easily avoid the *Lucas* standard by leaving the owner with some token use of the property?

The Court revisited the *Lucas* test in *Palazzolo*, where a state law restricting the development of wetlands allowed the owner to build only one house on his 18-acre tract. This diminished the value of the land from $3,150,000 to $200,000—a 94% reduction. Writing for the majority, Justice Kennedy rejected the owner's claim that this situation triggered the *Lucas* test: "A regulation permitting a landowner to build a substantial residence on an 18-acre parcel does not leave the property 'economically idle.'" *Id.* at 631.

h. Appropriate Remedy

What is the remedy for a regulatory taking? At one time, the remedy was thought to be limited to a judgment invalidating the regulation. But in *First English Evangelical Lutheran Church v. County of Los Angeles*, 482 U.S. 304 (1987), the Court held that the appropriate remedy was compensatory damages. It reasoned that the Takings Clause was designed "not to limit the governmental interference with property rights *per se*, but rather to secure *compensation* in the event of an otherwise proper interference amounting to a taking." *Id.* at 315.

i. Judicial Takings?

Suppose that A satisfies all the requirements under the law of State B to obtain title to C's land by adverse possession. If the supreme court of State B now changes the state's adverse possession law so that A's interest in the property is invalid, an argument can be made that the court has "taken" property from A and given it to C—a *judicial taking*.

Traditionally, the takings doctrine has been applied only to actions by the legislative and executive branches. The Supreme Court has never held that judicial action can constitute a taking. However, the Court did address the issue in *Stop the Beach Renourishment, Inc. v. Florida Department of Environmental Protection*, 560 U.S. 702 (2010). While holding that Florida property owners were not entitled to compensation when a state restoration project separated their private land from the water's edge (converting ocean-*front* lots into ocean-*view* lots), four justices indicated that they might endorse a cause of action for judicial takings. They suggested that the Takings Clause may bar the judiciary from ruling that an established private property right "no longer exists" unless just compensation is also provided. As Justice Scalia observed: "If a legislature *or a court* declares that what once was an established right of private property no longer exists, it has taken that property, no less than if the State had physically appropriated it or destroyed its value by regulation." *Id.* at 715. Although the case left the issue of judicial takings unresolved, it will probably spawn a flood of litigation. For a variety of interesting views on this topic, see *Symposium on Judicial Takings*: *Exploring the Boundaries of the Fifth Amendment*, 6 Duke J. Const. L. & Pub. Pol'y 1 (2011).

j. Aftermath of *Lucas*

On remand, the South Carolina Supreme Court ruled that background principles of state common law did not prohibit Lucas from building homes on his lots. The case was eventually settled. Lucas received $1,575,000 in exchange for conveying his lots to the Coastal Council. Ironically, the Council later sold the lots to a developer for $730,000 in order to recoup some of its expenses. A four-bedroom house was constructed on one of the lots, and a five-bedroom house was built on the other. After paying his mortgage and litigation expenses, Lucas was left with less than $100,000. For more information about the case, see Vicki Been, *Lucas v. The Green Machine: Using the Takings Clause to Promote More Efficient Regulation?*, in Property Stories 299 (Gerald Korngold & Andrew Morriss eds., 2d ed. 2009) and Oliver A. Houck, *More Unfinished Stories*: Lucas, Atlanta Coalition, *and* Palila/Sweet Home, 75 U. Colo. L. Rev. 331 (2004).

In practice, takings claims based on *Lucas* are rarely successful. One study found that plaintiffs prevailed in only 1.6% of the cases raising such claims. Carol Necole Brown & Dwight H. Merriam, *On the Twenty-Fifth Anniversary of* Lucas: *Making or Breaking the Takings Claim*, 102 Iowa L. Rev. 1847 (2017). For example, the court in *Shands v. City of Marathon*, 2023 WL 3214154, at 5* (Fla. Dist. Ct. App.) found a *Lucas* taking in the extreme situation where a zoning ordinance prohibited all uses of a privately-owned island in the Florida Keys "other than for beekeeping or personal camping."

2. Exactions: Essential Nexus and Rough Proportionality

Suppose developer D plans to build a tract of 50 homes on his 25-acre tract. D applies to City C for approval to subdivide the land. The City grants approval on the condition that D convey five acres of his land to the City as the site for a new elementary school. D believes that there will only be 60 children of elementary school age living in the subdivision at any one time. But the new school will serve 600 children. Is the City's demand for the school site an unconstitutional taking?

For many years, the infrastructure needed for new residential development was primarily financed with tax revenues. But many local governments began to shift these costs to developers, on the theory that they could pass them on to the home buyers who eventually would use the roads, sidewalks, parks, schools, and other facilities. Thus, governments began to require *exactions*—that the developer provide land or fees to offset the impacts of the project—as a condition of discretionary land use approvals.

Is there any limit on how much government may demand? The question surfaced in two important Supreme Court decisions which together provide our second categorical test: an exaction is a taking if either (1) there is no *essential nexus* between the exaction and a legitimate state interest or (2) the exaction is not *roughly proportional* to the project's impact.

In *Nollan v. California Coastal Commission*, 483 U.S. 825 (1987), the Commission approved a permit to build a new oceanfront home on condition that the owners grant an easement that allowed the public to cross their lot where it adjoined the public beach. Because the project would partly block the public's view of the beach from the highway in *front* of the house, the Court reasoned that a condition designed to address this impact (such as a height restriction) would be appropriate. But it found no *essential nexus* between the view problem and an easement allowing the public to walk along the beach *behind* the house. Accordingly, it held that the exaction was a taking.

Dolan v. City of Tigard, 512 U.S. 374 (1994) answered the question left open in *Nollan*: what degree of connection is required between the impact of the project and the exaction? The City approved the expansion of plaintiff's store on condition that she convey or *dedicate* two portions of her land: (1) land in the floodplain of the adjacent creek; and (2) land to be used as a link in a pedestrian/bicycle pathway. The *Nollan* standard was met because there was an essential nexus between these exactions and the project. But there was no evidence in the record demonstrating that each "required dedication is related both in nature and extent to the impact of the proposed development." *Id.* at 391. The Court ruled that the level of an exaction must be *roughly proportional* to the impact it was intended to address. For example, the requirement that the owner provide land for the pathway must be roughly proportional to the amount of increased customer traffic that the store expansion would produce.

Nollan and *Dolan* both involved exactions that required owners to convey interests in real property to public entities. Lower courts struggled with the question of whether these decisions also applied to fees. The Supreme Court resolved the controversy in *Koontz v. St. Johns River Water Management District*, 570 U.S. 595, 612 (2013), holding that "so-called 'monetary exactions' must satisfy the nexus and rough proportionality requirements of *Nollan* and *Dolan*." The four dissenters warned that the ruling "turns a broad array of local land-use regulations into federal constitutional questions" and "deprives state and local governments of the flexibility they need to enhance their communities—to ensure environmentally sound and economically productive development." *Id.* at 635–36. For a thought provoking article on the Court's exaction jurisprudence, see Lee Anne Fennell & Eduardo M. Peñalver, *Exactions Creep*, 2013 Sup. Ct. Rev. 287 (2014).

Finally, the exactions in *Nollan* and *Dolan* were imposed on specific projects following an individualized administrative review of the impacts of the particular project. But does the *Nollan-Dolan* test also apply to exactions imposed generally on projects by *legislation*? *Dolan* seemed to suggest that the answer was "no"; it distinguished certain precedents by noting that "they involved essentially legislative determinations classifying entire areas of the city, whereas here the city made an adjudicative decision to condition petitioner's application for a building permit on an individual parcel." *Dolan*, 512 U.S. at 385. Most courts have taken this position. *See, e.g., Am. Furniture Warehouse Co. v. Town of Gilbert*, 425 P.3d 1099 (Ariz. Ct. App. 2018); *but see Knight v. Metro. Gov't of Nashville & Davidson Cnty.*, 67 F.4th 816, 829 (6th Cir. 2023) (concluding that the test "applies just as much to legislatively compelled permit conditions as it does to administratively compelled ones").

3. Physical Appropriation of Property

Suppose R owns a 1,000 acre ranch in State W, which is located near an earthquake fault. The state adopts a regulation that permits government geologists to enter R's land—and other privately-owned lands which contain faults or are close to faults—one day every three years to conduct seismic testing. Is this a taking?

In *Loretto v. Teleprompter Manhattan CATV Corp.*, 458 U.S. 419, 426 (1982), the Court adopted its first categorical takings rule: "a permanent physical occupation authorized by government is a taking without regard to the public interests that it may serve." In that case, the Court concluded that a statute authorizing cable television providers to install permanent cables and other equipment on private property—in order to provide cable television service—was a taking. It reasoned that such an occupation effectively destroyed all of the owner's core property rights: "the government does not simply take a single 'strand' from the 'bundle' of property rights: it chops through the bundle, taking a slice of every strand." *Id.* at 435. In such an extreme case, it concluded, "the property owner entertains a historically rooted expectation of compensation." *Id.* at 441. But the Court emphasized that its "holding today is very narrow" and applied only to a "permanent physical occupation," while a temporary invasion was still governed by the *Penn Central* test. *Id.*

Under *Loretto*, State W's regulation above merely authorizes "temporary invasions" and thus is not a categorical taking. But the Court substantially expanded the *Loretto* approach in our next case, *Cedar Point Nursery v. Hassid*. As you read the case, consider whether the State W regulation would be a taking under the Court's current jurisprudence.

Cedar Point Nursery v. Hassid

Supreme Court of the United States

141 S. Ct. 2063 (2021)

CHIEF JUSTICE ROBERTS delivered the opinion of the Court.

A California regulation grants labor organizations a "right to take access" to an agricultural employer's property in order to solicit support for unionization. Cal. Code Regs., tit. 8, § 20900(e)(1)(C) (2020). . . . The question presented is whether the access regulation constitutes a *per se* physical taking under the Fifth and Fourteenth Amendments.

I

The California Agricultural Labor Relations Act of 1975 gives agricultural employees a right to self-organization and makes it an unfair labor practice for employers to interfere with that right. Cal. Lab. Code Ann. §§ 1152, 1153(a) (West 2020). The state Agricultural Labor Relations Board has promulgated a regulation providing, in its current form, that the self-organization rights of employees include "the right of access by union organizers to the premises of an agricultural employer for the purpose of meeting and talking with employees and soliciting their support." Cal. Code Regs., tit. 8, § 20900(e). Under the regulation, a labor organization may "take access" to an agricultural employer's property for up to four 30-day periods in one calendar year. . . . Two organizers per work crew (plus one addi-

> **FYI**
>
> The rights of private sector employees to organize into unions, participate in collective bargaining, and conduct strikes are guaranteed by the National Labor Relations Act of 1935. But "agricultural laborers" are excluded from the Act's protection. 29 U.S.C. § 152(3). During the late 1960s and early 1970s, the United Farm Workers campaigned for a similar California law to protect the rights of farmworkers; this eventually led to passage of the California Agricultural Labor Relations Act in 1975. The regulation at issue in this case was adopted in August, 1975.

tional organizer for every 15 workers over 30 workers in a crew) may enter the employer's property for up to one hour before work, one hour during the lunch break, and one hour after work. Organizers may not engage in disruptive conduct, but are otherwise free to meet and talk with employees as they wish.

Cedar Point Nursery is a strawberry grower in northern California. It employs over 400 seasonal workers and around 100 full-time workers, none of whom live on the property. According to the complaint, in October 2015, at five o'clock one morning, members of the United Farm Workers entered Cedar Point's property without prior notice. The organizers moved to the nursery's trim shed, where hundreds of workers were preparing strawberry plants. Calling through bullhorns, the organizers disturbed operations, causing some workers to join the organizers in a protest and others to leave the worksite altogether. Cedar Point filed a charge against the union for taking access without giving notice. The union responded with a charge of its own, alleging that Cedar Point had committed an unfair labor practice. . . .

Cedar Point Nursery
Click here for larger photo

[Cedar Point Nursery and another grower filed an action against Hassid and other members of the Board in their official capacities, alleging that "the access regulation effected an unconstitutional per se physical taking under the Fifth and Fourteenth Amendments by appropriating without compensation an easement for union organizers to enter their property." The district court granted the defendants' motion to dismiss, and the Ninth Circuit affirmed. Both courts held that the case was governed the multi-factor balancing test in *Penn Central Transportation Co. v. City of New York*, 438 U.S. 104 (1978), which the plaintiffs made no attempt to satisfy.]

II

A

The Takings Clause of the Fifth Amendment, applicable to the States through the Fourteenth Amendment, provides: "[N]or shall private property be taken for public use, without just compensation." The Founders recognized that the protection of private property is indispensable to the promotion of individual freedom. . . . This Court agrees, having noted that protection of property rights is "necessary to preserve freedom" and "empowers persons to shape and to plan their own destiny in a world where governments are always eager to do so for them." *Murr v. Wisconsin*, 582 U. S. ___, ___, 137 S.Ct. 1933, 1943 (2017).

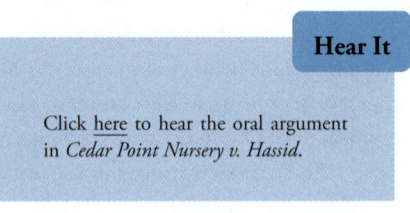

> **Hear It**
>
> Click here to hear the oral argument in *Cedar Point Nursery v. Hassid*.

When the government physically acquires private property for a public use, the Takings Clause imposes a clear and categorical obligation to provide the owner with just compensation. . . . The government commits a physical taking when it uses its power of eminent domain to formally condemn property. The same is true when the government physically takes possession of property without acquiring title to it. And the government likewise effects a physical taking when it occupies property—say, by recurring flooding as a result of building a dam. These sorts of physical appropriations constitute the "clearest sort of taking," *Palazzolo v. Rhode Island*, 533 U.S. 606, 617 (2001), and we assess them using a simple, *per se* rule: The government must pay for what it takes.

When the government, rather than appropriating private property for itself or a third party, instead imposes regulations that restrict an owner's ability to use his own property, a different standard applies. . . . To determine whether a use restriction effects a taking, this Court has generally applied the flexible test developed in *Penn Central*, balancing factors such as the economic impact of the regulation, its interference with reasonable investment-backed expectations, and the character of the government action.

Our cases have often described use restrictions that go "too far" as "regulatory takings." But that label can mislead. Government action that physically appropriates property is no less a physical taking because it arises from a regulation. . . . The essential question is not, as the Ninth Circuit seemed to think, whether the government action at issue comes garbed as a regulation (or statute, or ordinance, or miscellaneous decree). It is whether the government has physically taken property for itself or someone else—by whatever means—or has instead restricted a property owner's ability to use his own property. Whenever a regulation results in a physical appropriation of property, a *per se* taking has occurred, and *Penn Central* has no place.

B

The access regulation appropriates a right to invade the growers' property and therefore constitutes a *per se* physical taking. The regulation grants union organizers a right to physically enter and occupy the growers' land for three hours per day, 120 days per year. Rather than restraining the growers' use of their own property, the regulation appropriates for the enjoyment of third parties the owners' right to exclude.

The right to exclude is "one of the most treasured" rights of property ownership. *Loretto v. Teleprompter Manhattan CATV Corp.*, 458 U.S. 419, 435 (1982). According to Blackstone, the very idea of property entails "that sole and despotic dominion which one man claims and exercises over the external things of the world, in total exclusion of the right of any other individual in the universe." 2 W. Blackstone, Commentaries on the Laws of England 2 (1766). In less exuberant terms, we have stated that the right to exclude is "universally held to be a fundamental element of the property right," and is "one of the most essential sticks in the bundle of rights that are commonly characterized as property." *Kaiser Aetna v. United States*, 444 U.S. 164, 176, 179–180 (1979).

Given the central importance to property ownership of the right to exclude, it comes as little surprise that the Court has long treated government-authorized physical invasions as takings requiring just compensation. The Court has often described the property interest taken as a servitude or an easement.

For example, in *United States v. Causby* we held that the invasion of private property by overflights effected a taking. 328 U.S. 256 (1946). The government frequently flew military aircraft low over the Causby farm, grazing the treetops and terrorizing the poultry. The Court observed that ownership of the land extended to airspace that low, and that "invasions of it are in the same category as invasions of the surface." *Id.*, at 265. Because the damages suffered by the Causbys "were the product of a direct invasion of [their] domain," we held that "a servitude has been imposed upon the land." *Id.*, at 265–266. . . .

In *Loretto v. Teleprompter Manhattan CATV Corp.*, we made clear that a permanent physical occupation constitutes a per se taking regardless whether it results in only a trivial economic loss. New York adopted a law requiring landlords to allow cable companies to install equipment on their properties. 458 U.S. at 423. Loretto alleged that the installation of a ½-inch diameter cable and two 1½-cubic-foot boxes on her roof caused a taking. We agreed, stating that where government action results in a "permanent physical occupation of property, our cases uniformly have found a taking to the extent of the occupation, without regard to whether the action achieves an important public benefit or has only minimal economic impact on the owner." *Id.*, at 434–435. . . .

The upshot of this line of precedent is that government-authorized invasions of property—whether by plane, boat, cable, or beachcomber—are physical takings requiring just compensation. As in those cases, the government here has appropriated a right of access to the growers' property, allowing union organizers to traverse it at will for three hours a day, 120 days a year. The regulation appropriates a right to physically invade the growers' property—to literally "take access," as the regulation provides. It is therefore a *per se* physical taking under our precedents. Accordingly, the growers' complaint states a claim for an uncompensated taking in violation of the Fifth and Fourteenth Amendments.

C

. . . The Board and the dissent . . . contend that our decision in *PruneYard Shopping Center v. Robins*, 447 U.S. 74 (1980), establishes that the access regulation cannot qualify as a *per se* taking. There the California Supreme Court held that the State Constitution protected the right to engage in leafleting at the PruneYard, a privately owned shopping center. The shopping center argued that the decision had taken without just compensation its right to exclude. Applying the *Penn Central* factors, we held that no compensable taking had occurred. 447 U.S. at 83; cf. *Heart of Atlanta Motel, Inc. v. United States*, 379 U.S. 241, 261 (1964) (rejecting claim that provisions of the Civil Rights Act of 1964 prohibiting racial discrimination in public accommodations effected a taking).

The Board and the dissent argue that *PruneYard* shows that limited rights of access to private property should be evaluated as regulatory rather than *per se* takings. We disagree. Unlike the growers' properties, the PruneYard was open to the public, welcoming some 25,000 patrons a day. Limitations on how a business generally open to the public may treat individuals on the premises are readily distinguishable from regulations granting a right to invade property closed to the public.

III

The Board, seconded by the dissent, warns that treating the access regulation as a *per se* physical taking will endanger a host of state and federal government activities involving entry onto private property. That fear is unfounded.

First, our holding does nothing to efface the distinction between trespass and takings. Isolated physical invasions, not undertaken pursuant to a granted right of access, are properly assessed as individual torts rather than appropriations of a property right. This basic distinction is firmly grounded in our precedent. . . .

Second, many government-authorized physical invasions will not amount to takings because they are consistent with longstanding background restrictions on property rights. As we explained in *Lucas v. South Carolina Coastal Council*, the government does not take a property interest when it merely asserts a "pre-existing limitation upon the land owner's title." 505 U.S. at 1028–1029. For example, the government owes a landowner no compensation for requiring him to abate a nuisance on his property, because he never had a right to engage in the nuisance in the first place.

These background limitations also encompass traditional common law privileges to access private property. One such privilege allowed individuals to enter property in the event of public or private necessity. See Restatement (Second) of Torts § 196 (1964) (entry to avert an imminent public disaster); § 197 (entry to avert serious harm to a person, land, or chattels). The common law also recognized a privilege to enter property to effect an arrest or enforce the criminal law under certain circumstances. Because a property owner traditionally had no right to exclude an official engaged in a reasonable search, government searches that are consistent with the Fourth Amendment and state law cannot be said to take any property right from landowners.

> **Make the Connection**
>
> The regulation at issue in this case had been in effect for 46 years, long before Cedar Point Nursery purchased its land. Should it be viewed as a background principle of state property law under *Lucas v. South Carolina Coastal Council*?

Third, the government may require property owners to cede a right of access as a condition of receiving certain benefits, without causing a taking. In *Nollan v. California Coastal Commission*, 483 U.S. 825, 826 (1987), we held that "a permit condition that serves the same legitimate police-power purpose as a refusal to issue the permit should not be found to be a taking if the refusal to issue the permit would not constitute a taking." 483 U.S. at 836. . . .

Under this framework, government health and safety inspection regimes will generally not constitute takings. When the government conditions the grant of a benefit such as a permit, license, or registration on allowing access for reasonable health and safety inspections, both the nexus and rough proportionality requirements of the constitutional conditions framework should not be difficult to satisfy. See, *e.g.*, 7 U.S.C. § 136g(a)(1)(A) (pesticide inspections); 16 U.S.C. § 823b(a) (hydroelectric project investigations); 21 U.S.C. § 374(a)(1) (pharmaceutical inspections); 42 U.S.C. § 2201(*o*) (nuclear material inspections).

None of these considerations undermine our determination that the access regulation here gives rise to a *per se* physical taking. Unlike a mere trespass, the regulation grants a formal entitlement to physically invade the growers' land. Unlike a law enforcement search, no traditional background principle of property law requires the growers to admit union organizers onto their premises. And unlike standard health and safety inspections, the access regulation is not germane to any benefit provided to agricultural employers or any risk

> **Food for Thought**
>
> Suppose A refuses to sell his house to B because of B's race, which violates the Fair Housing Act as you saw in Chapter 7. B sues, and the court issues an injunction requiring A to sell the house to B. In effect, the injunction authorizes B to invade A's property without A's consent. Is this a taking under *Cedar Point Nursery*?

posed to the public. See *Horne* [*v. Department of Agriculture*, 576 U.S. 350, 366 (2015)] ("basic and familiar uses of property" are not a special benefit that "the Government may hold hostage, to be ransomed by the waiver of constitutional protection"). The access regulation amounts to simple appropriation of private property. . . .

* * *

The access regulation grants labor organizations a right to invade the growers' property. It therefore constitutes a *per se* physical taking. The judgment of the United States Court of Appeals for the Ninth Circuit is reversed, and the case is remanded for further proceedings consistent with this opinion.

JUSTICE BREYER, with whom JUSTICE SOTOMAYOR and JUSTICE KAGAN join, dissenting.

A California regulation provides that representatives of a labor organization may enter an agricultural employer's property for purposes of union organizing. . . . The question before us is how to characterize this regulation for purposes of the Constitution's Takings Clause. . . .

The Court holds that the provision's "access to organizers" requirement amounts to a physical appropriation of property. In its view, virtually every government-authorized invasion is an "appropriation." But this regulation does not "appropriate" anything; it regulates the employers' right to exclude others. At the same time, our prior cases make clear that the regulation before us allows only a temporary invasion of a landowner's property and that this kind of temporary invasion amounts to a taking only if it goes "too far." See, *e.g.*, *Loretto v. Teleprompter Manhattan CATV Corp.*, 458 U.S. 419, 434 (1982). In my view, the majority's conclusion threatens to make many ordinary forms of regulation unusually complex or impractical. And though the majority attempts to create exceptions to narrow its rule, the law's need for feasibility suggests that the majority's framework is wrong. With respect, I dissent from the majority's conclusion that the regulation is a *per se* taking. . . .

A

Initially it may help to look at the legal problem—a problem of characterization—through the lens of ordinary English. The word "regulation" rather than "appropriation" fits this provision in both label and substance. It is contained in Title 8 of the California Code of Regulations. It was adopted by a state regulatory board, namely, the California Agricultural Labor Relations Board, in 1975. It is embedded in a set of related detailed regulations that describe and limit the access at issue. . . . From the employers' perspective, it restricts when and where they can exclude others from their property.

At the same time, the provision only awkwardly fits the terms "physical taking" and "physical appropriation." The "access" that it grants union organizers does not amount to any traditional property interest in land. It does not, for example, take from the employers, or provide to the organizers, any freehold estate (*e.g.*, a fee simple, fee tail, or life estate); any concurrent estate (*e.g.*, a joint tenancy, tenancy in common, or tenancy by the entirety); or any leasehold estate (*e.g.*, a term of years, periodic tenancy, or tenancy at will). Nor (as all now agree) does it provide the organizers with a formal easement or access resembling an easement, as the employers once argued, since it does not burden any particular parcel of property. . . .

The majority concludes that the regulation nonetheless amounts to a physical taking of property because, the majority says, it "appropriates" a "right to invade" or a "right to exclude" others. It thereby likens this case to cases in which we have held that appropriation of property rights amounts to a physical *per se* taking.

It is important to understand, however, that, technically speaking, the majority is wrong. The regulation does not *appropriate* anything. It does not take from the owners a right to invade (whatever that might mean). It does not give the union organizations the right to exclude anyone. It does not give the government the right to exclude anyone. What does it do? It gives union organizers the right temporarily to invade a portion of the property owners' land. It thereby limits the landowners' right to exclude certain others. The regulation *regulates* (but does not *appropriate*) the owners' right to exclude.

> **Food for Thought**
>
> Does the law "take" the growers' right to exclude, as the majority argues? Or does it merely "regulate" the right to exclude, as the dissent asserts?

Why is it important to understand this technical point? Because only then can we understand the issue before us. That issue is whether a regulation that *temporarily* limits an owner's right to exclude others from property *automatically* amounts to a Fifth Amendment taking. Under our cases, it does not.

B

Our cases draw a distinction between regulations that provide permanent rights of access and regulations that provide nonpermanent rights of access. They either state or hold that the first type of regulation is a taking *per se*, but the second kind is a taking only if it goes "too far." And they make this distinction for good reason.

Consider the Court's reasoning in an important case in which the Court found a *per se* taking. In *Loretto*, the Court considered the status of a New York law that required landlords to permit cable television companies to install cable facilities on their property. We held that the installation amounted to a permanent physical occupation of the property and hence to a *per se* taking. See *id.*, at 441 ("affirm[ing] the traditional rule that a permanent physical occupation of property is a taking"). . . . In reaching this holding we specifically said that "[n]ot every physical invasion is a taking." *Id.*, at 435, n. 12. . . . We explained that the "permanence and absolute exclusivity of a physical occupation distinguish it from temporary limitations on the right to exclude." *Id.* And we provided an example of a federal statute that did *not* effect a *per se* taking—an example almost identical to the regulation before us. That statute provided " 'access . . . limited to (i) union organizers; (ii) prescribed non-working areas of the employer's premises; and (iii) the duration of the organization activity.' " *Id.*, at 434, n. 11 (quoting *Central Hardware Co. v. NLRB*, 407 U.S. 539, 545 (1972)). . . .

Now consider *PruneYard Shopping Center v. Robins*, 447 U.S. 74 (1980). We there considered the status of a state constitutional requirement that a privately owned shopping center permit other individuals to enter upon, and to use, the property to exercise their rights to free speech and petition. We held that this requirement was not a *per se* taking in part because (even though the individuals may have " 'physically invaded' " the owner's property) "[t]here [wa]s nothing to suggest that preventing [the owner] from prohibiting this sort of activity w[ould] unreasonably impair the value or use of th[e] property as a shopping center," and the owner could "adop[t] time, place, and manner regulations that w[ould] minimize any interference with its commercial functions." *Id.*, at 83–84; see also *Loretto*, 458 U.S. at 434 (describing the "invasion" in *PruneYard* as "temporary and limited in nature"). . . .

At the same time, *PruneYard*'s holding that the taking was "temporary" (and hence not a *per se* taking) fits this case almost perfectly. There the regulation gave non-owners the right to enter privately owned property for the purpose of speaking generally to others, about matters of their choice, subject to reasonable time, place, and manner restrictions. 447 U.S. at 83. The regulation before us grants a far smaller group of people the right to enter landowners' property for far more limited times in order to speak about a specific subject. Employers have more power to control entry by setting work hours, lunch hours, and places of gathering. On the other hand, as the majority notes, the shopping center in *PruneYard* was open to the public generally. All these factors, however, are the stuff of which regulatory-balancing, not absolute *per se*, rules are made. . . .

* * *

I recognize that the Court's prior cases in this area are not easy to apply. Moreover, words such as "temporary," "permanent," or "too far" do not define themselves. But I do not believe that the Court has made matters clearer or better. Rather than adopt a new broad rule and indeterminate exceptions, I would stick with the approach that I believe the Court's case law sets forth. "Better the devil we know . . . ." A right of access such as the right at issue here, a nonpermanent right, is not automatically a "taking." It is a regulation that falls within the scope of *Penn Central*. Because the Court takes a different view, I respectfully dissent.

Points for Discussion

a. **The Court's Rationale**

In effect, Chief Justice Roberts' opinion states that an owner has a right to exclude others—and thus almost any government interference with this right is a *per se* taking. But why? Unlike prior decisions such as *Lucas* and *Loretto*, there is no clear rationale for the Court's new test. *Lucas* and *Loretto* focused on (1) how severely the regulation affected property rights and (2) whether the owner would have a historically rooted expectation of compensation. Neither rationale clearly applies to the limited intrusions at issue in *Cedar Point Nursery*. For scholarly perspectives on the decision, see Bethany R. Berger, *Eliding Original Understanding in* Cedar Point Nursery v. Hassid, 33 Yale J.L. & Human. 307 (2022) and Lee Ann Fennell, *Escape Room: Implicit Takings after* Cedar Point Nursery, 16 Duke J. Const. L. & Pub. Pol'y 1 (2022).

b. **Invitation to Enter the Property**

One key fact distinguishes *Cedar Point Nursery* from all the precedents the Court cites—the owner's invitation to the employees. Those cases all involve situations where government obtains or authorizes a right of access over land occupied only by the owner. In *Cedar Point Nursery*, the owner voluntarily invited the employees to enter its land. Should this invitation make a difference? In *FCC v. Florida Power Corp.*, 480 U.S. 245 (1987), the respondent voluntarily leased space on its utility poles to a cable television company; but the federal government later used statutory authority to reduce the amount of rent due. The Court rejected the claim that this was a *Loretto* taking, explaining "it is the invitation, not the rent, that makes the difference." *Id.* at 252.

c. ***Cedar Point Nursery* Exceptions**

The Court's prior categorical takings decisions were narrowly focused. In contrast, the *Cedar Point Nursery* Court proclaimed a broad rule, and then sought to deal with its possible overreach by establishing three exceptions:

Isolated trespasses: It makes sense that rare governmental-authorized invasions should not rise to the level of takings. For example, the majority noted that a truck driver "parking on someone's vacant land to eat lunch" would be a trespass, not a taking. *Cedar Point Nursery*, 141 S. Ct. at 2078. But what counts as an "isolated" trespass? What if a government employee parked her truck on private land to each lunch three times each year?

Background restrictions on property rights: This provision is based on the exception in *Lucas*, although the Court seems to somewhat expand it by including "traditional common law privileges to access private property." *Id.* at 2079. Yet there is considerable uncertainty about what the exception encompasses. In his *Cedar Point Nursery* dissent, Justice Breyer pointed out that the *Lucas* Court only "defined a very narrow set of such background principles." *Id.* at 2088.

Conditions on government benefits: The final exception substantially expands the *Nollan-Dolan* rule outside of the exactions context and applies it to a wide range of government activities. It appears that government health and safety inspections will normally not be takings. But the concept that government can condition the grant of "certain benefits" on ceding a right of access raises the question of which benefits qualify. In his dissent, Breyer asked: "What about the benefit of having electricity? Of sewage collection? Of internet accessibility?" *Id.* at 2089.

d. Employee Housing

Suppose the Cedar Point Nursery workers lived on the employer's property. In *NLRB v. Babcock & Wilcox Co.*, 351 U.S. 105, 113 (1956), the Court indicated that the National Labor Relations Act would require a company to allow union organizers to enter its land when the employees lived on company land: "[I]f the location of the plant and the living quarters of the employees place the employees beyond the reach of reasonable union efforts to communicate with them, the employer must allow the union to approach his employees on his property." Would this be a taking under *Cedar Point Nursery*? If so, how does this decision affect the holding in *State v. Shack*, which you studied in Chapter 1? Is the holding in that case—now over 50 years old—a background principle of state property law?

e. Permits

Suppose California adopts a statute providing that any person or entity involved in growing plants for human consumption must obtain a permit from the state. One of the permit requirements is that the grower "must allow state workers to enter the workplace four times a year to talk with employees and inform them about their rights to join a union." The statute justifies this requirement on the basis that: "The police power permits the state to ensure that working conditions for employees involved in growing plants for human consumption are adequate in order to protect the public welfare, and unions can play an important role in helping to ensure that these conditions are adequate." Would this be a taking under the *Cedar Point Nursery* test? Why or why not?

f. Public Use?

After the Court determined that the regulation was a taking, California could arguably keep it in effect by compensating the affected property owners. An appraiser would presumably determine that the fair market value of the limited right to enter farm land for occasional union organizing is quite small. But the controversy raises a larger issue: would the regulation be a taking for *public use*? If not, it would be invalid regardless of the state's willingness to pay.

CHAPTER 14 Takings 943

g. Applying *Cedar Point Nursery*

Under the *Cedar Point Nursery* test, has a taking occurred in any of these situations?

> (1) State A adopts a statute which provides: "Any person may fly or otherwise operate a drone in the airspace over private properties owned by other persons so long as the drone remains at least 100 feet above the surface of such properties at all times."
>
> (2) A new law in State B provides that employees of a regional electric utility may enter residential property to fix malfunctioning electrical systems so that residents have the benefit of electricity, even if the malfunctions do not affect health or safety.
>
> (3) For over 100 years, a statute in State C has provided as follows: "Any person may enter unenclosed privately-owned land in this State unless the owner thereof has posted signs forbidding trespass (a) at intervals of 500 yards or less along its boundaries and (b) at all roads and trails entering the land."

h. Personal Property

Does *Cedar Point Nursery* apply to personal property? In *Horne v. Department of Agriculture*, 576 U.S. 350, 361 (2015), the Court held that a government price stabilization program which involved a "clear physical taking" of raisins violated the *Loretto* standard. Responding to the assertion that the Takings Clause provides less protection for personal property than real property, Chief Justice Roberts observed: "Nothing in the text or history of the Takings Clause . . . suggests that the rule is any different when it comes to appropriation of personal property. The Government has a categorical duty to pay just compensation when it takes your car, just as when it takes your home." *Id.* at 358.

i. Aftermath of *Cedar Point Nursery*

Appellate courts have begun to grapple with the scope of *Cedar Point Nursery*. An example is *Northwest Landowners Association v. State*, 978 N.W.2d 679 (2022), where owners challenged a state law which barred them from suing for trespass when the subsurface of their properties was invaded by fracking fluids from adjacent lands. Relying on *Cedar Point Nursery*, the North Dakota Supreme Court held that the law authorized physical invasions of plaintiffs' properties, and accordingly was a *per se* taking.

Conversely, in *Community Housing Improvement Program v. City of New York*, 59 F.4th 540 (2023), the Second Circuit rejected a claim by landlords and others that New York City's rent stabilization law which *inter alia* restricted evictions was a taking. It noted the *Cedar Point Nursery* statement that "[l]imitations on how a business open to the public may treat individuals" were distinguishable from regulations creating a right to invade property that was closed to the public. *Id.* at 551. The court stressed that the landlords had "voluntarily invited third parties to use their properties." *Id.*

Summary

- **Regulatory Takings.** While government may regulate an owner's use of her property under the police power, a regulation that goes "too far" is an unconstitutional taking. The Takings Clause is designed to prevent government from forcing certain owners to bear public burdens which in fairness and justice should be shared by the public as a whole.

- *Penn Central* **Test.** Under this test, three factors are evaluated to determine if a taking exists: the economic impact of the regulation on the owner; the degree of interference with the owner's reasonable investment-backed expectations; and the character of the government action. This is the general test used in most takings cases today. The Court has developed three categorical tests which supplement the *Penn Central* standard in special situations.

- **Defining the "Property."** In applying the *Penn Central* test, the court considers the whole parcel, not simply the portion which is affected by the regulation. However, determining what constitutes the whole parcel requires a balance of factors, including the treatment of the land under state and local law, the physical characteristics of the land, and the prospective value of the land.

- **Loss of All Economically Beneficial Use.** If regulation eliminates all economically beneficial or productive use of land, a taking will be found unless the regulation is justified by background principles of state property or nuisance law.

- **Rule for Exactions.** An exaction is a taking if either (a) there is not an essential nexus between the exaction and a legitimate state interest or (b) the exaction is not roughly proportional to the impact of the project.

- **Physical Appropriation of Property.** A regulation that results in a physical appropriation of property is a taking, unless a special exception applies: (a) the conduct is an isolated trespass; (b) the appropriation is consistent with longstanding background restrictions on property rights; or (c) the owner has ceded a right of access to the government as a condition of receiving certain benefits.

Test Your Knowledge

To assess your understanding of the material in this chapter, click here to take a quiz.

For More Information

For more information about the subjects covered in this chapter, please consult these sources:

- Carol Necole Brown & Dwight H. Merriam, *On the Twenty-Fifth Anniversary of* Lucas: *Making or Breaking the Takings Claims*, 102 Iowa L. Rev. 1847 (2017).
- *Looking Back on* Penn Central: *A Panel Discussion with the Supreme Court Litigators*, 15 Fordham Envtl. L. Rev. 287 (2004).
- Aziz Z. Huq, *Property Against Legality: Takings After* Cedar Point, 109 Va. L. Rev. 233 (2023).
- Frank I. Michelman, *Property, Utility, and Fairness: Comments on the Ethical Foundations of "Just Compensation" Law*, 80 Harv. L. Rev. 1165 (1967).
- John G. Sprankling, *Property and the Roberts Court*, 65 U. Kan. L. Rev. 1 (2016).
- William Michael Treanor, *The Original Understanding of the Takings Clause and the Political Process*, 95 Colum. L. Rev. 782 (1995).
- Danaya C. Wright, *A Requiem for Regulatory Takings: Reclaiming Eminent Domain for Constitutional Property Claims*, 49 Envtl. L. 307 (2019).

Index

References are to Pages

ABANDONMENT
Easements, termination of, 684–689
Finders' rights, 159–164, 177–178, 181–182
Landlords' rights, 488–494
Land use restrictions, 721–722
Nonconforming uses, 770–771, 773–774

ABSTRACTS OF TITLE, 571

ACCESSION, 45

ADVERSE POSSESSION OF PERSONAL PROPERTY
Demand and refusal approach, 196
Discovery rule, 189–194, 196
Generally, 185–197
Requirements for, 185–188
Statutory period, 187–188
Tacking, 188

ADVERSE POSSESSION OF REAL PROPERTY
Actual possession, 91, 96–97
Adverse and hostile possession, 92, 107–118
Bad faith test, 92, 108, 113
Claim of right, 92, 108
Color of title, 106–107
Continuous possession, 92, 97–98, 124
Disabilities, 125–126
Elements, 91–92
Exclusive possession, 92, 97
Generally, 90–126
Good faith test, 92, 108, 118
Government entity as owner, 126
Justifications for, 90–91, 98
Objective test, 92, 108, 117
Open and notorious possession, 92, 97
Statutory period, 92
Tacking, 119–124

AESTHETIC REGULATION, 792–800, 911

AIRSPACE RIGHTS, 126–133, 898–912

AMERICAN LAND TITLE ASSOCIATION, 599

ASSIGNMENTS, 470–479

BAILMENTS, 175

BODY PARTS, 35–46, 86, 261–262

CAPTURE RULE
Baseballs, 159–164
Domestic animals, 156–157
Generally, 8–14, 153–165
Natural gas, 13
Oil, 13
Pre-possessory interest, 162–163
Sunlight, 70, 75–76
Water, 70, 75–76, 142, 149
Wild animals, 8–14, 153–157

CAVEAT EMPTOR, 462, 532, 536–539

CC&Rs (See Common Interest Communities)

CERCLA (See Comprehensive Environmental Response, Compensation, and Liability Act)

CHAIN OF TITLE, 34, 568, 585–592

CHATTELS, 153–215

CIVIC REPUBLICAN THEORY, 5–6, 13

CIVIL RIGHTS ACT OF 1866, 428, 512, 714

CLEAN AIR ACT, 854

CLEAN WATER ACT, 829–838

CLIMATE CHANGE, 141, 853–861

CLOSING, 539–556

COASE THEOREM, 75, 721

COMMON INTEREST COMMUNITIES
CC&Rs (See Covenants, conditions, and restrictions below)
Covenants, conditions, and restrictions
    Abandonment, 721
    Changed conditions, 715–721
    Creation, 693–708, 772–723
    Defenses, 721–722
    Discrimination, 709–714
    Enforcement, 723–732
    Interpretation, 732
    Public policy, 722
    Unreasonableness, 723–732
Declarations, 722–723
Generally, 722–723, 733–739
Homeowners associations, 722–723, 733–739

COMMUNITY PROPERTY SYSTEMS, 387, 389–390

COMPREHENSIVE ENVIRONMENTAL RESPONSE, COMPENSATION, AND LIABILITY ACT (CERCLA), 838–847

CONCURRENT OWNERSHIP
Generally, 363–386, 390–397
Joint tenancy, 364–374
Ouster, 385
Partition, 374–382
Rights and duties, 382–386
Tenancy by the entirety, 365, 390–397
Tenancy in common, 364
Waste, 313–316, 328

CONDEMNATION (See Eminent Domain)

CONDITIONAL USES, 789

CONSERVATION EASEMENTS, 691–692

CONSTRUCTIVE EVICTION, 451–461

CONTINGENT REMAINDERS, 334–335, 338–341, 348–351

CONVERSION, 35–46, 159–163

COPYRIGHTS
Duration, 223–229
Fair use defense, 236–246
Generally, 217, 223–254
Infringement, 236–254
Requirements for, 229–236

COTENANTS (See Concurrent Ownership)

COVENANTS OF TITLE (See Title Covenants)

COVENANTS RUNNING AT LAW (See Real Covenants)

CURTESY, 387

CUSTOM, 157

CYBERSQUATTING, 285–286

DEATH
Community property systems, 390
Curtesy, 387
Death escrow, 549
Dower, 387–388
Escheat, 296–297, 304
Gifts causa mortis, 208–213
Intestate succession, 299, 303–304
Separate property systems, 389
Transfer on death deeds, 549
Wills (See Wills)

DEEDS
Acceptance, 546
Covenants, 557–565

Death escrow, 549
Deed as equitable mortgage, 623–629
Deed in lieu of foreclosure, 633
Delivery, 540–550, 583
Estoppel by deed, 565
Forgery, 583
Fraud, induced by, 583
General warranty deeds, 557–559
Merger, 526, 557
Quitclaim deeds, 110, 557
Requirements for validity, 540–546
Revocable deeds, 549–550
Special warranty deeds, 557–558
Statute of Frauds, 546
Statutory deeds, 565
Transfer on death deeds, 549

DEEDS OF TRUST, 609, 614, 618, 636–642

DEFEASIBLE ESTATES, 298, 319–332

DELIVERY
Deed to real property, 540–550, 583
Gifts of personal property, 198–213

DESTROY, RIGHT TO, 76–87, 313–316, 817–821

DISCLOSURE
"As is" clauses, 538
Caveat emptor, 462, 532, 536–539
Material defects, 531–538
Off-site conditions, 538–539

DISCRIMINATION
Civil Rights Act of 1866, 428, 512, 714
Equal Protection Clause, 709–714
Fair Housing Act, 420–429, 512, 714
Federal Housing Administration, 622, 713
Installment land contracts, 622
Leases, 420–429
Mortgages, 613, 713
Partition, 381–382
Racial covenants, 421, 709–715
Roommates, 430–435
Sales, 421–422, 428, 512
State legislation, 429
Zoning, 806–813

DOCTRINE OF DESTRUCTIBILITY OF CONTINGENT REMAINDERS, 345, 348–350

DOCTRINE OF WORTHIER TITLE, 345, 347–348

DOWER, 387–388

DRONES, 133

DUE PROCESS CLAUSE, 100, 410–414, 759–767, 843–848

EASEMENTS
Affirmative, 647
Appurtenant, 647, 649
Conservation easements, 691–692
Estoppel, easements by, 670–676
Express, 647–649
Generally, 646–692
Implied by prior existing use, 650–656
Implied from plat, 656
In gross, 647, 649
Interpretation of, 676–684
Irrevocable licenses, 670–676
Necessity, easements by, 657–662
Negative, 647, 691–692
Prescriptive, 662–669
Profit, 649
Statute of Frauds, 648
Termination, 684–691

EASEMENTS BY NECESSITY, 657–662

ELECTIVE SHARE, 389

EMINENT DOMAIN
Fifth Amendment, 85, 127, 863, 887
Future interests, 328
Generally, 85, 127–132, 863–884
Just compensation, 863, 870–871
Legislative deference, 870
Procedure for, 866
Public use requirement, 863–884
Rationale for, 863, 870
Takings Clause, 85, 127, 863, 887

ENDANGERED SPECIES ACT, 847–853

ENVIRONMENTAL LAW
Clean Air Act, 854
Clean Water Act, 829–838
Climate change, 141, 853–861
Comprehensive Environmental Response, Compensation, and Liability Act (CERCLA), 838–847
Endangered Species Act, 847–853
Green property theory, 821
Hazardous substances, 525, 604, 838–847
Public trust doctrine, 670, 821–828, 857–860
Wetlands, 821–838

EQUAL PROTECTION CLAUSE, 409–416, 709–714

EQUITABLE CONVERSION, 527–531

EQUITABLE DISTRIBUTION, 389–390, 403

EQUITABLE SERVITUDES, 645, 693, 701–707

ESCHEAT, 296–297, 304

ESTATES
Concurrent estates (See Concurrent Estates)
Fee simple absolute, 298, 300–305
Fee simple determinable, 319–320, 326
Fee simple subject to a condition subsequent, 320–321, 326
Fee simple subject to an executory limitation, 321–322
Fee tail, 298, 317–319
Feudalism, 295–298
Freehold estates generally, 298–332
Life estate, 198–202, 295–297, 305–316
Nonfreehold estates (See Nonfreehold Estates)

ESTOPPEL
Easement by estoppel, 670–676
Estoppel by deed, 565
Statute of Frauds, 519

EVICTION
Constructive eviction, 451–461
Good faith eviction, 501
Retaliatory eviction, 496–501
Self-help eviction, 501–508
Summary eviction, 507–508

EXACTIONS, 914, 930–931

EXCLUDE, RIGHT TO, 46–63, 931–944

EXCLUSIONARY ZONING, 806–813

EXECUTORY INTERESTS, 334–335, 342–344, 351

EXPRESS EASEMENTS, 642–647

EXTERNALITIES, 150, 157–158

FAIR HOUSING ACT, 420–429, 512, 714

FAIR USE DEFENSE, 236–246

FAMILY ZONING, 800–806

FEE SIMPLE ABSOLUTE, 298, 300–305

FEE SIMPLE DETERMINABLE, 319–320, 326

FEE SIMPLE SUBJECT TO A CONDITION SUBSEQUENT, 320–321, 326

FEE SIMPLE SUBJECT TO AN EXECUTORY LIMITATION, 321–322

FEE TAIL, 298, 317–319

FEUDALISM, 295–298

FIFTH AMENDMENT, 85, 127, 863, 887

FINDERS
Abandoned property, 159–165, 177–178, 181–182

Employee finds, 179–184
Generally, 165–184
Lost property, 165–175
Mislaid property, 165, 173–181
Shipwrecks, 178
Statutory approaches, 184
Treasure trove, 165, 184

FIRST AMENDMENT, 23, 62, 799–800

FIRST POSSESSION, 2, 8–14, 33

FIXTURES, 89

FORCED SHARE, 389

FORECLOSURE, 609, 634–642

FREEHOLD ESTATES (See Estates)

FUTURE INTERESTS
Created in transferees
    Executory interest, 334–335, 337, 342–343
    Remainder, 334–335, 337–341, 343
Doctrine of Destructibility of Contingent Remainders, 345, 348–350
Doctrine of Worthier Title, 345, 347–348
Eminent domain, 328
Marketability of land, 344–345
Retained by transferors
    Possibility of reverter, 327, 334–335
    Reversion, 334–336
    Right of entry, 327, 334, 336
Rule Against Perpetuities, 345, 350–360
Rule in Shelley's Case, 345–346

GENERAL WARRANTY DEEDS, 557–559

GHOSTS, 532–539

GIFTS
Acceptance, 198, 206
Causa mortis, 208–213
Delivery, 198, 204–206
Engagement rings, 207–208
Generally, 197–213
Intent, 198
Inter vivos, 197–208
Wills (See Wills)

GOOD FAITH IMPROVERS, 125

GRANTOR-GRANTEE INDEX, 567–569, 574–576, 585–588

GROUNDWATER, 142–143, 149

HAZARDOUS SUBSTANCES, 525, 604, 838–847

HEIRS, 299–300

HOLOGRAPHIC WILLS, 210, 311

HOMELESSNESS, 63, 435

HOMEOWNERS ASSOCIATIONS (See Common Interest Communities)

HORIZONTAL PRIVITY, 694–696, 701, 707

IMPLIED EASEMENTS BY PRIOR EXISTING USE, 650–656

IMPLIED EASEMENTS FROM PLAT, 656

IMPLIED WARRANTY OF HABITABILITY, 461–470

IMPLIED WARRANTY OF QUALITY, 538

INQUIRY NOTICE, 592, 597–598

INSTALLMENT LAND CONTRACTS, 618–623

INTELLECTUAL PROPERTY
Common law approach, 218–222
Copyrights, 217, 223–254
Moral rights, 85
Patents, 217, 254–270
Rights of publicity, 14–24
Trademarks, 217, 270–286
Trade secrets, 217, 286–291

Visual Artists Rights Act, 85–86

INTER VIVOS GIFTS, 197–208

INTESTATE SUCCESSION, 299, 303–304

IRREVOCABLE LICENSES, 670–676

JOINT TENANCY
Four unities, 364–365
Generally, 364–374
Right of survivorship, 364
Secret severance, 374
Severance generally, 365, 369–374
Straw person, 369

JUST COMPENSATION, 863, 870–871

JUS TERTII, 167

LABOR THEORY, 3, 13

LANDLORD AND TENANT
Abandonment, 488–494
Assignments, 470–487
Civil Rights Act of 1866, 428
Condition of premises, 448–470
Consent to transfer, 479–487
Constructive eviction, 451–461
Discrimination, 420–435
Eviction, 496–508
Fair Housing Act, 420–429
Implied warranty of habitability, 461–470
Leases, 419–420, 442–443, 450
Mitigation of damages, 488–494
Nonfreehold estates (See Nonfreehold Estates)
Possession, duty to deliver, 443–448
Rent control, 442–443
Retaliatory eviction, 496–501
Roommates, 430–435
Security deposits, 494–496
Selection of tenants, 420–435
Self-help eviction, 501–508
Statute of Frauds, 442
Subleases, 470–479

LATERAL SUPPORT, 141

LAW AND ECONOMICS, 4–5, 26, 54, 75, 150, 157–158, 721

LEGAL POSITIVISM, 1–2, 25, 28

LICENSES
Generally, 438, 649
Irrevocable (See Irrevocable Licenses)

LIFE ESTATES, 198–202, 295–297, 305–316

LOST PROPERTY, 165–175

MARITAL PROPERTY
Community property system, 387, 389–390
Curtesy, 387
Dower, 387–388
Married Women's Property Acts, 388
Premarital agreements, 403
Professional degrees, 397–404
Same-sex marriage, 409–416
Separate property system, 388–389
Tenancy by the entirety, 365, 390–397
Unmarried couples, 404–409

MARKETABLE TITLE, 520–526, 558, 604

MARRIAGE (See Marital Property)

MARRIED WOMEN'S PROPERTY ACTS, 388

MERGER, 526, 557

MISLAID PROPERTY, 165, 173–181

MORTGAGES
Acceleration, 612, 630
Antideficiency legislation, 635–636
Assuming, 613
Deed in lieu of foreclosure, 552, 633
Deeds of trust, 618, 636–642
Deficiency judgment, 635–641
Discrimination, 613
Due-on-sale clause, 612
Equitable mortgages, 623–629
Equitable redemption, 630
Equity of redemption, 615, 617
Foreclosure generally, 630–634

Future advances, 617, 633
Generally, 614–617
Installment land contracts, 618–623
Judicial foreclosure, 630
Liability of transferees, 613
Lien theory, 373, 614
Nonjudicial foreclosure, 631
Obligation, necessity for, 609–612
Power of sale, 615–616
Promissory notes, 610–612
Purchase money mortgages, 616, 633
Reinstatement, 630
Rents and profits, 617
Setting aside foreclosure sale, 634–635
Statutory right of redemption, 634
Subprime mortgages, 613
Taking title subject to, 613
Title theory, 373, 614
Usury, 627, 629

MOTHER HUBBARD CLAUSE, 569–574

NATURAL LAW, 1–2

NEGATIVE EASEMENTS, 647, 691–692

NONCONFORMING USES, 768–774

NONFREEHOLD ESTATES
Generally, 435–442
Periodic tenancy, 436–437
Tenancy at sufferance, 437–438
Tenancy at will, 436–441
Term of years tenancy, 436–437

NOTICE
Actual notice, 592
Constructive notice, 592
Inquiry notice, 592–598
Record notice, 566–592

NUISANCE
Private nuisance, 64, 68–76, 741–756, 766, 773, 895, 926
Public nuisance, 742, 854

OUSTER, 385

PARTITION, 374–382

PATENTS
Duration, 255
Generally, 217–218, 254–270
Infringement, 263–270
Requirements for, 255–263

PERIODIC TENANCY, 436–437

PERSONAL PROPERTY
Accession, 45
Adverse possession, 185–197
Bailments, 175
Conversion, 36–37
Finders, rights of, 165–184
Gifts, 197–213
Takings, 918, 943
Trespass to chattels, 55
Wild animals, 8–14, 153–157

PERSONHOOD THEORY, 6–7, 380–381

POSSIBILITY OF REVERTER, 327, 334–335

PREMARITAL AGREEMENTS, 403

PRESCRIPTIVE EASEMENTS, 662–669

PRIVATE NUISANCE, 64, 68–76, 741–756, 766, 773, 895, 926

PROBATE, 369, 549

PROFIT, 649

PROMISSORY NOTES, 610–612

PROPERTY RIGHTS
Bundle of rights metaphor, 24–26, 33, 556, 827
Right to destroy, 76–87, 313–316, 817–821
Right to exclude, 46–63, 931–944
Right to transfer, 26–46
Right to use, 63–76

PROPERTY THEORIES
Civic republican theory, 5–6, 13
First possession theory, 2, 8–14, 33
Green property theory, 821
Labor theory, 3, 13

Law and economics theory, 4–5, 26, 54, 75, 150, 157–158, 721
Personhood theory, 6–7, 380–381
Utilitarianism, 3–5, 13, 61, 64

PUBLIC DOMAIN, 224

PUBLICITY, RIGHT OF, 15–24

PUBLIC NUISANCE, 742, 854

PUBLIC PURPOSE TEST (See Eminent Domain)

PUBLIC TRUST DOCTRINE, 670, 821–828, 857–860

PUBLIC USE (See Eminent Domain)

QUIET TITLE, 95

QUITCLAIM DEEDS, 110, 557

REAL COVENANTS, 645, 693–702

REAL PROPERTY PURCHASE CONTRACTS
Closing, 539–556
Duty to disclose, 531–539
Equitable conversion, 527–531
Estoppel, 519
Generally, 512–526
Implied warranty of quality, 538
Marketable title, 520–526, 558, 604
Mortgages (See Mortgages)
Part performance, 518–519
Property descriptions, 517–518
Remedies for breach, 550–556
Statute of Frauds, 513–520
Title (See Title)

RECORDING ACTS
Acknowledgments, 578–583
Bona fide purchasers, 559, 577–598
First-in-time rule, 566–567, 577–578
Generally, 566–592
Mother Hubbard clause, 569–574
Notice (See Notice)
Notice jurisdictions, 577–578, 581
Race jurisdictions, 577
Race-notice jurisdictions, 578
Shelter rule, 584
Zimmer rule, 583

RECORDING SYSTEM
Chain of title, 34, 568, 585–592
Computerized records, 584
Generally, 566–598
Grantor-grantee index, 567–569, 574–576, 585–588
Marketable title acts, 575–576
Record notice, 566–592
Searching title, 567–569, 575–576, 585–588
Tract index, 569

RECORD NOTICE, 566–592

REGISTRATION OF TITLE, 584–585

REGULATORY TAKINGS (See Takings)

REMAINDERS, 334–335, 337–341, 343

REPLEVIN, 167–168, 195

RESTRAINTS ON ALIENATION, 306–311, 482–483, 487–488

RETALIATORY EVICTION, 496–501

REVERSIONS, 334–336

RIGHTS OF ENTRY, 327, 334, 336

RIGHTS OF PUBLICITY, 15–24

RULE AGAINST PERPETUITIES
Class gifts, 357
Classic snares, 357–358
Generally, 350–360
Lives in being, 350–352, 357
Rationale for, 350
Reforms to, 359
Savings clauses, 360
What-might-happen rule, 352, 356

RULE IN SHELLEY'S CASE, 345–346

RULE OF CAPTURE (See Capture Rule)

Index

SALES OF REAL PROPERTY
(See Real Property Purchase Contracts)

SAME-SEX COUPLES, 409–416

SECURITY DEPOSITS, 494–496

SELF-HELP EVICTION, 501–508

SEPARATE PROPERTY SYSTEMS, 388–389

SHELTER RULE, 584

SPECIAL EXCEPTIONS, 789

SPECIAL WARRANTY DEEDS, 557–558

SPECIFIC PERFORMANCE, 550–556

SPITE FENCES, 64–68

SPOT ZONING, 777–780

STATUTE OF FRAUDS
Deeds, 546
Electronic Signatures in Global and National Commerce Act, 519
Equal dignities rule, 518
Estoppel exception, 519
Leases, 442
Part performance exception, 518–519
Sales contracts, 513–520
Uniform Electronic Transactions Act, 519

STATUTE OF LIMITATIONS
Adverse possession of personal property, 187–188
Adverse possession of real property, 92
Title covenants, 560–565

STATUTE OF WILLS, 207

SUBJACENT SUPPORT, 141

SUBLEASES, 470–479

SUBSURFACE RIGHTS
Lateral support, 141
Ownership of subsurface, 134–141

Subjacent support, 141

TAKINGS
Average reciprocity of advantage, 895
Categorical tests, 913–944
Conceptual severance, 911, 924–926
Damages, 928
Denominator issue, 911, 924–926
Exactions, 930–931, 942
Generally, 887–944
Harm-benefit distinction, 898, 905, 919–920
History of, 887–888
Judicial takings, 928–929
Loss of all economically beneficial use, 914–929
Nuisance exception, 888, 895, 905, 919–920
Parcel, determination of, 911, 924–926
Penn Central test, 898–913
Personal property, 918, 943
Physical appropriation of property, 931–944
Takings Clause, 863, 881, 887
Temporary takings, 927–928
Transferable development rights, 903, 906, 910–911

TENANCY AT SUFFERANCE, 437–438

TENANCY AT WILL, 436–441

TENANCY BY THE ENTIRETY, 365, 390–397

TENANCY IN COMMON, 364

TERM OF YEARS TENANCY, 436–437

TITLE
Abstracts, 571
Bona fide purchasers, 559, 577–598
Chain of title, 34, 568, 585–592
Covenants, 557–565
First-in-time rule, 566–567, 577–578
Insurable title, 525–526
Insurance, 556, 598–605
Marketable title, 520–526, 558, 604
Notice (See Notice)
Opinions, 556, 566–598

Recording acts (See Recording Acts)
Recording system (See Recording System)
Record title, 525–526
Registration, 584–585
Relativity of, 24–25, 156, 166–167, 582
Search procedure, 567–569, 575–576, 585–588
Shelter rule, 584

TITLE COVENANTS
Future covenants, 558, 564–565
Generally, 557–565
General warranty deeds, 557–559
Present covenants, 558, 563–565
Quitclaim deeds, 110, 557
Rights of remote grantees, 564–565
Special warranty deeds, 557–558
Statute of limitations, 563–564

TITLE INSURANCE, 556–557, 598–605

TORRENS SYSTEM, 584–585

TOUCH AND CONCERN DOCTRINE, 694, 696, 701, 707

TRACT INDEX, 569, 591

TRADE DRESS, 277

TRADEMARKS
Dilution, 278–286
Generally, 217, 270–286
Infringement, 278–286
Requirements for, 270–277

TRADE SECRETS, 217, 286–291

TRAGEDY OF THE COMMONS, 157–158

TRANSFERABLE DEVELOPMENT RIGHTS, 903, 906, 910–911

TRANSFER, RIGHT TO, 26–46

TREASURE TROVE, 165, 184

TRESPASS, 46–63, 134–141, 936, 941

TRESPASS TO CHATTELS, 55

TROVER, 167–168

TRUSTS, 312, 359

UNMARRIED COUPLES, 404–409

USE, RIGHT TO, 63–76

UTILITARIAN THEORY, 3–5, 13, 61, 64

VARIANCES, 782–789

VERTICAL PRIVITY, 695–696, 701–702, 707

VESTED REMAINDERS, 338–341

VISUAL ARTISTS RIGHTS ACT, 85–86

WASTE, 313–316, 328

WATER RIGHTS
Groundwater, 142–143, 149
Surface water, 75–76, 142, 149–150

WETLANDS
Clean Water Act, 829–838
Generally, 817–838
Public trust doctrine, 670, 821–828, 857–860

WILLS
Attested wills, 312–313
Generally, 299
Holographic wills, 210, 306–311
Probate, 369, 549
Statute of Wills, 207

ZONING
Aesthetic regulation, 792–800
Amendments, 775–781
Amortization, 774
Comprehensive plans, 768
Conditional uses, 789
Constitutionality, 758–767
Exclusionary zoning, 806–813
Family zoning, 800–806
First Amendment, 799–800
General plans, 768
Group homes, 805

Growth controls, 806
Historic preservation, 82–83, 898–913
History of, 756–758
Inclusionary zoning, 812
Modern techniques, 789–791
New Urbanism, 790–792
Nonconforming uses, 768–774
Ordinances, 767–768
Signs, 800
Special exceptions, 789
Spot zoning, 780
Standard State Zoning Enabling
    Act, 758, 768, 774–775
Variances, 782–789
Vested rights, 774